# THE REFUGEE DEFINITION IN INTERNATIONAL LAW

# THE REFUGEE DEFINITION IN INTERNATIONAL LAW

HUGO STOREY

UNIVERSITY PRESS

Great Clarendon Street, Oxford, OX2 6DP,
United Kingdom

Oxford University Press is a department of the University of Oxford.
It furthers the University's objective of excellence in research, scholarship,
and education by publishing worldwide. Oxford is a registered trade mark of
Oxford University Press in the UK and in certain other countries

© Hugo Storey 2023

The moral rights of the author have been asserted

First Edition published in 2023

All rights reserved. No part of this publication may be reproduced, stored in
a retrieval system, or transmitted, in any form or by any means, without the
prior permission in writing of Oxford University Press, or as expressly permitted
by law, by licence or under terms agreed with the appropriate reprographics
rights organization. Enquiries concerning reproduction outside the scope of the
above should be sent to the Rights Department, Oxford University Press, at the
address above

You must not circulate this work in any other form
and you must impose this same condition on any acquirer

Public sector information reproduced under Open Government Licence v3.0
(http://www.nationalarchives.gov.uk/doc/open-government-licence/open-government-licence.htm)

Published in the United States of America by Oxford University Press
198 Madison Avenue, New York, NY 10016, United States of America

British Library Cataloguing in Publication Data
Data available

Library of Congress Control Number: 2023943381

ISBN 978–0–19–884264–4

DOI: 10.1093/oso/9780198842644.001.0001

Links to third party websites are provided by Oxford in good faith and
for information only. Oxford disclaims any responsibility for the materials
contained in any third party website referenced in this work.

The manufacturer's authorised representative in the EU for product safety is
Oxford University Press España S.A. of el Parque Empresarial San Fernando de
Henares, Avenida de Castilla, 2 – 28830 Madrid (www.oup.es/en).

# Foreword

Persecution—or the threat of it—traps the individual in a perilous situation. If an individual can no longer count on protection by his or her home country or, in the case of a stateless person, by the State in which he or she is habitually resident, then flight is often the only solution open to that person.

International law seeks to answer this problem. The Convention signed in Geneva on 28 July 1951[1] constitutes the cornerstone of the international legal regime for the protection of refugees. According to Article 1(A)(2) of the Geneva Convention relating to the Status of Refugees,

> [f]or the purposes of the present Convention, the term "refugee" shall apply to any person who: [ ... ] owing to well-founded fear of being persecuted for reasons of race, religion, nationality, membership of a particular social group or political opinion, is outside the country of his nationality and is unable or, owing to such fear, is unwilling to avail himself of the protection of that country; or who, not having a nationality and being outside the country of his former habitual residence as a result of such events, is unable or, owing to such fear, is unwilling to return to it.

That definition of the term 'refugee' in the Geneva Convention has been transposed almost verbatim into European Union law.[2]

The Mediterranean migration crisis and the war in Ukraine have highlighted the importance of a coherent approach, not only within the European Union but also worldwide, to the conditions that need to be satisfied in order for a third-country national or a stateless person to be considered a refugee.

Drawing on the author's judicial and academic experience, this book aims to shed light on the contours of refugee status, which are still all too obscure. In response to this lack of clarity, the author focuses on the definition set out in Article 1(A)(2) of the Geneva Convention. Without seeking to judge the merits of this definition in meeting its objective of protecting refugees as such, the author examines the meaning and content of each of the elements that make up the definition.

The main contents of the book is laid out in its individual chapters on each of the key elements of the refugee definition contained in Article 1A(2) of the Refugee Convention. These cover: nationality and statelessness; 'outside the country'; 'being persecuted'; internal protection alternative; the availment clause; Convention reasons;

---

[1] Convention Relating to the Status of Refugees (adopted 28 July 1951, entered into force 22 April 1954) 189 UNTS 137.
[2] Directive 2011/95/EU of the European Parliament and of the Council of 13 December 2011 on standards for the qualification of third-country nationals or stateless persons as beneficiaries of international protection, for a uniform status for refugees or for persons eligible for subsidiary protection, and for the content of the protection granted (recast) [2011] OJ L 337/9, Article 2(d) (EU Qualification Directive or QD).

and 'well-founded fear'. However, as demonstrated by its first three chapters—which address the definitional endeavour, rules of interpretation, and main approaches—the book has a broader aim. It seeks to take stock of a number of 'basic propositions' that can be transposed into a 'working definition' of the concept of 'a refugee', about which there appears to be a consensus, in the guidance provided by the Office of the United Nations High Commissioner for Refugees (UNHCR), in the case law of courts and tribunals—both national and supranational—and in academic circles. In conducting this task, the author seeks to maintain a distinction between these basic propositions and his own assessment of issues on which there continues to be a lack of consensus (his 'suggested propositions').

Animating all parts of the book but specifically reflected on in the concluding chapter are four main themes. One is that very considerable progress has in fact been made in resolving uncertainties and disagreements over the meaning of key terms and in ensuring that the refugee definition, for example, is interpreted in a way that retains its universal scope but is also sensitive to individual vulnerabilities. Thus, the book's analysis of the 'being persecuted' element highlights the great importance that is now attached to the need to take into account forms of persecution that are specific to certain categories of people, such as LGBTI-specific persecution and disability-specific persecution. The author thus supports the idea that the Convention is, fundamentally, a 'living' instrument.

A second theme of the book is an interrogation of the nature and status of the 'basic propositions' and how the study's working definition relates to existing sources of interpretative guidance, such as the 1979 UNHCR Handbook[3] or the series of Guidelines of the UNHCR on International Protection and existing attempts at codification in national and regional law. Special attention is further paid to judicial guidance and, in particular, to the case law of the Court of Justice of the European Union (CJEU) concerning the EU Directive on the conditions for granting refugee status.[4]

A third theme is more introspective. The author rigorously assesses the suitability of the 'basic propositions' and examines whether they meet the objective of ensuring clarity—and conversely of avoiding ambiguity—in the definition of the concept of a refugee.

A fourth theme is to explore whether there are sources of law or law-making mechanisms that might make it possible to achieve a common working definition of that concept in a more concrete form. The author draws concrete conclusions and recognises that academic proposals—such as those made in the present book—cannot bring about change on their own.

This well-structured and insightful work provides much food for thought. By comparing and contrasting different academic approaches to the task of defining the concept of a refugee, the author provides a comprehensive picture of the current state of

---

[3] UNHCR, Handbook on Procedures and Criteria for Determining Refugee Status and Guidelines on International Protection under the 1951 Convention and the 1967 Protocol Relating to the Status Of Refugees (Geneva, 2019, reissued in 2019) (UNHCR 1979 Handbook or 1979 Handbook).

[4] Directive 2011/95/EU of the European Parliament and of the Council of 13 December 2011 on standards for the qualification of third-country nationals or stateless persons as beneficiaries of international protection, for a uniform status for refugees or for persons eligible for subsidiary protection, and for the content of the protection granted (recast) (n 2).

thinking on that issue. That picture is further enhanced by the author's own observations on the matter. Those innovative observations are all the more useful as a basis for further discussion precisely because they are discursive rather than prescriptive in character, leaving space for others to build on the analytical work that has been done. By taking a step back and looking critically at his own ideas and proposals, the author manages to assess their value objectively and honestly, never shying away from expressing his own doubts as to their correctness or desirability where such doubts may appear justified.

The purpose of this book is not to propose that a new legal instrument should be drafted, nor even to posit that the definition of the concept of a refugee contained in the Geneva Convention needs to be modified. Rather, it suggests that certain aspects of that definition should be authoritatively interpreted, and thus clarified. This work thus provides precious impetus to moves to harmonise the interpretation of that concept and I wholeheartedly recommend it to anyone who has an interest in this subject.

Koen Lenaerts
President of the Court of Justice of the European Union
Luxembourg

# Preface and Acknowledgements

This book has been at once a labour of love and an unrelenting labour. Having found myself teaching and writing on aspects of the subject over the past thirty years, it gradually became more concrete an idea as I neared retirement age as a judge. Despite the labour, no matter how many times I look over its chapters, I still find deficiencies. I must hope that in large part this is due to the complexities of refugee law and that my book will nonetheless add something to the literature.

The book's contents reflect my own experience as a practitioner, refugee law academic and practising judge. Strongly shaping my book's call to achieve greater consensus have been the opportunities afforded me to collaborate with fellow judges from many countries in the context of conferences, workshops, and training events. The importance I attach in various chapters to setting out competing arguments and seeking to evaluate them is doubtless influenced by the adversarial nature of the asylum jurisdiction in the UK and the fact that representation can sometimes feature leading refugee law experts. But the benefits of such experience cannot imbue my own understanding with any special cachet. And as has properly been observed, 'horizontal judicial dialogue', though an important emerging source of learning, is for the most part neither any kind of state practice nor necessarily progressive.[5]

As this book was being finalised, Russia's war on Ukraine still rages. The longer-term implications of this event are likely to remain unclear for some time to come, but the challenges it poses both for refugee law and international law generally may be felt to make even more pressing the need for all working in these fields to redouble efforts to achieve greater clarity about the refugee definition.

This study is written and published in English, as are predominantly its references to books and articles. Still, my book tries to paint on a broader, transnational canvas. My background as a judge active in the International Association of Refugee and Migration Judges (IARMJ, formerly IARLJ) has caused me to acquaint myself with the ideas and thinking of a number of commentators, judicial and academic, who work and write in other languages. My involvement in training judges from other countries has exposed me to far more diverse understandings than otherwise. But of greatest importance in shaping my thinking has been my work as a judge during the 2006–2020 period when UK judges had to apply both EU asylum law and European-based human rights law. The first is subject to the authoritative guidance of the Court of Justice of the European Union (CJEU), a Court containing a heavy majority of judges from civil law jurisdictions; and the second is governed largely by the jurisprudence of the European Court of Human Rights (ECtHR), whose composition reflects an even

---

[5] Cathryn Costello, *The Human Rights of Migrants and Refugees in European Law* (OUP 2015) 326: '[w]hile the process of judicial dialogue has the potential to ensure enhanced human rights protection, it also has risks. It may wrongly give the impression of a human rights surfeit, or become iterative and mannered, rather than transformative.'

more diverse set of national judicial systems and legal cultures. In the field of asylum law, at least for those working in Europe, it is no longer possible anywhere, therefore, simply to apply a common-law approach. This in no way entails that I have expertise in civil law; it only means I have often had to engage with it and try to find synergies.

If this book is deemed useful it will be due in large part to the encouragement and support so graciously given by others.

I owe especial thanks to those who agreed to look over drafts of one or more chapters: David Allen, Roland Bank, John Barnes, Mark Blundell, David Cantor, Katelijne Declerck, Jean-Francois Durieux, Harald Dörig, Eric Fripp, Geoff Gilbert, Judith Gleeson, Guy Goodwin-Gill, Peter Lane, Hélène Lambert, Julian Lehmann, Liam McKenna, Lauren Neumann, Frances Nicholson, Jason Pobjoy, Ryszard Piotrowicz, Stephen Smith, John Stanley, Mark Symes, Jeff Walsh, Cornelius (Kees) Wouters, and Bostjan Zalar. Special thanks are due also to Koen Lenaerts for agreeing to write a foreword.

I have been lucky to have for the past thirty years a sounding board of judicial colleagues involved in the IARMJ. The lifeblood of this association's work has been conferences, seminars, and workshops aimed at improving judicial standards and practices and most important of all, the provision of training for judges working in this area. Within the Association's European Chapter, a number of us have been able to work together for the past nine years as an editorial team to produce judicial analyses and related materials on core asylum law subjects.

It is invidious to single out colleagues both within Europe and around the world, but among those not already mentioned who have particularly helped enhance my understanding of the myriad of issues thrown up by my chosen subject are: Mona Aldestam, Anders Andersson, Ahmed Arbee, David Baragwanath, Sean Baker, Hilkka Becker, Anna Bengsston, Johan Berg, Ledi Bianku, Holger Böhmann, the late John Bouwman, Bruce Burson, Mark Byrne, Eamonn Cahill, Jakub Camrda, Geoffrey Care, Cindy Carroll, Gaetan Cousineau, Anna-Celeste Carvalho, Jacek Chlebny, Maria Cristina Contini, Michael Creppy, Tjerk Damstra, Martine Denis-Linton, Sebastiaan de Groot, Isabelle Dely, Rolf Driver, Dora Dudas, Laurent Dufour, Tim Eicke, John Dyson, the late Roger Errera, Martina Flamini, Ed Grant, Rodger Haines, Goran Hakkinson, the late Henry Hodge, Michael Hoppe, Ella Kataeva, Kenneth Keith, Dominique Kimmerelin, Linda Kirk, Catherine Koutsopoulou, Joseph Krulic, Yann Laurans, Lars Bay Larsen, the late John Laws, Isaac Lenaola, the late Allen Linden, Allan Mackey, Florence Malvasio, Nurjehan Mawani, Esteban Lemus, Gaetan de Moffarts, Louise Moor, Peter Nedwed, Tony North, Juan Osuna, John Panofsky, Luca Perilli, Judith Putzer, Lori Rosenberg, Paul Schmidt, Lori Scialabba, Jolien Schukking, Eleanor Sharpston, Veronica Shaw, Peter Showler, James Simeon, Liesbeth Steendijk, Walter Stoeckli, Martin Treadwell, Majella Twomey and, Rebecca Wallace.

Other scholars or practitioners (not yet mentioned) who have helped me develop my ideas include Adrienne Anderson, Deborah Anker, Hemme Battjes, Celine Bauloz, Chaloka Beyani, Rachel Brett, Dr S Chelvan, Vincent Chetail, Cathryn Costello, Kathryn Cronin, Alice Edwards, Erika Feller, Michelle Foster, Madeline Garlick, Elspeth Guild, Gabor Gyulai, Kai Hailbronner, Jens Vedsted Hansen, Vanessa Holzer, Anja Klug, Hana Lupacova, Jane McAdam, the late Ian Macdonald, Francesco Maini, Paul Mahoney, Hugh Massey, Penelope Mathew, Madalina Moraru,

Violeta Moreno-Lax, Gregor Noll, Killian O'Brien, Clara Odofin, Maria O'Sullivan, the late Richard Plender, Michael Ross, Mathew Scott, Marina Sharp, Sarah Singer, Rick Stainsby, Daniel Thym, Ronan Toal, Rick Towle, Gillian Triggs, Volker Türk, and Frances Webber.

Names I particularly wish to mention are: Stephen Sedley, for his unwavering kindness and wonderful example throughout my judicial years; Guy Goodwin-Gill and Walter Kälin, who lent their support for my ideas for a book from the start; James Hathaway, for being an extraordinary pioneer (and for always patiently replied to questions about his position on certain issues); Nuala Mole who helped keep me apprised of ongoing human rights jurisprudence; David Cantor who gave me great practical and intellectual support; Frances Nicholson for her constant encouragement and editorial advice, and Michael Kirby, a former university friend, whose work as a judge on the Australian High Court and in the international arena has been an abiding source of inspiration to me.

I also owe a debt of gratitude to former UK judicial colleagues (not already mentioned) who provided real intellectual stimulus over the period I was reflecting on my subject: Mary Arden, Libby Arfon-Jones, John Barnes, Nihar Bird, Nicolas Blake, Doran Blum, Simon Brown, Gaynor Bruce, Russell Campbell, Melissa Canavan, Robert Carnwath, the late David Casson, the late Richard Chalkley, Jane Coker, Andrew Collins, Ken Craig, Bernard Dawson, Toby Davey, Elizabeth Davidge, the late Khurshid Drabu, John Dyson, Nadine Finch, Jill Frances, John Freeman, Nigel Froom, Devin Gill, Nathan Goldstein, Andrew Grubb, Brenda Hale, Chris Hanson, Henry Hodge, Jonathan Holmes, David Jackson, Catriona Jarvis, Satvinder Juss, Susan Kebede, John Keith, Razia Kekic, Peter King, Louis Kopieczek, Anna Landes, Clive Lane, Jim Latter, Fiona Lindsley, Vinesh Mandalia, Christine Martin, Chris Mather, Bernard McCloskey, Hugh Macleman, Richard McKee, Joanna McWilliam, Barbara Mensah, Joe Neville, Peter Moulden, Andrew Nicol, Mark Ockelton, Declan O'Callaghan, Mark O'Connor, Duncan Ouseley, David Parkes, David Pearl, Ian Peart, Jonathan Perkins, Julian Phillips, Sue Pitt, Melanie Plimmer, Madeleine Reeds, Helen Rimington, Jeremy Rintoul, Laurence Saffer, Stephen Sedley, Carol Scott-Baker, Paul Shaerf, Lesley Smith, Stephen Smith, Paul Southern, Paul Spencer, Joe Swaney, Deborah Taylor, Rebeccah Wallace, the late Susan Ward, George Warr, Lance Waumsley, Edward Woodcraft and David Zucker.

I have been fortunate to have the editorial assistance of Dr Noemi Magugliani, currently Lecturer in Law at the University of Kent and Research Fellow, British Institute of International and Comparative Law.

As always, however, the greatest thanks lie where the heart is, to my family, especially my wife Sehba and my youngest son, Xain, as well as to family friends (especially Lewis Bailey and Loretta Taylor) all of whom have encouraged, endured, cajoled, and commiserated in like measure.

Finally, I record my great thanks to Kathyrn Plunkett and all those at OUP who helped with the technical aspects.

# Outline of Contents

| | |
|---|---:|
| *Table of Cases* | xix |
| *Table of Legislation* | xxxvii |
| *List of Commonly Used Acronyms* | xli |
| 1. The Refugee Definition | 1 |
| 2. Interpretation | 60 |
| 3. Approaches, Ordering, Interrelationships, Modalities | 129 |
| 4. Nationality and Statelessness | 199 |
| 5. 'Outside the Country ...' | 259 |
| 6. 'Being Persecuted' and Serious Harm | 298 |
| 7. 'Being Persecuted' and Protection | 409 |
| 8. 'Being Persecuted' and the Internal Protection Alternative | 474 |
| 9. The Availment Clause: 'To Avail Himself of the Protection' | 545 |
| 10. Refugee Convention Reasons: 'For Reasons Of' | 586 |
| 11. 'Well-Founded Fear' | 663 |
| 12. Conclusions | 713 |
| *Selected Bibliography* | 745 |
| *Index* | 781 |

# Detailed Contents

| | |
|---|---|
| *Table of Cases* | xix |
| *Table of Legislation* | xxxvii |
| *List of Commonly Used Acronyms* | xli |

| | |
|---|---|
| 1  The Refugee Definition | 1 |
|   1  Aims of the Book | 2 |
|   2  The Refugee Definition in International Law | 8 |
|   3  Limits of the Refugee Definition | 25 |
|   4  Criticisms of the Refugee Definition | 27 |
|   5  Problems of Definition | 33 |
|   6  The Refugee Definition and Existing Learning | 38 |
|   7  Methodology and Outline of the Book | 55 |
|   8  Conclusions | 58 |
| 2  Interpretation | 60 |
|   Introduction | 61 |
|   1  Articles 31–33 of the Vienna Convention on the Law of Treaties 1969 (VCLT) | 62 |
|   2  Application of VCLT Rules to the Refugee Convention | 78 |
|   3  Interpretive Value of the Most Commonly Cited Sources | 107 |
|   4  VCLT Rules and the EU Asylum Law | 117 |
|   5  Conclusions | 121 |
| 3  Approaches, Ordering, Interrelationships, Modalities | 129 |
|   1  Main Approaches to the Refugee Definition | 130 |
|   2  The Human Rights Approach | 135 |
|   3  Criticisms of the Human Rights Approach | 147 |
|   4  Responses to Criticisms of the Human Rights Approach | 151 |
|   5  The Human Rights Approach: Advantages and Disadvantages of Specific Models | 170 |
|   6  The Human Rights Approach and International Law | 179 |
|   7  How Do Different Elements of the Refugee Definition Fit Together? | 181 |
|   8  Modalities of the Refugee Definition | 195 |
|   9  An Underlying Principle? | 196 |
|   10  Conclusions | 197 |
| 4  Nationality and Statelessness | 199 |
|   Introduction | 200 |
|   1  Background | 202 |
|   2  The International Law Framework | 206 |

|   |   |   |
|---|---|---|
| 3 Nationality and the Refugee Definition | | 212 |
| 4 Specific Issues | | 245 |
| 5 Nationality and Evidential Issues | | 250 |
| 6 Conclusions | | 256 |

5 'Outside the Country ...'    259
    Introduction    259
    1 'Outside the Country'    263
    2 'Outside the Country' and VCLT Rules    263
    3 'Outside the Country of Former Habitual Residence'    272
    4 Specific Issues    282
    5 Article 33(1) and Extraterritorial Application    288
    6 Conclusions    295

6 'Being Persecuted' and Serious Harm    298
    Introduction    299
    1 The Meaning of Being Persecuted in the Context of VCLT Rules    303
    2 The Meaning of Being Persecuted: Personal and Material Scope    321
    3 The Meaning of 'Being Persecuted': Modalities and Incidents    361
    4 Temporal Scope    402
    5 Conclusions    406

7 'Being Persecuted' and Protection    409
    1 Protection and the Notion of Surrogacy    410
    2 Persecution and Protection—Interrelationship    424
    3 Meaning of Protection    442
    4 Conclusions    471

8 'Being Persecuted' and the Internal Protection Alternative    474
    Introduction    475
    1 Basis in VCLT Rules and Textual Location    479
    2 The IPA Inquiry: Main Positions and Criticisms    493
    3 The IPA in International Human Rights Law (IHRL)    527
    4 Essential Elements of the IPA Test in Article 1A(2)—A Distillation    536
    5 Conclusions    542

9 The Availment Clause: 'To Avail Himself of the Protection'    545
    Introduction    545
    1 Availment    547
    2 History and Background    551
    3 Application of VCLT Rules    565
    4 The Availment Clause Reconsidered    572
    5 Conclusions    583

10 Refugee Convention Reasons: 'For Reasons Of'    586
    Introduction    587
    1 History and *Travaux Préparatoires*    590
    2 Approaches to Interpretation of the Reasons Clause    593

|  |  |
|---|---|
| 3 The Individual Reasons | 604 |
| 4 Causal Nexus ('for Reasons of') | 653 |
| 5 Conclusions | 659 |

## 11 'Well-Founded Fear'  663
1 Well-Founded Fear  663
2 VCLT Considerations  668
3 'Well-Founded Fear': The 'Subjective Element'  682
4 'Well-Founded Fear': The Objective Element  692
5 Conclusions  711

## 12 Conclusions  713
Introduction  714
1 Contents of the Working Definition  715
2 Nature and Status  724
3 How Does the Working Definition Represent Progress?  736
4 How Might Greater Clarity Be Achieved?  738

*Selected Bibliography*  745
*Index*  781

# Table of Cases

## INTERNATIONAL COURTS

### International Court of Justice

*Aegean Sea Continental Shelf (Greece v Turkey)*, Jurisdiction, Judgment
  [1978] ICJ Rep 3 .................................................... 72n.70
*Ahmadou Sadio Diallo (Republic of Guinea v Democratic Republic of the Congo),*
  Merits, Judgment [2010] ICJ Rep 639 ........................... 106n.295, 159n.176
*Ambatielos (Greece v United Kingdom)*, Judgment, Preliminary Objection
  [1952] ICJ Rep 28 ................................................... 66n.24
*Anglo-Iranian Oil Co (United Kingdom v Iran)*, Judgment, Jurisdiction
  [1952] ICJ Rep 93 ................................................... 66n.22
*Application of the Convention of 1902 governing the Guardianship of Infants*
  *(Netherlands v Sweden)*, Merits, Judgment [1958] ICJ Rep 55 ................. 69n.44
*Application of the Convention on the Prevention and Punishment of the Crime of*
  *Genocide (Bosnia and Herzegovina v Serbia and Montenegro)*, Judgment
  [2007] ICJ Rep 43 .............................................. 123–24n.385
*Application of the Convention on the Prevention and Punishment of the Crime of*
  *Genocide (Bosnia and Herzegovina v Serbia and Montenegro)*, Preliminary
  Objections [1996] ICJ Rep 595 ....................................... 378n.426
*Application of the International Convention on the Elimination of All Forms of*
  *Racial Discrimination (Georgia v Russian Federation)*, Judgment on preliminary
  objections [2011] ICJ GL No 140 ...................................... 69n.47
*Application of the International Convention on the Elimination of All Forms of*
  *Racial Discrimination (Qatar v United Arab Emirates)*, Preliminary objections
  [2021] ICJ 554 .................... 62n.7, 65n.15, 67n.37, 68n.42, 616n.174, 627n.253
*Armed Activities on the Territory of the Congo (the Democratic Republic of the*
  *Congo v Uganda)*, Judgment, Merits [2005] ICJ Rep 168 ............. 334n.178, 402n.556
*Asylum (Colombia v Peru)*, Merits, Judgment [1950] ICJ Rep 266 ........... 67n.37, 270n.55
*Avena and Other Mexican Nationals (Mexico v United States of America),*
  Judgment [2004] ICJ Rep 12 ............................................ 62n.5

*Barcelona Traction, Light and Power Company Limited (New Application, 1962)*
  *(Belgium v Spain)*, Judgment, Merits, Second Phase [1970] ICJ Rep 3 ............ 80n.123
*Border and Transborder Armed Actions (Nicaragua v Honduras)*, Jurisdiction,
  Admissibility [1988] ICJ Rep 396 ...................................... 66n.26

*Case Concerning Rights of Nationals of the United States in Morocco*
  *(France v United States)*, Judgment, Merits [1952] ICJ Rep 176 ........... 67n.37, 69n.50
*Case Concerning the Arbitral Award of 31 July 1989 (Guinea Bissau v Senegal),*
  Judgment [1991] ICJ Rep 53 ............................. 65n.15, 67n.31, 81n.132
*Certain Expenses of the United Nations (Article 17, paragraph 2, of the Charter),*
  Advisory Opinion [1962] ICJ Rep 159 .............................. 67n.32, 72n.65
*Competence of the General Assembly for the Admission of a State to the United Nations,*
  Advisory Opinions [1950] ICJ Rep 8 .................................... 67n.31

## xx  TABLE OF CASES

*Constitution of the Maritime Safety Committee of the Inter-Governmental Maritime Consultative Organization*, Advisory Opinion [1960] ICJ Rep 150 .............. 66n.28
*Corfu Channel (United Kingdom of Great Britain and Northern Ireland v Albania)*, Judgment [1949] ICJ Rep 24 ....................................... 66n.22, 69n.47

*Difference Relating to Immunity from Legal Process of a Special Rapporteur of the Commission on Human Rights*, Advisory Opinion [1999] ICJ Rep 62 ........... 443n.178
*Dispute regarding Navigational and Related Rights (Costa Rica v Nicaragua)*, Judgment [2009] ICJ Rep 213 .................................... 69n.50, 70

*Factory at Chorzów (Germany v Poland)*, Jurisdiction, Judgment [1927] PCIJ Series A No 9 ........................................ 39n.198, 229n.182

*Haya de la Torre Case (Colombia v Peru)*, Merits [1951] ICJ Rep 71. ................. 270n.55

*International Status of South-West Africa*, Advisory Opinion [1950] ICJ Rep 128...... 39n.199
*Interpretation of Peace Treaties with Bulgaria, Hungary and Romania*, Advisory Opinion (Second Phase) [1950] ICJ Rep 221 ................ 66n.24, 69n.48
*Interpretation of the Agreement of 25 March 1951 between the WHO and Egypt*, Advisory Opinion [1980] ICJ Rep 73. ..................................... 462n.278
*Interpretation of the Convention of 1919 Concerning the Employment of Women during the Night*, Advisory Opinion [1932] PCIJ Series A/B No 50 ............... 67n.35

*Jadhav Case (India v Pakistan)*, Merits [2019] ICJ GL No 168. ...................... 67n.31

*Kasikili/Sedudu Island (Botswana v Namibia)*, Judgment, Merits [1999] ICJ Rep 1045 .....69n.46

*Land and Maritime Boundary between Cameroon and Nigeria (Cameroon v Nigeria: Equatorial Guinea intervening)* [1998] ICJ Rep 275 ...............66n.26, 69n.45, 69n.50
*Land, Island and Maritime Frontier Dispute (El Salvador and Nicaragua (intervening) v Honduras)*, Judgment, Merits [1992] ICJ Rep 351 ................ 66n.27
*Legal Consequences for States of the Continued Presence of South Africa in Namibia (South West Africa) notwithstanding Security Council Resolution 276 (1970)*, Advisory Opinion [1971] ICJ Rep 16. ........... 69n.50, 106n.295, 157n.163
*Legal Consequences of the Construction of a Wall in the Occupied Palestinian Territory*, Advisory Opinion [2004] ICJ Rep 136 ................... 323n.123, 402n.556
*Legal Status of Eastern Greenland (Denmark v Norway)*, Judgment [1933] PCIJ Series A/B No 53 ............................................. 74n.88
*Legality of the Threat or Use of Nuclear Weapons*, Advisory Opinion [1966] ICJ Rep 2 ................................................. 67n.36, 378n.427
*Legality of Use of Force (Serbia and Montenegro v Belgium)*, Judgment, Preliminary Objections [2004] ICJ Rep 279 .................................... 67n.31

*Maritime Delimitation in the Area between Greenland and Jan Mayen (Denmark v Norway)*, Judgment [1993] ICJ Rep 38. ........................ 69n.45
*Maritime Delimitation in the Indian Ocean (Somalia v Kenya)*, Preliminary Measures [2017] ICGJ 508 ..................................... 64n.10
*Mavrommatis Palestine Concessions (Greece v United Kingdom)*, Objection to the Jurisdiction of the Court, Judgment [1924] PCIJ Series A no 2 ................ 573n.141
*Military and Paramilitary Activities in and against Nicaragua (Nicaragua v United States of America)*, Jurisdiction, Admissibility [1984] ICJ Rep 392 .........65n.18, 69n.44, 71n.60

TABLE OF CASES    xxi

*Nationality Decrees in Tunis and Morocco* [1923] PCIJ Ser B No 4 .................. 280n.103
*North Sea Continental Shelf Cases*, Judgment [1969] ICJ Rep 3 ............. 34n.175, 35n.183,
73n.83, 156n.161
*Nottebohm Case* (second phase) (Liechtenstein v Guatemala), Judgment
 [1955] ICJ Rep 4 ............................................... .207, 225–26, 229

*Oil Platforms (Iran v United States)*, Judgment, Preliminary Objection
 [1996] ICJ Rep 803 ......................................... 69n.45, 73n.78, 77n.108
*Oil Platforms (Iran v United States)*, Judgment, Merits [2003] ICJ Rep 161 ............. 69n.45,
73n.78, 77n.108

*Pulp Mills on the River Uruguay (Argentina v Uruguay)*, Judgment [2010] ICJ Rep 14 .... 63n.8

*Reparation for Injuries Suffered in the Service of the United Nations*, Advisory
 Opinion [1949] ICJ Rep 174 ............................................ 462n.278
*Reservations to the Convention on the Prevention and Punishment of the Crime
 of Genocide*, Advisory Opinion [1951] ICJ Rep 15 ...................... 70–71, 84–85

*South West Africa (Liberia v South Africa)*, Preliminary Objections, Judgment
 [1962] ICJ Rep 336 ........................... 67n.34, 72n.70, 72n.71, 73n.83, 102n.267
*Sovereignty over Pulau Ligitan and Pulau Sipadan (Indonesia v Malaysia)*
 [2002] ICJ Rep 645 ..................................................... 62n.5
*SS 'Lotus', France v Turkey* (Judgment) [1935] PCIJ Series A No 10 .................. 270n.52

*Territorial Dispute (Libya v Chad)*, Judgment, Merits [1994] ICJ Rep 6 ............... 67n.31
*Tunis and Morocco* (Advisory Opinion) [1923] PCIJ Series B No 4 ..................... 207

*United States Diplomatic and Consular Staff in Tehran (United States v Iran)*,
 Judgment [1980] ICJ Rep 33 .............................................. 66n.23

**Inter-American Court of Human Rights**

*Case of 'Las Dos Erres' Massacre v Guatemala*, Preliminary Objection, Merits,
 Reparations and Costs, Inter-American Court of Human Rights Series C
 No 171 (24 November 2009) ............................................. 446n.191
*Case of Luna Lopez v Honduras*, Merits, Reparations and Costs, Inter-American
 Court of Human Rights Series C No 269 (10 October 2013) .................. 577n.160
*Case of Río Negro Massacres v Guatemala*, Preliminary Objections, Merits,
 Reparations and Costs, Judgment, Inter-American Court of Human Rights
 Series C No 250 (4 September 4 2012) ..................................... 446n.191
*Case of Santo Domingo Massacre v Colombia*, Preliminary objections, Merits and
 Reparations, Inter-American Court of Human Rights Series C No 259
 (24 November 2009) ................................................... 402n.555
*Case of the Kichwa Indigenous People of Sarayaku v Ecuador*, Merits and Reparations,
 Judgment, Inter-American Court of Human Rights Series C No 245
 (27 June 2012) .......................................................... 343–44
*Case of the Yean and Bosico Children v Dominican Republic*, Preliminary Objections,
 Merits, Reparations and Costs, Inter-American Court of Human Rights
 Series C No 130 (8 September 2005) ...................................... 212n.84
*Case of Velásquez Rodríguez v Honduras*, Merits, Inter-American Court of Human
 Rights Series C No 4 (29 July 1988) ...................................... 364n.352
*Mayagna (Sumo) Awas Tingni Community v Nicaragua*, Judgment, Inter-American
 Court of Human Rights Series C No 79 (31 August 2001) ..................... 70n.53

xxii  TABLE OF CASES

*Proposed Amendments to the Naturalisation Provision of the Constitution of Costa Rica*,
  Advisory Opinion OINTER-AM4/84, Inter-American Court of Human Rights
  Series A No 4 (19 January 1984) ......................................... 207n.51
*The Institution of Asylum and its Recognition as a Human Right in the Inter-American
  System of Protection* (Interpretation and Scope of Articles 5, 22.7 and 22.8 in
  Relation to Article 1(1) of the American Convention on Human Rights),
  Advisory Opinion OC–25/18, Inter-American Court of Human Rights
  Series A No 25 (30 May 2018) ................................. 289n.147, 294n.173

European Court of Human Rights

*AA and Others v Sweden* App No 14499/09 (ECtHR, 28 June 2012) ................. 301n.11,
                                                                  435n.136, 436n.144
*AA v Switzerland* App No 58802/12 (ECtHR, 7 January 2014) ..................... 252n.306
*AAM v Sweden* App No 68519/10 (ECtHR, 3 April 2014) ................. 529–30, 531n.325
*Aktaš v Turkey* App No 24351/94 (ECtHR, 24 April 2003) ....................... 158n.170
*Al Sadoon and Mufdhi v United Kingdom* App No 61498/08
  (ECtHR, 4 October 2010) ................................................. 290n.152
*Al-Adsani v the United Kingdom* App No 35763/9 (ECtHR [GC],
  21 November 2001) .............................................. 73n.78, 74n.85
*Appleby and Others v United Kingdom* App No 44306/98 (ECtHR, 6 May 2003) ...... 160n.182
*Aslan and Atifa Muratovic v Denmark* App No 14923/03 (ECtHR,
  19 February 2004) ...................................................... 530–31n.322
*Assenov and Others v Bulgaria* App No 90/1997/874/1086 (ECtHR,
  28 October 1998) ........................................................ 394n.512
*Aydin v Turkey* App No 23178/94 (ECtHR [GC], 25 September 1997) .............. 157n.168

*Baba Ahmad and Others v United Kingdom* Apps Nos 24027/07, 11949/08, 36742/08,
  66911/09, and 67354/09 (ECtHR, 24 September 2012) ........................... 328
*Bankovic v Belgium* App No 52207/99 (ECtHR, 12 December 2001) ................ 577n.160
*Behrami v France & Saramati v France, Germany, and Norway* App Nos 71412/01 &
  78166/01 (ECtHR [GC], 2 May 2007) ......................................... 74n.85
*Biao v Denmark* App No 38590/10 (ECtHR [GC], 24 May 2016) ................... 380n.436
*BKA v Sweden* App No 1161/11 (ECtHR, 19 December 2013) ...................... 530n.313
*Bouyid v Belgium* App No 23380/09 (ECtHR, 28 September 2015) ................ 328n.140

*Catan and Others v Moldova and Russia* Apps Nos 43370/04, 8252/05 and
  18454/06 (ECtHR [GC], 19 October 2012) .................................. 464n.289
*Chahal v United Kingdom* App No 22414/93 (ECtHR, 15 November 1996) .............. 528
*Collins and Akaziebie v Sweden* App No 68411/08 (ECtHR, 17 May 2011) ........ 530–31n.322

*D v United Kingdom* App No 30240/96 (ECtHR, 2 May 1997) ............. 435n.136, 436n.144
*DH and Others v Czech Republic* App No 57325/00 (ECtHR [GC],
  13 November 2007) ...................................................... 339n.211
*DNM v Sweden* App No 28379/11 (ECtHR, 27 June 2013) ............... 439n.159, 530n.320

*Eremia v Moldova* App No 3564/11 (ECtHR, 28 May 2013) ....................... 357n.311
*Ergi v Turkey* App No 23818/94 (ECtHR, 28 July 1998) ......................... 383n.451
*Evans v United Kingdom* App No 6339/05 (ECtHR, 10 April 2007) ................ 160n.182

*F v United Kingdom* App No 17341/03 (ECtHR, 22 June 2004) .................... 160n.183
*FH v Sweden* App No 32621/06 (ECtHR, 20 January 2009) ............... 434n.135, 437n.149
*FN and Others v Sweden* App No 28774/09 (ECtHR, 18 December 2012) ............ 252n.306

TABLE OF CASES     xxiii

*Ghorbanov and Others v Turkey* App No 28127/09 (ECtHR, 3 December 2013) . . . . . . 350n.263
*Golder v the United Kingdom* App No 4451/760 (ECtHR, 21 February 1975) . . . . . . . . . . 73n.79
*Grimailovs v Latvia* App No 6087/03 (ECtHR, 25 June 2013) . . . . . . . . . . . . . . . . . . . . . 360n.328

*Hatton et al v United Kingdom* App No 36027/97 (ECtHR, 8 July 2003) . . . . . . . . . . . . . 176n.267
*Hida v Denmark* App No 38025/02 (ECtHR, 19 February 2004) . . . . . . . . . . . . . . . . 530–31n.322
*Hilal v United Kingdom* App No 45276/99 (ECtHR, 6 June 2001) . . . . . . . . . . . . . . . . . . . . . . 528
*HF and Others v France* App Nos 24384/19 and 44234/20 (ECtHR,
   14 September 2022) . . . . . . . . . . . . . . . . . . . . . . . . . . . . . . . . . . . . . . . . . . . . . . . . . . . . 291n.159
*HLR v France* App No 24573/94 (ECtHR, 29 April 1997) . . . . . . . 431n.114, 434n.135, 437n.149
*Husseini v Sweden* App No 10611 (ECtHR, 8 March 2012) . . . . . . . . . . . . . . . . . . . . . . . 530n.320

*Ibragim Ibragimov v Russia* Apps Nos 1413/08 and 28621/11 (ECtHR,
   28 August 2018) . . . . . . . . . . . . . . . . . . . . . . . . . . . . . . . . . . . . . . . . . . . . . . . . . . . . . . . 610n.137
*Ilascu and Others v Moldova and Russia* App No 48787/99 (ECtHR, 8 July 2004) . . . . . . . . . . 464
*Isayeva, Yusupova, and Bazayeva v Russia* Apps Nos 57947/00, 57948/00, and
   57949/00 (ECtHR, 6 July 2005) . . . . . . . . . . . . . . . . . . . . . . . . . . . . . . . . . . . . 401n.551, 402n.555
*İzzettin Doğan and Others v Turkey* App No 62649/10 (ECtHR, 26 April 2016) . . . . . . . 610n.133

*Jasinskis v Latvia* App No 45744/08 (ECtHR, 21 December 2010) . . . . . . . . . . . . . . . . . 360n.327
*Jersild v Denmark* App No 15890/89 (ECtHR, 23 September 1994) . . . . . . . . . . . . . . . . . . . 74n.85
*JK and Others v Sweden* App No 59166/12 (ECtHR [GC], 23 August 2016) . . . . . 109n.306, 350n.261

*KAB v Sweden* App No 886/11 (ECtHR, 5 September 2013) . . . . . . . . . . . . . . . . . . . . . . 402n.555
*Kart v Turkey* App No 8917/05 (ECtHR [GC], 3 December 2009) . . . . . . . . . . . . . . . . . . . . 72n.71
*Kerimova and Others v Russia* Apps Nos 17170/04, 20792/04, 22448/04, 23360/04,
   5681/05, and 5684/05 (ECtHR, 3 May 2011) . . . . . . . . . . . . . . . . . . . . . . . . . . . . . . . . 402n.555
*Khatsiyeva and Others v Russia* App No 5108/02 (ECtHR, 17 January 2008) . . . . . . . . . 402n.555
*Kokkinakis v Greece* App No 14307/88 (ECtHR, 25 May 1993) . . . . . . . . . . . . 610n.137, 611n.144
*Koua Poirrez v France* App No 40892/98 (ECtHR, 30 September 2003) . . . . . . . . . . . . . 176n.267

*LM and Others v Russia* Apps Nos 40081/14, 40088/14, and 40127/14
   (ECtHR, 15 October 2015) . . . . . . . . . . . . . . . . . . . . . . . . . . . . . . . . . . . . . . . . . . . . . . 401n.551
*Loizidou v Turkey* App No 15318/89 (ECtHR, 18 December 1996) . . . . . . . . . . . . . . . . . 164n.206
*López Ostra v Spain* App No 16798/90 (ECtHR, 9 December 1994) . . . . . . . . . . . . . . . . . . 346–47
*LR v North Macedonia* App No 38067/15 (ECtHR, 23 January 2020) . . . . . . . . . . . . . . 360n.328

*MA v Switzerland* App No 52589/13 (ECtHR, 19 April 2016) . . . . . . . . . . . . . . . . . . 254–55n.316
*Mamatkulov & Askarov v Turkey* App No 46827/99 (ECtHR [GC], 4 February 2005) . . . . . 74n.85
*Mastromatteo v Italy* App No 37703/97 (ECtHR, 24 October 2002) . . . . . . . . . . . . . . . . 702n.242
*ME v Sweden* App No 71398/12 (ECtHR, 26 June 2014) . . . . . . . . . . . . . . . . . . . . . . . . . 531n.323
*MN and Others v Belgium* App No 3599/18 (ECtHR, 5 May 2020) . . . . . . . . . . . . . . . . . . . 291–92
*MSS v Belgium and Greece* App No 30696/09 (ECtHR [GC], 21 January 2011) . . . . . . . . . . . 350
*MYH and Others v Sweden* App No 50859/10 (ECtHR, 27 June 2013) . . . . . . . . . . . . . . 530n.320

*N v Finland* App No 38885/02 (ECtHR, 26 July 2005) . . . . . . . . . . . . . . . . . . . . . . . . . . . 446n.192
*N v United Kingdom* App No 26565/05 (ECtHR [GC], 27 May 2008) . . . . . . . . . . . . . . . 435n.136
*NA v Finland* App No 25244/18 (ECtHR, 14 November 2018) . . . . . . . . . . . 434n.135, 437n.149
*NA v United Kingdom* App No 25904/07 (ECtHR, 17 July 2008) . . . . . . . . . . . . . . . . . . . 111, 391
*NANS v Sweden* App No 68411/10 (ECtHR, 27 June 2013) . . . . . . . . . . . . . . . . . . . . . . . 531n.325
*ND and NT v Spain* Apps Nos 8675/15 and 8697/15 (ECtHR [GC], 13 February 2020) . . . . . 295n.178
*Nencheva and Others v Bulgaria* App No 48609/06 (ECtHR, 18 June 2013) . . . . . . . . . . 360n.327
*NMB v Sweden* App No 68335/10 (ECtHR, 27 June 2013) . . . . . . . . . . . . . . . . . . . . . . . . . 532–33

*Odievfre v France* App No 4236/98 (ECtHR, 13 February 2003). . . . . . . . . . . . . . . . . . . . 160n.182
*Öneryildiz v Turkey* App No 48939/99 (ECtHR [GC], 30 November 2004) . . . 434n.130, 448n.202
*Opuz v Turkey* App No 33401/02 (ECtHR, 9 June 2009) . . . . . . . . . . . . . . . . . . . . . . . .467, 468–69
*Osman v United Kingdom* App No 23452/94 (ECtHR, 28 October 1998) . . . . . . . . . . . .160n.182, 445–46, 702n.242
*Othman (Abu Qatada) v United Kingdom* App No 8139/09 (ECtHR, 9 May 2012) . . . . 372n.394

*Paul and Audrey Edwards v United Kingdom* App No 46477/99 (ECtHR, 14 March 2002) . . . .702n.242
*Pretty v United Kingdom* App No 2346/02 (ECtHR, 29 April 2002) . . . . . . . . . . . . . . . . . 326n.135

*RC v Sweden* App No 41827/07 (ECtHR, 09 June 2010). . . . . . . . . . . . . . . . . . . . . . . . . . 710n.295
*RH v Sweden* App No 4601/14 (ECtHR, 10 September 2015) . . . . . . . . . . . . . . . . . . . . . . .468–69
*Ribitsch v Austria* App No 18896/91 (ECtHR, 4 December 1995) . . . . . . . . . . . . . . . . . 328n.140

*SA v Sweden* App No 66523/10 (ECtHR, 27 June 2013). . . . . . . . . . . . . . . . . . . . . . . . . . 439n.159
*Saadi v Italy* App No 37201/06 (ECtHR [GC], 28 February 2008) . . . . . . . . . . . . . . . . . . 710n.293
*Sadena Muratovic v Denmark* App No 14513/03 (ECtHR, 19 February 2004) . . . . . . . . 531n.323
*Salah Sheekh v the Netherlands* App No 1984/04 (ECtHR, 11 January 2007) . . . . . . 527–28, 532–33
*Savran v Denmark* App No 57467/15 (ECtHR [GC], 7 December 2021) . . . . . 435n.136, 436n.144
*Schuth v Germany* App No 1620/03 (ECtHR, 23 September 2010) . . . . . . . . . . . . . . . . . 160n.182
*Sejdic and Finci v Bosnia and Herzegovina* Apps Nos 27996/06 and 34836/06
  (ECtHR, 22 December 2009) . . . . . . . . . . . . . . . . . . . . . . . . . . . . . . . . . . . . . . . . . . . . . . . . 606
*Selmouni v France* App No 25803/94 (ECtHR, 25 November 1996). . . . . . . . . . . . . . . . 530n.315
*SHH v United Kingdom* App No 60637/10 (ECtHR, 29 January 2013). . . . . . . . . . . . . . 530n.313
*Sigurður A Sigurjónsson v Iceland* App No 16130/90 (ECtHR, 30 June 1993) . . . . . . . . . . 72n.71
*Singh and Ors v Belgium* App No 33210/11 (ECtHR, 2 January 2013) . . . . . . . . . . . . . . 255n.316
*Soering v United Kingdom* App No 14038/88 (ECtHR, 7 July 1989) . . . . . . . . . . . . . . . . . . 74n.85
*Sufi and Elmi v United Kingdom* Apps Nos 8319/07 and 1149/07 (ECtHR,
  18 November 2011) . . . . . . . . . . . . . . . . . . . . . . . . . . . . . . . . . . . . . . . . . . . . . . . . .338, 528, 532
*Sunday Times v United Kingdom* App No 6538/74 (ECtHR, 26 April 1979) . . . . . . . . . 367n.372

*Taskin et al v Turkey* App No 46117/99 (ECtHR, 10 November 2004) . . . . . . . . . . . . . . . 176n.267
*Thampibillai v the Netherlands* App No 61350/10 (ECtHR, 11 October 2011) . . . . . 530–31n.322
*TI v United Kingdom* App No 43844/98 (ECtHR, 7 March 2000) . . . . . . . . . . . . . . . . . . 365n.354
*Tyrer v the United Kingdom* App No 5856/72 (ECtHR, 25 April 1978) . . . . . . . . . . . . . . . 70n.53

*V v the United Kingdom*, App No 24888/94 (ECtHR [GC], 16 December 1999) . . . . . . . . . 72n.71
*Varnava and Others v Turkey* Apps Nos 16064/90, 16065/90, 16066/90 et al
  (ECtHR [GC], 18 September 2009) . . . . . . . . . . . . . . . . . . . . . . . . . . . . . . . . . . . . . . . . 402n.555
*Vincent v France* App No 6253/03 (ECtHR, 24 October 2006) . . . . . . . . . . . . . . . . . . . . 360n.328
*Von Hannover (No 2) v Germany* Apps Nos 40660/08 and 60641/08 (ECtHR,
  7 February 2012). . . . . . . . . . . . . . . . . . . . . . . . . . . . . . . . . . . . . . . . . . . . . . . . . . . . . . . 160n.182

*WM v Denmark* App No 17392/90 (14 October 1992) Commission Decision
  on Admissibility . . . . . . . . . . . . . . . . . . . . . . . . . . . . . . . . . . . . . . . . . . . . . . . . . . . . . . . 291n.161

*X and Y v Netherlands* App No 8978/80 (ECtHR, 26 March 1983) . . . . . . . . . . . . . . . . . 331n.160

*Z and T v United Kingdom* App No 27034/05 (ECtHR, 28 February 2006) . . . . . . . . . . . . . . . 611

**Court of Justice of the European Union**
Case C–135/08 *Rottman v Freistaat Bayern* [2010] ECLI:EU:C:2010:104. . . . . . . . . . . . 254n.314
Case C–234/17 *XC and Others v Generalprokuratur* [2018] ECLI:EU:C:2018:853. . . . . 708n.280

Case C-238/19 *EZ v Bundesrepublik Deutschland* [2020] ECLI:EU:C:2020:945 ...... 706n.268
Case C-255/19 *Secretary of State for the Home Department v O A*
[2021] ECLI:EU:C:2021:36 ............ 112n.326, 165n.211, 194n.339, 467, 680n.96, 727
Case C-280/21 *PI v Migracijos departamentas prie lietuvos Respublikos vidaus
reikalu miniterijos* [2023] EUECJ C-280/21 ........................97n.232, 109n.306,
645n.358, 650n.381, 650n.382
Case INTER-AM285/12 *Aboubacar Diakité v Commissaire général aux réfugiés
et aux apatrides* [2014] ECLI:EU:C:2014:39 .............................. 398n.530
Case C-31/09 *Nawras Bolbol v Bevándorlási és Állampolgársági Hivatal*
[2010] ECR I-05539. .................................... 11n.52, 117–18, 118n.358
Case C-349/20 *NB and AB v Secretary of State for the Home Department*
[2022] ECLI:EU:C:2022:151 ......................................... 11n.52, 707n.274
Case C-353/16 *MP v Secretary of State for the Home Department*
[2018] ECLI:EU:C:2018:276 ....................................... 340n.219, 434n.135
Case C-364/11 *El Kott* [2012] ECLI:EU:C:2012:826 ................. 11n.52, 124n.386
Case C-369/17 *Shajin Ahmed v Bevándorlási és Menekültügyi Hivatal*
[2018] EU:C:2018:713 .................................... 21n.103, 114–15, 119n.364
Case C-369/90 *Mario Vicente Micheletti and others v Delegación del Gobierno
en Cantabria* [1992] ECLI:EU:C:1992:295 ................................ 119n.363
Case C-380/17 *K and B v Staatssecretaris van Veiligheid en Justitie*
[2018] ECLI:EU:C:2018:877 ............................................... 708n.280
Case C-386/08 *Firma Brita GmbH v Hauptzollamt Hamburg–Hafen*
[2010] ECLI:EU:C:2010:91 ...................................... 119n.367, 120n.370
Case C-465/07 *Meki Elgafaji and Noor Elgafaji v Staatssecretaris van Justitie*
[2009] ECLI:EU:C:2009:94 ...................................... 196n.345, 364n.350
Case C-472/13 *Andre Lawrence Shepherd v Bundesrepublik Deutschland*
[2015] ECLI:EU:C:2015:117 ...................................... 87n.175, 373n.399
Case C-473/16 *F v Bevándorlási és Állampolgársági Hivatal*
[2018] ECLI:EU:C:2018:36 .................................................. 666n.8
Case C-481/13 *Criminal proceedings against Mohammad Ferooz Qurbani*
[2014] ECLI:EU:C:2014:2101 .................................... 119n.365, 366n.365
Case C-497/10 *Mercredi v Chaffe* [2010] ECLI:EU:C:2010:829 ................... 282n.110
Case C-507/19 *Bundesrepublik Deutschland v XT* [2021] ECLI:EU:C:2021:3 .......... 11n.52
Case C-542/13 *Mohamed M'Bodj v État belge* [2014] ECLI:EU:C:2014:2452 .......... 340–41,
393n.501, 434n.135
Case C-56/17 *Bahtiyar Fathi v Predsedatel na Darzhavna agentsia za bezhantsite*
[2018] ECLI:EU:C:2018:803 ........................ 118–19n.362, 368n.375, 706n.268
Case C-57/09 *Bundesrepublik Deutschland v B and D* [2010] ECLI:EU:C:2010:661 .... 118n.358,
118–19n.362, 119n.364
Case C-585/16 *Serin Alheto v Zamestnik-predsedatel na Darzhavna agentsia
za bezhantsite* [2018] EU:C:2018:584. ............................. 11n.52, 21n.103
Case C-621/21 *Intervyuirasht organ na DAB pri MS (Femmes victimes de violences
domestiques)* [2023] ECLI:EU:C:2023:314
Case C-63/09 *Axel Walz* [2010] ECLI:EU:C:2010:251 ..................... 62n.7, 119n.366
Case C-635/17 *E v Staatssecretaris van Veiligheid en Justitie* [2019]
ECLI:EU:C:2018:973 ..................................................... 710n.296
Case C-638/16 *X and X, Judgment* [2017] EU:C:2017:173 ........................291–92
Case C-652/16 *Nigyar Rauf Kaza Ahmedbekova and Rauf Emin Ogla Ahmedbekov v
Zamestnik-predsedatel na Darzhavna agentsia za bezhantsite*
[2018] ECLI:EU:C:2018:801 ...................... 386n.466, 638n.315, 680n.97
Case C-720/17 *Mohammed Bilali v Bundesamt für Fremdenwesen und Asyl*
[2019] ECLI:EU:C:2019:448 ................... 21n.103, 53n.261, 119n.364, 249n.295
Case C-756/21 *X v IPAT & anr* [2023] ECLI:EU:C:2023:523 ..................... 707n.274

xxvi    TABLE OF CASES

Case INTER-AM901/19 *CF, DN v Bundesrepublik Deutschland*, Opinion of
   Advocate General Pikamäe [2021] ECLI:EU:C:2021:116..................... 114n.341
Case C–91/20 *LW v Bundesrepublik Deutschland* [2021] ECLI:EU:C:2021:898........53n.261,
   99n.251, 109n.314
Joined Cases INTER-AM148/13 to INTER-AM150/13 *A and Others v Staatssecretaris
   van Veiligheid en Justitie* [2014] ECLI:EU:C:2014:2406........................665–66
Joined Cases C–175/08, C–176/08, C–178/08 and C–179/08 *Salahadin Abdulla
   and Others* [2010] ECR I-0000 ..... 21n.103, 118n.358, 118–19n.362, 216n.111, 699n.226
Joined Cases C–199/12 to C–201/12 *Minister voor Immigratie en Asiel v X and Y
   and Z v Minister voor Immigratie en Asiel* [2013] ECLI:EU:C:2013:720 ..... 118–19n.362, 368
Joined Cases C–391/16, C–77/17 and C–78/17 *M and Others v Commissaire général
   aux réfugiés et aux apatrides* [2019] ECLI:EU:C:2019:403 .........24n.125, 118–19n.362
Joined Cases C–71/11 and C–99/11 *Bundesrepublik Deutschland v Y and Z*
   [2012] ECLI:EU:C:2012:518....................... 99n.251, 173n.251, 333, 376–77,
   611–13, 680n.95, 703, 710n.294

United Nations Treaty Bodies

*Aalbersberg v Netherlands* (12 July 2006) Communication No 1440/2005,
   UN Doc CCPR/C/87/D/1440/2005....................................... 702n.242
*AT v Hungary* (26 January 2005) Communication No 2/2003,
   UN Doc CEDAW/C/36/D/2/2003........................................ 434n.135

*Billy et al v Australia* (22 September 2022) Communication No 3624/2019,
   UN Doc CCPR/C/135/D/3624/2019...................................... 344n.231

*Case of Besim Osmani v Republic of Serbia* (25 May 2009) Communication
   No 261/2005, UN Doc CAT/C/42/D/261/2005 ............................ 331n.158
*Case of Ioane Teitiota v New Zealand* (7 January 2020) Communication
   No 2728/2016, UN Doc CCPR/C/127/D/2728/2016............................. 346
*Case of Mohammad Munaf v Romania* (21 August 2009) Communication
   No 1539/2006, UN Doc CCPR/C/96/D/1539/2006......................... 291n.161
*Case of Natalia Schedko and Anton Bondarenko v Belarus* (3 April 2003)
   Communication No 886/1999, UN Doc CCPR/C/77/D/886/1999............. 331n.158
*Case of Peiris v Sri Lanka* (18 April 2012) Communication No 1862/2009,
   UN Doc CCPR/C/103/D/1862/2009...................................... 367n.371
*Case of Quinteros Almeida v Uruguay* (21 July 1983) Communication
   No 107/1981, UN Doc CCPR/C/19/D/107/1981........................... 331n.158
*Case of Similae Toala v New Zealand* (2 November 2000) Communication
   No 675/1995, UN Doc CCPR/C/70/D/675/1995.................. 374–75n.407, 564n.94
*Case of Sophie Vidal Martins v Uruguay* (2 April 1980) Communication
   No R.13/57, UN Doc Supp No 40 (A/37/40)............................... 564n.94
*Case of Toonen v Australia* (31 March 1994) Communication No 488/1992,
   UN Doc Doc CCPR/C/50/D/488/1992................................... 368n.376
*Case of Velasquez-Rodriguez*, Judgment, Inter-American Court of Human Rights
   Series C No 4 (29 July 1988) ........................................... 710n.293
*Case of Vuolanne v Finland* (2 May 1989) Communication No 265/1987,
   UN Doc CCPR/C/35/D/265/1987................................161n.190, 376–77
*Case of X v Tanzania* (18 August 2017) Communication No 22/2014,
   UN Doc CRPD/C/18/D/22/2014..................................... 360–61n.330
*Case of Y v Tanzania* (31 August 2018) Communication No 23/2014,
   UN Doc CRPD/C/20/D/23/2014..................................... 360–61n.330
*Case of Zephiniah Hamilton v Jamaica* (18 July 1999) Communication
   No 333/1998, UN Doc CCPR/C/66/D/616/1995........................... 360n.328

*Derksen (on behalf of Bakker) v Netherlands* (1 April 2004) Communication
   No 976/2001, UN Doc CCPR/C/80/D/976/2001 .......................... 176n.267

*Naveed Akram Choudhary v Canada* (17 December 2013) Communication
   No 1898/2009, UN Doc CCPR/C/109/D/1898/2009 ............... 431n.114, 434n.135
*Nystrom v Australia* (18 July 2011) UN Doc CCPR/C/102/D/1557/2007 ........... 230n.188

*Pillai et al v Canada* (25 March 2011) Communication No 1763/08,
   UN Doc CCPR/C/101/D/1763/2008 ...................................... 436n.144

*Sacchi et al v Argentina* (8 October 2021) Communication No 104/2019,
   UN Doc CRC/C/88/D/104/2019 ......................................... 346n.243

*Young v Australia* (18 September 2003) Communication No 491/2000,
   UN Doc CCPR/C/78/D/941/2000 ........................................ 176n.267

**Other Courts and Tribunals**

ACmHPR, *Shumba v Zimbabwe*, Communication No 288/2004 (2012). ........... 328n.139
*Award in Arbitration regarding the Iron Rhine ('Ijzeren Rijn') Railway between the
   Kingdom of Belgium and the Kingdom of the Netherlands*, decision of 24 May 2005,
   United Nations, Reports of International Arbitral Awards (UNRIAA),
   vol XXVII (sales No E/F.06.V.8) .......................................... 69n.47

*British Claims in the Spanish Zone of Morocco (Great Britain v Spain)*, decision
   of 1925, United Nations, Reports of International Arbitral Awards
   (UNRIAA), vol II, 615 .................................................. 435n.140
*Canevaro (Italy v Peru)* (1912) Scott 2 Hague Court Reports 284-96 ............... 226n.167
*Case concerning a dispute between Argentina and Chile concerning the Beagle Channel*,
   Report and Decision of the Court of Arbitration [1977] UNRIAA vol XXI ........ 68n.42

*Eritrea-Ethiopia Boundary Commission*, Decision Regarding Delimitation of the
   Border between the State of Eritrea and the Federal Democratic Republic
   of Ethiopia [2002] ....................................... 69–70, 72n.69, 108n.301

*Kabane v Parisi* (Decision of the Austro-German Mixed Arbitral Tribunal)
   Annual Digest of Public International Law Cases, 1929–1930 ................. 229n.182

*Malawi African Association and Others v Mauritania*, African Commission on
   Human and People's Rights, Communication Nos 54/91, 61/91, 98/93, 164/97,
   and 196/97 and 210/98 (2001) 8 IHRR 268 ................................. 564n.94
*Mergé Case (Italy v United States)* [1955] 22 ILR 443, Reports of International
   Arbitral Awards Vol XIV (10 June 1955) 236 .............................. 226n.167
*MOX Plant (Ireland v United Kingdom)*, Provisional Measures
   [December 2001] ITLOS Rep 95 ........................................... 74n.86

*Prosecutor v Blaškić (Tihomir)*, Case No IT-95-14-A, Appeal judgment [2004] ICL 34 ..... 308n.54
*Prosecutor v Naletilic and Martinovic* (Judgment) ICTY-98-34-T (31 March 2003) .... 603n.93

*Responsibilities and obligations of States sponsoring persons and entities with respect
   to activities in the area*, Advisory Opinion, Case No 17 [2011] ITLOS Rep 10 .... 641n.332

*Salem Case (United States v Egypt)* [1932] Reports of International Arbitral
   Awards Vol II (8 June 1932) 1163 ........................................ 226n.167

xxviii   TABLE OF CASES

*Robert John Lynch (Great Britain) v United Mexican States*, decision of
  8 November 1929, United Nations, Reports of International Arbitral
  Awards (UNRIAA), vol V 17. . . . . . . . . . . . . . . . . . . . . . . . . . . . . . . . . . . . . . . . . 450n.220

**Domestic Courts**

*1504584 (Refugee)* [2017] AATA 650 . . . . . . . . . . . . . . . . . . . . . . . . . . . . . . . . . . . . . . 280n.98
*1617142 (Refugee)* [2017] AATA 990 . . . . . . . . . . . . . . . . . . . . . . . . . . . . . . . . . . . . . . 278n.91
*203.332/0-VIII/22/98* [1998]. . . . . . . . . . . . . . . . . . . . . . . . . . . . . . . . . . . . . . . . . . . 355n.294
*6 K 338/17.A* [2017] . . . . . . . . . . . . . . . . . . . . . . . . . . . . . . . . . . . . . . . . . . . . . . . . . 355n.292
*A 11 S 1125/16* [2016]. . . . . . . . . . . . . . . . . . . . . . . . . . . . . . . . . . . . . . . . . . . . . . . . 357n.305

*A v Federal Asylum Review Board*, Case No 2003/20/0111 [2007] . . . . . . . . . . . . . . . . . . . 79n.115
*A-G v Refugee Council of New Zealand Inc* [2003] 2 NZLR 577 (CA). . . . . . . . . . . . . . . . 95n.216
*A4 213.316-0/2008/11E* [2011]. . . . . . . . . . . . . . . . . . . . . . . . . . . . . . . . . . . . . . . . . . 355n.292
*AA (Pakistan) v IPAT & Anor* [2018] IEHC 497 . . . . . . . . . . . . . . . . . . . . . . . . . . . . . 541n.380
*AAAD v Refugee Appeals Tribunal* [2009] IEHC 326 . . . . . . . . . . . . . . . . . . . . . . . . . . . 564n.94
*AAF v Federal Asylum Review Board*, Case No 99/20/0401 [2002]. . . . . . . . . . . . . . . . . . . 79n.115
*Abankwah v INS* [1999] 185 E3d 18 . . . . . . . . . . . . . . . . . . . . . . . . . . . . . . . . . . . . . . . 685n.140
*Abdel-Rahman v Gonzales* [2007] 493 F.3d 444. . . . . . . . . . . . . . . . . . . . . . . . . . . . . . 248n.288
*AC (Egypt)* [2011] NZIPT 800015 . . . . . . . . . . . . . . . . . . . . . . . . . . . . . . . . . . . . . . . 358n.316
*Adan (Lul Omar) v Secretary of State for the Home Department*
   [2001] 2 AC 477 . . . . . . . . . . . . . . . . . . . . . . . . . . . . . . . . . . . . . . . . . . 54n.263, 78n.113
*Adan v Secretary of State for the Home Department* [1997] 2 All ER 723 (CA) . . . . . . . . . . . . . 81
*Adan v Secretary of State for the Home Department* [1999] 1 AC 293 . . . . . 85, 86n.162, 117n.355,
                                                                   122n.380, 184n.293, 399–400
*Adjei v Canada (Minister for Employment & Immigration)*
   [1989] 2 FC 680. . . . . . . . . . . . . . . . . . . . . . . . . . . . . . . . . . . . 679n.85, 708n.282, 708n.285
*AF (Kiribati)* [2013] NZIPT 800413. . . . . . . . . . . . . . . . . . . . . . . . . . . . . . . . . . . . . . . . . . 347
*A-G v Zaoui and Inspector-General of Intelligence and Security*
   [2006] 1 NZLR 289. . . . . . . . . . . . . . . . . . . . . . . . . . . . . . . . . 83n.143, 97n.235, 107n.300
*AG and Others* [2006] EWCA Civ 1342 . . . . . . . . . . . . . . . . . . . . . . . . . . . . . . . . . . . . . 445n.184
*Agartha Smith v The Secretary of State for the Home Department*
   [2000] UK Immigration Appeal Tribunal, Appeal No 00TH02130. . . . . . . . . . . . . 257n.323
*Aguilera-Cota v INS* [1990] 914 F.2d 1375. . . . . . . . . . . . . . . . . . . . . . . . . . . . . . . . . . . 685n.141
*AH (Sudan) v Secretary of State for the Home Department* [2007] 3 WLR 832 . . . . . . 505, 515–17
*AH, GV and NM v SSHD* [2007] EWCA Civ 297 . . . . . . . . . . . . . . . . . . . . . . . . . . . . . 515n.251
*AL (Myanmar)* [2018] NZIPT 801255 . . . . . . . . . . . . . . . . . . . . . . . . . . . . . . . . . . . . . 237n.225
*Al-Harbi v INS* [2001] 242 F3d 882. . . . . . . . . . . . . . . . . . . . . . . . . . . . . . . . . . . . . . . . 685n.141
*Al-Khateeb v Canada (Citizenship and Immigration)* [2017] FC 31 (CanLII) . . . . . . . . . . 280n.96
*Alam v Canada (Minister of Citizenship and Immigration)* [2005] FC 4. . . . . . . . . . . . . 708n.285
*Ali v Canada (Minister of Citizenship and Immigration)* [1996] 119 FTR 258. . . . . . . . 339n.210
*Altawil v Canada (MCI)* [1996] FCJ 986 . . . . . . . . . . . . . . . . . . . . . . . . . . . . . . . . . . . . 574n.145
*Alvarez Lagos v Barr* [2019] No 17-2291. . . . . . . . . . . . . . . . . . . . . . . . . . . . . . . . . . . . 655n.402
*AM & AM (armed conflict: risk categories) Somalia CG* [2008] UKAIT 00091 . . . . . . . . 400n.546
*Amare v Secretary of State for the Home Department* [2005] EWCA Civ 1600 . . . . . . . . . . . . . 379
*AMM and Others (conflict; humanitarian crisis; returnees; FGM) Somalia CG*
   [2011] UKUT 445 (IAC) . . . . . . . . . . . . . . . . . . . . . . . . . . . . . . . . . . . . . . . . . . . . 524n.287
*Appellant S395/2002 v Minister for Immigration and Multicultural Affairs*
   [2003] HCA. . . . . . . . . . . . . . . . . . . . . . . . . . . . . . . . . . . . . . . . . . . . . . 333n.174, 613n.154
*Applicant A v Minister for Immigration and Ethnic Affairs* [1997] 190 CLR 225 . . . . . . . .78n.114,
                  82n.137, 86n.166, 86n.168, 87, 87n.171, 89, 103n.275, 105n.291,
                  113n.331, 122n.380, 162n.198, 188, 189, 381, 618n.618, 621, 633–34, 653

*Applicant S v Minister for Immigration and Multicultural Affairs*
  [2004] 217 CLR 387 . . . . . . . . . . . . . . . . . . . . . . . . . . . . . . . . . . . . . . . . . . . . . . .630–31, 636
*AQ (Myanmar)* [2021] NZIPT 801893. . . . . . . . . . . . . . . . . . . . . . . . . . . . . . . . . . . . 286n.133
*Argentina-Safeguard Measures on Imports of Footwear* [1999] AB–1999-7 . . . . . . . . . . 577n.163
*AS (Afghanistan) v Secretary of State for the Home Department* [2019] EWCA Civ 873 . . . . . .516n.255
*AS (Guinea) v Secretary of State for the Home Department & Anor*
  [2018] EWCA Civ 2234 . . . . . . . . . . . . . . . . . . . . . . . . . . . . . . . . . . . . . . . . . . . . . 709n.290
*Asghar case (Iran v United States)* [1990] 24 Iran-US CTR 242–43. . . . . . . . . . . . . . . . 226n.167
*Assange* [2012] UKSC 22 . . . . . . . . . . . . . . . . . . . . . . . . . . . . . . . . . . . . . . . 72n.69, 108n.301

*B & Ors v SSFCO* [2004] EWCA Civ 1344 . . . . . . . . . . . . . . . . . . . . . . . . . . . . . . . . 291n.161
*Bagdanavicius and Another* [2004] 1 WLR 1207. . . . . . . . . . . . . . . . . . . . . . . . . . . . . . . 427, 433
*Balazoski v Immigration and Naturalization Service* [1991] 932 F.2d 638 . . . . . . . . . 34n.171, 132
*Batayav v Secretary of State for the Home Department* [2003] EWCA Civ 1489 . . . . . . . . . . . . 390
*BG (Fiji)* [2012] NZIPT 800091 . . . . . . . . . . . . . . . . . . . . . . . . . . . . . . . . . . . . . . . 169n.233
*Bhatti v Canada* [1994] 84 FTR 145 . . . . . . . . . . . . . . . . . . . . . . . . . . . . . . . . . . . . . . . . . . 386
*BI (Afghanistan)* [2018] NZIPT 801220. . . . . . . . . . . . . . . . . . . . . . . . . . . . . . . . . . 509n.213
*BJU15 v Minister for Immigration and Border Protection* [2018] FCCA 1296 . . . . . . 698n.218
*Bocova v Gonzalez* [2005] 412 F.3d 257 . . . . . . . . . . . . . . . . . . . . . . . . . . . . . . . . . . . 132n.17
*Bouianova v Canada* [1993] FCJ No 576 . . . . . . . . . . . . . . . . . . . . . . . . . . . . . . . . . . . . .218–19
*Bringas-Rodriguez v Sessions* [2017] 850 F.3d 1051. . . . . . . . . . . . . . . . . . . . . . . 439–40n.162
*Bucur* [1997] 109 F.3d 399 . . . . . . . . . . . . . . . . . . . . . . . . . . . . . . . . . . . . . . . . . . . . 339n.213
*Butler v A-G* [1999] NZAR 205. . . . . . . . . . . . . . . . . . . . 86n.166, 186n.310, 488n.81, 570
*BV (Malaysia)* [2021] NZIPT 801914–916 . . . . . . . . . . . . . . . . . . . . . . . . . . . . . . . . . 278n.91
*BVerwG 1 C 31.18* [2019] . . . . . . . . . . . . . . . . . . . . . . . . . . . . . . . . . . . . . . . . . . . . . 710n.292
*BVerwG 1 C 36/04* [2005] . . . . . . . . . . . . . . . . . . . . . . . . . . . . . . . . . . . . . . . . . . . . . . 79n.115
*BVerwG 10 C 23.12* [2013] . . . . . . . . . . . . . . . . . . . . . . . . . . . . . . . . . . . . 679n.83, 698n.218
*BVerw G 10 C 25.10* [2011] . . . . . . . . . . . . . . . . . . . . . . . . . . . . . . . . . . . . . . . . . . . 700n.231
*BVerwG 10 C 33.07* [2008]. . . . . . . . . . . . . . . . . . . . . . . . . . . . . . . . . . . . . . . . . . . . 710n.292
*BVerwG 10 C 50.07* [2009]. . . . . . . . . . . . . . . . . . . . . . . . . . 247n.280, 282n.113, 283n.120
*BVerwG 9 C 21/00* [2001]. . . . . . . . . . . . . . . . . . . . . . . . . . . . . . . . . . . . . . . . . . . . . . 79n.115
*BVerwG 9 C 36/83* [1983]. . . . . . . . . . . . . . . . . . . . . . . . . . . . . . . . . . . . . . 679n.83, 680n.90
*BVerwG 9 C 434.93* [1994]. . . . . . . . . . . . . . . . . . . . . . . . . . . . . . . . . . . . . . . . . . . . 540n.375
*BZAAH v Minister for Immigration and Citizenship* [2013] FCAFC 72 . . . . . . . 274n.78, 280n.99
*BZADW v Minister for Immigration and Border Protection* [2014] FCA 541. . . . . . . . . . 374n.403

*Cai Luan Chen v Ashcroft* [2004] 381 F.3d 221 . . . . . . . . . . . . . . . . . . . . . . . . . . . . . . 132n.17
*Calado v Minister for Immigration and Multicultural Affairs* [1997] 81 FCR 59 . . . . . . . 606n.110
*Camara v A-G (US)* [2009] 580 F.3d 196 . . . . . . . . . . . . . . . . . . . . . . . . . . . . . . . . . . . . 665n.4
*Canada (AG) v Ward* [1993] 2 SCR 689 . . . . . . . . . . . . . . . . . . .24n.126, 83, 88, 90n.189, 104, 138,
                    223n.151, 365–66, 549, 558, 559, 596–99, 619, 678n.80, 685n.140
*Carranza-Hernandez v INS* [1993] 12 E3d 4 . . . . . . . . . . . . . . . . . . . . . . . . . . . . . . . 685n.140
*Case No 140222 Straravecka* [1999] . . . . . . . . . . . . . . . . . . . . . . . . . . . . . . . . . . . . . . . 679n.88
*Case No 2003/20/0181* [2006] . . . . . . . . . . . . . . . . . . . . . . . . . . . . . . . . . . . . . . . . . . . 79n.115
*Case No 312811 Chiporev* [1997]. . . . . . . . . . . . . . . . . . . . . . . . . . . . . . . . . . . . . . . . . 679n.88
*Cases Nos 210 509 and 210 619/I* [2019]. . . . . . . . . . . . . . . . . . . . . . . . . . . . . . . . . . . 358n.313
*Castro and Carranza-Fuentes v Holder* [2010] 597 F.3d 93 . . . . . . . . . . . . . . . . . . . . . 454n.241
*Castro-Martinez v Holder* [2011] 674 F.3d 1073 . . . . . . . . . . . . . . . . . . . . . . . . . . .439–40n.162
*Cece v Holder* [2013] 733 F.3d 662 (7th Cir) . . . . . . . . . . . . . . . . . . . . . . . . . . . . . . . 636n.311
*Chan v Canada (Minister of Employment and Immigration)* [1995] 3 SCR 593 . . . . . . .108n.305,
                                                          144n.84, 162n.198, 599, 621n.210
*Chan Yee Kin v Minister for Immigration and Ethnic Affairs* [1989] HCA 62. . . . . . 674, 676, 695n.202

*Chehade v Canada (Minister of Citizenship and Immigration)* [2017] FC 282.......... 564n.93
*Chen Shi Hai v Minister for Immigration and Multicultural Affairs*
 [2000] 201 CLR 293 .......... 92n.202, 131n.7, 393–94, 600, 657n.418, 684–85, 688–89
*Chen v Ashcroft* [2004] 113 Fed.Appx.135..................................... 339n.213
*CNDA No 10015655* [2011]............................................... 374n.403
*CNDA No 1102661* [2012]................................................ 280n.97
*CNDA No 16015675* [2017]............................................... 353n.283
*CNDA No 18031476* [2019]............................................... 355n.292
*CNDA Nos 363181 and 363182* [2014]...................................... 280n.98
*CRU18 v Minister for Home Affairs* [2020] FCAFC 129........................... 393n.504
*CV v Immigration and Protection Tribunal and CW v Immigration and Protection*
 *Tribunal* [2015] NZHC 510..........................................381–82n.444

*Dag (Nationality, Country of Habitual Residence, TRNC)* [2001] UKIAT 2........ 276, 279–80,
 281n.104
*Danian v Secretary of State for the Home Department* [1999] EWCA Civ 3000..... 404–5n.573,
 666n.10
*Demirkaya v Secretary of State for the Home Department* [1999] EWCA Civ 1654..... 388n.475
*Dhoumo v Board of Immigration Appeals* [2005] 416 F.3d 172 ..................... 267n.37
*Diatlov v MIMA* [1999] FCA 468........................................... 242n.255
*Doymus v Secretary of State for the Home Department* [2000] Unreported,
 IAT HX/80112/99................................................... 388n.475
*DQU16 v Minister for Home Affairs* [2021] HCA 10............................ 728n.10
*DS (Iran)* [2016] NZIPT 800788................146, 161n.190, 169n.233, 171n.243, 173n.251,
 175, 185n.301, 680n.98
*DT (No 2) v Refugee Appeals Tribunal & Ors* [2012] 1EHC 562 ..................... 247n.280

*E and Another v Secretary of State for the Home Department* [2003] EWCA Civ 1032 .....505n.185
*E1 432.053–1/2013/5E* [2013]............................................. 355n.292
*EB (Ethiopia) v SSHD* [2007] EWCA Civ 809 .................. 248n.288, 374n.403, 564n.94
*EBZ17 v Minister for Immigration and Border Protection* [2019] FCCA 79........... 700n.231
*El Assadi v Holder* [2011] 418 Fed Appx 484 (6th Cir)............................ 282n.110
*El-Ali v Secretary of State for the Home Department* [2002] EWCA Civ 1103 ......... 124n.386
*Elastal v Canada (Minister of Citizenship and Immigration)* [1999] FCJ No 328........ 282n.113
*Elian v Ashcroft* [2004] 370 F.3d 897, 901 (9th Cir)............................. 280n.96
*EMAP (Gang Violence—Convention Reason) El Salvador CG* [2022] UKUT 00335 (IAC) ....641n.333

*Fadli Dyli (Protection-UNMIK-Arif-IFA-Art1D) Kosovo CG* [2000] UKIAT 00001.... 449n.205
*FCS17 v MHA* [2020] FCAFC 68 ................................. 495n.121, 508n.205
*FER17 v Minister for Immigration and Multicultural Affairs* [2019] FCAFC 106 ...... 228n.178
*Fornah v Secretary of State for the Home Department (linked with Secretary of State*
 *for the Home Department v K)* [2006] UKHL 46.......... 81–82, 100, 112n.327, 122n.379,
 125, 127n.391, 625, 634–35, 656
*Fothergill v Monarch Airlines Ltd* [1981] AC 251 ............................... 113n.332
*FV v Refugee Appeals Tribunal & Anor* [2009] IEHC 268 .......................404–5n.573
*FX (Bangladesh)* [2020] NZIPT 801683...................................... 286n.133

*G (Appellant) v G (Respondent)* [2021] UKSC 9 ................................ 24n.125
*Ganze v Canada (Minister for Employment and Immigration)* [1993] FCJ 1062....... 699n.222
*Gashi and Nikshiqi* [1997] INLR 96 ......................................... 137n.50
*GE v The Refugee Appeal Tribunal and The Refugee Applications Commissioner*
 [2018] IEHC 564.................................................. 114n.341

TABLE OF CASES    xxxi

*Gebremedhin v Canada (Immigration, Refugees and Citizenship)* [2017] FC 497 . . . . . . 708n.285
*GM (Eritrea), YT (Eritrea) and MY (Eritrea) v Secretary of State for the
   Home Department* [2008] EWCA Civ 833. . . . . . . . . . . . . . . . . . . . . . . . . . . . . . . . . . . .708–9
*GP and Others (South Korean Citizenship)* [2014] UKUT 00391 (IAC). . . . . . . . . . . . . . 209n.69
*GRF(re), Nos AAO-0145, AAO-01462, AAO-01463* [2001] CRDD No 88. . . . . . . . . . . . 278n.91
*Gutierrez Gomez v Secretary of State for the Home Department*
   [2000] UKIAT 00007 . . . . . . . . . . . . . . . . . . . . . . . . . . . . . . . . . . . . . . . . . . . . . . . .645–47, 648

*Haile v Gonzalez* [2005] 421 F.3d 493. . . . . . . . . . . . . . . . . . . . . . 248n.288, 373–74n.401, 564n.92
*Halder v Canada (Citizenship and Immigration)* [2019] FC 922. . . . . . . . . . . . . . . . . . . 708n.285
*Hariri v Secretary of State for the Home Department* [2003] EWCA Civ 807. . . . . . . . . . . . . 390
*Hernandez-Avalos v Lynch* [2015] 784 F.3d 944  . . . . . . . . . . . . . . . . . . . . . . . . . . . . . . . . 655n.402
*HJ (Iran)* [2011] 1 AC 596 . . . . . . . . . . . . . . . . . . . . . . . . . . . . . . 149n.121, 333n.175, 385, 656n.410
*HJ (Iran) and HT (Cameroon) v Secretary of State for the Home Department*
   [2010] UKSC 31 . . . . . . . . . . . . . . . . . . . . . . . . . . . . . . . . . . . . . . . . . . . . . . . . . . . 704, 708n.283
*Horvath v Secretary of State for the Home Department* [2000] UKHL 37. . . . . . . . . 81, 87, 88, 90,
                                                  90n.189, 165n.208, 184–85, 186, 186n.306,
                                                  415, 419–21, 428–29, 433, 563, 565, 570
*Hou v Canada (MCI)* [2012] FCJ No 1083. . . . . . . . . . . . . . . . . . . . . . . . . . . . . . . . . . . . 404–5n.573
*Hoxha & Anor v Secretary of State for the Home Department* [2002] EWCA Civ 1403 . . . . .311n.64
*HS (Palestinian-return to Gaza) Palestinian Territories CG* [2011] UKUT 124 (IAC) . . . 280n.96
*Hysaj & Ors, R (on the application of) v Secretary of State for the Home Department*
   [2017] UKSC 82 . . . . . . . . . . . . . . . . . . . . . . . . . . . . . . . . . . . . . . . . . . . . . . . . . . . . . . . . 249n.294

*Immigration and Naturalization Service v Cardoza–Fonseca* [1987] 480 US 421  . . . . . . .34n.171,
                                                  103, 132, 675n.62
*Immigration and Naturalization Service v Elias–Zacarias* [1992] 502 US 478. . . . . . . . . . . . 391,
                                                  391–92n.491, 649n.379
*Immigration and Naturalization Service v Stevic* [1984] 467 US 407  . . . . . . . . . . . . . . . .312–13
*In re B (FC) (Appellant) (2002) Regina v Special Adjudicator (Respondent) ex parte
   Hoxha (FC) (Appellant)* [2005] UKHL 19 . . . . 44n.218, 50n.248, 78n.114, 87, 93, 122n.380
*In re Castioni* [1891] 1 QB 149. . . . . . . . . . . . . . . . . . . . . . . . . . . . . . . . . . . . . . . . . . . . . . . . .640–41
*In re Kasinga* [1996] WL 379826. . . . . . . . . . . . . . . . . . . . . . . . . . . . . . . . . . . . . . . . . . . . .393n.501
*In Re SP* [1996] WL 422990 BIA . . . . . . . . . . . . . . . . . . . . . . . . . . . . . . . . . . . . . . . . . . . . . 655n.402
*Islam v Secretary of State for the Home Department Immigration Appeal Tribunal
   and Another, Ex Parte Shah, R v* [1999] UKHL 20  . . . . . . . . . . . . .78n.114, 88n.180, 90n.189,
                                                  90n.191, 122n.380, 394–95

*JA (Child—Risk of Persecution) Nigeria* [2016] UKUT 00560 (IAC) . . . . . . . . . . . . . . . .357n.312
*Jacobellis v Ohio* [1964] 378 US 184  . . . . . . . . . . . . . . . . . . . . . . . . . . . . . . . . . . . . . . . . . . 620n.203
*Januzi v Secretary of State for the Home Department* [2006] UKHL 5. . . . . . . . .81n.125, 82n.137,
                                                  164n.201, 185n.298, 186, 186n.306, 481–82, 487, 502, 515–17
*Jasim v Secretary of State for the Home Department* [2006] EWCA Civ 342  . . . . . . . . . 524n.287
*Jerez-Spring v Canada (Minister of Employment and Immigration)* [1981] 2 FC 527 . . . 647n.370
*Jong Kim Koe* [1997] Aus FFC 1997 . . . . . . . . . . . . . . . . . . . . . . . . . . . . . . . . . . . . . . . . . . . 225n.161
*JV (Tanzania) v SSHD* [2007] EWCA Civ 1532. . . . . . . . . . . . . . . . . . . . . . . . . . . . . . . . . 374n.403

*K v Refugee Status Appeals Authority (No 2)* [2005] NZAR 441 . . . . . . . . . . . . . . . . . . . . .680n.93
*KA v Secretary of State for the Home Department* [2008] UKAIT 00042  . . . . . . . . . . . . 232n.198
*Kadoura v Canada (Minister of Citizenship and Immigration)* [2003] FCJ No 1328. . . . 281n.109
*Kaler v Minister of Employment and Immigration* [1994] FCTD No IMM-794-93. . . . 541n.380
*Karanakaran v Secretary of State for the Home Department*
   [2000] 3 All ER 449. . . . . . . . . . . . . . . . . . . . . . . . . . . . . . . . . . . . . . . 708n.282, 709, 711n.297

xxxii  TABLE OF CASES

*Katkova v Canada (MCI)* [1997] 130 FTR 192 .................................... 228n.178
*Katrinak v Secretary of State for the Home Department* [2001] EWCA Civ 832 ........ 386n.468
*Kaur v Canada (Minister of Citizenship and Immigration)* [2005] FC 1491 (Can FC) ...... .439n.161
*Kazemzadeh v A-G (US)* [2009] 577 F.3d 1341........................... 132n.15, 132n.17
*King v Bristow Helicopters* [2002] 2 AC 628................................ 62n.6, 72n.67
*KK and ors (Nationality: North Korea) Korea CG* [2011] UKUT 92(AC) ............. 209n.69
*Klinko v Minister of Citizenship and Immigration* [2000] 3 FC 327......... 643n.343, 648n.374
*Kotasz v Immigration and Naturalization Service* [1994] 31 F.3d 849................ 398n.532
*KS (benefit of the doubt)* [2014] UKUT 552 (IAC) .............................. 709n.291

*Lay Kon Tji v Minister for Immigration & Ethnic Affairs* [1998] 1380 FCA ...... 216n.112, 225,
228n.178, 250n.298
*Lazarevic v Secretary of State for Home Department* [1997] EWCA Civ 1007........... .313–14
*LK v Director-General, Department of Community Service* [2009] .................. 281n.107
*Long Hao Li v A-G (US)* [2011] 633 F.3d 136. ................................... 367n.370
*Lopes v Canada (Minister of Citizenship and Immigration)* [2010] FCJ 467........... 710n.292
*Luis Alonzo Sanchez-Trujillo and Luis Armando Escobar-Nieto v Immigration
and Naturalization Service* [1986] 801 F.2d 1571 ........................... 634n.295
*Luria v United States* [1913] 231 US 9....................................... 451n.221
*Luu the Truong v Chairman of the Refugee Status Review Bd* [2001] HCAL 3261....... 678n.80
*Lwin v Immigration and Naturalization Service* [1998] 144 F.3d 505 ................ 628n.257

*MA (Ethiopia-Eritrea-Mixed Ethnicity-Dual Nationality) Eritrea*
[2004] UKIA 00324 ..................................................... 228n.178
*MA (Ethiopia) v Secretary of State for the Home Department*
[2009] EWCA Civ 289................................................ 229n.181, 709n.290
*MA (Palestinian Territories) v SSHD* [2008] EWCA Civ 304..................... 280n.96
*MA (Somalia) v Secretary of State for the Home Department* [2010] UKSC 49 .......... 708–9
*Maarouf v Canada (Minister of Employment and Immigration)*
[1994] 1 FC 723................................................... 244n.266, 281n.109
*Mario v Secretary of State for the Home Department* [1998] ...................... 685n.140
*Marquez v Immigration and Naturalization Service* [1997] 105 F.3d 374............. 133n.18
*Matter of Acosta* [1985] A-24159781 ................. 594–95, 596–99, 627–30, 696n.204
*Matter of Mogharrabi* [1987] 19 I&N Dec 439.................................... 678n.81
*Maximilok v Canada (Minister of Citizenship and Immigration)* [1998] FTR 461 .... 247n.284
*Mazariegos v Immigration and Naturalization Service* [2001] 241 F.3d 1320.......... 511n.227
*MB (Internal Relocation—Burden of Proof) Albania* [2019] UKUT 392 (IAC)........ 540n.375
*Mbanza v Secretary of State for the Home Department* [1996] Imm AR 136 ........... 666n.10
*McKeel v Islamic Republic of Iran* [1983] 722 F.2d 582 .............................. 292n.166
*McPherson v Secretary of State for the Home Department* [2001] EWCA Civ 1955...... 422n.66
*Mei Fun Wong v Holder* [2011] 633 F.3D 64...................................... 132n.15
*Mgoian v INS* [1999] 184 F.3d 1029 ........................................... 685n.140
*MI (Fair Trial, Pre Trial Conditions) Pakistan CG* [2002] UKIAT 02239............. 372n.394
*MIEA v Guo* [1997] 191 CLR 559 ........................ 680n.91, 699n.220, 710n.292
*Minister for Immigration and Ethnic Affairs v Guo Wei Rong*
[1997] HCA 22 ................................................. 699n.220, 710n.292
*Minister for Immigration and Ethnic Affairs v Wu Shan Liang*
[1996] 185 CLR 259 ........................................... 700n.231, 711n.297
*Minister for Immigration and Multicultural Affairs v Ibrahim*
[2000] HCA 55 .................................................. 388n.475, 465n.292
*Minister for Immigration and Multicultural Affairs v Khawar*
[2002] 210 CLR 1 (Aus HC) ............................. 267n.38, 271n.63, 561–62

*Minister for Immigration and Multicultural Affairs v Respondents S152/2003*
  [2004] 222 CLR 1 (Aus HC) . . . . . . . . . . . . . . . . . . . . . . . 90n.191, 123n.383, 186n.309, 562
*Minister for Immigration and Multicultural Affairs v Savvin* [2000] 171A OR 483 . . . . . 241n.252
*Minister for Information v Haji Ibrahim* [2000] HCA 55 . . . . . . . . . . . . . . . . . . . . . . . . . 657n.418
*MS (Somalia)* [2019] EWCA Civ 1345. . . . . . . . . . . . . . . . . . . . . . . . . . . . . . . . . . . . . . . . . 50n.248
*MT (Palestininan Territories) v SSHD* [2008] EWCA Civ 304. . . . . . . . . . . . . . . . . . . . . 280n.96

*Najafi v Immigration and Naturalization Service* [1997] 104 F.3d 943 . . . . . . . . . . . . . . . . . . 611
*Ndjizera v Canada (Minister of Citizenship and Immigration)*
  [2013] FC 601 . . . . . . . . . . . . . . . . . . . . . . . . . . . . . . . . . . . . . . . . . . . . . . . . 708n.285, 710n.292
*Negusie v Holder* [2009] 555 US 511 . . . . . . . . . . . . . . . . . . . . . . . . . . . . . . . . . . . . . . . . . . 133n.18

*Okere v Minister for Immigration and Multicultural Affairs* [1998] 87 FCR 112 . . . . . . . . 599n.71
*Olvera v Canada (Minister of Citizenship and Immigration)* [2012] 2012 FC 1048. . . . . 643n.343
*ON v Refugee Appeals Tribunal & Others* [2017] IEHC 13. . . . . . . . . . . . . . . . . . . . . . . . 708n.284
*Oppenheimer v Cattermole (Inspector of Taxes)* [1976] AC 249. . . . . . . . . . . . . . . . . . . . . 210n.76
*Osorio v Immigration and Naturalization Service* [1996] 99 F.3d 928. . . . . . . . . . . . . . . 405n.577

*Paripovic v Gonzales* [2005] 418 F.3d 240. . . . . . . . . . . . . . . . . . . . . . . . . . . . . . . . . . . . . 281n.109
*Pathmakanthan v Holder* [2010] 612 F.3d 618. . . . . . . . . . . . . . . . . . . . . . . . . . . . . . . . . . 132n.17
*Perampalam v Minister for Immigration and Multicultural Affairs* [1999] 84 FCR 274 . . . . .525n.292
*Pham v Secretary of State for the Home Department* [2015] UKSC 19 . . . . . . . . . . . . . . 237n.232
*Prahastono v Minister for Immigration and Cultural Affairs* [1997] 77 FCR 260. . . . . . . 334n.184
*Pushpanathan and Canadian Council for Refugees (intervening) v Minister of Citizenship
  and Immigration, Appeal to Supreme Court* [1998] 1 SCR 982 . . . . . . . . . 88n.180, 103n.275

*QAAH of 2004 v Minister for Immigration & Multicultural & Indigenous Affairs*
  [2005] FCAFC 136. . . . . . . . . . . . . . . . . . . . . . . . . . . . .78n.114, 108n.304, 109n.311, 109n.313,
                                                                    110n.315, 112, 112n.328, 122n.380, 706n.270

*R (on the application of 'B') v Secretary of State for the Foreign and Commonwealth
  Office* [2005] EWCA Civ 1344 . . . . . . . . . . . . . . . . . . . . . . . . . . . . . . . . . . . . . . . . . . 290n.152
*R (Sivakumar) v Secretary of State for the Home Department* [2003] 2 All ER 1097 . . . . . . . . . 657
*R (ST, Eritrea) v Secretary of State for the Home Department* [2012] UKSC 12 . . . . . . . . . 266n.36
*R v Asfaw* [2008] UKHL 31 . . . . . . . . . . . . . . . . . . . . . . . . . . . . . . . . 82n.134, 86n.162, 107n.299
*R v Immigration Appeal Tribunal, ex parte Jonah* [1985] ImmAR 7 . . . . . . . . . . . . . . . . . . 130n.4
*R v Secretary of State for the Home Department, ex parte Adan and Aitsegeur*
  [1999] 3 WLR 1275 . . . . . . . . . . . . . . . . . . . . . . . . . . . . . . . . . . . . . . . . . . . . . . . . . . . . 35n.177
*R v Secretary of State for the Home Department, ex parte Adan*
  [1999] 1 AC 293 . . . . . . . . . . . . . . . . . . . . . . . . . . . . . . . . . . . . . . . . . . . . . 184n.293, 186n.306
*R v Secretary of State for the Home Department, ex parte S Jeyakumaran*
  [1994] Imm AR 45 . . . . . . . . . . . . . . . . . . . . . . . . . . . . . . . . . . . . . . . . . . . . . . . . . . . . 162n.198
*R v Secretary of State for the Home Department, ex parte Sivakumaran and
  Conjoined Appeals* [1988] AC 958 . . . . . . . . . . . . . . . . . 676n.66, 678–79, 698n.218, 708n.281
*R v Secretary of State for the Home Department, Immigration Appeals Tribunal,
  ex parte Anthonypillai Francis Robinson* [1997] Case No FC3 96/7394/D. . . . . . . . 108n.305
*R v Secretary of State for the Home Department, ex parte Milisavljevic*
  [2001] EWHC Admin 203. . . . . . . . . . . . . . . . . . . . . . . . . . . . . . . . . . . . . . . . . . . . . . . 228n.178
*R v Uxbridge Magistrates' Court and Another, ex parte Adimi* [1999] EWHC Admin 765 . . . 109,
                                                                                              109n.311, 121–22
*Radwan v Radwan* [1972] 3 All ER 1026 . . . . . . . . . . . . . . . . . . . . . . . . . . . . . . . . . . . . . . 292n.166
*Ram v Minister for Immigration and Ethnic Affairs* [1995] 57 FCR 565 . . . . . 113n.331, 345n.238

xxxiv  TABLE OF CASES

*Randhawa v Minister for Immigration* [1994] 124 ALR 265.............................481
*Re Minister for Immigration and Multicultural Affairs; ex parte MIAH*
  [2001] HCA 22 ......................................................................678n.80
*Re Minister for Immigration and Multicultural Affairs; ex parte Te*
  [2002] 212 CLR 162 (Aus HC) ...............................................267n.39
*Refugee Appeal No 2067/94* [1996] ..............................................228n.178
*Refugee Appeal No 1/92 Re SA* [1992] NZRSAA 5 .............................281n.109
*Refugee Appeal No 11/91* [1991] NZRSAA .......................... 487n.71, 565n.98
*Refugee Appeal No 1312/93 Re GJ* [1995] NZRSAA .............................631n.279
*Refugee Appeal No 70366/96 Re C* [1997] 4 HKC 236..........................81n.130
*Refugee Appeal No 71322/99* [2000] ............................................228n.178
*Refugee Appeal No 71427/99* [2000] NZRSAA ..................................131n.8
*Refugee Appeal No 71684/99* [2000] INLR 165 ............488n.81, 499n.142, 499n.145, 504,
                                                                   510n.220, 513–14
*Refugee Appeal No 72189/2000* [2000] NZRSAA ...............................344n.236
*Refugee Appeal No 72635* [2002] NZRSAA 33......... 231n.193, 281n.106, 281n.109, 283n.119
*Refugee Appeal No 72668/01* [2002] NZRSAA 11...............................699n.224
*Refugee Appeal No 73512* [2003] NZRSAA 7....................................278n.91
*Refugee Appeal No 74665/03* [2004] NZRSAA....................... 144n.84, 187n.313
*Refugee Appeal No 75694* [2006]................................................228n.178
*Refugee Appeal No 76044* [2008] NZAR 719....................................500, 513–14
*Refugee Appeal No 76339* [2010] NZAR 386...........................638–39, 641n.333
*Refugee Appeal Nos 73861 & 73862* [2005] NZRSAA................... 244n.268, 245n.271
*Regina v Immigration Officer at Prague Airport and Another, ex parte European*
  *Roma Rights Centre* [2004] UKHL 5................ 78n.114, 87n.171, 89n.186, 93n.206,
                    101, 103n.271, 103n.275, 107n.299, 122n.380, 266, 267, 271n.63, 293
*Regina, ex parte Petroff v Turnbull and Ors* [1971] 17 FLR 438......................292n.166
*Revenko v Secretary of State for the Home Department* [2000] EWCA Civ 500 .........78n.114,
                                              122n.380, 240n.245, 269n.49, 274n.74
*Rishmawi v Minister for Immigration and Multicultural Affairs* [1997] 77 FCR 421....242n.257
*RRT Case 1001549* [2010] RRTA 843............................................228n.178
*RT (Zimbabwe) and others v Secretary of State for the Home Department*
  [2012] UKSC 38 .......................................... 173n.251, 600, 708n.283

*S273 of 2003 v MIMIA* [2005] FMCA 983 .........................................680n.91
*Sale v Haitian Centers Council* [1993] 509 US 155 .......................81–82, 107n.299
*Saleh v US Department of Justice* [1992] 962 F.2d 234..............................678n.80
*Samut v Immigration and Naturalization Service* [2000] US App LEXIS 177 ..........382–83
*Sanchez-Jimenez v A-G (US)* [2007] 492 F.3d 1223 ..............................304n.33
*Sandralingham Ravichandran* [1996] Imm AR 97 ............................387–88n.474
*Savchenkov v Secretary of State for the Home Department* [1994] HX/71698/94 .......685n.141
*SB (refugee revocation; IDP camps) Somalia* [2019] UKUT 00358 (IAC)...............50n.248
*Secretary of State for the Home Department v Al-Jedda* [2013] UKSC 62..................218
*Secretary of State for the Home Department v SP (North Korea) and Others*
  [2012] EWCA Civ 114.........................................................209n.69
*Sepet and Bulbul v Secretary of State for the Home Department*
  [2003] UKHL 15.................................78n.113, 86n.164, 92–93, 100, 316
*Shi Liang Lin v US Dept of Just* [2007] 494 F.3d 296 .............................132n.17
*Sidhu v British Airways* [1997] AC 430.........................................113n.332
*Sivagnanam v Canada (Citizenship and Immigration)* [2019] FC 1540 ...............708n.285
*SN (Ghana) v International Protection Appeals Tribunal* [2019] IEHC 10............114n.341
*SR (Iran) v Secretary of State for the Home Department* [2007] EWCA Civ 460 .......709n.290
*SSHD v SC (Jamaica)* [2017] EWCA Civ 2112 ...................................540n.375
*Subramanian v Immigration Appeal Tribunal* [2000] Imm AR 173 ..................679n.89

*Surajnarain and Others v Minister of Citizenship and Immigration* [2008] FC 1165. . . . 401n.550
*SW (lesbians—HJ and HT applied) Jamaica CG* [2011] UKUT 00251 (IAC) . . . . . . . . . 355n.291
*SW v Federal Asylum Authority* [1998] 201.440/0–II/04/98 (Au UBAS). . . . . . . . . . . . . 282n.113
*SZATV v Minister for Immigration and Citizenship* [2007] 233 CLR 18. . . . . . . . . . . . . . 186n.312,
480–81, 487n.73, 562
*SZEOH v Minister for Immigration* [2005] FMCA 1178. . . . . . . . . . . . . . . . . . . . . . . . . . . 278n.91
*SZFDV v Minister for Immigration and Citizenship* [2007] 237 ALR 660. . . . . . . . . . . . . 487n.73
*SZJZN v Minister for Immigration and Citizenship* [2008] FCA 519. . . . . . . . . . . . . . . . . 666n.10
*SZOUY & Ors v Minister for Immigration* [2011] FMCA 347 . . . . . . . . . . . . . . . . . . . . . 228n.178
*SZTEQ v MIBM* [2015] FCAFC 39. . . . . . . . . . . . . . . . . . . . . . . . . . . . . . . . . . . . . . . . . . . 728n.14
*SZUNZ v Minister for Immigration and Border Protection* [2015] FCAFC 32 . . . . . 280n.98, 282n.113
*SZVKA v Minister for Immigration and Border Protection* [2017] 320 FLR 453 . . . . . . . 699n.223
*SZVYD v Minister for Immigration and Border Protection* [2019] FAC 648. . . . . . . . . . 370n.388

*Tahiri v Minister for Immigration and Citizenship* [2012] HCA 61. . . . . . . . . . . . . . . . . . . . . . 281
*Tarakhan v Canada (Minister of Citizenship and Immigration)* [1995] 105 FTR 128 . . . . 282n.110
*Tesfamichael v MIMA* [1999] FCA 1661 . . . . . . . . . . . . . . . . . . . . . . . . . . . . . . . . . . . . . . 564n.93
*Thabet v Canada (Minister of Citizenship and Immigration)* [1998] 4 FC 21 . . . . . . . . 283, 284–86
*The Secretary of State for the Home Department v MA (Somalia)*
[2018] EWCA Civ 994. . . . . . . . . . . . . . . . . . . . . . . . . . . . . . . . . . . . . . . . . . . . . . . . . 110n.318
*Thiel v Federal Commissioner of Taxation* [1990] 171 CLR 338. . . . . . . . . . . . . 78n.114, 122n.380
*Thirunavukkarasu v Canada (Minister of Employment and Immigration)*
[1994] 1 FC 589. . . . . . . . . . . . . . . . . . . . . . . . . . . . . . 487n.71, 495n.121, 541n.380, 565n.98
*Thompson v Secretary of State for the Home Department*, HX/78032/1996
(unpublished) . . . . . . . . . . . . . . . . . . . . . . . . . . . . . . . . . . . . . . . . . . . . . . . . . . . . . . . . 685n.142
*Tjhe Kwet Koe v Minister for Immigration and Ethnic Affairs*
[1997] 78 FCR 289 (Aus FC). . . . . . . . . . . . . . . . . 267n.41, 273–74, 275, 279–80, 280n.100
*Tretsetsang v Canada (Citizenship and Immigration)* [2016] FCJ No 615,
2016 FCA 175 . . . . . . . . . . . . . . . . . . . . . . . . . . . . . . . . . . . . . . . . . . . . . . . . . . . . . . . 219n.130

*US-UK Heathrow Airport Charges Arbitration* [1992] 102 ILR 215 . . . . . . . . . . . . . . . . 581n.172
*USA, Federal Reserve Bank v Iran, Bank Markazi Case A28* [2000-02] IUSCT Rep 5 . . . . . 581n.172

*Varga v Canada (Minister of Citizenship and Immigration)* [2013] FC 494 . . . . . . . . . . . 711n.297
*VwGH 95/20/0295* [1996] . . . . . . . . . . . . . . . . . . . . . . . . . . . . . . . . . . . . . . . . . . . . . . . . . 541n.381

*WA (Pakistan) v Secretary of State for the Home Department* [2019] EWCA Civ 302 . . . . . 613n.154
*Wackowski v Immigration and Naturalization Service* [1999] US App LEXIS 26590 . . . 397n.524
*Wiesbaden (Administrative Court in Wiesbaden)* [1983] IV/I E 06244/81. . . . . . . . . . . . 625n.239
*Williams v Canada (Minister of Citizenship & Immigration)* [2001] FCJ No 827 (TD) . . . . . . 219n.130

*X v Commissaire général aux réfugiés et aux apatrides* [2009] arrêt no 22144 . . . . . . . . . . 564n.92

*YB (Eritrea) v SSHD* [2008] EWCA Civ 360 . . . . . . . . . . . . . . . . . . . . . . . . . . . . . . . . . 404–5n.573
*YL (Nationality-Statelessness-Eritrea-Ethiopia) Eritrea CG* [2003] UKIAT 00016 . . . . . 281n.109
*YMKA ('Westernisation') Iraq* [2022] UKUT 16 (IAC) . . . . . . . . . . . . . . . . . . . . . . . . . . 612n.149
*Yugraneft Corp v Rexx Management Corp* [2010] 1 SCR 649. . . . . . . . . . . . . . . . . . . . . . 113n.332
*Yusuf v Canada* (Minister of Employment and Immigration) [1992] 1 FC. . . . . . . . . . . . 685n.142

*Zalzali v Canada (Minister of Employment and Immigration)* [1991] 3 FC 605 . . . . . . . . . . . . 549
*Zgnat'ev v Minister for Justice, Equality & Law Reform* [2001] IEHC 105 . . . . . . . . . . . . 678n.80
*Zolfagharkhani v Canada (Minister for Employment & Immigration)*
[1993] FCJ No 584 . . . . . . . . . . . . . . . . . . . . . . . . . . . . . . . . . . . . . . . . . . . . . . . . . . . 370n.387

# Table of Legislation

African Charter on Human and Peoples' Rights (adopted 28 June 1981, entered into force 21 October 1986) ... 413–14n.15

African Union Convention for the Protection and Assistance of Internally Displaced Persons in Africa (Kampala Convention) (adopted 23 October 2009, entered into force 6 December 2012).... 521n.270

Agreement by the Government of the United Kingdom of Great Britain and Northern Ireland, the Government of the United States of America, the Provisional Government of the French Republic and the Government of the Union of Soviet Socialist Republics for the prosecution and punishment of the major war criminals of the European Axis (adopted 8 August 1945, entered into force 8 August 1945) 82 UNTS 280................... 301n.11

American Convention on Human Rights (adopted 22 November 1969, entered into force 18 July 1978)........... 208n.57

Arab Convention on Regulating Status of Refugees in the Arab Countries (1994)......................... 22

Constitution of the International Refugee Organization (adopted 15 December 1946, entered into force 20 August 1948) 18 UNTS 3....264, 298–302, 551, 552–53, 592n.31, 604, 614, 639, 640, 668–69

Convention Against Torture and Other Cruel, Inhuman or Degrading Treatment or Punishment (adopted 10 December 1984, entered into force 26 June 1987) 1465 UNTS 85................324–25, 527–28n.302, 702n.243

Convention on Diplomatic Asylum (adopted 28 March 1954, entered into force 29 December 1954) .........294n.172

Convention on Rights and Duties of States adopted by the Seventh International Conference of American States (adopted 26 December 1933) 165 LNTS 19.................. 452n.230

Convention on the Elimination of All Forms of Discrimination against Women (adopted 18 December 1979, entered into force 3 September 1981) 1249 UNTS 13 ..... 101–2, 351–52, 353n.279

Convention on the Nationality of Married Women (adopted 20 February 1957, entered into force 11 August 1958) 309 UNTS 65.... 206–7

Convention on the Reduction of Cases of Multiple Nationality and on Military Obligations in Cases of Multiple Nationality (adopted 6 May 1963, entered into force 28 March 1968) ETS No 043.... 206–7, 209n.67

Convention on the Reduction of Statelessness (adopted 30 August 1961, entered into force 13 December 1975) 989 UNTS 175..... 48, 206–7, 255n.320

Convention on the Rights of Persons with Disabilities (adopted 13 December 2006, entered into force 3 May 2008) 2515 UNTS 3...... 358–59

Convention on the Rights of the Child (adopted 20 November 1989, entered into force 2 September 1990) 1577 UNTS 3 ..... 176n.266, 211, 357, 401–2n.554

Convention Relating to the Status of Refugees (adopted 28 July 1951, entered into force 22 April 1954) 189 UNTS 137....... v, 2, 8, 77, 200, 261
Article 1A(1)................. 9–10, 309
Article 1A(2)..... 2, 7–8, 9, 14, 26, 181–82, 300, 309, 310, 319, 442–43, 445, 449, 458, 545–46, 548–49, 587, 673–74, 705, 727

Article 1B.................... 26, 310
Article 1C....... 26, 93n.206, 268, 310–11,
    413, 442–43, 565–66, 568–69,
    675, 698, 699–700
Article 1D ....... 10–11, 26, 311, 458–345
Article 1E...... 26, 213n.87, 216, 230, 311
Article 1F.... 47n.238, 118n.358, 263n.17,
    311, 637–38, 640–41
Article 33........ .8, 106, 212, 241, 268–69,
    288–89, 292–93, 312–14, 319, 413,
    538–39, 562, 569, 654, 675, 705
Article 35........ 39–40, 108–11, 121–22,
    732, 740–41, 742
Article 38......... 39–40, 121–22, 739–40
Convention Relating to the Status of
    Stateless Persons (adopted 28
    September 1954, entered into force
    6 June 1960) 360 UNTS 117 ........ 48,
    206–7, 218n.128
Convention to Reduce the Number of
    Cases of Statelessness (adopted
    13 September 1973) ........... 209n.66
Council Directive 2004/83/EC of 29
    April 2004 on minimum standards
    for the qualification and status of
    third country nationals or stateless
    persons as refugees or as persons
    who otherwise need international
    protection and the content of the
    protection granted [2004]
    OJ L 304/12 ............... 20, 134n.24
Council of Europe Convention on the
    avoidance of statelessness in relation
    to State succession (adopted 19 May
    2006, entered into force 1 May 2009)
    CETS No 200 ................... 274n.75
Council of Europe Convention on
    preventing and combating violence
    against women and domestic
    violence (adopted 11 May 2011,
    entered into force 1 August 2014)
    CETS No 210................. 351n.267
Directive 2011/95/EU of the European
    Parliament and of the Council
    of 13 December 2011 on
    standards for the qualification
    of third-country nationals or
    stateless persons as beneficiaries
    of international protection, for
    a uniform status for refugees or
    for persons eligible for subsidiary
    protection, and for the content of

the protection granted
    (recast) [2011] OJ L 337/9
    ("EU Qualification Directive"
    or QD) ...... .v, 20–21, 99–100, 117, 134,
    138, 165, 166–67, 171–72, 195–96,
    216n.111, 252–53, 255n.316
Article 2(d) .............. 20–21, 79n.118
Article 2(e).................... 118n.358
Article 4 .... 404, 405, 696, 697, 706–7, 729
Article 5 ....................... 403–4
Article 6 ................ 340–41, 365–66
Article 7 ........ 428–29, 448, 459–60, 502
Article 8 ............... 477–78, 502, 729
Article 9 ....... 300–1, 331, 338, 352, 368,
    371, 373, 376–77, 387, 725
Article 10 ......... 602, 604, 609, 611–12,
    614–15, 624, 626–27, 645, 650, 659
Directive 2013/32/EU of the European
    Parliament and of the Council of 26
    June 2013 on common procedures
    for granting and withdrawing
    international protection [2013]
    OJ L 180 ............. 159n.179, 294–95
European Convention on Human
    Rights (adopted 4 November
    1950, entered into force
    3 September 1953).
Article 3 ...... 326–27, 328, 391, 427, 434,
    467, 505, 516, 528–29, 531–34
European Convention on Nationality
    (adopted 6 November 1997,
    entered into force 1 March 2000)
    ETS 166............... 206–7, 209, 254
Geneva Convention for the Amelioration
    of the Condition of the Wounded
    in Armies in the Field (22 August
    1864)........................ 591n.20
Geneva Convention relative to the
    protection of civilian persons in
    time of war (adopted 12 August
    1949, entered into force 21 October
    1950) 75 UNTS 287 ........... 301n.11
Instrumentos Regionales sobre
    Refugiados y temas relacionados,
    Declaración de Cartagena sobre
    Refugiados, Adoptado por el
    "'Coloquio Sobre la Protección
    Internacional de los Refugiados en
    América Central, México y Panamá:
    Problemas Jurídicos y Humanitarios"'
    (adopted 22 November 1984).......... 17,
    19–20, 214n.95, 261

International Convention on Maritime Search and Rescue (adopted 27 April 1979, entered into force 22 June 1985) 1405 UNTS 119. . . . 270n.57
International Convention on the Elimination of all Forms of Racial Discrimination (adopted 21 December 1965, entered into force 4 January 1969) 660 UNTS 19. . . . 101–2, 378n.428, 432n.122, 605–6, 614–15, 616
International Convention on the Suppression and Punishment of the Crime of Apartheid (adopted 30 November 1973, entered into force 18 July 1976) 1015 UNTS 243 . . . . . . . . . . . . . . . . . . . . 605–6
International Covenant on Civil and Political Rights (adopted 16 December 1966, entered into force 23 March 1976) 999 UNTS 171. . . . . . . 77, 143, 151, 154, 161, 169, 175–76, 177–78, 211, 342, 614–15
  Article 6 . . . . . . . 322–23, 335, 346, 384, 700
  Article 7 . . . . . . . . . . 324, 328, 331, 533, 534
  Article 18 . . . . . . . . . . . . . . . . . . . . . . . . . 608
International Covenant on Economic, Social and Cultural Rights (adopted 16 December 1966, entered into force 3 January 1976) 993 UNTS 3. . . . . . . 77, 143, 151, 154, 336, 337, 338–39, 340, 342
League of Nations, Additional Protocol to the Arrangement of the Convention concerning the Status of Refugees from Germany (14 September 1939) 198 LNTS 141 . . . . . 10
League of Nations, Arrangement Concerning the Extension to Other Categories of Certain Measures Taken in Favour of Russian and Armenian Refugees (30 June 1928) 89 LNTS 63 . . . . . . . . . 10
League of Nations, Arrangement Relating to the Issue of Identify Certificates to Russian and Armenian Refugees (12 May 1926) 89 LNTS 47 . . . . . . . . . . . . . . . . . . . . . . 10
League of Nations, Convention concerning the Status of Refugees Coming From Germany (10 February 1938) 192 LNTS 59 . . . . . . . 10, 234n.212

League of Nations, Convention on Certain Questions Relating to the Conflict of Nationality Law (adopted 13 April 1930, entered into force 1 July 1937) 179 LNTS 89, No 4137 . . . . . . . . . . . . . . . . . .206n.39
League of Nations, Convention Relating to the International Status of Refugees (28 October 1933) 159 LNTS 3663. . . . . . . . . . . . . . . . . .668n.19
League of Nations, Protocol Relating to a Certain Case of Statelessness (adopted 12 April 1930, entered into force 1 July 1937) 179 LNTS 115, No 4138 . . . . . . . . . . . . . . . . .206n.41
League of Nations, Provisional Arrangement concerning the Status of Refugees Coming from Germany (4 July 1936) 171 LNTS 395. . . . . . . . . . . 10
Nuremberg Charter (Charter of the International Military Tribunal) (adopted 8 August 1945) . . . . . . . . . . 301
Optional Protocol to the International Covenant on Civil and Political Rights (adopted 16 December 1966, entered into force 23 March 1976). . . . . . . . . . . . . .439n.160
Organization of African Unity (OAU), Convention Governing the Specific Aspects of Refugee Problems in Africa (adopted 10 September 1969, entered into force 20 June 1974) 1001 UNTS 45 ("OAU Convention"). . . . . . . . . . 17, 19, 214n.95, 261, 476–77
Protocol Relating to the Status of Refugees (adopted 31 January 1967, entered into force 4 October 1967) 606 UNTS 267 . . . . 2, 12, 261, 271
Regulation (EU) 2021/2303 of the European Parliament and of the Council of 15 December 2021 on the European Union Agency for Asylum and repealing Regulation (EU) No 439/2010 [2021] OJ L 468/1 . . . . . . . . . . . . . . . . . . .52n.257
Statute of the International Court of Justice (1945) TS No 993 . . . 115, 153–54
Statute of the International Criminal Court (adopted 17 July 1998, entered into force 1 July 2002) 2187 UNTS 90. . . . . . . . . . . . . 101, 308–9

Statute of the Office of the United
    Nations High Commissioner for
    Refugees (1950) . . . . . . . 13n.60, 672n.42
Treaty on the Functioning of the
    European Union (TFEU)
    [2016] OJ C202/1 . . . . . . . . . . . .118n.358
United Nations Convention on the Law
    of the Sea (adopted 10 December
    1982, entered into force 16
    November 1994) 1833 UNTS
    3 (UNCLOS). . . . . . . . . . . . . . . . .270n.57
Universal Declaration of Human
    Rights (adopted 10 December
    1948) UNGA Res
    217 A(III). . . . . . . . . . . . . . . 83, 135n.31,
        151–53, 207, 384, 413–14n.15, 591
Vienna Convention on Diplomatic
    Relations (adopted 18 April 1961,
    entered into force on
    24 April 1964) . . . . . . . . . . 290, 291n.155,
        547n.5, 574n.147
Vienna Convention on the Law of
    Treaties (adopted 23 May 1969,
    entered into force 27 January 1980)
    1155 UNTS 331. . . . . . . 4n.12, 7, 27, 130,
        151–55, 179, 213, 260, 291n.155
- Article 27. . . . . . . . . . . . . . . . . . . . .78n.113
- Article 31 . . . 63, 64–70, 71, 148–49, 157, 266
- Article 31(2) . . . . . . . . . . . . . . . . . . . 83–84
- Article 31(3) . . . .153–54, 271–72, 279–81
- Article 31(3)(b). . . . . . . . . . . . . . . 95–100
- Article 31(3)(c). . . . . . . . . . . . . . . . 73–74
- Article 31(4) . . . . . . . . . . . . . . . . . . . . . 74
- Article 32. . . . . . 63, 64–65, 74–75, 103–6,
        148–49, 154–55
- Article 33. . . . . . . . . . . . . . . 63–64, 76–77

# List of Commonly Used Acronyms

| | |
|---|---|
| 1954 Convention or CSSP54 | 1954 Convention Relating to the Status of Stateless Persons |
| 1967 Protocol | 1967 Protocol Relating to the Status of Refugees |
| AALCO | Asian-African Legal Consultative Organization |
| CEDAW | Convention on the Elimination of All Forms of Discrimination Against Women |
| CERD | Convention on the Elimination of All Forms of Racial Discrimination |
| CJEU | Court of Justice of the European Union |
| COI | Country of Origin Information |
| CRC | Convention on the Rights of the Child |
| CRS61 | 1961 Convention on the Reduction of Statelessness |
| EASO | European Union Agency for Asylum |
| ECHR | European Convention on Human Rights |
| ECOSOC | Economic and Social Council |
| ECtHR | European Court of Human Rights |
| EWCA | England and Wales Court of Appeal |
| ExCom | UNCHR's Executive Committee |
| HRC | United Nations Human Rights Committee |
| IACtHR | Inter-American Court of Human Rights |
| IARLJ | International Association of Refugee Law Judges |
| IARMJ | The International Association of Refugee and Migration Judges |
| ICCPR | International Covenant on Civil and Political Rights |
| ICESCR | International Covenant on Economic, Social and Cultural Rights |
| ICJ | International Court of Justice |
| IDP | Internally Displaced People |
| IFA | Internal Flight Alternative |
| IHRL | International Human Rights Law |
| ILC | International Law Commission |
| IPA | Internal Protection Alternative |
| IRL | International Refugee Law |
| IRO | International Refugee Organisation |
| MPSG | Membership of a Particular Social Group |
| NPA | National Protection Alternative |
| NZRSAA | New Zealand Refugee Status Appeals Authority |
| OAU | Organisation of African Unity |
| PCIJ | Permanent Court of International Justice |
| PSG | Particular Social Group |
| QD (recast) | Directive 2011/95/EU of the European Parliament and of the Council of 13 December 2011 on standards for the qualification of third-country nationals or stateless persons as beneficiaries of international protection, for a uniform status for refugees or for persons eligible for subsidiary |

| | |
|---|---|
| | protection, and for the content of the protection granted (recast) [2011] OJ L 337/9 |
| Refugee Convention or CRSR | 1951 Convention Relating to the Status of Refugees |
| RSD | Refugee Status Determination |
| The Hague Convention | 1930 Convention on Certain Questions Relating to the Conflict of Nationality Law |
| TLRS | James C Hathaway, *The Law of Refugee Status* (Butterworths Limited 1991) |
| TLRS2 | James C Hathaway and Michelle Foster, *The Law of Refugee Status* (2nd edn, CUP 2014) |
| UDHR | Universal Declaration of Human Rights |
| UNGA | United Nations General Assembly |
| UNHCR | United Nations High Commissioner for Refugees |
| UNHCR 1979 Handbook | Handbook on Procedures and Criteria for Determining Refugee Status |
| UNHCR Guidelines | UNHCR Guidelines on International Protection under the 1951 Convention and the 1967 Protocol Relating to the Status of Refugees |
| UNSC | United Nations Security Council |
| VCLT | 1969 Vienna Convention on the Law of Treaties |

# 1
# The Refugee Definition

| | | | |
|---|---|---|---|
| 1 | Aims of the Book | 2 | |
| 2 | The Refugee Definition in International Law | 8 | |
| | 2.1 The Refugee Convention and/or its 1967 Protocol | 8 | |
| |    2.1.1 Article 1A(2) refugee | 8 | |
| |    2.1.2 Article 1A(1) 'statutory' refugee | 9 | |
| |    2.1.3 Refugee assisted by other UN Agencies | 10 | |
| |    2.1.4 Recommendation E refugees | 11 | |
| |    2.1.5 Protocol relating to the Status of Refugees, 4 October 1967 | 12 | |
| | 2.2 The UNHCR Statute and Related Definitions | 13 | |
| |    2.2.1 Refugees under the Statute of the Office of the United Nations High Commissioner for Refugees (UNHCR Statute) | 13 | |
| |    2.2.2 'Persons of concern' to UNHCR and refugees | 14 | |
| |    2.2.3 UNHCR's 'good offices' and refugees | 15 | |
| |    2.2.4 Wider UNHCR understandings of the term 'refugee' | 17 | |
| | 2.3 Regional Definitions of Refugee | 19 | |
| |    2.3.1 Organisation of African Unity Convention (OAU Convention), 1969 | 19 | |
| |    2.3.2 Cartagena Declaration, 1984 | 19 | |
| |    2.3.3 EU Qualification Directive, 2004 and recast 2011 | 20 | |
| |    2.3.4 Bangkok Principles on the Status and Treatment of Refugees, December 1966 (Bangkok Principles) | 21 | |
| |    2.3.5 League of Arab States, Arab Convention on Regulating Status of Refugees in the Arab Countries, 1994 | 22 | |
| | 2.4 National Definitions of Refugee | 22 | |
| 3 | Limits of the Refugee Definition | 25 | |
| | 3.1 Temporal and Geographical Limitations? | 26 | |
| | 3.2 Exclusion and Cessation Clauses | 26 | |
| | 3.3 Limitations Inherent in Article 1A(2) Definition | 26 | |
| | 3.4 Limitations Imposed by International Law Framework (VCLT) | 27 | |
| 4 | Criticisms of the Refugee Definition | 27 | |
| | 4.1 Eurocentrism | 27 | |
| | 4.2 State-centrism | 28 | |
| | 4.3 Colonialist Roots | 28 | |
| | 4.4 Age and Gender Insensitivities | 29 | |
| | 4.5 Territorial Bias | 30 | |
| | 4.6 Perceived Need for Complementary Protection Regimes | 31 | |
| | 4.7 Ethical and Moral Drawbacks | 31 | |
| | 4.8 Perceived Redundancy and 'Under-Protectiveness' | 31 | |
| | 4.9 Lack of Any Treaty Monitoring or Similar Mechanism to Ensure Consistency/Convergence | 32 | |
| 5 | Problems of Definition | 33 | |
| | 5.1 Known Identity of the Definition's Beneficiaries? | 33 | |
| | 5.2 The Fact that a Definition Already Exists? | 34 | |
| | 5.3 Deliberate Vagueness? | 35 | |
| | 5.4 Further Definition Intrinsically Restrictive? | 37 | |
| | 5.5 The Notion of a 'Working Definition' | 37 | |
| 6 | The Refugee Definition and Existing Learning | 38 | |
| | 6.1 The Pillar of UNHCR Guidance | 39 | |
| |    6.1.1 UNHCR Handbook, 1979 | 41 | |
| |    6.1.2 ExCom Conclusions on the International Protection of Refugees | 44 | |
| |    6.1.3 UNHCR note, Interpreting Article 1 of the 1951 Convention Relating to the Status of Refugees, 2001 | 45 | |
| |    6.1.4 Guidelines on International Protection | 47 | |
| | 6.2 Case Law and the Judicial Pillar | 51 | |
| | 6.3 National Governmental Guidance | 53 | |
| | 6.4 Academic Guidance | 54 | |

*The Refugee Definition in International Law.* Hugo Storey, Oxford University Press. © Hugo Storey 2023.
DOI: 10.1093/oso/9780198842644.003.0001

| | | | | |
|---|---|---|---|---|
| 7 Methodology and Outline of the Book | 55 | 8 Conclusions | 58 |
| 7.1 Methodology | 55 | 8.1 Basic Propositions | 58 |
| 7.2 Outline of Book | 56 | 8.2 Suggested Propositions | 59 |

# 1 Aims of the Book

This book has essentially three aims: to explore why there continues to be such perceived lack of clarity about the meaning of the term 'refugee'; to consider to what extent continuing differences over interpretation of key elements of the refugee definition enshrined in Article 1A(2) of the 1951 Convention relating to the Status of Refugees (Refugee Convention or CRSR)[1] and its 1967 Protocol relating to the Status of Refugees (1967 Protocol)[2] can be resolved; and to seek to elaborate this definition by way of a list of basic propositions regarding its substantive contents. These aims reflect the belief that it is time for more concerted efforts to build on existing learning on the refugee definition, so as to recognise gains made in interpreting it and to achieve a more consistent approach to its application in refugee status determination (RSD). The focus of this study is thus deliberately narrow. It strives to concentrate as far as possible on the definition itself. It does not address (except incidentally) the cessation or exclusion clauses. It does not attempt to emulate major works and textbooks that provide a wider perspective. The history of the definition, although drawn on when relevant to interpretation, is not otherwise covered. Nor does the book cover issues of evidence assessment and/or procedures except in a limited way, e.g., when dealing with aspects of the 'being persecuted' and 'well-founded fear' elements of the definition.

Article 1A(2) states that the term 'refugee' shall apply to any person who:

[ ... ] owing to well-founded fear of persecution for reasons of race, religion, nationality, membership of a particular social group or political opinion, is outside the country of his nationality and is unable or, owing to such fear, is unwilling to avail himself of the protection of that country; or who, not having a nationality and being outside the country of his former habitual residence as a result of such events, is unable or, owing to such fear, is unwilling to return to it.

In the case of a person who has more than one nationality, the term 'the country of his nationality' shall mean each of the countries of which he is a national, and a person shall not be deemed to be lacking the protection of the country of his nationality if, without any valid reason based on well-founded fear, he has not availed himself of the protection of one of the countries of which he is a national.[3]

---

[1] Convention Relating to the Status of Refugees (adopted 28 July 1951, entered into force 22 April 1954) 189 UNTS 137 (CRSR51 or Refugee Convention).
[2] Protocol Relating to the Status of Refugees (adopted 31 January 1967, entered into force 4 October 1967) 606 UNTS 267.
[3] CRSR51 (n 1) Article 1A(2). The equally authentic French text reads: '[C]raignant avec raison d'être persécutée du fait de sa race, de sa religion, de sa nationalité, de son appartenance à un certain groupe social ou de ses opinions politiques, se trouve hors du pays dont elle a la nationalité et qui ne peut ou, du fait de cette crainte, ne veut se réclamer de la protection de ce pays; ou qui, si elle n'a pas de nationalité et se trouve hors du pays dans lequel elle avait sa résidence habituelle à la suite de tels événements, ne peut ou, en raison de ladite crainte, ne veut y retourner. Dans le cas d'une personne qui a plus d'une nationalité, l'expression "du pays dont

The 1967 Protocol did not alter the substantive contents of this definition, but did remove its temporal and geographical limitations.[4]

This definition is short enough to be written on tablets of stone. It is hard to think of any other international law text that so profoundly affects the lives of so many on a daily basis. Its brief words have often been the only thing standing between death and salvation. The international community, despite being divided on many matters, has broadly agreed to endow this definition with continuing legal power and effect (although it would be complacent to assume it will always do so). It has constructed this definition in declaratory terms, so that it inheres in the person.[5] Despite the crowded universe of treaties, case law, guidelines, commentaries, and studies that all of us involved with refugee law inhabit, it continues to occupy pride of place. Not one state party has denounced it.

Yet the text of Article 1A(2) is not self-explanatory. The Convention contains no definition of the key terms used either in this Article or in other provisions of Article 1. It is thus a definition in one sense, but not in another. It is the treaty definition, defining who is a refugee, but it is a definition whose key terms must be given form and content through interpretation.

Keeping the definition as simple as possible was doubtless one of the aims of the drafters. For sure, they wanted those seeking asylum to have the protection of a treaty set out in clear, simple terms—terms that would prove capable of adapting to the challenges ahead—but not so simple that they lacked effective application. They were of course mindful of the cumbersome nature of the enumerative approach to the refugee definition adopted in predecessor instruments, designed to deal with particular situations as they arose.

Hence it would doubtless come as a shock to the drafters to learn how massively litigated and argued over the refugee definition has become. Yet, perhaps, it has been inevitable that this should happen given that in the post-war period nation states consolidated their control of immigration and borders, and that for over a quarter of a century many countries of the global North have become more restrictionist in their approach to asylum and migration.

How then does this study fit in? Surveying the literature of refugee law, one cannot but be astonished at its diversity. Given how closely entangled refugee issues continue to be with the critical global issues confronting humankind—ranging from wars, inequality, environmental disasters, climate change, food insecurity, diseases (the COVID-19 pandemic included)—this diversity and the multiplicity, breadth, and scope of studies dealing with issues of refugee law and related fields, is sorely needed. Yet curiously, comparatively few studies deal comprehensively with the

---

*elle a la nationalité" vise chacun des pays dont cette personne a la nationalité. Ne sera pas considérée comme privée de la protection du pays dont elle a la nationalité, toute personne qui, sans raison valable fondée sur une crainte justifiée, ne s'est pas réclamée de la protection de l'un des pays dont elle a la nationalité.'*

[4] See sections 2.1.5 and 3.1 of this chapter.

[5] 'A person is a refugee within the meaning of the 1951 Convention as soon as he fulfils the criteria contained in the definition. [...] Recognition of his refugee status does not thereby make him a refugee but declares him to be one.' See UNHCR, Handbook on Procedures and Criteria for Determining Refugee Status and Guidelines on International Protection under the 1951 Convention and the 1967 Protocol Relating to the Status of Refugees (Geneva, 2019, reissued in 2019) (UNHCR Handbook or Handbook) para 28.

refugee definition. All leading textbooks cover it but rarely in depth.[6] Further, some of the studies that have gone into depth have not survived the dynamic development of the refugee definition,[7] which is indubitably a 'living instrument'. Some analyse the refugee definition primarily in the context of a particular national or regional law system.[8] Some barely cover all of the definition's key elements.[9] Some choose to approach it (in whole or in part) thematically.[10] Some prioritise advancing their own understandings without always explaining the state of the existing law.[11] Pervading many studies is also an air of almost resigned acceptance of discord—as if it is in the nature of the subject matter that the refugee definition will forever spawn diverse opinions and doctrinal disputes.

But in an area such as refugee law, too much diversity breeds uncertainty. When we come to the Refugee Convention as beginners (as we all first do), our thirst is surely for clarity and—to use a much-overworked term—at least some measure of legal certainty. Instead, almost as soon as we get started, we face a battery of questions. Consider just a few examples. Must all attempts at interpreting the definition's key terms actively apply 'rules' of interpretation set down in the Vienna Convention on the Law of Treaties (VCLT)?[12] Should the United Nations High Commissioner for Refugees (UNHCR) or leading judicial decisions on key elements of the refugee definition be taken to establish a settled 'state practice'? Where do we locate the critical analysis—in the 'being persecuted limb', the 'well-founded fear limb' or the 'protection limb'—of the definition? Is a human rights approach to the definition really necessary? By reference to what criteria do we determine a case of disputed nationality or statelessness? How do we establish the threshold at which an act becomes persecutory? What norms must we use to do that? Is persecutory intent essential to establish persecution? Is protection an integral part of the meaning of 'being persecuted'? Must protection be state protection? What qualities must protection possess in order to be effective? What is the threshold for deciding whether a state provides effective

---

[6] e.g. Guy S Goodwin-Gill and Jane McAdam (with Emma Dunlop), *The Refugee in International Law* (4th edn, OUP 2021) now furnish more concentrated analysis of it than did previous editions, but it still occupies only one chapter (ch 3).

[7] e.g. Atle Grahl-Madsen, *The Status of Refugees in International Law. Volume 1: Refugee Character* (Sijthoff 1966).

[8] e.g. Vigdis Vevstad, *Refugee Protection: A European Challenge* (Tano Aschehoug 1998); Deborah Anker, *Law of Asylum in the United States* (Thomson Reuters 2022 edn); Mark Symes and Peter Jorro, *Asylum Law and Practice* (2nd edn, Bloomsbury 2010); Karen Musalo, Jennifer Moore, and Richard Boswell, *Refugee Law and Policy: A Comparative and International Approach* (4th edn, Carolina Academic Press 2011); Kay Hailbronner and Daniel Thym, *EU Immigration and Asylum Law: A Commentary* (3rd edn, CH Beck-Hart Nomos 2022); Lorna Waldman, *The Definition of Convention Refugee* (2nd edn, LexisNexis 2019); Colin Yeo, Refugee Law (Bristol University Press 2022).

[9] Despite having, as its title, *Broadening the Edges: Refugee Definition and International Protection Revisited* (Martinus Nijhoff 1997), Pirkko Kourula's book contains virtually no treatment of the definition's meaning.

[10] e.g. Vanessa Holzer, *Refugees from Armed Conflict: The 1951 Refugee Convention and International Humanitarian Law* (Intersentia 2015); Efrat Arbel, Catherine Dauvergne, and Jenni Millbank (eds), *Gender in Refugee Law: From the Margins to the Centre* (Routledge 2014). Whilst addressing all elements, James C Hathaway and Michelle Foster, *The Law of Refugee Status* (CUP 2014) choose a thematic approach to serious harm: see their chapter 3.

[11] Hathaway and Foster (n 10).

[12] Vienna Convention on the Law of Treaties (VCLT) (adopted 23 May 1969, entered into force 27 January 1980) 1155 UNTS 331.

protection? Must the threshold for assessing protection in an internal protection alternative (IPA) be lower than in a person's home region? What measure or degree of causation is needed to establish a nexus to a Convention ground or reason? To what extent can 'membership of a particular social group' operate as a residual ground or reason? Must well-founded fear have a subjective and objective component? What light do the cessation and exclusion clauses of Article 1C and 1F shed on the inclusionary clauses of Article 1A(2)? How does Article 1A(2) correlate with Article 33?

All too often such questions harbour within themselves more questions. The problem is not that we have to address these and many more; but rather that it can too often seem like unstitching a tapestry without knowing how to weave it back together.

In the case of the Refugee Convention, charges of inconsistent, divergent, and diverse interpretation and application remain rife.[13] This state of affairs has been compounded by the lack of any activation of Article 38, which provides an inter-state mechanism for the International Court of Justice (ICJ) to settle disputes relating to its interpretation or application.[14] Various proposals have been made to remedy this lack, including the establishment of a specific treaty-monitoring body,[15] a review and monitoring subcommittee,[16] an independent international judicial commission,[17] a Supervisory Working Group, a Special Committee of Experts, or a regularised system of periodic reporting.[18] Lying behind judicial proposals in particular, has been a concern about an 'unacceptable degree of diversity in the interpretation of the Convention', which is seen to be at odds with a cluster of important legal principles, including the principle that like cases should be treated alike,[19] and the fact that the Convention

---

[13] e.g. Alexander Betts and Paul Collier, *Refuge: Transforming a Broken Refugee System* (Penguin 2017) 43, 46. Even within the EU, which has had a Qualification Directive in place since 2004 and a recast of it in place since 2011, a 2016 Commission survey found that there remained significant divergence in interpretation. See EU Evaluation Report of 2016 on the application of Directive 2011/95/EU (22 January 2019) 69 et seq. See also European Commission, 'Evaluation of the application of the recast Qualification Directive (2011/95/EU): Final Report' (2019). The diversity of national procedural rules also plays a significant role, even as regards the relatively harmonised procedures under the Common European Asylum System (CEAS): see e.g. UNHCR, 'Better Protecting Refugees in the EU and Globally' (2016).

[14] Karin Oellers-Frahm, 'Article 38 of the 1951 Convention/Article IV of the 1967 Protocol' in Andreas Zimmermann (ed), *The 1951 Convention Relating to the Status of Refugees and its 1967 Protocol: A Commentary* (OUP 2011) 1537–54.

[15] Oldrich Andrysek, 'Gaps in International Protection and the Potential for Redress through Individual Complaints Procedures' (1997) 9 IJRL 392, 393 et seq. Walter Kälin, 'Supervising the 1951 Convention Relating to the Status of Refugees: Article 35 and Beyond' in Erika Feller et al (eds), *Refugee Protection in International Law: UNHCR's Global Consultations on International Protection* (CUP 2003) 613, 639–49. James C Simeon, 'Strengthening International Refugee Rights through the Enhanced Supervision of the 1951 Convention and its 1967 Protocol' in Satvinder S Juss (ed), *The Ashgate Research Companion to Migration Law, Theory and Policy* (Ashgate Publishing 2013) 121.

[16] Kälin (n 15) 657–59.

[17] Anthony M North and Joyce Chia, 'Towards Convergence in the Interpretation of the Refugee Convention: A Proposal for the Establishment of an International Judicial Commission for Refugees' (2006) 25 Aust YBIL 105. They envisage that such a commission could be created under the supervisory mandate of the UNHCR.

[18] See Volker Türk, 'UNHCR's Supervisory Responsibility' (October 2002) UNHCR New Issues in Refugee Research, Working Paper No 67, 2. See also *Special Feature: Supervising the Refugee Convention* (2013) 26 J Refugee Stud 323–415; Simeon (n 15) 118.

[19] North and Chia (n 17) 107. They add: '[i]t is elementary common sense that a refugee, recognised as such pursuant to the definition in the Convention, should also be recognised as a refugee in another country using the same definition'.

is an instrument for the protection of the most vulnerable.[20] Undoubtedly, concerns about undue divergence have sometimes been overstated (dressing up failures of fact-sensitive application as failures of interpretation). It may be that such concerns are not unique to refugee law, arising in many other areas of public international law as well, e.g., international human rights law (IHRL).[21] It may well be that such concerns have yet to be properly vindicated by comprehensive empirical studies. But it is hard to view the present state of affairs as satisfactory. Can we reduce legal uncertainty and if so, how?

There is not an international 'state practice' crystallised enough to be able to discern a refugee definition in any fuller form, let alone one that has attained the status of customary international law. However, it is one of this book's themes, that in light of the learning that has accrued around the refugee definition, it is now possible to give it greater specificity and detail. This occupies a level of concord below state practice in the strict sense but is still identifiable as a body of learning about which there is substantial consensus—what the International Law Commission (ILC) has termed 'state practice in the broad sense'.[22]

My call throughout this book for greater 'definitional detail' is not new. Among those who have urged this in the past are Arboleda and Hoy who, having observed that 'divergent interpretation and application' are the 'rule' rather than the exception, exhorted in 1993 that:

> In resolving the problem of who is a Convention refugee in Western countries, a two-fold approach is called for. First, more specific criteria must be developed, in order to eliminate the ambiguities of the Convention definition as far as possible. Second, and most importantly, the Convention definition must be applied uniformly. Lacking such uniformity of application, the Convention definition is fast becoming over-legalistic, mired in juridical abstraction, removed from the reality facing refugees, and subject to the vagaries of national interests. Both steps are inter-dependent, though the second is predicated on the implementation of the first.[23]

---

[20] ibid 108: 'the Convention is designed to be a universal humanitarian instrument, offering a regime of international protection to the most vulnerable. In this respect, the aims and context of the treaty are fundamentally undermined if there are substantial differences between the views taken by states parties of their obligations. Obviously, the rights of the refugee are impaired. Further, other states parties may be forced to shoulder a heavier burden.' North and Chia conclude '[t]hat the degree of divergence appears to lead to dramatically different results of acceptance in neighbouring countries, offends the normative goals of equality before the law, certainty and stability. It does so with, one can only imagine, tragic consequences. In the arena of refugee law, we need to tilt the balance between consistency and divergence in favour of greater consistency.' See also *Special Feature: Supervising the Refugee Convention* (n 18); James C Simeon (ed), *The UNHCR and the Supervision of International Refugee Law* (CUP 2013). For a critique, see Guy S Goodwin-Gill, 'The Dynamic of International Refugee Law' (2013) 25 IJRL 651, 656–57.

[21] As discussed e.g. in various contributions in Carla M Buckley, Alice Donald, and Philip Leach (eds), *Towards Convergence in International Human Rights Law: Approaches of Regional and International Systems* (Brill Nijhoff 2016).

[22] See Chapter 2, n 69.

[23] Eduardo Arboleda and Ian Hoy, 'The Convention Refugee Definition in the West: Disharmony of Interpretation and Application' (1993) 5 IJRL 66, 76.

They concluded that:

> A refugee definition that is more precise will not alone ensure its own uniform application, even though it is the crucial first step to achieving such uniformity. It is also essential in helping fill the legal lacunae of international refugee law by better defining its parameters. This, in turn, paves the way for less ambiguous and more specific definitions of 'humanitarian' or 'de facto' status.[24]

To the modern-day reader, Arboleda and Hoy's call for 'uniformity' seems utopian. In light of the pluralities of the current international legal order and the highly fact-sensitive nature of RSD, the expectation can really only be for more convergent interpretation.[25] This does not mean abandoning the quest for a universal meaning; indeed, Chapter 2 argues that such a quest is enjoined by rules of interpretation prescribed by the VCLT. It is simply recognising that its achievement can never be complete. However, their call for greater precision is of a different order. There are at least several reasons to be more sanguine today about the prospects of achieving greater particularity, among them being the groundwork already done by UNHCR,[26] by case law, by the Michigan school;[27] the example afforded by the European Union (EU) asylum law in attempting to provide more flesh to the bone of the Article 1A(2) definition;[28] and the fact that a significant number of the debates that have arisen have been more or less settled.

One of the main contentions of this book is that it is possible to set out in clearer form a number of points of interpretation that are now accepted. Many of the main disagreements that have arisen over the past seventy years or so have to all intents and purposes been effectively resolved. This has resulted in clearer understandings, some of which can be enunciated as general propositions, i.e. those which have become widely accepted enough to stand as an agreed elaboration of the relatively few words enshrined in Article 1A(2). Desire on the part of scholars and others to continue evolving the refugee definition must not expunge past achievements nor readiness to learn from predecessors. It is high time the achievements and progress that have been made be seen to be what they have become—part of a further, working definition in this wider sense.

A paradox of refugee law is that despite the Article 1A(2) definition being consulted and applied daily by thousands of decision makers around the world, many studies of it, even ones written to guide decision makers, tend to the scholastic and theoretical. With that in mind, Betts and Collier criticise a focus on 'arcane disputes about how

---

[24] ibid 79.
[25] Consistently with the notion of convergent interpretation, Malcolm Evans has called for 'textured harmony' not 'monotone uniformity'. See Sir Malcolm D Evans, 'Co-existence and Confidentiality: The Experience of the Optional Protocol to the Convention Against Torture: Harmony and Human Rights: The Music of the Spheres' in Buckley et al (n 21) 542.
[26] Now brought together in one publication, the UNHCR Handbook and Guidelines on International Protection (n 5) were reissued February 2019, available at <https://www.refworld.org/docid/5cb474b27.html> accessed 2 April 2021.
[27] James C Hathaway, *The Michigan Guidelines on the International Protection of Refugees* (Michigan Publishing 2019).
[28] See section 2.3.3 of this chapter.

words in a treaty can be reinterpreted to fit today's challenges', which they say 'miss the central point which is the need to recognise that the refugee system is broken and the need is to build a new system'.[29] Certainly, there can often seem to be a disconnect between such studies and what decision makers—often state officials with no legal or academic expertise—apply and understand on the ground.[30] Commentators have rightly worried about 'over-formalism',[31] but few find it possible to avoid engaging themselves with the many conceptual issues seen to arise. This book is no exception in trying to ride this paradox, but seeks, with its concept of a 'working definition' to offer a possible pathway out of such ambivalences. The Refugee Convention may be part of a 'broken system', but ceasing to do what we can to make it work well in the absence of another is no solution either. Disputes about a legal definition can of course be 'arcane', but in the context of the Refugee Convention, so long as it remains the case that great numbers of decisions on refugee applications continue to be made around the world on a daily basis, the endeavour to achieve greater consensus on its interpretation is not arcane. It can be a matter of life or death.

## 2 The Refugee Definition in International Law

### 2.1 The Refugee Convention and/or its 1967 Protocol

2.1.1 Article 1A(2) refugee

By 'the refugee definition in international law', this book means the definition of refugee set out in Article 1A(2) of the Refugee Convention of 28 July 1951, as amended by the 1967 Protocol.

For the Convention drafters, this was the 'crux of the entire matter'[32] and the 'cornerstone on which the entire edifice of the Convention rested'.[33] That remains the case today. Whilst Articles 2–32 of the Refugee Convention set out various guarantees relating to the situation of refugees (and to some extent asylum-seekers)[34] they relate to their situation in the host state. Article 33 provides protection against non-refoulement but is limited to those who have established refugee status or are still awaiting a final decision on their application for refugee status.[35]

---

[29] Betts and Collier (n 13) 6.
[30] As highlighted by Goodwin-Gill (n 20) 652.
[31] Arboleda and Hoy (n 23) 82: 'An additional barrier to the uniform application of the Convention refugee definition is the problem of legal formalism.' See also Nicholas Blake QC, 'Entitlement to Protection: A Human Rights-based Approach to Refugee Protection in the United Kingdom' in Frances Nicholson and Patrick Twomey (eds), *Current Issues of UK Asylum Law and Policy* (Routledge 1998) 241: '[a] technical consideration of elements of the Convention definition of refugee, can rapidly turn an examination of a living instrument into an anatomical dissection of a dead one'.
[32] UN Ad Hoc Committee on Refugees and Stateless Persons, Ad Hoc Committee on Statelessness and Related Problems, First Session: Summary Record of the Second Meeting Held at Lake Success, New York, on Tuesday, 17 January 1930, at 11 a.m. (26 January 1950) UN Doc E/AC.32/SR.2, para 17.
[33] UN Conference of Plenipotentiaries on the Status of Refugees and Stateless Persons, Conference of Plenipotentiaries on the Status of Refugees and Stateless Persons: Summary Record of the Twenty-first Meeting (26 November 1951) UN Doc A/CONF.2/SR 21, 8.
[34] James C Hathaway, *The Rights of Refugees Under International Law* (CUP 2005) 154–70; James C Hathaway, *The Rights of Refugees Under International Law* (2nd edn, CUP 2021) 173–81.
[35] Walter Kälin, Martina Caroni, and Lukas Heim, 'Article 33, para 1' in Zimmermann (n 14) 1327–95.

It is well-settled that the refugee definition in Article 1A(2) continues to provide the primary legal foundation for the protection of refugees worldwide.[36]

Notwithstanding that there now exist multiple systems of protection against refoulement under international refugee law (IRL) and IHRL, the Refugee Convention and its definition of refugee continue to have primacy and to function as a form of *lex specialis*.[37] But it is not the only definition to be found in international refugee law. Before proceeding further, it is necessary to identify the other main definitions[38] and their status. They exist at international, regional, and national levels; they range from 'hard-law' definitions in treaty form to 'soft-law' definitions.

In approaching the subject of the refugee definition, it must not be overlooked that the ultimate authority for all refugee definitions at the international level emanates from the United Nations (UN). When in 1949 the UN set about establishing UNHCR, the United Nations General Assembly (UNGA) explicitly recognized 'the responsibility of the United Nations for the international protection of refugees'.[39] When establishing the Office of the High Commissioner, the Economic and Social Council (ECOSOC) and UNGA resolutions referred to the 'international protection of refugees'.[40]

### 2.1.2 Article 1A(1) 'statutory' refugee

That Article 1A(2) is not the only refugee definition at the international level is plainest from the fact that within the Refugee Convention itself, it is only the second of two categories of refugee, the first being those known as 'statutory refugees'[41] defined in Article 1A(1) as any person who:

> (1) Has been considered a refugee under the Arrangements of 12 May 1926 and 30 June 1928 or under the Conventions of 28 October 1933 and 10 February 1938, the Protocol of 14 September 1939 or the Constitution of the International Refugee Organization.

---

[36] The Declaration of the States Parties to the 1951 Convention relating to the Status of Refugees and/or its 1967 Protocol issued on 13 December 2001 preambular paragraph 7 reaffirmed that the Convention, as amended by the 1967 Protocol, 'has a central place in the international refugee protection regime'. In a 2019 Foreword to the UNHCR Handbook and UNHCR Guidelines on International Protection (n 5), Volker Türk notes that '[t]he centrality of the 1951 Convention and its 1967 Protocol to the refugee protection regime is reinforced in two seminal texts: the 2016 New York Declaration for Refugees and Migrants, and the Global Compact on Refugees, affirmed by the General Assembly in 2018'.

[37] Jane McAdam, *Complementary Protection in International Refugee Law* (OUP 2007) 1. The Refugee Convention has been described as the Magna Carta of refugee law: see Louise W Holborn et al, *Refugees, a Problem of Our Time: The Work of the United Nations High Commissioner for Refugees, 1951–1972* (Scarecrow Press 1975) 9, 99. See also The Editor's Desk, 'The Refugee Convention at 50 ... ' (2001) 123(2) Refugees, 2; and Judith Kumin, 'Gender: Persecution in the Spotlight' (2001) 123(2) Refugees, 12.

[38] This study does not seek to cover all definitions that have been advanced in international fora. Austin T Jr Fragomen, 'The Refugee: A Problem of Definition' (1970) 3 Case W Res J Int'l L 45, for example, notes a definition essayed by the Intergovernmental Committee for European Migration, circa 1969 encompassing 'victims of war or a disaster'. Goodwin-Gill and McAdam (n 6) 52–53 also offer a definition of 'refugees' for the purposes of general international law.

[39] UNGA Res 319 (IV) (3 December 1949).

[40] ECOSOC Res 248 (IX) (6 August 1949); UNGA Res 319(IV) (n 39). See also Holborn et al (n 37) 9, 99.

[41] Grahl-Madsen (n 7) 105–06; Stefanie Schmahl, 'Article 1A, para. 1' in Zimmermann (n 14) 251.

10 THE REFUGEE DEFINITION

In full, the instruments thus identified are the Arrangements of 12 May 1926 Relating to the Issue of Identity Certificates to Russian and Armenian Refugees;[42] the Arrangement of 30 June 1928 Concerning the Extension to Other Categories of Refugees of Certain Measures Taken in Favour of Russian and Armenian Refugees;[43] the Convention of 28 October 1933 (and 10 February 1938) Relating to the International Status of Refugees Coming from Germany;[44] the Protocol of 14 September 1939;[45] and the Constitution of the International Refugee Organisation.

Article 1A(1) effectively consolidates all the previous definitions contained in the interwar international instruments. It does so in order to ensure those previously considered a refugee under any of them remain a refugee for the Refugee Convention's purposes and that 'a formerly acquired refugee status remains valid without any need to renew it by means of the general definition in Article 1A para.2'.[46] It is now almost an entirely historical remnant. Article 1C also contains two 'ceased circumstances' clauses (Article 1C(5) and (6)) specifying respectively that they shall not apply to those falling within the Article 1A(1) definition who are 'able to invoke compelling reasons arising out of previous persecution for refusing to avail [themselves] of the protection of the country of nationality'; or, in the case of stateless persons, 'for refusing to return to the country of [their] former habitual residence'.[47]

In addition to Article 1A encompassing, therefore, two refugee definitions, the Convention and its Annexes can also be said to identify (without defining them) two further categories of refugee.

2.1.3 Refugee assisted by other UN Agencies
Article 1D of the 1951 Convention stipulates that:

> This Convention shall not apply to persons who are at present receiving from organs or agencies of the United Nations other than the United Nations High Commissioner for Refugees protection or assistance.
>
> When such protection or assistance has ceased for any reason, without the position of such persons being definitively settled in accordance with the relevant resolutions adopted by the General Assembly of the United Nations, these persons shall ipso facto be entitled to the benefits of this Convention.

---

[42] League of Nations, Arrangement Relating to the Issue of Identify Certificates to Russian and Armenian Refugees (12 May 1926) 89 LNTS 47.
[43] League of Nations, Arrangement Concerning the Extension to Other Categories of Certain Measures Taken in Favour of Russian and Armenian Refugees (30 June 1928) 89 LNTS 63.
[44] League of Nations, Convention concerning the Status of Refugees Coming From Germany (10 February 1938) 192 LNTS 59.
[45] League of Nations, Additional Protocol to the Arrangement of the Convention concerning the Status of Refugees from Germany (14 September 1939) 198 LNTS 141.
[46] Schmahl (n 41) 252. The UNHCR Handbook (n 5) states at para 33 that this provision was included 'in order to provide a link with the past and to ensure the continuity of international protection of refugees who became the concern of the international community at various earlier periods'.
[47] ibid 257.

The bare wording of Article 1D does not identify further who it covers but hidden in plain sight is the category of Palestinian refugees.[48] As the 1979 UNHCR Handbook explains: '[s]uch protection or assistance was previously given by the former United Nations Korean Reconstruction Agency (UNKRA) and is currently given by the United Nations Relief and Works Agency for Palestine Refugees In the Near East (UNRWA)'.[49] The Handbook further explains that '[w]ith regard to refugees from Palestine, it will be noted that UNRWA operates only in certain areas of the Middle East, and it is only there that its protection or assistance are given'.[50] Understanding the full meaning of the Article 1D formulation necessitates cross-reference to a number of UNGA resolutions, beginning with Resolution 194 of 11 December 1948 and the definition of (Palestinian) refugee applied by UNRWA,[51] which has changed over time, as well as recourse to the *travaux préparatoires* (hereinafter '*travaux*') which include extensive debate about the status of Palestinian refugees.[52] The significance of the intended focus on Palestinian refugees is reinforced by the fact, now well-established, that Article 1D is not merely an exclusion clause but also contains in its second paragraph a functional ('contingent')[53] inclusion clause identifying as refugees those in respect of whom protection or assistance has ceased for any reason.[54]

### 2.1.4 Recommendation E refugees

That the drafters saw their Article 1A(2) definition as non-exhaustive of the concept of refugee can be gleaned from the wording of Recommendation E contained in the Final Act of the Conference of Plenipotentiaries which adopted the 1951 Convention. This states that the Conference:

> *Expresses* the hope that the Convention relating to the Status of Refugees will have value as an example exceeding its contractual scope and that all nations will be guided by it in granting so far as possible to persons in their territory as *refugees and*

---

[48] 'Palestinian refugee' is used here as a generic term to refer to all generations and categories of Palestinian displaced populations. See further Susan M Akran, 'UNRWA and Palestine Refugees' in Cathryn Costello, Michelle Foster, and Jane McAdam (eds), *The Oxford Handbook of International Refugee Law* (OUP 2021) 644.
[49] UNHCR Handbook (n 5) para 142.
[50] ibid para 143.
[51] UNGA Res 194 (III) (11 December 1948). See also UNGA Res 302 (IV) (8 December 1949).
[52] Francesca Albanese and Lex Takkenberg, *Palestinian Refugees in International Law* (2nd edn, OUP 2020) 76–83, 85–122. See further UNHCR, Guidelines on International Protection (Guidelines) No 13: Applicability of Article 1D of the 1951 Convention relating to the Status of Refugees to Palestinian Refugees (December 2017) UN Doc HCR/GIP/17/13; Goodwin-Gill and McAdam (n 6) 153. Court of Justice of the European Union's rulings on Article 12(1)(a) of the Qualification Directive/Article 1D to date are: Case C-31/09 *Nawras Bolbol v Bevándorlási és Állampolgársági Hivatal* [2010] ECR I-05539; Case C-364/11 *El Kott* [2012] ECLI:EU:C:2012:826; Case C-585/16 *Serin Alheto v Zamestnik-predsedatel na Darzhavna agentsia za bezhantsite* [2018] EU:C:2018:584; Case C-507/19 *Bundesrepublik Deutschland v XT* [2021] ECLI:EU:C:2021:3; Case C-349/20 *NB and AB v Secretary of State for the Home Department* [2022] ECLI:EU:C:2022:151.
[53] Goodwin-Gill and McAdam (n 6) 185.
[54] UNHCR, Note on UNHCR's Interpretation of Article 1D of the 1951 Convention relating to the Status of Refugees and Article 12(1)(a) of the EU Qualification Directive in the context of Palestinian refugees seeking international protection (2013) 4–6; UNHCR, Guidelines No 13: Applicability of Article 1D (n 52).

12   THE REFUGEE DEFINITION

*who would not be covered by the terms of the Convention*, the treatment for which it provides.[55]

Jackson considers that this recommendation was intended to apply only to those not covered by Article 1A(2) by virtue of the 1951 dateline and the geographical limitation (later removed by the 1967 Protocol).[56] However, the 1979 UNHCR Handbook considers, without mention of any such restriction, that '[t]his recommendation enables States to solve such problems as may arise with regard to persons who are not regarded as fully satisfying the criteria of the definition of the term "refugee"',[57] and it has certainly been understood to go wider.[58]

### 2.1.5 Protocol relating to the Status of Refugees, 4 October 1967

It is overdue to refer in more detail to the 1967 Protocol, Article 2, which provides that:

> For the purpose of the present Protocol, the term 'refugee' shall, except as regards the application of paragraph 3 of this article, mean any person within the definition of article 1 of the Convention as if the words 'As a result of events occurring before 1 January 1951 and ...' and the words '... as a result of such events', in article 1 A (2) were omitted.

Article 3 states that the Protocol 'shall be applied without any geographical limitation'.

The 1967 Protocol requires specific mention here because, although a protocol, it is an independent instrument, Articles 2 and 3 of which amend the 1951 refugee definition.[59] Prior to the 1967 Protocol, for some sixteen years, the Article 1A(2) definition of refugee was subject to temporal and geographical restrictions.

Technically, therefore (leaving to one side the UNHCR Statute definition which is dealt with below), there are in fact two international instruments containing the definition of refugee that hold centre-stage. However, the Protocol's legal effect is not to alter the substantive refugee definition in Article 1A(2) but (as already indicated) simply to remove its temporal and geographical limitations. Accordingly, reference throughout this study to the 'Article 1A(2) refugee definition' means this definition as amended by the 1967 Protocol.

The great significance of the 1967 Protocol should not, however, be buried. It achieved the formal universalisation of the Article 1A(2) definition.

---

[55] This was a UK initiative, prompted by the deletion of a former article which would have allowed the Contracting States to add to the definition of the term 'refugee'. The UK representative explained that his delegation had felt that a general recommendation was called for to cover those classes of refugees who were altogether outside the scope of Article 1A. See UN, Final Act of the United Nations Conference of Plenipotentiaries on the Status of Refugees and Stateless Persons (25 July 1951) 189 UNTS 137, 148 (emphasis added).
[56] Ivor C Jackson, *The Refugee Concept in Group Situations* (Kluwer Law International 1999) 75.
[57] UNHCR Handbook (n 5) para 27.
[58] e.g. Jerzyv Sztucki, 'Who Is a refugee? The Convention Definition: Universal or Obsolete?' in Nicholson and Twomey (eds) (n 31) 57.
[59] Schmahl (n 41) 619.

## 2.2 The UNHCR Statute and Related Definitions

### 2.2.1 Refugees under the Statute of the Office of the United Nations High Commissioner for Refugees (UNHCR Statute)

Further complicating the international treaty picture, the Statute of the Office of the United Nations High Commissioner for Refugees (UNHCR Statute),[60] concluded on 14 December 1950, several months earlier than the Refugee Convention, contains its own, parallel, two-part definition of refugee. The purpose of the UNHCR Statute definition was to establish those persons to whom UNHCR competence extends. In common with Article 1 of the Refugee Convention, it sets out two categories of refugees. Provision 6A(i) of the Annex provides in identical terms to Article 1A(1) a definition of a 'statutory' refugee, and has the same consolidatory purpose. Provision 6A(ii) and B cover:[61]

> (ii) Any person who, as a result of events occurring before 1 January 1951 and owing to well-founded fear of being persecuted for reasons of race, religion, nationality or political opinion, is outside the country of his nationality and is unable or, owing to such fear or for reasons other than personal convenience, is unwilling to avail himself of the protection of that country; or who, not having a nationality and being outside the country of his former habitual residence, is unable or, owing to such fear or for reasons other than personal convenience, is unwilling to return to it.
> Decisions as to eligibility taken by the International Refugee Organisation during the period of its activities shall not prevent the status of refugee being accorded to persons who fulfil the conditions of the present paragraph;
> [ ... ]
> B. Any other person who is outside the country of his nationality, or if he has no nationality, the country of his former habitual residence, because he has or had a well-founded fear of persecution by reason of his race, religion, nationality or political opinion and is unable or, because of such fear, is unwilling to avail himself of the protection of the government of the country of his nationality, or, if he has no nationality, to return to the country of his former habitual residence.

The definition given in Provision 6A(ii) is not wholly identical to Article 1A(2). The juxtapositions[62] are of two different kinds. First, there are minor differences in substantive content. Provision 6A(ii) does not include 'membership of a particular social group' as one of the reasons for persecution. The Statute definition also includes persons who are outside their countries of origin because of a well-founded fear of being persecuted for 'reasons other than personal convenience'. They do not necessarily have

---

[60] UNGA Res 428(V) (14 December 1950) GAOR, 5th Session, Supplement No 20.
[61] The text here omits the cessation provisions.
[62] UNGA, Juxtaposition of Article 1 of the Draft Convention relating to the Status of Refugees with Chapter II, Paragraphs 6 and 7 of the Statute of the Office of the United Nations High Commissioner for Refugees: Note (21 May 1951). See also Interoffice Memorandum to Mr M Pagès, Director from P Weis, 'Eligibility of Refugees from Hungary' (9 January 1957) 22/1/HUNG [3], in UNHCR Archives Fonds 11 Sub-fonds 1, 6/1/HUN, cited in UNHCR, *The State of the World's Refugees: Fifty Years of Humanitarian Action* (OUP 2000) 30–31.

to show that their unwillingness to avail themselves of the protection of the country of origin (or of former habitual residence, if stateless) is owing to a well-founded fear.[63]

Second, in terms of temporal and geographical scope, Provision 6B extended the definition to those who were excluded by the temporal limitation set out in Provision 6A(ii).[64]

In addition, because the UNHCR Statute is not linked to the granting of a specific legal status but is concerned rather to identify those coming within the competence of the High Commissioner,[65] the latter's mandate is not limited in the same way as that of contracting states under the 1951 Convention and its 1967 Protocol, whose obligations only arise in respect of states who have become party to one or both.[66]

As a result, the Handbook envisaged that it was possible for a person to be both a Convention refugee under Article 1A(2) and a 'mandate refugee'.[67] However, as Aleinikoff has charted, the term 'mandate' is not strictly a legal term and is not to be confused with action within the competence of the High Commissioner under the Statute and UNGA resolutions, and over time reference to 'mandate refugees' has fallen away.[68]

2.2.2 'Persons of concern' to UNHCR and refugees
Paragraphs 9 and 3 of the Statute have enabled extension of the High Commissioner's protection and assistance role beyond those defined as refugees in the Statute, so as to accommodate 'persons of concern'.[69] In various resolutions, the UNGA has authorised the High Commissioner to assist such persons. It is clear that from early on this label was intended to encompass not only those whom the UNGA perceived as refugees ('refugees who are of [the High Commissioner's] concern') but also displaced

---

[63] UNGA, Juxtaposition (n 62) 47: 'Any person who, as a result of events occurring before 1 January 1951 and owing to well-founded fear of being persecuted for reasons of race, religion, nationality or political opinion, is outside the country of his nationality and is unable or, owing to such fear or for reasons other than personal convenience, is unwilling to avail himself of the protection of that country; or who, not having a nationality and being outside the country of his former habitual residence, is unable or, owing to such fear or for reasons other than personal convenience, is unwilling to return to it.'

[64] A 1957 memo by Paul Weis prompted by the Hungarian crisis set out the rationale for the applicability to the situation of both the 1951 Convention and the Statute: see UNHCR, *State of the World's Refugees* (n 62) 30–31. See also UNHCR Handbook (n 5) para 15: '[b]y virtue of these definitions the High Commissioner is competent for refugees irrespective of any dateline or geographic limitation'.

[65] Jackson (n 56) 7.

[66] UNHCR Handbook (n 5) para 63.

[67] ibid para 17: '[F]rom the foregoing, it will be seen that a person can simultaneously be both a mandate refugee and a refugee under the 1951 Convention or the 1967 Protocol. He may, however, be in a country that is not bound by either of these instruments, or he may be excluded from recognition as a Convention refugee by the application of the dateline or the geographic limitation. In such cases he would still qualify for protection by the High Commissioner under the terms of the Statute.' See also paras 35 and 36. The mandate has been particularly vital to UNHCR's role in situations of mass influx when the countries affected were not signatories to the Convention or Protocol.

[68] Thomas Alexander Aleinikoff, 'The Mandate of the Office of the United Nations High Commissioner for Refugees' in Vincent Chetail and Céline Bauloz (eds), *Research Handbook on International Law and Migration* (Edward Elgar 2014) 389, 390–93. See also Volker Türk, 'The Role of UNHCR in the Development of International Refugee Law' in Nicholson and Twomey (eds) (n 31) 153, 158.

[69] UNHCR, Note on the Mandate of the High Commissioner for Refugees and his Office (October 2013) available at <https://www.refworld.org/docid/5268c9474.html> accessed 28 March 2021.

persons[70] and other groups of people with protection needs whom he 'is called upon to assist in accordance with relevant resolutions of the General Assembly'.[71] In an oft-cited 1990 document,[72] 'persons of concern' were seen by UNHCR to be an umbrella term covering five main categories:

> (a) those who fall under the Statute definition and thus are entitled to benefit from the full range of the Office's functions; (b) those who belong to a broader category but have been recognized by States as being entitled to both the protection and assistance of the Office; (c) those to whom the High Commissioner extends his 'good offices', mainly to facilitate humanitarian assistance; (d) returning refugees, for whom the High Commissioner may provide reintegration assistance and a certain protection; and (e) non-refugee stateless persons whom UNHCR has a limited mandate to assist.[73]

As is clearest from (e), this categorisation is no longer confined to those understood to be refugees in even the broadest sense.

### 2.2.3 UNHCR's 'good offices' and refugees

Regarding category (c) above, the UNGA widened the reach of the High Commissioner's statutory competence by authorising him to use his 'good offices', originally for the benefit of 'refugees who do not come within the competence of the United Nations'.[74] The development of the UNHCR's 'good offices' doctrine, mainly under paragraph 9 of the Statute (which provides for further evolution of the High Commissioner's activities and functions via the UNGA),[75] has underlined again the

---

[70] See e.g. UNGA Res 2958 (XXVII) (12 December 1972). In 1975, a definition of the term 'displaced persons' was proffered by ECOSOC and confirmed by the General Assembly to connote 'victims of man-made disasters requiring urgent humanitarian assistance'. See UNGA Res 31/35 (30 November 1976). Whilst normally meant in this context to apply to externally displaced persons, in 1991 a Resolution of the UN Security Council Resolution 688 (1991) paragraph 2 of the Preamble, made reference to the 'flow of refugees towards and across international frontiers'. See UNSC Res 688 (1991) (5 April 1991).

[71] See e.g. UNGA Res 3143 (XXVIII) (14 December 1973). At 406, Aleinikoff (n 68) notes that 'the phrase first appeared as directly related to IDPs: General Assembly resolutions since the mid-1970s refer to 'refugees and internally displaced persons of concern to UNHCR', starting with UNGA Res 2958 (XXVII) (n 70) paras 2 and 3, and notes that '[s]ince 2000 (UNGA Res 55/76), reference is not made to 'refugees and internally displaced persons of concern to UNHCR' but rather to 'refugees and other persons of concern'. See also UNHCR, Consistent and Predictable Responses to IDPs—A Review of UNHCR's Decision-Making Processes (2005). UNHCR's mandate regarding stateless persons is also derived from UNGA Resolutions referring e.g. to the 1961 Statelessness Convention: see UNHCR, Note on the Mandate (n 69) 8–10.

[72] UNHCR, Population Movements Associated with the Search for Asylum and Refuge (4 December 1990) UN Doc EXCOM/WGSP/5.

[73] ibid. See also Matthew Seet, 'The Origins of UNHCR's Global Mandate on Statelessness' (2016) 28 IJRL 7.

[74] Grahl-Madsen (n 7) 107–08, citing UNGA Res 1167 (XII) (26 November 1957); UNGA Res 1388 (XIV) (20 November 1959); UNGA Res 1499 (XV) (5 December 1960); UNGA Res 1671 (XVI) (11 December 1961); and UNGA Res 1673 (XVI) (18 December 1961).

[75] UNHCR, Note on the Mandate (n 69). See also Türk (n 68) 153, 158. See further, Sadruddin Aga Khan, Lectures on Legal Problems Relating to Refugees and Displaced Persons delivered at the Hague Academy of International Law, 4–6 August 1976, 124–30, <https://www.unhcr.org/uk/admin/hcspeeches/3ae68fc04/lectures-prince-sadruddin-aga-khan-united-nations-high-commissioner-refugees.html>.

fact that the international community through the UN considers that the concept of refugee has a wider scope than that contained in the Refugee Convention and UNHCR Statute. Although only the definitions in the latter two instruments[76] operate as legal definitions at the level of international law, the UNGA has thereby enabled UNHCR to identify additional categories of persons as coming within their competence as so expanded.

The first occasion on which the UNGA requested the High Commissioner to use his 'good offices' was in Resolution 1167 (1957), to aid Chinese refugees in Hong Kong. Resolution 1673 (1958) generalised the intent of Resolution 1167 into a 'good offices doctrine': the High Commissioner was empowered to 'pursue his activities on behalf of refugees within his mandate or those for whom he extends his good offices'.[77] Resolution 1388 (XIV) of 20 November 1959, 'authorize[d] the High Commissioner, in respect of refugees who do not come within the competence of the United Nations, to use his good offices in the transmission of contributions designed to provide assistance to these refugees'. However, once again, the 'good offices' doctrine was never, even at the outset, confined wholly to refugees. It has gradually over time extended to a number of groups not in general considered by UNHCR to be refugees—not only internally displaced persons,[78] but also victims of man-made disasters and other persons in need of humanitarian assistance.[79]

However, it must not be thought that UNHCR's use of the 'good offices' mechanism in relation to those considered refugees in a broad sense always entailed that the recipients were not in fact refugees under the 1951 Convention or Statute. Jackson, for example, has observed when analysing use of the refugee definition in group situations in Asia during the period between 1975 and 1985, that this mechanism 'was being resorted to because that refugee status according to the UNHCR Statute was simply not being individually examined, and not because the person on whose behalf "good offices" were being extended were considered to fall outside the statutory definition'.[80] That has remained a feature of UNHCR's recognition of persons as refugees via prima facie determinations, although prima facie determinations have also sometimes been used in situations beyond the statutory definition.[81]

---

[76] Treating here the 1951 Convention and 1967 Protocol definition as a unity.
[77] Holborn (n 40) 439.
[78] UNHCR, Protection Aspects of UNHCR Activities on Behalf of Internally Displaced Persons (17 August 1994) EC/SCP/87; UNHCR, Note on the Mandate (n 69) 10.
[79] See e.g. the terms used in the following resolutions: UNGA Res 1673 (XVI) (n 74), 'refugees for whom [the High Commissioner] lends his good offices'; UNGA Res 2294 (XXII) (11 December 1967), 'refugees who are of [the High Commissioner's] concern'; ECOSOC Res 2011(LXI) (2 August 1976), endorsed by UNGA Res 31/35 (30 November 1976), 'refugees and displaced persons, victims of man-made disasters'; UNGA Res 36/125 (14 December 1981), 'refugees and displaced persons of concern to the Office of the High Commissioner'; UNGA Res 44/150 (15 December 1988) 'refugees and externally displaced persons'; and UNGA Res 48/118 (20 December 1993), 'refugees and other persons to whom the High Commissioner's Office is called upon to provide assistance and protection'.
[80] Jackson (n 56) 346, see also 322 et seq.
[81] Aleinikoff (n 68) 397; see also Jean-François Durieux, 'The Many Faces of "Prima Facie": Group-Based Evidence in Refugee Status Determination' (2008) 25 Refuge 152. Prima facie RSD can also be undertaken by states, as indicated in UNHCR's guidelines on this. See UNHCR, Guidelines No 11: Prima Facie Recognition of Refugee Status (24 June 2015) UN Doc HCR/GIP/15/11.

### 2.2.4 Wider UNHCR understandings of the term 'refugee'

As can be seen from its evolving 'persons of concern' and 'good offices' categories, UNHCR has itself always understood the term refugee to encompass not just those falling within the Article 1A(2) definition but those seen by the General Assembly and within its own organisation as refugees in a wider sense. From early on, UNHCR saw it as important to attach the 'refugee' label to persons fleeing conditions of civil disorder, even if they could not necessarily establish a Refugee Convention reason, beginning with those fleeing the Soviet invasion of Hungary in 1956 and those fleeing the Algerian war of independence.[82] It has recognised that this has created some 'ambiguities'. As it noted in the seminal 1994 Note on International Protection:

> It will be seen that the terminology employed for refugees who may not come within the terms of the 1951 Convention definition (and that in the UNHCR Statute) is neither consistent nor clear.
>
> The term 'displaced persons' has been used ambiguously for people displaced within and outside their country of origin; 'persons of concern' connotes nothing of the plight of refugees, and could refer to non-refugees of concern to the Office, such as returnees, asylum-seekers generally (because they may be refugees), and persons within their own country to whom the Office is requested to extend protection and assistance. In order to avoid these ambiguities and to convey clearly to the lay person the reality of coerced flight from one's country, the Office has in recent years adopted the usage of regional instruments such as the [Organisation of African Unity (OAU)] Refugee Convention and the Cartagena Declaration, using the term 'refugee' in the broader sense, to denote persons outside their countries who are in need of international protection because of a serious threat to their life, liberty or security of person in their country of origin as a result of persecution or armed conflict, or serious public disorder.[83]

Sztucki notes that in a 1997 publication, UNHCR stated that the term 'refugees' comprised: (i) those recognised as such by states parties to the Convention and/or the Protocol; (ii) those recognised as such under the OAU Convention and the Cartagena Declaration; (iii) those recognised by UNHCR as 'mandate refugees'; (iv) those granted residence on humanitarian grounds; and (v) those granted temporary protection on a group basis.[84] Piecing together various UNGA resolutions, ECOSOC resolutions, organisational practice, and implied powers, Volker Türk wrote in 1999 that:

> The term 'refugee' therefore covers all persons who are outside their country of origin for reasons of feared persecution, armed conflict, generalised violence, foreign aggression or other circumstances which have seriously disturbed public order, and who, as a result, require international protection.[85]

---

[82] Aleinikoff (n 68) 395–97. See also UNHCR, *The State of The World's Refugees* (n 62) ch 2.
[83] UNHCR, Note on International Protection (1994) UN Doc A/AC.96/830, para 32.
[84] Sztucki (n 58) 61, citing UNHCR, Refugees and Others of Concern to UNHCR: 1996 Statistical Overview (1997) 1.
[85] Türk (n 68) 156 cites UNHCR's Note on International Protection (n 83) paras 8, 10–11, 31, and 32 in particular. The UNHCR's Note on the Mandate (n 69) 1, replicates the same definition.

Developments since tend to suggest that UNHCR has moved even further from orienting its wider responsibilities around the concept of refugee to the view that it is better to organise conceptually around broader notions of international protection. Aleinikoff even questions the view sometimes expressed that UNHCR's 'core mandate'[86] continues to be refugees. He describes the evolution of UNHCR's mandate as:

> [ ... ] a story of consistent expansion along four dimensions: (1) the category of refugee (to include persons escaping generalised violence in their home countries, asylum-seekers and returnees); (2) growth of protection activities (including the supervisory responsibility); (3) massive increase in the provision of assistance (including provision of direct assistance by UNHCR); and (4) expansion of the categories of groups to whom the mandate extends (stateless persons and conflict-IDPs).[87]

For Crisp, this shift means that UNHCR is 'beginning to resemble an Office of the High Commissioner for Forced Migrants' concerned with 'people on the move'.[88] He lists, as persons who have been (or who are in the process of being) drawn into the ambit of UNHCR's policy concerns and operational activities: stateless people, internally displaced populations, irregular and stranded and survival migrants, populations affected by climate change, natural disaster victims, the urban displaced, and Palestinians outside the scope of UNRWA protection.[89] So far as concerns stateless persons, it should be noted that UNHCR's mandate also derives from separate UNGA resolutions referring, for example, to the 1961 Statelessness Convention.[90]

It remains UNHCR's view that some of the aforementioned categories (e.g. populations affected by climate change) may in certain circumstances fall within the Article 1A(2) definition,[91] but those falling outside it are no longer viewed as marginal. My purpose in drawing attention to this shift is not to evaluate its merits or demerits, but simply to chart how the concept of refugee, in its broader understanding, is increasingly becoming subsumed under protection-oriented categorisations.

---

[86] 'Core mandate' was a key term used in UNHCR, Note on the Mandate (n 69) 3.
[87] Aleinikoff (n 68) 410–13, 415. See also UNGA Res 64/127 (18 December 2009) para 18, which described 'protection of refugees' as the organisation's 'core mandate'.
[88] Jeff Crisp, 'Refugees, Persons of Concern, and People on the Move: The Broadening Boundaries of UNHCR' (2009) 26 Refuge 1, 73–4. This view rather obscures the role of the International Organisation for Migration (IOM), whose remit includes forced displacement: see International Organization for Migration, *Mission*, available at <http://www.iom.int/mission> accessed 9 June 2016.
[89] Crisp (n 88) 74–75.
[90] See UNHCR, Note on the Mandate (n 69) 8–10.
[91] UNHCR, Legal considerations regarding claims for international protection made in the context of the adverse effects of climate change and disasters (1 October 2020) available at <https://www.refworld.org/docid/5f75f2734.html> accessed 2 April 2021. See also UNHCR, *Legal considerations on refugee protection for people fleeing conflict and famine affected countries* (5 April 2017) available at <http://www.refworld.org/docid/5906e0824.html> accessed 2 April 2021.

## 2.3 Regional Definitions of Refugee

Then there are, of course, the regional refugee definitions.[92] The three most important are those established in Africa, Central and Latin America, and the European Union, but mention needs also to be made of the Bangkok Principles and the Arab Convention.

### 2.3.1 Organisation of African Unity Convention (OAU Convention), 1969

The 1969 Convention Governing the Specific Aspects of Refugee Problems in Africa (OAU Convention)[93] contains an expanded refugee definition. Its two-part definition incorporates the definition from Article 1A(2) but adds a second limb, applying the term 'refugee' to:

> [...] every person who, owing to external aggression, occupation, foreign domination or events seriously disturbing public order in either part or the whole of his country of origin or nationality, is compelled to leave his place of habitual residence in order to seek refuge in another place outside his country of origin or nationality.

Such an extended definition was felt necessary to address the specific refugee-producing situations arising in the context of decolonisation and the defence of the independence and territorial integrity of the Organisation's member states. Whilst only a regional definition, it is a treaty definition and as such 'hard-law'.[94]

### 2.3.2 Cartagena Declaration, 1984

The 1984 Cartagena Declaration on Refugees (Cartagena Declaration)[95] provides that:

> [T]he definition or concept of a refugee to be recommended for use in the region [that is, Central America] is one which, in addition to containing the elements of the 1951 Convention and the 1967 Protocol, includes among refugees persons who have fled their country because their lives, safety or freedom have been threatened by generalized violence, foreign aggression, internal conflicts, massive violation of human rights or other circumstances which have seriously disturbed public order.[96]

Although there are some differences, this formulation follows the same two-part approach as the OAU Convention, its first part setting out the Article 1A(2) definition, its second, an 'enlarged' definition.

---

[92] Focus here is confined to refugee definitions; there are also of course other regional instruments dealing with other aspects of refugee status: see UNHCR Handbook (n 5) paras 20–21; see generally, Part III: Regional Regimes in Costello et al (eds) (n 48).

[93] Organization of African Unity (OAU), Convention Governing the Specific Aspects of Refugee Problems in Africa (adopted 10 September 1969, entered into force 20 June 1974) 1001 UNTS 45 (OAU Convention). The OAU became the African Union in 2002.

[94] For recent analyses, see Marina Sharpe, 'Regional Refugee Regimes: Africa' in Costello et al (eds) (n 48) 279–95; *Special Issue on the OAU and Kampala Conventions* (2019) 31 IJRL 2/3.

[95] *Instrumentos Regionales sobre Refugiados y temas relacionados, Declaración de Cartagena sobre Refugiados, Adoptado por el 'Coloquio Sobre la Protección Internacional de los Refugiados en América Central, México y Panamá: Problemas Jurídicos y Humanitarios'* (adopted 22 November 1984).

[96] ibid Conclusion No 3.

Unlike the OAU Convention, the Cartagena Declaration, being only a non-binding declaration, is not 'hard-law'. However, as Reed-Hurtado has highlighted, it 'has gained legal force through its widespread incorporation, encouraged by the OAS General Assembly,[97] into national legal frameworks across the region'.[98]

### 2.3.3 EU Qualification Directive, 2004 and recast 2011

Next to consider is the refugee definition set out in the EU Qualification Directive (QD).[99] Originating in 2004, this directive was recast in 2011.[100] Unlike the other regional definitions mentioned so far, that given in the QD does not seek to expand the refugee definition beyond Article 1A(2) but rather to codify greater definitional details of its key terms. Nevertheless, it constitutes a definition of refugee in independent treaty form and, although this largely replicates Article 1A(2), it does not entirely do so.

Article 2(d) provides that:

> [ ... ] 'refugee' means a third-country national who, owing to a well-founded fear of being persecuted for reasons of race, religion, nationality, political opinion or membership of a particular social group, is outside the country of nationality and is unable or, owing to such fear, is unwilling to avail himself or herself of the protection of that country, or a stateless person, who, being outside of the country of former habitual residence for the same reasons as mentioned above, is unable or, owing to such fear, unwilling to return to it, and to whom Article 12 does not apply ....

Unlike Article 1A(2), this definition narrows the personal scope to third-country nationals and (among several other modifications) omits the second paragraph of Article 1A(2) dealing with multiple nationality. The Directive, however, proclaims that the Refugee Convention is the 'cornerstone' of its international protection regime[101] and contains several other direct or indirect references to Article 1A(2), including in its definition of 'acts of persecution' in Article 9(1)(a).[102] The Court of Justice of the

---

[97] See Organization of American States (OAS) General Assembly, Legal Status of Asylees, Refugees, and Displaces Persons in the American Hemisphere (9 December 1985) AG/Res 774 (XV–0/85).
[98] Michael Reed-Hurtado, 'The Cartagena Declaration on Refugees and the Protection of People Fleeing Armed Conflict and Other Situations of Violence in Latin America' (2013) UNHCR Legal and Protection Policy Series, 4–5; Jose H Fischel De Andrade, 'Regional Refugee Regimes: Latin America' in Costello et al (eds) (n 48) 321–23. According to De Andrade, even though the Declaration had 'an unprecedented impact in Latin America, both on policy, legal developments, and the conduct of protection policy advocacy; its practical, political and legal relevance, has 'with the passage of time ... become obsolete; except as "an effective advocacy model"'.
[99] Council Directive 2004/83/EC of 29 April 2004 on minimum standards for the qualification and status of third country nationals or stateless persons as refugees or as persons who otherwise need international protection and the content of the protection granted [2004] OJ L 304.
[100] Directive 2011/95/EU of the European Parliament and of the Council of 13 December 2011 on standards for the qualification of third-country nationals or stateless persons as beneficiaries of international protection, for a uniform status for refugees or for persons eligible for subsidiary protection, and for the content of the protection granted (recast) [2011] OJ L 337 (QD recast).
[101] ibid Recital (4).
[102] ibid Article 9(1); Recitals (14) and (23).

European Union (CJEU) has held that the QD is deemed to have been adopted 'to guide the competent authorities ... in the application of [the Refugee] Convention'.[103]

The plain intent of the Directive and its recast to offer interpretive guidance on the meaning of key terms of Article 1A(2) raises a complex issue, which will be discussed further in Chapter 2, regarding whether it amounts to an illegitimate modification of the terms of the Refugee Convention, contrary to Article 41 VCLT.[104]

It must not be forgotten that even though the QD does not offer an expanded definition of refugee, its creation of a regime of 'subsidiary protection' has important commonalities with those regions that have adopted expanded refugee definitions.

### 2.3.4 Bangkok Principles on the Status and Treatment of Refugees, December 1966 (Bangkok Principles)

The Bangkok Principles,[105] which constitute a non-binding instrument, were the result of deliberations by the Asian-African Legal Consultative Organization (AALCO), an intergovernmental body. The 1966 Principles were revised in 2001.[106] Article 1 of the Bangkok Principles is closely modelled on the OAU definition, and likewise adopts an essentially two-part definition, encompassing one part that closely follows the wording of Article 1A(2) and an additional category at paragraph 2 stating that:

2. The term 'refugee' shall also apply to every person, who, owing to external aggression, occupation, foreign domination or events seriously disturbing public order in either part or the whole of his country of origin or nationality, is compelled to leave his place of habitual residence in order to seek refuge in another place outside his country of origin or nationality.

Although dating from 1966, these Principles were only finally approved formally in 2001. Albeit only soft law, they have been seen to have an influence on the protection of refugees in Asia, where ratification of the international refugee instruments is limited.[107]

---

[103] Joined Cases C-175/08, C-176/08, C-178/08, and C-179/082 *Aydin Salahadin Abdulla and Others v Bundesrepublik Deutschland* [2010] EU:C:2010:105, para 52. See also Cases C-57/09 and C-101/09 *Bundesrepublik Deutschland v B and D* [2010] EU:C:2010:661, paras 93, 97; Case C-720/17 *Mohammed Bilali v Bundesamt für Fremdenwesen und Asyl* [2019] EU:C:2018:276, para 54, referring also to Case C-396/17 *Shajin Ahmed v Bevándorlási és Menekültügyi Hivatal* [2018] EU:C:2018:713, para 37.
[104] A question posed by Goodwin-Gill and McAdam (n 6) 66–67. See discussion in Chapter 2, section 4.2.
[105] Asian-African Legal Consultative Organization (AALCO), Bangkok Principles on the Status and Treatment of Refugees (31 December 1966) available at: <https://www.refworld.org/docid/3de5f2d52.html>
[106] UNHCR, 'Collection of International Instruments and Legal Texts Concerning Refugees and Others of Concern to UNHCR, vol. III: Regional Instruments: Asia, Middle East, Asia, Americas' (2007) 1187, para 2.
[107] Sébastien Moretti, 'Keeping Up Appearances: State Sovereignty and the Protection of Refugees in Southeast Asia' (2018) 17 European Journal of East Asian Studies 1, 3–30; Sébastien Moretti, 'Southeast Asia and the 1951 Convention Relating to the Status of Refugees: Substance without Form?' (2021) 33(2) IJRL 214; Vitit Muntarbhorn, 'Regional Refugee Regimes: Southeast Asia' in Costello et al (eds) (n 48) 428–49. See also Andreas Zimmermann and Claudia Mahler, 'Article 1 A, para. 2' in Zimmermann (n 14) 319–20.

### 2.3.5 League of Arab States, Arab Convention on Regulating Status of Refugees in the Arab Countries, 1994

This Convention[108] was adopted in 1994 but has not been ratified.[109] Casting its definition of refugee in similar fashion to the OAU Convention and Cartagena Declaration definitions, Article 1, in the second paragraph provides that:

> Any person who unwillingly takes refuge in a country other than his country of origin or his habitual place of residence because of sustained aggression against, occupation and foreign domination of such country or because of the occurrence of natural disasters or grave events resulting in major disruption of public order in the whole country or any part thereof.

It is the first regional instrument to include reference to 'natural disasters'.

From the above, it can be seen that notwithstanding a somewhat complex legal picture, it remains true that, along with the parallel provisions of the UNHCR Statute (and disregarding continuing provision in both instruments for 'statutory refugees' and the aforementioned incorporation in the first limb of the OAU Convention definition), the refugee definition in Article 1A(2) is the only one that exists in international treaty law. In addition, whilst all the regional definitions but for the EU seek to extend the refugee definition, all take Article 1A(2) as their cornerstone and starting-point.

## 2.4 National Definitions of Refugee

Despite the plain intent of Articles 35(2), 36, and 37 of the Convention to achieve a situation where the Article 1A(2) definition is applied in the national law of each contracting party,[110] national transpositions are not always faithful to the text. As a result, it remains the case, as Shacknove observed in 1985, there are 'dozens of definitions [of refugee] in effect within various jurisdictions'.[111]

Numerous UNGA resolutions[112] have urged all governments to facilitate the High Commissioner's function of international protection, by not only acceding to the 1951 Convention and the 1967 Protocol and considering regional instruments to complement it, but also by elaborating appropriate procedures at the national level for effective implementation.[113] The UNHCR Statute calls on contracting states to

---

[108] Arab Convention on Regulating Status of Refugees in the Arab Countries (1994). See also Marina Sharpe, *The Regional Law of Protection in Africa* (OUP 2018) 37.

[109] Maja Janmyr and Dallal Stevens, 'Regional Refugee Regimes: Middle East' in Costello et al (eds) (n 48) 339.

[110] UNGA Res 428(V) (14 December 1950) 2(a) and 8(f).

[111] Andrew Shacknove, 'Who Is a Refugee?' (1985) 95 Ethics 274–75.

[112] e.g. UNGA Res 2040 (XX) (7 December 1965); UNGA Res 2594 (XXIV) (16 December 1969); UNGA Res 2650 (XXV) (30 November 1970); UNGA Res 3454 (XXX) (1 December 1975); UNGA Res 31/35 (30 November 1976); UNGA Res 32/67 (8 December 1977).

[113] By Article 35(2), contracting states are obliged to provide 'information' about implementation. Article 36 obliges on contracting states to communicate to the Secretary-General of the UN 'the laws and regulations which they may adopt to ensure the application of this Convention'. See also Articles II and III of the 1967 Protocol (n 2).

co-operate over implementation and (like its Refugee Convention counterpart) obliges UNHCR to seek to obtain information from governments, including as regards 'the laws and regulations concerning' the number and conditions of refugees. In a significant number of Conclusions adopted by the member states of UNHCR's Executive Committee (ExCom), states have been urged to take legal and/or administrative measures to achieve effective implementation of the Refugee Convention and its 1967 Protocol.[114] The 2001 Global Consultations process was initiated with one of its primary objectives being a more complete implementation of these instruments.[115]

There has also been action taken at a regional level to achieve greater and more faithful national implementation. For example, the 1979 Pan-African Arusha Conference on African Refugees, made recommendations endorsed by the OAU and the UNGA.[116] With a view to ensuring their 'increased effectiveness', it was recommended that the 'various principles relating to asylum as defined in the 1969 OAU Refugee Convention and other relevant international instruments' should be incorporated into the national law of African states. This led to UNHCR producing guidelines to assist African states with this task.[117]

Nevertheless, as UNGA, UNHCR ExCom, and OAU initiatives convey, the matter of incorporation of the Article 1A(2) refugee definition at the national level is far from being straightforward, complicated by the fact that some countries expressly acknowledge the principle of asylum in their constitutions and in some national legal system, treaties have direct effect. In any event, there continues to be a significant problem of transpositions and/or revisions[118] that deviate from the text of Article 1A(2).[119]

---

[114] e.g. ExCom, Implementation of the 1951 Convention and the 1967 Protocol Relating to the Status of Refugees (13 October 1989) No 57 (XL); Marjoleine Zieck, 'Article 35/Article III1' in Zimmermann (n 14) 1507–10, 1524–25.

[115] UNHCR, Ministerial Meeting of States Parties to the 1951 Convention relating to the Status of Refugees and UNHCR's Global Consultations on International Protection: Background (2001) 2.

[116] Council of Ministers of the Organization of African Unity (6–20 July 1979) CM/Res 727 (XXXIII); UNGA Res 34/61 (29 November 1979).

[117] UNHCR, Guidelines for National Refugee Legislation, with Commentary (9 December 1980) HCR/120/41/80/GE.81–0013.

[118] On the restrictive nature of 2001 and 2014 amendments to the Australian Migration Act definition of refugee, see Linda Kirk, 'Island Nation: The Impact of International Human Rights Law on Australian Refugee Law' in Bruce Burson and David Cantor (eds), *Human Rights and the Refugee Definition* (Brill Nijhoff 2016) 49, 76–85.

[119] UNHCR, Note on Determination of Refugee Status under International Instruments (24 August 1977) EC/SCP/5, para 3. In this note, UNHCR observed that 'a definition of refugee status (or of analogous legal status, such as that of "asylee") is contained in the Constitution or in the ordinary legislation of a number of countries. Whereas a welcome trend has developed in recent years to include in such national legislation a definition close to the definition of the 1951 Convention or the 1967 Protocol, the national definitions of refugees are generally at variance, particularly if they were drafted in earlier periods, with those contained in international instruments adopted by the United Nations, or concluded under its auspices.' See also paras 23–24. Goodwin-Gill and McAdam (n 6) 45–50 discuss examples of municipal law implementation in Germany, Australia, France, the US, Canada, the UK, and Switzerland among other countries. They note at 49 the 'inclination of some States to tinker with international texts, or to 'legislate' particular interpretive approaches that are perceived to align more closely with national policy'. See also Eve Lester, 'National Constitutions and Refugee Protection' in Costello et al (eds) (n 48) 266–67, who notes the potential for an 'antagonistic relationship' between international refugee law and national constitutions. Incorrect transposition continues to be a problem even within some EU countries bound by EU asylum law: see European Commission, 'Evaluation of the application of the recast Qualification Directive (2011/95/EU): Final Report' (n 13).

Whether by virtue of Article 5 or otherwise, this is not problematic insofar as such definitions are more generous,[120] but has been extremely problematic where they are obviously or arguably more restrictive.[121]

The possibility, and sometimes the reality, of more restrictive codification points up the structural problem confronting applicants seeking recognition as a refugee under Article 1A(2). When they claim asylum within the territory of countries that are party to the Refugee Convention and/or its 1967 Protocol, their applications are dealt with under the national law of those countries. The refugee definition is only made operational through national law. National law provides the 'functional link' between the refugee definition and status.[122] It is national systems of law that ordinarily also provide, for instance, a refugee determination procedure (or delegate provision of same to UNHCR),[123] including procedures for appeal against refugee determination decisions etc. The absence of any procedural guarantees in the Refugee Convention means that the actual fate of asylum seekers and refugees turns heavily on the viability of national law. Further, the recognition they receive as a refugee is recognition under national law,[124] not at the universal level, albeit it remains as a matter of treaty law that the recognition of refugee status is a declaratory act, and the underlying status of refugee depends on a person having met the requirements set out in the refugee definition, not in national law.[125]

Another consequence of the variable implementation into national law of the refugee definition is that care must always be taken when having recourse to national case law as a source for interpretation, that the definition they apply is in fact Article 1A(2).[126]

---

[120] See for analysis of progressive Latin American legislation, Luisa Feline Freier, 'A Liberal Paradigm Shift? A Critical Appraisal of Recent Trends in Latin American Asylum Legislation' in Jean-Pierre Gauci et al (eds), *Exploring the Boundaries of Refugee Law* (2015 Brill Nijhoff 2015) 118–45.

[121] See UNHCR, 'Implementation of the 1951 Convention and the 1967 Protocol Relating to the Status of Refugees—Some Basic Questions' (15 June 1992) UN Doc EC/1992/SCP/CRP.10, para 9. Noted as one of three categories of obstacles to proper implementation was 'the clash of, or inconsistencies between existing national laws and certain Convention obligations; failure to incorporate the Convention into national law through specific implementation legislation; or implementing legislation which defines not the rights of the individuals but rather the powers vested in refugee officials.... Where the judiciary has an important role in protecting refugee rights, restrictive interpretations can also be an impediment to full implementation....' See also other references in Kälin (n 15) 631.

[122] Vincent Chetail, 'Are Refugee Rights Human Rights? An Unorthodox Questioning of the Relations between Refugee Law and Human Rights Law' in Ruth Rubio-Marin (ed), *Human Rights and Immigration* (OUP 2014) 51: 'As formulated the Refugee Convention fails to lay down a working system for determining who comes within the refugee definition. No specific procedure is explicitly mentioned in the Refugee Convention and as a result national law must provide the functional link' between the refugee definition and refugee status.'

[123] Bruce Burson, 'Refugee Status Determination' in Costello et al (eds) (n 48) 578, notes that 'RSD systems exist on a structural spectrum, with State-administered RSD at one end and [UNHCR] mandate RSD at the other. In between a variety of forms exist.'

[124] That remains the case even within the EU and under the QD (recast), as stated by Harald Dörig, 'Asylum Qualification Directive 2011/95/EU: Articles 1–10' in Hailbronner and Thym (n 8) 1231: '[i]t is still a national status'. See Council Directive 2011/95/EU (n 100) Articles 1–10.

[125] UNHCR Handbook (n 5) para 28. See also, Joined Cases C-391/16, C-77/17, and C-78/17 *M and Others v Commissaire général aux réfugiés et aux apatrides* [2019] ECLI:EU:C:2019:403, para 85; *G (Appellant) v G (Respondent)* [2021] UKSC 9, para 81.

[126] As noted in section 2.3 of this chapter, the Canadian Supreme Court in *Ward* was not interpreting Article 1A(2) verbatim. See *Canada (AG) v Ward* [1993] 2 SCR 689.

## 3 Limits of the Refugee Definition

A perennial question about the refugee definition that needs tackling is, what are its limits? Like all legal definitions, it serves as a mechanism for inclusion and exclusion,[127] but that still leaves the problem of identifying those limits. In the refugee law literature two particular perspectives, not necessarily at odds with one another, jostle for attention. One proclaims that because the Refugee Convention is a 'living instrument' its definition of refugee, through evolution of state practice, is capable of application beyond what was envisaged by its drafters. The other deposes that as time has gone on it has become increasingly plain that the definition's limitations have resulted in 'protection gaps' and that it increasingly needs complementing with wider protection mechanisms. Criticism of the definition's limitations will be briefly examined next, but it is first necessary to try and clarify what are its limits in legal terms.

That the Article 1A(2) refugee definition is not all-encompassing was unmistakably the view of the Convention's drafters and indeed that of the UNGA which enacted it in treaty form. All involved made clear that the definition was to be understood as broad and inclusive but not limitless.[128] As already noted, the fact that the definition was not intended to cover all refugees is also made clear by the terms of the Conference of Plenipotentiaries Recommendation E in the Final Act, which urges states parties to apply the Convention beyond 'its contractual scope' to other 'refugees 'who would not be covered by the terms of the Convention.' As also observed earlier, recognition by the UNGA that the UNHCR Statute and Article 1A(2) definitions do not exhaust their concept of refugee, has been long-standing.[129]

UNHCR has acknowledged the limitations of the Statute and Convention definition of refugee on many occasions.[130] The case law and wider literature also contains frequent recognition of the textual limitations. Thus, Jacqueline Bhaba wrote in 2002:

> [F]rom the outset, the refugee protection regime was intended to be restrictive and partial, a compromise between unfettered state sovereignty over the admission of aliens, and an open door for non-citizen victims of serious human rights violation. It was always clear that only a subset of forced transnational migrant persecutees were intended beneficiaries.[131]

It is possible to be more specific as to the precise nature of the definition's legal limits?

---

[127] Russell Sandberg, *Religion, Law and Society* (CUP 2014) 29.
[128] Terje Einarsen, 'Drafting History of the 1951 Convention and the 1967 Protocol' in Zimmermann (n 14) 56–58. Nehemiah Robinson, *Convention Relating to the Status of Stateless Persons: Its History and Interpretation, A Commentary* (UNHCR 1997) 8 describes the limits to the definition as being mainly due to the desire of the framers to reach unanimity and 'not to write a document which may be ideal in its wording but would not be acceptable to many governments'.
[129] See e.g. UNGA Res 1388 (XIV) (n 74); see further sections 2.2.2–2.4.4 in this chapter.
[130] e.g. UNHCR, Note on International Protection (n 83) para 30: '[h]owever liberally its terms are applied, some refugees fleeing the civil wars and other forms of armed conflict that are the most frequent immediate causes of refugee flight fall outside the letter of the Convention'.
[131] Jacqueline Bhabha, 'Internationalist Gatekeepers: The Tension between Asylum Advocacy and Human Rights' (2002) 15 Harv Hum Rts LJ 155, 167.

## 3.1 Temporal and Geographical Limitations?

As noted earlier, the refugee definition originally applied only to persons who met the terms of the definition '[a]s a result of events occurring before 1 January 1951', that is, events that had already transpired at the time of the Refugee Convention's creation. Additionally, by the terms of Article 1B, an option existed to confine those events to those occurring only in Europe before the cut-off date. The 1967 Protocol converted the refugee definition to one of 'universal' application by eliminating the restrictions on the place and date of circumstances that motivated their flight. Hence (save in relation to very few state parties) these limitations no longer obtain.[132]

## 3.2 Exclusion and Cessation Clauses

Clearly bespeaking the refugee definition's limited scope are the exclusion and cessation clauses set out at 1C, 1D, 1E, and 1F of the same Article. In relation to the exclusion clauses, these cover not only those excluded by Article 1F—individuals deemed to be undeserving of the protection which refugee status entails. They also encompass persons considered not to be in need of refugee status, either because they are already receiving protection or assistance from organs or agencies of the UN other than UNHCR (Article 1D),[133] or because the country in which they have taken up residence treats them equivalently to its own nationals (Article 1E). The Article 1C cessation clauses underline that the refugee definition is temporally contingent and does not extend to those persons who have ceased to be in need of international protection—e.g. because of a significant change in circumstances.

## 3.3 Limitations Inherent in Article 1A(2) Definition

There are also limitations inherent in key elements of the Article 1A(2) definition. Since these will be examined more closely in subsequent chapters, it will suffice to mention by way of illustration here that, even on the widest possible reading, the stated definition does not include, for example, all those who have a 'fear' of being persecuted: they must show that there is a *well-founded* fear. As will be explained below, persecution has been seen to require human agency, which often renders problematic its application to persons fleeing natural disasters.[134] Equally clear is that merely being able to show one faces a 'well-founded fear of being persecuted' is not enough: one must also show it is '*by reason of*' one of five enumerated reasons.

---

[132] For most up-to-date list, see <https://treaties.un.org/Pages/ViewDetails.aspx?src=TREATY&mtdsg_no=V-5&chapter=5&clang=_en>.

[133] However, Article 1D also contains a 'contingent inclusion clause': see Goodwin-Gill and McAdam (n 6) 153.

[134] See Chapter 6, sections 3.1–3.2, and also 2.2.5.

## 3.4 Limitations Imposed by International Law Framework (VCLT)

Limitations also flow from the Refugee Convention's status as a public international law treaty. As such, it must be interpreted in conformity with the rules set out in Articles 31–33 of the VCLT.[135] Whilst as will be seen from Chapter 2, these rules are to be flexibly applied, they do set a number of constraints on the scope of the meaning that can be derived from Article 1A(2)'s provisions.

## 4 Criticisms of the Refugee Definition

This book seeks to analyse the refugee definition rather than to evaluate its relative merits and demerits as a mechanism for international protection. But in order to help situate its role in refugee law and also to understand the wider environment in which its interpretation is conducted, it is salient to survey briefly the main criticisms of this wider kind that have been levelled at it, some of which overlap.

Criticisms of the refugee definition are legion. For the first two decades after 1951, the understandable focus of much of the criticism was, of course, on its temporal and geographical limitations.[136] The 1967 Protocol's elimination of these limitations answered those criticisms[137] but others abound.

### 4.1 Eurocentrism

The definition has been branded 'Eurocentric'. Lending some support for that label, the *travaux* record Monsieur Rochefort of France, for example, stating that '[i]n laying down the definition of the term "refugee", account had always been taken of the fact that the refugees principally involved had originated from a certain part of the world; thus, such a definition was based on historical facts'.[138] Even after the elimination of the temporal limits and geographical limitations accomplished by the 1967 Protocol, alleged Eurocentrism has remained as one of the most pervasive criticisms. Thus, Gervase Coles saw the definition as having been devised to address the particular problem at the time of 'new refugees', the majority of whom were from Eastern Europe. As such '[b]oth in its conception, and in practice, [its] ad hoc and partisan character ... was incontrovertible'.[139] Astri Suhrke has described the definition's persecution requirement as 'a product of Western liberal thinking and Western political supremacy in the 1950s' and has portrayed it as 'reflect[ing] particularist notions

---

[135] VCLT (n 12).
[136] Daniel J Steinbock, 'Interpreting the Refugee Definition' (1998) 45 UCLA Law Review 733, 739.
[137] See this chapter, section 3.1.
[138] UN Conference of Plenipotentiaries on the Status of Refugees and Stateless Persons (n 33) 15, remarks of Mr Rochefort of France.
[139] Gervase Coles, 'Approaching the Refugee Problem Today' in Gil Loescher and Laila Monahan (eds), *Refugees and International Relations* (OUP 1989) 374–75, cited in Matthew E Price, *Rethinking Asylum History, Purpose, and Limits* (CUP 2010) 58.

of needs and rights'.[140] In a similar vein, Jerzy Sztucki has noted that its definition is 'sometimes described as a Cold War product, "Eurocentric" and, if only for these reasons, obsolete'.[141] Even James Hathaway, who has done more than virtually anyone to portray the Convention as a universalist instrument, described it in his 1991 *The Law of Refugee Status*, as 'incomplete and politically partisan'.[142] It is now common to find the Convention described as working to protect the interests of Global North states.[143]

## 4.2 State-centrism

Even after the 1967 Protocol eliminated two key European-specific provisions, criticisms that the definition is based on Westphalian concepts of state sovereignty and is 'state-centric' have persisted. Thus, Sitaropolous has written that:

> Despite the positive and dynamic development from 1969 onwards in the African continent and in the Americas, the actual lack of a contemporary inter-continental treaty recognising the current forms and causes of refugee exodus has been a reflection of the predominant state-centric ideology in the international society, whose members' pragmatic interests have made it refuse to recognise, in effect, the reality of the modern world, and to accept *de jure* the novel post-1960 forms of forced migration.[144]

## 4.3 Colonialist Roots

Often underscoring the charge of state-centrism, some have criticised the Convention's character as a First World mechanism reflective of the history of colonialism and the domination of the Global North over the Global South. The foundational role colonialism and present day 'coloniality' have played in international law arrangements

---

[140] Astri Suhrke, 'Global Refugee Movements and Strategies of Response' in Mary M Kritz (ed), *U.S. Immigration and Refugee Policy: Global and Domestic Issues* (Lexington Books 1983) 159, cited in Price (n 139) 59. In 1997, Kourula (n 9) 353 noted that '[t]he prevalent view appears to be that the 1951 Convention definition is deficient, too narrow and unreceptive to the contemporary reality'. See also Susan M Akram, 'Orientalism Revisited in Asylum and Refugee Claims' (2000) 12 IJRL 7.
[141] Sztucki (n 58) 55; see also Betts and Collier (n 13) 6, 34–39.
[142] James C Hathaway, *The Law of Refugee Status* (Butterworths Limited 1991) 8.
[143] Rebecca Hamlin, 'The Politics of International Refugee Law and Protection' in Costello et al (eds) (n 48) 100.
[144] Nicholas Sitaropolous, 'Refugee: A Legal Definition in Search of a Principled Interpretation by Domestic Fora' (1999) 53 Hellenic Review of International Law, 158. See also T Alexander Aleinikoff, 'State-Centered Refugee Law: From Resettlement to Containment' (1992) 14 Michigan Journal of International Law 120, 122; Nevzat Soguk, *States and Strangers: Refugees and Displacements of Statecraft* (University of Minnesota Press 1999); Guy S Goodwin-Gill, 'The International Law of Refugee Protection' in Elena Fiddian-Qasmiyeh et al (eds), *The Oxford Handbook of Refugee and Forced Migration Studies* (OUP 2014) 44; T Alexander Aleinikoff and Leah Zamore, *The Arc of Protection: Reforming the International Refugee Regime* (Stanford Briefs 2019) 134.

for migration and asylum has been the subject of considerable study.[145] Perhaps the best-known summation of this type of criticism is to be found in the famous statement of Ambalavaner Sivanandan, '[w]e are here because you were there'.[146] Within this perspective, 'Western geopolitics' is seen as having contributed to the destabilisation of some of the countries from which people flee. Attention has been drawn to the paradox that laws discriminating against persons of diverse sexual orientation and gender identity, which were in many countries a colonial import, are now one basis for people seeking refugee status in former imperial countries with more inclusive laws.

## 4.4 Age and Gender Insensitivities

There is a significant body of literature that regards the Article 1A(2) definition, despite its universalist language, as reflective of patriarchal, androcentric, and societal attitudes of the day. This could be said to be implicit in the fact that ExCom felt it necessary to produce a number of Conclusions over the years highlighting that persecution can be gender-related.[147] That UNHCR chose to develop as its first set of *Guidelines on International Protection*, further guidance on gender-related persecution (No 1), and another specific set on child asylum claims (No 8) have been seen as probative of original insensitivities.[148]

---

[145] See e.g. B S Chimni, 'The Geopolitics of Refugee Studies: A View from the South' (1998) 11(4) JRS 350; Akram (n 140). For recent examples, see e.g. Lucy Mayblin, 'Colonialism, Decolonisation and the Right to Be Human: Britain and the 1951 Geneva Convention on the Status of Refugees' (2014) 27(3) Journal of Historical Sociology 423, 437; Lucy Mayblin, *Asylum after Empire: Colonial Legacies in the Politics of Asylum Seeking* (Roman & Littlefield International 2017); Ulrike Krause, 'Colonial Roots of the 1951 Refugee Convention and its Effects on the Global Refugee Regime' [2021] J Int Relat Dev. One aspect of such criticisms (not limited to the colonial context) concerns the apparent focus entailed by the refugee definition on the legal obligations of the physical state of origin, rather than on the external actors who may have caused or contributed to internal crises resulting in refugee flows (superpowers, global corporations, other states, etc.): see e.g. Mark Gibney, 'US Foreign Policy and the Creation of Refugee Flows', in Howard Adelman (ed), *Refugee Policy: Canada and the United States* (York Lanes Press, Toronto 1991) 87–90, 93–100; Aristide R Zolberg, Astri Sukrke, and Sergio Aguayo, *Escape from Violence: Conflict and the Refugee Crisis in the Developing World* (OUP, 1989) 260–63.

[146] See Colin Prescod, 'Remembering Ambalavaner Sivanandan' (Pluto Press, 2018) available at <https://www.plutobooks.com/blog/remembering-ambalavaner-sivanandan/> accessed 7 April 2021.

[147] ExCom Conclusion No 87 (1999). See also ExCom Conclusions: No 39 on Refugee Women and International Protection (1985); No 54 on Refugee Women (1998); No 64 on Refugee Women and International Protection (1990); No 73 on Refugee Protection and Sexual Violence (1993); No 77(g) on General Conclusion on International Protection (1995); No 105 on Women and Girls At Risk (2006). See also No 81(t) on General Conclusion on International Protection (1997).

[148] See Report of the UNHCR Symposium on Gender-Based Persecution (1997) 9 IJRL (Special Issue) 11. See also UNHCR, The International Protection of Refugees: Interpreting Article 1 of the 1951 Convention Relating to the Status of Refugees (2001) UN Doc A/AC.96/951, paras 29–32; UNHCR, Guidelines No 1: Gender-Related Persecution within the context of Article 1A(2) of the 1951 Convention and/or its 1967 Protocol relating to the Status of Refugees (2002) UN Doc HCR/GIP/02/01; UNHCR, Guidelines No 8: Child Asylum Claims under Articles 1(A)2 and 1(F) of the 1951 Convention and/or 1967 Protocol relating to the Status of Refugees (2009) UN Doc HCR/GIP/09/08; UNHCR, Guidelines No 9: Claims to Refugee Status based on Sexual Orientation and/or Gender Identity within the context of Article 1A(2) of the 1951 Convention and/or its 1967 Protocol relating to the Status of Refugees (23 October 2012) HCR/GIP/12/01. See further Jacqueline Greatbatch, 'The Gender Difference: Feminist Critiques of Refugee Discourse' (1989) 1 IJRL 518, 519–20; Joan Fitzpatrick, 'Revitalizing the 1951 Refugee Convention' (1996) 9 Harv Hum Rts LJ 229, 232–33; Alice Edwards, 'Age and Gender Dimensions in International Refugee

## 4.5 Territorial Bias

The Convention provides a definition of refugee premised on the concept of 'territorial asylum', meaning broadly protection accorded by a state to an individual who comes to seek it.[149] With the territorial dimension in mind, numerous criticisms assail this premise as an attempt to provide a (First World) geopolitically-minded solution to the plight of refugees. Matthew Price, for example, takes note of two particular criticisms voiced in the literature, one of 'proximity bias', the other of 'expatriate bias'.[150] Price writes that asylum has a 'proximity bias' because 'it is available only to refugees who manage to enter the territory of the state of refuge. But those refugees might not be the most in need of help.'[151] He says that '[t]his group is only a small subset of all of those who are in need of membership abroad, and may not be most in need'.[152] In rejecting moral arguments in defence of 'proximity bias', he highlights that women, children, and the poor are systematically disadvantaged by the requirement that they leave their country in order to gain protection abroad.[153] Although Price's argument overlooks perhaps that the vast majority of refugees are actually hosted in their region of origin by developing countries, the grim numbers of those who over the past decade have lost their lives just considering the seas close to Europe, especially the Mediterranean and English Channel, has lent it added force.

Price sees asylum's 'expatriate bias' to arise because 'it helps people by giving them assistance abroad, rather than in their states of origin'.[154] He describes its 'locus of relief' as being within Western states of refuge rather than in refugees' states or regions of origin. 'But that', he writes, 'is an extremely costly way to offer refuge.'[155]

The fact that regional human rights courts and treaty-monitoring bodies have seen basic guarantees such as the prohibition on ill treatment to have only limited extraterritorial effect has accentuated the perceived limitations of the refugee definition's protective scope.[156]

---

Law' in Feller et al (eds) (n 15) 46–80, who notes at 48 the view of a number of commentators that the normative structure of international law has allowed issues of particular concern to women to be either ignored or undermined. See also Arbel et al (n 10); Adrienne Anderson, 'Flawed Foundations: An Historical Evaluation of Domestic Violence Claims in the Refugee Tribunals' (2021) 45(1) MULR 1. On children, see Jason Pobjoy, *The Child in International Refugee Law* (CUP 2017) 17.

[149] Paul Weis, 'The United Nations Declaration on Territorial Asylum' (1969) 7 Canadian Yearbook of International Law 92, 136.
[150] Price (n 139) 164. Also called 'exilic bias': see Chimni (n 145); Seyla Benhabib, 'The End of the 1951 Refugee Convention? Dilemmas of Sovereignty, Territoriality, and Human Rights' (2020) 2 Jus Cogens 75.
[151] Price (n 139) 164.
[152] ibid 182. Price refers to criticisms of proximity bias made by Michael Walzer, *Spheres of Justice: A Defence of Pluralism and Equality* (Basic Books 1983) 51.
[153] Price (n 139) 184–85. The need to travel has also been seen to have helped spawn organized crime through smuggling and trafficking activities.
[154] ibid 164.
[155] ibid 183. This side of Price's argument underplays the fact that the vast majority of refugees are actually hosted in their region of origin in developing countries.
[156] e.g. Violeta Moreno-Lax, *Accessing Asylum in Europe: Extraterritorial Border Controls and Refugee Rights under EU Law* (OUP 2017) chs 8–10. See Chapter 5, section 5.6.

## 4.6 Perceived Need for Complementary Protection Regimes

Lying behind some criticism of the refugee definition is the fact that state practice has increasingly seen it as an inadequate legal instrument of protection. The very fact that so many states have had to devise schemes for temporary protection, humanitarian protection, and other forms of complementary protection[157] can be seen as a testament to this shortcoming. Linked to this, IHRL has been recognised as in general imposing wider protection obligations.[158] In this context, it has been seen of particular significance that within the EU it was decided that because so many member states had domestic laws or policies providing one or more forms of temporary or complementary protection, it was necessary to enact a specific directive on temporary protection and to institute in its asylum legislation a concept of international protection encompassing both refugee protection and 'subsidiary protection'.[159]

## 4.7 Ethical and Moral Drawbacks

There have been many and varied criticisms of the ethical basis of the Refugee Convention, some already voiced in other criticisms summarised in this section. Some of these highlight the lack of a moral case for treating persons in danger from their own states differently depending on whether they have crossed borders or have the ability to travel to other countries.[160]

## 4.8 Perceived Redundancy and 'Under-Protectiveness'

Criticisms that the refugee definition has become redundant have been levelled from multiple vantage points. In a 2001 editorial, Goodwin-Gill noted criticisms that 'the Convention is redundant ... functionally inefficient, overly legalistic, complex and difficult to apply'.[161] Doubtless the most prominent criticism in this context has been that

---

[157] See Jane McAdam, 'Complementary Protection' in Costello et al (eds) (n 48) 662–63; see also UNHCR, Conclusion on the Provision of International Protection Including Through Complementary Forms of Protection No 103 (LVI)—2005 (2005) UN Doc A/AC.96/1021.
[158] McAdam (n 37) 20–23.
[159] ibid 53–59; Hemme Battjes, *European Asylum Law and International Law* (Martinus Nijhoff 2006) 152–53, 193–95, 222–24, 274–76.
[160] For a survey of this and other criticisms of the definition's ethical basis and an attempted response, see Kristen Walker, 'Defending the 1951 Convention Definition of Refugee' (2003) 17 Geo Immigr LJ 583. See also Walzer (n 152); Shacknove (n 111); Joseph Carens, 'Who Should Get In? The Ethics of Immigration Admissions' (2003) 17 Ethics & International Affairs 95; David Miller, *Global Justice and National Responsibility* (OUP 2007); Sara L Zeigler and Rendra B Stewart, 'Positioning Women's Rights within Asylum Policy: A Feminist Analysis of Political Persecution' (2009) 30(1) Frontiers: Journal of Women Studies 115; Matthew J Gibney, *The Ethics and Politics of Asylum: Liberal Democracy and the Response to Refugees* (CUP 2014); Jaakko Kuosmanen, 'What's So Special about Persecution?' (2014) 17 Ethical Theory and Moral Practice 129. See also Seyla Benhabib and Nishin Nathwani, 'The Ethics of International Refugee Protection' in Costello et al (eds) (n 48) 114–33; David Miller and Christine Straehle (eds), *The Political Philosophy of Refuge* (CUP 2020); Daniel Kersting and Marcus Leuoth (eds), *Der Begriff des Flüchtlings: Rechtliche, Moralische und Politische Kontroversen. The Concept of the Refugee: Legal, Moral and Political Controversies* (JB Metzler 2020).
[161] Guy S Goodwin-Gill, 'Asylum 2001—A Convention and a Purpose' (2001) 13(1/2) IJRL 1, 1.

the refugee definition has increasingly over time created more and more 'protection gaps' and is 'under-protective'.[162] The kernel of such criticisms has been the view that as time has gone on there are more and more categories of persons in need of international protection who are not covered by the definition.[163] Thus in 1989, Isabelle R Gunning, noting that 'refugees fleeing war and civil strife now account for the greatest proportion of forced migrants', argued for the expansion of the refugee definition to include them.[164]

Among those raising such criticisms, Schabas has argued that '[a]lthough this is known as "complementary protection", the human rights regime governing non-refoulement has largely taken over that of the Refugee Convention, which is gradually becoming virtually superfluous'.[165] However, the growing dominion of the human rights regime has not always been seen to side-line the Refugee Convention entirely. For example, Chetail has argued that:

> In sum, human rights law has become the ultimate benchmark for determining who is a refugee. The authoritative intrusion of human rights has proved to be instrumental in infusing a common and dynamic understanding of the refugee definition that is more consonant with and loyal to the evolution of international law. It thus prevents the Geneva Convention from becoming a mere legal anachronism by adapting it to the changing realities of forced migration.[166]

## 4.9 Lack of Any Treaty Monitoring or Similar Mechanism to Ensure Consistency/Convergence

A final criticism to be mentioned here tracks back to what was said earlier about perceptions of undue divergence. It has been variously argued that the *de facto* lack of any international judicial mechanism (due to the inactivation of Article 38 of the Convention) or of any treaty-monitoring mechanism or other independent mechanism dooms the refugee definition to perpetual failure in achieving greater uniformity or at least convergence of interpretation.[167] For example, on the occasion of

---

[162] Cathryn Costello, *The Human Rights of Migrants and Refugees in European Law* (OUP 2016) 22, observes that 'most ethicists take the view that the CSR refugee definition is under-protective, and that those fleeing a wider range of existential threats should be afforded protection'. See also Betts and Collier (n 13) 43–47.

[163] UNHCR, Conclusion on the Provision of International Protection Including Through Complementary Forms of Protection No 103 (n 157). For an earlier resumé of protection gaps, see the Report of the Working Group on Solutions and Protection (12 August 1991) UN Doc EC/ECP/64.

[164] Isabelle Gunning, 'Expanding the International Definition of Refugee: A Multicultural View' (1989) 13(1) Fordham LJ 35, 85. Whilst sometimes expressing the same concern (e.g. in UNHCR, 'Note on International Protection' (n 83) para 21), UNHCR has increasingly taken the view that the refugee definition can include those fleeing war and generalised violence in certain circumstances: see UNHCR, Guidelines on International Protection No 12: Claims for refugee status related to situations of armed conflict and violence under Article 1A(2) of the 1951 Convention and/or 1967 Protocol relating to the Status of Refugees and the regional refugee definitions (2 December 2016) UN Doc HCR/GIP/16/12, 32.

[165] William A Schabas, 'Non-Refoulement' in OSCE and OHCHR, Expert Workshop on Human Rights and International Cooperation in Counter-Terrorism (2007) UN Doc ODIHR GAL/14/07, 23; see also Sztucki (n 58) 57.

[166] Chetail (n 122) 28. See further Chapter 3, section 6.2.

[167] See e.g. 'Special Feature: Supervising the Refugee Convention' (n 20); North and Chia (n 17). For a counterview, see Goodwin-Gill (n 20) 651, 656–57; Geoff Gilbert, 'UNHCR and Courts' (2016) 28 IJRL 623.

UNHCR's fortieth anniversary, it was observed that 'the interpretation of the criteria for granting refugee status and asylum displays almost as many variations as there are countries'.[168] More recent surveys tend to voice similar views, even within the EU where by virtue of the QD decision makers in all member states have been obliged to apply 'common criteria'.[169]

Important as these various criticisms are, their only remaining relevance for this study is when they impinge on issues of meaning and interpretation of the legal definition.

## 5 Problems of Definition

In light of one of the declared purposes of this book being to elicit further definitional detail, it is necessary to ask whether this represents a legitimate endeavour bearing in mind that this idea has met with a certain resistance over the years. What have been the main objections, and can they be refuted? These are questions which must be addressed at the outset. Notwithstanding that there has been relatively little sustained discussion on this subject, four main objections can be discerned in the literature to attempting further definitional detail: that it is a superfluous exercise since the definition's recipients are obvious—everyone knows who the definition is meant to benefit; that there is already a legal definition; that by its very nature the definition had to be cast in general terms having an inbuilt vagueness; and that in the nature of the underlying phenomena addressed by the definition, any attempt to define it further would be to unduly restrict it. Some of these objections overlap. Let us take each in turn.

### 5.1 Known Identity of the Definition's Beneficiaries?

It has been observed that one of the reasons the drafters themselves chose not to define key terms such as persecution, was because everyone knew what it meant;[170] this will be discussed in more detail in Chapter 6 on 'being persecuted' and serious harm. No more needs saying about this here since, whatever the truth of that understanding at the time, the post-1951 period has seen significant discord about the identity of persecutees—as the earlier discussion of UNHCR evolving understandings of the term made clear.

---

[168] Arboleda Hoy (n 23) 76, quoting Iain Guest and the Lawyers Committee for Human Rights, *The UNHCR at 40: Refugee Protection at the Crossroads* (The Committee 1991), cited also by North and Chia (n 17) 109.
[169] e.g. Roland Bank, 'Refugee Law Jurisprudence from Germany and Human Rights: Cutting Edge or Chilling Effect?' in Burson and Cantor (eds) (n 118) 156; European Commission, 'Evaluation of the application of the recast Qualification Directive (2011/95/EU): Final Report' (n 13); Julian Lehmann, '*Protection*' *in European Union Asylum Law: International and European Law Requirements for Assessing Available Protection as a Criterion for Refugee and Subsidiary Status* (Brill Nijhoff 2020) 115–22, 116, 162.
[170] e.g. Einarsen (n 128) 57; UNHCR, Interpreting Article 1 of the 1951 Convention (n 148) para 16.

34 THE REFUGEE DEFINITION

## 5.2 The Fact that a Definition Already Exists?

It was stated earlier that two of this book's objectives were to elucidate the meaning of the Article 1A(2) refugee definition and to consider the extent to which such elucidation can yield fuller definition. In a primary sense, there is and can only be one definition, that which is given, ready-made, in Article 1A(2). This is *the* refugee definition. It was a conscious choice by the drafters not to elaborate it further.[171] Hence it could be said that elucidation of its meaning must be confined to just that—elucidation. If the definition given therein is all the drafters chose to provide, can or should interpretation go further?

Such a view has superficial attraction, but it is in the nature of defining to go beyond the given. This is clear from dictionary definitions: e.g. the Oxford English Dictionary (OED) Online definitions of 'to define' and 'definition' include '[t]o set forth or explain what (a word or expression) means ... ' and '[t]he action of defining, or stating exactly what a thing is, or what a word means ... '.[172] Recognising that in logic there cannot be a second (legal) definition beyond the only one given does not render futile the attempt to achieve greater definitional detail. As noted by Muntarbhorn (citing Bayles), 'the fact that more often than not, there are lacuna within a certain definition is inevitably conducive to the quest for further definition to refine the existing definition'.[173] Indeed it is inherent in the very task of interpretation to go beyond the text.[174] Moreover, interpretation encompasses clarification.[175] Clarification contributes to a common background and understanding, minimising possible conflicts.[176]

The refugee definition is of a nature that cries out for further clarification, elucidation, and elaboration. It is at once simple and complex: simple because it condenses into very few words a multiple set of requirements for eligibility; complex because it clearly goes beyond the lay understanding of a refugee as someone needing protection from harm. Although (along with the UNHCR Statute's and the OAU Convention's incorporation of it as the first limb of its definition) it is the only legal definition operating globally, it is one that leaves its key terms undefined. That the drafters envisaged that it would need further interpretation is evident from Article 38 which created a mechanism for 'any dispute ... relating to ... interpretation' to be referred to the ICJ. Hence the quest to 'unpack' it could be said to be integral to what has been described as

---

[171] This is a view sometimes voiced in the case law, e.g. in *Balazoski v Immigration and Naturalization Service* [1991] 932 F.2d 638, 640, citing the US Supreme Court decision in *Immigration and Naturalization Service v Cardoza-Fonseca* [1987] 480 US 421, that it was germane that the drafters the 1951 Convention chose not to provide any further definition.
[172] Oxford English Dictionary Online, <oed.com>accessed March 2021.
[173] Vitit Muntarbhorn, 'Determination of the Status of Refugees: Definition in Context' (Symposium on the Promotion, Dissemination and Teaching of Fundamental Human Rights of Refugees, Tokyo, 7–11 December 1981) 83–90; UNHCR, Division of International Protection (February 1982) UNST/HCR/063.4/R4–E, 83–90; Michael D Bayles, 'Definitions in Law' in James H Fetzer, David Shatz, and George N Schlesinger (eds), *Definitions and Definability: Philosophical Perspectives* (Springer 1991). See also William L Davidson, *Logic of Definition* (Michigan 1896) 32; and Sitaropoulos (n 144) 157–60.
[174] Interpretation is 'the process of determining the meaning of a text or rule'. See Harvard Draft Codification of International Law (1935) 29 AJIL 653, 938–46.
[175] *North Sea Continental Shelf Cases*, Judgment [1969] ICJ Rep 3, Opinion of Judge Tanaka.
[176] Danae Azoria, '"Codification by Interpretation": The International Law Commission as an Interpreter of International Law' (2020) 31(1) EJIL 171, 176.

the endeavour to establish one 'true autonomous and international meaning'.[177] That endeavour goes to the heart of all treaty interpretation.[178]

## 5.3 Deliberate Vagueness?

It has often been noted that the refugee definition is vague, indeterminate, and generalised,[179] and for some this precludes efforts to make it more precise. In tackling this objection, it is important to recall how the drafters saw things. Whilst conscious of the 'complicated and delicate'[180] nature of their task, they doubtless coveted a clear definition. Thus, the US representative had urged that the categories of refugees to which the draft convention under discussion should apply should be 'clearly enumerated' and 'clearly and specifically determined'[181] and in committee the drafters had expressed their intention that the definition should 'state unambiguously to whom the convention would apply'.[182]

To modern-day readers, such expressions of intent might seem ironic, seeing that debates about the meaning of the definition still rage and that there is no settled 'state practice' in the form of agreement that is 'both extensive and virtually uniform in the sense of the provision invoked'.[183] Undoubtedly one of the reasons why the definition *even as it stands* has not achieved the status of customary international law (which requires an even higher standard than uniform state practice) is the perceived lack of agreement of this kind as to the meaning of its key elements. As noted by Sztucki, 'such an agreement is manifestly lacking in the case of the Convention definition of "refugee"'. He further notes that in 1994 UNHCR referred to '[v]arying interpretations of the refugee definition'. He ventures that 'nothing has changed in this respect since'. On the contrary, he states, 'subsequent practice demonstrates a wide variety of interpretations and application.'[184]

---

[177] *R v SSHD, ex parte Adan and Aitsegeur* [1999] 3 WLR 1275, 7.
[178] 'The practice of law operates on the assumption that there is one correct interpretation and this meaning has to be found.' (James Crawford, 'Chance, Order, Change: The Course of International Law, General Course on Public International Law (Volume 365)' (Brill 2013) Collected Courses of the Hague Academy of International Law, 119).
[179] See (n 187).
[180] UN Ad Hoc Committee on Refugees and Stateless Persons, Ad Hoc Committee on Statelessness and Related Problems, Status of Refugees and Stateless Persons—Memorandum by the Secretary-General (3 January 1950) UN Doc E/AC.32/2, 11.
[181] Alex Takkenberg and Christopher C Tabhaz, *The Collected Travaux Préparatoires of the 1951 Geneva Convention Relating to the Status of Refugees* (Dutch Refugee Council 1989) 10 (Collected Travaux).
[182] UN Ad Hoc Committee on Refugees and Stateless Persons, Ad Hoc Committee on Statelessness and Related Problems, First Session: Summary Record of the Third Meeting Held at Lake Success, New York, on Tuesday, 17 January 1950, at 3 p.m. (26 January 1950) UN Doc E/AC.32/SR.3, 9. The remarks continued:

> Since the responsibility of the United Nations would be committed with regard to refugees placed under its protection under that convention, the extent of that responsibility must be known in advance, and, to that end, it must be known what categories of refugees would be admitted to that protection. Too vague a definition, which would amount, so to speak, to a blank check, would not be sufficient. As the representative of Turkey has rightly pointed out, any unduly inexact definition would be likely to lead subsequently to disagreement to the convention to wish to know precisely to whom it should apply.

[183] *North Sea Continental Shelf Case* (n 175) paras 72, 74.
[184] Sztucki (n 58) 75, 78; see also Kourula (n 9) 43.

On the other hand, despite aspiring to clarity, the drafters were at pains to highlight that this did not mean imposing undue precision. They were clearly mindful that the legal definition they chose, being of a general nature, had to possess a degree of inexactitude. What they wished to avoid, the Ad Hoc Committee explained, was only 'unduly inexact definition'.[185] In thus acknowledging the need to strike a balance between exactitude and flexibility, the drafters could fairly be said to have simply being dutiful to the nature of treaty definitions in 'law-making' treaties,[186] such as the Refugee Convention. As noted by Sitaropolous:

> One of the fundamental characteristics of the established international legal refugee definition has been, as for all legal definitions of a general nature (synthetic-semantic definitions), a certain vagueness of its terminology, especially since the [United Nations Relief and Rehabilitation Administration] and [International Refugee Organisation]'s express introduction of the basic notion of persecution in their legal refugee conceptualisation. It is generally accepted in refugee law literature that the refugee definition['s] porousness, especially the one of the notion of persecution, was kept on purpose by the drafting state members of the 1951/1967 Refugee Convention, thus establishing a refugee definition which is 'prudently dubious'.[187]

Keeping in mind how the drafters viewed their work, the question remains whether the fact of vagueness and indeterminacy dooms the quest for further definitional detail. It is not obvious why this fact should negate such an attempt. Indeed, it could be argued that the drafter's choice of vague terms was predicated on the knowledge that those tasked with interpreting and applying it thereafter would be bound to add more contours in light of new developments. It has often been observed that it was because Article 1A(2) sought to address the problem of refugees in the future in a relatively open-ended way, that the definition has the character it has.[188]

In any event, it would be a mistake to regard definitions in 'law-making treaties' generally—or the Refugee Convention in particular—as having a fixed quantum of indeterminacy; in treaty law it is observably a question of degree in any particular case.[189] Indeed, one of the other main limbs of Article 1—Article 1A(1)—contains very little indeterminacy since its provisions are largely applicable only to predetermined groups. Later chapters contend that some elements of the Article 1A(2) definition are relatively determinate, others not.

---

[185] See UN Ad Hoc Committee on Refugees and Stateless Persons, Ad Hoc Committee on Statelessness and Related Problems (n 182).

[186] See Chapter 2, sections 1.4.1 and 2.5.1.

[187] Sitaropoulos (n 144) 157. He sources this quote to Mario Bettati, *L'Asile Politique en Question* (PUF 1985) 79, noting that Bettati categorises the legal refugee definition as one of the '*définitions prudemment incertaines*'. Sitaropoulos cites further Grahl-Madsen (n 7) 188; Guy S Goodwin-Gill, *The Refugee in International Law* (2nd edn, Clarendon Press 1996) 40. See also Hathaway and Foster (n 10) 102–05.

[188] Theodor Veiter, 'Begriffe und Definitionen zum Flüchtlingsrecht' (1983) 21 Association for the Study of the World Refugee Problem Bulletin 118, 118–19, cited by Sitaropoulos (n 144) 158.

[189] On 'law-making treaties' and use of generic terms, see Chapter 2, section 1.4.1; see also Helmut P Aust, Alejandro Rodiles, and Peter Staubach, 'Unity or Uniformity: Domestic Courts and Treaty Interpretation' (2014) 27 LJIL 75, 81.

## 5.4 Further Definition Intrinsically Restrictive?

Perhaps the main objection raised has been that to seek to define terms like 'persecution' and 'protection' would be to restrict their scope as the phenomena they identify are intrinsically protean. This appears to be the thrust of paragraphs 51–53 of the 1979 UNHCR Handbook.[190] Volker Türk and Frances Nicholson, echoing a number of eminent commentators, including Weis and Goodwin-Gill, have argued that attempts to define persecution 'could limit a phenomenon that has unfortunately shown itself all too adaptable in the history of humankind'.[191] This argument will be analysed further in Chapter 6, but given its general import it must be addressed here also.

As an argument against an 'absolutist' or 'fixed-list' approach to definition, it is extremely cogent, but legal definitions do not have to be of this character. Particularly if a human rights approach is taken to the definition, terms such as persecution can be given a definition at a general level of abstraction that allows for the fact that the nature of ill-treatment/persecution can change. Hence this objection really only bites against a 'static' or 'fixed list' approach to definition.[192] Further, this objection fosters an unacceptably eclectic approach to understanding of the definition's key terms. By insisting on seeking to understand them wholly in terms of the particular circumstances, it denies itself the ability to give such understanding any coherent conceptual underpinning. An approach to definition that treats meaning as wholly dependent on circumstances leaves unanswered what criteria underlie it. This problem will be explored further in the chapters on 'being persecuted' and serious harm and persecution and the internal protection alternative in particular.

Finally, one cannot overlook the fact that only rarely have the above objections prevented their proponents from making their own attempts at further elaboration of the definition. The quest for further definition is thus a legitimate one.

## 5.5 The Notion of a 'Working Definition'

Even though it is legitimate, therefore, to seek to achieve further definition, at least understood as further elaboration, the fact that a number of objections have been raised does represent a continuing obstacle to any attempt to proceed to try and construct a further definition in specific form, analogous to a draft legal text. Such objections demonstrate that there is no consensus in favour of such an attempt. And it would be fruitless to seek to advance any fixed position regarding the nature of

---

[190] See section 6.2 of this chapter.
[191] Volker Türk and Frances Nicholson, 'Refugee Protection in International Law: An Overall Perspective' in Erika Feller et al (n 15) 39; Paul Weis, *The Concept of Refugee in International Law* (UNHCR 1961); UN Doc HCR/INF/49, 22; Grahl-Madsen (n 7). See also sources cited in UNHCR, Interpreting Article 1 of the 1951 Convention (n 148) paras 16–22; Guy S Goodwin-Gill and Jane McAdam, *The Refugee in International Law* (3rd edn, OUP 2007) 93–94. See further Guy S Goodwin-Gill, 'Current Challenges in Refugee Law' in Gauci et al (eds) (n 120). Citing James Brierly's concern about the 'tyranny of phrases' in international law, he observes that '[i]f that is a problem with words which enjoy at least a measure of international consensus or agreement, how much greater it will be when glosses are overlaid on agreed text'.
[192] Michelle Foster, *International Refugee Law and Socio-Economic Rights* (CUP 2007) 81–82; Hugo Storey, 'Persecution: Towards a Working Definition' in Chetail and Bauloz (n 68) 461.

legal definitions anyway, since differences continue to abound in approaches taken to legal definition in the overarching legal jurisprudence.[193] In particular, there remains a real tension between what might be called the 'indicative' approach and the 'conceptual' approach.[194] Later on, this study takes issue with various kinds of indicative approaches to the refugee definition, viz. approaches that consider that all that can be achieved definitionally is providing examples and illustrations that are (in Grahl-Madsen's words, in relation to persecution) 'enumeration [that] should not be considered comprehensive or exhaustive'.[195] Taken on their own, such approaches are considered to lack any clear conceptual basis.

But whether or not the approach taken to the refugee definition is an 'indicative' or a 'conceptual' one, or a combination of the two, what is striking is that there is nonetheless discernible agreement about a number of basic propositions relating to the definition's key terms. It is in order to capture this consensus that this study utilises the notion of a 'working definition'. It is chosen not in order to accord any special conceptual status to this term, but to convey that the compilation of greater definitional detail serves as a building block for greater agreement about the one true meaning (the emphasis is on '*working ...* '). It reflects awareness that interpretation is a process of consolidation and systematising of agreed understandings. In the end, the fact of this type of consensus is more important than its philosophical underpinnings or precise status as 'further definition'. What is surely desired in the real world of RSD (alongside good quality decision-making) is more consistent decision-making, so that there is no 'asylum lottery' depending on the state in which a claim is assessed.[196] Whether by means of an indicative approach or a more conceptual one, or an admixture, progress should be measured in the coinage of that consensus.

Another advantage to deploying the notion of a working definition is that it helps counteract any attempt to understand the progress made as fixed. A working definition can only ever be a work in progress.

## 6 The Refugee Definition and Existing Learning

Before embarking on a quest for a more detailed definition, it is necessary to ask whether one is not already to hand in the existing learning. There are four possible sources: UNHCR guidance; case law; national governmental manuals/guidance notes; and academic studies. They interrelate in various ways and draw or rely on state practice (in the broad sense) in varying degrees, but are nevertheless distinct from one

---

[193] See Luther L Bernard, 'The Definition of Definition' (1941) 19 Soc F 500; Richard Robinson, *Definition* (OUP 1950); Herbert Lionel Adolphus Hart, *Essays in Jurisprudence and Philosophy* (Clarendon Press 1983) 275; Bayles (n 173); Muntarbhorn (n 173).

[194] These two terms are the author's oversimplified attempt to capture the manifold schools of thought on this issue.

[195] Grahl-Madsen (n 7) 216. See Chapter 6, 'Introduction: The Issue of Further Definition'.

[196] e.g. Jaya Ramji-Nogales, Andrew I Schoenholtz, and Philip G Schrag (eds), *Refugee Roulette. Disparities in Asylum Adjudication and Proposals for Reform* (New York University Press 2009); 'Turning the Asylum Lottery on its Head: A Critical Reflection on Ethnographies of Refugee Status Determination Processes' (International Workshop, University of Siegen, 13–14 December 2018). By 'lottery' in this context is meant in the RSD procedures, not in factors such as modes of travel, etc.

another.[197] In Chapter 2, all four will be examined with a view to gauging their value as sources applying VCLT rules of interpretation, but focus here is on their contents.

## 6.1 The Pillar of UNHCR Guidance

Article 35 of the Refugee Convention imposes on UNHCR a duty to supervise 'the application of the provisions of this Convention'. The Convention's only reference to 'interpretation' arises in Article 38 which identifies the ICJ as the arbiter of any disputes between state parties relating to interpretation.[198] Nevertheless, although application and interpretation are two conceptually distinct functions, the duty of supervising application must inevitably have regard to interpretive issues and is sufficiently wide to encompass the issuing of authoritative, albeit non-binding, guidance.[199] Hence any endeavour to provide a modern elaboration of the meaning of the refugee definition must first of all address the relevance of UNHCR's guidance as provided to date. In this context, there are four main UNHCR sources to consider: the 1979 UNHCR Handbook; the ExCom *Conclusions on the International Protection of Refugees* (Conclusions); the 2001 UNHCR note, *Interpreting Article 1 of the 1951 Convention Relating to the Status of Refugees*; and the ongoing series which began in May 2002, titled *Guidelines on International Protection* (Guidelines), of which there are thirteen to date.[200] Can it be said that these four sources already constitute the prized 'further definition' of Article 1A(2) which this book seeks to

---

[197] For further discussion, see Guy S Goodwin-Gill, 'The Search for the One, True Meaning ...' in Guy S Goodwin-Gill and Hélène Lambert (eds), *The Limits of Transnational Law: Refugee Law, Policy Harmonization and Judicial Dialogue in the European Union* (CUP 2010) 204; Goodwin-Gill (n 20); Gilbert (n 167). On state practice in the broad sense, see Chapter 2, n 69.

[198] The High Commissioner's supervisory responsibility is laid down explicitly in paragraph 8(a) of the Statute, in Articles 35 of the 1951 Convention and Article II of the 1967 Protocol, and requires the states parties to one or both of these treaties to cooperate with the High Commissioner in the exercise of his supervisory responsibilities. In his dissenting opinion in *Factory at Chorzów (Germany v Poland)*, Jurisdiction, Judgment [1927] PCIJ Series A No 9, Judge Ehrlich observed that 'interpretation, is [the process of] determining the meaning of a rule', while 'application, is the process in one sense, that of determining the consequences which the rule attaches to the occurrence of a given fact; in another sense, application is the action of bringing about the consequences which, according to a rule, should follow a fact'.

[199] In a study of the WTO Tribunal, Andrew D Mitchell and David Heaton, 'The Inherent Jurisdiction of WTO Tribunals: The Select Application of Public International Law Required by the Judicial Function' (2010) 31 Mich J Int'l L 559, comment at 570 that:'[t]he distinction between application and interpretation is not concrete and it may in some cases be difficult to determine whether a WTO Tribunal is applying international law or simply using international law to interpret a WTO provision. The answer to this question may not make a large difference from a practical perspective.' See also ILC, Report on subsequent agreements and subsequent practice in relation to the interpretation of treaties (2018) UN Doc A/73/10, Commentary on Conclusion 6, paras 3–6. On the authority of UNHCR guidance, see further Jane McAdam, 'Interpretation of the 1951 Convention' in Zimmermann (n 14) 79; Kälin (n 15) 611; Zieck (n 114) 1494–1500; Guy S Goodwin-Gill, 'The Office of the United Nations High Commissioner for Refugees and the Sources of International Refugee Law' (2020) 69 ICLQ 1. Drawing on the notion of 'sacred trust' articulated by the ICJ in the *International Status of South-West Africa, Advisory Opinion* [1950] ICJ Rep 128, Gilbert (n 167) 623, 635 argues that 'the standing of the organization in the international legal order with respect to its authority to pronounce on the meaning and scope of the 1951 Convention is stronger than that of any group of judges or committee members'.

[200] See further discussion in Chapter 2, section 3.2. A full list of the Guidelines is available in the Bibliography.

40  THE REFUGEE DEFINITION

explore? There are other, less-prominent UNHCR materials that also bear on the refugee definition,[201] but if these four do not achieve this, then recourse to such other materials can scarcely rectify the problem. Even if these four, individually or collectively do not furnish an authoritative elaboration of the refugee definition, it remains necessary to consider to what extent they should nevertheless be accorded a special role. Whilst for some scholars, UNHCR materials must play a key role,[202] for others[203] both the Handbook and other UNHCR sources of guidance are just part of the varied background of sources upon which proper interpretation of the definition must draw.[204]

---

[201] These include various Handbooks (e.g. *UNHCR Handbook* for the Protection of *Women and Girls*, January 2008), Notes (including the annual Note on International Protection), and court or tribunal-related interventions (third party *amicus curiae* briefs, oral interventions, public statements, or letters). Satvinder S Juss, 'The UNHCR Handbook and the Interface between 'Soft Law' and 'Hard Law' in International Refugee Law' in Satvinder S Juss and Colin Harvey (eds), *Contemporary Issues in Refugee Law* (Edward Elgar 2013) 31–67 highlights that UNHCR Eligibility Guidelines can also include interpretive guidance. A repository of UNHCR's court interventions is maintained in Refworld. Unless the rules of court determine otherwise, the interventions are made publicly available upon filing and can be accessed at <https://www.refworld.org/type,AMICUS,UNHCR,,,,0.html> accessed 10 April 2021. On court and tribunal-related interventions, see further: UNHCR, Remarks at the opening of the judicial year of the European Court of Human Rights (Strasbourg, 28 January 2011) available at <http://www.unhcr.org/refworld/docid/4d6377fe2.html> accessed 10 April 2021; Madeline Garlick 'International Protection in Court: The Asylum Jurisprudence of the Court of Justice of the EU and UNHCR' (2015) 34 RSQ 115; 'American Courts and the U.N. High Commissioner for Refugees: A Need for Harmony in the Face of a Refugee Crisis' (2018) 131(5) Harv L Rev 1399, 1399–420; and Gilbert (n 167) 623.

[202] Juss (n 201) 33–34, for example, states that 'for refugee law to become effective, the pronouncements of the UNHCR must be seen as having "ostensible" legal authority. Only in this way can scholars of refugee law succeed in rescuing the status of the Handbook, the "UNHCR Notes" and the UNHCR Eligibility Guidelines.'

[203] Whilst Hathaway and Foster (n 10) refer to provisions of the UNHCR Handbook frequently, their book contains only one index entry under the Handbook and does not treat it as having any special status.

[204] Hathaway sheds more light in *Rights* (2nd edn) (n 34). Whilst acknowledging UNHCR's valuable standard-setting and related legal work, he states at ibid 62 that '[t]he decline in the deference afforded to the Handbook is no doubt largely attributable to the increasing dissonance between some of its positions and those which have resulted from the intensive period of judicial activism in refugee law, which began in the early 1990s'. At ibid 66 he goes on to argue that with the advent of the Guidelines '[w]e thus find ourselves at a moment of significant normative confusion on the appropriate source of UNHCR institutional advice on the substance of international refugee law. With the advent of experienced national and regional judiciaries that have developed their own understandings of refugee law, there is less willingness than in the past simply to defer to the didactic expositions found in the UNHCR's Handbook and Guidelines. Judicial efforts to take account of UNHCR guidance are moreover complicated by the sheer volume of less-than-fully-consistent advice now emanating from the UNHCR, too often drafted at such a highly detailed level that its core content is difficult to discern. There is moreover understandable reticence to treat UNHCR published advice as authoritative when the agency itself often appears before courts to advocate particular views.' At ibid 57 he goes on to exhort that general principles of refugee law be codified in formal, and clearly authoritative, resolutions of ExCom. On the contents of the Handbook and other UNHCR materials as guidance, see further Jerzy Sztucki, 'The Conclusions on the International Protection of Refugees Adopted by the Executive Committee of the UNHCR Programme' (1989) 1 IJRL 285; Volker Türk, 'Introductory Note to UNHCR Guidelines on International Protection' (2003) 15 IJRL 303; Bryan Deschamp and Rebecca Dowd, 'Review of the Use of UNHCR Executive Committee Conclusions on International Protection' (UNHCR Policy Development and Evaluation Service 2008, PDES/2008/03) 5; Volker Türk and Rebecca Dowd, 'Protection Gaps' in Elena Fiddian-Qasmiyeh et al (eds), *The Oxford Handbook of Refugee and Forced Migration Studies* (OUP 2014) 278; Türk (n 18) 153–74; Kälin (n 15) 627–28; Hathaway (1st edn) (n 34) 112–18, 992–98; McAdam (n 199); Juss (n 201) 31–67; Goodwin-Gill (n 199) 1–41.

### 6.1.1 UNHCR Handbook, 1979

The best-known and most significant attempt to interpret key terms of the refugee definition remains the 1979 Handbook.[205] It states that it was issued at the request of member states of ExCom and pursuant to UNHCR's supervisory responsibility contained in paragraph 8 of the 1950 Statute of UNHCR in conjunction with Articles 35 and 36 of the 1951 Convention and Article II of its 1967 Protocol.[206] It is noteworthy—and contrary to what is often thought—that although reissued several times, its substantive contents have never (to date) been updated.

There is at least a strong argument that, at the time of its publication, this Handbook represented 'subsequent practice' within the meaning of Article 31(3) VCLT.[207] Even if it is felt to fail that test, there remains a strong case for treating its elaboration of the refugee definition in Part One as having continued for some time to codify widely held understandings of key terms. For several decades after it was issued, the Handbook was treated as authoritative by state parties. For ascertaining the meaning of key terms of this definition its Part One was the starting point and often the finishing point. Courts and tribunals frequently treated it as highly persuasive, albeit not binding.[208] At a time when there was no significant body of jurisprudence, it played a vital role in helping achieve some degree of international consistency of understanding, when national systems would have otherwise relied heavily on interpretation derived solely from their own national legal traditions. Further, UNHCR even today still continues to refer to the Handbook as the primary source of reference.[209] On the other hand, as will be discussed further in the next chapter (Chapter 2, section 3.2), even though courts and tribunals still do refer to it, they do so less often; they treat it primarily as a persuasive rather than a highly persuasive source; and they do not always concur with it.

This background also suggests that even if the Handbook cannot any longer be treated as providing in full an authoritative elaboration of the refugee definition's key terms, it certainly needs to be considered as a foundational reference-point.

It is useful to consider the Handbook's Part One guidance first as it stood in 1979 and second as it stands today.

Even as things stood in 1979, Part One of the Handbook contains some gaps. It does not identify the applicable rules of treaty interpretation as set out in the VCLT. There is nothing to indicate that it has considered each element of the definition by reference to VCLT rules, for example in terms of ordinary meaning, context, or object

---

[205] UNHCR Handbook (n 5).
[206] ibid, Foreword.
[207] See further Chapter 2, section 2.6.2.1.
[208] McAdam (n 199).
[209] e.g., in his 2019 Foreword to the UNHCR Handbook and Guidelines on International Protection (n 5), Volker Türk writes that the Guidelines 'complement and update the Handbook and should be read in combination with it'. In *UNHCR intervention before the United States Board of Immigration Appeals in the Matter of Michelle Thomas et al. (in Removal Proceedings)* (25 January 2007) UN Doc A-75-597-033/-034/-035/-036, available at <https://www.refworld.org/docid/45c34c244.html> accessed 26 March 2021, the Handbook is described as 'internationally recognized as the key source of interpretation of international refugee law'. In another intervention in January 2021 before the UK Supreme Court, UNHCR, *Submission by the United Nations High Commissioner for Refugees in the case G v G*, the Handbook is listed first as interpretive guidance and its contents are 'commend[ed]' to the court.

and purpose. The isolated references to the *travaux*, e.g. in paragraphs 36 and 100, appear to simply assume that the correct meaning is that furnished by the drafters themselves, an assumption not easily reconciled with the supplementary status accorded to *travaux* by VCLT rules.[210] Sometimes it enunciates a conclusion without any explanation (e.g. paragraph 104).

The Handbook's treatment of certain elements of the refugee definition is cursory. Thus, it provides no guidance on interpretation of the notions of nationality and statelessness. It contains a very important but short and isolated reference to non-state actors of persecution (paragraph 65). Its treatment of laws and related legal measures as capable of being persecutory is confined to a discussion of prosecution and punishment (paragraphs 56–60). In dealing with Refugee Convention reasons, it contains virtually no treatment of the issue of causal nexus (the closest it comes is in paragraph 81). Except in a glancing reference to political opinions sometimes being 'attributed' by the authorities to an applicant (paragraph 80), the Handbook does not articulate the important point that it may not matter in relation to any of the Convention reasons that a person does not actually possess specified characteristics if the persecutor attributes them to him or her. Its analysis of membership of a particular social group is limited to stating what such a group 'normally comprises' (paragraph 77). Overall, its treatment of the ('inclusionary') elements of the refugee definition is limited to Chapter II (paragraphs 32–110) and Chapter V of Part One (paragraphs 164–180 on 'Special Cases').[211]

It is also observable that numerous paragraphs confine themselves to issues of application rather than interpretation, by providing examples of concrete cases,[212] and/or mere illustrations. Sometimes the Handbook attempts to identify certain factors or considerations that are relevant when assessing key terms such as 'well-founded fear' (paragraphs 42–46) and 'political opinion' (paragraphs 85–86); yet at other times, most notably in relation to the key term 'persecution', it advances an approach to interpretation which maintains that save for a minimum core any attempt at definition beyond illustrative examples is fruitless (see paragraphs 51–54). Some of its text addresses problems of evidence, not interpretation (e.g. paragraph 93 on proving nationality).

Despite these omissions and limitations, the fact that the Handbook is an amalgam of direct attempts at defining certain terms and an illustrative/indicative approach can be said to furnish very much what one should expect of an explanatory commentary on key terms of a 'law-making' treaty.[213] In terms of its preference in many instances for an indicative approach, given the porous nature of certain key terms such as 'habitual residence', 'being persecuted', and 'protection', it may represent as much as could be expected of the definitional endeavour at that time, especially given that it was published before there was any sustained judicial engagement with the Article 1A(2)

---

[210] See Chapter 2, sections 1.8.1 and 2.9.1.
[211] Chapters III and IV of the UNHCR Handbook (n 5) are devoted to the cessation and exclusion clauses. Part Two is devoted to procedures (paras 189–219) and is concerned not with the substantive definition, but with procedures.
[212] As the Handbook itself identifies, '[i]t has also been sought to show how these definitions may be applied in concrete cases...'. See UNHCR Handbook (n 5) para 220.
[213] See Chapter 2, sections 1.4.1 and 2.5.1.

definition.[214] As emphasised earlier, the degree of precision to be expected of any legal definition is in part a function of the subject-matter and refugee cases can be highly fact-sensitive. It remains, however, that the Handbook had shortcomings at the time.

To be fair (and perhaps overlooked at times, even by UNHCR), the authors themselves acknowledge this, in the Handbook's Conclusion it is stated at paragraph 221 that:

> The Office of the High Commissioner is fully aware of the shortcomings inherent in a Handbook of this nature, bearing in mind that it is not possible to encompass every situation in which a person may apply for refugee status. Such situations are manifold and depend upon the infinitely varied conditions prevailing in countries of origin and on the special personal factors relating to the individual applicant.

But in any event the Handbook cannot be assessed by reference to matters of interpretation as they stood in 1979. Over forty years have passed and any present-day attempt to interpret the refuge definition must evaluate it in light of the accumulated experience gained since. As will be explained in Chapter 2, VCLT rules of interpretation as applied to the Refugee Convention require an 'evolutive' approach to be taken to its interpretation as a 'living instrument'.[215] This makes UNHCR's continued endorsement of the Handbook as the primary document for interpretation of the refuge definition a curiosity—especially given its own authors' awareness of its temporal limits: it could not, they observed, 'encompass every situation in which a person may apply for refugee status'.[216] To be true guidance, guidance must be current. Significantly, the process courts and tribunals typically use to establish UNHCR's position, is to consider what is UNHCR's *ongoing* guidance, referenced by the Guidelines on International Protection and/or other relatively recent UNHCR materials, with the Handbook often, if at all, a mere reference point.

Shortcomings in the Handbook's interpretation of key terms will be identified and analysed in this book's subsequent chapters, but in summary, it is evident that on certain matters modern refugee law either no longer follows the interpretations given in the Handbook or has come to see them as possessing 'equivocal authority',[217] or open to debate. Falling under this broad description are its positions on the following matters: its statement that subjective fear is an essential element of the concept of well-founded fear (paragraph 37); its statement that 'interpretations of what amounts to persecution are bound to vary' (paragraph 52); its treatment of persecution, which does not include any identification of gender-specific or child-specific or disability-specific forms of persecution (paragraphs 51–64); its extremely limited treatment of socio-economic persecution; the limiting of its treatment of the scope of 'political opinion' to opinions held regarding the authorities/government, without any consideration of them being held by non-state actors (paragraphs 80–86); its statement that the test for ascertaining whether there is protection in another part of the same

---

[214] See Chapter 2, section 3.2.
[215] See Chapter 2, section 2.5.3.
[216] UNHCR Handbook (n 5) para 221.
[217] The expression used by Juss (n 201) 41. See also Goodwin-Gill (n 187) 204, 224–27.

country (the 'internal flight alternative') concerns what an applicant did historically (whether 'he could have sought refuge in another part of the same country') and that it amounts to a 'reasonableness' test—'if under all the circumstances it would not have been reasonable to expect him to do so' (paragraph 91); its apparent assumption that refugees *sur place* are confined to those who have left their country of origin (paragraph 94–96); its apparent confinement of the test of protection of a country to diplomatic protection (paragraphs 97–100); its unqualified statement that a stateless person with more than one country of former habitual residence is not required to satisfy the criteria of fear of persecution in relation to all of them (paragraph 104); in the context of assessment of applicants with multiple nationality, its statement that the relevant test concerns whether 'nationality is ineffective' (paragraph 107); its adoption of a(n) '(ab)normalcy' requirement in order for persons fleeing armed conflict to qualify as refugees (paragraph 164); and its formulation of the test for assessing whether a deserter or draft evader can qualify for refugee status on the basis of disagreement with military action contrary to the basic rule so human conduct, as being 'military action ... [that] is condemned by the international community' (paragraph 171).[218]

In addition, there have been certain matters not covered which would almost certainly merit coverage in any modern-day equivalent of 'Chapter V on Special cases' (e.g. victims of trafficking; persons basing their claim on flight from 'natural disasters' or climate change events; and (possibly even) persons adversely affected by pandemics). Further, as the later Guidelines have come to highlight, there are numerous paragraphs that would now be written quite differently. That is particularly plain from the publication of Guidelines No 1 (Gender-related persecution);[219] No 2 (Membership of a Particular Social Group);[220] No 4 (Internal Flight);[221] No 6 (Religion-Based Refugee Claims);[222] No 8 (Child Asylum Claims);[223] No 9 (Claims based on Sexual Orientation and/or Gender Identity),[224] and No 12 (Armed Conflict).[225]

### 6.1.2 ExCom Conclusions on the International Protection of Refugees

As regards the ExCom's Conclusions on the International Protection of Refugees, there being 116 of them at the time of writing,[226] they warrant specific consideration

---

[218] There has also been significant disagreement about certain aspects of the Handbook's treatment of the cessation and exclusion clauses: on the former, see e.g. *In re B (FC) (Appellant) (2002) Regina v Special Adjudicator (Respondent) ex parte Hoxha (FC) (Appellant)* [2005] UKHL 19; on the latter, see e.g. Hathaway (1st edn) (n 34) 117–68; on both, see Hathaway and Foster (n 10) 490–94, 562–67, 588. See also Goodwin-Gill (n 187) 224–27.

[219] Guidelines No 1 (n 187).

[220] UNHCR, Guidelines No 2: Membership of a particular social group within the context of Article 1A(2) of the 1951 Convention and/or its 1967 Protocol relating to the Status of Refugees (7 May 2002) UN Doc HCR/GIP/02/01.

[221] UNHCR, Guidelines No 4: Internal Flight or Relocation Alternative Within the Context of Article 1A(2) of the 1951 Convention and/or 1967 Protocol Relating to the Status of Refugees (23 July 2003) UN Doc HCR/GIP/03/04.

[222] UNHCR, Guidelines No 6: Religion-Based Refugee Claims under Article 1A(2) of the 1951 Convention and/or the 1967 Protocol relating to the Status of Refugees (2004) UN Doc HCR/GIP/04/06.

[223] Guidelines No 8 (n 148).

[224] Guidelines No 9 (n 148).

[225] Guidelines No 12 (n 164).

[226] Available at: https://www.refworld.org/cgi-bin/texis/vtx/rwmain?page=search&skip=0&advsearch=y&process=y&allwords=&exactphrase=&atleastone=&without=&title=&category=&publisher=&type=EXCONC&monthfrom=&yearfrom=&monthto=&yearto=&coi=&coa=&language=&citation=

because they represent consensus resolutions of a formal body of government representatives that has gradually grown in number and is expressly responsible for 'providing guidance and forging consensus on vital protection policies and practices'.[227] Excom being the only global inter-governmental forum involved in developing international protection standards, there is a respectable argument that its Conclusions constitute 'subsequent practice' within the meaning of Article 31(3) VCLT at least at the time they were issued. Even if that is not the case,[228] their institutional basis in the UN system clearly means they are an important point of reference as evidence of state practice. However, few have any bearing on the refugee definition and even those that do—e.g. Conclusions No 39 Refugee Women (especially paragraph K), No 73 on Refugee Protection and Sexual Violence, No 105 on Women and Girls at Risk, No 107 on Children at Risk—have been more exhortatory than prescriptive.[229]

### 6.1.3 UNHCR note, Interpreting Article 1 of the 1951 Convention Relating to the Status of Refugees, 2001

Over the years, UNHCR has issued a number of notes dealing with one or more aspects of the refugee definition, but none that has sought to be comprehensive. Until the advent of the Guidelines, there is one publication, however, which, by virtue of its broadly phrased title, merits separate consideration, namely *Interpreting Article 1 of the 1951 Convention Relating to the Status of Refugees*.[230]

Several features of this publication have import here. First, it is not confined to inclusion; it covers cessation and exclusion as well as Article 1A(2). Second, it expressly describes the 1979 Handbook as continuing to provide 'the basic guidance of the Office on the interpretation of the refugee definition'. This deference is emphatic: the Handbook, it is stated, 'should be referred to for a full understanding of UNHCR's views on various interpretative issues'.[231] That in itself conveys that this 2001 document is not intended to stand on its own. Second, in the same paragraph it describes its immediate goal as seeking to 'elucidate contemporary issues in the interpretation of

---

[227] ExCom, General Conclusion on International Protection No 81 (XLVIII) (1997), contained in UN Doc A/52/12/Add.1. See also Türk and Dowd (n 204) 278. Türk (n 68) further states that '[a]lthough the Executive Committee has only an advisory function, upon UNHCR's request, concerning UNHCR's protection responsibilities, the annual conclusions on international protection have an important standard-setting effect. They document consensus of the international community on a specific protection matter and are usually worked out in close co-operation with UNHCR'. See also Sztucki (n 204) 285–318; Deschamp and Dowd (n 204) paras 26, 53, 70.

[228] Zieck (n 114) 1497, states that 'In view of the fact that the conclusions are adopted by a subsidiary organ of ECOSOC called upon to advise UNHCR rather than States which is not a treaty body or otherwise related to the 1951 Convention and/or the 1967 Protocol and does in particular not consist of all State parties to those instruments either, those conclusions cannot be categorized as "subsequent agreements between the parties" in the sense indicated.'

[229] ibid. Zieck mentions the following as ones that interpret the Convention and its Protocol: No 1 (1975), (f); No 6 (1977), (c); No 7 (1977), (a) and (c); No 12 (1979), (d) and (f); No 14 (1979), (a); No 15 (1979), (b); No 17 (1980), (g); No 47 (1988), (h) and (j); No 69 (1992); No 73 (1993), (d); No 94 (2002), (c). See also Hathaway (1st edn) (n 34) 113. Post-2002, Conclusions of relevance include: No 95 (LIV) (2003), No 98 (LIV) (2003), No 105 (LVII) (2006), No 107 (LVIII) (2007), No 110 (LXI) (2010); see UNHCR, 'Conclusions on International Protection Adopted by the Executive Committee of the UNHCR Programme 1975–2017 (Conclusion No 1–114)' (October 2017) UN Doc HCR/IP/3/Eng/REV.2017.

[230] UNHCR, Interpreting Article 1 of the 1951 Convention (n 148).

[231] ibid.

the terms of Article 1 of the 1951 Convention relating to the Status of Refugees, taking into account recent academic and jurisprudential developments'; it states that it 'discusses various topics that have become prominent in refugee law discourse since [the Handbook's] publication'. It refers at paragraph 25 to it '*now [being] generally agreed that imputed or perceived grounds, or mere political neutrality, can form the basis of a refugee claim*' (emphasis added), thereby identifying a point of interpretation only clarified since the Handbook—which, as already noted, made only one isolated reference to the doctrine of attribution. From each of these references it is clear that this note expressly sought to take account of developments since the Handbook. Further, it also portrayed itself as temporally limited, as a bridging publication designed in part to inform upcoming expert roundtables as part of the Global Consultations process (paragraph 1),[232] and in part to inform 'efforts currently underway in Europe to harmonise understanding of the refugee definition' (paragraph 6).[233]

These features alone disqualify it from performing the role of a self-standing or comprehensive source of authoritative guidance on all aspects of the refugee definition. Having said that, it makes several further important clarifications (which are in truth subsequent developments), in the understanding of the refugee definition. For example, it expressly identifies VCLT rules as those that should govern interpretation of the Refugee Convention (paragraphs 2–4); endorses a human rights approach to the refugee definition (paragraph 5);[234] affirms that the ongoing development of IHRL had 'helped advance the understanding of persecution' and that persecution includes 'gender-related' persecution (paragraphs 29–32); affirms UNHCR's view that the different elements of the refugee definition have to be approached holistically, applying an 'integrated' approach (paragraphs 7–9); maintains that for this reason a similar result could be achieved whether the notion of protection is understood as 'diplomatic' or 'national' protection (paragraph 35); expressly identifies the need to take into account 'the perspective of the persecutor' and (as already noted) clearly articulates the doctrine of attribution in considering 'political opinion' and other Convention reasons/grounds (paragraphs 25, 28); identifies (as again the Handbook had not done) that in UNHCR's view the 'causal link' provision should be understood to require only that the reason be 'a relevant contributing factor', not the sole, or dominant, cause' (paragraph 23); addresses the debate that had arisen in the literature regarding whether the correct approach to interpreting the Convention reason of 'particular social group' is a 'protected characteristics' approach or a 'social perception' approach;[235] and rejects

---

[232] ibid, para 1. It states that '[t]he results of these roundtables will help to refine or develop further the views of UNHCR, governments and other concerned actors on these issues'.

[233] At the time, the EU Member States were already developing intergovernmental agreements that would become precursors to the EU Qualification Directive (n 100). Para 6 of the Note refers to the Tampere Conclusions and footnotes cite the 'EU Joint Position on the Harmonised Application of the Definition of the term "refugee" in Article 1 of the Geneva Convention'.

[234] UNHCR, Interpreting Article 1 of the 1951 Convention (n 148) para 5: 'Human rights principles, not least because of this background, should inform the understanding of the definition of who is owed that protection.'

[235] This 2001 note (n 148) does not use these precise expressions but Guidelines No 2 (n 220), paras 6–7 confirm that these are the most commonly used. This note also makes clear that in fact the 'protected characteristics' approach encompasses both innate characteristics, historic status and also characteristics that 'though it is possible to change them, ought not be required to be changed because they are so closely linked to the identity of a person and/or are an expression of fundamental human rights' (para 27).

the approach that in order to qualify as a refugee, especially in the context of *sur place* claims, there is a 'good faith' requirement (paragraph 34). There are also a number of paragraphs that are obviously directed at vindicating the relevance of the refugee definition in response to contemporary criticisms—e.g. its analysis of armed conflict situations (paragraphs 20–22); and its elaboration of the distinction between prosecution and punishment in the context of military service (paragraph 18).

Overall, therefore, this document represents an important turn-of-the-century clarification of a number of issues of interpretation that were either not addressed in the 1979 Handbook (e.g. a forward-looking assessment of the internal protection alternative) or were not addressed adequately (e.g. the distinction between prosecution and punishment). Of especial importance was that it signalled UNHCR's adoption of a human rights approach based on VCLT rules.[236] However, it is professedly a timebound document intended to inform ongoing developments both in the EU region and in the context of the UNHCR Global Consultations on International Protection process that were in progress at the time. More than anything else, it stands as a connection point between the Handbook and the Guidelines, which were launched soon after.

### 6.1.4 *Guidelines on International Protection*

UNHCR's decision to launch a series, *Guidelines on International Protection*, in 2003 was one of the outcomes of the Global Consultation process embarked on in the context of the Convention's fiftieth anniversary and the start of the new millennium.[237] Being devoted to specific topics, the Guidelines could only constitute further guidance on a limited front, but as time has gone by, they have cumulatively traversed more of the terrain of the refugee definition. On certain elements of the definition, they furnish a far more detailed analysis than that given in the corresponding provisions of the Handbook. This applies particularly to Nos 2, 3, 4, 5, 12, and 13.[238] Also instructive is the way in which the Guidelines seek to add further detail to many of the Handbook's provisions on the inclusion clauses, namely by horizontal effect. Thus for example, Guidelines No 1 on Gender-Related Persecution, run through each of the elements of Article 1A(2) in turn, commenting on how they are to be understood and applied in the context of gender-based claims.

In 2003, Volker Türk noted that their issuance 'has been preceded by an analysis of State practice (including jurisprudence) and an examination of the applicable international legal framework'.[239] A key part of the Global Consultations was a series of expert meetings on themes that were taken up by the Guidelines. These meetings were preceded by an expert paper. Following criticism of its plans for 2013 guidelines on

---

[236] However, as analyzed in Chapter 3, section 2.1.2, since then there have been some UNHCR statements seemingly reverting to the 'circumstantial approach' of the 1979 Handbook.

[237] UNHCR, 'Agenda for Protection' (26 June 2002) UN Doc A/AC.96/965/Add.1.

[238] Guidelines No 2 (n 220); UNHCR, Guidelines No 3: Cessation of Refugee Status under Article 1C(5) and (6) of the 1951 Convention relating to the Status of Refugees (the Ceased Circumstances Clauses) (10 February 2003) UN Doc HCR/GIP/03/03; Guidelines No 4 (n 221); UNHCR, Guidelines No 5: Application of the Exclusion Clauses: Article 1F of the 1951 Convention relating to the Status of Refugees (4 September 2003) UN Doc HCR/GIP/03/05; Guidelines No 6 (n 222); Guidelines No 12 (n 164); Guidelines No 13 (n 52).

[239] Türk (n 204) 304.

military service, UNHCR introduced a methodology involving circulation of drafts, aimed at ensuring consultation with a wide range of interested parties. The 2013 Guidelines states that they are 'the result of broad consultations, provide legal interpretative guidance for governments, legal practitioners, decision makers and the judiciary, as well as UNHCR staff carrying out mandate refugee status determination'.[240] However, the Guidelines themselves do not always contain reference to case law.

On some matters the Guidelines identify a key area of disagreement and seek to reconcile it (e.g. No 4, paragraph 1).

In any case, some twenty years on, the Guidelines series are still a long way off addressing all the elements of the refugee definition: for example, there are still no Guidelines on the nationality and statelessness element,[241] on the well-founded fear element or on the availment clause. In addition, not all focus exclusively on one or more aspects of the refugee definition; most also cover cessation and exclusion and No 7 (on trafficking) also covers issues arising under the 1954 Convention Relating to the Status of Stateless Persons (CRSSP) and the 1961 Convention on the Reduction of Statelessness.[242]

There is a further problem, already highlighted. Each of the Guidelines expressly states that it is intended to 'complement'[243] the 1979 Handbook. The notion of the Guidelines *complementing* the Handbook embodies the claim that despite the former representing 'evolution' of interpretive understanding,[244] the two are consistent with one another and can co-exist as reliable guidance on the refugee definition.

Is that, however, a tenable position? Consider, for example, the main points the Guidelines have made that were absent from the Handbook, in particular as regards express identification of VCLT rules (No 2, paragraph 2; No 6, paragraph 4); application of a human rights approach (e.g. No 2, paragraphs 3, 6; No 4, paragraphs 24, 28; No 6, paragraphs 1–2, 11, 15, 20; and No 7, paragraph 14); recognition of gender-related persecution (No 1); provision of more analysis of non-state actors (No 1, paragraphs 11, 17, 19; No 2, paragraph 23; No 4, paragraph 7(1)(c); No 7, paragraphs 21–24); identification of the ability of the causal nexus to attach to both state and non-state actors (No 1, paragraphs 20–21); fuller acknowledgement of the role of the doctrine of attribution (No 6, paragraph 9); declaration that applicants cannot be expected to

---

[240] UNHCR, Guidelines No 10: Claims to Refugee Status related to Military Service within the context of Article 1A (2) of the 1951 Convention and/or the 1967 Protocol relating to the Status of Refugees (12 November 2014) UN Doc HCR/GIP/13/10/Corr.1, paras 5–9 seek to provide an up-to-date 'summary of state practice'. See also Guy S Goodwin-Gill, 'UNHCR's Protection Guidelines: What Role for External Voices?' (Refugee Studies Centre Seminar, 20 May 2015) available at: <https://www.rsc.ox.ac.uk/news/unhcr2019s-protection-guidelines-what-role-for-external-voices-guy-goodwin-gill>accessed 7 January 2022.

[241] In 2015, UNHCR posted a call for comments on a draft set of Guidelines on 'habitual residence' but the author has been advised by UNHCR that this did not proceed. There has been a separate Handbook on the protection of stateless persons: see UNHCR, Handbook on the Protection of Stateless Persons under the Convention Relating to the Status of Stateless Persons (2014)<https://www.refworld.org/docid/53b676aa4.html>.

[242] UNHCR, Guidelines No 7: The Application of Article 1A(2) of the 1951 Convention and/or 1967 Protocol Relating to the Status of Refugees to Victims of Trafficking and Persons at Risk of Being Trafficked (7 April 2006) UN Doc HCR/GIP/06/07, para 6.

[243] 'Complement' is the standard term used, although UNHCR, Guidelines No 4 (n 221) uses the term 'supplement'.

[244] See e.g. Guidelines No 2 (n 220) para 1.

conceal their religious or political views or other protected characteristics (e.g. No 4, paragraph 19); and synthesisation of two competing approaches to interpreting the term 'particular social group' (No 2, paragraphs 10–13).

Even if the Handbook text relating to *some* of these additional insights can perhaps be reconciled, can it seriously be suggested that the former embodies them all or that there are no points of difference between the two? To take an obvious point of difference highlighted by Hathaway, the Handbook directs attention (incorrectly) to the retrospective question of whether the applicant 'could have sought refuge in another part of the same country' (paragraph 91), whereas Guidelines No 4 on 'Internal Flight or Relocation Alternative' suggest (surely correctly) that the focus instead should be on 'whether the proposed area provides a meaningful alternative in the future' (paragraph 8).[245] The Guidelines nowhere identify any shortcomings in the Handbook. Given that guidance is surely about enunciating consistent and clear principles, this silence is erosive of the authority of UNHCR's overall guidance on interpretation.

That said, the Guidelines' contents still contain a considerable body of material that articulates matters about which there remains broad agreement and, in that way, represents at least important materials for building a modern comprehensive elaboration of the refugee definition.

It remains to consider whether, even if the Guidelines cannot do so on their own, UNHCR guidance materials taken *collectively* can be said to contain a further elaboration of the refugee definition. This is particularly pertinent because in UNHCR's *amicus curiae* briefs/interventions, its present-day formula is to describe its interpretive guidance as encompassing both the Handbook, the Guidelines, and also the ExCom Conclusions. Taking these materials cumulatively, it does at first sight appear possible to treat these and perhaps certain other UNHCR materials as a foundational body of material that includes a number of basic propositions relating to the refugee definition. However, further scrutiny does not bear this out.

An initial obstacle standing in the way of treating UNHCR guidance materials as authoritative *en bloc* has already been flagged, namely that UNHCR continues to insist that the Handbook is the primary source and that the others merely complement it. The logic of treating the Handbook as intact guidance is that, if there is any difference between it and other guidance, the former must prevail: that is the essence of complementarity. A second drawback is that, even if (taking this body of guidance collectively) it were somehow possible to say that it constitutes a comprehensive treatment of the refugee definition, it is nowhere, except that contained in Part One of the Handbook, set out in one place. Whilst there are other types of UNHCR materials post-Handbook that touch on the refugee definition, the very fact that they have not been incorporated into the new process of Guidelines leads to similar problems of co-existence. Indeed, it is not always clear where to find current UNHCR guidance. A third difficulty is that several of the Guidelines are now significantly out of date in certain respects, certainly in terms of addressing current case law. If one seeks to establish what UNHCR guidance is currently, one must look to other materials as well.

---

[245] Hathaway (2nd edn) (n 34) 64, fn 241.

Hathaway has noted further problems. Despite stating that the Guidelines were in principle intended to 'draw on' the expert advice received during the agency's Global Consultations process, they (in Hathaway's words) at time 'diverge' from even the formal conclusions reached through that process.[246] Other scholars have pointed out differences between the UNHCR Handbook and other UNHCR guidance materials.[247] Furthermore, courts and tribunals have not always agreed with the UNHCR position on one or more elements of the refugee definition, as expressed in either the Handbook, the Guidelines, or other UNHCR materials.[248]

Stepping back to survey the overall situation, it is difficult to disagree with Hathaway's conclusion that:

> More detailed guidance may sensibly be gleaned from a compendium of norms prepared by the agency itself, but that advice should rather be presented in a unified form that does not risk the confusion or conflicts of the present array of the Handbook, Guidelines and various other UNHCR papers. Mere preliminary thinking is best presented as such, with any effort at codification by the agency delayed until there is truly a clear and principled consensus achieved in the jurisprudence of the state parties.[249]

Given these problems of 'dissonance', as Hathaway terms them, UNHCR guidance cannot stand as ready-made authoritative guidance on key terms of the refugee definition. That said, it remains that UNHCR materials assist identification of provisions on which there has been broad consensus. In light of the special role given to UNHCR guidance by Article 35 of the Convention, it follows that it is not possible to say, absent UNHCR agreement, that any basic propositions are ones on which there has been substantial consensus. Mere enunciation of current guidance by UNHCR sources will not establish a proposition as one befitting this description; but it is a necessary condition.

To conclude, the UNHCR Handbook remains the most important attempt to provide a comprehensive elaboration of the meaning of the definition laid down in Article 1A(2). Until the ExCom Conclusions more directly address key elements of the refugee definition in substance (as Hathaway among others suggests they should do),[250] they can only play a background role. By virtue of the authoritative status attached to the Handbook by states and by courts and tribunals, especially in the 1980s and 1990s, it must remain as a foundational reference-point in any modern attempt to achieve a further elaboration based on either state practice or widespread consensus

---

[246] And of course, the more recent Guidelines have no integral connection with the Global Consultations.

[247] e.g. Juss (n 201) 49–52 identifies more than one difference between the Handbook's analysis of Article 1D and what was said by UNHCR in the 2002 'Note on the Applicability of Art. 1D of the 1951 Convention relating to the Status of Refugees to Palestinian Refugees' (October 2002).

[248] For example, in relation to Article 1F, the Guidelines No 5 (n 238) fail to address the fact that a significant body of case law has rejected a 'proportionality' approach. See Hathaway (2nd edn) (n 34) 64, fn 241; Hathaway and Foster (n 10) 563–67. On differences between the UNHCR position and case law on the cessation clauses, see *Hoxha* (n 218) on Article 1C(5) and (6); and on internal protection in the cessation context see, English Court of Appeal in *MS (Somalia)* [2019] EWCA Civ 1345; *SB (refugee revocation; IDP camps) Somalia* [2019] UKUT 00358 (IAC).

[249] Hathaway (1st edn) (n 34) 118.

[250] ibid. The author doubts they should do so unless they have input from eminent refugee law experts, judicial and non-judicial.

reflected in the practice of states and in the case law of leading courts and tribunals. This is true, notwithstanding that some of its guidance is now seen as 'equivocal' or deficient in one or more respect. In particular, where basic propositions as stated in the Handbook can be seen to remain valid, that enhances the value they have for modern purposes.

Despite the fact that they are some way off furnishing a comprehensive treatment of the key elements of the refugee definition, the *Guidelines on International Protection* series commenced in 2003, being issued under UNHCR's supervisory responsibility, should also serve as a primary reference point. And here as well, to the extent that they set out basic propositions of refugee law, these offer at least an essential reference-point for any modern attempt to provide a comprehensive elaboration of the definition. So far as concerns this book's objectives, this means that, subject to possible limited exceptions, only those propositions that have obtained UNHCR endorsement in the Handbook or Guidelines can qualify as 'basic propositions' about which there is substantial agreement. UNHCR guidance clearly constitutes a major pillar, but even taken compendiously, it cannot be said that it contains a ready-made further definition of key elements of the Article 1A(2) definition.

## 6.2 Case Law and the Judicial Pillar

Case law on the Article 1A(2) definition possesses obvious shortcomings as a ready-made body of learning regarding the refugee definition. It has no formal authority at the international level. In the absence of any activation by state parties of Article 38 of the Refugee Convention, there is no international court or UN treaty-monitoring mechanism in a position to issue authoritative rulings. Further, being based on decisions in individual cases, courts and tribunals tackle issues concretely and discretely; they never attempt an abstract or comprehensive treatment of the whole of the refugee definition. Even for those scholars who attribute a certain level of authority to leading cases, the result is therefore, what Gilbert has called, a 'multithreaded (and possibly incomplete) tapestry of authoritative analysis'.[251] Nor can it be overlooked that at times senior courts and tribunals have adopted quite restrictive interpretations of one or more aspects of the refugee definition. Additionally, even though case law has played a signal role in achieving consensus of many issues, leading courts and tribunals do not always agree over interpretation (as later chapters will document). Any attempt to achieve a working definition must draw heavily on case law, but there is no short cut to distilling from it points on which there is widespread judicial agreement.

At the same time, as will also be highlighted in Chapter 2, through a combination of sheer volume and the quality of some of the leading decisions, case law has come to hold a position of considerable importance in interpreting key terms, perhaps a position beyond that justified by the strict terms of Article 31(3) and/or Article 32 VCLT rules.[252] It too is now an indispensable pillar of refugee law. If, as is sometimes said, definitions belong to the definers, in the contemporary world the latter are very

---

[251] Gilbert (n 167) 634.
[252] VCLT (n 12).

often judges. What Hathaway described as the remarkable 'judicial activism' of the 1990s[253] has undoubtedly transformed the landscape of refugee law.[254] Whilst there are now fewer cases that tackle 'first principles' of the refugee definition, a very significant number of national legal systems provide a right of appeal against administrative decisions on refugee status by governmental authorities, resulting in greater judicial or quasi-judicial oversight. One way or another, various aspects of the refugee definition are scrutinised and tested daily in the world of actual cases. Unlike how it is for UNHCR RSD decision makers, interpretation of legal texts is judges' stock in trade. And in undertaking this interpretive task, as Hathaway has also observed, 'courts are increasingly (and appropriately) inclined to seek guidance from the jurisprudence of other state parties to the Convention'.[255] Adoption of a human rights approach to interpretation of the refugee definition (which as will become clear in Chapter 3 has become the dominant approach) has buttressed the judicial pillar, since the authoritative guidance on relevant human rights norms emanates in the main from the case law of regional human rights courts and the UN treaty-monitoring bodies.

Hathaway and Foster consider that '[a]s a matter of binding law, the task of determining the Refugee Convention's "truly autonomous and international meaning" has thus fallen principally to domestic decision-makers—officials, specialist tribunals and courts'. They portray the 'extraordinary judicial engagement with the Convention definition' as having created 'a rich comparative jurisprudence concerning the key terms of the refugee definition, which shows a determined effort to engage with the international and comparative nature of the refugee definition'.[256] There has also been a growing volume of 'transnational'/horizontal judicial dialogue' having some bearing on matters of interpretation.[257] Whether or not Hathaway and Foster are right to view case law as the principal source of guidance, it is indubitably the case that nowadays no interpretation of the refugee definition can be said to be widely agreed if it has not received substantial endorsement in case law.

---

[253] Hathaway (1st edn) (n 34) 116.
[254] Goodwin-Gill (n 187) 238, stating that 'national judgments, particularly of the higher courts, have contributed to identifying and understanding meaning and to the development of international refugee law'. His analysis also notes, however, various factors that make the precise value of jurisprudence contingent. See also Guy S Goodwin-Gill, 'Strategy and Strategic Litigation' (Keynote Address, Global Strategic Litigation Council Annual Conference, 12 April 2022) <http://www.kaldorcentre.unsw.edu.au/news/guy-s-goodwin-gill--strategy-and-strategic-litigation> accessed 6 June 2022.
[255] Hathaway (1st edn) (n 34); see also James C Hathaway, 'A Forum for the Transnational Development of Refugee Law: The IARLJ's Advanced Refugee Law Workshop' (2003) 15(3) IJRL 418, 418.
[256] Hathaway and Foster (n 10) 5.
[257] The most concrete form so far of such 'dialogue' has arisen in the context of the EU, with the publication by the European Asylum Support Office (EASO; now European Union Asylum Agency (EUAA)) of a number of 'Judicial Analysis' publications, including one on 'Qualification for International Protection' (2nd edn, January 2023). These have been developed by a transnational group of European judges utilising a drafting methodology which includes consultation with UNHCR and a judge from both the CJEU and the ECtHR. Most have been translated into more than one other European language. The entire series to date is available on the EUAA (formerly EASO) website. On transnational judicial dialogue in the refugee law context see Hélène Lambert, Jane McAdam, and Maryellen Fullerton (eds), *The Global Reach of European Refugee Law* (CUP 2013) 1–24. See further in Chapter 2. On the EUAA, see Regulation (EU) 2021/2303 of the European Parliament and of the Council of 15 December 2021 on the European Union Agency for Asylum and repealing Regulation (EU) No 439/2010 [2021] OJ L 468/1.

However, discussions about which source of guidance on the refugee definition is more important—case law or UNHCR guidance—must not be allowed to obscure the fact that they have become complementary pillars that mutually reinforce each other's importance. Indeed, the emergence of case law as a major force in refugee law has been actively promoted by UNHCR. As part of its commitment to the rule of law, UNHCR has been and continues to be in the forefront of promoting case-law driven developments.[258] The result is that there is now a steady daily stream of national cases that are posted on Refworld and other refugee-related websites addressing one or more aspects of the refugee definition (as well as many other provisions of the Refugee Convention). Although the UNHCR *Guidelines on International Protection* only rarely feature references to key cases, it was noted earlier that their drafting is based, inter alia, on a survey of case law.[259] On the judicial plane, even though UNHCR guidance has never been treated by judges as binding,[260] there is an unbroken line of judicial opinion that Article 35 of the Convention requires ongoing UNHCR guidance to be treated as highly persuasive. As the CJEU noted recently, UNHCR documents 'are particularly relevant in the light of the role conferred on it by the Geneva Convention.'[261]

In sum, international jurisprudence has now established itself as an indispensable major pillar, alongside UNHCR guidance.

## 6.3 National Governmental Guidance

Not to be underestimated as a relevant source is national governmental guidance. Such guidance primarily comprises guidance on how decision makers interpret the Convention definition of refugee. Where, however, national law contains provisions prescribing the meaning of one or more key terms of this definition, the nature of such guidance tends to be more ambivalent, typically combining instruction to apply the national law gloss with assertion that such gloss is fully in accordance with international meaning.

This study does not generally bracket what might be called the 'national governmental pillar' alongside UNHCR, judicial, and academic guidance for two main reasons. First, even though it sometimes embodies best practices, there are only a very limited number of such guidance/guidelines that are accessible, mainly emanating from countries with high volumes of asylum applications.[262] Second, even though as

---

[258] See UNHCR and IPU, 'A guide to international refugee protection and building state asylum systems: Handbook for Parliamentarians No 27' (2017), which has a section on appeals, available at <https://www.unhcr.org/3d4aba564.pdf> accessed 5 April 2021. Difficult though it is to reconcile with its frequent call for judicial supervision of governmental RSD, UNHCR has still not accepted that there should be an independent (as opposed to an internal) appeal against its own RSD decisions.
[259] See above section 6.1.4.
[260] See Chapter 2, section 3.2.
[261] *Bilali* (n 103), para 57; Case C-91/20 *LW v Bundesrepublik Deutschland* [2021] ECLI:EU:C:2021:898, para 56.
[262] On the US Citizenship and Immigration Services, 'Asylum Officer Basic Training Course: Asylum Eligibility', see Deborah Anker and Josh Vittor, 'International Human Rights and US Refugee Law: Synergies and Contradictions' in Burson and Cantor (eds) (n 118) 109, 116–17. Anker and Vittor note that in some respects these materials, which are updated from time to time, have taken a more principled approach to drawing on IHRL norms than have US judges. In the UK, see UK Home Office, 'Asylum decision-making guidance (policy instructions)', available at <www.gov.uk/government/collections/asylum-decision-mak

we shall see VCLT rules envisage that either national legislation or national guidance can constitute relevant evidence of 'subsequent practice', its very status as national guidance disqualifies it from constituting a truly universal definition. Applying VCLT rules, the premise for arriving at any definition of key terms of the refugee definition is to transcend national law.[263] Such guides can also be affected by having to interpret national legislation that has transposed or codified the Article 1A(2) definition inadequately. Although such guidance can be fairly described as constituting another 'pillar' of international refugee law, it can only be one of a subsidiary kind.

## 6.4 Academic Guidance

Refugee law has also reaped enormous rewards from the great quantity and rich quality of much of the academic literature; scholarship has often been a shining beacon. In relation to the refugee definition, academic studies serve at least three purposes: investigation of problems surrounding the definition, especially as regards how it is applied in practice (its 'investigative' role); identification of existing levels of agreement about key propositions (its 'digest' role); and enunciation of the writer's (or writers') own view as to what these propositions should be (its 'evaluative' role). The world of scholarship is often closely connected with the world of practice, in more ways than one. For example, leading courts and tribunals have drawn on leading academic studies when seeking to interpret key terms. Scholars in turn sometimes rely on judicial insights to support their own evaluations.

But again, academic studies offer no short cut. To take as an example, the most detailed study of the refugee definition in the English language literature, that by Hathaway and Foster,[264] clearly performs a major role in, inter alia, identifying various levels of agreement of disagreement over key aspects of the refugee definition, aided by their wide-ranging survey of case law and other sources. However, the priority for them is the evaluative task of arriving at a 'principled approach' that sometimes conflicts with prevailing understandings.[265] They continue for instance to endorse

---

ing-guidance-asylum-instructions> accessed 3 July 2023. For service instructions to German Federal caseworkers, see *Bundesamt für Migration und Flüchtlinge*, 'Dienstanweisung Asylverfahren', available at <https://www.asyl.net/fileadmin/user_upload/Gesetzestexte/DA-Asyl_21_02_2019.pdf> accessed 5 April 2021. See also for Australia, the Department of Home Affairs, 'Policy—Refugee and Humanitarian—Refugee Law Guidelines' (2017). Canada's Immigration and Refugee Protection Act, s 159(1)(h), provides statutory authority for the Chairperson of the Immigration and Refugee Board (IRB) to issue Guidelines, of which there are presently nine: <http://laws.justice.gc.ca/eng/acts/I-2.5/index.html>. These could also be considered to have quasi-judicial status, since the IRB is an independent authority.

[263] '[In] practice it is left to national courts, faced with a material disagreement on an issue of interpretation, to resolve it. But in doing so it must search, untrammelled by notions of its national legal culture, for the true autonomous and international meaning of the treaty' (*Adan (Lul Omar) v Secretary of State for the Home Department* [2001] 2 AC 477, per Lord Steyn at 515). In terms of the ability of such national guidance to constitute a relevant means of interpretation either under Article 31(3)(b) or Article 32 VCLT, another difficulty is, as Hathaway notes (2nd edn) (n 34), that it must comprise 'conduct in the application of the treaty' and not be official conduct motivated by expediency or self-interest.
[264] Hathaway and Foster (n 10).
[265] ibid 5: '[O]ur goal in this book is not simply to provide a digest or comprehensive assessment of the current state of transnational jurisprudence interpreting the Convention refugee definition. To the contrary, the analysis presented here is explicitly normative: we engage with the jurisprudence as a means of

an approach to the IPA that has been rejected by UNHCR and has attracted support from the courts and tribunals of only one country.[266] That does not necessarily mean their position is wrong, but it does highlight the fact that the purposes of academic endeavour can exist in tension and may not necessarily accord with either UNHCR or judicial guidance considered internationally. Every academic study continues to combine the aforementioned three purposes in their own way.

Whilst therefore, it might be possible to refer to an 'academic pillar', it is notable that scholars themselves do not propose this and recognise that the principal role of academic guidance is in helping drive the adoption by other key actors of better understandings on such matters as the refugee definition.

## 7 Methodology and Outline of the Book

### 7.1 Methodology

The existing corpus of refugee law is a rich repository of UNHCR materials, case law, state practices, scholarship, a growing number of guidelines, and an almost baffling plenitude of doctrinal disputes. That being so, this study does not seek to furnish a comparative law approach as such, although references to case law are plentiful. The author seeks to cite civil law jurisprudence where possible, but is mostly reliant on the refugee law literature in the English language, which continues to prioritise common law cases. The fact that leading common law cases sometimes feature citation of civil law cases mitigates the Anglo-Saxon bias to a degree, but this remains a limitation, especially now there are many more websites featuring civil law cases law with English summaries. In any event, refugee law has reached the stage where comprehensive citation of case law in relation to the entire refugee definition appears to be moving beyond the ken of any single author. It is no accident that, for example, the second edition of *The Law of Refugee Status* is now co-authored by Hathaway and Foster (who also seek to supplement their own analysis with detailed case references harvested by law students),[267] and that the Zimmermann *Commentary* is comprised of multiple chapters written by different authors.[268] The *Oxford Handbook of International Refugee Law*, with chapters by different authors, applies a similar *praxis*.[269]

However, the increasing number of studies making frequent reference to refugee case law in recent years does enable this author to draw on, rather than seek to imitate, them. Indeed, this book depends heavily on examination of what results these studies yield when it comes to identifying areas of agreement and disagreement. As a consequence, the approach of this study is more traditionally analytical.

positing and testing a comprehensive and principled analysis of the Convention refugee definition.' The predominantly academic-based *Michigan Guidelines*, which self-consciously have an evaluative purpose, are discussed further in Chapter 2, section 3.4.

---

[266] See Chapter 8.
[267] Hathaway and Foster (n 10).
[268] Zimmermann (n 14). The chapter on Article 1A(2) is co-authored by Zimmerman and Mahler.
[269] Costello et al (eds) (n 48).

Two of this book's main aims are: to provide a 'digest' of the learning on the Article 1A(2) definition in a particular form and to furnish the author's own evaluative analysis of the refugee definition. This book gives primacy to the 'digest' role, although taking it somewhat further, by not only trying to describe the learning but also seeking to extract from it a number of 'basic propositions' about which there can be said to exist a substantial consensus, so as to arrive at a 'working definition'. The rationale for a 'working definition' was set out earlier.[270] Framed in these terms, both aims reflect the belief that far more needs to be done to achieve greater clarity about the contents of the refugee definition.

In order to realise these aims, this study views it as of cardinal importance to endeavour to interpret each key element of the refugee definition, by explicitly applying the VCLT rules of interpretation. Achieving this is seen to require a detailed analysis of these rules both in general and with particular attention to efforts made so far to apply them explicitly to the Refugee Convention. To underline the central importance attached to these rules, each chapter on substantive elements of the Article 1A(2) applies a structured approach, going through the VCLT rules element by element, save when this is seen to cause unnecessary repetition. Doing so is also seen as critical to this study's attempt to identify 'basic propositions' about which there is substantial consensus, it being argued that they can be seen to reflect what the ILC has termed, 'state practice in the broad sense'.[271]

Applying VCLT rules in a structured way is also conceived as crucial to this book's other main aim, that of setting out and justifying the author's own views on each element of the refuge definition. Although secondary, the aim behind this evaluative exercise is generally to focus on the major issues about which there remains significant disagreements, by identifying the main arguments for and against and then by attempting the author's own evaluation in the form of a number of 'suggested propositions'. As far as possible, the aim is to demarcate this latter type of analysis from the elucidation of 'basic propositions'. Hopefully, this additional dimension offers a path to consideration of trends and in this way acknowledges the evolutionary nature of the refugee definition.

## 7.2 Outline of Book

Against the backdrop of this chapter, Chapter 2 (on Interpretation) explores the approaches that have been taken to the interpretative task that confronts all who seek to construe and apply the refugee definition. Reasons are given why the correct approach must be in conformity with VCLT rules and what more precisely this means in practice. Close attention is paid to how VCLT rules have been applied to the refugee definition and what in particular this means for UNHCR, judicial, and academic sources.

Chapter 3 (on 'Approaches, Ordering, Interrelationships, Modalities) first interrogates the main approaches taken to the refugee definition, namely the 'circumstantial approach', the 'subjective approach', the 'case-by-case' approach, and the 'human

---

[270] See above section 5.5.
[271] See Chapter 2, n 69.

rights approach'. It seeks to explain why and how the human rights approach to the definition of key terms in Article 1A(2) has become the dominant approach, albeit one that must always be pursued within the wider framework of international law. The question is asked, to what extent can a human rights approach admit of different interpretations and accommodate different versions, in particular the hierarchical and non-hierarchical approaches? An attempt is made to critically analyse recent attempts to move away from a human rights approach and to vindicate why a human rights approach should remain 'the only act in town'.

Chapter 3 also looks at the issue of the order in which elements of the definition should be tackled and then the problem of how the different elements of the definition fit together. Finally, it is explained why this study refers at various point to certain 'modalities', relating to personal, temporal, and material scope.

Chapters 4–11 then address, in turn, the key elements of the inclusion clauses of Article 1A(2):

Nationality and statelessness (Chapter 4)
'[O]utside the country' (Chapter 5)
'[B]eing persecuted' and serious harm (Chapter 6)
'[B]eing persecuted' and protection (Chapter 7)
'[B]eing persecuted' and the internal protection alternative (Chapter 8)
The availment clause (Chapter 9)
Convention reasons (Chapter 10)
'[W]ell-founded fear' (Chapter 11)

Whilst it is concluded in Chapter 3 that there is no prescribed order for dealing with the refugee definition's key elements, the order chosen in this study is justified in the following terms. In Chapter 3, the nationality and statelessness and 'outside the country' elements are dealt with first since they concern personal and territorial scope and, at least for decision makers, if personal and territorial scope are not established, it is not strictly necessary to analyse a refugee application further.

In relation to subsequent chapters addressing the definition's material scope, 'the being persecuted' element is tackled first, although divided into three segments: 'being persecuted and serious harm' (Chapter 6), 'being persecuted and protection' (Chapter 7), and 'being persecuted and the internal protection alternative' (Chapter 8). It is considered most logical and also textually apposite to only then deal in Chapter 9 with availment, because the availment clause is essentially about protection and so presupposes understanding of all aspects of its opposite—persecution. Chapter 10 on 'Convention reasons' then follows. 'Well-founded fear' is dealt with last mainly to underline that its meaning can best be understood by first having unpacked in full its object, namely fear *of* being persecuted etc. However, as is underlined in Chapter 3, this ordering is a matter of choice, since the definition itself does not impose one.

In each chapter (as explained above), an attempt is made to identify a number of basic propositions about which there is broad consensus and, in most instances, to venture 'suggested propositions' aimed at trying to resolve some of the continuing agreements of disagreement.

Chapter 12, the book's final chapter, draws together the various propositions identified as having been widely accepted and offers them as a 'working definition' in the hope that their cumulative contents can be seen to demonstrate that many disagreements have been effectively settled. Arguments for and against utilising such an approach are interrogated. Final reflections seek to explore new directions for study of the refugee definition in the future, bearing in mind that inevitably the definition will require further re-weaving in the light of ongoing challenges confronting those seeking international protection and all involved in refugee law.

## 8  Conclusions

Having identified that the refugee definition continues to be seen as prone to unduly diverse interpretations, this chapter has posed the question whether it is possible to do anything about this. In Part 1 it was argued that the goal of a more consistent, 'convergent' interpretation is within our grasp, that agreement has been reached about more than many think, and that it is now possible to elaborate, in the form of a 'working definition', basic propositions about the meaning of its key elements.

Part 2 of this Chapter explained why the definition of refugee in Article 1A(2) of the Convention and/or its 1967 Protocol, is rightly understood worldwide as the refugee definition. It then looked at other definitions of 'refugee' at the international level, both within the Refugee Convention itself and under the UNHCR Statute and under UNHCR's 'persons of concern' and 'good offices' doctrines. Brief mention was also made of the main regional definitions, along with some observations about national definitions, which do not always faithfully transpose the Article 1A(2) definition.

Part 3 set out the limits of the refugee definition in legal terms. Part 4 gave a brief summary of the main criticisms that have been made of this definition.

Part 5 sought to tackle the problems inherent in any attempt to provide a 'further definition' of a definition and to explain why this study instead uses the notion of a 'working definition'.

Part 6 considered to what extent governmental guides, UNHCR guidance, case law, or academic studies can be said to furnish a ready-made elaboration of the refugee definition. Whilst concluding that none fulfil this role, both UNHCR and judicial guidance were identified as indispensable pillars in establishing basic propositions that form part of a working definition.

Part 7 set out the book's methodology and gave an outline of contents, explaining the reasons for ordering the chapters in the way chosen. It concluded by reiterating the need, in any attempt to arrive at a greater level of agreement over the contents of the definition, to take stock of a number of 'basic propositions' that can be compiled into a 'working definition', alongside 'suggested propositions' aimed at proposing solutions to areas where there are still disagreements.

### 8.1  Basic Propositions

The purpose of identifying basic propositions essentially concerns the substance of the refugee definition, which we have yet to tackle, but it is worth asking whether any can be gleaned from this introductory chapter. The following is offered as being now the subject of wide agreement:

1. The two major pillars of interpretive guidance on the refugee definition are UNHCR guidance and the case law of courts and tribunals. However, governmental guidelines and academic materials continue to play a highly significant role.

## 8.2 Suggested Propositions

The following is offered as a suggested proposition, arising out of consideration of arguments for and against the quest for a 'further definition':

1. Valid concerns about seeking to define key elements of the refugee definition do not and must not defeat the endeavour to achieve a correct interpretation and to develop a 'working definition'. Such concerns have force only against absolutist or fixed-list approaches to definition.

# 2
# Interpretation

| | | | | |
|---|---|---|---|---|
| Introduction | | 61 | 2.6.1 Subsequent agreement | 93 |
| 1 Articles 31–33 of the Vienna | | | 2.6.2 Subsequent practice | 95 |
| Convention on the Law of Treaties | | | 2.7 Any Relevant Rules of | |
| 1969 (VCLT) | | 62 | International Law | 100 |
| 1.1 Good Faith | | 65 | 2.8 Special Meaning | 102 |
| 1.2 Ordinary Meaning | | 66 | 2.9 Article 32 VCLT | 103 |
| 1.3 Context | | 67 | 2.9.1 *Travaux préparatoires* (*travaux*) | 103 |
| 1.4 Object and Purpose | | 68 | 2.9.2 Other supplementary means | |
| 1.4.1 'Law-making treaties' | | 70 | of interpretation | 105 |
| 1.5 Subsequent Agreement and | | | 2.10 Article 33 VCLT and | |
| Subsequent Practice | | 71 | Interpretation of Treaties in More | |
| 1.6 Any Relevant Rules of | | | than One Language | 106 |
| International Law | | 73 | 3 Interpretive Value of the Most | |
| 1.7 Special Meaning (Article 31(4) | | | Commonly Cited Sources | 107 |
| VCLT) | | 74 | 3.1 Introduction | 107 |
| 1.8 Article 32 | | 74 | 3.2 UNHCR Materials | 108 |
| 1.8.1 Preparatory works or *travaux* | | | 3.2.1 Article 35 of the Refugee | |
| *préparatoires* (*travaux*) | | 75 | Convention | 108 |
| 1.8.2 Other supplementary means of | | | 3.3 Judicial Materials | 111 |
| interpretation | | 75 | 3.3.1 Case law | 111 |
| 1.9 Article 33 VCLT and Interpretation of | | | 3.3.2 Judicial analyses | 113 |
| Treaties in More than One Language | | 76 | 3.4 Academic Materials | 115 |
| 1.10 Significance of the VCLT Rules | | | 4 VCLT Rules and the EU Asylum Law | 117 |
| for Task of Interpretation | | 77 | 4.1 CJEU Approach to Interpretation | 117 |
| 2 Application of VCLT Rules to | | | 4.1.1 EU asylum law as evidence | |
| the Refugee Convention | | 78 | of state practice | 119 |
| 2.1 Introduction | | 78 | 4.1.2 'Conform interpretation' | 120 |
| 2.2 Good Faith | | 80 | 4.2 Conformity of EU Law Provisions on | |
| 2.3 Ordinary Meaning | | 80 | Refugee Definition with VCLT Rules | 120 |
| 2.3.1 Text as starting point | | 80 | 5 Conclusions | 121 |
| 2.4 Context | | 83 | 5.1 Conclusions: Key Features | 121 |
| 2.5 Object and Purpose | | 84 | 5.1.1 Relevance of Articles 38 and | |
| 2.5.1 Nature of the Convention's pur- | | | Article 35 of the Refugee | |
| poses: The Refugee Convention | | | Convention | 121 |
| as a 'law-making treaty' | | 84 | 5.1.2 Acceptance of VCLT as | |
| 2.5.2 Recourse to object and purpose | | 85 | customary international law | 122 |
| 2.5.3 Evolutive approach to interpret- | | | 5.1.3 The search for an autonomous | |
| ation: The Convention as | | | meaning | 122 |
| a 'living instrument' | | 86 | 5.1.4 Treaty interpretation as a unity | 122 |
| 2.5.4 Identification of the object(s) | | | 5.1.5 Good faith | 123 |
| and purpose(s) | | 86 | 5.1.6 Ordinary meaning | 123 |
| 2.5.5 Conclusions regarding different | | | 5.1.7 Context | 123 |
| objects and purposes | | 91 | 5.1.8 Object and purpose | 123 |
| 2.6 Subsequent Agreement and | | | 5.1.9 Subsequent agreement | |
| Subsequent Practice | | 93 | and practice | 124 |

*The Refugee Definition in International Law*. Hugo Storey, Oxford University Press. © Hugo Storey 2023.
DOI: 10.1093/oso/9780198842644.003.0002

| | | | | |
|---|---|---|---|---|
| 5.1.10 | Relevant rules of international law | 124 | 5.2 Interpretive Value of the Most Commonly Cited Sources | 125 |
| 5.1.11 | Special meaning | 124 | 5.3 Interpretive Value of EU Asylum Law | 126 |
| 5.1.12 | *Travaux* and other supplementary means of interpretation | 124 | 5.4 Flexibility | 126 |
| | | | 5.5 Link with Later Chapters | 127 |
| | | | 5.6 Basic and Suggested Propositions | 127 |

## Introduction

Very gradually, in the past two or so decades, refugee law has come to grasp the need not simply to strive for a universal definition of refugee but to do so by applying correct methods of interpretation. Over the first forty years of the life of the 1951 Convention relating to the Status of Refugees' (Refugee Convention or Convention), the refugee law literature contains virtually no reference to rules of treaty interpretation. Most notably, the 1979 United Nations High Commissioner for Refugees (UNHCR) Handbook on Procedures and Criteria for Determining Refugee Status under the 1951 Convention and the 1967 Protocol Relating to the Status of Refugees (UNHCR Handbook or Handbook) does not identify Vienna Convention on the Law of Treaties (VCLT) rules as the basis for its interpretive guidance on the Convention's provisions.[1] However, such identification is becoming more common, e.g. UNHCR materials do now sometimes identify and apply VCLT rules—see, for example, paragraph 2 of the UNHCR *Interpreting Article 1 of the 1951 Convention Relating to the Status of Refugees*, 2001; and significant coverage is now given to such rules in leading refugee law textbooks.[2] This reflects what is happening in the wider world of treaty interpretation.[3]

---

[1] Examples of studies not referring—or referring only glancingly—to VCLT rules (or their customary law predecessors) include Atle Grahl-Madsen, *The Status of Refugees in International Law. Volume 1: Refugee Character* (Sijthoff 1966); James C Hathaway, *The Law of Refugee Status* (Butterworths Limited 1991); Guy S Goodwin-Gill, *The Refugee in International Law* (2nd edn, Clarendon Press 1996) (albeit noting at ibid 34 that interpretation 'implies certain ground rules', and footnoting in this regard Article 31(1) VCLT, he thereafter refers to VCLT rules only sporadically, with the exception of a few prescient pages on *travaux préparatoires* (at ibid 366–38)); Jean-Yves Carlier et al, *Who Is a Refugee? A Comparative Case Law Study* (Brill 1997); Pirkko Kourula, *Broadening the Edges: Refugee Definition and International Protection Revisited* (Martinus Nijhoff 1997); Vigdis Vevstad, *Refugee Protection: A European Challenge* (Tano Aschehoug 1998); Deborah Anker, *Law of Asylum in the United States* (Thomson Reuters 2022); Lorne Waldman, *The Definition of Convention Refugee* (2nd edn, Lexis Nexis 2019). Early examples of scholars advocating a systematic application of VCLT rules to interpretation of the Refugee Convention include Daniel J Steinbock, 'Interpreting the Refugee Definition' (1998) 45(3) UCLA Law Review 733 and Nikolaos Sitaropoulos, 'Refugee: A Legal Definition in Search of a Principled Interpretation by Domestic Fora' (1999) 52 RHDI 151. One of the earliest authors to apply VCLT rules specifically to interpreting the term persecution was Ivor C Jackson, *The Refugee Concept in Group Situations* (Kluwer Law International 1999) 468–73.

[2] See e.g. James C Hathaway, *The Rights of Refugees Under International Law* (CUP 2005) 48–74. See also James C Hathaway, *The Rights of Refugees Under International Law* (2nd edn, CUP 2021) ch 2, 128–72; Andreas Zimmermann (ed), *The 1951 Convention Relating to the Status of Refugees and its 1967 Protocol: A Commentary* (OUP 2011); Jane McAdam, 'Interpretation of the 1951 Convention' in Andreas Zimmermann (ed), *The 1951 Convention Relating to the Status of Refugees and its 1967 Protocol: A Commentary* (OUP 2011) 75–115; Michelle Foster, *International Refugee Law and Socio-Economic Rights: Refuge from Deprivation* (CUP 2007) 40–75; James C Hathaway and Michelle Foster, *The Law of Refugee Status* (2nd edn, CUP 2014) 5–12. See also Guy S Goodwin-Gill, 'The Search for the One, True Meaning ...', in Guy S Goodwin-Gill and Hélène Lambert (eds), *The Limits of Transnational Law: Refugee Law, Policy Harmonization and Judicial Dialogue in the European Union* (CUP 2010) 204–41.

[3] Richard Gardiner, *Treaty Interpretation* (2nd edn, OUP 2015) 13–19 notes increasing endorsement of VCLT rules by the ICJ and other international courts and tribunals and national courts.

In a nutshell, such rules are important because the refugee definition is embodied in a treaty. Therefore, any progress in interpreting it must be based on recognised rules for interpreting treaties. The 'toolbox' that sets out the rules of treaty interpretation is the VCLT at Articles 31–33.[4] The rationale of what are commonly referred to as the 'VCLT rules'[5] is that of 'establishing the true meaning of a treaty'.[6] This book's devotion of a separate chapter to such rules reflects growing recognition of its fundamental importance to proper understanding of the refugee definition.

Accordingly, Section 1 outlines key features of the VCLT rules. Section 2 then looks at the way VCLT rules have been applied to the Refugee Convention. Two main questions are posed at the beginning of Section 2. First, what significance does application of such rules have for the task of seeking to identify the true meaning of key terms of the refugee definition? Second, are the VCLT rules a 'toolbox' that everybody interpreting such terms must use? Section 3 then examines the interpretive value of the most commonly cited sources; and Section 4 seeks to interrogate the interrelationship between VCLT rules and the EU law method of interpretation.

## 1 Articles 31–33 of the Vienna Convention on the Law of Treaties 1969 (VCLT)

The International Court of Justice (ICJ) considers that Articles 31–33 of the VCLT reflect customary international law, as does the academic literature.[7] Being customary

---

[4] Vienna Convention on the Law of Treaties (adopted 23 May 1969, entered into force 27 January 1980) 1155 UNTS 331. In the English-speaking literature, major studies of the VCLT include Arnold D McNair, *The Law of Treaties* (OUP 1960); Ian Sinclair, *The Vienna Convention on the Law of Treaties* (Manchester University Press 1984); Oliver Dörr and Kirsten Schmalenbach (eds), *Vienna Convention on the Law of Treaties* (Springer 2012); Anthony Aust, *Modern Treaty Law and Practice* (3rd edn, CUP 2013) ch 13; Eirik Bjorge, *The Evolutionary Interpretation of Treaties: A Commentary* (OUP 2014); Gardiner (n 3);James R Crawford, *Brownlie's Principles of Public International Law* (9th edn, OUP 2019).

[5] Studies that refer to 'rules' include Crawford (n 4) 365; Dörr and Schmalenbach (n 4) 521–604; Gardiner (n 3) 35–41. Gardiner notes that the ICJ also refers to 'rules', citing *Sovereignty over Pulau Ligitan and Pulau Sipadan (Indonesia v Malaysia)* [2002] ICJ Rep 625, paras 37 and 38, and *Case concerning Avena and other Mexican Nationals (Mexico v USA)* [2004] ICJ Rep 12, para 83. Aust (n 4) 205–26 prefers to refer to 'elements' or 'principles'. Jane McAdam (n 2) 75–115 argues that it is 'misplaced to describe Arts 31 and 32 VCLT as "rules" of treaty interpretation and that they are no more than logical devices for ascertaining the real area of treaty operation', citing Daniel P O'Connell, *International Law* (2nd edn, Stevens 1970) 253. She regards the principles of treaty interpretation in Arts 31 and 32 VCLT as 'merely guidelines' that facilitate a court's task.

[6] "The practice of law operates on the assumption that there is one correct interpretation and that this meaning has to be found' (James Crawford, *Chance, Order, Change: The Course of International Law, General Course on Public International Law (Volume 365)* (Brill 2013) in: *Collected Courses of the Hague Academy of International Law*, 13). See also Dörr and Schmalenbach (n 4) 522; UK case of *King v Bristow Helicopters* [2002] 2 AC 628, para 81.

[7] *Application of the International Convention on the Elimination of All Forms of Racial Discrimination (Qatar v United Arab Emirates)*, Preliminary objections [2021] ICGJ 554, para 75, which cites in support a number of other ICJ decisions; ILC, Report on subsequent agreements and subsequent practice in relation to the interpretation of treaties (2018) UN Doc A/73/10, 13, which notes that international courts and tribunals have acknowledged the customary character of these rules. The Court of Justice of the European Union (CJEU) has explicitly labelled Article 31 as a codification of general international law in Case C-63/09 *Axel Walz* [2010] ECLI:EU:C:2010:251, para 23. See also Sinclair (n 4) 141–42.

international law, the rules they elaborate are applicable in principle to treaties concluded both before and after the VCLT entered into force in 1980.[8]

It is well-established that Articles 31 and 32 VCLT envisage interpretation as a two-stage process. The text of Articles 31–33 reads:

ARTICLE 31
*General rule of interpretation*
1. A treaty shall be interpreted in good faith in accordance with the ordinary meaning to be given to the terms of the treaty in their context and in the light of its object and purpose.
2. The context for the purpose of the interpretation of a treaty shall comprise, in addition to the text, including its preamble and annexes:
   (a) any agreement relating to the treaty which was made between all the parties in connexion with the conclusion of the treaty;
   (b) any instrument which was made by one or more parties in connexion with the conclusion of the treaty and accepted by the other parties as an instrument related to the treaty.
3. There shall be taken into account, together with the context:
   (a) any subsequent agreement between the parties regarding the interpretation of the treaty or the application of its provisions;
   (b) any subsequent practice in the application of the treaty which establishes the agreement of the parties regarding its interpretation;
   (c) any relevant rules of international law applicable in the relations between the parties.
4. A special meaning shall be given to a term if it is established that the parties so intended.

ARTICLE 32
*Supplementary means of interpretation*
Recourse may be had to supplementary means of interpretation, including the preparatory work of the treaty and the circumstances of its conclusion, in order to confirm the meaning resulting from the application of Article 31, or to determine the meaning when the interpretation according to Article 31:
   (a) leaves the meaning ambiguous or obscure; or
   (b) leads to a result which is manifestly absurd or unreasonable.

Also relevant is Article 33:

ARTICLE 33
*Interpretation of treaties authenticated in two or more languages*
1. When a treaty has been authenticated in two or more languages, the text is equally authoritative in each language, unless the treaty provides or the parties agree that, in case of divergence, a particular text shall prevail.

---

[8] See e.g. *Pulp Mills on the River Uruguay (Argentina v Uruguay)*, Judgment [2010] ICJ Rep 14, para 65. See also UNGA Res 73/203 (20 December 2018), on 'Identification of Customary Law'; ILC, Report on subsequent agreements (n 7).

2. A version of the treaty in a language other than one of those in which the text was authenticated shall be considered an authentic text only if the treaty so provides or the parties so agree.

3. The terms of the treaty are presumed to have the same meaning in each authentic text.

4. Except where a particular text prevails in accordance with paragraph 1, when a comparison of the authentic texts discloses a difference of meaning which the application of articles 31 and 32 does not remove, the meaning which best reconciles the texts, having regard to the object and purpose of the treaty, shall be adopted.

Article 31 sets out the 'general rule of interpretation' (the first stage). Its crux is Article 31(1) which specifies four main elements: good faith, ordinary meaning, context, and object and purpose. Article 32 set out the 'supplementary means of interpretation' for use in certain circumstances only (the second stage).

The wording of Article 31 makes quite clear that its provisions are mandatory: paragraphs 1, 2, 3, and 4 of Article 31 employ the word 'shall'. They thus prescribe that certain factors must be taken into account. It remains, however, that (save for Article 31(4)) the VCLT rules are not prescriptive as to outcome. As regards the specific requirement in Article 31(3) to 'take into account' certain matters, this has been seen to reflect a stronger interpretive obligation than 'take into consideration' but a weaker obligation than 'apply'.[9]

In the first stage, the factors enumerated in Article 31 are examined in order to determine the ordinary meaning of the treaty terms in question. The factors mentioned in Article 32 are employed at the second stage of interpretation either to confirm an interpretation arrived at by an application of Article 31, or to determine the meaning when application of Article 31 'leaves the meaning ambiguous or obscure', or 'leads to a result which is manifestly absurd or unreasonable'.

Despite opting for a two-stage approach, the drafters clearly intended that the approach adopted would be a unitary one. In the words of the International Law Commission (ILC), '[t]he interpretation of a treaty consists of a single combined operation, which places appropriate emphasis on the various means of interpretation indicated, respectively, in Articles 31 and 32'.[10] This is referred to variously as the 'integrated'[11] or 'crucible'[12] or 'interactive' approach.[13]

In explication of the 'integrated' approach, it is often stressed that the considerations specified in Articles 31–32 are not absolute formulae, do not represent a hierarchy of methods, must be applied in a unified manner, and that their weight may

---

[9] Philippe Sands, 'Treaty, Custom and the Cross-Fertilisation of International Law' (1998) 1(1) Yale Human Rights and Development Law Journal 85. I am grateful to Jason Pobjoy for noting this point: see Jason Pobjoy, *The Child in International Refugee Law* (CUP 2017) 39, 104.

[10] See *Maritime Delimitation in the Indian Ocean (Somalia v Kenya)*, Preliminary Measures [2017] ICJ 508, 29, para 64; ILC, Report on subsequent agreements (n 7) 13. See also Crawford (n 4) 367.

[11] *Yearbook of the International Law Commission 1964 Volume II* (1965) UN Doc A/CN.4/SER.A/1964/ADD.1, 55, para 12.

[12] *Yearbook of the International Law Commission 1966 Volume II* (1967) UN Doc A/CN.4/SER.A/1966/Add.l, 219–20.

[13] ILC, Second report on subsequent agreements and subsequent practice in relation to treaty interpretation (26 March 2014) UN Doc A/CN.4/671, 20; cited in Hathaway (2nd edn) (n 2) 135.

depend on cumulative application.[14] However, there is a distinction between the criteria laid down in Article 31 and 32 since whilst together they list a number of 'means of interpretation', those in Article 31 *must* be taken into account. By contrast, those in Article 32 are only stated as ones that *may* be taken into account in the interpretation of treaties.

Another difference is that Article 31 is expressed in the singular as the '[g]eneral rule of interpretation' and Article 32 as '[s]upplementary means of interpretation'.

Further evincing their integrated character, the different elements of the provisions that comprise Articles 31–32 are not expressed as mutually exclusive categories. For example, Article 31(2) makes clear that a treaty's preamble is part of the treaty's context. At the same time, when considering the object and purpose of a treaty, the natural starting point is to look at the treaty's preamble.'[15]

## 1.1 Good Faith

Within Article 31(1), 'good faith' is an overarching principle indicating *how* the task of interpretation is to be undertaken.[16] Good faith implies the requirement to remain faithful to the intentions of the parties and, inter alia, to refrain from defeating them by a literal interpretation.[17] The principle has been applied in numerous decisions of the ICJ and its predecessor.[18] It has been the subject of widespread academic commentary.[19]

The VCLT does not define the term 'good faith' and in the drafting stages the ILC agreed with the Special Rapporteur that 'the concept of good faith, being difficult to express, had better left undefined'.

The Harvard Draft on the Law of Treaties identifies good faith as referring to 'the manner or spirit in which the obligation is to be performed—the degree of fidelity, strictness and conscientiousness manifested in the fulfilment of the promise made'.[20]

---

[14] Ivan A Shearer, *Starke's International Law* (11th edn, London Butterworths 1994) 435; Alexander Orakhelashvili and Sarah Williams (eds), *40 Years of the Vienna Convention on the Law of Treaties* (BIICL 2010) 120–21.

[15] *Case Concerning the Arbitral Award of 31 July 1989 (Guinea Bissau v Senegal)*, Judgment [1991] ICJ Rep 53; see also *Qatar v UAE* (n 7), Preliminary objections [2021] ICJ 554, para 84.

[16] Gardiner (n 3) 167–81.

[17] *Yearbook of the International Law Commission Volume I* (n 11) 326; *Volume II* (n 12) 211. See also McNair (n 4) 465; Mahmoud C Bassiouni, 'A Functional Approach to "General Principles of International Law"' (1990) 11(3) Michigan Journal of International Law 768.

[18] See e.g. *Military and Paramilitary Activities in and against Nicaragua (Nicaragua v United States of America)*, Jurisdiction, Admissibility [1984] ICJ Rep 392, 418, para 60; Bjorge (n 4) 8–9; Gardiner (n 3) 168–69.

[19] See eg Élisabeth Zoller and Suzanne Bastid, *La bonne foi en droit international public* (Pédone 1977); Alexander M Stuyt, 'Good Faith and Bad Faith' (1981) 28(1) Netherlands International Law Review 54; Michel Virally, 'Review Essay: Good Faith in Public International Law' (1983) 77(1) AJIL 130; Philippe Kahn, 'Les principes généraux du droit devant les arbitres du commerce international' (1989) JDI, 116; Shabtai Rosenne, *Developments in the Law of Treaties, 1945-1986* (CUP 1989) ch 3, 135–79; John F O'Connor, *Good Faith in International Law* (Dartmouth 1991); Robert Kolb, *La bonne foi en droit international public* (Graduate Institute Publications 2000); *Yearbook of the International Law Commission Volume II* (n 12) para 6.

[20] Harvard Law School, 'Draft Convention on the Law of Treaties' (1935) 29 AJIL Supp 653, 29, 98.

The impact of the good faith concept on other key elements of Article 31(1) is closely linked to what is known as the principle of effectiveness.[21] This principle has been seen to have two main senses when applied in the context of treaty interpretation. The first is the principle of '*effet utile*' according to which all provisions of the treaty must be supposed to have been intended to have significance;[22] a treaty should be given an interpretation which 'on the whole' will render the treaty 'most effective and useful' and in such a way that a reason and a meaning can be attributed to every part of the text.[23] The second main sense, which is sometimes termed the 'functional' approach, reflects the Latin maxim *ut regis magis valeat quam pereat*, i.e. that the treaty as a whole must be taken to have been concluded to achieve some intended effect,[24] serving to ensure, for example, that the text of the treaty is not read in a manner that leads to a result which is contrary to its object and purpose.[25]

The good faith principle cannot, however, be invoked to impose additional obligations upon the parties. As stated by the ICJ, the principle 'is not in itself a source of obligation where none would otherwise exist'.[26]

## 1.2 Ordinary Meaning

Article 31(1) is not concerned with 'ordinary meaning' per se but only with the 'ordinary meaning to be given to the terms of the treaty in their context and in the light of its object and purpose'. Nevertheless, its logic requires consideration of 'ordinary meaning' per se in order to differentiate it from what has been described as a modified or 'fully qualified' ordinary meaning.[27]

The import of the 'ordinary meaning' taken on its own is that words and phrases are in the first instance to be construed according to their plain and natural meaning.[28] Ordinary meaning is meaning that is 'regular, normal or customary'.[29] However, somewhat confusingly, it has been stated that ordinary meaning is not viewed from the layman's understanding, but from the point of view that a person reasonably informed on the subject matter of the treaty would reach regarding the terms used.[30]

---

[21] Gardiner (n 3) 179–81.
[22] This is the sense applied in *Corfu Channel (United Kingdom of Great Britain and Northern Ireland v Albania)*, Judgment [1949] ICJ Rep 24; and the *Anglo-Iranian Oil Co (United Kingdom v Iran)*, Judgment, Jurisdiction [1952] ICJ Rep 93, 105.
[23] *United States Diplomatic and Consular Staff in Tehran (United States v Iran)*, Judgment [1980] ICJ Rep 33.
[24] This was the sense applied in *Interpretation of Peace Treaties with Bulgaria, Hungary and Romania*, Advisory Opinion (Second Phase) [1950] ICJ Rep 221, 229; *Ambatielos (Greece v United Kingdom)*, Judgment, Preliminary Objection [1952] ICJ Rep 28, 45.
[25] *Yearbook of the International Law Commission Volume II* (n 12) 219.
[26] *Border and Transborder Armed Actions (Nicaragua v Honduras)*, Jurisdiction, Admissibility [1988] ICJ Rep 396, para 94; *Land and Maritime Boundary between Cameroon and Nigeria (Cameroon v Nigeria: Equatorial Guinea intervening)* [1998] ICJ Rep 275, para 39.
[27] *Land, Island and Maritime Frontier Dispute (El Salvador and Nicaragua (intervening) v Honduras)*, Judgment, Merits [1992] ICJ Rep 351, per Judge Torres Bernardez, cited in Hathaway and Foster (n 2) 8.
[28] *Constitution of the Maritime Safety Committee of the Inter-Governmental Maritime Consultative Organization*, Advisory Opinion [1960] ICJ Rep 150.
[29] Gardiner (n 3) 183, citing OED (1989).
[30] Dörr and Schmalenbach (n 4) 542; Gardiner (n 3) 193–94.

The usual practice of the ICJ is to treat ordinary meaning as the starting point.[31] Clear text may be deemed to be the expression of the intention of the parties.[32]

It has been frequently observed that in the nature of conventional or common usage there will often be more than one ordinary meaning,[33] and that this feature reinforces the need for the words and phrases of a treaty to be read in the light of the other specified elements, so as to assist the choice between the alternatives offered by ordinary meaning.[34]

Whilst it is generally assumed that ascertaining ordinary meaning is a routine matter, some have argued that clarity in treaty terms is always elusive. Thus, O'Connell has expressed doubts that any treaty provision is ever clear and unambiguous. Others argue rather that ordinary meaning can be ascertained by reference to context, object, and purpose.[35]

To divine ordinary meaning the most established method is to consult dictionary meanings. Dictionaries in general seek to catalogue all uses of words, not just their ordinary meanings, but their intended breadth makes them an obvious source of reference for ordinary meaning.[36]

## 1.3 Context

Whilst being part of a single rule that does not identify any hierarchy, 'context' is the only concept within Article 31 that is given a specific definition: it is restricted by Article 31(2) to the text, preamble, and annexes of the treaty, together with certain agreements and instruments relating to the treaty. The ICJ has treated a preamble as part of the context in a number of cases, especially to ascertain object and purpose.[37]

Paragraphs 2 and 3 of Article 31 draw a distinction between intrinsic and extrinsic means of interpretation: paragraph 2 setting out certain integral elements

---

[31] A recent example is *Jadhav Case (India v Pakistan)*, Merits [2019] ICJ GL No 168, paras 71–75; *Territorial Dispute (Libya v Chad)*, Judgment, Merits [1994] ICJ Rep 6, para 41; *Legality of Use of Force (Serbia and Montenegro v Belgium)*, Judgment, Preliminary Objections [2004] ICJ Rep 279, para 100; *Competence of the General Assembly for the Admission of a State to the United Nations*, Advisory Opinions [1950] ICJ Rep 8; cited in *Guinea Bissau v Senegal* (n 15); see also ILC, Draft Articles on the Law of Treaties with commentaries (1966) 220, para 11.

[32] See e.g. *Certain Expenses of the United Nations (Article 17, paragraph 2, of the Charter)*, Advisory Opinion [1962] ICJ Rep 159.

[33] John G Merrills, 'Two Approaches To Treaty Interpretation' (1971) 4(1) The Australian Year Book of International Law Online 55, 58.

[34] *South West Africa (Liberia v South Africa)*, Preliminary Objections, Judgment [1962] ICJ Rep 336. See also Aust (n 4) 208.

[35] e.g. Judge Anzilotti in *Interpretation of the Convention of 1919 Concerning the Employment of Women during the Night*, Advisory Opinion [1932] PCIJ Series A/B No 50, 383, referred to in O'Connell (n 5).

[36] Gardiner (n 3) 186. See also *Legality of the Threat or Use of Nuclear Weapons*, Advisory Opinion [1966] ICJ Rep 2.

[37] e.g. *Case concerning Rights of Nationals of the United States in Morocco (France v United States)*, Judgment, Merits [1952] ICJ Rep 176, 196; *Asylum (Colombia v Peru)*, Merits, Judgment [1950] ICJ Rep 266, 282; *Qatar v UAE* (n 7) para 84. See also Richard Gardiner, *Treaty Interpretation* (2nd edn, OUP 2015) 205–06: '[by] stating the aims and objectives of a treaty, as preambles often do in general terms, they can help in identifying the object and purpose of a treaty'; Makane Moïse Mbengue, 'Preamble', Max Planck Encyclopaedias of International Law (2006); Liav Orgad, 'The Preamble in Constitutional Interpretation' (2010) 8(4) International Journal of Constitutional Law 714.

'comprise[d]' by the context; and paragraph 3, listing extrinsic interpretative means to be used alongside ('together with ... ') the context.

It is important to note in relation to paragraph 2 that 'context' includes the whole text of a treaty, including its structure, content, and syntax. Conversely it need not necessarily be the whole text of the treaty; it can be just the particular portion in which the relevant word or phrases occur. Thus, the definition embraces what is sometimes referred to as 'systematic interpretation',[38] that is, interpretation based on consideration of whether other provisions of the same treaty shed light on a provision being interpreted.

The extrinsic interpretive means specified in 31(2)(a) and (b) would appear to be historically limited to proceedings surrounding the conclusion of the treaty. Agreements within the meaning of Article 31(2)(a) have been considered to encompass explanatory reports approved by the government experts involved in drafting conventions of the Council of Europe and adopted at the same time as the conventions and published with them.[39]

## 1.4 Object and Purpose

In contrast to the other elements of Article 31, which will differ when applied to a treaty's individual terms and provisions, 'object and purpose' pertains to the object and purpose of the treaty as a whole.[40]

The object and purpose criterion set out in Article 31(1) is sometimes equated with a 'purposive' approach to interpretation. More precisely, a purposive approach is one that utilises the object and purpose element in a particular way, in that it accords a key role to a treaty's object and purpose and is itself an approach that may take different forms, including one in which a treaty is to be regarded as a 'living instrument' and to be given a dynamic interpretation to reflect new situations.[41]

The search for a treaty's object and purpose is not necessarily confined to its text, although it has been common to look at a treaty's preamble.[42] However, it will always

---

[38] See e.g. Andreas Zimmermann and Claudia Mahler, 'Article 1A, para 2' in Zimmermann (n 2) 337.

[39] Aust (n 4) 211–12. The ILC, Report on subsequent agreements (n 7), in Commentary (3) on Draft Conclusion No 4 (page 28), states that: '[t]he phrase "in connection with the conclusion of the treaty" should be understood as including agreements and instruments that are *made in a close temporal and contextual relation with the conclusion of the treaty*. If they are made after this period, then such "agreements" and agreed upon "instruments" constitute "subsequent agreements" or subsequent practice under article 31, paragraph 3' (emphasis added).

[40] Jan Klabbers, 'Some Problems Regarding the Object and Purpose of Treaties' (1997) 8 Finnish Yearbook of International Law 138, 151–52; Gardiner (n 3) 213. See also Isabelle Buffard and Karl Zemanek, 'The "Object and Purpose" of a Treaty: An Enigma' (1968) 3 Austrian Review of International and European Law 311, 326.

[41] Sinclair (n 4) 131 (only for his remarks about emergent interpretation), cited in McAdam (n 2) 103; Gardiner (n 3) 213. See also Buffard and Zemanek (n 40) 326. The Preamble of a treaty is of relevance not just when considering 'context' but also object and purpose.

[42] *Case concerning a dispute between Argentina and Chile concerning the Beagle Channel*, Report and Decision of the Court of Arbitration [1977] UNRIAA vol XXI, paras 19–20. See also *Qatar v UAE* (n 7) para 84.

be necessary to consider the significance of a preamble in the context of the treaty's substantive provisions.[43]

The object and purpose of a treaty are also closely connected with the intention of the parties. In this context it is ordinarily the intention of the parties at the time the instrument was concluded that is apposite.[44] However, subsequent agreements and subsequent practice may also contribute to a clarification of the object and purpose of a treaty or reconcile invocations of the 'object and purpose' of a treaty with other means of interpretation.[45]

Further illustrative of the interactive role of the different elements, subsequent practice under Article 31(3)(b) may contribute to reducing possible conflicts when the 'object and purpose' of a treaty as a whole appears to be in tension with specific purposes of certain of its rules.[46]

The object and purpose element has been seen to be closely linked with the principle of effectiveness.[47] However, as the ICJ has observed,[48] the principle cannot be used to attribute to the provisions of a treaty a meaning which would be contrary to their letter and spirit.

The temporality of the object and purpose element of Article 31 has been the subject of disagreement. On the one hand, it is said that the principle to be applied is the principle of *contemporaneity* or *static interpretation,* by virtue of which treaty terms must be interpreted according to the meaning which they possessed at the time of its conclusion. On the other hand, the principle to be applied is said to be the evolutive or dynamic or 'living instrument' approach (sometimes called the 'always speaking' approach), which enjoins that a treaty is to be applied in the light of present-day conditions. The evolutive or 'living instrument' approach is closely associated with the principle of effectiveness, since it is inevitable that, in order to give effect to a treaty, reliance cannot solely be placed on the drafters, as they cannot foresee the issues that will arise in practice.[49]

The approach of the ICJ to the tension between the two approaches has been to identify certain criteria that make one or the other most apposite.[50] A high-profile

---

[43] Gardiner (n 3) 205–10.

[44] *Application of the Convention of 1902 governing the Guardianship of Infants (Netherlands v Sweden),* Merits, Judgment [1958] ICJ Rep 55; *Nicaragua v U.S.* (n 18) 270 et seq.

[45] *Maritime Delimitation in the Area between Greenland and Jan Mayen (Denmark v Norway),* Judgment [1993] ICJ Rep 38; *Oil Platforms (Iran v United States),* Judgment, Merits [2003] ICJ Rep 161; *Oil Platforms (Iran v United States),* Judgment, Preliminary Objection [1996] ICJ Rep 803; *Cameroon v Nigeria* (n 26).

[46] *Kasikili/Sedudu Island (Botswana v Namibia),* Judgment, Merits [1999] ICJ Rep 1045.

[47] See e.g. *Award in Arbitration regarding the Iron Rhine ('Ijzeren Rijn') Railway between the Kingdom of Belgium and the Kingdom of the Netherlands,* decision of 24 May 2005, United Nations, *Reports of International Arbitral Awards* (UNRIAA), vol XXVII (sales No E/F.06.V.8) para 49; *Corfu Channel* (n 22); and *Yearbook of the International Law Commission Volume II* (n 12) 219. See also *Application of the International Convention on the Elimination of All Forms of Racial Discrimination (Georgia v Russian Federation),* Judgment on preliminary objections [2011] ICJ GL No 140, paras 133–34; and Gardiner (n 3) 200–01.

[48] *Interpretation of Peace Treaties with Bulgaria, Hungary and Romania,* Advisory Opinion (Second Phase) (n 24) 318.

[49] Shearer (n 14) 437.

[50] *Case concerning Rights of Nationals of the United States in Morocco (France v United States)* (n 18) 189; *Dispute regarding Navigational and Related Rights (Costa Rica v Nicaragua)* paras 55–56. See also *South West Africa,* Advisory Opinion [1971] ICJ Rep 16, para 53 (at the beginning); and *Cameroon v Nigeria* (n 26) para 59.

arbitration case adopting the principle of contemporaneity was the *Eritrea-Ethiopia Boundary Commission* case in which Commissioners described the principle as requiring 'that a treaty should be interpreted by reference to the circumstances prevailing when the treaty was concluded. This involves giving expressions (including names) used in the treaty the meaning that they would have possessed at that time.'[51]

In *Navigational Rights,* when applying the evolutive method to the Spanish term '*comercio*', the ICJ shed important light of what criteria should be applied for deciding when to apply a contemporaneous or evolutive approach:

> [ ... ] where the parties have used generic terms in a treaty, the parties necessarily having been aware that the meaning of the terms was likely to evolve over time, and where the treaty has been entered into for a very long period or is 'of continuing duration', the parties must be presumed, as a general rule, to have intended those terms to have an evolving meaning.[52]

Thus, where a treaty uses generic terms and is of continuing duration, it appears broadly accepted that the approach to interpretation should be an evolutive one.[53]

1.4.1 'Law-making treaties'

It has been recognised that the character of a treaty may affect the question of whether the application of a particular interpretive principle, maxim, or method is suitable in a particular case.[54] 'Law-making treaties' have been defined by Visscher[55] as treaties the object of which is the laying down of common rules of conduct.[56] For the ICJ, such treaties concern those under which:

> [ ... ] the contracting States do not have any interest of their own; they merely have, one and all, a common interest, namely the accomplishment of those high purposes which are the *raison d'être* of the convention. Consequently, in a convention of this

---

[51] Eritrea-Ethiopia Boundary Commission, *Decision Regarding Delimitation of the Border between the State of Eritrea and the Federal Democratic Republic of Ethiopia* [2002].

[52] *Dispute regarding Navigational and Related Rights (Costa Rica v Nicaragua)*, Judgment [2009] ICJ Rep 213, para 66.

[53] The regional human rights courts have employed a 'living instrument' version of the evolutive approach to their respective human rights treaties: see e.g. *Tyrer v the United Kingdom* App No 5856/72 (ECtHR, 25 April 1978) 15; *Mayagna (Sumo) Awas Tingni Community v Nicaragua*, Judgment, IACtHR Series C No 79 (31 August 2001).

[54] UN, Third Report on the law of treaties, by Sir Humphrey Waldock, Special Rapporteur (1964) UN Doc A/CN.4/167 and Add.1-3, 55, cited by Hathaway (1st edn) (n 2) 72.

[55] Charles de Visscher, *Problèmes d'interprétation judiciaire en droit international public* (Pedone 1963) 128, cited by Hathaway (1st edn) (n 2) 72, and Hathaway (2nd edn) (n 2) 163.

[56] 'Law-making treaties' are recognised as one of four main types of international agreement: 'constitutive or organic agreements' relating to the constitutions of international organisations; 'law-making or legislative treaties' that lay down worldwide norms binding upon states; 'contractual agreements' between two or more states, regulating a limited area of their relations; and 'dispositive agreements' that refer to 'exchange[s] in relatively consummated transactions ... such as treaties of lease or cession and boundary treaties'. See Lung-chu Chen, *An Introduction to Contemporary International Law A Policy-Oriented Perspective* (1st edn, Yale University Press 1989) 265–66, cited in Sitaropoulos (n 1) 160. See also Crawford (n 4) 29; Catherine M Brölmann, 'Law-Making Treaties: Form and Function in International Law' (2005) 74 Nordic Journal of International Law 383.

type, one cannot speak of individual advantages to States, or of the maintenance of a perfect balance between rights and duties.[57]

Although use of this head of classification is not universal,[58] the criteria usually identified as comprising such treaties have a continuing relevance.

## 1.5 Subsequent Agreement and Subsequent Practice

Sub-paragraphs (a) and (b) of Article 31(3) are forward-focused. Their rationale is that the way in which a treaty provision is actually applied by the parties is usually a good indication of what they understand it to mean.[59] Subparagraph (a) of Article 31(3) concerns subsequent agreement. Subparagraph (b) concerns subsequent practice. The latter is similar to but not necessarily the same as the term 'state practice' (which of course is also one of the essential elements of *opinio juris* for the purposes of determining whether treaty provisions have the status of customary international law).[60]

The ILC considers that a 'subsequent agreement between the parties regarding the interpretation of the treaty or the application of its provisions' *ipso facto* has the effect of constituting an authentic interpretation of the treaty, whereas a 'subsequent practice' only has this effect if it 'shows the common understanding of the parties as to the meaning of the terms'. Thus, the difference between a 'subsequent agreement between the parties' and a 'subsequent practice ... which establishes the agreement of the parties' lies in the greater ease with which an agreement is established.[61]

According to Dörr and Schmalenbach, subsequent practice for Article 31(3)(b) purposes 'must constitute a sequence of acts or pronouncements, since "practice" cannot be established by one isolated incident'.[62] The interpretive value of that practice will always depend on the extent to which it is concordant, common, and consistent and thus sufficient to establish a discernible pattern of behaviour. On the other hand, they note that even though the practice requires agreement of the parties, 'that does not mean that every party must have individually engaged in practice .... It suffices, therefore that inactive parties should have accepted the practice set by other parties'.[63] 'Agreement' in this context 'would seem to mean acceptance, even tacit ... at the very minimum evidenced by the absence of any disagreement'.[64]

The constraint placed by the VCLT text on subsequent practice (it must be 'subsequent practice *in the application of the treaty* which establishes the agreement of the parties *regarding its interpretation*' (emphasis added)) is salient. It means that it is not

---

[57] *Reservations to the Convention on the Prevention and Punishment of the Crime of Genocide*, Advisory Opinion [1951] ICJ Rep 15, 26.
[58] Brölmann (n 56).
[59] *Air Service Agreement of 27 March 1946 (United States of America v France)* (1963) 54 ILR 303, cited by Aust (n 4) 215.
[60] *Nicaragua v U.S.* (n 18).
[61] See ILC, Report on subsequent agreements (n 7) Conclusion No 4.
[62] Dörr and Schmalenbach (n 4) 556.
[63] ibid 557–58.
[64] ibid 560.

enough to look at subsequent practice per se: also necessary is to show that this subsequent practice reflects a common understanding of the parties as to the meaning of the relevant treaty's terms. Dörr and Schmalenbach state that agreement 'presupposes knowledge or awareness of other parties of a certain practice'.[65]

The ILC's Conclusion 5 clarifies that subsequent practice encompasses case law ('conduct of a party in the application of a treaty ... in the exercise of ... judicial ... functions').[66] The Commentary on this Conclusion notes at (19) that domestic courts in particular, sometimes refer to decisions from other domestic jurisdictions and thus engage in a 'judicial dialogue' even if no agreement of the parties can thereby be established. Apart from being relevant under Article 32 (see section 1.8 below), such references may add to the development of a subsequent practice, particularly if endorsed by other senior domestic courts.[67]

Nonetheless, the relevance of case law emanating from courts and tribunals (international or domestic) within the context of the Article 31(3)(3) provisions has an important limit. It is not the case law that constitutes the state practice but rather the response of states to case law.[68]

The ILC has emphasised that subsequent practice 'in a broad sense', albeit not meeting the requirements of Article 31, may nonetheless be treated as relevant under Article 32.[69]

Subsequent agreement and subsequent practice may provide useful indications to the treaty interpreter for assessing, as part of the ordinary process of treaty interpretation, whether the meaning of a term is capable of evolving over time.[70]

The ILC Commentary observes that national legislation can be one form of subsequent practice and can therefore be an interpretive aid.[71] The Commentary, however, concludes that 'the possibility of amending or modifying a treaty by subsequent practice has not been generally recognized'.[72] The ILC has issued a Guide to Practice on Reservations to Treaties 2011 which, inter alia, distinguishes between modification of

---

[65] ibid. See especially *Certain Expenses* (n 32) 201, Separate Opinion of Judge Fitzmaurice.
[66] ILC, Report on subsequent agreements (n 7) 37. It must be borne in mind that Article 38(1)(d) of the ICJ Statute permits the Court to rely on judicial opinions and scholarly commentary, but only as *subsidiary* means of determining the content of international law. Those sources are not equivalent to the general practice of states.
[67] ILC, Report on subsequent agreements (n 7) Conclusion No 7(19).The importance of acceptance in other jurisdictions was emphasised by Lord Hope in *King v Bristow Helicopters* (n 6), cited by Goodwin-Gill (n 2) 221 (emphases added).
[68] See Serena Forlati, 'On Court Generated State Practice: The Interpretation of Treaties as Dialogue between International Courts and States' (2015) 20 Austrian Review of International and European Law 99, 101. Forlati cites Professor Zemanek's statement that 'it is ... not the Court's judgment that amounts to "subsequent practice", but the adoption by the parties of the specific interpretation by the Court of a protected right as correct'.
[69] ILC, Report on subsequent agreements (n 7) Commentary, Conclusion No 4, para 33. Thereby, in Brownlie's words, it can still have 'some probative value'. See Crawford (n 4) 368, citing *Eritrea-Ethiopia Boundary Delimitation* (n 51). See also *Assange* [2012] UKSC 22, para 109 (per Lord Kerr).
[70] *South West Africa* (n 34) 31. See also the *Aegean Sea Continental Shelf (Greece v Turkey)*, Jurisdiction, Judgment [1978] ICJ Rep 3, as regards the term 'territorial status'. See also ILC, Report on subsequent agreements (n 7) 37, Conclusion No 8(8)(18).
[71] *South West Africa* (n 34) 32–34. It cites, inter alia, *V v the United Kingdom*, App No 24888/94 (ECtHR [GC], 16 December 1999) para 73; *Kart v Turkey* App No 8917/05 (ECtHR [GC], 3 December 2009) para 54; *Sigurður A Sigurjónsson v Iceland* App No 16130/90 (ECtHR, 30 June 1993) para 35.
[72] ILC, Report on subsequent agreements (n 7) 63.

a treaty and an 'interpretive declaration'.[73] These Guidelines clarify that an interpretive declaration does not modify treaty obligations.[74]

## 1.6 Any Relevant Rules of International Law

The reference in Article 31(3)(c) to 'relevant rules' contains no restrictions and must therefore be taken to refer to all recognised sources of international law, including custom, general principles, binding resolutions of the UN Security Council (UNSC), other treaties, judicial decisions, and 'soft law' sources.[75] The term 'relevant' is an important but somewhat vague qualifier. Obviously included would be provisions of other treaties dealing with the same subject-matter or that are created to address the same or similar factual, legal, or technical problems.[76]

From being considered for a long time to be a 'dead letter',[77] this provision has been applied in more recent times in diverse circumstances.[78]

Article 31(3)(c) is often taken together with other elements of Article 31.[79] It has indeed been seen to embody the principle of 'systemic integration'.[80]

The most evident sticking point in relation to the scope of Article 31(3)(c) is that it concerns rules 'applicable' in the relations between the parties. Several different approaches have been advocated regarding this criterion.[81]

The approach taken, inter alia, by the ILC, is to treat the applicability criterion as relating to a rule that can be at least implicitly accepted or tolerated. It considers that focus should be on whether the relevant rules either expressed customary international law or 'where they provide evidence of the common understanding of the parties as to the object and purpose of the treaty under interpretation or as to the meaning of a particular term'.[82]

The ICJ has emphasised the importance of considering a treaty in the context of the wider international law context, in particular where there are other treaties dealing with similar subject matter, sometimes referred to as 'cognate treaties'.[83] From its

---

[73] ILC, Guide to Practice on Reservations to Treaties (2011) UN Doc A/66/10.
[74] ibid para 4.7.1.
[75] Dörr and Schmalenbach (n 4) 560–68; on treaties, see ILC, Report of the International Law Commission Fifty-eighth session (1 May–9 June and 3 July–11 August 2006) (2006) para 251(18); WTO, *Panel Reports, European Communities—Measures Affecting the Approval and Marketing of Biotech Products* (29 September 2006) WT/DS291/R.
[76] Dörr and Schmalenbach (n 4) 565.
[77] Gardiner (n 3) 304.
[78] ibid 304–17, 320–23. Cases often cited include the ICJ's *Oil Platforms (Iran v United States)* (n 45); and ECtHR cases such as *Al-Adsani v the United Kingdom* App No 35763/9 (ECtHR [GC], 21 November 2001).
[79] *Oil Platforms (Iran v United States)* (n 45); *Golder v the United Kingdom* App No 4451/760 (ECtHR, 21 February 1975).
[80] Campbell McLachlan, 'The Principle of Systemic Integration and Article 31(3)(c) of the Vienna Convention' (2005) 54(2) ICLQ 279.
[81] In the literature, four main approaches have been discussed but only three have gained any traction: see McLachlan (n 80) 314; Gardiner (n 3) 310–17.
[82] ILC, 'Fragmentation of international law: difficulties arising from the diversification and expansion of international law. Report of the Study Group of the International Law Commission, finalized by Martti Koskenniemi' (13 April 2006) UN Doc A/CN.4/L.682, paras 414–15.
[83] *North Sea Continental Shelf Cases*, Judgment [1969] ICJ Rep 3, 125, Separate Opinion of Judge Ammoun, cited by Hathaway (2nd edn) (n 2) 66; *South West Africa* (n 34).

approach to drafting of the VCLT, it appears the ILC foresaw such treaties as falling within Article 31(3)(c).[84] The ECtHR has expressly seen cognate treaties to contain 'relevant rules of international law applicable in the relations between the parties' in a number of cases.[85]

Whilst the relevancy requirement of Article 31(3)(c) is clearly wide enough to include comparative treaty interpretation, it is a principle that remains subject to the application of the provisions of Article 31 as a whole. Reference to the same term in another treaty will not necessarily assist if it has different objects and purposes.[86]

## 1.7 Special Meaning (Article 31(4) VCLT)

Article 31(4) is the only provision that is truly prescriptive: a special meaning 'shall' be given if it is established that the parties so intended. The term 'special meaning' has been construed to cover two different kinds of cases: where the terms of a treaty have a technical or special meaning due to the particular field the treaty covers; and where a term is used in a way different from the more common meaning.[87] This subparagraph prescribes that the burden of proof of a special meaning will rest on a party.[88]

Gardiner notes that 'the most common way in which a special meaning is indicated is by including a definition article in a treaty.'[89]

## 1.8 Article 32

Article 32 is concerned with the 'supplementary means of interpretation'. It appears that by separating Articles 31 and 32 into two stages, the drafters sought to ensure that the primary focus for interpreting a treaty was on the meaning of the text and that the role of supplementary means of interpretation was largely confined to 'confirming' the meaning resulting from the application of Article 31. They did not include in Article 31 any reference to the supposed intention of the parties as elicited in the *travaux*. At the same time, the ILC Commentary makes clear that the intention was not to draw a rigid line between the two Articles.[90] The ILC has more recently confirmed this understanding, noting that '[t]he interpretation of a treaty consists of a single combined

---

[84] Sinclair (n 4) 138–39, cited by Hathaway (2nd edn) (n 2) 66.
[85] See e.g. *Soering v United Kingdom* App No 14038/88 (ECtHR, 7 July 1989); *Jersild v Denmark* App No 15890/89 (ECtHR, 23 September 1994); *Al-Adsani v United Kingdom* (n 78); *Mamatkulov & Askarov v Turkey* App No 46827/99 (ECtHR [GC], 4 February 2005); *Behrami v France & Saramati v France, Germany, and Norway* App Nos 71412/01 & 78166/01 (ECtHR [GC], 2 May 2007) para 129 (decision as to the admissibility).
[86] *MOX Plant (Ireland v United Kingdom)*, Provisional Measures [December 2001] ITLOS Rep 95, para 51.
[87] Gardiner (n 3) 334.
[88] *Legal Status of Eastern Greenland (Denmark v Norway)*, Judgment [1933] PCIJ Series A/B No 53, ICGJ 303, 49; *Western Sahara*, Advisory Opinion [1975] ICJ Rep 12, para 116. Both are cited by Dörr and Schmalenbach (n 4) 569; Sinclair (n 4) 126–27; Gardiner (n 3) 296.
[89] Gardiner (n 3) 339.
[90] *Yearbook of the International Law Commission Volume II* (n 12) 220, para 10.

operation, which places appropriate emphasis on the various means of interpretation indicated, respectively, in Articles 31 and 32'.[91]

As noted earlier, the ILC has clarified that 'subsequent practice' that fails to meet the requirements of Article 31(3) may nevertheless constitute subsequent practice 'in the broad sense' falling under Article 32. The ILC notes that in this guise it may take various forms including:

> [ … ] a direct application of the treaty in question, conduct that is attributable to a State party as an application of the treaty, a statement or a judicial pronouncement regarding its interpretation or application. Such conduct may include official statements concerning the treaty's meaning, protests against non-performance or tacit acceptance of statements or acts by other parties.[92]

However, it considers that 'subsequent agreements' under Article 31(3)(a) will have 'greater interpretive value'.[93]

### 1.8.1 Preparatory works or *travaux préparatoires* (*travaux*)

The most commonly used supplementary means of interpretation are the 'preparatory works', usually referred to by their French rendering. It has been widely recognised that in practice treaty interpreters attach more significance to the *travaux* than appears strictly consonant with the two-stage process set out in Articles 31 and 32.[94]

The term 'preparatory work' is 'an omnibus expression' referring generally to all documentation that had a formative effect on a treaty's drafting,[95] including the circumstances of the conclusion of the treaty. It is widely understood to include written material, such as successive drafts of the treaty, conference records, explanatory statements by an expert consultant at a codification conference and uncontested interpretive statements by the chairman of a drafting committee, and ILC Commentaries.

It is recognised that the value of such materials will depend on a number of factors. Dörr and Schmalenbach state that the interpretive value of *travaux* 'will depend on its cogency, its accessibility, its direct relevance for the treaty terms at issue, the consistency with other means of interpretation, but also on the number of parties involved in the evolution of the particular materials'.[96]

### 1.8.2 Other supplementary means of interpretation

The wording of Article 32 admits of other supplementary means of interpretation without specifying any. However, such recourse is likewise to be confined to situations where reliance on the primary means produces an interpretation that (a) leaves the meaning 'ambiguous or obscure' or (b) leads to a result that is 'manifestly absurd

---

[91] ILC, Report on subsequent agreements (n 7) Conclusion No 2(5).
[92] ibid Conclusion No 4(35).
[93] ibid Conclusion No 4(33).
[94] See e.g. John Collier and Vaughan Low, *The Settlement of Disputes in International Law* (OUP 1999) 541–47, cited by Aust (n 4) 218.
[95] McNair (n 4) 411.
[96] Dörr and Schmalenbach (n 4) 577; see also Aust (n 4) 219.

or unreasonable'; and, in this context, the purpose is to determine the meaning, not simply to confirm it.

Supplementary means of interpretation include materials relating to the circumstances of conclusion of a treaty but also commentaries, explanatory reports, other governmental materials, judicial decisions, and academic writings. As noted earlier, the ILC has emphasised that there is an important interaction between Article 32 and Article 31(3)(b) VCLT.[97]

When considering the material scope of 'other supplementary means of interpretation', it must be recalled that Articles 31 and 32 do not enumerate exhaustively the factors which may be taken into account. Rather, they are intended to deal only with 'the comparatively few general principles which appear to constitute general rules for the interpretation of treaties'.[98]

There is therefore no intention of ruling out the use of other principles and maxims of interpretation which may be helpful in particular cases. The ILC has eschewed attempts to codify these, recognizing that 'the interpretation of documents is to some extent an art not an exact science'.[99] Such principles clearly include some discussed already, such as the principles of effectiveness and of evolutive/dynamic interpretation. Another principle, which could also be said to inhere in the notion of good faith or the *pacta sunt servanda* principle, is that of consistent or conform interpretation.[100] Other principles that have been mentioned include: *euisdem generis* (when general words follow special words, the general words are limited by the genus (class)); *lex specialis derogate legi priori* (a specific rule prevails over a general rule); the rule that exceptions to a general rule have, for the reason alone of being an exception, to be interpreted restrictively (*in dubio mitius*); the *expressio unius est exclusio alterius* rule (express mention of a circumstance or condition that excludes others).[101]

One important remark having a bearing on the methodology used in this book concerns Gardiner's comment on the distinction between 'reciting' and 'using' preparatory works. In his words, 'a narrative with provisions interwoven with preparatory work make the most coherent presentation of a reasoned interpretation'.[102]

## 1.9 Article 33 VCLT and Interpretation of Treaties in More than One Language

Article 33 enjoins that (unless the treaty provides, or the parties otherwise agree) where there is divergence between the texts, a particular text shall prevail. The default position is stated to be that the text is equally authentic or authoritative in each language in which it has been authenticated. Reflecting usual practice, Article 85 of the VCLT itself provides that for its own purposes various specified language texts

---

[97] Gardiner (n 3) 398–404; see above n 69.
[98] Gardiner (n 3) 405.
[99] *Yearbook of the International Law Commission Volume I* (n 11) 5, 54.
[100] Sir Hersch Lauterpacht, *The Development of International Law by the International Court* (Stevens 1958) 27–28, cited by Goodwin-Gill (n 2) 215.
[101] Aust (n 4) 220–21.
[102] Gardiner (n 3) 328.

are equally authentic. Paragraph 4 provides that where there is no provision for a particular text to prevail and when there is a difference of meaning between the authentic texts, or if meaning is ambiguous or obscure in one text, one must adopt the meaning that best reconciles the texts.

For the human rights treaties to which refugee law has often looked, the specific rules applied in relation to authentic versions are variable. For example, the twin 1966 Covenants, the International Covenant on Civil and Political Rights (ICCPR) and the International Covenant on Economic, Social and Cultural Rights (ICESCR), treat five languages as equally authentic: Chinese, English, French, Russian, and Spanish.[103] By contrast, the Refugee Convention stipulates only two authentic versions, in English and French.[104]

## 1.10 Significance of the VCLT Rules for Task of Interpretation

From the above analysis, we can glean that even though the VCLT rules are not exhaustive and not (save in one respect) binding as to outcome and do not necessarily lead to a correct result in every case,[105] they do constitute a set of generally applicable guidelines and furnish an 'essential infrastructure'.[106] Further, it is only by applying the VCLT rules that one can securely establish the true meaning of the key terms of this definition. These rules apply to all decision-making concerning interpretation of treaties such as the Refugee Convention, including at the national level, both administrative as well as judicial,[107] as well as to UNHCR Refugee Status Determination (RSD), which still takes place in many countries.

We can also discern that whilst the ICJ and other international arbitral tribunals treat Articles 31 and 32 as the rules they have to apply, they do not always assign them to their proper categories or 'pegs' as tools for interpretation.[108] The actual practice of treaty interpretation must always be to some degree an 'art' and treaty interpretation an 'inexact science'.[109] Nevertheless, the learning that has accumulated on the VCLT rules discloses the value of a structured approach.[110] According to this approach, the

---

[103] International Covenant on Civil and Political Rights (adopted 16 December 1966, entered into force 23 March 1976) 999 UNTS 171; International Covenant on Economic, Social and Cultural Rights (adopted 16 December 1966, entered into force 3 January 1976) 993 UNTS 3.

[104] Convention Relating to the Status of Refugees (adopted 28 July 1951, entered into force 22 April 1954) 189 UNTS 137, Article 46.

[105] ILC, 'Fragmentation of international law' (n 82). The report's author considers at para 17 that the conceptual framework in which to manage fragmentation is the VCLT: 'One aspect that does seem to unite most of the new regimes is that they claim binding force from and are understood by their practitioners to be covered by the law of treaties.'

[106] Gardiner (n 3) 6.

[107] Who in relation to cases in which they are required to interpret international law are sometimes referred to as 'natural judges'—see Antonios Tzanakopoulos, 'Domestic Courts as the "Natural Judge" of International Law: A Change in Physiognomy' in James Crawford and Sarah Nouwen (eds), *Select Proceedings of the European Society of International Law, Vol 3* (Hart Publishing 2010) 155–68.

[108] As observed by Frank Berman, 'Treaty "Interpretation" in a Judicial Context' (2004) 29(2) Yale Journal of International Law 315 when discussing the ICJ's approach in the *Oil Platforms* case. See also *Oil Platforms (Iran v United States)* (n 45) Separate Opinion of Judge Kooijmans, para 4.

[109] *Yearbook of the International Law Commission Volume II* (n 12) 5, 54.

[110] ILC, Report on subsequent agreements (n 7).

precise relevance of different means of interpretation must first be identified in any case of treaty interpretation before they can be 'thrown into the crucible' in order to arrive at a proper interpretation, by giving them appropriate weight in relation to each other.[111] This lends support to the value of considering each element of the VCLT rules in turn.

The accumulated learning on the VCLT rules also helps with such matters as what weight is to be accorded to different considerations.[112]

## 2 Application of VCLT Rules to the Refugee Convention

### 2.1 Introduction

Before proceeding to consider how VCLT rules are to be applied to the Refugee Convention, two matters need highlighting.

First, as was noted in the previous section, the ways in which the VCLT rules apply depend in some measure on the nature of the treaty concerned. There are cogent reasons for considering that the Refugee Convention is a fortiori a treaty whose interpretation must ensure it is consistent with VCLT rules. Perhaps more than any other global treaty, it stands in need of autonomous interpretation, i.e. one that is independent from national legal concepts, traditions, and terminologies.[113] The drafters envisaged that such interpretation would be ensured by Article 38, which provides for state parties to refer any disputes as to interpretation to the ICJ. But no state party has done so and it is thought highly unlikely, due to inter-state sensitivities, that any will.

Second, the need for consistency with VCLT rules raises the question as to whether this requires that they are expressly applied. In the common law world there has been growing acceptance that, when interpreting the Refugee Convention, the rules to be applied are those set out in the VCLT, since the latter represent customary international law.[114] However, in the civil law countries, it remains relatively unusual to find any express reference to the VCLT rules in decisions of courts and tribunals that concern

---

[111] ibid.

[112] ibid Commentary on Conclusion 9.

[113] Article 27 VCLT prohibits states parties from invoking the provisions of their internal law as justification for their failure to perform a treaty. The importance of an autonomous definition has been strongly voiced in common law cases and in the academic literature: see e.g. *Adan (Lul Omar) v Secretary of State for the Home Department* [2001] 2 AC 477, 515–56; *Sepet and Bulbul v Secretary of State for the Home Department* [2003] UKHL 15, para 6; *MPR v Refugee Status Appeals Authority* [2012] NZHC 567, para 15; Goodwin-Gill (n 2) 207–09.

[114] See *Revenko v Secretary of State for the Home Department* [2000] EWCA Civ 500; *R v Secretary of State for the Home Department, ex parte Adan and Aitsegeur* [1999] 3 WLR 1275; *Islam v Secretary of State for the Home Department Immigration Appeal Tribunal and Another, Ex Parte Shah, R v* [1999] UKHL 20; *European Roma Rights Centre and Ors v Immigration Officer at Prague Airport and Anor* [2004] QB 811 para 18; *In re B (FC) (Appellant) (2002) Regina v Special Adjudicator (Respondent) ex parte Hoxha (FC) (Appellant)* [2005] UKHL 19, para 22 (Keene LJ). McAdam (n 2) 82 cites *Applicant A v Minister for Immigration and Ethnic Affairs* [1997] 190 CLR 225, para 277 (Gummow); and *QAAH of 2004 v Minister for Immigration & Multicultural & Indigenous Affairs* [2005] FCAFC 136, para 74 (Kirby J), citing *Thiel v Federal Commissioner of Taxation* [1990] 171 CLR 338, 356.

interpretation of one or more elements of the refugee definition.[115] And within the Common European Asylum System (CEAS), the method of interpretation adopted by the Court of Justice of the European Union (CJEU), including when dealing with issues relating to the 1951 Convention, is expressly distinct from the VCLT rules. At the same time, whilst it would take a thorough comparative law survey to establish the precise situation, the author is not aware of any decisions of civil law courts or tribunals disputing that VCLT rules have customary law status or that they should govern interpretation of all treaties, including the Refugee Convention. In none of the civil law cases either has any dispute being raised to the general learning of common law courts and tribunals on the VCLT rules as applied to the Refugee Convention.

There are also several features of refugee case law in civil law countries that ameliorate their lack of VCLT referencing. Some comparative law studies that have been conducted indicate that courts and tribunals in such countries have regard to similar factors, especially ordinary meaning, object, and purpose.[116] Some civil law cases on refugee issues do refer to them indirectly, for example, when they cite or refer to sources that do expressly apply VCLT rules, in particular: (i) common law cases; (ii) UNHCR materials post-2001; and (iii) academic studies, especially post-2001.[117] Further, (iv), as is illustrated by CJEU jurisprudence and application of it (since the Qualification Directive (QD) came into force in 2006) by national courts and tribunals within the EU member states, it will be argued later in this chapter that the approach the CJEU takes to interpretation of the refugee definition[118] appears broadly consistent with a VCLT approach.[119] It nevertheless bears mention that whilst it is becoming more common for VCLT rules to be applied expressly in common law countries, it is still far from universal and, in addition, important international sources, such as UNHCR Guidelines on International Protection, still only refer to them sporadically.

None of this is to disregard the difficulties. The fact that VCLT rules have the status of customary international law,[120] means that even those states that have not ratified this treaty[121] are bound by them. Whether or not express reference is made to them

---

[115] In this respect the situation is typical of the broader world of treaty interpretation: see Gardiner (n 3) 14–20. Two exceptions known to the author are Germany and Austria, both of whose supreme administrative courts have made express reference to the VCLT in the context of the Refugee Convention. See German Federal Administrative Court decisions, *BVerwG 1 C 36/04* [2005] para 13, and *BVerwG 9 C 21/00* [2001] para 16; and the Austrian Supreme Administrative Court decisions *AAF v Federal Asylum Review Board*, Case No 99/20/0401 [2002]; *A v Federal Asylum Review Board*, Case No 2003/20/0111 [2007]; and *Case No 2003/20/0181* [2006]. I am grateful to Harald Dörig and Peter Nedwed for the German and Austrian references respectively.

[116] See e.g. the contributions contained in Goodwin-Gill and Lambert (n 2) regarding the practice of courts and tribunals in Belgium, France, Sweden, and Denmark.

[117] An example of a civil law case citing (i), (ii), and (iii) is the judgment of the Slovenian High Court, I U 411/2015-57 [2015]. An example of a civil law case citing (i) and (ii) is the judgment of the Supreme Administrative Court of Poland, II OSK 237/07 [2008].

[118] Article 2(d) of the EU Qualification Directive (recast) essentially replicates the definition of refugee in Article 1A(2) of the Refugee Convention. See Directive 2011/95/EU of the European Parliament and of the Council of 13 December 2011 on standards for the qualification of third-country nationals or stateless persons as beneficiaries of international protection, for a uniform status for refugees or for persons eligible for subsidiary protection, and for the content of the protection granted (recast) [2011] OJ L 337/9.

[119] See below sections 4.1.1–4.1.2.

[120] See above nn 8 and 114.

[121] As of 24 August 2022, 116 state parties have ratified the convention, and a further fifteen states have signed but have not ratified it according to the UN Treaty Collection database. See <https://treat

in the civil law or common law world, it is incumbent on states to ensure that all attempts at interpreting key terms of the refugee definition at least comport with VCLT rules. As a matter of international law, the task of achieving a universal definition of key terms cannot be served by reliance on national or regional systems using methods of interpretation contrary to rules of interpretation that have the status of customary international law. To apply VCLT rules expressly, facilitates consistency in interpreting the refugee definition and in that way enhances fairness and predictability in refugee status determination. In the absence of careful regard to the VCLT rules, interpreters can more easily fall into the trap of applying rules of interpretation based on national law, which can give rise to error and confusion.[122] However, the relative rarity of express application of VCLT rules in civil law countries does entail recognising from the outset that there is no global consensus about such application. What this means for the analysis that follows will be a matter addressed in the conclusion of this chapter.

## 2.2 Good Faith

Good faith has operated in two different ways in the context of the Refugee Convention. On the one hand, it has been seen to lend support for readings that place emphasis on object and purpose and pursue an evolutive approach.[123] On the other hand, it has been seen to place some limits on the circumstances under which it is justified to go beyond the constraints of ordinary meaning, context, and purpose. In relation to the latter, in *Roma Rights*, Lord Bingham cited ICJ authority for the proposition that the principle of good faith is not itself a source of obligation and stated that it could not be used to read into the refugee definition an obligation to treat a state's borders as extending to another country with which it has an agreement to conduct pre-entry controls.[124]

## 2.3 Ordinary Meaning

### 2.3.1 Text as starting point

Courts and tribunals have often deemed it as appropriate to take the Convention text as a starting point. For example, in *K and Fornah* Lord Bingham stated that 'the

---

ies.un.org/Pages/ViewDetailsIII.aspx?src=TREATY&mtdsg_no=XXIII-1&chapter=23&Temp=mtdsg3&clang=_en>.

[122] Tamara Wood, 'Interpreting and Applying Africa's Expanded Refugee Definition' (2019) 32(2/3) IJRL 290, 306 notes that '[a] disregard for the general rules of interpretation [set out in Article 31] is the key problem with existing understanding of the expanded refugee definition [in Africa] in both literature and practice'.

[123] See Goodwin-Gill (n 2) 216–17, referring to *Barcelona Traction, Light and Power Company Limited (New Application, 1962) (Belgium v Spain)*, Judgment, Merits, Second Phase [1970] ICJ Rep 3. He notes, inter alia, that it may sometimes require a '"reasonable interpretation" or a response more particularly in harmony with changed circumstances and evolving understanding'.

[124] *Roma Rights* (n 114) paras 30–31.

starting point of the construction exercise must be the text of the Refugee Convention itself, because it expresses what the parties to it have agreed'.[125]

Nevertheless, taking the Convention text as a starting point is not to be confused with a literalist approach that unjustifiably 'privileges' the text.[126] A literalist approach, as we have seen, is inconsistent with the 'integrated' approach to treaty interpretation reflected in the VCLT rules. It erroneously takes the text, not as a starting-point, but as the starting and finishing point. Yet a literalist approach has sometimes been applied by senior courts and tribunals. In *Sale*, for example, the US Supreme Court by a majority appeared to treat the element of 'ordinary meaning' as being both the starting and finishing point unless there is 'extraordinarily strong contrary evidence'.[127] In *Horvath*, the UK House of Lords ruled that persecution should be given its 'ordinary dictionary meaning'.[128] That assertion is difficult to square with the adoption in the same case of a human rights approach. In 1997 the New Zealand Refugee Status Appeals Authority justifiably criticised the approach of the English Court of Appeal to the meaning of persecution in *Adan*[129] for an 'overly literal approach to interpretation' that is 'contrary to established principles of treaty interpretation'.[130] Indeed, in light of such cases, Hathaway and Foster consider that 'overemphasis on literalism has led some courts to rely on (usually English) dictionaries, in order to construe the meaning of the convention—particularly, as is later discussed, to understand what kinds of harm legitimately fall within the notion of "being persecuted"'.[131]

However, in considering past practice, it would be wrong to portray as a 'literalist' approach decisions that merely treat ordinary meaning on its own as a starting point. The view that the ordinary meaning should be the starting point is not confined to the ILC Commission in its 1966 reports.[132] Hathaway indeed does not dispute that the text can be an appropriate starting point.[133] Taking it as a starting point should only be resisted if it is done without properly considering the other elements as part of an integrated exercise (this is the error committed by the majority in *Sale*, who treated it as both a starting and a finishing point). Thus, Lord Bingham's adoption of the text as a starting point in several UK cases went hand-in-hand with application of a unified approach, e.g. in *K and Fornah*, he considered that object and purpose was key to interpretation of the 'membership of a particular social group' ground and his judgments generally evinced a strong endorsement of the view that the Refugee Convention is

---

[125] *Fornah v Secretary of State for the Home Department (linked with Secretary of State for the Home Department v K)* [2006] UKHL 46, para 10 (Lord Bingham), referring also to *Januzi v Secretary of State for the Home Department* [2006] UKHL 5, para 4.
[126] McAdam (n 2) 82.
[127] *Sale v Haitian Centers Council* [1993] 509 US 155, paras 191 and 194 (Blackmun J), cited by McAdam (n 2) 84.
[128] *Horvath v Secretary of State for the Home Department* [2000] UKHL 37, 10.
[129] *Adan v Secretary of State for the Home Department* [1997] 2 All ER 723 (CA).
[130] *Refugee Appeal No 70366/96 Re C* [1997] 4 HKC 236, 264.
[131] Hathaway and Foster (n 2) 8.
[132] *Yearbook of the International Law Commission Volume II* (n 12). See e.g. *Guinea Bissau v Senegal* (n 15).
[133] Hathaway (2nd edn) (n 2) 170. His objection is to approaches that make it a 'privileged reference point'.

to be treated as a 'living instrument', taking stock of developments in international human rights law and standards.[134]

Even when the text is taken as a starting-point, though, there has been increasing recognition that often ordinary meaning provides limited interpretive assistance in the Refugee Convention context. Focusing on the treatment of the concept of 'being persecuted', it is apposite to recall that as long ago as 1997, Carlier et al found on the basis of a comparative survey that perusal of English, French, German, Dutch, and Spanish definitions of persecution, failed to yield a consistent approach to an understanding of the term as a matter of ordinary usage.[135] Undoubtedly one reason behind this growing recognition has been appreciation of the fact that some key terms of the refugee definition, such as 'being persecuted' are indeterminate.

A point often made in the literature is that the 1951 Convention, by virtue of its drafting history and eventual text, exemplifies a treaty that does not lend itself much or at all to ordinary meaning construction. Noting that it was the 'product of organisation and compromise', McAdam states that 'such compromises can lead to the adoption of deliberately ambiguous or nebulous phrasing'.[136] Recognition of this feature has clearly reinforced the need enjoined in any event by VCLT rules to take an integrated approach that considers the (unmodified) ordinary meaning together with the other elements set out in Articles 31–32. Certainly in the common law courts, there has been widespread acceptance of the need, when interpreting the Refugee Convention, to adopt an integrated or interactive approach, which treats the rules set out in Articles 31–32 VCLT as a non-hierarchical unity.[137] This is also the approach urged by leading scholars such as Hathaway.[138]

Whilst the need for a unified or interactive approach speaks strongly against literalism, it would nevertheless be incorrect to see a literal reading as always inapplicable. It cannot be excluded, a priori, at least, that some of the refugee definition's key terms lend themselves more than others to an ordinary meaning reading. Chapter 5 observes, for example, that (with good reason) most commentators have ascribed a literal meaning to the term 'outside' (as in 'outside the country').[139]

---

[134] This author would question whether the critique of the UK courts and tribunals for pursuing an unduly literal approach is entirely accurate, even in relation to the last two decades or so. For most of the time, UK courts and tribunals have pursued an approach that accords considerable weight to context, object and purpose(s). Where there have been tussles between judges of a literal bent and judges of a more purposive bent, the latter have tended to prevail. A good example is the case of *Asfaw* [2008] UKHL 31, which concerned interpretation of Article 31 and the issue of whether the prohibition on the imposition of penalties on refugees extended to those who sought to leave it illegally using another false passport. Finding that Article 31 should be read in this way, Lord Bingham applied an 'evolutionary approach' that did not confine the meaning of the expression 'on account of their illegal entry or presence' in Article 31(1) to the meaning the framers had in mind. It was his view that prevailed over that of Lord Rodger and Lord Mance (the latter who considered that a stricter, more literal, approach should be applied and who considered it significant that there was no extensive state practice sufficient to establish the agreement of the parties to such an interpretation).
[135] Foster (n 2) 48, citing Carlier et al (n 1) 702.
[136] McAdam (n 2) 86.
[137] See e.g. *Applicant A* (n 114); *Januzi* (n 125) para 4.
[138] Hathaway (2nd edn) (n 2) 134–37.
[139] See e.g. Hathaway and Foster (n 2) 20. See Chapter 5, sections 2.3–2.5.

## 2.4 Context

As was noted earlier, Article 31(2) distinguishes between context as text—sometimes called its 'core' meaning[140] (chapeau to Article 31(2))—and context in its extended sense as 'any agreement or instrument related to the treaty' (Article 31(2)(a) and (b)). At least in its core sense, context is an element that has been accorded a quite significant role in interpretation of the Refugee Convention. In applying it, courts and tribunals have dwelt particularly on the Convention's Preamble. The Canadian Supreme Court in *Ward v Canada* attached signal importance to the references in the Preamble to the UN Charter and the Universal Declaration of Human Rights (UDHR). They saw these references to encapsulate both the intention of the drafters and the objectives of the Convention.[141]

Courts and tribunals have regularly made reference to the context of the Refugee Convention, as including the entirety of its text or specific provisions, including its Preamble and annexes. A prime example within the Refugee Convention of utilising context by application of a 'systematic approach'[142] is the approach that has been taken to the interrelationship between Articles 1A(2) and Article 33 of the Convention.[143] Context in its core sense has also been important to interpretation of the phrase 'well-founded fear'.[144]

Some scholars have also seen context in a very extended sense as having important application to the Refugee Convention. According to Hathaway in 2005, Aust considered that the 1979 UNHCR Handbook was part of the context of the Convention, appropriately referenced under Article 31(2) VCLT, but that view appears as an isolated exception.[145] Hathaway himself only includes the Final Act of the conference which adopted the Refugee Convention and the Preamble as matters 'formally recognised as part of the context'. He expressly excludes the ExCom Conclusions on International Protection. At the same time, he appears to regard consideration of context as requiring that attention be paid to subsequent interpretive agreements and practice within the meaning of Article 31(3) VCLT and at one point refers to the ExCom Conclusions as 'imperfect elements of context'.[146]

That Article 31(2) VCLT encompasses the Final Act of the conference which adopted the Refugee Convention[147] is unexceptionable. However, the requirement

---

[140] Hathaway (2nd edn) (n 2) 140.
[141] *Canada (AG) v Ward* [1993] 2 SCR 689. See further, Ralf Alleweldt, 'Preamble to the 1951 Convention' in Zimmermann (n 2) 232.
[142] See above p. 68.
[143] See e.g. *A-G v Zaoui and Inspector-General of Intelligence and Security* [2006] 1 NZLR 289, paras 25–27, 29–30, cited by McAdam (n 2) 96; see also Zimmermann and Mahler (n 2) 346.
[144] James C Hathaway and William S Hicks, 'Is There a Subjective Element in the Refugee Convention's requirement of "Well-founded Fear"?' (2005) 26(2) Michigan Journal of International Law 505, 535–36. See Chapter 11, section 2.2.2.
[145] Hathaway (1st edn) (n 2) 54. It is not entirely clear that this was what Aust meant. He differentiated between 'explanatory reports', which 'should be seen as part of the "context" in which the conventions were concluded and "official" commentaries, which are later produced', putting the Handbook in the latter category: see now Aust (n 4) 211–12.
[146] Hathaway (2nd edn) (n 2) 144–45; see also Hathaway (1st edn) (n 2) 53–55; Hathaway and Foster (n 2) 8–9.
[147] Final Act of the United Nations Conference of Plenipotentiaries on the Status of Refugees and Stateless Persons (1954) 189 UNTS 37.

that the subsequent agreement must be 'regarding the interpretation of the treaty'[148] makes inclusion of any later instruments problematic.In any event, the case law has certainly made limited use of such an approach. McAdam's study, for example, does not note any example of it.[149]

## 2.5 Object and Purpose

In interpreting the refugee definition, the object and purpose element of the VCLT rules has widely been seen to play a major role.

2.5.1 Nature of the Convention's purposes: The Refugee Convention as a 'law-making treaty'

Consideration of object and purpose has been instrumental in the Refugee Convention being seen as a 'law-making treaty', especially given the ICJ's description in the 1951 *Genocide* case of law-making treaties being ones under which:

> [ … ] the contracting States do not have any interest of their own; they merely have, one and all, a common interest, namely the accomplishment of those high purposes which are the raison d'être of the convention. Consequently, in a convention of this type, one cannot speak of individual advantages to States, or of the maintenance of a perfect balance between rights and duties.[150]

In this regard, the *travaux* to the Refugee Convention also shed light. Its drafters agreed that 'the text of the Convention was not a treaty under which the Contracting States assumed certain obligations in exchange for certain advantages; it was rather a form of solemn declaration in order to benefit a third party'.[151]

In his 1999 article, Sitaropolous pointed out, by reference to the criteria set out by the ICJ in its advisory opinion on the *Genocide* case[152] that the 'law-making' features of the Refugee Convention were clear: it was an international agreement that did not seek to regulate inter-state but rather state-individual relations; its main purpose was not to benefit the state parties but 'on the contrary, to impose on them a general obligation of effective protection';[153] it was a multilateral convention of a special character, with a strong 'humanitarian and civilising purpose' and that it was ratified by the vast majority of states.[154] In a similar vein, Foster has written that

---

[148] See above p. 71.
[149] McAdam (n 2) 95–96.
[150] *Reservations* (n 57) 26.
[151] UN Conference of Plenipotentiaries on the Status of Refugees and Stateless Persons, Conference of Plenipotentiaries on the Status of Refugees and Stateless Persons: Summary Record of the Nineteenth Meeting (26 November 1951) UN Doc A/CONF.2/SR.19.
[152] *Reservations* (n 57).
[153] He cites an unpublished 1982 report for UNHCR by Goodwin-Gill, 'Implementation of Treaties: Obligations of conduct and result under the 1951 Convention Relating to the Status of Refugees'. See Sitaropoulos (n 1) 161.
[154] Sitaropoulos (n 1) 160–64.

'the Refugee Convention is far more akin to a law-making treaty than a contractual one.'[155]

### 2.5.2 Recourse to object and purpose

The relatively indeterminate nature of the literal text of the Convention has been seen to make recourse to object and purpose particularly apposite. Lord Lloyd in *Adan* [1999] noted that state parties had to make compromises in the process of negotiating the treaty which had resulted in a lack of precision. As a result, 'one is more likely to arrive at a true construction of Article 1A(2) by seeking a meaning which makes sense in the light of the Convention as a whole, and the purposes which the framers of the Convention were seeking to achieve, rather than by concentrating exclusively on the language'.[156] As noted by Steinbock, 'with a text as relatively amorphous as that of the refugee definition, some sense of its purpose is useful in deciding how to interpret its terms'.[157] He notes Brownlie's[158] observation that this is especially true when the textual approach leaves the decision maker with a choice of possible meanings.

McAdam observes that '[a]nalysis of the case law suggests that courts typically seek to determine the 1951 Convention's object and purpose by reference to the treaty text as a whole, and the Preamble in particular'.[159]

In arguing for an approach to interpretation of the Refugee Convention giving a key role to object and purpose, Hathaway urges a:

> [ ... ] 'merger' of the inquiry into a treaty's object and purpose with advancement of the more general duty to interpret a treaty in a way that ensures its effectiveness. Specifically, an interpretation of text made 'in the light of [the treaty's] object and purpose' should take account of the historical intentions of the parties, yet temper that analysis to ensure the treaty's effectiveness within its modern social and legal setting.[160]

Placing strong reliance on an object and purpose approach has undoubtedly tended to support arguments for a broad interpretation of key terms: thus, the identification of the humanitarian and/or human rights object and purpose of the Refugee Convention has been seen to warrant a 'broad approach to [interpretation] ... rather than a narrow linguistic approach'.[161]

Although McAdam and Hathaway and Foster, among others, maintain a concern that courts and tribunals in the common law world still apply an overliteral approach,

---

[155] Foster (n 2) 46. Foster cites Guy S Goodwin-Gill, 'Refugees and Responsibility in the Twenty-First Century: More Lessons Learned from the South Pacific' (2003) 12(1) Washington International Law Journal 23, 24–25; Nikolaos Sitaropoulos, *Judicial Interpretation of Refugee Status: In Search of a Principled Methodology Based on a Critical Comparative Analysis, with Special Reference to Contemporary British, French, and German Jurisprudence* (Sakkoulas 1999) 96. See also Hathaway (1st edn) (n 2) 72–73; Hathaway (2nd edn) (n 2) 163–65.
[156] *Adan* (n 129).
[157] Steinbock (n 1) 771; see earlier observation of McAdam (n 2).
[158] Steinbock (n 1) 771, citing Crawford (n 4) 632.
[159] McAdam (n 2) 91.
[160] Hathaway (1st edn) (n 2) 55; Hathaway (2nd edn) (n 2) 148, 156.
[161] *Adan* (n 129) 305; *Asfaw* (n 134) para 55.

viewed overall the jurisprudential trend is away[162] from reliance on dictionary definitions and towards stronger recognition that ordinarily the approach to interpretation should be one that applies a unified approach. Save perhaps in US case law, there is no longer any significant opposition to such an approach.

### 2.5.3 Evolutive approach to interpretation: The Convention as a 'living instrument'

Placing emphasis on object and purpose has helped drive the argument for application of an evolutive or dynamic approach to interpreting the Convention as a 'living instrument'.[163]

Although courts and tribunals deciding eligibility as a refugee have rarely noted the nuances to the evolutionary approach to interpretation as developed by the ICJ, for example (in treating it as dependent on whether or not the terms of a treaty are generic or evolutionary),[164] specific note has been made of the fact that the term 'being persecuted' was intended to be capable of encompassing future forms of harm.[165] In the wider refugee law literature, it has been viewed as of high importance that the state parties to the 1967 Protocol, by removing the temporal and geographical limitations on the scope of Article 1A(2), were confirming the acceptance made in the third preambular paragraph of the Preamble that 'it is desirable to revise and consolidate previous international agreements relating to the status of refugees and to *extend the scope and protection accorded by such instruments* by means of a new agreement'.[166]

One element of the refugee definition that has been seen by some to particularly lend itself to evolutive interpretation is the term 'membership of a particular social group',[167] with emphasis being placed on the fact that the drafters wished to ensure protection for groupings not foreseen at the time of drafting.[168]

At the same time, it would be wrong to conceive of the Convention's terms as requiring, in every instance, an evolutive interpretation. As noted earlier, case law and the wider literature have seen the literal meaning as still appropriate in some contexts.[169]

### 2.5.4 Identification of the object(s) and purpose(s)

Even though there is broad agreement that the Convention's 'object and purpose' is of high importance to its interpretation, it cannot be said that there is clear consensus about what it (or they) comprise(s). In the case law of common law countries, the Convention has largely been seen to manifest two main purposes—human rights protection and burden sharing—with each co-existing in tension, if not in outright conflict, with each other.[170]

---

[162] Foster (n 2) 47.
[163] *Sepet and Bulbul* (n 113) para 6.
[164] See above pp. 69–70.
[165] *Applicant A* (n 114); *Butler v A-G* [1999] NZAR 205, 217. Both cited by McAdam (n 2) 104.
[166] Hathaway and Foster (n 2) 9–10 (emphasis added).
[167] In *Applicant A* (n 114) 294, cited in McAdam (n 2) 104, Kirby J stated that the 'membership of a particular social group' concept was 'not a static one'.
[168] See Chapter 10, section 3.4.1.
[169] See above section 2.3.1.
[170] *Applicant A* (n 114) paras 247–48 See also *Roma Rights* (n 114) para 15. McAdam aptly summarises the overall position when she notes that: 'it is possible to discern various, and possibly conflicting, objects and purposes from the Preamble to the 1951 Convention. This is borne out in the jurisprudence, where courts

Whether or not these two purposes can be said to be the main ones will be addressed in section 2.5.5 below, but what is clear is that they are not the only ones that have been ascribed to the Convention.

There is also a lack of clarity about *where* one looks in order to divine the Convention's object and purpose. For Hathaway, the starting point for the search for the Convention's object and purpose should be the *travaux*,[171] whereas, according to Foster, the treaty's substantive provisions (along with its Preamble) shed light on its object and purpose since they reveal 'its overriding human rights purpose'.[172]

Let us turn then to the main objects and purposes that have been identified, (roughly) putting them in the order in which they have most commonly been referenced.

*2.5.4.1 Humanitarian or 'social and humanitarian' purpose*

In *Hoxha*, Lord Hope referred to the 'social and humanitarian nature of the problem of refugees' as being 'expressly recognised in the preamble to the convention'.[173] In *Shepherd*, the CJEU described the context of the EU Qualification Directive (whose regime of refugee protection is constructed around a definition or refugee largely replicating the wording of Article 1A(2)) as 'essentially humanitarian', as its objective is 'to identify persons who, forced by circumstances, genuinely and legitimately need international protection'.[174]

This objective is generally understood to straddle both securing the safety from persecution of refugees and the proper treatment of refugees (and to a limited extent asylum seekers) in the host state.

In identifying this purpose, courts and tribunals have reflected views widely expressed in the academic literature.[175]

When identifying a 'humanitarian' purpose, though, courts and tribunals, again reflecting the academic literature, have been careful to acknowledge its limits. Thus, in *Horvath*, Lord Hope stated that: '[i]t is important to note throughout that the humanitarian purposes of the Convention are limited by the tests set out in the article'. He then went on, by reference to observations made by Dawson J in the *Applicant A* case, to note that this purpose precluded persons fleeing epidemic, natural disaster, or famine, those fearing persecution but unable to show a Convention reason and those who could not show a need for surrogate protection.[176]

---

have sought to balance the 1951 Convention's humanitarian purpose, on the one hand, with its objective of facilitating burden-sharing among States of the refugee 'problem' on the other.' See McAdam (n 2) 91.

[171] Hathaway (1st edn) (n 2) 56; Hathaway (2nd edn) (n 2) 148–54.
[172] Foster (n 2) 46–47. In support of her view, see Lord Hope's statement in *Hoxha* (n 114) para 6.
[173] *Hoxha* (n 114) para 6.
[174] Case C-472/13 *Andre Lawrence Shepherd v Bundesrepublik Deutschland* [2015] EU:C:2015:117, para 32.
[175] Göran Melander, 'Refugee Policy Options—Protection or Assistance' in Göran Rystad (ed), The Uprooted: Forced Migration as an International Problem in the Post-War Era (Lund University Press 1990) 146–47; Karen Musalo, 'Irreconcilable Differences? Divorcing Refugee Protections from Human Rights Norms' (1994) 15 Michigan Journal of International Law 1179.
[176] *Applicant A* (n 114).

However, when identifying the 'humanitarian' purpose, it is not always clear whether courts and tribunals treat this as distinct from a human rights purpose. This creates a difficulty because at least at the theoretical level, the two concepts are distinct.

*2.5.4.2 Protection against serious harm*
Although not always identifying it as a purpose, some commentators have viewed the main aim of the Refugee Convention as being protection against serious harm (or some synonym thereof).[177] One prompt for that has been the reference in the third recital of the Preamble to the need 'to revise and consolidate previous international agreements relating to the status of refugees and to extend the scope and *protection* accorded by such instruments by means of a new agreement' (emphasis added). In addition, that is often how the Convention's objectives are described to the layman. For example, Wikipedia refers to its role as a 'shelter or protection from danger or distress'.[178]

*2.5.4.3 Protection of human rights*
Leading common law courts have seen protection of human rights as a primary purpose of the Convention. The Canadian Supreme Court in *Ward*, for example, saw the Convention's 'underlying objective' to be sought in the Preamble which voices 'the international community's *commitment to the assurance of basic human rights*, without discrimination'.[179] The immediate focus in this line of cases is on the protection of the human rights of individuals against threats of persecution in their country of origin, but it is clear that the judges also had in mind the protection of refugees by way of guaranteeing them certain rights and benefits in the host state. Indeed, for Lord Clyde in *Horvath* it was this latter focus that was its primary purpose:

> The purpose of the convention is to secure that a refugee may in the surrogate state enjoy the rights and freedoms to which all are entitled without discrimination and which he cannot enjoy in his own state.[180]

It is notable that in identifying a human rights purpose, courts and tribunals have attached significant weight to the views of certain scholars advocating the same, as can be seen most clearly in the Canadian and UK case law.[181]

---

[177] See e.g. Matthew E Price, *Rethinking Asylum History, Purpose, and Limits* (CUP 2010) 52 who describes the purpose of asylum as 'to shelter those exposed to persecution, but finds the distinctive feature of persecution lies in it being persecution inflicted for illegitimate reasons: see e.g. 108–09.
[178] Wikipedia, 'Refugee' <https://en.wikipedia.org/wiki/Refugee> accessed April 2021.
[179] *Ward* (n 141) (emphasis added); *Islam* (n 114) 639 (Lord Steyn). See also *Pushpanathan and Canadian Council for Refugees (intervening) v Minister of Citizenship and Immigration*, Appeal to Supreme Court [1998] 1 SCR 982, where Bastarache J referred to the 'overarching and clear human rights object and purpose' as being 'the background against which interpretation of individual provisions must take place'.
[180] *Horvath* (n 128) 508; McAdam (n 2) 92; Vincent Chetail, 'Are Refugee Rights Human Rights? An Unorthodox Questioning of the Relations Between Refugee Law and Human Rights Law' in Ruth Rubio-Marín (ed), *Human Rights and Immigration* (OUP 2014) 71; Vincent Chetail, 'Moving Towards an Integrated Approach of Refugee Law and Human Rights Law' in Cathryn Costello, Michelle Foster, Jane McAdam (eds), *Oxford Handbook of International Refugee Law* (OUP 2021) 208.
[181] See e.g. *Ward* (n 141) and *Horvath* (n 128).

Even though there are strong reasons to distinguish the human rights and humanitarian purposes at the theoretical level,[182] it is hard to disagree with Steinbock that the humanitarian object lacks specificity unless it is understood as being human rights-based.[183]

It would seem, however, that even those who propound a human-rights based understanding accept that it represents at root an articulation of the underlying purpose of protection against serious harm.

### 2.5.4.4 Burden-sharing

As adverted to earlier, in *Applicant A*, Dawson J considered that the preambular references in the Refugee Convention to equality and human rights had to be balanced against the fact that the fourth preambular paragraph recognises that 'the grant of asylum may place unduly heavy burdens on certain countries'.[184] For Lord Bingham, the Convention represents 'a compromise between competing interests, in this case between the need to ensure humane treatment of the victims of oppression on the one hand and the wish of sovereign states to maintain control over those seeking entry to their territory on the other'.[185] In this context, it is also important to bear in mind the historical origins of the Convention. It is premised on the duty of every state to respect the territorial integrity of others. It exclusively focuses on the obligations of asylum states.

Academic commentators who have highlighted this purpose include Martin.[186] In Martin's view, the purpose of the Convention is essentially to assign a scarce resource, namely asylum. He considers that 'the institution of asylum is not coterminous with human rights policy' and that the purpose of the Convention is not 'to express sympathy [or] to note human rights abuses whenever they appear, or to register disapproval of a practice'.[187]

### 2.5.4.5 Non-discrimination

Senior courts have frequently referred to the objective of non-discrimination, either as part of the corpus of human rights or on its own. They have extracted this purpose both from the first preambular paragraph and from the wording of Article 1A(2) ('being persecuted by reason of ... [the five Convention reasons]').[188]

---

[182] e.g. within international law, IHRL, and international humanitarian law are distinct branches.

[183] Steinbock (n 1) 803 refers to 'humanitarian purpose' as either equating with 'protection against human rights violations' or as being 'too vague to convey any additional meaning to the definition's terms'.

[184] Convention Relating to the Status of Refugees (n 104) Preamble. See further Claire Inder, 'The Origins of "Burden Sharing" in the Contemporary Refugee Protection Regime' (2017) 29(4) IJRL 523, 553.

[185] *Roma Rights* (n 114) para 15 (Lord Bingham).

[186] In David A Martin, 'The Refugee Concept: On Definition, Politics and the Careful Use of State Resources' in Howard Adelman (ed), *Refugee Policy: Canada and the United States* (Center Migration Studies 1991) 62.

[187] David A Martin, 'Major Developments in Asylum Law Over the Past Year: A Year of Dialogue Between Courts and Agencies' (2007) 84 Interpreter Releases 2069, 2072, cited in Kate Jastram, 'Economic Harm as a Basis for Refugee Status and the Application of Human Rights Law to the Interpretation of Economic Persecution' in James C Simeon (ed), *Critical Issues in International Refugee Law: Strategies toward Interpretative Harmony* (CUP 2010) 160.

[188] *Ward* (n 141); *Islam and Shah* (n 114); *Horvath* (n 128) para 508.

Since those who promote a prominent role for this purpose mainly fix on the reference to 'without discrimination' in the first preambular paragraph,[189] it is difficult to see that this purpose can be divorced from its human rights locus, since the term is used there in relation to the UDHR.

*2.5.4.6 Equality of treatment*
Another object that common law cases have identified is equality of treatment. For example, the Australian High Court has described the Convention's 'chief purpose' as being 'to impose obligations on the signatories to the Convention to provide protection and equality of treatment for the nationals of countries who cannot obtain protection from their own countries'.[190] The focus here appears to be on Articles 2–34 rather than Article 1A(2). In the absence of any distinct reasoning offered in these decisions for differentiating this principle from that of non-discrimination, it may be most appropriately considered as an alternative formulation of it.

*2.5.4.7 Surrogate protection*
Case law and academic writings have sometimes deemed one of the Convention's key purposes to be the provision of surrogate protection.[191]

Thus in *Horvath*, Lord Clyde, having noted Hathaway's model and the support for it voiced by the Canadian Supreme Court in *Ward*, concluded that:

> What the [Refugee Convention] seeks to achieve is the preservation of those rights and freedoms for individuals where they are denied them in their own state. Another state is to provide a surrogate protection where protection is not available in the home state. The convention assumes that every state has the obligation to protect its own nationals. But it recognises that circumstances may occur where that protection may be inadequate. The purpose of the convention is to secure that a refugee may in the surrogate state enjoy the rights and freedoms to which all are entitled without discrimination and which he cannot enjoy in his own state.[192]

Once again, as this example illustrates, the surrogacy purpose appears two-dimensional, having the goal of securing protection against persecution and securing the rights of refugees in host states.

In a more recent formulation of the human rights purpose, Hathaway has emphasised that insofar as the Convention's purpose is protection, it has a 'palliative' function.[193] He and Foster have also seen the objective of surrogate protection as instrumental to the internal protection alternative.[194]

---

[189] See e.g. David Cantor, 'Defining Refugees: Persecution, Surrogacy and the Human Rights Paradigm' in Bruce Burson and David Cantor (eds) *Human Rights and the Refugee Definition* (Brill Nijhoff 2016) 394; Matthew Scott, *Climate Change, Disasters, and the Refugee Convention* (CUP 2020) 115–16.

[190] *Minister for Immigration and Multicultural Affairs v Respondents S152/2003* [2004] 222 CLR 1 (Aus HC), para 53; *Islam* (n 114).

[191] See e.g. *Horvath* (n 128).

[192] ibid.

[193] See e.g. James C Hathaway, 'New Directions to Avoid Hard Problems: The Distortion of the Palliative Role of Refugee Protection' (1995) 8 Journal of Refugee Studies 293.

[194] See Chapter 8, n 136.

Understanding the principle of surrogacy as adding vital context to the Convention's object and purpose has also been seen to lend support for viewing it as a principle undergirding the refugee definition.[195]

It is clear that a close linkage is often made between the principle of surrogacy and the purpose of securing protection against persecution but mostly without any precise explanation of their interrelationship. On the one hand, the former on its own does not explain the nature of the surrogation, only the latter would seem capable of operating as a self-contained purpose. On the other hand, without the principle of surrogacy the purpose of securing protection against persecution might be said to lack specificity to the refugee context. It does not differentiate, for example, between internally and externally displaced persons in fear of persecution.

*2.5.4.8 Other purposes*
Any trawl of the wider literature quickly discloses that other purposes have also been canvassed. For example, Grahl-Madsen identifies the purpose of the Convention as providing shelter for those politically opposed to oppressive regimes;[196] Steinbock considers that the refugee definition centres around three related purposes which in different ways concern 'protection of the innocent';[197] Price identifies one key purpose as international sanction of the illegitimacy of home states' actions.[198]

At least some of the time such other purposes are seen to be closely tied to the non-discrimination purpose; certainly that is the case with Steinbock's analysis.[199]

2.5.5 Conclusions regarding different objects and purposes
Three main conclusions can be drawn from the foregoing analysis of how the VCLT rules regarding object and purpose have been seen to apply to the Refugee Convention and the refugee definition in particular.

First, there is broad recognition that the Convention has more than one purpose. However, a number of stated purposes appear in substance to be best understood as aspects of the human rights purpose. Thus the purpose of international protection/protection against serious harm essentially corresponds to either a humanitarian or human rights purpose or both; albeit theoretically distinct, the humanitarian purpose seems to lack specificity unless assimilated to the human rights purpose;[200] the principle of surrogacy has featured most prominently in articulations of a human rights approach; and the principle of equal treatment appears to constitute an aspect of the

---

[195] The notion or principle of surrogacy is further analysed in Chapter 7, section 1.
[196] Grahl-Madsen (n 1) 253.
[197] Daniel J Steinbock, 'The Refugee Definition as Law: Issues of Interpretation' in Frances Nicholson and Patrick Twomey (eds), *Refugee Rights and Realities: Evolving International Concepts and Regimes* (CUP 1999) 27–35.
[198] Price (n 177) 70–1; 108.
[199] Steinbock (n 197) 26.
[200] Given that within international law 'humanitarian' is a term of art (as demonstrated by the very term 'international humanitarian law') and that scholars sometimes contrast humanitarian with human rights purposes, it would be unsafe to merge these two objectives, notwithstanding that this has sometimes been done, especially in the case law. See further, Rachel Brett and Eve Lester, 'Refugee Law and International Humanitarian Law: Parallels, Lessons and Looking Ahead' (2001) 83(843) IRRC 713.

principle of non-discrimination, which in turn most naturally fits within the human rights purpose.

Second, though, reference here to 'human rights purpose' is not to be equated with the human rights approach. To take one example, the principle of surrogacy that often underlies the human rights approach appears capable of being embraced by human rights and non-human rights approaches to interpretation of the refugee definition; it does not in itself specify that the basis for the host state substituting its protection for that of the home state is because the latter has severely violated human rights.

Third, even though at least in the common law case law burden-sharing has been depicted as one of two main purposes—along with human rights—it appears effectively to operate as a qualification to a human rights/humanitarian approach rather than the other way around. The extent of any burden is necessarily a function of the scope of the refugee definition in terms of who under it qualifies as a refugee.[201] In addition, if the primary purpose was burden-sharing, the treaty would have been drafted in the language of contractual obligations concerned with sharing arrangements of those already defined as refugees. Put another way, burden-sharing cannot be the principal rationale for the definition of who is a refugee or, if it has an impact on the substance of the definition, it can only be in the form of setting a limit on its scope.

Fourth, the identification of multiple purposes does nevertheless point up a recurrent feature of the application of the VCLT rules to the Refugee Convention, namely that even diligent application of such rules is capable of resulting in variant interpretations. This complicates the goal of achieving consistency of approach. Further, even those invoking a specific object or purpose can sometimes construe its application in different ways. Consider for example, in relation to invocation of a human rights purpose, the ongoing debate in the case law and literature between those who consider that the internal protection alternative is to be assessed by reference to the 'endogenous' standards set out in Articles 2–33 of the Convention and those who consider that the standards have to be drawn from extraneous standards based on reasonableness/undue hardship or human rights.[202]

Also apparent is that there can be different views about the extent to which the Convention interpretation should embody any particular purpose. For example, despite the UK House of Lords broadly endorsing an evolutive approach to the refugee definition, Goodwin-Gill did not think it went far enough in that direction in *Sepet and Bulbul*.[203] He criticises their lordships for not being prepared to take account of

---

[201] The argument used here is similar to that expressed by Foster (n 2) 44–45, who in turn cites Kirby, J in *Chen Shi Hai v Minister for Immigration and Multicultural Affairs* [2000] 201 CLR 293. For Foster, the co-existence of the two purposes, the humanitarian and burden-sharing, strengthens the argument for a human rights approach as 'the emphasis is on the need for co-operation in order adequately to deal with the humanitarian problem' mindful of the need to prevent a repetition of the Second World War's affronts to humanity. It should also be noted that the wording of the fourth preambular paragraph deliberately fell short of identifying any specific obligation: see Inder (n 184) 553. See also Alleweldt (n 141) 236–38. The first substantive provision devoted to this principle was contained in Article 2 para (2) of the 1967 Declaration on Territorial Asylum; see also Article 2 para (4) of the OAU Convention and ExCom No 52 (XXXIX), Conclusion No 79 (XLVII), G.A. Res. 46/106, 16 December 1991. See further, B S Chimni, *International Refugee Law: A Reader* (UNHCR, Sage Publications, 2000) 146–51. Chimni also considers burden-sharing to be 'arguably a principle of customary international law'.

[202] See Chapter 8, sections 2.2 and 2.7.2.

[203] *Sepet and Bulbul* (n 113).

legal developments in the law relating to conscientious objection to military service since the 1979 UNHCR Handbook.[204]

## 2.6 Subsequent Agreement and Subsequent Practice

2.6.1 Subsequent agreement
Article 31(3)(a) mandates the taking into account, together with the context: '(a) any subsequent agreement between the parties regarding the interpretation of the treaty or the application of its provisions'. This element has one undoubted application to the Refugee Convention: by far the most important 'subsequent agreement' is the 1967 Protocol itself. As noted by the House of Lords in *Hoxha*, the fact that the parties were content in that Protocol to leave unamended the substantive provisions of the 1951 Convention was strong evidence that the parties' intentions remained the same in 1967.[205] Hathaway and Foster have seen the decision of states to supplement the Convention by a Protocol in 1967, as 'prospectively mandating a geopolitically inclusive and modern understanding of the refugee definition [which] is an extraordinarily powerful contextual indicator of the duty to interpret the definition in a broad and inclusive way, in line with the general duty of good faith interpretation'.[206]

In the Refugee Convention context, two other agreements appear prime candidates to fall within the terms of Article 31(3)(a), namely the Declaration of States Parties, issued at the December 2001 Ministerial Meeting of States Parties to mark the fiftieth anniversary of the Refugee Convention[207] and a meeting of Ministers in 2011 to mark the occasion of the Convention's sixtieth anniversary.[208] Two more recent instruments perceived to have a 'soft-law' importance are the New York Declaration for Refugees and Migrants, adopted in September 2016[209] and the Global Compact on Refugees affirmed by the UN General Assembly (UNGA) on 17 December 2018.[210] However, it is very hard to see that any of these instruments has made any real difference to the personal, material, or temporal scope of the refugee definition, save perhaps in reinforcing the core principle of *non-refoulement*; the enduring importance of

---

[204] Goodwin-Gill (n 2) 233. Guy S Goodwin-Gill and Jane McAdam (with Emma Dunlop), *The Refugee in International Law* (4th edn, OUP 2021) 126–32 note key developments since *Sepet and Bulbul*, including the Human Rights Committee case of *Yoon and Choi v Republic of Korea* (3 November 2006) UN Doc CCPR/C/88/D/1321–1322/2004, and the ECtHR case of *Bayatyan v Armenia* App No 23549/03 (ECtHR, 7 July 2011). At ibid 132, they conclude that two of the three findings in *Sepet and Bulbul*—on causation and conscience respectively—would not be sustained if the case law were considered today.

[205] Lord Hope considered that the fact that state parties had not amended Article 1C(5) in 1967 when the Protocol was concluded was 'eloquent of the continuing intention of the contracting parties to leave the proviso untouched'. See *Hoxha* (n 114). McAdam notes that a similar justification was used by Lord Bingham in *Roma Rights* (n 114) in relation to Article 33: see McAdam (n 2) 97.

[206] Hathaway and Foster (n 2) 9–10. Curiously, however, they treat this as a matter falling within the 'context' element of the Refugee Convention.

[207] UNHCR, Declaration of States Parties to the 1951 Convention and or Its 1967 Protocol relating to the Status of Refugees (16 January 2002) UN Doc HCR/MMSP/2001/09. This was the first occasion on which a meeting at the ministerial level of all state parties to the Refugee Convention and Protocol was convened.

[208] Ministerial Communiqué (8 December 2011) UN Doc HCR/MINCOMMS/2011/16, para 2.

[209] New York Declaration for Refugees and Migrants (9 September 2016) UNGA Res 71/1.

[210] UNGA Res 73/151 (17 December 2018); Report of the United Nations High Commissioner for Refugees, Part II: Global Compact on Refugees (2 August 2018) UN Doc A/73/12.

the Convention; the validity of a human rights approach; and the importance of age, gender, and other diversity considerations.[211]

According to Aust, the wording of Article 31(3)(a) is also broad enough to encompass subsequent agreements that relate to adjacent treaties and other international instruments. Thus, he observes that when interpreting Article 1F(c) of the Refugee Convention, which refers to the 'purposes and principles of the United Nations', it is legitimate to take into account the 1996 UNGA Declaration that terrorism is contrary to the purposes and principles of the United Nations.[212]

Within the refugee law literature there has also been some support for viewing Article 31(3)(a) as sufficiently broad to accommodate certain UNHCR materials. In the 2005 edition of *Refugee Rights*, Hathaway wrote that both the 1979 UNHCR Handbook and the ExCom Conclusions on International Protection are to be 'logically viewed as "subsequent agreement between the parties regarding the interpretation of the treaty or the application of its provisions"'.[213] He goes on to nuance this somewhat by stating that this cannot be technically correct since not all state parties are members of the ExCom at any given moment, and not all members of the ExCom are parties to the Convention or Protocol.[214] He maintains that they should nevertheless be treated as evidence of subsequent agreement between the parties to the Convention since the overwhelming majority of the more than sixty states (as were then represented) on the ExCom, are parties to the Convention or Protocol and all state parties are invited to observe and to comment upon draft proposals under consideration by it.[215]

The view that the Conclusions of the ExCom can be brought within the notion of 'subsequent agreement' merits closer scrutiny. Established in 1958, ExCom is mandated to review and approve the agency's programmes and budget, advise on international protection, and discuss a wide range of other issues with UNHCR and its intergovernmental and non-governmental partners. A 2014 study by Marion Fresia

---

[211] The 2001 Declaration did acknowledge 'the continuing relevance and resilience of the international regime of rights and principles'; and the 2016 New York Declaration and the Global Compact expresses commitment to the human rights of refugees and the importance of international human rights treaties. In para 4 of the Compact, international human rights and refuge law appear as overall guiding principles. See also para 13 of the Compact.

[212] Aust (n 4) 213.

[213] Hathaway (1st edn) (n 2) 54, fn 146.

[214] ibid.

[215] ibid. In the book's second edition, Hathaway (2nd edn) (n 2) 144, maintains that 'in practical terms, it is difficult to imagine how subsequent agreement among the state parties to the refugee treaties could be more effectively generated', but from his subsequent text it would appear that he envisages the Conclusions as 'subsequent practice'. He states that they are 'to be understood to exemplify state practice capable of establishing interpretive agreement among state parties to the Refugee Convention'. See also *A-G Refugee Council of New Zealand Inc* [2003] 2 NZLR 577 (CA) (New Zealand) para 100; Bryan Deschamp and Rebecca Dowd, 'Review of the Use of Executive Committee Conclusions on International Protection' (2008) UNHCR PDES/2008/03, para 86 (cited McAdam (2) 96); Marjoleine Zieck, 'Article 35/Article II1' in Zimmermann (n 2) 1497. Goodwin-Gill, 'The Office of the United Nations High Commissioner for Refugees and the Sources of International Refugee Law' (2020) 69(1) International and Comparative Law Quarterly 8–9 cites the description given of them by Elihu Lauterpacht and Daniel Bethlehem, 'The Scope and Content of the Principle of *Non-Refoulment*: Opinion' in Erika Feller, Volker Türk, and Frances Nicholson (eds), *Refugee Protection in International Law: UNHCR's Global Consultations on International Protection* (CUP 2003) 87, 148 as being 'expressions of opinion which are broadly representative of the views of the international community'. He concludes that they 'can be evidence of *opinio juris*'.

has noted that the Committee is the 'only specialised multilateral forum at the international level which contributes to the development of international standards relating to refugees'.[216] Fresia says of their Conclusions that that they 'have considerable moral and political authority for they are adopted by consensus by all ExCom member states'.[217] She notes that 'in legal terms they are considered as international soft law and are part of the "transnational legal order" telling states how they should treat the people living on their territory and leading to moral condemnation if not respected'.[218]

However, even though the Committee's number of state representatives has gradually enlarged since its original number of 24 (in 2007 its membership was seventy[219] and it is now 107),[220] which is still only around two thirds. In addition, although the Committee has adopted thematic 'Conclusions' on refugee protection providing guidance on asylum matters, they are often exhortatory in tone rather than declaring agreement; they have seldom touched issues of interpretation of the refugee definition; and UNHCR of course has provided its own guidance on the latter, e.g. in its 2001 note[221] and, of course, the Guidelines on International Protection.[222] Further, although ExCom is 'the Executive Committee of the UNHCR Programme' (and on that basis often termed the 'UNHCR ExCom'), it is in fact separate from UNHCR. These and related considerations lead Zieck to conclude (with considerable force in the view of this author) that this body's Conclusions cannot constitute 'subsequent agreement(s)'.[223]

### 2.6.2 Subsequent practice

Article 31(3)(b) mandates the taking into account, together with the context, of 'any subsequent practice in the application of the treaty which establishes the agreement of the parties regarding its interpretation'. It appears to have an important potential role in the context of the Refugee Convention, given that, as we have just seen, there is a tension in respect of what are its objects and purposes and that Article 31(3)(a), regarding subsequent agreements, seems to have little application. On the basis of our earlier analysis, this subparagraph constitutes a less demanding test since the criterion of applicability to the relations between the parties (which forms part of Article 31(3)(b) in relation to 'subsequent practice'), can be met by tacit acceptance.[224]

---

[216] Marion Fresia, 'Building Consensus within UNHCR's Executive Committee: Global Refugee Norms in the Making' (2014) 27(4) Journal of Refugee Studies 514.
[217] ibid.
[218] ibid.
[219] Guy S Goodwin-Gill and Jane McAdam, *The Refugee in International Law* (3rd edn, OUP 2007) 429.
[220] UNGA Res 75/162 on Enlargement of the Executive Committee of the Programme of the United Nations High Commissioner for Refugees (16 December 2020). For position as of August 2022, see <https://www.unhcr.org/excom-plenary-sessions.html>.
[221] UNHCR, The International Protection of Refugees: Interpreting Article 1 of the 1951 Convention Relating to the Status of Refugees (2001) UN Doc A/AC.96/951.
[222] A number (not many) of the ExCom Conclusions refer to such Guidelines. See e.g. ExCom Conclusion No 98 (LIV) Protection from Sexual Abuse and Exploitation (2003) and No 105 (LVII) Women and Girls at Risk (2006), available in UNHCR, Conclusions on International Protection Adopted by the Executive Committee of the UNHCR Programme 1975–2017 (Conclusion No 1–114) (October 2017) UN Doc HCR/IP/3/Eng/REV. 2017.
[223] Zieck (n 215) 1497.
[224] See above n 64.

96  INTERPRETATION

However, there are conflicting views in both the case law and scholarship about what refugee-related sources do fall within Article 31(3)(b) as illustrated by debates that have arisen about the relevance of UNHCR materials, which, alongside case law, represent the most likely candidate. This is well-illustrated by two English Court of Appeal cases. Whereas in *Adan and Aitsegeur*,[225] the Court considered the 1979 UNHCR Handbook to constitute good evidence of subsequent practice under Article 31(3)(b), a different constitution of the same Court later decided in *Hoxha*[226] that (the 1979 Handbook position notwithstanding) there was insufficient evidence to establish that the meaning of Article 1C(5) had been altered by state practice so as to apply not just to Convention refugees under Article 1A but also to refugees under Article 1A(2). To have been satisfied that there had been such a state practice, this Court noted, would have required 'very convincing evidence of a widespread and general practice of the international community'.[227] McAdam has noted that whilst courts frequently invoke the existence of state practice in the context of the 1951 Convention,[228] this is only rarely done by express reference to Article 31(3).[229]

*2.6.2.1 UNHCR Handbook and ExCom Conclusions as 'subsequent practice'?*
It is pertinent to ask at this point whether the UNHCR Handbook and the Excom Conclusions—the two sources most often seen to fall within Article 31(3)(b)—actually do so.

As already noted, there is a strong case for accepting the 1979 UNHCR Handbook as 'subsequent practice' as things stood between 1954 and 1979. The Handbook was developed in response to proposals of a Sub-Committee of ExCom in 1977 arising from a request from states to consider issuing guidance based on knowledge accumulated since the 1951 Convention entered into force in 1954. A precedent for issuing such guidance had been set by the Manual for Eligibility Officers produced by the International Refugee Organisation (IRO). Goodwin-Gill notes that UNHCR had already produced its own internal guide entitled 'Eligibility: A Guide for the Staff of the Office of the UNHCR (1962)' and its Legal Division had produced regular 'Eligibility Bulletins' and 'Legal Bulletins' under the directorship of Paul Weis until his retirement in 1967.[230]

However, whilst since then courts and tribunals worldwide continue to regard the Handbook as a valuable source of guidance to the present day,[231] it must seriously be doubted that it any longer constitutes 'subsequent practice'. First, although

---

[225] *Adan* (n 114) 1296F.
[226] *Hoxha* (n 114) para 47.
[227] ibid.
[228] McAdam (n 2) 97.
[229] ibid: 'it is rare for courts to refer expressly to Article 31, para 3(b) VCLT when explaining why they are making reference to [materials such as UNHCR materials, commentaries, comparative case law]'.
[230] Goodwin-Gill (n 2) 210. The ILC, Report on subsequent agreements (n 7) 40 notes that the UNHCR Handbook was 'prepared on the basis of a mandate to provide accounts on State practice in a particular field'.
[231] Goodwin-Gill (n 215) 18–20. For a recent CJEU reference, see Case C-280/21, *PI v Migracijos departamentas prie lietuvos Respublikos vidaus reikalu ministerijos* [2023] EUECJ C-280/21. Paragraph 27 describes the Handbook and Guidelines as 'particularly relevant in the light of the role conferred on the HCR by the Geneva Convention.'

frequently republished, the Handbook has never been updated. Further, as was noted in Chapter 1, the principle of evolutive interpretation dictates that any document written in 1979 cannot reflect developments that have unfolded since. Second, as we also saw in Chapter 1, especially in the past two decades or so, courts and tribunals and the wider literature have questioned the accuracy of the Handbook on a number of matters.[232]

In any event, whilst there has been much recognition in the case law and wider literature of the importance of the Handbook and ExCom Conclusions as sources of guidance,[233] there is hardly any reference in this regard to it/them constituting 'subsequent practice' within the meaning of Article 31(3)(b).[234] It is very difficult to pinpoint a particular moment in time when the Handbook ceased to constitute 'subsequent practice', but it most definitely fails the test currently.

Some of the hesitancy about identifying either UNHCR materials or other refugee law sources as falling within Article 31(3)(b) is linked to a wider concern about too ready endorsement of the conduct of state parties. For example, Hathaway cautions that:

> In the context of refugee and other international human rights treaties, expedient or other self-interested conduct by governments is distressingly common, thus taking much state practice under such accords outside the scope of Article 31's general rule of interpretation.[235]

Hathaway regards state practice in relation to the Refuge Convention as further limited by its specific character as a 'law-making treaty'.[236] Since 'law-making treaties' are treaties imposing obligations applicable for every civilised state, there is no place for individual advantages. These characteristics place such treaties outside the will of the contracting parties.

Hathaway points out that even so, state practice which does not meet the requirements of Article 31(3)(b), may still be considered as a residual supplementary means of interpretation under Article 32. He notes that the ILC has referred to this as subsequent practice 'in a broad sense'.[237]

Overall, conflicting views about the role of UNHCR materials under the Article 31(3)(b) rubric make it only possible to say that they constitute *evidence* relevant to the issue of whether there exists any subsequent practice and that they are in any event possible subsidiary means of interpretation under Article 32 VCLT.[238] There is no

---

[232] See Chapter 1, section 6.1.1.
[233] See cases cited by McAdam (n 2) 110–12.
[234] Even in *Zaoui* (n 143) paras 39–41, cited by McAdam (n 3) 97 the court appeared to limit its recognition to ExCom Conclusions being *evidence* of 'subsequent practice'.
[235] Hathaway (1st edn) (n 2) 70–71; Hathaway (2nd edn) (n 2) 161–67; Hathaway and Foster (n 2) 11.
[236] Hathaway (1st edn) (n 2) 72–73. See also Hathaway (2nd edn) (n 2) 162–63.
[237] Hathaway (1st edn) (n 2) 70–71; Hathaway (2nd edn) (n 2) 166. In the former he cites Gerald P McGinley, 'Practice as a Guide to Treaty Interpretation' (1985) 9 Fletcher Forum 211, 227 he cites McGinley's view that it may be admitted into evidence 'because practice represents the common-sense practical interpretation of the treaty under the varied contingencies of its ongoing operation'.
[238] ILC, Report on subsequent agreements (n 7), Commentary on draft Conclusion No 2, paras 10, 12, 16, 23, 25–35. In 33, the ILC refers to state practice 'in a broad sense'; in 34 and 35, to state practice 'in the broad sense'.

98  INTERPRETATION

consensus that they constitute 'subsequent practice'. It is the view of this author, however, already outlined in Chapter 1, that this aspect together with UNHCR's Article 35 supervisory responsibilities do warrant categorising 'UNHCR guidance' as one of the essential 'pillars' for understanding of the meaning of the refugee definition.[239]

### 2.6.2.2 Case law

Article 38(1)(d) of the ICJ Statute identifies judicial decisions and teachings as 'subsidiary means for the determination of rules of law'. The value of judicial decisions in helping form international custom and practice in general has been re-emphasised by the ILC in 2018.[240] We noted earlier that the ILC has identified that case law can potentially be a form of subsequent practice under Article 31(3)(b) and/or Article 32 VCLT.[241] Case law has certainly come to play a major role in refugee law as an aid to interpreting the refugee definition. As observed by Goodwin-Gill:

> Moreover, the growth in national refugee status determination procedures and the judicialisation of process have led the 1951 Convention to be one of the most litigated treaties at the domestic level, with courts and tribunals around the world engaged almost daily in a common purpose—elucidating the meaning of and applying the refugee definition and other Convention provisions relevant especially to admission, residence and non-removal.[242]

Yet there is virtually no support for seeing case law on the Refugee Convention as falling within any of the subparagraphs of Article 31(3)(b)[243] and only consensus that it is relevant evidence of subsequent practice and/or can come under Article 32 as a supplementary means of interpretation. A number of objections to treating refugee case law as coming under Article 31(3)(b) can be identified.

First, it has been pointed out that there is a lack of evidence that the state parties to the Refugee Convention have collectively embraced case law since many 'do not have either a refugee status procedure or a related body of jurisprudence'.[244] Second, case law is of variable quality. The sheer volume of cases nowadays stored on websites makes it increasingly hard to identify cases of importance.[245] A number of questions must always be asked of them, for example: what issue or issues was the judge addressing; are the conclusions of the judge accompanied by reasons; does the judge cite all relevant sources; is the decision of sufficient quality; is the reasoning based

---

[239] See Chapter 1, section 6.
[240] See Chapter V, 'Identification of Customary International Law', which states that judicial decisions 'may assist in collecting, synthesising or interpreting practice relevant to the identification of customary international law'.
[241] See above n 66, with reference to ILC, Report on subsequent agreements (n 7) Conclusion 5(1).
[242] Goodwin-Gill (n 215) 10–11.
[243] ibid 38: 'Conceivably, "subsequent practice" might include the decisions of national courts among the possible relevant juridical acts, but the requirements for such practice to give rise to a new, binding interpretation are so strict as to make that likelihood extremely remote.'
[244] ibid (with reference to ILC, Report on subsequent agreements (n 7) Conclusions Nos 10 and 13).
[245] As noted by Goodwin-Gill (n 2) 214, 'it has become harder to determine relative value and authority'. See also Goodwin-Gill (n 215) 14, noting that Refworld now houses over 12,000 cases: '[t]he judicial and administrative material could possibly be distilled quantitatively, but even then a clear outcome favouring one or other interpretation seems unlikely, and there is no doctrine of binding precedent by numbers'.

wholly or partly on national law; is the case cited one that has authority within the domestic legal system (and has not, for example, been overturned by a higher court); is the translation or translated summary reliable; and, of course, is its reasoning at least consistent with a proper application of VCLT principles (it may not be, for example, if it has applied an unqualified literal approach or relied solely on the *travaux*)? Further, national case law can contain divergent opinions and not furnish a consistent body of learning. 'Given the variety of jurisdictions and natural differences in the flows of asylum seekers', writes Goodwin-Gill, 'it is ... unlikely that national case law will ever produce universal consensus'.[246]

A third point that could also be made is that the decisions of the national judiciary, which is only one organ of a state, do not necessarily represent the position of that state, in terms of the (sometimes complex) configuration of executive, legislative, and judicial organs, even in a legal system based on precedent.

Obstacles in the way of refugee case law constituting 'subsequent practice' must not, however, obscure the evident fact that judicial decisions can sometimes constitute *evidence* of state practice.[247] This is of particular importance, given the close interaction the ILC envisages as existing between Article 31(3)(b) and Article 32 and its recognition that state practice in 'the broad sense', albeit falling short of qualifying under Article 31(3)(b), can come within the ambit of Article 32.[248] Further, case law can have a very significant role in state parties adopting legislation or policies—the shift to almost universal acceptance that there can be non-state actors of persecution being a prime example. In addition, both UNHCR and academic studies attach very significant weight to case law.

### 2.6.2.3 *Article 31(3)(b) and EU asylum law*

When considering 'subsequent practice' in the context of the Refugee Convention, special attention needs paying to the EU Qualification Directive (QD) which came into force in 2006 and its recast. Within the EU it is clear that there now exists a regional state practice bearing on the contents of the refugee definition. This takes two forms. First, there is the legislation itself. The QD and since 2011 the QD (recast) provide further definitional detail to key terms of the refugee definition,[249] in particular Article 9 but also Articles 5, 6, 7, and 8. Second, there is the further elaboration of key elements of the refugee definition provided in CJEU jurisprudence.[250]

Being only a regional instrument, it cannot be said that the QD (recast) constitutes 'subsequent practice' within the meaning of Article 31(3)(b) VCLT,[251] but the practice

---

[246] Goodwin-Gill (n 215) 16, disagreeing with Cecilia M Bailliet, 'National Case Law as a Generator of International Refugee Law: Rectifying an Imbalance within UNHCR Guidelines on International Protection' (2015) 29 Emory International Law Review 2059, where Bailliet argues that 'increased pluralistic references to national case law' will come up with a 'truly global assessment of protection standards as they evolve within refugee law tribunals around the world'.

[247] See above n 66.

[248] See above n 69.

[249] The definition of 'refugee' in Article 2(d) uses in large part the same wording as Article 1A(2) of the Convention. See Qualification Directive (n 118).

[250] See e.g. Joined Cases C-71/11 and C-99/11 *Bundesrepublik Deutschland v Y and Z* [2012] ECLI:EU:C:2012:518; Case C-91/20 *LW v Bundesrepublik Deutschland* [2021] ECLI:EU:C:2021:898, paras 32–33.

[251] Hathaway and Foster (n 2) 12.

of EU member states applying EU law is at least part of the evidential picture when considering the practice of states globally and certainly falls to be accorded weight within the ambit of Article 32. It is also possible to note decisions by non-EU courts and tribunals that have drawn, directly or indirectly, on EU asylum law.[252]

However, the above argument depends, in part, on the relevant EU state practice being in line with VCLT rules. That issue is dealt with separately in section 4 of this chapter.

## 2.7 Any Relevant Rules of International Law

This sub-head links to the provision in Article 31(3)(c) VCLT concerning any relevant rules of international law.

An important reason why this rule requires particular attention in the refugee law context is that one source of 'relevant rules of international law' can be treaties,[253] coupled with the evident fact that since the Refugee Convention was drafted there has been what one jurist has called the 'relentless rise in the use of treaties as a means for ordering international civil society'.[254] Almost all the international treaties of relevance, in particular the major human rights treaties, came later. Applying an evolutionary approach to the Refugee Convention, the importance of such other relevant treaties, sometimes referred to as 'cognate treaties' has proved very considerable. In *Sepet and Bulbul* Lord Bingham noted that:

> [ ... ] the reach of an international human rights convention is not forever determined by the intentions of those who originally framed it. Thus ... the House was appropriately asked to consider a mass of material illustrating the movement of international opinion, now a very significant period, since the major relevant conventions were adopted.[255]

One premise of what has become known as the human rights approach is that it is legitimate when interpreting the Refugee Convention to have regard to other international instruments that have a bearing on the same subject-matter, human rights treaties in particular. In *Fornah*, Baroness Hale stated that:

> State parties to the Refugee Convention, at least if they are also parties to the [ICCPR] and to the Convention on the Elimination of All Forms of Discrimination Against Women, are obliged to interpret and apply the Refugee Convention compatibly with the commitment to gender equality in these two instruments.[256]

---

[252] Hélène Lambert, 'Conclusion: Europe's Normative Power in Refugee Law' in Hélène Lambert, Jane McAdam, and Maryellen Fullerton (eds), *The Global Reach of European Refugee Law* (CUP 2013) 258–66.
[253] See above section 1.6.
[254] McLachlan (n 80) 283, cited in Gardiner (n 3) 323.
[255] *Sepet and Bulbul* (n 113) para 11.
[256] *Fornah* (n 125) para 86.

At the same time, courts and tribunals (properly reflecting general learning on the VCLT rules) have not seen recourse to other international instruments as warranting a simple transplantation of one meaning into another irrespective of context. This has been noted, for example, by Lord Steyn in *Roma Rights* in respect of the principle of non-discrimination and by scholars in respect of the meaning of persecution as set out in the Rome Statute.[257]

Focusing on treaties, Foster considers that the Article 31(3)(c) provision provides an 'even clearer justification for the use of "comparative treaty interpretation" as a method to ascertain the correct interpretation of key terms in the refugee definition'. Drawing on scholars who have analysed cross-fertilisation between treaties and the principle of 'systematic integration', she argues that this rule 'provides a further principled foundation for the argument of this book that refugee decision makers must ensure their understanding of the content and scope of international human rights law, especially socio-economic rights, is consistent with principles of international human rights law'.[258] She considers that '[h]uman rights treaties which have attained widespread membership are relevant "rules of international law" to which refugee decision-makers should have regard'.[259] She sees recourse to Article 31(3)(c) as affording more scope for International Human Rights Law (IHRL) because, unlike reliance in this regard on 'context' (which is limited to the UDHR), the former can be used to support reliance on a wider corpus of international law.[260] She draws on the decision of the ILC in its 2006 Report to treat Article 31(3)(c) as legitimising an approach that takes account of rules reflecting the 'common intention' of the parties to the treaty under consideration.[261]

For Foster, the relevant rules of international law can encompass treaties not in existence at the adoption of the Refugee Convention, by applying an evolutionary approach. She does not consider fatal to their relevance the fact that treaties have not been ratified by all or even a majority of the parties to the Refugee Convention:

> In practice, however, reference is most often made to the UDHR, ICCPR, ICESCR, a phenomenon which can be justified given the widespread membership of the ICCPR and the ICESCR, and the significant overlap between membership of those treaties and the Refugee Convention.[262]

She expresses agreement with Hathaway's latter-day acknowledgment that similarly widely accepted treaties, such as the Convention on the Elimination of All Forms of

---

[257] *Roma Rights* (n 114) para 43, cited in McAdam (n 2) 107; Goodwin-Gill and McAdam (n 219) 67 note that the definition of persecution in the Rome Statute of the International Criminal Court (adopted 17 July 1988), 2187 UNTS 3, Article 7(1) is 'specific to the context of art.7, namely "crimes against humanity", being acts "committed as part of a widespread or systematic attack directed against any civilian population, with knowledge of the attack"'.

[258] Foster (n 2) 52. Among the various rules of international law, she regards customary international law as being of little assistance since it requires state practice and *opinio juris* as essential elements (see ibid 54). See further on customary international law, Hélène Lambert, 'Customary refugee Law' in Costello et al (n 180) 240–57.

[259] Foster (n 2) 59.
[260] ibid.
[261] ibid 57.
[262] ibid 64; see also ibid 59, 63.

Discrimination Against Women (CEDAW), and the Convention on the Rights of the Child, and the Convention on the Elimination of All Forms of Racial Discrimination (ICERD) can also be properly said to reflect the common intentions of the parties with respect to fundamental rights. These specific conventions make significant contributions to a 'more complex understanding of equality, which go considerably beyond the [International Bill of Rights]'.[263] Foster then discusses the relevance of regional treaties, which she sees as having a valuable role when the relevant UN treaty-monitoring bodies overseeing the universal treaties 'have not yet considered the application of the specific right to the factual circumstances of the case'.[264]

Pobjoy shares a similar approach to application of Article 31(3)(c) to the Refugee Convention and considers that such an approach legitimises greater interaction between international refugee law and international law on the rights of the child.[265]

It has been less common for courts and tribunals and scholars to refer to relevant rules of international law not taking the form of treaties. Lauterpacht and Bethlehem appear to regard Article 31(3)(c) as also being in play in respect of general principles derived from human rights law, albeit considering that development in human rights is not by itself 'determinative of the interpretation of Article 33(1) of the 1951 Convention'.[266]

Academic materials have generally been seen not to fit easily within Article 31(3)(c).[267]

## 2.8 Special Meaning

As noted earlier, Gardiner observes that 'the most common way in which a special meaning is indicated is by including a definition article in a treaty'.[268] He, in fact, gives as an example the *Roma Rights* case in which Lord Bingham identified that the Refugee Convention 'gives a special meaning to "refugee"'.[269]

Lord Bingham also appeared to consider that the term 'refouler' in Article 33 was to be confined to its special meaning of 'return' rather than its ordinary meaning, in light of the failure of state parties in 1977 to agree to a widening of the 1951 Convention's scope.[270]

As regards identification of 'refugee' as having a special meaning, that of course does not assist with the meaning of its constituent elements.

In Chapter 4 of this book on Nationality and Statelessness it is argued that there is at least a case for the terms 'nationality of a country' and 'having no nationality' in Article 1A(2) being considered to have a special meaning. But even if that is accepted

---

[263] ibid 65.
[264] ibid 70.
[265] Pobjoy (n 9) 28–43 writes at 41: '[i]t seems that one would have little difficulty in establishing that the CRC, OPAC and OPSC are appropriate tools of reference for interpretation provisions of the [Refugee] Convention, particularly where the latter is applied to children seeking international protection.'
[266] Lauterpacht and Bethlehem (n 215) 113. See *South West Africa* (n 34) 16.
[267] Gardiner (n 3) 401.
[268] ibid 339.
[269] ibid 340.
[270] *Roma Rights* (n 114) para 18. See similarly, Gardiner (n 3) 340.

as correct, overall 'special meaning' has only played a peripheral role in interpreting the refugee definition.

## 2.9 Article 32 VCLT

As observed in section 1 of this chapter, Article 32 accords two roles for supplementary means of interpretation, including the *travaux*: a confirmatory role for the purpose of confirming the meaning resulting from the application of Article 31; and a determining role, when the interpretation according to Article 31 leaves the meaning ambiguous or obscure or leads to a result which is manifestly absurd or unreasonable.

### 2.9.1 *Travaux préparatoires (travaux)*
As noted earlier, the term used in Article 32—'preparatory work'—encompasses all documentation that had a formative effect on a treaty's drafting. In the context of the Refugee Convention, it commenced with GA Resolution 8(I) of 12 February 1946 and is primarily seen to comprise three sets of materials: (i) the drafting records and related documents of the Ad Hoc Committee on Statelessness and Related Problems constituted under ECOSOC Resolution 248(IX) B of 8 August 1949[271] (later renamed the Ad Hoc Committee on Refugees and Stateless Persons) (1950);[272] (ii) the proceedings of the Social Committee of ECOSOC in eight meetings between 31 July and 10 August 1950; and (iii) the Conference of Plenipotentiaries (1951) including successive drafts of the treaty text, written interventions by delegates, and minutes of meetings.[273]

Common law courts and tribunals have generally viewed the *travaux* as an important source for helping interpret the meaning of key provisions of the Refugee Convention. In *INS v Cardozo Fonseca*, for example, the US Supreme Court considered that in construing the meaning of 'well-founded fear' it was necessary to take account of the *travaux*.[274] Some academic studies see the *travaux* as having particular value with respect to the refugee definition. Einarsen, for example, considers that analysis of the *travaux* with respect to the refugee definition has particular value 'since its key provisions 'consists of a number of words and expressions which are inherently vague and broadly framed, and as such leave the meaning of the definition "ambiguous" within the meaning of Article 32(a) VCLT'.[275] Hathaway has argued that in the context of the Refugee Convention the *travaux* are of especial importance.[276]

---

[271] ECOSOC, Res 248 (IX) B (8 August 1949).
[272] Ad Hoc Committee on Statelessness and Related Problems, Thirty-third Meeting (Election of officers and preliminary discussion) (1950) UN Doc E/AC.32/SR.33, 1.
[273] McAdam (n 2) 99–100. In the context of the 1967 Protocol, identification of the precise contents of the *travaux* is less easy; but certainly encompasses the 1966 submission of proposals to ExCom, state responses to the proposal, and the submission of the final proposal by UNHCR to ECOSOC which consented and further submitted it to the UN Secretary-General: see Terje Einarsen, 'Drafting History of the 1951 Convention and the 1967 Protocol' in Zimmermann (n 2) 68–73. See also Robert F Barksy, 'From the 1965 Bellagio Colloquium to the 1967 Refugee Protocol' (2020) 32(2) IJRL 340.
[274] *Immigration and Naturalization Service v Cardoza-Fonseca* [1987] 480 US 421; *Roma Rights* (n 114) para 17; *Applicant A* (n 114) para 299; *Pushpanathan* (n 179) para 55.
[275] Einarsen (n 273) 49.
[276] Hathaway (1st edn) (n 2) 55–56; Hathaway (2nd edn) (n 2) 148–55.

On the other hand, there have been decisions decrying shortcomings of the *travaux*. In *Ward*, for example, La Forest J urged caution when considering the submissions of individual delegations made during the drafting process.[277] Some academic studies have observed that sometimes the *travaux* are either silent or uninformative[278] and that the *travaux* only involved twenty-six state parties.[279] Goodwin-Gill, for example, has consistently maintained that it would be contrary to the terms of the VCLT rules, which position the *travaux* as a 'supplementary' means of interpretation, to attach undue importance to them. He has urged caution in approaching interpretation based on original intent, given that 120 of the current state parties did not participate in the drafting and that international law has developed new understandings.[280]

Hathaway rejects such criticisms. He avers, inter alia, that noted shortcomings of *travaux* generally are not applicable in the case of the Refugee Convention since 'its preparatory work is carefully defined, approved by states, and published'.[281] He sees no difficulty in any event with the fact of 'shortcomings and blunders' since 'so long as recognised as such, [it] may actually help to elucidate the meaning of provisions ultimately adopted ... '.[282] He does not consider recourse to the *travaux* to be at odds with the dynamic approach that treats the Convention as a 'living instrument'.[283] Having noted that the ICJ has in practice relied on the *travaux* for diverse purposes and that several commentators regard the *travaux* as a source instrumental to interpreting a treaty in accordance with Article 31, Hathaway highlights what he describes as the low threshold for deeming the text of a treaty to be 'ambiguous or obscure'.[284]

But there remain analytical difficulties with Hathaway's approach. However much eminent jurists have insisted that Articles 31 and 32 must be read as a unity, the fact remains that only Article 31 sets out the 'rule' for interpretation of treaties and the means of interpretation set out in Article 32 are expressly described as 'supplementary'. It was noted earlier that in 2018 the ILC clearly saw the *travaux* as having lesser 'interpretive value' than sources falling within Article 31(3)(a).[285] As McAdam has observed, treating the *travaux* as a primary reference point risks elevating the particular intent of the parties at the time of the treaty's conclusion (and applying the principle of contemporaneity) over the object and purpose of the treaty understood as adaptable to new situations.[286]

---

[277] *Ward* (n 141). See also McAdam (n 2) 100.
[278] See observations by Lord Steyn and Lord Hoffman, cited in McAdam (n 2) 102.
[279] Goodwin-Gill (n 2) 209.
[280] ibid 238; see also Lauterpacht and Bethlehem (n 215); McAdam (n 2) 93.
[281] Hathaway (1st edn) (n 2) 56; see also Hathaway and Foster (n 2) 11; Hathaway (2nd edn) (n 2) 148–54.
[282] Hathaway (1st edn) (n 2) 56.
[283] ibid; see also Hathaway (2nd edn) (n 2) 149–54.
[284] Stephen M Schwebel, 'May Preparatory Work Be Used to Correct Rather Than Confirm the "Clear" Meaning of a Treaty Provision?' in Jerzy Makarczyk (ed), *Theory of International Law at the Threshold of the 21st Century: Essays in Honor of Krzysztof Skubiscewski* (Kluwer Law International 1996) 543, cited by Hathaway (n 2) 60; see also Hathaway (2nd edn) (n 2) 251.
[285] See ILC, Report on subsequent agreements (n 7); see above n 93.
[286] McAdam (n 2) 103. She cites, inter alia, Walter Kälin, 'Implementing Treaties in Domestic Law: from "Pacta Sunt Servanda" to "Anything Goes"?' in Vera Gowlland-Debbas (ed), *Multilateral Treaty-Making: The Current Status of Challenges to and Reforms Needed in the International Legislative Process* (Springer 2000) 115.

In any event, irrespective of the disagreements over the precise role of the *travaux*, McAdam's review of case law itself illuminates that recourse in refugee law to the *travaux* is made even when it does not meet the specific conditions set out in Article 32. She notes that in this regard, those referencing them follow the practice of the ICJ which likewise has often had recourse to *travaux* more widely. Actual practice also reflects, she writes, that reference to the *travaux* has been termed 'unavoidable' from a policy perspective.[287]

Partly with this backdrop in mind,[288] this study, when applying a systematic approach based on VCLT rules to interpretation of key terms of the refugee definition, often begins (out of turn) with the *travaux*. It is felt that generally readers benefit from knowing about origins before delving further.

2.9.2 Other supplementary means of interpretation

As noted earlier, Article 32 VCLT provides a non-exhaustive list of supplementary means of interpretation. These roughly sub-divide into interpretive principles and other interpretive materials.

*2.9.2.1 Interpretive principles*

One interpretive principle that has been applied in construing the element of the refugee definition concerned with Convention reasons or grounds is *euisdem generis*. The 'protected characteristics' approach in particular has considered that the meaning of 'particular social group' must be limited by the class indicated by the other four stated reasons of race, religion, nationality, and political opinion. As developed in the case law and literature, this approach is used to construe the phrase 'particular social group' with a non-ordinary meaning[289] informed by context, object, and purposes. However, some senior judges have criticised recourse to this principle in this context. The view in Australian decisions has rather been to apply a 'social perception' approach based primarily upon the ordinary meaning of the constituent words.[290]

Of particular importance in the context of the Refugee Convention is to keep in mind the rule against restrictive interpretation in the context of a multilateral treaty. On a number of occasions states have sought to interpret the refugee definition so as to make its scope narrower than its ordinary meaning—e.g. imposing a requirement that actors of persecution can only be state actors or precluding its material scope from ever covering those fleeing situations of armed conflict. As noted earlier,[291] the notion of restrictive interpretation has no role in the context of multilateral treaties.

---

[287] O'Connell (n 5) 263, cited by McAdam (n 2) 101. See also Gardiner (n 3) 377 who notes that 'a narrative with provisions interwoven with preparatory work may make the most coherent presentation of a reasoned interpretation'.

[288] And partly bearing in mind the observation of O'Connell (n 5) 263 that reference to travaux is 'unavoidable' from a policy perspective (cited by McAdam (n 2) 101).

[289] McAdam (n 2) 90. See further Chapter 10, section 3.4.2 of this book.

[290] *Applicant A* (n 114) para 295. See further Chapter 10, section 3.4.2.

[291] See above section 1.8.2.

*2.9.2.2 Interpretive materials*
In light of the residual and clearly non-exhaustive scope of Article 32, there has been strong support in refugee law for treating it as encompassing a wide range of materials, including those which may not fit—or not fit easily—within the specific terms of Article 31. This has been most clearly expressed in the academic literature.[292] Hathaway, for example, attaches particular importance to 'carefully reasoned national jurisprudence and the settled interpretive positions of expert treaty bodies'.[293] Given the importance to interpretation of the refugee definition of the human rights approach, particular note should be made of the mention by the ILC in its 2018 report of the fact that the authoritative opinions of UN treaty-monitoring bodies cannot be ignored in the interpretive process. Hathaway notes that this position has been supported by the ICJ, regional human rights courts, and senior national courts.[294] Similarly, Goodwin Gill notes that in his view, even though case law cannot come within Article 31(3)(b), it can still constitute 'supplementary means of interpretation' under Article 32.[295] This position fully accords with the ILC position, as outlined recently in 2018.[296]

The significant role of Article 32 as an anchor for UNHCR, judicial, and academic sources is dealt with in section 3 of this chapter.

## 2.10 Article 33 VCLT and Interpretation of Treaties in More than One Language

Article 33 concerns interpretation of treaties authenticated in two or more languages. The Refugee Convention provides at Article 46 that the English and French texts are equally authentic. The 1967 Protocol lists five languages as equally authentic: Chinese, English, French, Russian, and Spanish.

There have been limited occasions on which much has been seen to ride on the meaning of the text in English as compared to the French. Two significant examples are the meaning of 'well-founded fear' in Article 1A(2)[297] and, in the context of Article 33, the respective meanings of the English verb 'return' and the French verb 'refouler'.[298] The approach taken in both case law and the wider literature reflects awareness that Article 33(4) VCLT requires adoption, subject to certain conditions, of an approach that 'best reconciles the text'.

---

[292] See e.g. Hathaway (1st edn) (n 2) 71. Hathaway (2nd edn) (n 2) 166 underlines, however, that 'not even this broad reading of Art. 32 can be relied on to interpret a treaty by reference to any and all state practice since the only practice that is relevant is "conduct by one or more parties in the application of the treaty"'.
[293] Hathaway (2nd edn) (n 2) 167–70.
[294] Hathaway (2nd edn) (n 2) 168. In relation to the ICJ, he cites *Ahmadou Sadio Diallo (Republic of Guinea v Democratic Republic of the Congo)*, Merits, Judgment [2010] ICJ Rep 639, para 66; *Legal Consequences for States of the Continued Presence of South Africa in Namibia (South West Africa) notwithstanding Security Council Resolution 276 (1970)*, Advisory Opinion [1971] ICJ Rep 16 paras 109–12.
[295] Goodwin-Gill (n 2) 213–14.
[296] ILC, Report on subsequent agreements (n 7); see above n 69.
[297] See Chapter 11, section 2.2.4.
[298] e.g. in *Sale v Haitian Centers Council* (n 127) and in *Roma Rights* (n 114). The French text of Article 31 was considered by the House of Lords in the English Court of Appeal in *Asfaw* (n 134) para 89.

# 3 Interpretive Value of the Most Commonly Cited Sources

## 3.1 Introduction

Before we can draw conclusions regarding the overall impact of the VCLT rules on interpretation of the Refugee Convention, it is necessary to reflect further on a recurring paradox that has surfaced when discussing the application of these rules' different elements. Section 2 disclosed a tension between two positions. On the one hand, there is a lack of consensus about whether UNHCR and/or judicial materials fall within the scope of Article 31 at all. On the other hand, there is marked reliance on UNHCR materials, case law (and indeed academic sources) as providing valuable guidance for interpretation of key terms.[299] Sometimes these sources are noted as being supplementary means of interpretation within the meaning of Article 32, but more often such reliance on them is free-standing. Already in Chapter 1, this study has identified UNHCR and judicial materials as two main pillars of the interpretive endeavour. This poses the question: is it in line with VCLT rules to treat such sources as valuable guidance? There are several reasons for answering this question in the affirmative.

First, there are specific features of the Refugee Convention that create an acute need for recourse to such sources. In particular, there is the inactivation of Article 38 which has created an interpretive vacuum. There is also the fact that in relation to this treaty, there has been for some time a lack of state practice in the conventional sense regarding its interpretation.

Second, as we have seen, the VCLT rules are flexible and do not impose a particular result. Treaty interpretation remains an art and the rules broadly allow for the decision maker to attribute weight and/or significance to particular elements depending on the type of treaty concerned and the terms being interpreted. In this regard, it is significant that we have found, under the three subparagraphs of Article 31(3) in particular, that such sources meet some but not all of the requirements of each.

Third, even if such sources are considered to fall outside the strict scope of Article 31(3)'s provisions, the latter envisage that such sources can at least constitute *evidence* of 'subsequent practice' and relevant rules of international law.

Fourth, consideration of the potential role of such sources has come to form an integral part of modern attempts to apply the VCLT rules, orienting the way the interpretive exercise is conducted. As noted in Brownlie's *Principles*, subsequent practice by individual parties, falling short of meeting the requirements of Article 31(3), is nevertheless of 'some probative value'.[300]

Fifth, as noted earlier, even at a very minimum, such sources are capable of falling comfortably within Article 32 as supplementary means of interpretation.

Sixth, in view of the ILC understanding of the VCLT as an integrated set of considerations and also its emphasis on the interaction between Article 31(3)(b) and Article 32 when there is state practice 'in the broad sense' falling short of constituting

---

[299] As noted by McAdam (n 2) a good example of this way of referencing case law is the New Zealand Supreme Court case of *Zaoui* (n 143).
[300] Crawford (n 4) 368. Cited in support are *Eritrea-Ethiopia Boundary Commission* (n 51) 34–42, 66–74, 87–104, 110–13. See also *Assange* (n 69).

'subsequent practice', such sources have potentially a legitimate role in informing all aspects of the interpretive endeavour.

Having concluded that such sources are congruent with VCLT rules, the remaining question to be addressed is what interpretive value can be attributed to the three main sources that are looked to—UNHCR, judicial, and academic materials respectively?[301] In view of our earlier coverage, this can be done briefly.

## 3.2 UNHCR Materials

### 3.2.1 Article 35 of the Refugee Convention

As already noted, Article 35 confers a responsibility on UNHCR to supervise the *application*, not interpretation, of the Convention. UNHCR is generally careful not to claim that its materials on interpretation of the Refugee Convention have binding status, but as noted in Chapter 1, its supervision of application certainly endows its guidance with a special status.[302] It is important to consider different types of UNHCR documents and materials.

From the earlier treatment of such sources in Chapter 1 and in section 2 of this chapter (which looked at how such sources have been seen to fit within the various provisions of Articles 31–33 VCLT), the inherent value of such sources, the 1979 Handbook, UNHCR ExCom Conclusions and UNHCR Guidelines on International Protection in particular, will already be apparent.

McAdam's survey of the use of the UNHCR Handbook since it was published in 1979 conveys that courts and tribunals have seen it (sometimes along with other commentaries and explanatory documents) to be a useful aid to interpreting the Refugee Convention from a number of different aspects, principally: (a) as evidence of state practice; and (b) as an important source of guidance in its own right.[303] In the case of *Robinson* in the English Court of Appeal, for example, Lord Woolf MR described it as 'particularly helpful as a guide to what is the international understanding of the Convention obligations, as worked out in practice.[304] It is also salient that the Handbook continues to be drawn on by a number of national courts and tribunals as well as regional courts.[305]

---

[301] As noted in Chapter 1, governmental guidance materials, although also amounting to another interpretive pillar, is presently too limited in terms of the number of states who produce them and/or make them accessible and suffer from the drawback that of their nature they are concerned primarily with national interpretation.

[302] See p. 39.

[303] A notable decision identifying both aspects is the Australian High Court case, *QAAH* (n 113) paras 80–82 (per Kirby J). See further McAdam (n 2) 110–12.

[304] *R v Secretary of State for the Home Department, Immigration Appeals Tribunal, Ex parte Anthonypillai Francis Robinson* [1997] Case No FC3 96/7394/D, para 11, cited in McAdam (n 2) 111; *Chan v Canada (Minister of Employment and Immigration)* [1995] 3 SCR 593, 620.

[305] See e.g. Case C-280/21, *PI v Migracijos departamentas prie lietuvos Respublikos vidaus reikalu ministerijos*, 12 January 2023 [2023] EUECJ C-280/21, para 27 (which describes the Handbook and Guidelines as 'particularly relevant in the light of the role conferred on the [UNHCR] by the Geneva Convention'); *JK and Others v Sweden* App No 59166/12 (ECtHR [GC], 23 August 2016) para 93.

Nevertheless, as explained in Chapter 1,[306] subsequent developments in law and practice have revealed shortcomings in the Handbook which reduce its value as authoritative guidance.

The interpretive value of the ExCom Conclusions is well-demonstrated by McAdam's survey. For example, she notes that they 'are regularly invoked by the United Kingdom and New Zealand courts and have occasionally been referred to in Australia and Canada'.[307] However, in relation to Article 1A(2), as was observed earlier, it is difficult to identify many Conclusions that have a direct bearing on interpretation of its key terms, with the possible exception of those touching on the validity of a human rights approach and gender-related and child-specific and other diversity-related forms of persecution.[308]

The genesis of the UNHCR 'Guidelines on International Protection' and the evolving methodology underlying them has already been examined in Chapter 1.[309] As noted there, these Guidelines do not constitute the only guidelines UNHCR produces, as there has been a long-standing practice of producing documents setting out opinions and guidance on issues of interpretation (and of courts and tribunals having regard to them);[310] but by publishing the Guidelines together with the 1979 UNHCR Handbook,[311] UNHCR has identified them as an authoritative set of UNHCR materials on the Refugee Convention.

Whilst judicial references have sometimes appeared to deem recourse to the UNHCR Guidelines as limited to cases in which there is ambiguity or unclarity (in apparent reference to VCLT Article 32),[312] it would seem that they are regarded as relevant to the task of interpretation of key terms generally. As noted by Goodwin-Gill, the Guidelines have been cited by a significant number of courts and tribunals worldwide and also by the CJEU, ECtHR, and IACtHR.[313] In *Adimi*, for example, Simon Brown LJ considered that in light of Article 35(1) of the Convention, UNHCR's Guidelines with regard to the detention of asylum seekers 'should be accorded considerable weight'.[314]

There is also strong academic support for attaching significant weight to the Guidelines. Indeed, for Goodwin-Gill, '[t]hey are certainly no less authoritative than the Handbook, are much more up-to-date, and should be seen in the same light as

---

[306] See Chapter 1, section 6.1.1.
[307] McAdam (n 2). See also Fresia (n 216) and section 1.2.6.1 of this chapter.
[308] See Chapter 1 and Chapter 3.
[309] See Chapter 1, section 6.1.4. See also UNHCR Guidelines on International Protection—Consultation process (2019) available at <https://www.unhcr.org/protection/globalconsult/544f59896/unhcr-guidelines-international-protection-consultation-process.html> accessed 28 November 2020.
[310] See e.g. *R v Uxbridge Magistrates Court and Another, Ex parte Adimi* [1999] EWHC Admin 765; [2001] QB 667.
[311] The first eight are contained in UNHCR, Handbook on Procedures and Criteria for Determining Refugee Status and Guidelines on International Protection under the 1951 Convention and the 1967 Protocol Relating to the Status Of Refugees (Geneva, 2019, reissued in 2019) (UNHCR 1979 Handbook or 1979 Handbook).
[312] See e.g. Kirby J's observation in *QAAH* (n 113) that 'the UNHCR Guidelines and Handbook constitute a useful source of expertise that can aid the interpretation of provisions in the Convention that are ambiguous or unclear'.
[313] Goodwin-Gill (n 215) 18–22. For a recent CJEU acknowledgment of the interpretive value of UNHCR materials generally, Case C 91/20 *LW v Bundesrepublik Deutschland* (n 262) para 56. See also n 306.
[314] *Adimi* (n 310) 530; *QAAH* (n 113) para 80.

110 INTERPRETATION

equivalent work, such as the "General Comments" of the Human Rights Committee acknowledged in the jurisprudence of the International Court of Justice'.[315]

One of the great virtues of these Guidelines is that they have enabled UNHCR to continue to develop its legal interpretations in an incremental way and to focus on very specific issues arising in practice. However, the fact that UNHCR continues to reissue the 1979 Handbook unchanged alongside these Guidelines does pose difficulties, in particular that (as was noted in Chapter 1 and will be analysed further in ensuing chapters), the Handbook's analysis on some matters is no longer widely followed in either the case law or wider literature. Nor is it always clear to the readers of the post-2003 Guidelines, which often respond to new developments, how to treat the fact of their co-existence with a Handbook that only addressed such developments up to 1979.[316]

However, despite being consultative, the process used for development of the Guidelines is clearly not one that constitutes 'subsequent agreement' or 'subsequent practice' of state parties within the meaning of Article 31(3)(a) and (b) and they have sometimes been seen as of less persuasive value than the Handbook.[317]

In terms of UNHCR materials more generally, Goodwin-Gill has called in the past for a greater willingness to recognise what he terms the 'authority' which should attach to the Opinions and Guidelines of the UNHCR, using the word 'authority' to signify not 'competence to bind' but 'rather something similar to, perhaps stronger than [a] good faith obligation'.[318] More recently he goes further, exhorting that:

> If law-making is 'no longer the exclusive preserve of states', the task still remains of identifying the source and confirming its content and binding nature. In the field of international refugee law, that role now falls on UNHCR, both as the 'provider' of subsidiary means for the determination of rules of law, and as an authoritative interpreter of international agreements for the protection of refugees.[319]

When considering the use made of UNHCR materials, sight must not be lost of the fact that their influence on courts may arise either directly or indirectly. Indirect ways may include where courts and tribunals make reference to academic commentary that relies in turn on UNHCR sources or on UNHCR interventions. The world of refugee law is heavily interconnected. Be that as it may, the position taken in Chapter 1 of this study is that in terms of the meaning of key terms of the refugee definition, UNHCR materials can never be the last word. For UNHCR materials to achieve their place as a

---

[315] Goodwin-Gill (n 215) 21.
[316] See further pp. 48–49.
[317] e.g. in the English Court of Appeal, Arden, LJ wrote in *The Secretary of State for the Home Department v MA (Somalia)* [2018] EWCA Civ 994, para 57 that: 'I would treat the *Guidelines*, while perhaps not of the same persuasive authority as the UN Handbook, as an important text for the purposes of interpreting the provisions of the [EU Qualification Directive] replicating those in the Refugee Convention.'
[318] Goodwin-Gill (n 2) 240. For the meaning of this good faith obligation, he refers to Goodwin-Gill and McAdam (n 219) 430–32.
[319] Goodwin-Gill (n 215) 40.

major interpretive source in the contemporary world, their guidance needs to be confirmed in case law.[320]

In relation to UNHCR materials, it is pertinent to add a cautionary note. Some courts and tribunals and academics have expressed concern that UNHCR materials bearing on matters of interpretation may sometimes be unduly influenced by organisational policy objectives or stray into the realm of advocacy rather than being confined to pure interpretation. The ECtHR has had occasion to question whether UNHCR materials giving guidance on risks in specific countries can be accorded considerable weight. In *N.A. v UK*, for example, it stated, *à propos* of UNHCR Position Papers that:

> Thus in respect of the UNHCR, due weight has been given by the Court to the UNHCR's own assessment of an applicant's claims when the Court determined the merits of her complaint under Article 3 ... Conversely, where the UNHCR's concerns are focussed on general socio-economic and humanitarian considerations, the Court has been inclined to accord less weight to them, since such considerations do not necessarily have a bearing on the question of a real risk to an individual applicant of ill-treatment within the meaning of Article 3 ....[321]

In a similar vein, Goodwin-Gill has observed regarding UNHCR interventions that:

> [ ... ] it is one thing for UNHCR to focus its interventions on the interpretive possibilities of the Convention, working within the meaning of the words themselves, considered in context with due regard to object and purpose; but quite another to address recommendations to states in their law—and policy-making capacity, arguing for seriously progressive development, and for change and amendment beyond the meaning of words.[322]

He urges UNHCR to ensure it distinguishes carefully between positions which deal with matters of interpretation and those which are more in the form of recommendations for amendment.[323]

## 3.3 Judicial Materials

### 3.3.1 Case law

As already noted, UNHCR and other commentators have frequently attached considerable weight when interpreting the 1951 Convention to decisions of courts and tribunals, particularly at a senior level. That is apparent from each of the expert papers that precede the Guidelines as well as the various academic studies that make use of

---

[320] See pp. 51–53. See also Goodwin-Gill (n 215) 2, 12: '[ ... ] clearly the legal "products" of an organisation such as UNHCR need to be "received" or accepted; here, domestic courts are commonly the medium'.
[321] *NA v United Kingdom* App No 25904/07 (ECtHR, 17 July 2008) para 122.
[322] Goodwin-Gill (n 2) 219.
[323] ibid 240–41.

comparative jurisprudence on the Refugee Convention.[324] Whilst explicit references to decisions in other jurisdictions is far more marked in common law jurisdictions, it is clear that in those countries that have developed a significant body of case law, close attention is paid to leading decisions from around the world, judges everywhere being mindful that the Refugee Convention is an international instrument and that they are tasked with attempting to give it an international meaning. Even in the EU, the Opinions of Advocate Generals in asylum cases often refer to decisions of other courts and tribunals.[325]

Significantly, courts and tribunals themselves have identified the importance of case law in the context of the Refugee Convention as very much a function of two specific features of this treaty highlighted earlier: the lack of any supervision by a supranational court (arising out of Article 38's inactivation);[326] and lack of state practice in the strict sense.[327]

In addition, case law has been an important medium particularising how specific VCLT rules are to be applied. When a leading court rules, for example, that both 'context' and/or 'object and purpose' or Article 31(3) considerations point towards a particular approach to interpreting a key term, it is simultaneously providing an interpretation and lending support for one understanding of the VCLT rules or another. In this way it also helps ensure that interpretation of a treaty serves the rule of law that underpins the entire international legal order.[328]

Even assuming that judicial materials cannot qualify as a source under Article 31(3) VCLT and can only come within the ambit of 'supplementary means of interpretation' permitted by Article 32 (and are thus in general a source of less interpretive value), Article 32 can be invoked to 'determine' meaning when the interpretation according to Article 31 '(a) leaves the meaning ambiguous or obscure; or (b) leads to a result which is manifestly absurd or unreasonable'. As noted earlier, it is widely accepted that by their nature many provisions of the Refugee Convention are ambiguous and, as we have seen, application of various elements set out in Article 31 has not on its own always resulted in any consistent agreement as to their interpretation. According to Dörr and Schmalenbach, 'the elastic concept of ambiguity (or, for that purpose, of obscurity) clearly outweighs the—alleged—supplementary character of the integrative means identified in Article 32, before all of the *travaux préparatoires*'.[329]

However, assigning to case law a prominent role in interpretation of the Refugee Convention must always carry a note of caution. As Kirby J warned in *QAAH*, there is an especial need when considering comparative jurisprudence to take account of specific national circumstances.[330]

---

[324] Carlier et al (n 1); Hathaway and Foster (n 2); Goodwin-Gill and Lambert (n 2).
[325] See e.g. Opinion of Advocate General Hogan in Case C-255/19 *Secretary of State for the Home Department v OA* [2020] ECLI:EU:C:2020:342.
[326] *Fornah* (n 125) para 10.
[327] See e.g. *QAAH* (n 113) paras 54, 78 (emphasis added).
[328] On the role of judicial scrutiny as an important component of the rule of law, see Robert S Summers, 'The Principles of the Rule of Law' (1999) 74 Notre Dame Law Review 1691, 1694.
[329] Dörr and Schmalenbach (n 4) 584. See also Goodwin-Gill (n 215) 39 who highlights the relevance of the ICJ Statute.
[330] *QAAH* (n 113) para 46, and *Applicant A* (n 114) para 296 (Kirby J), referring to *Ram v Minister for Immigration and Ethnic Affairs* [1995] 57 FCR 565, 567, cited in McAdam (n 2) 109–10.

Also salient here are the points made earlier about the fact that the quality of judicial decisions is mixed, being a function of many variables, including not just the intrinsic merits of the decision; the fact that courts and tribunals can sometimes construe the refugee definition restrictively; the influence of national law and national legal culture; and the status of the courts in the national legal hierarchy among others.[331] There is the further dimension that when judges cite foreign cases this may amount to judicial selectivity or a 'justification exercise'.[332]

All this being said, as a *category* of relevant source materials, case law is clearly of major importance.[333]

### 3.3.2 Judicial analyses

In seeking to probe what interpretive weight is to be accorded to judicial materials, it is instructive to consider also judicial materials other than in the form of case law, in particular judicial analyses or guidelines. It has already been noted that the prime goal of interpretation of the Refugee Convention is to achieve a truly universal meaning. That presupposes national and regional law systems that ensure proper observance of Refugee Convention obligations and also a harmonised approach among the world's judiciaries.[334] It is beyond the scope of this book to explore the sea of literature on 'transnational judicial dialogue'[335] but effectively, for national courts and tribunals, judicial dialogue with their counterparts in other signatory states can be argued to be a necessity, if not an obligation, in the process of interpreting relevant provisions of international law.[336] Yet judicial dialogue when it happens is not necessarily unitary

---

[331] See this chapter, section 2.6.2.2. The 2018 ICJ Commentary (n 7) 58, notes that '[i]t may be appropriate, in a case in which the practice in different domestic jurisdictions diverges, to emphasize the practice of a representative group of jurisdictions and to give more weight to the decisions of higher courts'. In support, it cites: United Kingdom, House of Lords: *Fothergill v Monarch Airlines Ltd* [1981] AC 251, 275–76 (Lord Wilberforce); *Sidhu v British Airways* [1997] AC 430, 453 (Lord Hope). See also Canada, Supreme Court, *Yugraneft Corp v Rexx Management Corp* [2010] 1 SCR 649, para 21 (Rothstein J). See further, András Jakab, Arthur Dyevre, and Giulio Itzcovich (eds), *Comparative Constitutional Reasoning* (CUP 2017) 14–17.

[332] Letizia Lo Giacco, 'Swinging between Finding and Justification: Judicial Citation and International Law-Making' (2017) 6 Cambridge J Int'l & Comp L 27. See also Jeremy Waldron, 'Foreign Law and the Modern Jus Gentium' (2005) 119(1) Harv L Rev 129; Robert Reed, 'Foreign Precedents and Judicial Reasoning: The American Debate and British Practice' (2008) 124(2) Law Quarterly Review 253; Chloe Cheeseman, 'Harmonising Jurisprudence of Regional and International Human Rights Bodies: A Literature Review' in Carla M Buckley, Alice Donald, and Philip Leach (eds), *Towards Convergence in International Human Rights Law: Approaches of Regional and International Systems* (Brill Nijhoff 2017) 615–19.

[333] Goodwin-Gill (n 215) 30 considers that '[t]he value of judicial decisions at the national level thus falls somewhere between evidence of State practice and evidence of opinio juris, while also serving as "subsidiary means"'. See also Chapter 1, section 6.2.

[334] See Goodwin-Gill and Lambert (n 2) 2: 'Thus, the success of the harmonisation, as a tool for internal protection in the EU substantially depends on the development of common judicial understandings, principles and norms concerning refugee matters'; Hathaway (2nd edn) (n 2) 1–2: 'senior appellate courts now routinely engage in an ongoing and quite extraordinary transnational judicial conversation about the scope of the refugee definition and have increasingly committed themselves to find common grounds'.

[335] A helpful summation of different uses of the term 'judicial dialogue' is given in Madalina Moraru, Galina Cornelisse, and Philippe De Bruycker (eds), *Law and Judicial Dialogue on the Return of Irregular Migrants from the European Union* (Hart Publishing 2020) 24–25. See further, Antonios Tzanakopoulos, 'Judicial Dialogue as a Means of Interpretation' in Helmut Philip Aust and Georg Nolte (eds), *The Interpretation of International Law by Domestic Courts: Uniformity, Diversity, Convergence* (OUP 2016) 72.

[336] Goodwin-Gill and Lambert (n 2) ch 11. As pointed out earlier, application of Article 31(3) VCLT considerations will normally require consideration of case law: see above nn 66 and 75.

nor is it necessarily cogent[337] in content. Indeed, until recently, it was very difficult to point in the field of public international law to any specific substantive content to such dialogue, beyond citation of foreign cases.

Whilst citation of foreign cases remains the most concrete way in which judicial dialogue can express itself, the International Association of Refugee Law Judges (IARLJ, now renamed IARMJ) has shown since its inception a readiness to provide guidance on refugee law topics, albeit often brief and confined to specific topics.[338] But since 2014, within the CEAS, this association, has developed in partnership with the European Union Asylum Agency (EUAA, formerly the Asylum Support Office (EASO)) a series of publications on EU asylum law, in particular the *Qualification for International Protection Judicial Analysis*.[339] Whilst such judicial analyses are confined to EU asylum law, the latter is expressly based on 'accordance' with the Refugee Convention. Though certainly not constituting a harmonised judicial interpretation of the Refugee Convention worldwide, such analyses possess a number of features that warrant them being regarded as an important new source of evidence of 'state practice' regarding interpretation of the Refugee Convention (such was expressly recognised by the CJEU in *Shajin Ahmed*).[340] In particular, the transnational group of judges from EU member states who edit these materials are selected on the basis of criteria ensuring they are experts in the field of asylum law; secondly the drafts of each judicial analysis are developed in collaboration with researchers with expertise in refugee law; third, the drafts are the subject of a consultation procedure open to both judicial and civil society actors throughout the EU; fourthly, the drafts are the subject of comments by a judge of the CJEU as well as a judge of the ECtHR (UNHCR also provides comments); fifthly, they are periodically updated under a procedure which again involves, inter alia, obtaining feedback from national judges who make use of these publications either as a reference source or in training or both.[341] At the time of writing, IARMJ is actively discussing the development of 'Global Judicial Analyses' for use by

---

[337] See Cathryn Costello, *The Human Rights of Migrants and Refugees in European Law* (OUP 2016); Goodwin-Gill and Lambert (n 2); Jakab, Dyevre, and Itzcovich (n 331).

[338] Examples include endorsement of a human rights approach to persecution (see p. 138) and the study by Kate Jastram, Anne MacTavish, and Penelope Mathew, 'Violations of Socio-Economic Rights as a Form of Persecution and as an Element of Internal Protection' (2009) International Association of Refugee Law Judges, Human Rights Nexus Working Party Paper. There are other examples not directly concerned with interpretation of the Refugee Convention: see e.g. International Association of Refugee and Migration Judges, 'Judicial Criteria for Assessing Country of Origin Information (COI): A Checklist' (9 November 2006). By way of example of its use, the Administrative Court of Slovenia introduced in its case law, for the first time, a scheme of basic criteria for the assessment of country of origin information based on this checklist. See Administrative Court of Slovenia, Case No *U 2073/2006-10* [2006]. See also International Association of Refugee Law Judges, 'A Structured Approach to the Decision Making Process' (2016), prepared by Allan Mackey et al.

[339] European Union Asylum Agency (EUAA), 'Qualification for International Protection Judicial Analysis' (2nd edition, Produced by IARMJ-Europe under contract to the EUAA, January 2023).

[340] Case C-369/17 *Shajin Ahmed v Bevándorlási és Menekültügyi Hivatal* [2018] EU:C:2018:713, para 56. The same Judicial Analysis on Exclusion was recently referred to by the Irish High Court in *GE v The Refugee Appeal Tribunal and The Refugee Applications Commissioner* [2018] IEHC 564. See also *SN (Ghana) v International Protection Appeals Tribunal* [2019] IEHC 10. For references to other judicial analyses in the 'Professional Development Series (PDS) published by EUAA (formerly EASO), see e.g. Case C-901/19 *CF, DN v Bundesrepublik Deutschland*, Opinion of Advocate General Pikamäe [2021] ECLI:EU:C:2021:116.

[341] This methodology is set out in appendices to each of the judicial analyses: see e.g. EASO, Judicial Analysis on Ending International Protection (2nd edn, 2021) Appendix C.

members of courts and tribunals worldwide covering, inter alia, interpretation of the Refugee Convention.[342]

## 3.4 Academic Materials

It remains to consider what interpretive value is to be placed on academic materials. The ILC noted the importance in practice of 'teachings' and the work of publicists in 2018.[343]

When interpreting the Refugee Convention, courts and tribunals around the world have often relied heavily on academic sources. Chapter 1 refers to such materials as one of the pillars of interpretive guidance. Section 1 of this chapter outlining VCLT rules noted that the most obvious location within the VCLT rules for academic sources is Article 32 on supplementary means of interpretation. That they can be accommodated there is certainly in conformity with Article 38(4) of the ICJ Statute according to which 'subject to the provisions of Article 59, judicial decisions and the teachings of the most highly qualified publicists of the various nations, [are] subsidiary means for the determination of rules of law'.[344]

Just as the lack of a supervisory supranational court and state practice in the conventional sense has enhanced the interpretive value of UNHCR and judicial materials, these factors have also led to a very significant value being placed on academic materials. The most high-profile example has been the widespread citation by common law courts and tribunals, when developing a protection-based approach to interpreting 'being persecuted', of the human rights-based model outlined by James Hathaway in his 1991 publication.[345]

When considering academic sources, it is an important feature of the refugee law literature that scholars have typically made a great effort to refer to and link as far as possible their own analyses to comparative case law and UNHCR materials.

A very prominent role must also be accorded to leading academic journals devoted to refugee law and policy, in particular (in the English-speaking world) the International Journal of Refugee Law, which began in January 1989 under the editorship of Guy Goodwin-Gill and whose aims from the start included to 'stimulate research and thinking on refugee law and its development'.[346] But, focussing only on English language publications that have sought to offer a singular analysis of key elements of the refugee definition, there are four in particular that possess features tending to strengthen their efficacy as sources.

First to mention is the series of *Michigan Guidelines on the International Protection of Refugees*, recently published as a set of eight guidelines produced individually

---

[342] There was an earlier volume of training materials produced in 1998 under IARLJ auspices by the Mellon Foundation, but this was never taken further.
[343] ILC, Report on subsequent agreements (n 7) ch V, 'Identification of Customary International Law', Conclusion No 14, 150–51.
[344] Statute of the International Court of Justice (1945) TS No 993 Article 38; Gardiner (n 3) 401.
[345] James C Hathaway, *The Law of Refugee Status* (Butterworths Limited 1991). See further p. 135.
[346] Guy S Goodwin-Gill, 'Refugee Law and the Protection of Refugees' (1989) 1(1) IJRL 2.

between 1999 and 2017.[347] These are the fruits of a Colloquium process established in 1999 with the aim of furthering a 'truly transnational approach to international refugee law.' As described in the Preface to their recent all-in-one publication, each has been produced according to what is described as 'a rigorous methodology' involving some eighteen months of sifting, analysing, and organising relevant jurisprudence and scholarship from around the world so as to produce a comprehensive background study on the chosen topic, and then convening a small number of highly qualified external experts—including scholars, advocates, officials, judges, and a high-level observer from the UNHCR—who will have been invited beforehand to respond to the background study and then discuss alongside student contributors for three days of guided intensive reflection and debate. Each of the guidelines constitutes an unanimously agreed text. Four of the guidelines are devoted squarely to key interpretive issues relating to Article 1A(2): those on The Internal Protection Alternative (1999), Nexus to a Convention Ground (2001), Well-founded Fear (2004), and Risks for Reason of Political Opinion (2015).

The second to mention is the *Commentary* on the Convention edited by Zimmermann.[348] It covers all articles of the Convention and its 1967 Protocol, not just Article 1A(2), but its methodology exhibits three salient features from the point of view of interpreting the refugee definition. First, the majority of the individual contributors who author individual chapters (assisted by a team of students) are from civil law rather than common law countries, still a relative rarity in the world of English language refugee law literature. Second, each chapter analysing key provisions or different aspects of them seeks to broadly follow the ordering of the VCLT rules and in particular to include a section entitled 'State practice'. That is particularly evident in the main chapter dealing with Article 1A(2) by Zimmermann and Mahler. Third, the chapters on the individual articles routinely consider their interrelationship with other Convention provisions. These features add significantly to the global and VCLT-compliant character of this commentary's treatment of the refugee definition.

The third academic source of note is *The Law of Refugee Status* by Hathaway and Foster.[349] This is not only mentioned here because it is a second edition of one of refugee law's classics, or because both its authors are widely regarded as eminent in this field (although both are true), but because it too, in response to the felt need to render its analysis more transnational, exhibits a methodology designed to ensure a greater collective input in the form of copious footnotes drawing on a case law database (previously the refugeecaselaw.org database, now (since October 2014) RefLaw.org). The authors explain that they have been aided by advice from a panel of experts on international and comparative law who reviewed every draft chapter and convened twice.[350]

Another classic work is *The Refugee in International Law*, now in its fourth edition.[351] Albeit a work in the English language, it has permeated the world of refugee

---

[347] James C Hathaway, *The Michigan Guidelines on the International Protection of Refugees* (Michigan Publishing 2019).
[348] Zimmermann (n 2).
[349] Hathaway and Foster (n 2).
[350] ibid 12–13.
[351] Goodwin-Gill and McAdam (n 204).

scholarship. It has primarily been cited by courts and tribunals in common law countries, but its endeavour to identify refugee law as a distinct area of international law has made it an essential point of reference in refugee law literature worldwide. One of the features that makes it of particular importance is that each edition has sought, not simply to update, but also to critically engage with evolving case law and to refine its analysis of key points relating to the Refugee Convention and associated instruments in light of new developments. Its latest edition, for example, contains a specific chapter on 'Displacement Related to the Impacts of Disasters and Climate Change'.[352]

Nevertheless, judicial decisions clearly see parameters to reliance on academic materials, In part this is because much is more evaluative than descriptive of what the law is.[353] The judicial approach is to consider that it is always for judges to 'test' the force of academic ideas.[354] Further, whilst an immensely important source for ascertaining what matters are widely agreed and what are not, its heterogeneity means that for the most part focus has to be on what views the academic literature taken as a whole predominantly conveys.[355]

## 4 VCLT Rules and the EU Asylum Law

The EU Qualification Directive and the jurisprudence of the Court of Justice of the European Union potentially provides a valuable source of interpretive guidance on the refugee definition, since the former contains a definition of refugee that is virtually identical with Article 1A(2).[356] However, as was noted, that argument depends, in part, on the relevant EU asylum law practice being in line with VCLT rules. There are two distinct problems regarding this, one relating to methods of interpretation, the other to whether EU asylum law's codification of some elements of the refugee definition conforms to VCLT rules. These are addressed in order.

### 4.1 CJEU Approach to Interpretation

The CJEU accepts, subject to certain preconditions,[357] that it has jurisdiction to interpret key terms of the Refugee Convention. Nevertheless, generally and also specifically

---

[352] ibid 638–68.
[353] See Chapter 1.
[354] In *Adan* (n 114) para 53, Lord Hope noted that '[w]hile weight must be attached to the views of UNHCR in the light of its function under Article 35 of the Convention and to those academics who specialise in this field, their assertions appear never to have been tested judicially elsewhere in the courts of the states parties'.
[355] See above section 3.4.
[356] See Chapter 1, section 2.3.3.
[357] The preconditions are that the provisions of the QD and QD (recast) make direct or indirect *renvoi* to the Refugee Convention. As regards direct *renvoi*, Article 2(e) QD provides a definition of refugee that reproduces the wording of the first paragraph of Article 1A(2), although confining its personal scope to third-country nationals. Articles 9 QD also refers to Article 1A(2) and there are other references to provisions of the Refugee Convention in Articles 11 and 12 QD. On Article 11, see Joined Cases C-175/08, C-176/08, C-178/08, and C-179/08 *Salahadin Abdulla and Others* [2010] ECR I-0000, para 48. At para 34 of Case C-31/09 *Nawras Bolbol v Bevándorlási és Állampolgársági Hivatal* [2010] ECR I-05539, the Court noted in relation to a case concerned with Article 12(1)(a) of the QD, that '[a]s the Directive includes a reference to Article

in relation to EU asylum law, it applies an approach to interpretation that is identifiably different from the VCLT one.[358] Its own method of interpretation, combines a purposive with a 'meta-teleological' dimension,[359] which focuses not only on the object and purpose of the relevant provisions but also those of the EU regime as a whole, relying on the human rights standards contained in the Charter of Fundamental Rights (EU Charter) and the founding values of the organisation. As noted by Hemme Battjes, 'interpretation to wording and context are very much supplementary to the purpose. Moreover, it is not the purpose of the provision but rather the purpose of the Treaty as a whole that guides the interpretation.'[360] Thus in *Bolbol* the Court stated:

> The provisions of the Directive must [ ... ] be interpreted in the light of its general scheme and purpose, while respecting the Geneva Convention and the other relevant treaties referred to in point (1) of the first subparagraph of Article 63 EC. Those provisions must also, as is apparent from recital 10 in the preamble to the Directive, be interpreted in a manner which respects the fundamental rights and the principles recognised in particular by the [EU Charter] ....[361]

If the CJEU was strictly applying VCLT rules to the refugee definition in Article 1A(2), it would only be concerned with 'the general scheme and purpose' of the Geneva Convention, not of the EU treaties; and any recourse it had to human rights or other treaty norms would ordinarily be via the reference to them in the Preamble to the Geneva Convention (which refers to the UDHR), not, self-evidently, to the Charter.[362]

---

1D of the Geneva [Refugee] Convention, *the Court has jurisdiction to interpret the meaning of that article of the Convention*' (emphasis added). In relation to what might be termed indirect *renvoi*, the CJEU has made clear that it will also undertake interpretation of provisions of the Refugee Convention if its own EU asylum legislation contains provisions that are substantially equivalent: see Case C-57/09 *Bundesrepublik Deutschland v B and D* [2010] ECLI:EU:C:2010:661, para 72. In this case it was prepared to assume jurisdiction in relation to an Article 1F issue because it considered that provisions of Article 12(2) QD corresponded 'in substance' with those of Article 1F (para 71). In addition, there is a procedural requirement under the Consolidated versions of the Treaty on European Union and the Treaty on the Functioning of the European Union (TFEU) [2016] OJ C202/1, Article 267 that the referring court must ask its questions by reference to the EU legislation, not the Refugee Convention directly.

[358] As has been noted by commentators such as Dinah Shelton, 'Reconcilable Differences? The Interpretation of Multilingual Treaties' (1997) 20(3) Hastings International and Comparative Law Review 611, 631; Hemme Battjes, *European Asylum Law and International Law* (Martinus Nijhoff 2006) 42–46.

[359] Violeta Moreno-Lax, 'Of Autonomy, Autarky, Purposiveness and Fragmentation: The Relationship between EU Asylum Law and International Humanitarian Law', in David Cantor and Jean-François Durieux (eds), *Refugee from Inhumanity? War Refugees and International Humanitarian Law* (Brill 2014) 340–41, 311. See also Case C-901/19 *CF, DN v Bundesrepublik Deutschland*, Opinion of Advocate General Pikamäe (n 340) para 31, which identifies the method of interpretation as being 'to consider not only the wording of that provision but also the context in which it occurs and the objectives pursued by the rules of which it is part. It is therefore necessary to carry out a literal, systematic and purposive interpretation ...'.

[360] Battjes (n 358) 43.

[361] Case C-31/09 *Bolbol* (n 357) paras 37–38. See also Case C-176/08 *Abdulla* (n 357) paras 52–54; Case C-57/09 *B and D* (n 357) paras 76–78; Joined Cases C-199/12 to C-201/12 *Minister voor Immigratie en Asiel v X and Y and Z v Minister voor Immigratie en Asiel* [2013] ECLI:EU:C:2013:720, paras 39–40; Case C-56/17 *Bahtiyar Fathi v Predsedatel na Darzhavna agentsia za bezhantsite* [2018] ECLI:EU:C:2018:803, para 81; and Joined Cases C-391/16, C-77/17, and C-78/17 *M and Others v Commissaire général aux réfugiés et aux apatrides* [2019] ECLI:EU:C:2019:403, para 74.

[362] Even in areas where the CJEU has seen EU law to contain *lacunae*, e.g. in relation to nationality law, the CJEU has insisted on recourse to EU law requirements. In Case C-369/90 *Mario Vicente Micheletti and*

It must be open to question whether the CJEU is right not to align its approach to interpretation of the Refugee Convention more directly with VCLT rules, for several reasons.

First, its own primary law identifies the Refugee Convention as the cornerstone of EU asylum law. Article 78 TFEU stipulates that its asylum legislation must be 'in accordance with' the Geneva Convention and various recitals in the QD and in Directive 2013/32/EU (the recast Procedures Directive (PD)) etc. accord foundational pre-eminence to the Geneva Convention: see e.g. recital (4) of the QD (recast). Further, in relation to the QD, as the Court has itself stated, this instrument is deemed to have been adopted 'to guide the competent authorities ... in the application of [the Geneva] Convention'.[363]

Second, the CJEU itself recognises the importance of not letting national law or EU law get in the way of achieving 'uniform interpretation' of an international agreement.[364]

Third, Article 3(5) TFEU requires strict observance of international treaties and, by Article 21(2)(b), the Union's actions on the international scene should be in order to 'consolidate ... the principles of international law'.[365]

Fourth, the CJEU has held that 'even though the [VCLT] does not bind either the Community or all its Member States, a series of provisions in that convention reflect the rules of customary international law which, as such, are binding on the community institutions and form part of the Community legal order'.[366]

Thus, it might be thought that in the field of international refugee law, at least, the more the Court expressly applies VCLT norms of interpretation, the better it can achieve its own stated objective of 'uniform interpretation'.

However, as matters stand, the CJEU's expressly applies a different approach to interpretation. Can this be reconciled with VCLT rules? Three points can be made.

### 4.1.1 EU asylum law as evidence of state practice

First, there is nothing as such contrary to VCLT rules in a decision maker or court or tribunal referring to regional law sources. They can at least constitute evidence of 'subsequent practice' under 31(3)(b) VCLT and/or of 'state practice in the broad sense' under Article 32.[367] Thus, the fact that when interpreting terms of the refugee

---

*others v Delegación del Gobierno en Cantabria* [1992] ECLI:EU:C:1992:295, para 10, the Court stated that '[u]nder international law, it is for each Member State ... to lay down the conditions for the acquisition and loss of nationality', but added that in exercise of those powers, member states must 'comply with the rules of [EU] law'.

[363] Case C-57/09 *B and D* (n 361) paras 93, 97; Case C-720/17 *Mohammed Bilali v Bundesamt für Fremdenwesen und Asyl* [2019] ECLI:EU:C:2019:448, para 54, referring also to Case C-369/17 *Shajin Ahmed* (n 340), para 37.
[364] Case C-481/13 *Criminal proceedings against Mohammad Ferooz Qurbani* [2014] ECLI:EU:C:2014:2101, para 26.
[365] The CJEU has explicitly acknowledged this in Case C-63/09 *Axel Walz* [2010] ECLI:EU:C:2010:251, para 23.
[366] Case C-386/08 *Firma Brita GmbH v Hauptzollamt Hamburg-Hafen* [2010] ECLI:EU:C:2010:91, para 42.
[367] See above section 2.6.2.

definition the CJEU often cites the (regional) EU Charter when applying human rights principles is not in itself inconsistent with VCLT rules.

### 4.1.2 'Conform interpretation'

Second, as already noted when commenting on the dearth of references to the VCLT rules in civil law jurisdictions, what is essential is not express reference but interpretive methods that produce outcomes consistent with such rules. In this regard, it could be argued (with considerable force) that the Court's interpretation of Article 1A(2) has often been in substance consistent with an approach based on VCLT rules and has greatly strengthened international refugee law. It could also be pointed out that the Court's recourse to the Charter has in large part being, in substance, recourse to 'generic' IHRL rights, which is essentially in line with the human rights approach applied in international refugee law.[368] It does not look as if applying a VCLT approach would have produced a different outcome. Further, the Court's own conscious adoption of a doctrine of harmonious or conform interpretation of EU materials with international law would appear to ensure the same result.[369]

## 4.2 Conformity of EU Law Provisions on Refugee Definition with VCLT Rules

The other distinct problem concerns whether EU asylum law's codification of some elements of the refugee definition conforms to VCLT rules. Goodwin-Gill and McAdam raise as a possible argument that the QD could be seen to contain at least one 'illegitimate modification'[370] of the Refugee Convention contrary to Article 41 VCLT. They specify the delimitation in the directive of the personal scope of the refugee definition to 'third-country nationals'.[371]

Since Article 1A(2) is unrestricted in its personal scope, this study does not need to appraise this issue, although the author sees force in Goodwin-Gill and McAdam's critique of personal scope.[372] However, leaving aside the issue of personal scope, it is hard to see that anything in the QD or its recast constitutes a 'modification' in the requisite legal meaning of that term.[373] The QD appears analogous to national codification

---

[368] See Hugo Storey, 'What Constitutes Persecution? Towards a Working Definition' (2014) 25(2) IJRL 272, 278–79. Article 52(3) of the Charter also requires, in relation to the rights that it contains which correspond to rights guaranteed by the ECHR, 'the meaning and scope of those rights shall be the same as those laid down by the said Convention', although it is also added that [t]his provision shall not prevent Union law providing more extensive protection'.

[369] Case C-386/08 *Firma Brita GmbH v Hauptzollamt Hamburg-Hafen* (n 366) para 42.

[370] Goodwin-Gill and McAdam (n 204) 66 note that the phrase 'illegitimate modification' is used in the Commentary to draft Article 37, the precursor to Article 41.

[371] ibid 66–67.

[372] As Goodwin-Gill and McAdam (n 204) acknowledge, the QD's limitation of personal scope to 'third-country nationals' has to be read together with Protocol No 24 on asylum for nationals of Member States of the European Union as annexed to the Treaty on European Union (TEU) and the TFEU (recital 20 states that the QD (recast) is 'without prejudice' to this Protocol). Since this Protocol does allow for the possibility of applications for asylum by nationals of member states, the 'illegitimate modification' argument turns on whether this Protocol imposes too stringent procedural restrictions on such applications.

[373] See ILC, Guide to Practice on Reservations to Treaties (n 73) paras 1.1.6, 4.7.1

attempts and the ILC only regards these as modifications if they in fact go beyond the scope of 'interpretive declarations'.[374] Plainly the VCLT rules contemplate that state parties may enact domestic legislation seeking to interpret certain treaty provisions; that is not seen in and of itself as an illegitimate form of state practice; indeed, as noted earlier, the ILC has observed that it can be a form of subsequent state practice.[375] It is true that the EU legal order, being a grouping of states, is in a different position from a solitary state party to the Refugee Convention seeking to codify elements of the refugee definition in national legislation. However, both the terms of Article 41 and ILC guidance on treaty modification would seem to set a threshold for any issue arising as to illegitimate modification in terms of there being a need for other state parties to raise an objection. That has not happened so far. Thus, as Goodwin-Gill and McAdam recognise, this is presently an issue only at the 'theoretical level'.[376] Much more would be needed to advance any case that EU asylum law relating to the refugee definition, was an 'illegitimate modification' of terms of the Refugee Convention.

None of this is to say that there may be specific respects in which either provisions of the QD (recast) or interpretive rulings of the CJEU on aspects of the refugee definition that do not properly reflect (or achieve) the true international meaning. That, however, must be a matter of close analysis of specific provisions, not of formal breaches of VCLT rules.

## 5 Conclusions

### 5.1 Conclusions: Key Features

Having set out key features of the VCLT rules, this chapter sought in sections 2 and 3 to inquire into the extent to which they have been applied to the Refugee Convention and what such application has revealed. Section 4 sought to address pertinent questions concerning the alignment of EU asylum law with VCLT rules. Given the wide-ranging nature of these inquiries, it is salient to restate the main points that have emerged.

5.1.1 Relevance of Articles 38 and Article 35 of the Refugee Convention
The Refugee Convention provides for disputes regarding interpretation to be determined by the ICJ pursuant to Article 38, but this provision has never been activated. This fact has been seen to have created an interpretive vacuum needing to be filled by other sources. The conferral by Article 35 on UNHCR of supervisory responsibility for the application of the Refugee Convention has been seen to partially assist in filling this vacuum, since although the Article 35 responsibility concerns application, not interpretation of the Convention, these two functions are closely linked. Thus, in *Adimi*, Simon Brown LJ considered Article 35(1) provided a peg in its own right for 'accord[ing] considerable weight' to UNHCR's Guidelines with regard to the detention of asylum seekers.[377] Leading courts in the common law countries have also felt

---
[374] ibid para 4.7.1.
[375] 2018 ILC Commentary (n 7) 32–34. See above p. 72.
[376] Goodwin-Gill and McAdam (n 204) 67.
[377] *Adimi* (n 310) 530.

obligated to help fill this vacuum, mindful that all treaty interpretations must adhere to VCLT rules. Thus, in *Fornah*, Lord Bingham saw comparative case law as of importance precisely because of this vacuum.[378]

### 5.1.2 Acceptance of VCLT as customary international law

Turning to what has emerged regarding application of VCLT rules to the Refugee Convention, there has been broad acceptance that when interpreting the 1951 Convention the principles to be applied are those set out in the VCLT, since the latter represent customary law. Whilst such acceptance has mainly been voiced by senior courts in the common law world, similar observations have been made by German and Austrian courts.[379]

Express application of the VCLT rules to interpreting the refuge definition remains relatively rare outside of the common law tradition, but there are mitigating factors. These include the fact, indicated by some studies, that courts and tribunals in civil law countries have regard to similar factors, especially ordinary meaning, object and purpose, and extrinsic sources, notably UNHCR materials, academic materials, and to a lesser extent foreign cases.[380] Nevertheless the task of achieving a universal definition of key terms cannot be served by reliance on national or regional systems using methods of interpretation different from rules of interpretation that have the status of customary international law. Further, failure to expressly identify such rules cuts across widely embraced principles of transparency and consistency.

### 5.1.3 The search for an autonomous meaning

There is broad consensus that interpreting provisions of the Refugee Convention involves a search for an autonomous meaning as opposed to one coloured by national or regional norms. This principle has been seen as 'part of the very alphabet of customary international law'.[381]

### 5.1.4 Treaty interpretation as a unity

Again, although largely confined to the common law tradition, there has been widespread acceptance of the need, when interpreting the Refugee Convention, to adhere to an integrated or interactive approach, which treats the rules set out in Articles 31–32 VCLT as a non-hierarchical unity. In *S152*, Kirby J stated that 'treaties, like local texts, must be read as a whole, not word by isolated word'.[382] Key features that emerge under each of the VCLT rules can be summarised as follows.

---

[378] *Fornah* (n 125) para 10, cited in McAdam (n 2) 108. Goodwin-Gill (n 215) 11, notes that 'the absence of a centralised authority or treaty supervisory body in the traditional sense, means that such courts have particular responsibilities in compliance and development'.

[379] See *Revenko* (n 114). In addition to noting other UK cases that have made the same point (*Adan* (n 114); *Islam* (n 114); *Roma Rights* (n 114) para 18; *Hoxha* (n 114) para 22 (Keene LJ)), McAdam (n 2) 82 cites *Applicant A* (n 114) para 277 (Gummow); and *QAAH* (n 113) para 74 (Kirby J), citing *Thiel* (n 114) 356). For the German and Austrian case references see (n 115).

[380] See e.g. Goodwin-Gill and Lambert (n 116).

[381] *Adan* (n 113) 515–16.

[382] S152/2003 (n 190) para 109.

### 5.1.5 Good faith
In relation to '*good faith*', whilst this has rarely played a decisive role in interpreting provisions of the Refugee Convention, it has been seen as an important overarching principle.

### 5.1.6 Ordinary meaning
Although there is acceptance that an ordinary meaning is to be given to certain provisions (unmodified by the other VCLT rules), the case law and wider literature has increasingly seen the meaning of key terms to require recourse to other VCLT elements, in particular object and purpose. The shortcomings of applying an ordinary meaning approach to the Refugee Convention—and the consequent need for a unified approach—have become more and more apparent over time. One important reason for this shift has been fuller recognition of the indeterminacy and vagueness of many of its provisions.

### 5.1.7 Context
*Context i*n its core sense has proved an important element in terms of understanding the interrelationship between the refugee definition in Article 1A(2) and other provisions and the Preamble has proved of critical importance to the emergence of a object and purpose-driven human rights approach.

### 5.1.8 Object and purpose
Without doubt the *object and purpose* element has proved of major importance in both the case law and wider literature. There is a broad consensus that the Refugee Convention is an example of a treaty whose interpretation requires that a prominent place be given to the object and purpose element. Several facets of this element bear further comment.

First, consideration of the Convention's object and purpose has led a number of scholars to identify the Convention as a *'law-making'* treaty. However, this is not a feature highlighted either by UNHCR or by case law. In light of ongoing doctrinal debate about the propriety of reference to 'law-making treaties',[383] it cannot be said that there is universal agreement that the Refugee Convention is such a treaty, but it seems incontrovertible that the Convention falls under the general criteria identified by the ICJ in the *Genocide* case.[384] Its possession of these features, especially the fact of its universalism, lends support for the need for a broad approach to interpretation of terms.

Second, against the backdrop of the earlier discussions—in which it was identified that whether interpretation in temporal terms should adopt a static or dynamic approach depends on the nature of the particular treaty concerned—it can be said that there is widespread agreement that the Refugee Convention is a *'living instrument'* whose terms in the main[385] require an evolutive interpretation.

---

[383] See above section 1.4.1.
[384] *Application of the Convention on the Prevention and Punishment of the Crime of Genocide (Bosnia and Herzegovina v Serbia and Montenegro)*, Judgment [2007] ICJ Rep 43.
[385] The position of the English Court of Appeal in *El-Ali v Secretary of State for the Home Department* [2002] EWCA Civ 1103 (in which Philips LJ considered at para 58 that '[t]he ordinary meaning of the words "at present" [in Article 1D], when used in an agreement, whether concluded by individuals or by High Contracting Parties, is "at the time of the conclusion of this agreement"') was effectively overruled by the

124    INTERPRETATION

Third, regarding *purpose*, whilst the Refugee Convention has often been seen to have essentially two purposes—protection of human rights and burden-sharing—the case law and wider literature effectively treats the latter as no more than a limit on the former.

### 5.1.9 Subsequent agreement and practice

Aside from the example afforded by the 1967 Protocol, there has not been a common view as to what sources relevant to the Refugee Convention might constitute either '*subsequent agreement*' or '*subsequent practice*' within the meaning of Article 33(3)(a) and (b) respectively. There is, however, consensus that extrinsic sources such as UNHCR, judicial, and academic materials can (in addition to constituting supplementary means of interpretation under Article 32) provide at least evidence of state practice in the broad sense.

### 5.1.10 Relevant rules of international law

Here again, there remain sharp disagreements. Nevertheless, there is a growing recognition that it is permissible to treat '*relevant rules of international law*' as including cognate treaties. Once again, even amongst those who disagree about the ability of this element of Article 31(3) to strictly accommodate case law and UNHCR materials, there is increasing acceptance of the relevancy of such materials; the sticking point remains whether they constitute agreement between the parties.

### 5.1.11 Special meaning

Apart from the refugee definition itself, the Article 31(4) VLCT provision on '*special meaning*' has been seen to have limited application, although in a later chapter of this book it will be argued that there is at least an argument for considering that 'nationality' in one of the two senses deployed in Article 1A(2) has a special meaning.[386]

### 5.1.12 *Travaux* and other supplementary means of interpretation

In relation to the Refugee Convention, the Article 32 VCLT provisions regarding *the travaux and supplementary means of interpretation*, there is a clearly identifiable set of *travaux* materials. However, these are obviously of limited relevance since this provision defines them as 'supplementary' and the ILC regards them as of lesser 'interpretive value'. That said, since issues of intention are interwoven with other elements, the element of 'object and purpose' in particular, such materials can significantly impact on this element of Article 31(1) and reference to *travaux* materials is a well-established feature of case law and the wider literature, thus illustrating the close interconnection between different elements of the VCLT rules.

The difficulties in bringing UNHCR and judicial materials (and national guidance materials) within the strict terms of Article 31(3)(b)-(c) and the observable reality of

---

CJEU in Case C-364/11 *El Kott* [2012] ECLI:EU:C:2012:826. However, the respective analyses highlight that it cannot necessarily be assumed that every provision of the Refugee Convention requires evolutive interpretation.

[386] See p. 215 and Chapter 4, section 3.2.8.

the strong input made by refugee scholarship, lends added importance to the role of the provision in Article 32 for at least ensuring these sources are accepted as supplementary means of interpretation.[387]

Of particular import for the human rights approach is that the ILC has seen the authoritative opinions of human rights treaty-monitoring bodies to have interpretive value at least in the Article 32 context.[388]

## 5.2 Interpretive Value of the Most Commonly Cited Sources

Section 3 sought to tackle the 'paradox' that while refugee law now treats UNHCR, judicial, and academic materials as being of great importance as sources of interpretation, they are often not linked in any way with the VCLT rules or, if VCLT rules are mentioned, not always clearly linked to one element or the other. Given the ILC's clear understanding of the need for an integrated approach to the VCLT rules and its recognition of the interaction possible between Article 31(3)(b) and Article 32, it means it is now possible to say several things with confidence.

First, if nowhere else, UNHCR, judicial, and academic materials can fall within the ambit of Article 32 as supplementary means of interpretation. They have safe harbour there.

Second, as regards UNHCR materials, analysis confirms that they form one of the main pillars for interpreting the Refugee Convention and are to be accorded considerable weight. It is argued that there are cogent reasons for also according judicial materials very considerable weight as a source and regarding it as a second main pillar, subject to a number of important qualifications. It is noted that academic materials, particularly those that have adopted methods aimed at ensuring a transnational approach, are also playing a vital role.

Third, this chapter has highlighted that these three sources often intertwine with an effect that is mutually reinforcing overall. Thus, just as judges have generally accorded considerable weight to the UNHCR Handbook or Guidelines or both, UNHCR materials generally accord considerable weight to lead judicial decisions; UNHCR throughout its history has recognised jurisprudence to be a major way in which the meaning of the provision of the Refugee Convention is to be elucidated. Both these sources have often drawn on academic sources. Scholars in turn have sought to support their own interpretation by reference to UNHCR guidance and case law. A vivid example of this is the UK House of Lords decision in *K and Fornah* in which Lord Bingham sought support for the view that the family could constitute a particular social group from both the decisions of Australian, Canadian, and US cases and UNHCR's issuing of Guidelines on the topic. He also attached significant weight to academic sources, including the Michigan Guidelines.

Fourth, because focus throughout must be on treaty interpretation as a unity, consideration of such materials also requires assessment of the extent to which such materials might also constitute either subsequent practice or (much more commonly)

---

[387] Hathaway (2nd edn) (n 2) 167.
[388] ibid 167–70.

*evidence* of such and/or help reach conclusions on the proper application of other Article 31 considerations, such as ordinary meaning, context, and object and purpose, and relevant rules of international law.

The significant role of Article 32 as an anchor for UNHCR, judicial, and academic sources does, however, come with a caveat. This relates to the existence of multiple disagreements in the literature over the meaning of key terms of the refugee definition. It is possible to talk about state practice in the broad sense where such sources (at least UNHCR and judicial) align and reflect a consensus over their meaning. In this context, the Article 32 anchorage is of particular importance, at least where it helps to confirm or determine meaning within the terms of subparagraphs (a) and (b). However, where these sources are at odds with each other, then this anchorage offers much less help to the interpretive enterprise.

Finally, it remains important to recognise that identification by these main sources of widely accepted basic propositions regarding the refugee definition can stand without express reference to the VCLT rules. Although it remains highly desirable to be able to explain and demonstrate expressly the accordance of such propositions with VCLT rules, what ultimately matters is whether their contributions are consistent with VCLT rules.

## 5.3 Interpretive Value of EU Asylum Law

Section 4 sought to assess the interpretive value of EU asylum law, bearing in mind that its Qualification Directive contains a virtually identical definition of refugee and treats the Refugee Convention as the 'cornerstone' of international protection. Despite it being apparent that the CJEU adopts an idiosyncratic approach to interpretation (sometimes called 'meta-teleological'), it was concluded that its jurisprudence is broadly congruent with VCLT rules and has greatly strengthened international refugee law. Further, it was pointed out that there is nothing as such contrary to VCLT rules in a decision maker or court or tribunal referring to regional law sources, such as EU law. They can at least constitute evidence of 'subsequent practice' under 31(3)(b) and/or of 'state practice in the broad sense' under Article 32.[389] It was noted, however, that the restriction of the personal scope of its refugee definition to 'third-country nationals' may well amount to an 'illegitimate modification' of the Refugee Convention definition. Also noted was that it cannot be excluded that both the EU legislation and CJEU jurisprudence may sometimes diverge from the refugee definition's universal meaning.

## 5.4 Flexibility

One further feature highlighted in this chapter concerns the flexible character of VCLT rules. This can be seen as both a limitation and a virtue. The actual practice of

---

[389] See above p. 97.

treaty interpretation must always be to some degree an 'art' and treaty interpretation an 'inexact science'. There is no getting away from the fact that even when case law and the wider literature apply a principled approach to application of VCLT rules, this has not on its own resulted in any significant uniformity. Whilst McAdam's study confirms that courts and tribunals at least in the common law world increasingly apply a unified approach to treaty interpretation, she emphasises that it has not brought anything like certainty since 'it is possible to discern various, and possibly conflicting, objects and purposes from the Preamble to the 1951 Convention'.[390] It is observable how variable can be the way in which VCLT rules are seen to apply, especially when the text allows for a choice of meanings.

However, the fact that the VCLT rules are not prescriptive (save in one limited respect) does not mean they lack any structure. They do prescribe in several respects a specific type of approach, in particular the taking into account of seven core elements.[391] Further, they do constitute an 'essential infrastructure' comprising a set of generally applicable guidelines.[392] In this way they can at least narrow the field of possible meanings and solutions. As stated by Wood, '[a] principled interpretation of the definition's terms might yield a range of reasonable and justifiable views regarding its scope and meaning'.[393]

## 5.5 Link with Later Chapters

Now that the VCLT rules have been examined both generally and in specific relation to attempts so far to apply them to the Refugee Convention, the refugee definition in particular, we are in a position to commence from Chapter 4 onwards analysis of the various elements of the refugee definition applying a structured approach, varying slightly given the need to avoid repetition. Before then, however, it is necessary in Chapter 3 to consider several other preliminary matters, including the issue of approaches to the definition, an issue significantly influenced by VCLT considerations.

## 5.6 Basic and Suggested Propositions

In light of earlier remarks, it is not possible to identify any basic propositions relating to methods of interpretation. It is possible, however, to offer four suggested propositions:

1. Important contributions towards interpreting the meaning of key elements of the refugee definition have been made both by those who have expressly applied VCLT rules of interpretation and those who have not.

---

[390] *Fornah* (n 125).
[391] See above p. 77.
[392] Gardiner (n 3) 6. In its 2018 Commentary (n 7) the ILC noted at 22 that '[t]he interpreter needs to identify the relevance of different means of interpretation in a specific case and determine their interaction with the other means of interpretation by placing a proper emphasis on them in good faith, as required by the treaty rule to be applied.
[393] Wood (n 122) 304.

2. There is an increasing acceptance that in order to establish the true meaning of the key terms of Article 1A(2), the interpreter must actively apply VCLT rules.
3. A key feature of VCLT rules is that they confirm that treaty interpretation must strive to provide an autonomous, universally correct, meaning. Further, although not prescriptive as to outcome, they do constitute a set of generally applicable guidelines.
4. It follows that if any interpretive statements about key terms of the refugee definition are inconsistent with such rules, then they cannot be said to represent instances of the pursuit of a truly universal meaning.

# 3
# Approaches, Ordering, Interrelationships, Modalities

1. Main Approaches to the Refugee Definition — 130
   1.1 The 'Literalist Approach' — 130
   1.2 The 'Circumstantial Approach' — 131
   1.3 The 'US Subjective Approach' — 132
   1.4 The 'Case-by-Case' Approach — 134
   1.5 The Human Rights Approach — 134
2. The Human Rights Approach — 135
   2.1 History of the Human Rights Approach — 135
      2.1.1 Academic literature — 135
      2.1.2 UNHCR's role — 136
      2.1.3 Judicial endorsement — 138
      2.1.4 EU Qualification Directive — 138
      2.1.5 Reasons underlying the human rights approach — 139
      2.1.6 The human rights approach today — 140
   2.2 Variable Impact of the Human Rights Approach on the Refugee Definition — 141
   2.3 Different Types of Human Rights Approaches — 142
   2.4 Hierarchical Versus Non-Hierarchical — 142
      2.4.1 Hierarchical models — 142
      2.4.2 Non-hierarchical models — 143
3. Criticisms of the Human Rights Approach — 147
   3.1 VCLT Rules-Based Criticisms — 148
   3.2 Other Conceptual Criticisms — 149
   3.3 Empirical Criticisms — 150
4. Responses to Criticisms of the Human Rights Approach — 151
   4.1 VCLT-Based Criticisms — 151
      4.1.1 Ordinary meaning — 151
      4.1.2 Context — 152
      4.1.3 Object and purpose — 153
      4.1.4 Article 31(3) VCLT — 153
      4.1.5 Article 32 and the *travaux préparatoires* — 154
   4.2 Other Conceptual Criticisms — 155
      4.2.1 State accountability — 155
      4.2.2 Reliance on extraneous standards — 156
      4.2.3 Indeterminacy — 157
      4.2.4 Complexity — 158
      4.2.5 Conflict of rights — 159
      4.2.6 Lack of equivalency — 160
      4.2.7 Reliance on the surrogacy principle — 163
      4.2.8 UNHCR Handbook — 166
   4.3 Empirical Criticisms — 166
      4.3.1 Lack of entrenchment — 166
      4.3.2 Unclear contents and fragmentation — 168
      4.3.3 Failure to help with difficult issues — 169
      4.3.4 A set of criteria or merely illustrative standards? — 170
5. The Human Rights Approach: Advantages and Disadvantages of Specific Models — 170
   5.1 Advantages and Disadvantages of Hierarchical Models — 170
   5.2 Advantages and Disadvantages of the Non-Hierarchical Models — 172
      5.2.1 Foster's 2007 model — 173
      5.2.2 Hathaway and Foster's 2014 model — 174
      5.2.3 The New Zealand model in *DS (Iran)* — 175
      5.2.4 Evaluation — 175
   5.3 Other Models — 177
      5.3.1 Cantor's model — 177
      5.3.2 Scott's model — 178
6. The Human Rights Approach and International Law — 179
   6.1 The Primacy of International Law — 179
   6.2 The Refugee Convention as a Sub-Species of IHRL? — 180
7. How Do Different Elements of the Refugee Definition Fit Together? — 181
   7.1 The Nature of the Problem — 181
      7.1.1 The text — 181
      7.1.2 Ordering — 182

*The Refugee Definition in International Law.* Hugo Storey, Oxford University Press. © Hugo Storey 2023.
DOI: 10.1093/oso/9780198842644.003.0003

| | | | |
|---|---|---|---|
| 7.1.3 Interrelationship between the different elements | 183 | 7.4 The Principal Debates Revisited | 193 |
| 7.2 The Different Debates | 184 | 8. Modalities of the Refugee Definition | 195 |
| 7.2.1 Is this intermediary level of analysis necessary? | 185 | 8.1 Qualification Directive | 195 |
| 7.2.2 Arguments for and against the value or necessity of this type of inquiry | 187 | 8.2 Scope of Application *Ratione Personae, Ratione Materiae, Ratione Temporis* | 196 |
| 7.3 Proposed Solution | 191 | 9. An Underlying Principle? | 196 |
| 7.3.1 Underlying objectives | 191 | 10. Conclusions | 197 |
| 7.3.2 A high threshold | 192 | 10.1 Key Propositions | 198 |

# 1 Main Approaches to the Refugee Definition

Our study of the refugee definition has now reached its foreshores. But before proceeding to analyse the key elements of the refugee definition individually, there are several 'framework' matters that need attention first, since they impact on how such analysis should be undertaken. In light of the previous chapter's analysis of the Vienna Convention on the Law of Treaties (VCLT)[1] rules, we need to examine and evaluate the approaches that have been taken to the refugee definition, which include the human rights approach.

Prior to identification of a human rights approach, the refugee law literature rarely talked expressly about 'approaches'. Nevertheless, four other main approaches have been identified.[2]

## 1.1 The 'Literalist Approach'

The existence of a 'literalist approach' has already been noted when analysing the application of VCLT rules to the refugee definition. As its name denotes, this approach insists on basing interpretation of key terms, especially persecution, on ordinary meaning and dictionary definitions.[3] Such an approach was a prominent feature in the jurisprudence of the 1990s, especially in common law countries where, for example, persecution was interpreted by reference to Oxford English Dictionary definitions such as 'to pursue with malignity or injurious action'.[4] The superficial attractions of

---

[1] Vienna Convention on the Law of Treaties (VCLT) (adopted 23 May 1969, entered into force 27 January 1980) 1155 UNTS 331.

[2] The approaches outlined here are not exhaustive of alternatives that have been proposed. For example, in 1985 Jack Garvey argued that approaches based on humanitarian or human rights considerations were bound to fail and proposed instead a theory based on the inter-state principles of traditional international law in 1985: see Jack I Garvey, 'Toward a Reformulation of International Refugee Law' (1985) 26(2) Harv Intl LJ 483. The summary given here of other approaches broadly follows that given in James C Hathaway and Michelle Foster, *The Law of Refugee Status* (2nd edn, CUP 2014) 186–208 (TLRS2).

[3] James C Hathaway, *The Rights of Refugees under International Law* (CUP 2005) 49; James C Hathaway, *The Rights of Refugees under International Law* (2nd edn, CUP 2021); Hathaway and Foster (n 2) 190–93.

[4] As cited by Nolan J in *R v IAT, ex parte Jonah* [1985] Imm AR 7.

such an approach are obvious. If the meaning of the definition is seen to reside wholly or primarily in its literal text, the task of the decision maker is relatively simple, namely to establish the natural and ordinary meaning of the words set out in Article 1A(2).[5] However, as discussed in the previous chapter, this approach, when applied to the refugee definition, founders on the rock that there is virtually no clear or unambiguous ordinary meaning derivable from its text. In any event, proper application of VCLT rules requires considering 'ordinary meaning' alongside other elements such as context and object and purpose.[6] A further drawback from an international perspective is that dictionary definitions can vary from one national dictionary to another and competing definitions can be found, even within the same language.[7] They are ill-suited to interpreting a public international law treaty such as the Refugee Convention.[8]

## 1.2 The 'Circumstantial Approach'

Perhaps the most familiar approach is (what this author has elsewhere called)[9] the 'circumstantial approach'. It is most visible in the treatment given in paragraphs 51–53 of the UNHCR 1979 Handbook to the issue of the meaning of persecution. This approach cautions against developing general rules because what is meant by the definition's key terms, especially persecution, is said to depend on the circumstances of any particular case.[10] As the Handbook exemplifies, this approach does not reject an international law perspective; indeed it seeks to draw on international law standards wherever they are seen as appropriate to apply. However, it is insistent that application of such standards can only take matters so far, because of variability of the subject-matter. It treats such standards as indicative or illustrative rather than determinative. As such, it has been seen by Cantor to 'remain ... present' as a 'long-standing alternative' to the human rights approach and to be one that 'continues to be represented in ... UNHCR doctrine and in the scholarship'.[11]

---

[5] Hathaway (n 3); Hathaway and Foster (n 2) 190–93.
[6] As noted by Hathaway and Foster (n 2) 191. Rejection of a 'literalist approach' does not mean, however, that an ordinary meaning reading of a particular term might not sometimes be the right one.
[7] See e.g. Kirby J's statement in *Chen Shi Hai v MIMA* [2000] 201 CLR 293, para 108 that he was 'inclined to see more clearly than before the dangers in the use of the dictionary definitions of the word "persecuted" in the Convention definition'. See further Chapter 6, section 1.3.
[8] See Andreas Zimmermann and Claudia Mahler, 'Article 1A, para 2' in Andreas Zimmermann (ed), *The 1951 Convention Relating to the Status of Refugees and Its 1967 Protocol: A Commentary* (OUP 2011) 346. See also *Refugee Appeal No 71427/99* [2000] NZRSAA, in which Rodger Haines QC said such an approach lent itself to 'an unseemly ransacking of dictionaries for the *mot juste* appropriate to the case in hand', cited in Michelle Foster, *International Refugee Law and Socio-Economic Rights: Refuge from Deprivation* (CUP 2007) 48.
[9] Hugo Storey, 'Persecution: Towards a Working Definition' in Vincent Chetail and Céline Bauloz (eds), *Research Handbook on Migration and International Law* (Edward Elgar 2014) 465–69.
[10] UNHCR, Handbook on Procedures and Criteria for Determining Refugee Status and Guidelines on International Protection under the 1951 Convention and the 1967 Protocol Relating to the Status of Refugees (Geneva, 1979, reissued in 2019) para 52 (UNHCR Handbook or Handbook): '[d]ue to variations in the psychological make-up of individuals and in the circumstances of each case, interpretations of what amounts to persecution are bound to vary'.
[11] David Cantor, 'Defining Refugees: Persecution, Surrogacy and the Human Rights Paradigm' in Bruce Burson and David Cantor (eds), *Human Rights and the Refugee Definition* (Brill Nijhoff 2016) 393. He cites

Standing in the way of this approach are two main difficulties both of which were identified earlier in Chapter 1. First, an approach to definition that treats meaning as entirely dependent on circumstances leaves unanswered what are the criteria underlying it. In particular, if they are not always international law criteria, what are they and from whence do they come? Certainly, if the circumstantial approach is largely filled out by reference to international law standards, this shortcoming has limited impact, but it still leaves some definitional vacuum regarding what is left that is not to be defined by such criteria. Second, the premise on which this approach proceeds—that it is inherently wrong to seek to pin down a definition of refugee—is a false one, since it only stands as an objection to 'absolutist' or 'fixed list' approaches to definition.[12]

## 1.3 The 'US Subjective Approach'

A third approach is that which Hathaway and Foster have termed the 'subjective approach'. By this label they seek to capture the approach adopted in the US case law although they note that it has been instanced occasionally in Australian, UK, Austrian, and German case law.[13] Its essence is the basing of assessment of such matters as what harms are persecutory 'on a given decision-maker's personal assessment [of the severity of harms feared]'.[14] Whilst largely articulated in the context of considering the persecution element of the definition, this approach appears to have three main aspects. One is that since the drafters of the Refugee Convention chose to stipulate a definition of refugee in Article 1A(2), it cannot and should not be the subject of any further definitional endeavour. Thus, for the Seventh Circuit in 1991 in *Balazoski*,[15] citing the US Supreme Court decision in *I.N.S. v Cardoza-Fonseca*,[16] it was germane that the drafters of the 1951 Convention chose not to provide any further definition. A second aspect is that the terms of the refugee definition are seen as particularly ill-suited to further definition because of the changing nature of the phenomena they seek to address. Thus, the term persecution has been seen to have an 'ambiguous', 'elusive', and 'protean' character.[17] A third aspect is to see the meaning of key elements comprising the definition (particularly persecution) as best sought on a 'case-by-case' basis.

As regards the first aspect, undoubtedly correct though it is to view the 'refugee definition' as already given in Article 1A(2), such a stance gets refugee law nowhere in

---

Alice Edwards, 'Age and Gender Dimensions in International Refugee Law' in Erika Feller, Volker Türk, and Frances Nicholson (eds), *Refugee Protection in International Law: UNHCR's Global Consultations on International Protection* (CUP 2003) 50.

[12] Foster (n 8) 81–82; Storey (n 9) 461. See Chapter 1, section 5.4.
[13] Hathaway and Foster (n 2) 186–87.
[14] ibid 187.
[15] *Balazoski v INS* [1991] 932 F.2d 638, paras 641–42; see also *Hani Kazemzadeh v A-G (US)* [2009] 577 F.3d 1341, para 1357; *Mei Fun Wong v Holder* [2011] 633 F.3d 64.
[16] *INS v Cardoza-Fonseca* [1987] 480 US 421, paras 436–40.
[17] *Pathmakanthan v Holder* [2010] 612 F.3d 618, para 622; *Bocova v Gonzalez* [2005] 412 F.3d 257, para 263; *Cai Luan Chen v Ashcroft* [2004] 381 F.3d 221; *Shi Liang Lin v US Department of Justice* [2007] 494 F.3d 296; *Kazemzadeh v A-G (US)* [2009] 577 F.3d 1341; *Rios-Zamora v Sessions* [2018] 751 F.app 784.

terms of trying to elucidate the meaning of each of its key terms. Even the US Supreme Court has commented that a more comprehensive definition would be beneficial.[18] As regards the other two aspects, they certainly have a coherent rationale. If the phenomenon being addressed is protean, then seeking to elicit meaning on a 'case-by-case' basis does offer a concrete way of determining meaning, by enumerating specific features or criteria as one goes along on the basis of practical experience arising out of application. Such an approach is also in line with that sometimes taken to legal definitions more generally.[19] However, as noted above, the fact that key terms address a phenomenon that is always changing only operates against an absolutist notion of definition as a 'fixed list'. Further, as with the 'circumstantial approach', this approach fails to identify any clear criteria that underpin the gradual accretion of propositions attaching to it. As noted by Scott Rempell in 2013 about US case law:

> When the courts have attempted to provide a guiding framework for assessing persecution, the result has been an amalgamation of vague principles and general statements that are neither consistent nor entirely accurate. At times, certain courts have described the threshold for persecution as merely offensive conduct, while other courts require 'extreme' conduct. Some adjudicators believe one instance of harm is sufficient to establish persecution, while others require systematic abuse. The inconsistencies go on, and so does the confusion.[20]

In the same year, Deborah Anker's leading US textbook on asylum also portrayed the US jurisprudence on persecution as 'ad hoc and non-analytical'.[21] More recently, Anker has taken a more nuanced view, but she still perceives the US approach to exhibit 'general adherence to an "ad-hoc" approach'.[22] The underlying problem with such an approach is that when one asks what is the basis for adding a particular proposition to the case-by-case compilation, the answer is really no more than that it has been identified in the course of case law and found to be helpful or illuminating by other decision makers (and that it may sometimes become codified in national law or practices). In addition (and linked to this), because it is not governed by any clear criteria, it depends upon the subjective opinions of the judges concerned as to what content is given to it. This may sometimes yield a significant advance (e.g. when US case law began to recognise rape as a form of persecution), but it may sometimes represent a significant drawback (e.g. in the continued insistence at least by some US courts on the need to show persecutory intent) and is, in any event, in Anker's words 'non-analytical' in character. Despite Anker and Vittor seeming to suggest that US case law

---

[18] *Negusie v Holder* [2009] 555 US 511, para 524; see also *Marquez v INS* [1997] 105 F.3d 374, para 379, describing the 'largely ad hoc' approach to assessing persecution as 'unfortunate'.
[19] See Chapter 1, n 193.
[20] Scott Rempell, 'Defining Persecution' (2013) 2013(1) Utah Law Rev 283, 284.
[21] Deborah Anker, *Law of Asylum in the United States* (Thomson Reuters 2022) ch 4.4. On persecutory intent see Chapter 6, section 3.9.
[22] Deborah Anker and Josh Vittor, 'International Human Rights and US Refugee Law' in Burson and Cantor (n 11) 136.

is now integrating human rights norms more,[23] it is not clear how this alone can rectify the underlying analytical void.

## 1.4 The 'Case-by-Case' Approach

Brief mention should also be made of what was referred to in some civil law countries prior to the coming into force of the European Union's Qualification Directive (QD),[24] as the 'case-by-case' approach. Likewise indicative in character, this approach eschewed any attempt at further definition of key terms such as persecution, appearing to consider that gradually, through accumulation of cases, some definitional features can emerge.[25]

Mention of this approach can be brief because within the EU countries it has been overtaken since 2006 by the codification of several elements of the refugee definition in the QD and its recast.[26] In any event, adjudged on its own terms, it is almost indistinguishable from the US subjective approach and carries the same fundamental drawback in lacking any clear underlying criteria and thus rendering itself open to the criticism that it leaves decision makers having to essentially substitute their own personal assessment of whether a particular element of the definition is met.

## 1.5 The Human Rights Approach

At its simplest, the human rights approach is one according to which international human rights law (IHRL) is highly relevant for the interpretation of the refugee definition. Whilst in general understanding it is an approach that can take many different forms (ranging from ones in which it is seen as fundamental that the main elements of the refugee definition are construed by reference to underlying human rights standards through to ones that treat such standards as illustrative or non-exhaustive), its core rationale, so far as concerns approaches to the refugee definition, is that the meaning of key terms of the definition must be significantly informed by human rights standards.

Considering the first four approaches addressed above, it is readily apparent that none can serve as a valid approach to the refugee definition per se. Each has contributed—and still contributes—important insights regarding the definition, but none can demonstrate either sufficient accord with VCLT rules or a coherent approach to definition. Apart from the 'circumstantial' approach, none has ever gained

---

[23] ibid 110, 136–37.
[24] See Council Directive 2004/83/EC of 29 April 2004 on minimum standards for the qualification and status of third country nationals or stateless persons as refugees or as persons who otherwise need international protection and the content of the protection granted [2004] OJ L 304/12, now Directive 2011/95/EU of the European Parliament and of the Council of 13 December 2011 on standards for the qualification of third-country nationals or stateless persons as beneficiaries of international protection, for a uniform status for refugees or for persons eligible for subsidiary protection, and for the content of the protection granted (recast) [2011] OJ L 337/9 (QD (recast)).
[25] See e.g. report on France in Jean-Yves Carlier et al, *Who is a Refugee? A Comparative Case Law Study* (Brill 1997) 378.
[26] See (n 24).

significant international acceptance. And in the case of the 'circumstantial' approach, even if for a while it could be said to reflect an established approach, no significant discourse has developed seeking to consolidate the contents of such an approach. Even if it could be said to continue to underlie post-2003 UNHCR Guidelines,[27] it is clear that increasingly the latter, in step with UNHCR practice more generally, now has a stronger human rights orientation.

That leaves the human rights approach, which, over the past two decades, has become the dominant approach. Thus, if any approach is to succeed in establishing itself as the proper approach, it must either be the human rights approach or some other approach altogether. It is thus essential to examine the human rights approach in considerably more detail, considering first what it comprises, then what are the main criticisms that have been directed against it, and finally whether such criticisms can be overcome or whether we need to look elsewhere for an approach that would better serve the task of interpreting the refugee definition.

## 2 The Human Rights Approach

### 2.1 History of the Human Rights Approach

#### 2.1.1 Academic literature

The emergence of a human rights approach to the refugee definition is most commonly linked with the publication in 1991 of James Hathaway's *The Law of Refugee Status*,[28] in which he proposed interpretation of key refugee law concepts by reference to IHRL. However, the lineaments of such an approach can be traced further back. In a 1953 publication, *The Refugee in the Post-War World*, Jacques Vernant proposed that 'persecution' should be equated with 'severe sanctions and measures of an arbitrary nature, incompatible with the principles set forth in the Universal Declaration of Human Rights'.[29] In 1960, Paul Weis remarked on the importance of human rights to the definition of persecution.[30] In his major work on *The Status of Refugees in International Law* published in 1966, Grahl-Madsen noted the role of international human rights law as an aid to interpretation of the refugee definition.[31] Recourse to human rights in interpreting at least some elements of the refugee definition gained increasing support from scholars.[32] These included Goodwin-Gill in 1983,[33] Lapenna

---

[27] On the UNHCR Guidelines on International Protection, see Chapters 1, section 6.1.4 and 2, section 3.2.
[28] James C Hathaway, *The Law of Refugee Status* (Butterworths Limited 1991).
[29] Jacques Vernant, *The Refugee in the Post-War World* (Yale University Press 1953) 8.
[30] Paul Weis, 'The Concept of Refugee in International Law' (1960) 87(1) Journal du Droit International 928, 971.
[31] Atle Grahl-Madsen, *The Status of Refugees in International Law*. Volume 1: *Refugee Character* (Sijthoff 1966) 193. Intriguingly, in deciding not to treat the Universal Declaration of Human Rights (UDHR) as a reference point, he commented on the fact that it was non-binding and that its terms needed interpretation: see also ibid 194–95.
[32] See e.g. Hathaway (n 28) 104, who chronicles that in the 1980s there were a number of commentators noting the significant link between the refugee definition and IHRL.
[33] Guy S Goodwin-Gill, *The Refugee in International Law* (1st edn, OUP 1983) 38–46.

in 1984,[34] Shacknove in 1985,[35] Melander in 1987,[36] Coles in 1988,[37] Aleinikoff in 1991.[38] The supporting role of leading human rights jurists and scholars such as Louis Henkin between the 1960s and 1980s should not be underestimated.[39]

In the 1997 comparative case law study, *Who Is a Refugee?*,[40] Carlier proposed a 'Theory of Three Scales' for interpreting the 'well-founded fear of being persecuted' clause of the refugee definition. He identified the second level of risk as being concerned with the issue of the point at which persecution arises. He related this to 'the level of violation of human rights'[41] and observed:

> [ ... ] The more fundamental the right in question ... the less quantitively and qualitatively severe the treatment need be. The lower the priority attributed to the violated freedom (economic, social or cultural rights), the more quantitively and qualitatively severe the treatment must be.[42]

However, to concentrate solely on the pioneering work of academics would be misplaced. Other important milestones in the gradual emergence of the human rights approach to its current position as a dominant 'paradigm' have been UNHCR's growing support for it; its adoption by leading courts and tribunals around the world, both those in the common law world (Canada, the UK, Australia, and New Zealand especially); and its adoption by EU member states, following the coming into force of the QD.

### 2.1.2 UNHCR's role

There have been several strands to UNHCR's growing support for a human rights approach. Whilst in key respects the Handbook's text did not commit to a core human rights approach (e.g. in its 'circumstantial approach' to treatment of the definition of persecution),[43] there were certain passages which provided strong support for it.[44] For example, at paragraphs 68–73 the Handbook urged that the Refugee Convention's reasons of 'race' and 'religion' be understood in light of human rights law.

Another main strand has been statements of policy made in various UNHCR or UNHCR-related publications, addresses, and other materials. In 1981, in its Thirty

---

[34] Enrico Lapenna, 'Le réfugié et l'émigrant dans le cadre des droits et libertés fondamentaux' (1984) 22 AWR Bulletin 50.
[35] Andrew Shacknove, 'Who Is a Refugee?' (1985) 95 Ethics 274, 276–77.
[36] Göran Melander, *The Two Refugee Definitions* (University of Lund 1987).
[37] Gervase Coles, 'The Human Rights Approach to the Solution of the Refugee Problem: A Theoretical and Practical Enquiry' in Alan E Nash (ed), *Human Rights and the Protection of Refugees under International Law* (Institute for Research on Public Policy 1988) 196.
[38] Thomas A Aleinikoff, 'The Meaning of Persecution in United States Asylum Law' (1991) 3(1) IJRL 5.
[39] Louis Henkin, 'Refugees and Their Human Rights' (1994) 18 Fordham International Law Journal 1079, 1081.
[40] Carlier et al (n 25) 695–710; see also Jean-Yves Carlier, 'The Geneva Refugee Convention Definition and the "Theory of the Three Scales"' in Frances Nicholson and Patrick Twomey (eds), *Refugee Rights and Realities: Evolving International Concepts and Regimes* (CUP 1999) 41–45.
[41] Carlier et al (n 25) 696.
[42] ibid 704–05.
[43] See above section 1.2.
[44] Grahl-Madsen (n 31) 195.

second Session, the Executive Committee (ExCom) again stressed the importance of human rights in regard to asylum-seekers and characterised them as integral to UNHCR's work.[45] In 1998, ExCom adopted a Conclusion positioning the Refugee Convention as deriving directly from Article 14 of the Universal Declaration of Human Rights (UDHR). It observed that 'the refugee experience, in all its stages, is closely linked to the degree of respect by States for human rights and fundamental freedoms and the related refugee protection principles'.[46] In its 2001 publication on 'Interpreting Article 1 of the 1951 Convention',[47] UNHCR itself explicitly identified the Refugee Convention as a human rights instrument. It also emphasised that '[t]he human rights base of the Convention roots it quite directly in the broader framework of human rights instruments of which it is an integral part, albeit with a very particular focus'.[48] It stated that 'the strong human rights language' contained in the Preamble conveyed that 'the aim of the drafters [was] to incorporate human rights values in the identification and treatment of refugees, thereby providing helpful guidance for the interpretation in harmony with the Vienna Convention, of the provisions of the 1951 Convention'.[49] Also to be borne in mind in this context is that the *amicus curiae* interventions UNHCR has made in domestic and regional court proceedings have regularly encouraged national decision makers to make greater use of human rights norms.[50] Nevertheless, it must not be forgotten that in none of these materials is there specific endorsement of what might be called a 'core' human rights approach, namely one that purports to provide a self-contained explanatory framework based on human rights.

A further main strand in UNHCR's gradual shift towards a more human rights-oriented approach has been the approach taken in its Guidelines on International Protection. This was most clearly expressed first in the Guidelines on Religion-Based Claims issued in April 2004.[51] The Guidelines on Child Asylum Claims issued in 2009 also adopted a markedly human rights approach.[52] Once again, though, the extent of UNHCR's endorsement of such an approach in these Guidelines must not be overstated. In each instance, for example, they maintain the same position regarding the

---

[45] ExCom, Conclusion on International Protection No 22 (XXXII) (1981) UN Doc A/36/12/Add.121. However, as noted in Chapter 1, section 6.1.2, ExCom is not an organ of UNHCR but of the UN.
[46] Excom, Conclusion on International Protection No 85 (XLIX) (1998) UN Doc A/53/12/Add.1 para (g).
[47] UNHCR, The International Protection of Refugees: Interpreting Article 1 of the 1951 Convention Relating to the Status of Refugees (2001) UN Doc A/AC.96/951. One precursor was UNHCR, UNHCR and Human Rights, a policy paper resulting from deliberations in the Policy Committee on the basis of a paper prepared by the Division of International Protection (1997) UN Doc AHC/97/325. See also 1998 Note on International Protection (50th anniversary of UDHR <https://www.refworld.org/docid/3ae68d3d24.html> accessed 6 May 2023); Erika Feller, 'International Refugee Protection 50 years on: The Protection Challenges of the Past, Present and Future' (2001) 83(843) International Review of the Red Cross 581, 582: '[t]he refugee protection regime ... has its origins in general principles of human rights.'
[48] UNHCR, Interpreting Article 1 of the 1951 Convention (n 47) 2.
[49] ibid.
[50] Foster (n 8) 32 notes the UNHCR submission to the UKIAT in *Gashi and Nikshiqi* [1997] INLR 96, 104–05.
[51] UNHCR, Guidelines on International Protection (Guidelines) No 6: Religion-Based Refugee Claims under Article 1A(2) of the 1951 Convention and/or the 1967 Protocol relating to the Status of Refugees (2004) UN Doc HCR/GIP/04/06. See especially paras 2, 11, 15, and 20.
[52] UNHCR, Guidelines No 8: Child Asylum Claims under Articles 1(A)2 and 1(F) of the 1951 Convention and/or 1967 Protocol relating to the Status of Refugees (2009) UN Doc HCR/GIP/09/08. See especially paras 4, 5, 13, and 34.

concept of persecution—treating serious human rights violations as just one type of act that can constitute persecution.

It is also noteworthy that as a body responsible for refugee status determination in many countries, UNHCR's own training manuals have increasingly reflected the organisation's policy statements by recommending a human rights approach.[53]

### 2.1.3 Judicial endorsement

A further main milestone in the emergence of the human rights approach has been its adoption to a greater or lesser extent by leading courts and tribunals. Until the coming into force of the QD in October 2006, this emanated predominantly from the Anglo-Saxon case law, its start-point being most often ascribed to the decision of the Canadian Supreme Court in *Canada (A-G) v Ward* in 1993. Reflecting appreciation of this case law's global significance, in 1998 at its third world conference in Ottawa, the International Association of Refugee Law Judges (IARLJ)[54] passed a resolution advocating a human rights approach.[55]

### 2.1.4 EU Qualification Directive

A final major milestone in the rise to ascendancy of the human rights approach has been its legislative adoption in EU asylum law. Although only applicable within twenty seven member states,[56] the QD and its recast contain a definition of acts of persecution in Article 9(1) that enjoins a human rights approach.[57] Through the jurisprudence of the Court of Justice of the European Union (CJEU), the EU law position has also become extremely influential in neighbouring European countries and, in varying degrees, more widely.[58]

---

[53] For further references, see Brian Gorlick, 'Human Rights and Refugees: Enhancing Protection through International Human Rights Law' (2000) 69(2) Nordic Journal of International Law 117, 125–27. See also Bryan Deschamp and Rebecca Dowd, 'Review of the Use of UNHCR Executive Committee Conclusions on International Protection', April 2008 PDES/2008/03, paras 67–69 (on training modules).

[54] Now renamed the International Association of Refugee and Migration Judges (IARMJ).

[55] The resolution as amended and passed stated: 'The Human Rights Nexus Working Party recommends that the International Association of Refugee Law Judges encourages that the term persecution be interpreted by reference to accepted international human rights instruments.' See James C Simeon, '"Human Rights Nexus" Working Party: Rapporteur's Report' in IARLJ, *The Changing Nature of Persecution* (Institute of Public Law University of Bern 2000) 305. Subsequent IARLJ/IARMJ world conferences have frequently featured papers dealing with the relevance of human rights, see e.g. Kate Jastram, Anne Mactavish, and Penelope Mathew, 'Violations of Socio-Economic Rights as a Form of Persecution and as an Element of Internal Protection' (2009) IARLJ Human Rights Nexus Working Party Paper.

[56] Although no longer a member state, the UK continued under transitional arrangements to apply EU law relating to the refugee definition until June 2022. See now Nationality and Borders Act 2022, ss 30–38.

[57] Council Directive 2004/83/EC of 29 April 2004 on minimum standards for the qualification and status of third-country nationals or stateless persons as refugees or as persons who otherwise need international protection and the content of the protection granted [2004] OJ L 304/12. See now Directive 2011/95/EU of the European Parliament and of the Council of 13 December 2011 on standards for the qualification of third-country nationals or stateless persons as beneficiaries of international protection, for a uniform status for refugees or for persons eligible for subsidiary protection, and for the content of the protection granted (recast) [2011] OJ L 337/9 (QD (recast)). See Chapter 6, section 1.1.2.

[58] See Hélène Lambert, Jane McAdam, and Maryellen Fullerton (eds), *The Global Reach of European Refugee Law* (CUP 2013) 258–66.

### 2.1.5 Reasons underlying the human rights approach

It is salient to consider why courts and tribunals in particular should have been receptive to such ideas from the 1990s onwards. At least five reasons have played a part. Burson[59] has usefully identified four of them.

Within the body of international law, IHRL is considered to stand out because it offers a way of anchoring refugee status determination (RSD) in what states themselves have agreed in public international treaties are the appropriate standards for determining the scope of the duty of protection each state owes to it citizens. This also militates against a lapse into a purely utilitarian, rationalistic approach (the 'legitimacy justification').

Second, a HR approach can also be viewed as ensuring that decision makers make judgements overtly based on international law norms (the 'transparency justification').

Arguably, applying human rights norms to refugee assessment ensures the approach is an evolutive one that respects the status of the Refuge Convention as a 'living instrument' in conformity with VCLT rules. This ensures that the Refugee Convention continues to have practical application to the main refugee problems of the day (the 'dynamism justification').[60]

A human rights approach has also been seen to provide an antidote to subjectivity and to help ensure that decision makers base their decisions on objective standards, which promotes consistency by reference to a structured, disciplined framework (the 'consistency justification'). Commenting on this perspective, Chetail has observed that IHLR provides a universal and uniform set of standards—and thereby provides 'a particularly persuasive device for harmonizing the unilateral and frequently diverging interpretations of state parties'.[61] As against the 'subjectivity inherent in many of the key notions of the refugee definition', he views the human rights standards as offering 'a more predictable and objective normative framework for determining who is a refugee'.[62]

Casting the argument in terms of a 'consistency justification' is perhaps too narrow, since it is clear that commentators also regard it as important that human rights offer a value-system based on international law that recognises asylum-seekers as rights-bearers and as such protects refugee law decision-making against reduction to a pure utilitarian or instrumentalist or rationalistic calculus.[63] It may be useful therefore to see this aspect as a separate 'value-system justification'.

---

[59] See Bruce Burson, 'Give Way to the Right: The Evolving Use of Human Rights in New Zealand Refugee Status Determination' in Burson and Cantor (n 11) 29–31; see also Foster (n 8) 36–86.

[60] Burson (n 59) 30–31.

[61] Vincent Chetail, 'Are Refugee Rights Human Rights? An Unorthodox Questioning of the Relations Between Refugee Law and Human Rights Law' in Ruth Rubio-Marín (ed), *Human Rights and Immigration* (OUP 2014) 26.

[62] ibid. See also Vincent Chetail, 'Moving Towards an Integrated Approach of Refugee Law and Human Rights Law' in Cathryn Costello, Michelle Foster, and Jane McAdam (eds), *Oxford Handbook of International Refugee Law* (OUP 2021) 207.

[63] See e.g. Colin J Harvey, 'Taking Human Rights Seriously in the Asylum Context' in Frances Nicholson and Patrick Twomey (eds), *Current Issues of UK Asylum Law and Policy* (Routledge 1998) 215.

Seen against this backdrop, it was hardly surprising that refugee decision makers, especially members of courts and tribunals, should turn to IHRL. Within the framework of international law, IHRL treaties were the most obvious treaty counterparts also having a protective purpose and establishing individuals as rights holders to whom states owed certain obligations. Seen in this light, Hathaway's 1991 treatise, which offered the first developed human rights paradigm, expressed ideas whose time had come and ideas which judiciaries in countries suddenly faced with deciding significant numbers of asylum claims, readily embraced.

At the same time, it is also important not to overstate the extent of judicial endorsement of a human rights approach, certainly outside the context of common law countries and the European Union.[64]

### 2.1.6 The human rights approach today

It is widely acknowledged that today the human rights paradigm represents the dominant approach and occupies centre stage in present international refugee law (IRL). Illustrative of its growing rise, Steinbock wrote in 1997 that: '[i]ndeed, by providing tangible redress from certain basic human rights violations, the Refugee Convention and 1967 Protocol are, in actual effect, two of the foremost international human rights instruments'.[65] In 2002, Deborah Anker described the recognition of the Convention's 'international human rights roots' as refugee law's 'coming of age'.[66] In 2007, Michelle Foster observed that:

> One of the most significant developments in refugee law jurisprudence in recent years has been the well-documented move towards an understanding of 'being persecuted', as well as other elements of the definition, that is informed and understood in the context of international human rights standards.[67]

Summarising the contemporary picture, Chetail (although disagreeing that the Refugee Convention is a human rights treaty) wrote in 2014 that:

> In sum, human rights law has become the ultimate benchmark for determining who is a refugee. The authoritative intrusion of human rights has proved to be instrumental in infusing a common and dynamic understanding of the refugee definition that is more consonant with and loyal to the evaluation of international law. It thus prevents the [Refugee] Convention from becoming a mere legal anachronism by adapting it to the changing realities of forced migration.[68]

---

[64] See below section 4.3.
[65] Daniel J Steinbock, 'Interpreting the Refugee Definition' (1998) 45(3) UCLA Law Review 733, 736.
[66] Deborah Anker, 'Refugee Law, Gender and the Human Rights Paradigm' (2002) 15 Harv Hum Rts LJ 133, 135–36.
[67] Foster (n 8) 27, referring to a survey conducted by Jean-Yves Carlier and Dirk Vanheule and others of thirteen European states, Canada, and the USA charting references to human rights. See Jean-Yves Carlier and Dirk Vanheule (eds), *Europe and Refugees: A Challenge?* (Kluwer Law International 1997).
[68] Chetail (n 61) 19–72, 28; see also Chetail (n 62) 207.

## 2.2 Variable Impact of the Human Rights Approach on the Refugee Definition

Reference to a human rights approach to the refugee definition needs some qualification. As already noted, some proponents of a human rights approach can be identified in the literature, even though they do not adopt a 'core' human rights approach. Further, it is apparent that not all those who propound (or are seen to propound) such an approach necessarily mean to insist that IHRL norms should be applied with uniform intensity to each element of the refugee definition. The preponderant focus has been on a human rights inquiry into the 'being persecuted' and Convention reasons elements of the definition. Yet even in relation to these two elements, there is not full permeation. A human rights approach is not always applied to the issue of internal relocation/protection as an aspect of the 'being persecuted'/protection element.[69] Two leading proponents of a human rights approach, Hathaway and Foster, have rejected reliance on human rights concepts of due diligence.[70] In the literature on the Refugee Convention reason of 'particular social group', there remain strong differences over whether a human rights-driven 'protected characteristics' approach or a more sociological 'social perception' approach is the correct one, with the two sometimes being applied cumulatively.[71]

The issue of how and where to draw the line between those who can and cannot properly be said to pursue a human rights approach is not an easy one to resolve. So far as concerns lack of (uniform) application to different elements of the definition, this feature should not be seen as a shortcoming per se, since a contingent approach to how IHRL norms apply to each element of the refugee definition is a necessary consequence of a proper application of VCLT norms. These require each specific element of the definition to be analysed according to ordinary meaning, context, object, and purpose etc. As Chapter 2 notes, such an inquiry does not yield identical results. Later chapters on each individual element argue that adoption of a full or mainly IHRL framework is not appropriate for some elements (see e.g. Chapter 4 on Nationality and Statelessness) or is simply of very secondary relevance (see e.g. Chapter 5 on 'Outside the Country ...', which deals with 'being outside the country of nationality and country of former habitual residence'). It will also be apparent that in terms of reach or permeation, the human rights approach can be seen over time to be making further inroads, for example, having more of a role (although it will be argued still a secondary one) in the context of the nationality and statelessness provisions of the refugee definition. Nor must it be forgotten that IHRL is an evolving system and that may lead to further developments over time.

Be that as it may, recognition that the human rights approach should not be expected to have uniform application to each and every element of the refugee definition does not mean losing sight of its core identity. It is reasonable to expect that adoption of a human rights approach should mean that human rights norms will be applied unless there are cogent reasons for not doing so. In the last paragraph of section 3 of

---

[69] See Chapter 8, section 2.2.
[70] See pp. 428 and 436.
[71] See Chapter 10, section 3.4.

Chapter 8 of this book, for example, it is argued that application of a human rights approach to the internal protection alternative (IPA) should not extend to the adoption of the current approach of the European Court of Human Rights which applies an Article 3 ECHR threshold to the putative site of alternative protection. Requiring cogent reasons to be shown for any departure from, or failure to apply, a human rights approach is a criterion that preserves the distinct identity of the human rights approach. It also ensures its overall coherence and integrity.

## 2.3 Different Types of Human Rights Approaches

Having described the human rights approach in very general terms, let us briefly consider the main models that have been, or are being, advanced.

Every commentator who espouses a human rights approach applies their own version, bringing their own insights; that is to be expected of any application of a paradigm, certainly in the legal field. In this subsection, except in relation to the non-hierarchical approach (where it will be further explored in Foster's 2007 model, Hathaway and Foster's 2016 model, and briefly, the model developed in New Zealand by the International Protection Tribunal (IPT)), this study is not concerned with variations but with the main types of models. In this context, the main distinction that exists is between those embodying a hierarchical or a non-hierarchical approach. As will be explained, even sustaining that distinction involves some finessing, since several of the non-hierarchical theories do apply a certain element of differentiation (e.g. between the 'core' and 'periphery' or 'margin' of a human right) which at least arguably involve making hierarchical distinctions of sorts.

## 2.4 Hierarchical Versus Non-Hierarchical

### 2.4.1 Hierarchical models

The hierarchical model is primarily applied to the interpretation of the 'being persecuted' inquiry. Its essence is that in order to assess whether the harms feared cross the threshold to become persecution, the decision maker must attach more weight to certain categories of human rights (or human rights obligations) than others.

The hierarchical model surmises that a human right approach best conforms with the Convention's object and purpose, particularly since the Preamble 'commences with a specific reference to the interrelationships between refugee protection and international human rights law'.[72]

At its most general, the model can be expressed as a continuum. The more basic or fundamental the right that is said to be violated, the easier it will be for the applicant to establish a well-founded fear of being persecuted. Expression of the model in such terms is the crux of Carlier's 'Theory of the Three Scales'.[73] There are other variants of

---

[72] Hathaway (n 28) 105.
[73] Carlier et al (n 25) 105.

the hierarchical model,[74] but the only model that has been developed in any detail is Hathaway's 1991 model.

*2.4.1.1 Hathaway's 1991 model*
Notions of a hierarchy of human rights became prominent in the general human rights law literature, particularly in the 1980s,[75] but the classic expression of the hierarchical approach as applied to refugee law is contained in Hathaway's 1991 work,[76] in which he set out a fourfold hierarchy of obligations. Although Hathaway has now abandoned it, it remains as a major reference-point. He identified: (i) non-derogable International Covenant on Civil and Political Rights (ICCPR) rights, (ii) derogable ICCPR rights, (iii) International Covenant on Economic, Social and Cultural Rights (ICESCR) rights, and (iv) rights not codified in either Covenant.[77] As Foster has noted, this model is also sometimes expressed as a hierarchy of human rights, not specifically obligations.[78] It can be seen to have been applied most expressly in the past (but no longer) by the New Zealand tribunals.[79] But to a greater or lesser degree, it has been applied in some shape or form by courts and tribunals from a number of countries—albeit, outside of the EU, only ever a modest number.

2.4.2 Non-hierarchical models
The non-hierarchical approach concurs with the hierarchical approach in considering that a human rights approach conforms with proper application of VCLT rules, particularly given that 'human rights norms figure prominently in the Convention's preamble'.[80]

In departing from the hierarchical approach, the non-hierarchical approach takes as its premise that international law increasingly treats all human rights as equal, indivisible, and interdependent and that there are no clear or sufficient distinctions between different types of rights as set out in the ICCPR and ICESCR—or indeed the wider panoply of international human rights instruments—to warrant taking a hierarchical approach.

In two of its main formulations so far, that by Foster and that by Hathaway and Foster (Hathaway having changed his position meanwhile), this approach relies in part on a distinction between the core and the margin or periphery of rights.

---

[74] See Foster (n 8) 191–201.
[75] See e.g. Theodor Meron, 'On a Hierarchy of International Human Rights' (1986) 80(1) AJIL 1; Annika Tahvanainen, 'Hierarchy of Norms in International and Human Rights Law' (2006) 24(3) Nordisk Tidsskrift for Menneskerettigheter 191.
[76] Hathaway (n 28) 105.
[77] International Covenant on Civil and Political Rights (adopted 16 December 1966, entered into force 23 March 1976) 999 UNTS 171 (ICCPR); International Covenant on Economic, Social and Cultural Rights (adopted 16 December 1966, entered into force 3 January 1976) 993 UNTS 3 (ICESCR); Hathaway (n 28) 108–11.
[78] Foster (n 8) 120–23.
[79] Burson (n 59) 25–48.
[80] Hathaway and Foster (n 2) 193.

*2.4.2.1 Foster's 2007 model*

The first study to formulate a non-hierarchical model in any detail was Foster's 2007 publication, *International Refugee Law and Socio-Economic Rights*.[81] She argues in that book that Hathaway's hierarchical approach no longer reflects the state of human rights law.

Foster's non-hierarchical model proposes, in order to better align with the developing approach taken in IHRL, the adoption instead of a 'more principled method', namely the 'minimum core obligations' approach developed by the Economic, Social and Cultural Rights Committee (ESCR Committee) which identifies 'a minimum core obligation to ensure the satisfaction of, at the very least, minimum essential levels of each of the rights'.[82] The core or essence of a right is seen to comprise 'some essential element[s] without which it loses its substantive significance as a human right'.[83] The minimum core obligation is said to operate as an immediate obligation, alongside the duty not to discriminate and the duty to take steps towards progressive realisation of the ICESCR. She argues that such an approach is immanent in leading refugee law decisions by courts and tribunals.[84] She considers that the notion of core and periphery/margin helps explain why a risk of a violation of certain types of rights will always amount to persecution (for example the right to life and prohibition on torture), while other violations will amount to persecution in certain circumstances only. She argues that this is because, in respect of such rights, the core is entirely or almost entirely co-extensive with the right itself. By contrast, other rights, such as privacy, religion, free speech, and fair trial, may have an essential core and then a wider 'grey zone' or periphery, in which a violation of the right may occur, but such breach may not be sufficiently central to the right as to constitute persecution.[85]

*2.4.2.2 Hathaway and Foster's 2014 model*

The second main variant of the non-hierarchical approach is that set out by Hathaway and Foster in the second edition of *The Law on Refugee Status*.

This publication contends that 'an argument based on normative hierarchy is no longer defensible in light of the widely accepted principle that all human rights are universal, indivisible and interdependent and interrelated'.[86] They remark that since the adoption of the twin Covenants in 1966:

> [ ... ] the international community has agreed to additional treaties that elucidate in more depth the duties owed by states in a range of specific settings. Many of these are broadly subscribed to and thus fairly understood to serve as authoritative points of

---

[81] Foster (n 8). An early proponent of a non-hierarchical approach was Pirkko Kourula, *Broadening the Edges: Refugee Definition and International Protection Revisited* (Martinus Nijhoff 1997) 25.
[82] Foster (n 8) 163.
[83] ibid 196–97, citing Fons Coomans, *Economic, Social and Cultural Rights* (Advisory Committee on Human Rights and Foreign Policy of the Netherlands 1995) 18.
[84] Foster (n 8) 194–95, citing *Chan v Canada (MEI)* [1995] 3 SCR 593, 643–45; *Refugee Appeal No 74665/03* [2004] NZRSAA, para 909.
[85] Foster (n 8) 197–98.
[86] Hathaway and Foster (n 2) 203.

reference, in much the same way as the International Bill of Rights. In any event, the newer generation of treaties essentially complement and contextualise the general rights set out in the International Bill of Rights, showing how those generic standards apply in circumstances of specific vulnerability or need. There can thus be little objection to drawing upon them as a means of understanding the scope of serious harm presently recognised as impermissible.[87]

One of the main reasons advanced by the authors for jettisoning the hierarchical paradigm is their view that its central mechanism, namely the derogability criterion, fails to provide a principled basis for differentiation:

> [ ... ] non-derogability does not necessarily equate with normative importance or seriousness of harm. As the UN Human Rights Committee has explained, 'not all rights of profound importance ... have in fact been made non-derogable.' Derogability serves the quite distinct purpose of identifying those rights that both practically and as a matter of principle may be suspended for limited periods of time, during an officially declared national emergency. Some rights were made non-derogable in international law (such as the right not to be imprisoned for non-payment of debt) not because they are normatively superior to other rights but 'because their suspension is irrelevant to the legitimate control of the state in a national emergency' [citing HRC General Comment No 24]. Derogability thus does not provide a principled basis upon which to exclude a given right from the ambit of standards relevant to refugee law's assessment of serious harm.[88]

Another key reason they reject a hierarchical approach is that it has bred misunderstanding particularly as to the status of economic, social, and cultural rights. Some of the latter create immediate obligations; or have components that do; and Article 2(1) of the ICESCR, which provides that each state party undertakes to take steps to progressively achieve the full realisation of the Charter rights, cannot be used to negate the content of the substantive rights where what is at issue is discriminatory denial or withdrawal of rights.[89]

In place of Hathaway's 1991 model, they propose a modified paradigm comprising a three-step analysis: (i) establishing that the interest at stake is within the ambit of a broadly agreed human rights norm; (ii) inquiring whether 'the risk is nonetheless one deemed acceptable by reference to the scope of the right as codified' (this step focuses on whether the right is a limited one or requires emergency derogation rather than being an absolute one and acknowledges that a claim of relevant serious harm will not be made out where the facts show the harm feared was justified on the terms of the relevant human rights norm—because that norm was subject to a permissible restriction); and (iii) deciding whether the threat to the human rights norm is truly *de minimis* in the circumstances of a particular case. The advantage of this three-fold

---

[87] ibid 201.
[88] ibid 202–03.
[89] ibid 203–04; Michelle Foster, 'Economic Migrant or Person in Need of Protection? Socio-Economic Rights and Persecution in International Refugee Law' in Burson and Cantor (n 11) 241–47.

analysis is said to be that it avoids a priori, rigid classification of relevant harms and ensures attention to the particular circumstance of the specific individuals seeking protection.[90]

They develop their three-step analysis by considering its application to claims in three thematic categories: risk to physical security; threats to liberty and freedom; and infringements of autonomy and self-realisation, stating that:

> Our reliance on these three broad categories of rights rather than traditional hierarchical categories (in particular civil and political rights vs. economic, social and cultural rights) is in line with the now-established principle that all human rights are equal and indivisible. The flexibility of this framework moreover allows us to consider human rights risks in a more fluid way, reflecting the fact that categories of rights are not hermetically sealed, but are rather quite permeable in practice.[91]

Further, they emphasise that focus should now be on whether there is a real risk of actions that are serious denials of human rights.[92]

### 2.4.2.3 The New Zealand IPT model

Whilst the New Zealand IPT has stated that it adopts the Hathaway and Foster approach,[93] its own approach is not elaborated in the same terms entirely. In *DS (Iran)*, the IPT stated:

> **The Inquiry Re-framed**
> [203] The inquiry under the human rights approach to being persecuted should be understood as requiring the following sequential questions to be addressed once the claimant's credibility has been assessed and the facts found (the predicament question):
> (a) Does the claimant's predicament, as found, indicate there will be an interference with a basic human right or rights in the form of a restriction on its exercise or enjoyment? (the question of scope).
> (b) If there will be interference, does the right in principle permit any restriction? (the question of nature).
> (c) If restriction is in principle permitted, is the restriction at issue lawful in terms of the relevant limitation or derogation clause? (the question of legality).
> (d) If the restriction is not permitted in principle, or is permitted but applied unlawfully, will the breach of the right cause some form of serious harm to the claimant? (the question of impact).[94]

---

[90] Hathaway and Foster (n 2) 207.
[91] ibid.
[92] ibid 193, 195, 199.
[93] *DS (Iran)* [2016] NZIPT 800788.
[94] ibid paras 203–10.

## 3 Criticisms of the Human Rights Approach

Criticisms of the human rights approach are not new. In 1996, Grahl-Madsen noted with interest Vernant's 1953 outline of such an approach,[95] but seemingly rejected it because of the indeterminacy of UDHR provisions.[96] In 1999, Steinbock reflected critically that the Article 1A(2) definition makes no mention of human rights and that '[w]hile the identified purposes clearly serve to protect important human rights, it is also clear that they are not co-extensive with the entire body of human rights law'.[97] Even some advocating a human rights approach expressed doubts that it was workable. Kourula, for example, referred to 'the unhelpfulness of drawing up any particular lists of human rights violations'.[98] In 2007, Martin wrote that 'the institution of asylum is not coterminous with human rights policy' and that the purpose of the Refugee Convention is not 'to express sympathy, to note human rights abuses whenever they appear, or to register disapproval of a practice'.[99]

Surveying the literature, three things stand out. First, almost all the criticisms have been very ad hoc and piecemeal, comprising specific remarks on discrete points. It is only with Matthew Price's 2009 book, *Rethinking Asylum*,[100] that one finds a developed critique. Second, most of the piecemeal criticisms have been made by individuals who to a greater or lesser extent endorse a human rights paradigm. Thus Harvey in 2013 discerns an 'uneasy fit' between IHRL and refugee law (by virtue of the latter's particular concern with designated status) yet advocates pressing ahead with a human rights approach nonetheless.[101] In 2014 Chetail, whilst adamant that the Refugee Convention 'is a duty-based rather than a human rights-based instrument',[102] is equally adamant that 'human rights law has become the ultimate benchmark for determining who is a refugee'.[103] Indeed, even Price, who raises several criticisms, sees the human rights approach as illuminating what he calls the 'anti-brutality' component (which concerns core human rights recognised by customary international law) and grudgingly acknowledges that '[t]he human rights approach is helpful in giving additional texture to the concept of persecution and thereby promoting consistency of decision-making'.[104]

---

[95] Vernant (n 29).
[96] Grahl-Madsen (n 31) 194: 'some of the principles set forth in the Declaration may well give rise to serious difficulties of interpretation'.
[97] Daniel J Steinbock, 'The Refugee Definition as Law: Issues of Interpretation' in Nicholson and Twomey (n 40) 31, 35.
[98] See Kourula (n 81).
[99] David A Martin, 'Major Developments in Asylum Law Over the Past Year: A Year of Dialogue Between Courts and Agencies' (2007) 84 Interpreter Releases 2069, 2072.
[100] Matthew E Price, *Rethinking Asylum History, Purpose, and Limits* (CUP 2010); see also Matthew E Price, 'Persecution Complex: Justifying Asylum Law's Preference for Persecuted People' (2006) 47(2) Harv Intl LJ 413.
[101] Colin J Harvey, 'Is Humanity Enough? Refugees, Asylum Seekers and the Rights Regime' in Satvinder Juss and Colin J Harvey (eds), *Contemporary Issues in Refugee Law* (Edward Elgar 2013).
[102] Chetail (n 61) 28.
[103] ibid. See also Chetail (n 62) 207–09.
[104] Price (n 100) 114–15.

Third, it was only in 2016 that a study, namely that by David Cantor, mounted a fully-fledged, all-encompassing critique[105] in the book, *Human Rights and the Refugee Definition*, co-edited with Bruce Burson.[106] Having asked (with Burson) whether 'we have reached the limits of convergence and are now entering a phase of increasing regime-fragmentation',[107] Cantor proceeds in his own chapter to raise various doubts. He acknowledges at the outset that the human rights approach advanced by Hathaway and others offers 'a number of distinct advantages' over other proposed approaches, but at the same time makes clear that he regards its shortcomings as extensive and as requiring investigation of 'new theoretical models'.[108]

Given that in the wider world of law and political philosophy there is now much literature disavowing human rights law,[109] as well as long-standing debates over the extent to which human rights concepts provide normative justifications for the refugee definition,[110] the fact it has taken so long for a fully-fledged critique to emerge might seem surprising. However, it is worth recalling that for Thomas Khun, whose 1962 book introduced the notion of paradigms to the world of science and other disciplines, it was almost inherent in any 'paradigm shift' that it would be those working within the old paradigm who, faced with what they see as anomalies occurring suggestive of a serious and persistent failure in the *status quo*, would lead the call for a new one.[111]

In light of the above, it is convenient to focus predominantly on Cantor's critique, it being the only fully developed one to emerge so far, whilst at the same time noting that miscellaneous others have made the same or similar points.[112] The criticisms often overlap but can be conveniently classified into three main clusters, the first two being of a conceptual kind.

## 3.1 VCLT Rules-Based Criticisms

One main cluster of criticisms seeks to impugn the compatibility of a human rights approach with the rules of interpretation enjoined by Articles 31 and 32 of the VCLT. In

---

[105] Albeit known from his previous writings to be broadly supportive of an international law framework: see e.g. David Cantor, 'The Laws of War and the Protection of 'War Refugees': Reflections on the Debate and its Future Directions' (2014) 12(5) Journal of International Criminal Justice 931; David Cantor, 'Reframing Relationships: Revisiting the Procedural Standards for Refugee Status Determination in Light of Recent Human Rights Treaty Body Jurisprudence' (2015) 34(1) RSQ 79.

[106] Cantor (n 11).

[107] Bruce Burson and David Cantor, 'Introduction: Interpreting the Refugee Definition via Human Rights Standards' in Burson and Cantor (n 11) 11.

[108] Cantor (n 11) 356, 395.

[109] See e.g. Samuel Moyn, *The Last Utopia: Human Rights in History* (Harvard University Press 2010); Eric Posner, *The Twilight of Human Rights Law* (OUP 2014); Ben Golder, 'Beyond Redemption? Problematising the Critique of Human Rights in Contemporary International Legal Thought' (2014) 2 London Review of International Law 77; Samuel Moyn, *Not Enough: Human Rights in an Unequal World* (Harvard University Press 2018).

[110] See eg Price (n 100) 114–36.

[111] Thomas S Khun, *The Structure of Scientific Revolution* (50th Anniversary edn, University of Chicago Press 2012) 77–91.

[112] It should not be thought that the analysis here exhausts the range of criticisms (even Cantor's) that have been made; it does seek, however, to address the main ones.

the most forceful articulation of these complaints, Cantor[113] argues variously: that in terms of ordinary meaning, the text of Article 1A(2) of the Refugee Convention contains no human rights language[114] and Articles 2–34 enshrine protections based on traditional international law norms imposing duties on states rather than conferring refugee rights;[115] that in terms of context, the first two preambular paragraphs of the Convention do not evince a human rights reading since they are 'backward-looking' and focus on non-discrimination norms in the host state;[116] that in terms of object and purpose, the norms expressed are essentially social and humanitarian;[117] that Article 31(3) VCLT provides no separate legal basis for a human rights approach;[118] and that the *travaux préparatoires* (hereinafter *travaux*) do not show that the drafters intended the refugee definition to be given a human rights reading but rather crafted one based on pre-existing refugee instruments that pre-dated IHRL instruments.[119]

## 3.2 Other Conceptual Criticisms

Another main cluster of criticisms highlights other alleged conceptual problems not linked as such to VCLT considerations. The human rights approach is taken to task for: relying on a misconceived 'state accountability' model;[120] depending on extraneous standards that lack refugee specificity;[121] substituting one set of indeterminate terms for another (e.g. torture or inhuman and degrading treatment as one form of persecution);[122] being unduly complex, circuitous, and difficult for decision makers to negotiate;[123] being ill-suited to handling conflicts of rights;[124] wrongly assuming an

---

[113] Cantor (n 11) 371–76; see also Steinbock (n 97) 31, 35.
[114] Cantor (n 11) 369; Steinbock (n 97) 31–32.
[115] Cantor (n 11) 367; Chetail (n 61) 28.
[116] Cantor (n 11) 374.
[117] ibid 375.
[118] ibid 376–78.
[119] ibid 375.
[120] See e.g. Niraj Nathwani, *Rethinking Refugee Law* (Martinus Nijhoff Publishers 2003) 21, cited by Foster (n 8) 76. This criticism is not raised by Cantor.
[121] Cantor (n 11) 370, 375; Steinbock (n 97) 35; Martin (n 99) 2072; Price (n 100) 115; Harvey (n 101) 68–88; Gervase Coles, 'Refugees and Human Rights' (1992) 91 Bulletin of Human Rights 63. Both Steinbock and Price complain that a human rights approach is both 'over inclusive' and 'under inclusive'. Raza Husain, 'International Human Rights and Refugee Law: The United Kingdom' in Bruce Burson and David Cantor (n 11) 148–50 voices a similar criticism of the Hathaway and Pobjoy analysis of *HJ (Iran)* [2011] 1 AC 596. See James C Hathaway and Jason Pobjoy, 'Queer Cases Make Bad Law' (2012) 44(2) NYU Journal of International Law and Politics 315.
[122] Cantor (n 11) 386; Grahl-Madsen (n 31) 194; Price (n 100) 136; Jari Pirjola, 'Shadows in Paradise—Exploring *Non-Refoulement* as an Open Concept' (2007) 19(4) IJRL 639, cited by Kate Jastram, 'Economic Harm as a Basis for Refugee Status and the Application of Human Rights Law to the Interpretation of Economic Persecution' in James C Simeon (ed), *Critical Issues in International Refugee Law: Strategies toward Interpretative Harmony* (CUP 2010) 166. Vernant was also concerned about indeterminacy: see Vernant (n 29) 8, 15. On the relativism and indeterminacy of human rights concepts see further Jack Donnelly, 'The Relative Universality of Human Rights' (2007) 29 Human Rights Quarterly 281, 299; John Tobin, 'Seeking to Persuade: A Constructive Approach to Human Rights Treaty Interpretation' (2010) 23 Harv LJ 1, 1.
[123] Cantor (n 11) 380, 386–87; Foster (n 8) 85–86 notes Erika Feller's (head of UNHCR's International Protection Division's) concern that lack of expertise could make domestic judges reluctant to use a human rights approach (Foster goes on to reject this concern, as does this study below).
[124] Price (n 100) 120–22.

equivalency between IRL and IHRL norms;[125] being reliant on an extraneous concept of serious harm;[126] being too expansive[127] or too restrictive;[128] and imposing a 'principle of surrogacy' that lacks any clear foundation.[129] As noted earlier, Cantor also considers the fact that the UNHCR Handbook identified human rights standards (in his words) as 'illustrative rather than determinative', to mean that it 'remains present' as a 'long-standing alternative' that 'continues to be represented in such UNHCR doctrine and in the scholarship'.[130]

## 3.3 Empirical Criticisms

Finally, there is a cluster of criticisms of a more empirical and comparative nature. How, it is asked, can the human rights approach be a paradigm given that it has not in fact become entrenched and is really only utilised in the Global North;[131] and when it exhibits a 'sheer variety'[132] and fragmentation[133] and there is no agreement on what its contents actually consist of (hierarchically or non-hierarchically ordered norms; global human rights norms, or regional human rights norms, etc.);[134] and it does not

---

[125] Cantor (n 11) 383; David A Martin, 'Review of the Law of Refugee Status' (1993) 87(2) AJIL 335; Martin wrote at 350 that 'the fine gradations within the Covenants were adopted without any attention, so far as I am aware, to their possible application in the context of political asylum'; Price (n 100) 115, 120, 257. See also Patricia Tuitt, 'Human Rights and Refugees' (1997) 1 The International Journal of Human Rights 66, 69; Emma Haddad, 'Refugee Protection: A Clash of Values' (2003) 1 The International Journal of Human Rights 1, 14.
[126] Price (n 100) 116, 135; Cantor (n 11) 384–85.
[127] See e.g. Steinbock (n 65) 782; Matthew Scott, *Climate Change, Disasters, and the Refugee Convention* (CUP 2020) 118.
[128] Cantor (n 11) 386.
[129] ibid 357–72; Susan Y Kneebone, 'Refugees as Objects of Surrogate Protection: Shifting Identities' in Susan Y Kneebone, Dallal Stevens, and Loretta Baldassar (eds), *Refugee Protection and the Role of Law: Conflicting Identities* (Routledge 2014); Thomas A Aleinikoff and Leah Zamore, *The Arc of Protection: Reforming the International Refugee Regime* (Stanford University Press 2019) 48–52.
[130] Cantor (n 11) 393, citing Edwards (n 11) 50. Husain (n 121) 146–47, also considered this a valid point.
[131] Cantor (n 11) 381; Jastram (n 122) 171; Stephen Meili 'When do Human Rights Treaties Help Asylum Seekers?' (2014) 51(2) Osgood Hall Law Journal 627, discussed in James C Simeon, 'The Human Rights Bases of Refugee Protection in Canada' in Burson and Cantor (n 11) 106–07; Stephen Meili, 'Do Human Rights Treaties Help Asylum-Seekers: Lessons from the United Kingdom' (2015) 48(1) Vanderbilt Journal of Transnational Law 123. Roland Bank notes that despite the human rights approach embodied in Article 9 of the QD and CJEU case law, German jurisprudence due to constitutional traditions has 'stopped halfway': see Roland Bank, 'Refugee Law Jurisprudence from Germany and Human Rights' in Burson and Cantor (n 11) 176. See also Liliana Lyra Jubilut et al, 'Human Rights in Refugee Protection in Brazil' in Burson and Cantor (n 11) 217–18.
[132] Cantor (n 11) 392.
[133] Burson and Cantor (n 107) 11.
[134] Cantor (n 11) 378, 381; Martin (n 125) 350; Jastram (n 122) 167, 171. In the same Burson and Cantor volume, Cathryn Costello notes that sometimes IHRL can be less protective than refugee law and describes her analysis as demonstrating that 'the apparently less robust decentralised regime of refugee law has its own progressive dynamic, which leads human rights law just as much, if not more, than it follows human rights law': see Cathryn Costello, 'The Outer Edges of Non-Refoulement in Europe' in Burson and Cantor (n 11) 201, 209. Heaven Crawley observes that one of the reasons IHRL has not to date reconfigured the relationship between gender and international refugee law is that 'human rights law and discourse is itself gendered': see Heaven Crawley, '[En]gendering International Refugee Protection: Are We There Yet?' in Burson and Cantor (n 11) 322.

appear to result in more consistent decisions?[135] Does it really help, Cantor asks, with difficult cases?[136]

## 4 Responses to Criticisms of the Human Rights Approach

Having outlined the main arguments against the human rights approach, it is necessary to assess their merits and to reflect on what these demonstrate about the overall viability of the human rights approach.

### 4.1 VCLT-Based Criticisms

*À propos* the arguments against the human rights approach made by reference to the VCLT rules on treaty interpretation, there exist strong counterarguments based on the very same rules.

#### 4.1.1 Ordinary meaning
Turning first to the ordinary meaning, whilst the text of the refugee definition set out in Article 1A(2) and elsewhere in Article 1 does not expressly employ human rights language, it can only with difficulty be denied that the Convention read as a whole has a significant human rights density, as evidenced by the fact that Articles 2–34 enshrine a catalogue of refugee rights, most of them cast in the same human rights terminology employed in the 1948 UDHR and the 1966 twin Covenants. The argument of Cantor, Chetail, and others that Articles 2–34 are not formulated as human rights does not sit well with the fact that many of these provisions were indeed based in part on the UDHR and the draft ICCPR and ICESCR.[137] They may lack the status of human rights in pure form, but Hathaway is surely right to argue that refugee rights consist of 'an amalgam of principles' drawn from both refugee law and the human rights Covenants, and that refugee 'status' should be understood as comprising a combination of these.[138]

It is fair to say that some commentators have made too much of the human rights character of Articles 2–34, one example perhaps being Gorlick who hailed it as 'an extraordinary "Bill of Rights" for refugees'.[139] However, it still remains true that the Convention is a rights-granting instrument.[140] The objection that the Refugee

---

[135] Cantor (n 11) 383, 389; Jastram (n 122) 169.
[136] Cantor (n 11) 382; Price (n 100) 119.
[137] Jane McAdam, 'The Refugee Convention as a rights blueprint for persons in need of international protection' (July 2006) UNHCR New Issues in Refugee Research, Research Paper No 125, 7.
[138] Hathaway (1st edn) (n 3) 9; see also Hathaway (2nd edn) (n 3) 29.
[139] Gorlick (n 53) 122. See also Alice Edwards, who considers the Convention 'a rights-based and rights-granting instrument. Its coverage in Articles 2–34 is of the same nature as some rights granted under the various human rights instruments': Alice Edwards, 'Human Rights, Refugees, and the Right to Enjoy Asylum' (2005) 17(2) IJRL 293, 306; Tom Clark and François Crépeau, 'Mainstreaming Refugee Rights: The 1951 Refugee Convention and International Human Rights Law' (1999) 17(4) Netherlands Quarterly of Human Rights 389. See also Hathaway (1st edn) (n 3) 9.
[140] Edwards (n 139) 306.

Convention primarily creates obligations between states, not rights, overlooks that that is how rights arise within the principal IHRL instruments.[141]

It is true that nothing in the wording of the 'well-founded fear' or 'being persecuted' (or availment of protection) elements of the definition expressly suggests a human rights content. It is also plain that the drafters specifically rejected a French proposal to refer directly to the UDHR.[142] However, it would be wrong to portray the entirety of Article 1A(2) as devoid of any human rights traces. The formulation of the Convention reasons is virtually the same as that contained in the anti-discrimination provisions of the UDHR and the twin Covenants and indeed other major IHRL treaties. In any event, virtually none of the scholars who highlight the lack of human rights content to Article 1A(2) support a view that this provision should be interpreted purely by reference to ordinary meaning. Indeed, to do so would be contrary to the integrated approach to ordinary meaning, context, object, and purpose etc. embedded in Articles 31–33 VCLT. If there is thus a valid basis, at least in relation to some elements of the refugee definition, for going beyond ordinary meaning, on what basis could one exclude IHRL from relevant sources?

### 4.1.2 Context

The Preamble to the Convention opens with the following two paragraphs:

> **Considering** that the Charter of the United Nations and the Universal Declaration of Human Rights approved on 10 December 1948 by the General Assembly have affirmed the principle that human beings shall enjoy fundamental rights and freedoms without discrimination,
>
> **Considering** that the United Nations has, on various occasions, manifested its profound concern for refugees and endeavoured to assure refugees the widest possible exercise of these fundamental rights and freedoms,

Von Sternberg considers the 'framers' unambiguous reference' in the Convention preamble to the UDHR to indicate a desire for the refugee definition to evolve in tandem with human rights principles.[143]

As Cantor himself acknowledges, the drafters also saw the Convention as an articulation of the right to seek and enjoy asylum from persecution, guaranteed by Article 14 UDHR.[144] Accordingly, even if individual articles of the Convention are not considered to be human-rights-specific, the Convention is still entitled to be regarded

---

[141] Walter Kälin and Jörg Künzli, *The Law of International Human Rights Protection* (2nd edn, OUP 2019) 68.

[142] UN Ad Hoc Committee on Refugees and Stateless Persons, Ad Hoc Committee on Statelessness and Related Problems, First Session: Summary Record of the Second Meeting Held at Lake Success, New York, on Tuesday, 17 January 1930, at 11 a.m. (17 January 1950) UN Doc E/AC.32/SR.2, 10; UN Ad Hoc Committee on Statelessness and Related Problems, First Session: Summary Record of the Sixth Meeting Held at Lake Success, New York, on Thursday, 19 January 1950, at 11 a.m. (26 January 1950) UN Doc E/AC.32/SR.6, 7.

[143] See McAdam (n 137) 8, citing Mark R von Sternberg, *The Grounds of Refugee Protection in the Context of International Human Rights and Humanitarian Law: Canadian and United States Case Law Compared* (Martinus Nijhoff 2002) 314.

[144] Cantor (n 11) 375.

as a realisation of the international human rights project (a similar argument can be made by reference to the Convention's *travaux*—see below). Furthermore, Cantor's reliance on the 'backward-looking' formulation of the first two preambular paragraphs, as contrasted with the 'forward-looking' formulation of the remaining paragraphs of the Preamble, fails to engage with the normal rules governing the construction of preambles.[145] Whilst the first two preambular paragraphs do hark back, they do so to identify the Charter and the UDHR as sources of inspiration and thus guiding principles and purposes. If they were purely historic references, they would have no efficacy.

### 4.1.3 Object and purpose

As discussed in Chapter 2, identification of the object and purpose of the Refugee Convention has not proved straightforward. However, when it comes to the human rights approach, the wording of the opening two paragraphs of the Preamble has been seen to demonstrate that the promotion of human rights is a principal purpose of the Convention.[146]

As also explained in Chapter 2, the fact that the Refugee Convention is required by VCLT rules to be a 'living instrument' and to have its object and purpose construed in a dynamic way, further enhances the efficacy of a human rights approach which is intrinsically evolutive and has helped decision makers to interpret the refugee definition so as to take account of the growing number of international human rights treaties and of changing social and political conditions. Indeed, it is arguable that the ability of IRL to be responsive to new challenges has been largely due to taking a human rights approach.[147]

Cantor also voices criticisms of the strong reliance by proponents of a human rights approach on the principle of surrogacy as one of the Convention's purposes.[148] Since these go wider than discussion of object and purpose, they are addressed separately below.[149]

### 4.1.4 Article 31(3) VCLT

As we saw in Chapter 2, there is no consensus about the applicability of IHRL norms pursuant to Article 31(3)(a)-(c) VCLT (which concern subsequent agreement and practice and relevant rules of international law) to the refugee definition. However, whether Article 31(3) provides any kind of bridge to a human rights approach, this has never been the main element of the VCLT rules relied on. That said, Chapter 2 argues that even though human rights treaties or case law or UNHCR materials may not strictly come within the ambit of Article 31(3)(a)-(c), they do at least constitute evidence pointing towards identifying 'subsequent practice' and evidence of 'relevant

---

[145] See Chapter 2, n 37.
[146] Hathaway (1st edn) (n 3) 5; James C Hathaway, 'New Directions to Avoid Hard Problems: The Distortion of the Palliative Role of Refugee Protection' (1995) 8 Journal of Refugee Studies 293, 293. See Chapter 2, sections 2.5.4–2.5.5.
[147] Nicholas Blake QC, 'Entitlement to Protection: A Human Rights-based Approach to Refugee Protection in the United Kingdom' in Nicholson and Twomey (n 63) 258; see also Chetail (n 61) 70.
[148] Cantor (n 11) 361–78.
[149] See below section 4.2.7. See also Chapter 7, section 1.4.

rules'. Further, the Statute of the International Court of Justice (ICJ), at Article 38(1)(a) governing sources of international law, includes recognition of international conventions. At a bare minimum, such materials constitute supplementary means of interpretation under Article 32 VCLT.[150]

### 4.1.5 Article 32 and the *travaux préparatoires*

The assertion that the *travaux* offer little to indicate a human rights understanding of the Refugee Convention is broadly correct if focus is placed solely on statements made by the various drafters and on the fact that French proposals to refer in the definition to the UDHR were rejected.[151] It is important nonetheless to have regard to the historical background to the decision to draft a separate Refugee Convention. McAdam's study for UNHCR[152] has charted the ways in which the drafting work on the Refugee Convention took place within a wider interconnected context of international deliberations seeking to develop a body of international human rights law.

McAdam identifies that it was the Commission on Human Rights that was asked to draft a binding legal instrument in this area and that one of that instrument's purposes was described as being to implement Articles 14 and 15 of the UDHR, thereby firmly cementing the Convention's foundations in human rights law.[153] Many substantive provisions in Articles 2 to 34 were identified as taking their departure point from principles drawn from the UDHR and the embryonic ICCPR and ICESCR, collectively known then as the draft Covenant on Human Rights.

Early United Nations General Assembly (UNGA) resolutions also supported the Convention's underlying human rights ethos, with an emphasis on assisting the neediest, affirming basic principles relating to solutions, and recommending increased protection activities. For McAdam these features firmly establish the Convention as a 'specialist human rights treaty'.[154]

In any event, Chapter 2 shows that even if other cognate treaties, case law, and UNHCR materials do not fall within the strict terms of Article 31 VCLT, they certainly come within Article 32 and, as will be seen in subsequent chapters, interpretation of at least a good number of the key terms of the refugee definition acutely raise issues about whether application of Article 31 rules leave the meaning 'ambiguous or obscure' or lead to 'a result which is manifestly absurd or unreasonable'.[155]

Be that as it may, the VCLT-based criticisms that have been raised against the human rights approach do not wholly lack force. To regard the Refugee Convention in unqualified terms as one of the early examples of human rights treaties risks glossing

---

[150] See Chapter 2, section 3.1.
[151] James C Hathaway, 'International Refugee Law: Humanitarian Standard or Protectionist Ploy?' in Alan E Nash and John P Humphrey (eds), *Human Rights and the Protection of Refugees Under International Law. Proceedings of a Conference Held in Montreal, November 29–December 2, 1987* (The Institute for Research on Public Policy 1987) 185. See also UN Ad Hoc Committee on Refugees and Stateless Persons, Ad Hoc Committee on Statelessness and Related Problems, France: Proposal for a Draft Convention— Revision of Draft Article 12 of Document (25 January 1950) UN Doc E/AC/32/L.3.
[152] McAdam (n 137) 6–9.
[153] ECOSOC, Commission on Human Rights, Report of the Working Party on an International Convention on Human Rights (11 December 1947) UN Doc E/CN.4/56, 15.
[154] McAdam (n 137) 7–8.
[155] See p. 103.

over the lack of any specific mention in the core elements of the refugee definition of human rights norms. Further, Articles 2 to 34 are certainly not formulated as a catalogue of human rights in the conventional sense, since they are based on much earlier international standards applied to aliens. However, these criticisms do not gainsay that the Refugee Convention has a significant human rights density. The main criticisms levelled against this fact do not pass muster.

In considering the extent to which VCLT rules enjoin a human rights approach, it must also be borne in mind that in line with the structure of Articles 31 to 33 VCLT, it is also necessary to consider the holistic effect. It may be that taking each VCLT criterion separately a certain doubt can be cast—e.g. it may be the preambular paragraphs citing human rights do not quite bear the weight leading proponents have sought to place on them. It may be that the there are no relevant materials strictly falling within Article 31(3)(a)-(c). But under more than one of the VCLT rules, there is at least a strong argument for adopting a human rights approach.

## 4.2 Other Conceptual Criticisms

What is to be made of other arguments against the human rights approach of a conceptual kind not specifically based on VCLT considerations?

### 4.2.1 State accountability

So far as concerns the contention that the human rights approach relies on a misconceived 'state accountability' model that requires decision makers to go outside their jurisdiction and rule on matters of state liability under international human rights treaties for human rights failings,[156] this is sometimes combined with a broader critique of (over-)reliance within refugee law on the international law on state responsibility. This is addressed in more depth in Chapter 7. Here the discussion is confined to the specific criticism made of the human rights approach.

It is incontrovertible that decision makers, especially members of courts and tribunals, are often called upon to make evaluative judgements about the state of human rights in countries of origin (and/or about what Price terms failings of 'legitimacy').[157] However, it remains that, when applying IHLR norms to assessing refugee eligibility, refugee decision makers are not exercising any jurisdiction empowering them to hold such countries of origin to account.[158] Accountability, in jurisdictional terms, is solely a matter for the relevant supervisory human rights or other international organs. Refugee decision makers applying a human rights approach draw on IHRL as a source of standards. They may make assessments of the human rights record of the country of origin, but their decisions exercise no jurisdiction governing the human rights liability of countries of origin. That indeed reflects the underlying basis for the declaration

---

[156] See e.g. Nathwani (n 120) 21, 76–77.
[157] Price (n 100) 15.
[158] Foster (n 8) 75–78.

made by the UNHCR ExCom that the granting of refugee status is a 'peaceful and humanitarian act'.[159]

Further, in passing judgement on the extent of human rights violations in a country of origin, the refugee decision maker is not concerned with whether that country has ratified one or more human rights treaties (except insofar as it constitutes background evidence as regards state behaviour). The sole focus is on analysing the acts of the state in the light of human rights norms. If application of IHRL norms were made dependent on the extent of ratification of human rights treaties by countries of origin, that would create the grotesque paradox that the more a state refused to be bound by human rights treaties, the less recourse could be made to IHRL when considering victims of such a state's persecution.[160]

### 4.2.2 Reliance on extraneous standards

Criticisms deriding dependency on external standards have a number of manifestations, but in general, all ignore or forget the essential justifications for why recourse to IHRL provides a legitimate aid to interpreting the refugee definition. As noted earlier, by reference to Burson's taxonomy, such recourse helps decision makers avoid *renvoi* to national law, lack of transparency, and subjectivism. It also helps ensure that refugee status determination (RSD) is based rather on objective standards anchored in the norms that states have agreed to under 'cognate' international treaties and whose subject-matter—protection against harm—is most proximate to refugee decision-making. Such an approach is also in line with VCLT rules.[161]

Price and Cantor have also argued that the human rights approach breaks down because it relies on an extraneous notion of 'serious harm'; this point is also best addressed below in relation to lack of equivalency.

By raising the issue of whether the human rights approach binds IRL to an unnecessary dependency, Cantor's critique inevitably prompts the question of whether IRL should regard itself as *sui generis*, based on its own intrinsic terms.[162] Of course, the 1951 Convention needs to be interpreted as an individual treaty and in light of its specific terms, context and object(s), and purpose(s). Indeed, to do otherwise would be contrary to VCLT principles. It can also be accepted that as refugee law has developed, courts and tribunals have been able to apply their own insights, which have not always resulted from strict application of a human rights approach. A good number of the interpretive uncertainties that have arisen over the years have been largely resolved through specifically refugee law jurisprudence, not, at least observably, IHRL jurisprudence, and this development can fairly be said to show that refugee law has acquired a distinct identity of its own.

---

[159] UNHCR, Conclusion on the civilian and humanitarian character of asylum No 94 (LIII)—2002 (8 October 2002) UN Doc A/AC.96/973; ExCom, General Conclusion on International Protection No 99 (LV)—2004 (8 October 2004) UN Doc A/AC.96/1003.

[160] Foster (n 8) 77–78.

[161] *North Sea Continental Shelf Cases*, Judgment [1969] ICJ Rep 3, 125, Separate Opinion of Judge Ammoun, cited by Hathaway (1st edn) (n 3) 66; see also Foster (n 8) 36–40; Jane McAdam, 'Interpretation of the 1951 Convention' in Zimmermann (n 8) 104. See further Chapter 2, sections 1.6 and 2.7.

[162] Cantor (n 11) 375; for similar argumentation see Coles (n 121).

However, interpretation cannot be pursued *in vacuo* and must take place within the framework of international law. Refugee law's autonomy can only ever be relative. This has two consequences. First, whether or not IRL should or should not be interpreted through the prism of human rights law, it remains that IRL is part of public international law. Second, by virtue of Article 31 VCLT, which represents customary international law, the 1951 Convention cannot be interpreted in isolation from cognate treaties. The 1951 Convention is an international treaty with protective purposes. To cut IRL off, in the name of its distinctive status, from the most relevant sources of international law—other treaties that also have protective purposes—would be to forget that it operates within the framework of international law more generally. As the ICJ has stated it, 'an international instrument has to be interpreted and applied within the framework of the entire legal system prevailing at the time of the interpretation'.[163]

In addition, any rejection of the human rights approach that seeks to highlight the *sui generis* character of refugee law, must grapple with the risk this raises of opening the door to interpretive pragmatism. It would only make it easier for governments around the world, whenever the political winds blow harshly, to reinterpret it without regard to whether doing so was contrary to established norms of international law.

### 4.2.3 Indeterminacy

Cantor among others has expressed the view that the language of human rights treaties has the same abstract and indeterminate character as that found in the refugee definition and so simply adds one indeterminacy to another.[164] The indeterminate character of the refugee definition cannot be denied. But it is in the nature of 'law-making treaties' dealing with the subject-matter of protection against harms of various kinds and using 'generic' concepts,[165] that the wording is at a high level of abstraction.

Cantor may be right to suggest that terms to be found in the IHRL instruments, e.g. 'torture' and 'inhuman and degrading treatment', are indeterminate and that interpretation of such terms is not entirely uniform, but when tasked with applying international or regional treaty definitions, human rights adjudicative bodies—both the treaty-monitoring bodies at the international level;[166] the human rights courts at the regional level;[167] and courts and tribunals at the domestic level—have had no particular difficulty in identifying the contents of such terms and applying them in practice. Whilst there may be variations over time, as has been the case with the definition of torture,[168] this is an aspect of the fact that the term requires an evolutive approach to interpretation that strives for 'textured harmony' not 'monotone uniformity'.[169] IHRL

---

[163] *Legal Consequences for States of the Continued Presence of South Africa in Namibia (South West Africa) notwithstanding Security Council Resolution 276 (1970)*, Advisory Opinion [1971] ICJ Rep 16. See Foster (n 89) 229–52, 233.
[164] Cantor (n 11) 386.
[165] See Chapter 2, sections 1.4.1 and 2.5.1.
[166] e.g. the Human Rights Committee (HRC) and the Committee Against Torture.
[167] Most notably the European Court of Human Rights (ECtHR) and the Inter-American Court of Human Rights (IACtHR).
[168] See e.g. *Aydin v Turkey* App No 23178/94 (ECtHR [GC], 25 September 1997), in which the ECtHR held for the first time that rape could constitute torture.
[169] Sir Malcolm D Evans, 'Co-existence and Confidentiality: The Experience of the Optional Protocol to the Convention Against Torture. Harmony and Human Rights: The Music of the Spheres' in Carla M

has hammered/is hammering the relevant concepts into workable standards. It may be that IHRL often deploys open-ended terms, e.g. the notion of a 'minimum level of severity'[170] but case law has given their contours much more concrete shape.

Criticism citing indeterminacy also ignores that as refugee law jurisprudence has developed, decision makers are no longer working with key terms of the Refugee Convention as if they were a blank slate. Much of the indeterminacy of the text has been rendered determinate by case law or state practice (in the broad sense), much of it inspired by IHRL norms. For example, IHRL thinking undoubtedly fuelled acceptance that persecution can emanate from non-state as well as state-actors and that to be persecutory an act does not have to be motivated by malignant intent and that to avoid persecution persons cannot be expected to conceal aspects of their personality that are fundamental to them.[171]

### 4.2.4 Complexity

Price views the human rights approach as roundabout because it requires decision makers to apply and interpret two bodies of law and to struggle with the challenges internal to IHRL as well as IRL.[172] Human rights, he contends, are not 'self-defining'. With each of the human rights involved, he opines, similar interpretative problems arise.[173] Similarly, Cantor argues that the attempt to draw on human rights law shifts the 'interpretive exercise from the terms of the Refugee Convention to a complex new discursive terrain'.[174]

The human rights approach does entail addressing two bodies of law—IRL and IHRL. In this regard it can be said to jar with the viewpoint that the refugee definition should be relatively simple to apply and interpret. At the same time, the notion that the 1951 Convention can be interpreted in a vacuum is illusory. As already noted, such an approach would be contrary to VCLT rules. Second, this line of criticism begs the question of what should be required of decision makers in order to demonstrate that theirs is an objective interpretation as opposed to one based on subjectivism or reliance purely on national law criteria.[175] The only readily available objective legal norms capable of having universal application are human rights (or kindred international law) norms.

Further, under the human rights approach it will be rare for decision makers to be required to interpret, as opposed to straightforwardly bring to bear, IHRL. In

---

Buckley, Alice Donald, and Philip Leach (eds), *Towards Convergence in International Human Rights Law: Approaches of Regional and International Systems* (Brill Nijhoff 2016) 542.

[170] See e.g. *Aktaš v Turkey* App No 24351/94 (ECtHR, 24 April 2003) para 312; see further Kälin and Künzli (n 141).
[171] On each of these points see e.g. Zimmermann and Mahler (n 8).
[172] ibid 120–22.
[173] Price (n 100) 117–20.
[174] Cantor (n 111) 387.
[175] However, national law may sometimes prevent interpretation consistent with VCLT rules: see e.g. in Australia, Migration Act 1958, s 91R (as amended); Linda J Kirk, 'Island Nation: The Impact of International Human Rights Law on Australian Refugee Law' in Burson and Cantor (n 11) 49–85, 85. See also Guy S Goodwin-Gill and Jane McAdam, *The Refugee in International Law* (4th edn, OUP 2021) 45–50.

most applications, either the relevant human rights criteria will be set out accessibly in refugee jurisprudence or UNHCR materials or state practice (in the broad sense) or there will be clear criteria available from treaty-monitoring body 'General Comments'[176] or leading decisions of the relevant human rights courts.[177] The refugee decision maker will rarely if ever be starting from scratch. UNHCR materials and refugee law scholarship (and sometimes guidance produced by national governments) have also played a very significant role in seeking to concretise how particular human rights can be understood and brought to bear in a specific way in the refugee law context. In this way quite a lot of IHRL pertinent to IRL has been 'domesticated' by courts and tribunals applying a human rights approach and by UNHCR Guidelines, among other sources. No significant need has been felt to go outside the world of legal norms to consider what Price terms norms pertaining to 'legitimate' state conduct.

As regards the criticism voiced by Cantor and others[178] that having regard to two bodies of law places undue burdens on decision makers, two points are pertinent. First, it is long-recognised that to do RSD a certain level of expertise is required.[179] Having recourse to IHRL should not therefore require an expertise where there is none of any kind. Second, as already observed, much of IHRL has been 'domesticated' by courts and tribunals—and indeed UNHCR—when undertaking RSD. By and large, when refugee decision makers have recourse to IHRL they can proceed by identifying key cases or 'General Comments' made by the treaty monitoring bodies or UNHCR Guidelines; or they may find refugee cases that have already analysed such materials. The reference points are both tangible and accessible. Given the established prominence of IHRL jurisprudence within the body of international law, it is not unreasonable to expect refugee decision makers, certainly members of courts and tribunals, to have sufficient expertise in IHRL.

### 4.2.5 Conflict of rights

What of Price's criticism that human rights can be in conflict and so provide no solution? In assessing whether a state's action is persecutory, he argues, 'human rights lie on both sides of the balance'.[180] This criticism is perhaps a good illustration of how

---

[176] HRC, 'Working Methods, IX. General Comments/Recommendations', available at <https://www.ohchr.org/EN/HRBodies/CCPR/Pages/WorkingMethods.aspx> accessed 28 May 2021. For the comments of all the treaty bodies, see <https://www.ohchr.org/EN/HRBodies/Pages/TBGeneralComments.aspx>. In *Ahmadou Sadio Diallo (Republic of Guinea v Democratic Republic of the Congo)*, Merits, Judgment [2010] ICJ Rep 639, 663–64, para 66, the ICJ said that 'it should ascribe great weight to the interpretation adopted by this independent body that was established specifically to supervise the application of that treaty. The point here is to achieve the necessary clarity and the essential consistency of international law, as well as legal security, to which both the individuals with guaranteed rights and the States obliged to comply with treaty obligations are entitled.'

[177] A point made powerfully by Foster (n 8) 85–86.

[178] See e.g.Erika Feller, 'Address to the Conference of the International Association of Refugee Law Judges' (2001) 15(3) Georgetown Immigration Law Journal 381.

[179] See para 181 of the UNHCR Handbook (n 10). There are similar provisions in EU asylum law: see e.g. Directive 2013/32/EU of the European Parliament and of the Council of 26 June 2013 on common procedures for granting and withdrawing international protection [2013] OJ L 180 (Asylum Procedures Directive (recast)) Article 6. In the US, the AO Basic Training Course (AOBTC) mandates asylum officers to consider international human rights instruments: see Anker and Vittor (n 22) 116–17.

[180] Price (n 100) 121.

misconceptions can arise about how human rights norms are deployed in a legal context. Whilst there are schools of thought that deny there can be conflict between human rights,[181] it is a well-recognised feature of IHRL that if a conflict is seen to exist, it must be resolved by way of a decision in the particular case. The extensive case law demonstrates this to be routine for international human rights courts.[182]

### 4.2.6 Lack of equivalency

It is very hard to understand why critics consider that the lack of equivalency between the IRL and IHRL law systems constitutes an argument against the human rights approach. As explained in Chapter 2, an integral part of applying a VCLT approach is that the Refugee Convention must be considered within the wider framework of international law. Recourse to another legal system within this same framework cannot on its own give rise to error. Within the framework of international law, IHRL incontrovertibly constitutes the closest reference-point for at least some key elements of the refugee definition.

As regards the allegation of 'over-inclusivity', this seems mainly to rely on the flawed premise that the human rights approach treats any breach of human rights as persecutory, whereas IHRL on non-return cases has consistently applied a threshold of serious or sufficiently severe harm.[183] In asserting 'over inclusivity', Price states that 'it is hard to see how [violations of most rights listed in the ICCPR and ICESCR] could ever constitute serious harm' (he gives the example of the right to vote).[184] This wholly ignores that except where the absolute nature of the right makes its violation persecutory, the threshold of sufficient severity can be reached by an accumulation of measures, including violations of derogable rights.

As regards 'under-inclusivity', Price suggests, with reference to Hathaway's original four-fold hierarchy, that this schema 'would leave unprotected several categories of people who should be eligible for asylum', giving the example of those whose have met with arbitrary deprivation of property.[185] However, in the first place, violation of such rights was accommodated within category 4 of Hathaway's original hierarchy; and in the second place, one of the reasons why Foster (and now Hathaway) shifted

---

[181] Among the scholars who deny such conflicts see Jeremy Waldron, 'Rights in Conflict' (1989) 99(3) Ethics 503, 505; Christopher Wellman, 'On Conflicts between Rights' (1995) 14 Law and Philosophy 271, 277; Thomas M Scanlon, 'Adjusting Rights and Absolute Values' (2004) 72 Fordham Law Review 1477, 1477–79. Among those who consider conflicts of rights can arise, see Robert Alexy, *A Theory of Constitutional Rights* (OUP 2002).

[182] Stijn Smet, 'On the Existence and Nature of Conflicts between Human Rights at the European Court of Human Rights' (2017) 17(3) Human Rights Law Review 499, 502, notes the following cases: *Von Hannover (No 2) v Germany* Apps Nos 40660/08 and 60641/08 (ECtHR, 7 February 2012) para 100; *Evans v United Kingdom* App No 6339/05 (ECtHR, 10 April 2007) para 73; *Odievfre v France* App No 4236/98 (ECtHR, 13 February 2003) para 44; *Osman v United Kingdom* App No 23452/94 (ECtHR, 28 October 1998) para 116; *Appleby and Others v United Kingdom* App No 44306/98 (ECtHR, 6 May 2003) para 43; *Schuth v Germany* App No 1620/03 (ECtHR, 23 September 2010) para 57. See also Stijn Smet, *Resolving Conflicts between Human Rights: The Judge's Dilemma* (Routledge 2017).

[183] e.g. in *F v United Kingdom* App No 17341/03 (ECtHR, 22 June 2004), the ECtHR stated that '[on] a purely pragmatic basis, it cannot be required that an expelling contracting state only return an alien to a country which is in full and effective enforcement of all the rights and freedoms set out in the Convention'.

[184] Price (n 100) 116.

[185] ibid 117.

to a non-hierarchical approach was precisely to rectify possible disregard for, or downplaying of, such harms.[186]

*4.2.6.1 Reliance on the concept of serious harm*
A principal point levelled by critics viewing lack of equivalency as a flaw has focussed on the reliance within the human rights approach on the notion of serious harm. It has been said that placing reliance on this concept shows that the IHRL framework is deficient since serious harm is not a human rights concept. Thus, Price considers that the requirement that human rights violations be accompanied by serious harm 'dramatically curtails the scope of the human rights approach', since most human rights violations do not inherently constitute serious harm.[187] For Price, persecution should be defined as 'serious harm inflicted or condoned by official agents for illegitimate reasons'.[188]

Before addressing such criticisms, it must be acknowledged that the concept of serious harm is critical to the human rights approach. If violations of qualified rights such as the right to peaceful assembly and to freedom of association[189] were considered, per se, to amount to persecution, this would effectively undermine the universalism of the persecution standard. However, it is misleading to regard the concept of serious harm as extraneous to IHRL. In the jurisprudence on the prohibition of ill-treatment for example, international human rights organs have developed closely analogous notions of 'sufficient severity' of harm as human rights concepts. Thus, in relation to Article 7 ICCPR, it is well-established that to bring it within the range of harms proscribed by the prohibition against cruel, inhuman, or degrading treatment or punishment, the harm or harms concerned must be of sufficient severity or seriousness.[190] In any event, as flagged already, even if it is considered correct to regard the concept of serious harm as extraneous, that scarcely demonstrates that the human rights approach is flawed. Taking another legal system into account is not the same as adopting it lock stock and barrel.

It is also important to query Price's insistence that legitimacy should remain the 'touchstone for interpreting persecution' (which he calls 'the political conception of asylum').[191] Whilst one can describe the decisions refugee decision makers make as ones regarding legitimacy, it is not useful to do so, since to the extent that they are, they are exclusively confined to legitimacy as codified in IHRL or wider international law norms.[192] This point applies more widely to many ethical criticisms of the human rights approach.[193]

---

[186] Foster (n 8) 147–51; Hathaway and Foster (n 2) 229.
[187] Price (n 100) 116, 135.
[188] ibid 135.
[189] ICCPR (n 77) Articles 21 and 22.
[190] See *DS (Iran)* (n 93), which cites Elizabeth McArthur and Manfred Nowak, *The United Nations Convention Against Torture: A Commentary* (OUP 2008) 558; Kälin and Künzli (n 141) 320–33; see also *Vuolanne v Finland* (2 May 1989) Communication No 265/1987, UN Doc CCPR/C/35/D/265/1987, para 9.2.
[191] Price (n 100) 26.
[192] See further section 6.1 of this chapter.
[193] See e.g. Richard Rorty, 'Human Rights, Rationality, and Sentimentality' in Stephen Shute and Susan L Hurley (eds), *On Human Rights: The Oxford Amnesty Lectures 1993* (Basic Books 1993).

*4.2.6.2 Too expansive/too restrictive?*

Alongside allegations of over inclusivity and under inclusivity, have been concerns that the attempt to use human rights norms to interpret the refugee definition will lead to approaches that are too wide or too narrow.

In relation to the former, it has been argued that by virtue of IHRL's universal scope and constantly evolving character, to apply a human rights approach is too expansive. Thus, Daniel Steinbock expressed a concern that adoption of Hathaway's 1991 paradigm would mean that 'a large body of rights violations are equated with persecution' meaning that enormous numbers would qualify as refugees.[194]

Similarly, others have argued that a human rights approach opens or would open the 'floodgates' and impose burdens on states parties far beyond those they signed up for. Thus, Jastram has written in nuanced terms that as 'human rights law is used more widely as a point of reference in status determination, it will either be largely rhetorical or it will risk promoting fragmentation, as a result of the pressures on asylum'.[195]

At the opposite end of the spectrum, it has been argued that the human rights approach is too restrictive and constraining. Among the reasons given is that human rights law has normative gaps and that as a result the human rights approach to the 'being persecuted' element could result in the refugee definition failing to take account of changing circumstances, for example, the infinite capacity of actors of persecution to devise new ways to harm people.[196]

A separate argument alleging the same shortcoming, focuses on the results of its application. According to Cantor, 'in cases involving more subtle questions about the boundaries of persecution, recourse to human rights standards seems not infrequently to serve as a justification for a restrictive interpretation of this element'.[197]

In a sense, the co-existence of two opposite criticisms, that a human rights approach is too expansive on the one hand and too restrictive on the other, rather confirms that criticisms based on effects very much reflect the viewpoint of individual critics. It remains necessary, though, to evaluate them.

As regards objections that recourse to human rights norms makes for too expansive an approach to the refugee definition, it would appear that those who have voiced them often rely on the mistaken conception that ILR lacks the ability to assess when violations of human rights reach the level of sufficient severity to constitute persecution. In any event, as has been said on many occasions, the 'floodgates' argument has no basis in law.[198]

---

[194] Steinbock (n 65) 782; see also Scott (n 129) 118.
[195] Jastram (n 122) 171.
[196] See e.g. Edwards (n 11) 46–80, 48.
[197] Cantor (n 11) 386.
[198] Foster (n 8) 79 notes that whilst a human rights approach does carry the potential to expand the application of the refugee definition, 'any objection to such an outcome must be made on grounds of principle and not merely on the basis of some inchoate 'floodgates' concern. This is because, as the senior courts in the common law world have emphasised repeatedly, the floodgates argument is not a valid legal argument.' She cites *Applicant A v MIEA* [1997] 190 CLR 225, 241 (Gummow J); *Chan* (n 84) para 57; and *R v SSHD ex parte Jeyakumaran* [1994] Imm AR 45, 48.

So far as concerns the converse criticism—that a human rights approach is too restrictive– it is true that operating the human rights approach does carry with it certain constraints. However, first of all, the fact that IHRL self-consciously adopts an evolutive approach, treating human rights instruments as 'living instruments', endows it with a capacity to respond to changing circumstances and to constantly reassess how such circumstances impinge on existing understandings of the scope and application of IHRL norms. Secondly, whilst it is always possible, of course, to evaluate things from the premise that refugee law must necessarily be progressive or liberal, to operate as a viable body of law, there must always be rules and criteria and some winners and losers. If those who make this criticism mean to say that in order to ensure a progressive approach is achieved, IRL should break free from the framework of international law and the limits of state obligations under the 1951 Convention, then they need to make that explicit and accept the legal isolationism it might entail.

It is also important not to underestimate the capacity of IHRL to adapt under pressure from new ideas. For example, even assuming that some key developments in refugee law case law—e.g. that people cannot be expected to conceal their sexuality if at least one reason for their doing so is fear of ill treatment—have happened without reference to IHRL norms originally,[199] it clearly builds directly on the guarantees in IHLR of autonomy, self-realisation, and the 'development of the human personality'.[200] Between two closely related bodies of international law, both of whose underlying treaties constitute 'living instruments', there will always be some sort of *pas de deux*.

### 4.2.7 Reliance on the surrogacy principle

The surrogacy notion or principle is analysed in greater detail in Chapter 7, but it can be acknowledged here that in the abstract, the surrogacy principle is not an intrinsically human rights concept. Yet it is undoubtedly true that its espousal has been strongest by proponents of a human rights approach to the refugee definition and critics cannot be blamed for treating the two as almost inseparable.

Cantor's critique (highlighted here because it is the most extensive so far) of the strong reliance within the human rights approach on the 'surrogacy' notion is beguiling but ultimately unpersuasive.

Insofar as Cantor's critique seeks to portray the surrogacy model as relying on a relationship with the *host state* (which is seen to be a surrogate for national protection), for the most part the surrogacy model has rather based itself on an application of IHRL norms to the protection circumstances in the *country of the applicant's nationality or country of former habitual residence* (what Cantor calls 'internal protection'). Indeed, this model views it as erroneous to apply the standards prevailing in the host

---

[199] As seems to be suggested by Hussain (n 121), 149–50. Contrast Rodger Haines, 'The Intersection of Human Rights Law and Refugee Law: On or Off the Map? The Challenge of Locating Appellant 595/2002' (2004) IARLJ Australia/New Zealand Chapter Meeting, Sydney 9 June 2004, 39 who argues that in fact the IRL case law, starting with S395, simply gave recognition to IHRL thinking.

[200] See Hathaway and Foster (n 2) 260, citing UN Committee on Economic, Social and Cultural Rights (ESCR Committee), General Comment No 11 (10 May 1999) UN Doc E/1992/23, 22 and General Comment No 13 (8 December 1999) UN Doc E/C.12/1999/10, 1, 4.

state.²⁰¹ In applying IHRL standards, IRL has not sought to argue that the efficacy of internal protection (whose failure leads to the need for surrogate protection) is to be evaluated in light of the standards appropriate to the treatment of refugees by the host state.²⁰² It is simply incorrect to assert that somehow adopting a surrogacy model of internal protection ties the decision maker to having regard to standards applicable to refugees in host states.

In any event, to the extent that this body of criticism relies on the (related) point that most of the rights seen as necessary to protect refugees in host states compensate for the lack of external protection (diplomatic and consular protection),²⁰³ it is now well-established that whatever the textual reasons and the intentions of the drafters, it would render the refugee definition unworkable if it were read as being concerned primarily with external protection.²⁰⁴

An important premise of Cantor's approach is that the surrogacy model lacks correspondence with the concept of internal protection because the latter is grounded on possession of nationality (or its lack). This point fundamentally misunderstands what the refugee definition seeks to achieve by way of personal scope. In the first place, whilst it does treat the notion of nationality (and its lack) as a basic element or requirement to be satisfied in order to come within the refugee definition, the effect of Article 1A(2) is to cover all persons, both nationals or stateless persons.²⁰⁵ There is no person left outside its personal scope.

In the second place, the fact that a person is a national is entirely distinct from the issue of whether he or she faces a well-founded fear of persecution. In some cases, a person's nationality may well be a significant issue in establishing that they face a well-founded fear of persecution (e.g. where a country of origin targets stateless persons because of their national origins or in cases of denationalisation), but that does not belie the fact that the test of whether a person faces a well-founded fear of being persecuted is not limited in its application to persons who are nationals or citizens.

Third, it has come to be widely accepted that the state's duty to protect is not confined to those within its territory who are its nationals, but also extends to non-nationals.²⁰⁶

---

[201] See e.g. *Januzi v SSHD* [2006] UKHL 5, 16.
[202] The only exception has been the approach adopted by some (principally Hathaway and Foster, the *Michigan Guidelines on the Internal Protection Alternative*, 1999, and the New Zealand tribunals) of utilising in a limited context the standards set out in Articles 2–34 to inform the viability of an internal relocation or internal protection alternative, but this has not taken root in either the jurisprudence globally or in the refugee scholarship: see Chapter 8, section 2.7.2.
[203] Cantor (n 11) 358–62, 376.
[204] See Chapter 7, section 3.2.
[205] Michelle Foster and Hélène Lambert, *International Refugee Law and the Protection of Stateless Persons* (OUP 2019) ch 4.
[206] As noted by the ECtHR in *Loizidou v Turkey* App No 15318/89 (ECtHR, 18 December 1996) para 52: '[t]he obligation to secure ... the rights and freedoms set out in the Convention, derives from the fact of ... control [of territory]'. See also HRC, General Comment No 31: Nature of the General Legal Obligation Imposed on States Parties to the Covenant (26 May 2004) UN Doc CCPR/C/21/Rev.1/Add.13, para 10: 'the enjoyment of Covenant [ICCPR] rights is not limited to citizens of States Parties but must also be available to all individuals, regardless of nationality or statelessness, such as asylum seekers, refugees, migrant workers and other persons who may find themselves in the territory or subject to the jurisdiction of the State Party'.

Fourth, as Chapter 7 (on 'Being Persecuted and Protection') will hopefully make clear, state protection comprises not just negative obligations but positive obligations. In addition, contrary to what Cantor implies, the human rights approach to protection has resulted, not in a relatively minimalist notion of protection, but one that has to embody a number of qualities such as effectiveness, non-temporariness, and accessibility. Hence there is nothing contradictory or incongruous in seeking to interpret persecution or lack of protection by reference to human rights standards that pertain to all human beings.

As regards the criticism that the surrogacy model reduces assessment of refugee eligibility to a test of the 'capacity' or 'adequacy' of state protection (or of the extent to which applicants have sought to exhaust their domestic remedies with the authorities in their state),[207] as will be explained in Chapter 7, that overlooks that case law has shifted away from the first workings of the surrogacy model, for example as set out in the UKHL case of *Horvath*, to one of whether it is effective and whether it affords protection in the individual case.[208]

What is more, the development within IRL of a more demanding concept of protection has come about almost entirely through the application of IHRL-based notion of protection. This makes somewhat baffling Cantor's assertion that the standards applying to the duty on states to protect individuals from third party violations 'are not clearly specified by international human rights law'.[209] It is really only in IHRL that there is any basis in international law for a developed notion of state protection.[210]

Insofar as Cantor's argument seeks to question the notion that stable quasi-state entities can protect, it can certainly be conceded that the issue remains controversial.[211] But even assuming that notion is incorrect, by virtue of the development of an increasingly human rights content to the concept of protection (which is broadly reflected in Article 7 of the QD (recast)), very few existent non-state entities would be capable of qualifying as actors of protection. Powerful drug cartels or terrorist organisations such as ISIS are the most glaring example of entities that could never conceivably qualify; towards the other end of the spectrum, entities such as Somaliland may require more nuanced consideration.[212]

---

[207] Citing Goodwin-Gill and McAdam (n 175) 8–9, Cantor (n 11) 388 describes this as reflecting a 'well-developed scholarly critique'. See also Guy S Goodwin-Gill, 'Current Challenges in Refugee Law' in Jean-Pierre Gauci et al (eds), *Exploring the Boundaries of Refugee Law* (Brill Nijhoff 2015) 11–12.

[208] Burson (n 59) 42. In the same volume, Raza Husain notes that in the UK subsequent cases have 'honoured Horvath in the breach' (*Horvath v SSHD* [2000] UKHL 37) and goes on to suggest that the notion of 'effectiveness' in Article 7 QD has yet to be addressed fully. See Husain (n 121) 146, 154.

[209] Cantor (n 11) 389.

[210] Hugo Storey, 'The Meaning of "Protection" within the Refugee Definition' (2016) 35(3) RSQ 1. That is not to say that other areas of law, especially IHL, cannot also help inform a fully rounded concept of protection.

[211] See for a recent survey and analysis, Ben Saul, 'The Responsibility of Armed Groups Concerning Displacement' in Costello et al (n 62) 1138–56. In relation to the separate issue of whether the activities of civil society actors are relevant to the effectiveness of protection, see the CJEU judgment in Case C-255/19 *SSHD v O A* [2021] ECLI:EU:C:2021:36.

[212] See p. 460.

### 4.2.8 UNHCR Handbook

As regards Cantor's apparent suggestion that the 'illustrative' approach visible in the 1979 UNHCR Handbook remains and is 'still in existence and sometimes applied in practice', it has already been pointed out that UNHCR's approach is increasingly human rights oriented. Further, to the extent that there is any force in the worry about a 'determinative' approach to definition of key terms of the refugee definition, that really only bites against efforts to provide a 'static' or 'fixed list' approach to definition.[213] Nevertheless, Cantor's worry does need further consideration when seeking to identify the prerequisites of a human rights approach.[214]

## 4.3 Empirical Criticisms

The final cluster of criticisms are those that make empirical/comparative points.

### 4.3.1 Lack of entrenchment

Cantor considers the claim made that the human rights approach is the dominant paradigm to be belied by the fact that it remains unentrenched, being mainly used in countries of the Global North[215] and that in many countries of the world it is not applied. In a more recent contribution, Cantor (with Chikwanha) writes that only three African states expressly apply a human rights approach (Uganda, South Sudan, and Angola).[216] Absence of its use in Latin America has been noted in other studies.[217]

It is true the human rights approach, whilst properly called the dominant approach, has never been universalised. It must be conceded also that currently international refugee law jurisprudence is insufficiently inclusive; there is a real need for more reported cases from Latin America, Africa, and the Far East. That is counterbalanced somewhat by the fact that in more than fifty of the world's countries, RSD is done by UNHCR[218] who do, as explained earlier, increasingly apply a human rights approach. It is not the fault of the human rights approach that national systems have sometimes acted to deflect it e.g. Australia.[219] It is not the fault of the human rights approach

---

[213] Foster (n 8) 81–82; Storey (n 9) 461. See also p. 37.
[214] See section 4.3.4 of this chapter.
[215] He mentions 'parts of Europe, North America and Australia', see Cantor (n 11) 378–79; see also Hélène Lambert, Jane McAdam, and Maryellen Fullerton (n 58), whose contributions chronicle a mixed picture regarding permeation of this approach more widely.
[216] David Cantor and Farai Chikwanha, 'Reconsidering African Refugee Law' (2019) 31(2/3) IJRL 182, 222.
[217] However, David Cantor, 'European Influence on Asylum Practices in Latin America: Accelerated Procedures in Colombia, Ecuador, Panama and Venezuela' in Hélène Lambert et al (n 58) 71–80 notes that 'national jurisprudence contains no significant interpretation of the refugee definition .... Interviews in these countries showed that UNHCR constitutes the principal source of interpretive guidance.' This leaves open, though, that to the extent that UNHCR applies a human rights approach, so do national decision makers. See also Luisa Feline Freier, 'A Liberal Paradigm Shift? A Critical Appraisal of Recent Trends in Latin American Asylum Legislation' in Gauci et al (n 207) 140, who notes, inter alia, that '[t]he UNHCR endorse[d] the Argentine and Mexican refugee law as leading the vanguard of human rights based refugee legislation in the region'.
[218] See UNHCR, Refugee Status Determination, available at <www.unhcr.org/refugee-status-determination.html> accessed 28 May 2021.
[219] See Kirk (n 175) 78–85.

that in some countries the national legal culture of courts and tribunals continues to reflect a traditional reluctance to interpret the refugee definition via IHLR (e.g. as in Germany even with the binding EU law of the QD).[220] Furthermore, as regards the lack of jurisprudence from many of the world's countries, that is often a lack of *any* kind of jurisprudence on refugee law, human rights-based or otherwise. In addition, it remains the fact that at present there is not one country where judges have expressly rejected the human rights approach. Silence does not equal dissent.

Even in countries whose courts do not particularly apply a human rights approach, there sometimes can be a strong set of guidelines at the level of primary decision-making emphasising the importance of recourse to human rights norms. That is said to be the case in the US for example.[221]

Further, there may be various reasons why judges adjudicating asylum cases do not explicitly identify adoption of a human rights approach. For example, it might be excluded by national law at least in some respects (as in Australia).[222] For instance, it might not be compatible with the national legal culture or consistent with national codes governing judicial or quasi-judicial work to invoke IHRL norms or cite overseas cases.[223] It may not be part of the national legal culture to set out reasons relating to definitional aspects. It may even be because courts or tribunals do not make their decisions publicly available.[224] But such features do not necessarily mean that the judges concerned are unaware of or influenced by IHRL and the relevance of its norms to their deliberations, for example when they deal with cases concerned with the best interests of the child or sexual orientation. The regular activities held by international judicial associations such as the IARMJ would appear to indicate a significant volume of 'horizontal judicial dialogue' between judges across many countries.[225]

It must also be recalled that whilst the human rights approach is a paradigm, that does not mean it is a prescriptive grid. It is too purist to expect that a paradigm in the legal field only exists if it has crystallised through state practice into norms of customary international law. What is necessary for it to be viable is simply a substantial consensus at the level of state practice (at least in the broad sense), UNHCR guidance, case law, and scholarship, combined with the absence of any other credible alternative model(s) (we deal with the latter aspect below).

The truth of the matter is that far from the human rights approach having reached its zenith and to be now in decline, it is still in its relatively early stages. In the grand scheme of things, it is scarcely more than two decades that it has been acted upon. If there are currently divergent versions, then the challenge is not to abandon the paradigm but to reconcile them. Current political trends featuring populist rejection of

---

[220] See Bank (n 131) 156–79.
[221] Anker and Vittor (n 22) 116–19. See section 1.3 of this chapter.
[222] See Kirk (n 175) 85.
[223] In the US, see e.g. James W Leary, '"Outsourcing Authority?" Citation to Foreign Court Precedent in Domestic Jurisprudence & Refinement or Reinvention: The State of Reform in New York' (2006) 69(3) Albany Law Review 1. See also the 'treaty effectiveness' literature as discussed in e.g. Daniel W Hill Jr, 'Estimating the Effects of Human Rights Treaties on State Behavior' (2010) 72(4) The Journal of Politics 1161, 1169–73. For its application to refugee law, see Meili (n 131) 123.
[224] Tamara Wood, 'Who Is a Refugee in Africa? A Principled Framework for Interpreting and Applying Africa's Expanded Refugee Definition' (2019) 31(2/3) IJRL 290, 299.
[225] See Chapter 2, nn 66, 75, 336, and 339.

international law obligations altogether, might seem to provide all the more reason to hold fast to it.[226]

### 4.3.2 Unclear contents and fragmentation

Turning to the charges of unclear contents, lack of consistency, and 'fragmentation', Cantor argues that 'the sheer variety of human rights-based approaches to Article 1A(2) that are currently discernible in refugee law practice and scholarship calls into question the existence of a single "interpretive" paradigm'.[227] He writes that the 'human rights paradigm' 'is not cohesive but rather, across the different jurisdictions, seems to reflect a number of divergent understandings of the role of human rights in the interpretive exercise'.[228] It must again be acknowledged that there are differing versions of the human rights approach, e.g. (as already noted), some applying a hierarchical model, some applying a non-hierarchical model; some applying international human rights treaty norms, some applying regional human rights treaty norms (which have some differences); some confining the relevant IHRL norms to treaty norms, some extending them to soft-law instruments. However, it must be asked whether Cantor's expectation that the approach must embody 'a single interpretative paradigm' is warranted. That decision makers are sometimes applying the UN treaties, sometimes regional instruments, sometimes soft law instruments, does not gainsay the fact that there is broad consensus about the contents of the IHRL norms concerned. The fact that regional human rights treaties contain some differences (e.g. in the rights they set down as non-derogable) does create difficulties, but they are not in practice insuperable and have not led to significant deviation in the development of a consistent set of IHRL norms. To the contrary, there is considerable evidence that the standards applied by different international treaty-monitoring bodies and regional human courts and treaty-monitoring bodies are gradually converging.[229]

There are also cogent reasons for resisting the criticism of fragmentation. One, already noted, is that a certain level of diversity is to be expected of any viable paradigm and the existing levels of difference would appear to exist within tolerable limits. Whilst it is possible to weigh against the human rights approach that there are current tensions between hierarchical and non-hierarchical approaches and that some authors now speak about striking out in new directions,[230] those involved in these debates continue to share many assumptions. Indeed, it is hard to accept Cantor's view that his proposed non-discrimination framework is somehow distinct from a human rights framework given that non-discrimination is a foundational norm in customary international law.[231] As a customary norm, the non-discrimination principle has remained somewhat undefined. It is only within the framework of IHRL treaties that non-discrimination law has achieved any real specificity[232] and it could only be on the

---

[226] See Hugo Storey, 'The Human Rights Approach: Rising Sun or Falling Star' (2021) 33(3) IJRL 379.
[227] Cantor (n 11) 392.
[228] ibid 379; see also Jastram (n 122) 167, 171.
[229] Buckley et al (n 169).
[230] Cantor (n 11) 390–95; Scott (n 127) 112–31.
[231] Cantor (n 11) 390–94.
[232] See survey in Anthony Lester, 'Non-discrimination in International Human Rights Law' (1993) 19(4) Commonwealth Law Bulletin 1653.

basis of a non-discrimination norm having specificity that it would be possible to develop an alternative approach to the refugee definition.

Another reason to push back against the fragmentation accusation is that it is possible to discern in the unfolding debate between different human rights approaches (over, for example, the hierarchical and non-hierarchical approaches), a refinement of earlier understandings of the nature of the human rights emerging. Consider, for example, the clarifications made by the ESCR Committee regarding the minimum core obligations of certain economic and social rights.[233] It is realistic to expect more clarifications to emerge in IHRL and UNHCR doctrine, in the case law, and in the scholarship.

### 4.3.3 Failure to help with difficult issues

The co-existence of diverse versions of the human rights approach also impinges on the response to be given to Cantor's further point of criticism that the differences one finds in the human rights standards applied 'may be most likely on precisely those difficult issues where one might hope that recourse to human rights standards would provide a definitive and uniform answer'. He gives the example of the differing scope of the non-/derogability aspects of the right to freedom of religion in, respectively, the ICCPR and ECHR.[234] In response, at least two points might be made. First, his own analysis appears to recognise that at least in the past IHRL has been successfully drawn on to help tackle contentious issues.[235] Second, even assuming he is right in his analysis of this issue, it must be asked, why should we expect the human rights approach to provide definitive and uniform answers to the most difficult issues? If it is achieving broad consensus on a wide range of issues, should that not be the mark of success?

Even if IHRL law is failing to resolve certain important issues, it has helped clarify and frame many interpretive problems (consider, for example, the problem of whether conscientious objection to military service can found a claim for asylum).[236] On the issues that continue to be difficult, the human rights approach should be expected to offer informative answers—and it often does that. But if the paradigm could resolve all difficult questions, refugee law scholarship and new case law would be largely redundant. The existence of competing versions and applications of the human rights approach can be frustrating, but synthesis take time. And synthesis also requires commitment to achieving consensus.

Elsewhere in this book it is argued that over the past seventy years or so real progress has been made in agreeing on a number of basic propositions about the contents of the refugee definition. Quite often what runs through their articulation is the red thread of human rights concepts and values. If one concentrates on state practice (in

---

[233] See *DS (Iran)* (n 93) para 202: 'The discontinuance of the core/margin concept to describe the inquiry into the ambit of the right does not impact upon the continuing utility of the separate concept of a "minimum core obligation" for the purpose of claims based on violations of socio-economic rights.' See also *BG (Fiji)* [2012] NZIPT 800091, 93–109. This concept is said to provide 'greater specificity, legal determinacy and justiciability to the content of state obligations in respect of those rights which, unlike their civil and political counterparts, are subject to a progressive realisation provision'.
[234] Cantor (n 11) 382.
[235] ibid 353, 392.
[236] See Chapter 6, section 3.3.4.

the broad sense) and the progress made in agreeing on a number of key matters affecting the refugee definition, e.g. the ability of the definition to cover non-state actors of persecution and the shortcomings of interpretations based on the need to show 'persecutory intent', it has principally been arguments based on human rights law that have won these battles.[237] Additionally, the versatility and in-built dynamism of the human rights approach situates it as the approach most likely to yield greater analytical clarity and appropriate resolution of new issues as they arise.

### 4.3.4 A set of criteria or merely illustrative standards?

Cantor's belief that the UNHCR's 'illustrative' approach is still being utilised brings analysis back full circle, namely to the question of what can be said to constitute a human rights approach. The position taken earlier is that the term human rights approach can only strictly be applied to approaches that treat human rights as a determinative set of criteria to be applied to the refugee definition—what was referred to as a 'core' human rights approach. At a purely analytical level this must be correct, but it may be more prudent to regard that as an 'ideal-type'. As noted earlier, even adoption of a 'core' human rights approach does not entail invariable application of IHLR norms.[238] An alternative approach would be a 'big tent' understanding of the human rights approach as also encompassing theories that treat it as illustrative and non-exhaustive. The latter is more likely to accord with popular understanding. However, in order to retain any real sense of differentiation between approaches, it would still be reasonable to insist, in relation to any broad understanding, that to be classed as a human rights approach, it be one that regards recourse to human rights norms as having at least a substantial effect on refugee decision-making. Thus it does cover current UNHCR guidance, but does not cover, for example, the US 'subjective approach'.[239]

## 5 The Human Rights Approach: Advantages and Disadvantages of Specific Models

In addition to analysing the debates regarding the human rights approach at a general level, it is necessary to complement that with a brief analysis of the relative merits and demerits of the main types of human rights approaches.

### 5.1 Advantages and Disadvantages of Hierarchical Models

The key reasons why Hathaway's 1991 version gained such prominence have already been adverted to: it was squarely based on what states could be said to have subscribed

---

[237] For a human rights-based critique of persecutory intent see e.g. Karen Musalo, 'Irreconcilable Differences? Divorcing Refugee Protections from Human Rights Norms' (1994) 15 Michigan Journal of International Law 1179; see also Hugo Storey, 'What Constitutes Persecution? Towards a Working Definition' (2014) 25(2) IJRL 272, 278.
[238] See section 2.3.8 of this chapter.
[239] See section 1.3 of this chapter .

to in terms of international norms (in this respect, it was on a firmer footing than the UDHR which was non-binding); it also represented an example of an evolutive approach, taking into account the coming into being of the 1966 twin Covenants and other human rights treaties and the fact that it was commonplace at that time for hierarchical distinctions to be made between civil and political rights on the one hand and economic, social, and cultural rights on the other;[240] it provided an objective framework; and it furnished an identifiable catalogue of human rights.

Also seen as an advantage was that such an approach furnished a structured way of operationalising human rights norms in interpretation of key terms of the refugee definition. By virtue of the coming into force of the QD, whose Article 9 encapsulates a hierarchical approach, it now represented state practice at least in one important region. That development came on top of significant use made of the hierarchical approach in several common law countries.

One important feature of the hierarchical approach is that even though it attaches more weight to some categories of rights than others, it accepts that even rights not in the first category can give rise to persecution cumulatively. Thus, looking back at Hathaway's fourfold hierarchy as set out in 1991, the fact that the ICESCR rights rank only third in this hierarchy was clearly not understood to make them marginal to assessment of persecutory harm.[241]

The perceived disadvantages of a hierarchical model, Hathaway's in particular, include the following. There has been a concern that it results in a mechanistic approach and that it depends on untenable dichotomies between 'first generation' and 'second-generation rights' and between civil and political rights on the one hand and economic and social rights on the other. As articulated most forcibly by Foster, the hierarchical approach appears reliant on a system of categorisation that does not fit the permeable world of human rights law. The principal concept relied on to justify hierarchical ordering and to function as a metric of serious harm—derogation—'does not necessarily equate with normative importance or seriousness of harm, and attempts to identify those rights that are "fundamental", or "inalienable", and distinguish them from rights that are not, has proven impossible in the theory of human rights law'.[242] She points out that the ICESCR contains no distinction between derogable and non-derogable rights and that there is no binary distinction between duties of an immediate nature and those of progressive realisation.[243]

By its strong espousal of a hierarchical approach, the EU QD has been seen by Foster to demonstrate an unfortunate ongoing tendency to treat threats to civil and political rights as inherently more serious than threats to socio-economic rights. She considers that it 'risks retarding the progressive development of international refugee

---

[240] See Meron (n 75).
[241] Hathaway (n 28) 111.
[242] Foster (n 89) 244. See also Foster (n 8) 112–15, 175–81.
[243] Foster (n 8) 168–81; Shacknove (n 35) 695–705; Carlier (n 40). See also the analysis by Bruce Burson in *DS (Iran)* (n 93) 154–56. See also Ciara Smyth 'The Human Rights Approach to "Persecution" and Its Child Rights Discontents' (2021) 33(2) IJRL 238, 257 who argues that '[t]he hierarchical approach to human rights is deeply problematic from a child rights perspective'. She points out, inter alia, that all the rights in the CRC are non-derogable.

law by signalling a higher standard for measuring persecution than is justified at international law'.[244]

It has also to be noted that although hugely influential, Hathaway's 1991 model has been the only significant formulation of the hierarchical model. Although Carlier offered a distinct hierarchical model based on the 'Theory of Three Scales', it was never developed into a systematic theory.[245] Furthermore, outside New Zealand (until it was discarded by the New Zealand RSAA in 2005), the hierarchical model has not really been taken up in any systematic way in the jurisprudence or in the academic literature. By Article 9(1)(a), the QD has been seen to encapsulate a hierarchical approach because it requires that acts of persecution must 'be sufficiently serious by its nature or repetition as to constitute a severe violation of basic human rights, in particular the rights from which derogation cannot be made under Article 15(2) of the [ECHR]'. However, in point (a) 'basic human rights' are not confined to non-derogable rights. Further and in any event, Article 9(1)(b) of this same provision provides as an alternative that such acts can 'be an accumulation of various measures, including violations of human rights which is sufficiently severe as to affect an individual in a similar manner as mentioned in point (a)'. Therefore, the only real sense in which the Article 9 QD model can be described as hierarchical is in imposing (applicable under both (a) and (b) of Article 9(1)) a threshold of sufficient severity. That, however, does not in principle distinguish it from leading non-hierarchical models.[246]

## 5.2 Advantages and Disadvantages of the Non-Hierarchical Models

The non-hierarchical models, which have all evolved out of concerns about perceived disadvantages of the hierarchical models, still seek to apply an objective framework and one that enables identification to be made of specific rights engaged. Such models do better reflect the growing acceptance within IHRL that human rights are to be treated as equal, interdependent, and indivisible. They take stock of the growing body of IHRL instruments and the significant developments in case law via HR treaty-monitoring bodies (in both their decisions and their General Comments) and the regional human rights courts. The thematic approach adopted by Hathaway and Foster also fits well with contemporary classifications of human rights. Their approach also permits a more precise understanding of the particular contours of individual human rights: some being the subject of derogability clauses; some having express or implied limitations; some permitting restrictions on specified grounds; some imposing

---

[244] Foster (n 89) 244.
[245] See above section 2.4.1. According to his approach, '[t]he more fundamental the right in question... the less quantitively and qualitatively severe the treatment need be. The lower the priority attributed to the violated freedom (economic, social or cultural rights), the more quantitively and qualitatively severe the treatment must be.' See Shacknove (n 35) 704–05.
[246] On the position in New Zealand since 2005, see Burson (n 59) 36. As regards the concept of 'basic human rights', the CJEU held in *Y and Z*, para 64 that the right to religion (which is not a non-derogable right) was a 'basic right' (see also para 65). For further analysis of Article 9(1), QD, see Lehmann (n 315) 64: '[a]ccording to the [CJEU], it is the nature of the repression and its consequences rather than the substantive ambit of a right that forms the basis for identifying acts of persecution.'

minimum core obligations; others not. The core/periphery distinction can also be said to provide an intelligible basis for distinguishing between cases where the violation of a human right is or is not at the level of persecutory harm.

The non-hierarchical approach also ensures that there is no a priori downgrading of economic, social, and cultural rights when it comes to assessing violations of the human rights involved.

Given the criticisms that have been made of the application within refugee law of an extraneous concept of the seriousness or gravity of harm, it bears mentioning that the model advanced by Hathaway and Foster does ensure that this concept is operated conformably with the human rights jurisprudence of the main UN treaty-monitoring bodies and regional human rights courts.

Perceived disadvantages of the non-hierarchical approach include the following. Whilst it certainly helps ensure there is no mechanistic categorisation of rights (such that some are treated as intrinsically of a higher or lower order), it still depends nevertheless on recognition of the existing framework of human rights as contained in the major treaties and these do make distinctions between rights and between different levels of obligation. In the ICCPR, there is a key distinction between non-derogable and derogable rights. In the ICESCR, there is a key distinction between guarantees that impose an immediate obligation on states and ones that only require progressive realisation.[247] Further, despite representing that it has rejected such criteria, the non-hierarchical approach relies on taking careful account of the particular characteristics of each right (what is termed rather obliquely their 'inbuilt flexibility'),[248] which are sometimes non-derogable, sometimes subject to restrictions etc. Hathaway and Foster's non-hierarchical model still recognises in the second step of their recast model that: 'in limited and closely circumscribed situations, it may be necessary to disregard or suspend certain rights in the context of an emergency'.[249]

### 5.2.1 Foster's 2007 model

Difficulties that beset Foster's 2007 version include her heavy reliance on the core-periphery distinction. Her belief that there exists a broad consensus within IHRL on the core/periphery model has been undermined at least to some extent, not only by the critiques that have been advanced of it in IHRL, but by the lack of support it has received from refugee law scholars.[250] This distinction has also been rejected in leading cases, such as *RT (Zimbabwe)*,[251] *Y and Z*,[252] and *DS (Iran)*,[253] the last-mentioned which notes as one key problem that the term 'core' is used in different ways.[254] With reference to ECtHR case law, the IPT concludes that the core/margin analysis was

---

[247] See Hugo Storey, 'The Law of Refugee Status, 2nd Edition: Paradigm Lost' (2015) 27 IJRL 348.
[248] Hathaway and Foster (n 2) 205.
[249] ibid 207.
[250] Jastram (n 122) 168–69; Guy S Goodwin-Gill, 'The Dynamic of International Refugee Law' (2013) 25(4) IJRL 651, 655.
[251] *RT (Zimbabwe) and others v SSHD* [2012] UKSC 38, para 46; see also paras 42–52.
[252] Joined Cases C-71/11 and C-99/11 *Bundesrepublik Deutschland v Y and Z* [2012] ECLI:EU:C:2012:518, paras 62–63.
[253] *DS (Iran)* (n 93).
[254] ibid 190–96.

intended to perform an autonomous role not confined to the question of permissible limitation, and describes the relationship between the act and the right.[255] It notes that 'the concept and language of core/margin has, over time, become an unhelpful and confusing distraction and should no longer be used'.[256]

Foster has sought to respond to criticisms of the core/margin distinction advanced in her 2007 study. She rightly emphasises that it is based on the ESCR Committee's development of this distinction as an important tool to nuance the extent and scope of the rights violations in issue in any particular case,[257] but she offers no response to the criticisms that it is used in different ways and has garnered slender support in case law and scholarship.

It must be said, however, that if focus is kept on what constitutes a human rights approach in generic terms, the fact that Foster's model advocates a wider range of human rights being considered in order to establish the first step of a persecution assessment, may be enough in itself to justify the model. After all, in practice uses made of a human rights approach in case law and state practice rarely proceeds in a very structured fashion.

### 5.2.2 Hathaway and Foster's 2014 model

The main specific disadvantages of Hathaway and Foster's new non-hierarchical approach can be set out as follows. First, it is not clear that its central concepts of considering the 'impact on a right' and 'facets of a right' are sufficiently clear. They are not an integral a part of IHRL in the same way as 'sufficient severity' is. Second, it is not clear that, in continuing to rely on concepts such as sufficient seriousness or gravity of the harm, that they have entirely eliminated some hierarchisation, for example, when they recognise that infringements of 'a single core interest standing alone' such as the rights to food and shelter can give rise to serious harm.[258] Third, their reformulation creates a lack of clarity about thresholds of harm. They seem at times to suggest that even if the harm does not fall within the concept of ill-treatment, it can still constitute serious harm for the purposes of the refugee definition.[259] Such a suggestion leaves the puzzle as to what is serious harm if it is not at the level of severity to constitute ill-treatment or its cumulative equivalent? Are they in fact espousing a lower threshold of harm than that which Hathaway identified in 1991? Fourth, as already noted, their rejection of derogability creates the erroneous impression that they mean by a non-hierarchical approach a flatlining of rights, whereas what they in fact mean is that (as Hathaway himself formulated it in 1998), '[t]he interdependence and indivisibility of rights does not mean their legal equivalency'.[260] A further disadvantage is that Hathaway and Foster's reformulation still seeks to rely on a core/margin distinction in the third step

---

[255] ibid 195.
[256] ibid 199.
[257] Foster (n 89) 249–51.
[258] Hathaway and Foster (n 2) 235; and the reference to 'sufficiently serious' threshold at ibid 234. See also Foster (n 89) 249.
[259] Foster (n 89) 256.
[260] James C Hathaway, 'Human Rights and Refugee Law' in *The Realities of Refugee Determination on the Eve of a New Millennium: The Role of the Judiciary, 3rd Conference, October 1998, Ottawa, Canada* (IARLJ 1999) 88.

of their analysis. Although recast as merely a *de minimis* rule, it is not explained how it differs from the core/margin analysis outlined by Foster.

To summarise: the problem with the authors' attempt to revise the TLRS human rights paradigm is that for its clear workable structure they substitute a fungible, shifting threshold that sometimes gravitates towards the unanchored notion that the persecution threshold can be crossed even when the harm involved falls short of ill-treatment or its equivalent in the form of sufficiently severe violations of derogable rights. Arguably this direction of travel increases confusion.

### 5.2.3 The New Zealand model in *DS (Iran)*

The *DS (Iran)* approach was set out earlier.[261] Although describing itself as based on Hathaway and Foster's 2014 model, it is worth noting that this model's first two steps adhere more closely to the terminology of human rights treaties (focusing on 'interferences', at least in the context of rights with permissible limitations); and, unlike theirs, remain fully tied to the concept of serious harm. Whilst it too deploys the concept of 'impact', this is exclusively applied in relation to whether the harm amounts to serious harm. Also, in another contrast to Hathaway and Foster's formulation, it does not rely on any core/margin distinction.[262]

### 5.2.4 Evaluation

Whatever may have been the state of international opinion in 1991 or beforehand,[263] IHRL has now turned its face heavily against a hierarchical approach to the ranking of human rights and obligations arising therefrom. It is not just, as were the two main points invoked by Foster in her 2007 study, that the Vienna Declaration and Programme of Action had declared in 1993 that '[a]ll human rights are universal, indivisible and interdependent and interrelated' and that the UN actors responsible for economic, social, and cultural rights have concluded that 'the era of the hierarchization of human rights is more or less over and that a unified approach is to be sought in the interpretation of the relationship between the two major sets of rights'.[264] Fatally, for advocates of the view that the ICCPR rights are superior, this treaty's own treaty-monitoring committee, the HRC, has now adopted a unified approach. Whilst still according a role to non-derogable rights, it has stated in *General Comment No 24* that, 'there is no hierarchy of importance of rights under the Covenant'.[265] This doctrine has

---

[261] *DS (Iran)* (n 93); see above section 2.4.2.3.

[262] See ibid.

[263] Perhaps the genesis of the increasing shift from a hierarchical approach to a non-hierarchical one can best be traced back to Theodore Meron's observation in 1986 that 'to choose which rights are more important than other rights is exceedingly difficult'. See Meron (n 75). See also Ian Brownlie, *Principles of Public International Law* (6th edn, OUP 2003) 488, cited in Hathaway and Foster (n 2) 204.

[264] Foster cites, inter alia, Danilo Türk, 'The New International Economic Order and the Promotion of Human Rights: Realization of Economic, Social and Cultural Rights (Preliminary Report)' (28 June 1989) UN Doc E/CN.4/Sub.2/1989/19, para 26; Danilo Türk, 'The New International Economic Order and the Promotion of Human Rights: Realization of Economic, Social and Cultural Rights (Final Report)' (3 July 1992) UN Doc E/CN.4/Sub.2/1992/16, paras 26–27. See also ESCR Committee, General Comment No 3 (14 December 1990) UN Doc E/1991/23, para 8.

[265] HRC, General Comment No 24 on Issues Relating to Reservations Made upon Ratification or Accession to the Covenant or the Optional Protocols thereto, or in Relation to Declarations under Article 41 of the Covenant (4 November 1994) UN Doc CCPR/C/21/Rev.1/Add.6, para 10.

been further reiterated by the Committee on the Rights of the Child[266] and in HRC and regional human rights courts' case law.[267]

Rejection of hierarchical models within IHRL also comports with wider developments in international law. Dinah Shelton has highlighted that, especially with greater development of 'soft-law' instruments, there is 'an increasingly complex international system with variations in forms of instruments, means, and standards of measurement that interact intensely and frequently, with the common purpose of regulating behaviour within a rule-of-law framework'.[268] A more recent survey, having noted the lack of consensus regarding any hierarchy, concluded that: 'if a hierarchy of norms is ever to be found it will be based on the content of the norm reflecting the values that the norm was created to protect'.[269]

However, whilst the non-hierarchical models discussed above must therefore be seen to offer a better basis for further development of a human rights approach, it must be viewed as unfortunate that Hathaway and Foster have sought to focus their critique of the hierarchical approach so much on use of the derogability criterion, since, as their own reformulations demonstrate, this must remain a part of any human rights approach, for so long as IHRL deploys this criterion in treaties. These models have yet to furnish a comparably clear, workable structure.

Nonetheless, for the purposes of affirming a human rights paradigm, it remains that it is unnecessary to seek to decide conclusively between a hierarchical or non-hierarchical approach. The arguments for and against each model remain balanced, even though (in the view of this author) increasingly pointing against the former. It may be that the best way to approach both is to recognise that there are different ways of assessing the relative importance to be given to specific rights when considering whether the violation of the right or rights concerned is sufficiently serious to amount to persecution. For the hierarchical approach, the way advocated is to identify violations of some rights (non-derogable rights) as necessarily amounting to persecution (and only considering violations of others as persecutory if they are, cumulatively, sufficiently severe) whereas for the others it depends on whether violations of any right, taken on its own or cumulatively, reach a requisite threshold of serious (severe) harm. For the non-hierarchical approach, the approach taken is to consider the

---

[266] UN Committee on the Rights of the Child (CRC Committee), General Comment No 14 (2013) on the right of the child to have his or her best interests taken as a primary consideration (art 3, para 1) (29 May 2013) UN Doc CRC/C/GC/14, para 4. See also CRC Committee, General Comment No 5 (2003): General measures of implementation of the Convention on the Rights of the Child (27 November 2003) UN Doc CRC/GC/2003/5, para 6, stating that '[t]here is no simple or authoritative division of human rights in general or of Convention rights into the two categories'.

[267] For HRC cases, see e.g. *Young v Australia* (18 September 2003) Communication No 491/2000, UN Doc CCPR/C/78/D/941/2000; *Derksen (on behalf of Bakker) v Netherlands* (1 April 2004) Communication No 976/2001, UN Doc CCPR/C/80/D/976/2001. For ECtHR cases, see e.g. *Koua Poirrez v France* App No 40892/98 (ECtHR, 30 September 2003); *Hatton et al v United Kingdom* App No 36027/97 (ECtHR, 8 July 2003); *Taskin et al v Turkey* App No 46117/99 (ECtHR, 10 November 2004). For references in this and the preceding footnote, I am grateful to Tahvanainen (n 75).

[268] Dinah Shelton, 'Normative Hierarchy in International Law' (2006) 100(2) AJIL 291. Interestingly, TLRS2 leaves unresolved Foster's and Hathaway's differences regarding the relevance of soft-law sources: see Foster (n 8) 70–74.

[269] Tahvanainen (n 75) 194.

specific features of each right (which may include derogability but also cover permissible limitations) and ask about whether the impact of the interference in them constitutes serious harm. Yet from this summary it can be seen that both approaches accept that for there to be persecution the violation of the human right(s) involved must be sufficiently severe (or serious). Putting matters this way underscores that the two are not miles apart. Both approaches would appear capable in many cases, of achieving similar results. However, there remains a need for further clarification.

## 5.3 Other Models

Mention should be made of two other models that have been proposed in the context of ongoing debates regarding the human rights approach.

### 5.3.1 Cantor's model

The first is the model proposed by Cantor. In view of his extensive criticisms of the human rights approach, it is unclear whether it really constitutes a new human rights model, or is rather to be seen as a distinct alternative to a human rights approach. In any event it is convenient to consider it here, along with the expressly human rights-based model proposed by Matthew Scott, as there are similarities.

Critical to Cantor's new theoretical model is the concept of non-discrimination, which he describes as a 'free-standing principle of law that also underpins much of the framework of human rights law'. For him, it is the concept of discrimination expressed by the Convention reasons rather than the harm implicit in the element of persecuting that should form the starting-point for interpreting the refugee definition in Article 1A(2).[270] However, there are two particular problems with Cantor's analysis. First, in order for non-discrimination to perform the central organising role he advocates, it would have to be shown that it was a defining characteristic of persecution. As will be analysed in Chapter 6, that is a proposition that is exceedingly difficult to sustain. Second, even assuming he is correct, it is far from clear that this innovation creates the need for an alternative approach to a human rights one. As noted earlier, non-discrimination is embedded in human rights law or, in his own words, is a principle that 'also underpins much of the framework of human rights law'.[271] Indeed, it is more accurately seen as an essential part of human rights law. As noted by Greenberg,[272] racial, sexual, and religious discrimination are, certainly in terms of attention paid in treaty law, the overarching human rights concern of the international community. In the UN Charter, the UDHR and the main human rights treaties, the guarantees against discrimination are formulated as human rights guarantees. The ICCPR alone contains three articles which expressly forbid discrimination: Articles 2(1), 3, and 26 (Article 4 also prevents application of the derogation proviso in a discriminatory

---

[270] Cantor (n 11) 391.
[271] ibid 390–91; see section 4.3.2 of this chapter.
[272] Cited in Steinbock (n 65) 789.

178  APPROACHES, ORDERING, INTERRELATIONSHIPS, MODALITIES

fashion). For that reason, it has been said by one leading commentator that 'equality and non-discrimination constitute the dominant single theme of the Covenant'.[273]

This integral connection between human rights law and discrimination is of decisive importance when it comes to any application of a theoretical model based on non-discrimination. It is only within the framework of IHRL treaties that non-discrimination law has achieved any real specificity[274] and (as already noted) it could only be on the basis of a non-discrimination norm having specificity that it would be possible to develop an alternative approach to the refugee definition. Seen in this light, if Cantor's approach has any utility, it can really only be as a variation on existing human rights approaches, rather than an alternative to them. In any event, Cantor's suggested approach is presently just that—the merest outline of an alternative approach—not a fully developed theory or paradigm.

### 5.3.2 Scott's model

Mention should also be made of Matthew Scott's approach in his recent book, *Refugee Status Determination in the Context of 'Natural' Disasters and Climate Change*.[275] Later chapters will analyse some aspects of this approach more specifically, but focus here is on his argument that the organising principle for interpreting the personal scope of refugee definition should be the principle of non-discrimination, which he sees as permeating the definition of 'being persecuted' and not just being confined to the nexus clause. In Scott's analysis, 'being persecuted' is rather a 'condition of existence in which discrimination is a contributory cause of (a real chance of being exposed to) serious denials of human rights demonstrative of state protection'.[276] He thinks that treating non-discrimination as a foundational norm is particularly apposite to RSD because, like the concept of 'structural violence', the concept of systemic discrimination allows for a 'social paradigm' approach.[277]

Whatever is made of Cantor's approach, Scott's approach positions itself firmly within the human rights paradigm. In terms of personal scope, Scott's critique likewise only has a point if it is accepted that discrimination is a necessary condition of 'being persecuted' but, as is explained in Chapter 6,[278] that is a very difficult argument to uphold. If he is wrong about that, then the personal scope in terms of human rights violations is adequately limited by the Convention reasons and does not need some further limit. (Such further limit would also create the oddity of discrimination criteria being applied twice.)

To conclude, whilst there has been no attempt here to deal exhaustively with attempted alternatives to a human rights approach, it does not appear that there are any new theoretical models offered up so far that provide a viable alternative. The most that can be said is that there remains significant support for adopting, as have some of the leading textbooks, in particular Goodwin-Gill and McAdam's work, a relatively

---

[273] Bertrand G Ramcharan, 'Equality and Non-Discrimination' in Louis Henkin (ed), *The International Bill of Rights: The Covenant on Civil and Political Rights* (Columbia University Press 1981) 246.
[274] See survey in Lester (n 232).
[275] Scott (n 127).
[276] ibid 129.
[277] ibid 115.
[278] See Chapter 6, section 3.5.1.

noncommittal view towards the human rights approach, endorsing its key rationale but insisting on maintaining a critical approach when that is seen as justified, for example, in disparaging the strong reliance within the human rights approach on a surrogacy model.[279] That is not an unimportant fact, since it points strongly against espousal of a human rights approach if the latter is conceived as a strict set of criteria that cannot be deviated from.

The truth remains though that it is impossible to conceive of an analysis of the refugee definition uninfluenced by human rights law: as Chetail has written, 'the refugee definition has been critically reshaped by human rights law through a gradual process of pollination'.[280] Its in-built dynamism also positions it to be the most likely approach to resolve new issues as they arise.

## 6 The Human Rights Approach and International Law

### 6.1 The Primacy of International Law

Even though UNHCR has not embraced the human rights approach as an exhaustive set of criteria, it is fair to say that one reason for that is its recognition that there are other bodies of international law that have some relevance to refugee subject-matter. Thus, ExCom has noted that refugee law is a dynamic body of law which is 'informed by the object and purpose' of the Convention and Protocol 'and by developments in related areas of international law, such as human rights and international humanitarian law'.[281]

ExCom's formulation is instructive. Whilst the critique of the human rights approach for not being sufficient unto itself fails (insofar as that critique seeks to argue that there are higher value systems beyond international law based on legitimacy or moral and political ethics),[282] it remains correct that human rights is not exhaustive of the framework of relevant international law. The dynamic application of VCLT rules to different elements of the refugee definition sometimes requires an intensive human rights approach, but sometimes recourse to other areas of international law, such as the international law on nationality and statelessness and the law on statehood and state responsibility. Even in relation to the 'being persecuted' and protection elements of the definition, where human rights norms are widely seen to have most application, there can be contexts in which insights from international humanitarian law and even international criminal law can be instructive, such as in cases involving armed civilians or child soldiers.[283]

---

[279] Goodwin-Gill and McAdam (n 175) 8–9, 70–71. But see Chapter 7, section 1.4.
[280] Chetail (n 61) 23; Chetail (n 62) 207–09.
[281] UNHCR, Conclusion on the Provision on International Protection Including Through Complementary Forms of Protection No 103 (LVI)—2005 (07 October 2005) para (c).
[282] See e.g. Price (n 100) 136.
[283] For early extra-curial analyses of the relevance to IRL of both IHRL and international humanitarian law, see Roger Errera, 'Humanitarian Law, Human Rights and Refugee Law: The Three Pillars' in *The Asylum Process and the Rule of Law* (IARLJ 2006). For a recent survey of the principal debates, see Reuven (Ruvi) Ziegler, 'International Humanitarian Law and Refugee Protection' in Costello et al (n 62) 221–39.

Further, whereas (failing international anarchy) there will always be some body of international norms that recognisably comprise international law, it cannot be excluded that human rights might in the distant future be seen as a time-bound set of international law norms, subsequently replaced by others.[284] Even if the failure to prevent the growing inequalities generated by twenty first-century global capitalism and related failures seen by Posner and others to afflict human rights law do not herald its decline, there is always the possibility of extreme global events such as major wars, natural disasters and/or climate change, and/or epidemics/pandemics leading to the temporary or permanent abrogation of the Refugee Convention.

For these reasons it would be wrong to hold up the human rights approach to the refugee definition as a fixity. Today it is dominant, but it might not be even in a foreseeable future. An international law framework, by contrast, is far more likely to remain a permanent feature of world order, even if the world order becomes relatively dystopian.

None of this should deflect attention from the realistic prospect that the persistency of populism and anti-globalisation movements may lead to the Refugee Convention being increasingly seen as a threat to nation-states and global corporations and that it will become harder for decision makers to continue to apply a human rights approach without facing attack and resistance. In this author's view, that should be a powerful reason for not seeking to reject it.

## 6.2 The Refugee Convention as a Sub-Species of IHRL?

Brief attention needs paying to the view espoused by Chetail among others that the Refugee Convention has been subsumed by IHRL and that refugees should now be seen as just one example of persons who are at risk of human rights violations. Identification of the primacy of the international law framework makes clear why this view is misplaced. There are two main drawbacks to Chetail's analysis.

First, Chetail's notion that the Refugee Convention is somehow narrower and lacks the universalism of IHRL because 'the benefit of refugee status depends on the identification of a predetermined category of protected persons', does not withstand scrutiny.[285] It misrepresents the Convention's personal scope. Whilst the Refugee Convention distinguishes between nationals and stateless persons, these two categories between them exhaust all possibilities. Further, the Refugee Convention possesses a universalism in the most important sense: all persons able to meet the conditions set out in the definition stand to qualify as refugees. There are, it remains true, certain limitations to the scope of the refugee definition, for example, its requirement that applicants be outside the country and have a well-founded fear of being persecuted, but such limitations do not undermine the definition's regard for the dignity inherent in every human being.

Second, even within the body of IHRL law, it is apparent that in relation to persons seeking protection in other states because of dangers in their own, the Refugee

---

[284] As envisaged by Posner (n 109) 137–48.
[285] Chetail (n 61) 23; Chetail (n 62) 205.

Convention has primacy. The notion of the primacy of the Refugee Convention is not just a strong objective of the international community through the medium of treaties and global compacts, it is a true reflection of the international legal reality that when people flee their own countries and seek asylum in another, for most states in the world this gives rise to a binding obligation to assess, at least as a minimum, whether or not they are a refugee under the Refugee Convention. Significantly, in cases involving risk on return, both human rights treaty-monitoring bodies and the regional human rights courts see their own jurisdiction over persons in a refugee-like situation as complementary.[286]

## 7 How Do Different Elements of the Refugee Definition Fit Together?

Another 'framework' issue needing attention before proceeding to analyse the key elements of the refugee definition concerns conceptual organisation of the definition. It is hard to examine each element individually without any clear understanding of how they each fit together or of where the analysis of the definition as a whole is heading, or why. This problem is compounded by the fact that some of the most important studies of the definition contain quite strong views on how its various elements should be seen as fitting together. Two particular questions arise. The first stands on its own: in what order should the different elements of the definition be tackled? The second is: what is the interrelationship between the different elements? This second questions sometimes encompasses a further question, namely, in which element or elements of the definition should one 'locate' certain requirements?

### 7.1 The Nature of the Problem

#### 7.1.1 The text
To the question 'How Do the Different Elements Fit Together?' the text of Article 1A(2) definition furnishes no answer. Its wording is open-textured. It does not impose a particular ordering or step-by-step sequence, in the way sometimes expected of provisions of domestic law statutes. All the text reveals on its face is four main clauses:

'... owing to a well-founded fear of being persecuted'
'for reasons of race, religion, nationality, membership of a particular social group or political opinion'
'is outside the country of his nationality/or [for those not having a nationality] country of ... former habitual residence'
'and is unable or, owing to such fear, is unwilling to avail himself of the protection of that country; [or who, not having a nationality and being outside the country of his

---

[286] See *JK and Others v Sweden* App No 59166/12 (ECtHR, 4 June 2015) para 52.

former habitual residence as a result of such events, is unable, or, owing to such fear], is unwilling to return to it'

Although often called the 'well-founded fear' clause, the first clause in full also includes the most material element of the definition, that of 'being persecuted'.

The second clause in the above list, that setting out the Convention reasons, is clearly dependent on the 'being persecuted' element but in any event has a relatively simple structure, identifying five reasons and the need for them to have a nexus to persecution.

The third and fourth clauses in the above list harness together common provisions applying to nationals and non-nationals, with necessary variation in the fourth clause to deal with the inability of non-nationals to return. The third clause—'outside the country' (sometimes called the 'alienage' clause, although that terminology is not adopted in this study)[287] appears to be a self-contained and relatively discrete clause comprising just two elements: 'outside the country' and nationality (or its lack). That leaves the fourth clause, which is often referred to as the 'protection clause' but which this study prefers to term the 'availment clause'. It is expressed conjunctively ('and is ... ').

### 7.1.2 Ordering

Existing studies display significant variation in the order in which elements are tackled, as the following examples, limited to English language texts, show. The UNHCR Handbook deals first with 'well-founded fear of being persecuted' (and, within that clause, with 'well-founded fear' first), then Convention reasons (dealing first with the nexus requirement), then 'outside the country of his nationality', then the availment clause.[288] Zimmerman and Mahler, opt to follow the classic Commentary approach of taking each element as it arises in the wording of the definition.[289] Goodwin-Gill and McAdam do not deal with the Article 1A(2) elements in any particular order but state their view that:

> The Convention definition begins with the refugee as someone with a well-founded fear of persecution, and only secondly, as someone who is unable or unwilling by reason of such fear, to use or take advantage of the protection of their government...[290]

In their 2014 book, Hathaway and Foster deal first with 'alienage', then 'well-founded fear', then 'being persecuted' (divided into 'serious harm' and 'failure of state protection') then the 'nexus to civil or political status'.[291] The major studies published by Anker, by Symes and Jorro, and by Waldman each deal with 'well-founded fear', then

---

[287] Hathaway (n 28) 17–90. See p. 260.
[288] UNHCR Handbook (n 10).
[289] Zimmermann and Mahler (n 8).
[290] Goodwin-Gill and McAdam (n 175) 8—albeit they call the definition the 'emblematic paradigm of protection'.
[291] Hathaway and Foster (n 2).

'persecution', then 'reasons for the persecution'. Unlike Anker, Symes and Jorro add specific chapters on 'Protection against Non-state Actors and Internal Relocation' and 'Countries of Nationality and Habitual Residence'; Waldman adds specific chapters on 'outside the country' and 'inability or unwillingness to seek the protection of the country of nationality'.[292]

Lack of consensus about the precise order in which to analyse different elements of the definition is unsurprising. Even those who consider one or another clause to be core do not necessarily deal with it first. Unless it can be established that taking the elements in a particular order results in demonstrable error, it should be open to decision makers (and commentators) to tackle them in the order they see fit. If, as will be argued shortly, the definition is to be understood as interlocking and holistic in nature, then *a fortiori* all that is essential is that each key element is covered at some point, ideally with some analysis of how they interrelate.

That said, some order has to be chosen. That followed in this study does not adhere to the textual ordering because, for example, it is felt that this would entail tackling 'well-founded fear' first without any identification of the object of such fear.

Each of the chapters dealing with one of the key elements will say something more about ordering, but the following is an outline.

The two elements of the refugee definition tackled first are nationality and statelessness and that relating to 'outside the country', since they concern personal scope and, at least for decision makers, if personal scope is not established, there is no basis for proceeding to analyse a refugee application further.

Subsequent chapters then address the definition's material scope dealing first with 'being persecuted' (see immediately below), then the availment clause, then Convention reasons and finally the 'well-founded fear' element.

In the case of the 'being persecuted' element (reflecting the fact that it represents the core material component of the definition and the one which has been seen to require most attention), it is dealt with in three segments (each having its own chapter): 'being persecuted and serious harm', 'being persecuted and protection' and 'being persecuted and the internal protection alternative'. It is considered most logical and also textually apposite to only then deal with availment (in Chapter 9) because the latter is essentially about protection against persecution and so presupposes full understanding of its opposite—persecution. Whatever the precise boundary lines between the concepts of 'being persecuted' and the availment clause, they are closely connected. Chapter 10 on Convention reasons then follows. 'Well-founded fear' is dealt with last mainly to underline that its meaning cannot be understood without having unpacked in full its object, namely fear *of* being persecuted etc. Nevertheless, this ordering must remain a matter of choice, since, as highlighted earlier, the definition itself does not impose one.

### 7.1.3 Interrelationship between the different elements

The second question concerns the interrelationship between the different elements of the definition.

---

[292] Anker (n 21); Mark Symes and Peter Jorro, *Asylum Law and Practice* (LexisNexis 2003); Lorne Waldman, *The Definition of Convention Refugee* (2nd edn, Lexis Nexis 2019).

The silence of the Article 1A(2) text not only about ordering but about interrelationship between the different elements has resulted in numerous theories about how best the latter should be understood. In light of the lack of any clear internal structure, it is to be expected that commentators should seek to elicit one through interpretation. However, it is doubtful that anyone could have anticipated that efforts in this direction would spiral as they have into such a complex and tortuous set of theories forming what can fairly be described as an 'intermediary layer' between the reader and the definition's different elements.

## 7.2 The Different Debates

As alluded to earlier, the question about the interrelationship between the definition's different elements has two intertwining strands to it: one about which clause or 'limb' is to be regarded as of primary importance; and the other about where precisely, within different elements, different requirements of the definition should fit. The debates summarised below, some of which overlap, cover both aspects.

It will be necessary in the subsequent chapters on individual elements to address the extent to which any of the debates identified below are still ongoing or can be treated as resolved, but since 1951 we can discern the following:

- Debates about the 'fear test'. These have essentially been about whether one element of the 'well-founded fear of being persecuted' clause is availability of state protection. Through the common law case law, the view that it should *not* be treated as one element of this clause has become associated with the minority position taken by Lord Lloyd in *Horvath*.[293]
- Debates about the 'protection test'. Among the issues raised in these exchanges have been whether there can be protection against non-state actors of persecution,[294] whether protection is to be seen as part of the 'being persecuted' element or part of the 'well-founded fear' element or both,[295] or alternatively part of—or at least influenced by—the 'availment' limb.[296]
- Debates about the proper location or 'home' of the 'protection inquiry'—whether such inquiry is to be anchored in the 'well-founded fear of being persecuted' limb or is a test confined (as Lord Lloyd thought in *Horvath*) to the availment clause. There has also been debate about whether, within the 'well-founded fear of being

---

[293] *Horvath* (n 208). Lord Lloyd had previously argued for a sharp distinction between a 'fear test' and a 'protection test' in *R v SSHD, ex parte Adan* [1999] 1 AC 293.

[294] As explained by Laws LJ in *Adan* (n 293), at that time France and Germany subscribed to the 'accountability' theory, which limited the class of case in which an applicant may obtain refugee status to situations where the persecution alleged can be attributed to the state. See discussion in Kälin and Künzli (n 141); Zimmermann and Mahler (n 8) 364. See further, Chapter 6, section 3.2.2.

[295] *Horvath* (n 208); *Adan* (n 293).

[296] *Horvath* (n 208). See p. 430, which notes, inter alia, Lehmann's view that the protection analysis is essentially an aspect of the risk assessment forming part of the 'well-founded fear' limb.

persecuted' clause, the issue of protection should play a primary or secondary role.[297]
- Also interlinked with these two debates, are disputed positions about whether the internal protection alternative (IPA) should be located in the 'well-founded fear' or the 'being persecuted' elements of the 'well-founded fear of being persecuted' clause[298] and also about whether the IPA should be located rather in the availment clause (among those taking the latter position are Hathaway and Foster).[299]
- Debate about the proper location of the risk assessment—whether it is to be regarded as part of the 'well-founded fear' or the 'being persecuted' elements.[300]
- Debate about whether the non-discrimination criterion contained within the Convention reasons or nexus clause should also be seen as a component of the concept of 'being persecuted'. Almost all locate it in the nexus clause;[301] Scott, however, invokes some judicial observations to support his argument that it is also, and importantly, to be found in the 'being persecuted' element.[302]
- Although fundamentally only a debate about the meaning of the 'membership of a particular social group' element of the nexus clause, there have also been clashes between those who contend that the approach should be that of 'social perception' and those who say it should be that of 'protected characteristics'; and between those who say it can be either and those who say it must be both. The various debates over these issues have sometimes been seen to have ramifications for the entire unitary understanding of the refugee definition.[303]

Entangled with all of these debates are inevitably some of the wider questions already tackled in Chapter 2 and in section 1 of this chapter e.g. the question of whether and to what extent the refugee definition should reflect an international law and/or human rights approach[304] and what should be the role of preambular objectives other than protection of human rights.[305]

7.2.1 Is this intermediary level of analysis necessary?
Subsequent chapters will strive to examine how the above-mentioned debates have been resolved (if at all) or where the balance of opinion lies. Focus here, however, is not on how these debates should be resolved, but on how much if at all we need to evaluate and/or take notice of them.

As the footnotes to the above summary convey, this layer has not been particularly an academic creation. The prime movers have been judges. The most detailed and authoritative analyses of these issues have been made in leading judgments of senior

---

[297] *Horvath* (n 208). See also Guy S Goodwin-Gill and Jane McAdam, *The Refugee in International Law* (3rd edn, OUP 2007) 10; Goodwin-Gill and McAdam (n 175) 8.
[298] *Januzi* (n 201).
[299] Hathaway and Foster (n 2) 332–42.
[300] Scott (n 127) 100–07.
[301] See *DS (Iran)* (n 93).
[302] Scott (n 93) 113–31; see pp. 381–384.
[303] See p. 595.
[304] See also above sections 6.1–6.2.
[305] See Chapter 2, sections 2.4–2.5.

courts; indeed it seems that addressing them in detail has predominantly been a preoccupation of the common law jurisdictions, in UK cases such as *Adan*,[306] *Horvath*,[307] and *Januzi*,[308] and Australian cases such as *S152*[309] and New Zealand cases such as *Butler*.[310] The separate discussion of such issues in the academic literature of these issues has been largely a reaction to this amalgam of case law.

It is doubtful that anyone intended this meta-level of analysis to proliferate as it did. Indeed, if one looks again at *Horvath*, wherein (as we shall discuss in Chapters 6, 7, and 8) discussions about the different locations for the proper inquiry featured prominently, the judges concerned voiced a strong *cri de coeur* for simplicity and avoidance of technicality. They genuinely thought they were addressing such complexities purely in order to clear them out of the way so that judges could get on with the essential work. Thus, in *Horvath*, Lord Clyde stated that:

> [ ... ] it is obviously undesirable to heap onto the shoulders of the adjudicators and the members of the tribunals who already have a heavy burden of work an additional complexity in the unravelling of legal issues on the precise construction of the particular words used in the Convention.[311]

But whether or not instigated by judges, engaging in debate about where key elements fit continues (as we shall see) to be a noticeable feature of the refugee law literature.

It has to be conceded as well that what has driven at least some of the discussion at this 'meta'-level are very good intellectual reasons. For example, reflecting on the UK House of Lords decision in *Januzi*, it is hard to dispute the legitimacy of the desire expressed by their lordships in that case, by other judges in common law countries,[312] and also by some academics to at least explain how the IPA (still known in the UK as the 'internal relocation alternative') is to be read into the Article 1A(2) definition. The role of the IPA in the refugee definition is dealt with in Chapter 8, but assuming for the moment that the IPA concept is an essential element of the definition (about which there is now considerable but still not substantial consensus), there is an obvious question that arises. How in consistency does one say on the one hand that the refugee definition should be capable of being at least understood on the basis of the text (and expressed in a simple way that sets out all the essential conditions of refugeehood), yet on the other hand maintain that there is nothing at all in that text to indicate a condition requiring applicants to show there is no viable IPA?

Nevertheless, unresolved exchanges at this level have drawbacks. They can fairly be said to represent a disconnect between decision makers and scholars and/or a failure in the duty that falls on all to try and make things as clear and simple as much as possible. It is especially debates of this kind that have fuelled criticisms of refugee law for being too

---

[306] *Adan* (n 293).
[307] *Horvath* (n 208).
[308] *Januzi* (n 201). However, the conclusions in *Januzi* were broadly approved by the German Federal Administrative Court: see Chapter 8, n 184.
[309] *MIMA v Respondents S152/2003* [2004] 222 CLR 1 (Aus HC).
[310] *Butler v A-G* [1999] NZAR 205.
[311] *Horvath* (n 208).
[312] See e.g. Kirby J in *SZATV v MIC* [2007] HCA 40, 233 CLR 18, para 62.

arcane, too scholastic. Can anything be done to ensure debates of this order do not continue to play as much a role as they still do in refugee law?

7.2.2 Arguments for and against the value or necessity of this type of inquiry

The arguments in favour of the value and necessity of this type and level of inquiry fall into two main categories. One sees it as entailed by the need for analytical rigour. The other maintains that correctly locating definitional requirements within one or the other element or limb leads to avoidance of error.

*7.2.2.1 Analytical rigour*

The need for analytical rigour is well articulated by a 2003 New Zealand case in which the RSAA adopted a 'predicament' approach. It observed:

> It is essential to ensure that one element is not inadvertently given a function or meaning which more properly belongs to another.... Thus the question whether there is a Convention ground cannot sensibly be conflated or confused with the issue of risk (the well-foundedness element). Similarly, the question whether the anticipated harm can properly be described as 'being persecuted' is not an analysis which belongs in the assessment of risk.[313]

That the focus on the interrelationship between the definition's elements continues to be prominent is evident from two recent studies. Thus, Scott argues that refugee law has taken a wrong turning in giving a function and meaning to aspects of the 'well-founded fear' criterion and the nexus requirement that more properly belong to the 'being persecuted' element of the refugee definition.[314] Thus Julian Lehmann considers that the shift away from understanding 'protection of the country of nationality' in the availment clause as external protection and understanding it instead as internal protection, reinforced by a human rights approach, entails the conclusion that this clause 'does not circumscribe a criterion for refugeehood in addition to the Convention's requirements of a well-founded fear of being persecuted'.[315]

Yet is it in fact vital for the sake of analytical rigour to identify and demarcate different locations (whether they be clauses or different elements within clauses)? For a number of interrelated reasons, it is counterintuitive to treat them as such. First, there is the widely accepted need for a broad reading of the refugee definition, something highlighted by more than one of the Convention drafters.[316]

Second, as already explained in Chapter 2, the VCLT rules of interpretation require an integrated approach to various criteria. Applying them means recognising that textual or linguistic interpretation can rarely be determinative, particularly since (as explained in subsequent chapters), most if not all of the key terms in the refugee definition are either

---

[313] *Refugee Appeal 74665/03* (n 84) 48.
[314] Scott (n 127) chs 4–6.
[315] Julian Lehmann, *'Protection' in European Union Asylum Law* (Brill Nijhoff 2020) 70–72. See also Jessica Schultz, *The Internal Protection Alternative in Refugee Law* (Brill Nijhoff 2018).
[316] See Terje Einarsen, 'Drafting History of the 1951 Convention and the 1967 Protocol' in Zimmermann (ed) (n 8) 61.

ambiguous or can have more than one meaning. If textual interpretation cannot be determinative, then neither can be insistence on specific readings of key parts of the text, so as to make the case for locating the refugee definition inquiry in one element or clause or the other. This strongly suggests that the approach should not be overly technical or semantic.

Third, given that the Refugee Convention is either to be regarded as a human rights treaty or one strongly influenced by human rights norms,[317] it has become well-established that those interpreting it must apply the principle of dynamic or evolutive interpretation. At the heart of this principle is the desire to ensure a treaty is relevant to and responds to new circumstances. That is important because it means that it is not the kind of treaty where it is possible to insist on close adherence to the intentions of the drafters as evinced through the *travaux*.[318] We see this most clearly in the treatment of the concept of protection within Article 1A(2) where despite the drafters having primarily and expressly had in mind only 'external protection', it is now widely accepted that it is to be understood as encompassing both external and domestic protection and that indeed it is domestic or internal protection which is of primary importance.[319] Requiring would-be interpreters of the refugee definition to engage upon a meta-theoretical level of inquiry about where different elements are located, etc., does not fit well with the need for interpretation to be dynamic.

Fourth, perhaps most important of all, there is a wide acceptance that the approach to the refugee definition must be a holistic one.[320] As was stated by McHugh in *Applicant A*:

> The phrase 'a well-founded fear of being persecuted for reasons of . . . membership of a particular social group', is a compound conception. It is therefore a mistake to isolate the elements of the definition, interpret them, and then ask whether the facts of the instant case are covered by the sum of those individual interpretations. Indeed, to ignore the totality of the words that define a refugee for the purposes of the Convention [and the Act] would be an error of law by virtue of a failure to construe the definition as a whole.[321]

That in turn indicates that even if the definition can be broken down into clauses or elements, they cannot have strict boundary lines and indeed there may be respects in which the boundaries of each limb or element are malleable or may shift in order to have proper application. This is close to what Zimmermann and Mahler have in mind when discussing the treaty basis for IPA practice. They argue that both the 'well-founded fear of being persecuted' and the 'protection' approaches may be valid, but that these elements are intertwined in a way that renders the attribution of a clearly defined 'textual home' of the IPA test practically inconceivable.[322] Adoption of a

---

[317] See this chapter, sections 1.5 and 2.
[318] See Chapter 2, section 2.9.1.
[319] Walter Kälin, 'Non-State Agents of Persecution and the Inability of the State to Protect' (2001) 15(3) Georgetown Immigration Law Journal 428; Zimmerman and Mahler (n 8) 444; Goodwin-Gill and McAdam (n 175) 28. See further Chapter 7, section 3.2.
[320] See Chapter 2; UNHCR, Interpreting Article 1 of the 1951 Convention (n 47) refers to the need for a 'holistic and integrated analysis', paras 7–9, 58
[321] *Applicant A* (n 198) 256.
[322] Zimmermann and Mahler (n 8) 446–63.

holistic approach also makes it more possible to view different approaches to location as leading to similar results. UNHCR has taken that view in response to Hathaway and Foster's view regarding the location of the IPA inquiry:

> Some have located the concept of internal flight or relocation alternative in the 'well-founded fear of being persecuted' clause of the definition, and others in the 'unwilling ... or unable ... to avail himself of the protection of that country' clause. These approaches are not necessarily contradictory, since the definition comprises one holistic test of interrelated elements. How these elements relate, and the importance to be accorded to one or another element, necessarily falls to be determined on the facts of each individual case.[323]

A further argument against the value and necessity of particular views on interrelationship or location is the observable fact that whenever commentators identify one or other element as primary, they do not ordinarily suggest that as a consequence the refugee definition has to discard or jettison the other elements—rather they simply redistribute their role. Thus, those who adopted the 'fear' test and rejected the view of the majority in *Horvath* (for whom protection was an integral part of the concept of persecution (in non-state actor cases)), did not in fact say that as a result protection was irrelevant to the issue of whether there was a well-founded fear of persecution. Rather they saw it as a factor going solely to the issue of whether there was a real chance of persecution happening (see e.g. McHugh in *Applicant A*).[324] Thus Matthew Scott, although heaping virtually every element (the risk assessment, the protection test, the discrimination test) into the 'being persecuted' element, still requires that each of these elements be addressed.[325]

*7.2.2.2 Avoidance of errors in decision-making*
Another species of argument deployed in favour of locating various tests in certain clauses/elements is that it is necessary in order to avoid errors in decision-making.

A leading example is the discussion in Hathaway and Foster about the correct location of the IPA test. They contend that to link the availability of internal protection to the existence of 'well-founded fear' leads in practice to errors of approach. This, they contend, wrongly puts the onus of proof on an applicant; wrongly imposes a need to establish 'countrywide persecution'; focuses solely on whether the well-founded fear can be negated even if it requires hiding or concealment; and wrongly encourages the inquiry to move directly to the question of well-founded fear without first making factual findings about the substance of the claim.[326] For them the IPA test's 'logical location' is thus in the availment limb, and this is said to reinforce the protective purposes of the Convention. It is also in their view a way of ensuring the protection limb is given

---

[323] UNHCR, Guidelines on International Protection No 4: Internal Flight or Relocation Alternative Within the Context of Article 1A(2) of the 1951 Convention and/or 1967 Protocol Relating to the Status of Refugees (23 July 2003) UN Doc HCR/GIP/03/04, para 3.
[324] See *Applicant A* (n 198). This is close to the position taken in UNHCR, Interpreting Article 1 of the 1951 Convention (n 47) paras 35–36.
[325] Scott (n 127) 132.
[326] Hathaway and Foster (n 2) 332–42.

*effet utile*, as otherwise it is 'largely superfluous'.[327] They see its practical operation as avoiding the difficulties besetting the alternative approach of locating it in the 'well-founded fear' clause.

However, state practice as evidenced by case law shows that decision makers can commit the identified errors *irrespective* of where the IPA is understood to be located in the refugee definition.[328] Adopting the Hathaway and Foster approach to location does not immunise decision makers from making these types of errors. Conversely, the test appears capable of being construed and applied by those who locate the test in the 'well-founded fear of being persecuted' limb so that none of these errors is committed.[329] This book's Chapter 8, on 'Being Persecuted' and Internal Protection, reaches a similar conclusion on this matter.

Hence, it must at least be doubted that it is essential to see choices of location as inherently or as structurally predisposing decision makers to such errors since decision makers appear capable of making the identified errors whichever approach they adopt. To treat choice of location as a necessary condition for a proper understanding of the refugee definition is to risk reifying things.

*7.2.2.3 Testing the arguments*

One way of testing further whether such a level of inquiry is essential is to examine some widely accepted propositions and ask whether they depend for their viability on a particular view as to their location. Succeeding chapters refer to a number of different precepts regarding key elements of the refugee definition. For present purposes, let us consider just three of these that are well-known:[330]

- That actors of persecution can include non-state actors;
- That use of the phrase 'being persecuted' focuses inquiry on the predicament of the refugee, rather than necessarily on the motives of the actors of persecution;
- That the refugee assessment is forward-looking and requires a risk assessment.

In each instance (again anticipating conclusions we reach later in this book), we can safely say that their emergence as commonly accepted (or in the case of the 'predicament' focus, increasingly advanced) propositions has come about, not through endorsement of the view that they derive from one element or combination of elements of the Article 1A(2) definition, but directly through their own rationale or intrinsic cogency. Thus, the recognition of persecution by non-state actors came about primarily through concern that to confine it to state actors would leave out a whole swathe of asylum claims where persecution was demonstrably present. It did not result from any arguments about location of the refugee definition's different elements. Once it was accepted that non-state actors could be actors of persecution, so that issues had to be confronted not just about state complicity in failing to protect but also state inability,

---

[327] ibid 340.
[328] See p. 490; see also Schultz (n 315) ch 3, 85.
[329] ibid 86–87.
[330] See further Chapter 12, sections 1.6.1(4), 1.7.2(4), and 1.11.1(1).

the further step to embracing a 'predicament approach' focusing on the passive tense of 'being persecuted'[331] was a small one.

The endorsement of the view that Article 1A(2) requires a forward-looking assessment of risk primarily drew on the element of 'well-founded fear' but emphasised the fact that the definition as a whole was cast in the present tense. It was not identified by virtue of any locational inquiry.

The outcome of an examination of just three well-known propositions does not of course establish that the same is true for all others, but it does cast serious doubt on any notion that proper definition of key elements is in general dependent on correctly locating them within one or other clause or element of Article 1A(2). That is not to say that the emergence of such propositions has not benefitted from the deliberations of commentators whose works do grapple with issues of interrelationship and location; rather it is to try and place them in a proper context.

## 7.3 Proposed Solution

### 7.3.1 Underlying objectives

In order to achieve any resolution of the issue of whether analysis of the proper location of key elements of the refugee definition is valuable or necessary, we first need to articulate what should be our fundamental interpretive and doctrinal objectives? Drawing on major themes expressed in the jurisprudence, at least five principles can be identified:

- Simplicity;
- Consistency of interpretation;
- Quality of interpretation;
- Consolidation;
- Convergence.[332]

It would be wrong to suggest there is universal or unequivocal support for these principles—e.g. at the practitioner level some might prefer a fractured or at least a diverse jurisprudence on the basis that jurisprudential uncertainty can sometimes make it easier to help win cases, because there will always be decision makers/judges on one side of the debate or the other. In the present era, we must always bear mind also the climate of hostility in some quarters to the very existence of the Refugee Convention as an instrument of international protection. At the state level, anti-globalists see it as a threat to national sovereignty and the right to decide who is allowed into their countries. For them, consistent or harmonised interpretation is a threat because it limits the scope for states controlled by anti-globalist governments to break away and adopt

---

[331] But for doubts as to whether this proposition can be accepted as widely agreed, see pp. 363–364.
[332] Michael Waibel, 'Principles of Treaty Interpretation—Developed for and Applied by National Courts' in Helmut Phillipp Aust and Georg Nolte (eds), *The Interpretation of International Law by Domestic Courts* (OUP 2016) 9–33.

national definitions which are at odds with international consensus.[333] Additionally, to objections of all kinds can be added the understandable concern that none of these precepts must be allowed to fetter individual, fact-sensitive assessment.

Such concerns should not, however, undermine the virtues of these five principles.

We have already explained why avoidance of an over technical approach is both a necessary requirement of a VCLT approach to interpretation and a valid goal in itself, particularly given that the protection afforded by the 1951 Convention concerns individuals who need to be able to understand its key definition and find it accessible. Consistency of interpretation, and the cardinal rule of law principle of treating like cases alike (and unalike cases unalike) are vital to ensuring that application of the refugee definition is transparent and that it is not seen as a lottery depending on the vagaries of decision makers' individual preferences.[334] At the same time, consistency without quality would be self-defeating because it would be compatible with a system in which poor decisions were uniformly made.[335] If the approach to definition is to be an objective enterprise, then it must endeavour to reach a convergent view based on international law norms and on the best state practice. Without the principle of convergence, there is no principled reason why those who take opposing views about interpretation could not simply continue to adhere to their views even when state practice has begun to reveal a trend towards acceptance of one view or the other, or a synthesis.

### 7.3.2 A high threshold

In light of the above, my proposed solution is as follows:

(i) Flexibility. We should recognise that the open-textured nature of the clauses and terms set out in Article 1A(2) and the proper application of VCLT rules of interpretation mean that we cannot be too forensic and cannot expect elements of the definition to fit together in any precise or geometric way;

(ii) Holistic. We should acknowledge that whilst clarity is desirable about the function and location of different elements, it remains that the definition must be given a holistic interpretation;

(iii) No sharp edges. We should recognise that the clauses, elements and limbs can have shifting boundaries. Even those who have taken quite strong positions on the proper location of various tests, appear to recognise the need for a certain level of borrowing and shifting boundaries. Thus, for example, Hathaway and Foster in TLRS2 have no difficulty in seeing the 'protection inquiry' as firmly anchored in the 'being persecuted' element of the 'well-founded fear of being persecuted' limb, and in particular in seeing two of the essential qualities of 'state protection' as being ability and willingness to protect. But the

---

[333] See e.g. Chapter 7, n 196 on the imposition in the United States by the Trump administration of 'condonation' and 'complete helplessness' tests which effectively sought to reduce state protection standards so as to cover only extreme case of state failures.

[334] Anthony M North and Joyce Chia, 'Towards Convergence in the Interpretation of the Refugee Convention: A Proposal for the Establishment of an International Judicial Commission for Refugees' (2006) 25 Aust YBIL 105.

[335] Hugo Storey, 'Consistency in Refugee Decision-Making: A Judicial Perspective' (2013) 32(4) RSQ 112.

concepts of ability and willingness are only to be found expressly in the 'availment clause' of the definition.

(iv) <u>Broad correspondence, rather than precise location</u>. Observable practice being that decision makers can accept some propositions without being certain of their correct definitional location, we should not regard precise or 'correct' location as a precondition of correct interpretation. To take the clearest example, we can endorse forward-looking assessment of risk as a key element of the definition without taking a view about whether 'well-founded fear' constitutes a separate 'limb'. Accordingly, we should only require a broad level of correspondence between the different clauses and elements on the one hand and the key propositions of refugee law on the other.

(v) <u>Convergence</u>. We should respond to the disputes that have arisen (and still arise) about location in the same way as we ordinarily do to disputes as to the meaning of each element, that is, seek to resolve them by convergence where possible or otherwise by recognising that one side has the better of the argument. Sometimes this means accepting that an argument that has not won out should wither on the vine. We should seek to reduce differences and move on. Any area of international law wishing to progress must seek to build on state practice in this broad sense. Even if one side of the argument refuses to give way, it can at least be said that, through dialogue, both sides have been made more aware of what the perceived deficit is on their side and of the importance of overcoming it. That predisposes towards convergence.

(vi) <u>High threshold</u>. It remains legitimate to pose the 'how' question—how different elements of the definition fit together and where is the best location for different 'tests'. Without doing so, we would not have moved beyond particular interpretations, e.g., beyond the external protection approach and the accountability theory of protection.[336] We should nevertheless regard this question as one to which we only have recourse when a certain threshold is reached—when there is a demonstrable failure of approach that would result if we did not.

It must be acknowledged straightaway that reorienting refugee law away from preoccupation with issues of interrelationship and location will not be easy. For the present, any study of the refugee definition will inevitably have to engage with such issues to some extent in order to ensure they address all issues covered in the literature. That is certainly true of this book's subsequent chapters. It is hoped, however, that the above suggested criteria might help towards navigating a way out.

## 7.4 The Principal Debates Revisited

Circling back to the list given earlier of the principal debates regarding how the different elements of the refugee definition fit together, later chapters explain that in fact some of these debates can be taken for all intents and purposes to be over. Thus, in the 1990s, there was a considerable divide between those who took an 'accountability' and those who took a 'protection' view of what constitutes persecution.[337] Whilst the inner

---

[336] See Chapter 7, section 2.3.
[337] See Kälin and Künzli (n 141); Zimmermann and Mahler (n 8).

core of this debate concerned whether persecution could be by non-state actors, the arguments regarding it featured strongly opposing views as to how the 'well-founded fear' clause and the availment clause should be interpreted. The reason why the accountability view fell away in the end was chiefly because it was felt that to confine the definition to victims of state persecution would be too narrow and would fail to address the realities of non-state actor persecution.[338] As a result, this debate no longer features. It has been resolved. There is no longer any need for a meta-level of inquiry into it.

It can also be safely said that there is now a growing consensus that proponents of the original conception of the 'fear test' as being entirely separate from the protection test have lost the argument. The weight of argument preponderantly points to applying a holistic approach.[339]

As regards other debates, subsequent chapters will identify to what extent there is now either a consensus or at least a 'direction or travel' and will suggest whether indeed there needs to be any further treatment of them at the meta-level of inquiry. For example, although this chapter earlier rejected the viewpoint which seeks to regard errors of approach as inherently associated with a particular view of location, it cannot be excluded that proponents may be able to show more effectively than has been the case on present evidence that one location or the other regularly leads to certain types of errors or dependably yields less erroneous decision-making.

Why it would be wrong to rule out entirely that some debates still merit a meta-level treatment or inquiry is well-illustrated by a recent debate initiated by Goodwin-Gill and McAdam among others. They propose that the common reliance in the context of the protection enquiry on the notion of surrogacy should be revisited, arguing that it is 'an unnecessarily distracting and complicating factor, adding yet one more burden to the applicant in an already complex process'.[340] Their critique has clear implications for issues relating to the proper location of the protection inquiry and merits further scrutiny. While this study goes on to question aspects of this critique,[341] it is a good example of how important it will remain to keep an open mind about meta-level issues. Indeed, this chapter ends in Section 9 by posing a particular question regarding the principle of surrogacy.

It is also possible that new theories will emerge about location. But in the view of the author, most that have been identified and developed in the current literature do not meet the requisite threshold. They have not shown that unless a particular location is given that demonstrable error will result or that one approach or the other regularly leads to certain types of error.

The above approach is not intended to discourage refugee law scholars from being conceptually creative. For example, Scott's attempts to 'recalibrate' the refugee definition represent one of the most thoughtful contributions to refugee law in recent times. He says that he has attempted this recalibration out of concern to ensure the refugee definition responds to the contemporary challenge of climate change and man-made

---

[338] See Chapter 6, section 3.2.2.
[339] The CJEU judgment in *O A* (n 211) appears to apply such an approach.
[340] Goodwin-Gill and McAdam (n 297) 10–11; Goodwin-Gill and McAdam (n 175) 8–9.
[341] See Chapter 7, section 1.4.

'natural' disasters. However, anyone who invites us to engage at the 'meta' level of inquiry must expect that decision makers, especially courts and tribunals, will not take up that invitation willingly unless they can be persuaded that a failure to follow the proposed approach leads to demonstrable, unignorable error. Whilst it was primarily judges who first took refugee law down the road of focussing on this 'meta'-level of inquiry, any judge now looking at such debates is likely to be very reluctant to take the same road again (except by way of providing historical context).

Every encouragement should be given to innovative refugee scholarship but whether courts and tribunals or UNHCR or governments or the wider community of scholars will take on board anything they say must be a different matter. In order to ensure primary focus is on interpreting the key elements of the refugee definition, rather than on how they fit together, judges—and *a fortiori* other decision makers—are likely to set a high threshold for agreeing to move up to the meta-level.

## 8 Modalities of the Refugee Definition

Before leaving the subject of conceptual organisation, a little more needs to be said about references later in this book to 'modalities' of the refugee definition.

As is already clear, it is a feature of interpretation in the context of 'law-making treaties' such as the Refugee Convention (which provides a definition in generic, relatively indeterminate terms), to try and render it more determinate. The vast body of literature on refugee law offers an abundance of insights into how best to achieve that end. Congruent with what has been said already about different approaches to interrelationship and location, it is essential to avoid any unduly prescriptive approach to the interpretive exercise. At the same time, it is surely important to build on and improve what has gone before. That is why so much attention is paid in the wider literature to the EU experiment and the fact that since 2004 there is now one non-national example, albeit only in regional form, of an attempt to codify more definitional detail regarding key elements of the refugee definition: the QD and its recast.

### 8.1 Qualification Directive

Regardless of whether or not the substantive contents of this directive (and its recast) can be said to fully accord with the Refugee Convention, it is instructive to note the way that it has sought to identify some specific modalities to the definition. In particular, it is built around analysis of 'acts' and 'actors' of persecution and also seeks to identify 'actors of protection'. These developments are either in line with or mirror broader international law, e.g. IHRL law's concern with human agency as an aspect of violations of human rights;[342] and the international law of state responsibility's concern with acts or omissions as an aspect of establishing accountability for violations

---

[342] See pp. 363–364.

of international law.³⁴³ Later chapters grapple with arguments that reference to 'acts' and 'actors' is too restrictive and inconsistent with the need for a 'predicament' approach; but even if such arguments were accepted, deployment of such concepts in the QD (recast) has helped bring to the fore critical issues relating to, *inter alia*, agency and responsibility. As is argued in the later chapter on persecution, use of such modalities also helps make better sense of persecution as a human drama involving protagonists—persecutors and persecutees and often ineffective protectors.

## 8.2 Scope of Application *Ratione Personae, Ratione Materiae, Ratione Temporis*

One other set of concepts that have already been put to use and will be deployed later in this study are those represented by the terms relating to person (*ratione personae*), subject matter (*ratione materiae*), and time (*ratione temporis*). This study is not the place to consider the origins of such concepts in Roman law, canon law, continental, and some common law. Their deployment in this study derives directly from their continuing use in treaty interpretation, where they have primarily been employed to: (i) mark limits to the competence of states in relation to treaty obligations; (ii) help establish the jurisdiction of courts such as the ICJ to admit complaints; and (iii) help courts establish the scope of application of a treaty. These uses can overlap. Thus, for example, the regional human rights courts may decide not to treat a complaint as admissible if outside the treaty's personal scope or material scope.³⁴⁴ In this study such terms are primarily used in sense (iii) above, to help bring into focus issues of the scope of the refugee definition's application. However, only limited use is made of the *ratione temporis* concept (confined to issues of the extent to which the definition is forward-looking). The *ratione loci* concept does not have any obvious application to the refugee definition, although it is nevertheless found useful later in the chapter on the IPA (Chapter 8) to adopt the CJEU term, 'geographical scope'.³⁴⁵

# 9 An Underlying Principle?

Before leaving the subject of 'framework' matters pertaining to the refugee definition, it is pertinent to ask whether there can be said to be any principle or principles underlying the refugee definition as a whole. Chapter 2 examined the close interrelationship between the Convention purpose of protecting against persecution and the principle

---

³⁴³ See Chapter 6, n 338.
³⁴⁴ See Veijo Heiskanen, 'Jurisdiction v. Competence: Revisiting a Frequently Neglected Distinction' (1994) 5 Finnish Yearbook of International Law 1; Danio Campanelli, 'The United Nations Compensation Commission (UNCC): Reflections on Its Judicial Character' (2005) 4(1) The Law & Practice of International Courts and Tribunals 107; Dr Veijo Heiskanen, The Artefact of International Jurisdiction: Concept, History and Reality', lecture (26 October 2016) available at <https://blogs.ucl.ac.uk/law-journal/2016/11/08/the-artefact-of-international-jurisdiction-concept-history-and-reality/> accessed 2 November 2022.
³⁴⁵ Case C-465/07 *Meki Elgafaji and Noor Elgafaji v Staatssecretaris van Justitie* [2009] ECLI:EU:C:2009:94.

of surrogacy and this chapter earlier noted how central these two ideas have been to the development of the human rights approach.[346] At the same time, this study has already noted certain eminent scholars' rejection of the notion or principle of surrogacy. Not having as yet examined the individual elements of the definition, it would be premature to explore this issue further here, save to note that it is discussed in detail in Chapter 7 and explored further in the study's final chapter.[347]

## 10 Conclusions

In Section 1 this chapter identified five main approaches that have been taken to the refugee definition: the 'literal approach'; the 'circumstantial approach'; the 'US subjective approach'; the 'case-by-case' approach; and the human rights approach. Section 2 examined what is meant by a human rights approach; its history and rise to dominance; its main justifications; and the main versions of it that have been deployed. Section 3 looked at the main criticisms that have been ranged against it. Section 4 argued that criticisms of the human rights approach—both those based on VCLT principles and those identifying conceptual and empirical problems—do identify some real difficulties but fail to undermine significantly the overall viability of such an approach.

Section 5 explored the main specific types of human rights approaches, noting that that there are advantages and disadvantages to both the hierarchical and non-hierarchical models. It concludes that even though the non-hierarchal formulations appear to offer the way forward, they have not as yet furnished a comparably clear workable structure. More importantly, both models still possess a great deal in common.

Section 6 asked whether the human rights approach is to be equated with, or seen as exhaustive of, an international law approach. It concludes that primacy has to be given to an international law framework; the human rights approach should not be viewed as self-sufficient. Further, it takes issue with the view espoused by some that the Refugee Convention has indeed been subsumed by IHRL such that refugees should now be seen as just one example of persons who are at risk of human rights violations.

Section 7 addressed the conceptual organisation of the definition. It sought to analyse how they each fit together. This has become more important than before because some of the most influential analyses of the definition express quite strong views on such issues and indeed discourse on it has come to occupy a type of intermediary layer between the reader and the definition's individual elements. It is argued that as important as it is to reach a clear understanding of how the definition's key elements fit together, 'meta-level' inquiry should not be allowed to dominate analysis of the definition itself. In any event, the preponderance of argument is that the definition's key elements are to be understood as closely interrelated and their interpretation best approached holistically.

---

[346] See Chapter 2, section 2.5.4.7 and this chapter, section 4.2.7.
[347] See Chapters 7, section 1 and 12, section 2.6.1.

Section 8 explained why value is seen to lie in identifying modalities of the definition, by reference to the approach taken by the drafters of the QD, so as to identify 'acts' and 'actors' of persecution and 'actors of protection'.

Section 9 sought to explore the question whether there is (are) any principle(s) underlying the refugee definition.

## 10.1 Key Propositions

It remains to inquire whether any basic or suggested propositions can be derived from this chapter's contents. Given co-existing differences over approaches, views on interrelationship, ordering, and modalities, it cannot be said that there is any widespread agreement regarding any of these matters. In particular, it has to be recognised that important contributions to clarifying various aspects of the refugee definition have been made both by approaches to the refugee definition that apply IHRL norms and those that do not.

There are, however, several suggested propositions that flow from this author's own analysis, as follows:

1. The human rights approach to ascertaining the meaning of key terms of the refugee definition coheres well with VCLT rules of interpretation. It remains the dominant approach and the main criticisms made of it to date do not withstand scrutiny. Such an approach confirms that refugee law is a branch of law operating within the framework of international law. Whilst other approaches exist, it should be seen as the approach most likely to yield greater analytical clarity and appropriate resolution of new issues as they arise.

2. There is no fixed order for analysing the different elements of the refugee definition.

3. Whilst there exist differing views about which clauses or elements of the definition are key, there is a broad consensus that the definition's elements are to be understood as closely interrelated and their interpretation best approached holistically.

# 4
# Nationality and Statelessness
(*Nationalité et condition d'apatride*)

| | | | |
|---|---|---|---|
| Introduction | 200 | 3.2.10 Nationality's temporal dimension: nationality as actual nationality | 217 |
| Ordering | 201 | | |
| 1 Background | 202 | 3.2.11 Actual nationality and the date of decision | 220 |
| 1.1 Relative Neglect | 202 | | |
| 1.2 Why Nationality (or its Lack) Can Be a Problematic Issue | 204 | 3.2.12 The content of nationality and the issue of 'effective nationality' | 221 |
| 1.3 Disputed Nationality Cases | 205 | 3.3 'A Person who Has More Than One Nationality'/'*Personne qui a plus d'une Nationalité*' | 222 |
| 2 The International Law Framework | 206 | | |
| 2.1 The Basic Rules of International Law on Nationality | 206 | 3.3.1 Meaning | 222 |
| 2.1.1 Exclusive role of the state in determining nationality | 207 | 3.3.2 Multiple nationality and the concept of effective nationality | 224 |
| 2.1.2 Recognition at the international level | 207 | 3.3.3 The concept of effective nationality in international law | 225 |
| 2.1.3 Modes of acquisition of nationality | 208 | 3.3.4 Purported justifications for importing the concept of 'effective nationality' into the refugee definition | 226 |
| 2.1.4 Ways in which nationality is acquired | 209 | | |
| 2.1.5 Discretionary entitlement to or eligibility for nationality | 209 | 3.3.5 Difficulties | 227 |
| 2.1.6 Persons of indeterminate nationality | 210 | 3.3.6 Proposed solutions | 230 |
| | | 3.4 'Not Having a Nationality'/'*Personne qui n'a pas de Nationalité*' | 234 |
| 2.1.7 Loss of nationality | 210 | | |
| 2.1.8 Denationalisation | 210 | 3.4.1 Drafting history and *travaux préparatoires* | 234 |
| 2.2 The Human Rights Approach | 211 | | |
| 3 Nationality and the Refugee Definition | 212 | 3.4.2 Good faith | 235 |
| | | 3.4.3 Ordinary meaning | 235 |
| 3.1 Uses of the Term 'Nationality' in the Refugee Convention | 212 | 3.4.4 Context | 236 |
| | | 3.4.5 Object and purpose | 236 |
| 3.2 'Nationality' in the Term 'Country of Nationality' ('*Pays dont elle a la nationalité*') | 213 | 3.4.6 Article 31(3) and other VCLT considerations | 236 |
| | | 3.4.7 'Not having a nationality' and stateless persons | 237 |
| 3.2.1 Drafting history and *travaux préparatoires* | 213 | | |
| | | 4 Specific Issues | 245 |
| 3.2.2 Good faith | 214 | 4.1 Denationalisation and Arbitrary Deprivation of Nationality | 245 |
| 3.2.3 Ordinary meaning | 214 | | |
| 3.2.4 'Country of nationality' as a state | 215 | 4.2 Misuse of Nationality | 248 |
| 3.2.5 Context | 216 | 4.3 Voluntary Renunciation of Nationality | 249 |
| 3.2.6 Object and purpose | 216 | 5 Nationality and Evidential Issues | 250 |
| 3.2.7 Article 31(3) considerations | 217 | 5.1 Basic Propositions Regarding Nationality and Evidence Assessment | 251 |
| 3.2.8 Special meaning | 217 | | |
| 3.2.9 Article 32 | 217 | 5.2 Areas of Disagreement | 252 |

*The Refugee Definition in International Law.* Hugo Storey, Oxford University Press. © Hugo Storey 2023.
DOI: 10.1093/oso/9780198842644.003.0004

| | | | | |
|---|---|---|---|---|
| 5.2.1 | Actual nationality and documentary evidence | 252 | 5.2.4 Meaning of 'law' in the context of acquisition 'by operation of law' | 254 |
| 5.2.2 | Substantiation in the form of taking reasonable steps to assert a nationality | 252 | 5.2.5 Persons of indeterminate nationality | 255 |
| 5.2.3 | Duty of cooperation on the part of the determining authority | 254 | **6 Conclusions** | **256** |
| | | | 6.1 Basic Propositions | 257 |
| | | | 6.2 Suggested Propositions | 257 |

## Introduction

In any A B C of refugee law the first letter should be N for nationality ('*nationalité*' in the French). To come within the personal scope of Article 1A(2) of the 1951 Convention relating to the Status of Refugees (Refugee Convention),[1] it is necessary to establish that one either has a nationality or lacks it. In deciding whether a person is a refugee under the refugee definition,[2] the first question that should be asked is 'What is their nationality?' It arises first because unless and until nationality has been determined (or found to be lacking) it is not possible to ascertain the country by reference to which they claim to have a well-founded fear of being persecuted. It would be wrong, however, to infer from the deployment within Article 1A(2) of a nationality criterion that this restricts the universal scope of the definition, because it spans both nationals and non-nationals, who between them exhaust all possibilities.[3]

The first use of the term 'nationality' in the refugee definition relates to nationality as one of the five Convention reasons or grounds. In that context its meaning is broad, encompassing both nationality as a legal status and membership of a cultural, ethnic, or linguistic group. Use of the term in the latter context is dealt within Chapter 10.[4] Focus here is on the meaning of the term in each of its other uses within Article 1A(2).

---

[1] Convention Relating to the Status of Refugees (adopted 28 July 1951, entered into force 22 April 1954) 189 UNTS 137.

[2] Article 1A(2) of the Refugee Convention (n 1) defines a refugee as a person who: '[O]wing to well-founded fear of being persecuted for reasons of race, religion, nationality, membership of a particular social group or political opinion, is outside the country of his nationality and is unable or, owing to such fear, is unwilling, owing to such fear, is unwilling to avail himself of the protection of that country. In the case of a person who has more than one nationality, the term "the country of his nationality" shall mean each of the countries of which he is a national, and a person shall not be deemed to be lacking the protection of the country of his nationality if, without any valid reason based on well-founded fear, he has not availed himself of the protection of one of the countries of which he is a national.' For the equally authentic French text, see Chapter 1 (n 3).

[3] Stateless children born in the country of asylum may nevertheless fall outside the Article 1A(2) definition by virtue of never having lived in the country(ies) of their parents' former habitual residence: see pp. 277–278.

[4] See Atle Grahl-Madsen, *The Status of Refugees in International Law. Volume 1: Refugee Character* (Sijthoff 1966) 218–19; UNHCR, Handbook on Procedures and Criteria for Determining Refugee Status and Guidelines on International Protection under the 1951 Convention and the 1967 Protocol Relating to the Status Of Refugees (Geneva, 2019, reissued in 2019) (UNHCR Handbook or Handbook) paras 74–76; Paul Weis, *Nationality and Statelessness in International Law* (2nd edn, Dordrecht: Kluwer Academic Publishers Group 1979) 3, where Weis described the two different usages of the term nationality in the refugee definition as the 'politico-legal' and 'historico-biological' usages. See further Chapter 10, section 3.3.

This solely concerns nationality in the sense of legal status or more precisely, the legal relationship or legal bond between the individual and the state.[5]

## Ordering

Both 'country of nationality' and 'country of former habitual residence' are compound terms. Both designate what may loosely be termed the personal and the territorial scope of the refugee definition. Regarding personal scope, the key matter is nationality or its lack. With territorial scope, the key terms are 'country' and whether or not a person is 'outside' it. As explained above, personal scope is dealt with first because,

---

[5] Weis (n 4) 162; *Nottebohm Case (second phase) (Liechtenstein v Guatemala)*, Judgment [1955] ICJ Rep 4, 4. See also European Convention on Nationality (adopted 6 November 1997, entered into force 1 March 2000) ETS 166, Article 2 of which defines 'nationality' as 'the legal bond between a person and a State that does not indicate the person's ethnic origin'. In addition to the publications of Grahl-Madsen and Weis and the UNHCR Handbook mentioned immediately above (n 4), other refugee law materials dealing with this topic include: James C Hathaway, *The Law of Refugee Status* (Butterworths Limited 1991); Carol A Batchelor, 'UNHCR and Issues Related to Nationality' (1995) 14(3) Refugee Survey Quarterly 91; Carol A Batchelor, 'Stateless Persons: Some Gaps in International Protection' (1995) 7(2) IJRL 232; Ryszard Piotrowicz, 'Refugee Status and Multiple Nationality in the Indonesian Archipelago: Is There a Timor Gap?' (1996) 8 IJRL 319; Nehemiah Robinson, *Convention Relating to the Status of Stateless Persons: Its History and Interpretation, A Commentary* (UNHCR 1997); Mark Sidhom, 'Jong Kim Koe v Minister for Immigration and Multicultural Affairs: Federal Court Loses Sight of the Purpose of the Refugee Convention' (1998) 20(2) Sydney Law Review 315; Carol A Batchelor, 'Statelessness and the Problem of Resolving Nationality Status' (1998) 10(1–2) IJRL 156; Ryszard Piotrowicz, '*Lay Kon Tji v. Minister for Immigration & (and) Ethnic Affairs*: The Function and Meaning of Effective Nationality in the Assessment of Applications for Asylum' (1999) 11 Int'l J Refugee L 544; Kay Hailbronner, 'Nationality' in Thomas A Aleinikoff and Vincent Chetail (eds), *Migration and International Legal Norms* (TMC Asser Press 2003); Kay Hailbronner, 'Nationality in Public International Law and European Law' in Rainer Bauböck et al (eds), *Acquisition and Loss of Nationality Policies and Trends in 15 European States. Volume 1: Comparative Analyses* (Amsterdam University Press 2006); Guy S Goodwin-Gill and Jane McAdam, *The Refugee in International Law* (3rd edn, OUP 2007); UNHCR, 'Expert Meeting—The Concept of Stateless Persons under International Law: Summary Conclusions' (2010) (UNHCR 2010 Prato Conclusions); Andreas Zimmermann and Claudia Mahler, 'Article 1A, para 2', in Andreas Zimmermann (ed), *The 1951 Convention Relating to the Status of Refugees and Its 1967 Protocol: A Commentary* (OUP 2011); Jon Bauer, 'Multiple Nationality and Refugees' (2014) 47 Vanderbilt Journal of Transnational Law 905, 921; James C Hathaway and Michelle Foster, *The Law of Refugee Status* (2nd edn, CUP 2014); Alice Edwards, 'The Meaning of Nationality in International Law in an Era of Human Rights', in Alice Edwards and Laura van Waas (eds), *Nationality and Statelessness under International Law* (CUP 2014); UNHCR, Handbook on Protection of Stateless Persons (Geneva, 2014) (UNHCR 2014 Handbook or 2014 Handbook); Eric Fripp, *Nationality and Statelessness in the International Law of Refugee Status* (Hart Publishing 2016); Michelle Foster and Hélène Lambert, *International Refugee Law and the Protection of Stateless Persons* (OUP 2019); Hugo Storey, 'Nationality as an Element of the Refugee Definition and the Unsettled Issues of "Inchoate Nationality" and "Effective Nationality"' (2017) RefLaw, 1st part; Hugo Storey, 'Nationality as an Element of the Refugee Definition and the Unsettled Issues of "Inchoate Nationality" and "Effective Nationality"' (2019) RefLaw, 2nd part; Lorne Waldman, *The Definition of Convention Refugee* (2nd edn, Lexis Nexis 2019); Hélène Lambert, 'Stateless Refugees' in Cathryn Costello, Michelle Foster, and Jane McAdam (eds) (Costello et al), *Oxford Handbook of International Refugee Law* (OUP 2021) 797; Laura van Waas, 'The Intersection of International Refugee Law and International Statelessness Law' in Costello et al, 152; Guy S Goodwin-Gill and Jane McAdam, *The Refugee in International Law* (4th edn, OUP 2021) 669; Eric Fripp, 'Nationality, Protection, and "the Country of His Nationality" as the Country of Reference for the Purposes of Article 1A(2) of the 1951 Convention relating to the Status of Refugees' (2021) 33(2) IJRL 300; Eric Fripp, 'Statelessness, Inability or Unwillingness to Return, and the "Country of his Former Habitual Residence" as the Country of Reference for the Purposes of Article 1A(2) of the 1951 Convention relating to the Status of Refugees' (2022) 34(4) IJRL 327.

until it is determined whether someone is with or without nationality, no precise identification can be made of the type of country involved.[6]

## 1 Background

Despite nationality (or its lack) being an essential element of the refugee definition, its treatment in refugee law has been patchy. Alongside relative neglect has gone wariness that its meaning poses a number of challenges, not least the fact that it requires reference to rules found elsewhere in international law. Something needs to be said on these matters before proceeding to analyse its meaning and role in the refugee definition.

### 1.1 Relative Neglect

The 1979 UNHCR Handbook offers no real definition of nationality. When analysing the phrase 'is outside the country of his nationality', it simply states that '[i]n this context, "nationality" refers to citizenship'.[7] Given its clearly essential role as one element of the refugee definition, one would expect that every refugee law textbook would analyse nationality (or its lack) in some detail. Yet, until recently, at least in the English language, few did. For example, neither Grahl-Madsen,[8] nor the first three editions of *The Refugee in International Law*,[9] nor Zimmerman and Mahler,[10] say much about it at all. Anker's *Law of Asylum in the United States* confines virtually all of its references to nationality to the different context of nationality as a Convention ground or reason.[11] Now, however, there are several studies analysing this subject area in-depth, in particular Hathaway and Foster,[12] Fripp,[13] and Foster and Lambert.[14] These all build on important articles written in the 1990s by Carol Batchelor.[15] The latter-day studies have also done much to identify relevant case law, something which was previously a major problem.[16] At the same time, they also make clear that this is not an area where

---

[6] UNHCR 2010 Prato Conclusions (n 5) para 7.
[7] UNHCR Handbook (n 4) para 87.
[8] Grahl-Madsen (n 4) 15060, and (on multiple nationality) 257–58.
[9] Goodwin Gill and McAdam (n 5) 67–70 (on statelessness), 459 being the only substantive consideration.
[10] Zimmermann and Mahler (n 5) 441–42, 463–64, 461–62.
[11] Deborah Anker, *Law of Asylum in the United States* (Thomson Reuters 2022). See also Symes and Jorro (n 5), who do include a chapter on it—their Chapter 6.
[12] Hathaway and Foster (n 5) 49–75.
[13] Fripp (2016) (n 5) Chapters 2–6.
[14] Foster and Lambert (n 5) Chapters 2, 4, and 5.
[15] Batchelor, 'UNHCR and Issues Related to Nationality' (n 5); Batchelor, 'Stateless Persons: Some Gaps in International Protection' (n 5); and Batchelor, 'Statelessness' (1998, n 5).
[16] Foster and Lambert (n 5) 146–47, observe when analysing the issue of denial of nationality as persecution that '[a]n examination of the jurisprudence reveals three key challenges. First, many refugee law decision-makers appear unfamiliar with or unaware of the pertinent international law norms, and specifically the significant constraints imposed by human rights law on state discretion in relation to nationality laws. Second, many cases suggest a failure properly to apply modern human rights norms in practice. Third, even where a norm is properly identified and applied, there is a question as to whether denial of citizenship is sufficient on its own to constitute persecution.'

one can easily discern much clear state practice even in the broad sense. They also suggest that there is considerable scope for revisiting of leading decisions.[17]

It might be suggested that one reason for the limited treatment until recently is that the nationality element of the refugee definition is relatively straightforward and free of legal complexity, but, as we shall see, that is not the case. Another possible reason might be because nationality or statelessness is not a live issue in many asylum cases. Yet there are clearly acute problems that present themselves from time to time concerning nationality. One feature of the mass movement of people across the Mediterranean between 2015 and 2016 was the plight of many undocumented asylum seekers from Syria, whose first problem was establishing they were Syrian. In the context of this crisis, some European governments expressed concern at the incidence of applicants perceived to feign a nationality they did not possess to boost their asylum prospects.[18] There are no reliable estimates of how significant a problem this was, but clearly what underlay governmental concerns was available data showing that during this period persons of Syrian (and Eritrean and Iraqi) nationality had hugely better prospects of being granted refugee status than, for example, Egyptians, Nigerians, or Pakistanis.[19] To address concerns about misuse of nationality on the part of some applicants, some states have introduced methods of linguistic analysis or language testing, designed to establish where a person originates from and in that way gain a clearer picture of the likelihood that they are from the country they say they are.[20]

But long before, problems surrounding nationality, in particular denationalisation, constituted one of the major causes of people moving to claim asylum, indeed even before the Refugee Convention was enacted. As noted by Carole Batchelor over twenty years ago,[21] '[i]n many cases, the lack of nationality or being stripped of nationality and the rights generally associated with citizenship have been related to the decision to flee... As a result of the overlap between nationality status and other factors related to flight, many asylum seekers whose nationality is unclear or ineffective, or who have no nationality, come to UNHCR for assistance.'[22] It must also be borne in mind that dual or multiple nationality[23] has come to be viewed very differently than it was in the interwar years (when it was seen as a threat to international law norms that were based on persons having allegiance to one state only) and that it is only in recent decades that there has been a trend towards acceptance of multiple nationality.[24] A number

---

[17] ibid; see also 2–6.

[18] See e.g. statements made by a German interior ministry spokesman in Editorial, 'Refugee crisis: Many migrants falsely claim to be Syrians, Germany says as EU tries to ease tensions' (*The Telegraph*, 25 September 2015).

[19] EASO, 'Annual Report on the Situation of Asylum in the European Union' (2015).

[20] See further, Diana Eades, 'Applied Linguistics and Language Analysis in Asylum Seeker Cases' (2005) 26(4) Applied Linguistics 503; Peter L Patrick, 'Asylum and Language Analysis' in Susan K Brown and Frank D Beans (eds), *Encyclopaedia of Migration* (Springer 2013).

[21] Batchelor, 'UNHCR and Issues Related to Nationality' (n 5).

[22] ibid.

[23] This study uses the term 'multiple nationality'. As Alfred M Boll, *Multiple Nationality and International Law* (Brill Nijhoff 2006) 2, observes, this 'allow[s] for consideration of all issues related to dual nationals, while delineating the enquiry as far as the relevant issues in international law in the most appropriate and flexible sense'.

[24] Peter J Spiro, 'Dual Nationality and the Meaning of Citizenship' (1997) 46(4) Emory Law Journal 1411, 1412; Peter J Spiro, 'Dual Citizenship as Human Right' (2010) 8 Int'l J Const L 111; Edwards (n 5) 20–21; Boll (n 23) 1–4.

of reasons have led to this change of attitude, in particular growing recognition of the interests of immigrants in maintaining connection with their country of origin.[25]

Another major factor in bringing issues of nationality and statelessness to the fore has been the increased global interest in tackling statelessness, and the concomitant emergence of a recognisable area of law, 'statelessness law'.[26] The plight of the Rohingya has been seen to encapsulate major contemporary problems surrounding statelessness.[27]

## 1.2 Why Nationality (or its Lack) Can Be a Problematic Issue

It will assist the ensuing analysis to reflect briefly, as well, on why nationality can be a problematic issue.

One reason is the existential situation of asylum seekers as persons who often move without identity documents or who cannot produce such documents. Another factor, alluded to by Batchelor,[28] is that people seeking asylum may sometimes have no nationality or be of indeterminate nationality—e.g. because their countries of origin never recognised them as nationals or they were born in transit or were trafficked at an early age, never learning where they originated from. Or conversely asylum seekers may possess a second or multiple nationality of which they were never made aware.

There is another factor inherent in the legal concept. Nationality is not a physical or biological or cultural or ethnic fact but a legal one. Further, although it is typically proven by production of a passport or identity document, such documents themselves do not establish it as a legal fact; they are only declaratory of it. Additionally (leaving aside unusual cases where it is awarded as a privilege or favour),[29] nationality exists only insofar as an applicant meets the conditions for it as laid down in the law of the state/country concerned.

Yet a further factor to be added to the mix is that, ordinarily, refugee decision makers are not experts in the intricacies of nationality law (although they must try to ascertain nationality correctly). They have to make a multi-faceted assessment of an application of which nationality is but one element. Even decision makers at the level of courts and tribunals, who might be expected to have a better grasp of the international law rules governing nationality, may not always have sufficient training or familiarity with their complexities.

Another factor concerns potential misuse to which brief reference was made earlier.[30] If an applicant claims a nationality they do not have, or denies one they have, the result might be they are granted refugee status even though not in fact in genuine need of international protection. Concerns of this order have led some courts and

---

[25] Hailbronner (2003) (n 5) 80, cited by Fripp (2016) (n 5) 49.
[26] van Waas (n 5) 153.
[27] ibid 162–66.
[28] Batchelor, 'Stateless Persons: Some Gaps in International Protection' (n 5).
[29] See International Law Commission (ILC), Articles on Nationality of Natural Persons in Relation to the Succession of States (1999) Supplement No 10 (A/54/10).
[30] This term is borrowed from Hailbronner (2006) (n 5) 46, 48 and avoids somewhat loaded terms such as manipulation or abuse.

tribunals to regard such misuse as fatal to a claim for refugee status.[31] Whether that is the correct response is, however, another matter, considered later in this chapter. In any event, concerns of this kind must be kept in context. In most cases there is no issue as to whether a person is a national of a particular state; decision makers find no basis to doubt a person's claimed nationality.

## 1.3 Disputed Nationality Cases

That there can be legal complexities surrounding the issue of nationality as an element of the refugee definition is clear from case law. The main situations where nationality problems have posed particular difficulties for refugee status determination (RSD) are commonly referred to as 'disputed nationality' cases and have been identified as follows:

1) [T]hose where the applicant claims to have the nationality of state X but decision makers assess his/her only true nationality to be of state Y;
2) those where the applicant claims to have one nationality but decision makers consider he/she has more than one nationality; and
3) those where the decision maker does not accept that the applicant is a person 'not having a nationality'/stateless.[32]

Resolution of such disputes can have major—sometimes decisive—consequences for whether or not an applicant can qualify as a refugee. If someone fails to persuade the decision maker that they are nationals of state X, which may well be unsafe for them, they may then stand to be assessed by reference to state Y, which is safe for them; and so their claim may be rejected for that reason. If they have dual or multiple nationality, then they have to establish that they have a well-founded fear of being persecuted in both countries.[33] If someone claiming to be stateless is not determined to be such, it may be that their alleged country of nationality, unlike their country of former habitual residence, is safe for them and so they fail in their claim. Conversely a decision maker may consider someone stateless and reject their claim to be a national of unsafe country X, because their country of former habitual residence is safe. In relation to multiple nationality cases, the fact that there is potentially more than one nationality to assess obviously increases the room for dispute.

In considering whether an applicant's case falls to be treated as that of a stateless person, as opposed to that of a national, it is instructive to keep in mind the various causes of statelessness. UNHCR has identified them non-exhaustively as being of three kinds: (i) causes linked to the dissolution and separation of states and transfer of territory between states (e.g. the dissolution of the Soviet Union and Yugoslavia, and the post-colonial formation of States in Asia and Africa); (ii) technical causes through

---

[31] Concern about 'willful statelessness' has been a particularly prominent feature of Canadian case law: see Waldman (n 5) 406.
[32] IARMJ-Europe, 'Evidence and Credibility Assessment in the Context of the Common European Asylum System: Judicial Analysis' (2nd edn, 2023) s 5.1, 175–77.
[33] Unless able to show a valid reason for not availing themselves of the protection of a non-persecutory country of nationality: see below section 3.3.6.1.

the operation of citizenship laws or administrative practices; and (iii) discrimination and arbitrary deprivation of nationality.[34]

## 2 The International Law Framework

It makes sense to analyse next the basic rules of international law governing nationality and statelessness. Without some understanding of these, decision makers cannot respond adequately to cases requiring assessment of nationality and statelessness. Up to the present, the case law that has dealt with nationality and statelessness issues has often lacked any clear framework of analysis.[35]

### 2.1 The Basic Rules of International Law on Nationality

The international law on nationality is relatively limited. There remains no 'uniform international code regarding nationality'.[36] Much is still considered to be within the domain reserved to states' own municipal law.[37] In treaty terms, the most important international instruments are: the 1930 Hague Convention on Certain Questions relating to the Conflict of Nationality Laws (1930 Hague Convention),[38] which sought to codify the rules of customary international law on nationality;[39] the Protocol Relating to a Certain Case of Statelessness, also of 1930 vintage;[40] the Convention Relating to the Status of Stateless Persons, 1954 (CSSP54 or 1954 Convention);[41] the Convention on the Nationality of Married Women of 20 February 1957;[42] and the Convention on the Reduction of Statelessness, 1961 (CRS61).[43] These have been supplemented by certain regional instruments, in particular the Convention on Reduction of Cases of Multiple Nationality and Military Obligations in Cases of Multiple Nationality of May

---

[34] Inter-Parliamentary Union and UNHCR, Nationality and Statelessness: A Handbook for Parliamentarians No 22 (2014) 30–42. See also UNHCR and Asylum Aid, Mapping Statelessness in the United Kingdom (2011) 23–24. See also van Waas (n 5) 152–57.

[35] As noted by Foster and Lambert (n 5) 2–6.

[36] As Szymon Rundestein, among others, had hoped in 1930 would eventually materialise. See Weis (n 4) 87 and also discussion in Fripp (2016) (n 5) 20–21. For some commentators, there is no coherent definition of nationality in international law: see e.g. Malcolm N Shaw, *International Law* (5th edn, CUP 2012) 728.

[37] Ian Brownlie, 'The Relations of Nationality in Public International Law' (1963) 39 BYIL 284; *Tunis and Morocco* (Advisory Opinion) [1923] PCIJ Series B No 4.

[38] League of Nations, Convention on Certain Questions Relating to the Conflict of Nationality Law (adopted 13 April 1930, entered into force 1 July 1937) 179 LNTS 89, No 4137. The Convention entered into force having been ratified by nineteen states.

[39] Brownlie (n 37) 299.

[40] League of Nations, Protocol Relating to a Certain Case of Statelessness (adopted 12 April 1930, entered into force 1 July 1937) 179 LNTS 115, No 4138.

[41] Convention Relating to the Status of Stateless Persons (adopted 28 September 1954, entered into force 6 June 1960) 360 UNTS 117 (CRSSP54).

[42] Convention on the Nationality of Married Women (adopted 20 February 1957, entered into force 11 August 1958) 309 UNTS 65.

[43] Convention on the Reduction of Statelessness (adopted 30 August 1961, entered into force 13 December 1975) 989 UNTS 175 (CRS61).

1963,[44] the European Convention on Nationality of 1997,[45] and the Convention on the Avoidance of Statelessness in Relation to State Succession of 2006.[46]

Certain decisions of the Permanent Court of International Justice (PCIJ) and the International Court of Justice (ICJ) relating to nationality have been seen to have wide application, in particular the *Tunis and Morocco* case,[47] and the *Nottebohm* case.[48] However, ever since the Universal Declaration of Human Rights (UDHR)—which provide at Article 15 that everyone has 'the right to a nationality'[49] – developments in International Human Rights Law (IHLR) have come to play a role in imposing constraints on state discretion in this area.[50] The significance of IHRL in assessment of nationality is discussed further below.[51]

### 2.1.1 Exclusive role of the state in determining nationality

The general principle governing nationality determination is contained in the words of the opening sentence of Article 1 of the 1930 Hague Convention, which provides that: '[i]t is for each State to determine under its own law who are its nationals.'[52] As noted earlier, this is widely accepted as a customary international law norm.[53]

### 2.1.2 Recognition at the international level

The second sentence of Article 1 of the 1930 Hague Convention sets out a rule relating to recognition of national law: '[t]his law shall be recognised by other States in so far as it is consistent with international conventions, international custom, and the principles of law generally recognised with regard to nationality'.[54] This establishes an international law reference point.[55]

In addition to being enunciated in the aforementioned 1930 Hague Convention, these two propositions can be found in a number of international instruments, including the 1997 European Convention on Nationality (Article 3), and the case law of bodies such as the PICJ and its successor, the ICJ.

The requirement of consistency with general principles of international law does not mean that international instruments—or mechanisms established by international

---

[44] Convention on the Reduction of Cases of Multiple Nationality and on Military Obligations in Cases of Multiple Nationality (adopted 6 May 1963, entered into force 28 March 1968) ETS No 043.
[45] European Convention on Nationality (n 5).
[46] Council of Europe Convention on the avoidance of statelessness in relation to State succession (adopted 19 May 2006, entered into force 1 May 2009) CETS No 200.
[47] *Tunis and Morocco* (n 37).
[48] *Nottebohm* (n 5).
[49] Universal Declaration of Human Rights (UDHR) (adopted 10 December 1948) UNGA Res 217 A(III), Article 15.
[50] *Proposed Amendments to the Naturalisation Provision of the Constitution of Costa Rica*, Advisory Opinion OC-4/84, Inter-American Court of Human Rights Series (IAmCtHR) A No 4 (19 January 1984) 32.
[51] See below section 2.2.
[52] See Article 1 of the Hague Convention (n 38); see also *Tunis and Morocco* (n 37).
[53] In *Tunis and Morocco* (n 37), the PCIJ described this principle as a 'general principle': 'In general, therefore, questions relating to the enjoyment or non-enjoyment of its nationality fall solely within the domestic jurisdiction of the State.'
[54] The Hague Convention (n 38) Article 1.
[55] Without the general principles reflected in Article 1 of the 1930 Convention, there would be no law of nationality at the level of international law. That is because, as noted by Weis (n 4) at 29: 'there is ... not one definition of nationality as a conception of municipal law, but as many definitions as there are States'.

law instruments—can grant nationality to individuals who may have a claim. It is the state alone which bestows nationality through its internal law, and it is the state alone which determines the content of its nationality laws. In general, the second proposition in Article 1 of the 1930 Hague Convention has been understood to operate, not as a basis for negating the right of a state to determine who are its nationals, but only to decide whether or not to recognise such determinations in situations where they conflict with general principles—e.g. if the state in question arbitrarily grants nationality to nationals of another country or arbitrarily deprives a particular group of their nationality. Even given the impact of developing norms from human rights law relating to the right to a nationality and the right not to be arbitrarily deprived of it,[56] the international law framework remains relatively limited and is largely devoted to trying to rein in the grievous problems arising from conflicts of municipal nationality laws and events such as changes in sovereignty over territory and denationalisation by the state of nationality.[57]

### 2.1.3 Modes of acquisition of nationality

Debate continues about whether there are any rules governing the modes of acquisition and/or loss of nationality that have customary international law status.[58] Additionally, leading textbooks do not always classify the modes of acquisition and loss in the same terms. Nevertheless, it is widely accepted that in determining who qualifies for nationality,[59] states almost invariably fashion their nationality laws based on some combination of the following modes or methods of acquisition: *jus soli* (nationality based upon place of birth); *jus sanguinis* (nationality based upon descent); naturalisation (e.g. based on residency); succession (nationality being conferred as a result of state succession);[60] annexation and cession; and a residual category 'in any other manner, not inconsistent with international law'.[61] *Jus soli, jus sanguinis*, and naturalisation are the three main modes.[62]

It is often observed that such modes of acquisition reflect the fact that, in general, states do not grant nationality indiscriminately but by application of criteria that indicate a 'genuine and effective link' between the individual and the state.[63] However,

---

[56] e.g. UDHR (n 49) Article 15(1); American Convention on Human Rights (adopted 22 November 1969, entered into force 18 July 1978) Article 20.

[57] The classic example of transgression of limits imposed by international law is the wholesale and automatic attribution of nationality by one state over another state's nationals. See Brownlie (n 37) 295, cited in Edwards (n 5) 25.

[58] As regards the status of the two predominant modes, *jus soli* and *jus sanguinis* acquisition, compare Haro F van Panhuys, *The Role of Nationality in International Law* (Sijthoff 1930) 160–61; Hailbronner (2006) (n 5) with Weis (n 4) 96 and Brownlie (n 37) 303 on the other. See also Boll (n 23) 99.

[59] Sometimes another mode listed separately is the situation of inhabitants of a subjugated or conquered or ceded territory who may assume the nationality of the conquering state, or of the state to which the territory is ceded: see Ivan A Shearer, *Starke's International Law* (11th edn, London Butterworths 1994) 310.

[60] ILC (n 29).

[61] The wording here is taken from the ILC's Draft Articles on Diplomatic Protection. An example of acquisition based on the residual category is the Vatican where nationality is acquired only by holding office and residing in the Vatican City—see Oliver Dörr and Kirsten Schmalenbach (eds), *Vienna Convention on the Law of Treaties* (Springer 2012) 17; Hailbronner (2006) (n 5) 54.

[62] Edwards (n 5) 16. See also James R Crawford, *Brownlie's Principles of Public International Law* (9th edn, OUP 2019) 497.

[63] In *Nottebohm* (n 5) 23, the ICJ stated that: '[a]ccording to the practice of States, to arbitral and judicial decisions and to the opinions of writers, nationality is a legal bond having as its basis a social fact of

this does *not* mean that there is any free-standing test of nationality based on whether there is a genuine and effective link. If a state's nationality law only provides for nationality based on specific types of links (e.g. *jus soli* and/or *jus sanguinis*), there is no power on the international law plane to determine that someone can nevertheless qualify as a national on the basis of other types of links, even if genuine and effective.

### 2.1.4 Ways in which nationality is acquired

There are two main ways in which nationality is acquired. One is by operation of law or *ex lege* (or *ipso jure*).[64] The second way of acquiring nationality, by overt act, stands in sharp contrast to automatic or *ex lege* conferral or acquisition.[65] It requires a grant by the state following procedures determined by national law (usually requiring application).[66] Indeed, the literature indicates that in relation to the second mechanism, an important subdivision is made between: nationality which a person is *entitled* to acquire (non-discretionary or what I shall call 'entitlement acquisition'), usually on application; and nationality which an applicant *may* be able to acquire on application (what I shall call 'discretionary acquisition').

The distinction between *ex lege* acquisition and entitlement acquisition can be complicated in practice where, for example, state nationality law makes provision for *an application* for nationality by those automatically entitled to it. But unless the national law makes possession of nationality dependent on an application, those automatically entitled to it will have it *ex lege* 'by operation of law'.[67]

### 2.1.5 Discretionary entitlement to or eligibility for nationality

As regards the discretionary acquisition sub-category, it is inherent in its character that wherever the national law allows for discretionary granting of nationality, such applicants cannot be considered nationals until the application has been approved and completed and the nationality is bestowed by that state in accordance with its law.[68] Whether the same applies to those in the entitlement acquisition sub-category, is a separate matter addressed below.[69]

---

attachment, a genuine connection of existence, interests and sentiments, together with the existence of reciprocal rights and duties'.

[64] Batchelor (1998) (n 5) 171 (emphasis added).

[65] e.g. Protocol relating to a Certain Case of Statelessness (n 40) Article 1; CRS61 (n 43) Article 1(a), 4(a); Convention on the Reduction of Cases of Multiple Nationality and Military Obligations in Cases of Multiple Nationality (n 44) Article 2(2); Convention to Reduce the Number of Cases of Statelessness (adopted 13 September 1973) Article 1; 1997 European Convention on Nationality (n 5) Articles 6(1), 6(2)(a), 14.

[66] e.g. CRS61 (n 43) Articles 1(b), 4(1)(b); Convention on the Reduction of Cases of Multiple Nationality and Military Obligation in Cases of Multiple Obligation (n 44) Article 1; 1997 European Convention on Nationality (n 5) Articles 6(1)(a), 6(2)(b). Sometimes this modality is described as acquisition or loss of nationality 'by overt act' such as an application for naturalisation or declaration of renunciation.

[67] More problematic is what happens when a state's nationality law contains exceptions that entitle the state to deny nationality, e.g. on grounds of public health or security risk—as in the Law of Return (Israel) Statute 5710-1950: see Hathaway and Foster (n 5) 252. Whether that means that it is not possible to regard applicants in this situation as having such nationality 'by operation of law' is not straightforward.

[68] *KK and Ors (Nationality: North Korea)* Korea CG [2011] UKUT 92 (AC), para 83. See also *SSHD v SP (North Korea) and Others* [2012] EWCA Civ 114; *GP and Others (South Korean citizenship)* [2014] UKUT 00391(IAC). Whilst (as is noted later) there are some national cases which appear to espouse such a position, they appear to lack any established authority.

[69] See below pp. 218–220.

2.1.6 Persons of indeterminate nationality

Indeterminate (or 'doubtful') nationality is not a species of nationality. It is rather a description of a lack of evidence regarding nationality. For that reason, the position of persons deemed to be of indeterminate nationality is addressed below in the subsection on Nationality and Evidence.

2.1.7 Loss of nationality

Again, textbooks vary in the taxonomies they give for loss of nationality. *Oppenheim's International Law*[70] lists the primary means of loss of nationality as release, renunciation;[71] deprivation; expiration; and substitution.[72] More in keeping with the conceptual framework of the CRS61, loss of nationality refers to loss by operation of law, whereas deprivation refers to loss through administrative act.[73]

2.1.8 Denationalisation

Denationalisation is sometimes seen as a subcategory of deprivation of nationality, denoting, for example, deprivation as a penalty by a court following criminal conviction, but it is perhaps best treated in view of historical considerations as a means of loss of nationality in its own right. Denationalisation became the paradigm form of refugee creation in the aftermath of the First World War, when it was used for political reasons and took the form of mass denationalisation, depriving whole groups of nationals of their nationality (e.g. as used by Russia in 1921, the German *Reich* in respect of Jews in the 1930s, and smaller scale measures adopted by the Italian and Turkish authorities, but also, even after the defeat of Germany in 1945, by the governments of Czechoslovakia, Poland, Yugoslavia, Ukraine, Belarus, and Lithuania).[74]

Particularly in respect of denationalisation, principles of recognition have come to play a major role. Denationalisation was famously seen to be susceptible of control by general international law norms in the United Kingdom House of Lords case of *Oppenheimer v Cattermole*.[75] Whilst there remain jurisprudential and doctrinal differences, the clear trend is towards considering denationalisation, at least where it is animated by arbitrary or discriminatory objectives, as not being recognised by other states.[76]

---

[70] Robert Jennings and Arthur Watts (eds), *Oppenheim's International Law* (9th edn, OUP 2008), cited in Fripp (2016) (n 5) 31.
[71] Sometimes called 'expatriation': see Weis (n 4) 115–17.
[72] Fripp (2016) (n 5) 30, stating that expiration and substitution might be treated as subcategories of deprivation rather than separate concepts.
[73] Edwards (n 4) 21.
[74] 'Until well into the 1930s denationalisation in the sense of withdrawal of nationality or citizenship, was perceived as the paradigm refugee-creating situation confronting the international community.' See Fripp (2016) (n 5) 104. See also Claudena Skran, *Refugees in Interwar Europe: The Emergence of a Regime* (OUP 1995).
[75] *Oppenheimer v Cattermole (Inspector of Taxes)* [1976] AC 249.
[76] Edwards (n 5) 23.

## 2.2 The Human Rights Approach

As already noted, Article 15 of the 1948 UDHR (which has been described as 'a total innovation in the history of international law'),[77] provides that:

1. Everyone has the right to a nationality.
2. No one shall be arbitrarily deprived of his nationality nor denied the right to change his nationality.[78]

An increasing number of international and regional human rights treaties include provisions relating to nationality. For example, in 1966, Article 24(3) of the International Covenant on Civil and Political Rights (ICCPR) codified the right of every child to acquire a nationality.[79] Article 7 of the Convention on the Rights of the Child (CRC) also guaranteed the right of every child to acquire a nationality and obliged states to take measures where statelessness ensues.[80] As a result, the further development of the international law on nationality has become inevitably tied up with the development over time of IHRL and the greater importance placed within the latter system on the position of the individual.[81] In the words of Hélène Lambert:

> More recently, matters of nationality and nationality law as reserved domain have come to be counteracted by human rights law. A new rights conception of nationality has begun to emerge based on concepts of human dignity and humanity, and serious limitations on the denial and deprivation of nationality at least when viewed as an 'external act' touching on international obligations.[82]

However, the present extent of such human rights permeation of the international law on nationality must not be exaggerated. In key respects the element of the refugee definition dealing with nationality (or its lack) remains the leading example of a subject-area where human rights norms cannot play a primary role—and thus one where the proper framework is best described as an international law one rather than an IHRL one. That is for three reasons. First, the Convention's drafting reflects the state of international law relating to nationality at the time, which consisted almost solely of the rules drawn up within private and public international law; despite the enactment of the 1945 UN Charter and the UDHR, human rights norms were still relatively undeveloped. Second, the meaning of the term 'nationality' remains one that derives from the international law on nationality; notwithstanding the growing

---

[77] Guy S Goodwin-Gill, 'Deprivation of Citizenship resulting in Statelessness and its Implications in International Law: Opinion' (12 March 2014) 8–16, available at <https://www.kaldorcentre.unsw.edu.au/sites/kaldorcentre.unsw.edu.au/files/gsgg%202-deprivationcitizenshipintlawfinal.pdf> accessed 14 April 2021. See also Spiro (n 24) referring to the words of Nehemiah Robinson.
[78] UDHR (n 49) Article 15.
[79] International Covenant on Civil and Political Rights (adopted 16 December 1966, entered into force 23 March 1976) 999 UNTS 171, Article 24(3).
[80] Convention on the Rights of the Child (adopted 20 November 1989, entered into force 2 September 1990) 1577 UNTS 3. For a detailed treatment, see Foster and Lambert (n 5) 58–63.
[81] Weis (n 4) 3, cited in Fripp (2016) (n 5) 8–9.
[82] Hélène Lambert, 'Comparative Perspectives on Arbitrary Deprivation of Nationality and Refugee Status' (2015) 64 Int'l & Comp LQ 1, 7; see also Edwards (n 5) 11–43; Foster and Lambert (n 5) 77–90.

importance of applying human rights norms in some contexts, for example in cases of deprivation of nationality. Significantly, none of the regional human rights courts or treaty-monitoring bodies have sought to construct their own concept of nationality. Their approach is rather typified by the observation made by the Inter-American Court of Human Rights in *Case of the Yean and Bosico Children v Dominican Republic*, that '[t]he determination of who has a right to be a national continues to fall within a State's domestic jurisdiction'.[83] Increasing limits imposed on this right by human rights norms, cannot alter its core character. The main restrictions applicable in this context—the eschewal of arbitrariness, the prohibition on discrimination, and restrictions concerning the creation of statelessness—remain limited.[84]

Identification of the nationality element of the refugee definition as primarily based on the international law on nationality rather than on IHRL is important for a third, wider, reason. Whatever virtue the human rights approach might have in relation to other elements of the definition (e.g. the definition of 'being persecuted'), it can only have limited purchase in relation to determination of nationality. It would be wholly destabilising if refugee decision makers sought to create and apply notions of nationality divorced from international law principles and the practice of states relating to nationality; and it would create potential conflict of laws at every turn, also affecting exclusion and extradition matters. Human rights norms are playing an increasing role in determination of some nationality issues, for example deprivation of nationality, but so long as exclusivity of nationality law remains the established principle, they can only have a supplementary role.

## 3 Nationality and the Refugee Definition

### 3.1 Uses of the Term 'Nationality' in the Refugee Convention

The first paragraph of Article 1A(2) of the Refugee Convention uses the term 'nationality' three times; the second paragraph (dealing with multiple nationality) uses it another three. In the first paragraph, the first mention of the term is to identify nationality as one of the five Convention reasons ('being persecuted for reasons of ... nationality ...'); this is also the use of the term deployed in Article 33(1). As already noted, this use of the term to identify one of the five Convention reasons possesses a distinct meaning in tandem with the four other reasons and can be left to one side until Chapter 10.

Nationality is also of major importance to the construction of Article 1C, with five out of the six bases for cessation making reference to 'nationality'. Article 1E also contains an exclusion clause in respect of 'a person who is recognised by the competent authorities of the country in which he has taken residence as having the rights and obligations which are attached to the possession of the nationality of that country'.[85]

---

[83] *Case of the Yean and Bosico Children v Dominican Republic*, Preliminary Objections, Merits, Reparations and Costs, IAmCtHR Series C No 130 (8 September 2005) 140.
[84] See Jorunn Brandvoll, 'Deprivation of Nationality: Limitations on Rendering Persons Stateless under International Law' in Edwards and van Waas (n 4) 94–216.
[85] Refugee Convention (n 1) Article 1E.

The refugee rights regime contained in the Convention also includes references to nationality: there are references to nationals and nationality in the context of exceptional measures (Article 8) and wage-earning employment (Article 17).

In terms of the personal scope of the refugee definition, we are concerned solely with the references within Article 1A(2) to those who have a 'country of nationality', those 'not having a nationality' and those who have 'more than one nationality'. We shall also need to consider whether any light is shed on these usages by other uses of the term 'nationality' in the Refugee Convention.

We will first address the term 'country of nationality'. It is convenient to then deal with those who have 'more than one nationality', leaving those 'not having a nationality' until last.

## 3.2 'Nationality' in the Term 'Country of Nationality' (*'Pays dont elle a la nationalité'*)

### 3.2.1 Drafting history and *travaux préparatoires*

Looking first at the *travaux préparatoires* (hereinafter *travaux*) within the meaning of Article 32 of the Vienna Convention on the Law of Treaties (VCLT),[86] it appears that the term 'country of nationality'[87] was never debated by the Convention's drafters, and that this was because it was well-established that nationality in this context bore a technical meaning denoting the legal tie between the individual and the state.[88]

As noted earlier, in order to come within the personal scope of the refugee definition, a person must be either a national or a non-national. Whilst this differentiation matters in terms of identifying the relevant country of reference (and in the case of multiple nationals or stateless persons with more than one country of former habitual residence, the precise test of protection), it does not negate the description of the refugee definition as having universal application to all persons, since, between them, nationals and non-nationals exhaust the possible universe of persons.[89]

Although the *travaux* are only a supplementary means of interpretation, it is worth briefly identifying why the drafters chose nationality (or its absence) as the key criterion for personal scope. It is possible to read the *travaux* to the Refugee Convention as revealing some doubts about whether nationality was the right choice of criterion to apply in defining personal scope, given their awareness of recent and ongoing denationalisation measures creating large-scale statelessness. For some time, the drafters conceived of the personal scope in terms of stateless persons, subdividing the latter category into de jure and de facto stateless persons.[90] However, nationality had played

---

[86] Vienna Convention on the Law of Treaties (VCLT) (adopted 23 May 1969, entered into force 27 January 1980) 1155 UNTS 331, Article 32.
[87] And in the equally authentic French text, '*hors du pays dont elle a la nationalité*'.
[88] Robinson (n 5) 53; James C Hathaway, *The Rights of Refugees Under International Law* (CUP 2005) 144, both cited by Zimmermann and Mahler (n 5) 388.
[89] As regards the position of stateless children see p. 278. The situation of persons of indeterminate nationality is addressed below at section 2.1.6.
[90] Whilst not part of the *travaux*, the Recommendations of the Secretary General set out in 1949 made clear that it considered 'the possession of a nationality and the protection of a country of which they are nationals as the foundations of the status of foreigners'. See Ad Hoc Committee on Refugees and Stateless

a prominent part as a key criterion in predecessor international instruments[91] and the interstate system continued to have a firm hold at the time. Nationality was seen as a means of regulating relationships among and between sovereign states, giving rise, on the part of the state, to personal jurisdiction over the individual and creating duties upon states vis-à-vis other states. Focus on nationality also best matched the concern to ensure that refugee protection should only be made available to those who could not enjoy protection from their own states.[92] It should also be noted that even though the extended refugee definition in both the Organization of African Unity (OAU) Convention and the Cartagena Declaration did not strictly adhere to such a criterion,[93] both preserved the Article 1A(2) definition as one of its two limbs of the regional definition of refugee.

### 3.2.2 Good faith

The good faith element of Article 31 VCLT helps little with interpretation of the meaning of the terms 'nationality' and 'not having a nationality', except insofar as the legal duty on states parties to implement the Refugee Convention in good faith can be said to include facilitating the identification of those entitled to protection with a degree of legal certainty and the only widely accepted way for doing so is on the basis of the accepted international law definition of nationality as the legal bond between the individual and the state.[94]

### 3.2.3 Ordinary meaning

It has already been stated that the phrase 'country of nationality' within Article 1A(2) denotes the legal relationship or bond between an individual and a state. Some appear to describe this as its ordinary meaning.[95] That view encounters the difficulty that in common usage, there are at least two main meanings given to nationality, both broadly mirroring the same two main meanings attributed by common usage to the term 'nation'.[96] In a well-known passage, Paul Weis described the two senses of nationality in use as being 'a politico-legal term denoting membership of a State' and a 'historico-biological term denoting membership of a nation'.[97] By the former he clearly meant

---

Persons, A Study of Statelessness, United Nations, August 1949, Lake Success— New York (1 August 1949) UN Doc E/1112/Add.1.

[91] Claudena Skran, 'Historical Developments of International Refugee Law', in Zimmermann (n 5) 3–36.
[92] Hathaway and Foster (n 5) 49–50.
[93] Article 1(2) of the 1969 Organization of African Unity (OAU) Convention Governing the Specific Aspects of Refugee Problems in Africa (adopted 10 September 1969, entered into force 20 June 1974) 1001 UNTS 45 (OAU Convention) also applies the term 'refugee' to persons facing specified harms in their 'country of origin or nationality'. Similarly, conclusion 3 of the Cartagena Declaration (*Instrumentos Regionales sobre Refugiados y temas relacionados, Declaración de Cartagena sobre Refugiados, Adoptado por el 'Coloquio Sobre la Protección Internacional de los Refugiados en América Central, México y Panamá: Problemas Jurídicos y Humanitarios*') (adopted 22 November 1984) refers, not to 'country of nationality', but to 'their country'/'country of origin'. See also Arab Convention on Regulating Status of Refugees in the Arab Countries (1994) Article 1(2), cited in Fripp (2016) (n 5) 124.
[94] Edwards (n 5) 30; Foster and Lambert (n 5) 116.
[95] As Fripp seemingly does—see Fripp (2016) (n 5) 199, 205, 215.
[96] See e.g. Merriam Webster. Indeed, neither of the two uses identified in Oxford Dictionaries refer to legal status (they identify the two meanings as 'the status of belonging to a particular nation' and an 'ethnic group forming a part of one or more political nations').
[97] Weis (n 4) 3.

nationality as the legal bond between the individual and the state.[98] As we shall see, the latter sense he gave loosely corresponds to that to be given to nationality as one of the five Refugee Convention reasons.[99]

It is possible to argue that the drafters understood the term to have a technical meaning specific to the particular subject-matter covered by the Refugee Convention.[100] That appears to be the view taken (at least indirectly) by Foster and Lambert.[101]

At all events, either because the term 'nationality' possesses at least two meanings in common usage, or because it has a special meaning, it cannot easily be said that its 'ordinary meaning', even confined to the term 'country of nationality', is clear and unambiguous. Hence, in order to justify reading the term 'country of nationality' to mean the legal tie between an individual and a state, recourse must be had to other VCLT rules.

In considering the meaning of the term 'country of nationality' it is also necessary to heed the tense of the sentences in which it occurs. The present tense is used: '*is* outside the country of his nationality ... or who, *not having* a nationality ...'.[102] On a literal reading, the nationality that is referred to has to be nationality that is presently possessed, sometimes known as 'current' or 'actual' nationality.[103] However, without reference to context, and object and purpose, it is not possible to say that the tense alone establishes that nationality must be actual nationality.[104]

### 3.2.4 'Country of nationality' as a state

Once the term 'nationality' in the phrase 'country of nationality' is understood to mean the legal tie between the individual and the state, then in ordinary parlance the term can only denote a state, since it is only states that can confer nationality.[105] If one is without a nationality, however, the entity defined by the term 'country of former habitual residence' may not necessarily be a state.[106]

Understood as the legal tie between the individual and the state, nationality has sometimes been designated as 'formal' or 'de jure' nationality. Such designation is to be avoided since it fosters the erroneous notion that nationality has two subcategories,

---

[98] ibid.
[99] See Chapter 10, section 3.3.3.
[100] See Oliver Dörr, 'Article 31: General Rules of Interpretation' in Dörr and Schmalenbach (n 61) 521, 568, who notes, with reference to Article 31(4) VCLT, that where the terms of a treaty have a technical or 'special meaning' due to the particular field the treaty covers, 'the particular meaning may already appear from the context and object and purpose of the treaty' and the particular meaning is 'essentially the ordinary meaning in the particular context'.
[101] Although concerned with not having a nationality, Foster and Lambert (n 5) 106, contend that '[t]he background and context to the drafting, and adoption of both conventions [1951 and 1954 conventions] strongly suggests that the special meaning of "not having a nationality" was statelessness'.
[102] Refugee Convention (n 1) Article 1A(2).
[103] See Fripp (2016) (n 5) 200.
[104] See below section 3.2.10.
[105] This appears to be treated as a given in most case law; for a UK case that analyses the issue, see *Fadil Dyli (Protection—UNMIK—Arif—IFA—Art 1D)* Kosovo CG [2000] UKIAT 00001, [19]. Difficult issues may arise in the case of some countries, e.g. Taiwan and Kosovo, in relation to which there is dispute over whether they qualify as a state for international law purposes. It is beyond the scope of this study to analyse these.
[106] See pp. 273–274, 275–277, 279–281.

formal and 'de facto' or 'effective'. As explained below, this has led to considerable confusion in the literature: 'effective' or 'de facto' nationality is not nationality.[107]

### 3.2.5 Context

Whilst a treaty's context includes, inter alia, all its provisions,[108] neither of two other provisions having potential relevance to interpreting the meaning of 'country of nationality', namely Articles 1C and 1E, shed any light. It would be very odd if the concept of nationality at play in Article 1C differed, since cessation is essentially about whether relevant circumstances have arisen such that the same person *who has previously been accepted* as a national or stateless person *no longer* requires international protection.[109] Neither textual nor other VCLT considerations indicates that 'nationality' should here carry a different meaning. As regards Article 1E, there is no basis for considering that the use therein of the concept of nationality bears a different meaning either. There has been no sustained suggestion in the refugee literature or case law that the term 'nationality' possesses a different meaning in either of these articles.[110]

### 3.2.6 Object and purpose

It follows from what has been said in sections 3.2.2 and 3.2.5 regarding ordinary meaning and context, that to properly construe the meaning of the term 'nationality' within the phrase 'country of nationality', recourse must be had also to the Refugee Convention's object(s) and purpose(s). Additionally, the two concepts comprising the term 'country of nationality'—'country' and 'nationality'—require to be read together, since nationality at the level of international law only exists by virtue of an individual's membership of a state. As already noted, 'country of nationality' can only be a state since it is only a state that can confer nationality.

It is widely agreed that the Refugee Convention was drafted at a time when the Vattellian interstate understanding of international law was in the ascendant and individuals only had standing by virtue of being nationals (or subjects) and owing a duty of allegiance.[111] The Convention's purposes are predicated on the need for states to enter into treaty obligations to ensure protection of those with or without a nationality who are threatened with persecution. Reading 'nationality' as denoting the legal tie between the individual and the state also comports with the principle of surrogacy.[112]

---

[107] See below sections 3.2.12 and 3.3.3–3.3.6.
[108] See Chapter 2.
[109] See Joined Cases C-175/08, C-176/08, C-178/08, and C-179/08 *Salahadin Abdulla and Others* [2010] ECR I-0000, para 76. See now Directive 2011/95/EU of the European Parliament and of the Council of 13 December 2011 on standards for the qualification of third-country nationals or stateless persons as beneficiaries of international protection, for a uniform status for refugees or for persons eligible for subsidiary protection, and for the content of the protection granted (recast) [2011] OJ L 337/9 (QD (recast)), Article 11, which broadly mirrors Article 1C of the Refugee Convention.
[110] See Fripp (2016) (n 5) 324–25. However, for one judicial attempt to invoke Article 1C(3) and Article 1E to support the notion of 'effective nationality', see discussion below pp. 227–230 of *Lay Kon Tji v MIEA* [1998] 1380 FCA.
[111] Hailbronner (2006) (n 5); Johannes M Chan, 'The Right to a Nationality as a Human Right: The Current Trend Towards Recognition' (1991) 12(1/2) Human Rights Law Journal 1, 1; Spiro, 'Dual Nationality and the Meaning of Citizenship' (n 24) 1420–22.
[112] See Chapter 7, section 1.4.8.

### 3.2.7 Article 31(3) considerations

A similar observation applies in relation to the rules set out in Article 31(3) and/or 32 VCLT. Whether falling strictly within the category of 'subsequent practice', the view that nationality in this part of the definition denotes the legal tie between the individual and the state clearly constitute a subsequent practice in the broad sense.[113] In relation to the closely connected CSSP54, the UNHCR 2014 Handbook on Protection of Stateless Persons, which expressly bases itself on state practice (see paragraph 6), observes regarding the term 'nationality' that:

> [ ... ] the treaty's concept of national is consistent with the traditional understanding of this term under international law; that is persons over whom a State considers it has jurisdiction on the basis of nationality, including the right to bring claims against other States for their ill-treatment.[114]

### 3.2.8 Special meaning

Bearing in mind, as noted already, that commentators have seen Article 31(4) of the VCLT to have application where the terms of a treaty 'have a technical or "special meaning" due to the particular field the treaty covers',[115] there is a respectable argument for seeing both the terms 'nationality' and 'not having a nationality' as possessing such a meaning. However, there continues to be some uncertainty about the ambit of this element, in particular given the fact that the burden rests on the party asserting.[116] And it certainly cannot be said to be a position that has been broadly agreed.

### 3.2.9 Article 32

The relevance of the *travaux* has already been addressed.[117] Mention has already been made that at least in the broad sense, there would appear to be state practice (even if not strictly falling within Article 31(3)(b) or (c)) that treats nationality as the legal tie between the individual and the state.[118]

### 3.2.10 Nationality's temporal dimension: nationality as actual nationality

On the basis of the use of the present tense throughout Article 1A(2), 'nationality' must refer to a nationality that is actual or current. Whether that is also the position that results after application of VCLT rules in full is best analysed by reference to the debate that has arisen around Hathaway and Foster's adoption of the notion of 'inchoate nationality'.

In the second edition of *The Law of Refugee Status*, Hathaway and Foster identify themselves as proponents of the notion of 'inchoate nationality', which they define as 'automatic, non-discretionary access to citizenship' and as 'citizenship [that] actually

---

[113] See Chapter 2, section 1.5.
[114] UNHCR 2014 Handbook (n 5) para 52.
[115] See Chapter 2, section 1.7; Dörr (n 100) 568; Richard Gardiner, *Treaty Interpretation* (2nd edn, OUP 2010) 173–74.
[116] See Chapter 2 and Gardiner (n 115) 295–96.
[117] See above section 3.2.1.
[118] See above section 3.2.7.

exists in embryonic form and needs simply to be activated by means of a request that will clearly be acceded to'.[119] They seek to differentiate 'inchoate nationality' from what Germov and Motta call 'prospective' nationality.[120]

Taking account of the objects and purpose of the treaty, and also drawing particularly on the Canadian Federal Court case of *Bouianova*,[121] Hathaway and Foster accept that the use of 'is' in the refugee definition denotes present nationality, but contend that it can nevertheless be read purposively, in light of the Convention's objective of providing surrogate protection, to include those who have the nationality of a country available to them 'for the asking and could be acquired by means of a non-discretionary formality'[122] and thus can cover those with 'inchoate nationality' in this sense. In their view, where nationality is 'available for the asking', there is a 'strong substantive logic' to including those with an 'inchoate nationality' since it can reasonably be said that they have a 'genuine link' with that country.[123]

A first observation to make about this position is that it does not in any way represent endorsement for the view that nationality can include those who *may* be entitled to it—the discretionary category mentioned earlier. It is strictly confined to those who have mandatory entitlement to it.

A second observation is that it is contrary to the position taken by most leading textbooks,[124] by UNHCR, both in the 1979 Handbook and in its 2014 Handbook,[125] and by the United Kingdom's Supreme Court in *Al-Jedda* (which approved the UNHCR guidance).[126]

A third observation is that the jurisprudential basis of the 'inchoate nationality' approach is problematic. In particular, it appears to rely heavily on the Federal Court of Canada case of *Bouianova*,[127] even though the reasoning of that case is equivocal as to whether the applicant possessed Russian citizenship already. Further complicating matters, subsequent Canadian cases that have construed the *Bouianova* decision to mean that nationality could include (to use Hathaway and Foster's term) 'inchoate nationality' (e.g. *Williams*),[128] have sought to overlay it with requirements that relate

---

[119] Hathaway and Foster (n 5) 58, 63.
[120] Roz Germov and Francesco Motta, *Refugee Law in Australia* (OUP 2003) 147, cited in Hathaway and Foster (n 5) 57–58. The prospective nationality position has been criticised by UNHCR: see e.g. UNHCR's position on mixed Azeri-Armenian couples from Azerbaijan and the specific issue of their admission and asylum in Armenia (2003) 3, which states that: '[The text of Article 1A(2)] thus clearly states that what matters for the purposes of the inclusion clause is the nationality/ies that the persons actually possess/es not the nationality/ies that the person may eventually acquire', cited in Andrew Wolman, 'North Korean Asylum Seekers and Dual Nationality' (2012) 24(4) IJRL 793, 796.
[121] *Bouianova v Canada* [1993] FCJ No 576 (Bouianova).
[122] Hathaway and Foster (n 5) 57–64.
[123] ibid 58.
[124] See e.g. Robinson (n 5) 50; Grahl-Madsen (n 4) 158; Goodwin-Gill and McAdam (n 5) 88, 90.
[125] UNHCR Handbook (n 4) para 87; UNHCR 2014 Handbook (n 5).
[126] *SSHD v Al-Jedda* [2013] UKSC 62, para 34. The guidance endorsed by Lord Wilson—UNHCR, Guidelines on Statelessness No 1: The definition of 'Stateless Person' in Article 1(1) of the 1954 Convention relating to the Status of Stateless Persons (20 February 2012) HCR/GS/12/01—was incorporated into paragraph 50 of the UNHCR 2014 Handbook (n 5) virtually word for word.
[127] *Bouianova* (n 121).
[128] *Williams v Canada (MCI)* [2001] FCJ No 827 (TD); see also *Tretsetsang v Canada (Citizenship and Immigration)* [2016] FCJ No 615, 2016 FCA 175.

more to evidence than law. In addition, some have appeared to extend the approach by reference to vague tests going beyond that of 'mere formality'.[129]

A fourth observation is that Hathaway and Foster's approach appears to harbour formulations no less equivocal than those in *Bouianova*. Hence, they refer in a key passage to it as nationality (citizenship) which 'actually exists in embryonic form' needing simply to be 'activated'[130]—here the wording suggests they mean to denote a pre-existing nationality or *ex lege* nationality. Yet elsewhere they make clear that they see this concept as extending the meaning of nationality within Article 1A(2) *beyond* what a person possesses, and extending to persons who have 'access' to such nationality.[131]

A fifth observation is that at least on a strict literal interpretation such an approach confuses the issue of whether a person possesses nationality as a *matter of law* with the question of whether they could come to possess it as a *matter of fact*. If this approach is to prevail nevertheless, then it must be by way of an approach based on 'object and purpose'.

A sixth observation is that the notion does not appear to be relied on in other areas of public international law relating to nationality.

What then of Hathaway and Foster's view that their 'inchoate nationality' approach is consistent with the Convention's context, object and purpose? It is not clear that it is. Applying a literal current nationality approach ensures legal certainty as to which class of persons is identified, especially given that nationality in the context of the refugee definition concerns nationality that is acquired automatically and not as a matter of discretion. To assert (as they do) that the 'inchoate nationality' approach furthers the principle of surrogacy because those concerned have a 'genuine link' with the country concerned, is to engage in a predictive exercise which necessarily entails further assessment. That reduces legal certainty and increases the potential for subjective assessment.

Whilst not raised by Hathaway and Foster, it is salient to mention a separate argument that might be raised to suggest that the 'inchoate nationality' helps prevent a situation of (what the Canadian case law has termed 'optionality'),[132] whereby applicants may be able to manipulate their nationality to achieve refugee protection when they do not need it. The trouble with any such suggestion is that there is the possibility of misuse through optionality whichever approach is taken. Just as an applicant might be able under the 'actual nationality' approach to avoid being considered as a national of a safe country (e.g. because s/he has not yet made an application even though s/he appears to meet eligibility conditions), so an applicant under an 'inchoate nationality' approach may be able to avoid being assessed by reference to a safe country (e.g. if s/he is stateless and his/her country of former habitual residence is safe) but s/he has entitlement on application to nationality in another country that is unsafe.

A final reason for rejecting the 'inchoate nationality' approach is that one of its two main proponents, Michelle Foster, has now recanted. Her 2019 book with Lambert,[133]

---

[129] See cases cited by Foster and Lambert (n 5) 127–29.
[130] Hathaway and Foster (n 5) 58.
[131] ibid 57–58, 60.
[132] *Bouianova* (n 121) para 12; *Williams* (n 128) para 22.
[133] Foster and Lambert (n 5).

contains a strong critique of the 'inchoate nationality' approach as set out in Hathaway and Foster, pointing out that it is at odds with the definition's use of the present tense, at odds with the text of Article 1C (which does not refer to potential or possible acquisition either), has been rejected by UNHCR, and is inconsistent with general principles of international nationality law. She and Lambert argue that to suggest that international protection should be denied because nationality can/may be acquired in the future would undermine the basis of two general principles of international law (a state's duty to prevent arbitrary deprivation of nationality and a state's duty to eliminate provisions that permit the renunciation of a nationality without the prior possession or acquisition of another nationality).[134]

In a recent article, Fripp discusses the pros and cons of the 'inchoate nationality' approach and confirms the position taken in his 2016 book that the arguments against it strongly outweigh those in its support.[135]

Taking stock of the various arguments, the 'inchoate nationality' approach cannot be supported. Once it is accepted (as in logic it must) that persons possess nationality as a matter of law and that passports etc. are only (at best) declaratory of such nationality, then there is no need to resort to an 'inchoate nationality' approach to overcome what are essentially evidential issues. If, for example, a decision maker is satisfied (by looking at a country's nationality laws and surrounding materials about their operation) that applicant A possesses nationality of that country, then (assuming identity is accepted) the fact s/he may not have a passport or letter granting nationality should not necessarily matter. Similarly, the fact that s/he has not proceeded with an application for the relevant nationality is only relevant evidentially, since in such a scenario the result could only be confirmation of the fact of nationality.

As regards object(s) and purpose(s), it can be seen that there is a risk of misuse whichever approach is taken—the actual nationality or inchoate nationality approach. In any event, concerns about misuse are not a proper basis for applying an approach to nationality that departs from general international law. They are akin to those that arise in the context of claims based on bad faith, or could be said to be one example of them. Whilst there still remains controversy concerning the bad faith issue,[136] it is difficult to see that it can be used to read requirements into the refugee definition that are not there.

### 3.2.11 Actual nationality and the date of decision

Resolving that nationality means actual or 'present' nationality still leaves the matter of which precise point in time is to be taken as the 'present'—the date of decision or, as Zink and Grahl-Madsen argued in the context of cases of denationalisation, the point in time at which a person becomes a refugee (which was, in Grahl-Madsen's words, 'crossing the frontier or sur place').[137] The logic behind the latter view is that

---

[134] ibid 127–31. At 131, the authors note that '[o]ur view is that the alternative argument put forward in Hathaway and Foster ... needs to be revised'.
[135] Fripp (2021) (n 5) 311–21.
[136] See below p. 404.
[137] Grahl-Madsen (n 4) 185, citing Karl Friedrich Zink, *Das Asylrecht in der Bundesrepublik Deutschland nach dem Abkommen vom 28. Juli über die Rechtsstellung der Flüchtlinge under besonder Berucksichtigung der Rechtssprechung der Verwaltungsgerichte* (Dissertation, Erlangen-Nürnberg 1962) xxi, 32. Grahl-Madsen

since refugee status is declaratory,[138] it is incumbent on the decision maker to treat the 'present' as the date this happens, not the date on which it is 'declared' through a grant of refugee status by the host state. Whilst that argument has some force, it would result in significant uncertainty—requiring, for example, the decision maker to make a finding on precisely which date a person left their own country or when their *sur place* activity came to the adverse attention of the actors of persecution, facts which may not always be known even to the applicants. By contrast, fixing the date as that of the date of decision enables greater exactitude. But more importantly, to adopt the position taken by Zink and Grahl-Madsen would be at odds with VCLT rules. It would be contrary to ordinary meaning because Article 1A(2) is cast in the present tense, both in terms of the test of whether a person faces a well-founded fear of 'being persecuted' and in terms of nationality. Zink and Grahl-Madsen's view would require a decision maker to apply an historic, not an *ex nunc* test.

3.2.12 The content of nationality and the issue of 'effective nationality'
A source of some confusion in the refugee law literature has been recourse to the notion of 'effective nationality'.[139] As will be addressed in section 3.2.2, the principal role mooted for this notion has been in the context of persons with multiple nationality.[140] Given, however, that Hathaway and Foster also treat it as relevant to their 'inchoate nationality' understanding,[141] it is important to clarify that (whatever one makes of its role in the context of multiple nationals) the term 'nationality' within the phrase 'country of nationality', being concerned only with the legal tie between an individual and the state, is *not* concerned with whether or not nationality is effective. To construe it so would be to delimit the term 'nationality' to a particular type of nationality or some incident of it. As observed by Fripp, the concept of 'effective nationality' is a qualification of the concept of nationality, whereas the term 'nationality' is employed at Article 1A(2) without qualification.[142] Nothing in the object(s) or purpose(s) of the Refugee Convention requires the introduction of any qualification.[143] Nor is physical presence or the degree of closeness a person has with their country of nationality essential to deciding whether to treat them as a national of that country.[144] The 2014 UNHCR Handbook makes the point that:

> Nationality, by its nature, reflects a linkage between the State and the individual, often on the basis of birth on the territory or descent from a national and this is often evident in the criteria for acquisition of nationality in most countries. However, a

---

(n 4) also mentions as a possible candidate, the date of application, but there is no tenable argument for considering that point in time.

[138] UNHCR Handbook (n 4) para 28.
[139] Storey (2nd part) (n 5).
[140] See Fripp (2016) (n 5) 52–54.
[141] Hathaway and Foster (n 5) 59–64.
[142] Fripp (2016) (n 5) 170–72.
[143] ibid 170. See also Lambert (n 5) 809–12.
[144] Subject only to questions of recognition: see Fripp (2016) (n 5) 218.

person can still be a 'national' for the purposes of Article 1(1) despite not being born or habitually resident in the State of purported nationality.[145]

Conversely, even a close connection may not be enough.[146]

## 3.3 'A Person who Has More Than One Nationality'/'*Personne qui a plus d'une Nationalité*'

The second paragraph of Article 1A(2) provides that:

> In the case of a person who has more than one nationality, the term 'the country of his nationality' shall mean each of the countries of which he is a national, and a person shall not be deemed to be lacking the protection of the country of his nationality if, without any valid reason based on well-founded fear, he has not availed himself of the protection of one of the countries of which he is a national.[147]

### 3.3.1 Meaning

Application of VCLT considerations to this paragraph can conveniently be undertaken in the one place.

Although the *travaux* reveal that there was some discussion regarding the second paragraph, the drafters shed little light on its meaning. Considered in terms of the text, the first feature to note about this paragraph is that the use it makes of 'country of nationality' does not specify a meaning different from the term 'country of nationality' in the first subparagraph but simply clarifies how it applies when a person has more than one nationality. It expressly aligns its treatment of multiple nationals with the concept of nationality within the phrase 'country of nationality' employed in the first paragraph.

As a corollary, a second notable feature is that the wording of the second paragraph is predicated on the fact of dual or multiple nationality. Whatever is meant by its final sentence (and this is explored in greater detail in the next subsection), this paragraph is not about circumstances in which it might be appropriate to treat a multiple national as having just one nationality. Indeed, even the 1979 UNHCR Handbook statement at paragraph 107 (which is often relied on to justify recourse to the notion of 'effective nationality'),[148] makes very clear that the issue concerns whether persons who '*possess*' multiple nationality can be exempted by the additional requirement set out in this subparagraph from having to show that direct risk of being persecuted faces them in their country of plural nationality. The issue is not framed as being one about whether

---

[145] UNHCR 2014 Handbook (n 5) para 54.
[146] Fripp (2016) (n 5) 199 observes that had the drafters intended this, 'they could have achieved it by including a special meaning in the instrument itself, for instance, employing the words "a country to which he has a strong connection" or the language later adopted at article 12(4) [ICCPR 1966] "his own country". They did not do so.'
[147] Refugee Convention (n 1) Article 1A(2).
[148] See below section 3.3.3.

such multiple nationality exists. This might seem very obvious, but as we shall see in a moment the attempt to interpret this subparagraph by recourse to the notion of 'effective nationality' has tended to blur this fact. Such use inevitably carries the suggestion that, unless 'effective', the nationality concerned is not a nationality at all.

A third feature of this paragraph is that by stating that 'the term "the country of his nationality" shall mean each of the countries of which he is a national', its opening clause makes clear that the mere fact of multiple nationality does not exempt an applicant from the requirements set out in the first paragraph of having to establish in relation to their country of nationality, a well-founded fear of being persecuted, etc. If the first sentence had stopped at the end of the first clause, the result would have been to lay down an unqualified rule that an applicant with multiple nationality must establish a well-founded fear of persecution in each of the countries of their nationality. However, the first clause is qualified by the second clause, which can be termed the 'valid reason' clause.

Put another way, the second part of this paragraph makes it possible for a person whose second or multiple country of nationality is non-persecutory to nevertheless qualify as a refugee if able to show that in that country (or those countries) they would nevertheless be at indirect risk of persecution. Construing it in this way is also consistent with the principle of surrogacy.[149] The underlying rationale is that a person who is a national of country B as well as country A can demonstrate a need for surrogate protection even if only one of those countries of nationality is a persecutory country, but can only do so if able to demonstrate a 'valid reason based on well-founded fear' for not availing herself/himself of its protection.

On one possible view the 'valid reason based on well-founded fear' might be said to relate to fear of persecutory harm at the hands of state or non-state actors in the country (countries) of multiple nationality other than the country of origin. However, on closer analysis this would be illogical since, read thus, an applicant would either have no well-founded fear in his or her original country or have a well-founded fear in both/all. Read thus, the inclusion of this phrase would be redundant.[150]

Accordingly, the only meaning logically conveyed by the text and also consistent with the Refugee Convention's context, object and purpose is that this qualifying clause refers to well-founded fear in the *original* county of nationality against which the second or plural country of nationality (which cannot itself be a persecutory country) is unable to protect.[151] As developed further in section 3.3.6 below, there are two obvious sets of circumstances which could meet the requirements of this clause: where the country of multiple nationality, whilst non-persecutory, would (i) not admit the national to its territory; or (ii) where there was a real risk that this country would *refoule* the applicant. Whether there are any other circumstances is less certain but, in order not to breach the principle of surrogacy, they cannot be limitless.[152]

---

[149] As stated by the Supreme Court of Canada in *Ward*, '[t]he exercise of assessing the claimant's fear in each country of citizenship … accords with the principles underlying refugee protection. Otherwise the claimant would benefit from rights granted by a foreign state while home state protection had still been available'. See *Canada (AG) v Ward* [1993] 2 SCR 689, cited by Hathaway and Foster (n 5) 55.
[150] For a recent analysis of the 'valid reasons' provision, see Fripp (2021) (n 5) 327–34.
[151] ibid.
[152] See below section 3.3.6.

A fourth notable feature about the wording of the second paragraph is that it does not envisage any hierarchy of importance as between one nationality and another; there is nothing in the text to indicate that one should be treated as primary as compared with the others. That also comports with case law.[153]

Other VCLT considerations will be alluded to below where relevant but in essence they do not indicate the need for a different reading.

### 3.3.2 Multiple nationality and the concept of effective nationality

There has (as noted earlier) been significant support for giving the 'valid reason' clause a further gloss (drawing on object and purpose considerations in particular) by reference to the notion of 'effective nationality'.

The notion of 'effective nationality' has made its way into refugee law via the UNHCR 1979 Handbook,[154] which states at paragraph 107 in relation to multiple nationals that:

> In examining the case of an applicant with dual or multiple nationality, it is necessary, however, to distinguish between the possession of a nationality in the legal sense and the availability of protection by the country concerned. There will be cases where the applicant has the nationality of a country in regard to which he alleges no fear, but such nationality may be deemed to be ineffective as it does not entail the protection normally granted to nationals. In such circumstances, the possession of the second nationality would not be inconsistent with refugee status. As a rule, there should have been a request for, and a refusal of, protection before it can be established that a given nationality is ineffective. If there is no explicit refusal of protection, absence of a reply within reasonable time may be considered a refusal.[155]

The notion has been espoused to a greater or lesser degree by a number of academics, including Hathaway in *The Law of Refugee Status* (TLRS),[156] possibly Goodwin-Gill and McAdam in *The Refugee in International Law* in its third edition,[157] and Hathaway and Foster in TLRS2.[158]

---

[153] See e.g. *KK* (n 68) para 58.

[154] UNHCR Handbook (n 4).

[155] ibid para 107.

[156] Hathaway (n 5) 59: '[t]he major caveat to the principle of deferring to protection by a state of citizenship is the need to ensure effective, rather than merely formal, nationality. It is not enough, for example, that the claimant carries a second passport from a non-persecutory state if that state is not in fact willing to afford protection against return to the country of persecution. While it is appropriate to presume a willingness on the part of a country of nationality to protect in the absence of evidence to the contrary, facts that call into question the existence of basic protection against return must be carefully assessed.' See also Hathaway and Foster (n 5) 57. Despite citing *Jong Kim Koe* and *Tji* approvingly, they make an implied criticism of any equation of this notion with the view that 'the putative country of second citizenship is to be treated as a country of reference only if it provides protection against persecution and would ensure respect for human rights' (ibid 56–57).

[157] Goodwin-Gill and McAdam (3rd edn) (n 5) 67 (seemingly meaning to convey that this statement is contentious, the authors insert a footnote stating: 'Cf. Goodwin-Gill, G.S., *International Law and the Movement of Persons Between States* (Clarendon Press 1978), 46–49'; Piotrowicz (1999) (n 5)). The discussion in Goodwin-Gill and McAdam (4th edn) (n 5) 86–94 does not address the issue directly, although it does firmly endorse the notion of nationality as actual nationality.

[158] Hathaway and Foster (n 5): 'In cases of dual or multiple nationality, refugee status will only arise where the individual in question is unable or unwilling on the basis of well-founded fear, to secure the protection

There are very few reported cases dealing with the notion of 'effective nationality' in the context of claims to refugee status brought by persons of multiple nationality. The main two to have promoted and developed the application of the notion have been the Australian Federal Court decisions in *Jong Kim Koe*[159] and *Lay Kon Tji*,[160] both of which concerned persons from East Timor having Indonesian nationality and the issue of whether they could be denied refugee status on the basis that they also had Portuguese nationality.

In *Jong Kim Koe*, the Court drew on paragraph 107 of the UNHCR 1979 Handbook to conclude that where a dual national person does not have a well-founded fear of persecution in the country of second nationality, 'there remains the question whether the nationality is "effective", which in turn may lead to an inquiry as to the "availability" of protection.'[161]

In *Lay Kon Tji*, Finkelstein J went considerably further, concluding that 'effective nationality' means 'nationality that provides all of the protection and rights which a national is entitled to receive under customary or conventional international law';[162] and in light of that held that the Refugee Review Tribunal had erred in concluding that the Portuguese nationality of the applicant was an 'effective nationality'.[163]

3.3.3 The concept of effective nationality in international law

In the international law on nationality 'effective nationality' is an elusive term and has been used to mean different things. It has principally been applied in cases involving disputes between states as regards persons of multiple nationality, where it is primarily a 'method of distinguishing one or more nationalities from others on the basis of greater "effectiveness" in respect of some specified incident of nationality....'[164] Being a method of difference, it is sometimes termed the 'master' or 'dominant' nationality principle.[165] The notion of 'effective nationality' received its most high-profile

of any of the States of nationality. In this context, whether the link of nationality is effective in the sense of general international law will be a relevant consideration.'

[159] *Jong Kim Koe* [1997] Aus FFC 1997, cited in Hathaway and Foster (n 5) 57.
[160] *Lay Kon Tji* (n 110).
[161] *Jong Kim Koe* (n 159).
[162] *Lay Kon Tji* (n 110). Finkelstein J stated that '[t]he domestic protection that is to be accorded a national of a state is usually a matter governed by the domestic laws of that state. But according to international law, including conventional international law, a person is entitled to certain "fundamental" rights. Blackstone in his "Commentaries on the Laws of England" (18th ed) (1821) described them as the right to personal security, to personal liberty and to private property: Blackstone vol 1 at 128ff. A national is entitled to have his or her "fundamental rights" protected by the municipal laws of the state of his or her territory.' He interpreted para 107 of the Handbook to mean that 'the issue of "effective nationality" is explained in terms of equivalence to the protection normally granted to nationals. In other words, according to this view nationality will not be regarded as "effective" if, for example, the putative refugee will not receive the protection under the domestic laws of the state which all other nationals in fact receive'.
[163] ibid.
[164] Fripp (2016) (n 5) 52. See further Oliver Dörr, 'Nationality', *Max Planck Encyclopaedia of Public International Law*; Hailbronner, 'Nationality in Public International Law and European Law' (n 5); Ivan A Shearer and Brian Opeskin, 'Nationality and Statelessness', in Brian Opeskin, Richard Perrechoud, and Jillyanne Redpath-Cross, *Foundations of International Migration Law* (CUP 2012) 93–122; Jeffrey L Blackman, 'State Succession and Statelessness: The Emerging Right to an Effective Nationality Under International Law' (1998) 19(4) Michigan Journal of International Law 1141.
[165] Leading cases include *Canevaro (Italy v Peru)* (1912) Scott 2 Hague Court Reports 284–96; *Salem Case (United States v Egypt)* [1932] Reports of International Arbitral Awards Vol II (8 June 1932) 1163; *Mergé*

endorsement in the *Nottebohm* case.[166] Nottebohm was a German national who had settled in Guatemala in 1905. In October 1939 he had become a naturalised citizen of Liechtenstein and by doing so ceased to be German. Liechtenstein brought proceedings on behalf of Nottebohm for damages arising from the acts of Guatemala, which was seeking war reparations. Ruling that claim inadmissible, the ICJ held in a majority decision with strong dissenting opinions that Nottebohm lacked the real and effective links with Liechtenstein on the basis of which it could exercise diplomatic protection on his behalf.[167]

A second identifiable use has been to describe nationality that possesses a certain quality, e.g. to denote enjoyment by a national of some or all key rights and benefits that nationality may confer on a person. This use of the term is also seen to have been lent support by the reference in the ICJ's statement in the *Nottebohm* case to 'reciprocal rights and duties'.[168]

A third use equates the term to de facto nationality, meaning a nationality which does not exist in the formal (de jure) sense but exhibits some or all of the main features commonly seen to flow from possession of a nationality.[169]

### 3.3.4 Purported justifications for importing the concept of 'effective nationality' into the refugee definition

The main justification that has been given for importing the notion of 'effective nationality' into the refugee definition is that it best fits with the objects and purposes of the Refugee Convention and in particular the underlying principle of surrogacy. In this regard, Hathaway and Foster quote with approval the following passage from the *Jong Kim Koe* case:[170]

> To interpret 'nationality' for the purpose of Article 1A(2) as something of a 'merely formal' character ... instead of something effective from the viewpoint of a putative refugee, would be liable to frustrate rather than advance the humanitarian objects of the [Refugee] Convention. Nor would such a construction advance, in any practical

---

Case *(Italy v United States)* [1955] 22 ILR 443, Reports of International Arbitral Awards Vol XIV (10 June 1955) 236; *Asghar* case *(Iran v United States)* [1990] 24 Iran-US CTR 242–43.

[166] *Nottebohm* (n 5). It may be thought somewhat curious that the *Nottebohm* case has been cited to support the application of the notion of 'effective nationality' cases in dual nationality cases, when he was not a dual national, having lost his German nationality on acquiring Liechtenstein nationality.

[167] The ICJ in *Nottebohm* (n 5) drew on Article 5 of the 1930 Convention on Certain Questions Relating to the Conflict of Nationality Laws: 'Within a third State, a person having more than one nationality shall be treated as if he had only one. Without prejudice to the application of its law in matters of personal status and of any conventions in force, a third State shall, of the nationalities which any such person possesses, recognise exclusively in its territory either the nationality of the country in which he is habitually and principally resident, or the nationality of the country with which in the circumstances he appears to be in fact most closely connected.'

[168] The ICJ held that nationality may be lawfully bestowed only where there is a 'genuine link' between the granting state and the recipient of its nationality and that nationality should be understood as 'a legal bond having as its basis a social fact of attachment, a genuine connection of existence, interests and sentiments, together with the existence of reciprocal rights and duties'. See *Nottebohm* (n 5) 23.

[169] Fripp (2016) (n 5) 54.

[170] Hathaway and Foster (n 5) 57.

way, another object of the Refugee Convention, namely the precedence of national protection over international protection. That precedence has no obvious relevance where national protection is not effective.[171]

In the *Lay Kon Tji* case, also cited approvingly by Hathaway and Foster,[172] Finkelstein J additionally, sought support for applying it by way of a systematic reading of the Refugee Convention referencing Article 1C(3)[173] and Article 1E.[174]

3.3.5 Difficulties
However, recourse to the notion of 'effective nationality' in the context of the refugee definition has attracted significant criticism[175] and limited support in the case law.[176] Notwithstanding the imprimatur of the 1979 Handbook and endorsement by some leading scholars, it cannot be said to have become an established concept of refugee law. There are a number of difficulties with it.

One major drawback is the fact, already highlighted, that it is a highly porous notion. 'Effective' has no specific content. In the international law literature at least three different usages of the term subsist and, significantly, even within the context of interpretation of Article 1A(2), uses of the notion demonstrate quite varied views about what 'effective' means in this context.

Second, the way in which it has been applied in the context of interpreting Article 1A(2) risks its equation with the plainly erroneous idea that a person can only be said to have a nationality for the purposes of the Refugee Convention if they possess the full gamut of the rights and benefits normally accorded to nationals. This danger is particularly evident in the way in which Finkelstein, J sought to elaborate the concept in the *Lay Kon Tji* case when he concluded that:

---

[171] *Jong Kim Koe* (n 5) 57, no 236.
[172] Hathaway and Foster (n 5) 57.
[173] Article 1C(3) provides that the Convention shall cease to apply to anyone falling under its terms where he or she 'has acquired a new nationality and enjoys the protection of the country of his new nationality'.
[174] Article 1E excludes from the scope of the Convention anyone who has taken up residence in another country and is recognised by the competent authorities 'as having the rights and obligations attached to the possession of the nationality of that country'.
[175] Piotrowicz (1999, n 5); see also Piotrowicz (1996, n 5); Sidhom (n 5) 315; Fripp (2016) (n 5) 52–54, 217–35. See further Fripp (2021) (n 5) para 321 et seq.
[176] In addition to Australian cases from the 1990s, Wolman (n 10) 793–814 (who supports recourse to the concept of 'effective nationality' in the refugee law context) cites a number of New Zealand cases making use of the notion, including *Refugee Appeal No 75694* [2006] para 33; *Refugee Appeal No 71322/99* [2000] paras 20–26; *Refuge Appeal No 2067/94* [1996] paras 10–11. However, he acknowledges that 'in other countries, judges have been more reluctant to embrace an effective nationality analysis', citing, *inter alia*, in this regard the UK case of *KK* (n 68). Fripp (2016) (n 5) 225–29, cites as further cases applying the notion of 'effective nationally' the Canadian case of *Katkova v Canada* (MCI) (1997) 130 FTR 192; a UK High Court case, *R v SSHD ex p. Milisavljevic* [2001] EWHC Admin 203; and *MA(Ethiopia-Eritrea-mixed ethnicity-dual nationality)* Eritrea [2004] UKIA 00324, para 46. It should be noted in the Australian context that since the *Jong Kim Koe* case, the government has legislated to prevent recourse to any concept of 'effective nationality': see *RRT Case 1001549* [2010] RRTA 843 (21 September 2010); *SZOUY & Ors v Minister for Immigration* [2011] FMCA 347. There remains some uncertainty, though, as to whether that legislation has entirely displaced the concept. In *FER17 v MIMA* [2019] FCAFC 106, the Full Federal Court of Australia, whilst concluding that a 'national' in the Australian Migration Act meant actual nationality (para 64), deliberately did not address the issues addressed in *Lay Kon Tji* (n 110) para 57.

In my view, conformably with the views expressed in the United Nations Handbook and conformably with the purpose and object of the Refugee Convention, 'effective nationality' is a nationality that provides all of the protection and rights to which a national is entitled to receive under customary or conventional international law.[177]

Accepting this position of equivalency is tantamount to asserting that even people who can be protected by their country of nationality against persecution can qualify as refugees whenever they can show they will not obtain in their other country(ies) of nationality the full panoply of rights normally seen to attach to nationality. That is inconsistent with the qualifying requirement set out in the second paragraph of Article 1A(2) that a person must show a 'valid reason based on well-founded fear' for not availing himself of the protection of another country of nationality.

Such a position would also offend, not uphold, the principle of surrogacy, since it would result in refugee status being accorded to persons who have sufficient—albeit not absolute—protection available in the second country of nationality. A person could qualify simply because, for example, they were denied voting rights even when in a particular case such denial did not amount to persecutory conduct and had no impact on the ability of the person to be admitted to and to remain in such a state. It would also involve application of an entirely different concept of protection from the one used in the refugee definition otherwise.[178]

Third, this notion confuses the issue of nationality with the distinct issue of whether the state's treatment of its nationals is persecutory. If for example, nationality is said to be 'ineffective' because the usual benefits of nationality, whilst theoretically available, cannot in practice be accessed by the applicant, that may well go towards establishing a well-founded fear of being persecuted—and by reason of nationality or some other Convention reason.[179] But it does not negate the fact that the applicant is a national of the state in question. A destitute person with no passport and no access to benefits accorded to nationals generally is still a national.[180] To decline to equate nationality with a full panoply of rights and benefits that potentially attach to nationality does not affront any object and purpose of the Refugee Convention because international protection will be afforded to such persons if such deprivations can be shown to cross the threshold of persecution.

Fourth, although it could be said that the non-specific wording of paragraph 107 of the 1979 Handbook, which simply refers to protection 'normally granted to nationals',

---

[177] *Lay Kon Tji* (n 110).
[178] See Chapter 9, section 4.2.
[179] See e.g. *MA (Ethiopia) v SSHD* [2009] EWCA Civ 289, UK, para 43: 'the fact that it may, for example, prove to be impossible in practice to return someone seeking asylum has no relevance to the determination of their refugee status. But where the applicant contends that the denial of the right to return is part of the persecution itself, the Tribunal must engage with that question.' For further discussion see Foster and Lambert (n 5) Chapter 6, on 'Persecution by Denial of Nationality', 236–321.
[180] In emphasising that nationality is to be distinguished from rights of citizenship, which may be denied to persons who are nationals, Shearer (n 59) 309, observes that '[d]isabilities in citizenship, even of a serious nature, do not involve loss of nationality' and cites the case of *Kabane v Parisi* (Decision of the Austro-German Mixed Arbitral Tribunal) Annual Digest of Public International Law Cases, 1929–1930, 213 et seq, and the Austrian State Decision of the Austro-German Mixed Arbitral Tribunal in *Djevahirdijhian v Germany*, Annual Digest of Public International Law Cases, 1927–1928, 310 et seq. See also the 1930 Hague Convention (n 38) Articles 1 and 2.

gives some encouragement to use of the notion of 'effective nationality', it is important to bear in mind that it has not been endorsed by subsequent UNHCR publications addressing nationality and statelessness: e.g. in its 2014 Handbook, it is stated that '[t]here is no requirement of a "genuine" or an "effective" link implicit in the concept of "national" in Article 1(1) [of the 1954 Convention]'.[181]

Fifth, use of the notion fosters confusion as regards whether in multiple nationality cases any ineffectiveness in the other country(ies) of nationality nullifies that nationality. In international law, it is clear that in cases of disputes between states, a person of multiple nationality does not cease to hold these nationalities just because it is decided that for specific purposes they are to be treated as if they do not have that nationality.[182] Just because the ICJ decided in *Nottebohm* that Liechtenstein could not assert a right of diplomatic protection over Nottebohm did not mean that Nottebohm was a multiple national. Nor did it mean he was any less a national of Liechtenstein for all other purposes.[183]

Sixth, it is confusing for decision makers. They can be expected to be familiar with general principles of nationality law, but not to untangle mixed doctrinal messages. Pursuant to the 'effective nationality' view, they are being told, on the one hand, that in sole nationality cases 'country of nationality' (at least mostly) denotes simply the legal bond between an individual and the state; on the other hand, they are to be told that when it comes to multiple nationality cases a second, quite different, concept of nationality pertains, going beyond the 'merely formal'.[184] That is misconceived. In multiple nationality cases '(merely) formal' nationality still has a governing role in second paragraph cases; it is just that it is subject to a qualification designed to ensure the applicant is still not protected against indirect persecution.

This confusing aspect could be said to have deeper roots in the way in which general international law[185] seeks to combine two positions, asserting on the one hand that nationality is a formal legal concept and on the other hand that for the purposes of international recognition it must be based on 'genuine and effective' links. It is easily, and again wrongly, inferred, that if nationality must be based on genuine and effective links then it can be acquired by any such links, even if they are not one of the specified modes of acquisition that determine whether a person is a national for international law purposes. Thus, it might be thought that a person who has resided for a long time in country X should be treated as a national of country X, even if they have not applied for naturalisation based on discretionary criteria that include length of residence.[186] As noted earlier, the legal tie of nationality may have its basis in the notion of

---

[181] UNHCR 2014 Handbook (n 5) para 54.

[182] Boll (n 23) 113, notes the ILC observation in its draft rules on diplomatic protection (Report of the International Law Commission to the General Assembly, Fifty-fourth session, 176) that 'if the genuine link requirement proposed by *Nottebohm* was strictly applied it would exclude millions of people from the benefit of diplomatic protection as in today's world of economic globalisation and migration there are millions of people who have drifted away from their state of nationality and made their lives in states whose nationality they never acquire [,] or have [nationality] acquired by birth or descent from states with which they have a tenuous connection'.

[183] ibid 110. See analysis in Crawford (n 62) 499–504. At 501 it is noted, 'Nottebohm either had Liechtenstein nationality or none.'

[184] *Jong Kim Koe* (n 159).

[185] As illustrated by the *Nottebohm* case (n 5).

[186] This was similar to the error made by the UN Human Rights Committee in *Nystrom v Australia* (18 July 2011) UN Doc CCPR/C/102/D/1557/2007, when seeking to construe the phrase 'his own country'

an effective link and the existence of social attachments, associations etc., but, absent highly unusual circumstances, it only exists as a matter of law when a person possesses it by virtue of their state's nationality law based on one of the established modes of acquisition, primarily acquisition by birth, descent, residence, or a combination thereof.[187]

Finally, the attempted reliance by advocates of an 'effective nationality' concept on Articles 1C(3) and Article 1E has properly been found by Piotrowicz and others to be overstated.[188] It is inconsistent, for example, with the elaborations of these articles in the 1979 Handbook.[189]

Not all the above difficulties identify inherent flaws in the 'effective nationality' notion, but given it has primarily been imported into refugee law to help decision makers deal properly with multiple nationality cases, it is more than usually important to ascertain how it is said to help against the risk it carries of sowing confusion.

### 3.3.6 Proposed solutions

Given the identifiable pitfalls to applying the notion of 'effective nationality' in the refugee law context, it must be asked, are there better ways to give proper effect to the clear intent behind the text of the 'valid reason' clause of the second paragraph of Article 1A(2) to ameliorate the position somewhat for multiple nationals?

#### 3.3.6.1 The text of the second paragraph of Article 1A(2) revisited

Even though recourse to the concept of 'effective nationality' has been rejected, that is not to say that its proponents' starting point—the need to consider multiple nationality cases differently from sole nationality cases—is misplaced. As noted earlier there is obviously agreement that the second paragraph of Article 1A(2) contains a 'valid reason' clause. Hence there is a textual basis for not entirely equating the requirements to be applied in multiple nationality cases with those applied in sole nationality cases.[190] The question remains how this clause is to be interpreted.

Obviously if a person can establish that each of their countries of nationality is a persecutory country, they fully meet the refugee definition: if the other country/countries is/are persecutory, then by definition a person cannot avail themself of their protection. Hence to have any *effet utile* this qualifying clause can only apply to some other set or sets of circumstances limited to ones where (i) the other country of nationality is not persecutory, but yet (ii) there is a 'valid reason based on well-founded

---

within the meaning of Article 12(4) of the ICCPR, without any nexus to nationality in the accepted legal sense. I am grateful to Ryszard Piotrowicz for this observation.

[187] As articulated, for example, in Articles 1 and 2 of the Hague Convention (n 38).
[188] Piotrowicz (1999, n 5) 548–50.
[189] UNHCR Handbook (n 4) para 145.
[190] And also consistent with the Statement of Mr Fearnley of the United Kingdom, that 'persons with dual or even plural nationality would be considered as refugees only after it had been ascertained that they were either unable or unwilling to avail themselves of the protection of the governments of any of their nationalities'—see Summary of the Committee Meeting of the Economic and Social Council, UN Doc E/AC.7/SR.160 (18 August 1950). See also the Statement of Mr Henkin of the United States that 'so long as a person has one nationality and no reasons not to avail himself of the protection of the government concerned, he could not be considered as a refugee'.

fear' for not availing oneself of the protection of that state. The 'valid reason based on well-founded fear' can only refer to the persecutory country of origin.

### 3.3.6.2 Non-admission and refoulement (direct or indirect)

There are two sets of circumstances either of which plainly constitutes a valid reason, namely non-admission to one's country of nationality (which can also be intertwined with the issue of recognition by the state in question)[191] and the risk of refoulement. The former is material because if a person cannot access another country of nationality, then they are in the same position as persons of sole nationality: they are outside a persecutory country of nationality, with the only possible country that can afford them protection being the host state in which they are claiming refugee status.[192]

If it is established that a person will not be denied admission to their other country/countries of nationality, then another obvious material circumstance which could give rise to a well-founded fear of persecution would be if there was a real risk that that country/those countries would *refoule* them to a persecutory country of nationality. At general international law, states are not prevented from expelling nationals who have another nationality,[193] but they would stand in breach of Article 33(1) of the Refugee Convention if such expulsion would *refoule* them to any country of persecution.[194]

It is only fair to point out that proponents of the notion of 'effective nationality' have broadly recognised that non-admission and refoulement are two sets of qualifying circumstances (that is why it will be said at the end that there is consensus about these two instances). For example, Wolman observes that whilst the Australian case law may have involved a 'misguided expansion' of the concept of effective nationality, 'that does not mean that the principle itself—when properly understood as an evaluation of right of entry— should have also been dismissed'.[195] However, even on this reconstruction the notion of 'effective nationality' will still not serve, as it suffers from an open-ended material scope and it cannot conceptually be equated with one or two instances of it. The fact that Wolman on the one hand thinks 'effective nationality' can be reduced to two instances of it, whereas Finkelstein J in *Lay Kong Tji* regards it as covering the full gamut of rights and benefits normally associated with nationality, just illustrates the point made earlier, that being so porous the term is prey to varying interpretations. Further, identification of non-admission and indirect refoulement as two obvious sets of circumstances falling within the second paragraph's qualifying clause is not dependent on the notion of 'effective nationality' and hence there is no need to take a complex detour through other international law, borrowing from cases involving disputes between states.[196]

---

[191] See *Refugee Appeal No 72635* [2002] NZRSAA 33, cited in Fripp (2016) (n 5) 232.

[192] The duty of the State to (re-)admission of its nationals is of course (along with the right to diplomatic protection) one of the two rights traditionally attached to nationality in international law. See e.g. Weis (n 4) 47; Boll (n 23) 114–25, but that only reinforces the qualifying role it plays in the second paragraph of Article 1A(2).

[193] See William T Worster, 'International Law and the Expulsion of Individuals with More Than One Nationality' (2009) 14 J Int'l L & Foreign Aff 423.

[194] Fripp (2016) (n 5) 232.

[195] Wolman (n 120) 813, see also 809.

[196] Fripp (2016) (n 5) 54. Foster and Lambert (n 5) 112 state that 'we agree with the British tribunal's rejection [in *KA* [2008] 00042] of this argument on the basis that it appears ... to insert a quite unnecessary construct into the clear provisions of the Refugee Convention'. See also Fripp (2021) (n 5).

*3.3.6.3 Treatment of the second paragraph in existing in-depth studies*
It is instructive to consider how this study's above analysis of the second paragraph of Article 1A(2)[197] compares with the position taken in the three publications that have gone into more detail on this issue than any other books published in English, namely Hathaway and Foster's TLRS2, Fripp's book on *Nationality and Statelessness in in the International Law of Refugee Status*, and Foster and Lambert's *International Refugee Law and the Protection of Stateless Persons*.[198] All three take as their starting-point that the second paragraph of Article 1A(2) contains a qualifying 'valid reason' test, but seek to elaborate it different ways.

The reasons for rejecting Hathaway and Foster's reliance on the concept of 'effective nationality' were set out earlier. Here, one further point needs adding. Hathaway and Foster cite approvingly the open-ended formulation given by the Australian Federal Court in *Jong Kim Koe*, namely that adoption of the notion of effective nationality requires consideration of a 'range of practical questions' and they proceed to give the example identified in the *Lay Kon Tji* case, namely the 'recognition of the existence of nationality by the State of nationality'. Whilst I would accept that denial of recognition can be a material factor (at least if it would result in a refusal of admission), to invoke the notion of 'effective nationality' espoused in *Lay Kon Tji* risks real confusion, since that case adopts a broad equivalency approach of which they clearly disapprove.[199] Further, by treating the principle to be applied in individual cases as one of asking a 'range of practical questions', they wrongly imply that they support such questions being open-ended and as extending, for example, to rights and benefits that have no impact on the danger of non-admission or indirect persecution.[200]

Fripp's approach embodies a strong critique of any reliance on the notion of 'effective nationality' and takes to task the study by Hathaway and Foster for endorsing it. Much of this study's critique of this notion is consonant with his. However, what is to be made of his own alternative proposals?

One proposal set out by Fripp in his 2016 book is to advocate adoption of the notion of 'the National Protection Alternative' (NPA) or 'external protection alternative'.[201] Having noted that the second part of the second paragraph of Article 1A(2) only applies if it has been established that a person of multiple nationality faces persecution for a Convention reason in their home state, he proposes that the relevant standard for deciding whether there is adequate protection available in the second county of nationality is that of whether 'external relocation' would be unduly harsh or unreasonable.[202] He considers these standards align with those already applied in the context of the 'internal protection alternative' (IPA). He goes on to identify that the correct

---

[197] Which is much the same position set out by Sidhom as long ago as 1998, see Sidhom (n 5).
[198] Fripp (2016) (n 5); Foster and Lambert (n 5).
[199] Hathaway and Foster (n 5). At ibid 55–56, they had stated that '[t]he notion of effective nationality does not mean that the putative country of second citizenship is to be treated as a county of reference only if it provides protection against persecution and would ensure respect for human rights'.
[200] By contrast, the approach taken by Hathaway (n 5) 59 appears much closer to that taken here, namely limiting in practice the additional requirements to non-admission and non-refoulement. Interestingly, that is how this passage was understood by Sidhom (n 5) 3C. It has already been noted that Foster has now abandoned reliance on the 'effective nationality' concept: see Foster and Lambert (n 5) 112.
[201] Fripp (2016) (n 5) 230.
[202] ibid 234.

approach to the IPA requires it be shown in order to qualify as a refugee that an applicant does not have available an alternative part of the country where he or she is both safe from persecution and it is not unduly harsh or unreasonable to expect him or her to resettle there.[203]

Applied to the issue of multiple nationality, such an approach is problematic. That is primarily because there is no consensus within refugee law regarding the criteria to be applied when applying the IPA,[204] and hence it offers too contingent a basis for dealing with multiple nationality cases. Secondly, adoption (in his version of it) of a test of 'unduly harsh' or unreasonableness carries the danger of limitless expansion of the sets of circumstances in which protection could be considered inadequate beyond denial of admission and refoulement (direct or indirect) and beyond those warranted by either the text of the second paragraph or the Convention's object and purpose. Suppose, for example, an individual suffers from ill health and that in the alternative country of nationality they would only be able to access very basic treatment for their condition. Whilst on the basis of some case law at least that might well be unduly harsh or unreasonable, it would not on its own amount to a lack of adequate protection and may not, in particular, cause indirect refoulement. In a subsequent article, Fripp has rowed back significantly from this proposal.[205]

Fripp's second main proposal is that the qualifying clause should be seen as capable of applying to other protection-related circumstances. He describes that as encompassing:

> [...] a broad range of circumstances, difficult to categorise, without direct *refoulement* or refusal of admission by the non-persecuting State, closely [in which] conditions in a non-persecuting plural nationality State may be so adverse as to generate very significant pressure either to *refoulement* by others (the State or non-state agents) or to self-*refoulement*. For instance, the non-persecuting State may be subject to foreign occupation or international armed conflict, or there may be severe civil conflict or famine or epidemic disease. The non-persecuting State might also be subject to some form of wide-ranging ecological collapse, such as the loss of its territory to vulcanism or rising sea level. In such circumstances it seems wholly justified to interpret article 1A(2) as not displacing the entitlement to protection by reason of the existence of a non-persecutory State of nationality.[206]

It is significant that, unlike Fripp's other proposal based on an EPA, this proposal seeks to adhere closely to the concept of indirect refoulement. But, thus formulated, this proposal is really better understood as a sub-category of the second set of circumstances identified earlier as being plainly contemplated by the second paragraph's qualifying clause, namely those concerned with indirect refoulement.

---

[203] ibid 232–35.
[204] See Jessica Schultz, *The Internal Protection Alternative in Refugee Law* (Brill Nijhoff 2018) 17. See Chapter 8, 'Introduction'.
[205] Fripp (2021) (n 5) 331.
[206] Fripp (2016) (n 5) 222. At ibid 222–332, he argues that this proposal has been implicitly endorsed in a number of common law cases and by proponents of the 'effective nationality' approach. See also Fripp (2021) (n 5) 333.

Finally, in relation to the study by Foster and Lambert in their 2019 publication,[207] the approach taken in this study is broadly consonant with it. Whilst their book does not address the part of the refugee definition applying to persons with multiple nationality, the authors make clear that the nationality requirements of the refugee definition do not import any concept of 'effective nationality'. They endorse the view of the British tribunal in *KA*,[208] that this 'appears ... to insert a quite unnecessary construct into the clear provisions of the Refugee Convention'.[209]

## 3.4 'Not Having a Nationality' *'Personne qui n'a pas de Nationalité'*

In the case of persons not having a nationality, the words 'the country of nationality' in Article 1A(2) of the 1951 Refugee Convention are replaced by 'the country of his former habitual residence' and the expression 'unwilling to avail himself of the protection of that country' is replaced by 'unwilling to return to it'. Treatment is best split into two parts, looking first at the class of persons embraced by the term 'not having a nationality' and separately at what other specific requirements of the definition apply to them.

Manifestly the category of persons 'not having a nationality' is defined negatively, by the lack of a nationality. As already noted, when discussing the ordinary meaning of 'country of nationality', the present tense is used and that is maintained in respect of stateless persons by use of the (indicative present continuous) expression 'not having'.

### 3.4.1 Drafting history and *travaux préparatoires*

Close approximates of the term 'not having a nationality' had been used in predecessor refugee instruments, as had the term 'stateless'. For example, the 1938 Convention concerning the Status of Refugees coming from Germany employs both the terms 'not possessing any other nationality' and 'stateless persons'.[210]

Little light is shed by the *travaux* as to the meaning of this term. The United Nations General Assembly (UNGA) 'Draft Protocol relating to the Status of Stateless Persons' that accompanied early drafts of the Refugee Convention did not provide any definition of non-nationals.[211] In the meetings of the Conference of Plenipotentiaries on the Status of Refugees and Stateless Persons, the terms 'persons without nationality' and 'stateless persons' were used interchangeably without discussion or debate. Fripp considers that the preference for the phrase 'not having a nationality' reflected a desire to avoid confusion between different uses of the term 'stateless' employed prior to the 1954 Convention.[212]

---

[207] Foster and Lambert (n 5).
[208] *KA v SSHD* [2008] UKAIT 00042, para 7.
[209] Foster and Lambert (n 5) 112. See also Lambert (n 5) 809–12.
[210] League of Nations, Convention concerning the Status of Refugees Coming From Germany (10 February 1938) 192 LNTS 59, Article 38(1) differentiated two distinct streams of persons: (a) former and present German nationals; and (b) '[s]tateless persons' with a connection with Germany.
[211] UNGA, Draft Protocol relating to the Status of Stateless Persons (14 December 1950) UN Doc A/RES/429.
[212] Fripp (2021) (n 5); Fripp (2022) (n 5) 332–33.

As noted earlier, the decision to construct the refugee definition around the concept of 'country of nationality' was eventually seen to provide a more focussed basis than one based on de jure and de facto stateless persons.[213] Mr Henkin of the United States, during the Conference of Plenipotentiaries, stated that the draft Refugee Convention 'should not be based upon a confusion between the humanitarian problem of the refugees and the primarily legal problem of stateless persons, which should be dealt with by a body of legal experts, but should not be included in the proposed Convention'.[214] A distinction was drawn between two categories of stateless persons, Mr Rain of France noting that there were 'those who were also refugees, who would, of course, benefit from the draft convention, and those who were not refugees'.[215] The broader issues surrounding stateless persons, which had been addressed in a draft Protocol relating to the Status of Stateless Persons, originally attached to the Refugee Convention, were referred to a separate negotiating conference, which led, not in the event to a Protocol, but to the 1954 Convention as a self-standing treaty.[216]

### 3.4.2 Good faith

As noted at section 3.2.2, it could be said that there is a particular role when interpreting the meaning of the terms 'nationality' and 'not having a nationality' for the VCLT principle of good faith, given that the legal duty on states parties to implement the Refugee Convention in good faith, surely includes facilitating the identification of those entitled to protection, when such facilitation is most uncontroversially achieved by adopting the accepted understanding within international law that nationality denotes the legal tie between the individual and the state and that statelessness constitutes the lack of such a legal tie.[217]

### 3.4.3 Ordinary meaning

Even though in the phrase 'not having a nationality' the term 'nationality' would appear to have the same meaning as in 'country of nationality', the nature of the debates that have arisen in the literature make it necessary to analyse this phrase separately.

At section 3.2.3, in the course of analysing the ordinary meaning of nationality (as in 'country of nationality') mention was made of the argument that if the drafters understood the term to have a somewhat technical meaning that could be, in the context of the Refugee Convention, its ordinary meaning. On this view, the ordinary

---

[213] UN Ad Hoc Committee on Refugees and Stateless Persons, A Study of Statelessness (n 90). The study states that: 'i. Stateless persons de jure are persons who are not nationals of any State, either because at birth or subsequently they were not given any nationality, or because during their lifetimes they lost their own nationality and did not acquire a new one. ii. Stateless persons de facto are persons who, having left the country of which they were nationals, no longer enjoy the protection and assistance of their national authorities, either because their authorities refuse to grant them assistance and protection, or because they themselves renounce the assistance and protection of the countries of which they are nationals.'

[214] UN Ad Hoc Committee on Refugees and Stateless Persons, Ad Hoc Committee on Statelessness and Related Problems, First Session: Summary Record of the Second Meeting Held at Lake Success, New York, on Tuesday, 17 January 1930, at 11 a.m. (17 January 1950) UN Doc E/AC.32/SR.2, 6, 9.

[215] ibid 7–8. See further Zimmermann and Mahler (n 5) 461–62.

[216] See UN Ad Hoc Committee on Refugees and Stateless Persons, Report of the Ad Hoc Committee on Statelessness and Related Problems (17 February 1950) UN Doc E/1618; Batchelor (1998, n 5); Terje Einarsen, 'Drafting History of the 1951 Convention and the 1967 Protocol' in Zimmermann (n 5) 54–57.

[217] Foster and Lambert (n 5) 116.

meaning based on its technical meaning is the legal tie between the individual and the state and hence 'not having a nationality' should be taken to mean statelessness. That is the position taken, for example, by Foster and Lambert.[218] Given, however (as they acknowledge),[219] that treating the ordinary meaning of 'not having a nationality' as a technical or special meaning depends in part on consideration of background and context, it cannot be definitively concluded that a true meaning can be ascribed to this term without consideration of VCLT elements other than 'ordinary meaning'.

### 3.4.4 Context

Bearing in mind that the Refugee Convention and the contents of the CSSP54 were originally bundled together and that the third preambular paragraph of the latter confirmed that the former applied to stateless persons who were refugees, it is appropriate to read the two together. In this regard, the equation of persons 'not having a nationality' and stateless persons was confirmed by the eventual conclusion of a separate Convention on 'stateless persons' whose underlying purpose was to address other problems that they—the same group of people—faced.[220]

### 3.4.5 Object and purpose

As just noted, both the Refugee Convention and the CSSP54 were intended to address different aspects of the problems facing the same category of persons—stateless persons.[221]

### 3.4.6 Article 31(3) and other VCLT considerations

There is a strong basis for considering that the phrase 'not having a nationality' should be understood to denote statelessness as defined in the CSSP54, by reference to relevant rules of international law applicable in the relations between the parties in the form of customary international law, in view of the wide acceptance that the CSSP54 represents customary international law.[222] There is an integral interconnection between the two treaties.

Identifying the class of persons embraced by the phrase 'not having a nationality' as stateless persons *simpliciter* is the position taken in UNHCR materials, the great majority of case law, and in the wider literature.[223] Even if not comprising 'subsequent practice' within the strict confines of Article 31(3)(b), it clearly comprises state practice in the broad sense.[224] If the argument noted earlier as to whether nationality has

---

[218] ibid.

[219] ibid 106.

[220] ibid. In its Commentary upon the Draft Articles on Diplomatic Protection 2006, the ILC stated that the CSSP54 definition 'can no doubt be considered as having acquired a customary nature'. See ILC, Articles on Diplomatic Protection with commentaries (2006) 49.

[221] CRSSP54 (n 41) Preamble.

[222] Foster and Lambert (n 5) 107, cite the UNGA, 'Report of the International Law Commission: Fifty-Eight Session' (2006) UN Doc A/61/10, and also note that both the ILC and UNHCR endorse this position.

[223] UNHCR Handbook (n 4) paras 101–05; see also Foster and Lambert (n 5) 90–119; Lambert (n 5) 798–803; Fripp (2022) (n 5) 334–35. It should be noted, however, that although the New Zealand Immigration and Protection Tribunal in *AL (Myanmar)* [2018] NZIPT 801255, para 135 argues for treating the two classes of persons as mirroring each other, it disagrees that those denationalised should be treated as nationals under either Convention (paras 101–139): see below p. 247.

[224] See Chapter 2, n 69.

a special meaning has validity,[225] then it would seem to apply to its opposite—not having a nationality.

The relevance of the *travaux* in the context of Article 32 has already been addressed.[226]

At this point, however, it is necessary to specifically address arguments taking a different view than the analysis provided so far.

3.4.7 'Not having a nationality' and stateless persons
3.4.7.1 *Article 1A(2) and stateless persons*
It is possible to argue that whilst 'stateless person' works as a convenient paraphrase, it identifies a slightly narrower class of persons than qualify as 'stateless persons' under the CSSP54. The 1954 Convention employs the same negative definition in terms of the absence of nationality, but adds words that govern the approach to consideration of this status. Article 1 of the 1954 Convention provides that:

> For the purposes of this Convention, the term 'stateless person' means a person who is not considered as a national by any State under the operation of its law.[227]

The phrase 'under the operation of its law'[228] is not the same as, and is not to be confused with, the phrase 'by operation of law' as used in the general international law on nationality to denote *ex lege* or automatic acquisition of nationality.[229]

There are two possible respects in which this phrase creates difference. One is that the reference to 'its law' could be said to make the lack of nationality dependent on state determination regardless of rules governing recognition.[230] However, that would entail departure from Article 1 (second paragraph) of the 1930 Hague Convention.[231] On that ground alone it must be rejected. The second mooted difference, noted by Fripp, is that the reference to 'operation of its laws' may be read as extending beyond the strict law of the country of nationality and to legitimate, as conveyed by the UNHCR 2014 Handbook, reference to state practice.[232] This Handbook states that:

---

[225] See above section 3.2.8.
[226] See above section 3.4.1.
[227] CRSSP54 (n 41) Article 1.
[228] Which is to be distinguished from the concept of 'by operation of the law'. As stated in the UNHCR 2010 Prato Conclusions (n 5) para 15: '"under the operation of its law" should not be confused with "by operation of law", a term which refers to automatic (ex lege) acquisition of nationality. Thus, in interpreting the term "under the operation of its law" in Article 1(1), consideration has to be given to non-automatic as well as automatic methods of acquiring and being deprived of nationality.'
[229] As observed by Fripp (2016) (n 5) 43; Fripp (2022) (n 5) 334.
[230] A point made by Fripp (2016) (n 5) 216 (see also ibid 43). At ibid 235, he observes that the 1954 CRSSP54 (n 41) definition 'potentially extends beyond the source of nationality law under the Convention on Certain Questions Relating to the Conflict of Nationality Laws 1930 ... to include also absence of nationality according to "the operation of" its laws by the State'. The meaning of the phrase 'by operation of its laws' was considered in detail in *Pham v SSHD* [2015] UKSC 19, 24–29, 38 (per Lord Carnwath), 65 (per Lord Mance), but without any definitive conclusion being reached.
[231] The Hague Convention (n 38) Article 1; see section 2.1.2 in this chapter.
[232] But see the doubts expressed regarding such a reading by the Supreme Court justices in (n 230). See further Fripp (2016) (n 5) 41–43; Fripp (2022) (n 5) 334–35.

The reference to 'law' in Article 1(1) should be read broadly to encompass not just legislation but also ministerial decrees, orders, judicial case-law (in countries with a tradition of precedent) and, where appropriate, customary practice.[233]

Whilst, however, the issue of the meaning of this provision remains problematic,[234] it does not necessarily affect whether 'not having a nationality' denotes stateless persons. To compare Article 1(1) CSSP54 with the notion of acquisition of nationality by operation of law is not to compare like with like; the latter does not purport to define nationality or its lack but only to identify one mode of acquisition (or loss).[235]

As noted above, the position taken in the UNHCR 1979 Handbook—that the phrase 'not having a nationality' denotes 'stateless refugees'—continues to reflect the predominant view taken both in case law and the wider literature.[236]

Having concluded that the 'not having a nationality' phrase denotes stateless persons, it is necessary, second, to clarify the contours of its legal meaning. The term 'de facto stateless persons' has subsequently fallen away, because of increased recognition that as a matter of law being stateless means not having a nationality.[237] However, to the extent such language is still applied, it is clear that such persons are not stateless persons in legal terms. The correct position has been stated by Zimmerman and Mahler:

> The 'not having a nationality' clause only applies to *de jure* stateless persons. *De facto* stateless persons subject to persecution, who have formally retained the nationality of their home country but who are no longer considered as such by their country of origin, are already covered by the first part of Article 1A, para 2(1) since, due to their *de facto* statelessness, they are unable to avail themselves of the protection of their country of origin. They come within the scope *ratione personae* of Art.1A, para 2 in any cases, without the need to apply the 'not having a nationality' clause.[238]

A further clarification can be made, which arises as a corollary of the earlier analysis of nationality. By virtue of the negative definition given to stateless persons in Article 1A(2), it is not possible to construe the category of persons 'not having a nationality' as including those who have a nationality but lack most or all of the rights seen normally to attach to nationality. Put another way, it is not possible to read into the term nationality (in the phrase 'not having a nationality') any concept of 'effective nationality'.[239] The same points made earlier—when explaining why the term 'nationality'

---

[233] UNHCR 2014 Handbook (n 5) para 22.
[234] See e.g. discussion by Lord Carnwath in *Pham* (n 230) 24–29.
[235] In fairness, Fripp's main point appears to be that Article 1(1) CSSP54 is at odds with the opening sentence of Article 1 of the 1930 Hague Convention, which provides that: '[i]t is for each State to determine under its own law who are its nationals'. See Fripp (2016) (n 5) 235.
[236] UNHCR Handbook (n 4) paras 101–05; see also Foster and Lambert (n 5) 90–119; Lambert (n 5) 798–803.
[237] See the critique of Manley O Hudson, 'Report on Nationality, Including Statelessness' (21 February 1952) UN Doc A/CN.4.50, cited by Fripp (2016) (n 5) 97. However, a somewhat ambivalent reiteration of the concept was given in the UNHCR 2010 Prato Conclusions (n 5), cited by Fripp (2016) (n 5) 101.
[238] Zimmermann and Mahler (n 5) 462.
[239] As was noted in the UNHCR 2010 Prato Conclusions (n 5): '3. The issue under Article 1(1) is not whether or not the individual has a nationality that is effective, but whether or not the individual has a

in the phrases 'country of nationality' and 'more than one nationality' cannot mean 'effective' nationality—apply *mutatis mutandis* to consideration of persons who lack a nationality.

*3.4.7.2 The temporal dimension: 'not having a nationality'/statelessness and actual statelessness*

Just as the refugee definition deals with nationality in the present tense (and so is a test of 'actual nationality')[240] so the definition of 'not having a nationality' must also refer to actual lack of this status. As stated in the UNHCR 2014 Handbook at paras 14 and 50:

> 14. An individual is a stateless person from the moment that the conditions in Article 1(1) of the 1954 Convention are met. Thus, any finding by a State or UNHCR that an individual satisfies the test in Article 1(1) is declaratory, rather than constitutive, in nature....
>
> 50. An individual's nationality is to be assessed as at the time of determination of eligibility under the 1954 Convention. It is neither a historic nor a predictive exercise. The question to be answered is whether, at the point of making an Article 1(1) determination, an individual is a national of the country or countries in question. Therefore, if an individual is partway through a process for acquiring nationality but those procedures are yet to be completed, he or she cannot be considered as a national for the purposes of Article 1(1) of the 1954 Convention. Conversely, where requirements or procedures for loss, deprivation or renunciation of nationality have only been partially fulfilled or completed, the individual is still a national for the purposes of the stateless person definition.[241]

*3.4.7.3 Are stateless persons refugees ipso facto?*

As noted above, the 'not having a nationality' element concerns not just the issue of what class of persons is identified therein but what other specific requirements of the definition apply to them. In the academic literature there was early support for the view that stateless persons are not required to establish, in contrast to nationals, a well-founded fear of being persecuted (which I shall refer to as the 'ipso facto argument'). Grahl-Madsen contended that a stateless person 'need only substantiate that he is unable to return to the country in question, in order to win recognition as a refugee'.[242] As pressed in key cases before the Australian courts and the English Court of Appeal in *Revenko* (who closely analysed the former),[243] this argument was primarily based

---

nationality at all. Although there may sometimes be a fine line between being recognised as a national but not being treated as such, and not being recognised as a national at all, the two problems are nevertheless conceptually distinct: the former problem is connected with the rights attached to nationality, whereas the latter problem is connected with the right to nationality itself.'

[240] See above section 3.2.10.
[241] UNHCR 2014 Handbook (n 5) paras 14 and 52.
[242] Grahl-Madsen (n 4) 143–44.
[243] *Revenko v SSHD* [2000] EWCA Civ 500.

on a textual or literal reading of Article 1A(2) but also on the Convention's object and purpose and its *travaux*.

As regards the textual or literal argument advanced in support of the ipso facto argument (sometimes called the 'bifurcated view'),[244] it relied heavily on the precise wording of Article 1A(2) and the use of a semi-colon midway through the first paragraph of Article 1A(2).[245] According to this argument, the semi-colon has the effect that the phrase 'well-founded fear of being persecuted' in the first part of Article 1A(2) applies *only* to nationals and does not modify the text that comes after the semi-colon. According to this argument, the removal by the 1967 Protocol of the words in the square brackets means that Article 1A(2) has to be read as omitting the words in the square brackets, which has the effect of placing the stateless applicant in a preferential position, in that he or she is no longer required to link inability to return with particular events, and also no longer required to show that the well-founded fear of being persecuted is the reason for being outside the country of former habitual residence. It is seen as pertinent that in the second part of the clause the reference back to the first part of the paragraph is limited and the words 'such fear' appear to refer only to the word 'unwilling' and not to the word 'unable'.

A proper understanding of the Convention's context was also seen to lend further support to the ipso facto argument in that the eventual 1954 Convention did not deal with the stateless person whose lack of protection was manifest in an inability to return to some other country but rather 'covers only the situation of stateless persons admitted to residence or otherwise lawfully within State territory'.[246]

The Convention's object and purpose were also seen in this context to reside in the fact that, even though stateless persons require international protection as much as nationals, they are in a worse position, since they do not by definition enjoy the protection of a state.[247]

Also prayed in aid were the Convention's *travaux*. Goodwin-Gill in the aforementioned report filed in the *Revenko* litigation pointed out that the phrase 'as a result of such events' was inserted as a result of acceptance at the Thirty-fourth Meeting of the Conference of Plenipotentiaries of a United Kingdom proposal whose purpose was to ensure that those with and without a nationality were treated equally by reference to causal events, namely 'events occurring before 1 January 1951'.[248]

---

[244] Foster and Lambert (n 5) 93.
[245] For text of definition see above n 2.
[246] See Guy Goodwin-Gill, 'Revenko v Secretary of State for the Home Department: Report On Behalf of the Appellant' (UK Court of Appeal, Civil Division, 23 July 2000 (hereafter Report), para 27). See further *Revenko* (n 243).
[247] Goodwin-Gill (n 246) para 51. References to Goodwin-Gill's report are included here purely because of the clarity of its exposition; they are not to be taken to reflect his subsequent or current position. As noted by Foster and Lambert (n 5) 98, Goodwin-Gill's position as set out in the third edition of *The Refugee in International Law*, co-authored by McAdam (3rd edn) (n 5) 69–70, acknowledges that 'the view now generally accepted, and which makes sense in pursuit of a "single test" for refugee status is that no substantial difference is intended between stateless and other refugees'. See now, Goodwin-Gill and McAdam (4th edn) (n 5) 92.
[248] See Conference of Plenipotentiaries on the Status of Refugees and Stateless Persons: Summary Record of the Thirty-fourth Meeting (30 November 1951) UN Doc A/CONF.2/SR.34.

The reason why the above summary of the arguments in favour are cast in the past tense is that the ipso facto argument has clearly not survived close scrutiny.

As regards the *travaux*, if anything they provide powerful argument against the ipso facto reading. For example, Mr Hoare, the United Kingdom delegate, described the purpose of his amendment at the Twenty-third Meeting, as being that it 'was consequently to link stateless persons to those who were governed by the *twin conditions of a date and a well-founded fear of persecution as the motives for their departure*' and that his 'sole concern was to *make sure that the same criteria were applied to persons having nationality and to stateless persons*' (emphases added).[249] Nor is there anything in the *travaux* to the 1967 Protocol to suggest that stateless persons were to be considered on a different footing than nationals.

As regards the textual or literal argument, it is inconsistent with accepted grammatical principles.[250] In addition, as was pointed out by Clarke, LJ in *Revenko*,[251] it involves reading words into the text that are not there. In relation to context, acceptance of the 'bifurcated view' would create a disconnect between Article 1A(2) and Article 33. As noted by Pill, LJ in *Revenko*:

> I find it difficult to conclude that it was intended to open a door in Article 1A(2) by not requiring a well-founded fear, only substantially to close the door again in Article 33 by requiring a threat on account of a Convention reason to be established.[252]

Such an approach would also undermine the role of the 1954 Convention as a complementary treaty, rendering much of it superfluous.[253]

If the bifurcated view were correct, all stateless persons (having a country of former habitual residence they were unwilling to return to) would fall within the Article 1A(2) definition. Further, as noted by Foster and Lambert, the definition of a 'stateless person' for the purposes of the 1954 Convention contains no qualification in terms of persons admitted to residence or otherwise lawfully within state territory and not all the rights guaranteed by the 1954 Convention are conditioned on lawful stay (see e.g. Article 27).[254]

As regards the Convention's objects and purposes, Cooper J in *Rishmawi* wrote:

> Such a result would be unintended on the part of the framers of the Convention and inconsistent with the object of dealing only with persons who have been or who are being persecuted for a Convention reason or who have a well-founded fear of such persecution. It would also treat stateless persons in a substantially more favourable way in respect of obtaining refugee status than persons with a nationality and thus

---

[249] Conference of Plenipotentiaries on the Status of Refugees and Stateless Persons: Summary Record of the Twenty-third Meeting (26 November 1951) UN Doc A/CONF.2/SR.23.
[250] As was concluded by Justice Katz in *MIMA v Savvin* [2000] 171A OR 483, 501, 'the semi colon does not do the work of dividing the definition into two independent parts'.
[251] *Revenko* (n 243) para 92.
[252] ibid para 71.
[253] *Diatlov v MIMA* [1999] FCA 468, para 29.
[254] Foster and Lambert (n 5) 94.

would be inconsistent with the object of equality of treatment to all who claim refugee status.[255]

In light of what was said in Chapter 2 regarding Article 31(3) and Article 32 of the VCLT rules,[256] it is also pertinent to consider what view is taken on this issue by UNHCR. It does not support the bifurcated view. Paragraph 102 of the 1979 Handbook states that:

> [ … ] not all stateless persons are refugees. They must be outside the country of their former habitual residence for the reasons indicated if the definition. … Where these reasons do not exist, the stateless person is not a refugee.[257]

Leading courts have not supported the bifurcated view either.[258] As regards the wider literature, there has been at least one attempt by scholars to revive the view that Article 1A(2) provides distinctly less onerous criteria for stateless persons,[259] but this has been largely isolated and has not resulted in any change in the position taken by leading courts and tribunals.[260]

The bifurcated view can thus be effectively treated as having been definitively rejected.

### 3.4.7.4 Stateless persons and inability to return

It is important to note that although we have concluded that there is a broad symmetry between the situation of nationals and stateless persons so far as meeting the eligibility requirements set out in the refugee definition, that symmetry cannot be complete. The wording of the definition does make some distinction. In the case of nationals, it talks of the applicant being 'unwilling to avail himself of the protection of that country'. In the case of stateless persons, it talks only of being 'unable or, owing to such fear, is unwilling to return to it.' However, it would be incorrect to conclude that the question of the issue of availment of protection is irrelevant in the context of stateless persons for at least two interrelated reasons. First, if stateless persons are required to show a well-founded fear of being persecuted' in the same way as nationals, then as part of that requirement they have to establish that there would not be sufficient protection against such persecution.[261] Second, under IHRL, states owe duties to protect the basic human rights of all persons within their territory. Whilst there remain some differences in the content of the protection stateless persons can obtain applying IHRL norms, this is not

---

[255] *Rishmawi v MIMA* [1997] 77 FCR 421, 428.
[256] See p. 72.
[257] UNHCR Handbook (n 4) para 102.
[258] Foster and Lambert (n 5) 107.
[259] See Heather Alexander and Jonathan Simon, '"Unable to Return" in the 1951 Refugee Convention: Stateless Refugees and Climate Change' (2014) 26(3) Fla J Int'l L 531, 533, cited by Foster and Lambert (n 5) 92–93.
[260] Foster and Lambert (n 5) 96, note that 'senior courts have now uniformly rejected the argument that the hurdle for stateless persons to establish refugee status is any lower than for those with a nationality. Authority can be found in Australia, New Zealand, Canada, the US, the United Kingdom, France, Germany, Ireland, and in the EU Directive.'
[261] See Chapter 7, section 2.3 and Chapter 9, section 2.2.2.

an argument for differential treatment in respect of protection within the meaning of the refugee definition.

The heavy focus during the debate in the literature on the issue of whether the requirements of the refugee definition are less onerous for stateless persons requires further clarification of the meaning of the phrase 'unable to return'. Although this phrase forms part of the 'availment clause', its meaning is most sensibly addressed here as well.

A key question is whether, if the essence of the refugee predicament is that a person will face a real risk of persecution on return, how can s/he be considered a refugee if, as is often the case with stateless persons, s/he cannot be sent back to her/his country of former habitual residence in any event? The view that inability to return can exclude the possibility of protection under the Refugee Convention was most conspicuously advocated by Hathaway in TLRS. Therein he argued that returnability is determinative because 'where the stateless refugee claimant has no right to return to her country of first persecution or to any other state, she cannot qualify as a refugee because she is not at risk of return to persecution'.[262]

This position never gained any significant foothold in the case law on Article 1A(2) and suffers from inherent difficulties.

The drafting history indicates that while inability to return was seen as primarily a problem for stateless persons, it could also exist as a problem for nationals. The Australian Federal Court in *Rishmawi* makes reference to comments of the Ad Hoc Committee on the issue:

> The Committee agreed that for the purposes of this sub-paragraph and subparagraph A-29(c) and therefore for the draft convention as a whole, 'unable' refers primarily to stateless refugees, but includes also refugees possessing a nationality who are refused passports or other protection by their own government...[263]

In relation to the text itself, it would appear, at least reading Article 1A(2) as a whole, to envisage that inability to return can be problematic for both nationals and non-nationals.

In terms of object and purpose, a reading that made returnability determinative of refugee status would be at odds with the evident fact that the drafters clearly contemplated that stateless persons who have a well-founded fear of persecution were entitled to refugee status. As stated by Foster and Lambert after a close analysis of the drafting materials and the surrounding literature:

> [ ... ] a person's entitlement to refugee status—whether stateless or not—was never intended to be negated by a legal or factual inability to return to his or her country of origin at a particular point in time. On the contrary, the drafters were aware of the invocation of denationalisation as a tool of persecution in the decades that preceded the Refugee Convention's drafting. As observed by the Canadian Federal Court, a state 'could strip a person of his right to return to that country', as a 'final act of persecution'. To deny refugee status where the claimant did not have a legal right to return 'would

---

[262] Hathaway (n 5) 62.
[263] *Rishmawi* (n 255).

allow the persecuting state control over the claimant's recourse to the [Refugee] Convention and effectively undermine its humanitarian purpose'. Hence, to carve out an exception for those stateless persons who have no legally enforceable right to return to their country of origin or former residence would significantly undermine the objective and clear intentions of the drafters.[264]

To the extent that Article 31(3) and/or Article 32 VCLT entitle reference to UNHCR materials, the treatment of stateless persons in the 1979 Handbook clearly recognises that they can sometimes qualify as refugees.[265]

The position in the case law is encapsulated well by a 2005 decision of the NZ RSAA wherein it was stated:

> It cannot be, therefore, that *every* stateless person who is unable to return home is not a refugee since the inclusion clause contemplates some at least will be. Any attempt therefore to construct a definition of 'country of former habitual residence' or 'well-founded fear' that automatically excludes from the protection of the Convention every stateless person who is unable to return would appear to be at odds with the wording of Article 1A(2) and the underlying objectives and purpose of the Convention.[266]

Taking stock of the evolution of case law in Australia, Canada, New Zealand, the United States, and the UK, Foster and Lambert, conclude that:

> Where there is a question about returnability, decision-makers across all jurisdictions simply assess the claim on the hypothesis that return is possible, with the assessment focussing on the likely fate of the applicant should return be effected.[267]

As regards academic sources, it is noteworthy that Hathaway, who originally was one of the main proponents of the view that inability to return can exclude the possibility of protection, has recanted. In TLRS2, he and Foster acknowledge that the returnability criterion is not determinative.[268]

A requirement that an applicant be able in fact to return would also offend the principle of *ex nunc* assessment (assessment as at the date of hearing), which assumes hypothetically, in a forward-looking assessment, a return taking place, in relation to which by definition factors relating to the modality of return (unless relevant to risk) are irrelevant.[269]

There is, therefore, no principled basis on which it could be said that the reference to inability in the clause after the semi-colon (to a person not having a nationality '[being] unable or, owing to such fear, [is] unwilling to return to it [the country of his

---

[264] Hathaway and Foster (n 5) 100, citing, inter alia, *Marouf v Canada (MEI)* [1994] 1 FC 723.
[265] UNHCR Handbook (n 4) paras 97–105.
[266] *Refugee Appeal Nos 73861 & 73862* [2005] NZRSAA, para 78.
[267] Foster and Lambert (n 5)<IBT ch 4(1).
[268] ibid 102–03, citing Hathaway (n 156) 70.
[269] See *Refugee Appeal Nos 73861 & 73862* (n 266) 94. See Chapter 11, section 4.3.

former habitual residence'] should be construed to mean that inability to return negates risk on return.

None of this is to say that there may not be important issues in some types of cases arising that relate to inability to return. Indeed, in Chapter 5, with reference back to the earlier analysis of the 'valid reason' test applied by the second paragraph of Article 1A(2) to persons of multiple nationality,[270] it is argued that it would make sense to apply an analogous requirement to stateless applicants with more than one country of former habitual residence, where they have established a well-founded fear of persecution in one country of former habitual residence but would face, for example, non-admittance.[271]

*3.4.7.5 Stateless persons with more than one country of former habitual residence*
The meaning of the term 'country of former habitual residence' and how an applicant's country or countries of former habitual residence is/are to be identified will be addressed in Chapter 5, as will the interrelated issue of whether it is necessary for an applicant to establish a well-founded fear of persecution in relation to *every* country of former habitual residence.

## 4 Specific Issues

Whilst this study has now dealt with nationality and statelessness in the context of the refugee definition, its somewhat technical nature calls for some observations on selected issues that have given rise to particularly complex challenges.

### 4.1 Denationalisation and Arbitrary Deprivation of Nationality

The question has arisen whether those subject to denationalisation or arbitrary deprivation of nationality should or should not be seen to have lost their nationality for the purposes of refugee status determination. Disentangling the various views has become a task in itself.

On the one side there are those who have argued that such persons should continue to be seen as nationals. This viewpoint was forcefully articulated by Lauterpacht as long ago as 1948:

> [O]verwhelming considerations of fairness and equity demand that, in so far as the law allows, the victims of persecution should not be exposed to the hardships and losses attaching to a nationality of which they were deprived by a valid decree of the State responsible for the persecution.[272]

---

[270] See above section 3.3.6.1.
[271] See Chapter 5, section 4.2.
[272] Hersch Lauterpacht, *International Law, Being the Collected Papers of Hersch Lauterpacht*, Vol 3 (CUP 1977) 398, cited by Fripp (2016) (n 5) 64.

Grahl-Madsen notes the view of Zink that the 'country of nationality' should be understood in the sense of 'the country whose nationality he possesses, or whose nationality he has lost in connexion with leaving the country'.[273]

Recently the same view about the country of reference in such cases has been reasserted by Fripp in his book on *Nationality and Statelessness*. Fripp's argument has two main limbs. Firstly, he contends that it is the only way to respect international law principles on recognition; secondly that it is consonant with 'parallel interpretive policy or practice'.[274]

Having noted various ways in which the principle of non-recognition has been fortified in international law and international human rights standards since Zink and Grahl-Madsen among others had considered the issue,[275] Fripp argues that:

> [T]reating a denationalising State of origin as having ceased to be the reference state in favour of a non-national State of former habitual residence is additional prejudice to someone already the victim of a heinous form of state mistreatment—it adds a potential denial of international protection to the arbitrary removal of that individual's nationality and intuitively seems wrong.[276]

He considers that 'retaining focus in an appropriate case upon the state responsible for an arbitrary denationalisation prevents that state from escaping identification as the state responsible for a refugee-creating problem displacing a burden of protection on to other States'.[277] His impressive survey of non-recognition principles in the context of denationalisation seeks to recruit, inter alia, support for his position voiced by the German Federal Administrative Court in 2009 and the opinion expressed by one justice of the High Court of Ireland.[278]

No attempt will be made here to resolve fully debate on this issue, but there are several problems with Fripp's attempt to rely on considerations of recognition.

Dealing first with the reliance on the principle of non-recognition enshrined in the second sentence of Article 1 of the 1930 Hague Convention (see section 2.1.2. of this chapter), this provision has not resulted in international law establishing a straightforward position on the consequences of an act done by a state in the context of recognition of nationality. This is because (as Fripp himself acknowledges) the development of an international legal obligation to withhold recognition of illegal conduct 'has been hesitant and incomplete. States do not in practice acknowledge any general obligation

---

[273] Grahl-Madsen (n 4) 158–59 (where, inter alia, he cites Weis (n 4) 122). Grahl-Madsen also endorsed Zink's separate point that the relevant time for deciding whether a person is or is not denationalised is not the date of recognition or of application but the date when a person becomes a refugee by crossing the border 'or sur place'. However, if his underlying argument is that a state's arbitrary denationalisation should not be recognised, then it is irrelevant when it occurs.

[274] Fripp (2016) (n 5) 215. See also Fripp (2021) (n 5) 453.

[275] Fripp (2016) (n 5) 41.

[276] ibid 210.

[277] ibid 215.

[278] See BVerwG 10 C 50.07 [2009] 16–24. In *DT (No 2) v Refugee Appeals Tribunal & Ors* [2012] 1 EHC 562. Justice O'Keeffe granted leave to appeal to the Supreme Court of Ireland on exactly this point, but the latter eventually struck the case out for abuse of process on receipt of contradictory information about the claimant's nationality.

under international law permanently to withhold recognition of illegal acts or their consequences.'[279] Significantly, Fripp's own espousal of the non-recognition approach is heavily qualified, he advocates it only for dealing with some cases. Further, recourse to non-recognition in the asylum determination context goes beyond its typical role in international law, which is as an element in the determination of statehood and conditions for the establishment of formal relations.[280] A further complication is that on Fripp's own argument there thus exists a disjuncture between the Refugee Convention and the CSSP54, since the latter chose wording ('not considered as a national by any State under the operation of its law') intended to exclude considerations of recognition. That recognition is not relevant in the context of the CSSP54 is also clearly the view of UNHCR, whose 2014 Handbook states that to consider an individual who has been stripped of his or her nationality in a manner inconsistent with international law as nevertheless a 'national' for the purposes of Article 1(1) would be 'at variance with the object and purpose of the 1954 Convention'.[281]

Fripp's position could also be said to misunderstand the function of refugee status determination which is not to condemn the state of persecution.[282] Rather, its purpose is to provide a palliative mechanism for persons who are victims of persecution. In any event, states who arbitrarily deprive persons of their nationality can be held responsible for violations, certainly under modern IHRL law.[283]

What of Fripp's alternative limb based on 'parallel interpretive policy or practice'? Significantly, those coming to the same conclusion as Fripp include Goodwin-Gill and McAdam who argue for a 'straightforward, non-technical approach which leaves issues concerned with the international 'validity' of deprivation of citizenship as 'a matter for other tribunals'. They consider that '[i]n most cases it will be illogical to characterise the applicant for refugee status deprived of nationality as a stateless claimant ... what matters are the facts giving rise to well-founded fear of persecution, one of which may be the arbitrary or discriminatory deprivation of citizenship'.[284]

On the opposite side of the argument, a very different view is taken by, among others, Foster and Lambert. They contend that persons denationalised or arbitrarily deprived of their nationality stand to be considered as stateless persons. In their view, 'in by far the majority of cases involving denationalisation, decision-makers simply adopt this approach' and that 'the isolated instances in which this approach has not been implemented straightforwardly are anomalous, and are based on an incorrect assumption that there can only be one country of former habitual residence'.[285] They regard the opposite approach as at risk of assuming, incorrectly, that the country of former habitual residence must be confined to a person's 'last' country of former

---

[279] Jennings and Watts (n 70) 183, cited by Fripp (2016) (n 5) 55.
[280] Foster and Lambert (n 5) 124, cite observations to this effect in *Brownlie's Principles* (n 5) 147, 155–65.
[281] UNHCR 2014 Handbook (n 5) para 56. See also UNHCR 2010 Prato Conclusions (n 5): 'where a deprivation of nationality may be contrary to rules of international law, this illegality is not relevant in determining whether the person is a national ... rather, it is the position under domestic law that is relevant'. See also the UNHCR submissions to similar effect in *BD (Bhutan, Nepal)* [2018] IEHC 461.
[282] For a contrary view, see Matthew E Price, *Rethinking Asylum History, Purpose, and Limits* (CUP 2010).
[283] Lambert (n 82) 16–20.
[284] Goodwin-Gill and McAdam (4th edn) (n 5) 94.
[285] Foster and Lambert (n 5) 125–26. On the issue of multiple countries of former habitual residence, see Chapter 5, section 4.1.

habitual residence.[286] They submit that whilst any illegality on the part of the state withdrawing or depriving a person of nationality may be very relevant to the question of whether they face a well-founded fear of being persecuted, 'it does not bear on the question of the state of reference'.[287] A case giving detailed reasons for reaching the same conclusion is *AL (Mynamar)* [2018] NZIPT 801255, a decision of the New Zealand Immigration and Protection Tribunal. The reasoning deployed by the IPT in this case relies heavily on the wording of Article 1(1) of the CSSP54 which is seen to focus wholly on the issue of whether the state has acted under its national law and if that action takes the form of denationalisation or arbitrary deprivation, that has legal effects, irrespective of whether they are not recognised by the international community. The IPT relies, in addition, on the strong complementarity of the CSSP54 and the Refugee Convention.[288]

Given that both of the opposing views about the country of reference in such cases typically consider their reading to be justified in terms of considerations of ordinary meaning, context, object and purpose, and other VLCT considerations, it is the view of this author that even though Foster and Lambert seem to be on stronger ground, much remains to be clarified and that at present the main protagonists sometimes seem to be talking past each other.[289]

## 4.2 Misuse of Nationality

According to Hailbronner:

> Facilitating access to nationality for migrants has resulted in growing concern among states that more open access to nationality may be misused to evade immigration restrictions or escape expulsion or deportation. The misuse of nationality laws, therefore, has also become an issue of international co-operation. Thus, for instance, nationality has been renounced in order to escape deportation by acquiring the status of statelessness. States permitting this renunciation are generally acting in violation of public international law. A state's duty to respect the sovereignty of other states and their sovereign right to decide on the admission of foreigners implies a duty to accept a responsibility for a state's own citizens including an obligation to allow their return. This obligation could be easily overcome by a renunciation of nationality in order to prevent the return of a state's own citizens.[290]

---

[286] Foster and Lambert (n 5) 121–26. At 125, they cite, inter alia, *EB (Ethiopia) v SSHD* [2007] EWCA Civ 809; *Haile v Gonzalez* [2005] 421 F.3d 493; two French cases, CNDA Decision No 12013646-C [2013] and CNDA Decision No 09019611 [2011]; and several New Zealand decisions.
[287] Foster and Lambert (n 5) 126. See also Goodwin-Gill and McAdam (4th edn) (n 5) 94.
[288] *AL (Myanmar)* (n 223). See also *BD (Bhutan, Nepal)* (n 281) para 26 (Justice Humphreys).
[289] For example, both Goodwin-Gill and McAdam (4th edn) (n 5) 94 and Foster and Lambert (n 5) 126 take Fripp to task for relying on notions of opposability, but Fripp (2016) (n 5) 217 states opposability is 'not relevant'.
[290] Hailbronner (n 5) 46.

In certain circumstances fraud or misrepresentation can void nationality *ab initio*. National law may make specific provision for loss of nationality *ex lege* on such grounds.[291] However, whether opportunistic conduct amounts to fraud or misrepresentaton may depend very much on the circumstances, as is well-illustrated by several UK cases concerning persons who claimed to be from the former Republic of Yugoslavia (FRY) when in fact they were Albanian.[292]

Separate considerations may apply once an applicant has been granted refugee status. Given the object and purpose of the refugee definition, in particular that refugee status should only be granted to those who meet the underlying conditions, it may be that even where there is no fraud or misrepresentation, the grant of refugee status could be treated as a nullity if it materially depended on incorrect information in the first place.[293]

### 4.3 Voluntary Renunciation of Nationality

What is the position if a person, prior to a decision being made on whether they are a refugee, voluntarily renounces their nationality, something which is provided for by some domestic legal systems under their nationality laws? As recognised by the UNHCR in its 2014 Handbook at paragraph 161, '[s]ome individuals voluntarily renounce a nationality because they do not wish to be nationals of a particular State or in the belief that this will lead to grant of a protection status in another country'.[294] It is possible to envisage a situation, for example, where a person may take such action in order to create conditions for an asylum claim that would otherwise not exist, e.g. if they are a dual national and they voluntarily renounce their nationality with state A (where they face no risk of persecution), leaving them with only the nationality of state B (where they will face persecution).[295]

At the outset, it should be clarified that the issue here is voluntary action, not volition. There is no 'volition requirement' as regards the possession of a nationality: nationality continues to exist irrespective of the attitude of the individual to this.[296] Further, voluntary renunciation has no role if expressed simply as an opinion; it must be legally acted upon.

In broad terms, it might be said to be contrary to the object and purpose of the Convention if a person who is undeserving of international protection can by misuse

---

[291] At the level of treaty, Article 7(1) of the European Convention on Nationality (n 5) provides that one of the situations in which a State Party may provide in its internal law for the loss of its nationality *ex lege* is: 'b. acquisition of the nationality of the State Party by means of fraudulent conduct, false information or concealment of any relevant fact attributable to the applicant.'

[292] *Hysaj & Ors, R (on the application of) v SSHD* [2017] UKSC 82. See also Norwegian Supreme Court (Høyesterett, Norway), in judgment HR-2020-2408-A of 14 December 2020, which concerned whether the applicant could rely on having been issued with Eritrean nationality. See further UNHCR 2014 Handbook (n 5) paras 45–46.

[293] Case C-720/17 *Mohammed Bilali v Bundesamt für Fremdenwesen und Asyl* [2019] EU:C:2019:448, para 44. Although a decision on subsidiary protection, the Court's reasoning would appear to apply by analogy to refugee status.

[294] UNHCR 2014 Handbook (n 5) para 161. See Foster and Lambert (n 5) 126–32.

[295] See Hailbronner (2006) (n 5) 46.

[296] Hathaway and Foster (n 5) 62, citing *Lay Kon Tji* (n 110).

of nationality create the conditions for establishing refugeehood. This view could be said to be supported by the importance given by the drafters to voluntary action in relation to the criterion of 'unwillingness' in the availment clause and nationality in the context of the cessation clauses: see Articles 1C(1)–(2) and (4). For example, Article 1C(1) states that refugee status shall cease if '[h]e has voluntarily re-availed himself of the protection of the country of his nationality'. There is also a line of case law that has expressed concern about misuse or manipulation of nationality (or statelessness) in this context.[297] However, it is difficult to see that this concern should impinge on the analysis required by international law principles of nationality or statelessness. As stated by the Expert Meeting organised by UNHCR in May 2010 in Prato, in relation to the CSSP54:

> The definition in Article 1(1) refers to a factual situation, not to the manner in which a person became stateless. Voluntary renunciation of nationality does not preclude an individual from satisfying the requirements of Article 1(1) as there is no basis for reading in such an implied condition to the definition of 'stateless person'.[298]

The issue of voluntary renunciation is linked in some respects with that of refusal by applicants to take reasonable steps to apply for a nationality to which they appear to have some eligibility or entitlement. One of the bases for the idea that nationality should include potential nationality has been concern about 'country shopping' (the term used by the Canadian Federal Court in *Williams*).[299] However, as Fripp has observed, such a reading is not justified by the need for avoidance of abuse of the Refugee Convention.[300] Further, as noted earlier,[301] there is a potential for misuse whether one adopts a potential or actual nationality approach. In the next subsection, it is argued that requirements to take reasonable steps to acquire a nationality or to confirm an existing one have a proper place in the context of evidential considerations, but cannot affect whether or not a person is or is not a national.

## 5 Nationality and Evidential Issues

Albeit not strictly within the scope of this book, certain problems of evidence and credibility assessment impinge on the legal framework. As just noted in relation to case law that applies a 'reasonable steps' criterion, this particularly arises in the context of the requirements sometimes seen to apply to applicants in respect of proving their nationality or lack of it.

---

[297] In particular, *Williams* (n 128), in which Decary J, citing *Bouianova* (n 121), reasoned at [22] that 'If it is within the control of the applicant to acquire the citizenship of a country with respect to which he has no well-founded fear of persecution, the claim for refugee status will be denied.... It prevents the introduction of a practice of "country shopping" which is incompatible with the "surrogate" dimension of international protection recognised in *Ward*....'
[298] UNHCR 2010 Prato Conclusions (n 5) para 20.
[299] *Williams* (n 128).
[300] Fripp (2016) (n 5) 203–05.
[301] See above section 3.2.10.

This subsection aims to identify a number of basic propositions and then address remaining areas of disagreement where legal and evidential issues intersect.

Hathaway and Foster are surely right to say that '[t]he questions of nationality is to be treated like any other factual matter, with the applicant bearing the burden of proof in the context of a shared duty of fact-finding'[302] but, as their own coverage conveys, the precise way in which nationality is to be evidenced can give rise to real, sometimes intractable, difficulties.

The reasons why assessment of evidence concerning nationality can be fraught take us back to points noted earlier, in particular that nationality is not a physical or biological fact and in practice many asylum-seekers lack documentation which would otherwise make decision-making regarding it relatively straightforward. A further dimension of difficulty is that when assessing whether an applicant is a refugee, the duty of confidentiality prevents the host state from making the type of inquiries that could be made in the ordinary course of events.[303]

## 5.1 Basic Propositions Regarding Nationality and Evidence Assessment

It can be said, however, that the following rules are widely accepted in practice:

(i) Individuals are assumed to have a nationality as opposed to no nationality. This stems from the accepted fact that everyone originates from somewhere and the international order in very large part comprises a collection of individual states.

(ii) Substantiation of nationality will ordinarily be by way of an applicant's own testimony or production of documentary evidence such as a passport or identity card.[304] Production of a passport is widely regarded as *prima facie* evidence of possession of the nationality of the country of passport.[305] However, a passport or identity document is not a necessary requirement in order to establish nationality.

(iii) Further, precisely what type of documents will constitute good evidence will depend in part on the contents of the home State's nationality law. For example, birth certificates will be particularly relevant where the country of origin's nationality law confers nationality through *ius soli* or *ius sanguinis*; if a person has

---

[302] Hathaway and Foster (n 5) 54. See also UNHCR 2014 Handbook (n 5) para 89: 'In the case of statelessness determination, the burden of proof is in principle shared, in that both the applicant and examiner must cooperate to obtain evidence and to establish the facts.'

[303] UNHCR 2014 Handbook (n 5) para 95. See also Grahl-Madsen (n 4) 155.

[304] In *AA v Switzerland* App No 58802/12 (ECtHR, 7 January 2014) para 61, the ECtHR noted that: '[a]s previously held by the Court, the best way for an asylum seeker to prove his identity is by submitting an original passport. If this is not possible on account of the circumstances in which he finds himself, other documents might be used to prove his identity. A birth certificate could have value as evidence if other identity papers are missing'—see also *FN and Others v Sweden* App No 28774/09 (ECtHR, 18 December 2012) para 72.

[305] UNHCR Handbook (n 4) para 93; UNHCR 2014 Handbook (n 5) para 95. Shearer (n 59) 310, states that whilst there are authorities to this effect, 'there have also been decisions, both reported and unreported, that a passport is not to be relied on except in conjunction with other evidence of nationality, and is not conclusive on the question in the absence of such other evidence'.

acquired nationality through marriage, then the marriage certificate would be a document of particular importance.

Having identified some widely accepted propositions, it is important to consider remaining areas of disagreement.

## 5.2 Areas of Disagreement

### 5.2.1 Actual nationality and documentary evidence

The first area where disagreements exist concerns the issue of whether an applicant can only be considered to have a particular nationality if he or she possesses documentary evidence of it. It would be a misunderstanding of the legal notion of nationality to make possession of documentary evidence a necessary condition. If permitted to stand, such a view would also have a chilling effect on many claims made by asylum-seekers, substantial numbers of whom, as already noted, flee and arrive in host states without any documents. But it would also have the effect of allowing certain arguably undeserving applicants to succeed because, for example, they would be able to claim that since they lack satisfactory documentation of nationality of state X, they are not a national of that state, even when they in fact are. Such conduct may mean they are wrongly determined to be a national or former habitual resident of unsafe state Y, even though as a matter of law safe state X is their country of nationality. The reason why such a view is plainly erroneous in law can be gleaned from the basic propositions set out earlier. Nationality is a legal fact established by reference to national law, subject only to possible questions of recognition in a very limited range of cases. If a person fulfils the conditions laid down in national law that confer automatic entitlement, then they possess the nationality of that state as a matter of law, whether they or decision makers like it or not. A document such as a passport can at best only be declaratory of such nationality.[306]

It is important to note that this principle obtains whatever the basis for the acquisition of the nationality. A person only entitled to that nationality by virtue of discretionary provisions will not be a national as a matter of law unless and until such provisions have been applied to them by the state in question. However, once they have been processed and have been recorded in a state's procedures as having been granted nationality, then, again, they possess that nationality as a matter of law, whether or not they have satisfactory documentation. None of this is to say that an applicant's nationality can simply be accepted on their say so. There will remain to be addressed, of course, problematic issues regarding what evidence can be accepted in lieu of documentary evidence.

### 5.2.2 Substantiation in the form of taking reasonable steps to assert a nationality

There is also disagreement over whether it is right in certain circumstances to expect a person whom the determining authority considers a national of state X to take

---

[306] Fripp (2016) (n 5) 77.

reasonable steps to demonstrate it (e.g. by approaching that state's embassy for confirmation of their status as a national). This is the position seemingly taken for example in EU asylum law, by virtue of Article 4(3)(e) of the EU Qualification Directive (recast) which provides that an applicant 'may reasonably be expected to avail himself or herself of the protection of another country where he or she could assert citizenship'.[307] It is also the position akin to that taken in a range of national law cases (e.g. by the Canadian Federal Court of Appeal in the *Williams* case, which—again in the context of a second nationality case—held that in relation to nationality under automatic provisions of national law 'the test is better phrased in terms of "power within the control of the applicant"').[308]

There has been significant opposition to the requirement of reasonable steps both as formulated in Article 4(3)(e) QD(recast) and more widely.[309] If Article 4(3)(e) were to be read as setting down a rule for determining nationality, it would be highly problematic, imposing in effect a 'potential nationality' as opposed to an actual nationality understanding.[310] However, this provision is part of an article concerned with evidence assessment. When this provision and similar criteria relating to reasonable steps are read as being confined to evidence assessment, most if not all of the criticisms fall away.

On the basis of the earlier analysis rejecting the 'inchoate nationality' approach in favour of an 'actual nationality' approach, there is no bar to application of a reasonable steps requirement *prior to the making of a decision*. If an applicant is *still in the asylum process* awaiting a determination, then the requirement by a determining authority that they take reasonable steps to assert an *ex lege* (or pre-existing) nationality seems wholly unexceptionable, subject only to issues of procedural fairness.[311] That is because it is really just a matter of evidence assessment in the context of procedural requirements. If the question is identified at the interview/pre-decision stage, then a determining authority cannot be criticised for requiring the applicant to cooperate over the matter. Issues may arise here as to the extent to which the determining authority must itself actively cooperate in order to help the applicant take such steps and as to what happens if their result is inconclusive or there is delay, but in the end such matters remain evidential and/or procedural in nature. The critical point is that the failure of an applicant to take reasonable steps can only be a relevant factor up until the point of decision.[312] At the point of decision an applicant's nationality must be

---

[307] The interpretation of this provision has not yet been the subject of a reference to the CJEU. For an example of an attempt to codify reasonable steps provision in national law, see section 36(3) of the Australian Migration Act 2014 (as amended) (which refers to 'all possible steps').

[308] *Williams* (n 128), cited in Hathaway and Foster (n 5) 60.

[309] See e.g. UNHCR, 'Annotated Comments on the EC Council Directive 2004/83/EC of 29 April 2004 on Minimum Standards for the Qualification and Status of Third Country Nationals or Stateless Persons as Refugees or as Persons Who Otherwise Need International Protection and the Content of the Protection Granted' (30 September 2004) OJL 304.12. 15; Gregor Noll, 'Evidentiary Assessment in Refugee Status Determination and the EU Qualification Directive' (2006) 12 EPL, 295, 308; Hathaway and Foster (n 5) 60; Foster and Lambert (n 5) 113–19, 128.

[310] See above section 3.2.10.

[311] And possibly, if the approach of the CJEU in *Rottman* is followed, a principle of proportionality; see Case C-135/08 *Rottman v Freistaat Bayern* [2010] ECLI:EU:C:2010:104. See also UNHCR 2014 Handbook (n 5) paras 155–56, 158–59.

[312] If, however, the 'inchoate nationality' approach were accepted (but only if), then it would also seem unexceptionable for a determining authority, in response to an unreasonable failure by an applicant to take

assessed on the basis of what it is at that precise point in time. That is required by the actual nationality principle.

Yet it is crucial to recall the limited context in which such 'reasonable steps' can be expected. To be consistent with the principles of confidentiality and non-disclosure, it should be confined to cases in which the determining authority considers that there is a country of nationality where an applicant would have available protection and the applicant himself or herself does not claim such a country would be unsafe for them.

### 5.2.3 Duty of cooperation on the part of the determining authority

Whilst it can be accepted that at a general level there is a shared duty of cooperation on the part of the determining authority to help an applicant substantiate his application, it is difficult to see that this can be translated into a specific duty on the authority's part in every case to make inquiries of the applicant's home state to ascertain whether that state accepts the applicant as a national or not, especially given that it is bound to respect a duty of non-disclosure and confidentiality to the applicant.[313]

### 5.2.4 Meaning of 'law' in the context of acquisition 'by operation of law'

Another unclear area concerns the application and understanding of those cases in which it is accepted that a person has automatic entitlement to nationality 'by operation of law' but there is dispute about precisely what that law is. At root the issue here is a legal, not an evidential issue, but it arises as a difficulty in refugee status determination primarily as an issue about what types of evidence are relevant to ascertaining what is 'law' in this context.

There appears to be wide support for giving a broad definition to the term 'law' as it arises in the context of a person not having a nationality by operation of law under his or her state's nationality law.[314] That comports well with the definition of 'internal law' given in Article 2(d) of the 1997 European Convention on Nationality as meaning 'all types of provisions of the national legal system, including the constitution, legislation, regulations, decrees, case-law, customary rules and practice as well as rules deriving from binding international instruments'.[315]

That said, it is important to reflect on what is involved in any assessment of nationality or its lack in the context of RSD. Clearly it is an assessment that has to consider the individual circumstances of applicants and that may extend, for example, to taking

such steps, to conclude as a matter of evidence that that person has that nationality or does not have it for Article 1A(2) purposes.

---

[313] This is particularly the case under the EU QD (recast) because the wording of Article 4(3)(e) envisages action on the part of the applicant, not the member state. It is significant that the ECtHR, although identifying a duty on the contracting state to make inquiries in some contexts—see e.g. *Singh and Ors v Belgium* App No 33210/11 (ECtHR, 2 January 2013), did not do this in relation to nationality—see e.g. *AA v Switzerland* (n 304); *MA v Switzerland* App No 52589/13 (ECtHR, 19 April 2016) paras 60–63. For a different view, see Goodwin-Gill and McAdam (4th edn) (n 5) 90–91: '[a] claimant with a well-founded fear of being persecuted ought not to be denied protection as a refugee on the basis of specious assertions as to the availability of alternative protection; the burden therefore is on the authority that would deny refugee status to provide that the individual *is* in fact considered as a national by another State according to its law'.

[314] See e.g. *Pham* (n 230); UNHCR 2014 Handbook (n 5) para 22; Batchelor, 'Statelessness and the Problem of Resolving Nationality Status' (n 5).

[315] 1997 European Convention on Nationality (n 5) Article 2(d).

into account specific correspondence between them and their embassies. However, if the issue concerns how the nationality law of their home state operates in general, then correspondingly the evidence about that must predominantly be evidence at a general level. Because decision makers must reach a decision as authorities external to the state in question, their assessment must, it is submitted (save in unusual cases) confine itself to assessment of the state practice of the state concerned at a general level, to establish whether there are discernible general patterns—e.g. not to follow their own Constitution or their nationality legislation when it comes to a particular category of cases. Absent significant evidence that states do not ordinarily apply their own nationality law, how particular officials of one embassy might apply them should not be determinative.[316] Otherwise, there is too great a risk of refugee determination descending into a case-specific forensic examination of how a particular embassy or particular embassy official is likely to react to an application or to a request to confirm whether an applicant is one of its nationals. Such an exercise would also conflict particularly heavily with the principles of confidentiality and non-disclosure.

5.2.5 Persons of indeterminate nationality

It was noted earlier that indeterminate nationality is not a species of nationality. It is rather a description of a lack of evidence regarding nationality.

If the determining authority considers that by virtue of a lack of evidence, it cannot be clear what is a person's nationality—sometimes referred to as 'indeterminate nationality' cases[317]—then the most defensible position would appear to be to consider that there is a duty on that authority to assess the asylum claim on the assumption that the applicant is a national of one or more countries or is stateless. According to UNHCR, it is the country of former habitual residence.[318] According to Hathaway and Foster, this should be 'the country which it believes is most likely to be the applicant's true country of nationality'.[319] They see the underlying rationale as being that in order to ensure effective implementation of the Refugee Convention States Parties are required 'to undertake and complete an individual examination of each claim to asylum'.[320] As a result, '[t]o exclude *a priori* [an applicant] on the basis that he

---

[316] *KK* (n 68) para 60.
[317] See UNHCR, Guidelines on Statelessness No 4: Ensuring Every Child's Right to Acquire a Nationality through Articles 1–4 of the 1961 Convention on the Reduction of Statelessness (21 December 2012) UN Doc HCR/GS/12/04, paras 22–23: 'This term is used here as an umbrella expression for the classification of the nationality status as "unknown", "undetermined" or "under investigation". The term also covers cases where States do not classify a person as "stateless", but rather use a specific term based on their domestic law.'
[318] UNHCR Handbook (n 4) para 89: 'Where, therefore, an applicant alleges fear of persecution in relation to the country of his nationality, it should be established that he does in fact possess the nationality of that country. There may, however, be uncertainty as to whether a person has a nationality. He may not know himself, or he may wrongly claim to have a particular nationality or to be stateless. Where his nationality cannot be clearly established, his refugee status should be determined in a similar manner to that of a stateless person, i.e. Instead of the country of his nationality, the country of his former habitual residence will have to be taken into account ....'
[319] Hathaway and Foster (n 5) 54: 'If ... the applicant is unable to identify her citizenship or if her designation of the country of reference cannot be relied upon, the receiving state should proceed to assess risk in the state which it believes is most likely to be the applicant's true country of citizenship. Because the ultimate duty of the state is to assess whether or not the individual is a refugee, status may not lawfully be denied simply because the applicant's country of nationality was not properly identified by her.'
[320] *Agartha Smith v SSHD* [2000] UKIAT, Appeal No 00TH02130, para 47.

has failed to prove either a nationality or statelessness could undo the purpose of the Convention…, to protect fundamental rights and freedoms'.[321]

There is no reason to consider that approaching cases of indeterminate nationality in either of these proposed ways would impose undue burden on the determining authority, not at least if regard is had to the approach taken by UNHCR in relation to statelessness (but which would surely apply, *pari passu*, to nationality), namely that:

> The lack of nationality does not need to be established in relation to every state in the world. Consideration is only necessary of those States with which an individual has a relevant link, generally on the basis of birth on the territory, descent, marriage, adoption or habitual residence.[322]

## 6 Conclusions

It has been explained why the element of the refugee definition concerned with nationality and statelessness, which concerns its personal scope, has been dealt with first.

It has been argued that even though IHRL norms have come to impinge more on issues of nationality and statelessness than they did when the Convention was drafted, the primary framework for interpreting this element of the definition remains the international law on nationality, in particular the widely accepted rules pertaining to the various modes of acquisition of nationality and the main ways in which nationality is acquired and lost.

In relation to 'country of nationality', it was explained why the application of VCLT rules of interpretation requires construing the term to denote the legal bond between the individual and the state and why in temporal terms, 'nationality' must refer to current or actual nationality (not 'inchoate nationality').

As regards the second paragraph of Article 1A(2) dealing with multiple nationality, it was concluded that the meaning of the term 'nationality' in this context is the same, that the effect of the second paragraph of 1A(2) is that persons of multiple nationality must possess a well-founded fear of persecution in each country of nationality, unless they have 'valid reasons' for not availing themselves of their protection; and that interpretation of the additional requirement (or qualification) set out in the second subparagraph does not warrant importation of the concept of 'effective nationality'.

In relation to the phrase 'not having a nationality', it was argued that its meaning is to be equated with that of a stateless person as defined in Article 1 of the CSSP54 and that, in terms of temporal scope, the definition (like that of its opposite, 'nationality') is concerned with current or actual status, in this case as a stateless person.

After analysis of the competing arguments it was concluded that it can now be regarded as settled that stateless persons are not ipso facto refugees and that inability

---

[321] ibid para 197, citing UNHCR Handbook (n 4).
[322] UNHCR 2014 Handbook (n 5) para 92.

to return cannot be treated as determinative of refugee status since assessment of whether a person is a refugee is essentially a hypothetical one.

This section also sought to highlights selected issues that have proven difficult in relation to this element of the definition, namely illegal withdrawal or deprivation of nationality and denationalisation; misuse of nationality; and voluntary renunciation of nationality.

A final section, addressing nationality and evidential issues, highlighted areas where legal and evidentiary issues intersect.

## 6.1 Basic Propositions

Turning finally to consider, what basic propositions, if any, can be distilled from the above analysis, the following appear to be widely agreed:[323]

1. Establishing nationality or statelessness is an essential element of the refugee definition.
2. The primary framework for interpreting this element of the definition is the international law on nationality.
3. Nationality within the meaning of its main use in Article 1A(2) concerns the legal bond between the individual and the state.
4. In temporal terms, it concerns actual nationality.
5. In relation to the phrase 'not having a nationality', this can now be seen to identify stateless persons as defined in Article 1 of the Convention Relating to the Status of Stateless Persons (CSSP54). In parallel with the position that applies to nationals, the temporal scope of this term is actual status.
6. The effect of the second paragraph of 1A(2) is that a person of multiple nationality must have a well-founded fear of persecution in each country of nationality, unless there are 'valid reasons' for not availing himself or herself of their protection. Two obvious instances that would constitute valid reasons are non-admission and risk of refoulement to the country of persecution.
7. Assessment of inability to return requires a hypothetical inquiry into the situation a stateless person would face if returned.

## 6.2 Suggested Propositions

On the basis of this chapter's analysis, the following are proposed as suggested propositions that may assist in resolving ongoing debates:

1. Whilst IHLR norms have become more relevant to determination of nationality, the primary set of rules governing such determination remain those set out in the international law.

---

[323] For basic propositions concerning evidence and credibility assessment, see section 5.1 of this chapter.

2. Treating nationality as meaning actual nationality should not be extended to embrace 'inchoate nationality' or 'potential nationality'.
3. In relation to Article 1A(2), second paragraph, dealing with multiple nationals who can show 'valid reasons' why they are not required to show a well-founded fear of persecution in each country, there is no requirement for nationality to be 'effective'.

# 5
# 'Outside the Country...'
## ('Hors du pays...')

| | | | |
|---|---|---|---|
| Introduction | 259 | 3.5 Article 31(3) and Other VCLT Considerations | 279 |
| Ordering | 262 | 3.5.1 Habitual residence | 281 |
| Approach to Interpretation | 262 | 4 Specific Issues | 282 |
| A Human Rights Approach | 262 | 4.1 Multiple Countries of Former Habitual Residence | 282 |
| 1 'Outside the Country' | 263 | 4.2 Are Persons with Multiple Countries of Former Habitual Residence Subject to the Same Requirements as Multiple Nationals? | 284 |
| 2 'Outside the Country' and VCLT Rules | 263 | | |
| 2.1 Background and *Travaux Préparatoires* | 263 | | |
| 2.2 Good Faith | 266 | 4.3 Temporal Dimension | 286 |
| 2.3 Ordinary Meaning | 266 | 5 Article 33(1) and Extraterritorial Application | 288 |
| 2.4 Context | 268 | 5.1 Potential Relevance to Interpretation of 'Outside the Country' | 288 |
| 2.5 Object and Purpose | 270 | | |
| 2.6 Article 31(3) and Other VCLT Considerations | 271 | 5.2 *Travaux Préparatoires* | |
| | | 5.3 International Law Context | 289 |
| 3 'Outside the Country of Former Habitual Residence' | 272 | 5.4 Case Law and Academic Literature | 292 |
| 3.1 Background and *Travaux Préparatoires* | 272 | 5.5 Article 33(1) and Extraterritorial Immigration Controls | 293 |
| 3.1.1 Habitual residence | 273 | 5.6 Article 33(1): Extraterritorial Application via National and Regional Law | 294 |
| 3.2 Ordinary Meaning | 273 | | |
| 3.2.1 Habitual residence | 274 | | |
| 3.3 Context | 274 | 6 Conclusions | 295 |
| 3.3.1 Habitual residence | 275 | 6.1 Basic Propositions | 297 |
| 3.4 Object and Purpose | 275 | 6.2 Suggested Propositions | 297 |
| 3.4.1 Habitual residence | 277 | | |

## Introduction

The refugee definition requires that a person be 'outside the country of nationality' or, if 'not having a nationality' be 'outside … the country of his former habitual residence'. Both clauses make the 'outside the country' requirement a *sine qua non* for qualifying as a refugee. Together they form what this study terms the 'outside the country' element of the definition.

This element has received less analytical attention than any other part of the definition. The 1979 Handbook on Procedures and Criteria for Determining Refugee Status of the UN High Commissioner for Refugees (UNHCR Handbook or Handbook) devotes little space to it. In relation to nationals it states only that:

> It is a general requirement for refugee status that an applicant who has a nationality be outside the country of his nationality. There are no exceptions to this rule. International protection cannot come into play as long as a person is within the territorial jurisdiction of his home country.[1]

In relation to stateless persons, it simply says that they also 'must be outside the country of their former habitual residence … '.[2] The relative lack of analysis can be said to reflect the fact that there is less divergence in the literature over the meaning of the 'outside' element as compared with other elements, but it remains important to understand how the Vienna Convention on the Law of Treaties (VCLT)[3] rules are to be applied to this element and to address the main interpretive issues that have arisen.

Taken either on its own or in conjunction with the nationality and statelessness elements, this element is sometimes dubbed the 'alienage' requirement, a term popularised by Jaeger and Shacknove.[4] Whilst 'alienage' has the virtue of brevity, so does 'outside' and, unlike the latter, the former risks shifting attention away from the fact of physical separation from the country of origin to the applicant's status in the eyes of the host state and international community. Hence this study prefers adherence to the wording of the Convention text.

Some leading studies covering the refugee definition do not refer to the 'outside' element at all,[5] or if they do so, only briefly.[6] But its meaning is not unproblematic.

---

[1] UNHCR, Handbook on Procedures and Criteria for Determining Refugee Status and Guidelines on International Protection under the 1951 Convention and the 1967 Protocol Relating to the Status Of Refugees (Geneva, 2019, reissued in 2019) (UNHCR Handbook or Handbook) para 88. To this paragraph there is, however, a footnote relating to 'diplomatic asylum', a concept which will be addressed below at section 5.6.

[2] ibid para 2.

[3] Vienna Convention on the Law of Treaties (adopted 23 May 1969, entered into force 27 January 1980) 1155 UNTS 331.

[4] Gilbert Jaeger, 'The Definition of "Refugee": Restrictive versus Expanding Trends' (1983) World Refugee Survey 5, 5; Andrew Shacknove, 'Who Is a Refugee?' (1985) 95 Ethics 274, 275. See also James C Hathaway, *The Law of Refugee Status* (Butterworths Limited 1991) 29–63. It remains the preferred term employed by James C Hathaway and Michelle Foster, *The Law of Refugee Status* (2nd edn, CUP 2014) 17, who define it as the 'requirement of the definition—limiting status to an at-risk person who is "outside" her own country'.

[5] e.g. Deborah Anker, *Law of Asylum in the United States* (Thomson Reuters 2022); Lorne Waldman, *The Definition of Convention Refugee* (2nd edn, Lexis Nexis 2019).

[6] See e.g. Atle Grahl-Madsen, *The Status of Refugees in International Law. Volume 1: Refugee Character* (Sijthoff 1966) 151; Kees Wouters, *International Legal Standards for the Protection from Refoulement* (Intersentia 2009) 48–56; Andreas Zimmermann and Claudia Mahler, 'Article 1A, para 2' in Andreas Zimmermann (ed), *The 1951 Convention Relating to the Status of Refugees and Its 1967 Protocol: A Commentary* (OUP 2011) 441–42. The most comprehensive treatment in the English language literature is to be found in Hathaway and Foster (n 4) ch 1 on 'Alienage', 23–25. Both Eric Fripp, *Nationality and Statelessness in the International Law of Refugee Status* (Hart Publishing 2016), and Michelle Foster and Hélène Lambert, *International Refugee Law and the Protection of Stateless Persons* (OUP 2019) address the meaning of 'country of nationality' and 'country of former habitual residence', but barely touch on the 'outside' issues. That is also true of two recent articles by Eric Fripp: Eric Fripp, 'Nationality, Protection, and "the Country of His Nationality" as the Country of Reference for the Purposes of Article 1A(2) of the 1951 Convention Relating to the Status of Refugees' (2021) 33(2) IJRL 300; and Eric Fripp, 'Statelessness, Protection, and "the Country of his Former Habitual Residence" as Country of Reference for Purposes of Article 1A(2) Convention Relating to the Status of Refugees 1951' (2022) 34(4) IJRL 327.

Clearly the preposition 'outside' imposes a constraint. But whether it denotes a physical or territorial and/or jurisdictional separation—and/or whether it requires historic presence[7]—requires closer analysis.

The 1951 Convention relating to the Status of Refugees (Refugee Convention or CRSR)[8] and its 1967 Protocol relating to the Status of Refugees[9] is not alone in stipulating being 'outside the country' as an essential element of the definition.[10] So do the 1969 Convention Governing the Specific Aspects of Refugee Problems in Africa (OAU Convention),[11] and the 1984 Cartagena Declaration.[12]

It is against the 'outside the country' element of Article 1A(2) that critics of the Refugee Convention's limitations have directed their heaviest weaponry. It has been pointed out that by excluding from the scope *ratione loci* persons possessing all the characteristics of being a refugee but who have been unable to leave their country, the Convention has failed and continues to fail to address real needs.[13] It is complained that under the prevailing approach even those seeking to leave but actively prevented from doing so by their home state are excluded.[14] It has been pointed out that the number of internally displaced people (IDPs) exceeds that of refugees.[15] As explained

---

[7] Zimmermann and Mahler (n 6) 441 state that to be 'outside' a person must have 'cross[ed] the border of the respective home country'. Such a criterion would appear without justification to exclude persons who have acquired the nationality of a country *sur place* without ever having lived there: see below p. 264, p. 266, p. 268, and p. 271.

[8] Convention Relating to the Status of Refugees (adopted 28 July 1951, entered into force 22 April 1954) 189 UNTS 137.

[9] Protocol Relating to the Status of Refugees (adopted 31 January 1967, entered into force 4 October 1967) 606 UNTS 267.

[10] Luke T Lee, 'Internally Displaced Persons and Refugees: Toward a Legal Synthesis?' (1996) 9(1) Journal of Refugee Studies 27.

[11] Organization of African Unity (OAU), Convention Governing the Specific Aspects of Refugee Problems in Africa (adopted 10 September 1969, entered into force 20 June 1974) 1001 UNTS 45 (OAU Convention). Adopted by the Assembly of Heads of State and Government at its Sixth Ordinary Session in Addis-Ababa. The OAU became the African Union in 2002.

[12] *Instrumentos Regionales sobre Refugiados y temas relacionados, Declaración de Cartagena sobre Refugiados, Adoptado por el 'Coloquio Sobre la Protección Internacional de los Refugiados en América Central, México y Panamá: Problemas Jurídicos y Humanitarios'* (adopted 22 November 1984).

[13] See e.g. Lee (n 10); Hathaway and Foster (n 4) 21 cite, inter alia, James C Hathaway, 'Forced Migration Studies: Could We Agree Just to "Date"?' (2007) 20(3) Journal of Refugee Studies 349; Josh DeWind, 'Response to Hathaway' (2007) 20(3) Journal of Refugee Studies 381, 384. For a recent discussion of the literature, see Beaton (n 4). It has been much criticised in debates about the ethics of the refugee definition: see, in addition to Shacknove, e.g. Stephen R Perry, 'Immigration, Justice, and Culture' in Warren F Schwartz (ed), *Justice in Immigration* (CUP 1995) 94–135, 104; Matthew J Gibney, 'Liberal Democratic States and Responsibilities to Refugees' (1999) 93(1) American Political Science Review 169, 170–71; Joseph H Carens, *The Ethics of Immigration* (OUP 2013) 200–03; Matthew J Lister, 'Who Are Refugees?' (2013) 32(5) Law and Philosophy 645, 656–57; Serena Parekh, *Refugees and the Ethics of Forced Displacement* (Routledge 2017) 11–13; Eilidh Beaton, 'Against the Alienage Condition for Refugeehood' (2020) 39 Law and Philosophy 147; Elisabeth Brennen, 'RefLaw Primer: Alienage' (2021) RefLaw, available at <http://www.reflaw.org/?p=2765> accessed 22 April 2021. See further Chapter 1, sections 4.5 and 4.7.

[14] See e.g. Matthew E Price, *Rethinking Asylum History, Purpose, and Limits* (CUP 2010); Violeta Moreno-Lax, *Accessing Asylum in Europe: Extraterritorial Border Controls and Refugee Rights under EU Law* (OUP 2017).

[15] In 2021 UNHCR stated that globally there are 20,676,538 refugees under UNHCR's mandate, 4,176,545 asylum seekers, and 45,940,575 IDPs of concern to UNHCR. See UNHCR, Refugee Data Finder, available at <https://www.unhcr.org/refugee-statistics/download/?url=E1ZxP4> accessed 22 April 2021.

in Chapter 1, the primary focus of this study is how the existing refugee definition is to be interpreted, not to dwell on its perceived shortcomings. What must be engaged with, however, is whether, arising from these criticisms, there are valid reasons for interpreting the existing text differently.

## Ordering

It might be argued that the 'outside the country' requirements must necessarily be the first element of the refugee definition, since if persons are not outside it, they must fail for that reason, irrespective of whether they in fact have a well-founded fear of persecution for a Convention reason.[16] However, whilst this element clearly arises prior to any analysis of whether a person has a well-founded fear of being persecuted for a Convention reason, it would appear to be most appropriately tackled after the element of nationality (or lack of it), since it is only if there is a country of which an applicant is a national (or if stateless, a country in which he or she had former habitual residence) that it matters whether he or she is outside that country or not.

## Approach to Interpretation

One particular issue raised by this element of the definition is its suitability for an interpretation based primarily on context and object and purpose, given that (as we shall see) it has usually been seen as one element that (in whole or part) has an unambiguous ordinary meaning. On the basis of the analysis that follows, it remains essential to adopt an integrated approach to it taking into account ordinary meaning, context, object and purpose, alongside other VCLT rules.

## A Human Rights Approach

We have seen in the Chapter 4 that the meaning of the concepts of nationality and 'not having a nationality' as contained in relevant parts of Article 1A(2) is essentially informed by the international law governing nationality and statelessness, with only limited assistance to be derived from human rights norms. The analysis that follows indicates that in relation to the 'outside the country' element, human rights norms have an even more limited role. Although the Convention's object and purpose include respect for human rights, the meaning of both the 'outside the country' provisions can be derived without seeking to draw in any significant way on International Human Rights Law (IHRL) norms.

---

[16] See e.g. Jaeger (n 4) 5.

# 1 'Outside the Country'

The term 'outside the country' appears twice in Article 1A(2): once in relation to nationals and once in relation to stateless persons:

> [ ... ] is *outside the country of his nationality* and is unable, or owing to such fear, is unwilling to avail himself of the protection of that country; or who, not having a nationality and being *outside the country of his former habitual residence* ....[17]

Despite their parallel formulation, it cannot be assumed that the term 'country' in these two phrases has the same meaning. As explained in Chapter 4, the phrase 'country of nationality' clearly connotes the relationship between a national and a state (since only states can confer nationality).[18] By contrast, the term 'country' in the phrase 'country of ... former habitual residence' does not necessarily denote a state and even if the country in question is a state, those 'not having a nationality' do not have the same relationship with it as do nationals. Hence any analysis of the 'outside the country' element of the refugee definition must address the two phrases 'country of nationality', and 'country of ... habitual residence' separately to ascertain in each case what entity a person is required to be 'outside'.

# 2 'Outside the Country' and VCLT Rules

Let us consider the meaning of the key terms involved by reference to each of the main VCLT rules of interpretation. No specific sub-head is devoted to special meaning, as its relevance is more conveniently addressed when dealing with the other VCLT rules.

## 2.1 Background and *Travaux Préparatoires*

Previous refugee instruments referred to in Article 1A(1) were designed to ensure stable legal protection in the host country.[19] Unlike the Article 1A(2) definition, they did not textually apply any exclusive 'outside the country of origin' test. Concerning the 1933 Convention and its predecessors, Lee notes that 'the decisive criterion in determining the refugee status in all these definitions was the presence or lack of 'protection' by the Governments concerned'.[20]

There are differences over whether these instruments did not, however, implicitly require presence outside the country of origin. Goodwin-Gill, for example, has interpreted such outside presence as 'implicit in the objectives of the arrangements,

---

[17] Refugee Convention (n 8) Article 1A(2) (emphasis added). For the French text see Chapter 1, n 3. It also appears in Article 1F, in relation to serious non-political crimes.
[18] See Chapter 4, section 3.2.4.
[19] Claudena Skran, 'Historical Developments of International Refugee Law' in Zimmermann (n 6) 6–36.
[20] Lee (n 10) 31.

namely, the issue of identity certificates for the purpose of travel and resettlement'.[21] Contending otherwise, Lee argues, for example, that by pledging the contracting parties 'not to refuse entry to refugees at the frontiers of their countries of origin' (Article 3), the 1933 instrument 'confirmed the possibility that "refugees", like internally displaced persons, could also exist within the frontiers of their own country'.[22]

Lee also invokes the survey of the refugee question carried out by Hope Simpson in 1938 under the auspices of the Royal Institute of International Affairs which alluded to the 'many refugee movements of nationals both inside their own territory and into foreign territories'.[23] This definition included unsettled persons of Jewish origin or foreigners or stateless persons, who had resided in Germany or Austria, were victims of Nazi persecution, and were detained in Germany or Austria, even if they had never left Germany or Austria.[24]

Lee also points to a number of contemporary UN documents which did not differentiate between 'refugees' and 'internally displaced persons' and which regarded as refugees 'South Koreans driven from their homes as well as hundreds of thousands who had migrated southward seeking refuge within the area controlled by the United Nations Command forces'.[25] Clearly, however, the approach to internally displaced persons had changed by the time of the drafting of the 1951 Convention. Possibly a further background factor was that deliberations on its drafting took place at a time when the Cold War was taking hold and the crossing of the 'Iron Curtain' had become an issue.[26]

The International Refugee Organisation (IRO) Constitution required that a refugee be someone '*who has left, or who is outside of*, his country of nationality or of former habitual residence'.[27] Both these formulations envisage the necessity of physical separation from the country's territory.

Turning to the *travaux*, the early drafting of the 1951 Refugee Convention did not feature the term 'outside the country'; the favoured formulation was: 'has had to leave, shall leave or remains outside'. This wording presupposed previous departure from the

---

[21] Guy S Goodwin-Gill, *The Refugee in International Law* (1st edn, OUP 1983) 2–3. This view is maintained in Guy S Goodwin-Gill and Jane McAdam (with Emma Dunlop), *The Refugee in International Law* (4th edn, OUP 2021) 16.

[22] Lee (n 10) 31–32.

[23] John H Simpson, *Refugees: Preliminary Report of a Survey* (Royal Institute of International Affairs 1938) 4.

[24] Lee (n 10) 31–32.

[25] ibid 32. Lee cites UN Doc ST/DPI/SER.A/78 (29 September 1953) 14.

[26] ibid. Lee cites John R Bolton, 'Rethinking the Refugee Definition and the UN Role' (1992) The Second Annual Refugee Day, Office of the US Coordinator for Refugee Affairs, Department of State Publication 9952, 55–57.

[27] Constitution of the International Refugee Organization (IRO) (adopted 15 December 1946, entered into force 20 August 1948) 18 UNTS 3, Annex I, Part I, section A, para 1, provides that 'subject to the provisions of sections C and D and of Part II of this Annex, the term "refugee" applies to a person *who has left, or who is outside of*, his country of nationality or of former habitual residence' (emphasis added). However, there is some ambiguity as to whether paragraph 3 of the same section does not encompass certain persons who had not left or remained in Germany or Austria. It states that 'the term "refugee" also applies to persons who, having resided in Germany or Austria, and being of Jewish origin or foreigners or stateless persons, were victims of Nazi persecution and were detained in, or were obliged to flee from, and were subsequently returned to, one of those countries as a result of enemy action, or of war circumstances, and have not yet been firmly resettled therein'.

country of origin. However, this was replaced by the current text.[28] This change and the *travaux* discussions strongly suggest awareness on the drafters' part that a person could meet this requirement (at least in relation to a country of nationality) even if never having set foot in the country of origin.

The *travaux* also disclose that the drafters expressly rejected the notion that the refugee definition should cover 'internal refugees' (or 'national refugees' as they were also sometimes called). In response to a proposal made during a 1949 General Assembly meeting to consider including 'internal refugees', i.e. refugees who had not crossed a border, within the mandate of the proposed new refugee organisation, UNHCR, Eleanor Roosevelt stated that such persons' problems:

> [ ... ] should not be confused with the problem before the General Assembly, namely, the provision of protection for those outside their own countries, who lacked the protection of a Government and who required asylum and status in order that they might rebuild lives of self-dependence and dignity.[29]

There was clearly a concern that to include the internally displaced within the refugee definition might undermine the responsibility of their own country of care for their own population.[30]

The intention to confine assistance to those outside the country was confirmed by the observations made about the different situation of 'national refugees'. Reference was made to a number of examples of 'internal refugees' including Kashmiri and Indian refugees, mainland Chinese who had fled to modern-day Taiwan and the approximately eight million ethnic Germans from Central and Eastern Europe. In relation to the last-mentioned group, Henkin of the USA stated that his country considered them as 'normally under the jurisdiction of the German Government and it did not want to encourage that government to renounce all responsibility towards them by placing them under international protection.'[31]

During the Conference of Plenipotentiaries, Rochefort stated that the refugee definition was intended to exclude 'national refugees, such as those in Germany, India

---

[28] Zimmermann and Mahler (n 6) 326–27 note that in January 1950, during the 17th meeting of the Ad Hoc Committee on Statelessness and Related Problems, the suggestion of Mr Rain (France) that the paragraph should also include persons who had been outside the country before the persecution began was approved and included in the subsequent draft. The General assembly subsequently decided to drop the term 'leaving' altogether; and at the Conference of Plenipotentiaries (Conference of Plenipotentiaries on the Status of Refugees and Stateless Persons: Summary Record of the Twenty-third Meeting (26 November 1951) 8–10), 'the representative of Israel clarified that departure did not constitute a precondition for making a person a refugee'. At Zimmermann and Mahler (n 6) 442, they also refer in this connection to Report of the Ad Hoc Committee on Refugees and Stateless Persons, Second Session, Geneva, 14 August to 25 August 1950 (25 August 1950) UN Docs E/1850 and E/AC.32/8 (1950) 8. These considerations also represent strong grounding for acceptance of refugees *sur place*.

[29] Statement of Mrs Roosevelt of the United States, see 4 UN GAOR, Third Committee, Summary Records (2 December 1949) 110 (see also 473). See also the statement of Mr Henkin of the United States, available at Summary of the Committee Meeting of the Economic and Social Council, UN Doc E/AC.7/SR.160 (18 August 1950) 7.

[30] Hathaway and Foster (n 4) 18.

[31] See statement of Mr Henkin of the United States, UN Ad Hoc Committee on Statelessness and Related Problems, 1st Session, 5th Meeting (30 January 1950) UN Doc E/AC.32/SR.5, 5.

and Pakistan' as it was 'certain that the United Nations did not intend to include them in the refugee concept'.[32]

At a meeting of the Ad Hoc Committee established by ECOSOC, Rochefort (France) observed that:

> Whatever (definitional) formula might ultimately be chosen, it would not and could not in any event apply to internal refugees who were citizens of a particular country and enjoyed the protection of the government of that country. There was no general definition covering such refugees, since any such definition would involve an infringement of national sovereignty.[33]

Rochefort repeated the same point when arguing against the Belgian, Canadian, and Turkish draft.[34] Mrs Roosevelt likewise re-emphasised the point that it was only refugees who were outside their countries of origin who could be accorded protection 'under international auspices'.[35]

## 2.2 Good Faith

The 'good faith' element of Article 31 VCLT was seen by Lord Bingham in *Roma Rights* to have a bearing on the meaning of the 'outside' requirement. Citing ICJ authority for the proposition that the principle of good faith is not itself a source of obligation, he stated that it could not be used to read into the refugee definition an obligation to treat a state's borders as extending to another country with which it has an agreement to conduct pre-entry controls.[36]

## 2.3 Ordinary Meaning

In terms of ordinary meaning, the phrase 'outside the country of nationality' does not impose as a necessary condition that a person must have been inside that country in the past (by contrast, as is argued below, the wording of the phrase 'country of former habitual residence' manifestly does require historical presence, since its *sine qua non* is '*former* habitual residence'). Of course, typically, a person's claim for refugee status will be based on experiences or events that occurred in their country of origin, which means that he or she must have physically crossed the border of (or left a port or airport or other embarkation point in) their home country. Typically, also, such

---

[32] Conference of Plenipotentiaries on the Status of Refugees and Stateless Persons, Summary Record of the Twenty-fourth Meeting (27 November 1951) UN Doc A/CONF.2/SR.24, 17.

[33] Statement of Mr Rochefort of France in ECOSOC, Summary Record of the 172nd meeting held at the Palais des Nations, Geneva, on Saturday, 12 August 1950 (24 August 1950) UN Doc E/AC.7/SR.172, 98.

[34] See statement of Mr Rochefort of France in 5 UN GAOR (4 December 1950) 391, cited in Hathaway (n 4) 31.

[35] Statement of Mrs Roosevelt of the United States, 4 UN GAOR (29 November 1950) 363.

[36] *Regina v IO at Prague Airport and Another, ex parte European Roma Rights Centre* [2004] UKHL 5. See also *R (ST, Eritrea) v SSHD* [2012] UKSC 12, paras 30–31. See Chapter 2, section 2.2.

prior presence in the country of origin underlies even most claims raising a *sur place* element. For example, all three paragraphs of the 1979 UNHCR Handbook on refugees *sur place* claims (paras 94–96) are predicated on such prior presence. However, the 'outside the country' wording does not preclude refugees *sur place* who may not necessarily have ever lived in their country of origin before applying (e.g. if they were born in another state but acquired nationality of their country of origin by descent). Such scenarios have arisen in the case law.[37] Had the drafters intended to impose a requirement of historical presence and border-crossing, they could have used different words.[38]

The chosen formulation also avoids an applicant having to meet any presence or residence requirements in the country of *refuge*. Merely being 'outside' the country of origin is enough.

Reflecting the UNHCR Handbook, the broader jurisprudence and academic commentary,[39] Lord Bingham in *Roma Rights* considered that the phrase 'outside the country of nationality' to be unambiguous as a matter of ordinary meaning.[40] However, whilst as we have seen it is unambiguously the case that the country in this context can only be a state,[41] we also saw that the term 'nationality' lacks a clear, unambiguous ordinary meaning and requires interpretation taking into account its context, object and purpose, if not also its special meaning as a technical term in international law.[42] Further, in the context of this particular phrase—'outside the country of nationality'—because the entity involved can only be a state, it follows that the 'outside' element must mean outside of the territory of the state.

One of the essential components of statehood is a defined territory.[43] And, as correctly analysed by the UNHCR Handbook, territory in this context is a term that must be understood jurisdictionally. But that is already to acknowledge that 'territory' is also not a term that can be accorded a straightforward ordinary meaning, since it has several dictionary definitions, only one of which concerns territory as a legal status (the land or district lying round a city or town and under its jurisdiction).[44] Hence the phrase 'outside the country of nationality' cannot be accorded a straightforward ordinary meaning unless one assumes artificially that ordinary meaning is confined to a special meaning in international law. Interpreting the term thus requires recourse to context, object and purpose, and other VCLT considerations. Because the essence of the phrase depends on the meaning of 'nationality', and because the entity concerned can only be a state, its meaning must also derive from international law rules

---

[37] See e.g. *Dhoumo v Board of Immigration Appeals* [2005] 416 F.3d 172, which concerned the son of Tibetan parents of Chinese nationality born and raised in a refugee camp in India, cited by Hathaway and Foster (n 4) 52–53. There is also the phenomenon of stateless children who have never lived in their parent's country of former habitual residence, discussed below at section 3.4.

[38] See *MIMA v Khawar* [2002] 210 CLR 1 (Aus HC) para 62. Hathaway and Foster (n 4) 19 cite Jaeger (n 4) 5.

[39] See *Re MIMA; Ex parte Te* [2002] 212 CLR 162 (Aus HC); Guy S Goodwin-Gill and Jane McAdam, *The Refugee in International Law* (3rd edn, OUP 2007) 250.

[40] *Roma Rights* (n 36) para 16.

[41] '[T]he word "country" is used to designate a country capable of granting nationality', see *Tjhe Kwet Koe v MIEA* [1997] 78 FCR 289 (Aus FC), as cited by Hathaway and Foster (n 4) 53; see also Bolton (n 26).

[42] See Chapter 4, section 3.2.8.

[43] James R Crawford, *Brownlie's Principles of Public International Law* (9th edn, OUP 2019) 118–19.

[44] OED Online, accessed March 2021. The second meaning given is '[a] rising ground, hill, or eminence'.

governing the territorial jurisdiction of a state.[45] Identifying the defined territory of a state may not always be straightforward (e.g. when borders are disputed or when the country has had its territorial borders altered), but any difficulties must be resolved applying the rules of international law, as analysed in Chapter 4.

On analysis of the phrase 'outside the country of nationality', therefore, it is only really the preposition 'outside' that (applying an integrated approach) can be ascribed an ordinary meaning. Once the preposition 'outside' is considered in relation to its object—'country of nationality'—its meaning requires to be shaped significantly more by context, object and purpose, if not other VCLT considerations.

## 2.4 Context

It is possible to argue that the placement of the words '... owing to such fear' after the adverb 'outside' suggests that being outside has to be the result of an event occurring inside the home country giving rise to a 'well-founded fear of being persecuted'. If that is so, that could be said to point to the definition requiring past presence in the home state. However, such an interpretation would in effect require an unwarranted reading of the definition as an historic test of past persecution (see Chapter 6, section 4.1) and would in addition negate the well-established possibility of a sur place claim (see Chapter 6, section 4.2).

Bearing in mind that the 'context' includes other provisions of a treaty, it is relevant to consider three other provisions in the Refugee Convention namely Article 1A(1) (which identifies as one category of refugee those who were considered as a refugee under specified predecessor instruments), Article 1C, and Article 33(1). As to the first-mentioned, we have already noted that the IRO Constitution also (seemingly) made 'outside ... the country' a prerequisite of refugee status.[46] It is unlikely that the drafters intended 'outside' in Article 1A(2) to be interpreted any differently.

Article 1C contains cessation provisions that contemplate that a refugee may return to their country of origin (without necessarily ceasing to be a refugee),[47] but the alternative wording of Article 1C(4) ('He has voluntarily established himself in the country which he left *or* outside of which he remained owing to fear of persecution'(emphasis added)) implies that being 'outside' is a wider term than having left, and thereby lends some support for understanding the category of refugee as capable of including those who have never lived in their country of origin.

As regards other provisions of the treaty, the greatest attention has been paid to Article 33(1) which provides that:

> 1. No Contracting State shall expel or return *('refouler')* a refugee in any manner whatsoever to the frontiers of territories where his life or freedom would be

---

[45] Crawford (n 43) 192–230, 118.
[46] IRO Constitution (n 27) provides that 'subject to the provisions of sections C and D and of Part II of this Annex, the term "refugee" applies to a person *who has left, or who is outside of*, his country of nationality or of former habitual residence' (emphasis added).
[47] Refugee Convention (n 8) Article 1C(1) and 1C(4).

threatened on account of his race, religion, nationality, membership of a particular social group or political opinion.[48]

Two aspects of this provision have a potential bearing, notwithstanding that it is only concerned with those who are refugees (or still within the application process). First of all, there is the question of whether the reference to 'frontiers of territories' corresponds to the two entities identified in Article 1A(2) ('country of nationality' and 'country of... former habitual residence'). Secondly, there is the question of whether it is capable of having extra-territorial application and in this way making it possible for a person still inside their country of origin to meet the 'outside the country' requirements of Article 1A(2)—by applying for asylum within the diplomatic mission or other legation of a potential host country (usually referred to as 'diplomatic asylum'). Given its complex nature, the issue of possible extraterritorial application is dealt with in section 5 below.

As regards the choice on the part of the drafters to refer to 'frontiers of territories' in Article 33(1), it can possibly[49] be said to shed some limited light on the 'outside the country' phrases set out in Article 1A(2), in that the wording of Article 33(1) is clearly broader. Whereas in Article 1A(2) the focus is exclusively on protecting against return to the country/countries of origin in which a person has a well-founded fear of being persecuted for a Convention reason, in Article 33(1) the focus is on return to anywhere in the world.[50] The drafters were clearly concerned to ensure the universal scope of the non-refoulement obligation and to prevent indirect as well as direct *refoulement*. In addition, use of 'territories' rather than states or 'countries' suggests that what is in contemplation is the physical fact of territory, not the legal status of the place.[51] It will be argued below that, by contrast, even though the term 'country of... former habitual residence' can cover countries other than states, it cannot be understood in the purely physical sense of an(y) area of territory.

---

[48] Refugee Convention (n 8) Article 33(1).

[49] This possibility assumes that Article 33 of the Refugee Convention can be understood as relevant to the meaning of Article 1A(2), a matter that has not been universally accepted: see e.g. UK House of Lords in *Revenko v SSHD* [2000] EWCA Civ 500, para 113.

[50] '[T]he principle of non-refoulement applies not only in respect of the country of origin but to any country where a person has reason to fear persecution', see UNHCR, Note on Non-Refoulement (Submitted by the High Commissioner) (23 August 1977) EC/SCP.2. See also Elihu Lauterpacht and Daniel Bethlehem, 'The Scope and Content of the Principle of Non-Refoulement: Opinion' in Erika Feller, Volker Türk, and Frances Nicholson (eds), *Refugee Protection in International Law: UNHCR's Global Consultations on International Protection* (CUP 2003) para 114.

[51] Lauterpacht and Bethlehem (n 50); Goodwin-Gill and McAdam (n 39) 250; Wouters (n 6) 134. Walter Kälin, Martina Caroni, and Lukas Heim, 'Article 33, para 1' in Zimmermann (n 6) 1380-01; Goodwin-Gill and McAdam (n 39) point out that the original text read 'to the frontiers of their country of origin, or to territories'. They comment: '[p]resumably because the term "territories" also encompassed the "country of origin", the UK delegation proposed the simpler formulation "to the frontiers of territories", noting that "the amendment would not alter the purport" of the paragraph', see UN Ad Hoc Committee on Refugees and Stateless Persons, Ad Hoc Committee on Statelessness and Related Problems, First Session: Summary Record of the Twentieth Meeting Held at Lake Success, New York, on Wednesday, 1 February 1950, at 2.30 p.m. (10 February 1950) E/AC.32/SR.20, para 7.

## 2.5 Object and Purpose

The requirement for refugees to be persons 'outside' their country of nationality can be said to reflect the underlying purpose of ensuring that the refugee definition does not violate the principle of state sovereignty.[52] This principle is integral to the UN Charter and has as one of its essential elements, territorial sovereignty.

The concern to respect state sovereignty that lies behind the phrase 'outside the country' can also be seen as an expression of the principle of surrogacy.[53] It is only when a person is outside the territory of his or her state that the international community can consider them to be in a position to require protection as a substitute for that which their home state has failed to afford them. This understanding is reinforced by the statement set out at paragraph 88 of the 1979 Handbook that: '[i]nternational protection cannot come into play as long as a person is within the territorial jurisdiction of his home country'.[54]

Both these principles can be seen at work in the reasoning of the International Court of Justice in the *Asylum* case.[55] The Court saw the granting of territorial asylum as a 'normal exercise of the territorial sovereignty', specifically because the 'refugee is outside the territory of the State where the offence was committed, and a decision to grant him asylum in no way derogates from the sovereignty of that State'.[56]

Following from the fact that by the term 'country of nationality' the refugee definition clearly has in mind a state (or more precisely an entity capable of conferring nationality), it is necessary for an applicant to establish that he or she is 'outside' the state in international law terms. That means that a person is not 'outside' his country if he or she is still within the territorial waters or airspace of his/her state.[57] By the same token, it is not necessary for an applicant to show they have arrived in another country. Nor does the 'outside' element exclude persons who have reached land or territory that is not part of either their own state or any other state.[58] No obvious object or purpose

---

[52] SS 'Lotus', France v Turkey (Judgment) [1935] PCIJ Series A No 10, 18–19. See Hathaway (n 4) 31.

[53] See further Chapter 7, section 1.4.

[54] UNHCR Handbook (n 1); see also *Roma Rights* (n 36).

[55] *Asylum (Colombia v Peru)* (Judgment) [1950] ICJ 6, 274; see also *Haya de la Torre Case (Colombia v Peru)*, Merits [1951] ICJ Rep 71.

[56] The right to territorial asylum is also derived from the fundamental principle that the state has an exclusive right to exercise jurisdiction over individuals present in its territory (excluding individuals having jurisdictional immunity, e.g. diplomatic agents). The United Nations General Assembly has stated that the granting of asylum is a peaceful and humanitarian act, a normal exercise of state sovereignty, and that it should be respected by all other states. See UNGA, Declaration on Territorial Asylum (14 December 1967) UN Doc A/RES/2312(XXII).

[57] In the maritime environment, under the international law of the sea, no state has jurisdiction on the 'high seas', see United Nations Convention on the Law of the Sea (adopted 10 December 1982, entered into force 16 November 1994) 1833 UNTS 3, Articles 87(1) and 89 (UNCLOS); see also International Convention on Maritime Search and Rescue (adopted 27 April 1979, entered into force 22 June 1985) 1405 UNTS 119. In relation to territory, the fact that a person has boarded a ship having the (different) nationality exhibited by the flag it is entitled to fly does not mean they left the territory of their country of origin, since the ship remains under the jurisdiction of the country of origin. The same applies to persons who have boarded an aircraft registered in a country other than the state from which departure is pending. See further UNGA, Question of Diplomatic Asylum. Report of the Secretary-General (22 September 1975) available at <https://www.unhcr.org/en-ie/protection/historical/3ae68bf10/question-diplomatic-asylum-report-secretary-general.html> accessed 23 April 2021. See further Goodwin-Gill and McAdam (4th edn) (n 21) 329–49.

[58] Zimmermann and Mahler (n 6) 442.

would be served either by excluding from the 'outside' category those who have never lived in their own state.

A further purpose served by investing the phrase 'outside the country of nationality' with a meaning in terms of territorial jurisdiction is that it reinforces understanding of the Refugee Convention as a system intended to afford remedies to persons disadvantaged by the fact of being outside their own country.[59] In this regard, 'the alienage requirement ensures a match between the beneficiary class and the remedy provided by the Convention.'[60] This important feature of the Convention operates both to support a 'systematic' reading of the Convention (that is, looking internally and in this context taking Article 1A(2) in conjunction with Articles 2–34) and an object and purpose approach.

The relevant object(s) and purpose(s) underlying the term 'outside' in the phrase 'outside the country of former habitual residence' will be considered separately below.

## 2.6 Article 31(3) and Other VCLT Considerations

Assuming that unchallenged provisions of the 1979 Handbook continue to constitute either a 'subsequent agreement' or 'practice' within the meaning of Article 31(3), and/or state practice in the broad sense under Article 32,[61] its clear position—that the phrase 'outside the country of nationality' has to be applied as a territorial criterion—has already been outlined. No subsequent UNHCR materials have contradicted that.

The development of separate international arrangements for internally displaced persons since the coming into force of the 1951 Convention and its 1967 Protocol can be said to confirm that the international community never regarded the Article 1A(2) definition as covering them. This is further borne out by the UNGA measures taken from 1972 onwards to give UNHCR an extra-Convention mandate to provide material assistance to various groups of refugees within their national boundaries.[62]

The international jurisprudence has consistently proceeded on the assumption that 'outside the country' is to be construed in line with the 1979 UNHCR Handbook understanding.[63]

As already intimated, academic sources have been predominantly of one mind on this basic point, although, as already noted, not always considering that being 'outside' presupposes previous presence. In 1966 Grahl-Madsen stated that:

> The phrase 'is outside' means the same as the previous more elaborate draft phrase: 'has had to leave, shall leave or remains outside'. The chosen phrase consequently includes persons who have fled from their home country ('escapees') as well as those who have become refugees sur place....[64]

---

[59] See Hathaway and Foster (n 4) 20.
[60] ibid 22.
[61] See Chapter 2, n 69.
[62] See Chapter 1, n 71.
[63] Hathaway and Foster (n 4) 19, cite *Roma Rights* (n 36) and the Australian High Court case of *Khawar* (n 38) para 62.
[64] Grahl-Madsen (n 6) 151.

Zimmermann and Mahler, however, appear to confine the class to those who have left.[65] The role within Article 32 VCLT of the *travaux* was addressed earlier.[66]

## 3 'Outside the Country of Former Habitual Residence'

In turning to consider the preposition 'outside' within the phrase 'outside the country of former habitual residence', it is evident that, at least in the abstract, the country concerned is a different legal animal from 'country of nationality'. As we have seen, nationality denotes the legal bond between the individual and the state and gives rise to both rights and obligations specific to those possessing this status. Former habitual residence, by contrast, carries no parallel sets of rights and obligations.

### 3.1 Background and *Travaux Préparatoires*

In both the 1946 Constitution of the IRO, the draft Convention appended to the Report of the Ad Hoc Committee on Statelessness and Related Problems of 17 February 1950[67] and in the definition of refugee set out in the December 1950 Statute of the United Nations High Commissioner for Refugees,[68] the term 'country of former habitual residence' was used for those without a nationality in order to establish the country of reference for purposes of status determination. In its note to the Draft Convention, the Ad Hoc Committee on Statelessness and Related Problems stated that the phrase 'country of former habitual residence' meant, 'the country in which he had resided and where he has suffered or fears he would suffer persecution if returned'.[69]

From the *travaux* can be gleaned that the drafters considered the phrase 'country of former habitual residence' to be closely tied to the preceding phrase 'or, who not having a nationality'.[70]

The *travaux* lend particular support for the view that 'country of ... former habitual residence' was intended to have a wider meaning than state. Precisely how much wider is less clear. Hathaway and Foster consider that the countries the drafters had in mind were those that were either states or had the attributes of states.[71] Stateless persons

---

[65] Zimmermann and Mahler (n 6). That is also the position seemingly enjoined by the text of Article 5 of the Directive 2011/95/EU of the European Parliament and of the Council of 13 December 2011 on standards for the qualification of third-country nationals or stateless persons as beneficiaries of international protection, for a uniform status for refugees or for persons eligible for subsidiary protection, and for the content of the protection granted (recast) [2011] OJ L 337, which concerns international protection needs arising *sur place*. Paragraph (1) refers to 'events which have taken place since the applicant left the country of origin'. Paragraph (2) contains similar wording.
[66] See above section 2.1.
[67] UN Ad Hoc Committee on Statelessness and Related Problems, Report of the Ad Hoc Committee on Statelessness and Related Problems (17 February 1950) UN Docs E/1618 and E/AC.32/5.
[68] See Chapter 1 section 2.2.
[69] Ad Hoc Committee on Statelessness and Related Problems, Comments of the Committee on the Draft Convention (10 February 1950) UN Doc E/AC.32/L.32/Add.1.
[70] Ad Hoc Committee on Statelessness and Related Problems, Ad Hoc Committee on Statelessness and Related Problems, Memorandum from the Secretariat of the International Refugee Organisation (30 January 1950) UN Doc E/AC.32/1/16, 3, cited in Hathaway and Foster (n 4) 68.
[71] Hathaway and Foster (n 4) 67.

who have resided in their country of origin for a significant period of time could be said to 'have acquired *prima facie* the effective nationality of the host state'.[72] Whilst Hathaway and Foster may be right that the drafters had in mind the countries to which stateless person could be said to have an analogous tie of allegiance, it is less clear that such countries can be states only.

3.1.1 Habitual residence
The drafters' understanding of the expression 'habitual residence' is most conveniently addressed when discussing Article 31(3) VCLT considerations.

## 3.2 Ordinary Meaning

Whereas (as we have seen) the phrase 'outside the country of nationality' does not impose as a necessary condition that a person must have been inside that country in the past, the same does not apply, at least as a matter of textual construction, to the phrase 'outside the country of ... former habitual residence'. The literal wording of the latter manifestly requires historical (even if not immediate past) presence, since its *sine qua non* is '*former habitual* residence' (precisely what is meant by such residence will be addressed later).

Can, however, the term 'country' in the phrase 'country of ... former habitual residence' be said to possess a clear ordinary meaning? As with the word 'country' in 'country of nationality', it is hard to discern an ordinary meaning *simpliciter*, since both the term 'country' and the expression 'former habitual residence' lack a clear unambiguous ordinary meaning and so their interpretation too requires recourse to context, object and purpose, and other VCLT rules of interpretation. As regards dictionary definitions, they include but are not limited to the state. Other meanings given by the OED Online, for example, include: '[t]he land of a person's birth, citizenship, residence, etc.; one's homeland'; '[l]and, terrain, or a region of undefined extent, esp. considered with regard to its physical characteristics'; and '[a]n area of land of defined extent characterized by its human occupants or boundaries; a district or administrative region, typically one smaller than a nation or state'.[73] In each of these definitions entities such as Scotland in the United Kingdom and Catalonia in Spain and South Ossetia in Georgia are countries, albeit not states. Further, unlike the term 'country of nationality', the term 'country of ... former habitual residence' does not have a clear reference point for possibly investing it with a special or technical meaning, based on rules relating to the territorial jurisdiction of states. In contrast to the phrase 'country of nationality', there is no overt limit on the type of country that can be involved (except for it being necessary that it is for the applicant, their country of former habitual residence). As Tamberlin J stated in *Tjhe Kwet Koe v MIEA*:

> The language of Article 1A of the Convention itself draws a distinction between 'the country of nationality' and 'the country of former habitual residence'. The word

---
[72] Crawford (n 43) 521, cited by Hathaway and Foster (n 4) 66.
[73] OED Online, accessed 23 April 2021.

'country' in each of these expressions is used in a different sense. In the first phrase it is used to designate a country capable of granting nationality. In the second it is used to denote a country which need not have this capability but in which the individual resides. The concept of 'country' is broader than the concept of a State.[74]

According to Tamberlin J, a person's 'country of ... former habitual residence' need not be a state and the term 'country' within that phrase must be interpreted differently from 'country' in the phrase 'country of ... nationality'.

3.2.1 Habitual residence
Turning to the term 'habitual residence', it has a long vintage in international law.[75] The 1979 Handbook contains no analysis of its meaning, but appears at paragraph 103 to regard its correct definition to be that given by the drafters of the 1951 Convention (who, as we saw, defined country of former habitual residence as 'the country in which he had resided and where he had suffered or fears he would suffer persecution if returned').[76]

Almost self-evidently, the term 'habitual residence' is extremely flexible and has no specific, unambiguous ordinary meaning. Commentators on use of the term in the Hague Convention on International Child Abduction have noted that '[t]o preserve this versatility the Hague Conference has continually declined to countenance the incorporation of a definition'.[77] However, the Refugee Convention applies the descriptor 'former'. Its plain meaning (as noted earlier) unambiguously connotes an historical, past presence of some kind.

The significance or otherwise of the fact that the word 'country' is cast in the singular will be considered separately below when examining the issue of whether there can be multiple countries of former habitual residence.

## 3.3 Context

The word 'country' appears fifty-seven times in the Refugee Convention. It is qualified by words such as 'nationality', 'habitual residence', 'lawful residence', 'residence', and 'domicile'. According to the Australian case of *BZAAH*, its meaning must therefore be constant and the change in application 'comes via the qualifying words'.[78] However, this suggests an approach too wooden to comply with VCLT rules, which require an integrated approach to interpretation.

---

[74] *Tjhe Kwet Koe v MIEA* (n 41).
[75] Hathaway and Foster (n 4) 67, citing Paul R Beaumont and Peter E McEleavy, *The Hague Convention on International Child Abduction* (OUP 1999) 88, who trace its first use to the bilateral treaties of the 1880s. According to the Council of Europe Convention on the avoidance of statelessness in relation to State succession (adopted 19 May 2006, entered into force 1 May 2009) CETS No 200, Article 1, the term indicates a 'stable factual residence'; and does not imply a legal or formal qualification. See also Explanatory Report to the Council of Europe Convention on the avoidance of statelessness in relation to State succession (19 May 2006) para 10.
[76] UNHCR Handbook (n 1).
[77] Beaumont and McEleavy (n 75) 89, cited by Hathaway and Foster (n 4) 68.
[78] *BZAAH v MIC* [2013] FCAFC 72, para 40.

### 3.3.1 Habitual residence

The concept of 'habitual residence' is also used in articles other than Article 1A(2). Articles 12, 14, and 16 refer to the refugee's 'habitual residence'/'*résidence habituelle*'. No light is shed by Articles 14 and 16 on the meaning of the phrase in Article 1A(2), but Article 12(1) can be said to provide some insight since it juxtaposes the concepts of 'domicile' and 'residence': it provides that the personal status of a refugee 'shall be governed by the law of the country of his domicile, or, if he has no domicile, by the law of the country of his residence'.[79]

The Convention's provisions at Articles 2–34 demonstrate a clear understanding that in some contexts there can be a requirement for *lawful* residence or stay (e.g. Articles 10, 17, 18, 19, 21, 23, 24, 26, 28). By contrast, the term 'country of ... former habitual residence' contains no condition that the residence be lawful.

## 3.4 Object and Purpose

Reference was made when considering ordinary meaning to the reasoning of Tamberlin, J in *Tjhe Kwet Koe v MIEA* that '[t]o approach the term "country" in a narrow technical way would undermine the humanitarian purposes of the Convention by excluding some persons from its protection without any sound reason in principle for so doing'.[80] His conclusion that Hong Kong (although not a sovereign state) was the claimant's country of former habitual residence rested on a context, object and purpose approach to interpretation. Likewise, the United Kingdom's Immigration Appeals Tribunal (UKIAT) in *Dag*[81] felt it necessary to construe the phrase 'outside the country of ... former habitual residence' by applying a purposive approach. When considering whether Northern Cyprus could be a country of former habitual residence, it reasoned that:

> If the Convention is to be universal in application, it must be capable of affording protection to all those who cannot avail themselves of protection in the part of the world from which they come (to use a neutral phrase). It does so by providing a definition of refugee that applies to those of several nationalities, of one nationality, and of no nationality. But, even for those in the last category, there remains a condition, which is that the applicant establish (broadly speaking) a well-founded fear of persecution in the relevant part of the world. It cannot have been intended that those whose home is a part of the world that cannot formally claim to be a 'country' should be for this reason excluded from the benefits of the Convention. 'Country of ... former habitual residence' must therefore be capable of being understood to include not only a State of which the claimant could have been a national, but also a territory area whose status is in that sense doubtful.

---

[79] Refugee Convention (n 8) Article 12(1).
[80] *Tjhe Kwet Koe* (n 41).
[81] *Dag (Nationality, Country of Habitual Residence, TRNC)* [2001] UKIAT 2, para 31.

Having given as examples Hong Kong (governed from the United Kingdom at the time when *Tjhe Kwet Koe* was decided) and Bosnia-Herzegovina and Croatia (during the period prior to the breakup of the Socialist Republic of Yugoslavia), the UKIAT concluded:

> In the interests of universality, the phrase 'country of ... former habitual residence' must even be capable of applying to a new island arising in the sea, although, as Justinian points out, 'this rarely happens'.[82]

Nevertheless, whilst the argument for construing the term 'country' in the phrase 'country of ... former habitual residence' in a broad sense is compelling, it must be doubted that it encompasses any area of territory. At least applying an *eiusdem generis* approach, there must be something in common between the two entities concerned— country of nationality (state) and country of former habitual residence. Being an island in the sea would not in itself be enough. As noted earlier, the wording in Article 1A(2) is different from that employed in Article 33(1). In the latter, the drafters identified 'frontiers of territories' in a manner indicative that they wished to provide protection against refoulement physically anywhere in the world. Applying an object and purpose approach, the common strand in the Article 1A(2) context would appear to be that the country is one over which there is some authority exercising territorial control, since the internal protection component of the 'being persecuted' element of the refugee definition sets the task for a stateless person, just as much as a national, as being to establish that they cannot seek the protection of their country of origin.[83] Unless there is some authority exercising territorial control, there can be no ability to protect. Another possible consideration is that if the preposition 'outside' is to have an object which is easily identifiable in international law terms, that requires reference to an entity with territorial jurisdiction. It would be odd indeed if within the same definition 'outside' were to be read as requiring physical absence from the territory of a country (the latter being understood in jurisdictional terms) in one context but not in another.

Viewing 'country' as needing to be state-like (in at least having an authority exercising territorial control) could also be said to be indicated by the principle of surrogacy. In broad terms, this principle requires that stateless persons cannot qualify as refugees unless able to show that there is a failure of protection by the country to which they belong. Clearly such failure cannot be identical with that which may arise with nationals,[84] but even as stateless persons they are entitled to protection applying IHRL norms and (as will be analysed in Chapter 7) for *both* nationals and stateless persons, it is IHRL norms that govern the contents of that protection.[85] The impact on stateless persons of persecutory harm must be to deny them benefits akin to those possessed by nationals. As put by Hathaway and Foster, therefore, 'the fact of habitual

---

[82] ibid para 34.

[83] Notwithstanding that for stateless persons there is no availment of protection clause: see Chapter 9, section 1.

[84] For this reason Fripp (2022) (n 6) 330 considers that 'the concept of surrogate protection is less easy to apply directly in the case of stateless claimants'.

[85] On this point, I differ from Fripp (2022) (n 6) 330–31.

residence is understood to give rise to a bond between the stateless individual and a state that approximates in critical respects the relationship between a citizen and her state'.[86]

As with the term 'the country of nationality', the need for an object and purpose approach to interpreting the meaning of the phrase 'country of ... former habitual residence' is reinforced by the fact that most of the rights set out in Articles 2–34 were 'designed to compensate them for the traditional disadvantages of their alien status.... [T]hey are directly related to the predicament of being outside one's country of origin'.[87] They are (almost all) unrelated to the fact that the recipients possess or do not possess a nationality.

### 3.4.1 Habitual residence

The expression 'habitual residence' can be said to reflect a concern that there be more than a fleeting or transient connection with the country concerned.

It remains to consider whether the condition of being a country of *former* habitual residence' can be interpreted differently from this term's ordinary meaning, which is seemingly unambiguous in requiring previous residence. In a call in 2014 for comments on draft Guidelines on International Protection No 13 on 'the meaning of the phrase "former habitual residence" in Article 1A(2) of the 1951 Convention relating to the Status of Refugees as regards family members of stateless refugees born in the country of asylum', UNHCR attached a draft document which stated that:

> In order to give effect to the intention of the drafters of the 1951 Convention, which included affording protection to stateless refugees and their stateless refugee children, the object and purpose of the Convention and the legal principles of non-discrimination and family unity, and taking into account the realities of stateless refugee situations in which children are born in exile, UNHCR considers that the only interpretation of 'country of former habitual residence' for children born to stateless refugees is that their 'country of former habitual residence' is that of their parents.[88]

In consequence, the draft states that 'the only possible reading and application of the second sentence of Article 1A(2)—and to give effect to the object and purpose of the Convention—is to read the phrase as 'outside the country of former habitual residence of their parents'.[89] The draft argues that to do otherwise would lead to the unfavourable treatment of stateless refugee children compared with non-stateless refugee children, as for the latter, no distinction is made as to their place of birth. In relation to the

---

[86] Hathaway and Foster (n 4) 67. However, as argued earlier in this section, 'country' in this context does not necessarily have to be a state. Within EU law also, 'country' is a wider term than state: see e.g. Case C-632/20P *Kingdom of Spain v EU*, 17 Jan 2023 para 50.

[87] Hathaway and Foster (n 4) 21.

[88] UNHCR, Protection—Call for comments on: Guidelines on International Protection No 11: Prima facie recognition of refugee status (2014) para 2, available at <https://www.unhcr.org/544f5b0b6.pdf> accessed 23 April 2021.

[89] ibid.

principle of family unity, the draft considers this should be applied so that it protects the links between refugee parents and their children.

Whilst UNHCR did not proceed with this draft (and there are no longer current plans for Guidelines on this issue), Foster and Lambert in their 2019 book contend that there is 'limited authority for the proposition that in very particular circumstances a state may be properly understood as constituting a country of "former habitual residence" where it can be said that such a country is "the centre of [a person's] interests", although that person has not in fact resided there'.[90] They aver that:

> While this is difficult to reconcile with the ordinary meaning of 'residence', there is a convincing purposive argument that where an applicant has a right to return and reside in a state, the risk of being persecuted must be assessed in relation to that state in order to avoid a violation of the principle of non-refoulement. This is particularly the case in relation to stateless children born abroad who may be returned to their parents' country of former habitual residence even though they have never resided there. In such a context the Australian courts have accepted that where a child is born in Australia and 'had no nationality or country of former habitual residence, it was appropriate, sensible, practical and fair' to consider her or his claims against the country to which she may be returned, typically the parents' country of former habitual residence or nationality.[91]

Such a highly purposive reading, however, is one that would appear to go well beyond VCLT rules since, as noted earlier, the adjectives 'former' and 'habitual' in the phrase 'country of former habitual residence' plainly appear as a matter of ordinary meaning to require past physical presence. Further, whilst the drafters had as one of their objectives the protection of stateless persons, they did not intend to ensure that in unqualified terms. Limiting the personal scope to those with particular types of connection with a country of reference could also be said to be part of that purpose.

It cannot be denied that the situation of stateless children born in a host state is anomalous. The position taken here is that on a proper construction of the Article 1A(2) definition, they cannot establish a country of reference. If they do not fall within the Article 1A(2) definition, then they cannot come within the scope of Article 33(1). That said, international law does not leave them entirely unprotected. By virtue of the non-refoulement principle contained in IHRL, the host state cannot remove such a child to his or her parents' country of origin if that will contravene fundamental human rights, including the prohibition of ill-treatment and the right to respect for family life. Furthermore, state practice in applying family reunification principles and

---

[90] Foster and Lambert (n 6) 136–37.
[91] ibid 137. They cite French case *GRF(re)*, Nos AAO-0145, AAO-01462, AAO-01463 [2001] CRDD No 88; an Australian tribunal case, *1617142* (Refugee) [2017] AATA 990, para 56; *SZEOH v Minister for Immigration* [2005] FMCA 1178, para 9; and *Refugee Appeal No 73512* [2003] NZRSAA 7 (13 January 2003). See also *BV(Malaysia)* [2021] NZIPT 801914-916, [112]–[142]. A similar view is espoused by Sharelle Anne Aitchison, see Sharelle Anne Aitchison, 'A Teleological and Child-Sensitive Interpretation of a Country of Former Habitual Residence for Stateless Children Born Outside Their Parents' Country of Nationality or Former Habitual Residence' (2022) 4 Statelessness and Citizenship Review 7, 8. See further Fripp (2022) (n 6) 349, who considers this view inconsistent with Article 31 VCLT.

treating children as dependants can mean that stateless children's country of reference is effectively assimilated to that of their parents.[92]

## 3.5 Article 31(3) and Other VCLT Considerations

Recalling that the International Covenant on Civil and Political Rights (ICCPR) is among the treaties 'cognate' to the Refugee Convention, it is significant that the Human Rights Committee has stated, in relation to Article 12(4) of that Covenant (which stipulates that '[n]o one shall be arbitrarily deprived of the right to enter his own country'), that:

> The scope of 'his own country' is broader than the concept 'country of his nationality'. It is not limited to nationality in a formal sense, that is, nationality acquired at birth or by conferral; it embraces, at the very least, an individual who, because of his or her special ties to or claims in relation to a given country, cannot be considered to be a mere alien. This would be the case, for example, of nationals of a country who have there been stripped of their nationality in violation of international law, and of individuals whose country of nationality has been incorporated in or transferred to another national entity, whose nationality is being denied them. The language of article 12, paragraph 4, moreover, permits a broader interpretation that might embrace other categories of long-term residents, including but not limited to stateless persons arbitrarily deprived of the right to acquire the nationality of the country of such residence. Since other factors may in certain circumstances result in the establishment of close and enduring connections between a person and a country, States parties should include in their reports information on the rights of permanent residents to return to their country of residence.[93]

As noted earlier, the 1979 UNHCR Handbook at paragraph 101 saw fit to vindicate the definition of 'country of ... former habitual residence' given by the Ad Hoc Committee on Statelessness and Related Problems in the *travaux*, namely 'the country in which the person has resided and where he or she had suffered or fears he or she would suffer, persecution if returned thereto'.[94] We have already referred to paragraph 103 of the 1979 Handbook. However, neither in this or any other paragraphs pertaining to this part of the definition is there any elucidation of the meaning of the term 'outside' in this context. The Handbook does not seek to define the term 'habitual residence'.

The case law broadly supports the view that country of former habitual residence does not have to be a state. Reference has already been made to the Australian case of *Tjhe Kwet Koe* and the UK tribunal case of *Dag*.[95] Fripp has pointed out that this

---

[92] See further UNHCR, Guidelines on Statelessness No 4: Ensuring Every Child's Right to Acquire a Nationality through Articles 1–4 of the 1961 Convention on the Reduction of Statelessness (21 December 2012) UN Doc HCR/GS/12/04.
[93] UN Human Rights Committee (HRC), CCPR General Comment No 27: Article 12 (Freedom of Movement) (2 November 1999) UN Doc CCPR/C/21/Rev.1/Add.9, para 20.
[94] Ad Hoc Committee on Statelessness and Related Problems (n 67) 39, cited in Zimmermann and Mahler (n 6) 462.
[95] See pp. 275–276.

is also the position reflected in numerous United Kingdom decisions concerning Palestinians from the Occupied Palestinian Territories.[96] The French Cour Nationale du Droit d'Asile (CNDA) took a similar view of the term 'country' in a 2012 decision,[97] concerning a stateless person who had lived in Algeria but within a camp under the control of the partially recognised Sahrawi Arab Democratic Republic; and also in a 2014 decision[98] finding that the applicant's country of former habitual residence was Gaza which was under the exercise and control of the Palestinian Authority, albeit that Authority lacked the attributes of a state such as granting of nationality. However, the case law is not entirely unanimous, for example the Australian Federal Court case of *BZAAH* equates 'country' with 'state'.[99]

In terms of academic sources, whilst the predominant view appears to be that 'country' in this context is not confined to entities that are states,[100] some commentators equate them.[101] Others, Foster and Lambert for example, express concerns about treating 'country of ... former habitual residence' *eiusdem generis* with state. They consider that Hathaway's statement in *The Law of Refugee Status* that 'the stateless person must stand in a relationship to a state which is broadly comparable to the relationship between a citizen and her country of nationality'[102] risks adoption of the wrong test. On the other hand, the *eiusdem generis* principle does ensure focus is placed on the fact of both entities having a control function.

The question has arisen in the case law and literature as to whether the meaning of the term 'country' can be extended to cover colonies or dependent territories of sovereign states. On one view, it cannot because colonies or dependent territories are essentially part of the territory of the parent state for international law purposes.[103] However, in the refugee definition the requirement to show a 'country of ... former habitual residence' arises only in relation to stateless persons. If under relevant

---

[96] Fripp (2022) (n 6) 339–41 cites the following UK cases: *MA (Palestinian Territories) v SSHD* [2008] EWCA Civ 304; *MT (Palestinian Territories) v SSSHD* [2008] EWCA Civ 1149; *HS (Palestinian—return to Gaza) Palestinian Territories CG* [2011] UKUT 124 (IAC). He also cites *Al-Khateeb v Canada (Citizenship and Immigration)* [2017] FC 31 (CanLII); and *Elian v Ashcroft* [2004] 370 F.3d 897, 901 (9th Cir).

[97] *CNDA No 1102661* [2012] cited in Foster and Lambert (n 6) 133. The CNDA held that although not a state it was sufficient to make it a 'country' that its 'territory has the attributes of a state, such as defined borders, systems of law and a permanent identifiable community'.

[98] *CNDA Nos 363181 and 363182* [2014], cited in Foster and Lambert (n 6) 133. A similar view was taken regarding a stateless Palestinian from the West Bank by the Australian Refugee Tribunal in *1504584 (Refugee)* [2017] AATA 650, paras 26–27, cited by Foster and Lambert (n 6) 133.

[99] *BZAAH V MIC* (n 78) para 25. Foster and Lambert (n 6) 133 also cite the case of *SZUNZ v MIBP* [2015] FCAFC 32, doubting whether 'Western Sahara' could be considered a country. Whilst in consequence the case law cannot be said to reflect a unanimous view, there is substantial consensus that 'country' in this context is a wider term than 'state'. It is difficult to follow the reasoning given in the limited cases that take an opposing view. Thus, the court in *BZAAH* starts from the self-fulfilling premise that the Convention is designed around the inter-state system, disregarding the provision it makes for stateless persons.

[100] See e.g. Mary Crock and Laurie Berg, *Immigration Refugees and Forced Migration: Law, Policy and Practice in Australia* (The Federation Press 2011), relying on *Koe v MIEA* (n 41), cited Foster and Lambert (n 4) 133. See also Fripp (2022) (n 6) 340.

[101] See e.g. Mark Symes and Peter Jorro, *Asylum Law and Practice* (2nd edn, Bloomsbury 2010) 321, cited by Foster and Lambert (n 4) 133.

[102] Hathaway (n 4). Hathaway and Foster (n 4) 67, consider that the fact of habitual residence should be understood 'to give rise to a bond between the stateless individual and a state that approximates in critical respects the relationship between a citizen and her state'.

[103] *Nationality Decrees in Tunis and Morocco* (1923) PCIJ Ser B No 4, 7.

nationality legislation a person is a national of a sovereign state by virtue of having resided in a colony or dependent territory, then obviously they are not stateless, they are nationals of that country. But if they have resided there as stateless persons, then their residence within the colony or dependent territory as stateless persons should be sufficient to bring them within the personal scope of the refugee definition, so long as the authorities of the colony or dependent territory exercises sufficient control.[104]

As regards the concept of 'habitual residence', Article 31(3) and/or Article 32 considerations reinforce the view that to establish residence it is not necessary to establish domicile or permanent residence. That is the view expressed by UNHCR,[105] the case law,[106] and the academic literature.

3.5.1 Habitual residence

Precisely what is the nature and extent of 'habitual residence' has been variously expressed in the case law and background literature. In *Tahiri*, the High Court of Australia considered that assessing 'habitual residence':

[ ... ] involves a 'broad factual inquiry', factors relevant to which include 'the actual and intended length of stay in a state, the purpose of the stay, the strength of ties to the state and to any other state (both in the past and currently), [and] the degree of assimilation into the state.[107]

Grahl-Madsen wrote that the term 'describes a factual situation where a person has chosen a certain country as his or her centre of living at least of some duration but does not require any formal connection with that country of residence'.[108]

On the basis of this formulation, which has received broad agreement,[109] it is clear that in terms of the length of time necessary to show habitual residence, there is no fixed *minima* or *maxima*, although, applying an ordinary meaning approach, 'habitual' implies 'usual' and would appear in general to import that a brief visit or stay

---

[104] A different view is taken by the UK tribunal in *Dag* (n 81) at [37] (cited in Symes and Jorro (n 101) 232).
[105] UNHCR, Representation Stateless Persons before U.S. Immigration Authorities (August 2017), cited by Foster and Lambert (n 4) 108.
[106] Foster and Lambert (n 4) 135, cite, inter alia, *Refugee Appeal No 72635* [2002] NZRSAA 33.
[107] *Tahiri v MIC* [2012] HCA 61, para 16, citing its earlier decision in *LK v Director-General, Department of Community Service* [2009] HCA 9.
[108] Grahl-Madsen (n 4) 160. Fripp (2022) (n 6) 337 notes that earlier Weis had cited with approval a 1957 Austrian Supreme Court case concerning divorce in Austria by Hungarian refugees which had held that: 'habitual residence is the place in which a person uses to sojourn during some time even if not uninterruptedly. The intention to remain permanently is not relevant but only whether a person makes, in fact, a place the centre of their life, their economic existence and their social relations. This is also the case of the refugee who establishes residence in a place in order to clarify his or her future fate. Even if no permanent residence is planned, nevertheless residence until a definite settlement of his or her life can be carried out. Until such time, the place of residence of the refugee is the centre of their life, their economic existence and their social relations. It cannot be said of the plaintiff that she does not have her habitual residence in Austria.'
[109] Foster and Lambert (n 6) cite, inter alia, *Refugee Appeal No 1/92 Re SA* [1992] NZRSAA 5; *Refugee Appeal No 72635* (n 106); *Paripovic v Gonzales* [2005] 418 F.3d 240; *Kadoura v Canada (MCI)* [2003] FCJ No 1328; *Maarouf v Canada (MEI)* [1994] 1 FC 723; *YL (Nationality-Statelessness-Eritrea-Ethiopia) Eritrea CG* [2003] UKIAT 00016.

of short duration is insufficient.¹¹⁰ As regards the quality of the residence, bearing in mind the vagueness of the term and the object and purpose of the Convention, the term is flexible enough to accommodate periods of absence but does, as conveyed by this formulation, require that the person concerned must have resided in that country and have chosen that country as his or her centre of living.¹¹¹ It also helpfully avoids notions of (degrees of) permanence.

As regards the issue of whether residence must be lawful, Goodwin-Gill and McAdam write that:

> Habitual residence for a stateless person would necessarily seem to imply some degree of security, of status, of entitlement to remain and to return, which were in part the objectives of the inter-government arrangements of the inter-war period.¹¹²

The case law, on the other hand, is almost unanimous in rejecting legality of residence as a requirement.¹¹³

As regards the issue of whether the notion of 'former habitual residence' necessarily imports past physical presence, we have already noted some limited support for the contrary view in the case law and academic literature.¹¹⁴ Whilst this study considers this insufficient to override established understandings, it does suffice to show that there is no substantial consensus on the issue.

## 4 Specific Issues

Among the particular issues that have arisen concerning interpretation of 'country of former habitual residence' two merit specific treatment, one concerned with multiple countries, the other with the term's temporal dimension.

### 4.1 Multiple Countries of Former Habitual Residence

Does use of the singular 'country' in Article 1A(2) limit the term 'country of former habitual residence' to just one?

---

[110] Hathaway and Foster (n 4) 68, cite the following cases: *Tarakhan v Canada (MCI)* [1995] 105 FTR 128; *El Assadi v Holder* [2011] 418 Fed Appx 484 (6th Cir). Possibly out of step with the wider case law on habitual residence in international family law, the CJEU appears to regard a key indice as 'an adequate degree of permanence': see Case C-497/10 *Mercredi v Chaffe* [2010] ECLI:EU:C:2010:829.

[111] Goodwin-Gill and McAdam (n 39) 527. See now Goodwin-Gill and McAdam (n 21) 598.

[112] Goodwin-Gill and McAdam (n 39) 526, citing Ad Hoc Committee on Refugees and Stateless Persons, A Study of Statelessness, United Nations, August 1949, Lake Success—New York (1 August 1949) E/1112/Add.1, Introduction and Part 1. See now Goodwin-Gill and McAdam (n 21) 598.

[113] Hathaway and Foster cite an Austrian case requiring presence to be lawful: *SW v Federal Asylum Authority* [1998] 201.440/0-II/04/98 (Au UBAS), but it is a rare exception. Cases stipulating that legality is not a requirement include *BVerwG 10 C 50.07* [2009], cited by Hathaway and Foster (n 4) and Foster and Lambert (n 4) 138; *SZUNZ* (n 99); *Elastal v Canada (MCI)* [1999] FCJ No 328. See further Fripp (2022) (n 6) 335–39. See also (n 75).

[114] See Foster and Lambert (n 6) 136–37. There is also the 2014 draft UNHCR Guidelines that were not proceeded with: see above pp. 277–278.

The comments (noted earlier) of the Ad Hoc Committee on Statelessness and Related Problems (that 'former habitual residence' of a refugee, for the purposes of this convention, means the country in which he had resided and where he has suffered or fears he would suffer persecution if returned') would appear to suggest that country was intended to be singular.[115] However, considering the language of the text as at 27 September 1950, Fripp has noted, '[t]he use of a singular word "the", common to "the country of his nationality" as to "the country of his former habitual residence" does not exclude the possible existence of multiple countries of former habitual residence if 'the' is simply taken as referring singularly to each such country.'[116]

As regards context, there is a significant argument in favour of singularity based on the absence of any provision corresponding to Article 1A(2) second paragraph. However, as Fripp observes, 'this is explicable as necessary to exclude the contemporaneously established process of selecting a single 'effective' nationality.'[117]

Concerning object and purpose, it would be contrary to the principle of surrogacy if a stateless person was able to receive protection based on his or her country of former habitual residence if in fact he or she had another which was entirely safe but which could not be taken account of if the term was treated as singular.[118]

Considering Article 31(3) and/or Article 32 VCLT considerations, reference has already been made to the interpretation adopted in the 1979 UNHCR Handbook, that there can be multiple countries of nationality.

Case law does not exhibit consensus. On the one hand there are cases such as *Thabet* that have endorsed the 1979 UNHCR Handbook.[119] On the other hand, the German Federal Administrative Court) in a 2007 decision rejected the UNHCR position and that taken in *Thabet* on the basis that:

> [Stateless persons] would be positioned more advantageously than those with a nationality if they could claim a danger of persecution not only with reference to their last country of habitual residence, but also with reference to countries where they had their habitual residence before that.[120]

In the academic literature, there is significant endorsement of the view that there can be multiple countries of former habitual residence.[121] Fripp further considers that once it is accepted that there can be multiple countries of former habitual residence, 'it would seem that little space remains for any argument that there cannot have been two such countries at the same time—subject to appropriately careful consideration of the facts'.[122]

---

[115] Fripp (2022) (n 6) 343–47.
[116] ibid 343.
[117] ibid.
[118] See Hathaway and Foster (n 4) 72. Fripp (2022) (n 6) 345 notes that the wording of the US domestic statute (Immigration and Nationality Act (INA) s101(a)(42)(A), 8 United States Code (USC) 1101) states that 'any country in which such person last habitually resident ... ).
[119] *Thabet v Canada (MCI)* [1998] 4 FC 21. This approach was followed in *Refugee Appeal No 72635* (n 106) para 121.
[120] See *10 C 50.0* (n 113). See further discussion in Fripp (2022) (n 6) 345–46.
[121] See Grahl-Madsen (n 6) 160–63; Hathaway and Foster (n 4); Foster and Lambert (n 6).
[122] Fripp (2022) (n 6) 347.

## 4.2 Are Persons with Multiple Countries of Former Habitual Residence Subject to the Same Requirements as Multiple Nationals?

Must stateless persons with more than one country of former habitual residence establish, in the same way as multiple nationals, risk in every one of them? It was observed in Chapter 4 that Article 1A(2) contains a separate paragraph dealing with the position of those with more than one nationality and that such persons are required to show they have a well-founded fear of persecution in each of their countries of nationality save where there are valid reasons based on well-founded fear for not availing themselves of the protection of one of the countries of which they are a national.[123] Does this have analogous application to 'multiple' stateless persons?

The attempt to treat such persons analogously with multiple nationals runs up against the initial difficulty that Article 1A(2) contains no clause addressing the situation of those who have more than one country of former habitual residence. The absence of such a clause is one of the reasons given by UNHCR in its 1979 Handbook for considering it sufficient for a stateless person to establish a well-founded fear of persecution in just one of the countries of former habitual residence. The Handbook stated that:

> A stateless person may have more than one country of former habitual residence, and he may have a fear of persecution in relation to more than one of them. *The definition does not require that he satisfies the criteria in relation to all of them.*[124]

That is a significant argument based on the literal text and is one that is often made in relation to other attempts to read requirements into the Article 1A(2) definition. However, it is extremely difficult to square with the object and purpose and the *travaux* to the 1951 Refugee Convention. It is also not a view that has become established in the case law or in the academic literature generally.

The contrary view that both categories of person should be treated analogously has been most forcefully adopted by the Canadian Federal Court of Appeal in *Thabet*. In this case, Linden J stated that:

> Just as a person with more than one nationality cannot be found to be a Convention refugee unless he or she establishes that he or she is unwilling or unable to avail themselves of the protection of those countries, a stateless person must also pass a similar test. If the claimant has available a place of former habitual residence which will offer safety from persecution, then he or she must return to that country.[125]

The approach taken in *Thabet* has been endorsed by Hathaway and Foster and also by Fripp. Hathaway and Foster write that:

---

[123] Chapter 4, section 3.3.6.
[124] UNHCR Handbook (n 1) para 104 (emphasis added).
[125] *Thabet* (n 119). This approach was also followed in *Refugee Appeal No 72635* (n 106) para 121.

The *Thabet* test ensures that refugee status is recognised in the case of a stateless person denied the ability to continue to live in 'her own' country, owing to a risk of being persecuted there, yet respects the equally critical principle that surrogate protection is not owed when the applicant has a country fairly understood to be 'her own' that is both able and willing to afford national protection.[126]

However, echoing UNHCR's view, and opposing the *Thabet* view, Foster and Lambert consider that 'the fact that an explicit provision was introduced for dual nationals but not for non-nationals suggests precisely the opposite: that those without a nationality were not to be subject to the same requirement'.[127] In their view, the distinction made in the text of Article 1A(2) between nationals (who have to show they are unable or unwilling to avail themselves of *the protection* of their country of nationality) and non-nationals (where the question is simply whether the applicant is unable or unwilling 'as a result of such events', *to return to it*'—emphases added) is critical.

There is plainly no consensus on this issue, though in this author's view, Foster and Lambert's argument lacks force. Applying VCLT rules, ordinary meaning is only a starting point, and the wording of the treaty must be considered in terms of good faith, context, object and purposes among other rules as well. Additionally, in this instance the issue is not about the meaning of existing words but the significance of their omission. Further, there is no suggestion that the drafters intended to apply different rules for nationals and non-nationals in this context. Turning to consider object and purpose, reliance on this textual distinction clearly clashes strongly with the principle of surrogacy.

No doubt conscious that to be consistent with their support in other contexts for interpretation based on object and purpose, Foster and Lambert argue that the surrogacy principle prayed in aid by courts in cases such as *Thabet* cannot justify the extension of the multiple nationality provision to stateless persons 'since that principle rests on the supposition that the Refugee Convention was designed to intervene following "a breakdown of national protection"'.[128] However, this argument elides the notion of state protection with that of protection of nationals. The duty of the state to protect its population goes wider than protection of its nationals.[129] Nationality or citizenship affords residents greater rights and benefits, but in terms of protection within the meaning of the refugee definition—primarily protection against serious harm—states are obliged by IHRL norms to afford protection to *all* within their jurisdiction. Indeed, Foster and Lambert themselves chart the fact that IHRL has significantly enhanced the human rights of non-nationals.[130]

It is nevertheless possible to criticise both the *Thabet* test and Hathaway and Foster's endorsement of it for not wholly following through on the stated purpose of achieving symmetry so far as possible between those with more than one nationality and those

---

[126] Hathaway and Foster (n 4) 74; Fripp (2022) (n 6) 332.
[127] Foster and Lambert (n 6) 141.
[128] ibid 142.
[129] See Chapter 7, sections 3.8–3.9.
[130] They refer, inter alia, to Article 12(4) of the ICCPR and to the HRC, General Comment No 27 (n 93). See Foster and Lambert (n 6) 82–89, 167–73.

with more than one country of former habitual residence.[131] As explained earlier, the second paragraph of Article 1A(2) provides one exception to the requirement that multiple nationals must show a well-founded fear of being persecuted in each country of their nationality, namely where there is any valid reason based on a well-founded fear for not seeking to avail themselves of national protection.

Once it is accepted that the second paragraph of Article 1A(2) should be applied analogously, it would be inconsistent not to apply this exception also. Just as multiple nationals cannot be expected to show a well-founded fear of persecution in each country of nationality if there is any valid reason based on well-founded fear for not availing themselves of the protection of one of the countries of former habitual residence, so in respect of non-nationals such a requirement cannot be imposed if they have any valid reason based on well-founded fear for not availing themselves of the protection of one of the countries of former habitual residence. In each case the two most obvious issues are the same: will they be admitted to the country other than their persecutory country of origin. If not, they qualify as refugees. If they will be admitted, then focus must be on whether there is any real risk of indirect refoulement (if there is, they qualify as refugees). However, in the case of non-nationals, it is likely, at least in relation to the non-admission scenario, that it will be far easier for them to show that there are valid reasons, since, unlike nationals, they have no right to admission per se. But in respect of all cases based on a 'valid reason',[132] it will largely be a question of fact.[133]

To conclude, it is clear there remains no consensus on this issue. In this author's view, the key elements in any assessment of a claim to refugee status by a stateless person are essentially no different from those applicable to applicants with a nationality, namely, a well-founded fear of persecution attributable to the person's country of former habitual residence for a reason listed in Article 1A(2), and whether they are able to or willing to return to it, understood to mean in this context, whether protection is available there. The arguments in favour of applying an object and purpose approach of this kind to interpretation, as against insisting on a literal construction, would appear to carry the day.

## 4.3 Temporal Dimension

It is necessary to give specific attention to the issue of whether the country of former habitual residence must be fixed temporally. Applying an ordinary meaning approach, the term 'country of ... former habitual residence' would seem to require only that

---

[131] See Hathaway and Foster (n 4) 72–75, who, in analysing this matter, make no reference to the 'valid reasons' qualification.

[132] In parallel with the same arguments raised in relation to nationals, Fripp seeks to argue that both categories should benefit from a broader reading of the 'valid reason' exception: Fripp (2022) (n 6) 350–51. For criticisms of this position, see pp. 232–233.

[133] Some support for the approach taken here can be found in the New Zealand IPT decision in *AQ (Myanmar)* [2021] NZIPT 801893, although it draws on a more extensive 'protection elsewhere' analysis. And in this context (as in the context of multiple nationality—see Chapter 4, section 3.3.6) issues of inability to return can be highly material. See also *FX (Bangladesh)* [2020] NZIPT 801683, para 112.

the residence be 'former' without specifying when in time. However, there have been attempts to fix it in time at least indirectly, by reference to either the first country of former habitual residence or the last.

As regards the view that the country concerned can only be the place where the applicant *first* resided, in adopting this view Grahl-Madsen considered that '[t]he country from which a stateless person had to flee in the first instance remains the "country of his former habitual residence" throughout his life as a refugee, irrespective of any subsequent change of factual residence'.[134] However, reading the phrase in this way requires inserting a word—'first'—that is not there. In terms of object and purpose, it is, as Hathaway and Foster put it, 'unnecessarily restrictive' since it would exclude persons who had developed significant ties to a subsequent country or countries of habitual residence.[135] The drafters were clearly aware, when drawing up Article 1A(2), that stateless persons sometimes moved more than once outside their country of former habitual residence.[136] The 'first country' view is not one that has gained any traction in the case law.

As regards the opposite view that the 'country of former habitual residence' should be the *last* in time, there is no textual basis for construing it thus either. That would likewise amount to reading in an additional requirement not there in the text. Further, to construe the phrase in such a way would clash with the protective purpose of ensuring that stateless persons who have experienced past persecution can bring themselves within the personal scope of the Convention even though they may have since resided in another country before claiming asylum in the host state.[137] It is clear from the *travaux* that the drafters were concerned to ensure protection of stateless persons who had been subject to measures of denationalisation and they cannot have been unaware that such persons had sometimes moved to adjoining countries before going on to another to apply for asylum. The main line of case law has readily accepted that those denationalised are entitled to be assessed by treating the state that has stripped them of their nationality as their 'country of ... former habitual residence' without requiring them to show that they never resided anywhere else.[138] Foster and Lambert note that domestic legislation in the US and Germany require the country of former habitual residence to be the country of 'last habitual residence' or 'last country of former habitual residence'.[139] But these, of course, are best seen as examples of domestic legislation imposing criteria more stringent than those contained in Article 1A(2) and take matters no further as regards the issue of the international meaning.

Since, as noted earlier, 'habitual residence' does not require continuous physical presence, it would also appear possible for an applicant to have more than one country of former habitual residence at the same time.[140]

---

[134] Grahl-Madsen (n 6) 162.
[135] Hathaway and Foster (n 4) 73.
[136] See above section 4.1.
[137] Sometimes relocation may have been with the help of UNHCR, as in the *Refugee Appeal No 73512* (n 91) in which Uganda was found to be a country of former habitual residence for an Asian appellant and his family under threat from Idi Amin. See Foster and Lambert (n 6) 137.
[138] See above section 4.1.
[139] Foster and Lambert (n 6) 137.
[140] See Fripp (2022) (n 6) 346–47.

## 5 Article 33(1) and Extraterritorial Application

### 5.1 Potential Relevance to Interpretation of 'Outside the Country'

We observed earlier that neither of the two 'outside the country' phrases in Article 1A(2) can in their entirety be given a straightforward ordinary meaning, but must be read together with their context, object and purpose, and in light of other VCLT rules of interpretation. Given that the foregoing analysis posits that in these phrases the term 'country' has a legal jurisdictional meaning relating to the nature of the territory involved, it cannot be ruled out a priori that 'outside the country' might be read to permit diplomatic asylum.[141] There is some support for this in the literature. According to a 2003 article by Lauterpacht and Bethlehem, the reference in Article 33(1) to territories as opposed to 'countries' or states:

> [ ... ] suggests that the principle of non-refoulement will apply also in circumstances in which the refugee or asylum seeker is within their country of origin but is nonetheless under the protection of another Contracting State. This may arise, for example, in circumstances in which a refugee or asylum seeker takes refuge in the diplomatic mission of another State or comes under the protection of the armed forces of another state engaged in peacekeeping or other role in the country of origin. In principle, in such circumstances, the protecting State will be subject to the prohibition on refoulement to territory where the person concerned would be at risk.[142]

The fact that Article 33(1) contains no explicit territorial limitation has been viewed by some scholars to mean that IHRL norms can be used to establish responsibility of a diplomatic mission in such circumstances or indeed in a wider set of circumstances.[143] To analyse such contentions it is in order, once again, to apply VCLT rules, although in this instance it is unnecessary to address all of them one by one.

### 5.2 *Travaux Préparatoires*

The drafters conceived of Article 33(1) as applicable only to persons who had left their country of origin. There is nothing in the *travaux* to suggest that the drafters saw this provision as having application to persons who had not left their country of origin. They believed that '[t]here was no worse catastrophe for an individual who had

---

[141] Goodwin Gill and McAdam (n 39) 250.
[142] Lauterpacht and Bethlehem (n 50) para 114.
[143] See e.g. Kate Ogg, 'Protection Closer to Home? A Legal Case for Claiming Asylum at Embassies and Consulates (2014) 33 RSQ 81. This also appears to be the view taken by Moreno-Lax (n 14) 298–311: at ibid 308, she proposes that '[f]raming the issue not as a matter of diplomatic asylum, but rather access to territorial asylum may yield a more fruitful outcome'. For an analysis of Article 33(1) generally, see James C Hathaway, *The Rights of Refugees under International Law* (CUP 2005) 307–42; Hathaway and Foster (n 4); Wouters (n 6); Goodwin-Gill and McAdam (n 21) 308–27; Goodwin-Gill and McAdam (n 39) 201–84; Lauterpacht and Bethlehem (n 50) 87–164; Kälin, Caroni and Heim (n 51) 1327–95.

succeeded after many vicissitudes in leaving a country where he was being persecuted than to be returned to that country'.[144] According to Weis, they considered that:

> [ ... ] turning back a refugee to the frontiers of the country where his life or liberty is threatened on account of his race, religion, nationality or political opinion ... would be tantamount to delivering him into the hands of his persecutors.[145]

Since we have already found the 'outside' requirement to entail physical separation from a country in terms of territorial jurisdiction, there is no need to rehearse the general arguments arising under each of the VCLT rules *seriatim*. It is enough to focus on the particular argument advanced based on the notion of diplomatic asylum.

## 5.3 International Law Context

Whilst terminologies are not uniform,[146] international law generally distinguishes between two modalities of asylum: territorial asylum and extraterritorial asylum. Territorial asylum is asylum provided in the territory of the receiving (host) state. The precise scope of extraterritorial asylum is less certain, but is most commonly treated as referring to diplomatic asylum, namely asylum granted in embassies, legations, consulates, warships, and merchant vessels in foreign territory and is thus granted within the territory of the state from which protection is sought.[147] In the present context, we are only concerned with the situation in which asylum is sought by persons in-country. Unlike the situation in relation to territorial asylum (and unlike the situation on the high seas or where a person claims diplomatic asylum in a country outside their own), diplomatic asylum in this context presupposes that the person concerned is still in the territory of their own country. There have been high-profile examples in relatively recent times of foreign embassies giving some type of diplomatic asylum, e.g. in 1959 when some 800 political refugees sought asylum in embassies in Havana, in 1984 when six prominent members of the anti-apartheid movements sought asylum in the British Embassy in Durban ('the Durban Six'), in 1989 when the US embassy in

---

[144] Ad Hoc Committee on Refugees and Stateless Persons, Second Session: Summary Record of the Fortieth Meeting Held at the Palais des Nations, Geneva, on Tuesday, 22 August 1950, at 2.30 p.m. (27 September 1950) UN Doc E/AC.32/SR.40, 30–34.
[145] Paul Weis (ed), *The Refugee Convention 1951* (CUP 1995) 279.
[146] UNGA, Question of Diplomatic Asylum (n 57) para 1.
[147] Felice Morgenstern, 'Diplomatic Asylum' (1951) 67(267) Law Quarterly Review 362, 362. The Inter-American Court of Human Rights has defined 'diplomatic asylum' as '(ii) *Diplomatic asylum*: protection provided by a State within its legations, warships, military aircraft and camps, to persons who are nationals or habitual residents of another State where they are persecuted for political reasons, for their beliefs, opinions or political affiliation or for acts that may be considered political offences or related common crimes.' See *The Institution of Asylum and its Recognition as a Human Right in the Inter-American System of Protection (Interpretation and Scope of Articles 5, 22.7 and 22.8 in Relation to Article 1(1) of the American Convention on Human Rights)*, Advisory Opinion OC-25/18, Inter-American Court of Human Rights Series A No 25 (30 May 2018) paras 67(ii), 149. See further, Carroll N Ronning, *Diplomatic Asylum: Legal Norms and Political Reality in Latin American Relations* (Martinus Nijhoff 1965); Sinha S Prakash, *Asylum and International Law* (Springer 1971) 207–09; Eileen Denza, *Diplomatic Law: Commentary on the Vienna Convention on Diplomatic Relations* (4th edn, OUP 2018); Eileen Denza, 'Diplomatic Asylum' in Zimmermann (n 6) 1425–40; Crawford (n 43) 388–89; UNGA, Question of Diplomatic Asylum (n 57).

Beijing gave asylum to a prominent Chinese dissident and his wife, and in 1990, with mass invasions of foreign embassy premises in Albania.[148]

International law does not generally support the idea of a right to diplomatic asylum because, applying general principles of territorial sovereignty, a grant of diplomatic asylum interferes with the sovereignty of another state.[149] The international community has steadfastly eschewed inclusion of any provisions regarding it.[150] Nevertheless, the rule of the inviolability of a diplomatic mission, which is codified in the Vienna Convention on Diplomatic Relations 1961 (VCDR) at Article 22 means that acceptance onto embassy property can give rise to complex issues of responsibility[151] and some jurists have accepted that there is a legal right to grant asylum on grounds of humanity, in the case of violence or disorder (sometimes termed 'the humanitarian exception').[152]

The crux of the argument in support of the view that the 'outside the country' phrases set out in Article 1A(2) of the Convention could be construed so as to encompass a claim for asylum made in a diplomatic mission or other legation within that person's own country is that the premises of diplomatic missions form a part of the territory of the foreign state, and that diplomatic asylum is thus still asylum provided in the 'territory' of the state granting asylum.[153] If this view were correct, then it is arguable that the 'outside the country' requirement is met if the person concerned (albeit still inside the territory of his or her home state) has accessed some legal space that can be considered the territory of the foreign state—most commonly the diplomatic mission—and claimed asylum. However, this argument founders on several rocks. First, the International Law Commission, while drafting the VCDR,[154] rejected the theory of extraterritoriality as being based on a legal fiction and not reflecting

---

[148] Denza, 'Diplomatic Asylum' (n 147). On the Durban Six, see Susanne Riveles, 'Diplomatic Asylum as a Human Right: The Case of the Durban Six' (1989) 11(1) Human Rights Quarterly 139, 139.

[149] UNGA, Question of Diplomatic Asylum (n 57). Article 41(1) of the Vienna Convention on Diplomatic Relations (VCDR) imposes a duty on diplomatic missions 'not to interfere in the internal affairs of [the receiving] State'. See VCDR (adopted 18 April 1961, entered into force on 24 April 1964). A similar provision is contained in the Vienna Convention on Consular Relations (VCCR).

[150] Goodwin-Gill and McAdam (n 21) 327 note that a Uruguayan proposal to extend the right of asylum in the UDHR to diplomatic asylum was rejected—UN Doc A/C.3268, reproduced in UN Doc A/C/3/285/Rev.1 in UNGAOR Part 1 (3rd Session, 1948 Annexes 25). The drafters deliberately excluded the issue from the VCDR: see Crawford (n 147) 388–89.

[151] VCDR (n 149); Crawford (n 43) 389. The UNHCR Handbook, in a footnote to para 88 notes that '[t]he former notion of the "extraterritoriality" of embassies has lately been replaced by the term "inviolability" used in the 1961 VCDR'.

[152] Goodwin-Gill and McAdam (n 21) 310. At ibid 324, they cite Robert Jennings and Arthur Watts (eds), *Oppenheim's International Law* (9th edn, OUP 2008) and also *R (on the application of 'B') v Secretary of State for the Foreign and Commonwealth Office* [2005] EWCA Civ 1344, and *Al Sadoon and Mufdhi v United Kingdom* App No 61498/08 (ECtHR, 4 October 2010). They also note at ibid 325, footnote 115, that 'it is generally accepted that States may provide 'temporary refuge' in diplomatic premises to people fleeing unrest or pursued by violent mobs, etc' and cite, inter alia, Atle Grahl-Madsen, *The Status of Refugees in International Law. Volume II: Asylum, Entry and Sojourn* (Sijthoff 1972) 6, 46; Peter Porcino, 'Toward Codification of Diplomatic Asylum' (1976) 8 New York University Journal of International Law and Politics 435, 438; and Maarten den Heijer, 'Diplomatic Asylum and the Assange Case' (2013) 26(2) Leiden Journal of International Law 399. See also Denza (n 147) 1433–40.

[153] For a through treatment of the arguments for and against, see Gregor Noll, 'Seeking Asylum at Embassies: A Right to Entry under International Law?' (2005) 17(3) IJRL 542.

[154] VCDR (n 149).

actual reality or modern understanding of diplomatic relations.[155] Second, in accordance with General Assembly Resolution No 3321 (XXIX) of December 1974,[156] states were invited to submit their views on diplomatic asylum for inclusion in a report of the Secretary-General on the subject. This report was submitted to the General Assembly but no international instruments regulating this concept were adopted.[157]

Third, even though diplomatic missions or other legations do not fall wholly under the jurisdiction of the state in which they are located, it remains that states must refrain from exercising their territorial jurisdiction in the premises of their diplomatic missions.[158]

Fourth, whilst IHRL has developed an approach that accepts that states can be said to be under extraterritorial obligations in exceptional circumstances,[159] it is not under the same textual constraint imposed by the Article 1A(2) definition, namely requiring that a person be 'outside the country'. Extraterritorial obligations under IHRL derive solely from the jurisdictional scope provided in the IHRL treaties.[160]

Fifth, even though within IHRL jurisprudence some support can be found for the view that in exceptional circumstances diplomatic asylum can engage a contracting state's human rights obligations,[161] the mere fact of making an application for asylum outside the host state's territory cannot, of itself, engage host state responsibility. Pertinent in this context is the reasoning of the Strasbourg Court in *M.N. and Others v Belgium*,[162] which concerned Syrian nationals who had submitted applications for visas on humanitarian grounds, based on Article 25 of the EU Visa Code, at the Belgian embassy in Lebanon, with a view to applying for asylum in Belgium immediately upon their arrival in that member state and, thereafter, to being granted

---

[155] Neither the Vienna Conventions of 1961 and 1963 include the granting of asylum as a diplomatic or consular function.
[156] UNGA Res 3321 (XXIX), Question of Diplomatic Asylum (14 December 1974).
[157] UNGA, Question of Diplomatic Asylum (n 57) Introduction, para 2. At ibid para 302, the report identifies the numerous academic commentators who have abandoned the fiction of extraterritoriality.
[158] ibid para 310.
[159] Riveles (n 148). International human rights courts, for example the ECtHR, have been prepared to recognise in very limited circumstances that the contracting state, through the effective control of the relevant territory and its inhabitants abroad as a consequence of military occupation or through the consent, invitation, or acquiescence of the government of that territory, exercises all or some of the public powers normally to be exercised by that government: see e.g. European Court of Human Rights, *Ilascu and others v. the Republic of Moldova and Russia*, Application No. 48787/99, para 313. Other recognised instances concern cases involving the activities of a contracting state's diplomatic or consular agents abroad and on-board craft and vessels registered in, or flying the flag of, that state. In these specific situations, IHRL treaty provisions (sometimes drawing on customary international law principles) have recognised the extra-territorial exercise of jurisdiction by the relevant state (see Lord Bingham's review in *Roma Rights* (n 36)). For a recent elaboration (and slight development) of the ECHR jurisprudence, see *HF and Others v France* App Nos 24384/19 and 44234/20 (ECtHR, 14 September 2022) paras 184–215; 234–84. For the more functional approach of the HRC, see General Comment No 36 (2019): Article 6 (Right to Life) (3 September 2019) UN Doc CCPR/C/GC/35, para 63; and *AS and Others v Italy* (27 January 2021) Communication No 3042/2017.
[160] Goodwin-Gill and McAdam (n 39) 245; Goodwin-Gill and McAdam (n 21) 324. See also Ogg (n 143) 81.
[161] See *B & Ors v SSFCO* [2004] EWCA Civ 1344; *WM v Denmark* App No 17392/90 (14 October 1992) Commission Decision on Admissibility, para 1; *Case of Mohammad Munaf v Romania* (21 August 2009) Communication No 1539/2006, UN Doc CCPR/C/96/D/1539/2006, paras 14.2 and 14.5. See also Goodwin-Gill and McAdam, 3rd edn (n 39) 251–52, 356–57; Goodwin-Gill and McAdam (n 21) 81, 323–28.
[162] *MN and Others v Belgium* App No 3599/18 (ECtHR, 5 May 2020).

a residence permit with a period of validity not limited to ninety days (the same case has previously come before the CJEU in *X and X*).[163] The Grand Chamber stated that:

> [ ... ] the mere fact that an applicant brings proceedings in a State Party with which he has no connecting tie cannot suffice to establish that State's jurisdiction over him ... to find otherwise would amount to enshrining a near-universal application of the Convention on the basis of the unilateral choices of any individual, irrespective of where in the world they find themselves, and therefore to create an unlimited obligation on the Contracting States to allow entry to an individual who might be at risk of ill-treatment contrary to the Convention outside their jurisdiction....[164]

This reasoning would appear apt even in relation to a person seeking to apply for refugee status in their own country of origin to a diplomatic mission of a country with whom they have no connecting ties.

## 5.4 Case Law and Academic Literature

We noted earlier some support in the literature for treating Article 33(1) of the Convention as legitimising the right to diplomatic asylum. However, at least if read as of general application, the argument advanced by Lauterpacht and Bethlehem is against the weight of authority both judicial and academic.[165] So far as concerns the attempted reliance on the foreign embassy as being part of the territory of the sending state, this has never found significant support in the jurisprudence.[166]

The preponderance of the refugee case law and academic literature reflects the view that Article 33(1) considerations cannot negate the need for an applicant to show that they are 'outside the country'. Wouters aptly summarised the state of the learning on this issue as follows:

> [ ... ] the scope *ratione loci* of the prohibition on refoulement contained in Article 33(1) of the Refugee Convention depends on Articles 1A(2) and 33(1) of the Convention and the Convention as a whole. It is clear that Article 33(1) does not apply to people who are still within their country of origin. It is also clear that it does

---

[163] Case C-638/16 *X and X* (Judgment) [2017] EU:C:2017:173. Whilst measures by a state to block or hamper those in their territory from applying for a visa to leave for another country may engage that state's obligations to respect those persons' right to leave any country (e.g. under Article 12(3) of the ICCPR), it is far from clear that they can engage the extraterritorial responsibility of that other country: see further James C Hathaway, *The Rights of Refugees Under International Law* (2nd edn, CUP 2021) 354 and Goodwin-Gill and McAdam (n 21) 429–30.
[164] *MN and Others* (n 162) para 123.
[165] Lauterpacht and Bethlehem (n 50).
[166] See e.g. the English judgment, *Radwan v Radwan* [1972] 3 All ER 1026; the Australian judgment *Regina, ex parte Petroff v Turnbull and Ors* [1971] 17 FLR 438; and the United States judgment *McKeel v Islamic Republic of Iran* [1983] 722 F.2d 582.

apply to refugees who are within the host state's territory. In addition, Article 33(1) is applicable in situations where refugees find themselves outside their country of origin as well as outside the territory of a host State. This includes refugees who are at the border of a State, those intercepted on the high seas and those in the effective extra-territorial control of a State. Responsibility is then determined by the conduct of a State and the effect that conduct has on the refugee's right to be protected from refoulement.[167]

Also to be observed in this connection is that even if the view that diplomatic missions or other legations were jurisdictionally a part of the territory of the state whose refuge is sought were accepted, there remains another possible problem under the refugee definition of such persons establishing that they were 'outside' the *country*. Even if diplomatic missions could be regarded as self-contained jurisdictional enclaves belonging to the state whose refuge is sought, such enclaves are still *inside* the territory of the county of origin.

## 5.5 Article 33(1) and Extraterritorial Immigration Controls

The approach taken above to arguments based on asylum in diplomatic missions also applies to other potential modes of claiming asylum whilst still in the territory of the country of origin, such as legations, war vessels, commercial ships, military camps, aircraft, etc. This is best illustrated by considering a well-ventilated variation of the extraterritoriality argument concerning the exercise of immigration authority by a foreign country in the territory of the applicant's home state. That was the modality in the *Roma Rights* case.[168] In rejecting that this scenario could come within the Refugee Convention, Lord Hope observed that:

> Nobody now seeks to argue that the operations which were carried out at Prague Airport were in breach of article 33, even on the most generous interpretation that could be given to it. What the Convention does is assure refugees of the rights and freedoms set out in Chapters I to V when they are in countries that are not their own. It does not require the state to abstain from controlling the movements of people outside its borders who wish to travel to it in order to claim asylum. It lacks any provisions designed to meet the additional burdens which would follow if a prohibition to that effect had been agreed to. The conclusion must be that steps which are taken to control the movements of such people who have not yet reached the state's frontier are not incompatible with the acceptance of the obligations which arise when refugees have arrived in its territory.[169]

---

[167] Wouters (n 6) 56 (but see also 49).
[168] *Roma Rights* (n 36).
[169] ibid para 64.

## 5.6 Article 33(1): Extraterritorial Application via National and Regional Law

The position taken in section 5.5 of this chapter concerns the international law position. However, individual states are not precluded from applying a different approach within their national (or regional) law. Nothing in the refugee definition enshrined in Article 1A(2) prevents state parties or the international community from waiving the 'outside the country' requirement in their own law and practice.[170]

In addition to sometimes granting asylum on the basis of the humanitarian exception, a number of countries formally accept asylum applications or visa applications on asylum-related grounds at their embassies.[171]

In the context of the Americas, there is a specific international instrument, the Convention on Diplomatic Asylum.[172] However, this does not confer an individual right to receive diplomatic asylum; it confirms only that states retain the sovereign power to grant it.[173] Further, in its 2018 Advisory Opinion, the IACtHR, in addition to clarifying that diplomatic missions and foreign legations cannot be regarded as part of the territory of the sending state, ruled that even within the American region, 'the element of *opinio juris* necessary for the determination of a customary rule is not present, notwithstanding the State practice of granting diplomatic asylum in certain situations or granting some form of protection in their legations'.[174]

At the EU level, the Asylum Procedures Directive (recast) specifies that whilst it applies to all applications for international protection made in the territory 'including at the border, in the territorial waters or in the transit zones of the Member States ...', it

---

[170] At least arguably, Article 5 of the Convention permits state parties to provide more favourable treatment in relation to qualification as well as refugee rights: see Achilles Skordas, 'Article 5 (Rights Granted Apart from this Convention)' in Zimmermann (n 6) 669–706, 683, especially 685–86.

[171] In relation to practice in humanitarian cases, Goodwin-Gill and McAdam (n 21) 324–25 give the examples of the US, Canada, and the UK. Examples of 'in-country processing' include the resettlement of people from Vietnam during the late 1970s and the US Obama Administration's Central American Minors (CAM) program. At the international level, there has been the establishment of orderly departure procedures programs in collaboration with refugee-producing states, whereby refugees may make application within their country of origin for resettlement abroad under international auspices. Under the Orderly Departure Programme (ODP) administered by UNHCR, 'refugees' were airlifted from Ho Chi Minh City to Bangkok for onward journey to resettlement countries. The orderly departure program in the UK also formed the basis for in-country processing of asylum seekers in Russia, Cuba, and Haiti. For studies of the situation within the EU, see Gregor Noll and Jessica Fagerlund, 'Safe Avenues to Asylum? The Actual and Potential Role of EU Diplomatic Representations in Processing Asylum Requests' (2002) Danish Centre for Human Rights, available at <https://www.unhcr.org/3cd000a52.pdf> accessed 23 April 2021; Noll (n 153). In his 2005 study, Noll mentions Belgium, Germany, Italy, Ireland, and Luxembourg. He noted that a further six EU countries allowed access to their territory for protection reasons in exceptional cases (Austria, Denmark, France, the Netherlands, Spain, and the UK).

[172] Convention on Diplomatic Asylum (adopted 28 March 1954, entered into force 29 December 1954). The Convention has fourteen state parties: Argentina, Brazil, Costa Rica, Dominican Republic, Ecuador, El Salvador, Guatemala, Haiti, Mexico, Panama, Paraguay, Peru, Uruguay, and Venezuela. The reference in Article 41 VCDR to 'special agreements' has been seen to allow for bilateral recognition of the right to give asylum to political refugees within diplomatic missions: see Crawford (n 147) 388–89.

[173] *The Institution of Asylum*, Advisory Opinion OC-25/18 (n 147) paras 149 and 87.

[174] ibid para 162.

'shall not apply to requests for diplomatic or territorial asylum submitted to representations of Member States'.[175]

There has been exploration at the EU level of 'Protected Entry Procedures' which allow non-nationals to approach the potential host state outside its territory with a claim for asylum or other form of international protection and to be granted an entry permit in case of a positive response to that claim.[176] However, as Noll observes, '[n]either a homogenous state practice nor a corresponding *opinio juris* can be made out to support a right to access territory in order to seek asylum'.[177]

There are a number of countries outside the Americas and EU that make provision for diplomatic asylum, sometimes in conjunction with UNHCR. However, when such measures are taken, the state or the international partner concerned is not applying the refuge definition under Article 1A(2) but rather their national or regional law or other international agreement or simply executive prerogative. It becomes a different matter if the persons concerned subsequently leave the country of origin through such state measures, since then they can then be said to have fulfilled the Article 1A(2) requirement to be 'outside' from the moment of physical departure from that country's territorial jurisdiction.

An example at the national level of the waiving of the 'outside' requirement arose before the ECtHR in the case of *N.D. and N.T. v Spain*.[178] The Grand Chamber noted that Spanish law made provision for diplomatic asylum and indeed the existence of this domestic avenue of remedy was one of the reasons why it did not find a breach of Article 3 or Article 4 of Protocol No 4 in these cases.[179]

Measures of this kind, whether at the state, regional, or international level, do not, therefore, demonstrate the need for a different interpretation of 'outside the country'; they simply demonstrate that states may choose to allow other states and/or international agencies to assist with persons who are internal refugees and to waive this requirement in relation to them.

## 6 Conclusions

It can be seen that the 'outside' element of the refugee definition is relatively hard-edged. The analysis of this chapter broadly endorses the view expressed in the 1979 Handbook that the term 'outside' must be construed so as to require physical separation from the territory of a country, the latter being understood in jurisdictional terms. However, that entails recognition that the meaning of this element derives only in small part from a literal or ordinary meaning approach, since it is only really the preposition 'outside' that possesses such a meaning. It is only by applying an approach

---

[175] Directive 2013/32/EU of the European Parliament and of the Council of 26 June 2013 on common procedures for granting and withdrawing international protection [2013] OJ L 180, Articles 3(1) and 3(2).
[176] Noll (n 153) 543.
[177] ibid 547. Hailbronner takes a similar view: see Kay Hailbronner, 'Comments on the Right to Leave, Return and Remain' in Vera Gowlland-Debbas (ed), *The Problem of Refugees in the Light of Contemporary International Law Issues* (Martinus Nijhoff 1996) 115.
[178] *ND and NT v Spain* Apps Nos 8675/15 and 8697/15 (ECtHR [GC], 13 February 2020).
[179] ibid para 212.

based mainly on context and object and purpose that the 'country' aspects of both the 'country of nationality' and the 'country of former habitual residence' phrases can be interpreted satisfactorily.

As regards the expression 'country of nationality', it is a legal term of art designating a legal bond between the individual and the state. As such its meaning can be stated with some precision.

Despite also being a legal term of art, the expression 'country of former habitual residence' cannot be accorded the same precision, since the tie between a stateless person and their country of former habitual residence lacks the same legal content. There mostly appears to be agreement that in this latter expression the term 'country', whilst not confined to states, is limited to countries where there is an authority exercising territorial control.

The analysis of the concept of 'former habitual residence' reveals wide support for the view that 'habitual residence' is to be understood as a broad, flexible term that connotes a factual situation where a person has chosen a certain country as his or her centre of living and has some degree of security, of status, of entitlement to remain and to return, but does not require a fixed period of duration or any formal connection with that country of residence. The use of the adjectives 'former' and 'habitual', do, however, require that a person must have lived in the country previously. It would go beyond VCLT rules to 'read down' both of these adjectives so as to extend the scope of the term (as some have suggested) purposively even to certain persons such as stateless children who have never lived in their parents' country of origin.

There is significant level of agreement with the 1979 Handbook view that a stateless person can have more than one country of former habitual residence, but there remains disagreement as to whether such a person should be required to show they face a well-founded fear of being persecuted in each of the countries concerned. The position taken in this chapter is that there are sound reasons for considering that stateless persons with more than one country of former habitual residence should be subject to the same tests as those that apply to multiple nationals, namely that they must show a well-founded fear of being persecuted in each country, subject only to a similar 'valid reason' provision (which certainly encompasses those who face denial of re-admission or onward refoulement).

This chapter also seeks to analyse and evaluate disagreements that continue to exist over whether a country of former habitual residence must be the first or the last.

The final issue tackled in this chapter has been whether the phrase 'outside the country' when read together with Article 33(1) can be taken to include persons applying in-country for diplomatic asylum, at diplomatic missions, or other legations within the country of origin. It is concluded that this contention is contrary to a proper application of VCLT rules and has attracted little support. This remains the case, notwithstanding the existence of schemes permitting persons to apply for asylum to diplomatic missions within their country of origin. Being reliant on national law or separate regional or international agreements, these do not impinge on the international meaning to be given to the 'outside the country' element of the refugee definition.

Drawing together the main findings of this chapter, the following 'basic' and 'suggested' propositions can be identified.

## 6.1 Basic Propositions

1. The 'outside the country' requirement must be construed so as to require physical absence from the territory of a country, the latter being understood in jurisdictional terms.
2. In relation to nationals, they must be outside the territory of their state.
3. '[H]abitual residence' does not require domicile or permanent residence.
4. A person can have more than one country of former habitual residence.

## 6.2 Suggested Propositions

1. In the phrase 'country of former habitual residence', the 'country' need not be a state but must one in which there are actors controlling the territory or a substantial part of the territory of that country.
2. As regards the temporal dimension of the concept of former habitual residence, there is no sound basis for imposing either a first or last country requirement, notwithstanding some support in both case law and the wider literature for one or the other view.
3. Despite the lack of any provision for stateless persons that parallel those of the second paragraph of Article 1A(2) (which concerns persons with multiple nationality), the arguments for treating stateless persons as subject to analogous requirements outweighs arguments which favour giving stateless persons preferential treatment.
4. Whilst there is some support in the case law and academic literature for the view that in respect of stateless children born in the receiving country they can be treated as having the same country of former habitual residence as their parents, it is limited and requires a reading contrary to a proper application of VCLT rules of interpretation.

Three conclusions can therefore be drawn. First, it is only by applying an approach based mainly on context and object and purpose that the 'country' aspects of both the 'country of nationality' and the 'country of former habitual residence' phrases can be interpreted satisfactorily. Second, there mostly appears to be agreement that in this context the term 'country', whilst not confined to states, is limited to countries where there is an authority exercising territorial control. Third, as regards the 'former habitual residence' aspect, it would go beyond VCLT rules to 'read down' both of the adjectives—'former' and 'habitual'—so as to extend the scope of the term (as some have suggested) purposively even to certain persons such as stateless children who have never lived in their parents' country of origin.

# 6
# 'Being Persecuted' and Serious Harm
## ('Être persécutée' et préjudice grave)

| | | | | |
|---|---|---|---|---|
| Introduction | 299 | 2.3 Material Scope: Category-Specific Forms of Harm | 348 |
| Antecedents | 301 |
| The Issue of Further Definition | 302 | 2.3.1 Gender-specific persecution | 351 |
| 1 The Meaning of Being Persecuted in the Context of VCLT Rules | 303 | 2.3.2 Sexual orientation-based persecution | 353 |
| 1.1 *Travaux Préparatoires* | 303 | 2.3.3 Age- and child-specific forms of persecution | 355 |
| 1.2 Good Faith | 305 |
| 1.3 Ordinary Meaning | 305 | 2.3.4 Disability-specific forms of persecution | 358 |
| 1.3.1 Ordinary meaning as persistency? | 308 | 3 The Meaning of 'Being Persecuted': Modalities and Incidents | 361 |
| 1.3.2 A human rights reading? | 309 |
| 1.4 Context | 309 | 3.1 Acts of Persecution | 361 |
| 1.4.1 Articles 1A(1), 1B, 1C, 1D, 1F | 309 | 3.2 Actors of Persecution | 362 |
| | | 3.2.1 State actors | 364 |
| 1.4.2 Article 33(1) | 312 | 3.2.2 Non-state actors | 364 |
| 1.4.3 Articles 2–32 | 314 | 3.2.3 Ineffective protectors | 366 |
| 1.5 Object and Purpose | 315 | 3.3 Laws and Related Measures | 366 |
| 1.5.1 A human rights approach | 315 | 3.3.1 Laws persecutory in themselves | 367 |
| 1.5.2 Other approaches | 316 | 3.3.2 Discriminatorily applied laws | 369 |
| 1.6 Subsequent Agreement and Subsequent Practice | 317 | 3.3.3 Prosecution and punishment | 369 |
| | | 3.3.4 Military service laws and related measures | 372 |
| 1.7 Other Rules of International Law | 317 |
| 1.7.1 UNHCR | 318 | 3.3.5 Laws and measures denying nationality or the right to enter or return to one's own country | 373 |
| 1.7.2 Case law | 318 |
| 1.8 Special Meaning | 319 |
| 1.9 Article 32 VCLT | 319 | 3.4 Individual Assessment | 375 |
| 1.10 Article 33 and Authentic Versions | 319 | 3.5 Intensity | 376 |
| 1.11 Conclusions | 319 | 3.5.1 Persecution and discrimination | 379 |
| 1.12 The Human Rights Approach | 320 | 3.6 Actual or Threatened Harm | 384 |
| 2 The Meaning of Being Persecuted: Personal and Material Scope | 321 | 3.7 Indirect or Derivative Harm | 385 |
| | | 3.8 Duration | 386 |
| 2.1 Personal Scope | 321 | 3.9 Intentionality | 391 |
| 2.2 Material Scope: Main Types of Harm | 321 | 3.10 Individualisation (Individual and Group Persecution) | 396 |
| | | 3.10.1 Group persecution | 397 |
| 2.2.1 Physical violence and related harm | 321 | 3.10.2 Prima facie recognition | 398 |
| | | 3.10.3 Armed conflict and generalised violence | 399 |
| 2.2.2 Psychological and related forms of harm | 330 |
| 2.2.3 Socio-economic and cultural harms | 333 | 4 Temporal Scope | 402 |
| | | 4.1 Current Persecution | 403 |
| 2.2.4 Cultural harms | 342 | 4.2 *Sur Place* Persecution | 403 |
| 2.2.5 Environmental harm | 344 | 4.3 Past Persecution | 405 |

*The Refugee Definition in International Law.* Hugo Storey, Oxford University Press. © Hugo Storey 2023.
DOI: 10.1093/oso/9780198842644.003.0006

| 5 Conclusions | 406 | 5.2 Suggested | |
|---|---|---|---|
| 5.1 Basic Propositions | 407 | Propositions | 407 |

## Introduction

This is the first of three chapters devoted to the 'being persecuted' element of the refugee definition. It focusses on persecution as a form of harm. The aims are two-fold: to inquire what basic propositions about this aspect of the definition can now be taken as agreed upon; and to provide the author's own analysis of it.

The notion of 'being persecuted' (*être persécutée* in the French) lies at the heart of the refugee definition. Leading commentaries variously describe it as the 'core element' or the 'key' or 'lynchpin'[1] to the definition.

In analysing this key element, focus will mostly be on the noun 'persecution' rather than the actual words, 'being persecuted', for the reason that the noun names the quality inherent in the verb 'to persecute', but that said, the actual words are of key importance in some respects.

Following the same methodology applied in Chapters 4 and 5, it is necessary to begin analysis of the meaning of 'being persecuted' by consideration of how the Vienna Convention on the Law of Treaties (VCLT)[2] rules apply to it.

Since the essence of the human rights approach (which was discussed in Chapter 3) is to analyse key elements of the refugee definition by reference to International Human Rights Law (IHRL) norms, it might be thought more logical to move straight to examining how persecution arises in relation to violations of the various human rights. This is indeed the approach followed by Hathaway and Foster in the second edition of *The Law of Refugee Status* (TLRS2) who consider the application of the human rights framework to the sorts of claims most commonly made by organising their treatment into three thematic categories: risk to physical security, threats to liberty and freedom, and infringements of autonomy and self-realisation.[3] They contend that this approach better recognises the indivisibility and equality of human rights than the more traditional organising method chosen in the original *The Law on Refugee Status* (TLRS) which, based primarily around the twin 1966 UN Covenants, first addressed civil and political rights and then economic, social, and cultural rights.[4] However, in this chapter, whilst covering much of the same ground, organisational use is made of well-established distinctions based on personal scope (which is also addressed in the chapter on 'well-founded fear'), material scope, temporal scope. This chapter also seeks to identify and analyse well-recognised modalities and 'incidents' of the persecution concept. This will assist the aim of attempting later to identify basic propositions

---

[1] See e.g. Andreas Zimmermann and Claudia Mahler, 'Article 1A, para 2', in Andreas Zimmermann (ed), *The 1951 Convention Relating to the Status of Refugees and Its 1967 Protocol: A Commentary* (OUP 2011) 345, 353; Lorne Waldman, *The Definition of Convention Refugee* (2nd edn, Lexis Nexis 2019) 179.
[2] Vienna Convention on the Law of Treaties (VCLT) (adopted 23 May 1969, entered into force 27 January 1980) 1155 UNTS 331.
[3] James C Hathaway and Michelle Foster, *The Law of Refugee Status* (2nd edn, CUP 2014) 207.
[4] James C Hathaway, *The Law of Refugee Status* (Butterworths Limited 1991) 112–24.

of refugee law that can be said to be shared widely, irrespective of whether they are seen to be based on a human rights approach or an alternative approach.

Accordingly, having first considered the application of VCLT rules, this chapter will then look at personal and material scope; then at various modalities and incidents of the term's material scope (in terms of acts—intensity, severity, duration, nature of infliction (targeting), and actors); and then temporal scope (in terms of past persecution, current and future persecution, and *sur place* claims). Analysis of 'geographical scope', understood in terms of internal protection (or 'internal flight alternative', 'internal relocation alternative') is addressed separately in Chapter 8.

The Article 1A(2) definition provides at best only clues as to the modalities and incidents of refugeehood. Except when it comes to the Convention reasons[5] (which do identify why the persecution concerned is inflicted), it does not explicitly spell out who does what to who, where, when, or how. The definition employs the passive voice 'being persecuted', a formulation that a number of scholars and jurists have seized upon to highlight that it is concerned at root with 'protection against a condition or predicament—*being* persecuted'.[6] Be that as it may, this formulation clearly has in mind the two main *dramatis personae* involved, namely the persecutor(s) and the persecuted. As the Australian Federal Court put it in *Kord*, the 'use of the passive voice conveys a compound notion, concerned both with the conduct of the persecutor and the effect that conduct has on the person being persecuted'.[7] This observation, however, points up the importance of not allowing the characterisation of 'being persecuted' as a condition or predicament to obscure these features. And as a matter of plain grammar, one cannot easily describe all the modalities of 'being persecuted' in the passive voice. Otherwise, we would be saddled with contorted reference to actors of persecution as actors of '[the condition of] being persecuted' and actors of protection as actors of '[the condition of] being protected'.

In terms of *dramatis personae*, there is indeed, in non-state actor cases, a third protagonist integral to the notion of being persecuted, namely a state that is unwilling or unable to protect. If one surveys the literature on the refugee definition, it is essentially devoted to analysing the respective roles of these three protagonists.

Since 2004, with the introduction of the EU Qualification Directive (QD) there is now formal recognition for the first time in treaty form (albeit only regional in scope) of these different modalities.[8] Article 9 deals with 'acts' of persecution and Articles 6 and 7 deal with 'actors of persecution' and 'actors of protection' respectively. Regardless of whether this directive captures the international meaning of these

---

[5] See Chapter 10 on Refugee Convention Reasons.
[6] James C Hathaway and Jason Pobjoy, 'Queer Cases Make Bad Law' (2012) 44(2) NYU Journal of International Law and Politics 315.
[7] *MIMIA v Kord* [2002] 125 FCR 68.
[8] Council Directive 2004/83/EC of 29 April 2004 on minimum standards for the qualification and status of third country nationals or stateless persons as refugees or as persons who otherwise need international protection and the content of the protection granted [2004] OJ L 304/12. See now Directive 2011/95/EU of the European Parliament and of the Council of 13 December 2011 on standards for the qualification of third-country nationals or stateless persons as beneficiaries of international protection, for a uniform status for refugees or for persons eligible for subsidiary protection, and for the content of the protection granted (recast) [2011] OJ L 337/9 (QD (recast)).

modalities precisely, it provides a useful start-point for attempts to add further modal content to the definition of 'being persecuted'.

## Antecedents

The term 'persecution' is as old as human history. By the end of the nineteenth century, it had most frequently been used in the context of religious and political persecution, but not exclusively so.[9]

The 1951 Convention was not the first twentieth-century treaty to make use of the concept of 'persecution'. In the international criminal law/international humanitarian law context, the 1945 Nuremberg Charter included among the crimes against humanity 'persecution on political, racial or religious grounds'.[10] The 1948 London Charter of the International Military Tribunal[11] and Article 45 paragraph 4 of the 1949 Geneva Convention Relating to the Protection of Civilian Persons in Time of War also referred to it.[12] In the international human rights context, Article 14 of the 1948 Universal Declaration of Human Rights (UDHR) includes a right to seek 'asylum from persecution'.[13] Noting uses of the term 'persecution' by the United Nations Relief and Rehabilitation Administration and by military authorities in occupied Europe,[14] Grahl-Madsen reflected that during this period the term was 'in the air'.[15]

Within the field of refugee law, the most direct antecedent of its use in Article 1A(2) is of course the 1946 International Refugee Organization (IRO) Constitution. Among the latter's six categories of refugee were:

> [...] persons who, having resided in Germany or Austria, and being of Jewish origin or foreigners or stateless persons, were victims of Nazi *persecution* and were detained in, or were obliged to flee from, and were subsequently returned to, one of those countries as a result of enemy action, or of war circumstances, and have not yet been firmly resettled therein.[16]

---

[9] Matthew E Price, *Rethinking Asylum History, Purpose, and Limits* (CUP 2010) 24–51.

[10] Nuremberg Charter (Charter of the International Military Tribunal) (adopted 8 August 1945, entered into force 8 August 1945) Article 6(c). See also the earlier Allies' Declaration on the Persecution of the Jews (adopted 17 December 1942) 125 HL Debs 607–12 (Persecution of the Jews: Allies' Declaration).

[11] Agreement by the Government of the United Kingdom of Great Britain and Northern Ireland, the Government of the United States of America, the Provisional Government of the French Republic and the Government of the Union of Soviet Socialist Republics for the prosecution and punishment of the major war criminals of the European Axis (adopted 8 August 1945, entered into force 8 August 1945) 82 UNTS 280.

[12] Geneva Convention relative to the protection of civilian persons in time of war (adopted 12 August 1949, entered into force 21 October 1950) 75 UNTS 287.

[13] Universal Declaration of Human Rights (adopted 10 December 1948) UNGA Res 217 A(III).

[14] Administrative Memorandum Number 39 of the Supreme Headquarters, Allied Expeditionary Force (revised 16 April 1945).

[15] Atle Grahl-Madsen, *The Status of Refugees in International Law. Volume 1: Refugee Character* (Sijthoff 1966) 189.

[16] Constitution of the International Refugee Organization (IRO) (adopted 15 December 1946, entered into force 20 August 1948) 18 UNTS 3, Annex, pt I, s A(3) (emphasis added).

The IRO Constitution also incorporated 'persecution, or fear, based on reasonable grounds of persecution because of race, religion, nationality or political opinions' as one of three 'valid objections' to a refugee's repatriation.[17]

These provisions of the IRO Constitution built in turn on the 1938 Intergovernmental Committee on Refugees (IGCR), established at the Evian Conference in 1938 'to help victims of Nazi persecution in Germany and Austria, providing for their legal protection, maintenance and resettlement'.[18]

However, use of the concept in legal texts was not just familiar to the drafters from its earlier use in League of Nations and related instruments; it also had antecedents in national legal systems.[19] For example, there was reference to it in the British Aliens Act 1905[20] and the 1917 US Immigration Act.[21] By the 1940s, a number of national constitutions referred to it.[22] Further, as can be seen from the terms of the British Aliens Act, there was already some recognition that the concept required an individualised as opposed to a group-based assessment.[23]

## The Issue of Further Definition

The Refugee Convention contains no definition of the term 'being persecuted'. In Chapter 1, note was made of the two main reasons suggested for why the drafters did not provide one (because everyone knew what it meant; and because to define it would be to restrict the scope of something intrinsically protean).[24] It was also noted that, whatever the motives of the drafters, the issue ever since has been to what extent (if at all) the term can be defined further or, at least, given a meaning with more content. The position taken in Chapter 1 is that the attempt to achieve a further definition of this and other key terms of Article 1A(2) is both legitimate and enjoined by application of VCLT rules. However, such an endeavour must avoid seeking to offer a fixed or closed list definition and must not seek to lay down absolute criteria.

Even those who have warned against attempting further definition have sometimes sought to offer significant guidance as to its meaning. Thus, the UNHCR Handbook, having stated at paragraph 51 that '[t]here is no universally accepted definition of

---

[17] ibid. It should be noted that when the concept of persecution was added in this way it was as one element only of a broader definition. As stated by Ivor C Jackson, *The Refugee Concept in Group Situations* (Kluwer Law International 1999) 33; it did not 'exhaust' the refugee notion. It was 'resorted to as an element of "valid objections", i.e. the conditions under which a person already identified as falling within a refugee category could avail himself of the services of the organization'. Even *sub nomine* 'valid objections', it was not the only one. The category of 'objections of a political nature' judged by the organization to be 'valid'—was intended to be wider: see IRO, 'Manual for Eligibility Officers' (1987) paras 27–28, cited by Jackson at 37.

[18] *Yearbook of the United Nations, 1946–47* (United Nations 1947) 807, cited by Jane McAdam, 'Rethinking the Origins of "Persecution" in Refugee Law' (2013) 25(4) IJRL 667, 671, 679.

[19] McAdam (n 18) 671, argues that analysis of the drafting records of the refugee instruments of the first part of the twentieth century reveals that 'the express inclusion of 'persecution' in post-war instruments reflected pre-existing, underlying understandings about the 'preconditions' for refugeehood, rather than creating a fundamentally new conception of the refugee.'

[20] British Aliens Act 1905, s 1(3)(d).
[21] US 1917 Immigration Act, ch 29, s 3.
[22] See McAdam (n 18) 682.
[23] ibid 670.
[24] See Chapter 1, section 5.

"persecution" and various attempts to formulate such a definition have met with little success', proceeds to offer guidance as to its meaning. Thus, in the third edition of *The Refugee in International Law,* Goodwin-Gill and McAdam, despite stating that '[p]ersecution is a concept only too readily filled by the latest examples of one person's inhumanity to another, and little purpose is served by attempting to list all its known measures', proceed to identify as two key components 'the notion of individual integrity and human dignity' on the one hand and 'the manner and degree to which [individuals] stand to be injured'; on the other.[25] Their fourth edition follows the same approach, albeit noting that 'comprehensive analysis requires the general notion of persecution to be related to developments within the broad field of human rights'.[26]

A key task in this chapter is to see what meaning can be given to the term 'being persecuted' applying VCLT rules. On the strength of the conclusions to Chapter 3, the approach to this term's definition must be a human rights one but it will be important throughout to have regard to the meaning given the term by other approaches, in particular the 'circumstantial approach' and the 'US subjective approach'. Keeping in mind different approaches is vital to the inquiry into whether there are basic propositions that have achieved substantial consensus. In accordance with this objective, this chapter will seek to identify all the basic propositions that can be said to have been widely agreed in relation to this element. For convenience they are summarized at the end, along with 'suggested propositions' which condense this author's conclusions on certain unresolved issues.

## 1 The Meaning of Being Persecuted in the Context of VCLT Rules

### 1.1 *Travaux Préparatoires*

The analysis below will follow the ordering applied in Articles 31–32 of the VCLT rules, save for referring first to the 'supplementary means of interpretation' as constituted by the *travaux*, in order to best set the scene.

The *travaux* contain precious little assistance in respect of the 'being persecuted' element. As was noted by Mr Robinson of Israel, '[o]f the three factors governing the definition of the term 'refugee', practically no attention had been paid to the substantive requirements for qualification as a refugee.'[27]

Reference to persecution was first introduced by the United Kingdom in the form of the phrase 'well-founded fear of persecution' in 1950, in a revised draft to the Ad Hoc Committee on Statelessness and Related Problems.[28] Thereafter there were only two

---

[25] Guy S Goodwin-Gill and Jane McAdam, *The Refugee in International Law* (3rd edn, OUP 2007) 93–94; see also ibid 92–93 on 'protected interests'. At ibid 131, they state that '[p]ersecution ... is thus a complex of reasons, interests, and measures'.
[26] Guy S Goodwin-Gill and Jane McAdam (with Emma Dunlop), *The Refugee in International Law* (4th edn, OUP 2021) 69, 67–68.
[27] Conference of Plenipotentiaries on the Status of Refugees and Stateless Persons: Summary Record of the Twenty-second Meeting (26 November 1951) UN Doc A/CONF.2/SR.22.
[28] Ad Hoc Committee on Statelessness and Related Problems, *Comité spécial de l'apatridie et des problèmes connexes, Royaume-Uni: Texte remanié proposé pour l'article premier* (19 January 1950) UN Doc E/AC.32/

types of observations made on its meaning. The first were comments emphasising the need to eschew further codification of the term in order not to limit it.[29] The second were miscellaneous remarks identifying what the term could or could not cover. Thus, as to what the Convention definition *did* cover, there was an exchange between Mr Stolz of the American Federation of Labour (AFL) and Mr Rain of France. In reply to the former's concern about the lack of any specific mention of social and economic harms, Mr Rain said that he 'thought that the nature of the persecution should be described in very broad terms. In actual practice he felt sure that the people referred to by the AFL representatives would be recognised as refugees'.[30] As to what the Convention *did not* cover, during the Conference of Plenipotentiaries, Mr Robinson (Israel) stated that it was difficult to envisage that 'fires, floods, earthquakes or volcanic eruptions, for instance, differentiated between their victims on the grounds of race, religion or political opinion' and that the Convention did not cover 'all man-made events either ... for example, ... refugees fleeing from hostilities' unless they were otherwise covered by Article 1 of the 1951 Convention.[31]

Even though the drafters did not dissect it, it is clear that the paradigm of persecution they had in mind was that inflicted on the victims of the Nazi and Falangist regimes.[32] This lends some support for understanding persecution to be a 'strong word'.[33] Somewhat allied to this, the drafters clearly envisaged that persecution could take the form of both individual and group persecution. As stated by Jackson:

> It was, however, clear from the very outset, that international action on behalf of refugees might well relate to refugee groups despite the 'individual' form of these

---

L.2/Rev.1, para 1. The use of the noun 'persecution' continued to be used in subsequent drafts, including e.g. the internal working group definition which offered a compromise between a broad definition and geographical and temporal limitations: see Ad Hoc Committee on Statelessness and Related Problems, *Comité spécial de l'apatridie et des problèmes connexes, Texte provisoire de paragraphes a insérer dans le rapport sur la question et la suppression de l'apatridie, Proposé par le Président* (13 February 1950) UN Doc E/AC.32/L.36, cited by Terje Einarsen, 'Drafting History of the 1951 Convention and the 1967 Protocol' in Zimmermann (n 1) 55–56.

[29] Conference of Plenipotentiaries on the Status of Refugees and Stateless Persons: Summary Record of the Nineteenth Meeting (26 November 1951) UN Doc A/CONF.2/SR.19, 7–8, 17–18.

[30] Ad Hoc Committee on Statelessness and Related Problems, Seventeenth Meeting (Definition of the term 'refugee') (31 January 1951) UN Doc E/AC.32/SR.17.

[31] Conference of Plenipotentiaries on the Status of Refugees and Stateless Persons: Summary Record of the Twenty-second Meeting (26 November 1951) UN Doc A/CONF.2/SR.22, 6.

[32] As noted by Daniel J Steinbock, 'The Refugee Definition as Law: Issues of Interpretation' in Frances Nicholson and Patrick Twomey (eds), *Refugee Rights and Realities: Evolving International Concepts and Regimes* (CUP 1999) 18: '[ ... ] the Convention's inclusion of persecution for reasons of race, religion, and nationality speaks most directly to [the Nazi] persecutions of 1933–45'.

[33] *HJ (Iran) and HT (Cameroon) v SSHD* [2010] UKSC 31, para 12 (per Lord Hope); *Sanchez-Jimenez v A-G (US)* [2007] 492 F.3d 1223, 1232: 'Although the INA does not define "persecution", we have often repeated that "persecution is an extreme concept, requiring more than a few isolated incidents or verbal harassment or intimidation, and that mere harassment does not amount to persecution"' (citations omitted). See also *Bracic v Holder*, 603 F.3d 1027, 1034 (8th Cir.2010), cited in Deborah Anker, *Law of Asylum in the United States* (Thomson Reuters 2022) §4.4, 254.

refugee definitions. The travaux préparatoires ... contain numerous references to future 'groups' or 'categories' of refugees.[34]

## 1.2 Good Faith

This element of the VCLT rules has been invoked periodically to support interpretation of 'being persecuted', but only as a secondary factor.

## 1.3 Ordinary Meaning

The English word 'persecution' derives through the French from the Latin *persequi*, meaning to pursue or hunt or follow with hostile intent.[35] The task of determining whether 'being persecuted' can be interpreted by giving the term its ordinary meaning has most commonly been seen to require recourse to dictionaries,[36] specifically English and French dictionaries (the English and French versions of the Convention being the only two that are equally authoritative).[37] But even confining attention to dictionaries, it cannot be said that there is one ordinary meaning of the term. In English language dictionaries there is no single or uniform definition of 'persecution' or of 'to persecute'. For the verb 'to persecute', the Online Oxford English Dictionary[38] (OED) lists four meanings:

1. To seek out and subject (a person, group, organization, etc.) to hostility or ill-treatment, esp. on grounds of religious faith, political belief, race, etc.; to torment; to oppress.
2. To afflict, trouble, vex, worry; to harass; to pester, importune, or annoy persistently.
3. a. To chase, hunt, or pursue with intent to capture, injure, or kill.
   b. To follow up, pursue, prosecute (a subject); to carry out, go through with.
4. To prosecute (a person or suit) at law.

The Paperback Oxford Dictionary[39] gives two meanings: 'treat someone in a cruel or unfair way over a long period'; and 'persistently harass someone'. Other English

---

[34] Jackson (n 17) 85. See also Statement of Mr Henkin of the United States, Ad Hoc Committee on Statelessness and Related Problems, First Session: Summary Record of the Third Meeting Held at Lake Success, New York, on Tuesday, 17 January 1950, at 3 p.m. (26 January 1950) UN Doc E/AC.32/SR.3, paras 42–46.
[35] See Marriam-Webster dictionary, available at <https://www.merriam-webster.com/dictionary/persecute> (accessed 14 December 2021).
[36] See p. 81.
[37] Convention Relating to the Status of Refugees (adopted 28 July 1951, entered into force 22 April 1954) 189 UNTS 137, Article 46.
[38] OED Online, 2021 available at <https://www.oed.com>.
[39] Oxford Languages, *Paperback Oxford English Dictionary* (OUP 2012).

dictionaries use kindred expressions, sometimes ones that do not expressly specify anything about duration or intent: e.g. the Collins Dictionary defines it to mean 'cruel and unfair treatment of a person or group, especially because of their religious or political beliefs, or their race'.[40] French dictionaries exhibit similar variations.[41]

Dictionary definitions are also apt to change over time. Thus, the 1980 edition of the OED, 1989 provided the following list:

> To pursue, chase, hunt, drive (with missiles, or with attempts to catch, kill or injure); to pursue with malignancy or enmity and injurious action: espec to oppress with pains and penalties for the holding of a belief held to be injurious or heretical; [and] to harass, trouble, vex, worry; to importune.[42]

Taking stock of dictionary definitions, several points emerge. First, they identify at least five key characteristics, to which this study will give short descriptors:[43]

(i) Treatment that is unjust or unfair (the mistreatment component);
(ii) Treatment that is cruel or serious (the severity component);
(iii) Treatment that is persistent (the duration component);
(iv) Treatment that is inflicted by a human persecutor (the human agency component).
(v) Treatment that is inflicted for a reason (e.g. '... for the holding of a belief held to be injurious or heretical') (the discrimination component).

Second, they do not consistently list all five. Sometimes they identify only one or two of these characteristics. For example, not all identify persistency; some refer to episodic harm such as a single act of killing or injuring.

Third, they sometimes formulate these characteristics in different ways, e.g. where there is some reference to duration, this is not always expressed in the same terms: sometimes reference is made to persistency—'to persistently harass someone'—sometimes to mistreatment that is 'systematic'. As an example of the latter, the Wikipedia entry defines it as the 'systematic treatment of an individual or group by another individual or group'.[44]

---

[40] Collins Advanced English Dictionary (online), Harper Collins Publishers, available at <https://www.collinsdictionary.com/dictionary/english/persecution#:~:text=Persecution%20is%20cruel%20and%20unfair,political%20beliefs%2C%20or%20their%20race> accessed 4 June 2021.
[41] Jean-Yves Carlier, 'The Geneva Refugee Convention Definition and the "Theory of the Three Scales"' in Nicholson and Twomey (n 32) 44 observed that: '[i]n French, persecution is defined as a *traitement injuste et cruel infligé avec acharnement*' (unjust and cruel treatment relentlessly imposed) [citing Petit Robert dictionary] which can be rephrased as *'poursuites injustes et violentes'* (unjust and violent prosecution) [citing Littre dictionary] or as *'importunite conitnuelle'* (continuous harassment) [citing Petit Larousse dictionary]'.
[42] *Oxford English Dictionary, Vol XI* (2nd edn, Clarendon 1980) 591–92.
[43] The characteristics listed here are broadly comparable to the four characteristics identified by Francesco Maiani, 'The Concept of "Persecution" in Refugee Law: Indeterminacy, Context-sensitivity, and the Quest for a Principled Approach' (2010) Les Dossiers du Grihl, Les dossiers de Jean-Pierre Cavaillé, De la persécution. However, he goes too far in saying that: '[t]hey all highlight, ... four universally accepted characteristics of persecution', at least not if by that is meant necessary conditions.
[44] Wikipedia, available at <https://en.wikipedia.org/wiki/Persecution> accessed June 2021.

Likewise, in some dictionary renditions, the definition given conveys the severity of the treatment—'cruel', 'unfair' etc.—but in others it is ascribed an additional element, mistreatment inflicted for a specific reason.

There is also lack of consistency as regards whether the dictionary definitions denote an element of intention on the part of the persecutor. Clearly the second listed meaning in the 1980 OED, with its reference to pursuing 'with malignancy', strongly implies such an intent and the first meaning listed in the current Online OED, with its reference to the 'subject[ion of] (a person, group, organization, etc.) to hostility or ill-treatment, esp. on grounds of religious faith' might also be read to imply intent. It would appear that it was wording of this kind that prompted the Federal Court of Australia in *Ram* to consider that persecution required 'an element of motivation (however twisted) for the infliction of harm'.[45] However, not all the listed definitions state or necessarily imply anything about intent.

Does the fact of multiple meanings entail, as has been the view of some, that it is 'hardly possible' to give an ordinary meaning to the term?[46]

Given the lack of consistency, the answer must be yes, but it remains that almost all dictionary definitions do convey or imply that the mistreatment concerned is at the hands of human actors; it is not simply harm resulting from natural disasters etc. Further, whilst some dictionary definitions offer meanings that can denote mere harm (viz. those that deploy verbs such as 'harass' or 'trouble' or 'worry'), the majority denote something more than mere harm. That is to say, the dictionary definitions do support in general terms the frequent observation that 'persecution' is a 'strong word'.[47] That is understandable if one considers its bare essentials. Clearly it posits harm, but not just any harm will suffice. This feature could be said to be at least lend some support for later discussions highlighting the importance of the notion of the severity of harm.

Before leaving the topic of dictionary definitions, it must be noted that judicial appetite for reliance on them has lessened as time has gone on. Certainly the English-speaking materials of the 1990s in particular did bespeak a marked preference for interpreting the term based on that given as the first meaning in the Oxford English Dictionary of that time ('the action of persecuting or pursuing with enmity and malignity').[48] But in the twenty-first century there has been an increasing awareness worldwide that dictionary definitions in any language provide a problematic basis for ascribing meaning to this term.[49] As noted by Zimmermann and Mahler:

> [ … ] such a purely linguistic approach is to be criticised since any given dictionary might give a different meaning …. This jeopardises the understanding of this

---

[45] As noted by Michelle Foster, *International Refugee Law and Socio-Economic Rights: Refuge from Deprivation* (CUP 2007) 272.
[46] Jackson (n 17) 468, concludes that '[t]he literal context in which the term is employed, i.e. the wording of the refugee definition itself does not … shed any light on its meaning'.
[47] See above n 33.
[48] See e.g. *R v IAT, ex parte Jonah* [1985] ImmAR 7.
[49] See e.g. Kirby, J's statement in *MIMA v Khawar* [2002] 210 CLR 1 (Aus HC) para 108 that he was 'inclined to see more clearly than before the dangers in the use of the dictionary definitions of the word "persecuted" in the Convention definition'.

keystone concept since the result would merely depend on which dictionary best fits the case or the interests of the respective court.[50]

### 1.3.1 Ordinary meaning as persistency?

The perils of seeking to rely on dictionary definitions are well-illustrated by the recent attempt by Scott to argue that the meaning of 'being persecuted' is unambiguous and can be taken to require persistency.[51] In support he dwells on the examples of dictionary usages that convey persistency (e.g. 'To the glory of hys persecuted churche (1546)'). But his own analysis elsewhere notes that definitions of this kind co-exist with ones that do not.[52]

Whatever is made of Scott's overall approach to the meaning of 'being persecuted' when VCLT rules are applied as a unity, it is clear, as regards ordinary meaning, that selected examples do not establish lack of ambiguity. With (as we have seen) at least five characteristics variously woven into one or more of the most commonly given dictionary definitions, it really is impossible to imbue persecution with an ordinary meaning.

Before leaving the topic of ordinary meaning, there is the issue of what relevance if any, can be attached to the fact that there is another international treaty which both uses the term persecution and provides a definition of it: the 1998 Rome Statute of the International Criminal Court. Article 7, paragraph 2(g) of this instrument lists persecution as a crime against humanity and defines it as an 'intentional and severe deprivation of fundamental rights contrary to international law by reason of the identity of the group or collectivity'.[53] The reason why it is inappropriate to attempt any read-across to Article 1A(2) is not only that it is a definition drafted many years after the Refugee Convention, but also that it is one constructed for the purposes of identifying an international crime, a prerequisite for which is establishment of *mens rea* on the part of perpetrators.[54] The ICC Statute and the Refugee Convention have very different purposes.[55] As has been stated in a report for the International Law Commission (ILC), considerations of context and object may well lead to the same term having a different meaning and application in different treaties.[56] However, the fact that there is an existing definition found in an international treaty does underline

---

[50] Zimmermann and Mahler (n 1) 346. See also *Refugee Appeal No 71427/99* [2000] NZRSAA, in which Rodger Haines QC said such an approach lent itself to 'an unseemly ransacking of dictionaries for the *mot juste* appropriate to the case in hand', cited by Foster (n 45) 48.

[51] Matthew Scott, *Climate Change, Disasters, and the Refugee Convention* (CUP 2020) 94.

[52] ibid 109.

[53] Statute of the International Criminal Court (adopted 17 July 1998, entered into force 1 July 2002) 2187 UNTS 90.

[54] See *Prosecutor v Blaškić (Tihomir)*, Case No IT-95-14-A, Appeal judgment [2004] ICL 34.

[55] Goodwin-Gill and McAdam (3rd edn) (n 25) 100–01; Goodwin-Gill and McAdam (4th edn) (n 26) 73–74. See also Zimmermann and Mahler (n 1) 349. The latter cite, inter alia, the decision of the German Federal Constitutional Court, *2 B v R 1497/90* [1991]. See further Hathaway and Foster (n 3) 192.

[56] The report by William Mansfield on the Interpretation of Treaties in the Light of 'any Relevant Rules of International Law Applicable in Relations Between the Parties' (Article 31 (3) (C) of The Vienna Convention on the Law of Treaties), in the Context of General Developments in International Law and Concerns of the International Community (2004) 26 states that: '[a]s the International Tribunal for the Law of the Sea observed in another decision in the *Max Plant litigation*, considerations of context and object may well lead to the same term having different meaning and application in different treaties' (cited by Foster (n 45) 57).

how important to the ascertainment of meaning is consideration of a treaty's context and object and purpose, along with other VCLT considerations.

### 1.3.2 A human rights reading?

It has been said that there is no basis in Article 1A(2) for a human right reading of the term 'being persecuted'.[57] That is obviously true inasmuch as the wording does not as such refer to violations of human rights, but neither does it exclude a human rights understanding of the term. In any event, the clear conclusion is that there is no unambiguous ordinary meaning that can be ascertained. Hence other VCLT rules must play an important role.

## 1.4 Context

Article 31(2) VCLT specifies that the preamble is one of the sources for the context of a treaty. It is the contents of the first paragraph of the 1951 Convention's Preamble that provides the strongest support for the view that interpreting the refugee definition, including the key 'being persecuted' element, should be by reference to human rights norms. Precisely how this provision impacts on interpretation is dealt with below in the subsection on object and purpose.

Bearing in mind that 'context' also includes other provision of the same treaty, it is necessary to consider also the relevance to interpreting the term 'being persecuted' of other elements of Article 1A and to then consider Article 33(1) and also those provisions that establish refugee rights (Articles 2–32).

### 1.4.1 Articles 1A(1), 1B, 1C, 1D, 1F

Rather like the argument that the term 'being persecuted' was not defined because 'everyone knew' who it applied to, it is possible to argue that Article 1A(1) functions as a demonstration that to establish a well-founded fear of 'being persecuted' under Article 1A(2), an applicant has only to show that he or she is in the same or a comparable position as 'statutory refugees', as they are termed. However, whatever might have been the basis for maintaining such an argument in the first decade or so of the signing of the 1951 Convention, the third paragraph of the Preamble to the 1951 Convention makes clear that the purpose of the Convention is not simply to 'consolidate previous international agreements'; it is also to 'extend the scope of and the protection accorded by such instruments by means of a new agreement.' Likewise, the Preamble to the 1967 Protocol (which also forms part of the context of the Refugee Convention for VCLT purposes) contains an important acknowledgement of the fact that the refugee definition was meant to have ongoing application to 'new refugee situations'.[58]

---

[57] e.g. David Cantor, 'Defining Refugees: Persecution, Surrogacy and the Human Rights Paradigm' in Bruce Burson and David Cantor (eds) *Human Rights and the Refugee Definition* (Brill Nijhoff 2016) 371–6. See further Chapter 3, sections 3 and 4.

[58] Protocol Relating to the Status of Refugees (adopted 31 January 1967, entered into force 4 October 1967) 606 UNTS 267.

Some, albeit limited, aid as regards the meaning of the term 'being persecuted' can, however, be gleaned from other paragraphs of Article 1.

In relation to Article 1B, whilst it stands as evidence of the concern of the state parties to limit the scope of the refugee definition numerically, the geographical and temporal limitations it imposes do not impact on the conceptual contents of Article 1A(2). Both limitations were removed by the 1967 Protocol.[59]

Article 1C is replete with potential relevance to the Article 1A(2) definition of refugee because it uses some (or variants) of the same key terms that appear in the latter, in particular 'protection', 'country of nationality', and 'fear of persecution'. Adding to that, the very existence of cessation clauses can be said to demonstrate that persecution within Article 1A (2) must be understood as a contingent state of affairs and that changes in individual and/or country conditions can bring to an end the real risk someone faces of being persecuted and hence the need for international protection.[60] The clear reference in the first paragraph of Article 1C(5) to current persecution stands in juxtaposition with the express reference in the second paragraph to 'previous persecution'.

There is continuing debate as to whether the terms common to both Article 1A(2) and 1C should be interpreted so as to have the same or a 'parallel' meaning. Kneebone and O'Sullivan, for example, contend that there is no symmetry since protection in Article 1C must mean effective protection 'not limited to protection against persecution' or 'mere absence of fear of persecution'.[61] However, that is difficult to square with other commentaries (and the view adopted in this book) which consider that in Article 1A(2) the term 'protection' must equally be taken to denote effective protection (and be more than mere absence of persecution) anyway.[62]

Irrespective of whether the terms in common have the same or analogous meaning, several provisions of Article 1C underscore the centrality to the refugee definition of the concept of protection. Thus, Article 1C, paragraph 1 ('He has voluntarily re-availed himself of the protection of the country of his nationality') highlights the pivotal role played by the concept of protection of the country of nationality as an act capable in itself of refuting the existence of any continuing risk of persecution.

---

[59] Stefanie Schmahl, 'Article 1B' in Zimmermann, *Commentary* (n 1) 469, 473. Article 1, para 3 of the 1967 Protocol retains the option for States to keep the geographical constraints. There is no similar provision in the UNHCR Statute.

[60] The UNHCR, Handbook on Procedures and Criteria for Determining Refugee Status and Guidelines on International Protection under the 1951 Convention and the 1967 Protocol Relating to the Status of Refugees (Geneva, 2019, reissued in 2019) (UNHCR Handbook or Handbook) states at para 111 that the cessation clauses under Article 1C 'are based on the consideration that international protection should not be granted where it is no longer necessary or justified.' Paragraph 12(i) states that the cessation clauses are an aspect of the 'basic definition'. See also Susan Kneebone and Maria O'Sullivan, 'Article 1C' in Zimmermann (n 1) 485.

[61] Kneebone and O'Sullivan (n 60) 522–23, 528. For a different approach, seeking to derive affirmative rights from Article 1C(5) itself, see Georgia Cole, 'Cessation' in Cathryn Costello, Michelle Foster, and Jane McAdam (eds), *The Oxford Handbook of International Refugee Law* (OUP 2021) 1007–45, 1038.

[62] See p. 447 and p. 466. The CJEU discerns a strong 'parallelism' between the refugee definition and the cessation clauses: see Joined Cases C-175/08, C-176/08, C-178/08, and C-179/08 *Salahadin Abdulla and Others* [2010] ECR I-0000; Case C-255/19 *SSHD v O A* [2021] ECLI:EU:C:2021:36.

Similarly, under Article 1C, paragraphs 2 and 3, (voluntary) reacquisition of nationality and acquisition of a new nationality are seen as acts capable of negating any real risk of persecution.

As regards the second paragraph of Article 1C(5), UNHCR has argued that the 'compelling reasons' clause should be read as reflecting a broader humanitarian principle which should be applied in the context of Article 1A(2). Although the wording of Article 11(3) of the recast Qualification Directive accepts as much,[63] there has been no judicial consensus outside the EU law framework that such a provision, which is stated to concern statutory refugees, can be read into Article 1A(2).[64]

Article 1D also has potential relevance by virtue of its use of the term 'protection', although the actor of protection (and assistance) in this context is strictly confined to organs or agencies of the UN other than UNHCR. However, by virtue of Article 1D's personal scope applying to persons who are refugees (Palestinian refugees), there is no necessary linkage between this provision and the substantive requirements of the refugee definition set out in Article 1A(2), although an applicant excluded by Article 1D may still qualify as a refugee under Article 1A(2).[65]

Although Article 1E does not refer to protection, it could also be said to reinforce, in similar fashion to Articles 1B and 1C, the centrality to the refugee definition of the notion of protection. In this provision the fact of being recognized as having the rights and obligations which are attached to the possession of the nationality of the country in which they have taken up residence, is seen as sufficient to establish that an applicant does not need the benefit of Article 1A(2). That is so even if he or she remains as someone having a well-founded fear of being persecuted in their country of nationality (or habitual residence, if an applicant is stateless).[66]

Like Articles 1D and 1E, Article 1F operates as an exclusion clause whose effect is that the issue of whether a person qualifies as a refugee under Article 1A(2) is irrelevant. Even if an applicant meets all the requirements of the Article 1A(2) definition, they will not qualify as a refugee if falling within the Article 1F provisions. A corollary of this is that Article 1F reflects acceptance that persecutors can be persecuted. Whilst the commission, for example, of an international crime within the scope of Article 1F(a), has the effect of excluding a person from the scope of the refugee definition, it does not necessarily mean that they might not have a well-founded fear of being persecuted.[67] But this juxtaposition might be said to convey that, as much as the Convention drafters wanted to confine the class of refugees to those who met a certain criterion of legitimacy, they chose not to insert that into the definition of refugee in Article 1A(2).[68]

---

[63] QD (recast) (n 8).
[64] *Hoxha & Anor v SSHD* [2002] EWCA Civ 1403. See also Hathaway and Foster (n 3).
[65] Francesca P Albanese and Lex Takkenberg, *Palestinian Refugees in International Law* (2nd edn, OUP 2020) 105–24. See Chapter 1, section 2.1.3 and Chapter 7, section 3.10.3.
[66] Reinhard Marx, 'Article 1E' in Zimmermann (n 1) 573.
[67] Mutaz M Qafisheh and Valentina Azarova, 'Article 1D' in Zimmermann (n 1) 577.
[68] Article 2(d) of the QD (recast) (n 8) by contrast, does.

### 1.4.2 Article 33(1)

To regard Article 33(1) as having interpretive value in construing Article 1A(2) is certainly consistent with VCLT rules regarding context. There is an obvious reason to consider the relevance of Article 33(1) to interpreting the term 'being persecuted'. This resides in its reference to a person's 'life or freedom' being threatened ('on account of his race, religion, nationality, membership of a particular social group or political opinion'). The similarity of subject-matter has indeed been seized on by some as a reason to treat this phraseology as determinative of the meaning of 'being persecuted'. Such an approach has often been associated with the early analysis by Zink.[69] However, his approach was later lent partial support by Weis who (noting numerous instances in drafts of the Refugee Convention where persecution and *'life or freedom'* were used interchangeably), considered that this phrase was intended as a 'shorthand' for 'persecution' in Article 1A(2).[70] From one perspective, a 'shorthand' can be understood to capture the essence of a full definition. Be that as it may, treating Article 33(1) as informing the meaning of 'being persecuted' gives rise to several difficulties.

An initial difficulty is that if the drafters intended Article 33(1) to be the basis, one would have expected them to have made this clear, whereas examination of the *travaux préparatoires* discloses rather that they gave 'little thought' to the different formulations.[71]

A second difficulty with the approach of using Article 33(1) as the basis for definition, even when a broad definition is given to 'life or freedom', is that at best it does no more than substitute one set of indeterminate terms for another. Indeed, 'life or freedom' is a term that is particularly susceptible of competing understandings. At least in terms of ordinary meaning, it is capable of both a narrow and a broad reading. Thus, on the one hand, for Zink and the US Supreme Court in *Cardoza Fonseca*[72] and *Stevic*,[73] the words were to be understood narrowly as referencing threats to life or physical security or physical integrity. On the other hand, for others, it is possible, even on a purely literal construction to elicit a much broader approach.[74] Whereas 'life' would seem categorically a narrower term than persecution (it being easy to identify persecutory threats other than threats to life), the phrase is disjunctive, referring to 'life *or* freedom'. Being expressed in unqualified terms, 'freedom' is certainly capable of being read as a broader term than persecution, since it implies that threats to or interferences with any freedom might suffice, including with the exercise of a qualified right. Yet a mere interference with a qualified human right is not necessarily one likely to cause significant harm. Indeed, when discussing the *travaux*, Grahl-Madsen

---

[69] Karl Friedrich Zink, 'Zur Bestimmung des Begriffs "Verfolgung" im Sinne des Abkommens vom 28. Juli 1951 über die Rechtsstellung der Flüchtlinge' (1956) 2 Internationales Asyl-Colloquium.

[70] Paul Weis (ed), *The Refugee Convention 1951* (CUP 1995) 303, 341.

[71] Goodwin-Gill and McAdam (3rd edn) (n 25) 233, note that '[s]o far as the drafters of the [Refugee] Convention were aware of a divergence between the words defining refugee status and those requiring *non-refoulement*, they gave little thought to the consequences.'

[72] *INS v Cardoza-Fonseca* [1987] 480 US 421.

[73] *INS v Stevic* [1984] 467 US 407.

[74] Jackson (n 17) 473, considers that the drafters clearly intended a broad approach to this term's meaning. He states that the wording of Article 33(1)—in particular 'where his life or freedom would be threatened', 'would seem to be clearly inconsistent with the notion of "singling-out"'.

cites the statement of Sir Leslie Brass (United Kingdom) that 'threat to freedom was a relative term and might not involve severe risks'.[75] Canvassing a broad understanding, some commentators, e.g. Lauterepacht and Bethlehem, have argued that 'the threat contemplated in Article 33(1) [may be] broader than simply the risk of persecution ... [including] a threat to life or freedom [that] may arise other than in consequence of persecution'.[76]

By virtue of the possible range of approaches to the meaning of 'life or freedom', it must be doubted that the UNHCR Handbook and many other commentators are correct to consider that whilst persecution is broader than threats to 'life or freedom on account of race, religion, nationality, political opinion or membership of a particular social group', the latter are 'always persecution'.[77] That assertion is only true if 'life or freedom' is narrowly understood as concerned with physical security and integrity. It should also be observed that the position taken in the UNHCR Handbook is difficult to square with the prevailing view voiced by Weis, Grahl-Madsen, and others that the meanings of 'being persecuted' and [threats to] 'life or freedom' are interchangeable.[78]

A third problem is that there are unacceptable consequences to applying either an unduly narrow or an unduly broad interpretation of 'life or freedom' to the understanding of 'being persecuted'. If treated as fully furnishing the meaning of the term 'being persecuted', an approach based on a narrow understanding of 'life or freedom' could lend itself to denial of protection to persons who, whilst potentially at risk of persecution, do not face a threat to their 'life or freedom'. Such a scenario could happen if, for example, a decision maker was not prepared to construe economic proscription as a threat to life or freedom.[79] Conversely, if an unduly broad approach is taken, then that could potentially mean conferring the protection of non-refoulement to persons who do not need it.

However, also problematic is the mid-way position that regards the two terms—persecution and 'threat to life or freedom'—as 'interchangeable'. Such a position depends on the interpreter electing to read both terms as broadly synonymous. But even read thus, it does not follow that each is equally capable of informing the meaning of the other. Unlike Article 1A(2) which sets out the constituent elements of the definition of 'refugee', Article 33(1) only applies to those who are *already* 'refugees'. The personal scope of Article 33(1) is specified as applicable to 'a refugee'; those protected against refoulement are refugees as defined by Article 1A(2).[80] This entails, as stated by

---

[75] Grahl-Madsen (n 15) 193, citing UN Doc E/AC.32/SR/20, 14.
[76] Elihu Lauterpacht and Daniel Bethlehem, 'The Scope and Content of the Principle of Non-Refoulment: Opinion' in Erika Feller, Volker Türk, and Frances Nicholson (eds), *Refugee Protection in International Law: UNHCR's Global Consultations on International Protection* (CUP 2003) 124.
[77] See UNHCR Handbook (n 60) para 51; see also para 52.
[78] Grahl-Madsen (n 15).
[79] Scott Rempell, 'Defining Persecution' (2013) 2013(1) Utah Law Rev 283. He gives the example of the case of *Mirzoyan v Gonzales* [2006] 457 F.3d 217, in which the Second Circuit concluded that these interferences with her economic opportunities 'might constitute a 'substantial economic disadvantage', but her treatment is unlikely to constitute a 'threat to [her] life or freedom'.
[80] Save for the two exceptions specified in its second paragraph, namely, if a refugee poses a danger to the security of the country of refuge or if he or she constitutes a danger to the community of the country by virtue of having committed a particularly serous crime: see Walter Kälin, Martina Caroni, and Lukas Heim, 'Article 33, para 1' in Zimmermann (n 1) 1360.

Brown LJ in *Lazarevic*, that 'Article 1 must govern the scope of Article 33 rather than the other way around'.[81]

Properly recognising the limitations of seeking to use Article 33(1) to inform the meaning of Article 1A(2) does, however, point up the importance of consideration of object and purpose, in particular protection of refugees.[82]

At the same time, it cannot be ruled out that Article 33(1) has at least some analogical bearing on the interpretation of Article 1A(2). Both encapsulate in different ways a principle of non-refoulement and Article 33(1)'s wording does recognise that the prohibition of refoulement includes indirect refoulement ('in any manner whatsoever to the frontiers or territories'). In Chapter 4, it was noted that this principle may have a role to play in cases of persons who are multiple nationals or who have more than one country of former habitual residence. In Chapter 8, this feature will be seen to have potential implications for the development of the notion of an internal protection alternative (IPA).[83]

1.4.3 Articles 2–32

Is light shed on the meaning of 'being persecuted' by any other provisions of the Convention dealing with refugee rights?

Whilst there is considerable force in the argument that Article 2–32 demonstrate that the drafters were working within an overall framework of IHRL,[84] it is extremely hard to distil any specific ingredient of these rights that could be said to inform the meaning of 'being persecuted'. The core problem is that Articles 2–33 were intended to address the situation of refugees in the host country of asylum and were largely drawn from existing international law standards relating to aliens.

Nevertheless, note should be made of the approach of Hathaway and Foster and the Michigan Guidelines authors in relation to the issue of the internal protection alternative. They proceed on the premise that Articles 2–34 do shed light on the meaning of persecution, inasmuch as they argue that lack of access to standards equivalent to Articles 2–34 in another part of the country of origin can have the result that such persons are to be considered as at real risk of serious harm against which they are not adequately protected. However, in Chapter 8 this study finds their approach to lack cogency and to have received little support in the case law or wider literature.

Hence, little if any direct assistance can be drawn by reference to Article 2–33. Attempts to argue otherwise have not met with consensus.

---

[81] *Lazarevic v SSHD* [1997] EWCA Civ 1007. That this feature should not, however, prevent recourse to Article 33(1) as an aid to construction of Article 1A(2) was made clear by Pill and Clarke LJJ in *Revenko v SSHD* [2000] EWCA Civ 500, paras 69, 72, 111, 113–15.

[82] See Chapter 2, section 2.5; see further James C Hathaway, *The Rights of Refugees Under International Law* (CUP 2005) 305, 307; Kees Wouters, *International Legal Standards for the Protection from Refoulement* (Intersentia 2009) 57; Kälin, Caroni, and Heim (n 80) 1388–89.

[83] See Chapter 4, section 3.3.6.2 and Chapter 8, section 4.1.5.

[84] See Chapter 3, section 4.1.5.

## 1.5 Object and Purpose

1.5.1 A human rights approach
Given the inadequacies of seeking to define 'being persecuted' either in terms of its ordinary meaning or by reference to its context (Article 33(1) in particular), it becomes all the more vital to consider what meaning can be ascertained from the Convention's object and purpose. As set out in Chapter 2, the Convention can be said to have a number of objects and purposes, but the most basic is protection against persecution/serious harm[85] and in that context there are a number of cogent reasons for construing that purpose in human rights terms. Foremost is that the Preamble's first paragraph, by identifying the principle enshrined in the UDHR that 'human beings shall enjoy fundamental rights and freedoms without discrimination', bespeaks that persecution is about endangerment to such rights and freedoms.[86]

In terms of the relevance of this reference to human rights in the first preambular paragraph, it must also be observed that none of the other explicitly stated purposes— the reference in the fourth preambular paragraph to the fact that 'the grant of asylum may place unduly heavy burdens on certain countries' and to the need for 'international cooperation' or the reference in the fifth preambular paragraph to 'the social and humanitarian nature of the problem of refugees'—are capable on their own of generating a lexicon of meaning. At best the 'heavy burdens' clause acts as a fetter on too broad an understanding of the definition.[87] As often as not, the 'social and humanitarian' clause has been seen to reinforce the efficacy of a human rights approach,[88] but even when understood to embody a distinct purpose, it offers at most a background factor, requiring decision makers to bear in mind the broader framework of international efforts of a social and humanitarian nature. '[I]nternational cooperation' is a given premise. At best, therefore, the aforementioned clauses can be said to operate as influences at the margins of any elaboration of the definition—but not as shedding any light on its core contents in the same way as the first preambular paragraph.

As regards the second preambular paragraph, Goodwin-Gill[89] is undoubtedly correct to highlight that its reference to non-discrimination is concerned with the rights of refugees after they have fled their country of origin and focuses on treatment *in the host state* of those recognised as refugees and so it cannot be construed to identify a purpose relating to interpretation of persecution *in the country of origin*. Scott[90] has

---

[85] The third recital of the Preamble refers to the need 'to revise and consolidate previous international agreements relating to the status of refugees and to extend the scope and *protection* accorded by such instruments by means of a new agreement' (emphasis added).
[86] Mark R Von Sternberg, *The Grounds of Refugee Protection in the Context of International Human Rights and Humanitarian Law: Canada and United States Case Law Compared* (Martinus Nijhoff 2002) 314.
[87] See Chapter 2, section 2.5.5; see also e.g. Dawson J in *Applicant A v MIEA* [1997] 190 CLR 225; *Khawar* (n 49) para 47.
[88] See e.g. Kirby J in *Chen Shi Hai v MIMA* [2000] 201 CLR 293, para 308; UNHCR ExCom, Agenda for Protection (2003).
[89] Guy S Goodwin-Gill, 'Judicial Reasoning and "Social Group" after Islam and Shah' (1999) 11 IJRL 538.
[90] Scott (n 51) 125–26. See below section 3.5.1.

argued that this does not matter, as the reference to non-discrimination in the first preambular paragraph is 'far broader' and does offer an alternative object. However, it would be wholly artificial to isolate non-discrimination per se as the governing purpose when it occurs within a paragraph identifying what the UN Charter and the UDHR affirm.

Although the firm conclusion of this study is that the human rights approach to interpretation of 'being persecuted' is the only viable approach, it must be acknowledged that its adoption requires a considerable leap. What is being contended is not simply that the term 'being persecuted' can be construed to mean (sufficiently severe) violations of human rights but that such human rights are to be interpreted and applied in turn within the framework of IHRL. As voiced by Waller, LJ in a UK case when outlining Hathaway's theory:

> [ ... ] core entitlements [relevant to the meaning of 'being persecuted'] may be found by reference either to obligations under international law (obligations between states), or by reference to the human rights of individuals, for example pursuant to the Conventions on Human Rights, or as recognised by the international community at large.[91]

Nevertheless, we saw in Chapter 3 that such a leap coheres with the approach taken under the VCLT rules of interpretation of a treaty in three main ways. First, the VCLT rules require such interpretation to take place within the framework of international law. Second, more particularly, they endorse interpretation taking place by close reference to cognate treaties. That is why central to the human rights approach are the commonalities between the 1951 Convention and IHRL treaties.[92] Third, in the nature of the Refugee Convention, which deploys generic terms (including 'being persecuted'), it is a 'law-making treaty' requiring an evolutive approach to the meaning of its key terms.[93] This links to what was said earlier about the need for any definition of 'being persecuted' to be open-ended.

### 1.5.2 Other approaches

It must be acknowledged that other approaches to the interpretation of the refugee definition, especially the 'being persecuted' element—in particular the 'circumstantial approach', the 'US subjective approach' and the closely related 'case-by-case' approach—have also sought in whole or in part to base themselves on considerations of object and purpose. However, Chapter 3 gave reasons for rejecting each of these approaches, albeit it was intimated therein that in terms of the search for basic propositions about which there is broad consensus, they have mostly come to the same conclusions.[94]

---

[91] *Sepet and Bulbul v SSHD* [2003] UKHL 15, para 177.
[92] See e.g. p. 153, p. 154, p. 157, p. 158, p. 160, and p. 165.
[93] See Chapter 2, section 2.5.1.
[94] See p. 134.

## 1.6 Subsequent Agreement and Subsequent Practice

Article 31(3)(a) and (b) VCLT require the taking into account (together with the context) of subsequent agreement (between the parties regarding the interpretation of the treaty or the application of its provisions) and subsequent practice (in the application of the treaty which establishes the agreement of the parties regarding its interpretation) respectively. From the analysis in Chapter 2, it is clear that, apart from the 1967 Protocol itself, there has not been any subsequent agreement that touches on the meaning of 'being persecuted'. With regard to subsequent practice, we observed in that chapter that, whilst no sources appear to fall strictly within its terms either, this provision can be seen as lending a degree of legitimacy to cognate treaties, UNHCR materials, and case law, at least as sources of evidence of subsequent practice, or, failing that of state practice in the general sense falling within the ambit of Article 32 VCLT. None of this, however, enables any straightforward read-across from such sources to interpreting the 'being persecuted' element. They can be said to lend weight to an approach based on international law norms, IHRL norms in particular; they also help the process of trying to crystallise agreed propositions from UNHCR, judicial, and other materials that can be said to furnish evidence of emerging state practice; but they cannot furnish any agreed definition as such.

## 1.7 Other Rules of International Law

Article 31(3)(c) enjoins that interpretation take into account together with the context 'any relevant rules of international law applicable in the relations between the parties'. As outlined in Chapter 2, the importance of this VCLT provision is somewhat elusive in the context of the 1951 Convention. On a strict interpretation, it is difficult to identify the IHRL instruments as ones that are 'applicable in the relations between the parties' as none of the human rights law instruments is universally ratified.[95] However, this provision does at least confirm that interpretation must take place within the broader framework of international law and rules of possible relevance can include custom, general principles and, under certain circumstances, treaty provisions.

One proposition that can be inferred when considering the meaning of 'being persecuted' in the context of customary international law is that acts that would be a violation of peremptory norms against the infliction of harm must, by virtue of their gravity, ipso facto amount to persecutory conduct. That is one reason why acts of torture, for example, can be considered to constitute persecutory acts per se. The same goes for the customary law prohibition of deliberate targeting of civilian population. However, peremptory norms of this kind are few in number.[96]

As regards treaties, if it is accepted that this provision permits reference to them,[97] then of particular relevance here would be the international human rights treaties. On

---

[95] Cantor (n 57).
[96] For discussion of the role of customary international law in refugee law, see Hélène Lambert, 'Customary refugee Law' in Costello et al (n 61) 240–57.
[97] See Chapter 2, section 2.7.

this footing, Foster notes that Article 31(3)(c) offers 'at least an implicit justification for Hathaway's initial reference to the International Bill of Rights as an instructive tool for ascertaining the meaning of "being persecuted".'[98]

According to Scott, a relevant rule that should have a strong impact on interpretation of 'being persecuted' is the non-discrimination norm.[99] He considers non-discrimination to be both a norm of customary international law and a norm that a 'super-majority' of states have agreed to be bound in several human rights treaties.[100] However, it is only in treaties that the non-discrimination norm has been particularised. If non-discrimination is to be considered as falling within Article 31(3)(c) by virtue of a super-majority of states having agreed to be bound by it under treaty law, it is difficult to see why the same is not true of other human rights guarantees. In any event, whether strictly compatible with Article 31(3)(c), it remains that, in the words of the 2006 ILC Report, treaties can 'provide evidence of the common understanding of the parties as to the object and purpose of the treaty under interpretation'.[101]

### 1.7.1 UNHCR

To the extent that Article 31(3)(c) can be said, directly or indirectly, to justify recourse to UNHCR materials, the latter increasingly tend towards a human rights approach to the meaning of 'being persecuted'. In Chapter 3, it was noted that despite UNHCR still not definitively endorsing a human rights approach—and still on occasions reconfirming the 'circumstantial approach' to its meaning—the position taken in its 2001 publication on interpreting Article 1A(2) was predominantly a human rights one and its growing catalogue of Guidelines on International Protection continue that trend.[102]

### 1.7.2 Case law

Insofar as Article 31(3)(c) VCLT justifies recourse to jurisprudence, it cannot be said that the latter reflects a substantial consensus about the proper approach to interpretation of the 'being persecuted' element. A human rights approach is still not applied or scarcely applied in several of the world's regions, in particular Africa the Americas, and it was earlier noted that in the US the 'subjective approach' still holds sway, notwithstanding significant references in the US to IHRL norms.[103] At the same time, irrespective of what approach is taken to this particular VCLT provision, case law does appear to converge on a number of matters, as will be discussed further below.

---

[98] Foster (n 45) 56.
[99] Scott (n 51) 94, 116.
[100] ibid.
[101] International Law Commission (ILC), 'Fragmentation of international law: difficulties arising from the diversification and expansion of international law. Report of the Study Group of the International Law Commission, finalized by Martti Koskenniemi (13 April 2006) UN Doc A/CN.4/L.682, paras 414–15.
[102] See Chapter 3, section 2.1.2.
[103] See p. 133.

## 1.8 Special Meaning

As noted by Gardiner, the Article 1A(2) definition of refugee can in itself be classified as a 'special meaning' since it represents a treaty provision interpreting a key term. However, it does not assist with the meaning of its constituent elements.

## 1.9 Article 32 VCLT

So far as concerns Article 32, we have already considered what light is shed by the *travaux* as to the meaning of 'being persecuted'. It remains to consider what other 'supplementary means of interpretation' there are and what interpretive value they have.

By its terms, recourse to supplementary means of interpretation, including preparatory works, is apt when the procedure set out in Article 32 (a) leaves the meaning ambiguous or obscure; or (b) leads to a result which is manifestly absurd or unreasonable. As noted earlier, it is hard to deny that the ordinary meaning of the term 'being persecuted' is ambiguous.[104] But even assuming Article 32 can apply, an important difficulty is that it encompasses an abundance of potential materials, including UNHCR, judicial, and academic materials. Although as one would expect of a body of materials of such vast quantity and variety, it exhibits disagreements about many matters, it is nevertheless possible to distil from it a state practice in the broad sense[105] about a number of key propositions, including ones pertaining to the meaning of being persecuted.

## 1.10 Article 33 and Authentic Versions

As regards Article 33 VCLT, it is salient that the Refugee Convention stipulates that both English and French are authentic versions. However, as noted in Chapter 2, only two provisions with any possible relevance to Article 1A(2) have been seen to raise issues under this provision: the meaning of the verb to return/*refoule* in Article 33(1); and the meaning of 'well-founded fear' in Article 1A(2). Regarding the latter, whilst the French '*craignant avec raison d'être persécutée*' does shed light on the meaning of well-founded fear,[106] it does not point to any different reading of 'being persecuted' from the English version.

## 1.11 Conclusions

What emerges from consideration of the meaning of 'being persecuted' under VCLT rules is a mixed picture. On the one hand, such consideration clearly does not deliver its meaning on a plate. On the other hand, it does offer guidance in at least two

---

[104] See above section 1.3.
[105] See Chapter 2, n 69.
[106] See p. 663.

respects. First, it strongly indicates the need for approaching this term's meaning by reference to international law norms, IHRL norms in particular. Second, whilst it yields hardly any state practice in the strict sense, it does, by various routes, justify recourse to UNHCR, judicial, and academic materials and does thus legitimise the attempt to examine the extent to which these materials demonstrate agreement about a number of basic propositions.

## 1.12 The Human Rights Approach

Whilst, as just stated, VCLT rules strongly indicate the need to approach the meaning of 'being persecuted' by reference to international law norms, IHRL norms in particular, the limitations of such an approach must be recognised at the outset. Such an approach does not as such identify any specific content; it only identifies a framework of reference. At the same time, as we also saw in Chapter 3, the human rights approach has been considerably developed and made operational by reference to a known, ascertainable, and detailed set of objective norms. All versions of this approach have always seen the 'being persecuted' element as particularly amenable to such treatment. That is because all see the basic protection afforded by the refugee definition to be against serious violations or denials of human rights. The essential step in all versions is to understand persecutory acts accordingly.

In the nature of the existing corpus of human rights law, there are manifold human rights capable of being violated by interferences or threats that individuals can face and these may overlap.[107] Thus a threat to kill or injure someone can be translated as a potential violation of the right to life or the prohibition of ill treatment; a threat to shut down a newspaper can be rendered as a potential violation of the right to expression or the right to respect for private life, etc. More than one potential violation may arise in one and the same case. But to be able to conceptualise such harms as potential violation of human rights in this way, the decision maker must be aware of the contents of IHRL norms. At the time of the drafting of the twin Covenants—the International Covenant on Civil and Political Rights (ICCPR) and the International Covenant on Economic, Social and Cultural Rights (ICESCR)—the only international instrument seeking to identify human rights guarantees in any detail was the (non-binding) UDHR.[108] The position is radically different today. There is now a formidable array of international human rights instruments, nine global treaties, and a large body of 'soft-law' instruments. The essential components of each of the treaty instruments can be broken down into three: enumeration of certain human rights; mechanisms for establishing which of the rights in each treaty are absolute or qualified (mechanisms used include making distinctions between derogable and nonderogable rights, and between unqualified rights and rights that have permissible limitations and between rights of immediate obligation and others); and third, specification of treaty-monitoring mechanisms, if

---

[107] Walter Kälin and Jörg Künzli, *The Law of International Human Rights Protection* (2nd edn, OUP 2019) 36–49, 87–112. For reasons why this study chooses not to limit the human rights understanding of persecution to severe violation of 'basic' human rights, see p. 196–198.

[108] Although the drafters were aware of drafts of what became the 'International Bill of Rights'.

any.[109] It is beyond the scope of this book to identify the corpus of IHRL in the form of treaties in any detail, but if a human rights approach is to be taken to this element of the refugee definition, then it becomes essential that decision makers have at least a working knowledge of the different IHRL treaties and of the specific articles which identify various rights together with any separate provisions that constitute qualifications to such rights or establish treaty-monitoring mechanisms.

In light of the above, the remaining parts of this chapter focus strongly on a conceptualisation of 'being persecuted' in terms of serious violations of human rights. However, we cannot ignore that not everyone agrees with this conceptualisation. This entails that in seeking to establish what has come to be agreed about its meaning, our analysis must not leave out the contributions also made by non-human rights approaches.

## 2 The Meaning of Being Persecuted: Personal and Material Scope

In this part we look at personal scope (briefly) and then material scope, considering first the main types of harm and then the forms specific to particular categories of persons.

### 2.1 Personal Scope

Chapter 1 addressed and rejected criticisms that the refugee definition has a limited personal scope. Chapters 4 and 5 confirmed that the nationality and statelessness requirements ensure that both nationals and non-nationals can fall within the scope of the refugee definition. Hence the 'being persecuted' element of the definition is one capable of being established by 'any person'.[110]

### 2.2 Material Scope: Main Types of Harm

#### 2.2.1 Physical violence and related harm
The most tangible form persecutory harm can take is physical—in the form of killing, wounding, beating etc. Focus here is on actual or threatened harm to a person's physical integrity. This is sometimes referred to as the 'core meaning of persecution'.[111] In analysing the meaning of persecution, Grahl-Madsen first listed '[t]hreats to life, limb or physical freedom'.[112]

---

[109] See Kälin and Künzli (n 107) 179–258.
[110] See Chapter 1. See also Jackson (n 17) 470.
[111] Goodwin-Gill and McAdam (3rd edn) (n 25) 92.
[112] Grahl-Madsen (n 15) 201; section 1.4.2.

The refugee law literature has dealt with physical violence and related harm in great detail. This has not always been formulated in human rights terms,[113] but the latter has enabled decision makers to assess whether physical harm is persecutory by reference to specific international standards. As noted earlier, there is an interdependency among many human rights, but the two most important human rights engaged in the context of physical harm are the right to life and the prohibition of cruel, inhuman, or degrading treatment or punishment.

*2.2.1.1 Right to life*
In relation to the right to life, Hathaway and Foster state that '[t]he critical question, then, in a refugee status application is whether there is the forward-looking prospect of an arbitrary deprivation of life, in which case the risk of persecutory harm is established'.[114]

The UN Human Rights Committee (HRC) has stated that the right to life, as enshrined in Article 6 of the ICCPR, recognizes and protects the right to life of all human beings. They describe it as 'the supreme right from which no derogation is permitted, even in situations of armed conflict and other public emergencies'. However, as formulated in paragraph 1 of Article 6, it only guarantees against 'arbitrary' deprivation of life. Paragraphs 2, 4, 5, and 6 effectively exclude deprivation that is the consequence of a lawful use of force or that takes the form of an execution of a death penalty imposed by a court or is in accordance with International Humanitarian Law (IHL) in the context of an armed conflict.[115] In states parties that have not yet abolished the death penalty, death sentences are not to be applied except for the most serious crimes, and then only in the most exceptional cases and under the strictest limits. The death penalty cannot be imposed on children or pregnant women (Article 6 (5)).[116]

In its General Comment on Article 6, the HRC has made clear that the death penalty is automatically prohibited under the ICCPR if it is 'applied as a sanction against conduct whose very criminalisation violates the Covenant, including adultery, homosexuality, apostasy, establishing political opposition groups, or offending a head of state'.[117] Particularly important when applied in the refugee law context is the Committee's clarification that, regardless of whether states parties had ratified the Second Optional Protocol (OP2), 'States parties that abolished the death penalty cannot deport, extradite or otherwise transfer persons to a country in which they are facing criminal charges that carry the death penalty, unless credible and effective assurances against the imposition of the death penalty have been obtained.'[118]

The HRC has emphasised that the requirement set out in the second sentence of Article 6 (1), that the right to life 'shall be protected by law':

---

[113] Anker (n 33) §4.13, 300–06 details the main US case law on this category of harms which mostly does not analyse them in human rights terms.
[114] Hathaway and Foster (n 3) 209.
[115] Human Rights Committee (HRC), General Comment No 36 (2019): Article 6 (Right to Life) (3 September 2019) UN Doc CCPR/C/GC/35, paras 1–8; Kälin and Künzli (n 107) 261–62.
[116] By Protocols No 6 and 13 of the ECHR, contracting states to this convention have proscribed the death penalty whether imposed in wartime or peacetime.
[117] HRC, General Comment No 36 (n 115) para 36.
[118] ibid para 34.

[ … ] implies that States parties must establish a legal framework to ensure the full enjoyment of the right to life by all individuals as may be necessary to give effect to the right to life. The duty to protect the right to life by law also includes an obligation for States parties to adopt any appropriate laws or other measures in order to protect life from all reasonably foreseeable threats, including from threats emanating from private persons and entities.[119]

They clarify that 'States parties are obliged to take adequate preventive measures in order to protect individuals against reasonably foreseen threats of being murdered or killed by criminals and organized crime or militia groups, including armed or terrorist groups.'[120] Hathaway and Foster consider that the duty of the state to protect against privately inflicted risk to life includes risks of female infanticide, the burning of widows, dowry killings, and so-called 'honour killings'.[121]

*2.2.1.2 Armed conflict and generalised violence*
Of particular salience in refugee law has been the threat or actuality of killing during armed conflict. Even though the right to life in the ICCPR and regional human rights conventions is non-derogable, Kälin and Künzli observe that '[i]t is nonetheless accepted that loss of life attributable to lawful acts of war is not deemed to constitute arbitrary deprivation of life and hence is not a violation of the right to life'.[122] They cite in support the International Court of Justice's (ICJ) ruling in *Legality of the Threat or Use of Nuclear Weapons Case*, which refers to the complementarity of IHL and IHRL.[123] Applying IHL norms, there is no general prohibition on intentional killing in situations of armed conflict subject to the principle of distinction that the 'parties to the conflict must at all times distinguish between civilians and combatants' and that attacks must be directed against combatants and never against civilians unless and for such time as they take a direct part in hostilities.[124] Kälin and Künzli identify the following categories of deprivation of life that are prohibited in situation of war and armed conflict: the killing of a person '*hors de combat*'; deadly attacks on civilians; indiscriminate attacks; attacks not in accordance with the precautionary principle (according to which states, in advance of any attack, take steps to ensure that the prohibition of attacks on civilian objects and the prohibition of indiscriminate attacks are fully respected in practice); prohibited means of warfare; and the death penalty. Following on from the aforementioned ICJ ruling, the HRC has also asserted that 'both spheres of law are complementary, not mutually exclusive' and has relied on both bodies of law as providing a continuum of protection. Kälin has drawn on this

---

[119] ibid para 18.
[120] ibid para 21.
[121] Hathaway and Foster (n 3) 210.
[122] Kälin and Künzli (n 107) 271.
[123] *Legality of the Threat or Use of Nuclear Weapons*, Advisory Opinion [1966] ICJ Rep 2; see also *Legal Consequences of the Construction of a Wall in the Occupied Palestinian Territory*, Advisory Opinion [2004] ICJ Rep 136; *Armed Activities on the Territory of the Congo (the Democratic Republic of the Congo v Uganda)*, Judgment, Merits [2005] ICJ Rep 168, para 25.
[124] Kälin and Künzli (n 107) 271.

approach to articulate the relationship between the Refugee Convention and the law of armed conflict.[125]

Hathaway and Foster consider that, given IHL's 'powerful constraints' on the lawful use of armed force even in wartime, 'risk to a civilian's life will *usually* infringe the prohibition of arbitrary deprivation of life, thus amounting to serious harm for refugee law purposes'.[126] This is consistent with the fact that under IHL lethal force may be allowed in certain circumstances even as a first recourse if risks to civilians have been considered and the target is a legitimate military one.[127] However, the adverb 'usually' is salient; it cannot be taken for granted that the wars and armed conflicts being considered are ones that violate IHL norms, even though contemporary events demonstrate they very often are.

By virtue of there being many refugee claims brought by similarly situated persons fleeing armed conflict or generalised violence, this topic is addressed further below when analysing group persecution. There have been important developments within IHRL relating to threats to the right to life as a result of environmental degradation and/or climate change. These too are addressed separately below.[128]

### 2.2.1.3 Prohibition of torture, or cruel, inhuman, or degrading treatment

The prohibition of torture, or cruel, inhuman, or degrading treatment norm has undoubtedly been the most referenced and the most heavily mined IHRL norm in refugee decision making. As formulated in Article 7 ICCPR (and its regional equivalents), it is an absolute and non-derogable right. There are three sub-categories of ill treatment: torture; cruel or inhuman treatment or punishment; and degrading treatment or punishment. Case law accords these three distinct meanings, but to qualify as ill-treatment contrary to Article 7, it does not matter whether the act or measure is one or the other of these. It remains, however, that it furthers legal certainty to understand their respective contours. The forms of treatment that can cross the threshold of sufficient severity may be distinguished according either to the intensity or the purpose of a violation or a combination of both.[129] The HRC has stated that the prohibition in Article 7 relates not only to acts that cause physical pain but also to acts that cause mental suffering to the victim.

By virtue of Article 1(1) of the UN Convention against Torture, for severe physical or mental pain and suffering to qualify as torture, it must be shown to be 'intentionally inflicted'. However, it does not include pain or suffering arising only from, inherent in or incidental to lawful sanctions.[130]

---

[125] Walter Kälin, 'Flight in Times of War' (2001) 83 IRRC 629. For further discussion see Violeta Moreno-Lax, 'Systematising Systemic Integration: "War Refugees", Regime Relations, and a Proposal for a Cumulative Approach' (2014) 12(5) Journal of International Criminal Justice 907.

[126] Hathaway and Foster (n 3) 210 (emphasis added).

[127] Noam Lubell, 'Challenges in Applying Human Rights Law to Armed Conflict' (2005) 87(860) IRRC 737, 744–49.

[128] See below sections 2.2.5 (on environmental degradation) and 3.10.1 (on group persecution).

[129] Kälin and Künzli (n 107) 312–13.

[130] Convention against Torture and Other Cruel, Inhuman or Degrading Treatment or Punishment (CAT) (adopted 10 December 1984, entered into force 26 June 1987) 1465 UNTS 85. Kälin and Künzli (n 107) note, however, that the CAT definition 'does not fully correspond to what emerges from the ICCPR, the regional conventions, and international humanitarian and customary law. Whilst it excludes cases of torture by private actors in the absence of any involvement of the state, the other treaties oblige states to provide

All the circumstances of a case are taken into consideration, including the underlying purpose behind the infliction of treatment. The most detailed case law on torture derives from the regional human rights courts. Kälin and Künzli state that this case law has identified the following as torture: severe ill-treatment during custody and interrogation undertaken for the purpose of obtaining a statement or confession, of intimidating the victim or a third party, or of inflicting punishment; rape and other forms of sexual and gender-based violence by state agents in custodial or non-custodial circumstances; force feeding, not prompted by valid medical reasons or with the aim of forcing a person to stop his or her protest, and performed in a manner which unnecessarily exposes him or her to great physical pain and humiliation; repeated beatings and severe humiliation in pre-deportation custody; arbitrary and massive use of batons by masked members of a special unit in a prison camp with the aim of humiliating prisoners and breaking their physical and psychological resistance; the use of batons causing bone fractures in retaliation against attacks on police officers during a demonstration against police brutality; so-called 'capture-shock' treatment by CIA agents on the territory and in the presence of organs of a state party to the European Convention on Human Rights (ECHR), and the treatment of 'high-value' detainees in secret CIA prisons in Europe; psychological ill-treatment, including threats of violence during interrogation which may also be classified as torture especially when it aims to break the resistance of the accused.[131]

The prohibition of cruel, inhuman, or degrading treatment covers a wide range of ill-treatments which reach a certain level of severity. By contrast with torture, inhuman or degrading treatment may lack intent. According to Kälin and Künzli:

> Cases classified as *inhuman treatment* include specific conditions of detention on death row but not duration alone of said detention; sentencing a person to death after an unfair trial; the eight-month solitary confinement of a homosexual prisoner allegedly to protect him against assaults by fellow prisoners; threats of violence; beatings; and any use of physical force in detention that does not appear to be necessitated by the conduct of the person concerned; failure to provide medical treatment for a fatally ill person; lack of medical or psychiatric treatment for a prisoner entailing severe suffering; forced feeding of vomit-inducing products to secure evidence in a criminal procedure; medical tests with psychotropic drugs not yet authorized without the consent of the person concerned; extended incommunicado detention; the five-year-long detention of a fifteen-year old person in an adult detention centre; detention of a five-year old unaccompanied child in a closed transit centre without qualified personnel or surveillance appropriate to the child's age; continuation of administrative detention despite medical grounds for release; the eighteen-day administrative detention of a four-year old child and his parents without any efforts to end this measure of last resort; the involuntary hospitalisation in a psychiatric clinic that was not medically indicated; detention for several days without food and water; failure to

everyone with protection against torture also in the case of severe ill-treatment by private actors.' However, the HRC has not yet diverged from its application of the CAT definition.

[131] Kälin and Künzli (n 107) 314–15. For each example case law references are given.

inform detainees' relatives of their whereabouts or their execution as well as locations of the burial site; and destruction of the houses of complainants before their eyes by state agents or by private actors with the implicit consent of state agents.[132]

The prohibition on inhuman treatment has been of particular importance in gender-related refugee claims based on risk of rape, sexual slavery, enforced prostitution, sexual assault, female genital mutilation (FGM), forced pregnancy, forcible abortion, and sterilisation. Human rights law has particularly assisted in clarifying the nature of persecutory harm in physical form by identifying that ill-treatment can arise even where it arises in a family or domestic setting.[133]

Kälin and Künzli provide the following examples of *inhuman punishment* drawn from the case law of the treaty bodies and the regional human rights courts:

> [ ... ] any form of corporal punishment, even where it is imposed as a legally prescribed criminal penalty, irrespective of the act perpetrated; prolonged solitary confinement; the execution of a person by gas asphyxiation or by stoning and execution without prior notice as to the date of execution, but not a regular execution by lethal injection. According to the ECHR, coercing a military conscript suffering from knee disorders to undertake, as a disciplinary punishment, excessive physical exercises causing long-term health problems amounted to inhuman punishment in the specific case. Imprisonment in a severely overcrowded cell for several weeks where prisoners have as little space as three [metres] at their disposal, creates a presumption of inhuman punishment which can only be rebutted if sufficient freedom of movement within prison premises and adequate out-of-cell activities are available and the overall conditions of detention are adequate. Sentencing an adult to lifelong detention is not per se inhuman, except where no prospect whatsoever of an earlier (conditional) release exists because the sentence cannot be reviewed de iure or de facto after a certain lapse of time. In such a case, the violation already occurs at the time of the judgment imposing the sentence and not only when a later application for release is rejected. A 'grossly disproportionate sentence', even if not life-long, can also amount to inhuman punishment, but as highlighted by the ECtHR [(European Court of Human Rights)], this threshold will only be met on 'rare and unique occasions'. On the one hand, according to the [HRC], seventy-five years' imprisonment with hard labour imposed as a consequence of the commutation of a death sentence does not violate this prohibition. On the other hand, the Committee indicated in an obiter dicta that life imprisonment for economic crimes may amount to inhuman punishment.[134]

As regards *degrading treatment*, for it to occur the severity of the suffering imposed is of less importance than the humiliation of the victim, regardless of whether this is in the eyes of others or those of the victim himself or herself.[135] The suffering involved

---

[132] ibid 316. Again, they give case references for each example.
[133] Hathaway and Foster (n 3) 226–27, state that '[r]efugee law decision-makers embracing the human rights approach have thus recognised that subjection to "domestic violence" amounts to a risk of serious harm relevant to the "being persecuted" inquiry'.
[134] Kälin and Künzli (n 107) 317–18. Again, they give case references for each example.
[135] *Pretty v United Kingdom* App No 2346/02 (ECtHR, 29 April 2002) para 52.

has been defined by the ECtHR as 'degrading' because it is such as to arouse in the victim feelings of fear, anguish, and inferiority capable of humiliating or debasing them or because it affects a person's personality in a manner incompatible with Article 3 ECHR. Kälin and Künzli give the following examples of conduct explicitly classified by the case law of the treaty bodies and regional human rights courts as degrading treatment:

> [ ... ] strip searches in the presence of prison staff of the opposite sex; routine weekly strip searches without clear justification; gynaecological examination of a minor detainee carried out in a situation of heightened vulnerability and without her consent; slaps in the face by a police officer; the forced shaving-off of a prisoner's hair without objective justification; displaying a prisoner to the media in a metal cage or holding without proper justification, a defendant in such a cage with his hands handcuffed behind his back during a trial; harassment by prison warders involving repeated soaking of a prisoner's bedding; the chaining of an elderly prisoner to his hospital bed for a night without objective justification; the routine shackling of all prisoners with a life sentence since outside of their cell; being forced to stand in underwear in front of the battalion while being reprimanded as a disciplinary sanction during military service; refusal to undertake necessary and available genetic testing of a foetus suspected of being affected with an unidentified malformation during several weeks despite repeated requests and an entitlement to such tests as a matter of domestic law; eight consecutive condemnations to several months of detention each of a conscientious objector in a country that does not offer any civil service as an alternative; and, according to the ECtHR, also grievous and systematic discrimination on racist grounds. The treatment of a woman with a paralysed limb and suffering from kidney problems who was prevented from bringing the battery charger for her electric wheelchair into prison, had to sleep in the wheelchair, and was accompanied to the toilet by a male officer was also found to be degrading. According to the ECtHR, detention under particularly severe conditions and lack of medical care in a prison is degrading rather than inhuman treatment—in our view inappropriately and evidently on the basis of the 'degree of severity' theory.[136]

Examples of *degrading punishment* include public executions or certain forms of public punishment.[137]

In *R (Hoxha)*, Baroness Hale considered that a woman who had been raped by Serbian forces would be at risk on return of having to 'suffer the insult and indignity of being regarded by one's community ... as "dirty like contaminated" because one has suffered the gross ill-treatment of a particularly brutal and dehumanising rape'.[138]

Applying a human rights approach, the decisive criterion is that the ill-treatment attains a minimum level of severity. As noted earlier, the assessment of this minimum level of severity is relative: it depends on all the circumstances of the case, such as the duration of the treatment, its physical and mental effects and, in some cases, the

---

[136] Kälin and Künzli (n 107) 318–19. Again, case references are given for each example.
[137] ibid. As quoted here, the passage omits its (copious) footnotes.
[138] *Hoxha* (n 64) para 36, cited by Hathaway and Foster (n 3) 212.

gender, age, and state of health of the victim.[139] Further factors include the purpose for which the treatment is inflicted together with the intention or motivation behind it, as well as its context, such as an atmosphere of heightened tension and emotions. However, Kälin and Künzli rightly point out that the relativism reflected in this approach must have limits 'where physical force is used in custodial circumstances without objective justification, that is, treatment that may be viewed as unnecessary and therefore diminishes the victim's dignity, rendering the treatment inhuman'.[140]

From the above examples it can be seen that measures depriving a person of his/her liberty may involve an element of intense physical or mental suffering constituting inhuman or degrading treatment. However, the execution of an administrative decision or detention on remand or short-term detention may not in itself raise an issue under Article 7 ICCPR or its regional equivalents. Nor can this article be interpreted as laying down a general obligation to release a detainee on health grounds. Nevertheless, the state must ensure that a detained person is accommodated under conditions which are compatible with respect for human dignity and the manner and methods of the implementation of a measure must not subject the person to distress or hardship of an intensity exceeding the unavoidable level of suffering inherent in detention.[141]

Drawing on its previous case law, the ECtHR in its *Babar Ahmad and Others* judgment has suggested an illustrative list of factors that have been decisive for finding a violation of Article 3 ECHR arising out of ill-treatment of prisoners. The Court nevertheless underlined that 'all of these elements depend closely upon the facts of the case and so will not be readily established prospectively in an extradition or expulsion context'.[142]

As with the right to life, the HRC highlights the positive obligations engaged by the prohibition of ill-treatment, including having in place legislative, administrative, judicial, and other measures to prevent and punish acts of ill treatment.

The prohibition of ill-treatment can also be engaged by cases which concern severe environmental harm or deprivations of socio-economic rights. These are addressed in the separate subsections below on socio-economic and environmental persecution.[143]

*2.2.1.4 Modern slavery and trafficking*

Modern slavery and trafficking are universally recognised as forms of persecution, irrespective of whether a human rights approach is taken. But applying a human rights approach, these phenomena are forms of harm that, as well as constituting ill-treatment, give rise to specific violations against IHRL provisions prohibiting disappearances, slavery, and forced labour.[144] As noted by Hathaway and Foster, two forms of modern

---

[139] See e.g. *Aktaš v Turkey* App No 24351/94 (ECtHR, 24 April 2003) para 312. See also ACmHPR, *Shumba v Zimbabwe*, Communication No 288/2004 (2012), para 138, both cited by Kälin and Künzli (n 107) 320.

[140] Kälin and Künzli (n 107) 320. They cite *Ribitsch v Austria* App No 18896/91 (ECtHR, 4 December 1995) para 38, and *Bouyid v Belgium* App No 23380/09 (ECtHR, 28 September 2015) para 88.

[141] Kälin and Künzli (n 107). See also section 2.2.1.5 below.

[142] *Baba Ahmad and Others v United Kingdom* Apps Nos 24027/07, 11949/08, 36742/08, 66911/09, and 67354/09 (ECtHR, 24 September 2012).

[143] See below sections 2.2.3 and 2.2.5 respectively.

[144] See e.g. *M and Others v Italy and Bulgaria* App No 40020/03 (ECtHR, 31 July 2012) para 106.

slavery—trafficking for the purposes of labour and sexual exploitation and forced or underage marriage—are increasingly featuring in refugee claims.[145]

### 2.2.1.5 *Physical security and liberty: measures of arrest, detention, imprisonment, and holding in a closed institution*

Refugee law has long accepted that it would be far too narrow to restrict persecution to purely physical violence or harm, even if the latter for very good reason was uppermost in the minds of the 1951 Convention's drafters.[146] Following a human rights approach, the further scope envisaged can be considered in relation to physical security and liberty and then psychological and related forms of harm.

Although the drafters clearly recognised that deprivation of liberty and security could give rise to persecutory harm, there has been a long-standing reluctance to treat measures of arrest, detention, imprisonment, and holding in a closed institution as per se persecutory.[147]

Applying a human rights approach to such measures requires consideration of treaty provisions regarding the right to liberty and security of the person, pursuant to Article 9 ICCPR and similar provisions in the regional treaties. 'Liberty' in this context means 'freedom from confinement of the body' without free consent. Its deprivation (as noted earlier) can sometimes involve violations of the prohibition of torture, cruel or inhuman and degrading treatment of punishment, but not always.[148] With reference to case law, Kälin and Künzli identify five IHRL principles constraining the circumstances in which persons may be arrested, detained, or otherwise deprived of their liberty:

> (1) Only on grounds established by law. They must (2) be informed promptly of the reason for their arrest and (3) brought promptly before a judicial authority to determine the lawfulness of the deprivation of liberty. Anyone arrested, detained on suspicion of having committed a criminal offence must (4) be charged and brought to trial or must be released. Lastly, (5) anyone who has been the victim of unlawful deprivation of liberty has a right to compensation.[149]

They identify that in addition to arrest, deprivation of liberty can also include, inter alia, de facto apprehension not defined as such in domestic law; pre-trial detention or imprisonment on conviction; house arrest; coercive internment in locked-ward psychiatric hospitals; detention pending deportation or extradition; arrest as a disciplinary penalty in military service; internal exile to a small island without opportunity for normal social contact; and forcible placement of a legally incapacitated person in a social care home, where the inhabitants are under constant supervision and, even though visits to the neighbouring village are possible, remain not free to leave without explicit permission. Examples of breaches include arrest and detention for the

---

[145] Hathaway and Foster (n 3) 220, 224.
[146] Mark Symes and Peter Jorro, *Asylum Law and Practice* (2nd edn, Bloomsbury 2010) 99–102.
[147] Grahl-Madsen (n 15) 214.
[148] Kälin and Künzli (n 107) 451–58.
[149] ibid 451–53.

legitimate exercise of human rights such as the freedom of expression, of assembly, or of religion. Enforced disappearances by the state or *incommunicado* detention are seen to represent egregious breaches.[150]

However, even in relation to short-term detention, the authorities must still act on grounds and in accordance with procedures established by law, must not act in an arbitrary fashion, and cannot treat detainees in an inhumane or undignified way. In a state of emergency, states may be able to derogate from the right to liberty and security, but IHLR norms mandate states to take strict steps required by the exigencies of the situation and to act in a way that does not involve discrimination solely on the grounds of race, colour, sex, language, religion, or social origin. 'Only where there is compliance with these internationally identified norms will arrest and detention even in the context of a national emergency fail to be evidence of persecutory harm.'[151]

### 2.2.2 Psychological and related forms of harm

That mental, emotional, and psychological harm can be persecutory was clearly understood by the drafters and is well-captured in the case law and wider literature. Grahl-Madsen gave the example of a person facing being kept under more or less constant surveillance upon return to his home country who 'may argue that this will cause such a nervous strain that it more than equals a short-term imprisonment. Pressure to induce a person to become a police informer or a member of the ruling party may have to be judged in the same way.'[152] The 1979 UNHCR Handbook observes that individual feelings, opinions, and circumstances generally should be considered in evaluating whether actions or threats amount to persecution and indeed make it a requirement to qualify as a refugee that 'subjective fear' is shown.[153] The 2006 UNHCR Guidelines, when discussing the effect of past trafficking, state that: '[t]he nature of the harm previously suffered will also impact on the opinions, feelings and psychological make-up of the asylum applicant and thus influence the assessment of whether any future harm or predicament feared would amount to persecution in the particular case'.[154]

In the 2009 UNHCR Guidelines on Child Asylum Claims, it is noted in relation to children that they are 'more likely to be distressed by hostile situations, to believe improbable threats, or to be emotionally affected by unfamiliar circumstances'.[155] Waldman encapsulates well the Canadian case law on psychological harm in the

---

[150] ibid 452.
[151] Hathaway and Foster (n 3) 242–43; HRC, General Comment No 29: States of Emergency (Article 4) (31 August 2001) UN Doc CCPR/C/21/Rev.1/Add/11; in the ECHR context, see Guide of the European Convention on Human Rights: Derogation in time of emergency (April 2021) available at <www.echr.coe.int/Documents/Guide_Art_15_ENG.pdf> (accessed 25 January 2022).
[152] Grahl-Madsen (n 15) 216.
[153] UNHCR Handbook (n 60) para 52. UNHCR's position on subjective fear is critically analysed at Chapter 11, sections 3.1.1–3.1.4.
[154] UNHCR, Guidelines on International Protection (Guidelines) No 7: The Application of Article 1A(2) of the 1951 Convention and/or 1967 Protocol Relating to the Status of Refugees to Victims of Trafficking and Persons at Risk of Being Trafficked (7 April 2006) UN Doc HCR/GIP/06/07, para 16.
[155] UNHCR, Guidelines No 8: Child Asylum Claims under Articles 1(A)2 and 1(F) of the 1951 Convention and/or 1967 Protocol relating to the Status of Refugees (2009) UN Doc HCR/GIP/09/08, para 16.

heading 'Physical Harm Is Not Required in Order for a Person to Be a Victim of Persecution'.[156]

Recognizing that persecution can cover psychological as well as physical harm is wholly consonant with and supported by IHRL law. Thus in General Comment No 20, the HRC has stated that the proscription of ill-treatment in Article 7 of the ICCPR relates 'not only to acts that cause physical pain, but also to acts that cause mental suffering to the victim'.[157] This Committee's case law has emphasized that cruel and inhuman treatment encompasses psychological harm, irrespective of whether physical injury was sustained.[158] The UN Convention against Torture[159] (CAT) expressly includes mental pain or suffering as torture. In the jurisprudence of the ECtHR, it is well-established that mental suffering can amount to ill treatment contrary to Article 3.[160] Thus, to use terminology that has sometimes found its way into the discourse, IHRL norms have helped demonstrate that persecution encompasses both endogenous as well as exogenous harms.[161]

Within the EU, Article 9(2) of the QD (recast) contains an express recognition that acts of persecution can inter alia take the form of: '(a) acts of physical *or mental violence*, including acts of sexual violence' (emphasis added). As is emphasised in Article 4(3) of the same Directive, it is always necessary to consider the circumstances and susceptibilities of the particular applicant.[162] As noted by Hathaway and Pobjoy, with reference to leading cases of the HRC and the ECtHR, human rights law recognises that:

> While the *standards* of international human rights law are, of course, universal, this does not mean that their application is in any sense insensitive to the specific vulnerabilities of particular persons. To the contrary, the prohibition of cruel, inhuman or degrading treatment focuses on the nature of the harm experienced by each individual, requiring attention to be paid not just to what harm is threatened, but on the how that harm would impact on the applicant himself.[163]

---

[156] Waldman (n 1) 193.

[157] HRC, General Comment No 20: Article 7 (Prohibition of Torture, or Other Cruel, Inhuman or Degrading Treatment or Punishment) (12 May 2004) UN Doc HRI/GEN/1/Rev.7, para 5.

[158] Sarah Joseph, Jennifer Schultz, and Melissa Castan, *The International Covenant on Civil and Political Rights: Cases, Materials, and Commentary* (OUP 2000) 218–23. See also James C Hathaway and William S Hicks, 'Is There a Subjective Element in the Refugee Convention's Requirement of "Well-founded Fear"?' (2005) 26(2) Michigan Journal of International Law 505, 556–60. In *Case of Almeida de Quinteros v Uruguay* (21 July 1983) Communication No 107/1981, UN Doc CCPR/C/19/D/107/1981, para 14, the HRC determined that the mental anguish caused to a mother by the mysterious disappearance of her daughter violated Art. 7; see also *Case of Natalia Schedko and Anton Bondarenko v Belarus* (3 April 2003) Communication No 886/1999, UN Doc CCPR/C/77/D/886/1999. The jurisprudence of the UN Committee against Torture provides further support for this proposition: see e.g. *Case of Besim Osmani v Republic of Serbia* (25 May 2009) Communication No 261/2005, UN Doc CAT/C/42/D/261/2005.

[159] Convention Against Torture (n 130).

[160] QD (recast) (n 8). For recognition of mental violence in ECHR case law, see *Soering v United Kingdom* App No 14038/88 (ECtHR, 7 July 1989) para 100; *X and Y v Netherlands* App No 8978/80 (ECtHR, 26 March 1983).

[161] See Hathaway and Pobjoy (n 6).

[162] This doctrine is well-established in international human rights jurisprudence. See generally the discussion in Hathaway and Hicks (n 158) 545–46.

[163] Hathaway and Pobjoy (n 6) cite, inter alia, *Case of Vuolanne v Finland* (2 May 1989) Communication No 265/1987, UN Doc CCPR/C/35/D/265/1987, para 9.2, in which the HRC expressly affirmed that the

In the US case law, which does not generally apply a human rights approach, there has been a long-standing recognition that 'persecution may be emotional or psychological, as well as physical'.[164] In *Kahssai v I.N.S.*, the concurring judge observed that the emotional harm especially for a child arising from being present during beatings and threats against family members could be sufficient in and of itself to constitute atrocious persecution, even in the absence of direct physical harm.[165] Anker notes, with citation from US cases, that '[t]he emotional dimension of persecutory harm is apparent in cases of gender-based violence, especially those involving rape or FGM, which result in "severe and long-lasting" mental suffering and psychological harm'.[166]

Although it has been recognised that mental, emotional, and psychological harm can sometimes alone give rise to persecution, it has also often been seen to be an important factor in establishing cumulative harm (also to the fore in this context has been the recognition that persecution can be indirect).[167]

*2.2.2.1 Violations of freedom of thought, conscience, and religion or other fundamental beliefs or identity*

Closely tied to the notion of psychological harm are the concepts of human dignity,[168] identity, autonomy, and self-worth. Mental, emotional, or psychological harm tantamount to persecution can also arise when an individual faces threats to their fundamental beliefs or identity. Applying a human rights approach has fostered better understanding of the specific ways in which assaults on beliefs and identity and ways of life can give rise to persecutory harm, since IHRL specifically protects freedom of thought, conscience, and religion in the form of basic guarantees under the ICCPR and other IHRL instruments, including the right to respect for family and private life, the latter which also has an exterior as well as an interior dimension.[169] There are some aspects of the right to freedom of thought, conscience, and religion that are non-derogable,[170] but to the extent that such rights are derogable or qualified, a violation will not arise if the state has a legitimate basis for restricting its exercise, unless their denial nullifies the very existence of the right.[171] Freedom of religion, freedom of expression, assembly, and association may only be restricted for quite specific reasons prescribed by law and must meet the strict tests of proportionality and necessity.

---

meaning of Article 7 depends on 'all the circumstances of the case, such as the duration and manner of the treatment, its physical or mental effects as well as the sex, age and state of health of the victim'.

[164] Anker (n 33) §4.18, 326, citing *Mansour v Ashcroft* [2004] 390 F.3d 667.
[165] *Khassai v INS* [2004] 16 F.3d 323, cited in Anker (n 33) 216.
[166] Anker (n 33) §4.18, 276, citing, inter alia, *Lopez-Galara v INS* [1996] 99 F.3d 954.
[167] See below section 3.7.
[168] Human dignity is not defined in the major IHRL instruments and has been seen to have protean usages, but it encompasses at least two meanings, one relating to the intrinsic value of persons (so they are not treated as mere means) and one relating to conduct that respects other persons. See further Deryck Beyleveld and Roger Brownsword, 'Human Dignity, Human Rights, and Human Genetics' (1998) 61(5) The Modern Law Review 661, 665–66; George Kateb, *Human Dignity* (Harvard University Press 2011).
[169] Hathaway and Foster (n 3).
[170] HRC, General Comment No 22: Article 18 (Freedom of Thought, Conscience or Religion) (30 July 1993) UN Doc CCPR/C/21/Rev.1/Add.4, para 3.
[171] *Z and T v United Kingdom* App No 27034/05 (ECtHR, 28 February 2006); *Ullah, R (on the Application of) v Special Adjudicator* [2004] UKHL 26.

However, many types of coercion directed against persons because of their beliefs or identities may also involve a violation of absolute rights that prohibit ill treatment or of rights such as that to liberty and security of person where the restrictions are particularly constraining.

The US case law, which as we saw does not generally apply a human rights approach, has arrived at broadly similar conclusions. In relation to religious beliefs, for example, Anker notes that the Seventh and Eleventh Circuits 'have emphasised that '[a]sylum exists to protect people from having to return to a country and conceal their beliefs'.[172]

As regards identity, one key criterion long-established in the analysis of the Refugee Convention reason of 'membership of particular social group' is that people 'should not be required to change because it is fundamental to their individual identities or consciences'.[173] A wide range of beliefs has been considered fundamental, including beliefs relating to religion, marital and reproductive choice, and political and sexual orientation. Acts that compel a person to deny their basic identity (e.g. their ethnic or racial identity or gender identity) have been similarly regarded. This terminology has served as a helpful signpost to interpreting the term 'being persecuted'. It was at the heart of the important line of cases rejecting any 'concealment' criterion, beginning with the Australian High Court case of S395[174] and culminating in the Court of Justice of the European Union's (CJEU) judgments in *Y and Z* and in *X, Y and Z*.[175]

Wilsher terms the type of persecution involved in concealment or self-censorship cases, 'suppressive persecution'. He contrasts such cases with those of 'martyrs' who choose to act according to their fundamental values and/or identity. But for both, he writes, the resultant harm can amount to a serious violation of their human rights:

> Although the outcome of expulsion for martyrs would be imprisonment or violence, whilst that for the self-restrained would be concealment and fear, for both groups the real harm is the forcible denial of their freedom to exercise their human rights.[176]

### 2.2.3 Socio-economic and cultural harms

Sometimes overlooked by decision makers, the drafters of the Refugee Convention and leading commentators have always accepted that threats to socio-economic rights can give rise to persecution.[177] Reference was made earlier to the *travaux* exchange between Mr Stolz of the American Federation of Labour and the delegate of France acknowledging that economic and social reasons could found a claim to refugee

---

[172] Anker (n 33) §4.23, 347–48. She cites, inter alia, *Shan Zhu Qiu v Holder* [2010] 611 F.3d 403, and *Kazemzadeh v A-G (US)* [2009] 577 F.3d 1341.

[173] e.g. *Matter of Acosta* [1985] A-24159781; *Canada (AG) v Ward* [1993] 2 SCR 689. See Chapter 10, sections 2.1.4 and 3.4.4.

[174] *Appellant S395/2002 v MIMA* [2003] HCA 71, 40, per Kirby and McHugh JJ; see also *HJ (Iran)* (n 33) para 53.

[175] Joined Cases C-71/11 and C-99/11 *Bundesrepublik Deutschland v Y and Z* [2012] ECLI:EU:C:2012:518, para 78; Joined Cases C-199/12 to C-201/12 *Minister voor Immigratie en Asiel v X and Y and Z v Minister voor Immigratie en Asiel* [2013] ECLI:EU:C:2013:720, paras 70–71.

[176] Daniel Wilsher, '"Between Martyrdom and Silence": Dissent, Duress, and Persecution as the Suppression of Human Rights under the Refugee Convention' (2021) 33(1) IJRL 28, 32. See further *WA (Pakistan) v SSHD* [2019] EWCA Civ 302; Goodwin-Gill and McAdam (n 26) 98–99, 113–17.

[177] See Foster (n 45) 95, citing Grahl-Madsen (n 15) 86, 194, and Hathaway (n 4) at 121.

status.[178] Equally evident, the drafters plainly wished to deny refugee status to persons whose reasons for claiming were based on pure personal convenience or economic betterment.[179]

Early textbooks reflect recognition that persecution can encompass economic harm. Grahl-Madsen gave the example of 'economic proscription... so severe as to deprive a person of all means of earning a livelihood'.[180] The 1979 UNHCR Handbook noted that measures of discrimination capable of leading to consequences of a substantially prejudicial nature sufficient to amount to persecution included 'serious restrictions on [a person's] right to earn his livelihood' and 'access to normally available educational facilities'.[181]

On the other hand, for several decades the case law contained few affirmations of socio-economic persecution[182] and there have been no shortage of commentators who have taken the view that the 1951 Convention does not or should not encompass such forms of harm.[183] In a 2010 study, it was noted that instances where courts have accepted persecution can consist in socio-economic harm, e.g. in denial of employment or livelihood,[184] have been relatively limited.[185]

In the original model of a human rights approach espoused by Hathaway in TLRS, socio-economic harm was effectively given a limited role as a third-category obligation/right, notwithstanding that the ICESR and the ICCPR together formed the first (global) treaty incarnations of international human rights forming the 'International Bill of Rights'.

However, since TLRS was published, IHRL has moved on considerably. Applying a contemporary human rights approach has strengthened the case for adding socio-economic acts to the list of acts capable of constituting persecutory acts. The focus in this context is on violations of basic rights such as the right to work, education, housing, food, and health.

The core justification for inclusion of socio-economic harm as a potential form of persecution is that Article 1A(2) does not contain any restriction on the nature of the persecution. Even in doctrine and case law not applying a human rights approach, there is broad recognition of this core fact. However, applying a contemporary human rights approach clearly reinforces the need to avoid any such restriction in three principal (interrelated) ways.

---

[178] See p. 303; see also Hathaway (n 4) 103.
[179] Grahl-Madsen (n 15) 208; Anker (n 33) 300.
[180] Grahl-Madsen (n 15) 208 notes that even those who adopted a restrictive understanding of persecution, such as Zink, accepted that denial of every possibility of earning a living, could constitute persecution.
[181] UNCHR Handbook (n 60) para 54.
[182] Foster (n 45) 91, citing Hathaway (n 4) 123–24.
[183] See e.g. David A Martin, 'Review of the Law of Refugee Status' (1993) 87(2) AJIL 335, 351. See also Katharina Röhl, 'Fleeing Violence and Poverty: Non-Refoulement Obligations under the European Convention on Human Rights' (2005) UNHCR: New Issues in Refugee Research, Working Paper No 111, 3, who states that: 'the refugee definition in the 1951 Convention almost completely exclude[s] the violation of economic and social rights from the concept of persecution'.
[184] Foster (n 45) 94, cites the example of the Australian case *Prahastono v MICA* [1997] 77 FCR 260, 267.
[185] See Kate Jastram, 'Economic Harm as a Basis for Refugee Status and the Application of Human Rights Law to the Interpretation of Economic Persecution' in James C Simeon (ed), *Critical Issues in International Refugee Law: Strategies toward Interpretative Harmony* (CUP 2010).

First, IHRL embodies a recognition that sometimes absolute rights such as the right to life and the prohibition against ill-treatment can be violated by economic measures that on their own or cumulatively violate such rights, e.g. deliberate starvation of a group or deliberate poisoning of its water supply. Further, as Anker notes, '[e]conomic rights violations often have physical harm dimensions' and 'someone deprived of sufficient food, drinkable water essential medical care or suffering oil pollution, land flooding may suffer physical harm'.[186] Significantly, in its General Comment No 36 on the right to life, the HRC has written that: '[t]he duty to protect life also implies that States parties should take appropriate measures to address the general conditions in society that may give rise to direct threats to life or prevent individuals from enjoying their right to life with dignity' and has included amongst examples of such general conditions, 'degradation of the environment ... deprivation of indigenous peoples' land, territories and resources, the prevalence of life-threatening diseases, such as AIDS, tuberculosis and malaria, extensive substance abuse, widespread hunger and malnutrition and extreme poverty and homelessness'. The HRC states that the measures called for to address adequate conditions for protecting the right to life:

> [ ... ] include, where necessary, measures designed to ensure access without delay by individuals to essential goods and services such as food, water, shelter, health care, electricity and sanitation, and other measures designed to promote and facilitate adequate general conditions, such as the bolstering of effective emergency health services, emergency response operations (including firefighters, ambulance services and police forces) and social housing programmes.[187]

Second, whilst a human rights approach does not entail that socio-economic forms of harm necessarily qualify as persecutory,[188] the fact that IHRL guarantees cover social, economic, and cultural rights as well as civil and political rights and that all human rights are increasingly seen as 'indivisible, interdependent and interrelated',[189] certainly enhances the case for adding socio-economic forms of harm to a list of potentially persecutory acts.

Third, a human rights approach recognizes that the threshold of serious harm can be reached through the cumulative effect of lesser harms, discrimination in particular. Article 9(1)(b) of the QD (recast) recognises as one of two routes by which acts of persecution can arise 'an accumulation of various measures, including violations of human rights which is sufficiently severe as to affect an individual in a similar manner as mentioned in point (a)'.[190] Foster quotes from a decision of the New Zealand RSAA explaining that: '[t]he need to recognize the cumulative effect of threats to human rights is particularly important in the context of refugee claims based on discrimination'.[191] Her analysis of case law reveals that it is difficult to find consensus on any

---

[186] Anker (n 33) §4.27, 362–63.
[187] HRC, General Comment No 36 (n 115) para 26.
[188] Hathaway (n 4) 120: '[b]ecause socio-economic rights are intentionally defined in international law in terms of minimally acceptable standards, not every instance of unfairness broadly related to an enumerated right will support a finding of persecution'.
[189] Foster (n 45) 17.
[190] QD (recast) (n 8) Article 9(1)(b).
[191] *Refugee Appeal No 71427/99* (n 50) para 53(a) cited by Foster (n 45) 94.

more specific particularisation of relevant circumstances, but that 'the most common method by which claims based on the deprivation of economic and social rights have been successful is by reference to the principle that a fear of being persecuted may be established by an accumulation of a number of less serious violations'.[192]

Anker usefully particularises forms of economic harm so as to include fines and other economic penalties, denial of the right to work, demotion or other job-related consequences; denial of housing and means of living and support; and denial of health care and education.[193] Foster points out that applying a human rights approach entails recognising that the right to work is (in the words of the Committee on Economic, Social and Cultural Rights (ESCR Committee)) 'essential for realizing other human rights and forms an inseparable and inherent part of human dignity'.[194]

Foster is surely correct to see failure to refer to violations of internationally guaranteed socio-economic rights as having led to an overly restrictive understanding of 'being persecuted'.[195] She attributes continuing reticence to a lack of clarity in understanding the nature and method of implementing socio-economic rights and the misplaced notion of a normative hierarchy in which socio-economic rights invariably occupy an inferior place.

But her overall assessment of the case law and wider literature is that, despite continuing reticence:

[ ... ] refugee decision-makers have become increasingly willing to consider a range of socio-economic rights violations as capable of constituting persecution. In addition to the more traditional claims based on economic proscription, recent claims founded on severe discrimination in education, health care and a range of socio-economic rights related broadly to an adequate standard of living have been held to fall within the parameters of the Refugee Convention.[196]

It is difficult to disagree with Foster that approaches which rely in one way or another, on a notion of a hierarchy of rights or state obligations, have caused, in her words, 'a widespread tendency to undervalue socio-economic rights in refugee adjudication'.[197] She discerns a tendency to treat the fact that the violation of socio-economic rights, on Hathaway's 1991 model, is of third-level rights which as such require the need for a much higher level of violation[198] or to amount to a threat to a person's capacity to subsist. She maintains that framing the test this way disregards the fact that

---

[192] Foster (n 45) 94–111, 104. This is well-illustrated by what McHugh J wrote in *Chan Yee Kin v MIEA* [1989] HCA 62: 'persecution on account of race, religion and political opinion, has historically taken many forms of social, political and economic discrimination. Hence the denial of access to employment, to the professions and to education or the imposition of restrictions on the freedoms traditionally guaranteed in a democratic society such as freedom of speech, assembly, worship or movement may constitute persecution if imposed for a Convention reason.'
[193] Anker (n 33) §4.29, 373.
[194] UN Economic, Social and Cultural Rights Committee (ESCR Committee), General Comment No 18: The Right to Work (Art 6 of the Covenant) (6 February 2006) UN Doc E/C.12/GC/18, para 1.
[195] Foster (n 45) 81.
[196] ibid 110.
[197] ibid 124.
[198] ibid 127.

the types of harm concerned violate human dignity, even if they do not produce an immediate economic outcome or harm. She also rebukes a tendency to assume that socio-economic persecution can only arise in the form of cumulative harm and/or if combined with breaches of civil and political rights. Foster sees the error here as concentration on the 'value of the rights invoked rather than the *consequences of their breach* for the individual'.[199]

Foster also takes issue with the approach according to which economic, social, and cultural rights are of a different order from civil and political rights because they are essentially programmatic and do not impose any immediate obligations on states parties. This overlooks, she notes, that the 'programmatic' nature of these rights is not relevant to cases where a person's economic and social rights are actively withdrawn or where there is discrimination on a protected ground in the provision of such rights.[200] She points out that it is incorrect to portray all social, economic, and cultural rights as subject to resource constraints; this ignores that the ICESCR contains a number of core obligations from which states cannot derogate from to ensure the right of access to health facilities, goods, and services on a non-discriminatory basis, especially for vulnerable groups.[201]

The concern that Hathaway's 1991 model of four-fold hierarchy of obligations/rights has perhaps encouraged decision makers to think of violations of socio-economic rights as a lower-level order of rights (and hence as far more difficult for their violation to be seen to cross the threshold to become persecution) has now been acknowledged by Hathaway himself in his and Foster's second edition of TLRS. They make a strong case that IHRL has increasingly accepted and formulated clearer analyses of social and economic rights.[202] In a 2018 contribution, Foster notes further positive developments and seeks to address the continuing reticence she still perceives on the part of both advocates and decision makers in integrating violations of socio-economic rights more into their persecution analysis. She first addresses the alleged complexity of referencing socio-economic rights given that they include guarantees that depend on progressive realisation that are not easy for decision makers to apply. Such claims, she states, are 'unlikely, if ever, to come before refugee decision-makers' since the need to establish a nexus with a Convention reason entails that what is frequently involved is 'discriminatory withdrawal, deprivation or withholding of a right'. Second, she states that decision makers now have to hand far more materials focusing on arbitrary or discriminatory conduct, 'precisely the type of claim most relevant in refugee law'.[203]

It must be asked, where does greater referencing of social and economic rights leave claims from persons fleeing situations that have caused widespread socio-economic deprivation, e.g. floods, drought, fires, etc.? This will be addressed to some extent in the separate subsection on environmental harm, but two observations are in order here. First, in general terms, to demonstrate that socio-economic harms in such

---

[199] ibid 149.
[200] ibid 138.
[201] ibid 226.
[202] Hathaway and Foster (n 3) 204.
[203] Michelle Foster, 'Economic Migrant or Person in Need of Protection? Socio-Economic Rights and Persecution in International Refugee Law' in Burson and Cantor (n 57) 229–52.

large-scale situations amount to persecution, it would have to be shown that they are attributable to human agency on the part of state or non-state actors and that there had been a failure to protect, by act or omission.[204]

Second, it would seem essential, in order to establish lack of protection on the part of the state, that there is sufficient causal connection. Whilst this remains a relatively neglected topic, it would appear that, at least based on IHRL, the relevant causal test (not to be confused with the causal test used in establishing the Refugee Convention reasons) should be a 'sole or predominant cause' test as applied by the ECtHR in *Sufi and Elmi* in relation to Article 3 ECHR.[205] Applying this test, the Court went on to find that the drought in Somalia at the relevant time was 'primarily due to the direct and indirect actions of the parties to the conflict' and hence the dire humanitarian conditions crossed the threshold of Article 3 ECHR harm.

It is useful to have regard, as one significant source of state practice, to how acts of socio-economic harm might qualify as persecution under the terms of Article 9(1) of the QD (recast). It would appear that in order to qualify as acts sufficiently serious to constitute a severe violation of basic human rights, within Article 9(1)(a), it would have to be shown not only that the socio-economic harms were caused solely or predominantly by state or non-state actors but were also ones that threatened life and basic survival. Correspondingly, Article 9(1)(b) is capable of encompassing socio-economic harms which, even though not sufficiently severe violations in themselves, can cross that threshold when taken cumulatively, at least where such harms are solely or predominantly caused by human actors.

For both these reasons, to the non-exhaustive list of acts within the material scope of the definition of persecution as set out in Article 9(2) of this directive can be added 'socio-economic acts'. Notably the Australian legislation now includes a recognition of socio-economic persecution.[206]

### 2.2.3.1 Education-related harms

The ICESCR devotes two articles to the right to education, Articles 13 and 14. Article 13 (2)(a) guarantees the right to primary education. Primary education has two distinctive features: it is 'compulsory' and 'available free to all'. This same right is contained in Article 28 of the Convention on the Rights of the Child (CRC). According to Article 13(2)(b) ICCPR, secondary education 'shall be made generally available

---

[204] See Anker (n 33) §4.11, 236–50. However, human agency may not necessarily be required to establish lack of an internal protection alternative: see Chapter 8, section 4.1.5.

[205] *Sufi and Elmi v United Kingdom* Apps Nos 8319/07 and 1149/07 (ECtHR, 18 November 2011) para 282. See Chapter 8, section 4.1.5.

[206] Migration Act 1958, ss 5J(4)(b) and 91R(1)(b) (as amended) specify that persecution must involve 'serious harm' to the person; ss 5J(5) and 91R(2) then set out a non-exhaustive list of the type and level of harm that will meet the serious harm test. Among the examples specified are:

(d) significant economic hardship that threatens the person's capacity to subsist;

(e) denial of access to basic services, where the denial threatens the person's capacity to subsist;

(f) denial of capacity to earn a livelihood of any kind, where the denial threatens the person's capacity to subsist.

See further, Guide to Refugee Law in Australia: Chapter 4—Persecution, available at <http//www/aat.gov.au> (accessed 26 January 2022).

and accessible to all by every appropriate means, and in particular by the progressive introduction of free education'. Article 13(2)(c) provides that higher education 'shall be made equally accessible to all, on the basis of capacity'. Article 13(3) and (4) guarantee the right to educational freedom. In General Comment No 13 at paragraph 43, the ESCR Committee notes that:

> While the Covenant provides for progressive realization and acknowledges the constraints due to the limits of available resources, it also imposes on states parties various obligations which are of immediate effect. States parties have immediate obligations in relation to the right to education, such as the 'guarantee' that the right 'will be exercised without discrimination of any kind' (art. 2 (2)) and the obligation 'to take steps' (art. 2 (1)) towards the full realization of article 13.[207]

Kälin and Künzli consider that, 'unlike the right to a primary education, [the obligations to provide education at higher levels] 'are not justiciable and individually enforceable but are goals to be achieved progressively'.[208] Although analysing education under the heading of 'Autonomy and self-realisation', Hathaway and Foster consider that a violation of the right to primary education is 'in and of itself sufficient to constitute serious harm'. They cite in support the UNHCR Guidelines No 8[209] and both common law and civil law case law, including a decision of the Canadian Federal Court regarding a nine-year-old Afghani girl whose claim was that she would be deprived of the right to education on return.[210] They also consider that the right to education could be violated to a persecutory degree where children of a racial or ethnic group are consigned to clearly inferior educational facilities. That properly reflects IHRL case law.[211] Despite the more limited terms of the protection of the right to secondary education, they argue that it would violate IHLR norms if access was denied or withdrawn to secondary education on the basis of a Convention reason. They maintain that '[m]ost decision makers have thus sensibly refrained from distinguishing between primary and secondary education in articulating the principle that a denial of access to education can amount to serious harm, often speaking simply of the right of "children" to an education'.[212] However, they accept, in light of the case law, that the circumstances in which denial of access to tertiary education might qualify as persecutory harm are more limited, albeit citing US cases that have found persecutory the systemic exclusion of a protected groups such as 'the exclusion of Jewish students from German universities under the Nuremburg Laws' or a Romanian law 'forbidding [ethnic Hungarians] from [attending] college'.[213]

---

[207] ESCR Committee, General Comment No 13 (8 December 1999) UN Doc E/C.12/1999/10.
[208] Kälin and Künzli (n 107) 411.
[209] UNHCR Guidelines No 8 (n 155) para 36.
[210] Hathaway and Foster (n 3) 276–78; *Ali v Canada (MCI)* [1996] 119 FTR 258; see also Hathaway and Foster (n 3) 260.
[211] See e.g. *DH and Others v Czech Republic* App No 57325/00 (ECtHR [GC], 13 November 2007).
[212] Hathaway and Foster (n 3) 277.
[213] ibid, citing *Chen v Ashcroft* [2004] 113 Fed.Appx.135, para 139; *Bucur* [1997] 109 F.3d 399, paras 403–04. See also Foster (n 45) 223–26.

### 2.2.3.2 Health-related harms

That health-related harms may sometimes rise to the level of persecutory harm is not excluded by the refugee definition. Such an understanding is fortified by application of a human rights approach. First, in accordance with Article 12(1) of the ICESCR, states parties recognise 'the right of everyone to the enjoyment of the highest attainable standard of physical and mental health' and the right to health takes its place in this instrument alongside other social and economic rights. It has also been described by the ESCR Committee as a 'fundamental human right indispensable for the exercise of other human rights'.[214] The Committee has interpreted the right to health, as defined in Article 12(1), as an inclusive right 'extending not only to timely and appropriate health care but also to the underlying determinants of health, such as access to safe and potable water and adequate sanitation, an adequate supply of safe food, nutrition and housing, healthy occupational and environmental conditions, and access to health-related education and information, including on sexual and reproductive health'.[215]

Importantly, for application of a human rights approach, the right to health includes duties of an immediate nature, including the core obligations to 'ensure the right of access to health facilities, goods and services on a non-discriminatory basis, especially for vulnerable or marginalised groups'.[216]

That violation of such rights can sometimes have persecutory effects has been recognised in the refugee law jurisprudence and wider literature. As stated by the Australian RRT, 'access to medical care and treatment is a fundamental human right and ... actions amounting to an effective denial may constitute persecution'.[217] As with other cases involving vulnerable applicants, it is particularly important in assessing whether the harms involved cross the persecution threshold to take account of the individual circumstances. Whether denial of health care would suffice of itself or in combination with other factors (e.g. discriminatory measures) to amount to persecution will depend on the particular circumstances.

Foster identifies a number of different situations in which denial of health care could give rise to persecution. From her survey of case law, whilst there is broad consensus that denial of health care can potentially give rise to persecution, the circumstances in which that can happen have been seen to be relatively limited.[218] One particular reason why courts and tribunals have hesitated in their assessment of health cases is the difficulty in identifying intentional infliction of harm, either by act or omission. This difficulty has been addressed by the CJEU in two cases, *M'Bodj* and *MP (Sri Lanka)*. Although both concerned subsidiary protection status, not refugee status, the Court noted in *M'Bodj* that Article 6 QD sets out a list of those actors deemed responsible for inflicting persecution or serious harm, which 'supports the view that such harm must take the form of conduct on the part of a third party and that it cannot therefore simply be the result of general shortcomings in the health system of the country of origin'.[219]

---

[214] ESCR Committee, General Comment No 14: The Right to the Highest Attainable Standard of Health (Art. 12) (11 August 2000) UN Doc E/C.12/2000/4, para 1.
[215] ibid para 11.
[216] ibid para 43.
[217] Case No N95/08165/RRT [1997] para 9, cited by Foster (n 45) 227.
[218] Foster (n 45) 226–33.
[219] Case C-542/13 *Mohamed M'Bodj v État belge* [2014] ECLI:EU:C:2014:2452, para 35.

In *MP* the Court was concerned with a third country national who had been tortured by the authorities of his country of origin in the past. Even though there was no longer any risk of him being tortured again if returned to that country, he continued to suffer severe psychological after-effects resulting from the torture and according to the medical evidence those after-effects would be substantially aggravated and lead to a serious risk of him committing suicide if he were returned to his country of origin.[220] For the Court the question of whether such an applicant would experience intentional infliction of harm would turn on whether the authorities:

> [ ... ] notwithstanding their obligation under Article 14 of the Convention against Torture, are not prepared to provide for his rehabilitation. There will also be such a risk if it is apparent that the authorities of that country have adopted a discriminatory policy as regards access to health care, thus making it more difficult for certain ethnic groups or certain groups of individuals, of which MP forms part, to obtain access to appropriate care for the physical and mental after-effects of the torture perpetrated by those authorities.[221]

Whilst the CJEU's analysis is broadly in line with established principles regarding human agency, it is problematic that they have cast matters in terms of 'intentional infliction' of harm, since as will be addressed in section 3.9 of this chapter, ill treatment can arise without there necessarily been infliction that is intentional. It may be that the Court only meant here to identify human conduct attributable to the authorities of a state. If, however, they meant to treat persecutory intent as a necessary condition for an act of persecution, that would conflict with the growing body of case law and wider literature rejecting that position.[222]

The reasoning in *MP* does not exclude that, at least in certain circumstances, applicants who on return could face a serious deterioration in their health could establish persecutory harm—if there was a lack of care attributable to the state authorities. Even if lack of care attributable to the state authorities was not enough on its own, it could be in conjunction with other factors, e.g. other socio-economic measures of discrimination.

The COVID-19 pandemic particularly highlighted ways in which health-related harms can sometimes give rise to persecutory conduct. The UN Secretary General, António Guterres, said in February 2021 that:

> There has been a global crackdown on opposition activists and human rights defenders, increased attacks on journalists and moves to curb free speech, censor the media, roll out invasive tracking apps and put in place extreme surveillance measures, many of which are likely to far outlast the virus.[223]

---

[220] Case C-353/16 *MP v SSHD* [2018] ECLI:EU:C:2018:276.
[221] ibid para 57.
[222] See below section 3.9. For further discussion of the meaning of 'intentional' in this context, see *NM* [2021] UKUT 259, para 65.
[223] Annie Kelly and Pete Pattisson, '"A Pandemic of Abuses": Human Rights under Attack during Covid, says UN Head' (*The Guardian*, 22 February 2021). See also Bonavero Institute of Human Rights, 'A Preliminary Human Rights Assessment of Legislative and Regulatory Responses to the COVID-19 Pandemic across 11 Jurisdictions' (May 2020) Bonavero Report No 3/2020.

In an earlier United Nations report, it was noted that many countries affected by Covid-19 'were already facing humanitarian crisis because of conflict, natural disasters, and climate change'.[224]

In the context of a human rights approach, one of the main challenges in cases in which pandemic-related factors might form part of a claim to persecutory harm, arises when the human rights seen to be in jeopardy are derogable rights. There may be cases where the rights engaged include non-derogable rights, as, for example, when a pandemic is used by state actors as a pretext for targeting political opponents, e.g. by deliberately exposing them to highly infectious environments or deliberately withholding vaccines and/or medicines needed for treating pandemic sufferers from certain communities or ethnic groups supportive of opposition causes. However, if the rights involved are derogable, there are two particular problems. First these rights are subject to permissible restrictions which require a proportionality assessment, so that a state's efforts to protect their population against the pandemic will need to be balanced against the individual rights at stake. Second, issues may arise as to whether the state is justified in derogating from them on the basis that the pandemic situation has given rise to a public emergency. The ICCPR and the regional human rights instruments provide for derogations during a state of emergency and public health can be one possible basis for the declaration of such an emergency. Article 4(1) ICCPR provides that '[i]n time of public emergency which threatens the life of the nation and the existence of which is officially proclaimed, the states parties to the present Covenant may take measures derogating from their obligations under the present Covenant to the extent strictly required by the exigencies of the situation'.[225] Derogations comprising restrictions on rights for reasons of public health or national emergency must be lawful, necessary, and proportionate. Such requirements must mean, for example, that measures like mandatory quarantine or isolation of symptomatic people, need, at a minimum, to be carried out in accordance with the law.[226]

### 2.2.4 Cultural harms

There is virtually no refugee case law directly invoking violation of the cultural rights set out in the ICESCR. The two provisions of most potential relevance are the right to self-determination (Article 1) and Article 15. By Article 15, states are prohibited from interfering with the 'exercise of cultural practices and with access to cultural goods', and must ensure 'preconditions for participation, facilitation and promotion of cultural life' and access to cultural goods. Cultural rights may be exercised by a person (a) as an individual, (b) in association with others, or (c) within a community or group, as such.[227]

---

[224] UN COVID-19 Global Humanitarian Response Plan for COVID-19 (25 March 2020). See also UN Global Humanitarian Response Plan: COVID-19 (April–December 2020).

[225] International Covenant on Civil and Political Rights (ICCPR) (adopted 16 December 1966, entered into force 23 March 1976) 999 UNTS 171, Article 4(1).

[226] See HRC, General Comment No 29: States of Emergency (Article 4) (n 151); Council of Europe, Guide on Article 15 of the European Convention on Human Rights: Derogation in Time of Emergency (updated 30 April 2021).

[227] See ESCR Committee, General Comment No 21: Right of Everyone to Take Part in Cultural Life (Art 15, para 1a of the Covenant on Economic, Social and Cultural Rights) (21 December 2009) UN Doc E/C.12/GC/21, paras 6, 9, 42. *Legal Consequences of the Separation of the Chagos Archipelago from Mauritius in 1965*, Advisory Opinion [2019] ICJ Rep 95, paras 144–61. See further, Kathleen McVay, 'Self-Determination in

The right to take part in cultural life protects cultural diversity. Individuals have a right to freely determine their cultural identity. Moreover, these rights include the right to participate in the life of society, giving a wide reading to the term 'culture'.[228] States are required to take steps to avoid the adverse consequences that globalisation has on the right to take part in cultural life. The ESCR Committee has observed that cultural attributes can often be attacked or derided by states in attempts to favour one national, racial, or ethnic group over another. It sets out that violations can occur through the direct action of a state party or of other entities or institutions that are insufficiently regulated by the state party, including, in particular, those in the private sector. They can also occur through the omission or failure of a state party to take the necessary measures to comply with its legal obligations under this provision.[229]

The right of everyone to take part in cultural life is subject to limitations. Such limitations must pursue a legitimate aim, be compatible with the nature of this right and be strictly necessary for the promotion of general welfare in a democratic society. Limitations, if proportionate, may be necessary in certain circumstances, in particular in the case of negative practices, including those attributed to customs and traditions, that infringe upon other human rights. In this regard the Committee has noted that:

> A violation also occurs when a State party fails to take steps to combat practices harmful to the well-being of a person or group of persons. These harmful practices, including those attributed to customs and traditions, such as female genital mutilation and allegations of the practice of witchcraft, are barriers to the full exercise by the affected persons of the right enshrined in article 15, paragraph 1 (a).[230]

Clearly violation of cultural rights can sometimes occur alongside violations of other human rights, including environmental harm. Indeed, there is a close linkage between violations of cultural rights and some of the most egregious forms of persecution, e.g. genocide, and it is well-documented that minorities have sometimes been subjected to gross human rights violations, including the destruction of their cultural heritage. As an illustration of how violation of cultural rights might be relevant in assessing persecution, the Inter-American Court in *Case of the Kichwa Indigenous People of Sarayaku v Ecuador* found that the state violated the American Convention when it granted a permit to a private oil company to engage in oil exploration on the territory of the Kichwa Indigenous People of Sarayaku, without consulting the indigenous community. The oil exploration prevented the Sarayaku from accessing resources on their land and limited their right to cultural expression. The Court found violations of the right to communal property and the right to consultation, considering 'the serious impacts suffered by the [indigenous] People owing to their profound social and spiritual relationship with their territory' and the 'suffering caused to the People and to

---

New Contexts: The Self-Determination of Refugees and Forced Migrants in International Law' (2012) 28 Merkourios-Utrecht J Int'l & Eur L 36.

[228] ESCR Committee, General Comment No 21 (n 227) para 50(b).
[229] ibid para 63.
[230] ibid para 64.

their cultural identity'.[231] This example also illustrates the fact that cultural harm can sometimes interact with environmental harm. Where such harm causes individuals to cross borders, the fact that persecution may be involved may make the protection of the refugee definition of critical importance.

### 2.2.5 Environmental harm

It is often remarked that the drafters did not intend the Article 1A(2) definition to cover 'refugees from natural disasters' and that 'neither short-term ecological disasters nor long-term ecological changes were perceived as specific causes of displacement that should give rise to refugee status'.[232] Much-cited has been the observation of Dr Jacob Robinson (Israel) during the Conference of Plenipotentiaries in November 1951 that:

> The text of sub-paragraph (2) obviously did not refer to refugees from natural disasters, for it was difficult to imagine that fires, floods, earthquakes or volcanic eruptions, for instance, differentiated between their victims on the grounds of race, religion or political opinion. Nor did the text cover all man-made events.[233]

Both the 1979 UNHCR Handbook[234] and case law has seen such persons to ordinarily fall outside the scope of the refugee definition. Commentators have seen there to be an exceptional difficulty in seeking to assimilate natural disasters to a new form of persecution.[235]

Accommodating claims for refugee status based on environmental dangers may not be possible for reasons that are distinct from whether or not they amount to persecution. For example, they may fail because the individuals concerned may not have crossed an international border; or because the harm concerned, being 'slow-onset', does not meet the 'well-founded fear' requirement to show that the risk is real and not remote; or because, even if persecutory harm were accepted, it may not be inflicted for at least one of the five Convention reasons.[236]

Several main points have been raised against accepting environmental harm as persecutory harm.

First, (already familiar from previous discussion) there has been the concern that the notion of persecution presupposes human agency and, in the context of 'natural disasters' and climate change, that is not easily discernible. As McAdam has written,

---

[231] See *Case of the Kichwa Indigenous People of Sarayaku v Ecuador*, Merits and Reparations, Judgment, Inter-American Court of Human Rights (IAmCtHR) Series C No 245 (27 June 2012) paras 322–23. See also *Billy et al v Australia* (22 September 2022) Communication No 3624/2019, UN Doc CCPR/C/135/D/3624/2019, para 8.13.

[232] Einarsen (n 28).

[233] Conference of Plenipotentiaries on the Status of Refugees and Stateless Persons: Summary Record of the Twenty-second Meeting (n 27).

[234] UNHCR Handbook (n 60) para 39: '[t]he expression "owing to well-founded fear of being persecuted"—for the reasons stated ... rules out such persons as victims of famine or natural disaster, unless they also have well-founded fear of persecution for one of the reasons stated'.

[235] e.g. Michel Prieur, 'Draft Convention on the International Status of Environmentally-Displaced Persons' (2008) 4 Revue Européenne de Droit de l'Environnement 395.

[236] See e.g. *Refugee Appeal No 72189/2000* [2000] NZRSAA, concerning refugee claims brought by persons from Tuvalu.

'[p]art of the problem in the climate change context is identifying a "persecutor".'[237] Sometimes (and dubiously) this concern has gone hand in hand with the view that it is necessary to show persecutory intent.[238]

Second, it has been argued that, since the focus of the 'being persecuted' inquiry must be on acts or events of persecution, many cases of environmental harm would not qualify as they involve more complex processes, often prolonged or 'slow-onset' and focusing on the consequences of an event.

Third, there has been a concern about 'undifferentiated impact'. Thus, Zimmermann and Mahler write that:

> [ ... ] as a matter of general principle environmental disasters have a general impact on the population of a given area at large rather than individual or members of specific groups, who may accordingly find it difficult to claim that they have been exposed to acts of persecution. This is even more true since the effects of environmental problems commonly have a general influence on the living conditions of the overall population rather than being focused on a single person or members of a specific racial, religious, or other group, as defined in Article 1A, para 2 of the 1951 Convention.

At least in part what critics appear to have in mind here is that it is very difficult to show that the level of deprivation caused by such events amounts to harm that is sufficiently serious to amount to persecution.[239]

Fourth, there is the concern that in the case of persons fleeing 'natural disasters' or climate change, they would appear to still enjoy the protection of the state. As stated by Kälin and Schrepfer in a policy paper prepared for UNHCR, 'in the case of cross-border displacement caused by effects of climate change, the country of origin normally does not turn against affected people but remains willing to assist and protect them'.[240]

Each of these points needs contextualising. As regards human agency, it would be wrong to think that because there is not always some easily identifiable actors involved, that there is a lack of (sufficient) human agency. As Scott among others has observed, the literature of disasters and environmental degradation has underlined the need to place such events in a social and historical context within which policy choices made by governments and other actors may have played an instrumental role.[241] Further, as will be addressed below, it is not necessary, in order to establish the 'being persecuted' element of the refugee definition to show persecutory intent.[242] However, to fully align with IHRL, it would appear (at least on the basis of ECtHR case law), that claims based

---

[237] Jane McAdam, *Climate Change, Forced Migration and International Law* (OUP 2012) 45. See also Jane McAdam, 'Displacement in the Context of Climate Change and Disasters' in Costello et al (n 61) 832–47, 836; Goodwin-Gill and McAdam (n 26) 636–64, 643–45.

[238] As expressed by the full Federal Court of Australia in *Ram v MIEA* [1995] 57 FCR 565, 568 cited in Hathaway and Foster (n 3) 101. See further below section 3.9.

[239] McAdam (n 237) 43.

[240] Walter Kälin and Nina Schrepfer, 'Protecting People Crossing Borders in the Context of Climate Change: Normative Gaps and Possible Approaches' (2012) UNHCR, Legal and Protection Policy Research Series, PPLA/2012/01, 31–32.

[241] Scott (n 51) 7–8, 15.

[242] See below section 3.9.

on environmental harm must establish that such harm has human actors as a 'sole or predominant cause'.[243]

In relation to the concern raised about the need to focus on acts of persecution, it will be argued below that there is no basis for considering that the refugee definition requires a narrow concept of acts as single events or adoption of what some have termed the 'hazard paradigm'.[244]

As regards 'undifferentiated impact', there are several problem areas. One is that it would be wrong to assume that environmental harm is always undifferentiated. Environmental degradation can be used as a targeted instrument of oppression as happened with the Iraqi Marsh Arabs in the first Gulf War.[245] Another is that, even when impact is undifferentiated, there may be scenarios where the extent of the harm severely threatens everyone's non-derogable rights, such as the right to life and/or inhuman and degrading treatment. Thus, the Human Rights Committee decision in *Teitota v NZ*, identified that:

> Both sudden-onset events (such as intense storms and flooding) and slow-onset processes (such as sea level rise, salinization, and land degradation) can propel cross-border movement of individuals seeking protection from climate change-related harm. The Committee is of the view that without robust national and international efforts, the effects of climate change in receiving states may expose individuals to a violation of their rights under articles 6 or 7 of the Covenant, thereby triggering the *non-refoulement* obligations of sending states. Furthermore, given that the risk of an entire country becoming submerged under water is such an extreme risk, the conditions of life in such a country may become incompatible with the right to life with dignity before the risk is realized.[246]

A third problem area is that there seems no reason in principle, applying the concept of cumulative harm, why adverse effects caused by environmental harm to education, healthcare, adequate shelter, work, property, food, information, participation in public life etc. could not result in the deprivations involved cumulatively reaching the persecution threshold. Insofar as the human rights engaged by the facts of the case are qualified rights such as the right to respect for private and family life, there is a significant body of case law that has seen violations of such rights to arise in an environmental context. For example, there has been important ECHR jurisprudence on environmental damage, e.g. the case of *Lopez-Ostra v Spain*,[247] in which serious environmental damage and accompanying health problems were found to be a violation of

---

[243] *Sufi and Elmi* (n 205) para 282. On the related issue of shared responsibility, see *Sacchi et al v Argentina* (8 October 2021) Communication No 104/2019, UN Doc CRC/C/88/D/104/2019, para 10.10: 'In accordance with the principle of common but differentiated responsibility, as reflected in the Paris Agreement, the Committee finds that the collective nature of the causation of climate change does not absolve the State party of its individual responsibility that may derive from the harm that the emissions originating within its territory may cause to children, whatever their location.'
[244] Scott (n 51). See below section 3.1.
[245] As noted in *AF (Kiribati)* [2013] NZIPT 800413, para 58.
[246] *Case of Ioane Teitiota v New Zealand* (7 January 2020) Communication No 2728/2016, UN Doc CCPR/C/127/D/2728/2016, para 9.11. See also *Billy v Australia* (n 231) paras 8.3–8.8.
[247] *López Ostra v Spain* App No 16798/90 (ECtHR, 9 December 1994).

Article 8 ECHR. The African Commission on Human and Peoples Rights in *SERAC and CESR v Nigeria*, found that rights violated by the Nigerian government included the rights to health and food and shelter by virtue of the damage done to the environment of local communities, by the actions of an oil consortium, disposing toxic wastes into the environment and local waterways.[248] Such decisions strengthen the argument that violations of such rights could cumulatively give rise to persecutory harm.

Further, in a significant number of cases involving environmental harm, there may be other factors that taken cumulatively make the overall situation a persecutory one. As noted by UNHCR in its document on Climate Change and Disaster Displacement:

> There may be situations where the refugee criteria of the 1951 Convention or broader refugee criteria of regional refugee law frameworks may apply, for example if drought-related famine is linked to situations of armed conflict and violence—an area known as 'nexus dynamics...'.[249]

Finally, as regards, the issue of state protection, it is trite law that effective protection by a state requires that it is *both* willing and able to protect. Willingness on its own is not enough to negate a claim based on environmental harm. As Zimmermann and Mahler note, it remains that 'the requirements of persecution might be fulfilled when authorities in charge fail to adequately help a particular group of people to cope with environmental disasters'.[250] Further, the view that a state can provide effective protection by using best endeavours or due diligence has not won wide acceptance[251] and hence the fact that states seeking to respond to environmental harm 'do their best' is not to the point.

In light of the above analysis, the summary given by the NZ RSAA in *AF (Kiribati)* is one that commands respect. The RSAA stated that:

> What these observations illustrate is that generalised assumptions about environmental change and natural disasters and the applicability of the Refugee Convention can be overstated. While in many cases the effects of environmental change and natural disasters will not bring affected persons within the scope of the Refugee Convention, no hard and fast rules or presumptions of non-applicability exist. Care must be taken to examine the particular features of the case.[252]

---

[248] *Social and Economic Rights Action Center/Center for Economic and Social Rights v Nigeria* (7 May 2002) Communication No 155/96, ACHPR/COMM/A044/1, cited by Foster (n 45) 233.

[249] UNHCR, Climate change and disaster displacement, available at <www.unhcr.org/climate-change-and-disasters.htm> accessed 21 June 2021. This builds on a 2018 paper in UNHCR's Legal and Policy Protection Research Series by Sanjula Weerasinghe, 'In Harm's Way: International protection in the context of nexus dynamics between conflict or violence and disaster or climate change' (2018) UNHCR, Legal and Policy Protection Research Series, PPLA/2018/05. The Global Compact on Refugees, adopted by an overwhelming majority in the UN General Assembly in December 2018, directly addresses this growing concern. It recognizes that 'climate, environmental degradation and natural disasters increasingly interact with the drivers of refugee movements.' See Report of the United Nations High Commissioner for Refugees, Part II: Global Compact on Refugees (2 August 2018) UN Doc A/73/12. See further, Simon Behrman and Avidan Kent (eds) *Climate Refugees: Global, Local and Critical Approaches* (CUP 2022).

[250] Zimmermann and Mahler (n 1) 440.

[251] Goodwin-Gill and McAdam (3rd edn) (n 25) 10–12; Hathaway and Foster (n 3) 308–19.

[252] *AF (Kiribati)* (n 245) paras 63–65.

Applying a human rights approach, Scott has usefully mapped several types of situations where it may be possible for victims of such events to come within the scope of Article 1A(2) provided that the other requirements of the definition are fulfilled. He identifies two main categories: 'Category 2' cases, which concern scenarios where identifiable actors of persecution directly and intentionally inflict serious harm in the context of disasters and climate change; and 'Category 3' cases, which relate to other *ex-ante* and *ex post* failures of state protection.[253]

Accordingly, it is clear that as with socio-economic harms, environmental harms are acts capable of having the quality of persecutory acts and hence should be added to the iterative list of such acts. However, their capability of constituting persecutory acts remains highly context specific. Even on a human rights approach, it remains that there is no legal basis currently for recognition per se of 'environmental refugees' or 'climate refugees' in current international law.[254]

## 2.3 Material Scope: Category-Specific Forms of Harm

In addressing material scope up to this point focus has been on types of harm potentially applicable to *all* applicants for refugee status, e.g. physical and psychological forms of harm. However, it is also necessary, as part of the consideration of material scope, to consider forms of persecution that apply only to *some* categories of applicants—these are conveniently described as 'specific forms of persecution'.[255] It is necessary because the ability of the refugee definition to operate as a universal definition depends on at least two interrelated things being shown. First (as regards its personal scope), that it treats all persons as legal persons and as such entitled to be considered as to whether they qualify as a refugee in their own right (the chapeau to Article 1A refers to 'any person'); thus, for example, even though in other areas of law a child's rights may sometimes be assimilated to those of their parents, they are entitled to apply for refugee status in their own right and to receive, correspondingly, an individual assessment; they are not simply objects of protection.[256] Second, that it can be shown that Article 1A(2) has a protective role in relation to those with distinct protection needs and/or characteristics recognised in international treaty form to give rise to discrimination and unfair treatment, such as race, age, and gender. As explained by Alice Edwards in relation to the latter two examples, 'in order to ensure that international refugee law is applied in a non-discriminatory way to all individuals, age and

---

[253] Scott (n 51) 54–87. His Category 1 concerns 'Indiscriminate Adversity due to the Forces of Nature', see 48–54.

[254] As noted by UNHCR, Climate change and disaster displacement, available at <www.unhcr.org/climate-change-and-disasters.htm> accessed 21 June 2021. See further Simon Behrman and Avidan Kent (eds), *Climate Refugees: Global, Local and Critical Approaches* (CUP 2022).

[255] Consistent with the approach taken here, Article 9(2) of the QD (recast) combines enumeration of some acts of persecution that can apply to anyone (e.g. 'physical or mental violence'(Article 9(2)a)) with two that are specific to a subcategory of person, namely 'gender-specific and child-specific' forms of persecution: Article 9(2)(f) specifies that acts of persecution may include '(f) acts of a gender-specific or child-specific nature.'

[256] Jason Pobjoy, *The Child in International Refugee Law* (CUP 2017) 55.

gender approaches are vital components of any analysis'.[257] In relation to persecution, there must therefore be resistance to viewing persecutory harm in monolithic terms, with little regard to the vulnerabilities of the victim.[258]

Further, by virtue of the diversity of IHRL instruments, with key instruments addressing specific categories, e.g. children, women, trafficked persons, and persons with a disability, a well-formed body of IHRL has developed casting light on the nature of persecutory harm in the form of rights-violations specific to those categories. As pointed out by the UNHCR Guidelines on Gender, evolving international law standards can assist decision makers to determine 'the persecutory nature of a particular act'.[259]

Drawing upon earlier analyses, consideration of such specific forms bids understanding of three interrelated things: first, that the refugee definition requires individual assessment; second, that persecutory harm is relative in the sense that to be persecution it has to reach a certain threshold; and thirdly, that whether such a threshold is reached can depend very much on individual circumstances.

As regards *individual assessment*, by rejecting the previous group-based categorisation of refugees, the drafters inevitably committed decision makers to the need to make an individual-specific assessment. That principle is seen as an inherent feature in UNHCR, case law, and academic materials. Within the EU, it has been given expression in Article 4(3) of the QD, which, as noted earlier, requires that the assessment of an application for international protection is to be carried out on an individual basis.[260]

As regards the *relativity* of persecutory harm and the notion of a *threshold of sufficient severity*, it is a cardinal principle of a human rights-based approach that what amounts to a violation of a person's human rights sufficiently severe enough to constitute persecution will depend in part on how that harm impacts on them individually. Some measures will be sufficiently severe irrespective of who the person is, e.g. torture. But in relation to other measures, the same act may impact on a person differently depending on his/her personal circumstances and individual situation, including factors, particularly those relating to vulnerability, such as background, gender, and age.

---

[257] Alice Edwards, 'Age and Gender Dimensions in International Refugee Law' in Erika Feller et al (n 76) 49. See also Heaven Crawley, *Refugees and Gender: Law and Process* (Jordan Publishing Limited 2001); Rodger Haines, 'Gender-related persecution' in Erika Feller et al (n 76). See finally UNHCR, Guidelines No 2: Membership of a particular social group within the context of Article 1A(2) of the 1951 Convention and/or its 1967 Protocol relating to the Status of Refugees (7 May 2002) UN Doc HCR/GIP/02/01.

[258] Mary Crock et al, 'Where Disability and Displacement Intersect: Asylum Seekers and Refugees with Disabilities' (2012) 24(4) IJRL 735, 746.

[259] See e.g. UNHCR, Guidelines No 1: Gender-Related Persecution within the context of Article 1A(2) of the 1951 Convention and/or its 1967 Protocol relating to the Status of Refugees (2002) UN Doc HCR/GIP/02/01, para 9: '[w]hile female and male applicants may be subjected to the same forms of harm, they may also face forms of persecution specific to their sex. International human rights law and international criminal law clearly identify certain acts as violations of these laws, such as sexual violence, and support their characterisation as serious abuses, amounting to persecution. In this sense, international law can assist decision-makers to determine the persecutory nature of a particular act. There is no doubt that rape and other forms of gender-related violence, such as dowry-related violence, female genital mutilation, domestic violence, and trafficking, are acts which inflict severe pain and suffering—both mental and physical—and which have been used as forms of persecution, whether perpetrated by State or private actors.'

[260] Joined Cases C-148/13 to C-150/13 *A and Others v Staatssecretaris van Veiligheid en Justitie* [2014] ECLI:EU:C:2014:2406, para 57.

That this reflects the IHRL approach is clear from the formulation given by treaty-monitoring bodies and regional human rights courts of absolute rights, in particular the prohibition on ill-treatment. The ECtHR, for example, has emphasised that:

> [ … ] ill-treatment the applicant alleges that he will face if returned must attain a minimum level of severity if it is to fall within the scope of Article 3. The assessment of this level is relative, depending on all the circumstances of the case....[261]

The ECtHR has further reiterated that '[t]he assessment must focus on the foreseeable consequences of the applicant's removal to the country of destination, in the light of the general situation there and of his or her personal circumstances'.[262] In the Grand Chamber's judgment in *MSS v Belgium and Greece*, the Court stated that 'the assessment of this minimum … depends on all the circumstances of the case, such as the duration of the treatment and its physical or mental effects and, in some instances, the sex, age and state of health of the victim'.[263] Reflecting this common understanding, the CJEU noted in *Y and Z*:

> [ … ] it is apparent from the wording of Article 9(1) of the Directive that there must be a 'severe violation' of religious freedom having a significant effect on the person concerned in order for it to be possible for the acts in question to be regarded as acts of persecution....[264]

In similar fashion, national courts and tribunals around the world have developed case law which illustrates that certain acts may constitute persecution or serious harm when perpetrated against a child or an elderly person, where they might not for a comparably placed adult.

Vital as treatment of specific forms of persecution is, though, it must not turn into an attempt to redefine the general concept of persecution. Increased emphasis, for example, on the role of gender in persecution is not an argument for altering the meaning of the term 'being persecuted'; that meaning does not change depending on the subject matter.[265] It only serves to ensure that there is full understanding of all aspects of the applicant's claim of persecution.

In what follows, the objective is to summarise the state of the learning on some important specific forms of persecution. Coverage here must not be understood as a closed list. It does not address, for example, specific forms of persecution based per se on race, religion, nationality, membership of a particular social group, or political opinion, since they are already given formal recognition in the refugee definition (and

---

[261] *JK and Others v Sweden* App No 59166/12 (ECtHR [GC], 23 August 2016) para 79.
[262] ibid para 83.
[263] *MSS v Belgium and Greece* App No 30696/09 (ECtHR [GC], 21 January 2011) para 219. See also *Ghorbanov and Others v Turkey* App No 28127/09 (ECtHR, 3 December 2013) para 33.
[264] *Y and Z* (n 175) para 59.
[265] Zimmermann and Mahler (n 1) 406, properly reject the notion of 'a lowered standard of "persecution" for children'.

will be analysed in relation to Convention reasons in Chapter 10) and in that way have always been a backdrop to interpretation of the meaning of 'being persecuted'.[266]

### 2.3.1 Gender-specific persecution

UNHCR describes gender as referring to 'the relationship between men and women based on socially or culturally constructed and defined identities, status, roles and responsibilities that are assigned to one sex or another'.[267] The literature distinguishes between 'gender-related' and 'gender-specific' persecution.[268] The former relates to the experience of those who are persecuted because of their gender identity and status (mostly but not exclusively as women).[269] As recognised by the UNHCR Gender Guidelines, refugee claims based on differing sexual orientation also contain a gender element,[270] but the latter have come to be dealt with separately, as evidenced by the production in 2012 of further Guidelines on Sexual Orientation and/or Gender Identity. In addition, awareness has grown of the need for any definition of gender to take into account that some people now define themselves, and/or are defined, as non-binary and/or transgender and the fact that there are also people who have transitioned or are transitioning to a male or female gender.[271]

Gender-specific acts of persecution relate to forms of serious harm which are specific to gender. These predominantly (but not exclusively) concern women or girls. They may encompass physical, sexual, and psychological violence occurring in the family (including marital rape and sexual abuse of female children, bride-burning, suttee, dowry-related violence, FGM) or within the wider community, including rape, sexual abuse, sexual harassment, forced marriage, coerced family planning, punishment for transgression of social mores, intimidation at work or in educational

---

[266] Although in the case of race-specific forms of persecution, there has been a marked lack of attention to it in the case law and wider literature. Tendayi E Achiume, 'Race, Refugees, and International Law' in Costello et al (n 61) 43–59. At 44, Achiume identifies 'international refugee law scholarship's racial aphasia'.

[267] UNHCR Guidelines No 2 (n 257) para 3. The Council of Europe Convention on preventing and combating violence against women and domestic violence (CETS No. 210) defines 'gender' as Article 3(c) as 'the socially constructed roles, behaviours, activities and attributes that a given society considers appropriate for women and men'.

[268] Crawley (n 257) 7; Haines (n 257) 319; Nicole LaViolette, 'Gender-Related Refugee Claims: Expanding the Scope of the Canadian Guidelines' (2007) 19(2) IJRL 169, 182.

[269] UNHCR Guidelines No 2 (n 257).

[270] ibid para 16. See further on the gender element, Deborah Anker, 'Refugee Law, Gender and the Human Rights Paradigm' (2002) 15 Harv Hum Rts LJ 133; Alice Edwards, 'Transitioning Gender: Feminist Engagement with International Refugee Law and Policy 1950–2010' (2010) 29(2) RSQ 21; Efrat Arbel, Catherine Dauvergne, and Jenni Millbank (eds), *Gender in Refugee Law: From the Margins to the Centre* (Routledge 2014); Heaven Crawley, '[En]gendering International Refugee Protection: Are We There Yet?' in Burson and Cantor (n 57) 322; Adrienne Anderson and Michelle Foster, 'A Feminist Appraisal of International Refugee Law' in Costello et al (n 61) 66; Goodwin-Gill and McAdam (n 26) 107–13; Mathilde Crepin, *Persecution, International Refugee Law and Refugees: A Feminist Approach* (Routledge 2021); Adrienne Anderson, 'Flawed Foundations: An Historical Evaluation of Domestic Violence Claims in the Refugee Tribunals' (2021) 45(1) MULR 1.

[271] UNHCR, Guidelines No 9: Claims to Refugee Status based on Sexual Orientation and/or Gender Identity within the context of Article 1A(2) of the 1951 Convention and/or its 1967 Protocol relating to the Status of Refugees (23 October 2012) HCR/GIP/12/01; UNHCR, Policy on the Prevention of, Risk Mitigation, and Response to Gender-based Violence (2020) 5; Additional Principles and State Obligations on the Application of International Human Rights Law in Relation to Sexual Orientation, Gender Identity, Gender Expression and Sex Characteristics to Complement the Yogyakarta Principles (10 November 2017) (Yogyakarta Principles Plus 10).

institutions, forced prostitution or sexual exploitation and trafficking for such purposes, and discrimination against persons of diverse sexual orientation.[272] These example underscore that women often experience persecution differently from men.[273] Bearing in mind that persecution can result from an accumulation of harms in themselves falling short of serious harm, it is of particular importance that Article 1 of the Convention for the Elimination of Discrimination Against Women defines discrimination against women broadly as:

> [ ... ] any distinction, exclusion or restriction made on the basis of sex which has the effect or purpose of impairing or nullifying the recognition, enjoyment or exercise by women, irrespective of their marital status, on a basis of equality of men and women, of human rights and fundamental freedoms in the political, economic, social, cultural, civil or any other field.[274]

In addition to the Guidelines and other UNHCR materials, Article 9(2) QD (recast) includes as forms acts of persecution can take: 'acts of a gender-specific or child-specific nature'. A number of countries (including sometimes courts and tribunal themselves) have issued specific guidelines relating to gender-specific persecution.[275]

Gender-specific persecution typically reflects societal norms that treat women or girls or LGBTI+ persons as inferior and/or involve the abuse of power in society at large and/or in intimate relationships.[276] In the context of applications for refugee status made by women and girls, the UK House of Lords noted in *Fornah*[277] that 'women as a sex may be persecuted in ways which are different from the ways in which men are persecuted and ... they may be persecuted because of the inferior status accorded to their gender in their home society'.[278] In an earlier decision, *Islam and Shah*,

---

[272] Zimmermann and Mahler (n 1) 412–15. Historically, to denote gender-specific persecution, UNHCR has used the terms 'gender-based violence' or 'sexual and gender-based violence' (SGBV). Currently, it uses the term gender-based violence (GBV): see UNHCR, Policy on the Prevention of, Risk Mitigation, and Response to Gender-based Violence (n 271) 3. At 4, the Policy states that '[t]he term "Gender-Based Violence" ... is most commonly used to underscore how systemic inequality between males and females, which exists in every society in the world, acts as a unifying and foundational characteristic of most forms of violence perpetrated against women and girls'. On the need to see men as well as women as 'gendered subjects', see Noemi Magugliani, 'Trafficked Adult Males as (Un)Gendered Protection Seekers: Between Presumption of Invulnerability and Exclusion from Membership of a Particular Social Group' (2022) 34(4) IJRL 353, 357–58.

[273] ExCom, Refugee Protection and Sexual Violence No 73 (XLIV)–1993 (8 October 1993) paras d and e. See also the opinion of Advocate General Richard De La Tour in Case C-621/21, *Intervyuirasht organ na DAB pri MS (Femmes victimes de violences domestiques)* [2023] ECLI:EU:C:2023:314, para 56.

[274] Convention on the Elimination of All Forms of Discrimination against Women (CEDAW) (adopted 18 December 1979, entered into force 3 September 1981) 1249 UNTS 13, Article 1.

[275] QD (n 8); Zimmermann and Mahler (n 1) 411–12.

[276] See UNHCR, 'UNHCR Statement on the concept of persecution on cumulative grounds in light of the current situation for women and girls in Afghanistan: Issued in the context of the preliminary ruling reference to the Court of Justice of the European Union in the cases of *AH and FN v. Bundesamt für Fremdenwesen und Asyl* (C-608/22 and C-609/22)' (25 May 2023) available at <https://www.refworld.org/docid/646f0e6a4.html> accessed 26 May 2023.

[277] *Fornah v SSHD (linked with SSHD v K)* [2006] UKHL 46.

[278] ibid para 86.

violence against women in the form of domestic violence was identified as gender-based persecution.[279]

### 2.3.2 Sexual orientation-based persecution

It has taken refugee law globally some considerable time to recognise LGBTI+ persons as having valid protection needs.[280] There has been increasing recognition of the manifold ways in which LGBTI+ persons can face persecutory harm.[281] When considering such persons, the warning given by the High Court of Australia, that 'sexual identity is not to be understood ... as confined to particular sexual acts. It may, and often will, extend to many aspects of human relationships and activit[ies]',[282] is particularly apposite.[283] Definitions of sexual orientation and/or gender identity are set out in the Yogyakarta Principles.[284]

In a 2011 publication, 'Working with Lesbian, Gay, Bisexual, Transgender & Intersex Persons in Forced Displacement', UNHCR states that:

> LGBTI groups experience persecution and discrimination in distinct ways.
>
> **Lesbians** may suffer persecution based on both their gender and sexual orientation and may be exposed more frequently to honour crimes and rape at the hands of private actors, including family and community members. Their social and economic status may obstruct their access to asylum procedures, police, and other forms of protection and support in countries of asylum.
>
> **Gay men** tend to live more public lives and, as a result, are often at more immediate risk of harm, especially from State actors in countries where male same-sex conduct is a criminal offence. Gay men may be reluctant to reveal to authorities or service providers the sexual abuse they may have endured.
>
> **Bisexuality** is not well understood in many countries. Bisexual persons are attracted to people of the opposite as well as the same sex, but are persecuted because of their same-sex conduct. They consider their sexual orientation to be fluid and flexible, creating the misperception that their sexuality is a matter of choice, not identity.
>
> **Transgender persons** are often severely marginalized. They frequently experience abuse and discrimination from State authorities and hatred by family and community

---

[279] *Islam v SSHD Immigration Appeal Tribunal and Another, Ex Parte Shah, R v* [1999] UKHL 20. See also *Hoxha* (n 64) para 34. See also, Lee Hasselbacher, 'State Obligations Regarding Domestic Violence: The European Court of Human Rights, Due Diligence, and International Legal Minimums of Protection' (2010) 8(2) Northwestern Journal of Human Rights 190. The UN Committee on the Elimination of Discrimination Against Women, CEDAW General Recommendation No 19: Violence against women (1992), the UN General Assembly, Vienna Declaration and Programme of Action (12 July 1993) UN Doc A/CONF.157/23, and the United Nations, Beijing Declaration and Platform of Action, adopted at the Fourth World Conference on Women (27 October 1995) contributed to recognizing that especially women are particularly vulnerable to violence in the private sphere at the hands of private actors.

[280] Jenni Millbank, 'Sexual Orientation and Gender Identity in Refugee Claims' in Costello et al (n 61) 761–77, 761–62.

[281] Sometimes the term used is LGBT, LGBTI, LGBTQI, LGBTQI+, or SOGI (Sexual Orientation and Gender Identity). See (n 290).

[282] *S395/2002* (n 174) para 81.

[283] See also in the French National Court of Asylum Law, *CNDA No 16015675* [2017].

[284] Reference was made to these principles in *X and Y and Z* (n 175). They have now been complemented by the Yogyakarta Principles Plus 10 (n 271).

members; they are often subject to sexual abuse, by State as well as non-State actors. Frequently excluded from education and access to housing and employment, they may engage in survival sex work.

**Intersex individuals** may endure persecution because they do not conform to gender expectations, or are viewed as having a physical disability related to their atypical sexual anatomy. Family members of intersex persons are sometimes also abused. Intersex individuals may be subject to unwanted surgery to 'correct' their anatomy or have ongoing medical needs related to their condition.

As is clear from this summary, the risk of persecution in relation to LGBTI+ persons may arise as a result of laws and/or social practices that are persecutory and/or discriminatory and/or a failure by the authorities to protect LGBTI+ persons from persecution and/or discrimination by family members and others.[285]

Understanding LGBTI+ specific persecution may sometimes require assessment of whether applicants can be expected to avoid persecution on return by concealing their sexual identity. The fact that this concerns the notion of persecution and not just the risk of it is made clear by application of IHRL norms, which highlight that the right to express sexual orientation is one of the facets of the right to freedom of expression, human dignity, human autonomy, and private life. The act of being forced to renounce or conceal such expression can be persecutory.[286] Echoing the position that evolved in the senior common law courts,[287] the CJEU ruled in *X, Y and Z*, that when assessing an application for refugee status, 'the competent authorities cannot reasonably expect, in order to avoid the risk of persecution, the applicant for asylum to conceal his homosexuality in his country of origin or to exercise reserve in the expression of his sexual orientation'.[288] Although this principle has now been widely endorsed, there continues to be debates about its scope, in particular about whether applicants have to demonstrate that a 'material reason' for their concealment is fear.[289]

It may be important when assessing claims to refugee status by LGBTI+ persons based on their sexual orientation and/or gender identity, to consider the specific forms of persecution that can arise for different categories.[290] Examples include the

---

[285] With regard to criminalising homosexual acts in view of the discriminatory nature of such sanctions, see *X and Y and Z* (n 175) para 50.

[286] ibid para 70: '[i]n that connection, it is important to state that requiring members of a social group sharing the same sexual orientation to conceal that orientation is incompatible with the recognition of a characteristic so fundamental to a person's identity that the persons concerned cannot be required to renounce it'.

[287] See *S395/2002* (n 174) and *HJ (Iran)* (n 33). For an analysis of the latter, see Janna Wessels, '*HJ (Iran) and HT (Cameroon)*—Reflections on a New Test for Sexuality-based Asylum Claims in Britain' (2012) 24(4) IJRL 815.

[288] *X and Y and Z* (n 175) para 76.

[289] For a survey of the literature on this subject see Millbank (n 280) 761–77; Goodwin-Gill and McAdam (n 26). See also Wilsher (n 176) 28–53.

[290] See generally, UNHCR Guidelines No 9 (n 271) paras 10 and 20–25. Nuno Ferreira and Carmelo Danisi, 'Queering International Refugee Law' in Costello et al (n 61) 78–96, 81–82 state that 'we favour 'SOGI asylum claim' to 'LGBTIQ+ asylum claim', in order to focus on characteristics rather than Western-based identities and identifiers. See also Thomas Spijkerboer and Sabine Jansen, 'Fleeing Homophobia. Asylum Claims Related to Sexual Orientation and Gender Identity in Europe' (6 September 2011); Hathaway and Foster (n 3) 442–45; Arzu Guler, Maryna Shevtsova, and Denise Venturi (eds), *LGBTI Asylum Seekers and Refugees From a Legal and Political Perspective: Persecution, Asylum and Integration* (Springer 2019); Goodwin-Gill and McAdam (n 26) 113–17.

phenomenon, in respect of lesbians, of the risk of 'corrective rape'[291] or, for transgender persons, refusal to amend documentation to reflect their new gender, or involuntary prostitution, which have been found to amount to persecution.[292]

### 2.3.3 Age- and child-specific forms of persecution

Age is clearly a characteristic than can significantly affect whether harm inflicted on a person amounts to persecution. As noted by Edwards:

> For the elderly, their frailty or lack of mobility could also make threats rise to the level of persecution compared to more active persons, as they would be less able to avoid them or to escape.... Cumulative forms of discrimination against the elderly, including exclusion from social and economic life, could rise to the level of persecution in particular cases.[293]

Forms of persecution specific to elderly persons remain relatively undeveloped in the case law[294] and wider literature.[295] By contrast, awareness that persecution can take child-specific forms has accompanied the Refugee Convention from the outset.[296] That is not to say that such awareness has always been carried through into decision-making. As noted by Pobjoy, '[t]he refugee definition has traditionally been interpreted in an adult-focussed way'.[297] The 2009 UNHCR Guidelines on Child Asylum Claims state that although the refugee definition applies to all individuals regardless of their age, 'it has traditionally been interpreted in light of adult experiences. This has meant that many refugee claims made by children have been assessed incorrectly or overlooked altogether'.[298] At paragraph 15 the Guidelines observe that:

---

[291] See *SW (lesbians—HJ and HT applied) Jamaica* CG [2011] UKUT 00251 (IAC). See further Andrew Martin et al 'Hate Crimes: The Rise of "Corrective" Rape in South Africa' (ActionAid 2019).

[292] See e.g. Asylum Court (Asylgerichtshof, Austria) in *A4 213.316-0/2008/11E* [2011], concerning an Egyptian transgender woman, inter alia, unable to amend her Egyptian passport to her female identity; and Asylum Court (Asylgerichtshof, Austria) in *E1 432.053-1/2013/5E* [2013], a case involving involuntary prostitution. Other cases involving transgender persons, involve forms of persecution also faced by gay men or women. See e.g. French National Court of Asylum Law (CNDA, France) in *CNDA No 18031476* [2019], concerning an Algerian man seeking asylum on account of his sexual orientation and gender identity, who had arrived in France as a gay man, began medical treatment to become a transgender woman and who was recognised as a refugee; and Administrative Court Potsdam (Verwaltungsgericht Potsdam, Germany) in *6 K 338/17.A* [2017], concerning a bisexual, transgender Russian activist recognised as a refugee in Germany.

[293] Edwards (n 257) 65.

[294] But see Independent Asylum Senate (Unabhängiger Asylsenat, Austria) in *203.332/0-VIII/22/98* [1998].

[295] The treaty-monitoring bodies increasingly make reference to soft-law instruments such as the Vienna International Plan of Action on Aging, and the United Nations Principles for Older Persons: see e.g. ESCR Committee, General Comment No 21: Right of Everyone to Take Part in Cultural Life (Art 15, para 1a of the Covenant on Economic, Social and Cultural Rights) (n 227) paras 28–29.

[296] In the summary of conference proceedings of The Final Act of the United Nations Conference of Plenipotentiaries on the Status of Refugees and Stateless Persons (25 July 1951) UN Doc A/CONF.2/108/Rev/1, Pt IV reference was made to '[t]he protection of refugees who are minors, in particular unaccompanied children and girls, with special reference to guardianship and adoption'.

[297] Jason Pobjoy, 'Refugee Children' in Costello et al (n 61) 745–60, 749.

[298] UNHCR Guidelines No 8 (n 155) para 1. Earlier UNCHR guidance materials include: UNHCR Policy on Refugee Children (6 August 1993) UN Doc EC/SCP/82; Refugee Children and Adolescents' (1997). See also ExCom Conclusion No 84 (XLVIII) 'Conclusion on Refugee Children and Adolescents' (1997) and Conclusion No 107 (LVIII), 'Conclusion on Children at Risk' (2007).

While children may face similar or identical forms of harm as adults, they may experience them differently. Actions or threats that might not reach the threshold of persecution in the case of an adult may amount to persecution in the case of a child because of the mere fact that s/he is a child. Immaturity, vulnerability, undeveloped coping mechanisms and dependency as well as the differing stages of development and hindered capacities may be directly related to how a child experiences or fears harm. Particularly in cases where the harm suffered or feared is more severe than mere harassment but less severe than a threat to life or freedom, the individual circumstances of the child, including his/her age, may be important factors in deciding whether the harm amounts to persecution. To assess accurately the severity of the acts and their impact on a child, it is necessary to examine the details of each case and to adapt the threshold for persecution to that particular child.[299]

These Guidelines also state that substantive and procedural aspects of the assessment of a child's application for refugee status should be informed by the CRC.[300] The UN Committee on the Rights of the Child (UNCRC), which is the treaty-monitoring body for this treaty, has given guidance on a child-specific approach to the refugee definition in its General Comment No 6 at paragraph 74 as follows:

[ ... ] the refugee definition ... must be interpreted in an age and gender-sensitive manner, taking into account the particular motives for, and forms and manifestations of, persecution experienced by children. Persecution of kin; under-age recruitment; trafficking of children for prostitution; and sexual exploitation or subjection to female genital mutilation, are some of the child-specific forms and manifestations of persecution which may justify the granting of refugee status if such acts are related to one of the 1951 Refugee Convention grounds. States should, therefore, give utmost attention to such child-specific forms and manifestations of persecution as well as gender-based violence in national refugee status-determination procedures.[301]

Within Europe, Article 9(2) QD (recast) includes as forms acts of persecution can take: '(f) acts of a gender-specific or child-specific nature'. Globally, there are national guidelines requiring the taking into account of acts of a child-specific nature in several countries.[302]

The above-mentioned UNCRC General Comment and other sources disclose several important features. First, that children can be the subject of acts that are persecutory whether inflicted on them or adults, e.g. torture, inhuman and degrading treatment, slavery.[303] Second, that in addition to, or overlapping with this, there are child-specific forms of persecution. They can be subdivided into two main categories.

---

[299] UNHCR Guidelines No 8 (n 155) para 15.
[300] ibid paras 1, 13.
[301] See further Edwards (n 257) 57–59.
[302] QD (recast) (n 8). See also recital 28. As regards guidelines, Pobjoy (n 256) 118, mentions e.g. Australia DIAC, 'Refugee Law Guidelines' (March 2010); Canada, 'IRB Guideline 3–Child Refugee Claimants: Procedural and Evidentiary Issues' (1996) 8; and the UK UKBA, 'Processing Children's Asylum Claims' (2013).
[303] Pobjoy (n 256) 116–17 states that 'it is important to acknowledge that in a significant proportion of cases children will be threatened with a form of harm that is similar or identical to that faced by adults. A child may, for instance, be at risk of death, torture or cruel, inhuman or degrading treatment, involuntary

There are those that can only be (or are almost exclusively) inflicted on a child (e.g. forcible and/or underage military recruitment, forced underage marriage, infanticide, forced and/or underage marriage, discrimination against street children, forced child labour, child sexual abuse and exploitation, pre-puberty FGM; denial of primary education, separation from a parent because of discriminatory custody laws).[304] Then there are ones that might be considered mere harassment in the case of an adult but could cause serious physical or psychological harm amounting to persecution in the case of a child.[305]

In relation to psychological harm, Pobjoy's survey of jurisprudence leads him to observe that 'the age-sensitive approach has played a particularly significant role in claims involving psychological harm'. He also notes that 'although the jurisprudence is less developed, decision makers have also acknowledged that the denial of certain social, economic or cultural rights will have a greater impact on children than adults'.[306]

Once again, the significant development of treaty and soft-law IHRL norms relating to children has served to better identify and nuance the characteristics of child-specific persecution.[307] Case law has increasingly come to recognise this interconnection. In *Kim v Canada*, the Federal Court of Canada noted that '[i]f the CRC recognizes that children have human rights and that "persecution" amounts to the denial of basic human rights, then if a child's rights under the CRC are violated in a sustained or systematic manner demonstrative of a failure of state protection, that child may qualify for refugee status'.[308] The CRC contains a number of specific human rights of children. Breach of some of these rights may either by their nature or repetition constitute a violation of a basic human right or the accumulation of various measures may be considered an infringement of fundamental rights constituting persecution. Pobjoy considers that the CRC rights 'are tailored to take into account the fact that children experience harms in different ways to adults'.[309] UNHCR's 2009 Guidelines identify Articles 9, 19, 24, 27, 37, and 38 of the CRC as particularly relevant to a child-specific definition of persecution.[310]

Significantly, the regional human rights courts have recognised that the level of harm required to meet the threshold of ill-treatment can be more easily reached in the case of a child than in the context of an adult.[311] This is also a common theme in national case law.[312]

---

confinement, kidnapping or sexual assault. In these cases a failure to take into account the applicant's age in assessing the nature of the prospective harm is likely to be of limited importance.'

[304] There are also measures that are directed at the child, but may have repercussions later in life: e.g. discrimination because of illegitimacy.
[305] Higher Administrative Court of Baden-Wuerttemberg (Verwaltungsgerichtshof Baden-Württemberg, Germany) in *A 11 S 1125/16* [2016]. See also Pobjoy (n 256) 116–22; Zimmermann and Mahler (n 1) 408.
[306] Pobjoy (n 256) 120–21. See also Pobjoy (n 297) 749–53.
[307] In particular the Convention on the Rights of the Child (CRC).
[308] *Kim v Canada (MCI)* [2010] FC 720, para 51, cited by Pobjoy (n 256) 123.
[309] Pobjoy (n 256) 123, 126–56.
[310] UNHCR Guidelines No 8 (n 155) para 13.
[311] See e.g. *Eremia v Moldova* App No 3564/11 (ECtHR, 28 May 2013).
[312] See e.g. *JA (child—risk of persecution) Nigeria* [2016] UKUT 00560 (IAC); Council for Aliens Law Litigation (RVV/CCE, Belgium) in *Case No 170 821* [2016].

It should be noted, however, with regard to the relative nature of the notion of persecution, that some acts directed against young adults may have the same effect as when directed against minors.[313]

### 2.3.4 Disability-specific forms of persecution

In 2010, a report by the Director of the UNHCR New York Office estimated that some 40 million persons with disabilities worldwide were refugees or Internally Displaced Peoples (IDPs).[314] However, the ExCom Conclusions of the same year on disabled persons[315] did not address the issue of their eligibility under the refugee definition. Having surveyed the case law of mainly common law countries, Motz wrote in 2015 that 'most decision-makers do not yet expressly engage with a disability-sensitive interpretation of persecution'. She noted that nevertheless decision makers have seen the guidance given by paragraph 54 of the UNHCR Handbook (on the ability of cumulative discrimination to give rise to persecution) as having played an important role in cases involving disabled persons. She also found that in the case law of New Zealand, Australia, and Canada, 'a social model of disability is increasingly being recognised and a more general willingness to adopt a human rights-based approach to disability is being displayed'.[316] The references in the New York Declaration for Refugees and Migrants to 'the special needs of all people in a vulnerable situations ... including persons with disabilities' and similar references in the Global Compact on Refugees can be said to have added momentum to such a shift.[317]

Applying a human rights approach to persecution requires decision makers to have regard to IHRL norms dealing with disability, for example the 1971 Declaration on the Rights of Mentally Retarded Persons[318] and the 1975 Declaration on the Rights of Disabled Persons, the 2006 Convention on the Rights of Persons with Disabilities

---

[313] See e.g. Council for Aliens Law Litigation (RVV/CCE, Belgium) in *Cases Nos 210 509 and 210 619/I* [2019] 18. See also Pobjoy (n 297) 748.

[314] Cited in Michael A Stein and Janet E Lord, 'Enabling Refugee and IDP Law and Policy: Implications of the U.N. Convention on the Rights of Persons with Disabilities' (2011) 28(2) Arizona Journal of International and Comparative Law 401, 401.

[315] Conclusion on refugees with disabilities and other persons with disabilities protected and assisted by UNHCR No 110 (LXI)—2010 ExCom 61st session (12 October 2010) UN Doc A/AC.96/1095. See also Mary Crock, 'Protecting Refugees With Disabilities' in Costello et al (n 61) 785, where Crock writes that: '[d]isability is a broad concept, including physical impairments affecting gross motor through to fine motor functioning; varying degrees of cognitive impairments; and can encompass chronic illness and conditions that affect both physical and cognitive functioning'. She cites Barbara M Altman (ed), *International Measurement of Disability—Purpose, Method and Application* (Springer 2017).

[316] Stephanie A Motz, 'The Persecution of Disabled Persons' in Céline Bauloz and others (eds), *Seeking Asylum in the European Union: Selected Protection Issues Raised by the Second Phase of the Common European Asylum System* (Brill Nijhoff 2015) 168, 171. See also Stephanie A Motz, *The Refugee Status of Persons with Disabilities* (Brill 2020). For another survey of disability-related cases, mainly Canadian, see Crock (n 258). In Motz, 'The Persecution of Disabled Persons', 161, she notes that in *AC (Egypt)* [2011] NZIPT 800015, para 70, the New Zealand IPT considered that the large number of ratifications (105 at that time) made it 'appropriate to treat the CRPD as an international law treaty which identifies forms of serious harm and failures of State protection for the purposes of refugee status determination'. In ibid 193, she also argues that the UK has not yet applied a disability-sensitive approach because of its specific reservation to the CRPD in relation to immigration and asylum cases.

[317] New York Declaration for Refugees and Migrants (9 September 2016) UNGA Res 71/1, paras 23, 58; Global Compact on Refugees (n 249).

[318] UNGA Res 2856 (XXVI) (20 December 1971) UN GAOR, Supp No 29, UN Doc A/8429.

(CRPD),[319] and the Charter on Inclusion of Persons with Disabilities in Humanitarian Action. The most important of these is undoubtedly the CRPD, now signed or ratified by over 180 countries.[320] Its legal framework governing the special needs of disabled persons assists refugee law by identifying how specific forms of harm may impact in a severe or particularly severe way on disabled persons, so as to amount to persecution.[321] Crock considers that the non-discrimination formulation of the 'reasonable accommodation' principle enshrined in Article 2 CRPD[322] 'arguably creates a positive duty on States to acknowledge and address the unequal position of persons with disabilities. This is of critical importance as it demands change in both process and interpretation of refugee law.'[323]

Further, Article 11 CRPD requires states parties to take all necessary measures, in accordance with their international law obligations, 'to ensure the protection and safety of persons with disabilities in situations of risk, including situations of armed conflict, humanitarian emergencies and the occurrence of natural disasters'. Among other relevant provisions, Article 16(2) requires states parties to:

> [ ... ] take all appropriate measures to prevent all forms of exploitation, violence and abuse by ensuring, inter alia, appropriate forms of gender- and age-sensitive assistance and support for persons with disabilities and their families and caregivers, including through the provision of information and education on how to avoid, recognize and report instances of exploitation, violence and abuse.

Endowing disability rights with greater specificity, the CRPD Committee, as well as issuing state reports and dealing with individual cases under Article 5 of the Optional Protocol, has issued a number of General Comments, including No 6 on equality and non-discrimination.[324]

The relative nature of the assessment of whether acts are a severe violation of basic human rights is particularly important in the case of applicants who have a disability and/or a mental disorder.[325] An applicant's disability or mental disorder, either on its

---

[319] For the 1975 Declaration, see UNGA Res 3447 (XXX) (9 December 1975) UN GAOR, Supp No 34, UN Doc A/10034. The Convention on the Rights of Persons with Disabilities (CRPD) was adopted on 13 December 2006 during the Sixty-first session of the General Assembly by resolution A/RES/61/106. In accordance with its article 42, the Convention and its Optional Protocol opened for signature by all States and by regional integration organizations at United Nations Headquarters in New York on 30 March 2007.

[320] The Wikipedia entry (accessed 21 December 2021) states that '[a]s of December 2021, it has 163 signatories and 184 parties, 183 states and the European Union (which ratified it on 23 December 2010)'.

[321] See Foster (n 45) 73; Crock (n 315) 785–86; Carmine Conte, 'What about Refugees with Disabilities? The Interplay between EU Asylum Law and the UN Convention on the Rights of Persons with Disabilities' (2016) 18 European Journal of Migration and Law 327.

[322] CRPD (n 319) Article 2 states: 'Discrimination on the basis of disability' means any distinction, exclusion or restriction on the basis of disability which has the purpose or effect of impairing or nullifying the recognition, enjoyment or exercise, on an equal basis with others, of all human rights and fundamental freedoms in the political, economic, social, cultural, civil or any other field. It includes all forms of discrimination, including denial of reasonable accommodation.' Crock (n 315) 785, notes that whilst the duty to accommodate is qualified, 'the prohibition of discrimination is immediate and absolute'. See further CRPD Committee, General Comment No 6 (2018) on equality and non-discrimination (26 April 2018) UN Doc CRPD/C/GC/6, paras 23–27.

[323] Crock (n 315) 786.

[324] CRPD Committee, General Comment No 6 (n 322) 786.

[325] Crock et al (n 258) 742–43.

own, or in combination with other characteristics, may lead to their being targeted for persecution on account, for example, of stigmatisation, social prejudices, or beliefs held about particular types of disability such as autism or dwarfism or Down's Syndrome. For Crock, persons with disabilities are (along with children):

> [ ... ] another subset of asylum seekers who can experience harms in different ways because of their personal attributes; they can be particularly susceptible to injury, either because of their inherently precarious health status or because of their inability to take evasive or remedial action in the face of threatened harm. Persons with disabilities can also experience harms inflicted because they are identified as disabled.[326]

Human rights case law contains explicit recognition of the vulnerability of disabled persons to human rights violations. On the strength of that case law, it can be stated that disabled persons can be affected by human rights violations that are persecutory just as much and sometimes more than able-bodied persons, e.g. by virtue of torture or inhuman and degrading treatment. Some acts that might not constitute persecution for able-bodied persons may do so, if inflicted on persons with disabilities and mental disorders. Further, the latter's vulnerability may make them more likely to be targeted for persecutory acts. They may have a heightened exposure to torture or inhuman and degrading treatment in institutions or in domestic settings;[327] they may be more likely to experience involuntary detention and incarceration and suffer ill treatment as a result;[328] they may more often be targeted for sexual exploitation.[329] In other cases, their exposure to a real risk of persecution may arise through an accumulation of discriminatory measures, in particular (by reference to the CRPD), measures which involve denial of 'reasonable accommodation'.

There being as yet relatively little IHRL case law emanating from either the regional human rights courts or national courts or tribunals on risks arising in countries of origin for disabled persons claiming refugee or status or protection against refoulement, other IHRL sources, such as the decisions of the CRPD Committee, are likely to become more important to further augmenting a disability-sensitive approach to the 'being persecuted' element of the refugee definition.[330]

---

[326] Crock (n 315) 788.

[327] See *Jasinskis v Latvia* App No 45744/08 (ECtHR, 21 December 2010), concerning the death of a deaf and mute person in police custody; *Nencheva and Others v Bulgaria* App No 48609/06 (ECtHR, 18 June 2013), concerning the death of people with disabilities in care home or a psychiatric hospital. In *Aswat v United Kingdom* App No 17299/12 (ECtHR, 16 April 2012), the ECtHR held that the applicant's extradition to the US to face a period of pre-trial detention and his possible placement in a 'supermax' prison would be in violation of Article 3 on account of the severity of his mental illness (but see same case, 6 January 2015, decision on admissibility). See further Crock et al (n 258) 747.

[328] See *Case of Zephiniah Hamilton v Jamaica* (18 July 1999) Communication No 333/1998, UN Doc CCPR/C/66/D/616/1995, paras 3.1–3.2. See also e.g. *Vincent v France* App No 6253/03 (ECtHR, 24 October 2006); *Grimailovs v Latvia* App No 6087/03 (ECtHR, 25 June 2013); and *LR v North Macedonia* App No 38067/15 (ECtHR, 23 January 2020).

[329] *IC v Romania* App No 36934/08 (ECtHR, 24 May 2016).

[330] See e.g. *Case of X v Tanzania* (18 August 2017) Communication No 22/2014, UN Doc CRPD/C/18/D/22/2014, para 8.6, in which the CRPD Committee concluded that the author of the complaint, a national of Tanzania, had been a victim of a form of violence that exclusively targeted persons with albinism. Amongst the violations found was of the provision prohibiting torture or cruel, inhuman or degrading

## 3 The Meaning of 'Being Persecuted': Modalities and Incidents

It is useful to analyse the meaning of 'being persecuted' in terms of its 'modalities' and 'incidents'. Such terms are obviously not essential to the definition, but do help provide a more systematic coverage of key aspects of the term's material scope. Although 'temporal scope' can also be termed a modality, for convenience it is addressed separately in the next main subsection, as well as in Chapter 11.

### 3.1 Acts of Persecution

In analysing the term 'being persecuted', this study chooses to refer to *acts* of persecution. Although this term does not specifically identify acts or actors, it clearly rests on the existence of a transitive relationship between persecutors and 'any person' who faces 'being persecuted', in which the former act against the latter by inflicting or threatening to inflict persecutory harm.

In recent times, doubts have arisen about proceeding to render the definition of the compound notion of 'being persecuted' in terms of acts. These have sometimes been voiced by commentators who have advocated a 'predicament approach'.[331] Such doubts have led Scott to go one step further and call for a 'condition of existence' approach.[332] For Scott, focus on acts 'narrows the temporal scope of the refugee definition to the moment the harm is experienced, and thus detracts attention from the wider social context in which the risk of exposure to such acts arises'.[333] Scott highlights the point made in the New Zealand case law that the language of Article 1A(2) 'draws attention to the fact of exposure to harm rather than to the act of inflicting harm'.[334] However, as Scott acknowledges elsewhere (and the New Zealand case law confirms), 'being persecuted' does presuppose human agency and requires some transitive relationship in terms of identification of the human source of the harm to which there is exposure.[335] That being so, such criticisms really only point up a need to adopt a broad notion of 'acts' not necessarily limiting them to the moment of harm and recognising the wider

---

treatment or punishment and degrading treatment or punishment (Article 15 CRPD). The Committee concluded that 'the suffering experienced by the author owing to the lack of action by the State party that would allow the effective prosecution of the suspected authors of the crime, becomes a cause of re- victimization, and amounts to psychological torture and/or ill-treatment'. See similarly, *Case of Y v Tanzania* (31 August 2018) Communication No 23/2014, UN Doc CRPD/C/20/D/23/2014.

[331] Hathaway and Foster (n 3) 293, write that the Refugee Convention 'is concerned with protection against a condition or predicament—'being persecuted'. Such an approach has sometimes been followed in UNHCR Guidelines: see e.g. UNHCR, Guidelines No 10: Claims to Refugee Status related to Military Service within the context of Article 1A (2) of the 1951 Convention and/or the 1967 Protocol relating to the Status of Refugees (12 November 2014) UN Doc HCR/GIP/13/10/Corr.1, para 13.
[332] Scott (n 51) 129.
[333] ibid 96.
[334] ibid 107, citing *Refugee Appeal No 74665/03* [2004] NZRSAA, para 36.
[335] ibid 78, 108. As stated in *AF (Kiribati)* (n 245) para 54, '[t]he legal concept of 'being persecuted' rests on human agency'.

social context in which they can arise. There is no necessary conflict between a 'predicament approach' and focus on 'acts of persecution'.

It is possible to find support in the refugee law literature for the view that focus should not be exclusively on acts. Grahl-Madsen, for example, referred to 'acts *or circumstances* for which the government (or in appropriate cases, the ruling party) is responsible, that is, ... acts committed by the government (or the party) or organs at its disposal, or behaviour tolerated by the government in such a way as to leave the victims virtually unprotected by the agencies of the State'.[336] Goodwin-Gill and McAdam state that '[p]ersecution under the Convention is thus a complex of reasons, interests and *measures*. The *measures* affect or are directed against groups or individuals for reasons of race, religion, nationality, membership of a particular social group, or political opinion'.[337] However they take no issue with the QD's focus on acts of persecution. References to 'measures' or 'circumstances' therefore need only serve as a warning against construing acts in a narrow sense. All that is essential is that acts should be understood broadly so as to include conduct, measures, and circumstances.

A further reason why any conceptualisation of persecution in terms of acts requires a broad approach is that it is well-established both in the international law of state responsibility, in IHRL, and in refugee law that wrongful conduct may sometimes take the form of a failure to act.[338] As stated by Gleeson, CJ in *Khawar*, 'conduct may ... in certain circumstances, include inaction'.[339] Thus the ESCR Committee in General Comment No 15 recognises that violations of human rights can take the form of commission or omission.[340] The need in refugee law to respond properly to the phenomenon of non-state actor persecution underlines the importance of *renvoi* to international law because it contains the only available set of standards that furnishes a framework for linking failure to act with violations of a state's obligations or a breach of a legal duty, in particular under IHRL.

## 3.2 Actors of Persecution

What has just been said about 'acts' of persecution applies also to 'actors'. Although the drafters chose to cast the Article 1A(2) definition in the passive voice—'being

---

[336] Grahl-Madsen (n 15) 189 (emphasis added).
[337] Goodwin-Gill and McAdam (3rd edn) (n 25) 131 (emphasis added). See now Goodwin-Gill and McAdam (4th edn) (n 26) 71–72, 156.
[338] Article 2 of the ILC's Articles on Responsibility of States for Internationally Wrongful Acts 2001 (ARSIWA) conceives 'acts' as 'conduct consisting of an action or omission'; see also Article 15(1). Crawford has noted that '[c]ases in which the international responsibility of a State has been invoked on the basis of an omission are at least as numerous as those based on positive acts'. See James R Crawford, *The International Law Commission's Articles on State Responsibility: Introduction, Text and Commentaries* (OUP 2002) 82. A well-known example of omission in the form of failure to act arose in *United States Diplomatic and Consular Staff in Tehran (United States v Iran)*, Judgment [1980] ICJ Rep 33, paras 64–65, 68.
[339] *Khawar* (n 49) para 12.
[340] ESCR Committee, General Comment No 15: The Right to Water (Arts. 11 and 12 of the Covenant) (20 January 2003) UN Doc E/C.12/2002/11. Paragraph 43 states that '[v]iolations through *acts of omission* include the failure to take appropriate steps towards the full realization of everyone's right to water, the failure to have a national policy on water, and the failure to enforce relevant laws' (emphasis added).

persecuted'—they clearly conceived of persecution as something emanating from human actions and human actors.

There is a danger that some formulations of the predicament approach obscure this fact. Foster, for example, states that this approach 'focuses on the reason for the applicant's fear, rather than the reason for the persecutor's decision to harm the applicant'.[341] She goes on to say that '[t]he fact that the test is framed in the passive voice is significant, as it again underlines the focus on the predicament of the applicant, rather than on an assessment of the situation from the perspective of the persecutor'.[342] These comments prompt several responses. First of all, incorrect though it be to require it to be shown that a persecutor has intent or motivation to harm the applicant,[343] it must always be shown that the harm involved is inflicted by a human actor or actors. Secondly, whilst it is correct to say that the language does not focus on the mindset of the persecutor, the *effect* of the persecutor's conduct must surely always still be a key part of the situation to be analysed. By analogy, in discrimination law it is not necessary to establish intent because in the context of indirect discrimination the effect of the conduct can constitute discrimination irrespective of intent. Further, the seeming wish to omit any role for the 'perspective of the persecutor' is concerning. That omitting it entirely would be amiss is evident from the well-established role of the doctrine of attribution in the context of identifying reasons for persecution. If a persecutor perceives an applicant to have a particular characteristic (such as race) and that is a reason for that person having a well-founded fear of being persecuted, then that is all that matters. It is not necessary that the applicant in fact has such a characteristic.[344]

Third, there is a risk that such formulations can divert attention from the issue of responsibility for the predicament of persecution. Even though assessing whether persecution exists is not a matter of assigning fault or culpability, the IHRL framework depends upon a state being found to be violator of human rights to a sufficient level of severity. That is true even when the state concerned is a failed state. At international law, even a failed state remains bound by human rights obligations, so at least in the context of IHRL, inability does not mean that responsibility cannot be attributed.[345] Moreover, in terms of a human rights approach, it is only a violation that establishes a failure of state protection; mere 'denial' does not.[346]

However, there are at least two qualifications to the proposition that persecution presupposes human actors. First, it is entirely consistent with the refugee definition to not necessarily require identification of a specific or direct actor. Such an interpretation accurately reflects IHRL case law which recognises that systems or practices can result in diffusely inflicted adverse harm.[347] An acceptance that persecution can

---

[341] Foster (n 45) 271.
[342] ibid 273.
[343] See below section 3.9.
[344] See Chapter 10, section 4.4.
[345] See Chapter 7, section 3.11.
[346] Unless 'denial' is simply a synonym for violation: see p. 432.
[347] See *NA v United Kingdom* App No 25904/07 (ECtHR, 17 July 2008) para 16. Utilising the concept of 'structural violence' in the context of disasters, Scott (n 51) 30–31, writes that 'serious denials of human rights in "natural" disaster situations that appear as "nobody's fault" are instead understood as reflecting a condition of existence in which discrimination is a contributory cause of differential exposure and vulnerability to disaster-related harm'.

be indirect as well as direct is also important to the correct approach to the issue of whether it is necessary to establish persecutory intent.[348] In Chapter 8 on the internal protection alternative it will also be argued that harms arising from natural disasters that are not caused by human agency can nevertheless cause 'indirect refoulement' for which actors of persecution have responsibility.[349] Indirect human agency also feeds into the separate issue of attribution when it comes to establishing a Convention reason.[350]

Second (as already noted), in line with international law principles, identification of an actor of persecution does not necessarily require identification of a specific act or acts carried out by this person or body. This follows from the wide acceptance that violations of human rights can be caused by omissions as well as acts and that a failure to act is not always going to be directly attributable to specific individuals or groups in the same way as actual acts.[351]

### 3.2.1 State actors

Doubtless the drafters understood the paradigm actor of persecution to be the state or the authorities of the state or those they delegate to carry out their orders. The international law on state responsibility usefully clarifies that the state in this context includes not just police and army and border guards, but all manner of state officials— and state officials acting at all levels, including local authorities. Further, applying such principles, state actors can include actors whose acts can be attributed to the state even if acting extra judicially or otherwise outside the sphere of their authority and in contravention of the law of the state.[352] Integral to the exercise and operation of state power is also a system of laws and related measures.

### 3.2.2 Non-state actors

As regards ordinary meaning, there is nothing in the language of Article 1A(2) that restricts the meaning of 'being persecuted' to state actor persecution. To read into this provision a requirement that persecution be at the hands of the state only would be to impose an additional requirement not foreseen by the wording of the provision, contrary to the 'good faith' rules of interpretation.

In terms of object and purpose, given the underlying aim to secure protection,[353] it would be contrary to the Convention's object and purpose if human rights violations undertaken by non-state actors were to be exempt. Significantly within IHRL

---

[348] See below section 3.9.
[349] See Chapter 8, section 4.1.5.
[350] See Chapter 10, section 4.4.
[351] See e.g. *Budayeva and Others v Russia* Apps Nos 15339/02, 21166/02, 20058/02, 11673/02, and 15343/02 (ECtHR, 29 September 2008) para 142.
[352] ILC, Report on Responsibility of States for Internationally Wrongful Acts (12 December 2001) UNGA Res 56/83. According to James R Crawford, *Brownlie's Principles of Public International Law* (9th edn, OUP 2019) 524, these Articles have been 'much cited and have acquired increasing authority as an expression of the customary law of states'. See also *Case of Velasquez-Rodriguez*, Judgment, IAmCtHR Series C No 4 (29 July 1988). Anker (n 33) §4.9, 279–80, notes that the actions of a state's agents are also to be attributed to the state where the state actors are carrying out unofficial state policy or generally enhancing state power through persecutory action.
[353] See Chapter 2, sections 2.5.4–2.5.5.

jurisprudence, it is now well-established that ill-treatment can be inflicted by non-state actors.[354] Although only strong evidence of 'subsequent practice' up to the time of publication, the 1979 UNHCR Handbook at paragraph 65 points out that seemingly private acts of violence committed by the local populace 'can be considered persecution if they are knowingly tolerated by the authorities, or if the authorities refuse, or prove unable, to offer effective protection'.

As regards the *travaux*, they do not contain any discussions of the issue but certainly say nothing that confines actors of persecution to state actors;[355] it is widely agreed that the drafters clearly appreciated that acts of persecution could also be carried out by non-state actors.[356]

Whether considered as part of the evolutionary approach to object and purpose or under Article 31(3)(c) VCLT ('other relevant rules of international law') or as supplementary means of interpretation under Article 32 VCLT, there has been strong support for inclusion of non-state actors in the jurisprudence and in state practice (in the broad sense). The Canadian Supreme Court in *Ward* noted a number of academic authorities endorsing the position that actors of persecution could be private actors, including Grahl-Madsen.[357] Other common law jurisdictions followed the *Ward* approach.[358] In terms of evidence of state practice, it is significant that those European states that had originally adopted an 'accountability approach' (effectively construing 'being persecuted' as meaning 'being persecuted by the state')[359] subsequently abandoned it. The 'accountability approach' was holed beneath the water line by the 'Joint Position of 4 March 1996 on a harmonized application of the definition of the term "refugee" in Article 1 of the Geneva Convention of 28 July 1951, relating to the status of refugees',[360] which expressly recognized non-state actors of persecution, and then by the negotiations that led to the final text of the QD. Article 6 of the QD and its recast specifically identifies as one category of actors of persecution, non-state actors.[361] Notably, the drafters of Article 6 QD did not seek to delimit the categories of non-state actors of persecution to *de facto* state bodies: the text makes clear that even isolated

---

[354] See e.g. *NA v United Kingdom* (n 347) para 110: '[o]wing to the absolute character of the right guaranteed, Article 3 of the Convention may also apply where the danger emanates from persons or groups of persons who are not public officials'; *TI v United Kingdom* App No 43844/98 (ECtHR, 7 March 2000). See also August Refinish, 'The Changing International Legal Framework for Dealing with Non-State Actors' in Philip Alston (ed), *Non-State Actors and Human Rights* (OUP 2005); Robert McCorquodale (ed), *International Law Beyond the State: Essays on Sovereignty, Non-State Actors and Human Rights* (CMP Publishing 2011).

[355] A point noted in *Ward* (n 173) 713–14.

[356] See Zimmermann and Mahler (n 1) 362–65; Hathaway and Foster (n 3) 305.

[357] *Ward* (n 173) 713–15.

[358] See cases cited by Hathaway and Foster (n 3) 306.

[359] Principally Germany, France, Austria, and Switzerland. See Catherine Phuong, 'Persecution by Non-State Agents: Comparative Judicial Interpretations of the 1951 Refugee Convention' (2003) 4(4) European Journal of Migration and Law 521.

[360] Joint Position of 4 March 1996 on a harmonized application of the definition of the term 'refugee' in Article 1 of the Geneva Convention of 28 July 1951, relating to the status of refugees [1996] OJ L63/2. Less than a year earlier, a resolution adopted by the EU on 23 November 1995 had made it possible to avoid recognising as refugees individuals persecuted by non-State agents. France, Germany, Italy, and Sweden—as well as two other European States, Norway and Switzerland—had limited the application of the refugee definition in this way: see Pirkko Kourula, *Broadening the Edges: Refugee Definition and International Protection Revisited* (Martinus Nijhoff 1997) 99.

[361] QD recast (n 8).

individuals can be actors of persecution. To have held out against recognition of individual persecutors would have meant a failure to grapple with the fact that a victim's persecution is no less persecution just because it may be inflicted by only one person. And it is by dint of this recognition that refugee law has come to acknowledge, for example, that domestic violence can give rise to persecution.

At the same time, applying a human rights approach requires understanding that it is not the acts of the non-state actors that constitute persecution per se. As is explained in the next subsection, they only become persecutory if the state is unwilling or unable to protect the individual against such acts.[362]

Thus, we are now able to state that actors of persecution can include non-state actors as a basic proposition.[363]

### 3.2.3 Ineffective protectors

It was said earlier that the *dramatis personae* of the refugee definition include, in the context of cases featuring harms emanating from non-state actors, ineffective protectors. The topic of protection is the subject of Chapter 7, but one key point needs reiterating here. There are terminological difficulties with the position that acts of non-state actors cannot qualify as persecution unless the state (or a quasi-state entity) is unwilling or unable to protect against such acts. It entails that, lexically, reference to 'protection against persecution' cannot be correct. This has led proponents of the human rights approach to refer to 'serious harm' and to enunciate the proposition that 'persecution = serious harm + lack of state protection'.[364] Despite this awkwardness (which this chapter also embraces), there are strong reasons for considering that such an approach accords with VCLT rules and is enjoined by a human rights framework since, in IHRL, a human rights violation can only occur where a state has failed in its duty to protect an individual. This understanding also aligns with the language of Article 1A(2) as set out in its availment clause.[365] Such a reading is also supported by the approach taken by the CJEU when interpreting the QD and its recast.[366]

## 3.3 Laws and Related Measures

Acts of persecution arise within the context of a society in which there is (more or less) a system of laws or legal norms. The state is accountable for the conduct of all its organs and laws and for the policies they enact or maintain.[367] It is inherent in the sovereignty of a state that every government has the right to enact, implement, and

---

[362] See below section 3.2.3.
[363] Hathaway and Foster (n 3) 305–06, state that 'there is now relative uniformity in accepting the "protection" approach long-favoured by most common law jurisdictions'.
[364] See e.g. Refugee Women's Legal Group, 'Gender Guidelines for the Determination of Asylum Claims in the UK' (1998).
[365] See Chapter 9, section 4.
[366] O A (n 62) para 56.
[367] ILC, ARSIWA (n 352) Article 4(1).

enforce its own legislation.³⁶⁸ However, laws or systems of laws are never wholly neutral; to a greater or lesser extent, they reflect the policy of state institutions towards its populace.³⁶⁹ That may be true even of what the refugee law literature has referred to as 'laws of general application' (usually contrasted with laws addressing a specific group or groups).³⁷⁰ Even actions undertaken by private actors, e.g. by one side or the other in a local family or tribal feud, may sometimes be carried out through the medium of laws, e.g. the taking out of a summons which police must then enforce. Hence it is necessary in the refugee law context to focus particularly on when laws and related measures can be persecutory and on the different ways in which this can arise, including by way of prosecution. The analysis that follows seeks to apply a human rights approach to this subject. It must be acknowledged, however, that its treatment in the refugee law literature, whether applying a human rights approach or some alternative, has been and remains discursive and there appear to be only a limited number of propositions touching upon it that have achieved substantial consensus.

Under IHRL, states are under a duty to 'organise the governmental apparatus and, in general, all the structures through which public power is exercised, so that they are capable of juridically ensuring the free and full enjoyment of human rights'.³⁷¹ IHRL treaties identify rights which a state must treat as absolute and rights which are qualified; qualified rights are subject to restrictions that are prescribed or provided by law. In this regard, 'law' has been understood as an autonomous concept requiring predictability and foreseeability and precise criteria.³⁷² Thus, applying a human rights approach to laws and related measures requires identifying what right is engaged and then inquiring, what limitations (if any) on the right are permissible, and whether the laws exceed the scope of those limitations.

In the literature it is discussed that laws can be persecutory in two main ways: it is said they can be persecutory in themselves or in the way in which they are implemented.

### 3.3.1 Laws persecutory in themselves

What is to be made of the statements made by commentators on occasions that the national laws in a country of origin can sometimes be per se persecutory.³⁷³ For example, the 2008 UNHCR Guidelines on Gender state:

---

³⁶⁸ Goodwin-Gill and McAdam (3rd edn) (n 25) 103; Goodwin-Gill and McAdam (4th edn) (n 26) 124–25.

³⁶⁹ Harold J Berman and William R Greiner, *The Nature and Functions of Law* (Foundation Press 1980).

³⁷⁰ See e.g. UNHCR, Interpreting Article 1 of the 1951 Convention (n 24); *Long Hao Li v A-G (US)* [2011] 633 F.3d 136, 144–46. See also Goodwin-Gill and McAdam (n 26) 123–26. For further analysis see p. 370.

³⁷¹ *Case of Velasquez-Rodriguez* (n 352) para 166. See also *Case of Peiris v Sri Lanka* (18 April 2012) Communication No 1862/2009, UN Doc CCPR/C/103/D/1862/2009, both cited by Kälin and Künzli (n 107) 96.

³⁷² Kälin and Künzli (n 107) 92; HRC, General Comment No 34: Article 19 (Freedoms of Opinion and Expression) (12 September 2011) UN Doc CCPR/C/GC/34, para 25. See further *Sunday Times v United Kingdom* App No 6538/74 (ECtHR, 26 April 1979) para 49.

³⁷³ See e.g. Anker (n 33) §4.8, 268: 'Laws that punish the exercise of a fundamental, internationally protected human right, such as the right to protest peacefully or the right to the free exercise of religion, may be considered persecutory per se.'

18. A law can be considered as persecutory *per se*, for instance, where it reflects social or cultural norms which are not in conformity with international human rights standards.[374]

Examples often given include laws that de-nationalise a racial group or prohibit persons of a particular religion from practising their faith, racially discriminatory laws, and coercive family planning laws.

Referencing the ability of laws to be persecutory per se is an important way of identifying laws which on their face are repressive and/or discriminatory, e.g. Nazi-era Nuremburg laws. However, even in relation to such laws, it must still be established that they have an actual persecutory impact on individuals/groups in the society in which they are made. History furnishes examples of unenforced laws or laws that have always been or have become a 'dead letter' or are not otherwise put into practice. It is noteworthy that Article 9(2) of the QD (recast) does not adopt the proposition that laws per se can amount to persecutory acts and in the opinion of this author, that is a justifiable omission. The need for evidence of actual application has been highlighted by the CJEU in *X, Y and Z*. in relation to the criminalisation of homosexual acts.[375]

That said, rejection of the position that laws can be said to be persecutory on their face must not blind us to the fact that merely by being on a statute book an oppressive law may still sometimes exercise a malevolent influence. But that also is a matter of fact, not an eternal truth.[376] Goodwin-Gill and McAdam, in the context of a discussion of 'laws of general application', usefully phrase the question to be asked as being whether laws can be 'instruments of persecution'.[377] In this context, pertinent questions to be asked include whether there are any indications that the state's enforcement priorities are changing;[378] and whether the unenforced law has any secondary effects that rise to the level of persecution. Inquiry into such secondary effects needs to consider, inter alia, whether the law encourages public or private discrimination, whether the law prevents the state from responding to that discrimination and whether it causes psychological harm.[379]

---

[374] Albeit these Guidelines go on to say, '[t]he applicant, however, still has to show that he or she has a well-founded fear of being persecuted as a result of that law'.

[375] *X and Y and Z* (n 175) para 61. See also Case C-56/17 *Bahtiyar Fathi v Predsedatel na Darzhavna agentsia za bezhantsite* [2018] ECLI:EU:C:2018:803, para 96.

[376] As is reflected in UNHCR, Guidance Note on Refugee Claims Relating to Crimes of Lèse Majesté and Similar Criminal Offences (September 2015) paras 17–18. It is noteworthy that in *Case of Toonen v Australia* (31 March 1994) Communication No 488/1992, UN Doc CCPR/C/50/D/488/1992, in which the HRC found that the law of the Australian State of Tasmania which criminalised sodomy was in breach of the Covenant's right to privacy, this was because of its perceived impact on the applicant and those similarly placed. The Committee acknowledged that there had been no prosecutions under this law, but found that the applicant was nevertheless a 'victim' because 'the criminalisation of homosexuality in private has not permitted him to expose openly his sexuality and to publicise his views of reform of the relevant laws on sexual matters ...'

[377] Goodwin-Gill and McAdam (3rd edn) (n 25) 52; Goodwin-Gill and McAdam (4th edn) (n 26) 123. Recognising that 'laws of general application' can sometimes be oppressive could also be said to further evidence that discrimination is not a necessary ingredient of the meaning of being persecuted: see below section 3.5.1.

[378] *Sebastiao v Canada (MCI)* [2016] FC 803.

[379] See Samuel Rubinstein, 'Toward Principles for Refugee Claims Based on Unenforced Persecutory Laws' (RefLaw, 10 November 2020).

### 3.3.2 Discriminatorily applied laws

A second main way in which laws may constitute persecution arises when they are applied in a discriminatory or disproportionate way. This is reflected in UNHCR materials, including paragraph 59 of the 1979 Handbook. The UNHCR Gender Guidelines[380] give the examples of penal law that is applied to particular groups only or which is arbitrary in its formulation, or which is unlawfully executed. This mode is also recognised in in Article 9(2)(b) of the EU QD (recast).[381]

### 3.3.3 Prosecution and punishment

Under IHRL, states must prevent, investigate, and punish any violation of the fundamental human rights and if possible attempt to restore the right violated and provide compensation as warranted for damages resulting from the violation.[382] In the refugee law literature, much focus has understandably been placed on law enforcement in the form of prosecution or punishment, especially where laws are used to legitimise prosecution of individuals for alleged law-breaking or punishing them if found guilty through the justice system. Prosecution is indeed one of the meanings of the verb 'to persecute' still given in the OED Online.[383]

That state (or de facto state) persecution can sometimes take the form of prosecution is plain enough; history is freighted with examples. But to regard all prosecution as persecution would transgress the lawful domain of state sovereignty and the right of states to regulate their own governance through a system of law. The 1979 UNHCR Handbook at paragraphs 56–59 deals with the distinction between prosecution and punishment, emphasising that persons fleeing from prosecution or punishment are 'not normally refugees' and that the refugee definition is not designed to assist fugitives from justice. The Handbook also notes that nonetheless punishment that is excessive or penal may become persecution by virtue of its disproportionate character. The Handbook emphasises that it may be necessary to consider the laws of the country concerned so as to assess whether they are in conformity with accepted human rights standards, although more often it may not be the law but its application that is discriminatory. This approach has been endorsed by lead decisions of senior courts (e.g. the House of Lords in *Horvath*) and by many other commentators.[384] A useful guide[385] to demarcating prosecution and persecution, is given in the UNHCR publication, 'Interpreting Article 1 of the 1951 Convention Relating to the Status of Refugees':

---

[380] UNHCR, Guidelines No 1 (n 257).
[381] QD (recast) (n 8) Article 9(2)(b). In relation to a pending reference before the CJEU on this provision—C-608/22 and C-609/22—see above n 276.
[382] *Case of Velasquez-Rodriguez* (n 352) para 166.
[383] See p. 305.
[384] UNHCR Handbook (n 60) paras 59–60. Hathaway (n 4) 179, notes that: '[w]hile it is true that genuine criminality is not a form of civil or political status which attracts protection, the criminal law is not infrequently manipulated as a tool of persecution'. See also Hathaway and Foster (n 3) 244. See further, Anker (n 33) 220–24; Waldman (n 1) 216–48; Goodwin-Gill and McAdam (2nd edn) (n 26) 123–26.
[385] Save for what it states about laws being inherently persecutory: see above section 3.3.1.

In distinguishing the ordinary prosecution of offences from persecution, it is necessary to take into account and analyse at least some of the following factors:

Whether the law is in conformity with human rights standards or is inherently persecutory (for example where it prohibits legitimate religious belief or activity);

Whether implementation of the law is carried out in a manner which amounts to persecution based on a Convention reason.

Elements to be considered in this regard include: Whether persons charged under the law are denied due process of law for a Convention reason; Whether prosecution is discriminatory (for example where only members of certain ethnic groups are prosecuted); Whether punishment is meted out on a discriminatory basis (for example, the usual penalty is a six month prison term but those judged to hold a certain political opinion are routinely sentenced to a 1 year imprisonment); Whether punishment under the law amounts to persecution (for example where the punishment amounts to cruel, inhuman or degrading treatment).[386]

It is worthwhile reverting briefly to the notion of 'laws of general application', which for a certain period was the default way in refugee law to demarcate laws that could not be persecutory. In the phrase 'persecution, not prosecution', 'prosecution' was seen as a descriptor for the application of ordinary laws of general application in the context of a general system of justice. The premise of this analysis was that a state is entitled to enact and implement laws and to prosecute its citizens for violations so long as such laws are neutral. But from the start it was understood that this notion has many limitations. For example, a provision of a law of general application may be contrary to IHRL norms, e.g. a law which prevents anyone from leaving the country even in the absence of a public emergency. Or a neutral criminal law may be used for improper purposes, e.g. to bring false charges. Whilst efforts have been made to integrate the notion of 'laws of general application' with IHRL norms, this has required considerable qualifications to be made without any clear benefit in terms of clarity of approach.[387] Applying an object and purpose approach and more particularly a human rights approach serves to highlight that analysis in terms of 'laws of general application' is something of a blunt instrument even when it has been (sometimes perceptively) adapted for the refugee law context.[388] Within the framework of IHRL what matters is whether laws, of general or specific application, conform to basic human rights norms. The declining reference to laws of general application in contemporary case law likely reflects increased awareness of such limitations.

Another element of the prosecution dimension concerns determination of guilt or innocence through the judicial system and the issue of whether the trial involved was or would be fair. Within IHRL there are a number of provisions that guarantee justice

---

[386] UNHCR, Interpreting Article 1 of the 1951 Convention (n 24) para 18.

[387] Thus, in *Zolfagharkhani v Canada (MEI)* [1993] FCJ No 584, McGuigan J considered that an 'ordinary law of general application' had to be given a 'presumption of validity and neutrality'.

[388] In Australian refugee law, the status of 'laws of general application' that states are entitled to adopt is qualified by the requirement that they be 'appropriate to achieve a legitimate object'. See Michelle Foster and Hélène Lambert, *International Refugee Law and the Protection of Stateless Persons* (OUP 2019) 152. In the Australian case law, recourse to the notion of 'laws of general application' remains significant: see e.g. *SZVYD v MIBP* [2019] FAC 648.

in the sense of fair and reasonable outcomes of legal disputes, including: the right to an effective remedy in cases of an alleged violation of the human rights enshrined in the ICCPR (Article 2(3)(a)) and other relevant treaties; the right to have criminal charges and rights and obligations in a suit of law determined 'by a competent, independent and impartial tribunal established by law' (ICCPR, Article 14(1)); the right to equality before courts and tribunals (ICCPR, Article 14(1)); and the right to a fair and public hearing and to public pronouncement of the judgment (Article 14(1)). In the context of criminal offences, there is a presumption of innocence (ICCPR, Article 14(2)) and various rights of defence.[389] In this context, the proceedings have to be looked at as a whole, so as to include, for example, the aggregate of remedies provided under domestic law and the overall length of proceedings.[390]

Although often linked, separate issues can arise regarding punishment (as is recognised in Article 9(2) QD recast). Thus, punishment for violation of an ordinary law will not usually be persecutory but might be if the punishment is disproportionate.

It might be said that neither UNHCR, judicial, and academic materials nor Article 9(c) and (d) of the QD recast (which refer to 'prosecution or punishment, which is disproportionate or discriminatory punishment' and 'denial of judicial redress resulting in a disproportionate or discriminatory punishment') as such capture the phenomenon of prosecution which abuses basic human rights without necessarily having a discriminatory aspect. On a broad understanding of the concept of proportionality, however, the scope of formulations of this type can be extended to cover the type of non-discriminatory totalitarian context postulated in the later analysis of discrimination.[391] Their wording underlines the fact that even otherwise legitimate criminal legislation may constitute persecution if it lays down excessive punishment; and even the operation of legitimate laws may give rise to persecution if it leads to the imposition of excessive penalties.[392]

Also connected with punishment is the issue of the treatment that precedes or will result from the sentence of a court or tribunal. It may also be necessary to consider, for example, pre-trial detention conditions, during the investigation process. Potentially any stage of a prosecution process, either on its own or considered cumulatively, may involve ill-treatment that can render punishment persecutory. Paragraph 169 of the 1979 UNHCR Handbook notes that a deserter or draft-evader may qualify as a refugee if it can be shown that he would suffer disproportionately severe punishment for the military offence on account of his race, religion, nationality, membership of a particular social group, or political opinion.[393]

---

[389] Kälin and Künzli (n 107) 466–90.
[390] e.g. in the ECHR context see Guide on Article 13 of the European Convention on Human Rights Right to an effective remedy (updated on 31 August 2021) available at <www.echr.coe.int/Documents/Guide_Art_13_ENG.pdf> (accessed 26 January 2022).
[391] See below section 3.5.1.
[392] UNHCR Handbook (n 60) para 57: '[The distinction between prosecution and punishment] may, however, occasionally be obscured. In the first place, a person guilty of a common law offence may be liable to excessive punishment, which may amount to persecution within the meaning of the definition. Moreover, penal prosecution for a reason mentioned in the definition (for example, in respect of "illegal" religious instruction given to a child) may in itself amount to persecution'.
[393] UNHCR Handbook (n 60) para 169.

Whilst in certain circumstances the mere act of prosecution could be regarded as persecutory, it will ordinarily only be the fact that it results in disproportionate punishment that renders it sufficiently serious in character.

To conclude, in light of the preponderance of opinion that persecution should be given an international law-based reading, we should accept that the issue of prosecution should be analysed in human rights and international law terms. Crucial to this analysis is recognition that although it is primarily for states to enact their own systems of law and of crime and punishment, the matter of when prosecution is a legitimate response is essentially to be examined in international law terms. But applying this approach means that prosecution only transmutes into persecution if: (1) the law itself is contrary to IHRL norms (and is not merely a dead letter); (2) the law is applied in an arbitrary or discriminatory fashion; (3) there are failures in any trial process involved going beyond mere shortcomings and posing a threat to the very essence of the right to a fair trial (the test of flagrant denial); or (4) the trial at issue impinges on the applicant's basic human rights (e.g. lack of a fair trial for a minor motoring offence would not be persecutory).[394]

### 3.3.4 Military service laws and related measures

A cluster of specific issues have arisen in relation to military service laws. Given that a state has a right to self-defence and that one of the duties of a citizen is to perform military service if required, prosecution for refusal to perform military service does not in general constitute persecution.[395] The 2014 UNHCR Guidelines helpfully identify five main categories of cases where military laws might violate human rights norms: (i) conscientious objection where there is no civilian alternative; (ii) where service would involve recruits being exposed to conflicts contrary to basic rules of human conduct; (iii) where there are abusive conditions of military service; (iv) forced recruitment and/or conditions of service in non-state armed groups; and (v) unlawful child recruitment.[396]

In relation to conscientious objection, the UNHCR Guidelines note at paragraph 8 that the HRC case law has shifted from characterising the right as derived from the right 'to manifest' one's religion or belief (and thus as a right subject to certain restrictions in Article 18(3)), to viewing it as one that 'inheres in the right' to freedom of thought, conscience, and religion in Article 18(1) itself. It cannot yet be said that refugee case law worldwide has adjusted to this shift, but it is one that a human rights approach needs to make, in order to ensure an evolutionary approach to the refugee definition.[397]

---

[394] See e.g. *MI (Fair Trial, Pre Trial Conditions) Pakistan CG* [2002] UKIAT 02239. The ECtHR has held that 'flagrant denial' of a fair trial can in itself be a violation of Article 6 ECHR in an extra-territorial context: see e.g. *Othman (Abu Qatada) v United Kingdom* App No 8139/09 (ECtHR, 9 May 2012) paras 258–84.
[395] *MI* (n 394) para 5; *Sepet and Bulbul* (n 91). For US position, see Anker (n 33) §5.28, 389–91.
[396] UNHCR, Guidelines No 10 (n 331) paras 16–41.
[397] Goodwin-Gill and McAdam (n 26) 126–37. At 132, they call for earlier jurisprudence to be revisited in the light of IHRL developments. At 129–31, they note, however, a continuing difference between the Human Rights Committee and ECtHR approaches. See also Penelope Mathew, 'Draft Dodger/Deserter or Dissenter? Conscientious Objection as Grounds for Refugee Status' in Satvinder Juss and Colin J Harvey (eds), *Contemporary Issues in Refugee Law* (Edward Elgar 2013) 165–95.

As regards (ii), the UNHCR Guidelines herald a shift away from reliance in paragraph 171 of the 1979 Handbook's on a criterion linked to 'condemn[ation] by the international community' towards one based more directly on objective international law norms. In this respect it reflects the formulation contained in Article 9(2)(e) of the QD, which identifies as one type of harm arising in the context of performance of military service, 'prosecution or punishment for refusal to perform military service in a conflict, where performing military service would include crimes or acts falling under the exclusion clauses as set out in Article 12(2)'.[398] The reference to crimes or acts falling under the exclusion clauses highlights that in the military service context the relevant norms of international law are not confined to IHRL but also encompass international criminal law and IHL.

Goodwin-Gill and McAdam regard the approach of the EU to conscientious objection in Article 9(2)(e) of the QD (recast)—as interpreted by the CJEU in the case of *Shepherd*—as giving this notion 'a particularly narrow scope', but first of all Article 9(2) is a non-exhaustive list and secondly, there are other subcategories of Article 9(2) (e.g. Article 9(2)(b), (c), and (d)) capable of encompassing conscientious objection cases.[399]

### 3.3.5 Laws and measures denying nationality or the right to enter or return to one's own country

Two other particular type of laws and measures are selected for specific mention, namely those relating to a state's laws and practices governing nationality and those relating to rights to enter and return to one's own country.

It is a key element of state sovereignty that states have the right to determine who are its nationals. Nationality remains the principal basis on which individuals acquire rights as citizens which has led to the description of the right of nationality as the 'right to have rights'.[400] Being central to its sovereignty, the way in which a state adopts and operates its nationality laws and related measures has the potential to give rise to persecutory harm. Indeed, for the drafters of the 1951 Convention, the need for such an instrument had been underscored by the acts of denationalisation undertaken in the inter-war years as most glaringly perpetrated by the Nazi regime in the form of the Nuremburg laws during the Second World War.[401] Grahl-Madsen remarked that '[a]s

---

[398] QD (recast) (n 8). The exclusion clauses in the QD recast are closely based on those set out in Article 1D, 1E, and 1F of the Refugee Convention.

[399] Case C-472/13 *Andre Lawrence Shepherd v Bundesrepublik Deutschland* [2015] ECLI:EU:C:2015:117. At paras 47–56, the Court considered whether Article 9(2)(b)-(c) applied, albeit rejecting that they could in the circumstances of the present proceedings; see now also Case C-238/19 *EZ v Bundesrepublik Deutschland* [2020] ECLI:EU:C:2020:945. See further Goodwin-Gill and McAdam (n 26) 134. They cite Klaus Ferdinand Gärditz, 'Shepherd v Germany' (2015) 109(3) AJIL 623, 627–28, who urges that 'caution should be taken in transferring elements of the ECJ's interpretation into international refugee law'. In *BverwG 1 C 1.22* [2023], the German Federal Administrative Court held that Article 9(2)(e) QD (recast) can in certain circumstances cover the refusal to perform military service by applicants who are of compulsory military service age, belong to the group of those who are likely to be subject to military service, and for whom it is considerably probable that they will be called up in the near future (I am grateful to Michael Hoppe for this unofficial translation).

[400] *Perez v Brownell* [1958] 356 US 44, 64 (Earl Warren dissenting); see also Hannah Arendt, *The Origins of Totalitarianism* (Harcourt 1951) 177.

[401] In *Haile v Gonzalez* [2005] 421 F.3d 493, the US Federal Court of Appeal noted that denationalisation was one of the first steps taken by the Nazi regime against the Jews and cited Lucy S Dawidowicz, *The War*

de-nationalisation (deprivation of citizenship) for political, ethnic, or similar reasons incurs loss of civil rights, [it] too may be classified as persecution.'[402]

That de-nationalisation and other forms of deprivation of nationality can be persecutory has rarely been doubted in case law or the wider literature. Thus, in a 1995 judgment, the German Federal Administrative Court, citing in support the case law of other European states, noted that 'the court below correctly assumed that a deprivation of citizenship for reasons relevant to asylum may represent persecution'.[403]

Surveying the case law and wider commentary, Fripp identifies three main situations where a state through laws or other acts or omissions relating to nationality can perpetrate persecution: de jure or effective deprivation of nationality and core rights/incidents thereto; denial or withholding of nationality; and arbitrary exclusion of non-nationals. He points out that the growing importance of relevant human rights standards, especially Article 12(4) of the ICCPR, has helped clarify when nationality-related harm can be persecutory. Article 12(4) ICCPR provides: that '[n]o one shall be arbitrarily deprived of the right to enter his own country'.[404]

Foster and Lambert persuasively demonstrate that deprivation of nationality is not just capable of being an act of persecution but also that, especially in the context of denationalisation policies, it is often likely to be persecutory. In relation to statelessness, they point out that it is wrong to see denationalisation merely as a by-product of the legitimate exercise of state sovereignty when it can in many situations be understood to be the result of persecutory acts. They point to a 2017 UNHCR survey documenting that more than 75 per cent of the world's known stateless populations belong to minority groups and that '[d]iscrimination on the basis of ethnicity, race, religion or language is a recurrent cause of statelessness globally'.[405] However, to suggest as they do at certain points that deprivation of nationality is per se persecutory[406] would be a step too far, for two main reasons. Firstly, international law only proscribes *arbitrary* deprivation of nationality and continues to allow for the deprivation of nationality in certain circumstances.[407] Second, as is the case with all

---

*Against the Jews 1933-1945* (Bantam 1975) 67-69, discussing the Reich Citizenship Law of 1935, which stripped German Jews of their citizenship.

[402] Grahl-Madsen (n 15) 215.
[403] BVerwG 10 C 50.07 [2009]. The Court specifically cited *EB (Ethiopia) v SSHD* [2007] EWCA Civ 809, especially paras 54 and 75. See also *JV (Tanzania) v SSHD* [2007] EWCA Civ 1532; *BZADW v MIBP* [2014] FCA 541; *CNDA No 10015655* [2011], cited Foster and Lambert (n 388) 156. See also Chapter 4, sections 2.1.8 and 4.1.
[404] Fripp (n 15) 318-21.
[405] Foster and Lambert (n 388) 150, citing UNHCR, '"This is Our Home" Stateless Minorities and Their Search for Citizenships' (2017) Preface. They also cite UN Committee on the Elimination of Discrimination Against Women, CEDAW General Recommendation No 21: Equality in Marriage and Family Relations (1994) para 6: '[n]ationality is [thus still] critical to full participation in society'. See further Alice Edwards, 'The Meaning of Nationality in International Law in an Era of Human Rights' in Alice Edwards and Laura van Waas (eds), *Nationality and Statelessness under International Law* (CUP 2014) 40, where she notes that '[s]tateless persons are politically, socially and culturally marginalised'; Laura van Waas, 'The Intersection of International Refugee Law and International Statelessness Law' in Costello et al (n 61) 152-70; Hélène Lambert, 'Stateless Refugees' in Costello et al (n 61) 797-814.
[406] Foster and Lambert (n 388) 71-72, 89-90, 159-64.
[407] UN Human Rights Council, Human rights and arbitrary deprivation of nationality: Report of the Secretary-General (14 December 2009) UN Doc A/HC/13/34. As regards Article 12(4) ICCPR, the HRC has accepted that exceptions to it might arise where, for example, an act is held not arbitrary or a State

laws,[408] it is necessary to identify that any nationality-related measure has an adverse effect in practice: e.g. because it has (or would have) the effect of denying a national the right to enter or return to their country of nationality, or of rendering them subject to expulsion from their country of nationality, or denying them identity documents essential for accessing other civic rights, or exposing them to arbitrary detention or the right to work and to subsistence or to other discriminatory measures that cumulatively amount to serious harm. Factual circumstances may arise that might mean that deprivation of nationality is not persecutory, as can happen, for example, when an applicant possesses a second nationality.[409] Further, as in any refugee claim, it is necessary for an applicant to establish, not simply past denationalisation, but a forward-looking risk of relevant harm.[410]

In relation to the right to return (re-enter), it is well established that its denial may amount to an act of persecution.[411] Applying a human rights approach, arbitrary denial of a right to re-enter is contrary to Article 12(4) ICCPR and regional human rights equivalents. As noted by Foster and Lambert, 'although there are circumstances in which a state will not qualify as a person's 'own country' for the purposes of Article 12(4), once it does so there are no defences or exceptions that would justify the violation of Article 12(4)'.[412] Nevertheless, as with other laws, in order to establish that violation of the right to return is persecutory, it remains necessary to establish that it constitutes a sufficiently severe violation.

### 3.4 Individual Assessment

It is an axiom of refugee law that assessing whether a person is 'being persecuted' requires individual assessment. As already touched on, whether an individual fears persecution will depend on the particular circumstances of his or her case and that what is harm for one applicant may not necessarily be harm for another. Nevertheless, the requirement that fear be 'well-founded' (which will be addressed in Chapter 11) places some limits on the workings of this principle. Application of a human rights framework also places specific restrictions on its scope.[413] For example, the fact (albeit rare) that a person may accept that the authorities were justified in torturing him or her in the past, does not mean that that person was not the subject of a severe violation of their human rights. The fact that a woman expresses consent to be subjected to FGM

---

terminating nationality is held not to be an individual's 'own country' because the possession of nationality has been of a fleeting or purely technical matter: see *Simalae Toala v New Zealand* (2 November 2000) Communication No 675/1995, UN Doc CCPR/C/70/D/675/1995, cited by Fripp (n 15) 261.

[408] See above section 3.1.
[409] *BVerwG 10 C 50.07* (n 403) para 20.
[410] Hathaway and Foster (n 3) 251.
[411] *Marouf v Canada (MEI)* [1994] 1 FC 723; *MA (Ethiopia) v SSHD* [2009] EWCA Civ 289. For a recent ECtHR case on Article 3(2) of Protocol No 4 (the equivalent of Article 12(4) ICCPR), see *HF and Others v France* Apps Nos 24384/19 and 44234/20 (ECtHR [GC], 14 September 2022).
[412] Foster and Lambert (n 388) 168; they point out that nevertheless Article 12 may be subject to derogation in an emergency. See also Hathaway and Foster (n 3) 247–52.
[413] See Chapter 11, section 1.1.

does not negate the fact that FGM is a form of ill-treatment.[414] This principle is more fully understood by reference to analysis of intensity.

## 3.5 Intensity

As already noted, persecution is a 'strong word' and even though it cannot be ascribed an unequivocal ordinary meaning, its principal usages seek to differentiate it from mere harm and indicate that to be persecutory the harm has to possess a certain intensity or severity or gravity. Even asylum systems that have not defined persecution in human rights terms have generally recognized that persecution is an 'extreme concept', encompassing all treatment that is unfair, unjust, or unlawful, or oppressive; it is generally distinguished from low-level intimidation and harassment.[415]

To construe persecution to mean harm more serious than mere harm is also consistent with an object and purpose approach. To equate the term with mere harm would mean that a person could qualify as a refugee even when what they fear has no significant consequences for their everyday lives and does not cause or require them to seek international protection. That would also be contrary to the principle of surrogacy as it would entail recognising as refugees persons who do not in fact lack the protection of their home state.

Given that under Article 31(3)(b) VCLT, UNHCR, case law, and academic materials can at least constitute evidence of state practice (or constitute state practice in the broad sense under Article 32), it is notable that on this issue they reflect a broad consensus that persecution is more than mere harm. That understanding is shared by all main approaches, both the human rights approach and others.

As noted earlier, from the *travaux* it is clear that the paradigm the drafters had in mind were the victims of Nazi, Falangist, and other persecutions.[416] This is also indicative that the drafters wished by use of the concept of persecution to identify an aggravated form of harm such as was all too present in the Second World War and further back.

Accordingly, applying VCLT principles, we can derive that, to be persecutory, acts must have a certain level of intensity. Using the language of sufficient severity to describe this intensity matches closely with the human rights approach. As we have seen, contrary to the views of some critics that it requires the importation of extrinsic concepts of severity, IHRL has identified sufficient severity as a threshold that needs to be met to show ill-treatment.[417]

Linking back to the previous subsection, IHRL understands the notion of sufficient severity to require an assessment relative to the individual's circumstances. As noted by Kälin and Künzli, 'this threshold cannot be determined in the abstract but

---

[414] See e.g. *Collins and Akaziebe v Sweden* App No 23944/05 (ECtHR, 8 March 2007) in which the ECtHR noted that '[i]t is not in dispute that subjecting a woman to female genital mutilation amounts to ill-treatment contrary to Article 3 of the Convention.'

[415] See Anker (n 33) §4.4, 254, who cites several US cases to this effect.

[416] As noted by Steinbock (n 32) 18, 'the Convention's inclusion of persecution for reasons of race, religion, and nationality speaks most directly to [the Nazi persecutions of 1933–45].'

[417] See Chapter 3, section 4.2.2.

is heavily dependent on the circumstances involved'.[418] Thus the HRC has stated in *Vuolanne v Finland* that 'the assessment of what constitutes inhuman or degrading treatment falling within the meaning of article 7 depends on all the circumstances of the case, such as the duration and manner of the treatment, its physical or mental effects, as well as the sex, age and state of health of the victim' and proceeded in this case to find that there had not been any 'severe pain or suffering' or 'humiliation or debasement involved [exceeding] a particular level'.[419] The ECtHR has stated in respect of Article 3 (the prohibition on ill-treatment) that 'the standards of Article 3 of the Convention ... imply that the ill-treatment the applicant alleges he will face if returned must attain a minimum level of severity if it is to fall within the scope of Article 3' and that '[t]he assessment of this is relative, depending on all the circumstances'.[420] Under EU law the concept of sufficient severity has been codified within the definition of acts of persecution in Article 9 QD (recast). Under this definition there remains a lack of clarity as to the meaning of 'basic human rights' within the first limb (a) of this provision ('be sufficiently serious by its nature or repetition as to constitute a severe violation of basic human rights, in particular the rights from which derogation cannot be made under Article 15(2) of the [ECHR]'). But its second limb (b), which is in the alternative, provides for acts of persecution to arise cumulatively ('be an accumulation of various measures, including violations of human rights which is sufficiently severe as to affect an individual in a similar manner as mentioned in point (a)'). As a result, this article's definition of acts of persecution can fairly be summarised as requiring only a sufficiently severe violation of human rights. The critical criterion is the severity of the harm, not the 'basic' nature of the precise right(s) violated. For the CJEU, what is decisive is 'the severity of the measures and sanctions adopted or liable to be adopted against the person concerned'. This feature also calls into question whether Article 9(1) has fairly been characterised as deploying an hierarchical human rights approach.[421]

Whilst IHLR references to the notion of sufficient severity have been confined to the prohibition on ill-treatment, it is part and parcel of assessing human rights violations comprehensively that not all human rights violations automatically involve treatment that reaches a minimum level of severity. Thus, the HRC found in *Vuolanne v Finland* that to establish ill-treatment other elements must be involved than the mere fact of deprivation of liberty.[422] It is commonplace within the European system for example, for decisions to be made that whilst there has been a violation of qualified rights such as the right to respect for private and family life, there has not been a violation of the prohibition on ill treatment. By the same token, inherent in the case law on the prohibition of ill-treatment is recognition that whilst a violation of a qualified

---

[418] Kälin and Künzli (n 107) 319.
[419] *Vuolanne v Finland* (2 May 1989) Communication No 265/1987, UN Doc CCPR/C/35/D/265/1987, para 9.2. The African Commission on Human Rights has also applied a similar approach: see *Shumba v Zimbabwe* (n 139) para 138, cited in Kälin and Künzli (n 107) 320.
[420] *Hilal v United Kingdom* App No 45276/99 (ECtHR, 6 June 2001).
[421] *Y and Z*, joined cases C-71/11 and C-99/11, EU:C:2012:518, para 66. See also p. 196 and also European Union Asylum Agency (EUAA), 'Qualification for International Protection Judicial Analysis' 2nd edition (produced by IARMJ-Europe under contract to the EUAA, January 2023) 1.4.2.1–1.4.2.2.
[422] Kälin and Künzli (n 107) 320.

human right may not on its own reach the level of sufficiently severity, it may do so in cumulative fashion along with violations of other qualified human rights. Thus, both IHRL and refugee law embodying a human rights approach makes clear that it is only if violations of human rights attain a sufficient severity or disproportionality that they amount to persecution or ill treatment.[423]

There is the further dimension, most clearly posited by the human rights approach, that states in a situation of war or public emergency may be able to derogate from their responsibility for all but violations of non-derogable rights. As observed by the IACtHR, '[i]t cannot be denied that under certain circumstances the suspension of guarantees may be the only way to deal with emergency situations'.[424] Even under the non-hierarchical approach to human rights, this is a relevant dimension.[425] IHRL imposes very stringent conditions on the ability of states to derogate in full or in part from their derogable obligations under major human rights treaties However, where these are complied with, there will be far fewer human rights in play in the assessment of cumulative harm.

It needs briefly to be explained how assessment of the intensity of harm is to be conducted when what is involved is violations of peremptory norms of customary international law. In the case of a norm such as the prohibition of torture, it could be said that of itself a violation of this right should constitute persecution. The same could be said *a fortiori* of genocide[426] and the deliberate targeting of civilian population.[427] Such an understanding makes sense but does so because torture and genocide etc. are of their nature sufficiently severe acts. However, not all peremptory norms may necessarily have this feature. As can be seen from the example of non-discrimination, at least assuming this is accepted as a peremptory norm of customary international law, whether its violation involves the infliction of sufficiently serious harm will depend on which right or freedom it nullifies or impairs.[428] In any event, the International Law Commission in its study of peremptory norms has as yet only identified the prohibition of apartheid and racial discrimination as peremptory norms of general international law.[429] Further, outside the context of armed conflict and generalised violence and apartheid and racial discrimination, there are few (actual or putative) peremptory

---

[423] As noted by Jean-Yves Carlier, 'General Report' in Jean-Yves Carlier et al, *Who Is a Refugee? A Comparative Case Law Study* (Brill 1997) 6887.

[424] *Habeas Corpus in Emergency Situations*, Advisory Opinion OC-8/87, IAmCtHR (30 January 1987) paras 20, 27. See further HRC, General Comment No 29: States of Emergency (Article 4) (n 151); Guide on Article 15 of the European Convention on Human Rights Derogation in time of emergency (April 2021).

[425] See 176.

[426] *Application of the Convention on the Prevention and Punishment of the Crime of Genocide (Bosnia and Herzegovina v Serbia and Montenegro)*, Judgment [2007] ICJ Rep 43, para 161.

[427] *Legality of the Threat or Use of Nuclear Weapons* (n 123) para 78.

[428] This argument depends in part on what is the correct definition of discrimination for international law purposes. The HRC defines discrimination for the purposes of the ICCPR as '[a]ny distinction, exclusion, restriction or preference which is based on any ground such as race, color, sex, language, religion, political or other opinion, national or social origin, property, birth or other status, and which has the purpose or effect of nullifying or impairing the recognition, enjoyment or exercise by all persons, on an equal footing, of all rights and freedoms.' See also Article 1 International Convention on the Elimination of all Forms of Racial Discrimination (ICERD), and Article 2 CRC.

[429] ILC, Fourth report on peremptory norms of general international law (*jus cogens*) by Dire Tladi, Special Rapporteur (31 January 2019) UN Doc A/CN.4/727, paras 91–101.

norms that arise in the asylum field; and those that have been identified also constitute severe violations of IHRL.[430]

Reinforcing the validity of applying a threshold of sufficient severity is the fact that the object and purpose of the refugee definition as set out in Article 1A(2), whilst one derived from IHRL, is not the establishment of *any* human rights violation(s). As noted by Lord Hope in *HJ (Iran)*, the Convention's:

> purpose is to provide the protection that is not available in the country of nationality where there is a well-founded fear of persecution, not to guarantee to asylum-seekers when they are returned all the freedoms that are available in the country where they seek refuge. It does not guarantee universal human rights.[431]

Thus, whilst a human rights approach to interpretation of the 'being persecuted' element ensures that the concept is given a broad meaning, it also ensures that it continues to have recognisable limits rooted in the object and purpose of providing surrogate protection only when a state has failed to provide effective protection against persecution, not when a state has failed to provide effective guarantees against violation of every human right. If it were otherwise, there would be a real danger that persecution would be seen to arise in every case except where in their country of origin applicants enjoy a wide panoply of liberal democratic rights and freedoms. Such an approach would deny the evident fact that a significant number of states, if not indeed many, are generally stable and able to ensure effective protection to the generality of their population without oppression. As noted by Laws LJ in *Amare v Secretary of State for the Home Department*:

> The Convention is not there to safeguard or protect potentially affected persons from having to live in regimes where pluralist liberal values are less respected, even much less respected, than they are here. It is there to secure international protection to the extent agreed by the contracting States.[432]

It follows that when assessing the severity of human rights violations, the refugee decision maker is not conducting a comparative examination, to see, for example, to what extent the likely treatment facing an applicant on return will fall short of the human rights standards in the decision maker's own state. He or she is adjudging only whether the person concerned faces violations of international human rights norms of sufficient severity in their country of origin.

3.5.1 Persecution and discrimination
In the refugee law literature discrimination and persecution are seen as importantly different but closely linked. As noted by Dowd, discrimination:

---

[430] This is also true of customary international law more generally: see Lambert (n 96) 242.
[431] *HJ (Iran)* (n 33) para 15.
[432] *Amare v SSHD* [2005] EWCA Civ 1600, para 31, cited with approval by Lord Hope in *HJ (Iran)* (n 33).

[ ... ] is often used by decision makers to describe all treatment and incidents that fall short of persecution. It is sometimes used in the jurisprudence alongside—or even interchangeably with—'harassment', depriving it of independent meaning. In a commonly cited Canadian case, for example, the Federal Court said that 'the dividing line between persecution and *discrimination or harassment* is difficult to establish'.[433]

Dowd notes further that discrimination is an amorphous notion reliance on which has sometimes led to decision makers classifying forms of harm as mere 'discrimination' even when they may involve physical violence or other forms of human rights violations.[434]

This feature underscores the need to apply a human rights approach to *both* concepts.

Despite its frequent usage in international treaty law, there is no clear definition of the term discrimination. Kälin and Künzli state that:

[ ... ] the concept of discrimination under international law denotes specific and qualified cases of unequal treatment that have the purpose or effect of making adverse distinctions on the grounds of race, sex, birth, ethnic origin, religion, political opinion and other, similar reasons such as age or disability. These are all characteristics that define an 'individual' and thus are part of his or her identity.[435]

In the IHRL context, discrimination is understood to mean treating people in comparable situations differently, without an objective and reasonable justification.[436]

In seeking to evaluate the role of discrimination in the concept of 'being persecuted', it is necessary to address the argument that discrimination is a necessary condition of being persecuted. That is not the approach that has governed the preponderance of the case law and wider literature, but it is a view that has been advanced over the years, e.g. Steinbock wrote in 1997 that: 'the plain meaning of the term "persecution" in the refugee definition, read in light of its history, makes clear that persecution does not exist apart from a prohibited reason for the suffering that it produces'.[437] A similar

---

[433] Rebecca Dowd, 'Dissecting Discrimination in Refugee Law: An Analysis of its Meaning and its Cumulative Effect' (2011) 23(1) IJRL 28, citing *Sagharichi v Canada (MEI)* [1993] FCJ No 796 (QL), para 3 (emphasis added).
[434] Dowd (n 433) 34–36.
[435] Kälin and Künzli (n 107) 336.
[436] In relation to economic, social and cultural rights, the ESCR Committee stated in General comment No 20: Non-discrimination in economic, social and cultural rights (art 2, para 2, of the International Covenant on Economic, Social and Cultural Rights (2 July 2009) UN Doc E/C.12/GC/20, para 2 that: '[n]on-discrimination and equality are fundamental components of international human rights law and essential to the exercise and enjoyment of economic social and cultural rights'. At para 7, it defines discrimination as 'any distinction, exclusion, restriction or preference or other differential treatment that is directly or indirectly based on the prohibited grounds of discrimination and which has the intention or effect of nullifying or impairing the recognition, enjoyment or exercise, on an equal footing, of Covenant rights. Discrimination also includes incitement to discriminate and harassment'. The ECtHR distinguishes between 'direct discrimination' (which describes a 'difference in treatment of persons in analogous, or relevantly similar situations' and 'based on an identifiable characteristic, or "status" ' —see *Biao v Denmark* App No 38590/10 (ECtHR [GC], 24 May 2016), para 89) and 'indirect discrimination' (which describes disproportionately prejudicial effects of a general policy or measure which, though couched in neutral terms, has a particular discriminatory effect on a particular group—see *Biao v Denmark*, para 103).
[437] Steinbock (n 32) 758.

view has recently been voiced by Cantor (who has argued that persecution is instead to be viewed as 'an exacerbated form of discrimination that follows from the making of unjust distinctions recognised by the Convention grounds')[438] and by Scott (for whom discrimination is 'integral to the notion of being persecuted').[439]

The essence of the argument in favour of this view is that being persecuted cannot be understood in isolation from the Convention reasons and that in fact discrimination is a necessary condition for the phenomenon of persecution to arise. Attempted support is sought from judicial decisions, most notably passages in the UK House of Lords case of *Islam*, in particular one by Lord Hoffman,[440] and in the Australian case of *Applicant A*. In *Islam*, Lord Hoffman wrote that the concept of discrimination 'is concerned not with all cases of persecution, even if they involve denials of human rights, but with persecution which is based on discrimination'.[441] In *Applicant A*, McHugh J stated:

> Whether or not conduct constitutes persecution in the Convention sense does not depend on the nature of the conduct. It depends on whether it discriminates against a person because of race, religion, nationality, political opinion or membership of a social group.[442]

However, insofar as support is sought from such passages, there are many judicial observations to the contrary, sometimes within the same decision. Indeed, in *Islam* itself, Lord Hope stated that:

> [ … ] persecution is not the same thing as discrimination. Discrimination involves the making of unfair or unjust distinctions to the disadvantage of one group or class of people as compared with others. It may lead to persecution or it may not. *And persons may be persecuted who have not been discriminated against. If so, they are simply persons who are being persecuted.*[443]

Moreover, the very passage from his speech invoked to support the idea of discrimination as a necessary element of the persecution element contains the sentiment that in his opinion, the concept of discrimination is 'not concerned with all cases of persecution'.[444]

---

[438] Cantor (n 57) 392–94.

[439] Scott (n 51) 116. In lieu of the Hathaway and Foster definition, Scott argues that being persecuted 'entails a condition of existence in which discrimination is a contributory cause of (a real chance of being exposed to) serious denials of human rights demonstrative of a failure of state protection'. See further Mirko Bagaric and Penny Dimopoulos, 'Discrimination as the Touchstone of Persecution in Refugee Law' (2007) 3 Journal of Migration and Refugee Issues 14; Jean-Francois Durieux, 'Three Asylum Paradigms' (2013) 20 International Journal on Minority and Group Rights 147, 157; Andrew I Schoenholtz, 'The New Refugees and the Old Treaty: Persecutors and Persecuted in the Twenty-First Century' (2015) 16 Chicago Journal of International Law 81, 124.

[440] *Islam* (n 279).

[441] ibid.

[442] *Applicant A* (n 87). See also *MIMA v Respondents S152/2003* [2004] 222 CLR 1 (Aus HC), para 73.

[443] *Islam* (n 279) 20 (emphasis added).

[444] Contrary to Scott (n 51) 123, who considers that in this passage Lord Hoffman 'firmly situates discrimination within the "being persecuted" element of the refugee definition by first referring to the relevant discriminatory form of persecution among different forms, and second by locating that notion of

In any event, treating discrimination as a necessary condition of 'being persecuted' is inconsistent with a proper application of VCLT rules. One can readily agree that being persecuted cannot be understood in isolation from the Convention reasons: that is part of the well-accepted idea of a unified or holistic interpretation which sees the different elements of the refugee definition as interlocking and interconnected. But to assert that persecution is not persecution unless it is discriminatory is to stretch ordinary meaning, context, objects and purposes—and Article 31(3)(c) VCLT—too far.

Concerning Scott's argument that discrimination is 'inherent in the ordinary meaning of being persecuted',[445] it was noted earlier that the dictionary definitions of 'to persecute' include ones that make no use of a concept of discrimination.[446] In addition, even the definitions referencing discrimination, do not do so in definitive terms. Thus, the OED Online definition prefaces reference to the discriminatory elements (the 'grounds') with the adverb 'especially', not the adverb 'always'. Further, this definition, itself one of three, includes, as distinct usages, two definitions separated by a semi-colon that refer simply to 'to torment; to oppress'.

In relation to context, as Goodwin-Gill pointed out in 1999,[447] little support for such a reading can be derived from the Convention's second preambular paragraph as it concerns rights in the host state. As regards the reference to non-discrimination in the first preambular paragraph, it would be strange to construe it without noting that it refers to that norm as contained in the UN Charter and the UDHR. It is not affirmed as a free-standing peremptory norm.

This links to the significance of Article 31(3)(c) VCLT considerations. Even if non-discrimination can be said to qualify (by virtue of being a peremptory norm or otherwise) as one of the relevant rules of international law, its articulation as a rule or set of rules is primarily to be found in IHRL and so this argument works as much for the type of human rights approach advanced by Hathaway and Foster and others as it does for any discrimination-centric argument.

It has been suggested, for example by Scott, that making discrimination integral to the concept of 'being persecuted' has the benefit of precluding the reading in of a requirement to establish intention on the part of an actor of persecution, since discrimination can be established irrespective of the intention of those responsible for discriminatory acts or omissions. But the definition of 'being persecuted' that underpins the predominant human rights approach does not in any event draw on or entail acceptance that there is a requirement to establish intention,[448] so this argument is again at best effective against some approaches only.

Another drawback to treating discrimination as integral to the notion of 'being persecuted' is that it lends itself to assessments based on a comparative approach regarding

---

discriminatory persecution within the wider framework of IHRL. The NZIPT was surely right to conclude in *CV v Immigration and Protection Tribunal and CW v Immigration and Protection Tribunal* [2015] NZHC 510, para 103, that in this passage Lord Hoffman did not mean to treat persecution as being necessarily discriminatory.

[445] Scott (n 51) 116.
[446] ibid 122, as Scott himself acknowledges. See p. 305.
[447] Goodwin-Gill (n 89).
[448] See below section 3.9.

conditions in the country of origin rather than one based on IHRL norms directly. As will be shown later, it was application of a (misguided) comparative approach that led to some common law countries rejecting the view that group persecution could occur in situations of armed conflict and generalised violence (they requiring applicants to show they faced a risk 'over and above' those confronting other civilians); but such an error of approach has run wider, as illustrated by the US case of *Samut v I.N.S.* in which the judge stated: '[t]here is no evidence ... that [the claimant] ... faces a danger of persecution that is appreciably different from that faced by the hundreds of thousands of other Indo-Fijians still in Fiji'.[449] It can also be argued that the recognition that 'laws of general application' can sometimes be persecutory reflects acceptance that oppression can sometimes not discriminate.[450]

There is also a problem of self-contradiction. The main argument advanced as to why discrimination must be seen to be a necessary condition of being persecuted seems to be that to construe persecution more broadly (i.e. so it is not confined to discriminatory persecution) would dilute the distinctive quality of being persecuted so it becomes indistinguishable from being the victim of a human rights violation and would encompass all persons who are exposed to sustained or systemic denials of human rights, including 'all victims of natural disasters that result from failures by the state to fulfil its positive obligations to protect the right to life, health, property, and so forth from foreseeable hazards'.[451]

It is true that to reject discrimination as a necessary element of 'being persecuted' can have the consequence that applicants might be found to be victims of persecution, but still not be refugees unless able to establish a Refugee Convention reason. But that does not make the scope of *'being persecuted'* too wide. The limiting function is supplied by the requirement of a causal nexus to a Convention reason. Despite his struggles to advance a broader definition, Scott's approach risks in fact embracing a narrower one. If discrimination operates under the standard nexus approach as a way of delimiting the class of refugees, yet the scope of the 'being persecuted' element is still considered to be 'unduly broad', the implication is that there needs to be an additional limitation.[452]

Having rejected the view that discrimination is a necessary element of persecution, it remains to consider how the two concepts interact.

Unlike persecution, discrimination encompasses various levels of harm, not all of them serious (one can be discriminated against by someone, for example, even in relation to some very minor matter). Certainly, discrimination can sometimes be so serious that it constitutes persecution, e.g. when it takes the form of apartheid; however, it will far from always be so serious. Given that persecution involves serious harm, the two concepts—persecution and discrimination—cannot, therefore, be equated. As highlighted by the UNHCR Handbook analysis at paragraphs 53–55, discrimination does not amount to persecution unless it reaches a particular severity—identified

---

[449] *Samut v INS* [2000] US App LEXIS 177, cited in Hathaway and Foster (n 3) 174.
[450] See p. 370.
[451] Scott (n 51) 118.
[452] Another problem is that Scott himself acknowledges that adoption of his discrimination-based notion of 'being persecuted' would make no difference in practice in the vast majority of cases—see ibid 129.

therein as 'consequences of a substantially prejudicial nature' and identified within the human rights approach as sufficient severity.

As these paragraphs of the UNHCR Handbook illustrate, discrimination can be seen as an important indicator of whether persecution exists, even without reference to human rights violations, but the discrimination notion is sharpened by considering its human rights context. As Lord Steyn observed in *Islam*,[453] the reference in the 1951 Convention's preamble to the UDHR shows that counteracting discrimination was a fundamental purpose of the international human rights project, since Article 2 of the UDHR states:

> Everyone is entitled to all the rights and freedoms set forth in this Declaration, without distinction of any kind, such as race, colour, sex, language, religion, political or other opinion, national or social origin, property, birth or other status.[454]

The separate albeit interrelated duty of 'equal protection of the law', enshrined in both Article 7 of the UDHR and Article 26 of the ICCPR, requires equal protection in the exercise of the guaranteed rights and freedoms.

Consistent with the fact that discrimination can sometimes amount to a form of harm below the necessary threshold, it is an integral part of any analysis of human rights violations, both within IHRL and refugee law, to examine if discriminatory acts can give rise to serious harm when taken in conjunction with other measures.[455]

In IHRL case law, distinctions may be discriminatory unless based on objective and reasonable grounds.[456] Within refugee law itself, the New Zealand RSAA has stated that: '[i]t is recognised that various threats to human rights, in their cumulative effect can deny human dignity in key ways and should properly be recognised as persecution .... The need to recognise the cumulative effect of threats to human rights is particularly important in the context of refugee claims based on discrimination.'[457]

At the same time, applying a human rights approach to both concepts helps avoid treating discrimination as by definition about lesser forms of harm.

## 3.6 Actual or Threatened Harm

The refugee definition does not refer to threats of 'being persecuted' but neither does it prescribe that the persecution must be actual. Although doubtful that Article 33(1) materially assists with the meaning of 'being persecuted',[458] it is interesting that in the

---

[453] *Islam* (n 279) 639.
[454] UDHR (n 13) Article 2.
[455] This insight is also to be found in analyses that do not adopt an outright human rights approach, e.g. that given in the UNHCR Handbook (n 60) para 55, which notes that even where one discrimination does not on its own amount to persecution, it may do if taken cumulatively with others; see also, for the US approach, Anker (n 33) §4.35, 383–89.
[456] See p. 380. See also HRC, General Comment No 18: Non-discrimination (29 March 1996) UN Doc HRI/GEN/1/Rev.2, para 13, which states that: 'not every differentiation of treatment will constitute discrimination, if the criteria for such differentiation are reasonable and objective and if the aim is to achieve a purpose which is legitimate under the Covenant'.
[457] *Refugee Appeal No 71427/99* (n 50).
[458] See above section 1.4.2.

same context of considering risk on return, the drafters saw fit to refer to *threats* to life or freedom.[459] As was noted earlier, the mental, emotional, and psychological dimension to serious harm is part of the explanation of why persecution can sometimes consist in threats of serious harm and not their actuality.[460] In common sense, a threat as such may not be persecutory, but will be if its effect is sufficiently material.[461]

The notion of a threat of harm has to be understood broadly. A threat of harm may take the form of hostile words or gestures made to individuals but may also refer to the overall situation of harm likely to face an applicant on return.

In the context of future persecution the notion of threat goes wider than this, because the real risk of such persecution may arise even if the reality is that on return the actual harm fails to materialise. If the situation a person faces return to is a situation where they will have a threat over their head daily, that can constitute persecution even in the present and without it being decisive whether it is likely to materialise (this may also of course be true of the nature of past persecution). Through the discussion that arose in the UK Supreme Court case of *HJ (Iran)*, this has sometimes been referred to as 'the Anne Frank principle'. As described by Scott, this resides in the fact that Anne Frank 'might avoid being subjected to a specific act of persecution, but the discriminatory social context that forces her to hide [in Amsterdam] gives rise to the experience of being persecuted and thus having to hide in order to avoid exposure to feared acts of persecution'.[462]

This example underscores the close interconnection between persecution as threatened harm and the element of 'well-founded fear'.[463]

## 3.7 Indirect or Derivative Harm

Refugee law has long recognised that individuals can be subject to intense suffering as a result of fear that those close to them may suffer serious harm or of having to witness them doing so—sometimes referred to as 'vicarious persecution'. Grahl-Madsen pointed out as long ago as 1966 that:

> Even if, for some reasons, persecutory measures are applied to certain categories of persons only... so that members of such persons' families are not directly threatened, the latter may nevertheless claim to be indirect victims of (actual or potential) persecution. For, like the head of the family [who] is put to death, placed in a detention

---

[459] Emphasis added. The precise wording used is, 'where his life or freedom would be threatened'. See also Article 31(1) ('where their life or freedom was threatened').
[460] See p. 330.
[461] The Guide to Refugee Law in Australia (n 206) Chapter 4—Persecution, notes of the definition of persecution as serious harm in the Australian Migration Act (as amended), that 'a number of the instances of harm in ss 5J(5) and 91R(2) are expressed in terms of 'threat'. A 'threat' for the purposes of ss 5J(5) or 91R(2) would not normally be constituted by a mere declaration of intent. Rather, those sections contemplate that a person's livelihood or well-being will be jeopardised in a material way.' See further on threats, Anker (n 33) §4.19, 332–36.
[462] Scott (n 51) 106–09. For a critique, see pp. 703–704.
[463] On 'well-founded fear' generally, see Chapter 11.

camp, or deprived of his possibilities of earning a living, the members of his family will be seriously affected.[464]

As stated some time ago by the Federal Court of Canada in *Bhatti v Canada (Secretary of State)*, indirect harm may manifest itself in many ways 'ranging from the loss of the victim's economic and social support to the psychological trauma associated with witnessing the suffering of loved ones'.[465] Recital 36 of the QD (recast) states 'family members merely due to their relation to the refugee, will normally be vulnerable to acts of persecution in such a manner that could be the basis for refugee status'. The rationale behind this recital is that harm to one's family can have consequences not just for the person's psychological well-being but also for his or her material quality of life.[466]

The concept of indirect persecution is a corollary of the proposition that an applicant does not necessarily have to show an individualised threat of persecution.[467] As noted by Jerome J in *Bhatti*, '[b]y recognising that family members of persecuted persons may themselves be victims of persecution, the theory [of indirect persecution] allows the granting of status to those who might otherwise be unable to individually provide a well-founded fear of persecution'.[468]

However, as the *Ahemdebekova* case before the CJEU highlights, neither case law nor the wider literature supports the view that a person can establish persecution *merely* by virtue of a family relationship with a persecutee. In this case, the CJEU ruled that the refugee definition requires that an applicant faces a well-founded fear of being 'personally persecuted' and that 'an application for international protection cannot be granted as such on the ground that one of the applicant's family members has a well-founded fear of being persecuted or faces a real risk of suffering serious harm'.[469] Thus, the principle set out in recital 36 of the QD recast only creates a presumption which may be displaced by the particular circumstances of a case.

## 3.8 Duration

Does persecution need to be persistent or 'sustained or systemic'?

---

[464] Grahl-Madsen (n 15) 423–24.

[465] *Bhatti v Canada* [1994] 84 FTR 145, 147–48, cited by Waldman (n 1) 201. At ibid 202, Waldman notes a subsequent disagreement by the Federal Court of Appeal in *Pour-Shariati Canada (MEI)* [1997] 215 NR 174, 174–75, but considers this serves only as a qualification that persecution of one family member does not automatically give rise to a well-founded fear of persecution (ibid 203–04).

[466] QD (recast) (n 8). In Case C-652/16 *Nigyar Rauf Kaza Ahmedbekova and Rauf Emin Ogla Ahmedbekov v Zamestnik-predsedatel na Darzhavna agentsia za bezhantsite* [2018] ECLI:EU:C:2018:801, para 51, the CJEU observed that 'in carrying out the assessment of an application for international protection on an individual basis, account must be taken of the threat of persecution and of serious harm in respect of a family member of the applicant for the purpose of determining whether the applicant is, because of his family tie to the person at risk, himself exposed to such a threat'.

[467] See below section 3.10.

[468] *Bhatti v Canada* (n 465) 147–48. See also *Rafizade v Canada (MCI)* [1995] 92 FTR 55. See also *Katrinak v SSHD* [2001] EWCA Civ 832, para 23: '[i]t is possible to persecute a husband or a member of a family by what you do to other members of his immediate family. The essential task for the decision taker in these sort (sic) of circumstances is to consider what is reasonably likely to happen to the wife and whether that is reasonably likely to affect the husband in such a way as to amount to persecution of him'.

[469] *Ahmedbekova* (n 466) paras 49–50.

It was observed earlier that some of the dictionary definitions of persecution make reference to duration and/or persistency and this has been taken by some to indicate that it is integral to the term's ordinary meaning. However, as noted in the same discussion, ordinary meaning does not unambiguously make persistency a necessary condition, since not all dictionary meanings refer to duration or persistency.[470]

Bearing in mind that it is common for commentators to refer to 'acts' or 'measures' of persecution (and that within the EU Article 9 of the QD recast is concerned with 'acts of persecution'), it could be said to be implicit in such terms that persecution can sometimes take the form of a discrete moment or episode in time. However, as we have observed earlier, both 'acts' and 'measures' need to be given a broad meaning.[471] Neither narrow nor wide temporal limits can be inferred from use of such terms.

As regards object and purpose, it might be argued that since persecution is a strong word and that (at least in non-state actors cases) focus must be on a process or general situation, namely the willingness and ability of a state to protect against it, it makes sense to require it to have a persistent quality or be of a significant duration. Thus, Grahl-Madsen saw it as decisive to focus on 'the place of the offensive acts or atrocities in the general situation prevailing in the country of origin of the person concerned' and that '[i]f the atrocities which cause persons to flee are of relatively short duration only, for example, just an episode, and they are effectively put to an end by the government, there may hardly be any reason for considering the persons concerned political refugees'.[472] However (leaving aside that in this scenario he would appear to be considering persons who have not themselves been the victims of the atrocities), this is really only an example of a case in which an isolated incident is not probative of future risk because the government has 'effectively put an end' to the atrocities. It does not establish that isolated incidents against which the state failed to protect, could not be persecutory.

The highest profile version of the human rights approach, that first articulated by Hathaway in his 1991 book, very expressly views persistency as a necessary ingredient of persecution. For Hathaway in TLRS, 'persecution may be defined as the sustained or systemic violation of basic human rights demonstrative of a failure of state protection'.[473] It is this classic formulation that was adopted by the English Court of Appeal in *Ravichandran* and which continues to be employed widely.[474]

---

[470] See p. 306.

[471] See above section 3.1.

[472] Grahl-Madsen (n 15) 192.

[473] Hathaway (n 4) 104–05. Ethical theorists who have emphasised the persistency criterion include Jaakko Kuosmanen, 'What's So Special about Persecution?' (2014) 17(1) Ethical Theory and Moral Practice 129, 138.

[474] *Sandralingham Ravichandran* [1996] Imm AR 97. See e.g. Rodger Haines, James C Hathaway, and Michelle Foster, 'Claims to Refugee Status Based on Voluntary but Protected Actions: Discussion Paper No. 1 Advanced Refugee Law Workshop International Association of Refugee Law Judges Auckland, New Zealand, October 2002' (2003) 15(3) IJRL 430, 431 state: 'a fear of "being persecuted" is logically measured by reference to whether the applicant is genuinely at risk of the sustained or systemic violation of basic human rights, demonstrative of a failure of state protection'. See also *HJ (Iran)* (n 33); Hathaway (n 4) 112. This approach was first endorsed by the Supreme Court of Canada in *Ward* (n 173). It was formally embraced by the UK House of Lords: *Islam* (n 279) (Lord Hoffmann); *Horvath v SSHD* [2000] UKHL 37, para 495 (Lord Hope, for the majority), para 512 (Lord Clyde). See also *Sepet and Bulbul* (n 91) 862–63 (Lord Bingham); *Ullah, R (on the Application of) v Special Adjudicator* (n 171); *Do v SSHD* [2004] 2 AC 323, para 355 (Lord Steyn); and most recently the Supreme Court in *HJ (Iran)* (n 33) para 13 (Lord

However, the requirement that violations of human rights must always be 'sustained or systemic' and must involve some level of persistency or repetition has met with resistance in the case law and is extremely difficult to reconcile with a human rights approach. Under the latter framework, it is well-recognised that in the case of threats to life and ill-treatment, they can constitute serious harm which, if the state cannot protect against them, must constitute a violation of the right not to be ill-treated, even if they are isolated incidents. In the case of a single incident of evident severity, such as torture, to say that a person has not been ill-treated or persecuted as a result would entail requiring that something over and above a severe violation of a basic human rights had to be demonstrated. That would plainly be too restrictive.[475] As stated by Zimmermann and Mahler, with reference to case law that has rejected the persistency criterion, '[a]t least with regard to very basic rights a single incident should accordingly be regarded as sufficient to be tantamount to persecution and that 'persistency is a usual not a universal criterion of persecution'.[476]

In their 2014 work, Hathaway and Foster seek to rebut the criticisms levelled against the persistency criterion. They suggest that the famous definition given in the 1st edition has been misunderstood and that it was never meant to necessarily require a risk of repeated harm. They state that the 'sustained or systemic' wording 'has occasionally been misunderstood as necessarily requiring a risk of repeated harm (hence excluding one-off harm such as death). However, this has mostly now been understood to be an error.' They then cite a number of cases accepting that in some cases a single act of oppression may suffice.[477]

Given that Hathaway and Foster now accept the 'sustained and systemic' definition is defeasible, previous criticisms are perhaps now of largely scholastic interest, but in

Hope). As Hathaway and Pobjoy (n 6) have noted, it is not uniformly embraced in Australia, although it has been endorsed expressly by Justice Kirby and implicitly by Chief Justice Gleeson of the Australian High Court in *Khawar* (n 49) at 11 and 37-30 respectively. Although the United States approach to the interpretation of 'being persecuted' is not grounded in any particular framework, Deborah Anker and Josh Vittor, 'International Human Rights and US Refugee Law' in Burson and Cantor (n 57) 115, cite e.g. *Negusie v Holder* [1987] 555 US 421, with reference being made to international human rights instruments and norms. See also *Stenaj et al v Alberto Gonzalez* [2007] 227 Fed Appx 429, where the US Court of Appeals for the Sixth Circuit stated: '[w]hether the treatment feared by a claimant violates recognized standards of basic human rights can determine whether persecution exists'.

[475] As noted by Justice Kirby in *MIMA v Ibrahim* [2000] HCA 55, 'the notion of "systematic" conduct is a possible, but not a necessary element, in the idea of "persecution"'. See *Demirkaya v SSHD* [1999] EWCA Civ 1654; also, the UK Immigration and Asylum Tribunal case, *Doymus v SSHD* [2000] Unreported, IAT HX/80112/99. See further Hélène Lambert, 'The Conceptualisation of "Persecution" by the House of Lords: *Horvath vs Secretary of State*' (2001) 13(1) IJRL 16, 23, where she notes that the universality of the criterion of 'persistency' has been rejected explicitly by the UNHCR Handbook and by the European Union, and that it has not been adopted by most scholars, including Goodwin-Gill. Anker (n 33) 254–55, describes the US position as being that '[a]s with all forms of harm, physical violence must generally [NB: note not 'universally'] be serious or severe, repeated or capable of repetition. indicative of an underlying, systemic violation of rights in order to constitute persecutory harm'. Although the Australian Migration Act 2014 imposes a statutory test in s 5J(4)(c)/formerly s 91R(1)(c) for persecution to concern 'systematic [and discriminatory] conduct', this is presently interpreted to mean 'non-random' and 'does not displace the general proposition that a single act may suffice, as long as it is part of a course of systematic (in the sense of non-random) conduct'—see Guide to Refugee Law in Australia (n 206) ch 4. See further Goodwin-Gill and McAdam (4th edn) (n 26) 70.
[476] Zimmermann and Mahler (n 1).
[477] Hathaway and Foster (n 3) 195.

fact the expression of the definition in TLRS, with its reference to 'the need to show a sustained or systemic risk', was surely unequivocal. Further, it remains unclear what Hathaway and Foster's position, as clarified, is. To the extent that they appear to drive a distinction between risk and harm (they state that '[t]he ongoing risk may be one that manifests in a single harm'),[478] their own analysis treats the risk assessment as part of the 'well-founded fear assessment', an assessment downstream from the establishment of persecution. In addition, even their new formulation would on its face seem to still insist upon persistency: they state that 'a risk of being persecuted implies an element of persistence, relentlessness, or inescapability which is only present if the state is unwilling to or unable to protect against the risk of harm'.[479] Possibly what they have in mind is that the 'sustained or systemic' criterion is only an evidential one: thus they refer at one point to a risk of 'being persecuted' as 'requir[ing] evidence of a sustained or systemic denial of human rights demonstrative of a failure of state protection'.[480] But if it is evidential, then it is not a definitional requirement. Or possibly, what they mean to suggest is that since persecution is always a question of denial of human rights demonstrative of a failure of state protection, the latter must inevitably concern a process rather than an isolated episode.[481] That may very often be the case, but even in the context of state protection, it is possible to envisage a scenario that turns on an isolated failure. Consider, as an example of past persecution, a government who despite credible intelligence of an assassination attempt on an opposition leader at a rally, declines to arrange a police presence at it, with the result that that leader is attacked and physically maimed.

It may be thought that Article 9(1)(a) of the QD makes a better job of encompassing within the one definition both 'one-off' and repeated acts of serious harm (by use of the phrase 'by their nature or repetition').[482]

The New Zealand IPT in *DS (Iran)* has persuasively argued that, even though persistency is not a necessary condition,[483] the concept of 'sustained or systemic' denials of basic human rights demonstrative of a lack of state protection should retain rightful prominence in any further definition of the 'being persecuted' element since, even though not a 'test':

[126] [ ... ] the phrase serves to highlight critical elements of the 'being persecuted' component of the refugee definition. The referencing of human rights identifies the

---

[478] Scott (n 51) 99, considers that this is the distinction they seek to draw.
[479] Hathaway and Foster (n 3) 293.
[480] ibid 183. Similar equivocation can be found in some of the case law: see e.g. Mc Hugh J in *Chan Yee Kin v MIEA* (n 192) para 379. Despite accepting that '[a] single act of oppression may suffice', he goes on to reiterate the need for harm to be 'part of a course of systematic conduct'.
[481] That appears how they have been understood by the NZ IPT in *DS (Iran)* [2016] NZIPT 800788, para 126.
[482] In UNHCR, Interpreting Article 1 of the 1951 Convention (n 24) para 17, UNHCR notes that 'persecution comprises human rights abuses or other serious harm, often but not always with a systematic or repetitive element'.
[483] *DS (Iran)* (n 481) para 127: 'persecutory harm can, but must not, encompass multiple and ongoing violations of rights'.

role international human rights law plays in providing the overarching normative framework for analysis.

'Systemic' (not, as sometimes stated, systematic) identifies that 'being persecuted' arises because of an anticipated failure of the legal and other protection-relevant systems in the claimant's country of origin. Finally, 'sustained' can be seen to serve two functions. It references the enduring nature of the claimant's predicament arising from the failure of state protection in the country of origin. It also reminds decision-makers that persecutory harm can, but not must, encompass multiple and ongoing violations of rights.

The 'sustained or systemic' criterion can also be said to have a particularly significant role to play in claims to refugee status based, not on individual risk characteristics, but rather on membership of a class or category of persons ('group persecution'). It affords a way of testing to see if the harms feared are of such a nature that they are likely to impact on a significant number of persons. If, for example, a person bases his or her claim to fear persecution on the fact that he or she is a member of a sizeable ethnic group X, it defies logic that he or she should be able to succeed purely by pointing to one instance in the whole country of a person from this group meeting with harm. In such cases, it makes sense that applicants should be required to show that the scale and frequency of problems facing similarly situated persons are at a level where it is possible to say that the generality of such persons face harm. In the same vein, US regulations provide that an applicant can establish a well-founded fear by demonstrating the existence of a 'pattern or practice' of persecution of groups of 'similarly situated' persons: they focus exclusively on group-based characteristics of people 'similarly situated' to the applicant.[484]

In the UK, the Court of Appeal case of *Hariri* endorsed use of the notion of a 'consistent pattern of gross and systematic violation of fundamental human rights'.[485] However, in *Batayav*, which concerned whether the conditions of detention in the Russian penal system in which the appellant would be held would amount to ill treatment contrary to Article 3 ECHR, Sedley LJ added a prudent note of caution, stating that '[g]reat care' needed to be taken to such epithets as 'general' or 'systematic' of 'consistently happening':

> 38.... They are intended to elucidate the jurisprudential concept of real risk, not to replace it. If a type of car has a defect which causes one vehicle in ten to crash, most people would say that it presents a real risk to anyone who drives it, albeit crashes are not generally or consistently happening. The exegetic language in *Hariri* suggests a higher threshold than the IAT's more cautious phrase in *Iqbal*, 'a consistent pattern', which the Court in *Hariri* sought to endorse.[486]

Similar caution also underlines the US approach.[487]

---

[484] Anker (n 33) §2.12, 85–89.
[485] *Hariri v SSHD* [2003] EWCA Civ 807, para 8.
[486] *Batayav v SSHD* [2003] EWCA Civ 1489, para 38
[487] Anker (n 33) §2.12, 86–87.

In relation to application of a human rights approach, it is pertinent to mention that the need in such contexts to establish a practice or pattern has also been echoed by the ECtHR in considering the issue of whether generalised situations of violence can reach such a level that it can be said that all persons in a country or part of a country face a real risk of ill treatment contrary to Article 3. As the Court noted in *NA v United Kingdom*:

> Exceptionally, however, in cases where an applicant alleges that he or she is a member of a group systematically exposed to a practice of ill-treatment, the Court has considered that the protection of Article 3 of the Convention enters into play when the applicant establishes that there are serious reasons to believe in the existence of the practice in question and his or her membership of the group concerned .... In those circumstances, the Court will not then insist that the applicant show the existence of further special distinguishing features if to do so would render illusory the protection offered by Article 3.[488]

It may be, drawing on the insights of refugee law cases, that the Strasbourg Court's apparent requirement of a 'systematic practice' is too exacting a standard, but it does serve to illustrate the valid concern to base assessment of real risk to broad categories of persons on evidence of patterns or practices that are quantitatively and qualitatively significant.

The conclusion to be drawn as regards the incident of duration is that whilst it is not a necessary condition of persecution within the meaning of Article 1A(2) that it is 'sustained or systemic', this is a relevant criterion in a wide range of cases.

## 3.9 Intentionality

Another related issue, already touched on, concerns the need, or not, for a persecutory intent on the part of actors of persecution.[489] Persecutory intent is, of course, a necessary condition, of the definition of persecution in international criminal law, but there the crime itself must have a *mens rea*.[490] Within the Refugee Convention context, the highwater mark of the view that intent is a necessary condition of persecutory conduct was the US Supreme Court decision in *INS v Elias-Zacarias* which held that the refugee definition 'makes motives critical' and required claimants to establish the motives of alleged persecutors.[491]

---

[488] *NA v United Kingdom* (n 347) para 116.
[489] For background discussion, see Karen Musalo, 'Irreconcilable Differences? Divorcing Refugee Protections from Human Rights Norms' (1994) 15 Michigan Journal of International Law 1179; Hathaway and Foster (n 3).
[490] See Alice Edwards and Agnès Hurwitz, 'Introductory Note to the Arusha Summary Conclusions on Complementarities between International Refugee Law, International Criminal Law, and International Human Rights Law' (2011) 23(4) IJRL 856; Hathaway and Foster (n 3) 192–93; Goodwin-Gill and McAdam (4th edn) (n 26) 73–76.
[491] *INS v Elias-Zacarias* [1992] 502 US 478. Another case often cited for expression of the same view is the Australian Federal Court decision in *Ram* (n 238) para 568: 'Persecution involves the infliction of harm, but it implies something more: an element of an attitude on the part of those who persecute which leads to

As illustrated by the *Elias-Zacarias* case, the view that intention is a necessary condition of persecution is seen as entailed by the need to establish a causal nexus with one of the Convention reasons; it is considered that to satisfy the nexus clause, an applicant must establish that the perpetrator intends/intended to inflict persecution. In this conception, the role of the nexus clause is to link the Convention reason(s) to the persecutor's intention (which may, in non-state actor cases, sometimes be the intentions of state actors, sometimes non-state actors). The nexus clause is seen as requiring a decision maker to ask, 'why does the persecutor wish to harm (or withhold protection from) the applicant?'. However, as pointed out by Goodwin-Gill and McAdam, this interpretation appears to be influenced by US law which employs 'on account of' rather than the 'for reasons of' language of the refugee definition. Only the former, they contend, 'implies an element of conscious, individualised direction which is often conspicuously absent in the practices of mass persecution'.[492]

So far as the *travaux* are concerned, they provide no support for the view that intent was considered a necessary condition. As noted by Goodwin-Gill and McAdam, the *travaux* 'suggest that the only relevant intent or motive would be that, not of the persecutor, but of the refugee or refugee claimant: one motivated by personal convenience, rather than fear, might be denied protection'.[493]

To a degree, approaches which treat persecutory intent as a prerequisite appear to have been influenced by some dictionary definitions, which, based on the Latin root of the word, emphasise the idea that it is infliction of harm involving enmity or malignancy[494] (albeit the view that motives are critical does not necessarily entail that the intention be malevolent).[495]

However, as mainstream case law has highlighted, this perspective overlooks that to focus on the need for malignant intent would prevent recognition as persecutory of intrinsically harmful acts carried out by perpetrators in the belief they would help or benefit the victims (e.g. involuntary psychiatric treatment in certain circumstances, or 'corrective rape' of lesbians).[496] Such an approach is not borne out by the language of the Convention.

In any event, as we have seen, the wording of the refugee definition, by its use of the passive voice ('being persecuted') highlights not so much the act of inflicting harm as the exposure to harm. Although it was argued earlier that that does not make the mindset of the persecutor irrelevant, conceiving 'being persecuted' as a predicament

---

the infliction of harm, or an element of motivation (however twisted) for the infliction of harm. People are persecuted from something perceived about them or attributed to them by their persecutors.'

[492] Goodwin-Gill and McAdam (3rd edn) (n 25) 101–02; Goodwin-Gill and McAdam (4th edn) (n 26) 80–81.
[493] Goodwin-Gill and McAdam (3rd edn) (n 25) 102; Goodwin-Gill and McAdam (4th edn) (n 26) 81.
[494] See e.g. *R v IA, ex parte Jonah* (n 48). See also Carlier (n 41) 44, cited in Symes and Jorro (n 146) 86. Hathaway and Foster (n 3) 369 describe this as the 'intention plus animosity' requirement.
[495] As noted by the Australian Federal Court in *Ram* (n 238), cited in James C Hathaway and Michelle Foster, 'The Causal Connection ("Nexus") to a Convention Ground: Discussion Paper No. 3 Advanced Refugee Law Workshop International Association of Refugee Law Judges Auckland, New Zealand, October 2002' (2003) 15(3) IJRL 461, 463.
[496] See Foster (n 45) 48–49.

assists in understanding that what matters is the (threatened or actual) effects of a persecutor's conduct or actions, rather than their intention.[497]

Requiring persecutory intent is also at odds with the Convention's object and purpose which is to ensure the protection of victims of persecution, not to investigate the motives of the alleged persecutors.[498] Applying a human rights approach, it is instructive to note that IHRL does not consider that the intention of the perpetrator of human rights abuses is always essential for establishing whether ill treatment occurs; what matters is rather the nature of the act and its effect on the person concerned.[499] Human rights abuses can be direct or indirect.

It is notable that there has been increasing rejection of reliance on motives in UNHCR materials,[500] the case law,[501] in and in the academic literature.[502]

How extensive that rejection has been remains a matter of lively debate. Foster, writing in 2007, considered that notwithstanding such developments, 'the predominant approach in the common law jurisprudence as a whole undoubtedly remains one of requiring intent' and that 'it is only accurate to say that NZ has fully embraced the predicament approach'.[503] The position in Australia is certainly still represented as requiring persecutory intent,[504] but there remains no express rejection of the contrary position expressed by Kirby J in *Chen Shi Hai*,[505] or of the doubts about it expressed

---

[497] *Refugee Appeal No 72635* [2002] NZRSAA 33, citing *Chen Shi Hai* (n 49) paras 33 and 65.

[498] Foster (n 45) 263, 275–76; Hathaway and Foster (n 3) 370–73. See also UNHCR, An Overview of Protection Issues in Europe: Legislative Trends and Positions Taken by UNHCR (September 1995) European Series Volume 1(3) 1995/09, 62.

[499] See e.g. HRC, *Quinteros v Uruguay* (107/81) [9.68]; ECtHR, *Price v UK*, Reports 2001-VII, para 30. See also Kälin and Künzli (n 107) 313; Pieter van Dijk et al (eds), *Theory and Practice of the European Convention on Human Rights* (4th edn, Intersentia 2018) 418; Foster (n 45) 283.

[500] See UNHCR, Guidelines No 12: Claims for refugee status related to situations of armed conflict and violence under Article 1A(2) of the 1951 Convention and/or 1967 Protocol relating to the Status of Refugees and the regional refugee definitions (2 December 2016) UN Doc HCR/GIP/16/12, 32. See also UNHCR, Written Submission on Behalf of the UN High Commissioner for Refugees in the UK Court of Appeal in *Sepet* [2001] EWCA Civ 681, extracted in Jennifer Moore, Karen Musalo, and Richard A Boswell, *Refugee Law and Policy* (Carolina Academic Press 2018) 313–17, cited by Foster (n 45) 274.

[501] See e.g. Lord Rodger in *R (Sivakumar) v SSHD* [2003] 2 All ER 1097, para 41 ('the law is concerned with the reasons for the persecution and not with the motives of the persecutor.'); *NACM of 2002 v MIMIA* [2003] FCA 1554, para 63, cited in Foster (n 45) 276 and 280. See also the New Zealand case *Refugee Appeal No 72635* (n 497). In *NACM*, Madgwick J considered that to read in a requirement of persecutory intent would require a 'narrow, literalist approach ... disconsonant with the concerns properly to be imputed, as a matter of interpretation, to the framers of the Convention'. Anker (n 33) §4.7, 269–71, notes a significant shift in US case law away from requiring persecutory intent, as exemplified by *In re Kasinga* [1996] WL 379826, in which the Board found persecutory that the FGM feared by a Togolese girl was persecutory even though the persons performing or requiring FGM may have believed it was beneficial to the victim. One difficulty with the existing discourse is that intentionality can be understood in different ways. For example, it can be understood to denote subjective state of mind, as is clearly the case in the Australian case law: see e.g. *SZTAL v MIBP; SZTGM v MIBP* [2017] 347 ALR 405. Or, for example, it may simply denote conduct attributable to human agency: see e.g. C-542/13, CJEU (GC), judgment of 18 December 2014, *Mohamed M'Bodj v Etat belge*, EU:C:2014:2452, para 35. See further p. 341.

[502] See e.g. Foster (n 45); Zimmermann and Mahler (n 1).

[503] Foster (n 45) 280.

[504] See Guide to Refugee Law in Australia (n 206) ch 4, 4. *Dicta* by Burchett J in *Ram* (n 238) para 568, stating that there must be motivation, are said to have been widely approved by higher courts. For a recent example, see *CRU18 v Minister for Home Affairs* [2020] FCAFC 129, paras 46–48, albeit the Full Federal Court's reasoning in this case appears to rely on an outmoded dictionary definition approach.

[505] *Chen Shi Hai* (n 88) para 65.

by Madgwick J in the Australian Federal Court decision in *NACM* of 2002.[506] Further, Foster herself cites UK and Canadian cases rejecting the need to show persecutory intent.[507] Zimmermann and Mahler also refer to the issue as 'controversial' but state their conclusion that in the context of refugee law the issue of persecution 'centres on the question of the evidence of a human rights violation by reason of one of the enlisted ground and not on the intention of the perpetrator'.[508]

Foster points out that, especially in cases involving women or economic deprivation, an intentionality-based approach 'diverts attention from the wider societal context of discrimination and socio-economic disadvantage which frequently underlines the predicament of individual applicants, thus reducing persecutory motivation to personal and private matters'.[509]

Bearing in mind that the drafters clearly recognised that the refugee definition could encompass group persecution, it is noteworthy that requiring persecutory intent would cut across recognition that where there are general measures directed by state or non-state actors against groups, an applicant may have a well-founded fear of being persecuted merely by virtue of being a member of the group in question. As noted by Goodwin-Gill and McAdam:

> Where large groups are seriously affected by a government's political, economic, and social policies or by the outbreak of uncontrolled communal violence, it would appear wrong in principle to limit the concept of persecution to measures immediately identifiable as direct and individual.[510]

As regards non-state actor cases, Foster expresses concern about the tendency in some reported cases for decision makers to require it to be shown that the *state actors* intended the persecution. She links this with a failure to understand that in non-state actor cases, it can suffice, in order to establish lack of protection, that the state is either unwilling *or* unable to protect; it may not always be necessary to establish unwillingness to protect (sometimes called the 'bifurcated approach').[511] This point has force. Whilst sometimes a state's unwillingness (whether deliberate or a result of incompetence or ineptitude) may betoken intent, on the bifurcated approach it may be unnecessary to do more than establish a reason for inability to protect. Sometimes this may consist of a (non-intentional) failure to act.[512] As Lord Hoffman articulated matters in *Islam*, the failure of the state to protect Jewish shopkeepers in Nazi Germany

---

[506] *NACM of 2002* (n 501) para 66. It might also be said that the strong rejection in cases such as *Chen Shi Hai* (n 88) para 33 of the notion that the reason for persecution had to manifest animus or malignant intent should arguably have led the majority to recognise the inherent problems with any underlying concept of persecutory intent (as Kirby J did in para 65 of the same case): see Pobjoy (n 256) 160.

[507] Foster (n 45) 275–80. The UK case she cites at 278, containing the most categorical rejection of persecutory intent, is *Sepet and Bulbul* (n 91) para 92 (per Laws LJ, with whom Parker LJ agreed).

[508] Zimmermann and Mahler (n 1) 349–50. Hathaway and Foster (n 3) 369 highlight a German decision—BVerwG *10 C 52.07*, but also an Austrian Administrative Court decision, *M v Independent Federal Asylum Board* [2007], appearing to adopt a different view.

[509] Foster (n 45) 266; see also Hathaway and Foster (n 3) 372–73.

[510] Goodwin-Gill and McAdam (3rd edn) (n 25) 129; Goodwin-Gill and McAdam (4th edn) (n 26) 152.

[511] Foster (n 45) 201; Hathaway and Foster (n 3) 373.

[512] See e.g. *Assenov and Others v Bulgaria* App No 90/1997/874/1086 (ECtHR, 28 October 1998) para 102.

from gangs organised by an Aryan competitor did not in itself evince a motive on the part of the state, it was the fact that the state allowed such gangs, motivated by business rivalry and score-settling, to attack them unchecked.[513] As noted by Hathaway,[514] a state may 'not be bothered' to fulfil its obligations to protect a person or group of people because of who they are.

A requirement of persecutory intent also fits badly with the reality of refugee determination procedure. If persecutory intent were accepted as a necessary condition, then decision makers would be obliged to mind readers and conduct an inquiry into the motives of alleged persecutors who reside in a foreign country, a task which may entail a significant amount of speculation and conjecture. It is a task that has properly been termed 'extremely difficult or impossible to perform'[515] or as one 'beyond ascertainment even from the circumstantial evidence'.[516]

It can be concluded that in order to establish the 'being persecuted' element of the refugee definition there is no requirement of persecutory intent.

Rejecting persecutory intent as a requirement does not, however, negate the continuing need to establish a reason for the persecution (or in non-state actor cases, a reason for the failure to protect). Establishing such a reason is important not simply in order to establish a causal nexus with a Refugee Convention reason but in order to establish that acts said to be persecutory emanate from human actors. It will be just as mistaken in non-state actor cases to require intent to be established as in state cases, but it will still be essential to establish harm attributable to the non-state actor.

This last observation underlines that some formulations of the 'predicament approach' also harbour a risk of confusion between the applicant's and the persecutor's reasons.[517] In endorsing this approach, Foster, for example, states that it 'focuses on the reason for the applicant's fear, rather than the reason for the persecutor's decision to harm the applicant'.[518] But whilst as we have seen it is incorrect to require it to be shown that a persecutor has intent or motivation to harm the applicant, it still always needs to be established that the persecutor has a reason for inflicting such harm. To underline a point made earlier,[519] rejection of persecutory intent as a requirement must not obscure the need to establish a reason and one that is attributable to human agency. The predicament approach (at least as developed by Foster) risks losing sight of the fact that in assessing whether an act is persecutory it remains necessary to have regard to the perspective of the persecutor. What is decisive is not whether a person has particular characteristics but whether they will be ascribed to them by a potential persecutor. The doctrine of attribution (or imputation) is an integral part of refugee law.[520] But to ensure this doctrine has application, focus must not be placed exclusively on the predicament of the persecutee. Focus on the persecutor, however, does

---

[513] *Islam* (n 279).
[514] James C Hathaway, 'Food Deprivation: A Basis for Refugee Status?' (2014) 81(2) Social Research 327, 336; Hathaway and Foster (n 3) 370–72.
[515] *Chen Shi Hai* (n 88) para 313.
[516] *Refugee Appeal No 72635* (n 497) para 168.
[517] The same is true of Matthew Scott's 'condition of existence' approach: see Scott (n 51) 107.
[518] Foster (n 45) 271.
[519] See p. 363.
[520] *Ward* (n 173).

not necessarily mean focus on intention or motives; the central issue remains of the effects of the persecutor's actions. The perspective of the persecutor is a construct which makes it possible to have regard to intention and motives as evidence of reasons where appropriate but, where such evidence is not available, to infer from the surrounding facts that the persecutory act can be attributed to the persecutor. Thus, in a trafficking case, it may be justified to infer from the actions of the traffickers and other surrounding circumstances both that the traffickers would inflict serious harm on an applicant and that one of the contributing reasons would be because of the applicant's gender and/or age or social status.

These concerns about some formulations of the predicament approach aside, this author's own conclusions on the issue of persecutory intent are similar to those of UNHCR, leading scholars, and some jurists. However, despite a clear trend in the case law and wider literature away from the previous view which made persecutory intent a necessary requirement, there has still not been emphatic rejection of such a view by all leading courts. Accordingly, it would be premature to describe this rejection as an agreed basic proposition, even if it may only be a matter of time before such rejection is confirmed.

## 3.10 Individualisation (Individual and Group Persecution)

Under a human rights approach it remains the case that persecution has to be shown to affect an individual person. Not all violation of human rights will have equally serious consequences for different individuals. As noted earlier, there is broad acceptance of the need for the human rights approach to be applied *via* the principle of individual assessment which recognises that harm must be considered in terms of how it affects specific individuals. In Goodwin-Gill and McAdam's formulation, whether a human rights violation will amount to persecution will 'again turn on an assessment of a complex of factors, including (1) the nature of the freedom threatened, (2) the nature and severity of the restriction, and (3) the likelihood of the restriction eventuating in the individual case'.[521] Within the EU, Article 4(3) of the QD recast prescribes that the decision maker must take into account (alongside general circumstances) factors which include the individual position and personal circumstances of the applicant such as background, gender, and age.

In relation to this incident of persecution, vocabulary has been a real problem, as no available term is wholly without ambiguity. For example, what has been said above could be formulated as meaning that persecution has to be 'personal' or 'individualised'.[522] However, either or both of these descriptors might be construed by some to mean that a person has to be individually targeted; by others to mean that, even if not specifically targeted, they are personally or individually affected by a wider persecution. To take another example, 'targeting' might be understood to require a singling-out; alternatively, it might be understood as a more diffuse notion of adverse attention.

---

[521] Goodwin-Gill and McAdam (3rd edn) (n 25) 92; Goodwin-Gill and McAdam (4th edn) (n 26) 71.

[522] The CJEU in *Ahmedbekova* (n 466) paras 49 referred to the need for an applicant to have a 'well-founded fear of being personally persecuted'.

Gradually such ambiguities have largely been resolved in the case law and wider literature, although some blurred edges still remains. Two points in particular have solidified.

First, it is now well established that the need for persecution to be specific to the person does not mean that he or she has been individually targeted or 'singled out'. Despite emphatic rejection by early commentators such as Zink and Grahl-Madsen,[523] there was some support in early case law for a 'singling-out' criterion.[524] Understandably the latter came under heavy criticism[525] and never garnered any significant support.

Secondly, it is widely accepted that acts or measures can be said to be persecutory even though directed, not at a person individually, but at a group of which the individual is a member.[526] This invites closer attention to the concept of group persecution.

### 3.10.1 Group persecution

The drafters clearly envisaged that 'international action on behalf of refugees might well relate to refugee groups despite the "individual" form of these refugee definitions'.[527] As stated by Hathaway and Foster, '[t]he history and context of the Convention make clear that its protective ambit includes large groups of persons whose fear of persecution is generalised, not merely those who have access to evidence of particularized risk'.[528]

Indeed, not to have grasped this phenomenon would have risked the refugee definition being of aid only to an elite, e.g. high profile political dissidents subject to specific targeting.[529] Being individually persecuted by virtue of membership of a group is the essence of the concept of 'group persecution'.

One of the values of the intense debate that took place in the EU around the subsidiary protection provision set out in Article 15(c) of the QD was the clarification eventually provided by the CJEU that even violence that is 'indiscriminate' can give rise to serious harm against individuals. The core notion here is the same as in the context of group persecution under the refugee definition—that what harms the whole

---

[523] Endorsing rejection of this criterion by Zink, Grahl-Madsen (n 15) 213 observed that '[o]nce a person is subjected to a measure of such gravity that we consider it 'persecution', that person is 'persecuted' in the sense of the Convention, irrespective of how many others are subjected to the same or similar measures'.

[524] Among examples cited by Hathaway and Foster (n 3) 174, is *Wackowski v INS* [1999] US App LEXIS 26590.

[525] e.g. in *R v SSHD ex parte S Jeyakumaran* [1985] Unreported, QBD CO/290/84 (Taylor, J); see also James Crawford and Patricia Hyndman, 'Three Heresies in the Application of the Refugee Convention' (1989) 1 IJRL 152. The latter also note that, already in 1990, the US Asylum Regulations had explicitly dispensed with such a requirement and recognised that persecution could be established if an applicant could show a 'pattern or practice ... of persecution of a group persons similarly situated to the applicant'. See also Anker (n 33) §2.11, 84–85.

[526] Goodwin-Gill and McAdam (3rd edn) (n 25) 129; Goodwin-Gill and McAdam (4th edn) (n 26) 152–53; Zimmermann and Mahler (n 1) 369.

[527] Jackson (n 17) 85; Statement of Mr Henkin of the United States, Ad Hoc Committee on Statelessness and Related Problems, First Session: Summary Record of the Third Meeting Held at Lake Success, New York, on Tuesday, 17 January 1950, at 3 p.m. (n 34) paras 42–46.

[528] Hathaway and Foster (n 3) 175.

[529] ibid.

(civilians, an ethnic group, a family etc.) can in certain circumstances harm each of its constituent parts also.[530]

However, the existence of persecution merely by virtue of membership of a group is not a state of affairs established a priori. It depends on there being evidence establishing that the oppression directed at the group is such that it can be reasonably inferred that any individual member will suffer it too. As stated by Goodwin-Gill and McAdam in relation to the example of punishment under a law of general application, '[w]hether a well-founded fear of persecution exists will depend upon an examination of the class of persons in fact affected, of the interest in respect of which they stand to be punished, of the likelihood of punishment, and the nature and extent of the penalties'.[531] In such a situation, if a person is not specifically targeted, the evidence must suffice to indicate that the effect of the persecutory act (e.g. if aimed at a group) is reasonably likely to impact adversely on the applicant. Citing a US case, Zimmermann and Mahler state that '[t]he greater the risk to all members of the group and the more evidence there is confirming the persecution of the group as such, the less evidence of individualised persecution must be adduced by the refugee claimant'.[532]

### 3.10.2 Prima facie recognition

How does the concept of group persecution relate to what is known as 'prima facie recognition', a practice often applied in mass influx situations? This is a highly pertinent question, not least because this is the mechanism by which the majority of refugees in the developing world are granted status. For Jackson, the two concepts of group persecution and prima facie recognition have always overlapped and are in essence the same.[533] That view remains the subject of debate. According to Okoth-Obbo, prima facie recognition amounts to a merely provisional decision regarding refugee status.[534] For Jackson and Bonaventura and UNHCR in its 2015 Guidelines, by contrast, prima facie recognition, whilst presumptive, is nevertheless conclusive.[535]

It is unnecessary for the purposes of this book to seek to resolve this debate. It can certainly be said, however, that if prima facie recognition entails a finding of group persecution under the refugee definition, the language of this doctrine is somewhat odd. If, as the UNHCR Guidelines and other proponents of this view propound, prima facie recognition means that individual persecution of all those in the group is 'presumed' even though not 'individually established',[536] then it is surely still a prima facie

---

[530] Case C-465/07 *Meki Elgafaji and Noor Elgafaji v Staatssecretaris van Justitie* [2009] ECLI:EU:C:2009:94; Case C-285/12 *Aboubacar Diakité v Commissaire général aux réfugiés et aux apatrides* [2014] ECLI:EU:C:2014:39.

[531] Goodwin-Gill and McAdam (3rd edn) (n 25) 129.

[532] Zimmermann and Mahler (n 1) 369–70, citing *Kotasz v INS* [1994] 31 F.3d 849.

[533] Jackson (n 17) 464, chronicles that after the adoption of the UNHCR Statue and the Refugee Convention, the 1950/51 definitions were 'very liberally applied both as regards individuals and groups'.

[534] See George Okoth-Obbo, 'Thirty Years On: A Legal Review of the 1969 OAU Convention Governing the Specific Aspects of Refugee Problems in Africa' (2001) 20(1) RSQ 79, cited by Bonaventure Rutinwa, 'Prima Facie Status and Refugee Protection' (2002) UNHCR, New Issues in Refugee Research, Working Paper No 69, 3. Rutinwa himself sides with Jackson.

[535] UNHCR, Guidelines on International Protection No 11: Prima Facie Recognition of Refugee Status (24 June 2015) UN Doc HCR/GIP/15/11; Rutinwa (n 534) 6; Jackson (n 17) 375.

[536] Jackson (n 17) 375.

presumption, not something established in the individual case. Being a presumption, it can be rebutted, if, to use the language of paragraph 18 of the 2015 UNHCR Guidelines, 'there is evidence to the contrary in the individual case'. At paragraph 19, more than one example is given where evidence to the contrary concerns failure to meet the requirements of Article 1A(2).

### 3.10.3 Armed conflict and generalised violence

Situations of armed conflict or generalised violence can engender individual and sometimes group persecution. Given the Refugee Convention's origins in the Second World War, it is curious how refugee law has often struggled to accept that such situations can fall within the scope of Article 1A(2). There have been two main reasons for this. First, despite the drafters making clear that the refugee definition could cover group as well as individual persecution,[537] discussions of the limits of the definition (where there was a felt concern to ensure the definition did not create a 'blank cheque') sometimes identified persons fleeing armed conflict as an example of cases falling *outside* its limits. Oft cited in this regard is the statement from Mr Robinson, the Israeli representative, that there was 'no provision' in the refugee definition 'for refugees fleeing from hostilities unless they were otherwise covered by article 1 of the Convention'.[538]

This sentiment was echoed by UNHCR it its 1979 Handbook at paragraph 164 as follows:

> Persons compelled to leave their country of origin as a result of international or national armed conflicts are not normally considered refugees under the 1951 Convention or 1967 Protocol.[539]

Second, closely tied to the issue of the need to establish a Convention reason for persecution, the view took hold that in order to show persecution itself (not just the reasons for it) there was a need to show that the harms involved were over and above those arising in times of war—an 'exceptionality approach'.[540] This undoubtedly reflected prevailing conceptions of state sovereignty that included, as one of its core aspects, the right to self-defence and the right to require citizens in wartime to fight. It also reflected international humanitarian law and IHRL, neither of which proscribes killing in the course of war or armed conflict as such.[541]

One influential academic source expressing the view in the 1990s that those affected by armed conflict and generalised violence are not normally to be considered as refugees was Hathaway. Citing several contemporary scholars, he stated that: '[v]ictims of

---

[537] See p. 397.
[538] Conference of Plenipotentiaries on the Status of Refugees and Stateless Persons: Summary Record of the Twenty-second Meeting (n 27).
[539] UNHCR Handbook (n 60) para 164.
[540] Kees Wouters, 'Conflict Refugees' in Costello et al (n 61) 820–22. See also Hugo Storey, 'Armed Conflict in Asylum Law: The "War Flaw"' (2012) 31(2) RSQ 1; and Vanessa Holzer, 'The 1951 Refugee Convention and the Protection of Persons Fleeing Armed Conflict and Other Situations of Violence' (September 2012) UNHCR, Legal and Protection Policy Research Series, PPLA/2012/05; Goodwin-Gill and McAdam (n 26) 149–53.
[541] See Kälin and Künzli (n 107) 271. See p. 323.

war and conflict are not refugees unless they are subject to differential victimisation based on civil or political status'.[542] It was this insistence on differential victimisation that was subsequently drawn on (not necessarily accurately) in the decision of the UK House of Lords in *Adan*.[543] Lord Slynn of Hadley stated that in a situation where law and order had broken down and every group was fighting some other group or groups in an endeavour to gain power, 'the individual or group has to show a well-founded fear of persecution over and above the risk to life and liberty inherent in civil war.[544]

However, whilst this view came in for heavy criticism in two other common law jurisdictions[545] and whilst the UK Tribunal subsequently expressed the view that *Adan* had now to be read in light of later adoption by the same court of a human rights approach,[546] it still cannot be said that the state practice on this issue—either common law or civil law—has brought itself fully into line with international law norms.[547] Within Europe, one of the paradoxical effects of the EU's QD, is that even in situations of war and conflict that would appear to warrant a finding of persecution, decision makers have sometimes tended to treat such cases as falling solely under the 'subsidiary protection' regime, Article 15(c) of the QD in particular, disregarding potentially valid claims for refugee status.[548] At the same time, there is at least now much more consensus in the wider literature, as has been crystallised in the 2016 'Guidelines on International Protection No 12,[549] that applicants from countries beset by armed conflict and violence may satisfy all the requirements of the refugee definition. At paragraph 17, these Guidelines state that '[i]n situations of armed conflict and violence, an applicant may be at risk of being singled out or targeted for persecution. Equally, in such situations, entire groups or populations may be at risk of persecution.' At paragraph 22, there is express rejection of the comparative-based notion of 'differential risk':

> As mentioned in paragraph 17 of these Guidelines, a person may have a well-founded fear of persecution that is shared by many others, and of a similar or same degree. An applicant fleeing a situation of armed conflict and violence is not required to establish a risk of harm over and above that of others similarly situated (sometimes called a 'differential test'). No higher level of risk is required to establish a well-founded

---

[542] Hathaway (n 4) 185. His current, more nuanced, position is set out in Hathaway and Foster (n 3) 174–81.
[543] *Adan v SSHD* [1999] 1 AC 293; see also *Romain Kibiti v SSHD*.
[544] *Adan* (n 543).
[545] *Refugee Appeal No 71462* [1999] NZRSAA; and *Minister for Information v Haji Ibrahim* [2000] HCA 55.
[546] *AM & AM (armed conflict: risk categories)* Somalia CG [2008] UKAIT 00091.
[547] For a survey of case law, see Hathaway and Foster (n 3) 174–81. Among cases that have recognised persecution can occur in the context of civil war, they cite at ibid 177–78 a decision of the German Administrative Court in Wurzburg: *Ger.VG Wurzburg W K92.30416 446.11* [1994].
[548] See UNHCR, 'Safe at Last? Law and Practice in Selected EU Member States with Respect to Asylum-Seekers Fleeing Indiscriminate Violence' (July 2011). Madeline Garlick, 'Protection in the European Union for People Fleeing Indiscriminate Violence in Armed Conflict: Article 15(c) of the EU Qualification Directive' in Volker Türk, Alice Edwards, and Cornelis Wouters (eds), *In Flight from Conflict and Violence UNHCR's Consultations on Refugee Status and Other Forms of International Protection* (CUP and UNHCR 2017). This is paradoxical because the subsidiary protection regime was intended to provide protection that is 'complementary and additional to' refugee protection (recital 33).
[549] UNHCR, Guidelines No 12 (n 500).

fear of persecution in situations of armed conflict and violence compared to other situations.[550]

The UNHCR Guidelines underscore that IHRL also enjoins a non-comparative approach (to assessing in what circumstances situations of armed conflict and generalised violence can constitute persecution), in relation to the prohibition of ill treatment and protection of the right to life. They correctly note that under IHRL, such situations are capable of creating for individuals a real risk of severe human rights violations merely by being part of a particular group, as the ECtHR acknowledged in *NA v United Kingdom* could happen '[e]xceptionally, in cases where an applicant alleges that he or she is a member of a group systematically exposed to a practice of ill-treatment.'[551]

At paragraph, 13 the 2016 UNHCR Guidelines observe that:

Situations of armed conflict and violence frequently involve exposure to serious human rights violations or other serious harm amounting to persecution. Such persecution could include, but is not limited to, situations of genocide and ethnic cleansing; torture and other forms of inhuman or degrading treatment; rape and other forms of sexual violence; forced recruitment, including of children; arbitrary arrest and detention; hostage taking and enforced or arbitrary disappearances; and a wide range of other forms of serious harm resulting from circumstances mentioned, for example, in paragraphs 18 and 19 of these Guidelines.[552]

There continues to be debate over to what extent, if at all, the concept of 'being persecuted' in the context of armed conflict and generalised violence can be informed by IHL norms. Whilst this debate has clarified that IHL norms are not to be treated as a 'starting point' in such situations,[553] few contend that they have no role.

In the view of this author, the ongoing debate over this issue creates something of a dilemma for the human rights approach. Most, if not all, of the critics of the referencing of IHL norms in such situations appear to concur that at a general level a human rights approach needs to be taken to the meaning of 'being persecuted'. That being so, it cannot be ignored that when dealing with situations of armed conflict and generalised violence, IHRL itself has regard to IHL norms.[554] It is increasingly the

---

[550] ibid para 22. Among the cases cited in support is *Surajnarain and Others v Minister of Citizenship and Immigration* [2008] FC 1165, para 17.

[551] *NA v United Kingdom* (n 347) para 116; see also *Sufi and Elmi v United Kingdom* (n 205); and *LM and Others v Russia* Apps Nos 40081/14, 40088/14 and 40127/14 (ECtHR, 15 October 2015). Other ECtHR cases dealing with armed conflict where breaches of Articles 2 and 3 were at issue (but not in the context of risk on return) include *Isayeva, Yusupova, and Bazayeva v Russia* Apps Nos 57947/00, 57948/00, and 57949/00 (ECtHR, 6 July 2005) paras 168–200, building, inter alia, on *Ergi v Turkey* App No 23818/94 (ECtHR, 28 July 1998).

[552] UNHCR, Guidelines No 12: Claims for refugee status related to situations of armed conflict and violence (n 500) para 13.

[553] Reuven (Ruvi) Ziegler, 'International Humanitarian Law and Refugee Protection' in Costello et al (n 61) 226–27. After a survey of the recent literature, Ziegler considers that '[t]he healthy scepticism with which scholars and decision-makers approach references to IHL terms-of-art in refugee protection contexts [(earlier he highlights in this connection the term civilian)] is justified'. For a similar view, see also Goodwin-Gill and McAdam (n 26) 149–52.

[554] The most clear-cut example of such regard in the treaty context is Article 38(1) of the Convention on the Rights of the Child (adopted 20 November 1989, entered into force 2 September 1990) 1577 UNTS

case that IHRL itself has come to recognize that IHL rules—or close analogues of the same—can be relevant to interpretation of applicable human rights norms.[555] Further, IHLR works within the wider framework of international law and the latter regards the *lex specialis* as sometimes being, not IHRL, but IHL,[556] and in certain contexts international criminal law.[557] The two bodies of law—IHRL and IHL—are seen as complementary and reinforcing.[558] Critics of referencing of IHL norms in relation to persecution have done much to clarify the differences between IHL and international refugee law (IRL),[559] but cannot presumably mean to treat IHL norms as irrelevant to analysing situations of armed conflict in a refugee law context, especially when such norms have the status of customary international law and identify war crimes.[560]

## 4 Temporal Scope

It was noted earlier that for convenience (what may be termed) the modality of temporal scope would be addressed in a specific subsection. Also noted was that analysing 'being persecuted' in terms of 'acts' or 'measures' of persecution does not restrict the temporal scope of the refugee definition, unless such terms are read in unduly narrow fashion.[561] Since much relating to temporal scope will be covered in Chapter 11 on the 'well-founded fear' element of the refugee definition, what is said here can be kept very brief.

---

3: 'State parties undertake to respect and ensure respect for rules of international humanitarian law applicable to them in armed conflicts which are relevant to the child.'

[555] See e.g. *Isayeva, Yusopova, and Bazayeva v Russia* (n 551); *Sufi and Elmi v United Kingdom* (n 205) para 241; *Khatsiyeva and Others v Russia* App No 5108/02 (ECtHR, 17 January 2008); *Varnava and Others v Turkey* Apps Nos 16064/90, 16065/90, 16066/90, et al (ECtHR [GC], 18 September 2009) para 130; *Kerimova and Others v Russia* Apps Nos 17170/04, 20792/04, 22448/04, 23360/04, 5681/05, and 5684/05 (ECtHR, 3 May 2011) para 251; *KAB v Sweden* App No 886/11 (ECtHR, 5 September 2013) paras 77–79; *Case of Santo Domingo Massacre v Colombia*, Preliminary objections, Merits and Reparations, IAmCtHR Series C No 259 (24 November 2009) para 216. See also Orna Ben-Naftali (ed), *International Humanitarian Law and International Human Rights Law* (OUP 2011).
[556] In *Legality of the Threat or Use of Nuclear Weapons* (n 123) para 25. See also *Legal Consequences of the Construction of a Wall in the Occupied Palestinian Territory* (n 123) para 36; and *Armed Activities on the Territory of the Congo (the Democratic Republic of the Congo v Uganda)* (n 123) para 168.
[557] UNHCR Guidelines No 12 (n 500) para 15 state that IHL norms can help inform the meaning of the refugee definition. For a fuller treatment, see Storey (n 540); and Holzer (n 540). See further, Moreno-Lax (n 125); Ziegler (n 553) 221–39; Goodwin-Gill and McAdam (4th edn) (n 26) 151–52.
[558] See HRC, General Comment No 29 (n 424) and HRC, General Comment No 31: Nature of the General Legal Obligation Imposed on States Parties to the Covenant (26 May 2004) UN Doc CCPR/C/21/Rev.1/Add.13. See also Commission of Human Rights, Resolution 2005/63: Protection of the Human Rights of Civilians in Armed Conflicts (20 April 2005) UN Doc E/CN.4/RES/2005/63; and Human Rights Council, Report of the Office of the High Commissioner on the Outcome of the Expert Consultation on the Issue of Protecting the Human Rights of Civilians in Armed Conflict (2 June 2010) UN Doc A/HRC/11/40.
[559] See e.g. Ziegler (n 553) 222–24.
[560] Yet just such appears to be suggested by Ziegler (n 553) 225 ('when treaty norms are clearly designed to achieve different purposes, relying on an external norms risks undermining the treaty's object and purpose'). Wouters (n 540) 818 notes that the compulsory, forced, and voluntary conscription of enlistment of children into any kind of armed force or armed group and the use of children under the age of fifteen in hostilities qualifies as a war crime under the Rome Statute of the ICC, Arts 8(2)(b) (xxvi) and (e)(vii).
[561] See p. 361.

## 4.1 Current Persecution

It is often said that Article 1A(2) is future-oriented or forward-looking. The justification for this is that it is cast in the present tense and concerns fear. Being concerned with fear, the definition contemplates, as part of the condition of 'being persecuted',[562] what is to come. Understanding it as future-oriented is consistent with at least one of the ordinary meanings of that term and also accords with the Convention's object(s) and purpose(s) and with the principle of surrogacy. In contrast to Article 1A(1) dealing largely with statutory refugees, an almost entirely historical category, Article 1A(2) was clearly intended to be forward-looking, designed to provide for those who could demonstrate that their need for protection was current and ongoing. As noted by Hathaway and others in the *Michigan Guidelines on the Internal Protection Alternative*, April 1999:

> There is no justification in international law to refuse recognition of refugee status on the basis of a purely retrospective assessment of conditions at the time of an asylum-seeker's departure from the home State. The duty of protection under the Refugee Convention is explicitly premised on a prospective evaluation of risk. That is, an individual is a Convention refugee only if she or he would presently be at risk of persecution in the State of origin, whatever the circumstances at the time of departure from the home State.[563]

Reinforcing the centrality of the notion of current persecution, the first paragraph of Article 1C(5) identifies the point of cessation of refugee status as being 'because the circumstances in connexion with which he has been recognised as a refugee have ceased to exist' and this is contrasted in the second paragraph with 'compelling reasons arising out of previous persecution'.

## 4.2 *Sur Place* Persecution

It is a logical corollary of the focus in Article 1A(2) on current fear of persecution that a person can have such a fear arising out of events or his own actions that have occurred since departure from the country of origin.[564] As highlighted in the 1979 UNHCR Handbook, it is not necessary that a person must have left his country on account of a well-founded fear: '[a] person becomes a refugee "*sur place*" due to circumstances arising in his country of origin during his absence'. In addition, a person may become a refugee '*sur place*' as a result of his own actions.[565] Within Europe, the QD codifies both these scenarios: Article 5(1) QD (recast) states that a well-founded fear of being persecuted may be based on events which have taken place since the

---

[562] The same present passive voice is also employed in the French text of the Convention '*d'être persécutée*'.
[563] James C Hathaway, 'International Refugee Law: The Michigan Guidelines on the Internal Protection Alternative' (1999) 21(1) Michigan Journal of International Law 131, 131.
[564] Anker (n 33) 64–69.
[565] UNHCR Handbook (n 60) paras 95–96. See also Hathaway (n 4) 33–39; Goodwin-Gill and McAdam (3rd edn) (n 25) 63; Anker (n 33) §2.7, 75–80.

applicant left the country of origin; Article 5(2) states that a well-founded fear of being persecuted or a real risk of suffering serious harm may be based on activities which the applicant has engaged in since he or she left the country of origin.[566]

The first scenario (which is sometimes called 'objective refugees *sur place*') has not caused particular difficulties of interpretation.[567] The same cannot be said for the second (sometimes called the notion of 'subjective refugees *sur place*'). In respect of the latter, it could be said that the inclusion within the refugee definition of the notion of 'willingness' to avail oneself of protection confirms the role of voluntary choice and hence allows for *sur place* claims based on an applicant's own activities in the host state. However, it has given rise to divergent understandings, with some considering that such claims are subject to a requirement of 'good faith' that excludes opportunistic activities engaged in for the sole or main purpose of creating the necessary conditions for refugeehood.[568] Within the EU, it might have been thought that the wording of Article 4(3)(d) of the QD resolved the issue, in that it clearly contemplates that assessment of even opportunistic activities must still 'assess whether those activities would expose the applicant to persecution or serious harm if returned to that country'. However, some commentators consider the QD leaves the issue unclear.[569] UNHCR's position has strongly rejected the 'good faith' requirement. Thus, its Guidelines No 6 state that:

> Under all circumstances, however, consideration must be given as to the consequences of return to the country of origin and any potential harm that might justify refugee status or a complementary form of protection. In the event that the claim is found to be self-serving but the claimant nonetheless has a well-founded fear of persecution on return, international protection is required.[570]

Some states have introduced national law provisions that impose a good faith requirement, overriding domestic case law.[571] Save for New Zealand,[572] the case law in common law jurisdictions has rejected the good faith requirement. Leaving aside Grahl-Madsen, application of a good faith requirement has also been rejected in leading textbooks.[573]

---

[566] QD (recast) (n 8). The requirement in both Article 5(1) and (2) that the applicant must have 'left the country of origin' is arguably too narrowly drawn, as it is possible that an applicant may never have been in the country of origin: see p. 264, p. 266, p. 268, p. 270, and p. 271.
[567] Zimmermann and Mahler (n 1) 324–32; Goodwin-Gill and McAdam (4th edn) (n 26) 120–23. The latter note that the Convention does not specify where the threat of persecution must take place.
[568] Zimmermann and Mahler (n 1) 330–34; Goodwin-Gill and McAdam (4th edn) (n 26) 83–86, 120–03.
[569] Goodwin-Gill and McAdam (4th edn) (n 26) 85–86.
[570] UNHCR, Guidelines No 6: Religion-Based Refugee Claims under Article 1A(2) of the 1951 Convention and/or the 1967 Protocol relating to the Status of Refugees (2004) UN Doc HCR/GIP/04/06, para 36. See also UNHCR, Interpreting Article 1 of the 1951 Convention (n 24) para 34; UNHCR, *Amicus curiae* of the UNHCR on the interpretation and application of 'sur place' claims within the meaning of Article 1A(2) of the 1951 Convention Relating to the Status of Refugees (14 February 2017) paras 20, 28.
[571] See e.g. New Zealand Immigration Act 2009, s 134(3) and s 140; Australian Migration Act, as amended in 2014, s 91R(3), now s 5J(6). The effect of the latter would appear to be to require decision makers to disregard purely 'bad faith' *sur place* activities when assessing risk: see Guide to Refugee Law in Australia (2021) 17–23.
[572] See *Refugee Appeal No 2254/94 Re HB* [1994] NZRSAA.
[573] See e.g. *Danian v SSHD* [1999] EWCA Civ 3000; *YB (Eritrea) v SSHD* [2008] EWCA Civ 360; *FV v Refugee Appeals Tribunal & Anor* [2009] IEHC 268; *Hou v Canada (MCI)* [2012] FCJ No 1083. Under

## 4.3 Past Persecution

As already noted, Article 1A(2)'s notion of current persecution is juxtaposed with a specific reference to 'previous persecution' in Article 1C(5), second paragraph.

The requirement that persecution be current persecution has as another corollary that past persecution does not in itself show that one has a well-founded fear of 'being persecuted' in the present.[574]

That is not to say, of course, that past persecution is irrelevant and, as we shall note later, it can be a serious indication of the likelihood that acts of persecution will be repeated. The QD recast has codified this insight in Article 4(4):

> The fact that an applicant has already been subject to persecution or serious harm, is a serious indication of the applicant's well-founded fear of persecution or real risk of suffering serious harm, unless there are good reasons to consider that such persecution or serious harm will not be repeated.[575]

Some commentators have attempted to construe this provision to mean that establishing past persecution constitutes presumptive proof of future persecution and indeed in some national asylum systems that is the position;[576] but consensus on this further point is lacking.

In any event, there is no basis for considering that the concept of persecution should be different in relation to past or current persecution.[577]

---

this case law, however, applicants seen to act in bad faith face serious evidential hurdles in establishing well-founded fear. See also Grahl-Madsen (n 15) 248, 251–52; Hathaway and Foster (n 3) 88–90; Goodwin-Gill and McAdam (4th edn) (n 26) 83–86, 120-3; Penelope Mathew, 'Limiting Good Faith: "Bootstrapping" Asylum Seekers and Exclusion from Refugee Protection' (2010) 29 Australian Yearbook of International Law 135; IARLJ, 'A Manual for Refugee Law Judges Relating to the QD and APD'. It is possible this issue may be addressed by the CJEU in the pending preliminary reference, *J.F. v Bundesamt für Fremdenwesen und Asyl* (C-222/22): on the latter, see UNHCR, 'Statement on the interpretation of Article 5(3) of the EU Qualification Directive regarding subsequent applications for international protection based on *sur place* religious conversion: Issued in the context of the preliminary ruling reference to the Court of Justice of the European Union in the case of *J.F. v. Bundesamt für Fremdenwesen und Asyl* (C-222/22)' (3 February 2023) available at <https://www.refworld.org/docid/63dd3b214.html>.

[574] Encouraged by the exhortation in para 136 of the UNHCR Handbook (n 60), attempts have been made to argue that there is an exception relating to atrocious past persecution, which can be extrapolated from Article 1C(5) of the 1951 Convention which refers to compelling compassionate circumstances that militate against return for persons 'able to invoke compelling reasons arising out of previous persecution'. Such attempts have now been lent significant support by the introduction in the recast Qualification Directive recast of a clause which exempts from the cessation provisions 'a refugee who is able to invoke compelling reasons arising out of previous persecution for refusing to avail himself or herself of the protection of the country of nationality or, being a stateless person, of the country of former habitual residence' (Article 11(3)). However, this appears to be an example of European asylum legislators acting in effect under Article 5 of the 1951 Convention by creating more generous provision. In the text of the 1951 Convention, Article 1C(5) only applies to statutory refugees and hence it cannot impact on the Article 1A(2) definition. See *Adan* (n 543); and *Hoxha* (n 64).

[575] QD (n 8).

[576] e.g. in the US see Anker (n 33) 55, 69: 'Under U.S. law, past persecution is presumptive proof of future persecution.'

[577] ibid 70. At footnote 2, she cites *Osorio v INS* [1996] 99 F.3d 928, para 932, rejecting an immigration judge holding that the past persecution must be particularly severe to qualify an applicant for asylum.

## 5 Conclusions

This chapter, the first of three dealing with what most agree is the 'core element' of the refugee definition, has focussed on persecution as a form of harm.

In light of the discussion in Chapter 1 of 'further definition' of terms left undefined in Article 1A(2), it is reiterated that the principal objections to further definition of persecution bite only against certain approaches, in particular an 'absolutist' or 'fixed-list' approach.

Having reiterated the validity of seeking 'further definition' of key terms such as 'being persecuted', Section 1 considered what light is shed on the meaning of being persecuted by application of VCLT rules. It was concluded that there is no unambiguous ordinary meaning, although dictionary definitions do contain certain pointers. In terms of context on its own, it was concluded that other provisions of the Convention shed only limited light on the term's meaning and that attempts over the years to treat Article 33(1) of the 1951 Convention as determinative of the meaning of the term have rightly been discredited. Object and purpose was seen as the most important interpretive consideration in relation to the meaning of 'being persecuted', particularly (but not exclusively) by indicating the need for a human rights approach.

Section 2 concentrated on personal and material scope. With regard to personal scope, it was reiterated that the refugee definition is properly termed 'universal', at least since the removal by the 1967 Protocol of the temporal and geographical limitation. In relation to material scope, the main types of harm involved in acts of persecution were identified and analysed: physical violence and related harms; psychological and related harms; socio-economic harms; cultural harms; and environmental harms. Also analysed were the main specific forms of persecution, in terms of gender-specific, age- and child-specific, sexual orientation-specific, and disability-specific acts. Whilst in each instance the advantages of a human rights approach to these types of harm were highlighted, it was pointed out that alternative approaches have broadly identified them in similar fashion.

Section 3 focussed on the modalities of persecution in terms of acts of persecution and actors, both state and non-state, of persecution. Analysis was made of laws and related measures, these being the main structural medium through which state authorities ordinarily operate.

Part 4 analysed the main 'incidents' of persecution, considering the role of individual assessment; intensity (including the distinction between persecution and discrimination); actual or threatened harm; indirect or derivative harm; duration; intentionality; and individualisation (individual and group persecution).

Section 5 gave brief coverage of temporal scope, which is dealt with more fully in Chapter 11 on well-founded fear. It was explained why the 'being persecuted' element of the definition centres on current risk by means of a forward-looking assessment. Specific attention was given to one corollary of the concept of current persecution, namely *sur place* claims. Consideration was then given to the significance of past persecution.

It remains to consider, whether, drawing on the analysis set out in foregoing sections, it is possible to identify any 'basic propositions' that can be treated as having achieved wide agreement. Some consideration needs also to be given to whether the analysis carried out in this chapter yields any 'suggested propositions' that might assist the task of resolving issues that remain unsettled.

Drawing on this chapter's analysis, the following basic propositions can be identified.

## 5.1 Basic Propositions

1. The personal scope of the refugee definition is universal.
2. Determining whether an applicant is 'being persecuted' requires assessment relative to the individual.
3. The 'being persecuted' element requires human agency and is to be analysed in terms of acts or measures of persecution.
4. Actors of persecution can be state or non-state actors.
5. Laws and related measures (including laws of general application) can be persecutory in certain circumstances.
6. In order to rise to the level of the persecutory, harm must attain the level of sufficient seriousness or severity. Whilst discrimination can be persecutory in itself, more commonly it will not be persecutory unless established by reference to a number of cumulative harms.
7. Discrimination is not a necessary condition of 'being persecuted'.
8. Persecutory harm can be actual or threatened.
9. Persecutory harm can sometimes be indirect or derivative.
10. Acts or measures can be said to be persecutory even though directed, not at a person individually, but at a group of which the individual is a member.
11. The refugee definition allows for group persecution.
12. Among situations that can engender the phenomenon of group persecution are situations of armed conflict or generalised violence.
13. In terms of temporal scope, Article 1A(2) imposes a requirement of current persecution: it poses the hypothetical question of whether, if return were to take place now (*ex nunc*), persecution would arise.
14. It is a logical corollary of the focus in Article 1A(2) on current fear of persecution that a person can have a '*sur place*' fear, i.e. a fear arising out of events or his own actions that have occurred since the applicant has been outside the country of origin.
15. Past persecution does not in itself constitute 'being persecuted', but the fact that an applicant has already been subject to persecution is a serious indication of such, unless there are good reasons to consider that such persecution will not be repeated.

## 5.2 Suggested Propositions

On the basis of this author's own evaluation, the following would appear to be propositions offering a way forward in resolution of issues that remain unsettled.

1. Applying VCLT rules, interpretation of the meaning of 'being persecuted' requires giving priority to 'object and purpose' considerations.
2. Application of VCLT rules confirms that the human rights approach to the 'being persecuted' element of the refugee definition is the dominant approach.
3. The meaning of 'being persecuted' is usefully elucidated by considering the modalities of persecution, including in terms of acts and actors of persecution.
4. Use of the phrase 'being persecuted' focuses inquiry on the predicament of the refugee.
5. The human agency necessary for an act to be persecutory must be shown to be a substantial if not a predominant cause.
6. Understanding that different types of harms can be persecutory—especially physical and related harms; psychological and related harms; socio-economic, and cultural harms; and environmental harms—is enhanced by a human rights approach.
7. Harms carried out by non-state actors only become persecutory if the state is unwilling or unable to provide effective protection against such harms.
8. As part of the consideration of material scope, it is necessary to have regard to forms of persecution that are specific to certain categories of person, especially age- and child-specific persecution; gender-specific persecution; LGBTI+-specific persecution, and disability-specific persecution. Such consideration is vital in order to ensure that the 'being persecuted' element is interpreted in a way that is sensitive to individual vulnerabilities.
9. 'Persecutory intent' is not a necessary requirement of 'being persecuted'.
10. In *sur place* claims there is no requirement of 'good faith'.

# 7
# 'Being Persecuted' and Protection
## ('Etre persécutée' et protection)

1. Protection and the Notion of Surrogacy — 410
   1.1 The Notion of Surrogacy and VCLT Rules — 411
   1.2 Is Surrogacy a Key Principle? — 415
   1.3 Criticisms — 415
       1.3.1 Ordinary meaning — 416
       1.3.2 Primary purpose — 416
       1.3.3 Relationship between national and substitute protection — 416
       1.3.4 State responsibility — 417
       1.3.5 Impact on role of the individual — 417
       1.3.6 Unduly burdensome nature — 418
       1.3.7 Differences over location of the notion in elements of the refugee definition — 419
   1.4 The Notion of Surrogacy Re-Examined — 420
       1.4.1 Ordinary meaning — 420
       1.4.2 Purpose — 420
       1.4.3 Poor fit? — 421
       1.4.4 State responsibility — 421
       1.4.5 Displacement of the role of the individual? — 421
       1.4.6 Unduly burdensome — 422
       1.4.7 Location arguments — 423
       1.4.8 Conclusions on surrogacy — 424
2. Persecution and Protection—Interrelationship — 424
   2.1 Historical Background — 424
   2.2 Arguments Against Treating the Two Terms as Interdependent — 426
       2.2.1 Contrary to ordinary meaning — 427
       2.2.2 Contrary to how human rights law works — 427
       2.2.3 Reliance on misplaced state responsibility tests — 428
       2.2.4 Displacement of the importance of individual assessment — 429
       2.2.5 Unduly burdensome — 429
       2.2.6 The claimed advantage for understanding of causal nexus is illusory — 430
       2.2.7 Argument that protection considerations belongs in 'well-founded fear' limb — 430
   2.3 The Interrelationship Evaluated — 431
       2.3.1 Ordinary meaning — 431
       2.3.2 Does human rights law work like this? — 432
       2.3.3 Unwarranted reliance on state responsibility tests? — 435
       2.3.4 Displacement of individual assessment? — 438
       2.3.5 Unduly burdensome? — 439
       2.3.6 Is the causal nexus argument illusory? — 440
       2.3.7 Location of the protection test in the 'well-founded fear' element? — 441
3. Meaning of Protection — 442
   3.1 Multiple Uses — 442
   3.2 Connection with Protection in the Availment Clause — 443
   3.3 Background — 444
   3.4 The Human Rights Approach to Protection — 445
   3.5 Protection and State Structures — 448
   3.6 State Protection — 449
   3.7 Meaning of State and its Basic Duty to Protect — 449
       3.7.1 International law relating to state-individual relationship — 450
       3.7.2 International law on statehood — 452
       3.7.3 International law of state responsibility — 453
       3.7.4 Customary international law — 454
       3.7.5 Soft-law sources on protection — 455
   3.8 International Human Rights Law — 456
   3.9 The Duty to Protect — 457
   3.10 Protection Other than by the State — 458
       3.10.1 Main arguments against — 458
       3.10.2 Arguments evaluated — 458
       3.10.3 The significance of Article 1D protection — 458

| | | | | |
|---|---|---|---|---|
| 3.10.4 | Inherent problems with such entities in terms of stability, durability, etc. | 459 | 3.12 Effectiveness of Protection and the Role of Civil Society Actors | 466 |
| | | | 3.12.1 Evaluation | 468 |
| 3.10.5 | Lack of accountability | 460 | 3.12.2 The role of civil society actors and functions | 469 |
| 3.10.6 | Tension with the principle of surrogacy | 463 | **4 Conclusions** | **471** |
| 3.11 | Protection and Failed States | 463 | 4.1 Basic Propositions | 472 |
| 3.11.1 | Partially failed states | 464 | 4.2 Suggested Propositions | 472 |
| 3.11.2 | Fully failed states | 465 | | |

# 1 Protection and the Notion of Surrogacy

Having addressed in Chapter 6 the 'being persecuted' element of the refugee definition understood in terms of serious harm, attention turns in this chapter to analysing its interrelationship with the notion of protection against that harm. Here too the inquiry is animated by two main objects: to inquire what basic propositions there are regarding this aspect of the definition (if any) that can now be taken as agreed upon; and to provide the author's own analysis of it.

A most curious problem to start with is that although everyone talks about protection, it is not always clear from where within Article 1A(2) this term is to be derived. The obvious source would appear to be what this study calls the 'availment clause, which refers to a person being unable or unwilling to 'avail himself of the protection of that country' ('*ne veut se réclamer de la protection de ce pays*' in the French).[1] Yet by virtue of the concept being seen by many as integral to the meaning of 'being persecuted' in a different part of the definition, that is not always agreed.

There is broad agreement that protection is a concept at the heart of the refugee definition, but precisely how it is interrelated with persecution remains a bone of contention. There are two main views. One is that it is to be understood as a concept entirely distinct from persecution; the other is that it is to be understood as part of the meaning of being persecuted. Often seen as the principal anchor for the latter view is the notion of surrogacy. The essence of this notion is the idea that individuals are not in need of international protection if they can find protection in their home state. This notion has also been seen by some as relevant not simply to the concept of protection but to the refugee definition as a whole.

Given that there continues to be debate about whether the notion of surrogacy should play any role in interpreting the protection-related elements, or indeed any other elements of the refugee definition, it makes sense to explore it first. For some, the notion of surrogacy is to be understood as a principle, but this study will refer to it by the more neutral term 'notion' except where the context makes clear that principle, i.e. notion in a more developed form, is intended.

From the perspective of traditional international law on state sovereignty, which views the relations between the state and its citizens/population as the reserved

---

[1] The term is also used twice in the definition's second paragraph, dealing with multiple nationals: see Chapter 4, section 3.3.

domain of states, the need for surrogate protection represents an exception to this rule.[2] Writing in 1939, Jennings articulated this idea as follows:

> If a legal regime is to be established governing the status of refugees, the first step must be a definition of the term 'refugee'. The normal individual is a national of some state enjoying the protection of the government of that state. There are also some stateless persons who are not legally entitled to claim the protection of any state. A refugee may, or may not, be a stateless person. Quite often he remains a national of the state from which he has had to flee. The peculiarity of the refugee is that he does not in fact enjoy the protection of his state of origin, whether he is legally entitled to such protection or not. He is the victim of a pathological state of society in which the government which would normally form the link between him and international law not only fails to perform that function, but goes out of its way to embarrass him, so that he is actually in need of protection against it. It is this lack of protection, in fact, which is the test of a refugee adopted in all the arrangements and conventions.[3]

Expressed in this basic form, the notion of surrogacy has application regardless of whether the approach taken to it is human rights-based or not,[4] but in modern refugee law it has become closely intertwined with a human rights approach. It is sometimes described as 'substitute' protection, but this appears to be intended merely as a synonym.[5]

## 1.1 The Notion of Surrogacy and VCLT Rules

Treating the notion of surrogacy as relevant to interpreting the refugee definition has been seen to be supported by application of Vienna Convention on the Law of Treaties (VCLT)[6] rules, principally context and object and purpose, but also 'relevant rules of international law' and the *travaux préparatoires* (*travaux*).

Beginning for convenience with the *travaux*, both the Refugee Convention and its predecessor instruments have been widely viewed as conceiving international protection as surrogate protection, since they all envision refugee status as a consequence of

---

[2] Brid Ni Ghrainne, 'The International Protection Alternative Inquiry and Human Rights Considerations—Irrelevant or Indispensable' (2015) 27 IJRL 29, 32 describes the notion of 'surrogate' international protection as 'an exception to the normal principle of international law, that protection is usually the obligation of the country of nationality'.

[3] Robert Jennings, 'Some International Law Aspects of the Refuge Question' (1939) 20 BYIL 98, 111.

[4] There is also a strong argument that for the Convention's drafters surrogacy was conceived primarily in terms of external or diplomatic protection: see Chapter 9, section 2.2.1.

[5] See e.g. Pirkko Kourula, *Broadening the Edges: Refugee Definition and International Protection Revisited* (Martinus Nijhoff 1997) 206 who refers to 'the substitute protection of a State other than the county of origin'. The Court of Justice of the European Union (CJEU) has referred to 'the principle of the subsidiarity of international protection': see Case C-91/20 *LW v Bundesrepublik Deutschland* [2021] ECLI:EU:C:2021:898, para 32. The principle is not unique to refugee law—see e.g. International Commission on Intervention and State Sovereignty, 'The Responsibility to Protect' (2001).

[6] Vienna Convention on the Law of Treaties (VCLT) (adopted 23 May 1969, entered into force 27 January 1980) 1155 UNTS 331.

a lack of state protection.[7] It has also been argued that the decision of the Convention's drafters to exclude 'internal refugees' or 'national refugees', i.e. those internally displaced, reflected an underlying principle of surrogacy since, in the words of Rochefort (France), such persons were 'citizens of a particular country and enjoyed the protection of the government of that country'.[8]

Turning to *ordinary meaning*, whilst the literal text of the refugee definition makes no mention of the notion of surrogacy, it must be borne in mind that if the word 'state' in the availment clause is understood to mean 'home state', then the availment clause can at least be said to readily imply this notion, since it limits refugee status to those able to demonstrate that they are unable or unwilling to avail themselves of the protection of their home state.[9] Further, it has been argued, particularly in the context of the notion of an 'internal protection alternative' (IPA), that the need for surrogate protection is not triggered unless there is an absence of available protection elsewhere within the home state.[10]

In terms of *context*, the fact that in Article 1A(2) second paragraph, dealing with multiple nationals, the drafters saw fit to view an applicant's ability (without valid reasons) to avail himself of 'protection of one of the countries of which he is a national' as disqualifying him from refugee status also tends to support the surrogacy principle.[11] The same can be said for the Preamble's third paragraph (which refers to 'protection accorded by previous international agreements'); its final paragraph (which notes that the United Nations High Commissioner for Refugees (UNHCR) is charged with the task of 'providing for the protection of refugees'); and indeed the kindred Statute of the UNHCR (which refers to 'international protection' as the agency's function).[12] The invocation of 'international protection' can be seen of especial significance in this regard, since it implies a converse, national protection. The references

---

[7] Terje Einarsen, 'Drafting History of the 1951 Convention and the 1967 Protocol' in Andreas Zimmermann (ed), *The 1951 Convention Relating to the Status of Refugees and its 1967 Protocol: A Commentary* (OUP 2011) 44–46.

[8] ECOSOC, Summary Record of the 172nd meeting held at the Palais des Nations, Geneva, on Saturday, 12 August 1950 (24 August 1950) UN Doc E/AC.7/SR.172, 4. For a similar statement made by Mrs Roosevelt, see 4 UN GAOR, Third Committee, Summary Records (2 December 1949); cited by James C Hathaway, *The Law of Refugee Status* (Butterworths Limited 1991) 134. See also Andreas Zimmermann and Claudia Mahler, 'Article 1A, para 2', in Zimmermann (n 7) 448.

[9] Thus Hathaway (n 8) 125, states that the 'surrogate nature of international protection is clear from the text of the Convention itself, which limits refugee status to a person who can demonstrate inability or legitimate unwillingness 'to avail himself of the protection of [the home] state'. On the availment clause, see Chapter 9.

[10] See e.g. Jessica Schultz, *The Internal Protection Alternative in Refugee Law* (Brill Nijhoff 2018) 122 who cites as an exemplar of such an understanding the Australian Federal Court decision in *Randhawa v Minister for Immigration* [1994] 12 ALR 265 in which it stated that if asylum were allowed even if there was a domestic alternative, 'the anomalous situation would exist that the international community would be under an obligation to provide protection outside the borders of the country of nationality even though real protection could be found within those borders'. See p. 481.

[11] See p. 213, p. 218, p. 219, pp. 223–223, and p. 228. The 1979 Handbook dealing with this paragraph states that '[w]herever available, national protection takes precedence over international protection'. See UNHCR, Handbook on Procedures and Criteria for Determining Refugee Status and Guidelines on International Protection under the 1951 Convention and the 1967 Protocol Relating to the Status Of Refugees (Geneva, 2019, reissued in 2019) (UNHCR Handbook or Handbook) para 106.

[12] Statute of the Office of the United Nations High Commissioner for Refugees (1950) UNGA Res 428(v) (UNHCR Statute) ch1(1), para 8.

to protection at the international level presuppose that those seeking it lack it in their own country. Also relevant, as will be explained when addressing object and purpose, is the reference in the first preambular paragraph to human rights.

The cessation clauses could also be said to reflect the notion of surrogacy, in that these clarify that refugee status is only justified if there is a continuing need for international protection and that among the specified ways in which it ceases are when a person voluntarily re-avails himself of the protection of their country of origin (Article 1C(1)); or having acquired a new nationality, enjoys the protection of the country of his new nationality (Article 1C(3)); or when because of changed circumstances, he can no longer continue to refuse to avail himself of the protection of the country of his nationality (Article 1C(5)).[13] Insofar as Article 1E excludes persons who are recognised by the host state as 'having the rights and obligations of the nationality which are attached to the possession of the nationality of that state', it too can also be said to reflect the same underlying notion.

When it comes to *object and purpose*, providing protection at an international level to compensate for its lack at a national level can be understood as an almost self-evident object and purpose. Its rationale is buttressed by drawing on the reference in the Preamble to human rights, since this enables the trigger for surrogate protection to be seen as the failure of the home state to guarantee fundamental rights and freedoms without discrimination sufficient to prevent them from taking flight. It can also be said that the non-refoulement principle enshrined in Article 33(1) makes clear that the Convention's purpose is to prevent the refoulement of any person with a well-founded fear of persecution (and not falling within the exception set out in Article 33(2)) from being returned to any country that cannot protect them.[14]

The dynamic of the human rights framework has also been seen to dovetail with the principle of surrogacy since it rests on a similar notion, namely the subsidiarity of remedies for human rights violations, which requires domestic remedies to take precedence over recourse to human rights treaty remedies.[15]

In terms of Article 31(3) and/or Article 32 VCLT considerations, on the footing that regional arrangements, UNHCR, judicial, and academic sources can at least provide evidence of 'subsequent practice' and/or 'relevant rules of international law' or, if falling

---

[13] See *Applicant A v MIEA* [1997] 190 CLR 225, 233.
[14] Walter Kälin, Martina Caroni, and Lukas Heim, 'Article 33, para 1' in Zimmermann (n 7) 1335.
[15] See e.g. Universal Declaration of Human Rights (adopted 10 December 1948) UNGA Res 217 A(III) (UDHR) Article 8; International Covenant on Civil and Political Rights (adopted 16 December 1966, entered into force 23 March 1976) 999 UNTS 171 (ICCPR) Article 2(3)(a) (which imposes a duty on states to ensure 'that any person whose rights or freedoms as herein recognised are violated shall have an effective remedy'); and International Covenant on Economic, Social and Cultural Rights (adopted 16 December 1966, entered into force 3 January 1976) 993 UNTS 3 (ICESCR) Article 2(1). See also European Convention on Human Rights (adopted 4 November 1950, entered into force 3 September 1953) (ECHR) Article 13; African Charter on Human and Peoples' Rights (adopted 28 June 1981, entered into force 21 October 1986) (ACHPR) Article 7(1)(a) and Article 25. See further the UN Committee on Economic, Social and Cultural Rights, General Comment No 9: The domestic application of the Covenant (3 December 1998) E/C.12/1998/24, para 4, stating that: '[i]n general, legally binding international human rights standards should operate directly and immediately within the domestic legal system of each State party, thereby enabling individuals to seek enforcement of their rights before national courts and tribunals. The rule requiring the exhaustion of domestic remedies reinforces the primacy of national remedies in this respect. The existence

short of that, constitute supplementary means of interpretation under Article 32 VCLT,[16] it is significant that there is very considerable support in all four of the aforementioned sources for according the notion of surrogacy a key role. In EU asylum law, the EU Commission has identified the principle as a key aspect of the refugee definition.[17] The 1979 UNHCR Handbook appears to adopt it. Paragraph 106 states that 'wherever available, national protection takes precedence of international protection'.[18] Paragraph 65 states that:

> [ ... ] [whenever] the protection of the country of nationality is available, and there is no ground based on well-founded fear for refusing it, the person concerned is not in need of international protection and is not a refugee.[19]

Jurisprudence in both common law and civil law systems has long seen the notion to be of key importance (and thus to constitute a principle), the Canadian Supreme Court case of *Ward* being among the first to articulate it. La Forest J's statement in that case that '[t]he international community was meant to be a forum of second resort for the persecuted, a "surrogate" approachable upon failure of local protection' has become one of the most oft-quoted passages in refugee case law.[20] Among the many scholars who have given prominence to this principle are Paul Weis, writing in 1971,[21] Hathaway in his 1991 work, *The Law of Refugee Status* (TLRS), and Hathaway and Foster in the second edition of that work (TLRS2).[22]

All these sources also stand to be considered as supplementary means of interpretation under Article 32 VCLT (alongside the *travaux* which have already been mentioned).

Summing up the above analysis, attaching importance to the notion of surrogacy in seeking to elicit the meaning of the refugee definition can be said to be highly congruent with VCLT rules of interpretation.

and further development of international procedures for the pursuit of individual claims is important, but such procedures are ultimately only supplementary to effective national remedies.'

[16] See Chapter 2, n 69.
[17] EU Commission, Proposal for a Council Directive on minimum standards for the qualification and status of third country nationals and stateless persons as refugees or as persons who otherwise need international protection Proposal (2001) COM (2001)510, 18. See also *LW* (n 5) para 33; and Joined Cases C-175/08, C-176/08, C-178/08, and C-179/08 *Salahadin Abdulla and Others* [2010] ECR I-0000.
[18] 1979 UNHCR Handbook (n 11) para 106.
[19] ibid para 65. See also para 100 (last sentence).
[20] *Canada (AG) v Ward* [1993] 2 SCR 689. For a list of case law endorsing the principle of surrogacy, see Hathaway and Foster, *The Law of Refugee Status* (2nd edn CUP 2014) 288–97. The UK Supreme Court re-affirmed the principle in *HJ (Iran) and HT (Cameroon) v Secretary of State for the Home Department* [2010] UKSC 31 para 52 (per Lord Hope). See also *LW* (n 5) para 32.
[21] Paul Weis, 'Human Rights and Refugees' (1971) 10(1–2) Israel Yearbook on Human Rights 35, 48: 'the international community has created international agencies to provide a substitute for the national protection which those fleeing from persecution or fear of persecution—the refugees—are lacking, and has established multilateral treaties providing for basic minimum standards for the treatment of refugees'.
[22] See also, James C Hathaway, *The Rights of Refugees Under International Law* (CUP 2005) 4–5; Zimmermann and Mahler (n 8) 448.

## 1.2 Is Surrogacy a Key Principle?

It will be recalled that at the end of Chapter 3, the question was raised whether there was any principle or principles underlying the refugee definition as a whole, in particular the principle of surrogacy. This issue now needs interrogating further.

In many ways surrogacy as a principle explains itself. The international community was only prepared to define the term 'refugee' in the 1951 Convention and its 1967 Protocol on the footing that it was needed for those genuinely lacking national protection. Further, as we saw in Chapter 2, the notion informs understanding of the Convention's object and purpose.[23] It can be said to have particular importance in shaping the purpose of protection against persecution in a way that is consistent with the international legal order based on non-interference in the sovereignty of other states. Understood thus, it is a notion of great generality and well-suited therefore to operating as a principle underlying the definition as a whole.

However, it is not just seen as a foundational principle. La Forest J in *Ward*, for example, considered that it 'permeat[es] the interpretation of the various terms requiring examination'.[24] In Chapter 6 the notion was seen to have an impact on several aspects of the meaning of 'being persecuted'. In this chapter, the focus will be on its role in shaping the latter term's interconnection with the concept of protection. As will be explored in Chapters 9 and 10, the notion has also come to be viewed as the pivot for a modern understanding of the availment clause and its interconnection with the nexus clause. But in other chapters as well, the notion is understood to have a material bearing on interpretation of the meaning of other elements: various aspects of the definition's nationality and statelessness provisions; its 'outside the country' element; the internal protection alternative inquiry; more than one aspect of the Convention reasons element; and also of the 'well-founded fear' element.[25]

Given identification of the notion as a key principle, it is necessary to give careful consideration to the arguments for and against doing so.

## 1.3 Criticisms

Despite the apparent congruence of the notion of surrogacy with VCLT rules, the refugee law literature does not reflect any full agreement about its place. Critics range from those who say it has no place in refugee law to those who agree that, in some shape or form, it has some role to play (either as a notion or principle or both), but doubt its utility. Criticism of it tends to overlap considerably with criticism of subsuming

---

[23] Zimmermann and Mahler (n 8) 298.
[24] *Ward* (n 20).
[25] See p. 213, p. 218, p. 219, p. 223, p. 228, p. 270, p. 276, p. 283, p. 285, p. 376, p. 403, p. 426, p. 428, p. 429, p. 429, p. 434, pp. 438–439, p. 444, p. 458, p. 463, p. 469, p. 471, p. 484, p. 512, p. 522, p. 543, p. 558, p. 559, p. 569, p. 570, p. 577, p. 578, p. 582, p. 589, p. 603, and p. 683. See also p. 720, p. 721, and p. 728. For surrogacy as a purpose, see Chapter 2, sections 2.5.4–2.5.5. For the role of surrogacy in the human rights approach see Chapter 3, section 4.2.7.

national protection within the persecution element,[26] to which we shall come to next. This is understandable given that, as explained above, one of the three main substantive roles accorded to it concerns this claimed interrelationship.[27]

### 1.3.1 Ordinary meaning

Critics have picked up on the point that the notion is not identifiable from the text of the refugee definition and in the words of one, any reliance on it 'potentially adds a requirement to the words of the Refugee Convention definition'.[28]

### 1.3.2 Primary purpose

One of the main objections to the notion having a key role casts it as erroneously treating the primary purpose of the Refugee Convention as national protection rather than international protection. Thus, Kneebone contends that the 'primary purpose' of the Convention is the international duty to 'confer protection from persecution', which, she contends, is not a national duty.[29]

### 1.3.3 Relationship between national and substitute protection

For Cantor, among the 'conceptual limitations' to the notion of surrogacy is that it 'seems to be used to describe a relationship with the host state which replaces, or stands in for, that severed by the circumstances leading to refugeehood'.[30] As such he considers it a poor fit. He contends that since the Refugee Convention envisages national protection in terms of the citizen-state relationship based on nationality, a universalistic human rights-driven notion of surrogate protection lacks correspondence. Further, he regards the protection provided by Articles 3–34 of the Convention as not taking the form of human rights but rather of largely contingent rights pegged to the treatment of specific categories of nationals and aliens.[31] He argues that the notion of surrogate protection in the refugee context 'seems better to correspond to the role played by UNHCR in its statutory function of "international protection of refugees", which approximates more closely to the idea of standing in for the legitimate interests of the state in its nationals overseas'.[32]

---

[26] Thus, Kneebone's critique in Susan Y Kneebone, 'Moving Beyond the State: Refugees, Accountability and Protection' in Susan Y Kneebone (ed), *The Refugees Convention 50 Years On: Globalisation and International Law* (Routledge 2003, reissued 2018) 309, refers to 'the internal "surrogacy" concept'. See also Susan Y Kneebone, 'Refugees as Objects of Surrogate Protection: Shifting Identities' in Susan Y Kneebone, Dallal Stevens, and Loretta Baldassar (eds), *Refugee Protection and the Role of Law: Conflicting Identities* (Routledge 2014) 104, where she describes the target of her criticism as 'the "internal" surrogate protection approach'.

[27] See David Cantor, 'Defining Refugees: Persecution, Surrogacy and the Human Rights Paradigm' in Bruce Burson and David Cantor (eds), *Human Rights and the Refugee Definition* (Brill Nijhoff 2016) 363–64.

[28] Kneebone (2014) (n 26) 104.

[29] ibid. Kneebone states that the notion 'constructs the fleeing asylum seeker or refugee as the continuing responsibility of the home state, rather than as a person entitled to international protection'.

[30] Cantor (n 27) 364.

[31] ibid 367.

[32] ibid 365–66.

## 1.3.4 State responsibility

Kneebone avers that under a surrogate protection approach, first established in Canadian case law and 'transmuted' through transnational judicial conversations, application of the Convention definition risks becoming focused upon state accountability or complicity in the persecution, rather than upon the refugee applicant's 'well-founded fear of persecution' or the simple need for protection as a consequence of failure of state protection.[33] Burson[34] notes the warning voiced by the New Zealand IPT in *BG (Fiji)* that:

> The Tribunal is not a treaty supervisory body. It performs a fundamentally different function. It does not offer states guidance on the good faith discharge of treaty obligations. Nor is its task to apportion blame or to hold the relevant state accountable under international law for breaches of the claimant's fundamental rights....[35]

## 1.3.5 Impact on role of the individual

Kneebone sees the principle of surrogacy as turning refugees into 'objects' rather than subjects of international law.[36] Goodwin-Gill and McAdam,[37] among others,[38] likewise consider that the principle displaces the primary importance of the individual, leads away from individualised assessment and places undue burdens on the refugee claimant.[39] Observing that the Convention definition begins with the refugee as someone with a well-founded fear of persecution, and only secondly, as someone who is unable or unwilling, by reason of such fear to use or take advantage of the protection of their government, they remark that the emergence of the principle of surrogacy has resulted in 'the major premise [being] substituted by the minor':

> The words of article 1A(2) show that the fundamental question is that of risk of relevant harm, and in this context surrogacy is an unnecessarily distracting and complicating factor, adding yet one more burden to the applicant in an already complex process. Reading 'surrogacy' back into the refugee definition tends, as

---

[33] Kneebone (2014) (n 26) 104.
[34] Bruce Burson, 'Give Way to the Right: The Evolving Use of Human Rights in New Zealand Refugee Status Determination' in Burson and Cantor (n 27) 41–42.
[35] ibid. See *BG (Fiji)* [2012] NZIPT 800091, para 117.
[36] Kneebone (2014) (n 26) 98.
[37] Guy S Goodwin-Gill and Jane McAdam, *The Refugee in International Law* (3rd edn, OUP 2007) 10; Guy S Goodwin-Gill and Jane McAdam (with Emma Dunlop), *The Refugee in International Law* (4th edn, OUP 2021) 8–9.
[38] Daniel Wilsher, 'Non-State Actors and the Definition of a Refugee in the United Kingdom: Protection, Accountability or Culpability' (2003) 15(1) IJRL 68, 83 argues that 'the whole normative structure of the refugee definition then moves towards an examination of the extent to which the victim has been targeted or neglected by the State rather than the degree of risk of harm they face'. See also Cantor (n 27) 365; Schultz (n 10) 135; Thomas A Aleinikoff and Leah Zamore, *The Arc of Protection: Reforming the International Refugee Regime* (Stanford University Press 2019) 51–52.
[39] Wilsher (n 38) 444.

elements in the jurisprudence show, to downplay and even to trump the individual's fear of persecution, while giving preference to the state and its efforts to provide a reasonably effective and competent police and judicial system which operates compatibly with minimum international standards.[40]

They also regard the surrogacy approach as somewhat akin to the traditional perception of the nation-state/citizen relationship, where the individual is only with difficulty conceived of as a human rights holder.[41]

1.3.6 Unduly burdensome nature

In *Khawar*, McHugh and Gummow JJ stated that '[t]he "internal" protection and "surrogacy" protection theories as a foundation for the construction of the Convention add a layer of complexity to that construction which is an unnecessary distraction'.[42] We have already noted Goodwin-Gill and McAdam's view that surrogacy 'add[s] yet one more burden to the applicant in an already complex process'.[43]

Adding greater specificity to this line of criticism, a number of commentators have argued that the notion fosters a practice of requiring applicants to demonstrate they have first exhausted local and then higher-level domestic remedies so as to demonstrate that they cannot avail themselves of protection.[44] Often in tandem with this contention (and again illustrating the heavy overlap with criticisms of the approach of treating persecution and protection as interrelated), it is argued that it encourages the application of misplaced notions of state culpability and 'due diligence'. Kneebone considers that the principle of surrogacy rests on ill-suited notions of state accountability and complicity and risks causing a shift from focus on the well-founded fear of the applicant to the 'notional willingness' of the state of origin to combat the particular problem by taking 'reasonable steps'. She remarks that the surrogacy notion 'has been used to minimise the obligations of receiving states, particularly where non-state actors are the agents of persecution, and often when there is a group identity for those

---

[40] Goodwin-Gill and McAdam (3rd edn) (n 37) 11; Goodwin-Gill and McAdam (4th edn) (n 37) 9. See also Guy S Goodwin-Gill, 'Current Challenges in Refugee Law' in Jean-Pierre Gauci et al (eds), *Exploring the Boundaries of Refugee Law* (Brill Nijhoff 2015) 11: '[w]hile [seeing refugee protection as a 'surrogate' for national protection] might be a perfectly innocuous description of the international refuge protection regime as a whole (the international community steps in to provide what the national State will not or cannot), its effects become pernicious once surrogacy is somehow imagined as part of 'being a refugee', as opposed to simply a statement about practical consequences. I argue this position, not only because it introduces an irrelevant consideration not found in the text of the treaty, but principally because the 'surrogacy approach' diverts attention away from the individual asylum seeker, accords less weight to his or her personal circumstances and situation in context, and more weight to externalities, which are then perceived to bear on the *generality* of risk of harm, rather than on the *specific* risk to individuals.'
[41] Goodwin-Gill and McAdam (3rd edn) (n 37) 11; Goodwin-Gill and McAdam (4th edn) (n 37) 8.
[42] Goodwin-Gill and McAdam (3rd edn) (n 37) 73. See *MIMA v Khawar* [2002] 210 CLR 1 (Aus HC).
[43] Goodwin-Gill and McAdam (3rd edn) (n 37) 11; Goodwin-Gill and McAdam (4th edn) (n 37) 9.
[44] In relation to the internal flight alternative/internal protection alternative, Antonio Fortin, 'The Meaning of "Protection" in the Refugee Definition' (2000) 12(4) IJRL 548, 571 states that this notion 'constitutes an undue extrapolation into refugee law of the principle of exhaustion of local remedies embodied in human rights instruments'. See also Schultz (n 10) 130, who describes the exhaustion of local remedies rule as 'a problematic import into the realm of refugee law'; Julian M Lehmann, *'Protection' in European Union Asylum Law* (Brill Nijhoff 2020) 78.

individuals fleeing persecution'.[45] For Kneebone, espousal of the notion 'reveals the ability of the international community to avoid responsibility to significant groups of asylum seekers'.[46] Her survey of case law in Canada, the UK, and Australia particularly highlights the way in which the Canadian case law has erected unduly demanding burdens and standards of proof, e.g. in respect of there been a rebuttable presumption of state protection which the applicant has to disprove.[47]

In similar vein, Schultz argues that, in contrast to other human rights treaties which are concerned with securing internal protection to persons within a contracting state's jurisdiction, refugee law is concerned with international protection and, as a result '[t]he "due diligence" standard in human rights law introduces the question of whether reasonable measures have been taken, which is irrelevant to the refugee inquiry. Rather, the focus is forward-looking to the actual risk of harm, and the individual's well-founded fear on return'.[48] Cantor considers that the recourse to standards drawn from the international law of state responsibility results in their being minimalistic.[49]

It must not be thought, however, that criticism of the notion of surrogacy as 'an unnecessary distraction',[50] always means to allege that it disadvantages applicants. Sometimes it appears just to see the notion or principle to lack utility.

### 1.3.7 Differences over location of the notion in elements of the refugee definition

Also possibly adverse to endorsement of the notion of surrogacy is that, even among those who embrace it as a principle, there is no agreement over its proper location in the element(s) of the refugee definition. For some its home is in the availment clause. Thus, in *Horvath* Lord Lloyd stated that:

> [ ... ] the principle of surrogate protection finds its proper place in the second half of article 1A(2). If there is a failure of protection by the country of origin, the applicant will be unable to avail himself of that country's protection.[51]

Zimmermann and Mahler also appear to adopt this position.[52]

However, for others, Hathaway and Foster for example, the principle appears to be located primarily in the 'being persecuted' limb, but also, in relation to the internal protection alternative only, the availment clause.[53]

For yet others it has a more diffuse role. In *Horvath*, Lord Hope described the surrogacy principle as 'underl[ying] the issue of state protection' and envisaged both the 'fear test' and the 'protection test' as 'founded upon the same principle'.[54] The surrogacy

---

[45] Kneebone (2014) (n 26) 103–06; see also Wilsher (n 38) 99–100.
[46] Kneebone (2014) (n 26) 115.
[47] ibid 107–08.
[48] Schultz (n 10) 134.
[49] As noted below at p. 428, even Hathaway and Foster (who espouse the principle of surrogacy) reject importation of the 'due diligence' standard as applied in IHRL to refugee law. See Hathaway and Foster (n 20).
[50] *Khawar* (n 42), per McHugh J and Gummow J, para 73.
[51] *Horvath v SSHD* [2000] UKHL 37.
[52] Zimmermann and Mahler (n 8) 448.
[53] Hathaway and Foster (n 20).
[54] *Horvath* (n 51).

principle, he stated, 'has a part to play in the application of both tests to the evidence'.[55] It could also be said that the logic of the 'holistic approach', as endorsed by Lord Hope, requires treating the principle as having a role in the 'well-founded fear' limb as well.[56] That is what the Australian High Court in *S152/2003* construed the majority position in *Horvath* to be in considering that surrogate protection 'may be relevant to whether the fear is well-founded; and to whether the conduct giving rise to the fear is persecution; and to whether a person such as the respondent in this case is unable, or, owing to fear of persecution, is unwilling, to avail himself of the protection of his home state'.[57]

Differences are also discernible over what role the notion of surrogacy has within one or more elements of the definition. Lehmann considers that the notion is not an independent substantive criterion of refugeehood. Rather it 'reflects the purpose of the Convention to entrust refugees with surrogate, rights-based international protection'.[58] Kneebone considers the fact that the Australian High Court in *S152/2003* saw the principle as having a role in three limbs of the refugee definition as a cause of 'potential confusion'.[59]

So far as concerns reliance on the notion to justify IPA theories, it has been argued that some statements made in the *travaux* indicate to the contrary, in that the drafters envisaged that refugees from civil wars, such as Russian and Spanish refugees, were refugees even though they could presumably at some point have secured protection in a certain area of their home country.[60]

## 1.4 The Notion of Surrogacy Re-Examined

Whilst these objections to according a key role to the notion of surrogacy have to be weighed heavily, there are questions marks over their efficacy.

### 1.4.1 Ordinary meaning
The objection that the text of Article 1A(2) does not identify the notion of surrogacy is somewhat contingent. Assuming that 'being persecuted' is interpreted to have lack of internal (national) protection as one of its ingredients, it can be said to be identifiable without any words being added. In any event, it has never been a material contention of proponents of the principle of surrogacy that it forms part of the literal meaning of the refugee definition; it has always been justified by reference to other VCLT considerations.

### 1.4.2 Purpose
Kneebone's remark that the primary purpose of the Refugee Convention is international protection, not national protection, is primarily rhetorical. Asking about

---

[55] ibid.
[56] ibid.
[57] *MIMA v Respondents S152/2003* [2004] 222 CLR 1 (Aus HC), para 21, per Gleeson CJ, Haynes and Hayden JJ. See also La Forest J in *Ward* (n 24).
[58] Lehmann (n 44) 68–72.
[59] Kneebone (2014) (n 26) 105.
[60] Schultz (n 10) 128–29, where she cites the US proposal E/AC.32/SR.3 (1950) 10.

purpose(s) is essentially asking a 'why' question—why the Refugee Convention was enacted, etc. Of course, one can sensibly say the Convention's purpose—or even its primary purpose—is international protection, but that says nothing about why. The answer to the why question can only be that it was enacted precisely to do something about the lack of national protection against persecution/serious harm. Articulation of the principle of surrogacy in the context of the Refugee Convention has typically understood this interconnection: as stated by Lord Hope in *Horvath*, '[t]he general purpose of the Convention is to enable the person who no longer has the need for protection against persecution for a Convention reason in his own country to turn for protection to the international community.'[61]

### 1.4.3 Poor fit?

Whilst Cantor may be right that the drafters envisaged 'national protection' through the prism of the citizen-state relationship based on nationality, the notion of internal (national) protection as developed by application of a human rights approach treats *all* individuals within a state's territory as entitled to human-rights-based protection—citizens and non-citizens alike.[62] Further, by virtue of such an approach, the conduct of the home state is adjudged by objective standards based on International Human Rights Law (IHRL) norms, not national law standards.[63] In any event, contrary to what Cantor posits, it is not a necessary part of the surrogacy principle that the substitute protection—what he calls the 'external dimension' of the principle—must be 'identical to that for which it supposedly substitutes'.[64] Whilst Articles 2–34 are clearly intended to enshrine a catalogue of guarantees for refugees designed to address the main disabilities seen to flow from lack of national protection, they do so in a way designed to compensate for disabilities facing them in the host state. But even so, the protection they guarantee is sufficiently proximate to what residents normally receive from their home state and is thus properly described as 'back-up' or 'substitute' or 'surrogate'.

### 1.4.4 State responsibility

Concerns expressed about the notion or principle of surrogacy inclining decision makers to rely on misplaced concepts of state responsibility or accountability, being heavily connected with criticisms of the notion of protection as an aspect of the 'being persecuted' element of the definition, are best dealt with in section 2. It can simply be noted here that such concerns are found to lack cogency.

### 1.4.5 Displacement of the role of the individual?

The concern expressed by Goodwin-Gill and McAdam and others about the notion or principle of surrogacy displacing the individual or turning refugees into 'objects' is an

---

[61] *Horvath* (n 51); see also UNHCR Handbook (n 11) paras 65 and 100 (last sentence).
[62] Save for limited exceptions, e.g. ICCPR (n 15) Article 25, which limits rights to political participation to citizens; ECHR (n 15) Article 16, according to which states may restrict the political activities of aliens in connection to their rights under Articles 10, 11, and 14.
[63] Michelle Foster, *International Refugee Law and Socio-Economic Rights: Refuge from Deprivation* (CUP 2007) 77–78.
[64] Cantor (n 27) 365.

understandable reaction to the early international jurisprudence that sought to preserve the discretion of the state to choose how to comply with human rights obligations. As perhaps most acutely illustrated by the UK House of Lords case of *Horvath*, when dealing with the claim by a Roma family from Slovakia of racially motivated ill-treatment by skinheads, the principle was operated so as to conceptualise the protection test as one concerned only with whether the state had in place a system of protection, irrespective of whether that system would in fact protect specific individuals or groups. However, as demonstrated by the subsequent case law and certainly some state practice (e.g. as reflected in the 2011 amendment made to Article 7 of the EU Qualification Directive (QD recast)),[65] the principle does not have to be developed in this way and is now most often applied on the footing that assessment must always be made of whether protection is practical and effective in the individual case. As noted by the EU Commission in 2009, when proposing the aforesaid amendment to the QD, willingness and ability to protect have to be assessed 'in reality'.[66] As stated by Burson, with reference to New Zealand case law:

> The centrality of the concept of 'surrogacy' in New Zealand RSD has not, therefore, as Goodwin-Gill and McAdam feared, led to an approach under which the actions taken by the State are given preferential focus in the inquiry. Rather, the predicament of the claimant takes centre stage. Indeed, the approach taken in Horvath was expressly rejected because it concentrated not on the risk to the claimant but on the 'reasonable willingness of the state of origin to operate its domestic protection machinery'. Just as New Zealand refugee law has insisted on an entirely objective standard on the assessment of risk, so it has insisted on an objective assessment of the adequacy of State protection.[67]

Accordingly, treating surrogacy as an underlying principle need not entail substituting a minor for a major premise.

### 1.4.6 Unduly burdensome

Criticisms about undue burdens have primarily targeted reliance on a number of mooted criteria of protection (such as due diligence, exhaustion of domestic remedies) seen to derive from IHRL law and hence are best addressed when considering the protection-persecution interrelationship in the next section, although it can

---

[65] See below pp. 447–448.
[66] European Commission, Proposal for a Directive of the European Parliament and of the Council on minimum standards for the qualification and status of third country nationals or stateless persons as beneficiaries of international protection and the content of the protection granted (2009) COM(2009) 551 final, para 3.1.1: 'The mere fact that an entity is able to provide protection is not sufficient; it should also be willing to protect the particular individual. Inversely, mere "willingness to protect" is not sufficient in the absence of the "ability to protect". Subsequently the CJEU in *Abdulla* (n 17) paras 71, 89, 95 made clear the importance of individual assessment taking into account both general conditions and the individual's particular circumstance. On the need for protection to be practical and effective, see *McPherson v SSHD* [2001] EWCA Civ 1955, para 24.
[67] Burson (n 34) 42. Burson cites 72558/01 and 72559/01 (19 November 2002) para 107. In the same volume, Raza Husain notes that in the UK subsequent cases have 'honoured Horvath in the breach' and goes on to suggest that the notion of 'effectiveness' in Article 7 QD has yet to be addressed fully. See Raza Husain, 'International Human Rights and Refugee Law: The United Kingdom' in Burson and Cantor (n 27) 146, 154. See also *MA* [2018] EWCA Civ 994.

simply be noted here that such criticisms are found wanting.[68] As regards the criticism voiced in *Khawar* of the principle being an 'unnecessary distraction', which overlooks that as well as plays a foundational role, the principle has a substantive role in shaping the meaning to be given to key elements of the refugee definition, as summarised in section 1.4.8 below.

1.4.7  Location arguments
Whilst disagreements about the correct location of the notion or principle of surrogacy in the different limbs of the refugee definition are evident, it is hard to find anyone saying that the notion or principle has no role whatsoever. Thus, even Goodwin-Gill accepts that it represents 'a perfectly innocuous description of the international refuge protection regime as a whole (the international community steps in to provide what the national State will not or cannot)' as well as 'a statement about practical consequences'.[69] Another strong critic, Kneebone, directs her fire only against its 'transmutation' and seems content if it were to retain a role as part of the 'well-founded fear of being persecuted' part of the definition.[70] None appear to take issue, either, with its underlying rationale—that international protection is only justified if there is a lack of protection.

One view, as we have seen, is that the principle of surrogacy has relevance to the refugee definition but only as an underlying or foundational principle, not as part of any of the definition's substantive elements. It is possible in the abstract for a general principle to operate as an underlying purpose without also being treated as a substantive part of the definition, but (as is made clear in each of this book's chapters on individual elements of the definition) to confine it to such a role would obscure its interconnection with several aspects of the refugee definition.

It cannot be ignored that differences of view as to where to locate the principle of surrogacy exist and that they pose a problem for attempts to achieve greater consensus about the contents of the refugee definition, but if it is correct that the approach to the definition should be holistic (about which there is substantial consensus),[71] there should not be anything inherently confusing in postulating some role for it in all three of the main elements of the definition ('well-founded fear', 'being persecuted', and the availment clause).[72] Contrary to Kneebone's position, interconnectedness alone cannot be a cause of confusion.

There is no denying Schultz's point that the Convention drafters did appear to contemplate that certain cohorts of refugee met the requirements of refugee even though they presumably had an internal relocation alternative. Equally, however, as Zimmermann and Mahler have observed, the *travaux* reveal:

> [ ... ] a certain insistence on the exclusion of internally protected persons from the ambit of Article 1A, para 2 which allows the conclusion that the existence of sufficient

---
[68] See below sections 2.2.5 and 2.3.5.
[69] See above n 40.
[70] Kneebone (2014) (n 26) 114. See also Schultz (n 10) 120–35, who seeks to distinguish between the 'thin' and 'thick' perspectives on surrogacy and argues that only the 'thin' surrogacy perspective is justified.
[71] See pp. 192–192.
[72] As the majority of the Australian High Court held in *S152/2003* (n 57).

national protection was assumed to be inconsistent with the status as an internationally recognised refugee.[73]

### 1.4.8 Conclusions on surrogacy

From the above analysis, it can be concluded that there are valid reasons to question the efficacy of criticisms made of the role of the notion of surrogacy in explicating one or more elements of the refugee definition, although more needs to be done by those who accord it a key role to clarify its precise impact. Being only mid-way through analysing key elements of the refuge definition, it would be premature to state in full the ways in which this study considers the notion to play a substantive role in the refugee definition, but we can at this juncture summarise how the remainder of this chapter views the role it plays in clarifying the interconnection between persecution and protection. In this context, it operates as a limiting principle in relation to the material scope of the 'being persecuted' element. Not to apply it would mean that a person having a well-founded fear of serious harm could qualify as a refugee even though the state would provide effective protection.

It remains to consider where this leaves the matter of what if anything can be said to be agreed about the notion of surrogacy. All too apparent from the recital of criticisms and this study's attempts to address them, there is no agreement to it having any specific and/or substantive role as a principle. Nevertheless, there does seem on all sides to be agreement that persons are not in need of international protection if they can find protection in their home state, coupled with sometimes grudging acceptance that this idea has some bearing on the refugee definition. Beyond agreement on this somewhat anodyne proposition, there is clearly a long way to go.

## 2 Persecution and Protection—Interrelationship

Having analysed the notion of surrogacy, it is necessary to turn to the main subject of this chapter—persecution and protection's interrelationship. In probing this interrelationship, it is essential, as always, to consider VCLT rules but in this instance, these will be addressed together rather than element by element.

### 2.1 Historical Background

Closely linking persecution and protection is nothing new. Doing so is often associated with the human rights approach, but as Hathaway observed in his landmark treatise, TLRS, it is traceable back to the understanding of the Convention's drafters[74] and, as has often been noted, the same idea can be seen at work in the 1979 UNHCR

---

[73] Zimmermann and Mahler (n 8) 448. See pp. 265–266. See also Ni Ghrainne (n 2) 40; Hugo Storey, 'The Internal Flight Alternative Test: The Jurisprudence Re-examined' (1998) 10(3) IJRL 499, 503.
[74] Hathaway (n 8) 103–04.

Handbook[75] and in the writings of other early commentators such as Grahl-Madsen[76] and Weis, the latter who wrote later in 1995 that:

> At the very least, a connection exists between persecution and the failure on the part of states to observe certain human rights. The reference contained in the Preamble to the Convention concerning the principle that human beings all enjoy fundamental rights and freedoms may provide a context for advancing the view that the violation of certain rights may either constitute persecution per se, or evidence thereof.[77]

The human rights approach as developed by Hathaway subsumes protection within the meaning of the 'being persecuted' element. The explanation of this interconnection is most well-known in the common law world from Lord Hoffman's reference in *Islam* to the 'Jewish shopkeeper' scenario:

> Suppose oneself in Germany in 1935. There is discrimination against Jews in general, but not all Jews are persecuted. Those who conform to the discriminatory laws, wear yellow stars out of doors and so forth can go about their ordinary business. But those who contravene the racial laws are persecuted. Are they being persecuted on grounds of race? In my opinion, they plainly are. It is therefore a fallacy to say that because not all members of a class are being persecuted, it follows that persecution of a few cannot be on grounds of membership of that class. Or to come nearer to the facts of the present case, suppose that the Nazi government in those early days did not actively organise violence against Jews, but pursued a policy of not giving any protection to Jews subjected to violence by neighbours. A Jewish shopkeeper is attacked by a gang organised by an Aryan competitor who smash his shop, beat him up and threaten to do it again if he remains in business. The competitor and his gang are motivated by business rivalry and a desire to settle old personal scores, but they would not have done what they did unless they knew that the authorities would allow them to act with impunity. And the ground upon which they enjoyed impunity was that the victim was a Jew. Is he being persecuted on grounds of race? Again, in my opinion, he is. An essential element in the persecution, the failure of the authorities to provide protection, is based upon race. It is true that one answer to the question 'Why was he attacked?' would be 'because a competitor wanted to drive him out of business.' But another answer, and in my view the right answer in the context of the Convention, would be 'he was attacked by a competitor who knew that he would receive no protection because he was a Jew.'[78]

Subsuming protection within the 'being persecuted' element as part of a human rights approach is a perspective that has found substantial support in case law and the wider literature. Its two most high-profile proponents, Hathaway and Foster, dub

---

[75] UNHCR Handbook (n 11) para 65; see also para 98, '[s]uch denial of protection may confirm or strengthen the applicant's fear of persecution, and may indeed be an element of persecution', and para 166.
[76] Atle Grahl-Madsen, *The Status of Refugees in International Law. Volume 1: Refugee Character* (Sijthoff 1966) 189.
[77] Paul Weis (ed), *The Refugee Convention 1951* (CUP 1995) 8.
[78] *Islam v SSHD Immigration Appeal Tribunal and Another, Ex Parte Shah, R v* [1999] UKHL 20.

it the 'bifurcated approach' and adopt the well-known summary formula, persecution = serious harm + lack of state protection that was embraced by the House of Lords in *Islam*.[79] The value of such an approach in preventing an under inclusive interpretation of the nexus clause[80] has found wide support in the refugee law literature, having been adopted in UNHCR Guidelines[81] and in much of the case law and scholarship.[82] To exclude claims where the risk of harm from non-state actors could only be linked to the failure of the state to protect would be, as described by Lord Clyde in *Horvath*, anomalous and unsound.[83] It is significant that several of the leading cases dealing with this feature of the causal nexus have concerned claims by women whose countries of origin adopt discriminatory laws or practices based on gender.[84]

In addition to strong support in UNHCR, judicial, and academic materials, treating protection as an integral part of the 'being persecuted' element has also been supported by state practice within the EU, e.g. the QD (recast) in Article 9(3) foresees that the causal nexus can also link to lack of protection.[85] Article 6(c) states that acts of persecution can be carried out by 'non-State actors, if it can be demonstrated that the actors mentioned in (a) and (b), including international organisations, are unable or unwilling to provide protection against persecution or serious harm'.

The above considerations strongly indicate that treating protection as part of the meaning of 'being persecuted' is consistent with VCLT rules of interpretation.

## 2.2 Arguments Against Treating the Two Terms as Interdependent

At the same time, there has been long-standing resistance to the approach of treating the two concepts as interdependent. The objections voiced overlap heavily with those often made against the principle of surrogacy itself.

---

[79] ibid. See also Hathaway and Foster (n 20) 373; Heaven Crawley, *Refugees and Gender: Law and Process* (Jordan Publishing Limited 2001); Refugee Women's Legal Group (RLG), 'Gender Guidelines for the Determination of Asylum Claims in the UK' (1998) para 1.17; *Khawar* (n 42) para 31. See also *Refugee Appeal No 71427/99* [2000] NZRSAA.

[80] Hathaway and Foster (n 20) 294–97.

[81] See e.g. UNHCR, Guidelines on International Protection (Guidelines) No 2: Membership of a particular social group within the context of Article 1A(2) of the 1951 Convention and/or its 1967 Protocol relating to the Status of Refugees (7 May 2002) UN Doc HCR/GIP/02/01, para 22.'

[82] See Hathaway and Foster (n 20) 295. For a detailed exposition of the UK case law up to 2003, see Mark Symes and Peter Jorro, *Asylum Law and Practice* (2nd edn, Bloomsbury 2010) 192–207. See also Husain (n 67) 138, 144–55. US case law has long subscribed to the view that inability and unwillingness to protect is an integral part of the persecution concept: see e.g. *Matter of Acosta* [1985] A-2415978 222–23 (citing *McMullen v INS* [1981] F.2d 1312). See further Charles S Ellison and Anjum Gupta, 'Unwilling Or Unable? The Failure to Conform the Nonstate Actor Standard in Asylum Claims to the Refugee Act' (2021) 52 Colum Hum Rts L Rev 441, 460; Deborah Anker, *Law of Asylum in the United States* (Thomson Reuters 2022) §4.9, 274.

[83] *Horvath* (n 51) 23.

[84] See e.g. the House of Lords' decision in *Islam* (n 78).

[85] Directive 2011/95/EU of the European Parliament and of the Council of 13 December 2011 on standards for the qualification of third-country nationals or stateless persons as beneficiaries of international protection, for a uniform status for refugees or for persons eligible for subsidiary protection, and for the content of the protection granted (recast) [2011] OJ L 337/9 (QD (recast)), Article 9(3) states: '[i]n accordance with point (d) of Article 2, there must be a connection between the reasons mentioned in Article 10 and the acts of persecution as qualified in paragraph 1 of this Article or the absence of protection against such acts'.

### 2.2.1 Contrary to ordinary meaning

It has been argued that coupling the two concepts is contrary to an ordinary interpretation of the word persecution. Thus, with reference to a 1976 OED definition and mindful of the views expressed by some senior judges,[86] Wilsher submits that:

> Those who persecute 'pursue with enmity and ill-treatment'. This puts emphasis on the active nature of persecution. There would appear to be no reason why the actions of non-State actors should not fall within this definition. This would be consistent with common understandings of the meaning of the term. By contrast, to speak of 'persecution' being practised by an essentially passive State would appear to be inconsistent with the active nature of persecution.[87]

Insofar as the QD (recast) offers a guide to interpretation of the refugee definition, it could be argued that the literal wording of Article 7(2) and Article 6(c), both of which refer to 'protection against persecution' in fact points against treating the two concepts as interdependent, since it posits the two as distinct concepts. The same terminology has been applied by the Court of Justice of the European Union (CJEU), e.g. in *Abdulla* it referred to 'protection against acts of persecution'.[88]

### 2.2.2 Contrary to how human rights law works

Targeting Hathaway and Foster's embrace of a 'bifurcated approach' which construes persecution and protection as interdependent, it has been argued that human rights law does not in fact embody or justify such an approach. Aptly illustrating this objection, is the issue some commentators have taken with the UK House of Lords treatment of human rights in *Bagdanavicius*, in which Lord Brown stated, with reference to the prohibition of ill-treatment enshrined in Article 3 ECHR, that:

> Non-state agents do not subject people to torture or the other proscribed forms of ill-treatment, however violently they treat them: what, however, would transform such violent treatment into article 3 ill-treatment would be the state's failure to provide reasonable protection against it.[89]

Goodwin-Gill and McAdam cite with approval the following criticism by Andrew Clapham of Lord Brown's statement:

> The whole ethos of humanitarian protection argues against such a judgmental approach with regard to the receiving state.... [T]he only criterion under human rights treaty law is whether the person will be subject to a substantial risk of harm from

---

[86] Most notably, Lord Lloyd in (n 54) and McHugh J in *S152/2003* (n 57) paras 65, 77, both in a minority opinion.
[87] Wilsher (n 38) 80–81.
[88] *Abdulla* (n 17) para 59. See also Case C-255/19 *SSHD v O A* [2021] ECLI:EU:C:2021:36, paras 36, 43, 59.
[89] *Bagdanavicius and another* [2004] 1 WLR 1207, para 24.

the non-state actor. If there is such a risk, the human rights treaty obligation on the sending state should prevent such a state from sending individuals into harm's way.[90]

### 2.2.3 Reliance on misplaced state responsibility tests

It has been argued that applying a human rights approach that treats persecution and protection as interdependent requires an evaluation of state responsibility and state liability that is not the function of refugee law to make. Thus, Kneebone considers the surrogacy principle to be intertwined with ill-suited state accountability and state culpability approaches.[91] Wilsher writes that whilst human rights are 'clearly relevant to the issue of persecution' they 'should not define it in the sense of requiring State responsibility as a sine qua non'.[92] He considers that treating the two concepts as interdependent leads 'inexorably to a culpability test for the standard of protection required of the State'.[93] He states that:

> [ ... ] the decision in *Horvath* wrongly introduces into the refugee definition the need to establish State responsibility. In so doing it moves decisively away from the protection theory towards an interpretation based upon showing that the home State has breached the duty of protection it owes to its citizens.[94]

Along with others, Wisher also considers that such an evaluation brings in its train concepts such as 'due diligence' that impose undue burdens (see sections 2.2.3 and 2.3.3 below). Even the most prominent proponents of the 'bifurcated approach', Hathaway and Foster, consider that, notwithstanding recent developments, the IHRL concept of 'due diligence' cannot overcome three 'critical deficits'. These deficits are said to be: that its origins in international law concerned with state responsibility means that it is 'at odds with the conceptual basis of a palliative regime designed to protect individuals prospectively from a well-found risk of harm'; that 'the test is not designed to accommodate the particular challenges of refugee law because it is ultimately a duty of process, not of result and because it is largely retrospective'; and that both its content and scope remains vague.[95]

Matthew, Hathaway, and Foster consider that 'the due diligence approach tends to direct attention exclusively to a state's "willingness" to protect, and to eliminate consideration of whether it is "unable" to protect the applicant'.[96] Likewise, Schultz considers that the concept of due diligence is also prone to merging with the notion of 'whether reasonable measures have been taken'.[97] One of the main targets of the criticism made

---

[90] Andrew Clapham, *Human Rights Obligations of Non-state Actors* (OUP 2006) 335–41, cited Goodwin-Gill and McAdam (3rd edn) (n 37) 12; see also Goodwin-Gill and McAdam (4th edn) (n 37) 9.
[91] Kneebone (2014) (n 26) 104–05.
[92] Wilsher (n 38) 72.
[93] ibid 98.
[94] ibid 102.
[95] Hathaway and Foster (n 20) 314–15; see also Penelope Mathew, James C Hathaway, and Michelle Foster, 'The Role of State Protection in Refugee Analysis: Discussion Paper No. 2 Advanced Refugee Law Workshop International Association of Refugee Law Judges Auckland, New Zealand, October 2002' (2003) 15(3) IJRL 444, 450–51.
[96] ibid 451.
[97] Schultz (n 10) 134.

of the *Horvath* approach to protection is Lord Clyde's reference to the state needing to have a '"reasonable willingness" to operate a machinery for the protection, persecution and punishment'.[98] Concern has been expressed that it was this reference that served as the template for the drafting of Article 7(2) of the 2004 QD, which referred to protection being 'generally provided when the actors mentioned in paragraph 1 take reasonable steps to prevent the persecution or suffering of serious harm, inter alia, by operating an effective legal system for the detection, prosecution and punishment of acts constituting persecution or serious harm, and the applicant has access to such protection.'[99]

### 2.2.4 Displacement of the importance of individual assessment

Displacement of the importance of individual assessment has already been noted as a criticism of the principle of surrogacy and the same criticism has often been directed at treating persecution and protection as interdependent. Thus, Cantor maintains that subsuming internal protection under the persecution element:

> [ ... ] introduces the temptation for decision-makers to construe the concept of internal protection under the persecution element by reference to an 'objective' minimum standard that must be plumbed in order for the need for 'surrogate' protection to be made out, without real regard to the risk of persecution actually faced by the individual refugee.[100]

Although stated in relation to the principle of surrogacy, Goodwin-Gill and McAdam's point—that this principle appears to 'giv[e] preference to the State and its efforts to provide a reasonably effective and competent police and judicial system which operates compatibly with minimum international standards'[101]—would appear to bite also[102] against treating persecution and protection as interdependent.

### 2.2.5 Unduly burdensome

As already noted, when identifying criticism relating to state responsibility, rebuke of the notions of 'due diligence' and 'reasonable steps' has included the point that they place undue burdens on applicants. Concerns raised about such burdens are much like those raised in relation to approaches dependent on the notion of surrogacy, namely: seeming to rely on a presumption of state protection; and seeming to require the exhaustion of domestic remedies. Kneebone, for example, has argued, with reference to Canadian post-*Ward* case law in particular, that the 'internal surrogacy' approach can encourage decision makers to impose a presumption of state protection,

---

[98] *Horvath* (n 51) 134.
[99] Council Directive 2004/83/EC of 29 April 2004 on minimum standards for the qualification and status of third country nationals or stateless persons as refugees or as persons who otherwise need international protection and the content of the protection granted [2004] OJ L 304/12; Lehmann (n 44) 104.
[100] Cantor (n 27) 363–64.
[101] Goodwin-Gill and McAdam (3rd edn) (n 37) 11; Goodwin-Gill and McAdam (4th edn) (n 37) 9.
[102] Rather against their own later statement that '[f]ear of persecution and lack of protection are themselves interrelated elements'. See Goodwin-Gill and McAdam (3rd edn) (n 37) 30. See also Goodwin-Gill and McAdam (4th edn) (n 37) 70.

which adds an 'extra layer to interpretation of the Refugee Convention definition'.[103] Schultz considers that the concept of 'exhaustion of local remedies' is 'a problematic import' from human rights law into the realm of refugee law.[104]

In a similar vein, Wilsher has written that treating the two concepts as interdependent makes the burden upon a refugee in such cases 'much more onerous'. He argues that:

> Decision-makers are likely to be reluctant to find that a home State which is merely unable to prevent such harm is a co-author of the victim's persecution. Thus, despite a victim facing serious harm, it will be more difficult to establish that this amounts to 'persecution' because this would involve criticism of the home State when the latter might be actively trying to eradicate the harm.[105]

2.2.6 The claimed advantage for understanding of causal nexus is illusory
According to Cantor, the purported advantage of the model that subsumes internal protection within the persecution element in terms of the 'Jewish shopkeeper' scenario is illusory, 'since the same result is achieved by considering the context of background State or societal discrimination under the "for reasons of" element'.[106]

2.2.7 Argument that protection considerations belongs in 'well-founded fear' limb
Sometimes allied with one or more of the aforementioned arguments, sometimes advanced on its own, it has been submitted that, far from constituting one ingredient of the concept of persecution, (lack of) protection should be seen as having its home in a separate limb of the refugee definition, namely the 'well-founded fear' limb. This was the position taken by La Forest in *Ward*, by UNHCR in its 2001 publication,[107] by Fortin,[108] by McHugh J in *S152/2003*,[109] and (seemingly) by the New Zealand RSAA.[110] It is also the position seemingly taken by Kneebone[111] and by Lehmann, the latter who essentially frames the analysis of protection as a matter of the analysis of risk. For Lehmann the 'analysis of available protection is not a separate inquiry following the analysis of harm, but is linked to the notion of a well-founded fear.'[112] He also contends that in both IHRL and the IHRL-based system of subsidiary protection

---

[103] Kneebone (2014) (n 26) 108; see also Pia Zambelli, 'Knowing Persecution: Non-State Actors and the Measure of State Protection' (2020) 32(1) IJRL 28, who argues that a formulation whereby applicants must show a lack of State protection from persecution 'may have the accidental effect of increasing their evidential burden'.

[104] Schultz (n 10) 130. She cites, inter alia, Fortin's view (n 44) that the internal protection alternative 'constitutes an undue extrapolation into refugee law of the principle of exhaustion of local remedies embodied in human rights instruments and, de facto, entails an amendment to the refugee definition as it adds a new requirement to the inclusion clauses'.

[105] Wilsher (n 38).
[106] Cantor (n 27) 364.
[107] UNHCR, The International Protection of Refugees: Interpreting Article 1 of the 1951 Convention Relating to the Status of Refugees (2001) UN Doc A/AC.96/951, paras 15, 37.
[108] Fortin (n 44) 574.
[109] *S152/2003* (n 57) paras 32, 73, 77.
[110] *Refugee Appeal No 76044* [2008] NZAR 719.
[111] Kneebone (2014) (n 26) 114.
[112] Lehmann (n 44) 85.

set out in the QD, '[t]he analysis of available protection is framed as a matter of the analysis of risk, a risk that must be real, personal and foreseeable, and which goes beyond mere possibility'.[113] He cites as an example, *H.L.R. v France*, in which the ECtHR stated that 'it must be shown that the risk is real and that the authorities of the receiving state are not able to obviate the risk by providing appropriate protection'.[114] For Lehmann 'protection' is everything that reduces risk exposure to acts of persecuting or serious harm'.[115]

## 2.3 The Interrelationship Evaluated

Before seeking to evaluate the above criticisms, it is important to note that even though my own conclusion below is that they are not made out, it is clear that on this issue there is no consensus. This reality will need to be reflected in what is said at the end of the chapter about basic propositions.

### 2.3.1 Ordinary meaning
As was seen in Chapter 6,[116] linguistic considerations offer some pointers to interpreting protection as part of the meaning of 'being persecuted'; in particular the use of the passive voice ('being persecuted'), which can be said to convey that the term has to do with the combined effect of the conduct of two or more agents, in particular the persecutor and the persecutee. However, as was found in that chapter, the proper application of VCLT rules discloses that there is no (unqualified) ordinary meaning of 'being persecuted' and that context, object and purpose point and other VCLT considerations rather towards a human rights reading.[117] Thus, the crux of the issue turns on whether or not VCLT considerations other than ordinary meaning support treating protection and persecution as interdependent and, in particular, the 'bifurcated approach' of regarding persecution's two components as being serious harm + lack of state protection.

Before addressing the criticism that the 'bifurcated approach' is contrary to the way the human rights system works, two prefatory remarks are in order. First, it is hard to understand why, if a human rights approach is to be applied to the concept of persecution it should not also in consistency be applied to protection, even were the latter to be considered to be an independent concept. Second, it is important to recall that even though the 'bifurcated approach' postulates two ingredients, it is serious harm that provides the axis. As stated by Kirby J in *Khawar*, '[o]n its own, the failure of state protection is not capable of amounting to persecution. There must also be a threat or the actuality of serious harm, including from non-state agents'.[118]

---

[113] ibid 83.
[114] *HLR v France* App No 24573/94 (ECtHR, 29 April 1997) para 40. He also cites the HRC decision in *Naveed Akram Choudhary v Canada* (17 December 2013) Communication No 1898/2009, UN Doc CCPR/C/109/D/1898/2009, para 9.7.
[115] Lehmann (n 44) 91.
[116] See Chapter 6, section 1.3.
[117] See Chapter 6, sections 1.11–1.12.
[118] *Khawar* (n 42) para 122.

It is possible to pray in aid examples of key texts or decisions making use of language appearing to acknowledge that persecution and protection are independent of one another. The example was given earlier of Articles 7(2) and 6(c) of the QD and its recast making reference to 'protection against persecution', an expression also employed by the CJEU in *Abdulla*.[119] However, the CJEU has now made quite clear in *O A*, despite again echoing such language, that whether protection exists is a function of whether there is no well-founded fear of being persecuted.[120]

2.3.2 Does human rights law work like this?
Contrary to the understanding of critics, the answer to this question is yes. It is a predicate of the human rights approach in risk on return cases that ill treatment/serious harm and protection are interdependent. The principal reason is that once serious harm is conceptualised in terms of human rights violations, it inexorably follows that they must be causally linked to state conduct. That is because human rights are rights of individuals in relation to a state and in the international human rights system, states are the primary bearers of responsibility for securement of human rights.[121]

In a human rights analysis, even when it is non-state actors that inflict harm, that in itself is not a violation. A violation only arises as a result of state action or inaction. Under global and regional human rights treaties, human rights obligations fall almost exclusively[122] upon the state and only the state can breach a person's human rights; non-state actors alone cannot breach human rights.

Pausing here, it is necessary straightaway to address the apparent 'paradox' that such a coupling poses, namely that it seems to accord a contradictory role for the role of the state as both protector and violator of human rights. This paradox was identified succinctly by Gleeson CJ in *Khawar*, as follows:

> However, the paradigm case of persecution contemplated by the Convention is persecution by the state itself. Article 1A(2) was primarily, even if not exclusively, aimed at persecution by a state or its agents on one of the grounds to which it refers.

---

[119] *Abdulla* (n 66) para 58.
[120] *O A* (n 88) para 57: '[a]ccordingly, the Court has previously held that if the national concerned has, because of the circumstances existing in his or her country of origin, a well-founded fear of being personally the subject of persecution for at least one of the five reasons listed in Article 2(c) of Directive 2004/83, those circumstances establish that the third country in question does not protect its national against acts of persecution (see, to that effect, judgment of 2 March 2010, *Abdulla* (n 17) paras 57 and 58). A third country national who is in fact protected against acts of persecution within the meaning of that provision cannot, for that reason, be regarded as having a well-founded fear of persecution.'
[121] Walter Kälin and Jörg Künzli, *The Law of International Human Rights Protection* (2nd edn, OUP 2019) 69.
[122] There are isolated exceptions: see e.g. International Convention on the Elimination of all Forms of Racial Discrimination (adopted 21 December 1965, entered into force 4 January 1969) 660 UNTS 19, Article 5. See Kälin and Künzli (n 121) 72–85; Jan Arno Hessbruegge, 'Human Rights Violations Arising from Conduct of Non-State Actors' (2005) 11 Buffalo Human Rights Law Review 21; Andrew Clapham (ed), *Human Rights and Non-State Actors* (Edward Elgar 2013) 87–154, 96.

Bearing that in mind, there is a paradox in the reference to a refugee's inability or unwillingness to avail himself of the protection of his persecutor.[123]

The same paradox was also obliquely alluded to by Lord Clyde in *Horvath* when he stated that '[a]ctive persecution by the state is the very reverse of protection'.[124] Among academic commentators to find the paradox unacceptable, Wilsher writes that '[t]o say that a State is persecuting those it is trying to protect would appear to be both illogical and unpalatable'.[125] Awareness of this paradox is not exclusive to refugee law; it has been discussed within IHRL[126] as well in relation to risk on return cases and concern about it also underlies the critique mentioned earlier by Clapham of Lord Brown's analysis of Article 3 ECHR in *Bagdanavicius*.[127]

However, subsequent UK case law has clarified that it would be a misunderstanding to read *Horvath* as implying that protection was irrelevant when the state was the actor of serious harm. In *Svazas*, Browne LJ (with whom Stuart-Smith LJ agreed) stated that:

> The appellant's most extreme argument would be that the *Horvath* principle simply has no application in the event of persecution by officers of the State .... For my part, however, I would reject so extreme an argument: the question of the protection available in the home State seems to me of no less importance when State agents are involved as when the relevant ill-treatment is inflicted exclusively by non-State agents.[128]

In truth there is no real paradox. Referencing the state's failure to protect when it is the state itself that inflicts the harm is only a paradox when one forgets the distinction between the state as a body with international law obligations and the authorities in charge of it at any one time. In terms of a state's human rights obligations, it is the former that is determinative.

Further, recalling the backdrop to the enactment of modern human rights treaties, the predominant concern was to protect against violations by the authorities of a state and to do so by committing *states themselves* to an obligation to protect their populations against such violations. The power to harm necessitated the power—and obligation—to protect.[129] This understanding is closely connected with the concept of a state's positive obligations. A necessary (but not sufficient) condition for the ability of a state or state-like entity to protect is that it has laws and policies in place to ensure

---

[123] *Khawar* (n 42) para 22.
[124] *Horvath* (n 51).
[125] Wilsher (n 38) 98; see also Fortin (n 44) 574–75.
[126] e.g. Jack Donnelly, *Universal Human Rights in Theory and Practice* (3rd edn, Cornell University Press 2013) 33, sees the State as both 'principal violator' and 'essential protector' and observes that '[w]ith power and authority thus doubly concentrated, the modern state has emerged as both the principal threat to the enjoyment of human rights and the essential institution for their effective implementation and enforcement'.
[127] See e.g. Sirus Kashefi, 'Human Rights: A Relative, Progressive, Regressive, and Controversial Concept' (2011) 7(2) International Zeitschrift 74, referred to this as 'the paradox of human rights', and at ibid 78 poses the question, 'How can an institution be both the violator and the protector?'.
[128] *Svazas v SSHD* [2002] EWCA Civ 74, para 52.
[129] Conversely 'the power to protect ... included the power to persecute'. See *BVerfGE 80, 315* [1989], cited by Lehmann (n 44) 97.

regulation of *public* as well as private practices in a manner that ensures human rights protection.[130] Hence in IHRL terms it is axiomatic that states parties must protect against violations of human rights by their own agents.[131]

It is true that in the context of human rights claims based on risk of return, the only human rights treaty obligation(s) lies (lie) on the *sending* state (to refrain from sending individuals into harm's way), but that does not relieve the sending state from having to evaluate home state conduct in human rights terms. As stated by the ECtHR in *Salah Sheekh*, '[t]he establishment of any responsibility of the expelling State under Article 3 inevitably involves an assessment of conditions in the requesting country against the standards of Article 3 of the Convention'.[132]

Further the latter task, of assessing conditions in the home state, is not simply deciding (as Clapham opines) 'whether the person will be subject to a substantial risk of harm from the non-state actor'.[133] It also requires assessing whether *the home state* will or will not put people in harm's way by failing to provide effective protection against the real risk of human rights violations from such actors.[134] The case law of treaty-monitoring bodies and the regional human rights courts reveals that one critical question is always whether home state protection obviates the real risk of ill-treatment.[135]

Nevertheless, reference above to the fact that (in determining human rights claims based on risk of return) ultimate focus has to be on the sending state, is crucial. It highlights one of two fundamental differences from the ordinary domestic context of determining whether state or non-state actors have breached a person's enjoyment of human rights within the jurisdiction of the host state. One fundamental difference

---

[130] See HRC, General Comment No 35: Article 9 Liberty and Security of person (16 December 2014) UN Doc CCPR/C/GC/35, para 7. See also e.g. *Case of Velásquez Rodríguez v Honduras*, Merits, Inter-American Court of Human Rights (IAmCtHR) Series C No 4 (29 July 1988), para 166; *Öneryildiz v Turkey* App No 48939/99 (ECtHR [GC], 30 November 2004) paras 89ff; Kälin and Künzli (n 121) 87ff.

[131] HRC, General Comment No 31 (26 May 2004) UN Doc CCPR/C/21/Rev.1/Add.13, para 8: '[ ... ] the positive obligations on States Parties to ensure Covenant rights will only be fully discharged *if individuals are protected by the State*, not just *against violations of Covenant rights by its agents*, but also against acts committed by private persons or entities that would impair the enjoyment of Covenant rights in so far as they are amenable to application between private persons or entities ...' (emphasis added).

[132] *Salah Sheekh v the Netherlands* App No 1984/04 (ECtHR, 11 January 2007) para 136.

[133] Clapham (n 90).

[134] Goodwin-Gill and McAdam's lending of support for Clapham's critique support is difficult to square with their own understanding of protection and persecution as interrelated: see Guy S Goodwin-Gill, *The Refugee in International Law* (1st edn, OUP 1983) 38: 'Fear of persecution and lack of protection are themselves interrelated elements.' See also Goodwin-Gill and McAdam (3rd edn) (n 37) 29, 98–99; Goodwin-Gill and McAdam (4th edn) (n 37) 70.

[135] See e.g. HRC, *Kindler v Canada* (11 November 1993) Communication No 470/1991 UN Doc CCPR/C/48/D/470/1991, para 13.1: 'If a State Party extradites a person within its jurisdiction in circumstances such that as a result there is a real risk that his or her rights under the Covenant will be violated in another jurisdiction, the State party itself may be in violation of the Covenant.' See also *Naveed Akram Choudhary v Canada* (n 114) para 9.7; *HLR v France* (n 114) para 34; *NA v the United Kingdom* App No 25904/07 (ECtHR, 17 July 2008) para 110; *FH v Sweden* App No 32621/06 (ECtHR, 20 January 2009) para 102; and *JK and Others v Sweden* App No 59166/12 (ECtHR [GC], 23 August 2016) para 80. See further *AT v Hungary* (26 January 2005) Communication No 2/2003, UN Doc CEDAW/C/36/D/2/2003; *NA v Finland* App No 25244/18 (ECtHR, 14 November 2018) para 73. In the EU context, the CJEU has held in Case C-542/13 *Mohamed M'Bodj v État belge* [2014] ECLI:EU:C:2014:2452, para 35, in relation to the human-rights based subsidiary protection regime of Article 15(b) QD (recast), that attribution is relevant but only to assessing whether harm caused to an individual can properly be characterised as a violation of a state's obligation which must be understood as requiring human conduct. See also Case C-353/16 *MP v SSHD* [2018] ECLI:EU:C:2018:276, paras 51, 58.

is that although in risk on return cases it is still only the sending state that has the obligation to protect, a critical component of the assessment is whether there has been violation(s) of human rights by another state—the home state. Another fundamental difference arises from the fact that persecution when defined in human rights terms can only arise if the violation alleged amounts to one that is a sufficiently severe. Such a reading of persecution is again buttressed by the principle of surrogacy, which enjoins that individuals are not entitled to seek protection from another country unless the situation in their own represents a negation of the home state's basic duty to protect; and a mere violation of a qualified human right (unless sufficiently severe) will not suffice to establish that.[136] The same also applies to human rights claims based on risk of return, since in respect of them too the principle of surrogacy requires it to be established that the violation of an applicant's human rights would be sufficiently severe to require them to leave and/or not return to their home state. Put in more familiar language, the coupling of persecution and protection by application of a human rights approach does not entail the position that a violation of any human rights constitutes persecution.[137]

2.3.3 Unwarranted reliance on state responsibility tests?
In the view of this author, much of the concern expressed about recourse to concepts drawn from the international law of state responsibility[138] rests on a confusion. Whilst refugee status determination is not an adjudication of state responsibility,[139] the assessment that has to be made of the conduct of the home state may often require deciding whether or not that has been a (sufficiently severe) violation of human rights for which the home state is responsible. In the well-known words of Judge Huber in the *Spanish Zone of Morocco Claims (Spain v United Kingdom)*, '[r]esponsibility is the necessary corollary of a right. All rights of an international character involve international responsibility.'[140] To that extent, state responsibility *is* involved. It is important therefore not to seek to purge the notion of responsibility entirely by confusing the issue of a decision maker's jurisdiction with the subject-matter of their actual assessment. It is one thing to point out that it is not the task of refugee law decision makers to 'hold the relevant state accountable under

---

[136] However, the human rights jurisprudence has considered that the fact that because such refoulement cases 'do not concern the direct responsibility of the Contracting State for the infliction of harm', there is a need for a high threshold. See e.g. *Savran v Denmark* App No 57467/15 (ECtHR [GC], 7 December 2021) para 147; *N v United Kingdom* App No 26565/05 (ECtHR, 27 May 2008); *AA and Others v Sweden* App No 14499/09 (ECtHR, 28 June 2012); *D v United Kingdom* App No 30240/96 (ECtHR, 2 May 1997) paras 42–43. This threshold is less stringent in cases where the applicant faces a real risk of ill treatment in their home state for which human actors are the predominant cause: see *Sufi and Elmi v United Kingdom* Apps Nos 8319/07 and 1149/07 (ECtHR, 18 November 2011) paras 282–83.
[137] See Zimmermann and Mahler (n 8) 348.
[138] On the international law of state responsibility see Ian Brownlie, *System of the Law of Nations: State Responsibility. Part 1* (Oxford Clarendon Press 1983); James R Crawford, 'State Responsibility' *Max Plank Encyclopaedias of International Law* (2006).
[139] As noted in para 42 of the UNHCR Handbook (n 11) in relation to the objective 'well-founded' fear, it is stated that the 'authorities that are called upon to determine refugee status are not required to pass judgment on conditions in the applicant's country of origin'.
[140] *British Claims in the Spanish Zone of Morocco (Great Britain v Spain)*, decision of 1925, United Nations, *Reports of International Arbitral Awards* (UNRIAA), vol II, 615.

international law for breaches of the claimant's fundamental rights'.[141] That is entirely correct as a description of jurisdictional remit. However, it does not follow that refugee law decision makers must avoid assessing whether such breaches have taken or will take place. To the contrary, assessing whether there would be a violation of a home state's duty to protect human rights is at the heart of any human rights approach.

In insisting (in the face of eminent critics) that state responsibility does therefore have a role, it is important to reiterate its limits. First, what is involved is not an assessment under the international law of state responsibility;[142] it is only state responsibility rules applied *within the IHRL context*. To the extent that recourse is had here to some concepts familiar from the international law of state responsibility, it is confined to their deployment within IHRL. Second, IHRL case law on risk on return is only concerned with state responsibility in basic form. Thus, whilst attribution and accountability are involved, it is only in the basic form of assessing whether a state by act or omission is accountable for failure of human rights obligations. In particular, there is no reliance on the state responsibility requirements of culpability or liability or enforcement.[143] Whilst it would be apt therefore to describe what refugee decision makers sometimes do as 'indirect' assessment of state responsibility (or accountability),[144] that will only be the case so long as it is understood that they are not concerned with apportioning blame and have no jurisdiction to determine state culpability or liability.

What of the associated concern that focus on state responsibility brings in its train reliance on a misplaced 'due diligence' standard?[145] Within IHRL due diligence is an accepted standard. Thus, the Human Rights Committee has written in relation to Article 2 ICCPR that violation of this right could arise 'as a result of States Parties permitting or failing to take appropriate measures or to exercise due diligence to prevent,

---

[141] *BG (Fiji)* (n 35) para 117, cited by Burson (n 34) 41.

[142] The doctrine of state responsibility assigns liability to a state that breaches its international obligations. In its traditional sense, it provided remedies to a state for internationally wrongful acts committed by another state: see James R Crawford, *Brownlie's Principles of Public International Law* (9th edn, OUP 2019) 525ff. However, that is not to say that this body of law does not provide some assistance with defining the concept of a State: see below section 3.7.3.

[143] Contrast, ILC, Report on Responsibility of States for Internationally Wrongful Acts (12 December 2001) UNGA Res 56/83, Article 11. Some human rights treaties do however have mechanisms for enforcement against contracting parties in breach: see e.g. by Article 41 ECHR the ECtHR is empowered to make binding awards of damages and 'just satisfaction' (see also Article 46).

[144] By often only expressly excluding direct responsibility, the ECtHR has sometimes implied acceptance of 'indirect responsibility' (see e.g. *N v United Kingdom* (n 136); *AA and others v Sweden* (n 136) para 93). However, it held in *Salah Sheekh* (n 132) para 147 that: 'the existence of the obligation not to expel is not dependent on whether the risk of the treatment stems from factors which involve the responsibility, *direct or indirect*, of the authorities of the receiving state' (emphasis added). Whilst that is clearly true in relation to the obligation at issue (that of the sending state), it is apt to mislead in relation to analysis of treatment in the home state, since the norms applied to such treatment in the latter must surely be IHRL norms—in this instance, Article 3 ECHR. In the ICCPR context, e.g. in *Pillai et al v Canada* (25 March 2011) Communication No 1763/08, UN Doc CCPR/C/101/D/1763/2008, the HRC has clarified that the proper test was to ask whether deportation would necessarily and foreseeably expose a person to a real risk of *being killed or tortured* (in breach of ICCPR Article 7) (emphasis added). Of course, not all expulsion cases are confined to issues relating to treatment by the authorities of the receiving state: see e.g. *D v United Kingdom* (n 136); *Savran v Denmark* (n 136) para 131.

[145] See above p. 428.

punish, investigate or redress the harm caused by such acts by private persons or entities'.[146]

A human rights approach to the refugee definition is not and was never meant to be a mechanistic application of human rights criteria irrespective of the different context.[147] However, if it is to have normative consistency, cogent reasons should be advanced for any failure to apply such an approach, in particular that applying them conflicts with VCLT rules and/or with the integrity of the refugee definition. It would be anomalous for a human rights approach to pick and choose, without cogent reasons, what key concepts it likes and dislikes from IHRL.[148]

In this context, the main criticisms advanced against the application of a due diligence criterion in connection with the refugee definition are not made out. Thus, in relation to the charge that there is a temporal difference, with human rights law being concerned with past facts and refugee law with prospective facts, that is a half-truth. Whilst in cases brought by applicants against their own states, due diligence is ordinarily used in the context of a backward-looking assessment, that is not the case in human rights adjudication of risk on return cases. Both the human rights treaty monitoring bodies and the regional human rights courts have applied it in the non-refoulement context, as part of a forward-looking inquiry.[149] The concept is not conceptually tied to historic acts. Nor is the IHRL-based due diligence standard misplaced when it comes to assessing the availability of protection. Given that refugee law accepts that protection cannot be absolute, the assessment of whether it is effective must be based on some standards. UNHCR, for example, has applied a due diligence standard in its Guidelines on International Protection No 9, when stating that:

> State protection would normally neither be considered available nor effective, for instance, where the police fail to respond to requests for protection or the authorities refuse to investigate or punish (non-State) perpetrators of violence against LGBTI individuals with due diligence.[150]

Whilst the standard remains vague, it is not exclusively confined to process[151] and it has been developed in more recent IHRL case law so as to be both a fact-related (as

---

[146] HRC, General Comment No 31 (n 131). Hathaway and Foster (n 20) 309 themselves write that the due diligence standard, first adopted by the IACtHR in *Case of Velásquez Rodríguez v Honduras* (n 130), 'is now widely adopted in other regional bodies, as well as by the major international human rights treaty bodies, and is justified by reference to the language of "protect and ensure" in most treaties'.

[147] As emphasised, inter alia, by Burson (n 34) 47–48.

[148] See p. 142.

[149] See e.g. *Salah Sheekh* (n 132) para 136. Hathaway and Foster (n 20) 318, despite rejecting the due diligence approach, appear to acknowledge this fact when citing *HLR v France* (n 114) and *Salah Sheekh* (n 132); see also *NA v the United Kingdom* (n 135); *FH v Sweden* (n 135); *JK and Others v Sweden* (n 135); and *NA v Finland* (n 135) para 73.

[150] UNHCR, Guidelines No 9: Claims to Refugee Status based on Sexual Orientation and/or Gender Identity within the context of Article 1A(2) of the 1951 Convention and/or its 1967 Protocol relating to the Status of Refugees (23 October 2012) HCR/GIP/12/01.

[151] As noted by Goodwin-Gill, in Guy S Goodwin-Gill, 'State Responsibility and the "Good Faith" Obligation in International Law' in Malgosia Fitzmaurice and Dan Sarooshi (eds), *Issues of State Responsibility before International Judicial Institutions* (Hart Publishing 2004) 78, '[c]onduct and result overlap; torture, ill-treatment, arbitrary deprivation of life, and *refoulement*, are all examples of forbidden

opposed to formalistic) standard and one based, not on notions of 'best efforts' or 'adequacy', but on whether there is practical and effective protection.[152] There is no need, therefore to consider (as Hathaway and Foster seek to do) that the move in refugee law jurisprudence away from a formalistic assessment to one based on the practical availability and effectiveness of protection entails rejection of a due diligence standard; rather the two have evolved hand in hand. It remains that in the refugee law context, due diligence obligations of the home state are only indicators of the issue of the ability or willingness to protect against harm.

A similar observation can be made regarding reliance on notions such as 'reasonable willingness to protect' and 'reasonable steps'. It must be conceded that some case law has tended to conceptualise 'reasonable steps' so as to require minimal protection standards and that it has sometimes encouraged subjective decision making.[153] However, applying a human rights-based assessment based on objective norms, it always remains necessary to establish whether the level of protection is such as to amount to *effective* protection; and as long as kept within this framework, 'reasonableness' appears a workable test.[154] As Lehmann convincingly demonstrates, the amendments made in the QD (recast) to Article 7(2)—which added a new first sentence to Article 7(2) ('Protection against persecution or serious harm must be effective and of a non-temporary nature')—codify the position already taken by the CJEU that assessment of protection must have regard to an applicant's individual situation[155] and must make clear that (in Lehmann's words) 'the actual effectiveness of protection remains the relevant enquiry'.[156]

### 2.3.4 Displacement of individual assessment?

The points made earlier in response to this same criticism of the surrogacy approach apply here too. Treating persecution and protection as interdependent need not involve displacement of the importance of the individual applicant as a rights-bearer; the central issue remains whether an individual's human rights have been violated. The same response can be made in relation to Goodwin-Gill and McAdam's point that the surrogacy principle appears to 'giv[e] preference to the State and its efforts to provide a reasonably effective and competent police and judicial system which operates

---

conduct; but due process and accountability mechanisms are necessary, linked, but still separate bases for determining whether "protection" is available or effective'.

[152] As regards Hathaway and Foster's critique of a 'due diligence' standard, whilst they accurately identify use that has led historically to the 'adoption of the more formalistic due diligence standard, with its close connections with the principle of state responsibility', it is not clear that this is how it is used in IHRL. They themselves note in Hathaway and Foster (n 20) 313–34 that writers such as Lambert, Marks and Azizi, Heyman, Baillet, and Mullally invoke 'the more robust modern understanding of due diligence elaborated in more recent human rights jurisprudence—which places particular emphasis on the prevention of harm'. See also Neil McDonald, 'The Role of Due Diligence in International Law' (2019) 68(4) ICLQ 1041.
[153] See e.g. in the UK, *Horvath* (n 51); *MA (Ethiopia)* [2009] EWCA Civ 289 (per Elias LJ).
[154] It should be noted that reasonableness plays a part in Hathaway and Foster's own analysis: e.g. in Hathaway and Foster (n 20) 292, they state that '[r]efugee law is designed to interpose the protection of the international community only in situations where there is no reasonable expectation that national protection of human rights will be forthcoming'.
[155] *Abdulla* (n 17) paras 59, 68–71.
[156] Lehmann (n 44) 86.

compatibly with minimum international standards'.[157] That concern has force against approaches that focus unduly on formal criteria relating to whether a state has in place a system of laws etc., but it lacks force in relation to an approach that focuses on whether protection is practical and effective.

### 2.3.5 Unduly burdensome?

As already noted, the concern of Kneebone and others about the 'internal protection surrogacy' theory imposing unduly stringent burdens and standards was apt, at least in relation to the common law jurisprudence that took hold for a while following the *Ward* and *Horvath* cases, but in general terms the approach to protection in both the case law and wider literature has since evolved. Of the four main examples given of application said to impose unduly stringent standards, two have already been addressed ('due diligence' and 'reasonable willingness'). This leaves the presumption of state protection and the exhaustion of domestic remedies.

In relation to the presumption of state protection, whilst it is true that La Forest J in *Ward* did advance this notion, it should first be observed that this is not a test applied in IHRL and it is difficult to see that it has any inherent connection with the principle of surrogacy or the issue of the interdependency of persecution and protection either. Further, it has never taken root in international refugee law outside of Canada.[158]

So far as concerns exhaustion of domestic remedies, it is undoubtedly the case that in older refugee case law, courts and tribunals were prone to imposing such a requirement. However, there is virtually no evidence of human rights bodies applying this as a specific requirement when dealing with risk on return cases.[159] Within IHRL, it is a procedural rule going to competence to bring a human rights claim[160] and there is no analogue in the area of refugee law and hence no basis for its (alleged) importation.[161] In most jurisdictions there is growing acceptance that whilst failure to seek local protection can be relevant to the overall inquiry, whether that is significant will depend on a range of factors.[162]

---

[157] Goodwin-Gill and McAdam (3rd edn) (n 37) 11; Goodwin-Gill and McAdam (4th edn) (n 37) 9.

[158] Analysis of Canadian case law on persecution and protection in Lorne Waldman, *The Definition of Convention Refugee* (2nd edn, Lexis Nexis 2019) suggests that reliance on this presumption still persists, although there is now more focus on whether protection is 'effective' in the individual case. Zambelli (n 103) 32 reaches a similar conclusion. As regards the situation outside Canada, Hathaway and Foster note two British Court of Appeal cases from 2000 and 2003 and several old New Zealand cases invoking such a presumption, but also note its express rejection by the Australian Full Federal Court in *A v MIMA* [1999] 53 ALD 545 (Aus FFC) 554. In the UK, such a presumption has played no part in more recent case law on protection.

[159] For a clear case in which the ECtHR did not consider failure to seek local protection significant, see *N v Sweden* App No 23505/09 (ECtHR, 20 July 2010). See also *DNM v Sweden* App No 28379/11 (ECtHR, 27 June 2013); and *SA v Sweden* App No 66523/10 (ECtHR, 27 June 2013), both cited in Lehmann (n 44) 110.

[160] See e.g. Optional Protocol to the ICCPR (adopted 16 December 1966, entered into force 23 March 1976) Article 2.

[161] Even though according to Hathaway and Foster (n 20) 324, reliance on such a test has been 'particularly prevalent in Canada', they also note at ibid that in *Ward* the Supreme Court recognised that it would 'seem to defeat the purpose of international protection' if an applicant 'would be required to risk his or her life seeking ineffective protection of a state, merely to demonstrate that ineffectiveness' and at ibid 326 they cite several decisions of the Federal Court rejecting the test, including *Kaur v Canada (MCI)* [2005] FC 1491 (Can FC).

[162] See discussion of case law in Hathaway and Foster (n 20) 323–35. The same trend is observable in US case law: see e.g. *Bringas-Rodriguez v Sessions* [2017] 850 F.3d 1051, in which the *en banc* constitution of the

It is questionable whether Wilsher's concern that in non-state actor cases 'it will be more difficult to establish that this amounts to "persecution" because this would involve criticism of the home State when the latter might be actively trying to eradicate the harm' still reflects case law and practice.[163] In the early years of grappling with the issue of state protection in this context, decision makers did fall into the error of considering that protection existed if the state was 'doing its best'. It is true, as Lehmann documents,[164] that even in the EU, there continue to be some national decisions that exhibit this and related errors and that also appears to be the case with some Canadian decisions.[165] However, viewed overall, examples of such errors are now less in evidence and in the EU context they stand at odds with the fact that Article 7(2) of the QD (recast) requires protection to be effective. Whilst there continue to be shortcomings in judicial decision-making, these have not been shown to demonstrate any conceptual flaws in the 'bifurcated approach'.

### 2.3.6 Is the causal nexus argument illusory?

As regards Cantor's argument that the purported advantage of the model that subsumes internal protection within the persecution element in terms of the 'Jewish shopkeeper' scenario is 'illusory', it is hard to follow. He writes that:

> [ ... ] the same result is achieved by considering the context of background State or societal discrimination under the 'for reasons of' element,[166] but the premise of this scenario is precisely this context. As stated by Lord Hoffman, even though the Aryan shopkeepers were motivated by economic motives, 'the Nazi government pursued a policy of not giving any protection to Jews subjected to violence by neighbours'.[167]

---

9th Circuit court overruled *Castro-Martinez v Holder* [2011] 674 F.3d 1073, and other circuit precedent, to the extent the latter had introduced the construct that the failure to report private persecution to government authorities creates a 'gap' in the evidence or imposed a heightened evidentiary requirement to establish governmental inability or unwillingness to protect. At page 34, the *en banc* constitution stated: '[l]ike all other circuits to consider the question, we do not deem the failure to report to authorities outcome determinative, and we consider all evidence in the record'. See also *Zometa-Orellano v Garland*, 19 F.4th 970 (2021), USCA 6th Cir., 2 November 2021. In discussing New Zealand case law, Burson (n 34) 42 writes that: 'while it is recognised that under international human rights law there is an emphasis on the exhaustion of domestic remedies, and failure by the claimant to avail themselves of those remedies may, in certain instances be determinative of the state protection issue, this principle is to be applied with caution in the refugee law context.' Zambelli (n 103) 35 considers that 'Canadian refugee law and refugee law generally does not support any such "rule". There is no legal "duty" per se to seek police protection, let alone to complain to police oversight agencies.'

[163] Wilsher (n 38) 98.
[164] Lehmann (n 44) 77–83, 95–104, 115–22; but for more recent position within the EU, see ibid 112–15.
[165] Zambelli (n 103) n 17.
[166] Cantor (n 27) 364.
[167] ibid. In a footnote further explaining his criticism, Cantor appears to think that Hoffman's approach is also unnecessary since '[t]here is no need to subsume these considerations under the "persecution" element as part of the consideration of internal protection, which also fails to capture wider societal discrimination'. But this argument is no clearer. The Jewish shopkeeper scenario does entail that in assessing persecution one takes into account wider societal discrimination, but it does not 'subsume' the latter. Such discrimination continues to have a separate role in establishing the causal nexus.

If Cantor means to make the point that the causal nexus can be made out, without recourse to the internal protection notion, simply by viewing the Jewish shopkeeper experience of discriminatory persecution as a matter of fact, that idea still needs breaking down in order to identify an actor responsible for there being a Convention reason.

2.3.7 Location of the protection test in the 'well-founded fear' element?
The contention that the 'well-founded fear' element can on its own encompass protection considerations (which must in part be substantive requirements) must fail. Such a contention only begins to make sense if the 'well-founded fear' limb is merged with the '*of* being persecuted' limb;[168] but once that is done, its main premise is removed. To say, as does Lehmann, that '"protection" is everything that reduces risk exposure to acts of persecuting or serious harm' only makes sense by reading 'protection' as encompassing serious harm/persecution.[169] It is all very well noting (as does Lehmann) that in both IHRL and the IHRL-based system of subsidiary protection set out in the QD context, '[t]he analysis of available protection is framed as a matter of the analysis of risk',[170] but a risk analysis cannot on its own explain what it is that is being, or not being, obviated, namely the persecution.

It is unsurprising (and certainly not contradictory) therefore that leading proponents of the 'bifurcated approach' have had no difficulty in combining emphasis on the importance of risk reduction with adherence to the 'bifurcated approach'.[171] For Hathaway and Foster, '[t]he ultimate question is not, however, whether the home state has complied with any particular standard of conduct, but whether the result of even the best intentions and most diligent efforts is to reduce the risk of claimed harm below the well-founded fear threshold'.[172] Such an approach properly reflects the need to *combine* risk analysis with consideration of the substantive issue of protection and its effectiveness.

Indeed, what can be gleaned from analysis so far is that both critics and proponents alike of the view that the 'protection' test belongs in the 'being persecuted' element of the definition, agree on the importance of a holistic approach. That being the case, it is difficult to disagree with the position taken by UNHCR in its 2001 Note that:

> Whichever approach is adopted, it is important to recall that the definition comprises one holistic test of inter-related elements. How the elements relate and the importance

---

[168] See Chapter 3, section 7.1.3.
[169] Lehmann (n 44) 85, 91. So far as concerns Lehmann's parallel view (see ibid 70, 83–85) that human rights law also conceives of protection as being about risk-reduction (he invokes the ECtHR statement in *HLR* (n 114) that 'it must be shown that the risk is real and that the authorities of the receiving state are not able to obviate the risk by providing appropriate protection'), it suffers from the same difficulty; for the ECtHR it is still obviation in terms of the provision or not of appropriate protection.
[170] Lehmann (n 44) 83.
[171] See e.g. Rodger Haines, 'Gender-related Persecution' in Erika Feller, Volker Türk, and Frances Nicholson (eds), *Refugee Protection in International Law: UNHCR's Global Consultations on International Protection* (CUP 2003) 333.
[172] Hathaway and Foster (n 20) 319. At 318, they state that '[s]ince "being persecuted" is itself a bifurcated notion, comprising the twin elements of serious harm and a failure of state protection, the well-founded fear test logically applies to each of the elements of serious harm and failure of state protection'.

to be accorded to one or another element necessarily falls to be determined on the facts of each individual case.[173]

It is perhaps regrettable that the scholarship since has sometimes forgotten that agreement on the contents of the elements of the refugee definition is what is fundamental, not the precise location of the various tests.

Nevertheless, the lack of any agreement on this issue remains all too apparent. This will need to be borne in mind when considering at the end of this chapter, whether this subject area yields any basic proposition about which there is a substantial consensus.

## 3 Meaning of Protection

Having established that protection is best understood as an ingredient of the meaning of being persecuted, it remains to consider its content. Although as always the analysis must apply VCLT rules of interpretation, it will in this instance also avoid repetition to address them in substance as and when relevant, rather than element by element. As we have seen, this aspect of the refugee definition requires particular weight to be attached to the object and purpose of the Convention, the latter which are appropriately conceived as protection against sufficiently severe violations of human rights.[174]

### 3.1 Multiple Uses

Despite being used multiple times in the Refugee Convention, the term protection is nowhere defined.[175] Article 1A(2) employs the term three times: once in the first paragraph ('and is unable or, owing to such fear, unwilling to avail himself of the *protection* of that country'); and twice in the second paragraph ('In the case of a person who has more than one nationality ... a person shall not to be deemed to be lacking the *protection* of the country of his nationality, if without any valid reason based on well-founded fear, he has not availed himself of the *protection* of one of the countries of which he is a national.'). Article 1C (the cessation clause) employs it four times.[176] It also occurs twice in Article 1D (an exclusion clause); twice in Article 14; twice in the Preamble; once in paragraph 16 to the Schedule; and (effectively) three times in

---

[173] UNHCR, Note on International Protection (n 107) para 37.
[174] See Chapter 6, sections 1.3.2 and 1.5.1.
[175] Nor of course is the term 'being persecuted', although see Hugo Storey, 'Persecution: Towards a Working Definition' in Vincent Chetail and Céline Bauloz (eds), *Research Handbook on Migration and International Law* (Edward Elgar 2014) 459–518.
[176] Emphasis added. Article 1C provides: 'This Convention shall cease to apply to any person falling under the terms of Section A if: (1) He has voluntarily availed himself of the *protection* of the country of his nationality; or ... (3) He has acquired a new nationality, and enjoys the *protection* of the country of his new nationality; or (5) He can no longer, because the circumstances in connexion with which he has been recognised as a refugee have ceased to exist, continue to refuse to avail himself of the *protection* of the country of his nationality.

Provided that this paragraph shall not apply to a refugee falling under section A(1) of this Article who is able to invoke compelling reasons arising out of a previous persecution for refusing to avail himself of the *protection* of the country of nationality' (emphases added).

Annex B of the Final Act of the United Nations Conference of Plenipotentiaries on the Status of Refugees and Stateless Persons. Elsewhere,[177] this author has classified these different uses into three main categories (putting the places where they occur or may be said to occur in brackets):

(a) protection by the country of origin or home country, or what is most-often termed 'internal protection' (Article 1A(2) first paragraph (twice), Article 1C(1) and (5) … );
(b) protection by the host country of asylum or new nationality (Article IA(2), second paragraph, Article 1C(3), Article 14, para 16 to the Schedule);
(c) protection by the international community or organs or agencies thereof (Article 1D, Annex 1D, Preamble).

Whilst interpretation must be mindful of these different usages, we are primarily concerned here with protection within the context of Article 1A(2) first paragraph, i.e. (a) above.

The meaning of 'protection' in the context of (b) and (c) above is relatively uncontroversial, but the same cannot be said for the term 'protection' in Article 1A(2) first paragraph, since (as will be analysed in Chapter 9) some argue that it refers to internal protection, some that it denotes external protection only and some that it refers to both.[178]

## 3.2 Connection with Protection in the Availment Clause

As already noted, treating protection within the context of Article 1A(2) as an integral part of the 'being persecuted' element involves some inevitable overlap with analysis of the availment clause (which will be the focus in Chapter 9), but logically there is no way round this, since as we have seen, the meaning of the 'being persecuted' element cannot be fully elicited without clarifying its protection ingredient and (at least in the view of this author) the latter surely derives from the availment clause.

However, the fact that the actual term 'protection' is only used in the first paragraph of Article 1A(2) of the refugee definition within the availment clause inevitably raises the question as to what is the connection between the two. The meaning accorded to the term in Article 1A(2) first paragraph must surely be the same, irrespective of whether focus is on its role in the availment clause or on its implicit role in the 'being persecuted' clause. That is indeed widely agreed. There is not necessarily agreement that all uses of the term 'protection' in the Convention should have the same meaning, but here we are concerned with its use solely within Article 1A(2). Whilst a consequence of the 'bifurcated approach' to the meaning of 'being persecuted' is that protection is (an unstated) part of that term's meaning, it would be odd indeed if its meaning in this context could be any different from that accorded to it in the availment clause, especially since it is only in the availment clause that the term appears at all in the definition's first paragraph.

---

[177] Hugo Storey, 'The Meaning of "Protection" within the Refugee Definition' (2016) 35(3) RSQ 1.
[178] See Chapter 9, section 4.

At the same time, the wide acceptance that within both elements the concept of protection possesses the same meaning does raise in acute form whether this entails envisaging that a protection test arises twice or that there are two different protection tests.[179] Or does interpreting protection as part of the meaning of 'being persecuted' simply render the protection aspects of the availment clause otiose? In Chapter 9 it will be argued that the protection criterion in the availment clause has two distinct functions. First, in cases where a person has been able to establish a well-founded fear of being persecuted (by virtue of the unwillingness or inability of the state to protect internally), it functions as a way of ensuring a specific check on whether, nonetheless, protection in the form of external protection can cause the applicant *overall* to avail himself of protection. This constitutes a substantive requirement, albeit of limited applicability.[180]

Second, it expressly identifies that two necessary requirements for protection to exist are ability and willingness. Put another way, 'protection' in the availment clause identifies two essential qualities of protection. This reading does require treating the terms of the availment clause purposively as covering both an *individual's* ability and willingness to avail himself of protection and a *state's* inability or unwillingness, but such a reading is almost universally accepted as legitimate. This further role for the availment clause can also be said to constitute a substantive requirement, at least insofar as it identifies two qualities of protection that can be drawn on when interpreting protection as part of the 'being persecuted' concept. In both respects, the underlying principle of surrogacy operates to ensure focus on whether the protection sought will be of sufficient quality to substitute for the failure of internal protection.

## 3.3 Background

As has often been observed, there are few words more protean in meaning than 'protection' and the picture has only become more blurred by usages that have emerged since 1951. In a 2013 article, Dallal Stevens wrote:

> Not only does the literature refer to 'diplomatic protection', 'consular protection', 'surrogate protection' and 'international protection', but we are now confronted by 'subsidiary protection' (as in the Qualification Directive), 'complementary protection', 'effective protection',[181] 'humanitarian protection', 'temporary protection', 'internal protection', 'protection gaps', 'protection capacities' and 'protection space', to name

---

[179] See e.g. the concern of Cantor (n 27) 363 about introduction of a 'double protection hurdle'. As regards the accepted possibility that the same word can have different meanings within the same treaty, see p. 641 and Chapter 10, n 332. See also n 224 below.

[180] See Chapter 9, section 4.5. One example would be if the only reason an applicant would lack protection in his or her country of origin is because he lacks ID papers, but in fact he could obtain these from his country's embassy in the host country.

[181] 'Effective protection' has become linked with the concept of 'safe third countries': see Goodwin-Gill and McAdam (n 37) 393. See also Lisbon Expert Roundtable, 'Summary Conclusions on the Concept of "Effective Protection" in the Context of Secondary Movements of Refugees and Asylum Seekers' (December 2002).

but a few. It is unsurprising, then, that some misunderstandings as to the nature and meaning of protection might arise as a consequence.[182]

It is possible perhaps to identify a common theme to dictionary definitions of the term, namely, defence against, or shielding from, danger[183] but that takes matters very little further. Within the domain of refugee law, protection has always been understood as a 'term of art' whose meaning must be specific to the refugee context.[184]

### 3.4 The Human Rights Approach to Protection

As noted earlier, applying a human rights approach to the refugee definition entails applying it as far as possible to all its constituent elements.[185] What is entailed by endowing the concept of protection with a meaning informed by IHRL norms?

It is possible to conceive of the concept of protection within Article 1A(2) as a purely negative concept focusing on the *status negativus*, i.e. on shielding or safeguarding *against* serious harm. Certainly, it is often described as such.[186] That also appears to comport with its ordinary meaning. Viewing it purely negatively might also be thought to go some way to explaining the lack of any attempt in the text to spell out what it specifically means. However, on closer analysis, to construe protection as just a negative concept is incompatible with a human rights approach. According to the latter, 'being persecuted' is primarily to be understood that its terms of sufficiently severe violations of human rights and, as noted earlier, key human rights guarantees encompass both negative and positive obligations.[187] Further, in relation to the duty to protect (in contrast to the duty to respect), positive obligations are of particular importance.[188] On the logic of this approach, although 'being persecuted' and 'protection' are interdependent terms, protection must be more than a simple absence of persecution.[189]

That protection in IHRL must encompass positive as well as negative aspects is well-established[190] and is well-illustrated by the famous European Court of Human Rights

---

[182] Dallal Stevens, 'What Do We Mean by Protection?' (2013) 20(1) Intl J Min and Grp Rts 233, 246–47.

[183] Shorter Oxford Dictionary (1992): 'defence from harm, danger or evil'. See further Kourula (n 5) 203. The word's Latin root, *pro tegere*, means literally 'to cover in front'.

[184] Guy S Goodwin-Gill, 'The Language of Protection' (1989) 1(1) IJRL 6, 6. See also Jane McAdam, *Complementary Protection in International Refugee Law* (OUP 2007) 19, stating: '[t]here is no singular concept of "protection" in international law. Although "protection" forms the essence of States' obligations vis-à-vis refugees, the term itself is not defined in any international or regional refugee or human rights instruments. It is a term of art.' See also *AG and Others* [2006] EWCA Civ 1342, para 65.

[185] See Chapter 3.

[186] e.g. UNHCR, Note on International Protection (n 107) para 11: 'The question is whether the risk giving rise to the fear is sufficiently mitigated by available and effective national protection'. See also Kees Wouters, *International Legal Standards for the Protection from Refoulement* (Intersentia 2009) 99: 'The [protection clause] is linked to the element of well-founded fear within the definition, in the sense that availability of national protection negates or removes the risk or well-founded fear of being persecuted.'

[187] See Chapter 6, sections 1.3.2, 1.5.1, and 1.12.

[188] Kälin and Künzli (n 121) 95–104.

[189] Hathaway (n 8) 106.

[190] Manfred Nowak, *Introduction to the International Human Rights Regime* (Martinus Nijhoff 2003) 25–30; see also Foster (n 63) 160.

(ECtHR) judgment in *Osman v UK*. This was not of course a case related to the refugee context, but rather about a state's responsibility to ensure effective policing within its own jurisdiction in the context of Article 2 EHCR and its guarantee of the right to life. The Court concluded that:

> [ … ] the Convention may also imply in certain well-defined circumstances a positive obligation on the authorities to take preventive operational measures to protect an individual whose life is at risk from the criminal acts of another individual.[191]

Is it possible to provide any more specific content to what is involved in understanding protection as giving rise to negative and positive obligations on the part of the state, in the refugee law context?

As just highlighted, two of the essential qualities that protection must exhibit can be gleaned from the text of Article 1A(2) itself, namely the requirements derivable from the availment clause of ability and willingness.

Whilst the requirements of willingness and ability are normally developed in the context of analysis of protection against serious harm from non-state actors, there is no doubting that they are just as essential qualities for protection against state actors.[192] Unless a state is willing to protect against all manner of actors of serious harm it cannot be said to afford protection.[193] Certainly unwillingness to protect (understood as taking the form of either state policy, condonation by the state, or inaction by the state in the face of third party persecution)[194] is sufficient to establish inadequacy of state protection.

---

[191] *Osman v United Kingdom* App No 23452/94 (ECtHR, 28 October 1998) para 115. In similar vein, the HRC General Comment No 36 (2019): Article 6 (Right to Life) (3 September 2019) UN Doc CCPR/C/GC/35, emphasised at para 3 that 'the right to life has been too often narrowly interpreted'. In para 4, it has stated: '[p]aragraph 1 of article 6 of the Covenant provides that no one shall be arbitrarily deprived of life and that this right shall be protected by law. It lays the foundation for the obligation of States parties to respect and ensure the right to life, to give effect to it through legislative and other measures, and to provide effective remedies and reparation to all victims of violations of the right to life'. Paragraph 7 lays down that 'States parties must also ensure the right to life and exercise due diligence to protect the lives of individuals against deprivations caused by persons or entities whose conduct is not attributable to the State. The obligation of States parties to respect and ensure the right to life extends to reasonably foreseeable threats and life-threatening situations that can result in loss of life. States parties may be in violation of article 6 even if such threats and situations do not result in loss of life.' See also IAmCtHR in the following cases: *Case of 'Las Dos Erres' Massacre v Guatemala*, Preliminary Objection, Merits, Reparations and Costs, IAmCtHR Series C No 171 (24 November 2009) paras 73, 79, and 152; *Case of Río Negro Massacres v Guatemala*, Preliminary Objections, Merits, Reparations and Costs, Judgment, IAmCtHR Series C No 250 (4 September 2012) paras 56, 58–60, 63.

[192] As recognised by the ECtHR in *N v Finland* App No 38885/02 (ECtHR, 26 July 2005) para 164.

[193] See above section 2.3.2. See also recital 27 of the QD (n 85), which provides (albeit in the context of internal protection only) that '[w]here the State or agents of the State are the actors of persecution or serious harm, there should be a presumption that effective protection is not available to the applicant'. In *Horvath* (n 51), Lord Hope noted that in cases of persecution by the State surrogate protection was obviously necessitated. Hathaway and Foster (n 20) 301 cogently argue that 'a clear dichotomy between state versus non-state actor cases may be overly simplistic'.

[194] Hathaway and Foster (n 20) 297 identify three situations where unwillingness will arise: where the state is 'unequivocally responsible for the infliction of serious harm'; 'where the central government encourages or condones persecution carried out by subordinate or localized arms of the government'; and where there is 'the state's toleration or tacit encouragement of non-state actors'.

Even more so must be inability. A state being unable to protect at all renders irrelevant whether there is willingness.[195]

In light of the earlier discussion of the arguments for and against understanding protection as an integral part of the meaning of the term 'being persecuted', it will obviously be important to ensure that glosses are not given to the ability and unwillingness concepts that unduly restrict their meaning. For example, the imposition in the US by the Trump administration of 'condonation' and 'complete helplessness' tests effectively sought to reduce state protection standards so as to cover only extreme case of state failures.[196]

Within IHRL the concept of ability to protect must encompass, inter alia, provision of physical security as well as the existence of a system of laws and basic administrative structure and the enablement of individuals within their jurisdiction to exercise their rights.[197] The literature recognises a broad spectrum of cases—from, on the one hand those where the inability may be confined to one aspect of the state machinery or policy or where the state itself admits its failure to protect,[198] through to cases where the state is a 'failed state' and there is no functioning government.[199]

Three other qualities of protection can be gleaned from both the developing case law, the wider literature, and from the guidance set out in the EU QD (recast). Accessibility and effectiveness are qualities often associated with the distinct and seemingly more demanding protection regimes appropriate to Article 1C, but in truth they are just as necessary in the context of Article 1A(2) including in (but as we shall see, not confined to) the context of assessing whether there is effective protection in a person's home area. If there is no access to protection in a person's home area, it is not possible to say that such a person will or can receive protection there. If protection in the home area is not 'effective', it can hardly amount to a situation that reduces the level of risk to below that of being persecuted. As noted earlier, in seeking to consolidate the case law of the CJEU, the wording added by the QD (recast) drafters to Article 7(2) was designed to reinforce the fact that in assessing whether state actors have taken reasonable steps to

---

[195] As noted earlier, Article 1A(2) does not refer in terms to the inability or unwillingness of the state to protect but rather to the inability and unwillingness of the person 'to avail himself of the protection of that country'. But both terms are frequently used interchangeably to relate to either individual inability or unwillingness to avail oneself of protection or state inability or unwillingness to protect. For example, the 1979 UNHCR Handbook (n 11) para 98 states that: '[b]eing unable to avail himself of such protection implies circumstances that are beyond the will of the person concerned'; but at para 65 states that serious discriminatory or other offensive acts committed by the local populace 'can be considered as persecution if they are knowingly tolerated by the authorities, or if the authorities refuse, or prove unable, to offer effective protection'.

[196] See *Matter of AB* [2018] 27 I&N Dec 316, which required applicants fleeing nonstate persecution to establish their government 'condones' that persecution or is 'completely helpless' to stop it; vacated in *Matter of AB* [2021] 28 I&N. For a critical evaluation, see Ellison and Gupta (n 82) 507–11; Anker (n 82) §4.11, 299–300.

[197] See Chapter, section 7.7.4. Paragraph 18 of the HRC, General comment No 36 (n 191) provides that: '[t]he duty to protect the right to life by law also includes an obligation for States parties to adopt any appropriate laws or other measures in order to protect life from all reasonably foreseeable threats, including from threats emanating from private persons and entities'. See also *Case of Peiris v Sri Lanka* (18 April 2012) Communication No 1862/2009, UN Doc CCPR/C/103/D/1862/2009 and *Case of Velásquez Rodríguez v Honduras* (n 130) para 166, both cited by Kälin and Künzli (n 121) 96.

[198] Hathaway and Foster (n 20) describe such cases as 'rare' and, at footnote 109 cite, inter alia, the case of *Ward* (n 20).

[199] See discussion in Hathaway and Foster (n 20) 303–19.

provide protection, the overall test is whether protection is practical and effective in the individual case.[200]

Likewise, unless protection is of a non-temporary nature, it cannot be said to obviate the real risk of serious harm. The CJEU in *Adbulla* appeared to regard the non-temporary requirement as an element of the refugee definition[201] and it seems that amendment to include reference to this requirement in Article 7(2) of the recast of the QD was made partly with this ruling in mind.

In broad terms, Article 7 of the recast QD can be said to evince a strong state practice, at least in the EU, of requiring protection for the purposes of the refugee definition to denote not just the negation of persecution but a positive content in the form of securement against violation of basic human rights of sufficient severity so as to conform with at least the five aforementioned requirements.

### 3.5 Protection and State Structures

Recalling what was said earlier about the nature of the duty to protect imposed under IHRL, these five qualities, especially ability, willingness, and effectiveness, can indeed be said to entail a number of concrete manifestations in terms of how a state organises itself. As noted already, IHLR requires that states must put in place laws and policies to ensure regulation of *public* as well as private practices in a manner that ensures human rights protection.[202] As stated by Kälin and Künzli, citing *Velásquez-Rodríguez v Honduras*:

> The duty to protect not only requires authorities to take action if someone is threatened but also 'to organise the governmental apparatus and, in general, all the structures through which public power is exercised, so that they are capable of juridically ensuring the free and full enjoyment of human rights'. More generally, 'States must prevent, investigate and punish any violation of the rights recognised by the [applicable] Convention and, moreover, if possible attempt to restore the right violated and provide compensation as warranted for damages resulting from the violation.'[203]

The above list of qualities does not necessarily exhaust the field. Given the role played in the refugee definition by the internal protection alternative, it is necessary to raise in Chapter 8 the issue of whether or not there is a further quality of protection that must be required in the context of internal relocation.[204]

---

[200] See above p. 438.
[201] *Abdulla* (n 17) para 73.
[202] See HRC, General comment No 36 (n 191) para 18; General Comment No 35 (n 130) para 7; see also *Case of Velásquez Rodríguez v Honduras* (n 130) para 166; *Öneryildiz v Turkey* (n 130) paras 89ff; Kälin and Künzli (n 121) 87.
[203] Kälin and Künzli (n 121) 96, citing *Case of Velásquez Rodríguez v Honduras* (n 130) para 166.
[204] See pp. 512–513 in which this author doubts whether there is an additional quality.

## 3.6 State Protection

Thus far, the attempt has been to define protection in terms of its inherent qualities, but given it is a term of art within the context of the refugee definition, one highly dependent on text and context, it is necessary to ask more specific questions about agency—in particular, who holds or wields the power and the duty to protect? Is it just a state through a government or can it be other entities? Reference to the duty to protect is critical since (as analysed in the foregoing sections) it is a prerequisite of the human rights approach to the meaning of 'being persecuted' that persecution arises if a state has failed in its basic duty of protection to those within its jurisdiction against violations of human rights of sufficient severity.

Textually, the meaning of protection within Article 1A(2) is indissolubly linked with the entity said to afford protection—the 'country of nationality' (or for stateless persons, the 'country of … former habitual residence'). But the entity referred to is 'country' and the Convention does not contain any reference to 'state' when referring to a country of origin of a national or stateless person.

Arising from this observable lack of any mention of the state, there has been argument as to whether the use of 'country' instead of 'state' demonstrates that protection is simply to be understood as something afforded by a 'country' in a physical or geographical sense,[205] rather than by a country in a legal sense. That argument has been very properly rejected in leading decisions and commentaries.[206] Crucially, one of the two uses of the word 'country' in Article 1A(2) refers to 'country of nationality' and to be a 'country of nationality' the entity in question must be one that has the capacity to bestow nationality; and nationality in this context exclusively connotes the legal bond between an individual (a national) and a state.[207] As we shall see, that does not, however, entirely dispose of the issue of whether, in the case of de facto authorities, they can be said to protect in the name of the state as a matter of international law. But even if the answer is that they can in certain circumstances, it is clear that the paradigm of the protection envisaged in Article 1A(2) is state protection.

Three matters need further exploration here: first what is the meaning of the term 'state' in this context; can it be said to be a basic duty of the state to protect those within its jurisdiction and if so, what does it consist of (these two will be dealt with together); and thirdly, whether de jure 'state protection' is the only form that protection can take for the purposes of the Refugee Convention.

## 3.7 Meaning of State and its Basic Duty to Protect

In relation to the meaning to be accorded to the notion of the state, the refugee law literature affords limited assistance. In analysing the elements of Article 1A(2), the 1979 UNHCR Handbook, for example, scrupulously eschews the term. Very few refugee

---

[205] See e.g. *Fadli Dyli (Protection—UNMIK—Arif—IFA—Art1D)* Kosovo CG * [2000] UKIAT 00001, paras 12–13. For a critique of this geographical approach, see pp. 275–277 and pp. 279–280.
[206] e.g. Hemme Battjes, *European Asylum Law and International Law* (Martinus Nijhoff 2006) 248.
[207] See Chapter 4, section 3.2.4.

law textbooks tackle the matter of its meaning. Hathaway and Foster scarcely touch on the issue. As regards the basic duty of the state to protect, there appears to be wide agreement that there is such a duty and that it is central to understanding protection in the country of origin. However, the language in which this basic duty is expressed is relatively imprecise and amorphous. Thus, Hathaway and Foster refer variously to 'suitable guarantee of the individual's well-being';[208] 'a political community that has clear protective duties under international law'; 'the accountable protection of a political community';[209] 'the usual benefits of nationality';[210] (quoting from Goodwin-Gill),[211] 'protection [of a degree] normally to be expected of the government';[212] (quoting Shacknove),[213] 'protection of the citizen's basic needs'.[214] As noted elsewhere, the last-mentioned quote from Andrew Shacknove, like a similar one from Grahl-Madsen,[215] has been repeated down the years in the literature.[216] Sometimes the basic duty to protect is portrayed as confined to 'citizens' (as is implied by the phrase 'the usual benefits of nationality'); but sometimes it is worded so as to extend to the population at large, to include citizens and non-citizens.

Given that it was concluded in Chapter 3 that the meaning of key terms of the refugee definition must be sought within the framework of international law,[217] it is first necessary to ask what assistance if any can be elicited from this wider framework?

Within international law, however, there is no easily identifiable criteria. The six most immediate sources for the meaning to be given to the term 'state' and to the possible contents of any state duty to protect those within its jurisdiction would appear to be: the international law relating to the state-individual relationship; the law dealing with 'statehood' and recognition of states; the law dealing with 'state responsibility'; customary international law; soft-law sources; and IHRL.

3.7.1 International law relating to state-individual relationship
Given broad acceptance that the drafters worked within traditional understandings of state sovereignty,[218] state jurisdiction,[219] and the legal bond of nationality,[220] it is

---

[208] Hathaway and Foster (n 20) 289.
[209] ibid 292.
[210] ibid.
[211] Goodwin-Gill (n 134) 38–46.
[212] Hathaway and Foster (n 20) 294.
[213] Andrew Shacknove, 'Who Is a Refugee?' (1985) 95 Ethics 274. Grahl-Madsen (n 76) 99 describes a refugee as 'a person who is not being given the protection which a State normally may give to its nationals'; see also Anker (n 82) §4.8, 271.
[214] Hathaway and Foster (n 20) 294.
[215] ibid.
[216] e.g. McAdam (n 184) 20: 'The need for international protection is predicated on the breakdown of national protection—a lack of basic guarantees which States normally extend to their citizens.'
[217] See Chapter 3, section 6.
[218] Whilst the international law on state sovereignty largely concerns a state's status vis-à-vis other states, it has been recognised that it has other strands, including 'domestic sovereignty': see e.g. Stephen D Krasner, *Sovereignty: Organized Hypocrisy* (Princeton University Press 1999) 4.
[219] Crawford (n 142) 431–69.
[220] 'A man's nationality is a continuing legal relationship between the sovereign State on the one hand and the citizen on the other': see *Robert John Lynch (Great Britain) v United Mexican States*, decision of 8 November 1929, United Nations, *Reports of International Arbitral Awards* (UNRIAA), vol V 17, para 223. See also *Nottebohm Case (second phase) (Liechtenstein v Guatemala)*, Judgment [1955] ICJ Rep 4, 23.

necessary to ask what light do such understandings shed on the individual-state relationship? They derive from Western political and legal theory regarding the bond between the citizen and the state, variously conceived of in terms of allegiance, natural law, social contract, or the democratic will of the people, etc. Within this discourse, it is axiomatic that the state's duty to protect the individual is correlative to the allegiance that the individual owes to the state.[221] In such discourse the connection between the citizen and the state is fundamental and is at the heart of the notion of jurisdiction based on the nationality principle. As Shacknove has pointed out, within political and legal theory, such understandings have a long history. Thus, according to Hobbes, it was for a state to defend the citizen not only 'from the invasion of foreigners', but also from 'the injuries of one another'.[222] Shacknove depicts this tradition as one in which the state should provide such protection, and where it fails to, 'the bonds which constitute the normal basis of citizenship dissolve'.[223] The workings of such thinking can also be seen in Grahl-Madsen's[224] and Kimminich's[225] notion of 'broken bonds'. As noted earlier, Hathaway and Foster draw very much on this tradition: they paraphrase Shacknove's concept of state inability to protect as 'a breakdown of the protection to be expected of the minimally legitimate state'.[226]

At the same time, at the level of international law, traditionally focussed on interstate relations, the state's internal administrative and political system has been seen as the 'reserved domain' of states.[227] The underlying political and legal traditions having a bearing on this concept viewed the conduct of the state vis-à-vis individuals within its own jurisdiction as subject to some constraints,[228] but these did not amount to a state's *duty* to protect. As noted by Glanville Williams, within the classical understanding the state's duty to refrain from unlawfully interfering with the rights of individuals cannot be characterized as a 'duty of protection'.[229]

---

[221] Glanville Williams, 'The Correlation of Allegiance and Protection' (1948) 10(1) Cambridge Law Journal 54. In *Luria v United States* [1913] 231 US 9, Justice Van Devanter wrote that: '[c]itizenship is membership in a political society, and implies a duty of allegiance on the part of the member and a duty of protection on the part of the society. These are reciprocal obligations, one being a compensation for the other.'

[222] Thomas Hobbes, *Leviathan* (Bobbs-Merrill Co 1958) 142, cited by Shacknove (n 213) 278.

[223] ibid 279. For a late-nineteenth century example, see influential German legal and political philosopher, Georg Jellinek, *The Declaration of the Rights of Man and of Citizens: A Contribution to Modern Constitutional History* (authorized translation from the German by Max Farrand, revised by the Author, Henry Holt and Co 1901), who drew on Anglo-American political and legal history to argue that the state limits itself by recognizing and providing fundamental rights for individuals as a measure of inherent self-limitation; see Duncan Kelly, 'Revisiting the Rights of Man: Georg Jellinek on Rights and State' (2004) 22(3) Law and History Review 493. An early example of this concept being implicitly applied in a refugee context is the observation by Jennings (n 3).

[224] Grahl-Madsen (n 76) 79, 91–92, 100.

[225] Otto Kimminich, *Der internationale Rechtsstatus des Flüchtlings* (Heymann 1962) 492.

[226] Hathaway and Foster (n 20) 294. Criticisms made of this notion have mainly focussed on its allegedly 'state-centric' character: see e.g. Thomas A Aleinikoff, 'State Centred Refugee Law: From Resettlement to Containment' (1992) 14(1) Michigan Journal of International Law 120, 123; Niraj Nathwani, *Rethinking Refugee Law* (Martinus Nijhoff Publishers 2003) 14. See also Jennings (n 3).

[227] According to Lung-chu Chen, *An Introduction to Contemporary International Law: A Policy-Oriented Perspective* (Yale University Press 1989) 117, the 'reserved domain is usually understood to entail a state's "competence to prescribe and apply law to persons, things and events within a territorial domain to the exclusion of other states"'.

[228] Shacknove (n 213) 278.

[229] Williams (n 221) 58, subdivided protection as follows: 'protection of the individual against the activities of others (whether such protection takes the form of force or persuasion) and respect for the individual

### 3.7.2 International law on statehood

The international law bearing most directly on the meaning of the term state is that in relation to 'statehood'. Article 1 of the Montevideo Convention of 1933, which is broadly accepted as reflecting customary international law, defines the necessary conditions of a state as being: a) permanent population; b) defined territory; c) a government; and d) a capacity to enter into relations with other states.[230] Although being primarily concerned with states as subjects of international law and their relations with each other, this understanding of statehood furnishes several insights.[231]

First, it confirms that the 'state' is not to be confused with 'government'.[232] It has been by reliance on this distinction that refugee law has resolved the difficult issue of 'failed states'.[233] The fact that there may be no government in such states does not necessarily mean that the country concerned is no longer a 'state' at the level of international law.[234] The same has been said by the International Court of Justice in the *Genocide case* in respect of lack of control over territory.[235]

A second insight is that the international law on statehood diverges from classical political and legal theory in not being concerned for the most part with what a state 'ought' to be like or how it should be expected to behave. The criteria are minimalistic and purely factual and are intended to provide a simple means of identifying for the purposes of inter-state relations when a state comes into being and when it ceases to be a state; they are not concerned with a state's willingness to protect or whether it is accountable for its conduct.[236] Nor are they concerned with whether a state is effective.

---

by the sovereign in the course of his own activities. The first may be called positive or active protection: the sovereign exerts himself actively on behalf of the individual against fellow-citizens or foreigners. The second is negative protection, the absence of illegal interference with the individual by the sovereign himself and his officers.' He considered that negative protection did not involve a duty to protect: see Williams (n 221) 63–64.

[230] Convention on Rights and Duties of States adopted by the Seventh International Conference of American States (adopted 26 December 1933) 165 LNTS 19. Note, however, that Crawford (n 142) 118, considers that '[n]ot all the conditions are necessary, and in any case further criteria must be employed to produce a working definition'.

[231] James R Crawford, 'The Criteria for Statehood in International Law' (1976) 48(1) British Yearbook of International Law 93.

[232] Ivan A Shearer, *Starke's International Law* (11th edn, London Butterworths 1994) 118; Crawford (n 142) 119. However, it is common to find the two terms equated. For example, the UNHCR Handbook (n 11) refers at para 166 to 'the availability of effective protection on the part of the government of the country of origin'.

[233] Walter Kälin, 'Non-State Agents of Persecution and the Inability of the State to Protect' (2001) 15(3) Georgetown Immigration Law Journal 415, 430. See below section 3.11.2.

[234] Robin Geiss, 'Failed States: Legal Aspects and Security Implications' (2004) 48 GYIL 457, 465 notes that '[q]uite strikingly, the legal personality of States that have lacked an effective government over a significant period of time—in the case of Somalia, for example, the situation has persisted for more than thirteen years—has never been questioned'; see also Kälin (n 233) 430. Sarah Bressan, 'What's Left of the Failed States Debate?' (2020) Global Public Policy Institute.

[235] In the *Application of the Convention on the Prevention and Punishment of the Crime of Genocide (Bosnia and Herzegovina v Serbia and Montenegro)*, Preliminary Objections [1996] ICJ Rep 595, the ICJ held that it adheres to the declaratory view, in the sense that the failure to maintain effective control over territory does not extinguish the legal entity in the eyes of the United Nations.

[236] Crawford (n 231) '[i]t is sometimes said that 'willingness to observe international law' is a criterion for statehood. But it is particularly necessary to distinguish recognition from statehood in this context. Unwillingness or refusal to observe international law may well constitute grounds for refusal of recognition,

One of the four criteria is stated as being simply 'government'; it is not stated as being 'effective' government.

A third possible insight offered by the law on statehood stems from the less well-defined but nevertheless strong acceptance that it also denotes a system of laws and/or legal norms. In his famous article on criteria of statehood, James Crawford, despite rejecting the idea that 'legal order' is a necessary condition of statehood,[237] saw it as salient to mention observations by D'Entrèves that in traditional theory the state is composed of three elements, the people of the state, the territory of the state, and the so-called power of the state:

> All three elements can be determined only juridically, that is, they can be comprehended only as the validity and the spheres of validity of a legal order.[238]

However, in any event, the definition of statehood in the international law governing statehood is of limited value first because it primarily concerns states as subjects of international law and their relations with each other; and secondly, reflective of this fact, it says virtually nothing about the issue of whether a state has a basic duty to protect its own citizens and/or population and/or what it specifically comprises.

### 3.7.3 International law of state responsibility

A second international law source resides in the international law on state responsibility. We have already seen that the precise extent to which this body of law assists with interpreting the concept of protection as an ingredient of the meaning of 'being persecuted' has been a controversial matter,[239] but it remains that it does contain a definition of the state, Further, although, once again, its primary focus is on the relationship between states, not between a state and its citizens/population, it is seen as integral to the concept of responsibility in this context that there is definitional clarity as to which of its organs and personnel have agency.

This area of international law clarifies that 'state' is not just to be understood in terms of the formal institutions of a state, nor is it to be confined to those agents who have a monopoly on the use of force (the army, the police, the security forces), but also includes the legislature and judiciary: see The Draft articles on Responsibility of States for Internationally Wrongful Acts, with commentaries, 2001 (ILC Draft articles).[240] Indeed, under the ILC Draft articles there are three layers to state responsibility. First the state is held responsible for the conduct of all organs, instrumentalities, and officials which form part of its organisation and act in that capacity, whether or not they have separate legal personality under its internal law (Chapter II (7)). Second the conduct of organs or entities empowered to exercise governmental authority is attributable to the state

---

or for such other sanctions as the law allows, just as unwillingness to observe Charter obligations is a ground for non-admission to the United Nations. Both are, however, distinct from statehood.'

[237] ibid.
[238] Alessandro Passerin d'Entrèves, *The Notion of the State: An Introduction to Political Theory* (OUP 1967) 96.
[239] See above sections 2.2.3 and 2.3.3.
[240] ILC, Draft articles (n 143).

even if carried out outside the authority of the organ or person concerned contrary to instructions (Articles 5 and 7). Third, even conduct, not that of the state organ or entity, is nonetheless attributed to the state where it is carried out on the instructions of a state organ or under its direction or control (Article 8) (this includes recruitment or instigation of private persons or groups to act as 'auxiliaries' outside the official structure of the state: Commentary to Article 8). Such an approach to definition has proved helpful to refugee law in clarifying, for example, the notion of persecution at the hands of state actors, by making clear that this can include, in certain circumstances, acts perpetrated by private actors acting under the control of state organs or entities, even if they are rogue actors acting contrary to instructions:[241] It must also be borne in mind, as noted earlier, that IHRL has drawn on the international law on state responsibility to shape its own understanding of state accountability for human rights violations.

Nevertheless, the ability of the international law on state responsibility to inform the meaning of protection within Article 1A(2) suffers from two chief limitations. First, already pinpointed, whilst pertaining to the 'Rights and Duties of States', it contains very little about the duty of the state towards its own population. The most that can be gleaned from its case law is that the protection of *foreign* citizens requires a certain minimum threshold as regards the general security in the country of residence and of the justice system, so that it could not be merely illusory.[242] Second, this body of law is predominantly about attributing fault. Refugee law decision makers, by contrast, have no jurisdiction to adjudicate state responsibility and are not concerned with state culpability.[243]

### 3.7.4 Customary international law

It is also pertinent to consider whether customary international law shines any light on the meaning of the state and in particular on whether the state has a basic duty to protect those within its jurisdiction.

According to Conclusion 2 of the ILC's Draft Conclusions on Identification of Customary International Law, '[t]o determine the existence and content of a rule of customary international law, it is necessary to ascertain whether there is a general practice that is accepted as law (*opinio juris*)'.[244] Customary international law includes the core of rules binding on states and other entities that constitute the international *ius cogens* and that cannot be derogated from. Though there is no definitive list, in a 2019 report, Special Rapporteur Dire Tladi notes that the ILC has recognised the following as having attained the status of peremptory norms:

> the prohibition of aggression or aggressive force (sometimes referred to as 'the law of the Charter concerning the prohibition of the use of force'); the prohibition of genocide;

---

[241] Kälin and Künzli (n 121) 69. However, both in UNHCR materials and in case law applying this understanding, it is hard to find any express reliance on the ILC Draft Articles: see e.g. UNHCR Guidelines No 9 (n 150) para 34. See also Hathaway and Foster (n 20) 301, where they cite a German Federal Administrative Court case, *A A S* 1116/11 [2013], and *Castro and Carranza-Fuentes v Holder* [2010] 597 F.3d 93. An important case on rogue state actors is *Svazas* (n 128) (per Sedley LJ), paras 15–21.
[242] Arbitrator Max Huber in *British Claims* (n 142).
[243] Hathaway and Foster (n 20) 301. See above sections 2.2.3 and 2.3.3.
[244] ILC, 'Draft conclusions on identification of customary international law' (2018) Report of the ILC: Seventieth Session, UN Doc A/73/10.

the prohibition of slavery;the prohibition of apartheid and racial discrimination; the prohibition of crimes against humanity;the prohibition of torture; the right to self-determination; and the basic rules of international humanitarian law.[245]

At paragraph 123 of the same report, the Special rapporteur added:

Beyond the list here proposed, other norms that have been cited as norms of *jus cogens*, and whose *jus cogens* status enjoys a degree of support, include the prohibition of enforced disappearance, the right to life, the principle of non-refoulement, the prohibition of human trafficking, the right to due process (the right to a fair trial), the prohibition of discrimination, environmental rights, and the prohibition of terrorism.[246]

Lambert has argued that customary law also includes: the prohibition of arbitrary deprivation of liberty; the right to leave any country; and the right to family reunification (by derivation from the right to respect for family life).[247]

But whilst it is possible to deduce from the customary law norms (either as listed by Tladi or as supplemented by Lambert above) that the state has a basic duty to protect its own citizens/population against specified forms of harm, such as genocide, slavery, apartheid (perhaps even arbitrary deprivation of liberty; the right to leave any country and the right to family reunification) etc., even when taken collectively such norms identify a duty to protect against the most serious of harms only.[248] The subset of harms protected against is, in relative terms, still extremely narrow, far narrower than the concept of protection as envisioned within Article 1A(2) of the 1951 Convention. '[B]eing persecuted' is clearly a broader term than subjection to the most egregious violations of international law. Customary international law cannot be used to ground a basic international law duty owed by states to protect those within their jurisdiction except in a narrow sense.

### 3.7.5 Soft-law sources on protection

For completeness, mention should also be made of soft-law sources on protection, and two in particular.

A relatively recent development of the UN and other bodies has been the 'Responsibility to Protect' (R2P) doctrine. This doctrine reflects a shift away from the citizen-state model, since within R2P protection is to be afforded to 'populations', a

---

[245] ILC, 'Fourth report on peremptory norms of general international law (*jus cogens*) by Dire Tladi, Special Rapporteur' (2019) UN Doc A/CN.4/727, para 60. See also ibid para 137 (Draft conclusion 24).
[246] ibid para 123.
[247] Hélène Lambert, 'Customary Refugee Law' in Cathryn Costello, Michelle Foster, and Jane McAdam (eds), *The Oxford Handbook of International Refugee Law* (OUP 2021) 242.
[248] Although the Special Rapporteur's list of norms that have been also 'cited' as attaining the status of peremptory norms include the right to life, his own discussion of it identifies only this right's bare essentials as having a peremptory character. As stated in ILC, Fourth report (n 245) para 128, '[t]here is also some support for the peremptory character of the right to life, or at least the prohibition on the arbitrary deprivation of life (right not to be arbitrarily deprived of life)'. As such, it would seem difficult to seek to extract from this assessment, a detailed set of positive obligations to protect life. Kälin and Künzli (n 121) 6, likewise include in their list of peremptory norms only the prohibition of 'arbitrary killing' ('for example, genocide, slavery, torture, and inhuman and degrading treatment; systematic racial discrimination, arbitrary killing, or taking hostages and collective punishment')'.

term that includes both nationals and non-nationals of the state. However, its parameters are also carefully limited to protection from a narrow subset of dangers only. Its first pillar proclaims that '[e]ach individual state has the responsibility to protect its populations from genocide, war crimes, ethnic cleansing and crimes against humanity. This responsibility entails the prevention of such crimes, including their incitement, through appropriate and necessary means.'[249]

Another influential soft-law source is the conclusions of the 1996 'Protection Workshop' convened by the International Committee of the Red Cross (ICRC) one of whose aims was to arrive at an agreed definition of 'protection' for use in humanitarian work. It concluded that:

> The concept of protection encompasses all activities aimed at obtaining full respect for the rights of the individual in accordance with the letter and the spirit of the relevant bodies of law (i.e. human rights, humanitarian and refugee law).[250]

Protection activity was defined as '[a]ny activity—consistent with the above-mentioned purposes—aimed at creating an environment conducive to respect for human beings, preventing and/or alleviating the immediate effects of a specific pattern of abuse, and restoring dignified conditions of life through reparation, restitution and rehabilitation.'[251] In viewing protection as encompassing responsive action, remedial action, and environment-building action, the Workshop used a diagram known as the 'ICRC protection egg' to illustrate the overlapping and holistic nature of protection from a humanitarian perspective.[252] Such an approach certainly overcomes the narrow approach of R2P but self-confessedly seeks to identify a wider concept of protection than that contained in refugee law on its own.[253]

## 3.8 International Human Rights Law

Last but far from least, it remains to consider IHRL, which is one further branch of international law. If any adequate answer is to be found to the key question posed

---

[249] 'The Responsibility to Protect' (n 5) xviii: 'sovereign states have a responsibility to protect their own citizens from avoidable catastrophe—from mass murder and rape, from starvation—but that when they are unwilling or unable to do so, that responsibility must be borne by the broader community of states'. See further Brian Barbour and Brian Gorlick, 'Embracing the Responsibility to Protect: A Repertoire of Measures including Asylum for Potential Victims' (2008) 20 IJRL 533; Anne Orford, *International Authority and the Responsibility to Protect* (CUP 2011); Jared Genser, 'The United Nations Security Council's Implementation of the Responsibility to Protect: A Review of Past Interventions and Recommendations for Improvement' (2018) 18(2) Chicago Journal of International Law 420.

[250] International Committee of the Red Cross, 'Conclusions of the 1996 International Humanitarian Law and Protection Workshop' (1996).

[251] ibid.

[252] I am indebted to Dallal Stevens' article (n 182) for this reference.

[253] For other notable examples of attempts to concretise criteria of protection see Galloway and Acton's IANLaw 2010 World Justice Project's Rule of Law Index and the Fragile States Index (FSI; formerly the Failed States Index). The latter is an annual report published by the US think tank, the Fund for Peace, and the American magazine *Foreign Policy* from 2005 to 2018, then by *The New Humanitarian* since 2019.

earlier—whether there is indeed a firm basis in international law for the refugee law notion that a state has a basic duty to protect—it must primarily be sought in IHRL.

Although IHRL also lacks any precise definition of the state, it too has drawn on notions to be found in general international law, the law on state responsibility in particular.[254] But it has not stopped there and has gone on to make absolutely central the fact that states have a duty to secure fundamental human rights. Of particular importance (given that the Refugee Convention's drafters dealt separately with nationals and non-nationals) is that its personal scope is also (like R2P's), unambiguously wider than for example in the state responsibility context. Except in very limited respects, IHRL imposes obligations on states in respect of everyone within their jurisdiction, non-citizens as well as citizens. Article 2(1) ICCPR stipulates that '[e]ach State Party to the present Covenant undertakes to respect and to ensure to all individuals within its territory and subject to its jurisdiction the rights recognized in the present Covenant, without distinction of any kind, such as race, colour, sex, language, religion, political or other opinion, national or social origin, property, birth or other status'.[255]

## 3.9 The Duty to Protect

It can be concluded (leaving aside soft law sources) that the only bodies of international law that come close to establishing the duty of a state to protect its own population are customary international law and IHRL. However, customary international law norms protect only against the most egregious acts of serious harm. They draw the boundaries *too narrowly* for the purposes of interpreting an international instrument based on risk of persecution.

How helpful a template is IHRL? It might be said that the duty to protect enshrined in various IHRL instruments draws the boundaries *too widely*, since IHRL imposes a duty on states to secure protection against all human rights violations. However, that difficulty is overcome by the accepted approach taken within IHRL in risk on return cases, when the claimed human rights violations primarily concern likely treatment of applicants in their home state. As explained above, in this special context, the applicant is required to show that the human rights violations in the home state would be of a sufficient severity and, correspondingly, that the protection afforded by their home state would be insufficient to prevent the serious harm/ill treatment underpinning such violations.[256] Accordingly, when the focus is the home state/country of origin to which the applicant faces refoulement, the basic duty to protect its population is not a duty to prevent violation of any human rights but only to secure individuals against

---

[254] Kälin and Künzli (n 121) 69 write that: 'the types of human rights violations attributable to the state may be inferred from the rules of international law governing *state responsibility*'. Arguably the Preamble of the American Convention on the Forced Disappearance of Persons (1994) 22 ILM 1529 draws on the international law of state responsibility to reinforce the need for protection against forced disappearances to extend to acts of 'agents of the State or ... persons or groups of persons acting with the authorisation, support, or acquiescence of the State'.
[255] See also ICESCR (n 15) Article 2(1).
[256] See above section 2.3.2.

sufficiently severe violations.[257] This being so, IHRL does offer a concrete source for giving meaning and content to the basic refugee law idea of protection as afforded by a state.

## 3.10 Protection Other than by the State

Given earlier rejection of the attempt to construe the term 'country' in Article 1A(2) as a purely geographical notion, does it follow that protection within the meaning of Article 1A(2) must always be state protection? Hathaway and Foster among others argue that the only protection capable of qualifying as effective protection under the refugee definition is state protection.[258] In the context of making this argument they appear to have in mind protection afforded by state actors understood as part of a government.

### 3.10.1 Main arguments against
The main arguments Hathaway and Foster and others[259] direct against the idea of protection other than by the state are as follows; that it misunderstands the role of Article 1D (which does identify protection other than by a state); that any such entities cannot exhibit essential qualities such as stability, durability etc.; and that such entities lack accountability in international law. They take strong issue with the recognition within the EU QD of the ability of parties or organisations, including international organisations, to be 'actors of protection' under Article 7.[260] Another argument (not always made explicit) is that the idea runs contrary to the principle of surrogacy understood as back-up 'national protection' provided only by state parties to the Refugee Convention.[261]

### 3.10.2 Arguments evaluated
In an important respect, this entire line of argument contains a puzzle. On the one hand, it regards any de facto entity as falling outside the concept of state for refugee determination purposes. On the one hand (as we will come to), when it comes to claims for refugee status brought by applicants from 'failed states', it seems to recognise that a state can still exist at the level of international law even if there is no or no accepted entity—government or otherwise—in power. This puzzle is explored further in section 3.11.

### 3.10.3 The significance of Article 1D protection
An obvious difficulty for the approach that protection must mean state protection (particularly bearing in mind VCLT considerations relating to context) is that Article 1D of

---

[257] ibid.
[258] Hathaway and Foster (n 20) 291–92.
[259] ibid 289–92; Maria O'Sullivan, 'Acting the Part: Can Non-State Entities Provide Protection Under International Refugee Law?' (2012) 24(1) IJRL 85.
[260] In *Abdulla* (n 17) para 74. The position taken by the EU on this issue is not unique. e.g. Anker (n 82) §4.9, 277–78 cites several US cases accepting that the concept of 'state' may include de facto regimes.
[261] Hathaway and Foster (n 20) 291.

the Refugee Convention recognises that protection can be afforded by at least one category of entity(ies) other than the state of nationality,[262] namely 'protection or assistance of organs or agencies other than UNHCR protection or assistance' (Article 1D).[263] The fact that one and the same article of the Refugee Convention (Article 1) refers to more than one species of protection, might seem to afford some basis for considering that its core meaning is broad and that 'protection of the country of nationality' in Article 1A(2) and 'protection or assistance' in Article 1D are both to be understood as just adjectival manifestations of a core set of protective activities conceived in functional terms. Hathaway and Foster seek to overcome this apparent difficulty by maintaining that Article 1D is an isolated exception to the paradigm of state protection. It is significant in their view that the rights and obligations that accrue to persons in receipt of UNRWA protection are 'broadly analogous' to those of citizens. Surely, however, the same could be said about at least some de facto state entities—that their protection is 'broadly analogous' to state protection? As strong as the argument of Hathaway and Foster may be for the idea that the paradigm of domestic protection within the Refugee Convention is state protection,[264] it remains that at the abstract level, protection in Article 1 is a genus of which the state is only one species.

Doubt also exists regarding the other arguments brought by Hathaway and Foster, and O'Sullivan,[265] among others, for rejecting the notion that protection does not necessarily have to be state protection.

3.10.4 Inherent problems with such entities in terms of stability, durability etc.
One main rationale for rejecting the notion that protection can be afforded by entities other than a state through a government is that in practice such entities are unlikely to have the necessary qualities of stability and durability etc. Thus, UNHCR has been heavily critical of the wording of Article 7(1) of the QD, which (as noted above) defines 'actors of protection' to include both 'the State' (7(1)(a)) and 'parties or organisations, including international organisations, controlling the State or a substantial part of the territory of the State' (7(1)(b)). UNHCR has pointed out that non-state actors normally only exercise authority in a state on a temporary or transitional basis and have a limited ability to enforce the rule of law.[266] Likewise, O'Sullivan has highlighted

---

[262] The precise phrase refers to 'protection or assistance'.
[263] Despite the use of the plural in Article 1D ('organs or agencies'), Hathaway and Foster argue, like many other commentators, that the only entity capable of fulfilling that function is UNRWA: Hathaway and Foster (n 20) 509–22.
[264] ibid 463.
[265] Maria O'Sullivan, 'Territorial Protection: Cessation of Refugee Status and Internal Flight Alternative Compared' in Satvinder S Juss (ed), *The Ashgate Research Companion to Migration Law, Theory and Policy* (Routledge 2013) 222.
[266] For UNHCR's rejection of the ability of UN bodies to protect, see Madeline Garlick, 'UNHCR and the Implementation of Council Directive 2004/83/EC on Minimum Standards for the Qualification and Status of Third Country Nations or Stateless Persons as Refugees or as Persons who Otherwise Need International Protection and the Content of the Protection Granted (The EC "Qualification Directive")' in Karin Zwaan (ed), *The Qualification Directive: Central Themes, Problem Issues, and Implementation in Selected Member States* (Wolf Legal Publishers 2007) 65. It must be noted, however, that UNHCR has generally avoided

the fact that such actors are very often unstable entities quite unable to deliver effective or durable protection.[267]

However, powerful as it is, the assertion that such entities can at best only prevent immediate threats of harm is based on historical practice. Being only a matter of contingent fact, it cannot be used to refute at the level of theory the notion that protection can be afforded by actors other than state actors. In any event, one has only to think in recent times of entities that seek to operate as de facto regimes such as the authorities in control of Somaliland in Somalia or of the Kurdistan region of Iraq which according to reputable country reports[268] have in recent times (arguably) proved at least relatively stable and durable.

### 3.10.5 Lack of accountability

The other main objection, however, is made at the level of theory and has to do with accountability. Echoing many commentators on this point,[269] Hathaway and Foster consider the idea that non-state entities can protect as 'misconceived' for the following reason:

> Even if a clan or militia were able to prevent the immediate threat of harm, indeed even if it operated its own version of what the EU refers to as an 'effective legal system', the 'protection' afforded would be subject to little, if any, accountability at international law.[270]

---

any categorical rejection of protection being afforded by non-state entities. For example, the UNHCR, Guidelines No 4: Internal Flight or Relocation Alternative Within the Context of Article 1A(2) of the 1951 Convention and/or 1967 Protocol Relating to the Status of Refugees (23 July 2003) UN Doc HCR/GIP/03/04, para 16 states defeasibly that '[t]he general rule is that it is inappropriate to equate the exercise of a certain administrative authority and control over territory by international organisations on a transitional or temporary basis with the national protection provided by States. Under international law, international organisations do not have the attributes of a State.' The same defeasible language is used in para 17: 'Similarly, it is inappropriate to find that the claimant will be protected by a local clan or militia in an area where they are not the recognised authority in that territory and/or where their control over the area may only be temporary. Protection must be effective and of a durable nature. It must be provided by an organised and stable authority exercising full control over the territory and population in question.'

[267] O'Sullivan (n 259) 107 states that: '[t]here are a number of reasons why non-state actors may not be able to protect citizens in the same way as states: clans and militias are typically more vulnerable to overthrow by opposing clans and militias, and non-state bodies usually operate as "protectors" when the state has failed or there is ongoing civil war within a country. In such situations, a non-state actor may have only a tenuous hold of power.' See also Hathaway and Foster (n 20) 289–91; and ECRE, 'Actors of Protection and the Internal Protection Alternative: European Comparative Report' (2014) 34.

[268] According to Landinfo, '[a]lthough no state has recognised its independence, Somaliland currently functions as an independent state with its own territory, population, laws and institutions'. In addition, it notes that 'the security situation in Somaliland has generally been peaceful and stable.' See <https://landinfo.no/en/>, accessed 12 July 2021. In relation to the Kurdistan region of Iraq, EASO has noted that the 2016 Fact-Finding Mission report by the Danish Immigration Service (DIS) stated that in areas controlled by the KRG, their police and military units 'have the potential to provide very effective security'. See the EASO, Country of Origin Information Report: Iraq, Actors of Protection (2018) para 8.2, 75.

[269] See e.g. UNHCR, 'UNHCR Statement on the "Ceased Circumstances" Clause of the EC Qualification Directive' (14 August 2008).

[270] Hathaway and Foster (n 20) 291–92.

For Hathaway and Foster among others, it is only really acts carried out by state actors that can qualify as protection within the meaning of Article 1A(2) because it is only states that can be held accountable at international law.[271]

Leaving aside that in other contexts Hathaway and Foster have roundly rejected the relevance of the law of state responsibility,[272] there are, however, a number of difficulties with this 'accountability' approach.

First, whilst it is true that states have accountability at international law, the human rights approach is primarily concerned with accountability for human rights violations under IHRL law.[273] But within this context a state is responsible for human rights violations even if it is a failed state with no functioning government. That indeed must be the basis for Hathaway and Foster's (widely shared)[274] view that applicants from failed states can establish refugee eligibility.[275] Having regard to the 'the most straightforward example of a failure of state protection', namely 'where there is no state or the state has completely or effectively failed', they write (with reference to the example of a decision of the French Refugee Appeals Commission regarding Somalia) that:

> In such a case it is immaterial whether a person is at risk of serious harm by a clan, tribe or organisation controlling all or large parts of the state, or a more localised non-state actor such as a family member. The fact that there is no state available to offer protection means that there is a clear need for surrogate protection.[276]

Yet if a state can be accountable for a failure of state protection even when there is no government in control, why should that be any less the case when there are de facto actors in control? In both scenarios the failure is the responsibility, in IHLR terms, of the state concerned. It is not the identity of actors as either state or de facto state actors that is determinative, but the overall inability of the state to protect and its failure thereby to secure human rights. Significantly, whilst Article 7(1)(b) of the QD (recast) recognises that non-state actors in the form of 'parties or organisations, including international organisations' can be actors of protection, it does so only insofar as such entities control the state.[277] They are entities existing within the self-same state.

---

[271] O'Sullivan (n 259) cites the following sources as supporting the accountability approach: UNHCR, Annotated Comments on the EC Council Directive 2004/83/EC of 29 April 2004 on Minimum Standards for the Qualification and Status of Third Country Nationals or Stateless Persons as Refugees or as Persons Who Otherwise Need International Protection and the Content of the Protection Granted (OJ L 304/12 of 30.9.2004) (2005); ECRE, 'Information Note on the Council Directive 2004/83/EC' (2004); Battjes (n 206) 249; Jane McAdam, 'The Qualification Directive: An Overview' in Zwaan (n 266) 1.
[272] See e.g. Hathaway and Foster (n 20) 314.
[273] Hathaway (n 8) 104, cites approvingly Chooi Fong's words in her article, 'Some Legal Aspects of the Search for Admission into Other States of Persons Leaving the Indo-Chinese Peninsula in Small Boats' (1981) 52(1) BYIL 53, 92, that: '[t]he concept of persecution is usually attached to acts or circumstances for which the government ... is responsible ... [and which] leave the victims virtually unprotected by the agencies of the State'.
[274] But not universally shared, see below n 292.
[275] Hathaway and Foster (n 20) 308–09.
[276] ibid.
[277] QD (recast) (n 85) Article 7(1)(b) refers to such entities 'controlling the State or a substantial part of the territory of the State'.

Second, entities other than states with governments can be accountable at international law, at least in limited respects. IHRL considers that in certain circumstances de facto state entities can have a duty to protect against human rights violations. So too international organisations, the UN for example, can have responsibility for the conduct of their organs or agents.[278] The HRC has held that the UN Interim Administration Mission in Kosovo was responsible for the human rights situation in that part of Serbia.[279] Significantly, the HRC has seen such organisations to be effectively exercising power delegated by the relevant state parties. Thus, in General Comment No 31 (2004), it stated:

[ ... ] a State party must respect and ensure the rights laid down in the Covenant to anyone within the power or effective control of that State Party, even if not situated within the territory of the State Party.... This principle also applies to those within the power or effective control of the forces of a State Party acting outside its territory, regardless of the circumstances in which such power or effective control was obtained, such as forces constituting a national contingent of a State Party assigned to an international peace-keeping or peace-enforcement operation.[280] Transnational corporations and businesses, armed opposition groups, international and nongovernmental organisations can be accountable in some circumstances.[281] That such circumstances are extremely limited does not alter the fact that states with governments are not the only accountable entities.[282]

---

[278] *Difference Relating to Immunity from Legal Process of a Special Rapporteur of the Commission on Human Rights*, Advisory Opinion [1999] ICJ Rep 62, 88–89; see also *Reparation for Injuries Suffered in the Service of the United Nations*, Advisory Opinion [1949] ICJ Rep 174, 179; *Interpretation of the Agreement of 25 March 1951 between the WHO and Egypt*, Advisory Opinion [1980] ICJ Rep 73. The ILC Draft Articles on the Responsibility of International Organisations (n 143) para 87, state at Article 3 that to be held responsible for their international wrongful acts, international organisations must have international legal personality, and at Article 4 that such acts must fulfil two requirements: they must be attributable to the organisation concerned, and must entail a violation of an international legal obligation incumbent on that organisation.

[279] HRC, Concluding Observations on Kosovo (Serbia) (14 August 2006) UN Doc CCPR/C/UNK/CO/1. Cited by Wouters (n 186) 398, who notes that the responsibility of the United Nations Mission in Kosovo (UNMIK) for the protection and promotion of human rights in Kosovo is based on the UNSC Res 1244 (10 June 1999) UN Doc S/RES/1244(1999), para 11(j).

[280] HRC, General Comment No 31 (n 131) para 10. See also Wouters (n 186) 374.

[281] See Clapham (n 90) 271–316; Philip Alston and Ryan Goodman, 'Non-State Actors and Human Rights' in Philip Alston and Ryan Goodman, *International Human Rights Law* (OUP 2013) 1461–515. Non-state actors have obligations under various IHL instruments. Article 3 common to the Geneva Conventions applies to organized armed groups in their capacity as parties to a non-international armed conflict; the 1977 Additional Protocol II to the Geneva Conventions, the Hague Regulations, the Convention for Protection of Cultural Property in the Event of Armed Conflict, and customary international law also impose obligations on organised armed groups. There are also a number of instruments outside the law of armed conflict that impose obligations on non-state actors, including the Terrorism Suppression Conventions and the Genocide Convention. The practice of the UN Security Council has also imposed obligations on non-state actors, including in the context of counter-terrorism, arms embargoes, and access to humanitarian assistance: see e.g. UNSC Res 1474 (2003) UN Doc S/RES/1474 (2003), where the UNSC stressed 'the obligation of all States and *other actors*' to comply with its previous resolution imposing an arms embargo in Somalia. See Ben Saul, 'The Responsibility of Armed Groups Concerning Displacement' in Costello et al (n 247) 1138–56.

[282] See Jans Klabbers 'The Accountability of International Organisations in Refugee and Migration Law' in Costello et al (n 247) 1157–73.

Third, refugee law has never seen the thresholds of serious harm and effective protection to vary depending on whether or not the relevant home state is or is not a signatory to international human rights treaties;[283] at best that is only part of the evidence as to the level of risk. The focus has almost always been on what the state does in fact by way of protection or lack of it. In the context of assessing whether there is a well-founded fear of being persecuted in an applicant's country of origin, accountability cannot depend on the contingency of whether or not a state has ratified an international human rights treaty. In any event, although still limited, the ways in which de facto actors can be held to be accountable in international law for failures of protection are increasing.[284]

Fourth, Hathaway and Foster's approach deviates from that which they elsewhere deem the correct approach, namely one that considers that the test for whether or not there is effective protection should be a factual one based on results and actual performance.[285]

### 3.10.6 Tension with the principle of surrogacy

It is certainly true that, Article 1D (and countries of former habitual residence) aside, the system of obligation established by the Refugee Convention rests on states alone providing the back-up or substitute protection.[286] But, as noted already,[287] the principle of surrogacy does not logically entail that the substitute be an exact substitute. Indeed, even where, for example, the international community has settled on a protection system not based at a state level, as it has done in Article 1D, the protection afforded would still be surrogate.

## 3.11 Protection and Failed States

Given that in the course of the above analysis reference has been made to different scenarios in which state protection appears problematic, it will assist to address two such scenarios further: first when a state loses control over part of its national territory and there exist de facto authorities; second, when there is no functioning government at all. In relation to both, it will be argued that the difficulties they cause in the context of a refugee law understanding of protection can be largely resolved by taking a human rights approach.

---

[283] Hathaway and Foster (n 20) 199–200.
[284] Clapham (n 90) 503; Andrea Bianchi (ed), *Non-State Actors and International Law* (Routledge 2009); Saul (n 281).
[285] Hathaway and Foster (n 20) 314, 319, 323, 332.
[286] Even when UNHCR does refugee status determination (RSD), that is ordinarily done with the consent of the host state concerned. Bruce Burson, 'Refugee Status Determination' in Costello et al (n 247) 578 considers that 'RSD systems exist on a structural spectrum, with State-administered RSD at one end and mandate RSD at the other'.
[287] See above section 1.4.3.

### 3.11.1 Partially failed states

In the first scenario (which I shall term the 'partially failed state scenario'), the state has lost control over part of its national territory and there exist de facto authorities (who may or may not be under the control of another state occupying part of the territory). The presenting problem here is that some consider that individuals at risk of serious harm at the hands of such 'private' actors, are not victims of human rights violations because under the international law on state responsibility the state is not accountable for strictly private actions.[288] However, this scenario is accommodated by a human rights approach. As the ECtHR decided in *Ilascu and Others v Moldova and Russia* in relation to Moldova vis-à-vis the de facto authorities in control in Transdniestria:

> [ ... ] even in the absence of effective control over the Transdniestrian region, Moldova still has a positive obligation under Article 1 of the Convention to take the diplomatic, economic, judicial or other measures that it is in its power to take and are in accordance with international law to secure to the applicants the rights guaranteed by the Convention.[289]

It is important to note in light of this example why it can be vital in terms of a human rights approach, to acknowledge that de facto state actors can protect. At least for approaches that limit state protection to effective protection by governmental authorities, the danger is that claims for refugee status brought by persons from regions where the writ of the governmental authorities does not run, will be rejected on the basis that any real risk of serious harm is not attributable to any formal state authorities. But on the human rights approach, such failure may still involve a violation of human rights. Here international law and IHLR have marched together to reduce the protection gap. As analysed by Kälin and Künzli (discussing certain exceptions to the rule that the state will not be held accountable for the actions of non-state groups in civil wars and similar circumstances):

> [ ... ] during an international armed conflict, a civil war or a revolution the authority of the state may collapse completely and in the resulting power vacuum private groups without formal authority begin to discharge state functions, such as laying the

---

[288] The ILC Commentary on Article 11(1) of the ILC Draft Articles on State Responsibility states that '[t]he acts of private persons or of persons acting ... in a private capacity are in no circumstances attributable to the State'.

[289] *Ilascu and Others v Moldova and Russia* App No 48787/99 (ECtHR, 8 July 2004) para 331; see also paras 333, 351. This approach was confirmed by the Grand Chamber in *Catan and Others v Moldova and Russia* Apps Nos 43370/04, 8252/05 and 18454/06 (ECtHR [GC], 19 October 2012) paras 109–10. See also *Loizidou v Turkey* App No 15318/89 (ECtHR, 18 December 1996) para 52. Kälin and Künzli (n 121) 124, note that a similar approach was taken by the HRC with respect to Georgia (Abchasia and South Ossetia) and Moldova (Transdniestria). See HRC, Concluding Observations on Georgia (2007) UN Doc CCPR/C/GEO/CO/3/CRP.1, para 6; HRC, Concluding Observations on Moldova (2016) UN Doc CCPR/C/MDA/CO/3, paras 5–6. In relation to Palestine, see also *Mangisto and al-Sayed v the State of Palestine* (23 March 2023) Communications Nos 67/2019 and 69/2019, UN Docs CRPD/C/28/D/67/2019 and CRPD/C/28/D/68/2019, para 8.8. In such situations states may, in addition, incur responsibility for the acts of armed groups under general international rules of attribution (Articles 9 and 10 ILC Draft Articles on State Responsibility (n 143)).

foundations for a rudimentary police force and judicial authority or collecting taxes. If, in such circumstances, private actors violate human rights while exercising de facto governmental authority, the violations are attributable to the state concerned. The authorities of said state, however, must genuinely be incapable of functioning in the area in question and the assumption of de facto governmental authority must appear to be necessary in the circumstances.[290]

Viewed in this light, 'we need not', as Clapham has observed, 'abandon human rights thinking in the absence of a government ready to carry out all the traditional functions of statehood'.[291] Consideration of this scenario strongly indicates that as regards accountability, refugee law should move in tandem with human rights law.

### 3.11.2 Fully failed states

The second problematic scenario concerns (what I shall term 'the fully failed state scenario') a state that has no functioning government. The question already raised about such a state needs scrutinising further here: if there are no state actors, how can it be considered that individuals at risk of serious harm from private actors are at risk of human rights violations? A limited number of commentators and judges have concluded that in such circumstances, individuals fall out with the refugee definition.[292] However, so long as there is a state at the level of international law, it follows from the human rights approach to the refugee definition that such a state remains bound by human rights obligations throughout the absence of an effective government.[293] The fact that there are no specific state actors to whom failure to protect can be attributed does not negate the responsibility of the state for human rights violations; it simply

---

[290] Kälin and Künzli (n 121) 71. See also Hans-Joachim Heintze, 'Are De Facto Regimes Bound by Human Rights?' in IFSH (ed), *OSCE Yearbook 2009* (Baden-Baden 2010) 267–75; Jonte van Essen, 'De Facto Regimes in International Law' (2012) 28 Merkourios-Utrecht J Int'l & Eur L 31; Anthony Cullen and Steven Wheatley, 'The Human Rights of Individuals in De Facto Regimes under the European Convention on Human Rights' (2013) 13(4) Human Rights Law Review 691; Lucia Leontiev, 'The Application of International Human Rights Law in De Facto States' in Sebastian Relitz (ed), *Obstacles and Opportunities for Dialogue and Cooperation in Protracted Conflicts* (Leibniz Institute for East and Southeast European Studies 2018).

[291] Clapham (n 90) 14.

[292] Kälin (n 233) 430, gives the example of Ben Vermeulen et al, *Persecution by Third Parties* (University of Nijmegen 1998) 24–26. In *Minister for Immigration v Ibrahim* [2000] 204 CLR 1, there was disagreement over this issue. Gummow J for the majority appeared doubtful that the Refugee Convention did not apply if there is no effective state (ibid para 141). McHugh J in the minority considered at ibid para 69 that '[w]here the State has disintegrated, as appears to have been the case in Somalia, so that there is no State to prevent the persecution of a person by private individuals or groups, that persecution will fall within the definition of refugee just as it would if an existing government had failed to protect that person from the persecution'. The current position in Australia appears to accept that where there is no functioning government, applicants can be considered to lack protection for Refugee Convention purposes: see Guide to Refugee Law in Australia, available at <http:/www/aat/gov.au> accessed 30 January 2022.

[293] Zimmermann and Mahler (n 8) 368, note that a 'failed State remains bound by human rights obligations even when the government has fallen apart. [ . . . ] To exclude those situations from the notion of "persecution" would make it most difficult to obtain refugee status where the risk would be the most obvious.' As noted above, this also appears to be the logic of Hathaway and Foster's analysis of such states.

means that there is by definition a general inability to guarantee the protection of the population.[294] As stated by Kälin:

> [ ... ] a collapse of governmental power does not terminate the existence of a State. Failed States remain subjects of international law even if they no longer have any functioning authorities: they usually do not terminate their membership in international organizations; their territory cannot be annexed by another state as stateless land, and an invasion of this territory still constitutes, according to the UN Charter, a violation of the prohibition of the use of force and it leads to an interstate armed conflict in the sense of 1949 Geneva Conventions on humanitarian law. Thus, States without governments just represent an extreme case of a situation of inability to protect because authorities are not just too weak to do so, but are totally lacking. In such situations, victims of persecution by non-state actors are *unable* to get external protection because the State no longer has functioning embassies and consulates abroad, or, even if such institutions still exist, will be too weak to effectively provide the necessary diplomatic and consular protection effectively.[295]

This last quotation points up that one of the underlying problems affecting the debates on this subject is an awkwardness of language, 'state' sometimes being understood as its government and sometimes as an entity at the level of international law. Greater precision of language will be key in any future attempts to resolve them.

## 3.12 Effectiveness of Protection and the Role of Civil Society Actors

Whilst in foregoing sections analysing the role of state protection this chapter has taken the position that protection (within the meaning of Article 1A(2) first paragraph) can be afforded by entities other than a state, this has been on the basis that such an entity must be either a de facto state or an international organisation meeting certain qualitative requirements. Barring these exceptions, there can be no other actors of protection. Civil society or other private actors cannot therefore qualify as actors of protection.

However, earlier it was pointed out that, under the internal protection approach, effectiveness of protection has become a central criterion, capturing on the one hand the need to establish that to be truly able and willing to protect, the home state must be able to deliver effective protection.[296] This issue is not made easy by the porous nature of the term 'effective' whose meaning clearly depends heavily on context. But in any event, if effectiveness is a central criterion, the question arises of how does

---

[294] See Geiss (n 234) 489: '[h]uman rights, even though they remain legally in force throughout the absence of an effective government, are thus insufficient to guarantee the protection of the population'. It is possible that one of the reasons why early jurisprudence sometimes considered that the refugee definition did not apply to failed states was that the UNHCR Statute para 6(B) refers to 'protection *of the government* of the country of his nationality' (emphasis added). However, any possible argument based on this must confront the counter-argument that the 1951 Convention definition did not replicate this.
[295] Kälin (n 233) 430.
[296] See above pp. 446–448.

one measure or gauge whether the protection (which can only be provided by state or de facto state authorities) is effective? The very term 'effective protection' suggests the existence of a threshold between protection that is effective and protection that is ineffective. Applying well-established principles relating to assessment of refugee claims,[297] assessing effectiveness would appear to require a rounded assessment encompassing both individual assessment and assessment of the general circumstances in the country of origin, including the extent to which the state or de facto state authorities are generally able or unable to afford protection.

On the issue of effectiveness at the general level, there have been two sharply contrasting approaches: on the one hand there is the view that any protective functions performed by civil society actors are irrelevant to the issue of whether protection is effective; on the other hand, there is the view that to treat them as irrelevant would be contrary to a rounded or holistic approach.

This controversy has been the subject of both judicial and academic consideration. Up until 2020, one prominent position taken in the case law was that assessment of the effectiveness of protection had to be considered holistically, taking into account all types of protective acts whether carried out by state or non-state actors. However, that was flatly rejected by the CJEU in *O A*.[298] The CJEU's judgment in *O A* considers that the issue of effective protection is to be confined solely to assessment of what the state or parties or organisations controlling the state or a substantial part of the territory of the state provide or fail to provide. In particular, the Court held that provision by private actors of security or social and financial support is 'irrelevant' to the issue of whether actors of protection provide effective protection.[299]

It is too early to tell whether courts and tribunals outside the EU will follow this CJEU ruling, although it is likely to have strong persuasive effect.

The issue of whether civil society actors have any role in assessing the effectiveness of protection has also been the subject of academic debate. It is argued by Hathaway and Foster with reference to a number of Canadian cases that because the protection within Article 1A(2) must be state protection, this means that it must consist of acts that emanate from state organs, not civil society or 'non-governmental' organisations. In relation to the specific example of women's shelters, they argue that:

> [ ... ] the availability of forms of assistance and relief such as those providing material relief, psychological support, and other remedies essential to victim recovery is irrelevant to the question of whether there is an ability on the part of the state to provide protection.[300]

Hathaway and Foster[301] cite a Strasbourg case, *Opuz*, which they say reaches a similar conclusion in the context of human rights law.[302]

---

[297] As set out, for example, in Article 4 QD (recast) (n 85).
[298] *O A* (n 88).
[299] ibid paras 48, 52–53, 63.
[300] Hathaway and Foster (n 20) 329–30.
[301] ibid 300.
[302] ibid 171–72. See *Opuz v Turkey* App No 33401/02 (ECtHR, 9 June 2009).

### 3.12.1 Evaluation

The reasoning of the CJEU in relation to which entities can constitute *actors* of protection is cogent, but neither the Court's judgment in *O A* nor the prior Advocate General's Opinion give any clear reasons for considering that *effectiveness* of protection is not to be assessed holistically. As to why protective functions or acts carried out by civil society actors in relation to social and financial support are said to be irrelevant, the Court's only reason is a circular one—that such acts are 'inherently incapable of either preventing acts of persecution or of detecting, prosecuting and punishing such acts and, therefore, cannot be regarded as providing the protection required by Article 11(1)(e) of Directive 2004/83, read together with Article 7(2) of that directive'.[303] In relation to provision of security, the Court's principal reason is that assessing well-founded fear of persecution requires verification, 'having regard to that refugee's individual situation, that the actor or actors in question who are providing protection, within the meaning of Article 7(1), have taken reasonable steps to prevent the persecution, that they therefore operate, inter alia, an effective legal system for the detection, prosecution and punishment of acts constituting persecution'.[304]

However, even assuming that the sine qua non of effective protection is 'preventing acts of persecution or of detecting, prosecuting and punishing such acts', it is possible to hypothesise situations where social and financial support and/or security functions performed by civil society actors might play a role in at least preventing persecution. Consider for example, a victim of domestic violence, now divorced, whose claim is she would face persecution at the hands of the ex-spouse's family. Would decision makers applying ordinary criteria of assessment[305] want to say that it was irrelevant if, for example, there was evidence that the woman concerned had remarried into a wealthy family that employs effective private security? Possibly such circumstances might not be considered enough ultimately to reduce the level of risk. Such considerations on their own would be far from establishing that she would not be at risk of ineffective protection. However, at the same time, how could such considerations be deemed irrelevant? The Court's reasoning is all the more problematic because in *O A* they expressly concluded that protection was to be seen as part and parcel of the assessment of well-founded fear of being persecuted.[306]

As regards the reasons given by Hathaway and Foster for concluding that the protective acts of civil society actors are irrelevant, it is perhaps unfortunate that *Opuz* should be cited as illustrative of the Strasbourg approach because there are other ECtHR cases taking a different view of protection by civil society actors that are both more recent and (unlike *Opuz*) deal specifically with the non-refoulement context. In *RH v Sweden*,[307] for example, the Court concluded at that in RH's case she would

---

[303] *O A* (n 88) para 46.
[304] ibid para 38.
[305] e.g. those set out in Article 4 QD (recast) (n 85).
[306] *O A* (n 88) para 58: 'the same circumstances that establish that the third country concerned does not protect its national against acts of persecution explain why it is impossible for that national, or why he or she justifiably refuses, to avail himself or herself of the protection of his or her country of origin in terms of that provision, that is to say, in terms of that country's ability to prevent or punish acts of persecution'; see also para 51.
[307] *RH v Sweden* App No 4601/14 (ECtHR, 10 September 2015).

not face a real risk of ill treatment contrary to Article 3 because the evidence was that she had access to 'both family support and a male protection network',[308] despite observing that:

> Women are unable to get protection from the police and the crimes are often committed with impunity, as the authorities are unable or unwilling to investigate and prosecute reported perpetrators. It is also clear that women are generally discriminated against in Somali society and that they hold a subordinate position to men.[309]

That aside, for Hathaway and Foster to say that the availability of assistance in the form of women's shelter is 'irrelevant' is odd for several reasons. First, on their own account, the question of whether the protection test is satisfied is a factual one that does not relate to whether the state has conducted itself according to certain standards but is rather about the result.[310] On a factual approach, whether women's shelters contribute to the effectiveness of state protection should surely depend on the particular circumstances: if, for example, they are de facto prisons or do not ensure effective security or do not provide for eventual transition to life in the wider society, they will not do so; but in other cases they might so contribute. Second, Hathaway and Foster's own position elsewhere (properly) avoids embracing the overly narrow notion that the state is limited to the acts of police or security forces.[311] Elsewhere they appear to accept that the state is also a system comprised of laws and social mores and that in essence ineffective protection is at core a breakdown of the 'political community'.[312] In general parlance, 'political community' is a term that encompasses both state and civil society bodies.[313] Third, it appears to rely on a narrow and reductive (sometimes called 'statist') approach which considers that in order to decide whether a state protects, one focuses exclusively on what is actively done by state actors or those acting under their control or supervision. Yet the nature and type of the protective functions carried out by state actors is at least to some extent a function of the overall situation in the society in which they operate. For example, (other things being equal) greater protective activity by state actors against crime will be required in countries with a high crime rate than in countries with a low one.

3.12.2 The role of civil society actors and functions

In order to understand why the approach, such as that advocated by Hathaway and Foster, confining effectiveness of protection exclusively to state actors is narrow and reductive, consider a hypothetical example concerning a state in which persons from ethnic minorities face a real risk of serious harm from extreme right wing racist groups. Although the state does not take positive steps to protect the ethnic

---

[308] ibid para 73.
[309] ibid para 70.
[310] Hathaway and Foster (n 20) 319.
[311] ibid 297–98.
[312] ibid 292.
[313] For a discussion of the interrelationship between civil society and political community in political theory and sociology, see Craig Calhoun, 'Civil Society and the Public Sphere' in Michael Edwards (ed), *The Oxford Handbook of Civil Society* (OUP 2011) 311–23.

minorities against such groups, there is an extremely well-organized and effective umbrella of civil society organisations whose impact is such that racist groups never feel able to attack or effectively threaten anyone. The simple fact of the matter is, in this hypothetical example, that ethnic minorities are safe and have their basic human rights secured and there is no reason to consider that will change. Yet on Hathaway and Foster's analysis, and contrary to the principle of surrogacy, they would qualify as refugees.

The objection that may be made to the above critique of Hathaway and Foster is that it seeks to say that there are no dividing lines between state and non-state actors, between the spheres of state and civil society. But the above critique does not reject that there are such dividing lines, only that they are not dichotomies. Given that state and civil society actors operate within the same state system, it is almost inevitable that the actions of each sphere will affect the other and that their interaction will affect the overall level of protection.

It must be underlined again, however, that none of this is to say that civil society actors can ever be 'actors of protection' within Article 7(1) EU QD (recast). So, in the above hypothetical example, where the anti-racist civil society organisations are strong (and assuming there are anti-racist laws in place), the *overall answer* is still that there is effective protection provided by the state; it is just that because of the overall level of protection in the country, the state actors have not had/do not need to take any positive steps on this front. They have still gone about providing police, security, administration, a system of laws, etc., but because the threat from the racists has been resolved by non-state actors, they have not had to do anything else in relation to the racist groups. Even though civil society actors cannot be state actors, the protective functions they can sometimes perform may reduce or obviate the need for specific protective steps by state actors in the first place. Ultimately, assessment of whether the level of protection in a country of origin is or will be sufficient to comply with human rights norms must surely be about overall assessment of thresholds of harm and protection based on a holistic approach to evidence as to what happens in the country of origin at all levels: state, central government/local government, civil society, tribe, clan, workplace, family, individual.

Such an approach also accords with the holistic approach to assessment of country conditions that is required in order to ascertain whether other aspects of the refugee definition are satisfied. When one analyses the situation in the country of origin for the purposes of identifying persecutory harm, one does not simply look at the situation as regards government institutions and services, political institutions, and the police and justice system etc. One also looks at the social structures and support systems. Indeed, Article 4 of the EU QD (recast) enjoins an approach that takes into account 'all relevant facts as they relate to the country of origin ...'. The 'laws and regulations of the country of origin and the manner in which they are applied' is only given as an example. Not to apply a similar approach to assessment of the effectiveness of protection against that harm makes no sense.

Recognition of the need for a holistic approach both to persecution and protection can also be discerned in some UNHCR materials. Significantly when examining the question of internal flight or relocation the UNHCR Guidelines on International Protection No 4 emphasises that in assessing whether it is reasonable to expect a person to relocate, regard must be had, inter alia, to whether ties of family, clan, tribe, ethnic, religion, culture enable protection.[314]

A holistic approach is also congruent with the ICRC approach to 'protection activities'. For example, when analysing the extent to which situations of armed violence and conflict can undermine the ability of the state to provide protection, one does not leave the civil society situation out of the picture. Even outside the context of armed violence and conflict, it is important not to impose on the refugee definition a concept of state that is really based on one type of state—the interventionist state. In countries in which the state plays an interventionist role in ensuring basic services and livelihoods, it will obviously be right to focus on state institutions, but in states where the state plays a limited role in the organisation of society, it would even more seriously distort the protection analysis to focus purely on what is done by governmental organs.

As regards Hathaway and Foster's position, it must be asked, given that they accept that a holistic approach must be taken to the meaning of key terms of the refugee definition, including 'being persecuted' and that they consider that protection is an ingredient of the meaning of this term, why they should not straightforwardly apply a holistic approach to protection also.[315]

## 4 Conclusions

Taking stock of arguments that have been advanced for and against, this chapter has found that surrogacy is indeed a principle underlying the refugee definition and is of particular importance in giving meaning to the notion of protection against persecution. At the same time, this is not a matter on which there is widespread agreement. Consideration of arguments for and against is also found to lead to the conclusion that protection is indeed an ingredient of the meaning of 'being persecuted'. Applying a human rights approach, protection has been found to possess both positive and negative qualities. Whilst within the refugee definition the paradigm of protection is state protection, it has been concluded that it can also include de facto state entities subject to important qualitative requirements. It is concluded that despite strong arguments been ranged against it, including by the CJEU, it remains arguable that in assessing the effectiveness of protection, the protective functions of private or civil society actors have at least some relevance.

In the course of interrogating the meaning of protection this chapter has sought to describe and analyse the main issues over which there has been disagreement. Nevertheless, in keeping with the methodology outlined in this book's opening chapter, it is necessary to examine what if any propositions can be distilled regarding the protection aspects of the 'being persecuted' element that can be considered as widely agreed. Given the emphasis throughout on there being a number of debates that remain unresolved, there appear to be a limited number of possible candidates.

---

[314] UNHCR, Guidelines No 4 (n 266) para 30, see also para 29.
[315] In addition to endorsing a 'holistic reading of the refugee definition', Hathaway and Foster (n 20) 122–81 advocate an approach to assessment of well-founded fear that takes all evidence into account.

472  'BEING PERSECUTED' AND PROTECTION

However, consistent with the foregoing analysis, the following basic propositions suggest themselves.

## 4.1 Basic Propositions

1. Persons are not in need of international protection if they can find protection in their home state.
2. A state has a basic duty to protect those within its jurisdiction.
3. In addition to willingness and ability, the qualities protection provided by actors of protection must include being accessible, effective, and non-temporary.

## 4.2 Suggested Propositions

The very fact that there are still so few (basic) propositions that have achieved substantial consensus and that much of this chapter has been taken up with examining a number of disagreements in the refugee law literature demonstrates that a lot more has yet to be done to achieve a greater level of accord. The following are only the suggestions that flow from this author's own analysis and evaluation of the main disagreements:

1. Notwithstanding recent criticisms to the contrary, surrogacy is a principle underlying the refugee definition.
2. Treating protection as an integral part of the meaning of 'being persecuted' is at once consistent with VCLT rules of interpretation and with the dynamics of human rights law. It is particularly important as a way of ensuring that the refugee definition fully addresses harm emanating from non-state actors and properly recognises that connection may be made with a Convention reason either by reference to the non-state source of harm or the state's inadequate response.
3. As case law and wider learning has developed, it is clear that treating protection as an integral part of the meaning of 'being persecuted' does not entail applying misplaced notions of state responsibility and does not displace the role of individual assessment or impose undue evidential burdens on applicants. However, the notion of state responsibility as embodied in IHRL remains essential to a human rights approach to persecution and protection.
4. Whilst the notion that a state has a basic duty to protect is widely endorsed, it is only international human rights law that has given it concrete content in terms of a set of negative and positive obligations that states (or de facto state entities) must meet in order to avoid sufficiently severe violations of human rights.
5. Applying a human rights approach, protection within the meaning of Article 1A(2) must possess not just the negative quality of countering serious harm; it must also possess several positive qualities. In addition to two qualities constructively indicated by the wording of Article 1A(2) first paragraph—willingness and

ability to protect—protection must at least also be accessible, effective, and non-temporary. To accord with IHRL, these qualities entail that states have a duty to organise the governmental apparatus (and indeed all the structures through which public power is exercised), so that they are capable of securing human rights and the rule of law. In the refugee law context, the duty to protect imposed by human rights law, requires that the state protects against sufficiently severe violations of human rights.
6. There remains no consensus about whether or not states with governments are the only entity that can provide protection under Article 1A(2). However, whichever view is taken, it is clear that no entity can meet the requirements of protection outlined above unless they exhibit the aforementioned five qualities of protection, including a stable and enduring character.
7. There is powerful judicial and academic support for the view that in assessing the threshold of the effectiveness of state actor activities, no account can be taken of the role of private civil society actors, but how that view can be reconciled with a holistic approach to assessment of well-founded fear of persecution remains moot.

# 8
# 'Being Persecuted' and the Internal Protection Alternative
## ('Etre persécutée' et l'alternative de protection à l'intérieur du pays)

| | | | |
|---|---|---|---|
| Introduction | 475 | 2.7.5 IPA as an implied limit on Article 1A(2) | 521 |
| 1 Basis in VCLT Rules and Textual Location | 479 | 2.7.6 IPA as an implied limit on the right to refugee status | 522 |
| 1.1 VCLT Rules | 480 | 2.8 Conclusions on Main Approaches | 522 |
| 1.1.1 *Travaux préparatoires* | 480 | 2.8.1 Home area | 523 |
| 1.1.2 Good faith | 480 | 2.8.2 Causal nexus | 524 |
| 1.1.3 Ordinary meaning | 480 | 3 The IPA in International Human Rights Law (IHRL) | 527 |
| 1.1.4 Context | 482 | 3.1 Conclusions on IHRL IPA Analysis | 534 |
| 1.1.5 Object and purpose | 484 | 4 Essential Elements of the IPA Test in Article 1A(2)—A Distillation | 536 |
| 1.1.6 Article 31(3) VCLT | 485 | 4.1 Substantive Contents | 536 |
| 1.1.7 Article 32 VCLT and supplementary means of interpretation | 486 | 4.1.1 Risk in the home area | 536 |
| 1.1.8 Conclusions on VCLT rules | 486 | 4.1.2 Significance to any IPA assessment of state actor persecution | 537 |
| 1.2 Textual Location Within the Refugee Definition | 487 | 4.1.3 Accessibility | 537 |
| 1.2.1 'Well-founded fear' | 487 | 4.1.4 Absence of well-founded fear of persecution in the IPA | 538 |
| 1.2.2 The 'protection clause'/availment clause | 488 | 4.1.5 Absence of risk of indirect refoulement | 538 |
| 1.2.3 'Being persecuted' | 489 | 4.1.6 Non-temporariness | 539 |
| 1.2.4 Holistic approach | 490 | 4.1.7 Individual assessment | 539 |
| 1.2.5 Evaluation | 490 | 4.1.8 Forward-looking assessment | 539 |
| 2 The IPA Inquiry: Main Positions and Criticisms | 493 | 4.1.9 Causal nexus | 540 |
| 2.1 UNHCR and the 'Reasonableness' Test | 494 | 4.2 Procedural Contents | 540 |
| 2.2 Michigan Guidelines on the Internal Protection Alternative | 497 | 4.2.1 Burden of proof resting on the RSD authority? | 540 |
| 2.3 Human Rights Approach | 501 | 4.2.2 Burden of raising as an issue | 540 |
| 2.4 1998 UN Guiding Principles on Internal Displacement | 506 | 4.2.3 Duty to give notice | 541 |
| 2.5 Implied Limit on Article 1A(2) | 506 | 4.2.4 Burden of specific identification | 541 |
| 2.6 Implied Limit on the Right to Refugee Status | 507 | 4.3. Conclusions on Essential Elements of the IPA Test in Article 1A(2) | 541 |
| 2.7 Evaluation of Different Approaches | 507 | 5 Conclusions | 542 |
| 2.7.1 UNHCR Guidelines No 4 | 507 | 5.1 Basic Propositions | 543 |
| 2.7.2 Michigan Guidelines or MGs | 509 | 5.2 Suggested Propositions | 543 |
| 2.7.3 Human rights approach | 513 | | |
| 2.7.4 1998 UN Guiding Principles on Internal Displacement | 520 | | |

# Introduction

The notion of the Internal Protection Alternative (IPA) has vexed refugee law for decades.[1] Despite having become a regular feature of refugee law decision-making, levels

[1] Hugo Storey, 'The Internal Flight Alternative Test: The Jurisprudence Re-examined' (1998) 10(3) IJRL 499, 524; Bill Frelick, 'Down the Rabbit Hole: The Strange Logic of Internal Flight Alternative' (1999) World Refugee Survey 22; UNHCR, 'Relocating Internally as a Reasonable Alternative to Seeking Asylum (The So-Called "Internal Flight Alternative" or "Relocation Principle")' (1999) UNHCR Position Paper, paras 13–17; 'The Michigan Guidelines on the Internal Protection Alternative' (MGs) (1999) 21(1) Michigan Journal of International Law 134, 135; Gaetan de Moffarts, 'Refugee Status and the Internal Flight or Protection Alternative' (2002) 2 (unpublished copy on file with the author—this is an update of the 1997 paper, 'Refugee Status and the "Internal Flight Alternative" (Refugee and Asylum Law: Assessing the Scope for Judicial Protection: International Association of Refugee Law Judges, Second Conference, Nijmegen, January 1997) 123–38); European Legal Network on Asylum, 'Research Paper on the Application of the Concept of Internal Protection Alternative' (2000); Sir Kenneth Keith, 'The Difficulties of "Internal Flight" and "Internal Relocation" as Frameworks of Analysis' (2001) 15 Georgetown Immigration Law Journal 433; Ninette Kelley, 'Internal Flight/Relocation/Protection Alternative: Is it Reasonable?' (2002) 14(1) IJRL 4, 42; Reinhard Marx, 'The Criteria of Applying the "Internal Flight Alternative" Test in National Refugee Status Determination Procedures' (2002) 14 IJRL 179; Hugo Storey, '"From Nowhere to Somewhere": An Evaluation of the UNHCR 2nd Track Global Consultations on International Protection: San Remo 8–10 September 2001 Experts Roundtable on the IPA/IRA/IFA Alternative' in *IARLJ Conference 2002* (Victoria University of Wellington 2003) 359; 'Summary Conclusions: Internal Protection/Relocation/Flight Alternative' (Expert roundtable organized by the United Nations High Commissioner for Refugees and the International Institute of Humanitarian Law, San Remo, Italy, 6–8 September 2001) in Erika Feller, Volker Türk, and Frances Nicholson (eds), *UNHCR Global Consultations, Refugee Protection in International Law* (UNHCR 2003) 418–19 (Global Consultations Summary Conclusions); James C Hathaway and Michelle Foster, 'Internal Protection/Relocation/Flight Alternative' in Erika Feller, Volker Türk, and Frances Nicholson (eds), *UNHCR Global Consultations, Refugee Protection in International Law* (UNHCR 2003) 357–417, 360; UNHCR, Guidelines on International Protection (Guidelines) No 4: Internal Flight or Relocation Alternative Within the Context of Article 1A(2) of the 1951 Convention and/or 1967 Protocol Relating to the Status of Refugees (23 July 2003) UN Doc HCR/GIP/03/04; Guy S Goodwin-Gill and Jane McAdam, *The Refugee in International Law* (3rd edn, OUP 2007) 123–26; UNHCR, Interpreting Article 1 of the 1951 Convention Relating to the Status of Refugees (2001); Andreas Zimmermann and Claudia Mahler, 'Article 1A, para 2', in Andreas Zimmermann (ed), *The 1951 Convention Relating to the Status of Refugees and Its 1967 Protocol: A Commentary* (OUP 2011) 445–61; Jonah Eaton, 'The Internal Protection Alternative under European Union Law: Examining the Recast Qualification Directive' (2012) 24(4) IJRL 765; Penelope Mathew, 'The Shifting Boundaries and Content of Protection: The Internal Protection Alternative Revisited' in Satvinder Juss (ed), *The Ashgate Research Companion to Migration Law, Theory and Policy* (Ashgate 2013) 204; AIDA, 'Mind the Gap: An NGO Perspective on Challenges to Accessing Protection in the Common European Asylum System' (Annual Report 2013–14); Gina Clayton, '"Even If ... ": The Use of the IPA in Asylum Decisions in the UK' (2014) Asylum Aid; James C Hathaway and Michelle Foster, *The Law of Refugee Status* (2nd edn, CUP 2014) 332–61; Jessica Schultz, 'The European Court of Human Rights and Internal Relocation: An Unduly Harsh Standard?' in Jean-Pierre Gauci, Mariagiulia Giuffre, and Lilian Tsourdi (eds), *Exploring the Boundaries of Refugee Law* (Brill Nijhoff 2015) 31–49; Brid Ní Ghráinne, 'The International Protection Alternative Inquiry and Human Rights Considerations—Irrelevant or Indispensable' (2015) 27 IJRL 29; Kay Hailbronner and Daniel Thym, *EU Immigration and Asylum Law A Commentary* (2nd edn, Hart Publishing 2016) 1157–64; Chao Yi, 'Contextualizing the Reasonableness Test of Internal Relocation in International Refugee Law: Empirical Analysis of Decisions of the Administrative Appeals Tribunal of Australia Concerning Afghanistan, Pakistan, Bangladesh, India, and Sri Lanka' (2017) 20 Gonzaga Journal of International Law 138; Jessica Schultz, *The Internal Protection Alternative in Refugee Law: Treaty Basis and Scope of Application under the 1951 Convention Relating to the Status of Refugees and Its 1967 Protocol* (Brill Nijhoff 2018); Jessica Schultz and Terje Einarsen, 'The Right to Refugee Status and the Internal Protection Alternative: What Does The Law Say?' in Bruce Burson and David Cantor, *Human Rights and the Refugee Definition* (Brill Nijhoff 2019); Jessica Schultz, 'The Internal Protection Alternative and Its Relation to Refugee Status' in Satvinder Juss (ed), *Research Handbook on International Refugee Law* (Edward Elgar 2019) 126; Lorne Waldman, *The Definition of Convention Refugee* (2nd edn, Lexis Nexis 2019) 444–81; Julian Lehmann, 'Protection' in European Union Asylum Law (Brill Nijhoff 2020) 142–95; Brid Ní Ghráinne, 'The Internal Protection Alternative' in Cathryn Costello, Michelle

of disagreement over the concept remain high.[2] The simplicity of the core idea contrasts sharply with the complexity of the debates. If the concept can be stripped down to one basic question (if someone is unsafe where they live, can they be safe by moving elsewhere internally?), how is it that it should cause such division? Just about the only advance immediately visible is the growing accord that the term 'internal protection alternative' is to be preferred to the two other most popular descriptors—'internal flight alternative' (IFA) and 'internal relocation alternative'.[3] In recognition of this, the term generally employed throughout the rest of this chapter is 'internal protection alternative' or 'IPA'.

This study chooses to address the IPA notion as the last of three chapters addressing the 'being persecuted' (*'dêtre persécutée'* in French) element of the refugee definition. The main reason for this choice, which is addressed further in 2.2.3 of this chapter when considering location of the IPA notion in the refugee definition, is that this best reflects its material role. However, as highlighted in Chapter 3, there is no prescribed order for dealing with the definition's different elements. The concept can be described as concerned with the definition's 'geographical scope', so long as that is understood to refer to the interior of a country's territory only.

Despite there now being widespread (although not universal)[4] agreement that it is an integral part of the refugee definition,[5] acknowledgement of this in most of the academic literature has been grudging, especially in view of its origins, which Hathaway and Foster in 2003 described as 'inauspicious' and 'suspect'.[6] They highlight, as do others, that until the mid-1980s,[7] there was no practice of routinely denying asylum on the grounds that protection could be secured in another part of the home state. Others have fastened on the fact that the drafters nowhere articulated the doctrine.[8] It

---

Foster, and Jane McAdam (eds), *The Oxford Handbook of International Refugee Law* (OUP 2021) 695–710; Guy S Goodwin-Gill and Jane McAdam (with Emma Dunlop), *The Refugee in International Law* (4th edn, OUP 2021) 144–53.

[2] Ní Ghráinne (2021) (n 1) 696–97.
[3] The main reasons that have led to this consensus are that '*internal flight*' wrongly suggests a backward-looking (only) inquiry and wrongly implies that 'flight' has to be involved; and that the term 'relocation' in '*internal relocation alternative*' unduly emphasises ability to move, too readily suggests voluntary rather than forced movement, and is also used in the asylum law of EU countries in a different context, to denote EU-administered programmes to transfer protection applicants away from certain member states: see Hathaway and Foster (n 1) 334–35; Schultz (2018) (n 1) 16. These three labels are not necessarily exhaustive. Schultz notes isolated examples of countries that have used or still use other names such as 'internal asylum' or 'internal resettlement'.
[4] Schultz (2018) (n 1) 22. Schultz considers that the IPA 'is neither an inherent part of the refugee concept nor a limit on refugee status compelled by the "surrogate" role of refugee law'; but at ibid 389 she considers that her study 'establishes a narrower scope for IPA application under the Refugee Convention than is usually conceived . . .'.
[5] Ní Ghráinne (2021) (n 1) 695; Zimmermann and Mahler (n 1) 445, 448–49; Goodwin-Gill and McAdam (3rd edn) (n 1) 123–26.
[6] Hathaway and Foster (2003) (n 1) 360, 359; see also Eaton (n 1) 766–68, who describes it as a 'state-created' doctrine of 'dubious lineage'.
[7] In fact, Marx (n 1) 181, and Schultz (2018) (n 1) 11–12, trace its origin earlier, identifying a Dutch decision of May 1977 (confirmed by the Dutch Council of State in *Turkish Christian* [1978] Rechtspraak Vreemdelingenrecht (RV) 1978 N 30 (Dutch Council of State)) and German jurisprudence, including a decision from 1978.
[8] Schultz (2018) (n 1) 126–29.

has been noted that although paragraph 91 of the United Nations High Commissioner for Refugees (UNHCR) Handbook[9] is often seen as the first important endorsement of the concept's legitimacy, UNHCR's then Director of Protection, Gilbert Jaeger, saw its explicit insertion in the Handbook as designed to exclude as far as possible incipient IPA practice.[10] The position of the UNHCR on the doctrinal basis of the concept subsequently shifted more than once.[11] For some, application of the IPA concept requires a human rights approach, for others it is conceptually at odds with such an approach. Schultz, for example, considers that it 'exists in tension with the right to leave one's country, freedom of movement, non-discrimination, and the right to return to one's home when the dangers giving rise to displacement have subsided.'[12] She ventures that it is 'undeniably problematic that IPA practice usually results in internal displacement for the refugee claimant rather than a durable solution.'[13] '[B]eing forced to abandon one's place of habitual residence', she writes, 'enhances vulnerability to human rights harms'.[14] Emphasis has also been placed on the fact that the doctrine is not applied in the extended refugee definition set out in the Organisation of African Unity (OAU) Convention or in the Cartagena Declaration.[15]

The codification of a version of the IPA doctrine in Article 8 of the recast Qualification Directive (QD recast), which came into force in October 2006, might have been thought to entrench its role in the refugee definition to some degree, albeit it is only a European Union (EU) instrument. However, the article in both its original[16]

---

[9] UNHCR, Handbook on Procedures and Criteria for Determining Refugee Status and Guidelines on International Protection under the 1951 Convention and the 1967 Protocol Relating to the Status Of Refugees (Geneva, 2019, reissued in 2019) (UNHCR Handbook or Handbook).

[10] Schultz (2018) (n 1) 12, 138–39.

[11] Ní Ghráinne (2021) (n 1) 699. She notes that whereas in 1995 (in its 'Information Note on Article 1 of the 1951 Convention' (1 March 1995)) UNHCR accepted that the IPA test was relevant to whether an applicant's fear is well-founded, in 1999, in its 'Position Paper on Relocating Internally as a Reasonable Alternative to Seeking Asylum (The So-Called "Internal Flight Alternative" or "Relocation Principle")' (1999) available at https://www.refworld.org/docid/3ae6b336c.html accessed 9 December 2021, UNHCR stated that the IPA principle 'rests on understandings which are basically at odds with those underlying the fundamental refugee protection principles'. Although the UNHCR Guidelines No 4 treat the concept as '[p]art of the holistic assessment of refugee status' (II.A, paras 6–7), it also notes that the question of whether an applicant has an IPA is a matter that '*may*... arise as part of the refugee status determination': see Guidelines on International Protection No 4 (n 1) (para 2) (emphasis added).

[12] Schultz (2018) (n 1) 7.

[13] ibid.

[14] ibid 8.

[15] Organization of African Unity (OAU), Convention Governing the Specific Aspects of Refugee Problems in Africa (adopted 10 September 1969, entered into force 20 June 1974) 1001 UNTS 45 (OAU Convention), Article I(2). Article I(2) specifically supplements the Article 1(1) definition of a refugee as follows: 'every person who, owing to external aggression, occupation, foreign domination or events seriously disturbing public order in either part or the whole of his country of origin or nationality, is compelled to leave his place of habitual residence in order to seek refuge in another place outside his country of origin or nationality'. The 1984 Cartagena Declaration, which specifically refers to Article I(2) of the OAU Refugee Convention, has generally been understood to reflect a similar position by virtue of its refence in conclusion III to the necessity of 'bearing in mind ... the precedent of the OAU Convention (article 1, paragraph 2)'; see further Marina Sharp, *The Regional Law of Refugee Protection in Africa* (OUP 2018) 36, 60–62. However, for a different view about the role of the IPA in the OAU, see Tamara Wood, 'Protection and Disasters in the Horn of Africa: Norms and Practice for Addressing Cross-Border Displacement in Disaster Contexts' (2013) The Nansen Initiative, cited in Ní Ghráinne (2021) (n 1) 701.

[16] Council Directive 2004/83/EC of 29 April 2004 on minimum standards for the qualification and status of third country nationals or stateless persons as refugees or as persons who otherwise need international protection and the content of the protection granted [2004] OJ L 304/12 (QD).

and recast[17] form still leaves its application as a matter for the discretion of each member state[18] and a 2019 European Commission Report found there were still significant differences in member state interpretation and application.[19] Those who have criticised certain aspects of Article 8 include UNHCR, European Council on Refugees and Exiles (ECRE), and a number of academics.[20]

As well as disquiet about the doctrine at a conceptual level, there has been frequent complaint about the way it is applied. Thus, Kelley wrote in 2002 that '[t]he concept is at times misapplied and inconsistently applied both within and across jurisdictions'.[21] UNHCR's Guidelines on International Protection No 4: Internal Flight or Relocation Alternative (Guidelines No 4) saw their task as resolving the numerous inconsistencies of approach.[22] Yet, over a decade later Zimmermann and Mahler observed that 'State practice is quite far from being uniform on this matter and across jurisdictions.'[23] Schultz refers to a 'persistent lack of consensus concerning the IPA's treaty basis and its scope of application'.[24] Lack of consistency over application of the IPA concept has also been widely seen as one of the main reasons for disparate recognition rates, especially in Europe.[25] In addition, the concept's application is seen to have been state-driven: thus Schultz avers that '[t]here is little doubt that application of the IFA ... concept is used in state practice as a tool to restrict the inflow of refugee claimants'.[26]

Have doubts about the doctrines' dubious lineage sometimes gone too far? That would seem to be the case, at least in relation to the contention that the notion was wholly unknown to the Refugee Convention drafters. That contention is difficult to square with what Zimmermann and Mahler have called a 'certain insistence' in the

---

[17] Directive 2011/95/EU of the European Parliament and of the Council of 13 December 2011 on standards for the qualification of third-country nationals or stateless persons as beneficiaries of international protection, for a uniform status for refugees or for persons eligible for subsidiary protection, and for the content of the protection granted (recast) [2011] OJ L 337/9 (QD (recast)).

[18] Draft proposals by the Commission, transforming the QD into a Qualification Regulation, to reformulate article 8 as a mandatory provision: see European Commission, Communication from the Commission to the European Parliament and the Council, Towards a reform of the Common European Asylum System and enhancing legal avenues to Europe (2016) COM(2016) 197 final. This is opposed, inter alia, by UNHCR: see UNHCR, Comments on the European Commission proposal for a Qualification Regulation (2016) 15–17.

[19] European Commission, Evaluation of the application of the recast Qualification Directive (2011/95/EU): Final Report (2019) 72–79.

[20] UNHCR, Comments on the EC's proposal for a Directive the European Parliament and of the Council on minimum standards for the qualification and status of third country nationals or stateless persons as beneficiaries of international protection and the content of the protection granted (21 October 2009) 6–7; ECRE, Information Note on the Directive 2011/95/EU. Perhaps the strongest academic criticism has been that of Eaton (n 1) 791: '[t]he application of the internal protection alternative under the Qualification Directive is incompatible with the standards of the Refugee Convention and international law'; see also Eaton (n 1) 777.

[21] Kelley (n 1) 4.

[22] UNHCR Guidelines No 4 (n 1).

[23] Zimmermann and Mahler (n 1); see also Goodwin-Gill and McAdam (3rd edn) (n 1) 124.

[24] Schultz (2018) (n 1) 18.

[25] See the studies cited in Schultz (2018) (n 1) 6; see also Clayton (n 1); Lehmann (n 1) 164–70, cites cases indicating that even within EU member states applying Article 8, case law is still divergent. See also Ní Ghráinne (2021) (n 1) 696–97.

[26] Schultz (2018) (n 1) 159.

*travaux préparatoires* (*travaux*) 'on the exclusion of internally protected persons from the ambit of Article 1A, para 2'.[27]

But in any event, many aspects of the understanding we have today of the refugee definition did not fully emerge until the last twenty to thirty years (for example the modern understanding that applicants cannot be expected to conceal their basic identities)[28] and no less is thought of them because they were (or might have been) incognisant to the drafters or early case law or scholarship. The Refugee Convention is a 'living instrument' and changing objective circumstances sometimes require decision makers, in order to respond appropriately, to grapple with the meaning of key terms anew. This aspect has been seen by Hathaway and Foster to be very much to the fore in relation to the IPA, given that the 1980s onwards did present challenging new circumstances:

> These legitimate concerns notwithstanding, it must be conceded that the move to embrace IFA rules in recent years may also be explained by the growing number of persons seeking asylum since the late 1980s who are fleeing largely regionalized threats (including many internal armed conflicts) rather than monolithic aggressor States. The changing nature of the circumstances precipitating flight may have allowed the consideration of the possibility of securing protection within one's own State in a way not previously available when the aggressor was usually a central government.[29]

At all events, what ultimately matters is whether or not the doctrine is integral to a modern understanding of the refugee definition and, as already noted, almost all agree that it is.

## 1 Basis in VCLT Rules and Textual Location

Given that the IPA has become integral to the modern understanding of the refugee definition, it is instructive to consider the various approaches to the doctrine. Before examining them, two questions crucial to a proper understanding of the IPA concept must be posed: to what extent is it consistent with the Vienna Convention on the Law of Treaties (VCLT) rules of interpretation to apply this concept as part of the refugee definition; and where, if at all, is the concept to be located in the refugee definition?

---

[27] Zimmermann and Mahler (n 1) 448. They cite Hathaway's observation in James C Hathaway, *The Law of Refugee Status* (Butterworths Limited 1991) 133–34: 'For instance, during the 1951 Conference on Plenipotentiaries it was considered that the provisions of the 1951 Convention were not intended to apply to 'national refugees, such as those in Germany, India and Pakistan.' See Conference of Plenipotentiaries on the Status of Refugees and Stateless Persons, Summary Record of the Twenty-fourth Meeting (27 November 1951) UN Doc A/CONF.2/SR.24, Statement of Rochefort (France). Hathaway and Foster also cite Reinhard Marx's discussion of 'national refugees' in Reinhard Marx, 'Article 1E' in Zimmermann (n 1) 575–77. Even in the interwar period there was a strong focus on national protection. Thus Sir John Hope Simpson, *Refugees: Preliminary Report of a Survey* (Royal Institute of International Affairs 1938) 1, wrote that since all definitions had certain inherent deficiencies, it was important to keep in view the 'essential quality' of the refugee as one 'who has sought refuge in a territory other than in which he was formerly resident as a result of political events which rendered his continued residence in his former territory impossible or intolerable'.

[28] See p. 333.

[29] Hathaway and Foster (2003) (n 1) 360.

## 1.1 VCLT Rules

To varying degrees, each of the main schools of thought on the IPA seeks either to anchor their particular approach to one or more VCLT rules or to argue that the concept has no treaty basis at all. In considering how such rules should apply to IPA issues, this chapter will follow their ordering as set out in Articles 31 and 32 VCLT except in relation to the *travaux* which are addressed first in order to set the scene.

### 1.1.1 *Travaux préparatoires*

As already presaged, views on whether the drafters intended the IPA concept to be part of the refugee definition are deeply divided. On the one hand, Schultz argues that debates during the *travaux* accepted the need for the refugee definition to cover all types of refugees known at the time, including persons whose risk was presumably contained within one part of a country. From her own reading of the *travaux*, she says, 'I found no indication that the drafters were concerned with cases where the risk of persecution was limited to a certain area of the country of origin.'[30] On the other hand, as already noted, Zimmermann and Mahler think 'otherwise'.[31]

It being difficult to resolve this difference, it will suffice to note that even Schultz accepts that '[i]t is *debatable* whether the drafters of the Convention were incognisant of [the scenario of] 'refugee claimants fleeing regionalised threats, including by non-state actors'.[32] However, as a result, all that can safely be concluded is that the *travaux* do not clearly demonstrate either acceptance or non-acceptance by the drafters of the IPA concept.

### 1.1.2 Good faith

In the most extensive study of the IPA concept so far, Schultz does not invoke the principle of good faith to any particular effect when analysing VCLT considerations relevant to it.[33] Possibly, insofar as the principle denotes fidelity to the intentions of the parties,[34] it could be argued that the drafters did not intend the concept to be part of the definition, but as we have just seen, the *travaux* contain observations pointing for and against validation of the concept. However, if the view were taken that to treat the IPA concept as integral to the refugee definition amounted to imposing an additional legal obligation, then the good faith principle might have some purchase.[35]

### 1.1.3 Ordinary meaning

There is wide accord that there is no explicit basis in the text of Article 1A(2) for the IPA concept, but opinions differ on what can or cannot be read into the text. Thus the New

---

[30] Schultz (2018) (n 1) 43.
[31] Zimmermann and Mahler (n 1) 448. See also Storey (n 1) 503; Ní Ghráinne (2021) (n 1) 40. Ní Ghráinne (2021) (n 1) at 697 also notes that the lack of mention at the time of drafting was not surprising, 'considering that the traditional assumption was that State sovereignty extended over the whole of the State and that States were the primary actors of persecution'.
[32] Schultz (2018) (n 1) 153 (emphasis added).
[33] ibid 22–79.
[34] See p. 65.
[35] See p. 76.

Zealand RSAA, quoting Kirby J's observations in the Australian High Court case of *SZATV*, considered that the IPA has 'a fragile footing in the text of the ... Convention' and that its origins are therefore 'suspect'.[36] According to Schultz, accommodating IPA practice within the definition entails understanding the phrase 'protection of that country' as 'protection of that country anywhere', which is arguably (in Fortin's words) 'a (de facto) amendment to the refugee definition'.[37] She emphasises that this would appear to conflict with the principle, voiced by Kirby J in *SZATV*, that one must not 'read into [the Convention's] provisions qualifications, limitations and exceptions that are not there'.[38]

For some others, however, the IPA can be inferred from the word 'country'. As advanced by Zimmermann and Mahler, '[a] *contrario* it may be argued that where a country is providing protection from persecution, be it only in parts of its territory, the person concerned does not fall within the criteria of "refugee" as contained in Article 1A, para. 2'.[39] This perspective builds on points made in leading cases, in particular *Randhawa*, in which the Australian Federal Court stated that the focus of the Convention definition is not upon the protection that the country of nationality might be able to provide in some particular region, but 'upon a more general notion of protection by that country'.[40] If it were otherwise, the Court said, 'the anomalous situation would exist that the international community would be under an obligation to provide protection outside the borders of the country of nationality even though real protection could be found within those borders'.[41] As restated by Ní Ghráinne, if, within that country, obtaining its 'protection' is merely a question of relocating, it implies that inability or unwillingness to return is for reasons extrinsic to those set out in the Refugee Convention and that the claimant is therefore not a refugee.[42] This also appears to be the viewpoint of Lord Bingham in *Januzi*, although his reasoning focuses as much on the requirement of 'well-founded fear':

> The Refugee Convention does not expressly address the situation at issue in these appeals where, within the country of his nationality, a person has a well-founded fear of persecution at place A, where he lived, but not at place B, where (it is said) he could reasonably be expected to relocate. But the situation may fairly be said to be covered by the causative condition to which reference has been made: for if a person is outside the country of his nationality because he has chosen to leave that country and seek asylum in a foreign country, rather than move to a place of relocation within his own country where he would have no well-founded fear of persecution, where the protection of his country would be available to him and where he could reasonably be expected to relocate, it can properly be said that he is not outside the country of

---

[36] *Refugee Appeal No 76044* [2008] NZAR 719.
[37] Schultz (2018) (n 1) 140, quoting Antonio Fortin, 'The Meaning of "Protection" in the Refugee Definition' (2000) 12(4) IJRL 548, 571.
[38] *SZATV v MIC* [2007] 233 CLR 18, para 67.
[39] Zimmermann and Mahler (n 1) 446.
[40] *Randhawa v Minister for Immigration* [1994] 124 ALR 265.
[41] ibid para 8.
[42] Ní Ghráinne (2015) (n 1) 32; Ní Ghráinne (2021) (n 1) 698.

his nationality owing to a well-founded fear of being persecuted for a Convention reason.[43]

In focusing more on well-founded fear, the reasoning in *Januzi* is akin to that expressed by Nehemiah Robinson in his 1953 Commentary, namely that the refugee criteria would rule out 'happenings of a local character ... which are being combatted by the authorities because in such cases there would be no reason for a person possessing a nationality to be unwilling to avail himself of the protection of his country'.[44]

Just as some have sought to argue that the IPA concept effectively reads into the refugee definition words not there, it is equally possible to argue that if the drafters had intended to exclude the notion, they would have chosen wording akin to that used in the OAU Convention, namely 'in *either part or the whole of* his country of origin or nationality'.[45]

### 1.1.4 Context

There have been divergent views regarding what light is impliedly shed by other elements of the Article 1A(2) definition, the Preamble, and other articles of the Convention on the IPA concept. On one view, the structure of the Convention is to exhaustively set out exceptions to the scope of refugee protection for those who do meet the criteria for refugee status in Articles 1D, 1E, and 1F and from this fact it is deduced that introducing any IPA concept is impermissible.[46] For those who, by contrast, consider that the IPA has a definitional role, particular emphasis is placed on other provisions of Article 1A(2). Some, as we have already noted, see the source of the concept in the definition's requirement that the fear of persecution must be 'well-founded'.[47] The reasoning here is that if the source of the persecution could be avoided by relocating internally, then the fear is not well-founded. Others see the nucleus of the concept to reside in the 'protection clause'.[48]

Other provisions of the Convention have also been seen to have some bearing. For proponents of the Michigan Guidelines on the Internal Protection Alternative (MGs), who also consider the concept to have its source in the 'protection clause',[49] it is of high importance that the Convention includes Articles 2–33 which in their view 'suggest' a set of standards that can be appropriately linked directly with the protection clause and thus applied to assessing whether there is a viable IPA. This enables, it is said, an approach that is thus tied directly to the Convention text. 'Protection' as conceived by the 1951 Convention, they write, 'includes legal rights of the kind stipulated in the Convention itself'.[50] The point has been made, independently of reliance on the MGs' approach, that Articles 2–33 represent the second of two dimensions to the Refugee

---

[43] *Januzi v SSHD* [2006] UKHL 5, para 7.
[44] Nehemiah Robinson, *Convention relating to the Status of Stateless Persons: Its History and Interpretation, A Commentary* (UNHCR 1997) 46.
[45] OAU Convention (n 15) (emphasis added). For the text of Article I(2) of this Convention see (n 15).
[46] See e.g. Schultz (2018) (n 1) 382.
[47] See e.g. Fortin (n 33) 564–65; *Januzi* (n 43) para 7; see below section 1.2.1.
[48] See e.g. Hathaway and Foster (2014) (n 1) 339–42.
[49] MGs (n 1).
[50] Hathaway and Foster (2003) (n 1) 405.

Convention—one the non-refoulement obligation which is a negative obligation not to return; and the other the positive obligation to facilitate assimilation/integration.[51] This perspective could be said to point to a need for any IPA analysis to ensure that it reflects a concern for assimilation in any alternative location. Hathaway and Foster also deem that protection must be given a positive content as 'affirmative protection' so that it is a 'context-specific touchstone'. They note that the Preamble identifies one of the Convention's key purposes as being to 'revise and consolidate previous international agreements relating to the status of refugees and to extend the scope of *and protection accorded by such instruments* by means of a new agreement'.[52]

Specific mention also needs to be made of Article 33. Despite divergent viewpoints, there is a quite significant level of agreement that Article 33 has a role to play in informing the contents of the IPA concept, in that it helps identify the existence of a requirement of 'indirect refoulement'. Emphasis is directed in this regard to the phrase 'in any manner whatsoever' in Article 33(1) which mandates that: '[n]o Contracting State shall expel or return ("refouler") a refugee in any manner whatsoever to the frontiers of territories where his life or freedom would be threatened'. This phrase is seen to be strongly indicative of the need for a broad rather than a narrow assessment of the applicant's predicament, which would continue to arise if an applicant were compelled by conditions in an IPA, to return to his or her home area.[53] As expressed by Ní Ghráinne:

> Article 33 is just one of two provisions of the Refugee Convention that limits the power of states to expel aliens and thus it is logical to have recourse to article 33 when determining whether an asylum seekers may be sent to an IPA. As article 33 applies to asylum seekers, it arguably expresses a general principle of protection that can and should be factored into the IPA inquiry.[54]

Such diverse views about the relevance of context are difficult to reconcile; most depend at least in part on the validity of their underlying arguments. Thus, the MGs' approach depends to a degree on the strength of its arguments for rejecting the human rights approach (as usually understood), the latter which draws on International Human Rights Law (IHRL) norms directly. Likewise, the view that to apply the IPA would amount to applying a *de facto* exclusion clause depends on a particular reading of other elements of the definition—either 'protection' or 'well-founded fear'—and on the argument that the 'well-founded fear' element of the definition is established by a real chance of being persecuted in the home area.

---

[51] Jean François Durieux, 'Three Asylum Paradigms' (2013) 20(2) International Journal of Minority and Group Rights 147, 157.
[52] Hathaway and Foster (2003) (n 1) 405 (emphasis added).
[53] ibid 401; Zimmermann and Mahler (n 1) 452 emphasise that it can only apply by analogy since this obviously cannot be considered refoulement within the strict meaning of the term. They refer to it as a lack of a risk of 'internal refoulement' and '[t]here must not be a danger of an equivalent to refoulement'. See also Eaton (n 1) 770–71, who uses the term 'constructive refoulement'; Ní Ghráinne (2015) (n 1) 47–48; Ní Ghráinne (2018) (n 1) 709. However, Marx (n 1) 197–98 has argued that reliance on Article 33(1) is 'problematic' since, among other things, the concept of 'indirect refoulement' already has a different established meaning as part of a proper interpretation of Article 33(1) to denote forcible removal by a State to a third State where refoulment is likely.
[54] Ní Ghráinne (2015) (n 1) 47–48 considers it consistent with the 'reasonableness' inquiry.

As regards recourse to the notion of 'indirect refoulement', Marx is right to worry that if treated as a condition implicit in Article 33(1), it courts confusion with the established notion of 'indirect refoulement' meaning the return by a host state of applicants to another state which then returns persons to their home state,[55] but it remains that it does reflect the underlying Convention principle, with possible application by analogy, that individuals cannot be compelled to face return internally to persecutory conditions.

Overall, the Convention's context appears to offer some secondary support to differing views.

1.1.5 Object and purpose

When it comes to object and purpose, appraisal of the potential relevancy of the IPA tends to be made on two levels, one primary, the other secondary. At the primary level, the core of the IPA concept is viewed by many to reside in the notion or principle of surrogacy, the latter being seen to embody a basic principle of refugee law, namely that international protection only comes into play when national protection within the country of origin in unavailable. This is the understanding most commonly applied in the case law and wider literature.[56] However, Schultz considers that whilst the principle of surrogacy has a place in its 'systemic aspect' (related to the state's ability and willingness to protect from the original harm), there is no justification for also investing it with a 'territorial aspect' (related to the possibility of state protection elsewhere in the country of origin). She considers that the protection available in an IPA can by definition only be partial, since it impairs choice of residence and freedom of movement.[57]

At a secondary level, the fact that the Preamble identifies human rights as a fundamental objective is seen to be of particular importance to proponents who urge that a human rights approach is taken to the IPA concept. Included in this context are proponents of the MGs who, as identified earlier, construe their own Articles 2–33 (or 'refugee rights') approach as based on a 'subset' of basic human rights.[58]

Taking a different approach, Schultz considers that the reference in the Preamble to human rights would be compromised by a 'broad exclusion practice like the IPA' because (i) 'the concept rests in tension with a humanitarian regime predicated on finding solutions to forcible displacement'; (ii) because 'burden-sharing and international cooperation in addressing the refugee "problem" are weakened by IPA

---

[55] Marx (n 1) 197–98; see also *TI v UK* App No 43844/98 (ECtHR, 7 March 2000).

[56] See e.g. De Moffarts (n 1) 367, 358–59 (cited in Hathaway and Foster, 'Internal Protection/Relocation/Flight Alternative' (n 1)); Kelley (n 1) 8; Ní Ghráinne (2015) (n 1) 32; Eaton (n 1) 769; Zimmermann and Mahler (n 1) 448. Schultz (2018) (n 1) 4 considers that UNHCR does not recognise surrogacy as a principle of refugee law, This study disagrees: see p. 414.

[57] Schultz (2018) (n 1) 125.

[58] See Hathaway and Foster (2003) (n 1) 408: '[t]he required standard is not respect for all human rights, but rather provision of the rights codified as the 1951 Convention's endogenous definition of "protection" in Articles 2–33. In general terms, these standards impose a duty of non-discrimination vis a vis citizens or other residents of the asylum country and refugees in relation to a core subset of civil and socio-economic rights'. See also *Refugee Appeal No 76044* (n 36) para 147. Although Hathaway and Foster (2014) (n 1) 360 describe Articles 2–33 as 'clear, legal human rights norms', elsewhere in their elaboration they generally prefer to identify them as refugee rights.

practice, which shifts the burden of displacement back to the county of origin'; and (iii) because 'variable outcomes in IPA cases undermine the consistent treatment of claims the Convention aims to promote'.[59]

The wide divergence in views as to how the IPA concept is impacted by reference to object and purpose illustrates (once again) with one exception that the points made depend very much on the force of the underlying arguments about how the refugee definition is to be construed. In Chapter 3 of this book, it has been argued that the reference in the Preamble's first paragraph to human rights is particularly relevant to identification of object and purpose, but, as can be seen from the reading given this by the 1999 MGs, the import of this reference can be construed in more ways than one.

If Schultz's objections were valid, they would pose a serious obstacle to acceptance of the IPA concept. However, their validity is open to doubt. The human rights approach is not based on defining 'being persecuted' as a violation of any human right and violation of freedom of internal movement, is only relevant as a factor going to whether, intrinsically or cumulatively, the threshold of sufficient severity has been breached.[60] 'Burden-sharing' is only shifted improperly back to the country of origin if decision makers have misapplied the IPA concept. If they have applied it correctly (to find an applicant has a viable IPA), there is no genuine need for international protection. If return of failed asylum-seekers to burdened countries of origin is an international malady, that is not for the refugee definition to solve. Whilst IPA may amount to forcible displacement, what matters for refugee law purposes remains the gravity of any harm attendant upon relocation. '[V]ariable outcomes' in refugee decisions is not in itself a reason to impugn the basic concept of an IPA. However, Schultz's observation that an IPA protection can only be partial because it impairs choice of residence and freedom of movement,[61] remains of potential relevance to later analysis of indirect refoulement.[62]

### 1.1.6 Article 31(3) VCLT

In view of the significant divergences, at least in the wider literature, it is difficult to hold that the IPA concept can find support within the strict terms of Article 31(3) VCLT either in relation to 'subsequent practice' or as a 'relevant rule of international law'. On the one hand, there are factors pointing to there being a state practice in the broad sense, which might at least fall within the ambit of Article 32,[63] in particular: the

---

[59] Schultz (2018) (n 1) 153–54.
[60] See Chapter 6, section 3.5. There is also the issue of whether displacement from one area of a country necessarily violates the (derogable) right to freedom of movement in the country as a whole, as set out in the ICCPR Article 12 (1) (which provides that '[e]veryone lawfully within the territory of a State shall, within that territory, have the right to liberty of movement and freedom to choose his residence'). In *CR1026 v The Republic of Nauru* [2018] HCA 19, paras 45–48 at para 45, the High Court of Australia considered in relation to complementary protection that 'a rational choice to relocate from [the home area] to another place to avoid the risk of harm in the former is not a denial of freedom of movement but a manifestation of its exercise'. This reasoning would appear to ignore that forced displacement does limit the ways in which freedom of movement may be exercised and in this sense is always at least a partial denial of the right.
[61] Schultz (2018) (n 1) 125.
[62] See below section 4.1.5.
[63] See Chapter 2, n 69.

reference to the concept in the 1979 UNHCR Handbook;[64] the fact of significant consensus in the case law that the concept is now an inherent part of the refugee definition;[65] and the fact that most states with any published refugee case law now apply it. On the other hand, pointing in the opposite direction, there are two particular aspects that speak loudly against treating it as state practice even in the broad sense. First, UNHCR continues to endorse its Guidelines No 4 and these do not unambiguously state that the IPA concept is a necessary element;[66] nor does the other most influential attempt to articulate guidelines—the MGs.[67] Second, even though within the EU there is now a strong regional state practice regarding the refugee definition, the existing text of the QD (recast) continues to leave it as a matter of discretion for member states as to whether to apply it.[68] Schultz, therefore, is surely right to observe that state practice regarding it is hardly 'concordant, common and consistent' enough to imply the agreement of all parties regarding this interpretation.[69] Similar considerations apply to the argument that the doctrine constitutes a relevant rule of international law.

1.1.7  Article 32 VCLT and supplementary means of interpretation

The relevance of the *travaux* has already been addressed. In relation to other supplementary means of interpretation, it was observed when considering UNHCR, judicial, and academic sources that they do not appear to disclose a 'subsequent practice' within the strict confines of Article 31(3) recognising the IPA concept as an integral part of the refugee definition, although there is certainly mounting evidence of wide acceptance. Even though the case for there being a state practice in the broad sense (within the ambit of Article 32) is stronger, it is still not fully established.

1.1.8  Conclusions on VCLT rules

Interpreting the Refugee Convention through the prism of the rules contained in the VCLT does not yield a wholly clear picture as regards whether the IPA is an integral part of the refugee definition. In particular, we have noted that even the case for saying that there is now a state practice to this effect in the broad sense (falling within Article 32 VCLT) is not fully established. Hence there is still not substantial consensus for the

---

[64] The case for considering the Handbook to represent state practice as things stood in 1979 is discussed in Chapter 1, section 6.1.1.

[65] Ní Ghráinne (2015) (n 1) 50; Ní Ghráinne (2021) (n 1) 695.

[66] See UNHCR Guidelines No 4 (n 1) para 2: 'The question of whether the claimant has an internal flight or relocation alternative *may*, however, arise as part of the refugee status determination process' (emphasis added). See also the conditional language of paras 4 and 6. As regards continuing endorsement of Guidelines No 4, see e.g. UNHCR, Guidelines No 12: Claims for refugee status related to situations of armed conflict and violence under Article 1A(2) of the 1951 Convention and/or 1967 Protocol relating to the Status of Refugees and the regional refugee definitions (2 December 2016) UN Doc HCR/GIP/16/12, para 41.

[67] MGs (n 1) para 7.

[68] Schultz (2018) (n 1) 145–52. Hailbronner and Thym (n 1) 1159 write in 2016 that Italy and Spain had not transposed Article 8 into their national legislation and that it is not applied in Italy and in Spain is left to the discretion of the asylum authorities. The European Commission, Evaluation of the application of the recast Qualification Directive (2011/95/EU): Final Report (n 19) 72–79, notes at 73 that '[a]lmost all Member States' laws had transposed Article 8, except for *Italy, Spain* and *Sweden*. While *Italy* also in practice had never applied this concept and generally refused to do so' (emphasis added).

[69] Schultz (2018) (n 1) 145–52.

proposition that the IPA is an integral part of the refugee definition. In consequence, it still cannot be said to form part of the working definition of its key elements.

Nevertheless, as will be reflected in the 'suggested propositions' set out at the end of this chapter, this author considers there to be cogent reasons for viewing the IPA to have a sufficient conceptual basis in the Article 1(A)(2) definition of a refugee. Whilst there remain numerous respectable arguments for and against treating it as consistent with one or more particular element of the VCLT rules, on balance the IPA appears adequately grounded in treaty interpretation.

## 1.2 Textual Location Within the Refugee Definition

Divergence over what constitutes a proper approach to the IPA analysis has often extended also to precisely where it is to be located in the refugee definition. The refugee law literature reveals four positions on this: three explicit and one implicit.

### 1.2.1 'Well-founded fear'

The longest-standing position is that taken by UNHCR, who see its location as being primarily in the 'well-founded fear' element of the definition.[70] It is also the position taken, at least historically, in most of the common law case law, for example by the Canadian courts,[71] the UK House of Lords in *Januzi*,[72] and the Australian courts.[73] Although the heading to Article 8 of the QD (recast) is 'Internal Protection', its text has also been considered by some to locate the analysis in the well-founded element of the Convention definition.[74]

Locating the IPA analysis in the 'well-founded fear' element has met with particular dissent from Hathaway and Foster and other proponents of the 1999 MGs, who consider it suffers from numerous deficiencies, including: encouraging the false notion of countrywide persecution; encouraging determination of the issue of IFA without examining in full the claimant's individual circumstances;[75] pre-empting the analysis

---

[70] Thus UNHCR Guidelines No 4 (n 1) cross-refer to UNHCR, Interpreting Article 1 (n 1), which at para 12 describes it as '[o]ne aspect of the well-founded fear element'. However, in both these documents, UNHCR urges that a 'holistic approach' be taken.

[71] *Zalzali v Canada (MEI)* [1991] 3 FC 605, paras 614–15; *Thirunavukkarasu v Canada (MEI)* [1994] 1 FC 589; *Refugee Appeal No 11/91* [1991] NZRSAA. However, the leading case, *Rasaratnam v Canada (MEI)* [1992] 1 FC 706, clearly treats the concept as inherent in the 'protection'/availment clause; see Waldman (n 1) 448–50.

[72] *Januzi* (n 43); see also *AH (Sudan) v SSHD* [2007] 3 WLR 832.

[73] *Randhawa* (n 40) para 13; *SZATV* (n 38) and *SZFDV v MIC* [2007] 237 ALR 660, para 61 (per Kirby J). In relation to *SZATV*, it is often noted, however, that Kirby J stated at para 63 that 'locating the inquiry in well-foundedness strains the language of the Convention and justifiably attracts the cogent criticism that approaching the problem in this way 'involves building an edifice of reasoning on a very scant textual foundation'.

[74] As noted by Chairperson Haines in *Refugee Appeal No 76044* (n 36) para 115. In the QD (recast), Article 8 is one of the provisions that underwent significant revision: see Eaton (n 1) 767–68, 776–80. Article 8 QD (recast) states that '[a]s part of the assessment of the application for international protection, Member States may determine that an applicant is not in need of internal protection if in a part of the country of origin, he or she (a) has no well-founded fear of being persecuted …; or (b) has access to protection against persecution… as defined in Article 7'. See also Lehmann (n 1) 143–70.

[75] Hathaway and Foster (2003) (n 1) 371; Hathaway and Foster (2014) (n 1) 339–40.

of a well-founded fear of being persecuted;[76] imposing an extremely onerous burden on refugee applicants;[77] and predisposing decision makers to require applicants to conceal fundamental beliefs and opinions.[78] Hathaway and Foster also aver that 'to collapse internal protection considerations into the "well-founded fear" element of the definition makes the protection clause largely superfluous.'[79]

1.2.2 The 'protection clause'/availment clause

Another view, most prominently voiced by Hathaway and Foster in their 2003 report,[80] is that the test should be located in what they refer to as the 'protection clause' (which this study terms the availment clause) and its 'protection' wording. This has received less support in the case law,[81] but some significant backing in the academic literature.[82] For Hathaway and Foster and others, such an approach overcomes (the aforementioned) perceived drawbacks to the 'well-founded fear' location. Hathaway and Foster contend that analysing the concept instead as a 'protection alternative' provides structure and encourages a logical, methodical approach to the determination process. It is thus, they opine, of considerable assistance to decision makers as well as to applicants:

> A protection-based understanding of IFA reinforces the fact that once the applicant has established a well-founded fear in one location, she is entitled to the full weight of the establishment of a prima facie case. In this way, the IFA analysis is understood as akin to an exclusion enquiry such that the evidentiary burden is then on the party asserting an IFA to establish that it exists.[83]

Location in this clause has been criticised by some on various counts. One concern has been directed at a version of it that construes 'protection' as subject to an ill-suited 'due diligence' test. Thus, Eaton has suggested that under a *Horvath*[84] 'due diligence' construction of protection, the IPA inquiry fails to focus on whether the IPA will be effective in the individual case. Such an approach, he suggests, could encourage decision makers to require applicants 'to show country-wide failure of due diligence, engaging in a rather speculative exercise of looking for a domestic authority somewhere in the country of origin willing to operate a criminal justice system'.[85] In relation to Hathaway and Foster's version, one issue seen as problematic is how this can be

---

[76] Hathaway and Foster (2003) (n 1) 370–71.
[77] ibid 337–38.
[78] ibid 338–39.
[79] ibid 340.
[80] Hathaway and Foster (2003) (n 1) 393. Significantly, however, they agree that the inquiry begins with ascertaining well-founded fear.
[81] This view has most notably been espoused in the New Zealand case law: see *Butler v A-G* [1999] NZAR 205 and the Authority's subsequent decision in *Refugee Appeal No 71684/99* [2000] INLR 165.
[82] See e.g. Lehmann (n 1) 148–49, 170. Waldman's analysis, for example, appears to proceed on this premise: see e.g. Waldman (n 1) 445.
[83] Hathaway and Foster (2003) (n 1) 370.
[84] *Horvath v SSHD* [2000] UKHL 37.
[85] Eaton (n 1) 786.

squared with their own protection-oriented approach to the meaning of 'being persecuted' as comprising serious harm + lack of state protection.[86]

### 1.2.3 'Being persecuted'

Another possible textual home is the 'being persecuted' limb. Somewhat curiously, this is not often explicitly addressed in the literature, largely because (it may be presumed) when UNHCR refers to the 'well-founded fear' limb or element of the definition they mean 'well-founded fear' taken together with 'being persecuted'.[87] In any event, the human rights approach to the meaning of 'being persecuted', so as to treat protection as an integral part of this term (see Chapter 7), strongly implies specific consideration of the IPA primarily within the 'being persecuted' element. Dealing with it in this context is seen by this study to best reflect its material role (this is indeed why this study chooses to treat the IPA as one of three chapters devoted to the 'being persecuted' element).

Hathaway and Foster do not explicitly consider location within the 'being persecuted' element of the definition. Their critique is directed more broadly at location within the 'well-founded fear of being persecuted' limb. However, it is clear that for them the only permissible location is in the 'protection'/availment clause. They see this clause as the only one which refers to protection and which provides a 'context-specific touchstone' comprising 'the provision of legal entitlements and rights of the kind set by the Convention'.[88]

It is unclear, however, that it needs to be a case of either/or. Treating the concept of 'protection' within the availment clause as central to the IPA inquiry does not preclude the latter's location in the 'being persecuted' element, since (as we saw) this element includes a notion of internal (in the sense of national) protection.[89] In essence, if protection is essential to the meaning of persecution and the focus of the refugee assessment is on considering whether protection *of the country* is available, then that must encompass consideration of whether there is any part of the country where such protection is available. Further, if within this context protection is not simply a negative concept but also a positive concept requiring the actor(s) of protection to exhibit certain qualities, including effectiveness, accessibility, and non-temporariness (which is the analysis given in Chapter 7), then it would appear that the dominant concerns raised in the literature on IPA can and should be accommodated within the 'being persecuted' element without recourse to any concepts that go beyond it—whether reasonableness or 'meaningful protection'. That, however, is a matter that will require

---

[86] Hemme Battjes, *European Asylum Law and International Law* (Martinus Nijhoff 2006) 250; Storey (2003) (n 1) 377.

[87] UNHR Guidelines No 4 (n 1) para 3, describe the main division as being between those who have located the concept 'in the 'well-founded fear of being persecuted' clause of the definition' and [in the availment clause]. See also Lehmann (n 1) 147–48 who, whilst referring explicitly to the possible location of the IPA in the 'being persecuted' limb, proceeds to elide it with the 'well-founded fear' element. One author who has particularly emphasised the overlapping of the different locations proposed, is Rebecca Wallace, 'Internal Protection Alternative in Refugee Status Determination: Is the Risk/Protection Dichotomy Reality or Myth: A Gendered Analysis' in Satvinder Juss and Colin Harvey (eds), *Contemporary Issues in Refugee Law* (Edward Elgar 2013).

[88] Hathaway and Foster (2014) (n 1) 335–61.

[89] See e.g. pp. 425–426.

further consideration when seeking to assess the different approaches to the IPA analysis in section 2 of this chapter.

### 1.2.4 Holistic approach

The fourth main approach is to regard the concept's location as falling within the well-founded fear, the 'being persecuted', and the availment elements as part of a holistic assessment.[90] As already noted, that appears to be the alternative position endorsed by UNHCR, despite their own preference for location in the 'well-founded fear' clause (understood as encompassing 'well-founded fear of being persecuted').

It is clear from Hathaway and Foster's approach that they consider such a holistic approach would obscure the particular saliency of the location of the IPA in the availment clause. For the human rights approach, by contrast, either location in the 'well-founded fear' clause (understood as comprising a 'well-founded fear of being persecuted'); or the 'being persecuted' element; or a holistic approach, would be permissible.

### 1.2.5 Evaluation

It is perhaps best to begin with practicalities. As glimpsed already, one of the reasons why the issue of location of the IPA test has loomed large is because it has been seen to lead to different outcomes in individual cases. Hathaway and Foster, for example, cite Lord Carswell's observation in *Januzi* that the choice between the 'well-founded fear' and 'protection'/availment clause approaches to location 'may be critical, for it may lead to different results in individual cases'.[91] In the view of this author, two main difficulties attend this perspective. First (irrespective of which location is favoured), the concern about different outcomes rests on an 'ideal type' of decision-making not applied in practice. Whether in the common law or civil law world, decision makers (including judges) make their IPA analysis without apparent regard to issues of definitional location. Very few refer to this issue. That is not to say that issues of location are not salient, but it does sound a warning note against accepting concerns about location as essential. As was discussed in Chapter 3, section 7, letting 'meta-level' analysis intrude unnecessarily into refugee law is fraught with problems.

The second difficulty is that it is doubtful that those who have expressed concern about disparate outcomes in IPA decisions are right to view mere textual location of the test in the 'well-founded fear' clause as producing or tending to produce mistakes of the kind they identify—e.g. commitment to a countrywide persecution requirement;[92] a propensity to 'pre-empt the analysis of well-founded fear in the first region by moving directly to the question of an IFA';[93] or a predisposition to impose

---

[90] Schultz (2018) (n 1) 3, treats the 'well-founded fear' and 'holistic approach' as one and the same, but such equation risks glossing over key points made only by the 'holistic approach'.
[91] *Januzi* (n 43) para 65 (Lord Carswell).
[92] Hathaway and Foster (2003) (n 1) 368–69. At the very least, UNHCR clearly rejects such an approach: see UNHCR Guidelines No 4 (n 1) para 6.
[93] Hathaway and Foster (2003) (n 1) 370; Hathaway and Foster (2014) (n 1) 338–39. Their concern that the 'reasonableness' approach encourages decision makers to pre-empt the analysis of well-founded fear in the place of origin seems to ignore the very strong emphasis the UNHCR Guidelines No 4 place on the need for individual assessment of risk in both the home area and the IPA. For an analysis of why it is wrong to treat this type of mistake as inherent in the well-founded fear or holistic approaches, see Kelley (n 1) 8–9. Given that Hathaway and Foster (2003) (n 1) 409 accept that 'in the hands of experienced and thoughtful

a concealment requirement.[94] Even taking full cognisance of various studies done of the use of the IPA in case law, they reveal[95] relatively few examples of such pitfalls and certainly not enough, in comparative law terms, to demonstrate a structural failure.

What of, however, the conceptual issues?

As regards the view that the IPA inquiry should be located in the 'well-founded fear' clause, it needs to be highlighted that, whatever is made of it, it does not entail that no protection inquiry of any kind is made. That is clearest from the terms of the UNHCR Guidelines No 4. This requires mention because one of the main objections to location of the IPA inquiry in the 'protection'/availment clause was raised by Fortin who argued that 'protection' therein referred solely to *diplomatic protection*. He made clear nonetheless that *internal protection* still falls to be addressed in the context of the 'well-founded fear' limb.[96] Nor does locating the IPA in the 'well-founded fear' clause necessarily 'collapse' the definition so as to make the 'protection clause' superfluous, since the test of internal protection made within the former clause at least draws on some of the latter's constituent concepts—(in)ability and (un)willingness to avail oneself of protection in particular.[97] Further, sight must not be lost of the fact that UNHCR, the most prominent proponent of location in the 'well-founded fear' clause, also considers that this position is consistent with a holistic approach which sees the IPA inquiry as linking to both this clause and the 'protection'/availment clause. Indeed, what essentially appears meant by UNHCR's own understanding is that the IPA inquiry is to be located not in the 'well-founded fear' clause in isolation, but the wider clause 'well-founded fear of being persecuted', which obviously enfolds the persecution inquiry and interconnects heavily with the protection inquiry.

As noted above, locating the IPA analysis in the 'being persecuted' element fits well with an approach that treats protection as an integral part of the meaning of 'being persecuted'. Within this approach the consideration of whether protection is effective must incorporate an assessment of whether the unwillingness or inability of the state to protect is confined to a part or parts of the country of origin. It must be acknowledged, however, that to treat protection as an integral part of the meaning of 'being persecuted' is already to acknowledge a close interconnection between the 'being persecuted' limb and the availment clause, since it is only the latter that expressly deploys the concept of protection.[98]

As regards location in the 'protection'/availment clause, Eaton's concerns about this encouraging a misplaced 'due diligence' approach (which he associates with the

---

decision makers, we believe the results will be largely the same [as under our approach]', it might rhetorically be asked why it is thought other approaches are *conceptually* erroneous. At the very least, it is clear that the UNHCR Guidelines No 4 (n 1) condemn any such tendency: see UNHCR, 'Relocating Internally as a Reasonable Alternative to Seeking Asylum' (n 1) para 18.

[94] Hathaway and Foster (2014) (n 1) 338. Whilst case law in the past has been guilty of imposing such a requirement, this stemmed from a general error in understanding the 'being persecuted' notion, not from any specific feature of IPA analyses under the 'well-founded fear' limb.
[95] ibid. Hathaway and Foster, for example, cite relatively few examples, and these include several quite old cases.
[96] Fortin (n 33) 574.
[97] Indeed, Hathaway and Foster (2003) (n 1) 379–81, seem to acknowledge this tacitly.
[98] See p. 578.

*Horvath* case), seem somewhat contingent. Hathaway and Foster's own work is a testament to the fact that choice about where to locate this clause is not inherently tied to any 'due diligence' notions that displace focus away from whether protection is effective.[99] If one accepts their logic of regarding 'protection' in the availment clause as concerned with the refugee rights contained in Articles 2–33, then their approach has an obvious appeal since then, as they say, the IPA analysis could be seen as expressly rooted in the availment clause. However, if that assumption is incorrect, then their whole approach lacks any content distinct from the protection inquiry they see as being an integral part of the 'being persecuted' inquiry. How, furthermore, does it comport with a holistic approach?[100]

From one perspective, the holistic approach must be right, given the interlocking nature of the refugee definition's elements and the fact that 'well-founded fear' surely requires to be read in conjunction with its object, namely 'being persecuted'.[101] As Kelley notes:

> To be well-founded, the claimant must fear persecution for reasons of a Convention ground and establish that there is an objectively valid basis for it. The latter involves considerations of the basis for the fear and whether protection from the risk of persecution is available. If protection is available, either in the original area or the IFA, then the fear is not well-founded and refugee status is denied. However, where there is a legitimate fear of persecution for a Convention ground, which cannot be assuaged by effective protection, the claim is established.[102]

In light of the above, this author sees considerable justification in Zimmermann and Mahler's view that 'both the concept of a lack of "well-founded fear of persecution" and that of "protection" cover scenarios where the person possesses an internal flight alternative'; that the two concepts represent 'two sides of the same coin'; that 'both views prove to be able to provide appropriate results';[103] and that 'both elements also prove to be intertwined in a way that renders the attribution of a clearly defined "textual home" of the test practically inconceivable'.[104]

In any event, it is hard to see how it is not an improvement on the two alternatives if the advantages of both can be preserved. Since Hathaway and Foster themselves acknowledge that even in their protection-oriented approach more than one criteria requires consideration of well-founded fear,[105] there seems realistic scope for merging the two.[106]

---

[99] Hathaway and Foster (2003) (n 1) 332–61. They expressly reject the importation of due diligence notions into refugee law: see p. 428.
[100] Storey (2003) (n 1) 372.
[101] See pp. 441–442.
[102] Kelley (n 1) 8.
[103] Zimmermann and Mahler (n 1) 447–48.
[104] ibid 458.
[105] Hathaway and Foster (2003) (n 1) 342.
[106] Zimmermann and Mahler (n 1) 447 argue for a two-stage approach: '[a]ccordingly, an in-depth analysis is required on whether the persecution feared is clearly limited to a specific geographical area (which relates more to the well-founded character of the fear) and whether effective protection is available in other parts of the country (which in turn centres more on the protection question)'. In order to illustrate this

Locating the IPA analysis in the 'being persecuted' limb is consistent with a holistic approach so long as it is accepted that its location there does not preclude the need for an overall assessment. Indeed, since much of the argument relating to the location of the IPA concept in the 'well-founded fear' limb is in reality about the more inclusive 'well-founded fear of being persecuted' limb, the significance of both the 'well-founded fear' and the 'being persecuted' inquiry has already been accommodated.

Perhaps what matters most about the ongoing debate over the proper location of the test is that virtually all share the same belief that the concept cannot operate as an independent or 'stand-alone' test. All accept, in the words of Sir Kenneth Keith, that it must be 'tied back' to the existing elements of the refugee definition.[107] That said, the critical question remains whether any of the main approaches actually succeed in doing that, given that at least two of them (the UNHCR Guidelines No 4 approach and the MGs' approach) insist on developing a test—for the former, 'reasonableness'; and for the latter, 'affirmative protection'—that potentially goes beyond the scope afforded by the existing elements of the refugee definition.

## 2 The IPA Inquiry: Main Positions and Criticisms

Our discussion so far has alluded in passing to several schools of thought regarding the IPA. It is time to consider them in more detail. Each has been thoroughly aired in the literature, often categorised in different ways. The main approaches[108] can conveniently be grouped under six heads: UNHCR 'reasonableness' test; MGs; human rights approach; UN Guiding Principles on Internal Displacement; implied limit on Article 1A(2); and implied limit on refugee status. Following a brief description, analysis is attempted of these approaches' relative merits and demerits.

Before turning to look at each approach, it is important to reiterate the principal conclusion from the previous discussions of the concept's textual home or location in the refugee definition. Notwithstanding continuing disagreements as to what that is, most accept that it must be located *somewhere* within Article 1A(2) and that it is not, to use UNHCR's words, an 'independent' or 'free-standing' element. Accordingly, one key question that must be borne in mind throughout what follows is the extent to which each school of thought actually adheres to that acceptance.

---

view, they refer to Hathaway and Foster (2003) (n 1) 357, 371, who cite *Refugee Appeal No 70951/98* [1998] NZRSAA.

[107] *Butler* (n 81).
[108] They are not exhaustive of all that have been proposed. For example, Lehmann (n 1) 174–76 advocates a combination of a refugee rights approach (using Articles 2–33 of the Convention) with a human rights approach.

## 2.1 UNHCR and the 'Reasonableness' Test

Mention has already been made of the 1979 UNHCR Handbook which leading court decisions have seen as the staging post for modern adoption of the IPA doctrine. Paragraph 91 states:

> The fear of being persecuted need not always extend to the whole territory of the refugee's country of nationality. Thus in ethnic clashes or in cases of grave disturbances involving civil war conditions, persecution of a specific ethnic or national group may occur in only one part of the country. In such situations, a person will not be excluded from refugee status merely because he could have sought refuge in another part of the same country, if under all the circumstances it would not have been reasonable to expect him to do so.

Yet, it was not until 1995 that UNHCR set out in explicit terms its position on appropriate application of what it called the 'notion of internal flight alternative'—in its March 1995 'Information Note on Article 1 of the 1951 Convention' (UNHCR 1995 Information Note). In this Note, it stated that the 'underlying assumption' for the application of the notion is 'a regionalized failure of the State to protect its citizens from persecution'.[109] This was closely followed by further confirmation of the role of the notion in the UNHCR, Regional Bureau for Europe, an Overview of Protection Issues in Western Europe (UNHCR 1995 Overview).[110] The next UNHCR pronouncement on the topic came in 1999 in a paper entitled, 'Relocating Internally as a Reasonable Alternative to Seeking Asylum—The So-Called "Internal Flight Alternative" or "Relocation Principle"' (UNHCR 1999 Position Paper). As already noted, this took a more sceptical position.[111] In its influential 2001 Note, UNHCR emphasised, inter alia, that the 'internal flight alternative' was not a separate element of the refugee definition but was part of the 'well-founded fear' assessment.[112]

Not long after, cognisant that debates and disagreements about the notion continued to swirl, UNHCR chose to address the topic in the second track of Global Consultations to mark the Convention's fiftieth anniversary. These resulted in Guidelines No 4. The latter confirm the view that when the IFA issue arises, it does so as 'part of the refugee status determination process'.[113]

In face of 'divergent practices' the UNHCR Guidelines No 4 purport both to consolidate state practice and provide 'a more structured approach to analysis of this aspect of refugee status determination', one that views the IFA test as part of the holistic assessment of a claim to refugee status, 'in which a well-founded fear of persecution

---

[109] UNHCR, 'Information Note on Article 1 of the 1951 Convention' (1995) para 6.
[110] UNHCR, Regional Bureau for Europe, An Overview of Protection Issues in Western Europe: Legislative Trends and Positions Taken by UNHCR (1995) 1(3) European Series.
[111] UNHCR, Position Paper on Relocating Internally as a Reasonable Alternative to Seeking Asylum (n 11). At para 7, it stated that '[t]he internal relocation notion, which advocates staying within the borders of one's own country and trying to find safety there, rather than leaving and seeking asylum abroad, rests on understandings which are basically at odds with those underlying the fundamental refugee protection principles'; compare, however, para 18.
[112] UNHCR, Interpreting Article 1 of the 1951 Convention (n 1) paras 12–15.
[113] UNHCR Guidelines No 4 (n 1) para 2.

for a Convention reason has been established in some localised part of the country of origin'.[114] They reiterate in this context the point made in the 2001 publication on Article 1 that the concept is not a 'stand-alone' element of the refugee definition[115] and application of the concept requires individual assessment.[116] They treat it as axiomatic that the Convention definition does not require that an applicant's fear of persecution need always extend to the whole territory of the refugee's country of origin.[117] The IFA assessment is seen to require two main sets of analyses, a 'relevance analysis' and a 'reasonableness analysis', the latter embodied in the question, '[c]an the claimant, in the context of the country concerned, lead a relatively normal life without facing undue hardship?' They state that '[i]f not, it would not be reasonable to expect the person to move there'.[118] At paragraph 23, the 'reasonableness test' is described as:

> [ ... ] a useful legal tool which, while not specifically derived from the language of the 1951 Convention, has proved sufficiently flexible to address the issue of whether or not, in all the circumstances, the particular claimant could reasonably be expected to move to the proposed area to overcome his or her well-founded fear of being persecuted. It is not an analysis based on what a hypothetical 'reasonable person' should be expected to do. The question is what is reasonable, both subjectively and objectively, given the individual claimant and the conditions in the proposed internal flight or relocation alternative.[119]

In relation to the reasonableness analysis, the Guidelines state:

> 28. Where respect for basic human rights standards, including in particular non-derogable rights, is clearly problematic, the proposed area cannot be considered a reasonable alternative. This does not mean that the deprivation of any civil, political or socio-economic human right in the proposed area will disqualify it from being an internal flight or relocation alternative. Rather, it requires, from a practical perspective, an assessment of whether the rights that will not be respected or protected are fundamental to the individual, such that the deprivation of those rights would be sufficiently harmful to render the area an unreasonable alternative.[120]

The UNHCR Guidelines No 4 garnered considerable approval in subsequent jurisprudence, most notably from the UK House of Lords in *Januzi*.[121] The common law

---

[114] ibid para 7.
[115] ibid para 2.
[116] ibid para 4: 'A consideration of internal flight or relocation necessitates regard for the personal circumstances of the individual claimant and the conditions in the country for which the internal flight or relocation alternative is proposed', citing UNHCR, Interpreting Article 1 of the 1951 Convention (n 1) para 12.
[117] ibid para 4.
[118] ibid para 7.
[119] ibid para 23.
[120] ibid para 28.
[121] *Januzi* (n 43); *Rasaratnam* (n 71); *Thirunavukkarasu* (n 71) para 12; *SZATV* (n 38). However, a 2014 amendment to the Migration Act 1958 was intended to preclude a reasonableness test: see Goodwin-Gill and McAdam (4th edn) (n 1) 148. See also *FCS17 v MHA* [2020] FCAFC 68; and Guide to Refugee Law in Australia, ch 3, 25–27.

jurisprudence has tended to prefer to describe the test as one of 'undue hardship' but has seen this term as interchangeable with the UNHCR concept of 'reasonableness'.[122]

Yet from early on, the 'reasonableness test' also attracted criticism. Hathaway and Foster took early UNHCR versions of it to task for being subjective, amorphous, unstructured, vague, indeterminate, and arbitrary. They saw its arbitrariness to be illustrated by it having produced wide inconsistencies between jurisdictions. They criticised its proneness to an 'unfocused and open-ended inquiry that is not anchored in the language or object of the 1951 Convention'.[123] This author said of the synonymous test of 'undue hardship' that '[i]f [it] is not in turn underpinned by human right norms, then it can mean all things to all men'.[124] Marx contended that the reasonableness consideration must be anchored in a protection analysis 'relating to the protection offered by the Convention and not just as a discretionary or amorphous consideration'.[125] In the second edition of *The Law of Refugee Status*, Hathaway and Foster, now taking direct aim at the UNHCR Guidelines No 4, repeat their 2003 criticisms.[126]

On the other hand, some commentators have seen the UNHCR approach as capable of being read as a human rights approach.[127] Summarising the various criticisms made of the reasonableness standard by those who take a human rights approach, Kelley has written that as generally understood this standard:

[ ... ] has led to an expansion of the factors considered relevant to evaluating whether a proposed area is an IFA. Claimant specific factors have included such things as the claimant's age, gender, family status and employment experience. Conditions in the proposed IFA that have been found relevant include such things as the state of the administrative, economic and judicial infrastructure and the social and economic quality of life in the area. The widening of the relevant criteria has enabled the IFA determination to flexibly respond to individual circumstances. But it has not resulted in consistent jurisprudence within and between jurisdictions leading some to conclude that the whole concept of reasonableness as it has been applied is simply not adequate, being too vague and open to subjective interpretations to lead to consistent and rational jurisprudence in the area. In fact, the indeterminacy of the approach has been the subject of international attention and the focus of some higher court decisions, notably in Canada and New Zealand, which has led to a rethinking of the relevant criteria.[128]

Zimmermann and Mahler remark of the 'reasonableness' test that 'the standard is neither anchored in the text of the 1951 Convention nor in other binding instruments of

---

[122] *Januzi* (n 43) para 1.
[123] Hathaway and Foster (2003) (n 1) 387. They cite criticisms to this effect from, among others, Frelick (n 1) 23.
[124] Storey (2003) (n 1) 368.
[125] Marx (n 1) 206.
[126] Hathaway and Foster (2014) (n 1) 352.
[127] See e.g. Ní Ghráinne (2015) (n 1) 46–51; Hailbronner and Thym (n 1) 1164.
[128] Kelley (n 1) 24.

international law. It therefore, per se, provides little authoritative guidance but rather bears the inherent risk of fragmentation in refugee decision-making.'[129]

## 2.2 Michigan Guidelines on the Internal Protection Alternative

The MGs[130] first appeared in 1999. Despite being thus several years prior to the UNHCR Guidelines No 4 (and undoubtedly influencing their contents), they are dealt with second because they specifically contrast their position with the 'reasonableness' approach taken by UNHCR in earlier UNHCR publications. The MGs have become closely associated with the report produced by Hathaway and Foster in 2003[131] for the UNHCR Global Consultations process ongoing at that time, in which they set out the case for adoption of the MGs in more detail.

Having said that '[o]ur analysis is based on the requirements of the Refugee Convention, and is informed primarily by the jurisprudence of leading developed states of asylum',[132] the MGs view the IPA inquiry to be 'inherent in the Convention's requirement that a refugee not only have a well-founded fear of being persecuted', but also be 'unable or, owing to such fear, [be] unwilling to avail himself of the protection of [her or his] country'.[133] The MGs do not say it expressly, but they too clearly reject any notion that an applicant must show persecution countrywide.[134]

The MGs construe the IPA inquiry to be 'predicated on the existence of a well-founded fear of persecution for a Convention reason in at least one region of the asylum-seeker's state of origin, and hence on a presumptive entitlement to Convention refugee status'.[135] In Hathaway and Foster's 2003 report, this predicate is described as a 'prima facie' case for refugee status:

> Yet serious harms falling short of persecutory conduct may nonetheless be relevant to the assessment of IPA. This is because a person under consideration for IPA has already prima facie satisfied the 'well-founded fear of being persecuted' (inclusionary) language of the 1951 Convention. The decision maker is now engaged in what amounts to an inquiry into exclusion from refugee status on the grounds that the applicant (like a person with an actual or de facto second nationality) does not in fact require surrogate international protection. In a fundamental sense, the question is whether the IPA can amount to an adequate substitute for the refugee status

---

[129] Zimmermann and Mahler (n 1) 455.
[130] See MGs (n 1).
[131] Hathaway and Foster (2003) (n 1) 203.
[132] MGs (n 1) para 6.
[133] ibid para 11.
[134] Hathaway and Foster (2003) (n 1) 337 expressly criticise the 'countrywide' persecution approach. A notable US case in which such an approach was adopted is *Matter of Acosta* [1985] A-24159781, but it is not consistent with the later US Asylum Regulations. See further Deborah Anker, *Law of Asylum in the United States* (Thomson Reuters 2022) §2.13, 90–91; Goodwin-Gill and McAdam (4th edn) (n 1) 146.
[135] MGs (n 1) para 14; see also para 12. If the notion of 'presumptive entitlement' is accepted, it would appear to mean that the burden of proof shifts to the refugee determining authority: see Reinhard Marx, 'Interner Schutz von Flüchtlingen nach Art. 1a Nr. 2 GFK (Art. 2 Buchst. d) RL 2011/95/EU' (2017) 13 Zeitschrift für Ausländerrecht und Ausländerpolitik 303, 309–11 (cited Lehmann (n 1) 153).

otherwise warranted in the asylum country. Critically, this inquiry is predicated on the fact that the person being considered for IPA has already been found to have a well-founded fear of being persecuted.[136]

The MGs state at paragraph 13 that the IPA analysis can be broken into three parts, but Hathaway and Foster in 2003 re-adjust it so as to require four analytical steps:

> First, is the proposed IPA accessible to the individual—meaning access that is practical, safe, and legal? Secondly, does the IPA offer an 'antidote' to the well-founded fear of being persecuted shown to exist in the applicant's place of origin—that is, does it present less than a 'real chance' or 'serious possibility' of the original risk? Thirdly, is it clear that there are no new risks of being persecuted in the IPA, or of direct or indirect refoulement back to the place of origin? And, fourthly, is at least the minimum standard of affirmative State protection available in the proposed IPA?[137]

At first sight, notwithstanding the efforts of the MGs' authors to differentiate their approach from the UNHCR Guidelines No 4, the framework they propose for answering the first three questions appears to closely resemble the latter.[138] Hathaway and Foster's fourth step,[139] however, represents a radical departure from previous understandings, all of which had focussed on application of norms drawn either from general notions of a 'relatively normal life' and/or 'reasonableness' and/or 'undue hardship' or from norms drawn from IHRL. Albeit described by their main proponents as manifesting a 'human rights approach'[140] (and being understood by at least some courts to be such), the MGs stake themselves on a highly distinctive application of 'refugee rights' drawn directly from Articles 2–33 of the Refugee Convention itself, *not* from IHLR. Paragraph 21 states that when determining the existence of an IPA, reference should be made to the rights that make up what the MGs interpret the Refugee Convention's 'endogenous' definition of protection to be, specifically Articles 2–33. Paragraph 22 states that 'at a minimum … conditions in the proposed site of internal protection ought to satisfy the affirmative, yet relative, standards set by the textually explicit definition of the content of protection' (a shorthand used for this conception is 'affirmative protection').[141] It is stated at paragraph 23 that, if these guidelines are followed, there is no additional duty to assess the 'reasonableness' of the IPA.

In elaborating this fourth step, which they acknowledge to be the 'most conceptually challenging', the MGs' authors see it as necessitated by shortcomings in prevailing human rights approaches. Hathaway and Foster, seeking to develop the approach in the MGs more fully, note that '[i]t may be that decision makers fear that "fundamental rights and freedoms" is an unmanageably vague notion. Moreover, it may be thought

---

[136] Hathaway and Foster (2003) (n 1) 402; see also 370: '[i]n this way, the IFA analysis is understood as akin to an exclusion inquiry such that the evidentiary burden is then on the party asserting an IFA to establish that it exists'.
[137] ibid 389.
[138] Regarding Step 1, see UNHCR Guidelines No 4 (n 1) para 7.1.a. Regarding Steps 2 and 3, see para 7.1.d.
[139] MGs (n 1) para 20–24.
[140] See MGs (n 1) para 21, and Hathaway and Foster (2003) (n 1) 408–09.
[141] Hathaway and Foster (2014) (n 1) 360.

that a rights-based approach travels considerably beyond the requirements of the 1951 Convention text.'[142] It was because they considered that 'there is no consensus that any risk to even a core, internationally protected human right is tantamount to a risk of "being persecuted" ',[143] that the MGs' authors:

> [ ... ] determined that reference could instead be made to the rights which comprise the 1951 Convention's own definition of 'protection'. Since the rationale for IPA analysis is to determine whether an internal site may be regarded as affording a sufficient answer to the applicant's well-founded fear of being persecuted such that the presumptive remedy of protection in an asylum State is not required, then there is a logic to measuring the sufficiency of IPA 'protection' in relation to the actual protective duties of asylum states. The required standard is not respect for all human rights, but rather provision of the rights codified as the 1951 Convention's endogenous definition of 'protection' in Articles 2–33. In general terms, these standards impose a duty of non-discrimination vis-a-vis citizens or other residents of the asylum country and refugees in relation to a core subset of civil and socio-economic rights, including, for example, freedom of religion, freedom of movement, access to courts, and rights to work, social assistance, and primary education.[144]

According to the New Zealand case law of the same vintage, the 'added attraction' of using Articles 2–33 was 'that it provides a decision-maker with an identified, quantified and standard set of rights common to all State parties, thereby facilitating consistent and fair decision-making'.[145]

Unsurprisingly, the decision of the MGs (and the New Zealand RSAA) not to apply IHRL norms to the IPA analysis has attracted heavy criticism both from those advocating a human rights approach and those advocating a 'reasonableness' approach. Thus Kelley has argued that applying the more limited range of rights recognised by the MGs would lead to more consistency but that they are narrower than the UNHCR criteria.[146] Critics have seen the framework of the MGs to: confuse criteria for inclusion in refugee status with the rights attaching to status following inclusion;[147] constitute a bad conceptual fit, as Articles 2–33 'take account of the special needs of a particular class of foreigners [and] cannot be adopted to rule the legal status of nationals within their country of origin';[148] overlook or downplay that the rights under Articles 2–33 make no reference to protection from persecution and only accrue after

---

[142] Hathaway and Foster (2003) (n 1) 406; A similar point was made by Chairperson Haines in *Refugee Appeal No 71684/99* (n 81) in which it was stated that 'the difficulty with requiring correspondence with other major human rights instruments ... is that no uniform and ascertainable standard of rights for refugees has emerged on which state parties to the Refugee Convention are agreed. Insistence on these human rights instruments would also potentially involve measuring the proposed site of internal protection against a standard which is possibly unobtainable in many states party to the Refugee Convention.'
[143] Hathaway and Foster (2003) (n 1) 407–08.
[144] ibid 408–09.
[145] *Refugee Appeal No 71684/99* (n 81) para 62.
[146] Kelley (n 1) 35–36, 40; see also Storey (2003) (n 1) 376.
[147] *Januzi* (n 43) (per Lord Bingham).
[148] Marx (n 1) 203.

a person has satisfied the criteria of the refugee definition;[149] be susceptible to the same type of vagueness seen to plague the terms 'reasonable' and 'unduly harsh';[150] endorse a comparative threshold based on the level of national protection accorded to citizens and or aliens, which could sometimes be lower than even core basic human rights standards;[151] embody a hierarchy of rights dependent on the increasing level of connection with the host state, levels which have no analogues in an applicant's country of origin;[152] and amount to *de lege ferenda* based on case law in just one country— New Zealand.[153] The MGs' approach was expressly rejected by the UK House of Lords in *Januzi*.[154] There has also been criticism of the notion endorsed by the MGs and Hathaway and Foster that an IPA has to be premised on prima facie acknowledgement of a well-founded fear of persecution, which is said to represent a misreading of the refuge definition.[155] It has been canvassed that insistence, in the context of the IPA, on the contents of the concept of protection being *additional to* that otherwise deployed in the refugee definition, sows conceptual confusion.[156]

Hathaway and Foster's main retort to these criticisms has been to emphasise that the MGs '[do] not suggest a literal interpretation of Articles 2–33 in considering internal protection, but rather that decision makers seek inspiration from the kind of interests protected by these Articles'.[157] As regards the criticism that the MGs endorse lesser standards than IHLR, Lehmann (in seeking to argue for a combined Articles 2–33 and human rights approach) points out that at least some of the standards enshrined in Articles 2–33 still exceed human rights law—he mentions Articles 17–18 on access to the labour market and Article 23 on welfare.[158]

The principal New Zealand response to the rejection of the MGs' approach by the UK House of Lords in *Januzi* was set out in *Refugee Appeal No 76044*. Chairperson Haines reiterated the point that the MGs were not meant to be read literally or applied slavishly,[159] and that specific identification of a 'core subset' of human rights, namely the rights in Articles 2–33, was preferable to the approach of applying human rights norms more broadly. He reiterated criticisms of the reliance in the UNHCR Guidelines No 4 on the 'subjective' metric of reasonableness. He also criticised the decision of their lordships in *Januzi* to locate the IPA inquiry in the 'well-founded fear' test.[160]

---

[149] Ní Ghráinne (2015) (n 1) 40: '[t]o treat those rights as a standard that forms part of the refugee definition would be premature and would possibly entail extending the reach of the refugee definition beyond that which was envisaged by its drafters'.
[150] See above p. 496.
[151] Storey (2003) (n 1) 378–79; Eaton (n 1) 774, 789; see also Kelley (n 1) 34–35.
[152] Storey (2003) (n 1); Ní Ghráinne (2015) (n 1) 40–41.
[153] Storey (2003) (n 1) 361; Ní Ghráinne (2015) (n 1) 42.
[154] *Januzi* (n 43) paras 15, 19.
[155] Michael Barutciski, 'Tensions Between the Refugee Concept and the IDP Debate' (1998) 3 Forced Migration Review 11, 12 has argued that it would amount to an unwritten exclusion clause since it would entail an inquiry into whether someone who was prima facie a refugee should lose that status by the application of the internal protection principle.
[156] Storey (2003) (n 1) 377; Ní Ghráinne (2015) (n 1) 39–40.
[157] Hathaway and Foster (2003) (n 1) 409; Hathaway and Foster (2014) (n 1) 357.
[158] Lehmann (n 1) 172.
[159] *Refugee Appeal No 76044* (n 36) paras 140, 147, 176.
[160] ibid paras 138, 163–69.

Concern has also been expressed about the seeming inconsistency between the approach taken by Hathaway and Foster to the IPA inquiry and that which they take to the 'being persecuted inquiry'. Battjes argues that their approach to the IPA inquiry involves a concept of protection that is different from the concept employed in the state protection limb of the 'being persecuted' inquiry.[161] Hathaway and Foster's reply to that is that in the latter limb, the 'failure of state protection element ... is directly connected to the serious harm and the inability of the state to prevent that harm'.[162]

## 2.3 Human Rights Approach

Given especially that Hathaway and Foster represent the MGs approach as a type of human rights approach, it is important to clarify that what is normally meant in refugee law (and in this book) by a human rights approach is the application of IHRL norms to the refugee definition and in particular to assessment of whether in the applicant's home country they have a well-founded fear of being persecuted, persecution being understood as serious harm + lack of state protection.[163] Without intending at this point to reject Hathaway and Foster's view that the *MGs* embody a (different) human rights approach, in order to avoid confusion I shall refer to their approach as a 'refugee-rights-based' approach.

What then of the human rights approach understood in the usual sense? Although widely noted as one of the main approaches, it has not as yet been cast into the form of guidelines in the same way as the UNHCR Guidelines No 4 and the MGs have been. The scholar who has sketched the human rights approach in the most detail so far is Kelley.[164] Advocating a holistic approach that views the IPA inquiry as part of the refugee definition, she echoes rejection by the UNHCR and the MGs of the notion that persecution must be shown countrywide. This notion, she writes, 'stems from misreading the definition, essentially adding a requirement that the claimant fear being persecuted "throughout the entire country", which cannot be sustained on either a two-part or holistic approach to Article 1(2)(A)'. For a human rights-governed IPA inquiry, she considers it essential that a determination of whether the applicant is at risk of persecution in the displacement area precedes a determination of whether the applicant has an IFA. This follows, she writes, 'from the fact that the IFA is a place where the claimant can access meaningful protection, necessitating first a determination of "protection from what?"'. She views the nature of the persecution feared, the circumstances that gave rise to that fear and prompted flight from the original area, as all being relevant considerations in the determination of whether the alternative locale is an IFA.[165] For Kelley, an IFA inquiry 'first determines whether there is a serious possibility that the persecutor will persecute the claimant in the IFA'.[166] This initial stage requires, inter alia, consideration of the facts that form the basis of the reasons for the original fear and also 'includes an assessment of whether state protection from

---

[161] Battjes (n 86) 250; Storey (2003) (n 1) 377.
[162] Hathaway and Foster (2014) (n 1) 355.
[163] ibid.
[164] Kelley (n 1)./IBT>
[165] ibid 8–12.
[166] ibid.

that form of persecution is available'. If this initial stage concludes that there is no possibility of persecution in the IFA:

> [ ... ] then the second stage of the inquiry would go on to determine whether meaningful protection is otherwise available in that area. The benchmark for that determination should be whether the claimant's basic civil, political, and socio-economic human rights, as expressed in the Refugee Convention and other major human rights instruments, would be protected there.[167]

The human rights approach to the IPA has occupied an ambiguous place in the case law and wider literature. For example, the UNHCR Guidelines No 4 have sometimes been seen to embody a human rights approach; and other times seen as an alternative to it; the MGs reject a 'general' human rights approach[168] but purport to apply a particular one.[169] In one of the leading cases, *Januzi*, Lord Bingham rejects the human rights approach in terms, but then approves the UNHCR Guidelines No 4, quoting a passage from the latter often seen to encapsulate a human rights approach.[170] He also makes clear that an IPA will not exist if that would cause an infringement of the non-derogable human right prohibiting ill treatment.[171]

Clearly, therefore, the human rights approach to the IPA inquiry has not always been easy to identify, nor has it attracted consensus. That said, whilst within the EU, the Court of Justice of the European Union (CJEU) has yet to address Article 8 of the QD (recast) as such, it would appear, on the strength of its analysis in *Abdulla*,[172] that it takes a human rights approach to the underlying concept of protection. In relation to the provision governing actors of protection (Article 7(2)), this Court stated in *Abdulla—although* only in the context of evidence assessment under Article 4(3)— that decision makers 'may take into account ... the extent to which basic human rights are guaranteed in that country'.[173] A number of scholars, most notably Kelley, have advocated a human rights approach and indeed Zimmermann and Mahler, having reviewed the literature, conclude that the '[n]eed to consider at the very least certain core human rights of a non-derogable nature and moreover further human rights standards enjoining general recognition among States illustrates that any approach to internal relocation has to be based on human rights to a certain extent'.[174]

In outlining a human rights framework, and having noted case law and other evidence of support for it,[175] Kelley states that:

---

[167] ibid 8–12, 36–44.
[168] MGs (n 1) para 20.
[169] This is how Hathaway and Foster appear to construe their reliance on the refugee rights set out in Articles 2–33—see Hathaway and Foster (2003) (n 1) 408–09.
[170] *Januzi* (n 43)/IBT> para 20.
[171] ibid para 19.
[172] Joined Cases C-175/08, C-176/08, C-178/08, and C-179/08 *Salahadin Abdulla and Others* [2010] ECR I-0000.
[173] ibid para 71; see also *AK (Article 15(c)) Afghanistan* CG [2012] UKUT 163 (IAC), para 240.
[174] Zimmermann and Mahler (n 1) 458; see also Kelley (n 1) 39–40; Storey (1999) (n 1) 529–30; and Hugo Storey, 'Persecution: Towards a Working Definition' in Vincent Chetail and Céline Bauloz (eds), *Research Handbook on Migration and International Law* (Edward Elgar 2014).
[175] Kelley (n 1) 36–40.

It is true that there is not a core consensus regarding the scope and extent of the positive obligations imposed on the state signatories to the major international rights treaties. A human rights analysis will not give a formulaic framework with predictable group outcomes. What it will do is at least provide a benchmark against which the claim of the refugee claimant, regarding why relocation is 'unreasonable', can be assessed. It would require the refugee to show what rights he or she will not be accorded in the IFA and in what way they are fundamental to him or her. It would recognize the individual character of the IFA assessment, which is entirely in keeping with the refugee determination more generally. If the country of origin is unable to protect the individual from a deprivation of a human right, fundamental to him or her, the area cannot be an appropriate IFA. In other words, it will not be reasonable to expect the person with an established risk of persecution for a Convention refugee reason in one part of the country to relocate to another area of harm. So for example, at its most obvious, persons who could show good grounds for fearing they would be killed in the IFA, or that they would face torture or other brutal treatment there, could point to Articles 3, 5, and 7 of the [Universal Declaration of Human Rights] UDHR48 and the non-derogable right not to be arbitrarily deprived of life and not to be subjected to torture, or cruel, inhuman, and degrading treatment found in Articles 6 and 7 of the *International Covenant on Civil and Political Rights* (ICCPR66).[176]

From this and kindred passages it can be seen that Kelley thinks that the human rights approach can build on UNHCR's 'reasonableness' analysis by more fully underpinning this concept specifically with human rights norms. She gives the example of the differing views taken in the case law and wider literature over whether family life considerations are or can be relevant to an IPA analysis:

What is often overlooked however is the recognition in Article 16(3) of the UDHR48 and Article 23 of the ICCPR66 that the family is the 'natural and fundamental unit of society and is entitled to protection by the society and the State' and Article 10 of the *International Covenant on Economic, Social and Cultural Rights* (ICESCR66) which provides that the 'widest possible protection and assistance should be accorded to the family ... particularly for its establishment and while it is responsible for the care and education of dependent children'. Moreover Article 9 of the CRC89 states that 'state parties shall ensure that a child is not separated from his or her parents against their will' except where such separation is in the best interests of the child. There is no consensus of opinion regarding the parameters of 'family', however, all would agree that at a minimum 'family' includes the 'nuclear family'. The international recognition of the protection to be accorded the family would militate against the reasonableness of requiring a refugee claimant, particularly a spouse or a dependant child from resettling in a proposed area without their spouse or parent respectively. It may also support a finding against the relocation of any dependant (elderly, disabled) to an area where they would not have other family members and where the latter are central in the provision of physical care, economic support and protection from exploitation.[177]

[176] ibid 39–40.
[177] ibid 41.

A different version of the human rights approach is offered by Ní Ghráinne. Whilst agreeing with critics that the attempt to apply a 'general' human rights approach to the IPA is flawed because of indeterminacy, she considers that it can nevertheless provide a proper grounding to the IPA if human rights considerations form part of the IPA analysis 'only to the extent that respect for such rights is a necessary ingredient of protection from the persecution feared, or that lack of such rights may result in indirect *refoulement*'.[178]

We have already noted two of the main criticisms of the human rights approach, those voiced by the MGs and their main proponents, Hathaway and Foster, namely that it is overbroad and lacks state party consensus.

In much the same way as the reasonableness-based UNHCR Guidelines No 4 and the refugee rights-based MGs have been criticised for failing to provide clear enough criteria and parameters, the human rights approach has also been criticised for lack of determinacy. Chairperson Haines in *Refugee Appeal No 71684/99* coupled both these points of criticism when he stated that 'no uniform and ascertainable standard of rights for refugees has emerged on which state parties to the Refugee Convention are agreed'.[179] Haines also added a further point, namely that '[i]nsistence on these human rights instruments would also potentially involve measuring the proposed site of internal protection against a standard which is possibly unobtainable in many states party to the Refugee Convention'.[180] He added that the programmatic nature of many of the economic, social, and cultural rights set out in the ICESCR added to the lack of clarity.[181]

But rejection of the human rights approach in similar terms has also come from critics of the MGs' refugee-rights approach. Schultz has prayed in aid Cantor's critique of a human rights approach for shifting the refugee analysis to 'a parallel field of no less contested or complicated understandings'.[182] She also echoes the concern expressed by Alice Edwards that any approach predicated on human rights risks exclusion of factors that cannot be captured in a human rights analysis.[183]

As already intimated, the most notable judicial criticism of the human rights approach has come from the UK House of Lords in *Januzi*, who considered broad-based human rights concerns to be 'irrelevant'.[184]

The House of Lords judges also expressed concern that such an approach would produce the unwanted outcome that applicants from a 'poor and backward country' could benefit from their 'accident of persecution or to take the advantage of past

---

[178] Ní Ghráinne (2015) (n 1) 35–36, 46–47, 48; Ní Ghráinne (2021) (n 1) 709–10.
[179] *Refugee Appeal No 71684/99* (n 81) para 177.
[180] ibid para 57. For similar criticisms, see Lehmann (n 1) 173.
[181] *Refugee Appeal No 71684/99* (n 81) paras 57–59.
[182] Schultz (2018) (n 1) 105; for a response to this criticism, see Chapter 3, section 4.2.2.
[183] ibid. She cites Alice Edwards, 'Age and Gender Dimensions in International Refugee Law' in Erika Feller, Volker Türk, and Frances Nicholson (eds), *Refugee Protection in International Law: UNHCR's Global Consultations on International Protection* (CUP 2003) 72; see also Schultz and Einarsen (n 1) 311–12.
[184] *Januzi* (n 43) para 54. Whilst focus here is placed on a UK case it appears that a similar approach was taken at the time by the German courts: see Lehmann (n 1) 154–55, 164: '[i]n Germany, jurisprudence post-2004 neatly ties in with practice on the substantive level ('*Existenzminimum*') focusing on the ability to survive economically, and does not in practice consider other human rights concerns'.

persecution to achieve a better life in the host country or become the 'lucky ones'.[185] A similar point has been made in academic studies.[186]

In addition to being assailed for being overbroad, a human rights approach has sometimes been criticised for being unduly narrow. The gravamen of the decision of the House of Lords in *AH (Sudan)* was that, at least if the applicable human rights standard was taken to be prohibition of non-derogable rights (in particular, ill-treatment, as exemplified by Article 3 of the European Convention on Human Rights (ECHR)), then that would clearly be too restrictive. As started by Baroness Hale:

> Further, although the test of reasonableness is a stringent one—whether it would be 'unduly harsh' to expect the claimant to return—it is not to be equated with a real risk that the claimant would be subjected to inhuman or degrading treatment or punishment so serious as to meet the high threshold set by article 3 of the European Convention on Human Rights.... Obviously, if there were a real risk of such ill-treatment, return would be precluded by article 3 itself as well as being unreasonable in Refugee Convention terms. But internal relocation is a different question.[187]

Significantly, however, the caveat to their lordships' view that the less demanding standard of 'reasonableness' was to be used was that, if the lack of respect for human rights in the IPA poses threatens an applicant's life or exposes him to the risk of inhuman or degrading treatment or punishment, that could never be reasonable. Indeed, it was precisely because there was seen to be a real risk to non-derogable rights in a proposed IPA that Lord Hope remitted the appeals of the three Sudanese appellants in *Januzi*.[188]

The reason why close attention is paid here to the UK case law regarding this point will become clearer in section 2.7.3 below, when attempting to identify and put to rest a widely held misconception about this matter.

Concern about a human rights approach being unduly narrow has also been expressed by reference to the underlying notion of protection on which it is seen to depend. Thus, Mathew has argued that adoption of a human rights approach would unduly narrow the IPA inquiry down to a purely negative assessment based on absence of persecution. She considers that 'to frame the inquiry as being whether any person has their rights respected in the IPA undermines the notion of protection, almost emptying it of content. It deprives protection of any positive meaning other than absence of persecution, suggesting that a human rights limbo for victims of persecution is acceptable.'[189]

---

[185] *Januzi* (n 43) para 19; see also paras 27, 32, and 41 per Lord Brown. See also *E and another v SSHD* [2003] EWCA Civ 1032, paras 24 and 37 (per Lord Philips MR). Such judicial concerns have been voiced by other European courts and tribunals: for the position in Germany, see Reinhard Marx, *Handbuch zum Flüchtlingsschutz: Erläuterungen zur Qualifikationsrichtlinie* (2nd edn, Luchterhand Verlag GmbH 2012) 137, cited in Lehmann (n 1) 175.

[186] See e.g. Ryszard Piotrowicz, 'Comment on the Draft Summary Conclusions' (2001), stated by Hathaway and Foster (2003) (n 1) 407 to be on file with them.

[187] *AH (Sudan)* (n 72) para 20 (per Baroness Hale).

[188] *Januzi* (n 43) paras 24–60.

[189] Mathew (n 1) 201.

## 2.4 1998 UN Guiding Principles on Internal Displacement

Whilst advocated by only a small number of scholars,[190] the 1998 UN Guiding Principles on Internal Displacement (IDP Guiding Principles)[191] have been seen to be at least worth considering as a potential benchmark for standards to be applied to home states in the context of assessing IPA, given that both the IDP and refugee scenarios involve displacement.[192] As stated by Ní Ghráinne, '[a]fter all, if an asylum seeker is forced to relocate to a safe place within his or her country of origin, in effect, he or she will become internally displaced'.[193] The advantage of treating these IDP Guiding Principles as a benchmark could be said to reside in the fact that they represent a strong international consensus about how international law standards should be brought to bear on the problem of internal displacement.[194] They are largely based on existing legal provisions consistent with international law.

## 2.5 Implied Limit on Article 1A(2)

In the course of her book on the IPA, Schultz argues that a narrow scope for IPA practice exists in cases in which an applicant's unwillingness to return lacks a reasonable relationship to his or her well-founded fear. She argues that this can properly be understood as an implied limit on the application of Article 1, one that only narrowly limits the substantive scope of Article 1A(2).[195] She considers that, unlike other readings which make central the state's ability or willingness to protect, this reading keeps the claimant's well-founded fear of persecution the focus of the refugee status assessment.[196] In this understanding, the IPA concept 'conditions the claimant's unwillingness to accept meaningful protection by the home state with a requirement of reasonableness'.[197]

---

[190] See e.g. Elizabeth Ferris, 'Internal Displacement and the Right to Seek Asylum' (2008) 278(3) Refugee Survey Quarterly 76; Monette Zard, 'Towards a Comprehensive Approach to Protecting Refugees and the Internally Displaced' in Anne Bayefsky (ed), *Human Rights and Refugees, Internally Displaced Persons and Migrant Workers* (Martinus Nijhoff 2006) 34–39, both cited in Schultz (2018) (n 1) 106.

[191] UN Guiding Principles on Internal Displacement (1998) UN Doc E/CN.4/1998/53/Add.2.

[192] Barutciski (n 155) 12; Hathaway and Foster (2003) (n 1) 407; Ferris (n 190) 88; Ní Ghráinne (2015) (n 1).

[193] Ní Ghráinne (2015) (n 1) 37.

[194] Walter Kälin, 'The Guiding Principles on Internal Displacement—Introduction' (1998) 10 IJRL 557, 562; Catherine Phuong, *The International Protection of Internally Displaced Persons* (CUP 2004) 64. The Guiding Principles must also be seen to have influenced the evolution of IHRL; see e.g. the discussion by David Cantor, 'The IDP in International Law? Developments, Debates, Prospects' (2018) 30(2) IJRL 191, 208–09.

[195] Schultz (2018) (n 1) 22, 382.

[196] ibid 382.

[197] ibid 161–62.

## 2.6 Implied Limit on the Right to Refugee Status

Schultz in both her book and in an article with Einarsen[198] has also suggested a further approach. According to this, the IPA analysis would only arise *after* a person has been determined to be a refugee. Once the criteria for refugee status are met, whenever a well-founded fear of persecution in the home area has been established but there appears to be a viable IPA, the rights and benefits attached to that status may be denied under certain conditions. Doubtless influenced by Hathaway and Foster describing the IPA analysis in 2003 as 'akin' to an exclusion inquiry,[199] she submits that an 'implied limit' approach can be drawn from usage made within IHRL of a proportionality analysis associated with the doctrine of 'implied limits' in human rights and constitutional law. She writes:

> Under this approach, the IPA is analogous to the exclusion clauses elsewhere in Article 1. However, unlike these other exceptions, it directly follows from the doctrine of implied limits in human rights law that a proportionate relationship must exist between the state aim of preserving restricted resources for international protection and the impact on the individual claimant from a human rights and humanitarian perspective.[200]

An 'implied limit' approach appears to be taken in a very small number of countries.[201]

## 2.7 Evaluation of Different Approaches

### 2.7.1 UNHCR Guidelines No 4

Not all of the criticisms made of the UNHCR Guidelines No 4 seem justified. As regards the alleged 'flexible' or 'fungible' character of the reasonableness standard,[202] the fact that the Guidelines aim to apply a holistic approach consciously seeking to marry different approaches to the IPA inquiry, suggests that it is capable of being adapted to fit other approaches offering greater determinacy.[203] Furthermore, criticisms of the 'reasonableness' test as being too 'fungible' and 'flexible' fail to take account of the fact that some of its components are accepted on all sides as identifying specific requirements. Thus, as noted by Kelley, its first step, the necessity of being able to access the

---

[198] Schultz and Einarsen (n 1) 274, 288–98. Schultz (2018) (n 1) 114–15 notes that Jean Yves Carlier, *Droit d'asile et des refugies* (Brill Nijhoff 2008) 159–60 has also proposed an approach based on limiting refugee status, albeit through the different theoretical route of identifying the IPA as an implied territorial exception to the principle of non-refoulement.

[199] Hathaway and Foster (2002) (n 1) 370.

[200] Schultz (2018) (n 1) 383.

[201] ibid 158–59. Schultz states that this is the position under Norwegian legislation. The European Commission, Evaluation of the application of the recast Qualification Directive (2011/95/EU): Final Report (2019) 76, observes that three member states 'assessed the option of an IPA after the status had been determined (BE, DE, FR)'. This observation is not sourced and its accuracy is doubtful.

[202] Hathaway and Foster (2003) (n 1) 368–88; Hathaway and Foster (2014) (n 1) 353.

[203] One such example being Kelley's attempt to reposition reasonableness as a standard to be applied within the context of a human rights approach.

IPA, is widely recognized as a fundamental component of any valid IPA inquiry and has not led to much confusion or inconsistency in the case law.[204] Further, when decision makers seek to avoid the reasonableness criterion, there can be a tendency for analogous criteria to creep back in.[205]

One of the most intriguing criticisms of the UNHCR Guidelines No 4 made by Hathaway and Foster is that, despite insisting that the IPA test is not an independent test but simply part of the test of 'well-founded fear of being persecuted', these Guidelines appear to endorse the threshold for reasonableness as including humanitarian-based criteria that go wider.[206] This is not a criticism they repeat in terms in TLRS2, but it prompts this question: if the 'reasonableness test' is not an independent test, then should not the only difference from other key requirements of the refugee definition (which include safety) be confined to those factors that relate to the *impact of relocation*—that is, those that bear specifically on the ability of claimants to relocate and to access an IFA? Unless the test is circumscribed in some such way, it does appear to reify certain criteria not linked to persecution or protection as so defined in the refugee definition itself.

A further question, which brings to the surface both distinct and related issues, concerns whether the UNHCR position embodies a human rights approach. As noted in Chapter 3, since 2001 UNHCR has increasingly moved towards adopting a human rights approach to the refugee definition generally[207] and, alighting on several references in the UNHCR Guidelines No 4 to human rights, some commentators have portrayed them as effectively endorsing such an approach, notwithstanding treating 'reasonableness' as key. For example, Ní Ghráinne notes that the reasonableness inquiry places focus on whether adequate protection of fundamental civil, political, and socio-economic rights is available in the proposed area of relocation.[208] At a minimum, Guidelines No 4 make very clear in paragraph 28 that '[w]here respect for basic human rights standards, including in particular non-derogable rights, is clearly problematic, the proposed area cannot be considered a reasonable alternative'.[209] Hence it would certainly be wrong to say that the 'reasonableness' test reduces assessment to a purely relativistic notion of ability to live 'a relatively normal life'.

However, it is open to some doubt that these Guidelines can accurately be said to represent a human rights approach as they stand. For example, they appear to bracket human rights equally alongside other, seemingly distinct, criteria: thus in paragraph 24 they state that '[i]n answering this question, it is necessary to assess the applicant's personal circumstances, the existence of past persecution, safety and security, respect for human rights, and possibility for economic survival'.[210] Even paragraph 28, bearing the subhead 'Respect for human rights', is sandwiched between sub-heads on

---

[204] Kelley (n 1) 33; Ni Ghráinne (2015) (n 1) 706.
[205] See Guide to Refugee Law in Australia, ch 3, 27, which notes, with reference to the Federal Court decision in *FCS17* (n 121) applying s 5J(1)(c) of the Migration Act as amended, that 'the introduction [in this case] of concepts such as a "likely inability to find food, shelter or work" would appear to move the relocation assessment under the refugee criterion back towards [the reasonableness] standard'.
[206] See Hathaway and Foster (2003) (n 1) 388. See also *Refugee Appeal No 76044* (n 36) paras 138, 161.
[207] See Chapter 3, section 2.1.2.
[208] Ní Ghráinne (2021) (n 1) 707–08.
[209] UNHCR Guidelines No 4 (n 1) para 28.
[210] ibid para 24.

'Safety and security' and 'Economic survival' as if they were three equally relevant but distinct sets of factors. Further, as just noted, the Guidelines appear to endorse reliance on criteria that go beyond the core concept of well-founded fear of being persecuted. Specifically, the Guidelines insist on describing the key test in terms of ability to live 'a relatively normal life' without requiring any reference to human rights except as a seeming minimum floor.[211] The Guidelines appear to maintain that 'reasonableness' requires *going beyond* respect for human rights.

Finally, there is an oddity about the Guidelines' presentation. They say they reflect a 'more structured approach' and insist that the IPA analysis is only 'part of the holistic assessment of refugee status',[212] but then fail to note at the end that, having analysed the IPA in the way outlined, the decision maker must then take stock of its implications for the holistic assessment of risk on return to the home state.

### 2.7.2 Michigan Guidelines or MGs

The volume and extent of the criticisms of the MGs on the Internal Protection Alternative should not obscure the evident fact that three steps out of its four-step framework of analysis articulate a number of widely accepted key principles and could reasonably be said to do so in much more conceptually consistent and targeted form than the UNHCR Guidelines No 4. Criticisms alleging that the MGs are susceptible to the same type of vagueness that plagues the term 'reasonable', seem largely to miss the mark; if Articles 2–33 are the applicable standards, they are singularly identifiable. But in the view of this author, many other points raised against the MGs remain cogent. The conceptual oddity of applying norms specially devised to protect refugees in *host states* to the predicament of individuals in their *home state* cannot be understated. It flouts observable reality for the MGs (at least as regards Step 4) to describe their being (at a time when only one country's case law had taken the same view) 'informed primarily by the jurisprudence of leading developed states of asylum'.[213] Proponents of the MGs have failed to explain how their application could not result in anomalous acceptance of a viable IPA in countries where, although the comparative criteria set out in Articles 2–33 were met, conditions fell below core minimum basic human rights protection. To assert that by invoking Articles 2–33 the MGs *interpret* the Refugee Convention's definition of protection[214] would make sense in relation to the (international) protection of refugees in the *host state*, but simply cannot, without a leap of faith, be said to interpret the notion of internal (in the sense of national) protection.

For the MGs' authors, it is of especial importance that Articles 2–33 are 'legal rights'[215] concerned with integration and assimilation, yet if that is so, then they have to be taken on their face. It is uncontroversial that almost all the rights set out in

---

[211] ibid paras 6, 7 II(a), 20, 23, 28, 30. See critique in *Refugee Appeal No 76044* (n 36) paras 163–76.
[212] UNHCR Guidelines No 4 (n 1) paras 1, 7, 8.
[213] MGs (n 1) para 6. The New Zealand case law continues to endorse the approach taken in the MGs, although in *BI (Afghanistan)* [2018] NZIPT 801220, para 51 the Tribunal noted the 'caveat' that 'in the site of IPA, the claimant cannot be expected to forego his or her basic human rights in order to avoid the risk of being persecuted or being exposed to other forms of serious harm'. See also *Refugee and Protection Officer v BA (Nigeria)* [2022] NZHC 706.
[214] Hathaway and Foster (2003) (n 1) 409.
[215] ibid 405.

Articles 2–33 are inherently defined in comparative terms: with slight variations, the standard set is either treatment at least as favourable to that accorded to nationals (e.g. Articles 6, 14, 15, 16, 17, 20) or the same treatment as is accorded to aliens generally (Articles 7, 13, 18). Further, by means of these comparative standards, their integrative character is hierarchically organised, depending on increasing levels of attachment to the host state.[216] Despite their integrative host-country specific character, proponents of the MGs insist that this aspect can be disregarded when applying it to the situation in the home state.[217] However, seeking to extract from such rights more general non-discrimination or integrative norms is surely contrary to their incremental structure.[218]

There is also a palpable discord between on the one hand the claim that the 'refugee rights' approach ensures the application of an 'identified and quantified' set of rights and on the other hand the insistence by Hathaway and Foster (when defending the MGs' approach against critics) that its approach is not to be literally applied but only treated as a source of inspiration.[219]

Re-reading the MGs and Hathaway and Foster's exposition of them, this author is struck again by what a counter-intuitive step this represented back in 1999. Here, in stark text, two of the foremost proponents of a human rights approach to the key concept of 'being persecuted'—and to the refugee definition generally—elected to disapply it for reasons which, if they are correct, stood to undermine this entire approach. They disapply a human rights approach in its normal understanding because of an asserted lack of 'consensus' about IHRL standards. Yet that did not preclude Hathaway from advancing a human rights approach in 1991 and nor has it stopped him and Foster[220] from holding fast to such an approach since. Even on Hathaway and Foster's own analysis of Articles 2–33, it is hard to follow why it is considered apposite to draw on (what they term) a 'core subset' of IHRL norms but not 'IHRL norms more generally'.[221] To represent them in the margins as a human rights-based approach or to imply that they incorporate a particular rather than a 'general' human rights approach, is to invert existing understandings of a human rights approach as one based on IHLR norms applied to the home state. It is highly ironic but perhaps to be expected that some critics of the MGs regard its adoption of a special approach to the IPA as confirmation that difficulties with a human rights approach to the refugee definition *in general* are 'inherent'.[222]

---

[216] As noted by Hathaway himself in James C Hathaway, *The Rights of Refugees Under International Law* (CUP 2005) 156–60; James C Hathaway, *The Rights of Refugees Under International Law* (2nd edn, CUP 2021) 176–81.
[217] Hathaway and Foster (2014) (n 1) 357. At footnote 436, Hathaway and Foster cite *Refugee Appeal No 76044* (n 36). At para 140, the latter states that 'it is not relevant in this context to engage with the levels of attachment at which these rights would otherwise operate or with the stipulated comparator groups'.
[218] Storey (1999) (n 1) 377.
[219] ibid 380.
[220] Foster's own book, Michelle Foster, *International Refugee Law and Socio-Economic Rights: Refuge from Deprivation* (CUP 2007) 75–86 contains a strong refutation of precisely the same type of objections against using of ICESCR norms as a benchmark voiced by Chairperson Haines in *Refugee Appeal No 71684/99* (n 81).
[221] Hathaway and Foster (2003) (n 1) 408.
[222] Storey (2003) (n 1) 377.

Another problem is that even on the MGs' approach, it includes as one step in its IPA inquiry an assessment that unmistakeably requires application of a human rights approach in its ordinary understanding. Step 2 headed 'Antidote' in Hathaway and Foster's 2003 report[223] and called a 'second criterion', 'Negation of original risk', in the second edition of TLRS2,[224] requires 'measuring the degree of risk in the IPA in the usual "well-founded fear" test, that is, whether there is a "reasonable possibility", "reasonable chance" or "real chance" of being persecuted in the IPA'.[225] There is no suggestion whatsoever that the protection inquiry in this context means anything other than assessing protection as an integral part of the 'being persecuted' inquiry, the latter being conceived in human rights terms. This means that at least one necessary component of the MGs' IPA inquiry must apply a human rights-based approach in the usual sense, not in the Articles 2–33 sense. What this means is that in actuality the MGs offers a hybrid of two different approaches to assessing IPA viability.

Also, very much open to question is the position taken in the MGs and confirmed by Hathaway and Foster in their 2003 report regarding the 'presumptive entitlement' or prima facie possession of refugee status.[226] It is one thing to state that the IPA analysis is predicated on acceptance that a person faces a well-founded fear of persecution in their home area against which the state cannot or will not protect them. That understanding builds properly on the reality that any IPA analysis presupposes that a person faces persecution in their home area. It is another thing entirely, however, to describe such a person as having established, even only prima facie, a well-founded fear of persecution under the refugee definition. The refugee definition ties protection to 'protection of the country'.[227] A home area is not a country; a geographical sub-unit of a country is not a country. Lack of protection in one part of a country is not equivalent to lack of protection in the country as a whole. On Hathaway and Foster's own understanding, 'country' has to be understood to denote a politically sovereign state capable of conferring nationality.[228] To take an extreme example, suppose an applicant has established they will face a well-founded fear of persecution in their home area from a lone individual, but their home area is a tiny town in a huge country with a loose federal structure. If in virtually every other part of this country the applicant could live safely and in full enjoyment of their rights of citizens, how could it sensibly be said that he or she has a 'presumptive entitlement' to refugee status? Contrary to a holistic approach to the refugee definition, the 'presumptive entitlement' approach depends on treating the 'well-founded fear' criterion as concerned with a sub-unit of the country, not the country as a whole.

Hathaway and Foster rely on the analysis of Sedley LJ in *Karanakaran* who averred that to regard a viable IPA as negating a well-founded fear of persecution would render meaningless the requirement in the availment clause that the applicant 'owing to such fear, is unwilling to avail himself' of home state protection. Sedley LJ wrote that 'if the

[223] Hathaway and Foster (2003) (n 1) 392.
[224] Hathaway and Foster (2014) (n 1) 343–44.
[225] Hathaway and Foster (2003) (n 1) 392.
[226] Supported by the New Zealand tribunal in *Refugee Appeal No 76044* (n 36).
[227] *Randhawa* (n 40); see also *Mazariegos v INS* [2001] 241 F.3d 1320, 1327, cited indeed by Hathaway and Foster (2014) (n 1) 332.
[228] Hathaway and Foster (2014) (n 1) 291.

simple availability of protection in some part of the home state destroyed the foundation of the fear or its causative effect, this provision would never be reached.'[229] Sedley LJ's interpretation is correct in noting that the availment clause makes clear that in assessing protection the existence of a well-founded fear must remain causative, but such causation must still be established in the context of the protection of the country, not the geographically abridged home area.

The same point applies if analysis is framed in terms of national protection or internal protection. The MGs contend that 'it is neither logical nor realistic to find that the fact that the state can protect the person in some other region of the country (region 'B') means that she no longer has a well-founded fear of being persecuted in region A'.[230] To reiterate, that is surely true, at least to the extent that, irrespective of relocation, the well-founded fear of persecution in the *home region* has been established and it is not extinguished by relocation. But acknowledging this point does not entail accepting a presumptive lack of *national* protection. Hathaway and Foster contend that 'to hold that the availability of alternative internal protection removes the well-founded fear of being persecuted involves a legal fiction which has concrete detrimental ramifications for refugee applicants'.[231] But on a proper understanding of the 'being persecuted' inquiry, it is not a question of protection 'removing' the well-founded fear of being persecuted, but of assessing that, by virtue of a viable IPA, the persecution in the home area will not constitute a well-founded fear of being persecuted through lack of *national* protection. Hathaway and Foster are right to argue, in favour of the MGs' approach, that it is linguistically more natural[232] to refer to the ill treatment in the home area as 'a well-founded fear of being persecuted' full-stop, but their own approach to the 'being persecuted inquiry' is based on a rejection of that linguistic point. Insistence on it wrongly converts the factual issue of the precise relationship between any regionalised 'well-founded fear' and national protection into one of law.

The notion of presumptive entitlement also invites the criticism that Hathaway and Foster, by thereby treating the IPA analysis as akin to an unwritten exclusion clause,[233] commit themselves to a breach of the principle that a public international law treaty cannot impose restrictive clauses beyond those set out expressly. The Refugee Convention does not identify IPA as an exclusion clause. In any event, Hathaway and Foster themselves are insistent that the IPA analysis is part of the (inclusionary) assessment of refugee status.

It is also difficult to square the logic of the approach the MGs take to the notion of protection within the IFA context with that which Hathaway and Foster take to protection *in the context of the 'being persecuted' inquiry*. The latter treats protection as an integral part of the concept of being persecuted. But under this inquiry, protection (as an integral part of the 'being persecuted' test) cannot just be the negation of serious

---

[229] Hathaway and Foster (2003) (n 1); see also Schultz (2018) (n 1).
[230] Hathaway and Foster (2003) (n 1) 367. This view is not confined to proponents of the MGs: see e.g. Sedley LJ in *Karanakaran v SSHD* [2000] 3 All ER 449; Battjes (n 86) 24; and Carlier (n 198) 145.
[231] Hathaway and Foster (2003) (n 1) 372.
[232] ibid.
[233] ibid 370. In Hathaway and Foster (2014) (n 1) 340–41, they prefer to describe it as 'akin to a cessation inquiry'.

harm; it must also possess positive qualities.[234] This leaves unclear how or in what way the 'affirmative', 'meaningful' protection they say is vital in the *IPA context* goes further.

There is much the same oddity in the structure of the MGs as that contained in the UNHCR Guidelines No 4. Despite offering an 'analytical framework for the IPA that is to be 'carried out in full conformity with the requirements of the Refugee Convention',[235] the MGs likewise confine the steps of its inquiry to assessing the IPA without addressing how the results of that inquiry are to be fed back in to the (decisive) issue of whether an applicant requires international protection against the risk of persecution in their own country.

### 2.7.3 Human rights approach

As already noted, the human rights approach remains to be fully developed in guidelines akin to those of UNHCR or the MGs; although Kelley's study offers a basic structure.[236]

This author was an early advocate of a human rights approach being taken to the IPA and in my own current assessment, the shortcomings just outlined in the other two main approaches strengthen the case for a human rights approach, albeit it would have to be one that ensures what both the other two main approaches promise but fail to deliver, namely fully tying back the IPA analysis to the refugee definition. Not all versions of a human rights approach as usually understood would necessarily do that. There is also presently an obstacle in the way of applying IHRL norms straightforwardly to the IPA analysis under the refugee definition posed by current Strasbourg case law.[237]

Turning to criticisms that have been levelled, and addressing first of all the rebuke that any 'general human rights approach' to the IPA analysis 'might be thought unwieldy and potentially too broad and over-inclusive',[238] it has already been observed in Chapter 3 that the human rights approach has become the dominant approach applied to the refugee definition as a whole and criticisms of it for being overbroad or over-inclusive were argued to be misplaced.[239]

Similarly, in relation to the criticism that the human rights approach to the IPA requires decision makers to draw on norms that lack universal state ratification and are not ascertainable or obtainable, that must (if correct) be as true for the application of IHRL norms to the 'being persecuted' inquiry as for their application to any protection inquiry. In any event, even Hathaway's original human rights approach as famously set out in *The Law of Refugee Status* (TLRS), which sought to rely on IHLR norms primarily in treaty form, did not base itself on the argument that there was consensus in the form of universal state ratification of these treaties or on any express acceptance by states parties that the norms they enshrine could be applied in the context of the refugee definition.[240] Furthermore, Hathaway and Foster have confirmed that to their

---

[234] See further Chapter 7, section 3.4.
[235] MGs (n 1) paras 1, 4–5.
[236] Kelley (n 1).
[237] See below pp. 532–533.
[238] Hathaway and Foster (2014) (n 1) 354, citing Hathaway and Foster (2003) (n 1) 406–08.
[239] See pp. 162–163.
[240] Hathaway (n 27) 106.

understanding the human rights framework *is* ascertainable by reference to rights set out in major IHL treaties especially those subject to a wide, 'super-majority' ratification.[241] As regards obtainability, the further comment by Chairman Haines in Refugee Appeal No 76044 that '[i]Insistence on these human rights instruments would also potentially involve measuring the proposed site of internal protection against a standard which is possibly unobtainable in many states party to the Refugee Convention',[242] introduces unnecessary confusion. The human rights approach has never based itself on a test of whether countries of origin are parties to either the Refugee Convention or human rights treaties: lack of ratification of one or both is at best only relevant evidence of human rights failings.[243] Its focus has always been on what the human rights performance of countries of origin is in fact.[244] An approach based on state party ratification would in any event make a mockery of assessment based on objective norms drawn from IHRL since the worse the ratification record of a home state the less applicants could establish persecution.[245] If, on the other hand, Chairman Haines meant to highlight the point that the human rights approach is too demanding, that must be true also for its application to the 'being persecuted' inquiry (which he supports).

The incongruity of Hathaway and Foster—and Haines—endorsing such a critique cannot be underplayed. These three find no difficulty in applying a human rights approach to the inquiry into 'well-founded fear of being persecuted' in the home area (and even as we have seen, to Step 2 of their 4-Step IPA framework of analysis); in doing so they have not been deterred by objections that such an approach is too broad or over-inclusive. They have not accepted that a human rights approach entails considering that breaches of *any* human right engage the refugee definition's threshold of serious harm, but have cogently explained that 'being persecuted' requires more than a violation of any human right and requires a breach (or breaches) that cross a threshold of impermissible serious harm or sufficient seriousness.[246] Concerns of the order voiced by Schultz, relying on Cantor's worry about a human rights approach displacing analysis to a 'complex, parallel field' and Edwards' worry about such an approach failing to capture all aspects of persecution were addressed and rejected in Chapter 3.[247]

There is a more general concern about Hathaway and Foster's commitment to applying a human rights approach to the assessment of 'being persecuted' in the home area but disapplying it to assessment in any IPA. If the refugee definition is concerned with national protection, why should a human rights approach to such protection suddenly cease to apply simply because the geographical focus shifts to another part of the same country? As noted earlier, the human rights approach is not applied with uniform intensity to all elements of the refugee definition,[248] but treating geographical

---

[241] Hathaway and Foster (2014) (n 1) 200–08.
[242] *Refugee Appeal No 71684/99* (n 81) para 57.
[243] See e.g. Foster (n 220) 54–67; Mathew (n 1) 205 notes that 'the Refugee Convention has never operated on the basis of reciprocity. The inquiry into refugee status is not about whether the state of origin is party to particular human right treaties.' Hathaway and Foster (2014) (n 1) 200 make a similar point.
[244] Storey (2003) (n 1) 377.
[245] See Foster (n 220) 54–67.
[246] See e.g. Hathaway and Foster (2014) (n 1) 196, 206–07.
[247] See pp. 158–159 and p. 163.
[248] See p. 141.

distribution of persecution within a country as determinative of whether or not to apply a human rights approach makes no sense. Its absurdity is well-illustrated by the hypothetical example of a case involving two applicants joined in the same appeal case in which IPA is an issue, one for whom region A is their home area and one for whom region A is a potential IPA. Despite it being the same area of the country, under Hathaway and Foster's analysis, their cases stand to be considered under two distinct sets of standards.

What then of the criticism made by Lord Bingham in the passage from *Januzi* quoted earlier (relating to a hypothetical 'poor and backward country') and also by academic commentators such as Piotrowicz which regards any attempt to apply human rights standards to the IPA (other than securement of non-derogable rights) as anomalous since it would mean according applicants a superior level of human rights protection over the rest of the population? In one respect, it is important to bear in mind that Lord Bingham's observations regarding this were directed against the MGs' approach based on the refugee rights set out in Articles 233,[249] rather than on the human rights approach as normally understood, but it still remains to be evaluated.

As regards the nature of the comparative exercise, it is first necessary to clarify that in *Januzi* the House of Lords discussed two variants of it in the same case: one being a comparison between the place of habitual residence and the putative IPA; and the other being that identified as 'standards prevailing generally in the country of nationality' and the putative IPA.[250] In the subsequent case of *AH (Sudan)*, Baroness Hale, rejected the approach of the Court of Appeal which was to rely on the first variant (a comparison between the place of habitual residence and the putative IPA).[251] She clarified that it was the second variant that was the proper standard of comparison, that is, 'standards prevailing generally in the country of nationality'.[252]

What is to be made of the criticism voiced in *Januzi* and *AH (Sudan)* concerning the relevance to this comparative exercise (as thus clarified) of human rights standards? If the comparative exercise contemplated by their lordships—comparing the putative IPA with 'standards prevailing generally in the country of nationality'—were simply to be taken as it stands, such an exercise would be highly problematic since it would entail accepting that even in a country where what is a 'relatively normal life ... in the context of the country concerned'[253] is (let us hypothesise) an abject Hobbesian 'war of all against all', an IPA would be viable if it was even slightly better than those standards, even though individuals there still faced intolerable conditions.

But in the same way as UNHCR's exposition of reasonableness as denoting a 'relatively normal life' has to be read in light of what its Guidelines state about 'respect for basic human rights',[254] the above passage from *Januzi* cannot be read simply as it stands. In both *Januzi* and *AH (Sudan)* the House made very clear their view that an

---

[249] As Lord Bingham noted in *AH (Sudan)* (n 72) para 5.
[250] See Lord Bingham in *Januzi* (n 43) paras 5, 13, and 20; see also Lord Brown, concurring, para 39.
[251] *AH, GV and NM v SSHD* [2007] EWCA Civ 297, paras 36–39.
[252] *AH (Sudan)* (n 72) para 27. However, this does not appear to have been entirely agreed by Lord Bingham at para 13; see also Lord Brown, *Januzi* (n 43) para 39.
[253] As noted by Eaton (n 1) 789.
[254] UNHCR Guidelines No 4 (n 1) para 28.

IPA could *never* be viable if conditions in the IPA fell below basic human rights norms such as the prohibition of ill-treatment.[255]

It is therefore somewhat ironic that concerns voiced in *Januzi* and *AH (Sudan)* about comparative living standards should be seen as counting against a human rights approach per se, because their lordships clearly endorsed an approach which treats protection against violation of non-derogable rights exemplified by Article 3 ECHR[256] as an objective standard below which no IPA can fall if it is to be viable. This proviso makes plain that an IPA inquiry cannot solely be about whether an applicant would be worse off or better off than others living in the IPA but must ensure the protection of at least non-derogable rights is available.[257] At best, therefore, the critique voiced in *Januzi* and *AH (Sudan)* works only against an approach that considers violations of derogable human rights to be relevant in a broader sense, even if they do not, on their own or cumulatively, amount to sufficiently severe violations/ serious harm.

At this point, however, the *Januzi/AH (Sudan)* approach runs into self-contradiction because on their lordship's own analysis an IPA can be unreasonable or unduly harsh even if does not constitute such sufficiently severe violations. In Baroness Hale's words, 'although the test of reasonableness is a stringent one—whether it would be 'unduly harsh' to expect the claimant to return—it is not to be equated with a real risk that the claimant would be subjected to inhuman or degrading treatment or punishment so serious as to meet the high threshold set by article 3 of the European Convention on Human Rights.'[258]

Upon closer analysis it can be seen that the self-contradictory nature of their lordships' analysis in *Januzi/AH(Sudan)* stems from a fundamental misunderstanding about the different situation of an applicant with a putative IPA as compared with other individuals whose home is in that area. It entirely disregards the significance of the fact that in any IPA case an applicant has established a well-founded fear of being persecuted in their home area, that is, somewhere else. To describe this as an 'accident of persecution' entirely overlooks that such an applicant's life has been severely disrupted. When an applicant faces internal relocation, they are not in the same position as other individuals living in the alternative area. It may be, after an individual assessment of their case, that the situation they face in the alternative area may be found not to be unreasonable or unduly harsh or (the preferred approach in this study) insufficiently violative of their human rights, but at a conceptual level their situation cannot

---

[255] See e.g. the last sentence of *Januzi* (n 43) para 19. A purely comparative or relativistic approach would not only be conceptually flawed but also in any event at odds with earlier House of Lords authority in *Horvath* (n 84), which endorsed a human rights approach to 'being persecuted'. For further discussion of the comparative approach, see *AS (Afghanistan) v SSHD* [2019] EWCA Civ 873.

[256] Although Baroness Hale in *AH (Sudan)* (n 72) focuses on Article 3 ECHR, she clearly had in mind Lord Hope's reference in *Januzi* (n 43) to 'the most basic of human rights that are universally recognised— the right to life, and the right not to be subjected to cruel or inhuman treatment' (at para 54); and in broad terms both would have been aware that Lord Hope in *Horvath* (n 84) had approved Hathaway's understanding that 'persecution is most appropriately defined as the sustained or systemic failure of state protection in relation to one of the core entitlements which has been recognised by the international community'. Hence their position is not necessarily limited to non-derogable rights but does require (as does Hathaway) any violation of basic human rights to cross a threshold of sufficient severity.

[257] Schultz (2018) (n 1) 105.

[258] *AH (Sudan)* (n 72) para 20 (per Baroness Hale).

be straightforwardly compared with others living in the alternative area who do not face a well-founded fear of being persecuted anywhere.

Second, whilst the *Januzi/AH (Sudan)* analysis correctly identifies that assessment of an applicant's situation *in an IPA* must apply a threshold *lower than serious harm* or sufficiently severe violations of human rights,[259] it incorrectly concludes that the assessment of whether such an applicant lacks *national protection* as a result has also to entail a lower threshold.

However, if understood as focussing on *conditions in the IPA*, the 'reasonableness' test is not one that goes beyond the confines of the refugee definition. It would only go beyond the confines of the refugee definition if the assessment of reasonableness was also applied to the overall issue of *national protection*. As long as the reasonableness test is confined to conditions in the IPA, it can properly be 'tied back' to the refugee definition. The combination of well-founded fear of being persecuted in one's home area and the lack of reasonableness of conditions in the putative IPA will often justify a conclusion that there is overall a lack of national protection. But that will not always be so.

It is necessary next to turn to the criticism that application of a human rights approach to IPA analysis would involve too limited a notion of protection and would unduly narrow the IPA inquiry down to a purely negative assessment based on absence of persecution. Thus, Mathew, it will be recalled, contends that 'to frame the inquiry as being whether any person has their rights respected in the IPA undermines the notion of protection, almost emptying it of content. It deprives protection of any positive meaning other than absence of persecution, suggesting that a human rights limbo for victims of persecution is acceptable'.[260] This criticism has echoes of the insistence made by proponents of the MGs that protection in the IPA context must be 'affirmative protection'.[261]

It is hard to understand how, of all approaches, a human rights approach would result in a 'human rights limbo', but to the extent that this criticism is aimed at application to assessment of an applicant's situation *in the IPA* of a standard or threshold of serious harm, it must be valid, for the reasons just given—the threshold applied in such a context must be lower. However, this criticism also invites misunderstanding of the key concepts at work in any assessment of refugee status concerned with an IPA scenario. Whatever qualities protection must possess in the IPA context does not mean that the essential requirement of the refugee definition, to show serious harm + lack of state protection, is displaced or alters its meaning. Mathew's criticism embodies two misunderstandings. First, it overlooks that even in the context of the inquiry into whether or not an IPA is free of persecution, that inquiry must encompass whether there is protection that embodies positive as well as negative qualities—in particular that it is effective and that the authorities are able and willing to protect against the serious harm. Second, it deflects attention away from the fact that any wider notion of protection involved is confined to the adjustments that must be made to accord proper recognition of the fact of displacement from a place of persecution and consequent

---

[259] *AH (Sudan)* (n 72) para 22 (Baroness Hale), paras 41, 43 (Lord Brown).
[260] Mathew (n 1) 201.
[261] MGs (n 1) paras 20–22; Hathaway and Foster (2014) (n 1) 350–61.

steps that must be taken to access and live in any IPA without conditions there being such as to give rise to a real risk that they would compel the applicant to return to their home area. Put another way, it is justified to say that analysis of a putative IPA requires recourse to a meaning of protection 'additional to' that contained in the refugee definition—and 'affirmative' protection remains as good a label as any to describe it— but *only* so long as that is understood solely to denote adjustments that are required by the particular exigencies of an internal protection alternative. These adjustments do not mean that protection against serious harm in the applicant's *country* must be understood as meaning protection in a wider sense.

*2.7.3.1 Reasons for lowering the threshold of serious harm in the putative IPA*
At this point, it is necessary to spell out in more specific terms the basis for making certain adjustments to the relevant threshold of harm in the IPA context. There are three main reasons why they are called for. We are still primarily concerned with evaluation of the human rights approach, but the points that will be made here would appear equally valid for ongoing efforts to strengthen or modify the other main approaches, the UNHCR Guidelines and the MGs on IPA in particular.

*2.7.3.2 Established risk in the home area*
First, to equate the threshold for protection in the IPA with the threshold of protection in the home area would ignore the fact that an applicant only stands for consideration under an IPA inquiry if a real risk of ill treatment in their home area has already been established. Applicant A, for whom such a risk has been established, cannot be equated with Applicant B, for whom such risk in their home area has not been established (although the MGs' approach overeggs this point by portraying it as a 'presumptive' or 'prima facie' entitlement to refugee status, this underlying point regarding risk in the home area remains valid). One corollary of home area persecution is that the applicant's right to internal freedom of movement in his or her country has already been partially impaired.[262]

*2.7.3.3 The need to take steps to access an IPA*
Second, in order for an IPA to be viable it must be accessible which entails that an applicant can safely and legally travel there, gain admittance, and settle there. Again, these are steps an applicant only has to take because of displacement from their home area. In some cases, none of the steps may be too difficult, but in others they will and the need to take them into account must be a structural feature of any IPA analysis.

*2.7.3.4 Avoidance of indirect refoulement*
Third, unless conditions in the IPA are tolerable for an applicant, he or she would be placed at real risk of being compelled to return to their home area—back into

---

[262] This bears out the value of Schultz's observations regarding the context of any IPA inquiry, that it always entails that an applicant will already face partial denial of his human rights relating to freedom of movement (caused by being displaced from his or her home area). However, her reference to the 'right to return' is hard to follow since that right arises vis a vis a country, not a sub-region. See Schultz (2018) (n 1).

the lion's mouth (this can loosely be called the principle of indirect or 'constructive' refoulement).

The notion of indirect refoulement clearly goes wider than mere absence of a real risk of persecution (or in MGs' terms, being an 'antidote to' persecution).[263] Whereas (as explained in Chapter 6) an individual cannot be said to have a well-founded fear of persecution unless they face serious harm inflicted by human actors,[264] the principle of indirect refoulement does not necessarily require human agency. If, for example, what an applicant would face in the IPA is not persecution, but intolerable conditions caused by 'natural' disasters (e.g. fire, flood, earthquakes) such conditions, even though not persecutory might well be dire enough to compel him or her to return to their home area, which by definition is a site of persecution. Applying the notion of indirect refoulement, they would still qualify as a refugee because considering their position in their *home state as a whole*, conditions in the putative IPA area would compel them to return to face the well-founded fear of persecution in their home area.[265] This analysis also affords a (limited) basis for treating environmental and/or climate change factors as relevant considerations within the compass of the refugee definition. However, even thus formulated, this notion entails a high standard clearly distinguishable from criteria based on compassionate or humanitarian considerations.

Together these three sets of considerations explain why the IPA operates as an ameliorative concept compensating for the home area persecution and the geographical displacement. As such, assessing its viability does require more than establishing that there will there be an absence of persecution in that area (even when that is understood as involving serious harm plus lack of state protection in both the negative and positive sense).

However, to repeat, applying this reduced threshold to assessment of conditions in the *IPA* does *not* mean, when assessing whether overall there is *national protection* such as to qualify a person as a refugee, that the standard is more extensive than serious harm or sufficient severity of the violations of human rights.

It remains a difficulty for the human rights approach to map precisely how a threshold of human rights violations in the IPA less than that of sufficient severity is to be identified and applied in practice. Similar difficulties afflict the UNHCR Guidelines No 4 and its concept of 'reasonableness'. They do not afflict the MGs' concept of affirmative protection understood in terms of violations of Articles 2–33 as much (albeit since they cannot be applied literally, these are not hard edged either), but as explained earlier, such a standard is untenable in any event. The notion of indirect refoulement does provide some assistance here in shaping the inquiry, which then becomes one focussing on whether shortcoming in human rights protection would compel an applicant to return to their home area.[266]

---

[263] MGs (n 1) para 15.
[264] See p. 361 and p. 363.
[265] Persecution might nevertheless be involved even in climate change scenarios, if, e.g. the fires or floods or droughts etc. are predominantly caused by human agency: see Chapter 6, section 2.2.5. See also Anker (n 134) §2.13, 92–93. The MGs (n 1) para 19 and Hathaway and Foster (2014) (n 1) 348 state a similar position regarding the principle of indirect non-refoulement to that set out here.
[266] A similar (but not identical) position is taken by Brid Ní Ghráinne (2015) (n 1) 48, who observes that '[h]uman rights considerations ... form part of the IPA analysis only to the extent that respect for such

Also of assistance is the very nature of the human rights standards that are to be applied. The example given by Kelley is instructive. With reference to relevant provisions of the ICCPR and Convention of the Rights of the Child (CRC), she argues that the international recognition of the protection to be accorded the family:

> [ … ] would militate against the reasonableness of requiring a refugee claimant, particularly a spouse or a dependant child from resettling in a proposed area without their spouse or parent respectively. It may also support a finding against the relocation of any dependant (elderly, disabled) to an area where they would not have other family members and where the latter are central in the provision of physical care, economic support and protection from exploitation.[267]

Even if such recognition would not in itself negate a viable IPA, it is likely that it would if considered in terms of the risk of indirect refoulement. Seen in this light, the challenges in applying a human rights assessment to the putative IPA should be no more and no less than those that face applying such an assessment to the refugee definition generally.

To recapitulate, in order to be workable any human rights approach to the IPA inquiry would need to adhere closely to the criteria that have already been clarified through state practice in the wide sense (and as are summarised at the end of this chapter under 'basic propositions'). A human rights approach that diverged from these criteria (e.g. one that considered that an IPA could be unviable because of breaches of human rights that had a minor impact on a person's way of life and well-being and that would not compel him or her to return to their home area) would obviously not fit this description.

2.7.4 1998 UN Guiding Principles on Internal Displacement
Whilst the Guiding Principles have an important role in influencing and 'reshaping' some of the norms of IHRL, their inutility as a benchmark for determining refugee status is evident. It should not matter that they are a composite, avowedly drawn not just from IHRL but from international humanitarian law. But some of the principles are clearly more extensive than could be justified in interpreting the refugee definition.[268] Ní Ghráinne gives the examples of Principle 16 (denial of the right to visit the grave sites of deceased relatives), Principle 21 (arbitrary confiscation of property), and Principle 29 (restitution for property loss). She concludes that '[r]refugee status granted on the basis of risk inconsistent with the Guiding Principles could go

---

rights is a necessary ingredient of protection from the persecution feared, or that lack of such rights may result in indirect refoulement'.

[267] Kelley (n 1) 41.
[268] Phuong (n 194) 61. Walter Kälin, 'Internal Displacement' in Costello et al 2021 (n 1) 854 notes that '[b]esides the fact that IDPs remain within their own country, this notion differs conceptually from the refugee definition in article 1A(2) of the Refugee Convention in several important respects. It only requires that flight is predominantly forced, leaving no or little room for choice. In particular, it is not necessary that it is motivated by a well-founded fear of persecution based on specific reasons. Rather, the list of circumstances that may trigger displacement is non-exhaustive.'

far beyond what was intended by the drafters of the Convention, as the risk of such harms would not create an entitlement to refugee status'.[269] Whilst the fact that these Guidelines are non-binding rules[270] is not an insuperable problem,[271] it does reduce their viability as a benchmark when compared with IHLR benchmarks derived from international treaty obligations.

Notwithstanding that these Principles are increasingly seen as an important source of soft law, the idea of using them as a benchmark for IPA in refugee law has gained little or no traction. Schultz observes that '[t]he Principles have not been accepted in any jurisdiction as the basis for the IPA test'.[272]

### 2.7.5 IPA as an implied limit on Article 1A(2)

Schultz's proposed notion of IPA as an 'implied limit' on Article 1A(2) reading seeks to build on the understanding voiced by Robinson in his 1953 Commentary that the refugee criteria would 'rule out happenings of a local character ... which are being combatted by the authorities', because in such cases there would be no reason for a person to be unwilling to accept the home country's protection.[273] It also comports well with the view that the IPA analysis relates primarily to the 'well-founded fear' element of the refugee definition, since it hinges the issue of whether there is a viable IPA on whether it reduces the level of risk below the usual threshold of serious possibility and in that way entitles the conclusion that the fear has failed to be well-founded with respect to the country as a whole.[274] Its requirement of 'reasonableness' is described as dependent on understanding fear as having both subjective as well as objective elements and fastens therefore on the issue of unwillingness. However, Schultz herself notes several drawbacks to this reading. It introduces an additional condition for refugee status (because on its reading the availment clause has to be read as adding a requirement not there, namely—in her own words—'unable or, owing to the fear of persecution, *reasonably* unwilling to avail him or herself of home state protection/ return to the country of origin').[275] It opens the door for an overly broad application of the IPA concept. It potentially burdens the applicant with the duty of disproving an IPA. Formulating the IPA as an implied limit 'leaves the boundaries of the limits unclear'.[276] The reasonableness ingredient of the '*reasonable* unwillingness' criterion is one that she herself considers, in her critique of the UNHCR Guidelines No 4, to be unstructured.[277] It can be added that there is no support in case law, UNHCR sources, or the wider literature for such an approach and it is unclear whether there is any country that applies it. In any event, in her article with Einarsen, Schultz confirms that

---

[269] Ní Ghráinne (2015) (n 1) 37.
[270] But within the African Union, see African Union Convention for the Protection and Assistance of Internally Displaced Persons in Africa (Kampala Convention) (adopted 23 October 2009, which entered into force 6 December 2012).
[271] Because soft-law sources can provide a treaty aid to interpretation: see p. 73.
[272] Schultz (2018) (n 1) 108.
[273] Robinson (n 44) 46.
[274] Schultz (2018) (n 1) 138–39.
[275] ibid. Schultz and Einarsen (n 1) 286 conclude that 'the IPA limit to refugee status does not seem necessary to uphold the purpose of the Refugee Convention as required by the doctrine of implied limits'.
[276] Schultz (2018) (n 1) 383.
[277] ibid 139.

this proposed limit 'does not seem necessary to uphold the purpose of the Refugee Convention as required by the doctrine of implied limits'.[278]

### 2.7.6 IPA as an implied limit on the right to refugee status

What of Schultz's argument in favour of an implied limit on the right to *refugee status* which she considers to arise in cases in which an applicant's unwillingness to return lacks a reasonable relationship to his or her well-founded fear?[279] The fact that it is only applied in a very small number of countries is one factor telling against it. But on a conceptual level, Schultz herself (again) appears to articulate well the main objection to such an approach, namely that it amounts to an implied exclusion clause despite the treaty exhaustively identifying those in Articles 1D, 1E, and 1F. 'Because these exceptions explicitly delimit the group of persons to whom the Convention regime applies', she writes, 'it is arguable that no further limits should be permitted without an amendment to the treaty itself.'[280] It is also, she writes, 'unclear whether general concerns related to immigration control legally justify a limitation on the rights established or inferred from the text of the Refugee Convention'.[281] Her own suggested alternative, framing the legitimate state aim as 'the preservation (or efficient use) of a state's finite resource base for protection', might arguably be said to embody a Convention purpose and to protect the integrity of the refugee protection regime and also to be 'the least intrusive means' for achieving the legitimate interests in preserving scarce resources. But this approach completely upends refugee status determination. It is based on an untenable premise (that there is no justification for treating the IPA as an inherent part of the refugee definition) and even if correct, offers a solution that is irrelevant to the refugee definition and at best provides an alternative way of accommodating surrogacy-driven concerns about the need for international protection to benefit only those in need.

## 2.8 Conclusions on Main Approaches

Taking stock of the main approaches, it is obviously an unhappy state of affairs that there should still be such divergence over a subject area that has an everyday impact on Refugee Status Determination (RSD). Some of the debates, which began in earnest in the 1990s, seem to continue unabated. In the face of this state of affairs, this author has two main reactions.

The first is simply to state this author's own view that of the three main approaches, the human rights approach is the only one that is consistent with the broader direction of refugee law. However, (in agreement with Kelley) it is considered that such an approach can utilise much of the guidance given in the UNHCR Guidelines No 4. The MGs, by contrast, are unlikely to ever gain significant support in judicial or UNHCR

---

[278] Schultz (2019) (n 1) 286.
[279] See above section 2.6.
[280] Schultz (2018) (n 1) 152.
[281] ibid 159.

sources and its proponents have not been able to overcome the major criticisms directed at its final requirement or step.

One cannot point, in the same way as is possible with the UNHCR Guidelines No 4 and the MGs, to a fully developed statement of the human rights approach, but valuable pointers to such an approach have already been developed in the literature (particularly by Kelley). The approach taken in the UNHCR Guidelines No 4 cannot as things stand overcome the criticisms levelled at the subjective nature of its 'reasonableness' test, but given that already in these Guidelines there is partial recourse to human rights norms (as an apparent minimum floor) and that the UNHCR has moved since 2003 towards a more explicit human rights approach to the refugee definition generally,[282] there are good reasons to consider that either updated UNHCR Guidelines more directly based on a human rights approach, or production by others of specific human rights IPA guidelines would overcome most if not all of the current objections to the approach in the Guidelines. In particular, along the lines Kelley suggests, so long as the notion of 'reasonableness' is recast in purely human rights terms and properly tied back to the refugee definition, such a synthesis should be possible (the fact, as noted in section 3 of this chapter that IHRL case law utilises a 'reasonableness' concept would also point further in that direction). This author fully recognises, however, that the MGs' authors are unlikely to abandon their now-entrenched positions.

The second reaction is that despair at divergent approaches must not blind us to the quite remarkable extent to which the debates, in the course of exchanging musket fire, have crystallised agreement around a number of basic propositions relating to the contents of the IPA. Although each approach (certainly the MGs) tends to present such propositions as only valid within their own theoretical framework, that is visibly not so. For example, despite heavy criticism of the UNHCR approach, Hathaway and Foster in TLRS2 acknowledge that all but one of the criteria or steps they advocate broadly correspond to those set out in the UNHCR Guidelines No 4.[283] This observation regarding commonalities will be built on in section 4 of this chapter.

2.8.1 Home area

Mention should be made next of a discrete issue intermingled in all variety of approaches to the IPA, namely the concept of place of origin/region of origin or home area/region.

It is at first sight curious, given how central it is to the IPA concept, that notions such as 'place of origin' or 'home area' or 'home region' have not been closely analysed in the IPA literature. It is after all the obverse of the 'alternative' part of the country forming the putative IPA. There is no agreed terminology to describe the home area—e.g. the UNHCR Guidelines No 4 refer to 'original area', 'original area of persecution', or 'part of the country'.[284] The MGs refer variously to 'part of the country', 'locality', 'place',

---

[282] See Chapter 3, section 2.1.2.
[283] Hathaway and Foster (2014) (n 1) 342 (at footnote 333). Indeed, they suggest that the MGs likely inspired the contents of the 'relevance analysis' set out in UNHCR Guidelines No 4 (n 1). They state that the latter analysis 'involves issues such as accessibility, whether the agent of persecution would likely reach the applicant in the alternative region, and whether the applicant would be exposed to any new risks of persecution there'.
[284] UNHCR Guidelines No 4 (n 1) paras 8, 11, 20, 21.

'region'.[285] Article 8 of the QD (recast) uses the expression 'part of the country'.[286] The terms used in case law are just as various.[287] What seems to lie behind the preference for such general terms and their diversity is a healthy reluctance to erect any particular test or tests, or to tie the concept to particular requirements, e.g. 'habitual residence'. Decision makers may confront situations which might warrant describing a part or area of the country as a person's home area other than the fact of residence over a significant period of time, e.g. ties of kinship, marriage, tribe, clan, even religion. Indeed, '[i]n some cultures', as Schultz has noted, ' "home" may not be a fixed geographic space, but shift over time, or have multiple *loci*'.[288] It does not seem necessary, either, that an applicant have only one home area. This is not to say that it is not of key importance for decision makers to identify a home area, even if not always with precision (see below section 4.2.4). Doing so is central to assessing whether there is a well-founded fear of being persecuted anywhere in the applicant's country of origin. But it is to say that identification should be left as a fact-sensitive exercise unencumbered by any fixed criteria.

2.8.2 Causal nexus

Earlier analysis of the main approaches to the IPA did not encompass their treatment of the issue of the role within the IPA inquiry of the requirement to show a Convention reason and a causal nexus between the two. That is principally because their analysis of this issue has been scant; indeed, some treatments of the IPA do not address it at all. Whilst this study has yet to tackle the Convention reasons and the nexus clause (that is the subject of Chapter 10), it is appropriate to consider this issue insofar as it affects the IPA inquiry.

*2.8.2.1 The main approaches*

In the UNHCR Guidelines No 4, the only reference to the role of Convention reasons for persecution is in a paragraph examining a 'new risk of serious harm' in an IPA:

> If the claimant would be exposed to a new risk of serious harm, including a serious risk to life, safety, liberty or health, or one of serious *discrimination*, an internal flight or relocation alternative does not arise, irrespective of whether or not there is a link to one of the Convention grounds.[289]

All but one of the references in the MGs to Convention reasons are confined to the context of identifying the need, as a prerequisite for any IPA analysis, for the applicant to have established a well-founded fear of persecution for a Convention reason in the place of origin.[290] However, in setting out the first of two ways in which an IPA will be

---

[285] MGs (n 1) paras 3, 12, 14, 18.
[286] QD (recast) (n 17).
[287] This study mainly uses the term 'home area' which is sometimes used in the UK case law: see e.g. *Jasim v SSHD* [2006] EWCA Civ 342, para 16; *AMM and others (conflict; humanitarian crisis; returnees; FGM) Somalia CG* [2011] UKUT 445 (IAC), para 225.
[288] Schultz (2018) (n 1) 254.
[289] UNHCR Guidelines No 4 (n 1) para 20.
[290] MGs (n 1) paras 12, 14, 15.

rendered unviable if there exists additional risk of, or equivalent to, persecution, the MGs state that:

> First, the asylum-seeker may have an independent claim in relation to the proposed site of internal protection. If the harm feared is of sufficient gravity to fall within the ambit of persecution, the requirement to show a nexus to a Convention reason is arguably satisfied as well. This is so since but for the fear of persecution in one part of the country of origin for a Convention reason, the asylum-seeker would not now be exposed to the risk in the proposed site of internal protection.[291]

In their 2003 report, Hathaway and Foster elaborate on the position if the IPA is 'persecution-free' but conditions in it would compel the applicant to return to their place of origin to face the original persecutors. They give the example of an applicant who has already been found to face a well-founded fear of being persecuted for a Convention reason in their original place but for whom the harm faced in the proposed IPA takes the form of generalized threats to life or physical security associated with war, or to generalized extreme economic deprivation on a variety of fronts (for example, lack of food, shelter, or basic health care) that have no Convention nexus. They highlight that:

> The only reason—albeit an indirect reason—that she or he now faces the prospect of a threat to life or physical security in the proposed IPA is therefore the flight from the place of origin on Convention grounds which has led him or her (via the asylum State) now to be confronted with a harm within the scope of persecution. The risk now faced is therefore a risk faced 'for reasons of' the Convention ground which initiated the original involuntary movement from the home region. This is because the nexus criterion in the refugee definition requires only a causal relationship between a protected factor (race, religion, nationality, political opinion, membership of a particular social group) and the persecutory risk. If the protected ground is a contributing factor to the risk of being persecuted, then Convention status is appropriately recognized.[292]

---

[291] ibid para 18.
[292] Hathaway and Foster (2003) (n 1) 401–02. At 402, footnote 146, they cite in support the German Federal Administrative Court Decision *BverwG C 45.92* [1993] (unofficial translation); they also cite James C Hathaway, 'The Michigan Guidelines on Nexus to a Convention Ground' (2002) 23(2) Michigan Journal of International Law 207; and Storey (n 1) 527. Earlier at 400 (footnote 141), Hathaway and Foster (2003) (n 1) cite the Full Court of the Federal Court of Australia decision in *Perampalam v MIMA* [1999] 84 FCR 274: '[i]t cannot be reasonable to expect a refugee to avoid persecution by moving into an area of grave danger, whether that danger arises from a natural disaster (for example, a volcanic eruption), a civil war or some other cause. A well-founded fear of persecution for a Convention reason having been shown, a refugee does not also have to show a Convention reason behind every difficulty or danger which makes some suggestion of relocation unreasonable.' A similar view is taken by Marx (n 1) 197: '[w]hile the level of risk in one or more IFAs must be shown to be uniformly intense, the continuing directness of the cause of a Convention risk need not be. All that matters is that there continues to exist a serious possibility that conditions in the IFA would either re-expose the claimants to direct risk, cause them to accept, or be forced to accept, undue hardship, or cause them to suffer infringement of core fundamental human rights.'

From this analysis (with which this author agrees) it can be deduced that unless an applicant can establish a well-founded fear of persecution for a Convention reason in their home area or region, the need for an IPA inquiry does not arise. They will have failed to establish a key requirement of being a refugee. At least two caveats are in order. First, it must be borne in mind that if one applies (as do Hathaway and Foster along with many others) a 'bifurcated' approach to the causal nexus,[293] then in non-state actor cases establishing a Convention reason in the home region is easier than under the approach that requires a direct link with the reason(s) of the persecutor.[294] Second, in line with our earlier analysis of 'home area',[295] it may be important to avoid any rigid understanding of what constitutes an applicant's home region or original area. For example, if they originally lived in a home area where they faced persecution at the hands of a criminal gang but then moved and resettled in an area where, after a while, they became targeted for persecution for a Convention reason from new actors of persecution, it is arguable that the area of resettlement has become their home area.

Proponents of a human rights approach appear to concur with the position taken regarding Convention grounds in the UNHCR Guidelines No 4 and in the MGs.[296]

*2.8.2.2 Evaluation*

The view which is shared by the three most common approaches—viz. that the causal nexus issue only arises in relation to the home area or region—would seem to be incontrovertibly correct, for several reasons.

First, when analysing an applicant's situation in his or her home area, the terms of the refugee definition require not just that they establish a well-founded fear of persecution but well-founded fear of persecution for a Convention reason. It is only if an applicant has established risk in the home area in this sense that the RSD authority is entitled to raise the possibility of an IPA. If an applicant, whilst able to establish a well-founded fear of being persecuted in their home area, cannot establish a Convention reason connected to persecution in that area, then they have not met this requirement and there is no basis for proceeding with an IPA inquiry.

Second, to require a person to establish in addition that the risk(s) faced in any IPA were for a Convention reason would clearly be too stringent. There may, of course, be evidence of the existence of such a Convention reason in the IPA as well—either by virtue of the risk there being a continuation of the same risk (e.g. from the original persecutors) or a new source. But even if the risk is an entirely new one, it will remain the case that the fear of persecution applicants face is sufficiently causally linked to their predicament in the home area—so long as its effect would be to compel that person to return to their home area. That is so irrespective of whether or not the conditions in the IPA identify persecutors (or ineffective protectors) who have a Convention reason.

A third reason is that approaching matters in this way reflects almost universal practice. It is consistent, for example, with the position taken by the UNHCR Guidelines

---

[293] Hathaway and Foster (2014) (n 1).
[294] See Chapter 10, section 4.3.
[295] See above p. 523.
[296] See e.g. Kelley (n 1) 44, 23; Storey (2003) (n 1) 371.

No 4,[297] and also by Article 8 QD (recast)[298] as well as by academic commentators.[299] It comports as well with this study's own analysis of the relevance of the notion of indirect refoulement.[300]

The upshot of the above analysis is that so far as concerns the causal nexus, it does not need to form part of the IPA inquiry itself, although the existence, for example, of a new source of persecution based on racism or other Convention reason, may well add evidential weight to the intolerability of the conditions in the IPA.

It must be re-emphasised, however, that attaching causal nexus to the original place of persecution, is not tantamount to accepting that establishing risk of persecution in that place creates a 'presumptive entitlement' to refugee status, since the refugee definition requires it to be shown that return to the *country of origin* (not just to their home area) will give rise to a well-founded fear of being persecuted.

## 3 The IPA in International Human Rights Law (IHRL)

This book is not concerned with the IPA in IHRL as such, but it is still necessary to analyse its essential elements because applying IHRL norms is integral to the human rights approach to the refugee definition. In the case of the IPA, this poses certain difficulties, as this concept, as developed within IHLR cases dealing with risk on return, has plainly borrowed to some extent from existing international refugee law (IRL) case law on the same subject. Further, with the exception of the ECtHR,[301] the regional human rights courts and the relevant treaty-monitoring bodies have still to flesh out much content to the IPA concept used in risk on return cases.[302] Nevertheless, the

---

[297] UNHCR Guidelines No 4 (n 1) para 20: 'If the claimant would be exposed to a new risk of serious harm, including a serious risk to life, safety, liberty or health, or one of serious discrimination, an internal flight or relocation alternative does not arise, *irrespective of whether or not there is a link to one of the Convention grounds*' (emphasis added).

[298] As noted by Lehmann (n 1) 174, 'Article 8 requires the absence of a 'well-founded fear of being persecuted', omitting the requirement of a nexus to a Convention ground'.

[299] Eaton (n 1) 770, notes a 'consensus ... that the original persecution that led the asylum applicant to flee cannot continue and that they should not face life threatening harm in the area of relocation, even if that threat is not related to one of the enumerated grounds in article 1(A)(2) of the Refugee Convention (in other words, persecution without a nexus to a convention ground)'.

[300] See below section 4.1.5.

[301] First use by the Strasbourg organs can be dated at least back to 1986 in the European Commission of Human Rights case law: see cases cited by Lehmann (n 1) 151 (at footnote 28).

[302] In its Concluding Observations on Norway (cited in Kees Wouters, *International Legal Standards for the Protection from Refoulement* (Intersentia 2009)) 399), the UN Human Rights Committee (HRC) said, in relation to a report on Norway, that '[t]he State Party should apply the so-called internal relocation alternative only in cases where such alternative provides full protection for the human rights of the individual'. See HRC, Concluding observations of the HRC: Norway (25 April 2006) UN Doc CCPR/C/NOR/CO/5, para 11. Other important cases in which the HRC has addressed the internal flight alternative include *Case of BL v Australia* (16 October 2014) Communication No 2053/2011, UN Doc CCPR/C/112/D/2053/2011, para 7.4; and *Case of SYL v Australia* (11 September 2013) Communication No 1897/2009, UN Doc CCPR/C/108/D/1897/2009, paras 8.1–8.4. In *Case of Alan v Switzerland* (8 May 1996) Communication No 21/1995, UN Doc CAT/C/16/D/21/1995, the Committee Against Torture (CtteAT) addressed the claim of a rejected Kurdish asylum seeker from Turkey. The Committee, having concluded that the agent of persecution was the Turkish State itself, found that there was no safe area for the applicant inside Turkey. In *Case of Orhan Ayas v Sweden* (12 November 1997) Communication No 97/1997, UN Doc CAT/C/21 D/097/1997, the CtteAT considered whether there was a place of refuge within the country 'for an applicant fearing torture if returned' (cited in Lehmann (n 1) 151). Other CtteAT cases addressing IPA, but containing no analysis of

ECtHR's treatment of the IPA concept (which it continues to call the 'internal flight alternative') has not simply been derivative from IRL. Indeed, its judgment in *Salah Sheekh*,[303] which is widely seen as the *locus classicus* of the IHLR notion of IPA, was instrumental in persuading the EU legislator to amend Article 8 of the QD (recast) when it was recast in 2011.[304] At all events, it remains essential to inquire in the first instance if the criteria developed within the IHRL IPA analysis are at least broadly consistent with those applied to the IPA concept within IRL. Secondly, it is necessary to ask whether there can be any straightforward application of the IHRL IPA criteria to the refugee definition context.

Analysing this subject is also necessary for another reason. It helps crystallise the central conundrum for any human rights approach within IRL to the IPA concept. This conundrum is as follows. If (as has been argued earlier) the existence of a viable IPA within the Article 1A(2) definition does not necessarily require it to be established that there has been a violation of a non-derogable rights such as Article 7 ICCPR/ Article 3 ECHR (or violations of equivalent severity), how can IHRL on risk on return (as it seems currently to do) necessarily require such a violation? On the logic of the human rights approach, the human rights concepts to be applied should ordinarily have the same scope as those formulated in IHRL.

Before considering the ECtHR analysis in the case of *Salah Sheekh* more closely,[305] its treatment of the IPA concept pre-*Salah Sheekh* should be briefly summarised. It is mostly fact-specific but in *Chahal* the Court rejected the UK Government contention that the applicant would have a viable IPA because it considered that the background evidence showed that someone with his profile would be at risk from the Punjab security forces acting either within or outside state boundaries. The Court also attached significance to the fact that attested allegations of serious human rights violations had been levelled at the police elsewhere in India.[306] In *Hilal*, the Court rejected the UK Government's argument that an 'internal flight' option existed in mainland Tanzania for an applicant fleeing persecution in Zanzibar. The Court reasoned that '[t]he police in mainland Tanzania may be regarded as linked institutionally to the police in Zanzibar as part of the Union and cannot be relied on as a safeguard against arbitrary action'.[307] However, it was not until *Salah Sheekh* that the Court sought to delineate relevant legal principles in its analysis.

The Court's usefully restated the findings it made in *Salah Sheekh* in *Sufi and Elmi v United Kingdom* as follows:

---

it, include: *Case of Hayden v Sweden* (16 December 1998) Communication No 101/1997, UN Doc CAT/C/ 21/D/101/1997; *Case of BSS v Canada* (17 May 2004) Communication No 183/2001, UN Doc CAT/C/32/ D/183/2001, para 11.5; *Case of SSS v Canada* (5 December 2005) Communication No 245/2004, UN Doc CAT/C/35/D/245/2004, para 8.5.

[303] *Salah Sheekh v the Netherlands* App No 1948/04 (ECtHR, 11 January 2007) para 141.
[304] Schultz (2018) (n 1) 263; Lehmann (n 1) 159.
[305] *Salah Sheekh* (n 303) para 141.
[306] *Chahal v United Kingdom* App No 22414/93 (ECtHR, 15 November 1996) para 98.
[307] *Hilal v United Kingdom*, App No 45276/99 (ECtHR, 6 June 2001) para 67.

The Court recalls that Article 3 does not, as such, preclude Contracting States from placing reliance on the existence of an internal flight alternative in their assessment of an individual's claim that a return to his country of origin would expose him to a real risk of being subjected to treatment proscribed by that provision .... However, the Court has held that reliance on an internal flight alternative does not affect the responsibility of the expelling Contracting State to ensure that the applicant is not, as a result of its decision to expel, exposed to treatment contrary to Article 3 of the Convention .... Therefore, as a precondition of relying on an internal flight alternative, certain guarantees have to be in place: the person to be expelled must be able to travel to the area concerned, gain admittance and settle there, failing which an issue under Article 3 may arise, the more so if in the absence of such guarantees there is a possibility of his ending up in a part of the country of origin where he may be subjected to ill-treatment ....[308]

An important backdrop to the Court's assessment of both the applicants' home area and any putative IPA is their clarification of the threshold to be applied in situations where dire humanitarian conditions are involved. The Court reasoned that if the dire humanitarian conditions in Somalia were solely, or even predominantly attributable to poverty or to the state's lack of resources to deal with a naturally occurring phenomenon (such as drought), then decision makers would have to apply to the Article 3 assessment the higher ('very exceptional') threshold set out in health cases such as *N v United Kingdom*.[309] The Court concluded in *Sufi and Elmi*, that the crisis in Somalia at that time was predominantly due to the direct and indirect actions of the (human actor-warlord) parties to the conflict and hence the correct approach was the one adopted in *M.S.S. v Belgium and Greece*, which requires the decision maker to have regard to an applicant's ability to cater for his most basic needs, such as food, hygiene, and shelter, his vulnerability to ill-treatment, and the prospect of his situation improving within a reasonable time frame.[310]

When it came to applying the IPA principles thus summarised to the applicants' cases, the Court concluded that in the putative IPA the applicants would not have a viable alternative location unless they had close family connections there: '[i]f [a returnee] has no such connections, or if those connections are in an area which he could not safely reach, the Court considers that there is a likelihood that he would have to have recourse to either an IDP or refugee camp.'[311]

The most important case since in which the ECtHR has set out its thinking on the IPA is that of *A.A.M. v Sweden*. Having reiterated the principles set out in *Sufi and Elmi*, the Court stated at paragraph 73 that:

> Internal relocation inevitably involves certain hardship. Various sources have attested that people who relocate to the Kurdistan Region may face difficulties, for instance,

---

[308] *Sufi and Elmi v United Kingdom* Apps Nos 8319/07 and 11149/07 (ECtHR, 18 November 2011) para 266.
[309] In *N v United Kingdom* App No 26565/05 (ECtHR [GC], 27 May 2008) the Court held at paras 42–44 that humanitarian conditions would give rise to a breach of Article 3 of the Convention only in 'very exceptional cases' where the humanitarian grounds against removal were 'compelling'.
[310] *Sufi and Elmi* (n 308) para 283.
[311] ibid para 294.

in finding proper jobs and housing there, not the least if they do not speak Kurdish. Nevertheless, the evidence before the Court suggests that there are jobs available and that settlers have access to health care as well as financial and other support from the UNHCR and local authorities. In any event, there is no indication that the general living conditions in the KRI for an Arab Sunni Muslim settler would be unreasonable or in any way amount to treatment prohibited by Article 3. Nor is there a real risk of his or her ending up in other parts of Iraq.[312]

In the above paragraphs, three things are apparent. First, it can be seen that the Court applies a type of reasonableness standard—applied in this example to general living conditions. However, it is treated as equivalent to the Article 3 ECHR ill-treatment standard. Understanding it thus is also consistent with other cases in which the Court has said that socio-economic and humanitarian considerations do not 'necessarily have a bearing, and certainly not a decisive one' on the question of whether an applicant would face a real risk of ill-treatment in areas considered as an alternative flight option.[313] Second, it would appear that a key criterion brought to bear is whether or not conditions would cause indirect refoulement.[314]

A third feature of IHRL case law, based on ECtHR examples, is that in the case of applicants who have established a well-founded fear of ill treatment in their home area from *state authorities*, there should be a presumption against an IPA that will need to be rebutted by decision makers. Such a position is consistent with the general approach in IHLR in response to scenarios in which state actors are involved in ill treatment.[315] Put another way, the Court considers that the benefit of any doubt regarding the potential of the government of the home state for continued persecution in the alternative region should be resolved in favour of the asylum applicant.[316]

The Strasbourg jurisprudence on the IPA has been the subject of criticism, most recently from Schultz[317] and Lehmann,[318] the former who considers that the jurisprudence demonstrates 'an unduly restrictive set of criteria for the IPA assessment' and to thus represent a 'problematic precedent'.[319] Whilst much of Schultz's criticism is aimed at Strasbourg decisions that fail to apply the standards set out in *Salah Sheekh*,[320] one can extract from her book and other published pieces that she perceives four main deficiencies in the Court's general approach: that in a number of cases the Court has placed reliance on, or simply taken for granted,[321] non-state agents of protection;[322]

---

[312] *AAM v Sweden* App No 68519/10 (ECtHR, 3 April 2014) paras 73–74; see also para 68.
[313] See e.g. *SHH v United Kingdom* App No 60637/10 (ECtHR, 29 January 2013). See also *NMB v Sweden* App No 68335/10 (ECtHR, 27 June 2013); *BKA v Sweden* App No 1161/11 (ECtHR, 19 December 2013).
[314] See e.g. *AAM v Sweden* (n 312) para 68; *NMB v Sweden* (n 313) para 37.
[315] See e.g. *Selmouni v France* App No 25803/94 (ECtHR, 25 November 1996).
[316] *JK and Others v Sweden* App No 59166/12 (ECtHR, 23 August 2016) para 122.
[317] Schultz (2018) (n 1) 297–309.
[318] Lehmann (n 1) 176–95. Lehmann argues that the IPA doctrine in IHRL embodies lower standards.
[319] Schultz (2018) (n 1) 298, 318; see also Schultz (2015) (n 1) 31.
[320] As an example of misapplication, she cites *MYH and Others v Sweden* App No 50859/10 (ECtHR, 27 June 2013); *DNM v Sweden* App No 28379/11 (ECtHR, 27 June 2013); *Husseini v Sweden* App No 10611 (ECtHR, 8 March 2012).
[321] She gives the example of *NANS v Sweden* App No 68411/10 (ECtHR, 27 June 2013) para 38, where the Court assumed that the Kurdish Regional Government could provide protection to Iraqi nationals.
[322] In addition to *Salah Sheekh* (n 303) para 140 (where the court suggested that clan protection would suffice to make return to Somaliland and Puntland relatively safe generally) and *Sufi and Elmi* (n 308) (in

that it has failed to include a criterion of durability;[323] that it does not consider the impact of factors relating to security, family life, private life, gender, age, health and past persecution, etc.;[324] and that:

> In addition to reinforcing an overly narrow approach to the serious harm assessment, the Strasbourg jurisprudence also encourages a conflation in State practice of Article 3 harms with the additional 'reasonableness' analysis required in most jurisdictions.[325]

What of Schultz's first criticism decrying the Court's reliance on protection by non-state actors? It is unfortunate that her criticism here treats all kind of non-state actors in the same bracket, as there is a clear distinction to be made between de facto state actors on the one hand and other types of non-state actors on the other. In relation to the former, reasons were set out in Chapter 7 for considering that the IHRL approach to de facto state actors is consistent with international law norms and that the notion of protection within the refugee definition can encompass de facto state actors, albeit, because of the demanding criteria connected with the protection concept, instances of such protection will be rare.[326]

What of the situation of at least some other types of non-state actors, in particular entities such as clans that perform security functions and civil society entities such as families and community organisations that provide assistance and/or support, e.g. women's shelters? Schultz's criticism here raises the same issues discussed in Chapter 7. In the latter, it was argued that whilst such actors clearly cannot constitute actors of protection, it remains moot whether the CJEU was correct in *O A* to consider their protective functions are 'irrelevant' to the issue of the effectiveness of protection.[327] In this connection, it was pointed out that the Strasburg Court has viewed the protective functions of such non-state actors as relevant to assessment of whether an applicant's circumstances give rise to a real risk of ill treatment. Schultz's criticism is in line with

---

which the Court considered that close family connections might constitute adequate protection in some cases), she cites *Thampibillai v the Netherlands* App No 61350/10 (ECtHR, 11 October 2011); *Hida v Denmark* App No 38025/02 (ECtHR, 19 February 2004); *Sadena Muratovic v Denmark* App No 14513/03 (ECtHR, 19 February 2004); *Aslan and Atifa Muratovic v Denmark* App No 14923/03 (ECtHR, 19 February 2004); *Collins and Akaziebie v Sweden* App No 68411/08 (ECtHR, 17 May 2011) paras 80–81; *AA and Others v Sweden* App No 14999/09 (ECtHR, 28 June 2012); and *RH v Sweden* App No 4601/14 (ECtHR, 10 September 2015) paras 73–74.

[323] Schultz (2018) (n 1) 305–06, with reference to *Sufi and Elmi* (n 308) paras 272–77. She goes on to raise another deficiency, which concerns the Court's treatment of the issue of concealment of sexual or religious orientation (in *ME v Sweden* App No 71398/12 (ECtHR, 26 June 2014) and *Z and T v United Kingdom* App No 27034 (ECtHR, 28 February 2006)), but these cases do not address the IPA concept specifically and she does not address more recent case law on this issue.

[324] Schultz (2018) (n 1) 307–08.

[325] Schultz (2015) (n 1) 45; Schultz (2018) (n 1) 307–09. In the latter she refers to the case of *NANS v Sweden* (n 321) para 38, but its wording is very similar to that used in *AAM v Sweden* (n 312). For a slightly different criticism, see Lehmann (n 1) 182: '[a]lthough the court has in some few cases used the language of reasonableness in connection with internal relocation, it is clear that reasonableness does not amount to a requirement separate from the Article 3 threshold'.

[326] See pp. 459–460.

[327] Case C-255/19 *SSHD v O A* [2021] ECLI:EU:C:2021:36. See further Chapter 7, section 3.12.

the approach taken in *O A* and with some leading academics, including Hathaway and Foster, but the matter cannot be regarded as settled.

As for Schultz's second criticism, it is true that the ECtHR has not as yet identified durability or non-temporariness as a requirement for protection in the same way as the CJEU has (at least in the Article 7 QD (recast)). It must also be accepted that the Court has not always seemed to recognise the durability criterion implicit in their own requirement that an applicant must be able to 'settle' in a putative IPA. At the same time, the ECtHR's actual approach to the facts of the case in both *Salah Sheekh* and *Sufi and Elmi* indicate that it treats this criterion as part of the overall assessment that has to be made. Thus, in *Salah Sheekh* it saw as important the lack of evidence of any 'substantial' change for the better.[328] So in *Sufi and Elmi* the Court treated as relevant that there was very little prospect of the situation facing minority clan members improving 'within a reasonable time frame'.[329]

As regards Schultz's third main criticism, it does not appear to do justice to the fact that the Court's constant Article 3 EHCR jurisprudence makes clear that, in any kind of Article 3 case, individual assessment is paramount and that the standards guaranteed by this article 'imply that the ill-treatment the applicant alleges he will face if returned must attain a minimum level of severity if it is to fall within the scope of Article 3. The assessment of this is relative, depending on all the circumstances of the case.'[330] If one examines cases such as *Salah Sheekh, Sufi and Elmi*, and *A.A.H.*, the Court does take into consideration in each instance precisely the kind of wide-ranging factors Schultz considers imperative for any IPA analysis, whether under refugee law or Article 3. The fact that in the course of this assessment it adopts some kind of 'reasonableness' test tends to reinforce that.

It remains to consider Schultz's fourth criticism alleging that the Strasbourg Court has conflated the Article 3 ECHR and reasonableness standards. This author considers it entirely accurate. In both *Salah Sheekh* and *Sufi and Elmi* the Court plainly treats the key criterion as being whether the applicant would be exposed to a real risk of treatment contrary to Article 3 ECHR *in the internal protection area*.[331] It is just possible to suggest that the Court's formulation in cases such as *NMB* (which refers to whether the general living conditions in IPA 'would be unreasonable *or* in any way amount to treatment prohibited by Article 3')[332] treats 'reasonableness' and Article 3 as alternatives. However, as *NMB* illustrates, this formulation is accompanied by a conclusion that the issue is whether or not the applicant 'may reasonably relocate to the [IPA], *where he will not face such a risk*'.[333] The reason why this position is erroneous is that if an Article 3 threshold is applied to the *IPA*, this would mean that the assessment of risk on return to the *home country* would in fact be higher than Article 3, since it fails to factor in the existing deficit in human rights protection in the home area and the consequent circumstances of an applicant having to seek access to a place where he or she can settle and where conditions will not compel them to return to their home

---

[328] *Salah Sheekh* (n 303) para 147. See also *Hilal* (n 307) paras 66–67.
[329] *Sufi and Elmi* (n 308) para 291.
[330] ibid para 213.
[331] *Salah Sheekh* (n 303) para 145; *Sufi and Elmi* (n 308) paras 266, 277.
[332] See e.g. *NMB v Sweden* (n 313) para 43 (emphasis added).
[333] ibid para 46 (emphasis added).

area. It would effectively be to require applicants to show they face a real risk of such ill treatment in every part of their country. It also runs contrary to the Court's own acceptance of the notion of indirect refoulement in a number of cases concerned with internal relocation (including the *NMB* case),[334] since under this notion what matters is simply whether an applicant would be compelled by the conditions in the alternative area to return to their home area. Factors that might compel such internal refoulement cannot be necessarily limited to Article 3 harms.

There is a further strong reason for questioning the approach taken to date by the Strasbourg Court. Although the case law of the Human Rights Committee (HRC) concerning IPA is less developed, it very noticeably takes a different approach. Its approach is much more in line with that taken in much of refugee law, of considering that the threshold in the putative IPA is the lesser standard of reasonableness (or some analogue). Thus, in *BL v Australia*, which concerned an applicant originating from Touba, Senegal, the Committee concluded that:

> [ ... ] it was not shown that the authorities in Senegal would not generally be willing and able to provide impartial, adequate and effective protection to the [applicant] against threats to his physical safety, and that it would not be unreasonable to expect him to settle in a location, especially one more distant from Touba, where such protection would be available to him. Provided that the [applicant] would only be returned to such a location where [Australia] determines that adequate and effective protection is available, the Committee cannot conclude that removing him to Senegal would violate [Australia's] obligations under article 6 or 7 of the Covenant.[335]

What can be said about the error this study discerns in the Strasbourg analysis, however, is that it is capable of being corrected without abandonment of the Court's underlying position that the ultimate Article 3 ECHR question must always be whether an applicant's claim that a return to his *country of origin* would expose him to a real risk of being subjected to treatment proscribed by that provision.[336] It simply requires the Court to clarify that, in determining whether there is a viable IPA, the threshold of harm *in the IPA* does not necessarily have to be at the Article 3 level. This also provides the answer to the conundrum identified earlier: whilst the analysis of risk on return cases within IHRL must confine itself to the Article 7 ICCPR or Article 3 ECHR standard, this does not have to entail that, for there to be a *viable IPA*, conditions in it must be at an Article 7 ICCPR or Article 3 ECHR threshold; it is only the applicant's circumstances in the country as a whole that have to meet this threshold. The ultimate standard is still tied back to Article 7 ICCPR or Article 3 EHCR. The same applies, *pari passu*, in relation to the IPA analysis within the refugee definition.

A second question posed at the outset of the analysis of the IPA within IHRL is whether it can be applied straightforwardly to the IPA analysis within the refugee

---

[334] ibid para 39: 'Nor is there a real risk of his or her ending up in the other parts of Iraq.'
[335] *Case of BL v Australia* (n 302) para 7.4 (emphasis added). See also concurring opinions at Appendix 1–II. See further *Case of SYL v Australia* (n 302) paras 8.1–8.4; and discussion in High Court of Australia, *CR1026* (n 60) paras 34–37.
[336] >*Sufi and Elmi* (n 308) para 266.

definition. The fact that the ECtHR's case law on IPA currently takes a misconceived approach to the necessary threshold of harm in the IPA means that there cannot be any straightforward application of its criteria to the context of the refugee definition. This does reduce its value as a benchmark for IPA assessment in the Refugee Convention context. It presently stands as an example where there are cogent reasons for failing to take the ECtHR case law as instructive (namely because it is different from that applied by the HRC and exhibits a misconception). However, this qualification does not mean refraining from applying to IPA analysis a human rights approach conceived of in terms of application of IHRL norms at a general level—recourse to concepts of sufficiently severe violations of human rights etc. Nor does it mean refraining from applying all the other specific criteria developed within IHRL on risk on return cases. It only means declining to apply one specific criterion currently applied by the ECtHR. Accordingly, it remains possible to develop a more coherent IPA analysis that is still strongly based on a human rights approach.

### 3.1 Conclusions on IHRL IPA Analysis

Three main points emerge from an analysis of the IPA concept in IHRL.

The first is that presently the case law of the ECtHR, which has developed an IPA concept more fully than other regional human rights courts and the UN treaty-monitoring bodies, has severely limited itself from achieving a coherent position by insisting on requiring the threshold of harm in the IPA to be at the level of ill treatment as prohibited by Article 3 ECHR. This entails that whatever analysis is conducted of the situation of the IPA in terms of violations of other human rights, derogable human rights in particular, it will always run up against the need to meet an unduly high threshold, that of ill-treatment, in the IPA.

The second observation is that IHRL has nevertheless succeeded in clarifying three important matters: (i) the key importance of accessibility—making clear that unless an applicant can safely and legally travel to and gain admittance to an IPA, it cannot be said to be a viable alternative; (ii) that in order to be viable an IPA must also be a place where an applicant must be able to settle, that is have some stability of existence. Although it has not expressly identified non-temporariness as a criterion, it has made clear that it is not sufficient that an IPA is purely a temporary state of affairs; and (iii) it has frequently applied the notion of indirect refoulement, thereby effectively recognising that one essential condition for any IPA to be viable is that conditions there do not drive an applicant back to their home area.

A final point is that it is possible to identify a number of basic propositions which form part of the IPA analysis. In the context of IHRL elaboration (mostly by the ECtHR so far) it would seem that such propositions are capable of standing on their own, irrespective of differences between the ECHR and the HRC over the issue of the threshold of harm in the IPA. IHRL, of course, has only to apply to the home state as a whole a straightforward assessment of violation of the non-derogable right (set out in Article 7 ICCPR or Article 3 ECHR) prohibiting ill-treatment; it does not have to wrestle with how various definitional clauses—'well-founded fear', 'being persecuted', protection, causal nexus—interact and what is the precise meaning of each.

The basic propositions that can be distilled from IHRL IPA analysis in risk on return cases are as follows:

> That it is well-established that persons will not be in need of international human rights protection if they can obtain protection by moving elsewhere within their own country;[337]
>
> That as with any other Article 7 ICCPR/Article 3 ECHR assessment, it is necessary to undertake a holistic assessment that takes account both of general country conditions and individual circumstances;[338]
>
> That the issue of an IPA only arises if there is a finding of real risk of ill treatment in a person's home area or region;[339]
>
> That in order for an IPA to be viable it must be shown to be accessible (which entails, *inter alia*, that they are able to travel to it and gain admittance to it);[340]
>
> That in order for an IPA to be viable it must be established that an applicant can settle there;[341]
>
> That in relation to an IPA, an assessment must be made as to whether the situation there is likely to change substantially, so as to render it unsafe;[342]
>
> That there is a need to ensure that there is no continuing risk of ill treatment in the IPA;[343]
>
> That in this context it is important to have regard to the reach of the actors of harm and whether they have the resources or wherewithal to pursue an applicant outside their home area;[344]
>
> That in this context, risk can emanate either from the original actors of harm locating them or from fresh sources of harm;[345] and
>
> That in assessing risk, consideration has to be given to the risk of indirect refoulement.[346]

To this list should be added the evident fact that, unlike the case in IRL:

> There is no requirement in any part of the Article 7 ICCPR/Article 3 ECHR analysis—whether focussed on the home area or IPA—to establish that the risk of ill treatment is for a specified reason or causally linked to it.

It will be observed shortly that whilst not identical, this list significantly resembles those extractable from each of the main approaches to the IPA within IRL.[347]

---

[337] ibid para 35.
[338] ibid para 213.
[339] This is not stated expressly but is implicit in the Court's statement about indirect refoulement e.g. *Salah Sheekh* (n 303) para 141 and *Sufi and Elmi* (n 308) para 266; see also *Hilal* (n 307) para 66.
[340] *Sufi and Elmi* (n 308) paras 266, 294.
[341] ibid.
[342] *Hilal* (n 307) paras 66–67; *Salah Sheekh* (n 303) para 147; *Sufi and Elmi* (n 308) paras 291.
[343] *Chahal* (n 306) paras 106–07; *Hilal* (n 307) para 67.
[344] *Chahal* (n 306) paras 98, 100, 104, 107; *Hilal* (n 307) paras 66–67.
[345] This is not stated explicitly but is implicit in *JK and Others* (n 316) 121.
[346] *Salah Sheekh* (n 303) para 141. In *Sufi and Elmi* (n 308) the Court considered that conditions in the proposed IPA(s) would compel the applicants to either return to their home area or go into IDP or refugee camps where COI indicated that conditions would be contrary to Article 3: see paras 266, 285.
[347] See above section 2.8.

## 4 Essential Elements of the IPA Test in Article 1A(2)—A Distillation

Having analysed the IPA concept in the refugee definition and also in IHRL we must now ask whether it is possible to derive any common position on key elements in the former. We have just seen that it is possible to extract a number of basic propositions animating the IPA concept in IHRL. We must now ask whether this is possible for IPA analysis under Article 1A(2) as well, notwithstanding the greater number of legal requirements set out in the latter.

From sections 2 and 3 of this chapter, it will be apparent that despite discord over approaches to the IPA concept and the use of quite diverse vocabularies to conceptualise it, there appears to be a great deal of common ground in terms of basic propositions. That seems a point lost in some of the scholarship.[348] The purpose here is to identify these commonalities and then consider their wider implications. We shall deal first with the substantive content of the test. In what follows 'risk' is used as a shorthand for well-founded fear of persecution. The term IPA can comprise either a part or parts of the country.

It is arguable the following list could be longer and include in particular acceptance that where the risk emanates from state actors, there is a presumption against a viable IPA, but whilst this proposition is shared by each of the four main approaches and have received significant support,[349] it has not received full support in the case law[350] or wider literature.[351] For that reason alone they could not be said to be widely agreed. It is also arguable the following list could include other propositions such as that there is no requirement to establish countrywide persecution, but it effectively precludes any such a notion in any event.

### 4.1 Substantive Contents

#### 4.1.1 Risk in the home area

Even though consensus is lacking about what constitutes an applicant's home area,[352] there is agreement that the issue of an IPA only comes into play once the decision maker has accepted (or is prepared to assume) that an applicant has a well-founded fear of persecution in their home area or region.[353] In concrete terms, this is a prerequisite for there to be any IPA inquiry.

---

[348] A notable exception is Ní Ghráinne (2021) (n 1) 697 who argues that using VCLT rules of interpretation, 'it is nonetheless possible to distil a minimum binding standard of relevant IPA criteria from both State practice and the text of the Refugee Convention itself'. She identifies three criteria: '(i) that the proposed IPA must be accessible to the applicant, (ii) there is no risk of exposure to the original risk of persecution, and (iii) there must be no new risk of persecution or of refoulment in the proposed IPA, and the conditions there must not be so unreasonable as to risk driving the individual to a place where there is a risk of persecution.'
[349] See e.g. Zimmermann and Mahler (n 1) 451–52.
[350] As noted by Ní Ghráinne (2021) (n 1) 703.
[351] See e.g. Storey (2003) (n 1) 369.
[352] See above section 4.1.1.
[353] UNHCR Guidelines No 4 (n 1) para 16; Hathaway and Foster (2014) (n 1) 316; Kelley (n 1) 22–23; Waldman (n 1) 445. Kelley describes this condition as 'Persecution in the Displacement Area First',

### 4.1.2 Significance to any IPA assessment of state actor persecution

Whilst the main approaches agree in considering that where the risk in the home area emanates from state actors, there is a presumption against an IPA elsewhere,[354] this has not met with full agreement in the case law.[355] However, what can be seen as a commonality is that when persecution in the home area emanates from state actors, this places greater difficulties in the way of assessing an IPA to be viable.[356]

### 4.1.3 Accessibility

There is now a substantial consensus that there can be no viable IPA unless it is accessible; an applicant has to be able to get there and live there. This operates in effect as a precondition for any IPA. It would go too far to say that there is also consensus about precisely what contents is to be given to the concept of accessibility, but as refugee law has evolved, there is increasing acceptance that accessibility entails three specific requirements: that it is safe for the applicant to travel to the IPA;[357] that the applicant must be able to gain admittance;[358] and that the applicant must be able to settle there.[359]

As was noted earlier, there is no legal requirement for an applicants to show they have tried to relocate internally prior to leaving their country of origin, although it may be a relevant evidential factor. However, given that their application for refugee status is made outside their country of origin, the question inevitably arises as to the route of travel to any putative IPA. It is still not possible to say that there is broad consensus regarding this matter, as it is seen to depend a great deal on the part of the country to which an applicant faces return and individual host state practices regarding points of return in the home state in question. However, there does appear increasing acceptance that since applicants in an IPA context cannot be expected to return to their home area (because they face there a well-founded fear of persecution), accessibility must entail assessing possible alternative routes *to* any IPA. It is no surprise therefore that case law on IPA analysis has increasingly included consideration of the point of return (border point, port, or an airport etc.) and of how an applicant can get from there to the IPA area. The underlying reasoning is clearly that if there is

---

commenting '[c]onceptually, a determination of whether the claimant faces a serious possibility of persecution in the displacement area precedes a determination of whether the claimant has an IFA. This follows from the fact that the IFA is a place where the claimant can access meaningful protection, necessitating first a determination of "protection from what?".'

[354] See e.g. QD (recast) (n 17) Recital 27.
[355] Ní Ghráinne (2021) (n 1) 703.
[356] 'Summary Conclusions: Internal Protection/Relocation/Flight Alternative' (n 1) para 2.
[357] UNHCR Guidelines No 4 (n 1); MGs (n 1) para 20; QD (recast) (n 17) Article 8(1)(b); Zimmermann and Mahler (n 1) 450–51: '[o]ther part of the country of origin possibly qualifying as an area of relocation needs to be practically, safely and legally accessible for the applicant'; Hailbronner and Thym (n 1) 1161–62; Waldman (n 1) 450; Ní Ghráinne (2021) (n 1) 706–07. There is not, however, any evident consensus as to what constitutes legal accessibility: see Marx (n 1) 186.
[358] See e.g. Federal Administrative Court, *BVerwG 1 C 4.20* [2021] DE:BVerwG:2021:180221U1C4.20.0, para 18; Council of State (*Conseil d'État*, France), *Ms DF No 332491* [2012] FR:CEASS:2012:332491.20121221; *Paxi v Canada (MCI)* [2016] FCJ No 887.
[359] UNHCR Guidelines No 4 (n 1) para 20; QD (recast) (n 17) Article 8(1)(b); Hailbronner and Thym (n 1) 1162; Waldman (n 1) 466–78 (he cites case law referencing 'a secure substitute home'). It is possible to also treat non-temporariness as a precondition, but this is listed later.

no safe route, then the IPA is not accessible. Since only a route of travel is concerned, it makes sense that the essential criterion is limited to safety, as it is not a matter of living there.

### 4.1.4 Absence of well-founded fear of persecution in the IPA

An applicant cannot be considered to have a viable IPA unless there is a part (or parts) of the country in which he or she will not have a well-founded fear of being persecuted. Otherwise, he or she would go from a frying pan into a fire. This proposition is variously expressed in the main approaches[360] but the common underlying concept is shared by all—that in one way or another any alternative place must at least be 'persecution-free'. Thus understood, this proposition covers two scenarios: (i) that the IPA negates the original risk; and (ii) that it does not constitute or contain any new risk.

As regards (i), it is incontrovertible that if in an IPA the applicant will still face risk from the original persecutor(s), it cannot be viable.[361] It is accepted that this requires a consideration, inter alia, of whether the original persecutor(s) has/have the will and the wherewithal/reach to pursue or otherwise take an adverse interest in the applicant in the IPA.[362]

As regards (ii), this requires assessing any potential new sources of risk.[363] Not to assess those would subvert the basic idea of the IPA concept.

### 4.1.5 Absence of risk of indirect refoulement

Although not everyone derives it from Article 33(1) of the Convention, all agree with the proposition that for there to be a viable IPA there must be an absence of a risk of indirect (or 'constructive') refoulement.[364] Once again, although expressed variously,[365] the common underlying idea is that an IPA cannot be viable if conditions there are

---

[360] UNHCR Guidelines No 4 (n 1) paras 15–16 (they refer to the alternative site needing to provide an 'antidote to well-founded fear of persecution in the place of origin'); Hathaway and Foster (2003) (n 1); Hathaway and Foster (2014) (n 1) 344; Kelley (n 1) 22–23; Waldman (n 1) 461–64; Ní Ghráinne (2021) (n 1) 707: 'The criterion that there must be effective protection from the original risk of persecution is well-established in State practice.' Mathew (n 1) 192 terms this the idea of a 'persecution-free zone'. In several jurisdictions this is sometimes referred to as the 'safety' limb. Although simpler, this usage is avoided by some because of concerns expressed about the way this has sometimes been understood by courts and tribunals. Thus, Hathaway and Foster, 'Internal Protection/Relocation/Flight Alternative' (n 1) 383–84 abjure reference to 'safety' because in practice it has produced highly questionable results in particular cases, and has been interpreted as meaning considerably less than protection. They consider that 'safety' is not a term found in the 1951 Convention and has a fungible content that has proved a dangerous distraction, leading some states to return applicants to face the risk of war and other serious dangers.

[361] 'Summary Conclusions: Internal Protection/Relocation/Flight Alternative' (n 1) para 4; UNHCR Guidelines No 4 (n 1); QD (recast) (n 17) Article 8(1)(b); Zimmermann and Mahler (n 1) 451–52; Hailbronner and Thym (n 1) 1161.

[362] UNHCR Guidelines No 4 (n 1) paras 7(1)(c), 18; MGs (n 1) para 15; Hathaway and Foster (2014) (n 1) 345–46.

[363] 'Summary Conclusions: Internal Protection/Relocation/Flight Alternative' (n 1) para 4; UNHCR Guidelines No 4 (n 1) para 7 (1)(d), 13, 20; MGs (n 1) paras 17–79, refer to there being 'no additional risk of, or equivalent to, persecution'; Hathaway and Foster (2014) (n 1) 348–50; the QD (recast) (n 17) Article 8(1)(a), refers to 'no well-founded fear of being persecuted' (emphasis added); Zimmermann and Mahler (n 1) 452–53; Hailbronner and Thym (n 1) 1161; Waldman (n 1) 445–46; Kelley (n 1) 22, 40, 43; Ní Ghráinne (2021) (n 1) 708–09.

[364] Ní Ghráinne (2021) (n 1) 708–09.

[365] UNHCR Guidelines No 4 (n 1) para 19; Kelley (n 1) 34; Zimmermann and Mahler (n 1) 452: '[t]here must be not a danger of an equivalent to refoulement'. This is sometimes referred to in the jurisprudence as

sufficiently adverse to compel the applicant to attempt return to the home area,[366] notwithstanding that he or she is at risk there. Again, whilst there is no agreed formulation, integral to this idea is that such adverse conditions do not necessarily themselves have to constitute a well-founded fear of persecution, since the only issue is whether they will in fact have the effect of causing an applicant to return to the original site of persecution. It should be noted, however, that although there seems broad acceptance of this logic,[367] there is still no wide endorsement of one of its obvious implications, namely that it is unnecessary to show that the adverse conditions are caused (or predominantly caused) by human actors ( e.g. the cause may just be a natural disaster).

4.1.6 Non-temporariness

Once again, although framed in diverse terminologies,[368] the various approaches concur that an IPA will not be viable if it will only offer a temporary or unstable haven.[369] For UNHCR and the MGs, this requirement is best described as durability, but in light of the refusal of the CJEU in *Abdulla* to adopt UNHCR's proposal to term it thus,[370] the proposition is cast in this more neutral form.

4.1.7 Individual assessment

There is broad agreement that deciding the question of whether an applicant has a viable IPA requires an individual assessment. Studies have drawn attention to occasional examples of attempts by courts and tribunals to rely on generalised assessments, but increasingly the principle of individual assessment has come to be seen as necessary to apply to all elements of the refugee definition, including the IPA.[371]

4.1.8 Forward-looking assessment

There is consensus that what is involved in an IPA inquiry is a forward-looking assessment.[372] As a corollary, there is no requirement that an applicant must have tried to move to the IPA prior to departure, although this may in particular cases be relevant to evidence assessment.

---

'constructive refoulement': see e.g. Ní Ghráinne (2021) (n 1) 708. On the principle of equivalence: see Storey (2003) (n 1) 364.

[366] Or possibly another area in which they will face persecutory treatment.
[367] e.g. Ní Ghráinne (2021) (n 1) 710 considers that the requirement of reasonableness 'can be incorporated into the prohibition of constructive refoulement', thereby giving it a strong treaty-based underpinning.
[368] UNHCR Guidelines No 4 (n 1); QD (recast) (n 17) Article 8 (entailed by Article 8(1)(b)); Hailbronner and Thym (n 1) 1163; Waldman (n 1) 446.
[369] Ní Ghráinne (2021) (n 1) 704–05.
[370] Lehmann (n 1).
[371] 'Summary Conclusions: Internal Protection/Relocation/Flight Alternative' (n 1) para 1; UNHCR Guidelines No 4 (n 1) para 12; QD (recast) (n 17) Articles 4, 8(2); Marx (n 1) 196–99; Eaton (n 1) 770; Kelley (n 1) 43; Zimmermann and Mahler (n 1); Hathaway and Foster (2014) (n 1) 347; Ní Ghráinne (2015) (n 1) 46–50; Waldman (n 1) 446, 470, 474, 480; Hailbronner and Thym (n 1) 1163; Schultz (2018) (n 1) 387.
[372] UNHCR Guidelines No 4 (n 1) para 8; Kelley (n 1) 13, 43; QD (recast) (n 17) Article 8(2); Zimmermann and Mahler (n 1) 449–50; Hailbronner and Thym (n 1) 1160.

### 4.1.9 Causal nexus

As regards causal nexus, this requirement is met once an applicant has established a well-founded fear of persecution on account of a Convention reason in their home area.

## 4.2 Procedural Contents

The importance of procedural contents to the IPA cannot be underestimated. As noted by Eaton, '[w]hile the arguments over IPA have been extensive, the core concerns are often procedural and evidentiary'.[373] This has been reflected in the earlier elaboration of each of the main approaches, although they do not always share the same list.

Notwithstanding some degree of consensus over several procedural requirements, it cannot presently be said that there is substantial consensus. Given as well that the Refugee Convention is silent about procedures to be used by refugee decision makers for determining refugee status, it would be wrong therefore to venture a list of accepted procedural propositions. The following points do represent, though, where the main discussions on evidential matters have reached so far.

### 4.2.1 Burden of proof resting on the RSD authority?

Although there has been some support in state practice and in the wider literature for the view that the burden of proof in the IPA inquiry rests on the RSD authority,[374] there is a significant body of case law that disagrees.[375]

### 4.2.2 Burden of raising as an issue

There is considerable backing for the view that the burden rests on the RSD authority to identify the IPA as a live issue. UNHCR considers that in regard to the IPA inquiry, the 'usual rule', that he who alleges must prove, applies.[376] Hathaway and Foster consider such a proposition can be derived from the accepted fact of risk in the home area. Whilst the case law mostly supports both propositions,[377] there have been decisions that have declined to accept it, one of the difficulties being that in certain cases an applicant may have already raised it in their asylum application.[378]

---

[373] Eaton (n 1) 769.

[374] Schultz (2018) (n 1) 279–80 notes cases from Poland and Sweden. There is a Commission Proposal to introduce a Qualification Regulation which includes such a provision: see above n 18.

[375] Schultz (2018) (n 1) 276–81 cites UK, New Zealand, Canadian, and US case law and/or practice. See also *BVerwG 9 C 434.93* [1994], cited Hailbronner and Thym (n 1) 1165. For the position in Canadian case law (which broadly considers the onus to remain on the applicant) see Waldman (n 1) 457. For recent UK cases, see *SSHD v SC (Jamaica)* [2017] EWCA Civ 2112, and *MB (Internal relocation—burden of proof) Albania* [2019] UKUT 392 (IAC). See also Ní Ghráinne (2021) (n 1) 703. On US case law, however, Anker (n 134) §2.14, 93 observes that '[w]here the government is the agent of harm, the burden is on the DHS to establish by a preponderance of the evidence that, under all the circumstances, it would be reasonable for the applicant to relocate'.

[376] UNHCR Guidelines No 4 (n 1) para 6; MGs (n 1) para 26; however, Kelley (n 1) 11 (at footnote 19) notes some case law taking a different view.

[377] See e.g. Canadian cases cited in Waldman (n 1) 451–54.

[378] See discussion in Schultz (2018) (n 1) 280–81.

### 4.2.3 Duty to give notice

In its Guidelines No 4, UNHCR state that '[b]asic rules of procedural fairness require that the asylum-seeker be given clear and adequate notice that [the IPA application] is under consideration'.[379] Most, but not all, case law has followed suit.[380]

### 4.2.4 Burden of specific identification

Linked to adequate notice is the notion that the burden rest on the RSD authority to identify a specific part or parts of the country considered to offer a viable IPA. In their 2003 report, Hathaway and Foster, considered that procedural fairness dictated that 'at a minimum, the applicant must be given clear and adequate notice that the adjudicating authority intends to canvass the possibility of denying status on internal protection grounds. This includes specific notice as to the specific location which is proffered as an IPA, with adequate opportunity to prepare a case in rebuttal.'[381] In the 2003 Guidelines, UNHCR states that (as part of the burden on the decision maker to establish that an IPA is relevant) 'it is up to the party asserting this to identify the proposed area of relocation and provide evidence establishing that it is a reasonable alternative for the individual concerned'.[382] However, there has not been unanimity about this. Some leading cases are adamant that there is such a requirement.[383] Others are more nuanced, emphasising that it is too demanding to require precise identification.[384]

## 4.3. Conclusions on Essential Elements of the IPA Test in Article 1A(2)

It can be seen that whilst the existence of a list of basic propositions covering most of the contents of the IPA concept represents a significant development, it is still more

---

[379] 'Summary Conclusions: Internal Protection/Relocation/Flight Alternative' (n 1) para 7. Support for a similar proposition can also be sourced from IHRL, the principles of effective remedy, and the 'right to be heard' in particular, Schultz (2018) (n 1) 283; see also Hathaway and Foster (2003) (n 1) 414–15.

[380] See e.g. *Rasaratnam* (n 71); *Thirunavukkarasu* (n 71); and other Canadian cases cited in Waldman (n 1) 450–54. However, Waldman notes a decision by Cullen J in *Kaler v MEI* [1994] FCTD No IMM-794-93, considering that the requirement was only that an applicant had had 'ample opportunity to speak to the IFA issue'. In *AA (Pakistan) v IPAT & Anor* IEHC 497, Humphrey J doubted that there was such a duty; but in *NNM* [2020] IEHC 590, Burns J cited Clark J in *KD (Nigeria) v RAT* [2013] IEHC 481, para 11 to the contrary.

[381] Hathaway and Foster (2003) (n 1) 414–15, who cite in support *Thirunavukkarasu* (n 71) 595–96 and an Austrian Administrative Court, *VwGH 95/20/0295* [1996].

[382] UNHCR Guidelines No 4 (n 1) para 34.

[383] See e.g. Kelley (n 1) 11 (at footnote 19). However, Waldman (n 1) 454 regards the judicial position in Canada as being now quite clear—that the decision maker must clearly identify the geographical areas that are being considered.

[384] See e.g. *Refugee and Protection Officer v BA (Nigeria)* [2022] NZHC 706 (in which the Court was satisfied that Lagos served as an unarticulated proxy for the rest of Nigeria) and (in the context of complementary protection) *CR1026* (n 60) para 40: 'it will [not] be necessary in every case for a decision maker to identify with precision the proposed place of relocation and undertake the analysis of reasonableness in relation to that precise place. In some cases it may be that the reliable information available to the decision maker demonstrates that the risk of harm of the kind described in Arts 6 and 7 of the ICCPR exists only in one place or area, or a couple or few places or areas, within the applicant's country of nationality, and that elsewhere the country is relevantly risk free. In such cases, it is accurate to say that the burden would be upon the applicant for complementary protection, once sufficiently alerted to the significance of the information available to the decision maker, to present reasons why it would nonetheless be unreasonable to expect the applicant to relocate to any place beyond the affected places or areas.'

limited than some commentators would wish. For example, it does not include the notion that the IPA must provide 'additional' protection beyond protection against persecution. Whilst that is strongly advocated by the MGs and is also integral to the UNHCR notion of 'reasonableness', it cannot be said to have been attained broad consensus, due to the continuing debates over the concepts of protection and 'being persecuted'. In particular, it is to be doubted that 'protection against persecution' can properly be limited to a mere absence of serious harm. As we addressed in Chapter 7, even in the 'being persecuted' inquiry, protection has positive as well as negative qualities. If that is correct, then the contrast between it and 'affirmative protection' cannot be as stated at least in the MGs.

## 5 Conclusions

This chapter has set out why the IPA analysis has justifiably been accepted by most to be an integral part of the refugee definition. It has been found to have sufficient anchorage in VCLT rules and is particularly enjoined by the principle of surrogacy, since international protection should not be required if internal protection is available.

After close analysis of the three main approaches to the IPA concept—the 'reasonableness' analysis set out in UNHCR Guidelines No 4; the Michigan Guidelines; and the human rights approach—it has been concluded that the human rights approach is the most coherent, although it appears possible that the UNHCR Guidelines No 4 could be adapted to bring them more in line with such an approach without too much difficulty.

One key conclusion reached in this chapter is that treating the relevant standard of protection within the refugee definition as a whole as being a sufficiently severe violation of human rights does *not* mean that such a level of violation must be shown *in the IPA*. Conversely, accepting that the threshold of human rights violations necessary to establish a viable *IPA* is *less than* the serious harm/sufficient severity threshold does not mean accepting that the standard is less when it comes to placing the IPA analysis into the holistic assessment needed to determine whether, within the meaning of Article 1A(2), there is *national* protection against persecution. To maintain otherwise would conflict with the agreed position in all the main approaches that the IPA is not an independent concept, and that the IPA analysis must be 'tied back' to the key terms of the refugee definition. The IPA is only part of the assessment of whether protection against serious harm is available in the applicant's country.

The analysis in this chapter also has implications for the controversial issue of whether protection in the IPA must have some *additional* quality beyond that in play when assessing well-founded fear of being persecuted in the home area. Given the position reached in Chapter 7 that protection as an ingredient of the meaning of 'being persecuted' must embody several positive qualities (and thus be more than the mere negative quality of the absence of persecution),[385] the precise ambit of the avowed notion of 'affirmative protection' (as applied in particular in the MGs) still lacks clarity.

---

[385] See pp. 445–446.

The claimed contrast between a (supposedly) wholly negative concept of protection in play in the 'being persecuted' inquiry and affirmative protection is a false one, since even within the 'being persecuted' inquiry, protection must be shown to have positive as well as negative qualities. However, it remains valid to describe the test of protection in the IPA context as additional, so long as it is strictly understood to function as an amelioration for the deficits in protection terms, caused by the need to relocate away from the persecution arising in an applicant's home area, to access somewhere else, and to settle there. In this context, the principle that the requisite conditions in the IPA must be such as to not compel an applicant to return to their home area (albeit that is still a high test), has an important role, since it may require protection against non-persecutory harms.

That there continue to be significant disagreements about approaches to the IPA test and its proper textual 'home' must be a cause for concern, given that the concept is one to which refugee decision makers frequently have recourse and that the refugee definition should be easily understandable. However, upon examination it is clear that despite such disagreements there is very considerable consensus about the substantive contents of the IPA test. This fact should be seen to represent an important level of progress towards greater consensus regarding the refugee definition. In light of the above discussion the following basic propositions, followed by several suggested propositions, can be identified:

## 5.1 Basic Propositions

1. IPA analysis requires an individual assessment.
2. IPA analysis is forward-looking.
3. The IPA analysis is premised on a prior finding of well-founded fear of being persecuted for a Convention reason in the home area.
4. An IPA must, as a precondition, be safe in the sense that it is both free from a well-founded fear of persecution and accessible.
5. The conditions in the IPA must not be such as would compel an applicant to return to the home area.
6. In cases that call for an IPA analysis, the causal nexus requirement of the refugee definition is satisfied simply by virtue of an applicant being able to show a well-founded fear of being persecuted for a Convention reason in their home area.

## 5.2 Suggested Propositions

1. The concept of IPA is an integral part of the refugee definition. It would be contrary to the principle of surrogacy if an applicant could qualify as a refugee even though he or she had a viable IPA.
2. The IPA analysis must be tied back to the refugee definition; it is not a test independent of whether an applicant has a well-founded fear of being persecuted in their country of origin.

3. An IPA must, as a precondition, be accessible (increasingly understood to mean that it must be safe practically and legally to travel to, gain admittance into, and settle in).
4. To be a viable IPA, the alternative part or parts of the country must be a place in which the applicant can settle. Settlement means stay that is more than temporary.
5. Accepting that harms at a lesser threshold than ill-treatment can establish that there is no internal protection in *a part of the country* should not mean that assessment of whether there is protection against persecution in *the country as a whole* is assessed at a lower threshold also.
6. In order to ensure that the IPA analysis is tied back to the refugee definition, it is vital that IPA analysis contains a final stage in which the assessment of risk in any putative IPA is incorporated into the overall assessment of whether there is a well-founded fear of being persecuted in the country of origin.
7. Ordinarily the refugee status determining authority has:
   (i) the burden of raising IPA as an issue;
   (ii) the duty to give notice that an IPA is under active consideration; and
   (iii) a duty to specifically identify (but not necessarily precisely) a part or parts of the country that are said to afford a viable IPA.

# 9
# The Availment Clause: 'To Avail Himself of the Protection'
## ('Se Réclamer de la Protection')

| | | | |
|---|---|---|---|
| Introduction | 545 | 3.3 Context | 568 |
| 1 Availment | 547 | 3.4 Object and Purpose | 569 |
| 1.1 Inability and Unwillingness | 548 | 3.5 Article 31(3) VCLT | 571 |
| 1.2 'Or, Owing to Such Fear' | 550 | 3.6 Article 32 VCLT | 571 |
| 1.3 'Protection of the Country of Nationality' | 550 | 3.7 Article 31(4): Special Meaning | 572 |
| 1.4 Return | 550 | 4 The Availment Clause Reconsidered | 572 |
| 2 History and Background | 551 | 4.1 Difficulties with the External Protection Reading | 573 |
| 2.1 Predecessor Instruments | 551 | 4.2 Difficulties with the Internal Protection Reading | 576 |
| 2.2 *Travaux Préparatoires* | 553 | 4.3 A Non-Substantive Role? | 578 |
| 2.2.1 Protection as external protection | 553 | 4.4 The Availment Clause as Combining Internal and External Protection | 579 |
| 2.2.2 Relevance of internal protection | 554 | 4.5 Practical Consequences: The Way Forward | 581 |
| 2.2.3 Role of protection as additional requirement in its own right | 555 | 5 Conclusions | 583 |
| 2.3 Post-1951 Understandings | 556 | 5.1 Basic Propositions | 584 |
| 3 Application of VCLT Rules | 565 | 5.2 Suggested Propositions | 584 |
| 3.1 Good Faith | 565 | | |
| 3.2 Ordinary Meaning | 565 | | |

## Introduction

[ ... ] and is unable or, owing to such fear, is unwilling to avail himself of the protection of that country; or who, not having a nationality and being outside the country of his former habitual residence is unable, or, owing to such fear, is unwilling to return to it.

[ ... ] *et qui ne peut ou, du fait de cette crainte, ne veut se réclamer de la protection de ce pays; ou qui, si elle n'a pas de nationalité et se trouve hors du pays dans lequel elle avait sa résidence habituelle, ne peut ou, en raison de ladite crainte, ne veut y retourner.*[1]

---

[1] Convention Relating to the Status of Refugees (adopted 28 July 1951, entered into force 22 April 1954) 189 UNTS 137, Article 1A(2).

*The Refugee Definition in International Law.* Hugo Storey, Oxford University Press. © Hugo Storey 2023.
DOI: 10.1093/oso/9780198842644.003.0009

This portion of the refugee definition is mostly referred to as the 'protection' or 'availment' clause/limb/branch. Neither is strictly accurate since textually the references to availment and protection apply only to nationals; for stateless persons the focus is solely on return. However, to propose a different shorthand would just add confusion. Given the controversy over the meaning of 'protection', this study uses the more neutral 'availment' tag.

In the previous three chapters, it was concluded that a human rights approach needs to be taken to the 'being persecuted' element of the refugee definition and that taking such an approach requires interpreting this element as a severe violation of human rights, an approach that presupposes ineffective state protection.[2] It was also argued that in analysing the meaning of the concept of protection it was necessary to look to the availment clause as both the locus of this concept and the source for two qualities of protection, namely ability and willingness to protect. Notwithstanding the inevitable overlap with some of the analysis in the previous three chapters, it remains necessary to consider the availment clause of the definition in its own right by application of the Vienna Convention on the Law of Treaties (VCLT) rules. Consideration must also be given to how this part of the definition fits with other elements.

The availment (or protection) clause of the refugee definition has been subject to highly divergent interpretations and great uncertainty persists about its meaning and role. Whether, however, this divergence and uncertainty has had a practical impact on the outcome of cases is a separate matter addressed towards the end of this chapter.

Disagreements over interpretation of this clause have been of various kinds. Historically the main debate about the meaning of the clause took the form of a clash between the 'accountability' versus the 'protection' theories.[3] As we shall see, this has largely been resolved, but division has remained firstly over whether the clause denotes 'external' or 'internal' protection and secondly over whether it is to be given a 'narrow(er)' or 'wider' meaning. A further dimension to the debate concerns whether it is a separate element of the definition in the sense of setting out a substantive requirement (or substantive requirements) that must be fulfilled. For some it is a separate element but for others it has at best only a vestigial role. Among those who view it as a separate element, there are differences over its relative importance, some seeing it, for example, as secondary. Among those who do not accept that it is a separate element, there are some who nevertheless see it as encapsulating the main purpose of the definition, namely surrogate protection. In addition, some textbooks scarcely address this clause in its own right.[4] That there is still such lack of clarity after more than seventy years about this clause might be thought a highly unsatisfactory state of affairs.

---

[2] See e.g. p. 366 and pp. 441–442.

[3] Guy S Goodwin-Gill, *The Refugee in International Law* (2nd edn, Clarendon Press 1996) 72–73; Walter Kälin, 'Non-State Agents of Persecution and the Inability of the State to Protect' (2001) 15(3) Georgetown Immigration Law Journal 415. See also Jennifer Moore, 'Whither the Accountability Theory: Second-Class Status for Third-Party Refugees as a Threat to International Refugee Protection' (2001) 13(1) IJRL 32; Reinhard Marx, 'The Notion of Persecution by Non-State Agents in German Jurisprudence' (2001) 15 Georgetown Immigration Law Journal 447; Catherine Phuong, 'Persecution by Third Parties and European Harmonization of Asylum Policies' (2001) 16 Georgetown Immigration Law Journal 81, 82–83; James C Hathaway and Michelle Foster, *The Law of Refugee Status* (2nd edn, CUP 2014) 303–06; Guy S Goodwin-Gill and Jane McAdam (with Emma Dunlop), *The Refugee in International Law* (4th edn, OUP 2021) 28–30, 70–9.

[4] See e.g. Jean-Yves Carlier et al, *Who Is a Refugee? A Comparative Case Law Study* (Brill 1997).

Already from the above summary it will be apparent that in existing analyses of this clause a number of key terms are deployed, not always with a clear meaning. It is helpful therefore to start by clarifying what is meant by some of the main terms in use.

As regards 'internal protection', what is meant in this context (not to be confused with the 'internal protection alternative') is national protection, that is the protection afforded by a state to its own citizens and other persons within its own territory.

'External protection' is used to encompass both diplomatic and consular protection, although *stricto sensu*,[5] 'diplomatic protection' has played virtually no part even from the beginning. The focus of the report that heavily influenced the work of the drafters of the 1951 Convention, namely *A Study of Statelessness*,[6] was those actions that consular representatives undertake in order to ensure better standards of treatment for the nationals of the country abroad, in particular the provision of 'administrative assistance', meaning the issuance and authentication of certificates, the issuance and renewal of passports, and so forth.[7]

With regard to references to 'narrow' or wider' meanings, what is meant depends heavily on context. Accordingly, all that can be said in general is that the term 'wider' in this chapter will be taken to mean protection that includes both internal and external protection.

In the remainder of this chapter, analysis will focus on the specific components of the availment of protection clause that bear on its scope; a brief summary of the different views taken about it both prior to and after the coming into force of the 1951 Refugee Convention; a detailed treatment of the notion of protection by applying VCLT rules; an evaluation of the two main views that have been taken as to the meaning of 'protection' in the availment clause; and some reflection of what impact different interpretations have had on the outcome of decisions. At the end, an attempt is made to distil basic propositions that have achieved wide acceptance, followed by a number of suggested propositions arising out of evaluation of the main debates over meaning.

## 1 Availment

What sense is to be accorded to the verb 'avail' depends very much on what meaning is ascribed to 'protection'. The latter term will be analysed later, but it can simply be noted here that in dictionary definitions, 'to avail oneself' means to use or take advantage;[8] read literally, it conveys some action—or the opportunity to take action—on the

---

[5] According to a 1997 International Law Commission (ILC) Working Group report (Yearbook of the ILC, 49th session, Doc A/52/10, para 177) diplomatic protection had two different senses: 'diplomatic protection' properly so called, that is, a 'formal claim made by a State in respect of an injury to one of its nationals which has not been redressed through local remedies'; and 'certain diplomatic and consular activities for the assistance and protection of nationals as envisaged by articles 3 and 5 respectively of the Vienna Convention on Diplomatic Relations of 1961 and the Vienna Convention on Consular Relations of 1963'.

[6] Ad Hoc Committee on Refugees and Stateless Persons, A Study of Statelessness, United Nations, August 1949, Lake Success—New York (1 August 1949) E/1112/Add.1.

[7] Antonio Fortin, 'The Meaning of "Protection" in the Refugee Definition' (2000) 12(4) IJRL 548, 554.

[8] OED Online defines 'to avail oneself' as 'to benefit oneself or profit by; to take advantage of, turn to account'<https://www.oed.com> accessed 27 July 2021.

part of an individual. This makes sense in relation to significant aspects of consular protection, since nationals outside their own country typically approach the consular authorities representing that country for a passport or a certificate of citizenship.[9] However, if protection is to be ascribed a wider meaning, then it must be seen to also encompass acts or omissions on the part of the *authorities* of the home state, whether they take place within its own territory or abroad operating diplomatic and/or consular activities.

The availment clause breaks down into two main components, one relating to nationals, the other to stateless persons. For nationals, the relevant clause is:

> [ … ] and is unable or, owing to such fear, is unwilling to avail himself of the protection of that country.

For stateless persons, the relevant clause is:

> [ … ] or who, not having a nationality and being outside the country of his former habitual residence, is unable or, owing to such fear, is unwilling to return to it.

For both nationals and stateless persons, there are requirements to show inability or unwillingness. However, whereas in relation to unwillingness the applicant must show it is 'owing to' a well-founded fear of persecution, in relation to inability there is no such requirement. Both nationals and stateless persons are required to be 'outside the country'. However, whereas for nationals the requirement is that they are unable or unwilling to avail themselves of the protection of the country, for stateless persons there is no requirement relating to protection; rather they have to show that they are unable or unwilling to return. Under the wording of both provisions ('unable or, … unwilling') it is sufficient for being granted refugee status that one of the alternatives (being unable/unwilling) is present.

## 1.1 Inability and Unwillingness

Regarding the terms 'unable' and 'unwilling' the 1979 United Nations High Commissioner for Refugees (UNHCR) Handbook, states that:

> 98. Being *unable* to avail himself of such protection implies circumstances that are beyond the will of the person concerned. There may, for example, be a state of war, civil war or other grave disturbance, which prevents the country of nationality from extending protection or makes such protection ineffective. Protection by the country of nationality may also have been denied to the applicant. Such denial of protection may confirm or strengthen the applicant's fear of persecution, and may indeed be an element of persecution.

---

[9] Atle Grahl-Madsen, 'Protection of Refugees By Their Country of Origin' (1986) 11 Yale Journal of International Law 362, 363.

99. What constitutes a refusal of protection must be determined according to the circumstances of the case. If it appears that the applicant has been denied services (e.g., refusal of a national passport or extension of its validity, or denial of admittance to the home territory) normally accorded to his co-nationals, this may constitute a refusal of protection within the definition.

100. The term *unwilling* refers to refugees who refuse to accept the protection of the Government of the country of their nationality. It is qualified by the phrase 'owing to such fear'. Where a person is willing to avail himself of the protection of his home country, such willingness would normally be incompatible with a claim that he is outside that country 'owing to well-founded fear of persecution'. Whenever the protection of the country of nationality is available, and there is no ground based on well-founded fear for refusing it, the person concerned is not in need of international protection and is not a refugee.[10]

La Forest J in *Ward* stated that 'unable' means 'physically or literally unable', whereas 'unwilling' means that 'protection from the state is not wanted for some reason, though not impossible'.[11] He noted in this context that originally the draft version of the refugee definition linked 'unwilling' with applicants who were entitled to seek the protection of their state, whereas 'unable' was used in connection with stateless individuals. However, when the definition was revised to its current form, 'unable' was used in connection with both nationals and stateless persons.

La Forest J also appeared to approve the additional interpretation given earlier by the Canadian Federal Court in *Zalzali* that:

[ ... ] the natural meaning of the words 'is unable' assumes an objective inability on the part of the claimant, and the fact that 'is unable' is, in contrast to 'is unwilling', not qualified by 'by reason of that fear' [the Canadian version of Article 1A(2)'s 'owing to such fear' clause], seems to me to confirm that the inability in question is governed by objective criteria which can be verified independently of the fear experienced, and so independently of the acts which prompted that fear and their perpetrators.[12]

Even though *Zalzali* and *Ward* are examples of cases subscribing to an 'internal protection' reading, the former's construction of the meaning of 'is unable' as denoting an objective inability would seem pertinent to either an internal or external protection reading.[13]

---

[10] UNHCR, Handbook on Procedures and Criteria for Determining Refugee Status and Guidelines on International Protection under the 1951 Convention and the 1967 Protocol Relating to the Status Of Refugees (Geneva, 2019, reissued in 2019) (UNHCR Handbook or Handbook) paras 98–100 (emphases in original).
[11] *Canada (AG) v Ward* [1993] 2 SCR 689.
[12] *Zalzali v Canada (MEI)* [1991] 3 FC 605.
[13] An example of 'inability' in the context of consular protection would be where a state provided no consular facilities.

## 1.2 'Or, Owing to Such Fear'

The fact that the definition already requires in the opening words of the first paragraph that a person show they are outside their country owing to a well-founded fear of persecution ('owing to a well-founded fear of being persecuted') raises the question as to what additional role if any, does this further element—'owing to such fear'—play? The specific answer appears to depend very much on the view taken of the meaning of the availment clause overall, but the words on their face suggest (as does the UNHCR Handbook's interpretation of them in paragraph 100) that an applicant has to show a causal link between any unwillingness (on the part of nationals, to seek protection; or in the case of stateless persons, to return) and the well-founded fear of persecution.[14]

## 1.3 'Protection of the Country of Nationality'

Issues relating to 'country of nationality' were dealt with in Chapter 4 (on Nationality and Statelessness). 'Protection' is obviously a key component of the availment clause. The position taken in Chapter 7, section 3.2 was that whatever meaning the concept of protection has in the refugee definition, it must essentially be unitary. However, when considering the concept's actual location in the availment clause, there remains to be explored the issue of its scope and in particular whether it concerns external rather than internal protection or both.

## 1.4 Return

'Return' in the context of the availment clause relates solely to return of a stateless person to the country of former habitual residence. This issue was addressed in more detail in Chapter 4.[15] There is wide acceptance that since the material issue concerns inability or unwillingness [to return], it covers both legal as well as practical obstacles to return.[16] Further, there is now strong acceptance that Article 1A(2) requires a hypothetical assessment of risk on return, asking what would happen if a person were returned. As stated by Foster and Lambert, '[w]here there is a question about returnability, decision-makers across all jurisdictions, simply assess the claim on the hypothesis that return is possible, with the assessment focusing on the likely fate of the applicant should return be effected'.[17]

---

[14] Andreas Zimmermann and Claudia Mahler, 'Article 1A, para 2' in Andreas Zimmermann (ed), *The 1951 Convention Relating to the Status of Refugees and Its 1967 Protocol: A Commentary* (OUP 2011) 444 (see also ibid 323–24).

[15] See pp. 242–245.

[16] Ardi Imseis, 'Statelessness and Convention Refugee Determination: An Examination of the Palestinian Experience at the Immigration and Refugee Board of Canada' (1997) 31(2) University of British Columbia Law Review 317; Michelle Foster and Hélène Lambert, *International Refugee Law and the Protection of Stateless Persons* (OUP 2019) 99–103.

[17] Foster and Lambert (n 16) 102.

## 2 History and Background

### 2.1 Predecessor Instruments

The wording of the availment clause is a borrowing: virtually the same or similar formulations can be found in the main predecessor instruments.[18] As noted by Skran, the League of Nations instruments were confined to specified groups of refugees and all contained definitions that imposed two requirements: first, a certain national or ethnic origin; and second, a lack of protection by the country of origin.[19] And in all these instruments 'protection of the Government' meant external protection, that is, diplomatic and consular protection abroad.[20] Correspondingly, for those who met both requirements, the envisaged substitute protection was the issuing of refugee travel documents, certification of identity, civil status, profession, etc.

That 'protection' continued to have the same meaning of external protection even in the immediate predecessor instrument—the International Refugee Organisation (IRO) Constitution—is confirmed by Holborn's definition of a refugee under it as:

> [ ... ] a person who has no consul or diplomatic mission to whom to turn, and who does not benefit from reciprocal agreements between countries maintaining friendly relations which protect the nationals of one country living on the territory of another.[21]

For 'protection' in these predecessor instruments to denote external protection made complete sense for two main reasons.

First, such an approach was entirely in accord with these instruments' group-based classification of refugeehood. Once a person could establish mere membership of a particular category—e.g. Russian, Armenian, Assyrian, Assyro-Chaldean, Turkish, etc.—the only remaining issue was whether there was some obvious reason not to grant them protection. As noted by Jackson in relation to all these definitions:

> In showing that he was without national protection, the individual applicant was not per se required to justify his refugee status according to the substantive reasons why he had left or did not wish to return to his country of origin, *since these reasons were already implicit in the determination of the refugee character of the group to which he belongs, which created a 'presumption' in favour of individual refugee status*. It was, however, still necessary for the individual to establish that he did not enjoy the protection of his country of origin.[22]

---

[18] See Claudena Skran, 'Historical Developments of International Refugee Law' in Zimmermann (n 14) 9–30.
[19] Claudena Skran, *Refugees in Inter-War Europe: The Emergence of a Regime* (OUP 1995).
[20] ibid 110.
[21] Louise W Holborn, *The International Refugee Organization: A Specialized Agency of the United Nations: Its History and Work 1946–1952* (OUP 1956) 311.
[22] Ivor C Jackson, *The Refugee Concept in Group Situations* (Kluwer Law International 1999) 22–23 (emphasis added).

Jackson noted discussions identifying concern that the wide group-based definition should not lead to 'false refugees', e.g. persons who did not in fact have substantive reasons for leaving the specified countries of origin. It was recognised that the loss of nationality could sometimes be due merely to a conflict of nationality laws or free choice. The Representative of Czechoslovakia had stated during the international Conference of 8 and 9 February 1938, leading to the adoption of the 1938 Convention that the draft provision 'should [not] be applicable to persons who left Germany for other than political, religious or racial reasons, e.g. persons prosecuted for breaches of the common law or offense against revenue regulations'.[23] It was this concern that resulted in the formula used in the 1938 Convention imposing the specific qualification, 'persons who leave Germany for reasons of purely personal convenience are not included in this definition'.

A second reason why it made sense for protection to be construed as external protection in these instruments was that at the time external protection was extremely meaningful and consequential for refugees, as without it they could be in a vulnerable and inferior position. Unlike ordinary aliens, who could still turn to their country of nationality for diplomatic and consular protection, refugees were aliens 'in every country'. As was stated in a note from the Director General of the IRO in 1950:

> A refugee is an anomaly in international law, and it is often impossible to deal with him in accordance with the legal provision designed to apply to aliens who receive assistance from their national authorities. When the ordinary citizen goes abroad, his own national authorities look after him and provide him with certain advantages. If he resides in a foreign country, the organisation of his entire legal and economic life depends upon his possession of a nationality. The refugee who enjoys no nationality is placed in an abnormal and inferior position which not only reduces his social value but destroys his self-confidence.[24]

Denial of external protection could cause vulnerability to expulsion (for illegal stay); inability to get a passport or other national identity document; inability to move freely internally or to move to another country; and denial of access to the labour market. Even civil acts like marriage and divorce, conclusion of contracts, and acquisition and possession of real estate could be problematic. As Kälin has observed, '[c]ontemporary refugees themselves emphasized the crucial role of diplomatic and consular protection by pointing out that they 'enjoy no legal protection such as is accorded to the citizens of every country by their diplomatic representatives. This imposes a heavy burden on their lives.'[25]

There is another feature of the predecessor instruments already touched on, but needing underlining, given the ongoing debate about whether the availment clause has now only a vestigial role. In all of them, lack of protection featured as an independent basis on which to achieve refugeehood.[26] Indeed, under the Constitution of

---

[23] League of Nations Document Con.C.S.R.A./p.v.4 (1938) 12, cited in Jackson (n 22) 24 (at footnote 38).
[24] Cited by Fortin (n 7) 559.
[25] Kälin (n 3) 419. He cites Skran (n 19) 103 (quoting a letter from Russian Refugee Organizations in London to Lord Kobert Cecil of 13 August 1923).
[26] Skran (n 18).

the IRO, lack of state protection provided an alternative basis upon which to qualify for relief.[27]

## 2.2 Travaux Préparatoires

### 2.2.1 Protection as external protection

There are also significant indications that the drafters of the 1951 Convention likewise understood the availment of protection formulation imported from predecessor instruments to denote (wholly or mainly) external protection.[28] The 1949 Report of the Secretary-General, *A Study of Statelessness*, stated that:

> The conferment of a status is not sufficient in itself to regularize the standing of stateless persons and to bring them into the orbit of the law; they must also be linked to an independent organ which would to some extent make up for the absence of national protection and render them certain services which the authorities of a country of origin render to their nationals resident abroad.[29]

The Ad Hoc Committee set up shortly after remarked that 'unable' refers primarily to stateless refugees but includes also refugees possessing a nationality who are refused passports or other protection by their own government. Mr Robinson of Israel pointed out that what was designated in the draft convention as stateless de facto (in contrast to those who were stateless de jure), 'was in effect merely the lack of diplomatic protection'.[30] Mr Henkin, during a discussion on proposals for wording of this clause, noted that:

> [ ... ] 'protection' was a term of art, and meant diplomatic protection, which, could only be given by the country of nationality and not by the country of habitual residence. Hence, refugees included persons with a nationality who were *unwilling* to avail themselves of the protection of the government of the country of their nationality or those who were unable to enjoy such protection because their government refused it, and persons who had no nationality and were thus *unable* to avail themselves of the protection of any government.[31]

---

[27] See Charles S Ellison and Anjum Gupta, 'Unwilling or Unable? The Failure to Conform the Nonstate Actor Standard in Asylum Claims to the Refugee Act' (2021) 52 Colum Hum Rts L Rev 441, 456.

[28] The two main studies that have looked at what the *travaux préparatoires* disclose concerning the meaning of protection in the availment clause are by Fortin (n 7) and Kälin (n 3). Guy S Goodwin-Gill and Jane McAdam, *The Refugee in International Law* (3rd edn OUP) 22 (at foonote 30) note that the external protection reading has 'solid historical roots'. See also Goodwin-Gill and McAdam (n 3) 21 (at footnote 31).

[29] The report was submitted in two parts: UN Doc E/1112 (1 February 1949) and UN Doc E/1112/Add.l (n 6), submitted to the eighth and ninth sessions of ECOSOC, respectively. The passage above is to be found at 68 (see Fortin (n 7) 560 (at footnote 35)).

[30] UN Ad Hoc Committee on Refugees and Stateless Persons, Ad Hoc Committee on Statelessness and Related Problems, First Session: Summary Record of the Fourth Meeting Held at Lake Success, New York, on Wednesday, 16 January 1950, at 11 a.m. (26 January 1950) UN Doc E/AC.32/SR.4, cited by Fortin (n 7) 561 (at footnote 41).

[31] ECOSOC, Official Records, First Session, Summary Record of the Hundred and Sixtieth Meeting of the Social Committee (1950) UN Doc E/AC.7/SR.160, 6–7, cited by Fortin (n 7) 562 (at footnote 45).

Mr Humphrey, Acting President and personal representative of the Secretary General, drew attention to the fact that although both in the Secretary-General's Study and in Council resolution 116 (VI) D, reference was made only to stateless persons:

> [ ... ] it clearly emerged from the text of the first part of the Study that what was primarily contemplated was the protection of the so-called *de facto* stateless persons or refugees, in other words, persons, who for certain reasons, found themselves outside the border of the countries of which they were legally nationals, and who either could not or did not wish to avail themselves of the diplomatic protection of those countries.[32]

In light of Skran's and their own study of the *travaux*, Zimmermann and Mahler conclude that the notion of 'unable' 'refers primarily to two groups, namely on the one hand stateless refugees, and on the other hand refugees who, while legally possessing a nationality, are nevertheless refused passports or other protection by their government'.[33] They explain that a person is 'unable to avail himself of protection of that country' if that country 'would de facto not extend its protection to this very person upon his or her return, thus having the effect of the refugee not being able to successfully seek protection from persecution'.[34] The term 'unwilling' was in turn 'considered to refer to refugees who refuse to accept the protection of their respective home government'.[35]

Hathaway and Foster[36] have suggested that the references denoting external protection are scant and mainly relate to the period prior to when the drafters decided that statelessness would be dealt with in a separate instrument. However, if the latter decision was meant to signal a shift to a different understanding of protection, one would expect that would have been remarked upon during the discussions about this separation.

### 2.2.2 Relevance of internal protection

At the same time, one can discern three interrelated ways in which the drafters can be taken to have been mindful of the relevance of protection in the sense of internal protection.

First, the understanding of the refugee as someone who 'does not in fact enjoy the protection of his state of origin' was well-entrenched in predecessor instruments and

---

[32] Conference of Plenipotentiaries on the Status of Refugees and Stateless Persons: Summary Record of the 1st Meeting, held at the Palais des Nations, Geneva, on Monday, 2 July 1951 (19 July 1951) UN Doc A/CONF.2/SR.1, 5, cited by Fortin (n 7) 562–63.

[33] Zimmermann and Mahler (n 14) 443 refer to UN Ad Hoc Committee on Refugees and Stateless Persons, Report of the Ad Hoc Committee on Statelessness and Related Problems (17 February 1950) UN Doc E/1618, and UN Ad Hoc Committee on Statelessness and Related Problems, 1st Session, 5th Meeting (30 January 1950) UN Doc E/AC.32/SR.5; Nehemiah Robinson, *Convention Relating to the Status of Stateless Persons: Its History and Interpretation, A Commentary* (UNHCR 1997) 44.

[34] Zimmermann and Mahler (n 14) 443.

[35] ibid.

[36] James C Hathaway and Michelle Foster, 'Internal Protection/Relocation/Flight Alternative' in Erika Feller, Volker Türk, and Frances Nicholson (eds), *UNHCR Global Consultations, Refugee Protection in International Law* (UNHCR 2003) 374–75.

was said by Jennings in 1939 to have permeated all the arrangements and conventions concluded up to that time.[37] In opening the general debate in 1951, the High Commissioner for Refugees stated that, '[a] vital right for the refugee was that to *be protected from being returned to a country where his life or freedom would be threatened*'.[38]

Second, the drafters always clearly understood that more was at stake for refugees than mere absence of external protection and that the root of their problem was lack of protection in their home state. They may not have articulated this understanding in the same graphic way Grahl-Madsen did in his early commentary, when he urged that the lack of diplomatic or consular protection be seen as 'but a symptom of a political controversy, a deep-rooted conflict between the State and the individual, which means that the normal relationship between a State and its national (or resident) has turned into its negation, namely the relation between an oppressor (or political avenger) and his (actual or potential) victim.'[39] But the drafters' concern to prevent refoulement to home states clearly reflects an understanding of the need to focus on the likely situation facing an applicant in his or her home state.[40]

Third, and closely linked to the above, implicit in the approach taken to the notion of protection as external protection was that the beneficiaries of refugee status could be presumed to be persons who also lacked internal protection. As Grahl-Madsen termed it, '[s]ince the international community was generally aware of repression in such countries, it was unnecessary to expound on this denial of protection in the definitions'.[41] The salient point was that the person concerned was not in good standing with the new government of his home country, and the concept of denial of protection came to express this idea.[42] In similar vein, Kälin wrote that '[o]bviously, in these cases, the country of origin's denial of diplomatic and consular protection abroad was taken as sufficient evidence that the State had severed the relationship of trust and loyalty between itself and the individual'.[43]

### 2.2.3 Role of protection as additional requirement in its own right

What also emerges from the above analysis is that the drafters continued to treat the issue of protection as an additional requirement in its own right. As is clear from the statement made by Mr Henkin cited earlier, the protection requirement was understood to be *part of* the definition of a refugee.[44] Significantly, the eventual text adopts

---

[37] Robert Jennings, 'Some International Law Aspects of the Refuge Question' (1939) 20 BYIL 98, 111.
[38] Conference of Plenipotentiaries on the Status of Refugees and Stateless Persons: Summary Record of the 2nd Meeting, held at the Palais des Nations, Geneva, on Monday, 2 July 1951 (20 July 1951) UN Doc A/CONF.2/SR.2, 17 (emphasis added).
[39] Atle Grahl-Madsen, *The Status of Refugees in International Law. Volume 1: Refugee Character* (Sijthoff 1966) 98.
[40] Grahl-Madsen went on to warn against obscuring 'this basic 'ailment' with 'lack of protection, which, like so many other symptoms, are ambivalent.' See ibid 101–02. In his 1986 article, Grahl-Madsen (n 9) 375 attributed this notion to Otto Kimminich's work—see Otto Kimminich, *Der internationale Rechtsstatus des Flüchtlings* (Heymann 1962) 33–48).
[41] Grahl-Madsen (n 9) 373.
[42] ibid.
[43] Kälin (n 3) 420.
[44] See (n 31): 'Hence, refugees included persons with a nationality who were unwilling to avail themselves of the protection of the government of the country of their nationality or those who were unable to enjoy such protection because their government refused it, and persons who had no nationality and were thus unable to avail themselves of the protection of any government.'

the same conjunctive wording. Article 1A(2) requires there to be a 'well-founded fear of being persecuted' *and* that [any person] is unable or, owing to such fear, is unwilling to avail himself of the protection of that country' (emphasis added).

## 2.3 Post-1951 Understandings

The post-1951 debates about whether the availment clause concerns external or internal protection (or both) are quite a saga. Leading commentators writing in the years immediately following the signing of the Convention, saw protection as external protection. Thus Weis wrote in 1953 that 'two conditions are essential for the quality of refugee: residence outside the country of nationality or former nationality, and lack of diplomatic protection by any State'.[45] That this was the notion of protection seen to have been intended by the text of Article 1A(2) was confirmed in 1953 by Heuven Goedhart, the first United Nations High Commissioner for Refugees[46] and, in 1962, in an internal UNHCR 'Eligibility Guide'.[47]

Grahl-Madsen's major 1966 study, building mainly on German, French, and Austrian cases, likewise concluded that this part of the definition referred to 'external protection', in the sense of diplomatic or consular protection.[48] However, as noted earlier, in one of the earliest indications of disquiet with the implications of such a reading, he also voiced concerns about its overall role in the refugee definition, given that 'a person is a refugee because there is something basically wrong with the political relationship between him and the government of his home country'.[49] Despite taking the view that protection in the availment clause meant external protection, Grahl-Madsen also identified this narrow reading to have the following problem scenario:

> It is rather clumsy language when the Convention provides that in order to qualify as a 'refugee', a person must be unwilling to avail himself of protection 'owing to' fear of being persecuted upon his eventual return to the country of his nationality, yet he may have nothing to fear at the hands of the members of the foreign service of that country. The Convention would, in fact, largely be rendered meaningless if a person's claim to refugee status should depend on whether the diplomats or consular officers of his home country were likely to persecute him should he ever ask them for protection or assistance.[50]

---

[45] Paul Weis, 'Legal Aspects of the Convention of 28 July 1951 Relating to the Status of Refugees' (1953) 30 BYIL 480, cited by Grahl-Madsen (n 39) 96. See also Kälin (n 3) 425 (at footnote 74).
[46] Gerrit Jan van Heuven Goedhart, 'The Problem of Refugees' (1953) 82 Recueil des Cours 284, 286.
[47] Regarding the inability of persons possessing a nationality to avail themselves of the protection of their country, this guide stated that: '[a] person possessing a nationality is deemed to be unable to avail himself of the protection of his country if his request for what may be called normally granted protection has been refused. This protection may be diplomatic or consular in character.' See UNHCR, 'Eligibility. A Guide for the Staff of the Office of the United Nations High Commissioner for Refugees', cited by Fortin (n 7) 565 (at footnote 55) and 566 (footnote 57).
[48] Grahl-Madsen (n 39) 254–61, 381–85.
[49] ibid 100–01.
[50] Grahl-Madsen (n 39) 257; also discussed in Fortin (n 7) 575–76. In the same passage, Grahl-Madsen's proposed solution was to maintain that: '[t]he meaning of the phrase [the unwilling ... phrase] can only be that in order to be considered a "refugee", a person must be unwilling to avail himself of the protection

In 1979 the High Commissioner for Refugees, Poul Hartling, emphasized that lack of protection [in the sense of normal consular and diplomatic protection] of the refugee and the need to establish a substitute system of protection was very much linked with the manner in which the refugee was to be defined.'[51] The 1979 UNHCR Handbook on Procedures and Criteria for Determining Refugee Status seemingly followed suit. In several paragraphs devoted to the availment clause, although not defining 'protection', the Handbook gave as the only examples that:

> If it appears that the applicant has been denied services (e.g. refusal of a national passport or extension of the validity, or denial of admittance to the home territory) normally accorded to his co-nationals, this may constitute a refusal of protection within the definition.[52]

However, reflective of a wider ambivalence, in an earlier paragraph dealing with 'non-state agents', the Handbook also appeared to recognise that persecution could arise as a result of ineffective protection within the country of origin:

> Where serious discriminatory or other offensive acts are committed by the local populace, they can be considered as persecution if they are knowingly tolerated by the authorities, or if the authorities refuse, or prove unable, to offer effective protection.[53]

A similar position was taken by UNHCR in a March 1995 document on Agents of Persecution.[54]

Goodwin-Gill's major work, *The Refugee in International Law*, first published in 1983, noted without demur interpretations of the availment clause adopting an internal protection understanding, and stated that:

> Fear of persecution and lack of protection are themselves interrelated elements. The persecuted clearly do not enjoy the protection of their country of origin, while evidence of the lack of protection on either the internal or external level may create a presumption as to the likelihood of persecution and to the well-foundedness of any fear.[55]

of the State of which he is a national, and this unwillingness must be based on well-founded fear of being persecuted upon his eventual return to the territory of that State, not on reasons of personal convenience, business considerations, or the like'.

---

[51] Poul Hartling, 'Concept and Definition of "Refugee": Legal and Humanitarian Aspects', Inaugural Lecture at the Second Nordic Seminar on Refugee Law, University of Copenhagen (23 April 1979) 8, referring to the definition in Article 1A(2), cited by Kälin (n 3) 426 (at footnote 79).

[52] UNHCR Handbook (n 10) para 99.

[53] ibid para 65. See also ibid para 100, which addresses the meaning of the term 'unwilling'. It concludes that '[w]henever the protection of the country of nationality is available, and there is no ground based on well-founded fear for refusing it, the person concerned is not in need of international protection and is not a refugee'.

[54] UNHCR, Agents of Persecution—UNHCR Position (1995) para 3. See also UNHCR Regional Bureau for Europe, An Overview of Protection Issues in Western Europe: Legislative Trends and Positions Taken by UNHCR (1995) I European Series 3, 28–30. Both are cited by Kälin (n 3) 423 (at footnote 63).

[55] Guy S Goodwin-Gill, *The Refugee in International Law* (1st edn, OUP 1983) 38; see Goodwin-Gill and McAdam (n 28) 30–31; Goodwin-Gill and McAdam (n 3) 70.

By contrast, Hathaway's *The Law of Refugee Status* (TLRS) took an approach to the availment clause that unequivocally construed protection as internal protection. Without any engagement with the external protection approach as advanced by Weis and Grahl-Madsen and others, he stated that: 'there is a failure of protection where a government is unwilling to defend citizens against private harm, as well as in situations of objective inability to provide meaningful protection'.[56] Elsewhere he made clear that in adopting this approach he drew on both academic and judicial precedents. In respect of the former, he noted the perspective advanced by Shacknove and others that primary status had to be given to the 'municipal relationship between an individual and her state' and that persecution essentially concerns the breakdown of the protection to be expected of the minimally legitimate state.[57] He also referred to a number of Canadian cases that had clearly taken the same path of automatically recasting the availment clause into a test of a government's inability and unwillingness to protect.[58]

Drawing on analyses by Hathaway and Goodwin-Gill among others, the Canadian decision in *Ward*[59] represents the first definitive statement at a supreme court level[60] of the view that the primary object and rationale of the refugee definition is the principle of surrogacy. According to this view, refugee protection compensates for lack of internal protection. The Court treated the availment clause's concepts of ability and willingness as straightforwardly pertaining to the authorities in the country of origin. It is interesting to note, however, that in *Ward*, La Forest J did not in terms reject the submission of the Canadian Council of Refugees that 'protection' in this part of the definition concerned only external protection and he seemed in one paragraph to suggest that such a reading would be appropriate because internal protection was to be addressed in the well-founded fear of persecution element.[61]

In the second edition of *The Refugee in International Law*, published in 1996, Goodwin-Gill, having noted that '[l]ack of protection by the government of the country of origin is already an element in the statutory definition of the refugee', stated that:

'Protection' here implies both 'internal protection', in the sense of effective guarantees in matters such as life, liberty, and security of person; and 'external protection', in

---

[56] James C Hathaway, *The Law of Refugee Status* (Butterworths Limited 1991) 127. Significantly, whilst he clearly derived the notion of internal protection from the wording of the availment clause (see ibid 133) Hathaway's treatment of it is part of his chapter (ch 4) on persecution.

[57] ibid 133, citing Andrew Shacknove, 'Who Is a Refugee?' (1985) 95 Ethics 274, 277. Hathaway (n 56) 125, also sought to derive this position from Grahl-Madsen's observation in Grahl-Madsen (n 39) 97–101, that primary status is to be accorded to the municipal relationship between an individual and her state.

[58] Hathaway (n 56) 124–33.

[59] *Ward* (n 11).

[60] In ibid, the SC upheld the internal protection approach taken by the Federal Court in such cases as *Zalzali* (n 12) 609–10.

[61] See ibid: 'The Council for Refugees and the Board argued, convincingly in my view, that there is simply no need for a judicial gloss of the meaning of "unwilling" and "unable". As the Council argued, there is a clear distinction between the state's being unable to protect its citizens while they are situated in that state (which is considered in the "fear of persecution" analysis) and the individual's being "unable" to avail him or herself of that protection, which refers to the relationship between the individual and the state outside the country.'

the sense of diplomatic protection, including documentation of nationals abroad and recognition of the right of nationals to return.[62]

UK courts followed *Ward*. In *ex parte Adan*,[63] Lord Lloyd of Berwick also endorsed the Hathaway approach. In *Butler*,[64] Keith J of the New Zealand Court of Appeal made clear his support for an internal protection reading. In *Horvath*, fully accepting the analysis in *Ward* and its endorsement of Hathaway's interpretation, Lord Hope stated that '[i]f the principle of surrogacy is applied, the criterion must be whether the alleged lack of protection is such as to indicate that the home state is unable or unwilling to discharge *its* duty to establish and operate a system for the protection against persecution of its own nationals'. Lord Lloyd of Berwick added that 'the principle of surrogate protection finds its proper place in the second half of Article 1A(2). If there is a failure of protection by the country of origin, the applicant will be *unable to avail himself* of that country's protection.'[65]

Writing in 2000, Nathwani excoriated reliance placed on the notion of diplomatic protection for interpreting the availment clause. He depicted it as having been sidelined by developments in international human rights law.[66] His conclusion was that '[w]e should interpret the Convention dynamically and take account of these changed circumstances; in this sense, Weis' theory has been overtaken, if it was ever adequate'.[67] In October the same year, Walter Kälin gave a speech to the International Association of Refugee Law Judges (IARLJ) Conference in Bern, Switzerland in which he concluded that, despite the strong evidence that the Convention's drafters intended the availment clause to refer to external protection, such considerations should be overridden by an object and purpose approach, such that 'protection' is to be understood in the wide sense to incorporate internal protection. He wrote that:

> These changes provide strong reasons for an interpretation of the text of Article 1A(2) CSR51 giving the notion of 'protection' in the 'unable to avail himself...' clause an extended meaning that also covers internal protection. This presents a logical extension of the original idea of the drafters of the 1951 Convention that regarded persecution and lack of protection as the two core requirements of the refugee definition.[68]

He considered that, applying an evolutive approach, the diplomatic protection meaning intended by the drafters stood to be revisited. For him:

> [ ... ] this clause has lost much of its original meaning as the function of diplomatic and consular protection has fundamentally changed since the 1951 Convention was

---

[62] Goodwin-Gill (n 3) 16. See also Goodwin-Gill and McAdam (n 3) 28, 156–58.
[63] *R v SSHD, ex parte Adan* [1999] 1 AC 293.
[64] *Butler v A-G* [1999] NZAR 205, para 32.
[65] *Horvath v SSHD* [2000] UKHL 37 (emphases in original).
[66] Niraj Nathwani, 'The Purpose of Asylum' (2000) 12(3) IJRL 354, 358: 'The importance of the lack of diplomatic protection in explaining refugee law might have been plausible in the 1960s. Because of the lack of binding and effective human rights standards, the only protection for the alien seemed to be the diplomatic protection of the country of origin. However, the picture has changed drastically. In today's light, the institution of diplomatic protection is often seen as an ineffective instrument'.
[67] ibid.
[68] Kälin (n 3) 428.

drafted. Although such protection remains important in many regards, it has lost its original function of securing basic rights to aliens at a time when international human rights were virtually non-existent.[69]

Notwithstanding such trends, UNHCR did not discard an external protection reading of the availment clause entirely nor did it wholeheartedly adopt the Hathaway reading. So much is clear from its April 2001 publication, Interpreting Article 1 of the 1951 Convention Relating to the Status of Refugees.[70] Its paragraph 35 stated that there had been 'much debate' over whether in the availment clause 'protection' meant external or internal protection. Having recalled that there was both textual and historical evidence in favour of the external protection reading, this note observed at paragraph 36 that:

> Despite this apparent clarity, there now exists jurisprudence that has attributed considerable importance in refugee status determination to the availability of state protection inside the country of origin, in line with the first view described above. This somewhat extended meaning may be, and has been, seen as an additional—though not necessary—argument in favour of the applicability of the Convention to those threatened by non-state agents of persecution.

This mostly critical view of the internal protection reading as advanced by Hathaway and others followed on from this note's earlier observation at paragraph 15 that:

> Consideration of effective national protection is, in UNHCR's view, neither a separate nor a seminal issue, but rather one of a number of elements concomitant to determining refugee status in certain cases, particularly those involving a fear of persecution emanating from non-state agents. The question is whether the risk giving rise to the fear is sufficiently mitigated by available and effective national protection from that feared harm. Where such an assessment is necessary, it requires a judicious balancing of a number of factors both general and specific, including the general state of law, order and justice in the country, and its effectiveness, including the resources available and the ability and willingness to use them properly and effectively to protect residents.

Whilst not entirely clear, it appears that UNHCR's own view as expressed in this note was that internal protection considerations were best considered and determined as an element of the well-founded fear test and that, as a result, it remained appropriate to confine protection within the availment clause to mean external protection, since ultimately external protection could not be said to be available if it exposed an applicant to risk of being returned.[71]

---

[69] ibid 427–28.
[70] UNHCR, Interpreting Article 1 of the 1951 Convention Relating to the Status of Refugees (2001) UN Doc A/AC.96/951.
[71] ibid, footnote 81.

Despite in this way intimating its support for the external protection view, UNHCR concluded that there is a place for both approaches:

> It has been suggested above that the internal protection element is best considered and determined as an element of well-foundedness of fear. It has been argued elsewhere that the last phrase of Article 1A(2) may be given more contemporary content by reinterpreting it in the following fashion: if the country of origin is unable to provide protection against persecution (whether the inability be despite best efforts of a weak state or on account of the total failure of the state), then the victim will fear persecution in case of return and therefore has good reason to be unwilling, owing to that fear, to avail him or herself of the protection of that country. These approaches are, in effect, not contradictory. Whichever approach is adopted, it is important to recall that the definition comprises one holistic test of inter-related elements. How the elements relate and the importance to be accorded to one or another element necessarily falls to be determined on the facts of each individual case.[72]

The following year, 2001, saw the publication of an influential article by UNHCR Senior Legal Adviser, Antonio Fortin espousing an external protection approach, the unpublished version of which, as already observed, the UNHCR note had already endorsed.[73]

In April 2002, the Australian High Court in *Khawar* sought to address the continuing ambivalence in the case law and wider literature. Having noted that protection could have a narrow or a wider meaning, Gleeson CJ accepted that historical and textual analysis carried out by Grahl-Madsen and Fortin and others pointed to a (narrow) external protection reading. However, with reference to the paradigm case of persecution by the state, he echoed Grahl-Madsen's concern that sight not be lost of the underlying breach in the relationship between the applicant and his or her home government:

> But accepting that, at that point of the Article, the reference is to protection in the narrower sense, an inability or unwillingness to seek diplomatic protection abroad may be explained by a failure of internal protection in the wider sense, or may be related to a possibility that seeking such protection could result in return to the place of persecution. During the 1950s, people fled to Australia from communist persecution in Hungary. They did not, upon arrival, ask the way to the Hungarian Embassy.[74]

Gleeson CJ's acceptance in the above paragraph that 'at that point' in the Article the reference is to diplomatic protection, indicated his thinking that it was unnecessary, in order to accord due weight to internal protection, to read the availment clause other than narrowly. That is consistent with his opinion that the Federal Court was correct in concluding in this case that (internal) protection was part of the meaning of 'being

---

[72] ibid para 37.
[73] Fortin (n 7).
[74] *MIEA v Khawar* [2002] 210 CLR 1 (Aus HC), para 22.

persecuted'. For Gleeson CJ's two colleagues, McHugh and Gummow JJ, the matter was clear-cut. They were adamant that:

> The reference then made in the text to 'protection' is to 'external' protection by the country of nationality, for example by the provision of diplomatic or consular protection, and not to the provision of 'internal' protection provided inside the country of nationality from which the refugee has departed.[75]

They considered that to import 'internal protection' into this (availment) portion of the definition would be to 'add a layer of complexity to that construction which is an unnecessary distraction'.[76]

In *S152*, the Australian High Court subsequently interpreted *Khawar* as having endorsed an external protection approach.[77] Several years later in *SZATV*, Kirby J felt impelled by this line of authority to follow suit, although making clear his own reasons for preferring Hathaway's internal protection approach.[78]

2003 saw the publication of UNHCR's *Global Consultations on International Protection*. In the chapter they contributed on the internal protection alternative, Hathaway and Foster describe the external protection view as an attempt 'to force a narrow, decontextualized reading of "protection" onto the 1951 Convention'.[79] They portray such a view as 'out of step with most contemporary pronouncements of UNHCR as manifested in its official documents... materials and interventions in domestic adjudication'.[80] In the same year, however, Daniel Wilsher sought to defend Fortin's position, albeit arguing that its underlying strength rested on Article 33(1) and the principle of non-refoulement.[81]

In 2006, the UK House of Lords (per Lord Carswell) described 'adaptation to modern conditions' as having led to a 'shift in meaning' towards reading the availment clause to refer to internal protection.[82]

In 2011, in *Abdulla*, the Court of Justice of the European Union (CJEU) proceeded without discussion to automatically equate the meaning of the availment clause (which Article 2(c) of the Qualification Directive (QD) had largely replicated in its definition of refugee) with internal protection.[83]

---

[75] ibid para 62.
[76] ibid paras 66–67.
[77] *MIMA v Respondents S152/2003* [2004] 222 CLR 1 (Aus HC). Significantly Gleeson CJ, Haynes, and Heyden JJ noted at ibid para 20 that: '[b]ecause it is the primary responsibility of the country of nationality to safeguard those rights and freedoms, the international responsibility has been described as a form of "surrogate protection". "Protection" in that sense has a broader meaning than the narrower sense in which the term is used in Art 1A(2) but, so long as the two meanings are not confused, *it is a concept that is relevant to the interpretation of Art 1A(2)*' (emphasis added). McHugh's separate opinion in the same case, whilst holding fast to the external protection reading of the availment clause, accepted that internal protection was relevant to the issue of well-founded fear: see ibid para 101.
[78] *SZATV v MIC* [2007] 233 CLR 18, para 60.
[79] Hathaway and Foster (n 36) 357–417.
[80] ibid.
[81] Daniel Wilsher, 'Non-State Actors and the Definition of a Refugee in the United Kingdom: Protection, Accountability or Culpability' (2003) 15(1) IJRL 68.
[82] *Januzi v SSHD* [2006] UKHL 5, para 66.
[83] Joined Cases C-175/08, C-176/08, C-178/08, and C-179/08 *Salahadin Abdulla and Others* [2010] ECR I-0000, para 69: 'Those circumstances [existing in his country of origin] form the reason why it is impossible for the person concerned, or why he justifiably refuses, to avail himself of the "protection" of his country of

For Zimmermann and Mahler, in their contribution to the major 2011 Commentary on the 1951 Convention, the historical evidence pointing to ascription of an external protection meaning was seen to have given way to an object and purpose approach affording protection in this clause with a wide meaning.[84]

Whilst in 2014, in the second edition of *The Law of Refugee Status*, Hathaway and Foster strongly endorse the approach in *Horvath*, they in fact say little more than that they agree that the 'diplomatic protection' view 'has scant judicial or academic support'.[85] They describe it as resting on 'an illogical premise, since, as explained by Mathew, the "litmus test for refugee status is clearly not whether a person can approach their embassy for consular assistance, but whether they are willing to return home"'.[86] They also suggest that for them the protection clause is now largely superfluous unless it is utilised as a home for internal protection alternative analysis: '[a]ssessing internal protection analysis under the rubric of the protection limb', they write, 'is not only respectful of the Convention's text and overarching goals, but also abrogates the practical difficulties inherent in the well-founded fear approach'.[87]

In 2016, Fripp, summarising the state of the academic literature, described Zimmermann and Mahler's conclusion as 'generally consistent with the treatment of the issue by Goodwin-Gill and McAdam and by Hathaway and Foster'.[88]

Two recent studies appear to doubt that the availment clause has any continuing role. Thus, Aleinikoff and Zamore have forcibly argued that 'the "protection" element of the refugee definition is "unnecessary"' and is 'a historical relic' that has been 'largely superseded by persecution as the core concept; and plays no significant role in modern interpretation' (they also take issue with the 'modern standard account' which sees international protection as surrogate protection).[89] Lehmann in his 2020 work, whilst accepting that a modern reading requires interpreting the 'protection clause' to embody the notion of 'surrogacy', sees this as demonstrating that this clause does not contain an 'independent substantive condition' and that (in language reminiscent of UNHCR's 2001 note) linkage within the clause to well-founded fear 'implies that the clause does not circumscribe a criterion for refugeehood in addition to the Convention's requirement of a well-founded fear of being persecuted'.[90] However,

---

origin within the meaning of Article 2(c) of the Directive, that is to say, in terms of that country's ability to prevent or punish acts of persecution.' Whilst *Abdulla* was a cessation case, the CJEU made clear at para 69 that protection in that context meant the same as in the refugee definition. This approach was confirmed in Case C-255/19 *SSHD v O A* [2021] ECLI:EU:C:2021:36, paras 36, 42, 56, 58.

[84] Zimmermann and Mahler (n 14) 444–45.
[85] Hathaway and Foster (n 3) 340.
[86] ibid.
[87] ibid. See also Penelope Mathew, 'The Shifting Boundaries and Content of Protection: The Internal Protection Alternative Revisited' in Satvinder Juss (ed), *The Ashgate Research Companion to Migration Law, Theory and Policy* (Ashgate 2013) 191.
[88] Eric Fripp, *Nationality and Statelessness in the International Law of Refugee Status* (Hart Publishing 2016) 325, states that '[i]n Article 1A(2) CSR51, "protection" does not mean "diplomatic protection" but "protection from persecution"'.
[89] Thomas A Aleinikoff and Leah Zamore, *The Arc of Protection: Reforming the International Refugee Regime* (Stanford University Press 2019) 43, 48, 52.
[90] Julian Lehmann, '*Protection*' *in European Union Asylum Law* (Brill Nijhoff 2020) 70. He also considers (in n 207) that Zimmermann and Mahler (n 14) 445 appear to take the same view.

in contrast to Aleinikoff and Zamore, the true role of this clause, for him, is to 'reflect... the purpose of the Convention to entrust refugees with surrogate, rights-based international protection'.[91]

Before concluding this (thus far chronological account) of the competing arguments, there are three other important facets not yet mentioned. The first is that, throughout these debates, no issue appears to have been taken with the examples given in paragraphs 120–124 of the UNHCR 1979 Handbook of situations in which there may be issues relevant to determining refugee status regarding whether a person has availed themselves of diplomatic or consular protection. The second is that there has been a small but seemingly steady stream of cases in which diplomatic and consular protection have been live issues. These have largely concerned either (i) situations in which the authorities of the country of origin have taken diplomatic or consular action amounting to (either on its own or in conjunction with other factors) persecutory conduct towards an individual who is outside their country of origin, e.g. by denationalising them[92] or cancelling passports or other identity documents; or (more commonly) (ii) situations in which the diplomatic or consular officials of a state have refused an individual a passport (or renewal of a passport), identity document, or other assistance services.[93] The outcome of these cases has depended very much on their own facts but on occasions has resulted in a finding that the lack of diplomatic or consular protection is evidence of lack of internal protection.[94] Significantly, the courts or tribunals have largely proceeded on the explicit or implicit basis that such cases can be analysed by applying the availment clause and its wording. Just as significantly, they

---

[91] Lehmann (n 90) 241.

[92] See e.g. *EB (Ethiopia) v SSHD* [2007] EWCA Civ 809, paras 54, 71; *MA (Ethiopia) v SSHD* [2009] EWCA Civ 289, para 43; German Federal Administrative Court *BVerwG 10 C 50.07* [2009] paras 16–23; *Haile v Gonzalez* [2005] 421 F.3d 493. For all these references, see Fripp (n 88) 296–317. Hathaway and Foster (n 3) 251 note that past denationalisation may not suffice to establish current risk. Denationalisation will only involve consular authorities when applicants are outside their country of origin.

[93] The case examples given by Grahl-Madsen almost all concern passports: see below n 112. For recent case law, see e.g. *V03/16458* [2004] RRTA 592, applying *Tesfamichael v MIMA* [1999] FCA 1661. Where withholding such documents constitutes a denial of the right of return, that has been seen to be an act that 'may in itself constitute an act of persecution by the state' (see *Maarouf v Canada (MEI)* [1994] 1 FC 723); see also *Thabet v Canada (MCI)* [1998] 4 FC 21. For all these references, see Fripp (n 88) 296–313. See also *Chehade v Canada (MCI)* [2017] FC 282, para 20, cited Foster and Lambert (n 16) 170 (at footnote 173); Belgian Aliens Litigation Council, *X v Commissaire général aux réfugiés et aux apatrides* [2009] arrêt no 22144; *AAAD v Refugee Appeals Tribunal* [2009] IEHC 326, para 86; last two, cited by Foster and Lambert (n 16) 171 (at footnote 181).

[94] Given the human rights approach to the concept of persecution, it is also pertinent that the UN Human Rights Committee (HRC) has confirmed in a number of cases concerned with Article 12 of the International Covenant on Civil and Political Rights (ICCPR) that refusal of a national passport whilst resident outside one's country can violate this right: see e.g. *Case of Sophie Vidal Martins v Uruguay* (2 April 1980) Communication No R.13/57, UN Doc Supp No 40 (A/37/40); and that deprivation of nationality was seen in *Case of Similae Toala v New Zealand* (2 November 2000) Communication No 675/1995, UN Doc CCPR/C/70/D/675/1995, as potentially within the Covenant's remit because of the potential loss of the right to enter. See also HRC, CCPR General Comment No 27: Article 12 (Freedom of Movement) (2 November 1999) UN Doc CCPR/C/21/Rev.1/Add.9, para 19; *Malawi African Association and Others v Mauritania*, African Commission on Human and People's Rights, Communication Nos 54/91, 61/91, 98/93, 164/97, and 196/97 and 210/98 (2001) 8 IHRR 268; and *Modise v Botswana*, African Commission on Human and Peoples' Rights, Decision on the Merits, Communication No 97/93 (2002) 9 IHRR 209, cited by Fripp (n 88) 284. See further Hathaway and Foster (n 3) 249–52.

have not for the most part linked such assessments to any specific position on whether protection in the availment clause exclusively denotes external protection.

The third matter is that, in the course of debating these issues, some sources that have embraced an internal protection reading have seen it as important to identify precisely in which part or limb of the Article 1A(2) definition is the correct textual 'home' or location of the internal protection inquiry. Hathaway, and Hathaway and Foster, for example, locate this inquiry in the 'being persecuted' limb;[95] in *Horvath*, however, Lord Hope appeared to locate it in both the 'well-founded fear' limb and the availment clause;[96] whereas McHugh J in *S152/2003* argued that it should be located solely in the 'well-founded fear limb', a position which he also understood UNHCR to have taken in its 2001 note.[97] In addition, Hathaway and Foster, most prominently, have contended that the availment clause is the logical textual home for the 'internal protection alternative' analysis.[98]

## 3 Application of VCLT Rules

Having set out the history and background to the availment clause, we must turn to see what understanding of it is yielded by application of VCLT rules of interpretation (we shall return to the significance of the *travaux* when considering Article 32 VCLT). Many of the analyses of this clause discussed in the previous section have, of course, sought to apply such rules to a greater or lesser extent, but it is instructive to consider their application in the one place.

### 3.1 Good Faith

This element of the VCLT rules has not been seen to offer any direct assistance to interpreting this part of the definition.

### 3.2 Ordinary Meaning

As was noted in Chapter 7, 'protection' is a classic example of a word that has multiple meanings depending on the context in which it is used.[99] On its own

---

[95] Hathaway and Foster (n 3) 294–95.
[96] *Horvath* (n 65). Lord Lloyd (ibid 589), on the other hand, considered that this principle 'finds its proper place in the second half of article 1A(2). If there is a failure of protection by the country of origin, the applicant will be unable to avail himself of the country of protection.'
[97] UNHCR, Interpreting Article 1 of the 1951 Convention (n 70). Albeit an arch-proponent of the external protection reading, Fortin was also of the view that internal protection had to be assessed as part of the 'well-founded fear' test: see p. 667.
[98] Hathaway and Foster (n 36) 365–81 remark at ibid 365 that 'courts have frequently recognised that the clearest textual home for IFA is the protection clause', citing *Thirunavukkarasu v Canada (MEI)* [1994] 1 FC 589; *Refugee Appeal No 11/91* [1991] NZRSAA; and *Randhawa v Minister for Immigration* [1994] 124 ALR 265.
[99] See pp. 442–443. See also Fripp (n 88) 159–60. Hugo Storey, 'The Meaning of "Protection" within the Refugee Definition' (2016) 35(3) Refugee Survey Quarterly 1, 4–9.

it does not identify whether its scope concerns external or internal protection or both. In terms of dictionary definitions, the OED Online gives as the first meaning: '[t]he action of protecting someone or something; the fact or condition of being protected; shelter, defence, or preservation from harm, danger, damage, etc.; guardianship, care; patronage'.[100] As noted in Chapter 7, the word has no obvious common meaning across its various usages in the 1951 Convention. Whilst those in Article 1C could be said to broadly mirror the protection concept at work in Article 1A(2), the term is used in Article 1D without reference to something afforded by a country; the reference in the Preamble to (UNHCR) 'protection of refugees'—is plainly different; as is (again) the usage in Article 14 which refers to protection of refugee rights in the host state.[101] Within the wider refugee literature, the word also has multiple meanings.[102]

Considering the status of the availment clause as a whole in textual terms, it has already been pointed out that the conjunctive wording of Article 1A(2) points to it being considered to constitute an additional requirement in its own right and hence that an applicant does not qualify as a refugee unless this requirement is met.[103]

There are also several textual indications that have been seen to point to an external protection reading.

First, there is the fact that the clause uses different wording for stateless persons than it does for nationals: the test for stateless persons is not, as it is for those with a nationality, willingness or ability to avail of the protection of the state; it is simply whether the applicant is unable or unwilling to return there. If protection is understood as external protection, this makes perfect sense because stateless persons are not entitled to the diplomatic protection of any country and so cannot, by definition, be able or willing to avail themselves of such protection. This was precisely the point voiced by Henkin in the *travaux*.[104] If, however, the word were taken to mean internal protection, there would arguably have been no need for such differentiation. As Fortin notes, '[h]ad the term "protection" in the refugee definition connoted the protection accorded by States within their territory, it would certainly not have been necessary to differentiate between nationals and stateless persons, as the latter are entitled to the internal protection of their country of residence'.[105]

Second, coming as this clause does immediately after mention of the requirement that a person must be 'outside the country', the most natural construction is that its availment requirement relates to actions of nationals in host states. In Fortin's words, 'the only protection that can be made available to persons who are outside their country of nationality, or to which such persons can resort, is diplomatic protection'.[106]

---

[100] OED Online, <https://www.oed.com> accessed 25 July 2021.
[101] Paragraph 16 of the schedule to the Convention refers to the 'protection of the diplomatic or consular authorities of the country that has issued a refugee's travel document'. See p. 443.
[102] Dallal Stevens, 'What Do We Mean By Protection?' (2013) 20(1) International Journal on Minority and Group Rights 233.
[103] See above p. 553.
[104] ibid.
[105] Fortin (n 7) 564.
[106] ibid 564–65. See also UNHCR (n 70).

It is true that if read as meaning 'internal protection', protection can still be said to be available or not, on the basis of a forward-looking assessment of the likely actions of the authorities in the country of origin upon any hypothetical return, but that requires a more indirect path of reasoning.

Third (which is particularly relevant to any choice between an internal and external protection reading), the text refers to actions or possible actions *by an applicant*. This fits well with the realities of external protection because, as we have seen, it will ordinarily be action on the part of an individual, in seeking to obtain an identity document for example, that establishes whether external protection is available or not; whereas in order to construe the term as meaning internal protection, one has to recast inability and unwillingness to include actions (or omissions) on the part of the authorities as well.

In light of the above considerations, there simply cannot be said to be an ordinary meaning that unambiguously points to either an internal or external protection reading. If one applies in full the view that ordinary meaning is what a person reasonably informed on the subject matter of the treaty would reach regarding the terms used,[107] that does arguably tend to support reading it as external protection, since there are strong grounds for considering that this was the contemporary meaning for those engaged in the drafting of treaties on refugees.[108] However, as McAdam has noted, 'there is no singular concept of 'protection' in international law. Although 'protection' forms the essence of states' obligations vis-à-vis refugees, the term itself is not defined in any international or regional refugee or human rights instruments. It is a term of art.'[109] Further, neither the 1951 Convention nor its predecessor instruments contain a definition of protection and given the generic nature of the term, neither external nor internal protection can safely be said to comprise the 'regular, normal or customary' meaning.[110] Although some have assumed that applying a literal reading inevitably identifies internal protection, it does not. It is also capable of identifying external protection.[111]

Given the absence of any clear ordinary meaning, any better understanding of the scope of the protection concept in the availment clause must be achieved by reference to other VCLT rules. Whilst it might be said that the conjunctive wording linking the availment clause with the earlier parts of the definition points strongly to the clause as a whole being understood as a substantive requirement in its own right—an integral part of the definition of refugee—the central role in it of the protection concept makes it difficult to establish that separately from the issue of the meaning of that concept.

---

[107] Oliver Dörr and Kirsten Schmalenbach (eds), *Vienna Convention on the Law of Treaties* (Springer 2012) 542; Richard Gardiner, *Treaty Interpretation* (2nd edn, OUP 2015) 193–94.
[108] See above pp. 553–554.
[109] Jane McAdam, *Complementary Protection in International Refugee Law* (OUP 2007) 19. See also Guy S Goodwin-Gill, 'The Language of Protection' (1989) 1(1) IJRL 6. See also p. 443.
[110] Gardiner (n 107) 183, citing OED (1989).
[111] It must be doubted, therefore, whether Kälin (n 3) 427, or Hathaway and Foster (n 36) 380, or Zimmermann and Mahler (n 14) 444, are right to assume that a literalist or ordinary meaning view clearly supports an internal protection construction.

## 3.3 Context

As noted in Chapter 7, section 3.1, the term 'protection' is used elsewhere in the Convention. It is not necessary to rehearse its various usages here, since it is really only Article 1C that has been seen to offer any significant assistance in interpreting this clause.

The provisions of Articles 1C would appear potentially to shed light on the scope of the concept of protection within the availment clause because 1C(1) and (5) both refer expressly to availment of protection and 1C(3) also refers to enjoyment of protection. However, if light is shed, it would appear to shine both ways. On the one hand, it seems that both the drafters' understanding, and interpretations adopted thereafter by UNHCR especially, point strongly to treating protection in these provisions to mean external protection. Thus, almost all of the cessation cases discussed by Grahl-Madsen concern issues regarding individuals seeking renewal of passports.[112] All but one of the examples given in paragraphs 120–124 of the UNHCR Handbook concern external protection;[113] only paragraph 125, which concerns visits to a refugee's former home country, could be said to intrinsically concern internal protection.[114]

On the other hand, the context of Article 1C—cessation—is one that necessarily places sharp focus on actions undertaken by refugees in a host state in relation to their home country; and to a very great extent (except in relation to returns) the only available medium through which such actions can take place is by receiving diplomatic or consular assistance. By contrast, Article 1A(2) because of its forward-looking character can arguably be said to necessitate consideration of protection in all its aspects. Further, even in the more limited context of assessment envisaged in Article 1C, it has always been the case that availment has ultimately to be assessed by reference to what it demonstrates about an applicant's fear of persecution. Thus the UNHCR Handbook's analysis of cessation, in identifying three essential factors—voluntariness, intent, and actual re-availment—proceeds on the basis that assessment ultimately requires focus on whether the applicant continues to have a well-founded fear of persecution.[115] Whilst this Handbook maintains that obtaining or renewing a passport creates a presumption that an applicant intends to avail himself of the protection of the country of his nationality, this on its own understanding[116] can be rebutted by

---

[112] Grahl-Madsen (n 39) 381–92. Goodwin-Gill and McAdam (n 28) 136 note that the evidence as to availment 'comprises all such actions by the refugee as indicate the establishment of normal relations with the authorities of the country of origin, such as registration at consulates or application for and renewal of passports or certificates of nationality.'

[113] For Fripp (n 88) 326, 'emphasis on documentation rather than the identification of the underlying meaning is unfortunate, because whilst ambiguous overall a part of it again seems to suggest "diplomatic protection"'.

[114] Even Hathaway and Foster (n 3) 464–70, who generally regard the meaning of protection in Article 1 to be read widely so as to include internal protection, describe Article 1C(1) as deriving from a 'highly formalistic' understanding limited to diplomatic consular assistance and to be thus a clause that will 'rarely be applicable'. At ibid 469, they state that '[t]he purpose of Art.1(C)(1) is to withdraw refugee status where there is evidence of diplomatic or consular protection'.

[115] UNHCR Handbook (n 10) paras 119–23; see also UNHCR, Guidelines on International Protection No 3: Cessation of Refugee Status under Article 1C(5) and (6) of the 1951 Convention relating to the Status of Refugees (the 'Ceased Circumstances' Clauses) (10 February 2003) UN Doc HCR/GIP/03/03.

[116] Hathaway and Foster (n 3) 467–48 (correctly in this author's view), do not accept that there is such a presumption.

evidence that there continues to be a well-founded fear of persecution, e.g. because authorities in the host state have required him or her to take action to obtain a certificate of nationality, for example.[117] In addition, it could be said that the wording of Article 1C(5) requires that any continued refusal to avail oneself of protection is directly tied to whether or not 'the circumstances in connection with which he has been recognised as a refugee' have changed and thus inevitably requires assessment of internal as well as external protection. That is certainly how case law and the wider literature on this provision has always proceeded. Indeed, for some, it is entirely about internal protection. Thus Fripp concludes that, even in relation to Article 1C(1) (which he agrees with Hathaway and Foster derives from formalistic understandings of protection as external protection), '[o]n the best interpretation [ ... ], re-availment of the protection of his country of nationality means re-availment of internal protection from persecution for a Convention reason'.[118]

Although not using the language of protection, it might be mooted that Article 33(1) casts some light. If, despite its very different wording from Article 1A(2), the prohibition in Article 33(1) that '[n]o Contracting shall expel or return ("refouler") a refugee in any manner whatsoever to the frontiers or territories where his life or freedom would be threatened [ ... ]' is to be read as having an 'interchangeable' meaning with Article 1A(2) (as Weis among others has contended),[119] that points away from understanding the availment clause as denoting internal protection because Article 33(1) is not confined to harms threatened in the state/country of origin; it covers 'territories', which may sometimes be places other than the applicant's country of origin.[120] At least one commentator has seen Article 33(1) to offer a valid way of developing the external protection understanding.[121]

There is still the significance of the Convention's reference to human rights in the first preambular paragraph, but this only arises as part of interpretations based on object and purpose.

All in all, context provides little or no help with interpretation.

### 3.4 Object and Purpose

As regards whether the availment clause is to be understood as an additional requirement in its own right, treating it as such would appear to cohere well with the purpose of protection against sufficiently severe violations of human rights, if not also with the principle of surrogacy.

---

[117] UNHCR Handbook (n 10) para 121; see also Grahl-Madsen (n 39) 370; Joan Fitzpatrick and Rafael Bonoan, 'Cessation of Refugee Protection' in Erika Feller, Volker Türk, and Frances Nicholson, *International Law: UNHCR's Global Consultations on International Protection* (CUP 2003) 524.

[118] Fripp (n 88) 331; Hathaway and Foster (n 3) 463; Susan Kneebone and Maria O'Sullivan, 'Article 1C' in Zimmermann (n 14) 486.

[119] See p. 312 and p. 313.

[120] See Kälin (n 3) 418: 'Regarding context, Article 33(1) CSR51 is relevant insofar as it implicitly defines "persecution" by stating that no refugee shall be returned "to the frontiers *of territories where* his life or freedom would be threatened on account of any of the relevant motives of persecution"' (emphasis added).

[121] Wilsher (n 81) 109–10.

Proponents of the external protection reading of the availment clause have not obviously sought to support it by reference to object and purpose. Proponents of the internal protection approach, by contrast, lean heavily on this element of the VCLT rules, which includes an understanding of the Convention as a 'living instrument'.[122] Amongst scholars, Hathaway in 1991, Nathwani in 2000, Kälin in the same year, Hathaway and Foster in 2003 and 2014, and Zimmermann and Mahler in 2011 have all argued that applying a dynamic approach to interpretation requires interpreting the notion of protection in the availment clause to mean internal protection. In this context, the external protection approach is seen to overlook that changes in international relations over time have made diplomatic protection much less effective.[123]

Amongst leading cases, the Canadian Supreme Court in *Ward*, the UK House of Lords in *Horvath* and *Januzi*,[124] and the New Zealand Court of Appeal in *Butler* have all seen the object and purpose of the Convention to require reading protection as internal protection.

However, the result of application of the object and purpose element of the VCLT rules to this portion of the refugee definition is not wholly an open and shut matter. Closer inspection of the various arguments put forward reveals a more mixed picture. Yes, there is very substantial agreement that the refugee definition must accord a crucial role to the notion of internal protection—protection against acts or omissions of the government within the country of origin. But in pointing towards an internal protection reading, such arguments simultaneously raise the question of duplication and/or redundancy. If, internal protection is an integral part (and thus a substantive requirement) of the meaning of 'being persecuted' it could be said to be illogical to require the very same thing to be shown under the protection clause. This concern has led some to consider the object and purpose of the availment clause not to lie in identifying internal protection (or external protection) but in identifying the notion or principle of surrogacy as underlying the entire definition.[125]

Further, as regards object and purpose, although not advanced in this way in the literature, there is a plausible argument that the external protection approach is *also* consonant with an object and purpose reading, since for leading proponents of this approach the centrality of internal protection has already been achieved by locating it in the 'being persecuted' element (or indeed, as La Forest J and UNHCR among others have sometimes seemed to favour, the 'well-founded fear' limb). If that is the case, there is no obvious need to for the availment clause to also reflect the same object and purpose.

Against this argument, it could be said to be very odd were the definition to be read as on the one hand making lack of internal protection a key requirement and yet, in the only place in the refugee definition where the term 'protection' is actually used, to

---

[122] See p. 86.
[123] Nathwani (n 66) 359, citing Rosalyn Higgins, *Problems and Process: International Law and How We Use It* (Oxford Clarendon Press 1994) 53. See also Kälin (n 3) 428.
[124] *Ward* (n 11); *Butler* (n 64); *Horvath* (n 65); *Januzi* (n 82).
[125] Lehmann (n 90) 241. Lehmann considers that the influence of human rights law has meant that the external protection reading has become outdated and as a result 'the protection clause reflects the purpose of the Convention to entrust refugees with surrogate, rights-based international protection'.

accord it a narrower meaning.[126] Reverting to the discussion by the Australian High Court in *Khawar*,[127] to criticise the 'inject[ion]' of an internal protection reading into the availment clause might be said to be wholly back to front because the only place in the refugee definition from which the 'internal protection' reading of the 'being persecuted' element can be derived is the concept of protection in the availment clause.

## 3.5 Article 31(3) VCLT

Leaving aside strong reasons for doubting that the 1979 UNHCR Handbook any longer represents 'subsequent practice',[128] its analysis of protection is in any event inconclusive. It offers only illustrative examples relating to the scope of the concept, one of which appears to relate to diplomatic or consular protection ('e.g., refusal of a passport or extension of its validity'), the other which might be understood to refer to internal protection but only at a stretch ('denial of admittance to the home territory').[129] On the other hand, as much-noted in the literature, its analysis of the availment clause co-exists with its clear recognition of internal protection in the context of its paragraph 65 analysis of 'Agents of persecution', wherein it states, in relation to non-state agents, that persecution 'also exists where [the authorities of a country] prove unable to offer effective protection'.[130]

Turning to other possible candidates for 'subsequent practice', even on the assumption that post-1979 UNHCR, judicial, and academic materials could qualify as relevant sources under this VCLT provision, our earlier chronicling of post-1951 understandings shows that there have been considerable internal tensions as to meaning within UNHCR; ambivalent understandings in some of the academic studies (most notably Grahl-Madsen); as well as open disagreements amongst both judges and academics.

Much the same problem fatally undermines any attempt to derive either an internal or external protection interpretation from 'relevant rules of international law'.

## 3.6 Article 32 VCLT

When already considering the *travaux* above, it was found that they indicated first that the drafters understood protection in the availment clause to be an additional requirement to that set out in the first part of the Article 1A(2) definition, and secondly that they mostly appeared to construe it to mean external protection.[131]

---

[126] See, in relation to the 'internal protection alternative', Storey (n 99) 7: 'This might be thought to represent something of an interpretive conjuring trick. On the one hand, words not there (protection, (in)ability, (un)willingness) are read into the "being persecuted" limb, whereas the second limb of the definition where these words do actually appear are treated as an irrelevance except in the secondary context of assessing whether there is a viable internal relocation or protection alternative. In terms of protection in a person's home area, it is treated as completely irrelevant.'
[127] See above pp. 561–562.
[128] See Chapter 2, section 6.1.1.
[129] UNHCR Handbook (n 10) para 99.
[130] ibid para 65. See also ibid para 100.
[131] See above pp. 553–554.

As regards other supplementary means of interpretation, what was said earlier regarding Article 31(3) VCLT applies just as strongly here. Given the many disagreements it cannot be said that there is any state practice in the broad sense one way or the other.[132]

## 3.7 Article 31(4): Special Meaning

In support of his view that protection in this portion of the refugee definition meant external protection only, Fortin argued not only that such an understanding was based on an ordinary meaning analysis and grounded in the *travaux*, but also that:

> [ ... ] the authors of the definition specifically assigned to the term 'protection' the special meaning of 'diplomatic protection', namely, the protection accorded by States to their nationals abroad. It is submitted that this is the sense in which the term must be understood, in conformity with the rule of interpretation laid down in Article 31(4) [VCLT], which provides: '[a] special meaning shall be given to a term [of a treaty] if it is established that the parties so intended'.[133]

This contention has not received any significant support in the case law or literature and faces two main problems, even leaving aside the high evidential hurdle.[134] First, whilst as Fortin documents, there are a significant number of instances in which the drafters identified that by protection in this context they meant 'external protection', they did not seek to define the term. Gardiner notes that 'the most common way in which a special meaning is indicated is by including a definition article in a treaty'.[135] Second, the mooted 'special meaning' of 'diplomatic protection' fails to grapple with the problem that even Grahl-Madsen (a supporter of the external protection view) as well as critics such and Nathwani and Hathaway and Foster have highlighted, namely that it has never been 'diplomatic protection' *stricto sensu* that the external protection reading of the availment clause depends upon, but rather consular protection.[136] To accord it the special meaning of 'diplomatic protection' would heavily obscure this fact.

## 4 The Availment Clause Reconsidered

It can be seen that whilst for the most part sources concur in viewing the availment clause as an additional independent requirement of the refugee definition, the issue of whether it connotes external or internal protection or both has been a source of real controversy at least in a doctrinal context (we shall leave to later to consider its

---

[132] See Chapter 2, n 69.
[133] Fortin (n 7) 551; see also ibid 563.
[134] See p. 74.
[135] Gardiner (n 107) 339.
[136] See e.g. Grahl-Madsen (n 9) 374.

impact on actual decision-making). It was found difficult to resolve this latter issue by reference to ordinary meaning or context or other VCLT considerations. Matters seem thus to ride very much on the outcome of applying an object and purpose approach and one that applies an evolutive approach.

## 4.1 Difficulties with the External Protection Reading

As regards the external protection view, this chapter has already noted a number of difficulties. In recapitulating in the one place these and others that have been made it is convenient to draw on Hathaway and Foster's identification of several of them.[137]

First, despite the term protection appearing multiple times in the Convention, it is nowhere defined as diplomatic or external protection.[138]

Second, even though Hathaway and Foster may underplay the significant number of references in the *travaux* appearing to imbue the term with the meaning of diplomatic or consular protection,[139] they are certainly right to say that there was 'in fact very little discussion dedicated to the meaning of the "protection" aspect of the definition at all'.[140]

Third, it is misleading for proponents of the external protection view to portray the external protection involved as 'diplomatic protection'. The term 'diplomatic protection' in international law has largely been confined to inter-state action in respect of claims made by one state concerning an injury to one of its nationals as against another state. Even though the International Law Commission's formulation might be said to incorporate consular services as a type of diplomatic protection, this remains, in Hathaway and Foster's words, a 'modified and extended' understanding.[141]

A fourth difficulty identified is that it is inconsistent with an 'object and purpose' interpretation since diplomatic protection is a discretionary right possessed by a state whose exercise may have no bearing on the ability of a state to protect its nationals internally.[142]

A fifth point, closely linked to this, is that diplomatic protection does not necessarily bear any relationship whatsoever to the question of whether a state would wish to protect an individual against a well-founded fear of being persecuted.[143] In this regard,

---

[137] Hathaway and Foster (n 36) 373–81. They, in turn, draw heavily on Nathwani's analysis—see Nathwani (n 66).
[138] Hathaway and Foster (n 36) 373–74.
[139] ibid 374–75; see above pp. 553–554.
[140] ibid 375.
[141] ibid 376 (at footnote 63). They note that 'diplomatic protection' was described in the Report of the ILC on the work of its Forty-ninth session, 12 May–18 July 1997, Official Records of the General Assembly, Fifty-second session, Supplement No 10 (1997) UN Doc A/52/10, para 178, as a 'term of art' bearing the (narrow) meaning given to it in *Mavrommatis Palestine Concessions (Greece v United Kingdom)*, Objection to the Jurisdiction of the Court, Judgment [1924] PCIJ Series A no 2.
[142] Hathaway and Foster (n 36) 376–77.
[143] Citing Grahl-Madsen's problem scenario (see above p. 556), Hathaway and Foster state that '[i]ndeed, the diplomatic protection thesis allows the unilateral action of the State of nationality to remove the refugee's right to protection, a position irreconcilable with Article 1C(1) which denies status only where the refugee voluntarily re-avails him or herself of the protection by the State of nationality'. To similar effect, see also Nathwani (n 66) 358: '[i]f diplomatic protection were a crucial criterion for determining refugee status, the

Hathaway and Foster highlight the passage from Grahl-Madsen's book, which offers what I have described earlier as a 'problem scenario'. This posits a person who whilst fearing non-state actors, is on good terms with the government of his or her country and would thus have no problems in obtaining external protection in the form of consular assistance etc.[144]

Sixth, if the availment clause is understood to connote diplomatic and consular protection, it is left unclear how stateless persons are to be assessed. There is no 'protection' clause in this part of the refugee definition that relates to stateless persons. Yet surely even for such persons there can be cases where their availment or not of diplomatic or consular services of their country of origin may be a live issue. Being stateless, they may have no 'right' to expect diplomatic or consular protection, but some countries do make services available to mere residents, e.g. in furnishing identity documents; and human rights violations can arise from failures of this kind by states to respect the right of return to one's own country (even for stateless persons).[145]

It is possible to identify counter-arguments in relation to each of these difficulties. If the Convention contains no definition of protection as external protection, neither does it define the term as internal protection. One cannot disregard the significant number of references in the *travaux* appearing to invest the term with the meaning of diplomatic or consular protection.[146] Even though proponents of an external protection reading have not helped their cause by identifying the crux of this term as being about 'diplomatic' rather than consular protection, the latter has been accepted as one type of diplomatic protection. Whilst diplomatic protection might only be a discretionary right of states, it is arguably consistent with an object and purpose approach to consider that state parties might wish to have regard to what actions applicants take in relation to diplomatic and consular services where they exist.[147] Even though Grahl-Madsen himself did not offer a specific resolution of his problem scenario,[148] his answer can be inferred from his own emphasis on the need to apply the clause keeping in mind that its underlying rationale must always be the lack of such protection available

State of origin might grant diplomatic protection over the head of the refugee and, thus, obstruct the grant of asylum to the refugee'.

[144] Hathaway and Foster (n 36) 377 (at footnote 66).
[145] Fripp (n 88) 320 notes, with reference to *Maarouf* (n 93) and *Altawil v Canada (MCI)* [1996] FCJ 986, and *MA (Palestinian Territories) v SSHD* [2008] EWCA Civ 304, that 'protection from arbitrary expulsion is not restricted to stateless persons, but applies very acutely in their case because stateless persons may not have any route of admission to another State or territory. It is strongly arguable that a State may breach the protected human rights of an individual who is subjected to expulsion or exclusion even if no duty to grant citizenship arises.' See also HRC, General Comment No 27: Article 12 (Freedom of Movement) (n 94) para 19. The 1967 European Convention on Consular Functions expressly recognises a protection role for the consuls of a refugee's State of habitual residence: see Goodwin-Gill and McAdam (n 28) 447 (at footnote 142); Goodwin-Gill and McAdam (n 3) 513.
[146] See above pp. 553–554.
[147] At least insofar as diplomatic protection is understood to encompass consular protection, it would also be incorrect to portray the latter as entirely limited to a (discretionary) right of states: the 1963 Vienna Convention on Consular Relations includes certain consular rights for individuals: see e.g. Article 36(1) as discussed in *Avena and Other Mexican Nationals (Mexico v United States of America)*, Judgment [2004] ICJ Rep 12.
[148] Grahl-Madsen (n 39) 98 also observed that: 'lack of protection is only relevant if it is caused by a deep-rooted political controversy between the authorities and the individual'.

in the home state. So far as concerns the lack of any 'protection' analysis of stateless persons, it can be argued that for them protection only becomes relevant once there is an issue about return and Article 1A(2) caters for this by requiring in their case inability or unwillingness to return.[149]

However, whatever is made of the arguments one way or another, two points stand out. One is that, for the proponents of the external protection reading, the debate has rarely been a binary one. It is almost always fully accepted by them that the refugee definition must contain an internal protection analysis *somewhere*. Leading proponents have advanced it on the footing that 'internal protection' has already to be addressed in the well-founded fear and/or 'being persecuted' limbs.[150] Hence, the divergence between the two views is much less than is often represented.

The other point is that, even taking the external protection view at its highest, it represents a very limited test, certainly in the modern historical context. In essence, its main proponents understand it to be an additional check on whether the applicant's dealings or lack of them with the consular authorities of their home state confirm or disconfirm that they continue to have a well-founded fear of being persecuted. Thus Grahl-Madsen, despite ambivalence about the importance of this clause,[151] saw it to have application, both in relation to inability and unwillingness, as follows. In relation to inability, he identified three contexts: 'protection may be refused expressly or tacitly, as when a passport is denied or even cancelled'; 'the government of the country of origin may not be recognized by the government of the country of refuge'; and 'the two countries may be at war with each other'.[152] In relation to unwillingness, he appeared to see it as being a simple matter of whether or not an applicant was unwilling to ask for diplomatic or consular assistance.[153] The 1979 UNHCR Handbook's treatment is in similar terms.[154] According to the 2001 UNHCR note:

> [ … ] it may surely be legitimate for a person who fears non-state agents not to accept diplomatic protection outside the country as this would provide the country of origin with the possibility of lawfully returning him or her to that country. This would expose the refugee to the feared harm and therefore would make his or her unwillingness to avail of such external protection both reasonable and 'owing to such fear' of persecution.[155]

Whilst accepting that the availment clause could arguably be 'omitted from the definition without seriously affecting the integrity of the concept', Fortin (for much the

---

[149] Zimmermann and Mahler (n 14) 445.
[150] Thus, in *Khawar* (n 74), Gleeson CJ expressly endorsed internal protection being raised earlier in the definition (see ibid paras 30–31) and McHugh and Gummow JJ were prepared to proceed on a similar basis (see ibid paras 84–87). Their main concern was that the notion of internal protection should not be 'injected' into the availment clause: see ibid para 66. Fortin (n 7) also considered that assessment of internal protection had a place, but was to be located in the 'well-founded fear' limb.
[151] Saying on the one hand that '[t]he denial of diplomatic protection by one's country of origin is the crucial characteristic of refugee status', and on the other that '[d]enial of protection is, in fact, a symptom rather than the disease itself'. See Grahl-Madsen (n 39) 370, 375.
[152] ibid 373.
[153] ibid 256–57.
[154] UNHCR Handbook (n 10) paras 98–100.
[155] UNHCR (n 70) para 81; see also para 35.

same reasons as set out in UNHCR's 2001 note) still considered it could have a role, even in the case of persecution by non-state actors:

> The answer to the question of why should persons who fear persecution by non-State agents be prevented from availing themselves of the protection of the diplomatic or consular authorities of their country of nationality, is that enjoyment of such protection provides the host country with the possibility of lawfully returning them to that country. And it is apparent that such possibility is incompatible with, and indeed amounts to the negation of, refugee status.[156]

For Wilsher, in state persecution cases, it can simply be inferred that external protection will not be forthcoming: '[t]hus a person who has left their country due to State persecution can legitimately say that because of this, they are unwilling to seek diplomatic protection from the same State authorities'.[157]

### 4.2 Difficulties with the Internal Protection Reading

Drawing on our earlier analysis, the internal protection reading has the following discernible difficulties.

First, such a reading does not sit well with most of the requirements of Article 31 VCLT. It cannot be said that there is an unambiguous ordinary meaning of internal protection; if anything, textual/syntactical considerations point to an external protection reading. An internal protection reading gets no specific support from a consideration of context. Given the lack of agreement in the UNHCR, judicial, or academic literature, Articles 31(3) and (4) VCLT offer no bolster to such a reading. As regards Article 32 (VCLT), the *travaux* contain significant materials pointing in favour of an external protection reading and the lack of agreement noted in the Article 31(3)(b) VCLT context is no less marked under the subsidiary Article 32 aegis.

Second, whilst consideration of object and purpose provides strong support for an internal protection reading, that does not mean, as just explained, that the opposite (external protection) reading is inconsistent with the Convention's object and purpose. Since the main proponents of the external protection view accept that there is an internal protection analysis to be conducted elsewhere in the refugee definition, this could be said to demonstrate sufficient support for the objective of ensuring surrogate protection. As long as an internal protection analysis is conducted somewhere else in the definition (either in the well-founded fear element or the 'being persecuted' element, or both), confining the scope of the availment clause to a check on whether an applicant's relations with consular authorities of their home state confirm or disconfirm a well-founded fear of being persecuted, would appear consonant with an object and purpose-based understanding.

---

[156] Fortin (n 7) 575–76.
[157] Wilsher (n 81) 108–09. In relation to non-state actors, Wilsher does not accept the approach of Fortin (n 7) and UNHCR (n 70), arguing instead that they could simply benefit from the principle of non-refoulement set out in Article 33. It is not clear to this author that this addresses the underlying problem.

Third, the internal protection reading involves not simply reading the term 'protection' in a particular way but inverting the text's transitive rendering of the individual-state relationship. Whereas the text sees ability or unwillingness to avail as qualities of an applicant, the internal protection reading effectively treats ability or unwillingness as (also being) qualities of state authorities. This is not necessarily an insuperable difficulty, as courts and tribunals have devised various ways of ensuring both types of relationships are addressed.[158] However, it is arguable that some of the problems that have arisen with protection analyses, e.g. over whether their reliance on a principle of surrogacy makes them too state-centric, have gained a foothold due to uncertainties over to what extent the applicant-related words of the text still have application.[159]

Fourth, linked to this, just as proponents of the external protection view have weakened their cause by portraying the issue as being about 'diplomatic protection' (rather than consular protection), in a similar way some proponents of the internal protection view have weakened theirs by not making clear whether their own position understands internal protection to concern protection in *both* its internal and external aspects. Logically, the internal protection view entails the wider view, since at international law a state is responsible for the acts of all its organs at home and abroad, including those carried out by diplomatic and consular services in foreign territories.[160]

Fifth, perhaps the most troublesome, there is the drawback that in the main versions of the internal protection reading, it becomes difficult to follow what independent role—or indeed any role—they leave for the availment clause to play in the refugee definition, since they also treat internal protection as an integral part of the 'being persecuted' limb and/or the 'well-founded fear' limb.[161] Whether dealt with under either or both of these limbs, the same issue arises of potential redundancy/irrelevancy of the availment clause. If in order to establish persecution or 'well-founded fear', it is necessary to establish lack of protection, then the availment clause might appear to be either repetitive or otiose.[162] Whilst it cannot be excluded that even a major clause in a treaty definition contains a clause that is otiose, it is a general principle of law that interpretation should strive to give treaty provisions an *effet utile*.[163]

To each of these difficulties, strong counter-arguments can be raised, the most important of which is that state practice (in a broad sense) has increasingly shifted

---

[158] e.g. in *A v MIMA* [1999] 53 ALD 545 (Aus FFC), para 38.

[159] See p. 444 and Chapter 7, n 195. A similar point is made by Wilsher (n 81) 83, who sees a cardinal error of the *Horvath* (n 65) approach to be that 'the whole normative structure of the refugee definition then moves towards an examination of the extent to which the victim has been targeted or neglected by the State rather than the degree of risk of harm they face'.

[160] ILC, Draft articles on Responsibility of States for Internationally Wrongful Acts (2001) Article 4(1); HRC, General Comment No 31: Nature of the General Legal Obligation Imposed on States Parties to the Covenant (26 May 2004) UN Doc CCPR/C/21/Rev.1/Add.13, para 4; Case of *Luna Lopez v Honduras*, Merits, Reparations and Costs, Inter-American Court of Human Rights Series C No 269 (10 October 2013) para 119; *Bankovic v Belgium* App No 52207/99 (ECtHR, 12 December 2001) para 71.

[161] See e.g. Wilsher (n 81) 82–83.

[162] For Wilsher (n 81) 109, though, it is only the 'unwilling' criterion that would be rendered otiose. For a categorical statement of the view that the availment clause (or at least its concept of protection) is redundant, see Aleinikoff and Zamore (n 89) 43, 48, 52.

[163] On *effet utile*, sometimes known as the principle of effectiveness, see Gardiner (n 107) 180. Cases he cites include the Appellate Body of the WTO in *Argentina-Safeguard Measures on Imports of Footwear* [1999] AB-1999-7, para 81 that 'a treaty interpreter must read all applicable provisions of a treaty in a way that gives meaning to all of them, harmoniously'.

away from the external protection approach towards an internal protection approach. That is so in relation to UNHCR, judicial, and academic sources. Regarding judicial sources, perhaps the most important development so far is that the CJEU has clearly adopted an internal protection approach.[164]

## 4.3 A Non-Substantive Role?

Given matters noted earlier, it must not be overlooked that the external protection reading is capable of endowing the availment clause with a substantive role, albeit a limited one. It will be argued below that an internal protection reading is capable of doing the same. However, the possibility has also to be considered of according the clause some lesser, non-substantive role.

One recent attempt to identify a non-substantive role for the availment clause is that by Lehmann. He posits that this clause is not an 'independent substantive criterion', but that it still has a valuable function, namely that of identifying surrogacy as a 'rule underlying the 1951 Convention's refugee definition'.[165] There are at least two interrelated drawbacks to this view. First, in order to conceptualise surrogacy as a rule underlying the definition, it must be tied to something in it, and that can only be a protection-related element (wherever located). Second, on his own analysis the availment clause could only hold this role because the protection-related element is that of internal protection. 'Rather than containing an independent substantive condition for refugee status', he writes:

> [ ... ] the protection clause then points to the broken human rights protective relationship, and to the Convention's objects and purpose of granting international protection in order to restore rights protection, earlier referred to as a bond between individual and state. In a modern reading, this bond is (surrogate) enfranchisement of refugees with human rights under the 1951 Convention concurrently.[166]

But if the clause is about internal protection, then it becomes unclear why surrogacy does not function as part of its meaning also. It also begs the question of the derivation of the protection element of 'being persecuted'. To suggest it does not derive from the only part of the definition that contains the concept, appears to imply (anomalously) that it has more than one meaning within the refugee definition.

In any event, this study's earlier analysis has indicated that both as a matter of ordinary meaning and of state practice in the broad sense, the availment clause has widely been understood to comprise an additional substantive requirement. It is true that such understanding has sometimes described that addition in terms of surrogacy, e.g. by Lord Lloyd in *Horvath* who stated that 'the principle of surrogate protection finds its proper place in the second half of article 1A(2). If there is a failure of protection by the country of origin, the applicant will be unable to avail himself of that

---

[164] See *Abdulla* (n 83) para 69; and *O A* (n 83), para 56.
[165] Lehmann (n 90) 71; see also ibid 70, 72, 241.
[166] ibid 70, 72.

country's protection.'[167] However, there has been far stronger support for viewing its additional role as deriving from the need for a holistic approach to the refugee definition. If a holistic approach is taken, then it is not excluded that the notion also has a role in relation to the 'being persecuted' and/or the 'well-founded fear' elements of the definition. One is also driven back to the importance of understanding the notion of protection within the refugee definition as having a unified meaning; otherwise the risk arises of treating the Article 1A(2) definition as applying different concepts of protection. One further factor is that not to give the availment clause a substantive role would also be in tension with the principle of *effet utile* or effectiveness.

## 4.4 The Availment Clause as Combining Internal and External Protection

On the strength of the analysis thus far, there are two positions, both of which are problematic. On the one hand, if the scope of the protection concept in the availment clause is taken to just connote external protection, the result would seemingly appear to be that the internal protection analysis (which proponents of the external protection reading agree must arise somewhere within the Article 1A(2) definition), has to be seen as employing a different underlying meaning of protection. Not only would it be incongruous to apply two meanings of protection within the one article but such a reading would require treating the only place where the term appears as entirely divorced from the predicament of lack of internal protection, contrary to the strong trend towards understanding protection as essentially about internal protection. On the other hand, to interpret the availment clause as being solely concerned with internal protection seemingly jars with the fact that, even though less common, cases can still arise where issues that are manifestly concerned with external protection are relevant, concerned with, for example, issuing of a passport—issues that may significantly impact on whether or not a person has a well-founded fear of being persecuted.

The question arises, however, whether these two competing views exhaust the field. It seems apparent from the foregoing analysis that both the external and internal protection approaches have sought to recognise in one way or another that the *refugee definition* must consider protection in both its internal and external aspects. Although reading the debates it can sometimes appear otherwise, neither side emphatically maintains that protection is to be read exclusively as external or internal. Building on this insight, it must be asked whether there is any coherent way of seeking to reconcile the two approaches or at least to arrive at an understanding of the meaning of the availment clause that accommodates both approaches—what has sometimes been referred to as a 'wider' meaning of protection.

Given the strong doctrinal nature of the disagreements it is not easy to see how this might be done, but in principle it does seem possible to understand the availment clause as encompassing both internal and external protection. As noted earlier, the functions of a state encompass not just protection of those living within its territory,

---

[167] *Horvath* (n 65).

but also extra-territorial jurisdiction exercised through diplomatic and consular officials acting as agents of the state.[168] Further, to treat the availment clause as connoting external and internal protection also resolves the problem of disparate definitions. By this means protection within Article 12A(2) can be understood to have a uniform meaning.

One immediate obstacle to reading the availment clause as connoting both external and internal protection is that alluded to earlier—that it appears duplicatory. As noted earlier, leading proponents of both readings agree that the internal protection analysis must arise somewhere within the definition. But if it arises either in the well-founded fear or being persecuted elements or both, then how can it make sense for it to arise again under the availment clause? It might seem that duplication can only be avoided either by treating the clause as vestigial, having no real functionality, or investing it with some quite different role. Treating it as vestigial appears to flout the principle of *effet utile*. Another possible role claimed for this clause is that it provides a home for the 'internal protection alternative' analysis. This was explored in Chapter 8 and the analysis there rejected such a role and pointed out that, in any event, it has not attracted widespread support.

The only other viable possibility would be to accept that whilst protection in this clause connotes both external and internal protection, the clause can for practical purposes be seen to permit a division of labour. It can still be treated as the appropriate place in which to consider external protection, whilst deeming the internal protection dimension as best addressed as part of the earlier well-founded fear or being persecuted elements or both. This solution depends on the understanding that internal protection is not a test 'injected' into these other elements *ex cathedra*, but is rather a borrowing from the availment clause. It also builds on the need for the refugee definition to employ a unitary meaning of the concept of protection against the backdrop that the only mention of the term in the definition's text is in the availment clause. Self-contradiction is avoided if the definition is treated in a holistic way. Essentially, it amounts to saying that even though the availment clause is the source of the protection concept for all purposes under the refugee definition, it makes best sense to treat its internal aspects under the well-founded fear of persecution clause, so that when it comes to applying the availment clause on its own, the only aspect left to consider is external protection. Strengthening this conception of the availment clause, is the fact that not only do proponents of both approaches treat internal protection as a necessary requirement, but they take as their premise that internal protection must be interpreted by reference to the criteria of ability and unwillingness—terms only located in the availment clause. This was one of the main points made in Chapter 7.

On the logic of the above approach the internal protection approach can remain faithful to the fact that that external protection is one of the functions of the state, although accepting that this is most appropriately addressed under the availment clause. That is important because proponents of the internal protection reading appear never to have disputed that from time to time issues impacting on the ability of a state to provide national protection against serious harm can turn on whether its diplomatic or

---

[168] See above p. 577.

consular officials acting outside the territory of the state take or fail to take any action, e.g. refusing to issue a passport.

Another objection that might be made to such a solution is that it fails to grapple with Grahl-Madsen's problem scenario, in that it would mean that someone who is at real risk of persecution in his or her home state could nevertheless be found not to qualify as a refugee if the home state's consular authority was willing and able to provide him with consular services, e.g. by issuing him or her with a passport and/or identity documents. However, as Grahl-Madsen himself implies, one obvious solution to the problem would be to say that in such a case it would be a sufficiently safe inference on the evidence that notwithstanding that diplomatic or consular protection was forthcoming, an applicant would have reasonable grounds for being unwilling to avail himself or herself of such protection.[169]

One final matter needing mention concerns the emphasis placed above on the availment clause being linked conjunctively with earlier parts of the Article 1A(2) definition. In this context, it must not be forgotten that the earlier parts include the nexus clause setting out the Convention reasons. The linkage, that is to say, is not just to the 'well-founded fear of being persecuted' element but also to the causal nexus with the Convention reasons.[170] That adds force to the reasons for continuing to see the availment clause as having a substantive role.

## 4.5 Practical Consequences: The Way Forward

In the course of this chapter's analysis of the availment clause a number of possible roles have been identified. In considering these, it should first be recalled that there is very wide agreement that the approach to the refugee definition should be holistic, and the different elements be seen as interdependent. It is part of the principle of effectiveness in treaty interpretation that different parts of a treaty definition must be interpreted harmoniously.[171] That is important, because this strongly suggests that it would be wrong to approach the definition with the fixed idea that each of its main elements must comprise a strictly compartmentalised set of necessary conditions or substantive requirements; there is nothing wrong as such with one element being treated as a source for another, for example.

Second, applying VCLT rules of interpretation, there is nothing untoward as such about applying an object and purpose reading that has the effect of reading down the actual text of a clause in whole or in part.[172] Even so, it would be perverse to treat the availment clause as irrelevant if some substantive function or role or *effet utile* of interpretation of the refugee definition can sensibly be assigned to it.

Third, another feature tending to confirm the efficacy of a holistic approach is that most of the case law has not seen it to make any practical difference whether the

---

[169] Grahl-Madsen (n 9) 257; this is also Fortin's proposed solution: Fortin (n 7) 575–76.
[170] See Zimmermann and Mahler (n 14) 323–24; see also Chapter 10, section 4.
[171] See p. 66 and p. 67.
[172] See Gardiner (n 107) 208, where he cites *US-UK Heathrow Airport Charges Arbitration* [1992] 102 ILR 215. However, object and purpose cannot be used to counter clear substantive provisions: see *USA, Federal Reserve Bank v Iran, Bank Markazi Case A28* [2000–02] IUSCT Rep 5, cited in Gardiner (n 107) 219.

external protection or internal protection understandings of the concept of protection are viewed as arising under one limb or the other of the refugee definition. As noted already, this is because on both the external and internal protection readings, there has been broad recognition that both aspects have to be addressed somewhere within the refugee definition.

On the strength of the above analysis, several possible interpretations of the availment clause can be eliminated in fairly short terms. Although in the course of the debates it has sometimes been represented that proponents of one side or the other seek to take a binary position—that it is exclusively a requirement to show the unavailability of external protection or exclusively a requirement to show the unavailability of internal protection—we have seen that in fact neither side of the debate adopts such a position. Both sides acknowledge that the refugee definition needs to consider protection in both its external and internal aspects.

It is also relatively straightforward to eliminate the proposal that it has no role and is therefore irrelevant (because anachronistic or vestigial, irrelevant,[173] or duplicatory/repetitive[174] etc.); or alternatively that (Lehmann's proposal) it has a role, not as an independent substantive requirement, but as an expression of an underlying rule of surrogacy.[175] As regards the former, it would be contrary to the principle of effectiveness to treat the clause as having no role and such a possibility should only fall to be considered if there was no coherent alternative. As regards Lehmann's proposal, even though it accords the clause some role, it fails to explain how the notion of surrogacy can be treated as separate from the concept of protection (wherever located in the definition).

That really only leaves the possibility of construing the availment clause as connoting both external and internal protection. This has the highly important advantage that protection is given a uniform meaning. However (as we have seen), it is only workable if the clause is limited in practice to an external protection inquiry, with the internal protection inquiry being conducted, in order to prevent duplication, under the well-founded fear or being persecuted elements, or both.

Confessedly, the position just outlined involves a somewhat tortuous construction, yet sight must not be lost of the evidently greater pitfalls involved in taking any other position, such as treating protection as having two different meanings within the same definition or endorsing the view that the clause is either duplicatory or redundant. It is also one whose end-result does in fact conform very closely to what was seen as state practice, at least up until the time of the 1979 UNHCR Handbook was first published. In the Handbook, the clause is seen to have a role only in a limited number of cases concerned with whether denial of services by diplomatic or consular authorities (or authorities responsible for deciding on admission) constitutes a 'refusal of protection'. The proposed solution is also within the scope of the approach adopted by UNHCR's 2001 note, which envisages that once lack of internal protection by the state apparatus within the country is established,[176] there only needs to be a check that external

---

[173] Lehmann (n 90) 140.
[174] Wilsher (n 81) 108–12.
[175] See above p. 563.
[176] Drawing here on the wording of UNHCR (n 70) para 35.

protection does not assuage the well-founded fear of persecution. In addition, such a position is also consistent with the preponderance of case law, at least to the extent that it endorses the need to ascertain somewhere within the refugee definition whether there is protection internally and externally.

It remains that the above position is not reducible to that taken by UNHCR or the case law. The difference is that the availment clause is not seen as having only a limited role in cases in which external protection issues have a material bearing on well-founded fear of being persecuted. It is also seen as the source for the underlying concept of protection and also two of its essential qualities, namely ability and willingness to protect. The latter help shape the concept of internal protection in play in the 'well-founded fear of being persecuted' clause (for these purposes it matters not whether the internal protection test is seen to arise under either the 'being persecuted' or the well-founded fear elements of this clause).[177] Viewing it in this way as a source for key concepts in another part of the definition leaves it with a substantive role in the overall definition. In order to show that an applicant in the context of non-state actor cases, will not receive effective protection, establishing that the authorities are either 'unable' or 'unwilling' to protect, has come to be seen as indeed a necessary requirement in order to qualify as a refugee.[178]

However, in terms of the structuring of decision-making, the clause, thus interpreted, does have very limited scope, since (to repeat) in practice the test of external protection only has application in cases where action or inaction on the part of the state's diplomatic or consular authorities outside the country is at least one material factor in the applicant's case to have a well-founded fear of being persecuted. Ordinarily, as noted by Grahl-Madsen, Fortin, and others, a finding of a lack of internal protection (in the sense of the protection afforded by the home state's authorities within its own territory) would justify an inference, without further ado, that there was also a lack of protection by the authorities of the home state outside its territory, in the form of diplomatic or consular protection.

Finally, it has been mentioned several times that there remain differences of view as to which clause or 'limb' of the refugee definition is the appropriate 'home' for assessing the protection issue. However, the approach taken in UNHCR's 2001 note, in seeking to accommodate different approaches and to aspire to convergence, is surely the best way forward.

## 5 Conclusions

This chapter has sought to analyse the constituent elements of the availment clause by application of VCLT rules. Part 3 (The Availment Clause Reconsidered) sought to evaluate the two main views that have been expressed (the external protection view and the internal protection view). The conclusion was reached that divergences remain, but that the only tenable position is to consider the clause to connote both external and internal protection.

---

[177] See pp. 441–442.
[178] See p. 444.

A prominent theme of this chapter is that the availment clause has substantive content. Being the only element of the refugee definition that uses the term 'protection', it should be treated as the main source for use made of the protection concept elsewhere in the definition, in particular in the 'being persecuted' (or the 'well-founded fear of being persecuted') element. The clause is not therefore redundant. Within the refugee definition protection must have a unified meaning and the best way to underline that is to treat the availment clause as the primary locus of that meaning. That does not mean, however, that the internal aspects cannot be addressed within the 'being persecuted' (or 'well-founded fear of being persecuted') element and does not preclude the availment clause being confined in practice to the concept's (now quite limited) external aspects. Even though the external aspects are now quite limited they too continue to have substantive content.

In line with the methodology applied throughout this study it is necessary to ask whether there are any basic propositions regarding this particular element of the refuge definition that can be gleaned from the foregoing analysis. In contrast to the position found in relation to several of the definition's other elements, the continuing existence of polarised positions in the case law and wider literature over the availment clause means there are few matters that, drawing on this chapter's analysis, can be said to have achieved substantial consensus. But there are some. These are listed first below. The author's own understanding of this clause also provides some suggested propositions, which are listed second.

## 5.1 Basic Propositions

1. Protection encompasses both internal and external aspects (the latter being understood as diplomatic and consular protection).
2. Internal protection (in the sense of protection within the country of origin) is a crucial component of the refugee definition.
3. Inability and unwillingness (which are both concepts expressly identified in the availment clause) are key requirements for assessing the availability of protection.
4. In terms of external protection, it remains the case that issues of inability and unwillingness on the part of applicants in relation to diplomatic and consular protection can sometimes be ones that need to be addressed in determining whether someone meets the requirements of the refugee definition.

## 5.2 Suggested Propositions

1. The approach of reading the availment clause as connoting external protection exclusively suffers from numerous difficulties, most notably that it would entail operating two different concepts of protection within Article 1A(2). The approach of reading the clause as connoting internal protection exclusively also

suffers from numerous difficulties, most notably that it involves duplication, given that all agree that an internal protection inquiry must take place within either the well-founded fear or the being persecuted elements of the definition, or both.

2. The only feasible approach is to read the availment clause as connoting both internal and external protection but to understand its internal protection dimension as being most appropriately conducted within either the well-founded fear or being persecuted elements, or both.

# 10
# Refugee Convention Reasons: 'For Reasons Of'
## (*'Du fait de'*)

| | | | |
|---|---|---|---|
| Introduction | 587 | 3.1.3 Evaluation | 606 |
| Human Rights Approach | 589 | 3.2 Religion | 607 |
| Role Within the Refugee Definition | 590 | 3.2.1 Origins and *travaux préparatoires* | 607 |
| 1 History and *Travaux Préparatoires* | 590 | 3.2.2 Article 31 and other Article 32 VCLT considerations | 607 |
| 1.1 Cognate Treaties | 591 | 3.2.3 Right to freedom of religion | 609 |
| 1.2 Predecessor Instruments Dealing with Refugees | 591 | 3.2.4 Proselytism | 611 |
| 1.3 *Travaux Préparatoires* | 592 | 3.2.5 *Forum internum/forum externum* | 611 |
| 2 Approaches to Interpretation of the Reasons Clause | 593 | 3.2.6 Doctrinal knowledge | 612 |
| 2.1 General Observations | 593 | 3.2.7 Discretion/concealment | 612 |
| 2.1.1 Limitations of ordinary meaning | 593 | 3.2.8 Evaluation | 613 |
| 2.1.2 The issue of an underlying theme | 593 | 3.3 Nationality | 613 |
| | | 3.3.1 Origins and *travaux préparatoires* | 613 |
| 2.1.3 The concept of non-discrimination and a human rights approach | 595 | 3.3.2 Article 31 and other Article 32 VCLT considerations | 614 |
| 2.1.4 Protected characteristics? | 596 | 3.3.3 Evaluation | 616 |
| 2.1.5 Interrelationship between the Convention reasons and the meaning of persecution | 599 | 3.4 Membership of a Particular Social Group | 617 |
| | | 3.4.1 Origins and *travaux préparatoires* | 617 |
| 2.2 Common Features | 599 | 3.4.2 Article 31 and other Article 32 VCLT considerations | 618 |
| 2.2.1 Limiting role | 600 | 3.4.3 Types of PSGs—three examples | 622 |
| 2.2.2 Non-hierarchical character | 600 | 3.4.4 'Protected characteristics' and 'social perception' approaches revisited | 624 |
| 2.2.3 Need for a reason-specific analysis | 600 | 3.4.5 Agreed key features | 633 |
| 2.2.4 Overlapping character | 600 | 3.4.6 Evaluation | 638 |
| 2.2.5 Individualised basis | 601 | 3.5 Political Opinion | 638 |
| 2.2.6 No requirement of discretion/concealment | 601 | 3.5.1 Origins and *travaux préparatoires* | 639 |
| 2.2.7 The doctrine of attribution: imputed or perceived reasons/grounds | 602 | 3.5.2 Article 31 and other Article 32 VCLT considerations | 640 |
| 3 The Individual Reasons | 604 | 3.5.3 Key features | 643 |
| 3.1 Race | 604 | 3.5.4 Evaluation | 647 |
| 3.1.1 Origins and *travaux préparatoires* | 604 | 4 Causal Nexus ('for Reasons of') | 653 |
| | | 4.1 The Nature of the Causal Link | 654 |
| 3.1.2 Article 31 and other Article 32 VCLT considerations | 605 | 4.2 Causal Nexus and Persecutory Intent | 657 |

*The Refugee Definition in International Law.* Hugo Storey, Oxford University Press. © Hugo Storey 2023.
DOI: 10.1093/oso/9780198842644.003.0010

| | | | |
|---|---|---|---|
| 4.3 'Bifurcated Nexus' | 658 | 5 Conclusions | 659 |
| 4.4 Causal Nexus and the Doctrine of | | 5.1 Basic Propositions | 661 |
| Attribution | 659 | 5.2 Suggested Propositions | 661 |

# Introduction

According to Article 1A(2) of the 1951 Convention, a refugee is a person who has a well-founded fear of being persecuted 'for reasons of race, religion, nationality, membership of a particular social group or political opinion' ('*du fait de sa race, de sa religion, de sa nationalité, de son appartenance à un certain groupe social ou de ses opinions politiques*' in the French version).

The clause as a whole is sometimes referred to as the 'Convention reasons' or 'Convention grounds' clause and sometimes as 'the nexus clause' or 'nexus element' or 'nexus requirement'.[1] The reasons or grounds are often referred to as 'the prohibited (or enumerated) reasons'/'prohibited (or enumerated) grounds'. When used in its broad sense, the 'nexus clause' incorporates a twofold test: (i) the requirement to show a Convention reason; and (ii) the need to show some causal relationship between that reason and the feared persecution (the 'causal nexus' requirement). In relation to (i), an applicant who can establish a well-founded fear of being persecuted but no Convention reason, cannot qualify as a refugee. In relation to (ii), an applicant who can establish a well-founded fear of being persecuted but cannot establish that the Convention reason for it is causally related, will also fail to qualify as a refugee.[2] Conversely, if an applicant cannot establish a 'well-founded fear of being persecuted', it will not assist that they fulfil the twofold test of the nexus clause.

In terms of ordering, the refugee definition does not prescribe any specific sequence for addressing its different elements. However, the fact that this element requires a causal nexus to exist between it and the 'well-founded fear of being persecuted' means that it is best understood as a qualifying clause, limiting the types of persecution that are covered in the definition. Mainly for that reason this study only turns to it now, after the interrelated 'being persecuted' and protection elements have been analysed. However, in whichever order the different elements are tackled, they must be considered holistically.

The need to strive for a universal meaning of the refugee definition applies just as much to the Convention reasons as to other elements of the definition. Despite being seemingly the definition's most straightforward part (save for the MPSG reason),[3] the reasons clause has provoked myriad conceptual difficulties. For some it holds the key to the rest of the definition's meaning.[4]

---

[1] See e.g. Andreas Zimmermann and Claudia Mahler, 'Article 1A, para 2' in Andreas Zimmermann (ed), *The 1951 Convention Relating to the Status of Refugees and Its 1967 Protocol: A Commentary* (OUP 2011) 372; Deborah Anker, *Law of Asylum in the United States* (Thomson Reuters 2022) §§5.2–5.87, 401.
[2] See *Fornah v SSHD (linked with SSHD v K)* [2006] UKHL 46.
[3] e.g. in ibid Lord Bingham said that '[t]he four Convention grounds most commonly relied on (race, religion, nationality and political opinion), whatever the difficulty of applying them in a given case, leave little room for doubt about their meaning'. Contrastingly, the analysis given in this chapter would suggest that problems of meaning have arisen in relation to each of the other four reasons as well.
[4] See discussion below p. 590 on Scott's views.

The development within international protection law of complementary protection regimes has brought into sharp relief the question of what place is occupied within the Article 1A(2) definition by the requirement of a Convention reason. There are now several forms of international protection for those fleeing persecution that do not depend on being able to show the harm feared is for reasons of one or more of the five enumerated reasons—or indeed any reasons at all. At the global and regional levels, there are human rights treaty provisions preventing refoulement to conditions that would give rise to a real risk of ill treatment[5] or torture.[6] The Convention Governing the Specific Aspects of Refugee Problems in Africa applies an expanded refugee definition which provides, as a separate basis for qualifying, a clause which contains no requirement to show reasons.[7] Within the context of the European Union Qualification Directive (QD), 'international protection' status is accorded to beneficiaries of subsidiary protection, who are defined as those in respect of whom there are substantial reasons for believing they are at real risk of serious harm, without any requirement to show reasons.[8] Many states apply various forms of complementary protection which again do not require reasons to be shown for the harms feared.[9] Some of the questioning as to whether the 1951 Refugee Convention is still fit for purpose has focused on the contrast between these legal regimes and the 1951 Convention's limiting effect of requiring Convention reasons.[10]

It remains universally accepted, however, that the 1951 Convention continues to be the cornerstone of the international protection regime.[11] Prospects of a revised Convention remain dim. Further, the emergence of complementary protection regimes has not always meant that it no longer matters if a person cannot meet the refugee definition. For example, not all EU member states accord equal rights and benefits to beneficiaries of subsidiary protection as opposed to refugee status, especially as regards family reunion, and as a result there continues to be very active litigation on the part of persons granted subsidiary protection status but denied refugee protection[12] and often, in that context, issues surrounding

---

[5] See e.g. International Covenant on Civil and Political Rights (ICCPR) (adopted 16 December 1966, entered into force 23 March 1976) 999 UNTS 171, Article 7.

[6] See e.g. Convention Against Torture and Other Cruel, Inhuman or Degrading Treatment or Punishment (adopted 10 December 1984, entered into force 26 June 1987) 1465 UNTS 85, Article 3.

[7] Organization of African Unity (OAU), Convention Governing the Specific Aspects of Refugee Problems in Africa (adopted 10 September 1969, entered into force 20 June 1974) 1001 UNTS 45 (OAU Convention). See also *Instrumentos Regionales sobre Refugiados y temas relacionados, Declaración de Cartagena sobre Refugiados, Adoptado por el 'Coloquio Sobre la Protección Internacional de los Refugiados en América Central, México y Panamá: Problemas Jurídicos y Humanitarios'* (adopted 22 November 1984).

[8] Directive 2011/95/EU of the European Parliament and of the Council of 13 December 2011 on standards for the qualification of third-country nationals or stateless persons as beneficiaries of international protection, for a uniform status for refugees or for persons eligible for subsidiary protection, and for the content of the protection granted (recast) [2011] OJ L 337/9, Article 15 (QD (recast)).

[9] See Jane McAdam, 'Complementary Protection' in Cathryn Costello, Michelle Foster, and Jane McAdam (eds), *The Oxford Handbook of International Refugee Law* (OUP 2021) 662–63.

[10] See p. 31.

[11] See pp. 8–9.

[12] See e.g. Case C-91/20 *LW v Bundesrepublik Deutschland* [2021] ECLI:EU:C:2021:898, paras 52–62. For analysis of the Convention reasons in EU asylum law, see EUAA, 'Judicial Analysis on Qualification for International Protection', Directive 2011/95/EU (2nd edn, 2023), section 1.6.

Convention reasons can remain at the forefront. Outside the EU, similar problems continue to arise in relation to persons who are accepted by governments as eligible for some form of complementary protection but who seek to maintain their claims to qualify as refugees.[13]

Before analysing the Refugee Convention reasons, it is necessary to address two general issues.

## Human Rights Approach

In previous chapters it has been argued that the approach to the meaning of key elements of the refugee definition should be based on international law norms, primarily international human rights law (IHRL) norms. An holistic approach has been seen to be required which treats the different elements of Article 1A(2) as closely interlocking. A holistic approach does not necessarily mean that each element of the refugee definition has to embody a uniform quantum of human rights content; it must depend in part on how susceptible each element is to a human rights reading. But in the case of the reasons clause, a human rights approach has been seen as particularly apposite. Indeed it was the early encounters with the concept of MPSG, first in US case law and then in Canadian case law,[14] that resulted in the wider adoption of the human rights approach to the Article 1A(2) definition as a whole. The reasons element of the definition, more than any other, has been seen to link closely to the fundamental human rights norm of non-discrimination. This still leaves though the matter of precisely how a human rights analysis materialises in relation to this reason. Daley and Kelley contend that whereas the focus of the human rights analysis with respect to persecution is on whether the harm feared amounts to persecution, when it comes to the Convention reasons, the focus must be not on the harm threatened but on 'the human right being exercised, or sought to be exercised, free of the threatened harm'.[15] The close linkage that has sometimes been made between the principle of surrogacy as articulated within the human rights approach and the nexus clause will be addressed further in section 4.3 of this chapter.

At the same time, this study has also been at pains to underline that the contributions to developing a more detailed understanding of the contents of the refugee definition have come from a number of approaches, not just a human rights approach. There will be need to revert to this point in this chapter's conclusions regarding agreed basic propositions.

---

[13] Jane McAdam, *Complementary Protection in International Refugee Law* (OUP 2007); Michelle Foster, *International Refugee Law and Socio-Economic Rights: Refuge from Deprivation* (CUP 2007);Guy S Goodwin-Gill and Jane McAdam (with Emma Dunlop), *The Refugee in International Law* (4th edn, OUP 2021) 285–354; McAdam (n 9) 670–71.
[14] *Matter of Acosta* [1985] A-24159781; *Canada (AG) v Ward* [1993] 2 SCR 689.
[15] Krista Daley and Ninette Kelley, 'Particular Social Group: A Human Rights Based Approach in Canadian Jurisprudence' (2000) 12 IJRL 148, 173–74.

## Role Within the Refugee Definition

Although not beset with the type of argumentation about location that has arisen in relation to the 'well-founded fear of being persecuted' and 'protection' clauses,[16] analysis of the MPSG element of the reasons clause has led to sharp debate about the extent to which its underlying criteria should be taken to infuse other elements of the definition, in particular the 'being persecuted' element. Thus, Matthew Scott has argued that an essential ingredient of the concept of persecution is discrimination.[17] This debate was addressed in Chapter 6 and one of the points made was that if this argument were right, it would cause major difficulties for application of the nexus clause, as decision makers would in effect have to ask a mostly circular question: 'Is the discriminatory conduct for a discriminatory reason?'.

Article 1A(2) specifies five reasons for persecution. According to some early studies these five are not intended to impose any limits on the kinds of persecution covered by the refugee definition and the reasons clause can operate as a 'catch-all' clause. Thus, Aleinikoff wrote in 1991 that in the *travaux préparatoires* (*travaux*) 'there was virtually no discussion of the kinds of persecution that would qualify an individual for refugee status' and that '[t]he history of the Convention thus provides no support for a narrow reading of the grounds of persecution, but rather displays an intent to write a definition of refugee broad enough to cover then-existing victims of persecution'.[18]

Yet whilst (as we shall see) this line of argument has garnered some support, there is no escaping that at least textually the definition is exhaustive, specifying five reasons only and that these impose limits both on the type of persecution and the conditions under which a Convention reason can be established. That the reasons element impose limits was also the starting-point of the failed attempts by the 1977 United Nations Conference on Territorial Asylum to add further reasons.[19]

As with other elements of the definition, this chapter seeks to apply the Vienna Convention on the Law of Treaties (VCLT) rules of interpretation, mindful, of course, that it is an element that has become renowned for its blurred edges and lack of clarity.

## 1 History and *Travaux Préparatoires*

The decision of the drafters to include a requirement to show reasons was not made *ex cathedra*. Several factors formed a backdrop.

---

[16] See e.g. p. 184 and p. 441.
[17] Matthew Scott, *Climate Change, Disasters, and the Refugee Convention* (CUP 2020) 118–28.
[18] Thomas A Aleinikoff, 'The Meaning of Persecution in United States Asylum Law' (1991) 3(1) IJRL 5, 11.
[19] Report of the United Nations Conference on Territorial Asylum (1977) UN Doc A/CONF.78/12. James C Hathaway, *The Law of Refugee Status* (Butterworths Limited 1991) 138 notes that this conference 'would have been prepared to recognise "foreign occupation or domination"'.

## 1.1 Cognate Treaties

By the time of the drafting of the United Nations High Commissioner for Refugees (UNHCR) Statute and the Refugee Convention, references to prohibited grounds of discrimination had become an established part of international law.

Customary international law has recognised the principle of non-discrimination in various respects ever since the first Geneva Convention of 1864 mandated humane treatment 'without any adverse distinction founded on race, colour, religion or faith, sex, birth or wealth, or any other similar criteria'.[20] The London Charter of the International Military Tribunal had proscribed 'persecution on political, racial or religious grounds'.[21] The 1949 Geneva Conventions[22] include prohibition of adverse distinction founded on sex, race, nationality, religion, political opinion, or any other similar criteria.[23] The Minorities Treaties under the League of Nations established a principle whereby nationals belonging to racial, religious, or linguistic minorities were to enjoy freedom from discrimination and the same treatment in law and in fact as other nationals.[24]

Prior to 1951, international human rights law treaties had also firmly established the principle of non-discrimination. The 1945 UN Charter promoting human rights and fundamental freedoms contains a number of provisions ensuring that guaranteed rights are to be enjoyed 'without distinction as to race, sex, language or religion'.[25] As well as the right to seek and enjoy asylum from persecution, the Universal Declaration of Human Rights 1948 (UDHR) enshrines the principles of equal treatment (Preamble, paragraph 1, Articles 1, 7, 10) and non-discrimination. Article 2 states that '[e]veryone is entitled to all the rights and freedoms set forth in the Universal Declaration without distinction of any kind, such as race, colour, sex, language, religion, political or other opinion, national or social origin, property, birth, or other status'.

## 1.2 Predecessor Instruments Dealing with Refugees

The various refugee instruments drawn up in the interwar years recognised that the main causes of refugee flows were rooted in persecution visited on people on account

---

[20] Geneva Convention for the Amelioration of the Condition of the Wounded in Armies in the Field (22 August 1864) Article 3(1).

[21] Agreement for the Prosecution and Punishment of the Major War Criminals of the European Axis, and Charter of the International Military Tribunal (8 August 1945) Article 6 lit c).

[22] Convention for the Amelioration of the Condition of the Wounded and Sick in Armed Forces in the Field; Convention for the Amelioration of the Condition of the Wounded, Sick, and Shipwrecked Members of Armed Forces at Sea; Convention Relative to the Treatment of Prisoners of War; and Convention Relative to the Protection of Civilian Persons in Time of War.

[23] See common Article 3; Article 12 of First and Second Conventions respectively; see also Article 16 of Third Convention and Article 13 of the Fourth Convention.

[24] The Minorities Treaties refer to the treaties, League of Nations Mandates, and unilateral declarations made by countries applying for membership in the League of Nations and United Nations. Most of the treaties entered into force as a result of the Paris Peace Conference: see Carole Fink, 'Minority Rights as an International Question' (2000) 9(3) Contemporary European History 385.

[25] UN Charter (adopted 26 June 1945, entered into force 24 October 1945) Articles 1(3)(1)(b), 55c, 13b, 76c.

of their membership of groups closely linked to national or social origin or race or religion.[26] A 1938 resolution of the Intergovernmental Committee for Refugees had made reference to 'persons ... who must emigrate on account of their political opinions, religious beliefs and racial origin'.[27] Grahl-Madsen noted that paragraph 32 of Administrative Memorandum Number 39 of the Supreme Headquarters, Allied Expeditionary Force, revised, 16 April 1945, identified persons 'persecuted because of their race, religion or activities in favour of the United Nations'.[28] So far as concerns racial origin, the persecution of Jews and other specific groups had been specifically noted in 1938.[29] As regards political opinion, events of the nineteenth century had seen the political *émigré* emerge as the paradigm example of a refugee. Events of the first half of the twentieth century had demonstrated that political motives lay behind many of the major forced displacements that occurred. The term refugee and 'political refugee' were often used interchangeably.[30]

The International Refugee Organisation (IRO) Constitution definition of a refugee identified six protected categories, including persons who were considered refugees before the outbreak of the Second World War 'for reasons of race, religion, nationality or political opinion'.[31]

## 1.3 *Travaux Préparatoires*

In the *travaux*, there were significant references to the Convention reasons, especially within the Ad Hoc Committee on Statelessness and Related Problems when the definition listed only four reasons (race, religion, nationality, and political opinion). However, none elaborated on their meaning; that appears to have been taken for granted by virtue of their adaptation from earlier refugee instruments. The UNHCR Statute adopted by the General Assembly on 14 December 1950,[32] was confined to these four reasons.[33] It was only during the deliberations of the Conference of Plenipotentiaries taking place in July 1951, that it was decided to add the fifth reason (curiously placed fourth in the resultant text) of 'membership of a particular social group'. The Swedish delegate proposed adding this reason, his explanation being that '[s]uch cases existed, and it would be as well to mention them explicitly'.[34]

---

[26] e.g. in the 1926 Arrangements relating to Russian and Armenians and the 1928 Arrangements for refugees of Assyrian, Assyro-Chaaldean, Syrian, Kurdish and Turkish origin. See Terje Einarsen, 'Drafting History of the 1951 Convention and the 1967 Protocol' in Zimmermann (n 1) 44.
[27] Intergovernmental Committee on Refugees, Resolution of the Committee (14 July 1938) (cited in Hathaway (n 19) 136).
[28] Atle Grahl-Madsen, *The Status of Refugees in International Law. Volume 1: Refugee Character* (Sijthoff 1966) 217.
[29] Einarsen (n 26) 44.
[30] Paul Weis (ed), *The Refugee Convention 1951* (CUP 1995); Jacques Vernant, *The Refugee in the Post-War World* (Yale University Press 1953) 6, cited in Einarsen (n 26) 35.
[31] Constitution of the International Refugee Organization (IRO) (adopted 15 December 1946, entered into force 20 August 1948) 18 UNTS 3, Article 6, Part 1(A) at (c).
[32] As an Annex to General Assembly Resolution 428 (V).
[33] Statute of the Office of the United Nations High Commissioner for Refugees (1950) UNGA Res 428(v) 6A(ii).
[34] UN Conference of Plenipotentiaries on the Status of Refugees and Stateless Persons: Summary Record of the Nineteenth Meeting (26 November 1951) UN Doc A/CONF.2/SR.19, 13.

The lack of discussion about meaning of the Convention reasons seems mainly due to the fact that the drafters saw the definition as reflecting the realities of persecution that had taken place in the previous decades and did not envisage in this regard that future developments would have a markedly different character.[35] However, indication that this clause did impose some form of limit can be gleaned from the discussion that occurred over whether victims of natural disasters and environmental problems could qualify. Robinson (Israel) commented that it was difficult to envisage that 'fires, floods, earthquakes or volcanic eruptions, for instance, differentiated between their victims on the grounds of race, religion or political opinion'.[36]

## 2 Approaches to Interpretation of the Reasons Clause

### 2.1 General Observations

What implications do the basic VCLT rules have for analysing the Convention reasons and their associated nexus requirement? Several observations of a general kind are in order first regarding the reasons considered collectively.

2.1.1 Limitations of ordinary meaning
An initial observation is that whilst we shall later see that in terms of VCLT rules, the ordinary meaning of each of the five reasons indicates that they are to be given a broad construction evoking a strong social content, it is one that in each case is marked by significant indeterminacy. Exclusive reliance on ordinary meaning, also leaves unanswered obvious questions such as 'Why were these five reasons chosen?' and 'What do they have in common?'. These features have understandably fuelled concerns to draw on other VCLT considerations.[37] It was perhaps inevitable, therefore, that the wording of this clause would be seen to lend itself to application of the *eiusdem generis* rule.

2.1.2 The issue of an underlying theme
Second, as regards the issue of commonalties, two main approaches can be discerned. One is simply to take the reasons as they stand, without seeking to impose any unifying theme. The other is to seek to identify such a theme. Examples of the former include

---

[35] 'The new refugees from the East after the Second World War fitted the already well-known category of political persecution', according to Einarsen (n 26) 67. See also Daniel J Steinbock, 'Interpreting the Refugee Definition' (1998) 45(3) UCLA Law Review 733, 768.

[36] Conference of Plenipotentiaries on the Status of Refugees and Stateless Persons: Summary Record of the Twenty-second Meeting (26 November 1951) UN Doc A/CONF.2/SR.22, 6.

[37] The UNHCR expert roundtable on Membership of a Particular Social Group in 2001 concluded that '[t]he ground must be given its proper meaning within the refugee definition, in line with the object and purpose of the Convention': see Erika Feller, Volker Türk, and Frances Nicholson (eds), *Refugee Protection in International Law: UNHCR's Global Consultations on International Protection* (CUP 2003) 313. Significantly, even though urging in *Applicant A v MIEA* [1997] 190 CLR 225 that the clause's key words be afforded an ordinary meaning, at least two of the justices (Brennan CJ and McHugh) considered object and purpose played a significant part in establishing their meaning. The *eiusdem generis* doctrine was earlier identified as one of the general principles widely seen to fall within the ambit of Article 32 VCLT: see p. 105.

the 1979 UNHCR Handbook whose analysis of the reasons does not refer to any unifying theme.[38] Kirby J's opinion in *Applicant A* was that 'it is difficult to find a genus which links the categories of persecution unless it be persecution itself'. Endorsing the criticisms of Graves and Fullerton, Kirby J observed further that: '[s]ome of the groups to which the definition applies are voluntary; others are not. Some are cohesive; others are not. Some are homogeneous; others are not. Some involve immutable characteristics; others do not. Some involve characteristics central to the members' identities; others do not.'[39]

Nevertheless, the approach of seeking an underlying theme has held sway for a considerable period of time. Early commentators saw the reasons as denoting forms of fundamental socio-political disenfranchisement[40] or as constituting 'the major grounds for discrimination or oppression'[41] or as linked by 'common victimisation'[42] or as 'forms of civil and political disenfranchisement'.[43] In the course of analysing the MPSG reason, Hathaway in his 1991 study endorsed the approach taken by the United States Board of Immigration Appeals in *Matter of Acosta*, which, applying the doctrine of *eiusdem generis*, held that each of the five grounds 'describes persecution aimed at an immutable characteristic: a characteristic that either is beyond the power of an individual to change or is so fundamental to individual identity or conscience that it ought not be required to be changed'.[44] Earlier he had ventured his own view that the element that distinguishes refugees from other persons at risk of serious harm is their 'socio-political situation and resultant marginalisation'.[45] In his General Report in *Who Is a Refugee?* Carlier, reflecting on this work's comparative study of case law, stated, *à propos* of the 'five causes of persecution', that '[t]heir common characteristic is that they are the basis for discriminatory treatment'.[46] Sternberg has argued that rather

[38] An example of an academic study that chooses simply to elaborate the five reasons without exploring any underlying linkage is Vigdis Vevstad, *Refugee Protection: A European Challenge* (Tano Aschehoug 1998) 72–85. In Niraj Nathwani, *Rethinking Refugee Law* (Martinus Nijhoff Publishers 2003) 79–80. Like Nathwani, Mark R Von Sternberg, *The Grounds of Refugee Protection in the Context of International Human Rights and Humanitarian Law: Canada and United States Case Law Compared* (Martinus Nijhoff 2002) 8–9 disagrees with Hathaway's designation of 'civil or political status' as a unifying basis because the definition does not link the reasons to lack of protection but only to persecutors. Thomas A Aleinikoff, 'Protected Characteristics and Social Perceptions: An Analysis of the Meaning of "Membership of a Particular Social Group"' in Feller et al (n 37) 270, whilst ultimately endorsing an approach that seeks to combine the 'protected characteristics' and 'social perception' approaches, is critical of the attempt to treat non-discrimination as the lynchpin.

[39] *Applicant A* (n 37). It is to be noted that he came to a different view later in *Applicant S v MIMA* [2004] 217 CLR 387.

[40] Louise W Holborn, *The International Refugee Organization: A Specialized Agency of the United Nations: Its History and Work 1946–1952* (OUP 1956) 47–48, cited in Hathaway (n 19) 136.

[41] Austin T Jr Fragomen, 'The Refugee: A Problem of Definition' (1970) 3 Case W Res J Int'l L 45, 54 (cited in Hathaway (n 19) 136).

[42] See Isi Foighel, 'The Legal Status of the Boat People' (1979) 48 Nordisk Tidsskrift for International Relations 222, 223.

[43] Hathaway (n 19) 137, 141. See also Michael G Heyman, 'Redefining Refugees: A Proposal for Relief of the Victims of Civil Strife' (1987) 24 San Diego L Rev 449, 453 (cited in Hathaway (n 19) 137); Hathaway (n 19) 140, notes Canadian decisions viewing the grounds as concerned with civil and political status: e.g. *Rajudeen v MEI* [1985] 55 NR 129 (FCA).

[44] Hathaway (n 19) 160–61.

[45] ibid 136 et seq.

[46] Jean-Yves Carlier et al, *Who Is a Refugee? A Comparative Case Law Study* (Brill 1997) 712. Not all scholars have seen the reasons to have a single underlying theme. Grahl-Madsen (n 28) 217, for example, saw them as falling under two main headings: 'reasons which are beyond the control of the individual,

than civil and political status, the common factor is 'any component of the claimant's persona which defines her relationship either to the State, or to some important social aggregate within that larger national community'.[47] Reaffirming the position taken in Hathaway's 1991 study, Hathaway and Foster have confirmed that the unifying idea is 'socio-political disenfranchisement defined by reference to core norms of non-discrimination law'.[48]

Taking a broad-brush approach, it is difficult to exclude any of these proposed understandings of the unifying theme. This means that deciding which best fits turns heavily on which offers the most coherent and objective framework.

2.1.3 The concept of non-discrimination and a human rights approach
Treating the underlying norm of the reasons clause as non-discrimination has increasingly become the dominant view. Applying the *eiusdem generis* doctrine[49] in conjunction with other elements of the VCLT rules, it is this norm that constitutes the most obvious linkage between the five reasons. Considering context, this norm is specifically identified in the Convention Preamble. In addition, the principle is given prominence in the Convention's treatment of refugee rights.[50] As we have seen, courts and tribunals from early on saw non-discrimination as an underlying theme. As also noted earlier, the non-discrimination norm already played a part in pre-existing public international treaty provisions.[51]

In terms of object and purpose (and reflecting the fact that the mention of non-discrimination in the Preamble connects it with the Charter and the UDHR),[52] the making of a linkage with the concept of non-discrimination has been seen to facilitate a human rights approach. As Hathaway noted in 1991, '[g]iven the prevailing primacy of the civil and political paradigm of human rights, it was contextually logical that marginalisation should be defined by reference to norms of non-discrimination'.[53] The highwater mark of this type of linkage was the UK House of Lords' decision in *Islam* in which Lord Hoffman stated:

> [ ... ] the concept of discrimination in matters affecting human rights and freedoms is central to an understanding of the Convention. It is concerned not with all cases of persecution, even if they involved denials of human rights, but with persecution which is based on discrimination. And in the context of a human rights instrument, discrimination means making distinctions which principles of fundamental human rights regard as inconsistent with the right of every human being to equal treatment

namely race, nationality, membership of a particular social group, and—in certain respects—religion'; and 'reasons of an individual character: political opinion and active religion'.

[47] Sternberg (n 38) 230.
[48] James C Hathaway and Michelle Foster, *The Law of Refugee Status* (2nd edn, CUP 2014) 390–91.
[49] See p. 76 and p. 105.
[50] Article 3 provides that: '[t]he Contracting States shall apply the provisions of this Convention to refugees without discrimination as to race, religion or country of origin'. See James C Hathaway, *The Rights of Refugees Under International Law* (CUP 2005) 239–60.
[51] See p. 591.
[52] ibid.
[53] Hathaway (n 19) 136.

and respect. The obvious examples based on experience of persecution in Europe which would have been in the minds of the delegates in 1951, were race, religion, nationality and political opinion. But the inclusion of 'particular social group' recognised that there might be different criteria for discrimination *in pari materia* with discrimination on the other grounds, which would be equally offensive to principles of human rights ... ).[54]

The drafters' late addition of 'membership of a particular social group' demonstrates at least a doubt on their part that the other four reasons sufficiently covered the forms of discrimination that had led to persecution previously. It was also a step towards reconciling the limited list approach taken inter-war with the somewhat more open-ended formulations of the non-discrimination principle found, for example, in international humanitarian law and IHRL.

Whilst identifying a unifying theme has led to more than one approach being taken to the nature of the common characteristics, all sides broadly agree that the reasons[55] refer to characteristics or beliefs typically shared by many others in social groups or other collectivities.[56] Applying such an approach also allows for an evolutive understanding. That is important because, as Steinbock among others have highlighted, there is little to suggest that the drafters intended the MPSG category, for example, to encompass gender-based inequalities or that they intended it to extend much beyond social class. Yet an evolutive approach has enabled it to do so.[57]

It is important to note, however, the following caveat. Viewing the five reasons as sharing an underlying theme does not necessarily determine the precise contents of each reason. It further remains possible to read each reason as having a varying impact depending on the circumstances obtaining in any particular society. Moreover, at least two of the reasons—religion (in relation to the holding of a religious belief) and political opinion—do not seem to necessarily entail a group context. In addition, it must not be assumed that applying a human rights approach entails requiring those who come within the five categories to themselves embody human rights values. Indeed, a human rights approach points towards broad and inclusive definitions.

### 2.1.4 Protected characteristics?

In the literature the topic of whether there is an underlying theme has often been linked with what has become known as the 'protected characteristics'[58] approach to

---

[54] *Islam v SSHD Immigration Appeal Tribunal and Another, Ex Parte Shah, R v* [1999] UKHL 20; see also *Fornah* (n 2) para 20, per Lord Bingham of Cornhill.
[55] Save possibly that of political opinion: see p. 653.
[56] This seems broadly the view taken by Goodwin-Gill and McAdam (n 13) 95–123.
[57] Steinbock (n 35) 778; see also Goodwin-Gill and McAdam (n 13) 101.
[58] UNHCR, Guidelines on International Protection (Guidelines) No 2: Membership of a particular social group within the context of Article 1A(2) of the 1951 Convention and/or its 1967 Protocol relating to the Status of Refugees (7 May 2002) UN Doc HCR/GIP/02/01, para 6 which notes that this is sometimes referred to as the 'immutability' approach. The Guide to Refugee Law in Australia (2021) 38–39 notes that according to dictionary definitions 'innate' refers to characteristics that are 'inborn; existing or as if existing in one from birth'; 'inherent in the essential character of something'; or 'arising from the constitution of the mind, rather than acquired from experience'; whereas 'immutable' is defined as 'not mutable; unchangeable; unalterable; changeless'. It is noted that immutable characteristics may include 'attributes acquired during

construction of the MPSG reason. Whereas the other main approach to this reason—the 'social perception' approach[59]—does not necessarily assert any common theme underlying it and the other four, the 'protected characteristics' approach has based its rationale on non-discrimination being the theme underlying all five reasons. All the main versions of this approach consider that this underlying theme derives from the categories set out first in the US case of *Acosta*[60] and endorsed by the Canadian Supreme Court in *Ward*. In *Ward*, La Forest J identified three possible categories which he accepted as coming within the notion of a particular social group:

(1) groups defined by an innate or unchangeable characteristic;
(2) groups whose members voluntarily associate for reasons so fundamental to their human dignity that they should not be forced to forsake the association; and
(3) groups associated by a former voluntary status, unalterable due to its historical permanence.[61]

La Forest J explained that:

The first category would embrace individuals fearing persecution on such bases as gender, linguistic background and sexual orientation, while the second would encompass, for example, human rights activists. The third branch is included more because of historical intentions, although it is also relevant to the anti-discrimination influences, in that one's past is an immutable part of the person.[62]

Given that the judges in *Acosta* and *Ward*[63] (whose formulation was later taken almost word for word into Article 10(d) of the QD)[64] saw themselves as identifying features common to or underlying all five reasons, it is pertinent to examine very briefly: (a) whether the other reasons do in fact reflect these particular features; and (b) whether the *Acosta/Ward* sub-categories are conceptually clear. It is arguable that the answer to both questions should be no. These questions will arise again when later considering the MPSG reason in detail.

To address these questions, it is first necessary to situate where each of the other four reasons is understood to fit within the *Acosta/Ward* framework. Leading cases do not make this entirely clear, but the general position appears to be as follows. In the case of race, this term, at least in respect of one of its core meanings, would appear to relate exclusively to the *Ward* category (1)—'innate' or 'unchangeable' or 'immutable' characteristics.[65] Whilst religion and political opinion can be understood as quintessentially

one's life, such as the health status of being HIV positive, or a certain experience such as being a child soldier, sex worker or victim of human trafficking'. See discussion further below at p. 627 and pp. 628–629.

[59] UNHCR Guidelines No 2 (n 58) para 7. See further below pp. 630–632.
[60] *Acosta* (n 14).
[61] *Ward* (n 14).
[62] ibid.
[63] ibid.
[64] QD (recast) (n 8).
[65] Although as underlined in section 3.1 below this does not mean that the meaning of race is biological or based on physical characteristics.

characteristics or beliefs that are so fundamental to identity or conscience that a person should not be forced to renounce them (and so belonging in *Ward* category (2)), it is noteworthy that at least one scholar, Grahl-Madsen, considered that political opinion and 'active religion' did not fall within this category[66] and that in UNHCR guidance and other materials, political opinion has been understood to have virtually no qualitative restrictions.[67] Nationality, which as will be explained below has in the context of the Convention reasons to be given a broad ethnographic meaning, appears difficult to classify since although for many it is effectively unalterable, it can be changed and is at the discretion of states.[68]

The *Acosta/Ward* categories are not themselves entirely clear. Taken on its own, (1) (groups defined by an innate or unchangeable characteristic) appears potentially to apply to an infinite variety of groups. Notwithstanding the apparently narrow understanding of this category by La Forest in *Ward* (he referred to 'such bases as gender, linguistic background and sexual orientation') its broad wording appears to go far wider. As regards (3) (groups associated by a former voluntary status, unalterable due to its historical permanence), it is not clear how this is distinct from (1); but in any event,[69] taken literally, it again would seem capable of covering a bewilderingly large number of groups. Only (2) (groups whose members voluntarily associate for reasons so fundamental to their human dignity that they should not be forced to forsake the association) would appear to contain any hard-edged delimitation. But even here it is unclear what it means (or what (3) means) by voluntary association/voluntary status, in particular whether it amounts to a requirement of actual voluntary association or can be met simply by reference to how the group would be perceived.[70] Two years after *Ward*, La Forest J in *Chan* sought to clarify this issue by noting that the association need not be formal nor was the applicant required to associate voluntarily with other members of the designated group:

---

[66] Grahl-Madsen (n 28) 217. It must be said, however, that his subsequent analysis fails to make clear why these two categories do not qualify as 'reasons beyond the control of the individual'. The Australian Department of Home Affairs' Refugee Law Guidelines, re-issued in 2017, describe 'fundamental' as synonymous with a 'necessary base or core' or of 'central importance'. Acts of certain kinds are said to be 'fundamental to identity or conscience' where they are of central importance to the identity or conscience of the group. They link the term 'conscience' to aspects such as religion, political opinion, or moral beliefs.

[67] This feature is discussed below at pp. 643–644.

[68] See Grahl-Madsen (n 28) 217; *Acosta* (n 14); Sternberg (n 38) 51–52. However, the ICJ in *Application of the International Convention on the Elimination of All Forms of Racial Discrimination (Qatar v United Arab Emirates)*, Preliminary objections [2021] ICGJ 554, para 81 states that in contrast to race, colour, and descent, which were 'characteristics that are inherent at birth', nationality 'is a legal attribute which is within the discretionary power of the State and can change during a person's lifetime', citing *Nottebohm Case (second phase) (Liechtenstein v Guatemala)*, Judgment [1955] ICJ Rep 4, 20 and 23.

[69] Goodwin-Gill and McAdam (n 13) 104 observe (citing *Ward*) that: 'Given that "one's past is an immutable part of the person", the third category belongs essentially to the first.'

[70] ibid 104–05. Having noted that the Court in *Ward* said that group (3) was included 'because of historical intentions', they state: '[h]owever, there is no evidence to suggest that those apparently intended to benefit from the social group provision, the former capitalists of eastern Europe, were ever formally associated with one another. They may have been, but equally they may not. What counted at the time was the fact that they were not only *internally* linked by having engaged in a particular type of (past) economic activity, but also *externally* defined, partly if not exclusively, by the perceptions of the new ruling class.' (emphases in the original).

In order to avoid any confusion on this point let me state incontrovertibly that a refugee alleging membership in a particular social group does not have to be in a voluntary association with other persons similar to him or herself. Such a claimant is in no manner required to associate, ally, or consort voluntarily with kindred persons. The association exists by virtue of a common attempt made by its members to exercise a fundamental human right.

However, leaving aside that the majority in *Chan* did not endorse such reasoning, this attempt at clarification leaves unanswered the question, what constitutes a 'common attempt' to exercise a fundamental human right if voluntary association is not required? Potentially this amounts to a Trojan horse, letting in the approach to which the 'protected characteristics' approach contrasts itself—the social perception approach. A further doubt about any attempt to apply the *Acosta/Ward* framework to interpret all five reasons is that the notion of 'membership' is only expressly mentioned in relation to 'particular social group'. Whilst it has been widely recognised that (typically at least) the other reasons concern groups, at least definitionally, membership as such would not seem critical to their existence.[71]

Later, in the section on MPSG, this study casts doubt on whether the *Acosta/Ward* categories even work for the MPSG reason, but in light of the above difficulties, its efficacy as an overall framework for the Convention reasons *en bloc* must be doubted.

### 2.1.5 Interrelationship between the Convention reasons and the meaning of persecution

A next observation is that whilst there is wide agreement that the Convention norm of non-discrimination underpins the Convention reasons, attempts to argue that this norm also forms part of the meaning of 'being persecuted' have largely been resisted. This was a principal conclusion of this book's analysis in Chapter 6, which considered, inter alia, the contrary view advanced most recently by Matthew Scott[72] which attempts to treat persecution as an exacerbated form of discrimination. It was considered that, especially if a human rights approach is taken to the refugee definition, core entitlements to protection against serious violations of human rights are clearly something different from the Convention reasons.[73]

## 2.2 Common Features

Irrespective of whether each of the five reasons reflects an underlying theme of some kind, it is necessary to ask what specific features, if any, can they be said to have in common?

---

[71] See *Okere v MICA* [1998] 87 FCR 112, paras 115–17.
[72] Scott (n 17). See pp. 380–383.
[73] ibid. See also Nathwani (n 38) 80–81. Richard Buxton, 'A History From Across The Pond' (2012) 44 International Law and Politics 391, 394, observed that attempts to conflate the nexus requirement with the analysis of 'being persecuted' can lead in some contexts to a distorted understanding of both, as was noted in *Refugee Appeal No 71427/99* [2000] NZRSAA, para 52.

### 2.2.1 Limiting role

Notwithstanding the view of some early commentators, there is a broad consensus that the five enumerated reasons do constitute a limit of some kind on the type of persecution covered by the definition and on when the reasons can be engaged. That reflects not only the text but also the evident fact that if they did not constitute a limit of some kind, they would be superfluous and have no *effet utile*.

### 2.2.2 Non-hierarchical character

There is no logical basis, on either textual or other grounds, for regarding one or other reason as more important or fundamental than another. As noted by Lord Dyson in *RT (Zimbabwe)*, 'the well-founded fear of persecution test set out in the Convention does not change according to which Convention reason is engaged'.[74] If one or more reasons tend to predominate in certain types of cases, this is best understood as a function of the social and political context of the case. Thus, for example, Holzer[75] has noted that the grounds of race and religion and nationality are particularly relevant in contemporary armed conflict situations.

### 2.2.3 Need for a reason-specific analysis

All sources highlight the importance of understanding the specific characteristics of each reason. Thus, in *Chen Shi Hai v Minister for Immigration and Multicultural Affairs*, the Australian High Court observed that:

> 24. The need for different analysis depending on the reason assigned for the discriminatory conduct in question may be illustrated, in the first instance, by reference to race, religion and nationality. If persons of a particular race, religion or nationality are treated differently from other members of society, that, of itself, may justify the conclusion that they are treated differently by reason of their race, religion or nationality. That is because, ordinarily, race, religion and nationality do not provide a reason for treating people differently.
>
> 25. The position is somewhat more complex when persecution is said to be for reasons of membership of a particular social group or political opinion. There may be groups—for example, terrorist groups—which warrant different treatment to protect society. So, too, it may be necessary for the protection of society to treat persons who hold certain political views—for example, those who advocate violence or terrorism—differently from other members of society.[76]

### 2.2.4 Overlapping character

All sources concur in recognising that the Convention reasons are not mutually exclusive and must be understood as capable of overlapping when applied to individuals' particular circumstances. For example, the 1979 UNHCR Handbook notes that:

---

[74] *RT (Zimbabwe) and others v SSHD* [2012] UKSC 38.

[75] Vanessa Holzer, *Refugees from Armed Conflict* (Intersentia 2015) 183; Vanessa Holzer, 'The 1951 Refugee Convention and the Protection of Persons Fleeing Armed Conflict and Other Situations of Violence' (September 2012) UNHCR, Legal and Protection Policy Research Series, PPLA/2012/05, 28–29; see also Sternberg (n 38) 83.

[76] *Chen Shi Hai v MIMA* [2000] 201 CLR 293.

It is immaterial whether the persecution arises from any single one of these reasons or from a combination of two or more of them. Often the applicant himself may not be aware of the reasons for the persecution feared. It is not, however, his duty to analyse his case to such an extent as to identify the reasons in detail.... Usually there will be more than one element combined in one person, e.g. a political opponent who belongs to a religious or national group, or both, and the combination of such reasons in his person may be relevant in evaluating his well-founded fear.[77]

In a similar vein, the UNHCR Guidelines on MPSG note that the Convention reasons are not mutually exclusive and may overlap. They give the example of an applicant who claims that she is at risk of persecution because of her refusal to wear traditional clothing. 'Depending on the particular circumstances of the society', they note 'she may be able to establish a claim based on political opinion (if her conduct is viewed by the State as a political statement that it seeks to suppress), religion (if her conduct is based on a religious conviction opposed by the State) or membership in a particular social group.'[78]

The overlapping character of the Convention reasons might also be said to further demonstrate the interlocking nature of the definitional elements of the Article 1A(2) definition.[79]

### 2.2.5 Individualised basis

By virtue of the fact that the refugee definition is cast in individualistic terms,[80] an applicant need only show that one of the five reasons was causative of his or her persecution, not that all members of that person's race, religion, political opinion, nationality, and particular social group are at risk. As expressed by UNHCR in the Guidelines on MPSG:

> An applicant need not demonstrate that all members of a particular social group are at risk of persecution in order to establish the existence of a particular social group. As with the other grounds, it is not necessary to establish that all persons in the political party or ethnic group have been singled out for persecution.[81]

### 2.2.6 No requirement of discretion/concealment

In Chapter 6, it was noted that the Article 1A(2) definition nowhere imposes a requirement of concealment or behaviour modification.[82] In logic, this understanding must

---

[77] UNHCR, Handbook on Procedures and Criteria for Determining Refugee Status and Guidelines on International Protection under the 1951 Convention and the 1967 Protocol Relating to the Status Of Refugees (Geneva, 2019, reissued in 2019) para 66 (UNHCR Handbook or Handbook).
[78] UNHCR Guidelines No 2 (n 58) para 4.
[79] See pp. 192–193.
[80] See p. 672.
[81] UNHCR Guidelines No 2 (n 58) para 17. As noted by Goodwin-Gill and McAdam (n 13) 99–100: '[i]t is not necessary that those persecuted should constitute a minority in their own country, oligarchies traditionally tend to resort to oppression'.
[82] See p. 333.

be applied—and is now widely applied—to the reasons clause as well. For example, requiring persons to seek to hide their race or ethnic identity or nationality or MPSG, or to practise their religion in secret, or to hide or dissemble their political opinion, is contrary to basic principles of human rights. The UNHCR Guidance Note on Sexual Orientation,[83] for example, justifiably maintains that 'requiring a person to conceal his or her sexual orientation and thereby to give up those characteristics, contradicts the very notion of "particular social group" as one of the prohibited grounds in the 1951 Convention'.[84]

### 2.2.7 The doctrine of attribution: imputed or perceived reasons/grounds

It is a long-established axiom of refugee law that what matters ultimately when assessing the risk of being persecuted for a Convention reason is not who or what people *are* but how they are *perceived* by the actors of persecution. Thus, it is not necessary, in order to demonstrate a risk for a Convention reason, that a person possesses in reality the racial, religious, national, political, or group characteristics in question; it is enough that s/he will be perceived to possess those characteristics. This is known variously as the doctrine (or principle) of attribution or imputability or perception. Whilst the 1979 UNHCR Handbook only referred to this doctrine in the context of political opinion[85] and whilst (curiously) the 2002 Guidelines on MPSG[86] make no mention of it, it was made explicit in the 2001 note on 'Interpreting Article 1'[87] and in the Guidelines on Trafficking,[88] Child Asylum Claims,[89] Sexual Orientation/Gender Identity,[90] and Military Service.[91] Within the EU, Article 10 of the EU QD contains a specific provision giving direct legal effect to this doctrine. Article 10(2) provides:

> 2. When assessing if an applicant has a well-founded fear of being persecuted it is immaterial whether the applicant actually possesses the racial, religious, national, social or political characteristic which attracts the persecution, provided that such a characteristic is attributed to the applicant by the actor of persecution.[92]

---

[83] UNHCR Guidelines No 9: Claims to Refugee Status based on Sexual Orientation and/or Gender Identity within the context of Article 1A(2) of the 1951 Convention and/or its 1967 Protocol relating to the Status of Refugees (23 October 2012) HCR/GIP/12/01.

[84] ibid para 32.

[85] UNHCR Handbook (n 77) para 80.

[86] UNHCR Guidelines No 2 (n 58).

[87] UNHCR, Interpreting Article 1 of the 1951 Convention Relating to the Status of Refugees (2001) para 25.

[88] UNHCR Guidelines No 7: The Application of Article 1A(2) of the 1951 Convention and/or 1967 Protocol Relating to the Status of Refugees to Victims of Trafficking and Persons at Risk of Being Trafficked (7 April 2006) UN Doc HCR/GIP/06/07, para 29.

[89] UNHCR Guidelines No 8: Child Asylum Claims under Articles 1(A)2 and 1(F) of the 1951 Convention and/or 1967 Protocol relating to the Status of Refugees (2009) UN Doc HCR/GIP/09/08, paras 46–47.

[90] UNHCR Guidelines No 9 (n 83) para 41.

[91] UNHCR Guidelines No 10: Claims to Refugee Status related to Military Service within the context of Article 1A (2) of the 1951 Convention and/or the 1967 Protocol relating to the Status of Refugees (12 November 2014) UN Doc HCR/GIP/13/10/Corr.1, para 48. Several paragraphs embody a distinction between 'real or perceived' reasons: see e.g. paras 37–39.

[92] QD (recast) (n 8).

The rationale for the doctrine of attribution is rarely doubted but is, in any event, strongly indicated by the principle of surrogacy. If applicants were viewed as unable to establish a Convention reason even though the very basis for their persecution was one of the definition's five enumerated characteristics, that would mean denying refugee status to many genuinely lacking national protection. Whether or not they actually possess one or more such characteristics is immaterial to that predicament.

Universal support for the doctrine of attribution does highlight though a tension (or paradox) underlying *all* of the Convention reasons. On the one hand, the doctrine of attribution bids us to heed primarily the world of appearance or perception rather than reality—how a person is perceived by the persecutor.[93]

On the other hand, if focus is placed at all times entirely on the world of appearance or perception, that would legitimise an approach that had no necessary linkage to the objective circumstances prevailing in the country of origin. It would also blur clear understanding of what underlies persecutors' perceptions. Albeit what actors of persecution perceive is crucial to deciding whether someone will face persecution, what they perceive as persecutory only makes sense by reference to the actual circumstances and patterns of understanding obtaining in their country. Their perception may not accord with reality but there will often be something rooted in reality driving it. This insight demonstrates, it is submitted, that any attempt at definition of any of the five reasons in terms of a pure 'social perception' approach—in this case considering nothing but the perception of the persecutor—would make it impossible to explain the root basis for the persecution. Ultimately there has to be some correlation between the underlying reality of the reason and the societal perceptions about it.

Framing matters in this way strongly suggests that the tension between these two approaches cannot be resolved by adopting one and rejecting the other but must aim for a synthesis. Any synthesis must give effect to the existence of key features of human society rooted in basic ethnographical, linguistic, and cultural differences. For that reason, some help may be derived from UNHCR's attempt in Guidelines No 2 at a synthesis of the two approaches to the MPSG reason, so that the 'protected characteristics' approach is seen to denote the 'core' of the concept. Whether, however, that justifies UNHCR and other's acceptance that the 'social perception' approach has a free-standing role to play—designed to address the exceptional cases in which certain characteristics are merely imputed by the persecutors (or in the case of particular social group, by society) to a victim of persecution[94]—is another matter, dealt with in section 3.4.4 below.[95] What can be stated, however, is that perception must ultimately

---

[93] Zimmermann and Mahler (n 1) 387. They note that the same tension has arisen in the international criminal law jurisdiction when dealing with the differently defined concept of persecution within the statutes of the international criminal tribunals. Thus, in *Prosecutor v Naletilic and Martinovic* (Judgment) ICTY-98-34-T (31 March 2003), the ICTY Trial Chamber stated that '[t]he targeted group must be interpreted broadly, and may, in particular, include such person who are defined by the perpetrator as belonging to the victim group due to their close affiliations or sympathies with the victim group. The Chamber finds this interpretation consistent with the underlying ratio of the provision prohibiting persecution, as it is the perpetrator who defines the victim group while the targeted victims have no influence on the definition of their status.'

[94] See Tillmann Löhr, *Die kinderspezifische Auslegung des völkerrechtlichen Flüchtlingsbegriffs* (Nomos Verlag 2009) 142, cited by Zimmermann and Mahler (n 1) 393.

[95] See below p. 626 especially.

always be a secondary route, otherwise the result is an inversion of the worlds of appearance and reality.

## 3 The Individual Reasons

In previous chapters, it has been argued that valuable groundwork for establishing a more detailed working definition of 'being persecuted' and other key elements of the Article 1A(2) definition has now been laid by the drafters of the Qualification Directive and its recast, which, although a regional instrument, provides a useful starting point for a truly global understanding of the refugee definition. Article 10 on 'Reasons for Persecution' is indeed the most detailed of its definitional provisions (each of its paragraphs are quoted below when addressing individual reasons).[96]

Drawing in this way on Article 10, however, does not mean endorsing its precise terms; indeed, this study goes on to expressly reject its cumulative listing of MPSG criteria;[97] it is used here only as a major modern reference-point. All attempts to codify the meaning of the MPSG reason (or indeed any other element of the refugee definition), whether at the national law or regional law level,[98] must be subjected to close scrutiny as to whether they reflect the term's international meaning.

### 3.1 Race

3.1.1 Origins and *travaux préparatoires*
The inclusion of race as a prohibited ground in international treaties and in predecessor refugee instruments was noted earlier.[99] It can be added here that the London Charter of the International Military Tribunal had identified 'persecution on racial grounds' as a punishable crime against humanity.[100]

Neither in the deliberations on the interwar refugee instruments or the IRO Constitution was there any particular discussion of the meaning of the term 'race'; its meaning appears to have been taken to be self-evident, with the recent history of Jewish victims of Nazi persecution in the forefront of everyone's minds.[101]

---

[96] QD (recast) (n 8). This is a 'recast' of the earlier Council Directive 2004/83/EC of 29 April 2004 on minimum standards for the qualification and status of third country nationals or stateless persons as refugees or as persons who otherwise need international protection and the content of the protection granted [2004] OJ L 304/12. The wording of Article 10(1)(d) in the recast Directive represents a slight change from that in the original Directive: there is now the added requirement in 10(1) for gender-related aspects to be 'given due consideration' combined with the deletion of the previous statement that gender creates no presumption of membership of a group.
[97] See below p. 638.
[98] See p. 729. Exemplifying a codification based on highly politicised and restrictionist domestic policy considerations, in 2018, the Trump administration had imposed a ruling that victims of domestic violence and gang violence did not qualify as a PSG. This was reversed in June 2021 by Attorney General Garland: see *Matter of LEA* [2021] Interim Decision #4018, 28 I&N Dec 304 (AG); and *Matter of AB* [2021] Interim Decision #4019, 28 I&N Dec 307 (AG).
[99] See pp. 591–592.
[100] Zimmermann and Mahler (n 1) 376.
[101] Grahl-Madsen (n 28) 217.

3.1.2 Article 31 and other Article 32 VCLT considerations

In language which continues in this regard to reflect the view of leading commentators, the 1979 Handbook states that race has to be understood 'in its widest sense to include all kinds of ethnic groups that are referred to as "races" in common usage'.[102] In ordinary usage, race is an elusive concept. There is no definitive dictionary definition and the entry in the current OED Online (as one example) signifies a marked shift away from earlier definitions that had defined the notion in terms of physical characteristics.[103] As was said earlier in relation to the Convention reasons *en bloc*, to make any significant progress in arriving at an international law meaning we have to consider ordinary meaning alongside other VCLT elements.

As regards context, in addition to its place as a reason in Article 1A(2) and Article 31(1), race is one of three grounds identified in the non-discrimination provision of Article 3 which governs refugee rights, but this tells us nothing about meaning.

Having regard to object and purpose, the fact that the Preamble refers to human rights prompts consideration of whether assistance for interpreting the term 'race' can be derived from IHRL. As noted by the 1979 Handbook, persecution for reason of race has been internationally condemned as a fundamental assault on human dignity incompatible with the most elementary and inalienable human rights.[104] Confirming this reason's underpinning in international law and in human rights law, various international treaties (mostly) post-dating the Refugee Convention proscribe racial discrimination, e.g. the Convention for the Elimination of All Forms of Racial Discrimination (ICERD)[105] and the International Convention on the Suppression and Punishment of the Crime of Apartheid.[106] Within the framework of international law, race is seen to be interconnected with the concept of ethnicity and other concepts relating to colour, descent, or national or ethnic origin. Article 1(1) of ICERD states that '[i]n this Convention, the term "racial discrimination" shall mean any distinction, exclusion, restriction or preference based on race, colour, descent, or national or ethnic origin which has the purpose or effect of nullifying or impairing the recognition, enjoyment or exercise, on an equal footing, of human rights and fundamental freedoms in the political, economic, social, cultural or any other field of public life'. In General Comment No 20, the Committee on Economic, Social and Cultural Rights has stated that '[t]he use of the term "race" in the Covenant or the present general comment does

---

[102] UNHCR Handbook (n 77) para 68.
[103] The most relevant entry (n 6.d) states: '[a]ccording to various more or less formal attempted systems of classification: any of the (putative) major groupings of mankind, usually defined in terms of distinct physical features or shared ethnicity, and sometimes (more controversially) considered to encompass common biological or genetic characteristics'. Contrast the 1989 OED which included as one of the senses (n 2.d), '[o]ne of the great divisions of mankind, having certain physical peculiarities in common'.
[104] UNHCR Handbook (n 77) para 69. At para 68, the Handbook notes that '[d]iscrimination for reasons of race has found world-wide condemnation as one of the most striking violations of human rights'.
[105] International Convention on the Elimination of all Forms of Racial Discrimination (ICERD) (adopted 21 December 1965, entered into force 4 January 1969) 660 UNTS 19.
[106] International Convention on the Suppression and Punishment of the Crime of Apartheid (adopted 30 November 1973, entered into force 18 July 1976) 1015 UNTS 243. This Convention makes it unlawful to engage in 'inhuman acts' for the purpose of achieving racial hegemony of one racial group over another. The list of proscribed acts includes '[p]ersecution of organizations and persons, by depriving them of fundamental rights and freedoms, because they oppose apartheid' (Article II(f)).

not imply the acceptance of theories which attempt to determine the existence of separate human races'.[107]

A similarly broad approach is taken in IHRL jurisprudence. For example, in *Sejdic and Finci v Bosnia and Herzegovina*, the Grand Chamber of the ECtHR has observed that race and ethnicity are related and overlapping concepts. The Court noted that the concept of ethnicity 'had its origin in the idea of social groups marked by common nationality, tribal affiliation, religious faith, shared language, or cultural and traditional origins and backgrounds'.[108] Whilst distinguishing between the two concepts, the Court proceeded on the basis that in the context of examining grounds of discrimination, ethnic origins could be considered alongside race, stating in the same paragraph '[d]iscrimination on account of a person's ethnic origin is a form of racial discrimination'.[109]

Although it is a statement of the obvious, it is also relevant to note, given issues that have arisen in relation to some of the other reasons, that the category of race is not based on any qualitative criteria regarding whether those of a particular race think or act in conformity with any particular system of values.

Having regard to Articles 31(3) and 32 VCLT considerations, UNHCR learning, case law (sparse as it has been) and leading academic commentaries have supported a broad understanding of 'race'.[110] Accurately reflecting in this regard not just EU but global state practice, at least in the broad sense,[111] Article 10(a) QD specifies that '(a) the concept of race shall in particular include considerations of colour, descent, or membership of a particular ethnic group'.

### 3.1.3 Evaluation

What is stated in these above-mentioned sources accurately reflects the position taken in the bulk of the literature. Grahl-Madsen, for example, noted that 'the term "race" as used in Article 1A(2) is a social more than an ethnographic concept and is applicable

---

[107] ICERD (n 105); UN Committee on Economic, Social and Cultural Rights (ESCR Committee), General comment No 20: Non-discrimination in economic, social and cultural rights (art. 2, para. 2, of the International Covenant on Economic, Social and Cultural Rights (2 July 2009) UN Doc E/C.12/GC/20, para 19).

[108] *Sejdic and Finci v Bosnia and Herzegovina* Apps Nos 27996/06 and 34836/06 (ECtHR, 22 December 2009).

[109] ibid para 43. Walter Kälin and Jörg Künzli, *The Law of International Human Rights Protection* (2nd edn, OUP 2019) 357, take issue with the emphasis placed by the ICERD Committee on self-identification of the individuals concerned (see CERD General Recommendation VIII Concerning the Interpretation and Application of Article 1, Paragraphs 1 and 4 of the Convention Identification with a Particular Racial or Ethnic Group (22 August 1990) UN Doc A/45/18). They consider it an approach which is 'adequate in many cases but insufficient in other situations as the history of racial discrimination and the social mechanisms leading to it indicate that the worst cases of racism are often based on insinuated or assumed membership in a racial or ethnic group'. For analysis of the concept of ethnicity, see Kathleen McVay, 'Self-Determination in New Contexts: The Self-Determination of Refugees and Forced Migrants in International Law' (2012) 28 Merkourios-Utrecht J Int'l & Eur L 36, 38.

[110] Zimmermann and Mahler (n 1) 376–78; Hathaway and Foster (n 48) 394–97 cite *Horvath v SSHD* [2000] UKHL 37; *Calado v MIMA* [1997] 81 FCR 59. Lorne Waldman, *The Definition of Convention Refugee* (2nd edn, Lexis Nexis 2019) 314, cites the Canadian case of *Rajudeen v Canada (MEI)* [1984] FCJ No 601 55 NR. In *SZEGA v MIMIA* [2006] FCA 1286, para 19, the Australian Federal Court held that caste did not come within the meaning of the reason of race. For US case law see Anker (n 1) §5.85, 666–72. See also Eileen Pittaway and Linda Bartolomei, 'Refugees, Race and Gender: The Multiple Discrimination against Refugee Women' (2001) 19(6) Refuge 21.

[111] See Chapter 2, n 69.

whenever a person is persecuted because of his ethnic origin'.[112] However, given that, as Goodwin-Gill and McAdam have noted, '[p]ersecution on account of race is all too frequently the background for refugee movements in all parts of the world',[113] it is a cause of real concern that there has been strikingly little refugee case law addressing the meaning of race.[114] The contrast with the vast jurisprudence on MPSG is staggering. The fact that 'many racial or ethnic claims are framed and decided under other grounds'[115] is one reason for this but acutely poses the question, why not frame them under this reason on its own or as well? The quest for a truly universal approach to the refugee definition will forever be impeded if there is not a greater reckoning with the relative neglect of race and ethnicity.[116]

## 3.2 Religion

### 3.2.1 Origins and *travaux préparatoires*

The drafters of the Convention were well aware of the scourge of religious persecution not just from large-scale persecution suffered by Jews in the Second World War but from the late nineteenth century pogroms of Jews in the western areas of the Russia Empire and of Armenian Christians in Ottoman Turkey. We have already noted the inclusion of 'religion' as a proscribed ground of discrimination in early human rights instruments, including the UN Charter and the 1948 UDHR. In the Refugee Convention's *travaux*, it appears that its meaning was taken for granted or not seen as requiring any debate.[117] Grahl-Madsen notes that race and religion had been considered in the Records of Headquarters First Allied Airborne Army (SHAEF) Administrative Memorandum Number 39, which was aimed at helping the Jewish victims of Nazi persecution some of whom were persecuted because of their race, some because of their Jewish religion, and some for both reasons.[118] Frequently made has been the observation that religion is often mixed in with other reasons.[119]

### 3.2.2 Article 31 and other Article 32 VCLT considerations

In ordinary usage, religion too is an elusive concept. Dictionaries proffer several definitions with significant variations. The OED Online, for example, contains definitions

---

[112] Grahl-Madsen (n 28) 218. See also Hathaway and Foster (n 48) 396–97.
[113] Goodwin-Gill and McAdam (n 13) 96.
[114] Carlier et al (n 46) 657; Zimmerman and Mahler (n 1) 377; Anker (n 1) 535; Waldman (n 110) 313–17.
[115] Anker (n 1) 536; Susan M Akram, 'Orientalism Revisited in Asylum and Refugee Claims' (2000) 12 IJRL 7; von Sternberg (n 38) 21; Hathaway and Foster (n 48) 396–97; see also Waldman (n 110) 314.
[116] See Christopher Kyriakides et al, 'Introduction: The Racialized Refugee Regime' (2019) 35(1) Refuge 3, 5; Tendayi Achiume, 'Race, Refugees, and International Law' in Costello et al (n 9) 52–53, who notes that the ICERD 'is largely absent in litigation on behalf of refugees that nonetheless relies on other international human rights treaties' and diagnoses 'international refugee law scholarship's racial aphasia'.
[117] Karen Musalo, 'Claims for Protection Based on Religion or Belief' (2004) 16(2) IJRL 170, cited in Zimmermann and Mahler (n 1) 381.
[118] Grahl-Madsen (n 28) 216–17.
[119] Jeremy Gunn, 'The Complexity of Religion and the Definition of "Religion" in International Law' (2003) 16 Harv Hum Rts LJ 189, 208 notes that '[i]n many asylum cases it may be difficult to determine whether the alleged persecution is a result of religious, gender, political, or even cultural factors—or perhaps some combination thereof'. See also Anker (n 1) §5.69, 638 and Akram (n 115).

that include 'particular system of faith and worship', '[a] pursuit, interest, or movement, followed with great devotion'; and '[b]elief in or acknowledgement of some superhuman power or powers (esp. a god or gods) which is typically manifested in obedience, reverence, and worship; such a belief as part of a system defining a code of living, esp. as a means of achieving spiritual or material improvement'.[120] Jeremy Gunn's seminal study notes that 'no one definition of religion has garnered a consensus, and the definitional enterprise, as well as the debate over the very need for definitions, continues in full vigor'.[121] As was said in earlier general comments, to make any significant progress in arriving at an international law-related meaning of such a reason, we have to consider the ordinary meaning alongside other requirements of the VCLT rules.

There are other references to religion in Article 33(1) and Article 3 of the Convention, but they tell us nothing about meaning. In terms of object and purpose, however, light is shed by IHRL within which religion is seen as an internationally protected activity or status, closely linked to the basic rights to freedom of thought, conscience and religion, i.e. internationally protected activities or statuses. Article 18 of the ICCPR provides that everyone shall have the right to freedom of thought, conscience, and religion.[122] The Declaration on the Elimination of All Forms of Intolerance and of Discrimination Based on Religion or Belief adopted in 1981,[123] and the Declaration on the Rights of Persons belonging to National or Ethnic, Religious and Linguistic Minorities 1993,[124] reinforce the fact of international recognition of the need for persons facing harm to receive protection on account of this reason. However, these only help with the meaning of religion indirectly.

The UNHCR Guidelines No 6 are in part an attempt to respond to the uncertainty over the meaning of this reason.[125] It points up that this reason has to be interpreted in light of the fact that the right to religious freedom is more contextualised compared to some other guaranteed rights in international law. It emphasises that to be consistent with the approach to definition of the other Convention reasons, religion must be given a broad construction so that it encompasses not just its primary sense, (i) religion in the form of belief, but also (ii) religion in the form of identity, and (iii) religion as a way of life.[126] It must also be taken to include the right not to hold a religious belief, either individually or as a member of a group which does not hold a religious belief, such as humanists. These three senses are seen to highlight religion's close connections with family, society, ethnicity, race, and nationality. In relation to beliefs, the

---

[120] OED Online <https://www.oed.com>accessed 12 August 2021.
[121] Gunn (n 119) 191. A similar concern underlies the UNGA, Interim report of the Special Rapporteur on freedom of religion or belief (17 July 2009) UN Doc A/64/159, cited in Zimmermann and Mahler (n 1) 379.
[122] ICCPR (n 5).
[123] See Declaration on the Elimination of All Forms of Intolerance and of Discrimination Based on Religion or Belief (25 November 1981) UN Doc A/RES/36/55.
[124] Declaration on the Rights of Persons belonging to National or Ethnic, Religious and Linguistic Minorities (4 March 1994) UN Doc A/RES/48/138.
[125] UNHCR Guidelines No 6: Religion-Based Refugee Claims under Article 1A(2) of the 1951 Convention and/or the 1967 Protocol relating to the Status of Refugees (2004) UN Doc HCR/GIP/04/06, para 1; Zimmermann and Mahler (n 1) 370.
[126] Zimmermann and Mahler (n 1) 200–05.

UNHCR Guidelines state that: '[b]eliefs may take the form of convictions or values about the divine or ultimate reality or the spiritual destiny of humankind. Applicants may also be considered heretics, apostates, schismatics, pagans or superstitious, even by other adherents of their religious tradition and be persecuted for that reason.' The term is not seen to be limited to belief in the existence of divine forces or supernatural powers.[127]

Article 10(b) of the QD (recast) also adopts a broad definition, albeit without any clear differentiation of these three senses. It states that:

> [ ... ] the concept of religion shall in particular include the holding of theistic, non-theistic and atheistic beliefs, the participation in, or abstention from, formal worship in private or in public, either alone or in community with others, other religious acts or expressions of view, or forms of personal or communal conduct based on or mandated by any religious belief.'

### 3.2.3 Right to freedom of religion

Applying a human rights analysis, neither the freedom of thought and conscience nor the freedom to have or adopt a religion or belief of one's choice is subject to limitation. This means that there can be no restrictions on the freedom to hold beliefs.[128] However, religion cannot encompass every self-identification of a religious belief or motivation. For example, the refusal to fulfil certain legal duties, e.g. tax obligations, military service obligations, is generally not held to be protected by the relevant provisions governing freedom of religion.[129] In relation to the (qualified) freedom to manifest belief, in order to count as a manifestation, the act in question must be intimately linked to the religion or belief and so may not cover acts or omissions which do not directly express the belief concerned or which are only distantly connected to a precept of faith.[130]

The role of the doctrine of attribution in refugee law necessitates reading the term religion even more broadly than is dictated by ordinary meaning and object and purpose. As noted by Gunn, 'the relevant issues for adjudicators may not be the religious beliefs or religious activities from the perspective of religious communities or academics studying religion, but the attitudes of those who are causing the religious persecution'.[131]

Employing a broad definition, religion embraces not just well-established religions such as Hinduism, Christianity, Islam, Buddhism, Judaism, and the less mainstream religions, e.g. Jehovah's Witness, Pentecostalist faiths. It enables it to be applied to traditional religions or to religions and beliefs with institutional

---

[127] UNHCR Guidelines No 6: Religion-Based Refugee Claims (n 125).

[128] UN Human Rights Committee (HRC), General Comment No 22: Article 18 (27 September 1993) UN Doc CCPR/C/21/Rev.1/Add.4, 8; *SAS v France* App No 43835/11 (ECtHR [GC], 1 July 2014).

[129] Zimmermann and Mahler (n 1) 386. In the *Case of Pretty v United Kingdom* App No 2346/02 (ECtHR, 29 July 2002) para 82, the ECtHR observed that not all opinions or convictions constitute beliefs in the sense protected by Article 9(1) ECHR and noted that the applicant's claim was essentially a belief in personal autonomy, which was a restatement of an Article 8 right (the right to private life).

[130] e.g. in relation to Article 9 ECHR, see ECtHR, Guide on Article 9 of the European Convention on Human Rights Freedom of thought, conscience and religion (2021) para 28.

[131] Gunn (n 119) 199; see also Anker (n 1) §5.79, 655–57.

characteristics or practices analogous to those of traditional religions.[132] Thus, it also encompasses relatively recent belief systems such as Rastafarianism.[133] In certain contexts, it may not even be necessary for an individual to self-identify their belief-system as a religion.[134] Religious belief need not necessarily be sincere.[135] Further, it is a general feature of a broad definition of religion that it does not seek to impose qualitative criteria appertaining to whether a religion or follower of a religion is ethically good or bad.

Understanding religion in international law and/or human rights terms reinforces the need to construe it as protecting not only religious adherents but persons who do not wish to be forced to follow a religion[136] or who wish to change their religion.[137] It also means that it can be seen to encompass the rights of non-theists as well as theists, non-believers (atheistic or agnostic) as well as believers.[138]

In contrast to the right to hold or not to hold a religious belief, the right to manifest religion or belief in worship, observance, practice, and teaching is subject to permissible restrictions.[139] In terms of manifestation, none of the international law/human rights instruments attempts to define it exhaustively. It certainly includes worship, observance, practice, and teaching, but wisely the text of Article 10(1)(b) of the QD (recast) allows for unspecified other manifestations of religious belief ('shall in particular include').[140] IHRL permits governments to place proportionate restrictions on the manifestation of theistic or non-theistic beliefs, where such restrictions are necessary for the protection of 'public safety, order, health, or morals or the fundamental rights and freedoms of others'.[141] The UNHCR Guidelines cite as examples of possible permissible restrictions, 'measures to prevent criminal activities (e.g. ritual killings), or harmful traditional practices and/or limitations on religious practices injurious to the best interests of the child, as judged by international

---

[132] HRC General Comment No 22 (n 128) para 2.

[133] *Case of Gareth Anver Prince v South Africa* (31 October 2007) Communication No 1474/2006, UN Doc CCPR/C/91/D/1474/2006, paras 7.2–7.3. On non-traditional religions, see *İzzettin Doğan and Others v Turkey* App No 62649/10 (ECtHR, 26 April 2016).

[134] Anker (n 1) §5.67, 641, gives the example of Falun Gong.

[135] ibid §5.72, 649. She cites, inter alia, *Fessehaye v Gonzalez*, 414 F.3d 746, 756 (7th Cir.2005: '[o]ne's religion is inherently a personal experience not reasonably subject to verification' (internal quotation omitted).

[136] Hathaway (n 19) 148, who refers to this phenomenon as 'indirect prevention of religious practice'. See *Okere* (n 71).

[137] Article 12(1) expressly provides for a right to change one's religion; see UN Human Rights Committee, General Comment No 18: Non-discrimination (29 March 1996) UN Doc HRI/GEN/1/Rev.2, para 5. For the same position taken under Article 9 ECHR, see *Kokkinakis v Greece* App No 14307/88 (ECtHR, 25 May 1993) paras 31, 33, 44, 48–49. See also *Ibragim Ibragimov v Russia* Apps Nos 1413/08 and 28621/11 (ECtHR, 28 August 2018); European Court of Human Rights, Guide on Article 9 (n 130).

[138] HRC General Comment No 22 (n 128) para 2; Kälin and Künzli (n 109) 420–21.

[139] Anker (n 1) §5.72, 643 notes though that the distinction between the absolute right to hold beliefs and the manifestation of beliefs is not always clear-cut in practice, as the holding of a religious belief can be closely connected with practicing a belief, by attending services, etc.

[140] QD (recast) (n 8). The ECtHR has held that applicants claiming that an act falls within their freedom to manifest their religion or beliefs are not required to establish that they acted in fulfilment of a duty mandated by the religion in question, so long as there is a sufficiently close and direct nexus between the act and the underlying belief which must be determined on the facts of each case: see e.g. *Eweida and Others v United Kingdom* Apps Nos 48420/10, 59842/10, 51671/10, and 36516/10 (ECtHR, 15 January 2013) para 82.

[141] ICCPR (n 5) Article 18(3); ECHR, Article 9. See further, Kälin and Künzli (n 109) 420–28; and *SAS v France* (n 128).

law standards' as well as 'criminalisation of hate speech, including when committed in the name of religion'.[142]

Even though IHRL permits governments to place reasonable restrictions on manifestations of the practice of religion, it does not in terms permit them to prevent persons from bearing witness in words and deeds. As stated by *Najafi v INS*, '[i]f one is a believer in a religious faith, one would presumably wish to practice that faith. Religious adherence could take the form of attending services, meeting with others of the same faith, personal prayer, or openly sharing one's beliefs'.[143]

It is helpful to complete this analysis of religion by considering certain aspects which have caused problems in the case law.

### 3.2.4 Proselytism

In general terms, proportionate and lawful restrictions do not extend to curbing the right to practice one's religion or the right to evangelise. Freedom to manifest one's religion comprises, in principle, *the right to attempt to convince and convert other people*, for example through 'teaching', failing which, moreover, 'freedom to change [one's] religion or belief', enshrined in Article 9 of the Convention, would be likely to remain a dead letter'.[144] However, arguably the right is limited to a reasonable manifestation of religious beliefs in practice. In the context of considering Article 9, the ECtHR held in *Z and T v United Kingdom* that whilst the freedom of religion includes the right to seek to convince one's neighbours, this right does not extend to 'improper proselytism'.[145] For the Court the crucial issue for the purposes of assessing risk of refoulement remained whether the religious activity or conduct will attract sufficiently serious harm.[146]

### 3.2.5 *Forum internum/forum externum*

Intersecting with IHLR understandings, the question has arisen in refugee law whether interference with religious freedom only constitutes persecution where it can be shown that such interference affects the core or essential elements of the religious identity of the person concerned, sometimes known as the '*forum internum*'. In rejecting this position, the CJEU in *Y and Z* made reference to Article 10 QD (recast), concluding that any distinction between 'forum *internum*' and 'forum *externum*':

> [ ... ] is incompatible with the broad definition of 'religion' given by Article 10(1)(b) of the Directive, which encompasses all its constituent components, be they public or

---

[142] UNHCR Guidelines No 6 (n 125) para 15. HRC General Comment No 22 (n 128) para 7 states that 'no manifestation of religion or belief may amount to propaganda for war or advocacy of national, racial or religious hatred that constitutes incitement to discrimination, hostility or violence'.

[143] *Najafi v INS* [1997] 104 F.3d 943, cited in Anker (n 1) 414.

[144] ECtHR, Guide on Article 9 (n 130) para 124, citing *Kokkinakis v Greece* (n 137) and *Larissis and Others v Greece* Apps Nos 140/1996/759/958–960 (ECtHR, 24 February 1998).

[145] *Z and T v United Kingdom* App No 27034/05 (ECtHR, 28 February 2006) para 326. See more generally, Peter G Danchin, 'Of Prophets and Proselytes: Freedom of Religion and the Conflict of Rights in International Law' (2008) 49 Harv Intl LJ 249; Tad Stahnke, 'Proselytism and the Freedom to Change Religion in International Law' (1999) Brigham Young University Law Review 251, 276–77.

[146] Cited by Zimmermann and Mahler (n 1) 365 with the comment, 'the ECtHR expressed its doubts concerning the far-reaching scope of Article 9 ECHR within the refugee context'.

private, collective or individual. Acts which may constitute a 'severe violation' within the meaning of Article 9(1)(a) of the Directive include serious acts which interfere with the applicant's freedom not only to practice his faith in private circles but also to live that faith publicly.[147]

Thus, in deciding whether persecution is on account of religion, regard must be had to any element of the right to religion, whether core or peripheral.

Separately, by virtue of the fact that persecution and the reasons for it have to be considered from the point of view of the persecutor (the doctrine of attribution), allowance has to be made for a claim based on this Convention reason being advanced by someone who in fact has either peripheral religious beliefs or indeed no religious beliefs or ones an applicant has not expressed.[148]

### 3.2.6 Doctrinal knowledge

One of the most vexed issues surrounding the Convention reason of religion concerns the extent to which, if at all, decision makers should require an applicant to demonstrate a certain level of doctrinal knowledge in order to be able to show religious persecution. It is correctly observed that people can identify with a religion without necessarily having detailed knowledge about it and that in any event what matters is the perspective of the persecutor.[149] However, except in cases of attribution, it is not immediately obvious why a person who has in truth no interest in the religion concerned should be able to win a claim based on religious persecution.

### 3.2.7 Discretion/concealment

Another thorny issue already touched on when outlining the common features of the five Convention reasons,[150] concerns persons whose claim is based, not on persecutors targeting them on return for their religious beliefs or activities, but on their being expected by decision makers, in order to avoid such targeting, to conceal those beliefs or to abstain from those activities (religious self-censorship). This has been an issue that has long divided opinion.[151] In a decision that accurately reflects the growing trend in international law jurisprudence on this issue, the CJEU held in *Y and Z v* that:

> [ ... ] where it is established that, upon his return to his country of origin, the person concerned will follow a religious practice which will expose him to a real risk of

---

[147] Joined Cases C-71/11 and C-99/11 *Bundesrepublik Deutschland v Y and Z* [2012] ECLI:EU:C:2012:518, para 63.

[148] Zimmermann and Mahler (n 1) 387. It is for this reason that the UNHCR Guidelines No 6 (n 125) para 9 caution against approaches to Article 1A(2) that conceive the Convention reason of religion as being satisfied only if the applicant can establish the sincerity of their beliefs or a certain way of life.

[149] See further UNHCR Guidelines No 6 (n 125) paras 28–33; *YMKA ('Westernisation') Iraq* [2022] UKUT 16 (IAC) para 32. See also Anker (n 1) §5.77, 650–53. By reference to a case brought by a claimant testifying that he did not wish to fight in the Iranian Army because of his religious beliefs, Waldman (n 110) 320 observes that '[t]hus, if the person's conduct is guided by his or her religious beliefs, then even if the conduct itself does not involve directly practising the person's religion, it will be sufficient to sustain a claim, if the conduct results in persecution'.

[150] See above sections 2.1.2 and 2.2.

[151] Gunn (n 119).

persecution, he should be granted refugee status, in accordance with Article 13 of the Directive. The fact that he could avoid that risk by abstaining from certain religious practices is, in principle, irrelevant.[152]

This is consistent with the reasoning applied by UNHCR in its Guidelines on International Protection No 6. These observe that 'the Convention would give no protection from persecution for reasons of religion if it was a condition that the person affected must take steps—reasonable or otherwise—to avoid offending the wishes of the persecutors. Bearing witness on words or deeds is often bound up with the existence of religious convictions.'[153] A similar view has been taken by the Australian and UK courts in cases concerning persons compelled to conceal their sexual and political orientation where at least one of the reasons for them doing so is fear of persecution.[154]

3.2.8 Evaluation
It can be seen that when considering application of the reason of religion, care must be taken to bear in mind three facets—religion as belief, religion as identity, and religion as a way of life. Application of VCLT considerations points strongly to interpreting the term religion by applying a human rights approach. Whilst a human rights approach supports reading the term 'religion' broadly—so that it encompasses both the 'core' and the 'periphery' of the right to freedom of religion and extends, for example, even to atheistic beliefs—it does place some limits on the right to manifest one's beliefs, as can be seen, for example in cases concerned with 'improper proselytism'. At the same time, notwithstanding the benefits of a human rights approach, it is notable that case law that has not overtly applied a human rights analysis as such, has sometimes managed to come to broadly similar conclusions.[155]

## 3.3 Nationality

3.3.1 Origins and *travaux préparatoires*
Reference has already been made to nationality as a proscribed ground of discrimination under IHRL.[156] From the start, IHRL included provisions relating to nationality in both its legal and sociological meaning. The 1948 UDHR declares at Article 15 that 'everyone has the right to a nationality' and proscribes its arbitrary deprivation and denial of the right to change one's nationality. There, its primary if not exclusive meaning is a legal one. But Article 2 of this same instrument guarantees rights and freedoms 'without distinction of any kind, such as ... national or social origin'.

---

[152] *Y and Z* (n 147) para 79. For further analysis, see p. 333.
[153] UNHCR Guidelines No 6 (n 125) para 13. See also Anker (n 1) §5.72, 643.
[154] *Appellant S395/2002 v MIMA* [2003] HCA 71; *HJ (Iran)* [2011] 1 AC 596; *RT (Zimbabwe)* (n 74); *WA (Pakistan) v SSHD* [2019] EWCA Civ 302, para 60.
[155] See Musalo (n 117), who analyses United States, Canada, Australia, and New Zealand. For the evaluation in the US, see Anker (n 1) §§5.69–5.84, 636–66. Although Anker herself applies a human rights approach, the US case law she cites mostly does not; for the US case law approach generally, see Chapter 3, section 1.5.3. Waldman's survey of Canadian cases in Waldman (n 110) 318–28, includes ones that expressly apply a human rights analysis and ones that simply treat the concept as broad.
[156] See above pp. 591–592.

As noted earlier, predecessor refugee instruments regarded protection of those unable to enjoy the protection of their country of nationality (or those who were stateless) as instrumental and that concern carried through into the eventual form given to the availment clause in Article 1A(2).[157] In this context, the legal meaning of nationality was clearly intended. Yet there was also recognition of nationality as a prohibited ground of discrimination. In the IRO Constitution, nationality was one of the four reasons (along with race, religion, political opinion) set out in the definition of refugee at Annex 1, Part 1, section A, paragraph 1.[158] The 1950 Statute of the Office of the United Nations High Commissioner for Refugees set out a definition of refugee at article 6A(ii) containing the same four reasons.

Nationality as one of the Convention reasons was included from early on in the drafting process, it featuring in the Ad Hoc Committee's 23 January 1950 definition. In relation to the meaning of the concept of 'nationality' in the context of the nexus clause, the *travaux* are silent. However, near-contemporary analyses considered that nationality as a Convention reason was always understood to be a term clearly conveying a broad, sociological, concept of nationality—what Weiss referred to as 'a historico-biological' one.[159]

### 3.3.2 Article 31 and other Article 32 VCLT considerations

As we saw in Chapter 4, within the availment clause nationality is a term which has a formal meaning, to designate the legal tie between the citizen and the state. This is also one of the senses of the term listed in most dictionary definitions.[160] However, other dictionary definitions include, for example, '[n]ational origin or identity' and 'group of persons belonging to a particular nation; a nation; an ethnic or racial group'.[161] The very fact that the term nationality is also used in the phrase 'protection of the country of nationality' to denote a legal tie between the individual and the state,[162] demonstrates that ordinary meaning itself cannot resolve which of the above senses is apposite in the context of the reasons clause. Hence other elements of the VCLT rules must come more into play.

Considering meaning in relation to other elements of the VCLT rules brings matters back to the instrumental role of the *eiusdem generis* rule. In order to be read *in pari materiae*, at least with race, the meaning of nationality must be wider, so as to refer to membership of an ethnic or linguistic group, the latter possessing attributes also sometimes identified with race.[163]

Bearing in mind the relevance to context and object and purpose of human rights norms, conceiving of nationality in terms of ethnic, cultural, or linguistic groups also marches well with the provisions in IHRL instruments prohibiting discrimination

---

[157] See pp. 551–552 and pp. 554–555.
[158] IRO Constitution (n 31).
[159] Paul Weis, *Nationality and Statelessness in International Law* (2nd edn, Kluwer Academic Publishers Group 1979) 3.
[160] See e.g. OED Online, 2021 available at <https://www.oed.com> accessed 6 August 2021, sense 3.a. See further pp. 214–215.
[161] OED Online, <https://www.oed.com> accessed 6 August 2021.
[162] See pp. 213–217; see also Eric Fripp, *Nationality and Statelessness in the International Law of Refugee Status* (Hart Publishing 2016) 4–5.
[163] Sternberg (n 38) 27. See above p. 605 and pp. 605–606.

against minorities. For example, Article 1(1) of the Declaration on the Rights of National, Ethnic, Religious or Linguistic Minorities declares that 'States shall protect the existence and the national or ethnic, cultural, religious and linguistic identity of minorities within their respective territories and shall encourage conditions for the promotion of that identity.'[164] Article 1 ICERD prohibits race discrimination based, inter alia, on 'national or ethnic origin'.[165] Similar provisions are to be found in the ICCPR (Article 2, paragraph 1) and the general non-discrimination clause of the ICESCR prohibits distinction, inter alia, on the basis of 'national or social origin'.[166] Consolidating this understanding, Article 10(c) of the QD (recast) provides that: 'the concept of nationality shall not be confined to citizenship or lack thereof but shall in particular include membership of a group determined by its cultural, ethnic, or linguistic identity, common geographical or political origins or its relationship with the population of another State'.[167]

In relation to Article 31(3) and/or Article 32 VCLT considerations, there has been a substantial consensus from early commentaries through to the present that 'nationality' in this context is to be given a broad meaning encompassing both the formal legal sense and the wider sociological sense (Weis's 'historico-biological' sense).[168] The 1979 UNHCR Handbook set out that:

> The term 'nationality' in this context is not to be understood only as 'citizenship'. It refers also to membership of an ethnic or linguistic group and may occasionally overlap with the term 'race'. Persecution for reasons of nationality may consist of adverse attitudes and measures directed against a national (ethnic, linguistic) minority and in certain circumstances the fact of belonging to such a minority may in itself give rise to well-founded fear of persecution.[169]

The Handbook, however, cautions against understanding nationality to relate solely to minorities, noting that '[w]hereas in most cases persecution for reason of nationality is feared by persons belonging to a national minority, there have been many cases in various continents where a person belonging to a majority group may fear persecution by a dominant minority'.[170]

---

[164] The United Nations Declaration on the Rights of Persons Belonging to National or Ethnic Religious and Linguistic Minorities (18 December 1992) UN Doc A/47/135. See also Article 3.

[165] ICERD (n 107).

[166] According to the ESCR Committee's General comment No 20 (n 107) para 24: ' "National origin" refers to a person's State, nation, or place of origin. Due to such personal circumstances, individuals and groups of individuals may face systemic discrimination in both the public and private sphere in the exercise of their Covenant rights.'

[167] QD (recast) (n 8).

[168] See e.g. Grahl-Madsen (n 28) 218–89, 89; Patricia Hyndman, 'The 1951 Convention Definition of Refugee' (1987) 9 HRQ 49, 70.

[169] UNHCR Handbook (n 77) para 74. See also UNHCR Guidelines No 1: Gender-Related Persecution within the context of Article 1A(2) of the 1951 Convention and/or its 1967 Protocol relating to the Status of Refugees (2002) Doc HCR/GIP/02/01, para 27; Guidelines No 7 (n 88) para 36; Guidelines No 8 (n 89) para 41.

[170] UNHCR Handbook (n 77) para 76. See also Fripp (n 162) 153–54.

Hathaway and Foster, with reference to stateless persons, highlight that in the reasons clause nationality has been recognised to 'extend both to persons who do, and those who do not, have the relevant attributes set by the Convention'.[171]

Even confined to its formal meaning, denoting the legal tie between an individual and a state, nationality can be fundamental to a person's life. It has been described as 'the right to have rights' in view of the fact that it may not only endow people with identity but entitle them to enjoy many civil and political rights.[172] Fripp usefully identifies a number of scenarios where possession of a nationality in the formal sense could give rise to persecution, including where the country is dominated by non-nationals, where military occupation or political domination by a foreign state occurs, where a state has more than one class of national, and where oppression occurs in the context of an attempt to remove rights by the creation of a false situation of state succession.[173]

The importance in the context of the reasons clause of the need for a broad reading of nationality encompassing both its formal and sociological senses entails that caution must be exercised in focussing too narrowly on the precise variations found in some other international instruments. Whilst, for example, there are valid reasons found by the ICJ relating to the *travaux* and object and purpose of ICERD for construing the term 'national origin' to preclude the legal tie of nationality,[174] to seek to transfer that construction to the Refugee Convention context would be unduly restrictive, at odds with the latter's object and purpose and contrary to UNHCR, judicial, and academic approaches.

As with race, another self-evident feature of a broad definition of nationality, encompassing both its legal sense and in its 'historic-biological' sense, is that it does not seek to impose any qualitative criteria relating to whether those of a particular nationality (or without one) think or conduct themselves according to any particular set of values.

### 3.3.3 Evaluation

Whilst case law on the nationality reason is relatively sparse,[175] it has for a long time supported a broad reading.[176] It has not caused much debate in case law or UNHCR and academic materials. It is uncontroversial that it must be given a broad reading,

---

[171] Hathaway and Foster (n 48) 397 see also Fripp (n 162) 146–47, 150–51.

[172] UNHCR and Inter-Parliamentary Union, 'Nationality and Statelessness: Handbook for Parliamentarians', cited by Zimmermann and Mahler (n 1) 387. Goodwin-Gill and McAdam (n 13) 100 note that nationality 'may, for example, be relied on in claims by children who are denied the right to a nationality at birth or access to education or health services'. They cite UNHCR Guidelines No 8 (n 89) para 41.

[173] Fripp (n 162) 146–47. See also Hugo Storey, 'Are Those Fleeing Ukraine Refugees?', in Sergio Carrera and Meltem Ineli-Ciger (eds), *EU Response to the Large-Scale Displacement from Ukraine: An Analysis on the Temporary Protection Directive and Its Implications for the Future EU Asylum Policy* (European University Institute (EUI) 2023) 113–15.

[174] In *Qatar v United Arab Emirates* (n 68), the ICJ held that in Article 1, paragraph 1 of ICERD the term 'national origin' refers to a person's bond to a national or ethnic group at birth (para 81) and does not encompass current nationality (para 88).

[175] Sternberg (n 38) 27; Fripp (n 162) 149.

[176] See cases listed for each selected country under 'nationality' in Carlier et al (n 46); Hathaway and Foster (n 48) 397–99; Fripp (n 162) 149–55; Waldman (n 110) 329–31.

going beyond the more formal notion applied elsewhere in the refugee definition, which denotes the legal tie between the individual and the state. Its broader, sociological, meaning extends not just to minorities but applies to membership of an ethnic or linguistic or cultural group. Furthermore, it encompasses stateless persons.

## 3.4 Membership of a Particular Social Group

MPSG has become renowned as the 'ground [or reason] with the least clarity'.[177] As Lord Bingham noted in *Fornah*:

> The four Convention grounds most commonly relied on (race, religion, nationality and political opinion), whatever the difficulty of applying them in a given case, leave little room for doubt about their meaning. By contrast, the meaning of 'a particular social group', for all the apparent simplicity and intelligibility of that expression, has been the subject of much consideration and analysis.[178]

The reason is also undoubtedly the one that has attracted the most scholasticism. Some leading court decisions on it might easily be mistaken for philosophical discourses. On some interpretations, identifying a PSG is a given; on others, only those able to get through the eye of a needle can qualify. As will be evident from the earlier analysis, this reason has also been the lightning rod for most of the debates about the reasons' common features. As already observed, much of the debate regarding this reason has pitted two approaches against each other—the 'protected characteristics' approach and the 'social perception' approach.[179]

### 3.4.1 Origins and *travaux préparatoires*

It was noted earlier that the introduction of the reason of MPSG came late in the drafting process, at the Conference of Plenipotentiaries, at the behest of the Swedish delegate, Sture Petrin, but his only recorded comments were extremely non-specific, he stating that 'experience had shown that certain refugees had been persecuted because they belonged to particular social groups' and that 'persons ... might be persecuted owing to their membership of a particular social group. Such cases existed, and it would as well to mention them explicitly [sic]'.[180]

It would be wrong, however, to regard the late inclusion as entirely unexpected since, as noted earlier, IHRL instruments had already begun to frame non-discrimination guarantees in broad terms, Article 2 of the UDHR guaranteeing entitlement to rights and freedoms 'without distinction of any kind' and making clear, by the use of the

---

[177] UNHCR Guidelines No 2 (n 58) para 1; Michelle Foster, 'The "Ground with the Least Clarity": A Comparative Study of Jurisprudential Developments Relating to "Membership of a Particular Social Group"' (2012) UNHCR Legal and Protection Policy Research Series, 25. See also Foster (n 13) 293.
[178] *Fornah* (n 2) para 11.
[179] See above p. 596.
[180] Conference of Plenipotentiaries on the Status of Refugees and Stateless Persons: Summary Record of the 3rd meeting, held at the Palais des Nations, Geneva, on Tuesday, 3 July 1951 (19 November 1951) UN Doc A/CONF.2/SR.3.

phrase 'such as', that the list then given was open-ended. In addition, its list included 'national or social origin, property, birth *or other status*'.[181] Delimitation to just four reasons was not, therefore, an undoubted given. On the other hand, it seems apparent that the drafters did not want to follow the open-ended list approach taken in the UDHR. Goodwin-Gill and McAdam consider that the initial intention behind the Swedish intervention was the protection of bourgeois or landowners who became victims of the 'restructuring' of socialism in socialist states.[182] It could also be added, as noted in Chapter 6, that the drafters clearly recognised the phenomenon of group persecution.[183] At all events, the drafting discussions shine little light on meaning.[184]

3.4.2 Article 31 and other Article 32 VCLT considerations
Supporters of the 'social perception' approach have particularly hailed the importance of an ordinary meaning reading. Dawson J in *Applicant A*, for example, drew heavily on dictionary definitions of 'social', 'group', and 'particular'.[185] Those sympathetic to this approach have made the point that if the 'protected characteristics' approach[186] were right, one would have expected the drafters to specify the need for the group to be based on immutable or human rights affiliations.[187] However, even if ordinary meaning is weighed heavily, it clearly yields little insight into meaning, since it is prodigiously vague. To take Dawson J's own presentation of such definitions in *Applicant A*:

> A 'group' is a collection of persons ... the word 'social' is of wide import and may be defined to mean 'pertaining, relating, or due to ... society as a natural or ordinary condition of human life'. 'Social' may also be defined as 'capable of being associated or united to others' or 'associated, allied, combined' .... The word 'particular' in the definition merely indicates that there must be an identifiable social group, such that a group can be pointed to as a particular social group ....[188]

Given that an ordinary meaning approach yields very little, other VCLT considerations must be to the fore.[189]

Considering first of all, context, the recommendations of the Final Act of the Conference of Plenipotentiaries included reference to the 'unity of the family, the natural and fundamental group of society'.[190] However, of far greater importance as

---

[181] Goodwin-Gill and McAdam (n 13) 100 (emphasis added). They note that during debates on the UDHR the USSR stressed the importance of abolishing 'differences based on social conditions as well as the privileges enjoyed by certain groups in the economic and legal fields'.
[182] ibid 100–01.
[183] See p. 397.
[184] Zimmermann and Mahler (n 1) 390–91. See also Daniel Compton, 'Asylum for Persecuted Social Groups: A Closed Door Left Slightly Ajar' (1987) 62 Washington Law Review 913, 925–26.
[185] *Applicant A* (n 37).
[186] Aleinikoff (n 38) 294.
[187] ibid.
[188] *Applicant A* (n 37).
[189] As the Australian High Court in *Applicant A* (n 37) recognised in any event.
[190] Convention Relating to the Status of Refugees (adopted 28 July 1951, entered into force 22 April 1954) 189 UNTS 137, Annex 1, B.

regards context has been the Preamble's first paragraph identifying human rights and non-discrimination as guiding principles, linked heavily to object and purpose.

Turning to object and purpose, it was remarked upon earlier that the reference in the Preamble to human rights and non-discrimination has been seen to provide a guiding principle for interpretation of all five reasons.[191] In order to facilitate a more specific understanding of this feature, senior courts in the common law world have applied an *eiusdem generis* approach so as to find that such membership must be understood *in pari materiae* with the other reasons.[192] A logical corollary of the *eiusdem generis* approach to this reason is that MPSG cannot be construed as a residual category deliberately intended as a 'catch-all'.[193] If it was, then enumeration of the other four reasons would have been superfluous and there would be no effective delimitation of the prohibited grounds of discrimination. On the *eiusdem generis* approach as applied in leading common law decisions, the meaning of MPSG must be informed (and possibly underpinned) by the unifying concept of non-discrimination. Within this perspective, inclusion of MPSG enables decision makers to consider and deal with some forms of discrimination less demarcated than the four classic reasons.

In order to give shape and content to the non-discrimination norm, the Canadian Supreme Court in *Ward* linked it with the theme of 'defence of human rights'.[194] The human rights approach has been developed more fully by, among others, Hathaway, and Hathaway and Foster.[195] Utilising defence of human rights and non-discrimination norms in tandem also enables this element of the refugee definition to be seen as an evolving one drawing on a wide range of developments in treaty law, thereby providing a safety valve over time for identification of new types of persecution.

Moving on to Article 31(3) VCLT considerations, some early commentators saw the MPSG reason as entirely—or almost entirely—open-ended. Grahl-Madsen said the term was 'of broader application than the combined notions of racial, ethnic and religious groups, and in order to stop a possible gap, the Conference felt that it would be as well to mention this reason for persecution explicitly'.[196] It was, he wrote, 'appropriate to give the phrase a liberal interpretation. Whenever a person is likely to suffer persecution merely because of his background, he should get the benefit of the present provision'.[197] He gave the examples of '[n]obility, capitalists, landowners, civil servants, businessmen, professional people, farmers, workers, member of a linguistic or other minority, even members of certain associations, clubs, or societies'.[198] As

---

[191] e.g. Guy S Goodwin-Gill, 'Judicial Reasoning and "Social Group" after Islam and Shah' (1999) 11 IJRL 538; see also McHugh J in *Applicant A* (n 37) para 401.

[192] Sometimes the relevant rule of interpretation has been seen to be the less stringent *noscitur a sociis* rule of construction (the meaning of a word may be known by words accompanying it). See Aleinikoff (n 38) 290 (at footnote 116).

[193] A 'catch-all approach' to MPSG was emphatically rejected by Australian High Court in *Applicant A* (n 37).

[194] See La Forest J, *Ward* (n 14) at 739.

[195] Hathaway (n 19) 160–61; Hathaway and Foster (n 48) 423. In her 2012 study, Foster (n 177) 74 observed that '[t]he principled basis proffered by this approach is reference to well accepted principles of human rights law, which are objectively identifiable and comprehensible, and hence provide a transparent and consistent basis on which to decide a MPSG claim'.

[196] Grahl-Madsen (n 28) 219.

[197] ibid.

[198] ibid 219–20.

noted earlier, the 1979 UNHCR Handbook made no attempt to link this reason with the other four, save to note that it 'may frequently overlap with a claim to fear of persecution on other grounds'.[199] It confined itself to an illustrative definition suggestive of a sociological approach: '[a] 'particular social group' normally comprises persons of similar background, habits or social status'.[200] A 1985 conclusion of the UNHCR Executive Committee also suggested a sociological approach, which included women who had transgressed social mores.[201] Helton considered it a 'catch-all clause' and 'safety-net'.[202] That perspective comported with the view of some early US cases which considered that any attempt to discern specificity was misguided and that the application of the criteria should be left to decision makers on the basis that they will recognise persecuted social groups when they see them.[203]

In 1991, Hathaway advanced an approach to the MPSG reason which sought to build on the application in the US decision in *Acosta* of an *eiusdem generis* approach.[204] This approach was subsequently endorsed by the Supreme Court in *Ward* (see following paragraph). However, another eminent scholar, Goodwin-Gill, continued to maintain a more nuanced approach. He saw the concept as encompassing 'people in a certain relation or having a certain degree of similarity, or a coming together of those of like class or kindred interests'.[205] 'For the purposes of the Convention definition', he wrote, 'internal linking factors cannot be considered in isolation, but only in conjunction with external defining factors, such as perceptions, policies, practices and laws.'[206] Nor did he agree that the qualities the groups possessed should be confined to those over which individuals have no control. The concept could include groups defined by factors that may involve a good deal of individual choice, such as economic activity, education, and shared aspirations. He considered that the definition should also include groups based on 'ethnic, cultural, and linguistic origin; education; family background; economic activity; shared values, outlook, and aspirations'.[207]

As discussed earlier, those applying a 'protected characteristics' approach have seen the commonalities residing in the other four reasons to have been aptly summarised by the US case of *Acosta*[208] and the Canadian Supreme Court case of *Ward*. As observed

---

[199] UNHCR Handbook (n 77) para 77.
[200] ibid.
[201] ExCom, Conclusion on refugee women and international protection No 39 (XXXVI) (18 October 1985) para (k): 'States, in the exercise of their sovereignty, are free to adopt the interpretation that women asylum-seekers who face harsh or inhuman treatment due to their having transgressed the social mores of the society in which they live may be considered as a 'particular social group' within the meaning of [the 1951 Convention].'
[202] Arthur Helton, 'Persecution on Account of Membership in a Social Group as Basis for Refugee Status' (1983) 15 Columbia Human Rights Law Review 39. To similar effect, see the 'common victimisation' theory of Foighel (n 42).
[203] Gummow J in *Applicant A* (n 37) cites as examples *Roth v United States* [1957] 354 US 476, paras 489–92; *Jacobellis v Ohio* [1964] 378 US 184, para 197.
[204] Hathaway (n 19) 160–1.
[205] Guy S Goodwin-Gill, *The Refugee in International Law* (1st edn, OUP 1983) 30.
[206] Guy S Goodwin-Gill, *The Refugee in International Law* (2nd edn, Clarendon Press 1996) 362.
[207] ibid 363; see also Guy S Goodwin-Gill and Jane McAdam, *The Refugee in International Law* (3rd edn, OUP 2007) 362–66; Goodwin-Gill and McAdam (n 13) 105–06. A similar approach was proposed by Maureen Graves, 'From Definition to Exploration: Social Groups and Political Asylum Eligibility' (1989) 26 San Diego Law Review 739.
[208] *Acosta* (n 14).

earlier, the list given in *Ward* defines PSG as composed of: (1) groups defined by an innate or unchangeable characteristic; (2) groups whose members voluntarily associate for reasons so fundamental to their human dignity that they should not be forced to forsake the association; and (3) groups associated by a former voluntary status, unalterable due to its historical permanence.[209] The Court linked (3) closely with (1), observing that it was included 'more because of historical intentions' but also because 'one's past is an immutable part of the person'.[210]

The position taken by those applying a contrasting 'social perception' approach has been in essence that to be a PSG, a group must have social cognisability.[211] This approach appears to have two main versions, often intertwining. On one version, all that matters is that a group can be said to be identified or 'cognised' in some way as a group. That is, for example, the position taken by Aleinikoff, when defending the 'social perception' approach against its apparent inclusion of 'trivial' groups such as philatelists or rollerbladers.[212] The other main version (which will later be referred to as the 'difference version') considers that to be a PSG the group must share a common, uniting characteristic that distinguishes or sets its members apart from the rest of society. The *locus classicus* of this approach is the Australian High Court case of *Applicant A*.[213]

Surveying the history up to 2011, Mahler and Zimmerman noted that the view expressed early on that MPSG was an open-ended category soon came under heavy challenge, resulting in 'an emerging consensus on the necessity to elaborate a definition as sharp as possible, providing the 1951 Convention ground of "social group" with a well-shaped, independent meaning'.[214] That may be an accurate description of intention. The reality has been very different. There have been significant divergences among courts and administrative agencies over the meaning of the term and the proper approach to be taken to it.[215] Compounding the problem is that VCLT rules do not easily point one way or the other. As noted by Foster, 'both the social perception and protected characteristics approaches could be said to represent the outcome of an application of the rules of treaty interpretation'.[216] The UNHCR Guidelines on MPSG sought to overcome the difficulties posed for interpretation by proposing that the 'protected characteristics' and the 'social perception' approaches be merged by treating them as alternates. Even though of the two main approaches the former has become more entrenched in the case law and wider literature,[217] the 'social perception' approach has not gone away, as recognised by the UNHCR Guidelines, Australian case law, and the

---

[209] *Ward* (n 14) paras 33–34.
[210] ibid. In the subsequent case of *Chan v Canada (MEI)* [1995] 3 SCR 593, paras 642–46, La Forest J (in the minority) sought to modify (2): see above pp. 598–599.
[211] Aleinikoff (n 38) 294.
[212] ibid 299–300.
[213] *Applicant A* (n 37) paras 265–66; see also para 264.
[214] Zimmermann and Mahler (n 1) 391. In this regard they refer, inter alia, to Löhr (n 94) and Vevstad (n 38) 75, Goodwin-Gill and McAdam (n 207) 74; and UNHCR Guidelines No 2 (n 58) para 3.
[215] As demonstrated by the survey of case law in Aleinikoff (n 38). There is also the further dimension that even decision makers in precedential systems applying one approach or the other may not apply them in practice: see, regarding the *Ward* framework, Daley and Kelley's (n 15) observation at 165, that in Canada it is 'rarely applied'.
[216] Foster (n 177) 12.
[217] Aleinikoff (n 38) 300.

academic literature.[218] To complicate matters further, in the US, a social perception-type criterion, namely 'social distinction', has gained a foothold, even though sometimes seen (somewhat confusingly) as another way of stating the *Acosta* test.[219]

### 3.4.3 Types of PSGs—three examples

Leaving aside the issue of the divergent approaches to the MPSG analysis (addressed further below), it is also clear from the extensive surveys undertaken of case law and the wider literature, that very diverse views have been expressed about which types of groups can constitute PSGs and such views have also evolved over time. Whilst this study does not seek to replicate the breadth of coverage of types in other studies,[220] it will assist understanding to briefly examine three of the main types of potential PSG that are often discussed and to identify one main point of difficulty that has arisen about their interpretation, as it will be important to this chapter's conclusions.

#### 3.4.3.1 Women

Under the weight of evolving UNHCR guidance, judicial pronouncements, and academic opinion,[221] objections to recognising that women can constitute members of a PSG have gradually fallen away. Reflecting the growing consensus that at least in certain circumstances, a group defined simply as 'women' can constitute a PSG, Article 10(1)(d) of the QD (recast), although falling short of express identification, states that '[g]ender related aspects, including gender identity, shall be given due consideration for the purposes of determining membership of a particular social group or identifying a characteristic of such a group'.[222] Recital 30 further reinforces this requirement:

> It is equally necessary to introduce a common concept of the persecution ground 'membership of a particular social group'. For the purposes of defining a particular social group, issues arising from an applicant's gender, including gender identity and sexual orientation, which may be related to certain legal traditions and customs, resulting in for example genital mutilation, forced sterilisation or forced abortion, should be given due consideration in so far as they are related to the applicant's well-founded fear of persecution.[223]

UNHCR's Guidelines No 1 consider that women are a 'clear example of a social subset defined by innate and immutable characteristics'.[224] Nevertheless, the same Guidelines

---

[218] See e.g. Breanna Cary, 'Differing Interpretations of the Membership in a Particular Social Group Category and Their Effects on Refugees' (2016) 41 Okla City U L Rev 241, 276–77. However, she ultimately endorses the UNHCR Guidelines' approach.

[219] *Matter of MEVG* [2014] 26 I&N Dec 227; *Matter of WGR* [2014] 26 I&N Dec 208, both discussed in Anker (n 1) 429–35. See also *Matter of ERAL* [2020] 27 I&N Dec 767; *Matter of HLSA* [2021] 28 I&N Dec 228. Whilst in the US context the social distinction test sees itself as working within the *Acosta* framework, Anker (n 1) §5.44, 520–36 expresses strong doubt that it is consistent with the *eiusdem generis* principle upon which *Acosta* is based.

[220] See e.g. Foster (n 177); Hathaway and Foster (n 48) 436–61; Anker (n 1) 436–505.

[221] e.g. in the UK, see *Islam* (n 54) and *Fornah* (n 2).

[222] QD (recast) (n 8).

[223] ibid.

[224] UNHCR Guidelines No 1 (n 169) para 30.

express evident wariness about suggesting that women are a PSG per se in all cases[225] as do other more recent UNHCR materials. A similar wariness can be detected in Article 10(d) of the QD (recast). It prefaces its acknowledgment that 'gender-related aspects' are to be given due consideration, with the qualifier '[d]epending on the circumstances in the country of origin'. Whilst there appears to be some support for the opposite view—that women are a PSG per se[226]—it is arguable that such a view would empty this Convention reason of content. If they were considered to be a PSG a priori, then the drafters would have included as one of the Convention reasons, sex or gender. They did not.

*3.4.3.2 Sexual orientation*

A similar dynamic has characterised UNHCR, judicial, and academic materials on sexual orientation. Sexual orientation can be viewed as either an innate and unchangeable characteristic, or as a characteristic that is so fundamental to human dignity that the person should not be compelled to forsake it. It is also a characteristic that is often 'socially cognisable'.[227] The UNHCR Guidelines No 9 (which expressly sought to 'harmonise' existing understandings),[228] note that '[w]hether applying the "protected characteristics" or "social perception" approach, there is broad acknowledgment that under a correct application of either of these approaches, lesbians, gay men, bisexuals and transgender persons are members of "particular social groups" within the meaning of the refugee definition'.[229] This wording might appear to suggest that UNHCR's position is that such groups are to be understood as forming a PSG per se. However, an earlier paragraph quotes a passage from the MPSG Guidelines stating that 'the term membership of a particular social group should be read in an evolutionary manner, open to the diverse and changing nature of groups in various societies and evolving international human rights norms'.[230]

---

[225] UNHCR Guidelines No 2 (n 58) in which the language is rather that women 'can' be a PSG: see e.g. para 6.
[226] Laura Sheridan Mouton, *Gender-related Asylum Claims and the Social Group Calculus: Recognizing Women as a 'Particular Social Group' Per Se* (The Committee on Immigration and Nationality Law of Association of the Bar of the City of New York 2003). This can also be prescribed in some national case law: see Michelle Foster, 'Why We Are Not There Yet: The Particular Challenge of "Particular Social Group"', in Efrat Arbel, Catherine Dauvergne, and Jenni Millbank (eds), *Gender in Refugee Law: From the Margins to the Centre* (Routledge 2014) 17–45 at 25–28.
[227] However, it will sometimes be difficult to say that sexual orientation is 'socially cognisable', e.g. in the case of someone who has 'come out' whilst in the host country but would be fearful of expressing their orientation upon return. Including such an example within the social perception approach may require treating it as a given that if they did express their orientation such applicants would then be socially cognisable.
[228] UNHCR Guidelines No 9 (n 83) para 4.
[229] ibid para 46.
[230] ibid para 44. See also UNHCR, 'Statement on Membership of Particular Social Group and the Best Interests of the Child in Asylum Procedures Issued in the context of the preliminary ruling reference to the Court of Justice of the European Union in the case of K., L. v. Staatssecretaris van Justitie en Veiligheid (C-646/21)' (21 June 2023) para 4.1.2, available at <https://www.refworld.org/docid/6492f5f54.html>; Catherine Dauvergne, 'Women in Refugee Jurisprudence' in Cathryn Costello et al (n 9) 738 considers that the uncertainty over whether women as such will be considered a PSG 'is a marked contrast with groups defined on the basis of sexual orientation or non-binary gender identity'. However, the solution to this inconsistency may be that both types of group be required to meet a relevancy or 'contextual requirement'.

In contrast to this ambivalent stance, Article 10(1)(d) of the QD (recast) is premised on explicit rejection of the notion that sexual orientation groups are per se PSGs. This provision states that '[d]epending on the circumstances in the country of origin, a particular social group might include a group based on a common characteristic of sexual orientation...'[231]

*3.4.3.3 Age and children*

That the 1951 Convention was mindful of the special situation of minors can be gleaned from the recommendation in the Final Act of the UN Conference of Plenipotentiaries for governments to take special measures protecting the refugee's family, including '[t]he protection of refugees who are minors, in particular unaccompanied children and girls, with special reference to guardianship and adoption'.[232] The UNHCR Guidelines No 8 on Child Asylum Claims notes that '[a]lthough age, in strict terms, is neither innate nor permanent as it changes continuously, being a child is in effect an immutable characteristic at any given point in time'.[233] This understanding has been endorsed in case law and the wider literature[234] although in the US there have been some decisions refusing to accept that age is an immutable characteristic.[235] The 'social perception' approach has also largely treated children as at least capable of being a PSG.[236]

However, with children and other age-based groups as well, there is a similar ambivalence as to whether the mere fact of age being an immutable characteristic means that, for example, children or old people are members of a PSG per se. Arguably, on either the 'protected characteristics' approach or the 'difference' version of the social perception approach, it is also necessary to show that there is some element of discrimination affecting those groups, which in turn is also always context-specific.

3.4.4 'Protected characteristics' and 'social perception' approaches revisited
Closer examination can no longer be delayed of the sharp divide on a fundamental issue of approach to interpretation as between the 'protected characteristics' (or internal) approach and the 'social perception' (or external) approach.[237] As noted earlier, the former approach is said to be based on whether a group is united by either an immutable characteristic or by a characteristic fundamental to their human dignity.[238] The latter approach appears to have two main versions. One requires mere 'social cognisability'. The other requires social cognisability establishing that the group is identified in some way as distinguished or 'set apart' from society at large as a distinct

---

[231] UNHCR Guidelines No 9 (n 83) para 44.
[232] Final Act of the United Nations Conference of Plenipotentiaries on the Status of Refugees and Stateless Persons (1954) 189 UNTS 37, B (2).
[233] UNHCR Guidelines No 8 (n 89) para 49.
[234] See e.g. Jason Pobjoy, *The Child in International Refugee Law* (CUP 2017) 175–78.
[235] See Anker (n 1) §5.6, 612; Pobjoy (n 234) 181–82.
[236] Pobjoy (n 234) 181–82.
[237] For a detailed study of the two approaches up to 2002, see Aleinikoff (n 38). He explains at 270 that the 'protected characteristics' label is intended to cover all the categories identified in *Ward*.
[238] See above pp. 596–597.

group, based on the characteristics relied upon.[239] Under the latter version (which can for convenience be termed the 'difference version'), it is not sufficient, therefore, that a group is purely 'statistical' or shares a demographic factor.[240]

Evidence that the two approaches have been seen as antithetical is readily to hand: e.g. in UNHCR's observations in its 2002 Guidelines on International Protection[241] and in the analysis conducted by Lord Bingham in *Fornah* (drawing on the same).[242] The issue of how they relate to one another is thrown into sharp relief by the fact that in some jurisdictions, e.g. in the US (sometimes) and in the EU, the two approaches have been applied cumulatively—this is discussed further below.[243]

Having surveyed the literature, Zimmermann and Mahler state that there are two main positions taken as to the interrelationship between the two main approaches. The first is what they describe as the 'Combined Alternative Approach' (which is UNHCR's position). This allows for either to apply. The second is the 'Combined Cumulative Approach' (which treats them as both cumulatively necessary conditions for establishing a PSG).[244] In relation to the 'Combined Alternative Approach', they write:

> This proposed merger has been criticized as being overly broad, but has also found support. It has to be noted, however, that in most cases the two proposed approaches will reach the same result, as people sharing innate, unalterable, common characteristics or characteristics of fundamental importance to identity, and thus protected by human rights norms, will often by the same token also be perceived as a group

---

[239] One of the landmark decisions outlining this approach was *Wiesbaden (Administrative Court in Wiesbaden)* [1983] IV/I E 06244/81; see Maryellen Fullerton, 'Persecution Due to Membership in a Particular Social Group: Jurisprudence in the Federal Republic of Germany' (1990) 4 Geo Imm L J 381, 408; Maryellen Fullerton, 'A Comparative Look at Refugee Status Based on Persecution Due to Membership in a Particular Social Group' (1993) 26 Cornell Int'l LJ 505. However, according to Aleinikoff (n 38) 283, the German Federal Administrative Court has adopted a 'protected characteristics' approach. The principal decision in the common law world to which reference is made for a 'social perception' approach is that of the Australian High Court in *Applicant A* (n 37) paras 265–66. Aleinikoff (n 38) 274, notes that two of the judges in *Islam* (n 54)—Lords Hope (with the majority) and Millett (in dissent)—'adopted language closer to the social perception approach of the High Court of Australian in *Applicant A*'. Another decision he considers to have adopted a social perception approach is *Ourbih* Case No 171858 [1997] Conseil d'État, SSR (see Aleinikoff (n 38) 281, 296—for further French references see Foster (n 13) 11). Aleinikoff (n 38) 298, also considers that Goodwin-Gill embraces a social perception approach. Approaches associated with the 'social perception' approach include those applying two tests gradually introduced into US case law post-*Acosta* (n 14): the 'social visibility' and the 'social distinction' tests: see Anker (n 1) §5.43, 516–20; Hathaway and Foster (n 48) 431; Cary (n 218) 252–66; and Fatma E Marouf, 'The Emerging Importance of "Social Visibility" in Defining a Particular Social Group and Its Potential Impact on Asylum Claims Related to Sexual Orientation and Gender' (2008) 27 Yale Law & Policy Review 47. Marouf also states at 74 that the UK AIT applied a social perception approach in *SB* [2008] UKAIT 00002, para 53. For a critique of the social perception approach, see James C Hathaway and Michelle Foster, 'The Causal Connection ("Nexus") to a Convention Ground: Discussion Paper No. 3 Advanced Refugee Law Workshop International Association of Refugee Law Judges Auckland, New Zealand, October 2002' (2003) 15(3) IJRL 461, 489–91. See also Foster (2014) (n 226) 32–37.

[240] For a detailed discussion of the 'social perception' overlay applied in some US case law, see Anker (n 1) §5.44, 520–36; Cary (n 218) 252–66.

[241] After extensive 'Global Consultations': see p. 47.

[242] *Fornah* (n 2) para 16.

[243] See below p. 638.

[244] Zimmermann and Mahler (n 1) 392–93.

by society. Different conclusions may, however, be drawn from these different approaches in those rather exceptional cases in which a certain characteristic is merely imputed by society to a victim of persecution and the imputed characteristic is not covered by another 1951 Convention ground.[245]

Describing the 'Combined Alternative Approach' as a merger is not entirely helpful since its premise is that either approach is valid in itself, something which will be questioned below. It has to be asked whether either approach rests on a proper foundation. The position taken in this study is that neither approach taken on its own is internally consistent—since inquiry into the existence of a PSG must incorporate both an internal and external dimension.[246]

Before proceeding further, it is necessary to consider in more detail how the two approaches were dealt with in the UNHCR Guidelines of May 2002, which followed extensive 'Global Consultations'. These Guidelines contain the following proposal:

> B. *UNHCR's Definition*
> 10. Given the varying approaches, and the protection gaps which can result, UNHCR believes that the two approaches ought to be reconciled.
> 11. The protected characteristics approach may be understood to identify a set of groups that constitute the core of the social perception analysis. Accordingly, it is appropriate to adopt a single standard that incorporates both dominant approaches:
> *a particular social group is a group of persons who share a common characteristic other than their risk of being persecuted, or who are perceived as a group by society. The characteristic will often be one which is innate, unchangeable, or which is otherwise fundamental to identity, conscience or the exercise of one's human rights.*

These Guidelines observe that if the two approaches are binary then certain groups which should qualify might not be treated as constituting a PSG. They posit a case in which the 'social perception' approach might recognize as PSGs associations based on a characteristic that is neither immutable nor fundamental to human dignity—such as, perhaps, occupation or social class. They give the specific example of an applicant owning a shop or participating in a certain occupation in a particular society where that was neither unchangeable nor a fundamental aspect of human identity.[247]

Worries that each of the approaches taken on their own can leave protection gaps were also voiced by the UK House of Lords in *Fornah*. By this time there was the further development to consider that the text of Article 10 of the QD (recast), if read literally, seemed to adopt the position that in order to show a PSG an applicant had to satisfy *both* the 'protected characteristics' and 'social perception' tests. Article 10(1)(d) provides that:

> [ ... ] a group shall be considered to form a particular social group where in particular: members of that group share an innate characteristic, or a common

---

[245] ibid.
[246] A similar position was taken by Goodwin-Gill and McAdam (n 207) 73–86, and is maintained in Goodwin-Gill and McAdam (n 13) 100–19.
[247] UNHCR Guidelines No 2 (n 58) para 9, 13.

background that cannot be changed, or share a characteristic or belief that is so fundamental to identity or conscience that a person should not be forced to renounce it, *and* that group has a distinct identity in the relevant country, because it is perceived as being different by the surrounding society.[248]

The House of Lords chose to read Article 10(1)(d) of the QD (recast) as not imposing a cumulative requirement (notwithstanding its use of the conjunctive 'and' when setting out both the protected characteristics and the social perceptions formulations) and endorsed UNHCR's attempt to regard them as alternates. In Lord Bingham's opinion, to read them conjunctively would be unduly stringent.[249] This Court's analysis, in turn, has attracted significant criticism.[250]

### 3.4.4.1 'Protected characteristics' approach

There are several drawbacks to the 'protected characteristics' approach[251] as presently understood.

First, it utilises a one-sided understanding of the actual character of the other reasons. On the basis of our earlier analysis of the first three reasons, applying a *eiusdem generis* approach should mean recognising that none of them is actually purely innate. Thus 'race' for Convention purposes may be defined by ethnicity or cultural or linguistic distinctiveness, and frequently overlaps with other Convention grounds. It is not confined to innate categories of a biological or scientific nature.[252] Thus as a matter of treaty interpretation 'nationality' is not ordinarily understood to be innate.[253] Neither can the other four reasons easily be seen to concern unchangeability. It is at least not straightforward to see religion and nationality as unchangeable given the observable fact that people can change their religion and can sometimes change their nationality or have it changed by state measures. Shoehorning them within *Acosta/Ward* categories (1), (2), or (3) may sometimes require applying a historical test.[254] As will be made clear below, similar difficulties apply, *a fortiori*, to political opinion.[255] That is not simply because (on a literal reading) political opinion can change/be changed, but because, unlike the *Acosta/Ward* category (2), it is not defined in a value-laden way. 'Political opinion' does not only cover those who can show voluntary association for reasons so fundamental to their human dignity that they should not be forced to forsake the association. Certainly, within the political opinion category there is a sub-set

---

[248] Their lordships were considering the QD, but this part of Article 10 of the QD (recast) is in the same terms.

[249] *Fornah* (n 2) para 16.

[250] See Zimmermann and Mahler (n 1) 394 who cite criticisms by Hruschka/Löhr and Löhr.

[251] Hathaway and Foster (n 48) 426–27. They in fact prefer to call this approach the *eiusdem generis* approach, but this terminology is not followed here, as the latter seems too generic and (as we shall see) does not sufficiently distinguish it from one of the two versions of the 'social perception' approach.

[252] See above pp. 605–606.

[253] See *Qatar v United Arab Emirates* (n 68) para 81. Indeed, it could be argued on the basis of what is said in this paragraph that 'nationality' is not unchangeable. The ICJ states that nationality 'is a legal attribute which is within the discretionary power of the State and can change during a person's lifetime'—see *Nottebohm* (n 68) 20 and 23.

[254] On this basis category (3) itself, being an historical category associated by a former voluntary status, could be said to be either immutable or unchangeable or both: see Goodwin-Gill and McAdam (n 13) 104.

[255] See below p. 653.

of cases where the threat to freedom of expression is fundamental to human dignity, but it is not confined to them.[256]

A second drawback concerns the 'protected characteristics approach's identification of one of its subcategories as 'groups whose members voluntarily associate for reasons so fundamental to their human dignity that they should not be forced to forsake the association' (*Acosta/Ward*'s Category 2). We have already observed that there has not always been clarity about whether this means actual or assumed voluntary membership. Further, in either case, it is not clear how this test is compatible with *Acosta/Ward*'s overriding immutable characteristic test.[257] Category 2's reliance on a fundamental purpose, would also appear to be too restrictive. As Hathaway accepts, the corollary of this category's criterion is that 'membership in a voluntary association defined by a non-fundamental purpose, such as recreation or personal convenience, would normally be seen to be outside the scope of the notion of a particular social group'.[258] Thus, applied to economic classes, what will be decisive applying the *Acosta/Ward* category (2) is if their situation is avoidable without affront to their human dignity. Hathaway gives the example of the poor who as a class might constitute a PSG if membership, though nominally voluntary, 'is the only means of ensuring basic subsistence, an interest protected under core norms of human rights law'.[259] What then about economic classes outwith this criterion? Their exclusion might not matter if there was scope for inclusion under categories (1) and (3), but, as explained above, these two categories increasingly seem more disparate than *Acosta/Ward* seem to assume. The question then is can—or should—category (2) bear the burden of being the only possible unifying category under this framework.

A third main drawback is that the 'protected characteristics' approach does not consistently follow through on what this study has called 'the contextual requirement', which is ultimately a type of relevancy criterion. According to this requirement, each of the specified grounds can only actually operate as a Convention reason if in the society in question it has a distinct social significance. Race may not be relevant if everyone in the society in question shares the same race. The same with nationality—after all, everyone has either a nationality or is stateless—and we saw that both nationals and stateless persons can fall within the scope of the nationality reason.[260] Whilst likewise in relation to MPSG an innate or unchangeable characteristic will be *capable* of comprising a PSG, does it make sense to include it even if it has no societal significance? To take the example of category (1), immutable characteristics, possession of such immutable characteristics such as eye colour, or left-handedness, is not considered ordinarily to give rise to MPSG. It will only be

---

[256] See below p. 643.
[257] See e.g. *Lwin v INS* [1998] 144 F.3d 505, para 512 (finding that the immutable characteristic and voluntary association tests are incompatible); Nancy Kelly, 'Gender-Related Persecution: Assessing the Asylum Claims of Women' (1993) 26 Cornell International Law Journal 625, 651; Peter C Godfrey, 'Defining the Social Group in Asylum Proceedings: The Expansion of the Social Group to Include a Broader Class of Refugees' (1994) 3 Journal of Law and Policy 257, 267–68. See also Mouton (n 226).
[258] Hathaway (n 19)168.
[259] ibid 167.
[260] See above p. 616.

when eye colour or left-handedness is understood as significant within a particular society, that such a characteristic gives rise to an actual PSG. Save in relation to the doctrine of attribution, each of the Convention reasons must surely identify a material reality. If everyone in country X is white Caucasian and an applicant for refugee status from that country is white Caucasian, it is at least challenging to see how he or she could ever show a Convention reason based on race. Since for the 'protected characteristics' approach, the underlying principle is non-discrimination, the presence or absence of a discriminatory element must be dependent on historical time and place. By failing to expressly identify a contextual requirement as necessary, leading proponents of the 'protected characteristics' approach appear to endorse an absolutist understanding that it is the innate or unchangeable or non-renounceable characteristic per se that constitutes the PSG.

The lack of a relevancy criterion also links with the criticism noted earlier that each of the *Acosta/Ward* subcategories, as formulated, lacks coherent outer limits. For example, the definition of a PSG as always including a group of persons who share an innate characteristic other than their risk of being persecuted would mean, if taken literally, treating as members of a PSG every permutation of human beings who shared some biological or genetic or other kind of innate characteristic. To make sense in the context of the Refugee Convention, one must read into this limb of *Ward*'s category (1), 'a group of persons who share an innate ... characteristic *having societal significance*'.[261] In relation to *Acosta/Ward*'s category (2), if, as La Forest J acknowledged in *Chan*, it is not necessary after all for the members of the group to have associated, all that is left (outside the context of attribution) is the characteristic of being fundamental to human dignity which would mean that this reason could include all whose human rights might be engaged.[262] This may not in itself be a fatal criticism, but it is clear from Hathaway and Foster's analysis, for example, that they consider that category (2) can, merely by virtue of being able to identify a human right to which such groups relate, encompass a very wide range of groups, e.g. economic and social classes,[263] students,[264] groups defined by reference to occupation.[265] This makes sense if their approach incorporates a contextual requirement, but this is not always how they formulate matters—e.g. they state that 'a correct application of the *eiusdem generis* approach, would result in the inclusion of occupation-based groups per se within the ambit of the particular social group category'.[266] The dilemma for this approach is clear from their discussion of the 'wealthy'. Despite having noted that 'property' is recognised as a prohibited ground of discrimination at international law, they appear to conclude that such a group will not constitute a PSG because wealth is not a characteristic fundamental to human dignity that is non-renounceable.[267] Yet the same logic should also surely apply to certain categories they wish to include such as students and (to take another example they discuss) taxi drivers. Just as 'wealth per se is not a

---

[261] *Ward* (n 14) (emphasis added).
[262] See *Chan* (n 210); see also Aleinikoff (n 38) 270.
[263] Hathaway and Foster (n 48)453.
[264] ibid 455.
[265] ibid 457.
[266] ibid.
[267] ibid 458.

protected interest in international law,[268] neither is 'studenthood' nor a particular occupation such as taxi-driving.

Adding a contextual criterion to the 'protected characteristics' approach is not imposing an undue restriction; it is simply recognising that it is only groups with shared innate or unchangeable or renounceable characteristics having some context-specific social significance that have relevance in a refugee context. Hathaway and Foster recognise this feature very well when giving the example of philatelists and rollerbladers not being properly considered as a PSG unless there is something non-trivial about their situation.[269] Yet they fail to acknowledge that this means according a role at the conceptual level for a social dimension. Essential to the transformation from non-triviality is, therefore, societal significance. Adding such a requirement is not necessarily the same as accepting that a PSG can be constituted merely by external perception (which is the position taken by some variants of the 'social perception' approach),[270] but it does mean recognising that 'protected characteristics' can only sensibly give rise to a Convention reason by virtue of societal significance.

It is pertinent to consider here the critique mounted by Hathaway and Foster of the reference by one of the two main 'social perception' approaches to the objectivity of this test in terms of 'third-party' assessment. They highlight the emphasis placed by the Australian High Court in *Applicant S* on drawing conclusions 'as to whether the group is cognisable within the community from "country information" gathered by international bodies and nations other than the applicant's country of origin.'[271] For Hathaway and Foster, 'it is surely patently clear that country information is not generally prepared specifically for refugee law purposes, and hence is incapable of addressing the refugee law specific issue of "social perception"'.[272] Yet their own approach surely depends crucially at various points on country information, e.g. they cite with approval a summary account of 'a wide variety of circumstances' in which family members threatened with retaliation or coercion can constitute PSGs.[273] It is a general feature of country of origin information that much of it is not tailored to the refugee law context, but that does not mean it is not a vital tool.[274] To take just two examples, it will sometimes be needed in order to establish what is the innate or unchangeable characteristic; or sometimes to establish whether this characteristic is relevant.

*3.4.4.2 Social perception approach*

Although not as entrenched as the 'protected characteristics' approach, the 'social perception' approach has attracted support from notable scholars, including Aleinikoff,

---

[268] ibid.
[269] ibid 433.
[270] Foster (n 177) 15, 75.
[271] *Applicant S* (n 39) para 35; Hathaway and Foster (n 48) 428.
[272] Hathaway and Foster (n 48) 435.
[273] ibid 447.
[274] ibid 122, the authors observe earlier that 'country data is normally a critical means of both putting an applicant's evidence in context, and more generally of ensuring a complete understanding of relevant risks'. They do not say anything to suggest why in assessing risk, the MPSG element should be somehow off limits.

and continues to play a role in US and Australian case law particularly.[275] It must also be observed that for those countries that apply a 'Combined Cumulative Approach' (to use Zimmermann and Mahler's categorisation set out earlier), they are applying both 'social protection' criteria and 'protected characteristics' criteria.[276]

A presenting problem in seeking to analyse this approach is a lack of clarity about what it actually comprises. As noted earlier, on one version of it all that is necessary to establish a PSG is that it is cognisable. That is the position taken by Aleinikoff, for example, when defending the inclusion of philatelists and rollerbladers against the accusation of triviality.[277] The other version is that which has been solidified by the Australian High Court in *Applicant S*. In this version mere cognisability is not enough. It must also be shown that the PSG is 'set apart' from the rest of society.[278]

Taking the first version, it has the difficulty that the category of groups that could be included within this approach is infinite and mere perception of them seems insufficient to demarcate those of relevance in the context of the nexus clause. It provides no principled basis for excluding any group that is perceived to be a group no matter how unrelated to anything to do with the context of the refugee definition.[279] On its logic, it can be applied to any group. Hathaway and Foster give the example of 'philatelists or roller-bladers'.[280] Aleinikoff has sought to argue that including such 'trivial' groups should not be seen as a difficulty, since in certain circumstances such groups could face persecution.[281] However, as his own analysis accepts, the likelihood of persecution cannot in itself be a criterion for whether a group is a PSG or not.

What then of the other main version of the 'social perception' approach, expressed most notably by judges of the Australian High Court in *Applicant S*? Whilst it avoids the problem of undue open-endedness, it only does so by applying a criterion of difference—the quality of being 'set apart' or 'distinguished' from the rest of society. In one respect, adoption of this criterion could be said to draw this version very close to the 'protected characteristics' approach. Both seek to identify common characteristics, the only difference being that, in the former it matters (whereas in the latter it does not) whether the characteristics are innate/unchangeable/non-renounceable or otherwise. However, the principle of difference, thus stated, is also undifferentiated and raises the same problem of undue open-endedness afflicting the other version.

---

[275] Aleinikoff (n 38) 297–301. He also regards Goodwin-Gill's approach as falling within this camp. It must be noted, however, that the US case law largely continues to see its 'social distinction' approach as operating within the *Acosta* framework: see above n 219.

[276] Goodwin-Gill and McAdam (n 13) 118 write that in light of the EU Commission's 2019 Report on the application of the QD (recast), 'most member States apply the two approaches covered in Article 10(1)(d) cumulatively, and … only five apply them alternatively (Greece, Ireland, Italy, Latvia, and Lithuania)'. In light of recent CJEU judgments, the latter five countries must be seen to be failing to apply binding EU law: see below n 315.

[277] Aleinikoff (n 38).

[278] *Applicant S* (n 39).

[279] According to *Refugee Appeal No 1312/93 Re GJ* [1995] NZRSAA: 'by making societal attitudes determinative of the existence of the social group, virtually any group of persons in a society perceived as a group could be said to be a particular social group'.

[280] Aleinikoff (n 38) 299; Hathaway and Foster (n 48) 433.

[281] Aleinikoff (n 38) 299: '[t]he triviality, or not, of the shared group characteristic therefore ought not to be relevant for Convention purposes'.

Whether or not it is applied objectively, e.g. by way of what the Australian case law terms 'third party perspectives',[282] or subjectively, e.g. by societal perceptions within the society, it is possible, as stated, to identify an infinite number of differences and in turn an infinite number of groups. This version only makes sense if read as meaning discriminatory difference(s) in the context of a particular society. In other words, this version is only coherent if understood as also underpinned by a *eiusdem generis* approach based on the human rights norm of non-discrimination. Yet if this is its underpinning, then the question arises as to what extent this version can then give shape and content to this norm. If it adopts a human rights approach to assessing difference,[283] then it is no longer an approach clearly distinct from the 'protected characteristics' approach. If it does not adopt a human rights approach, then it is vulnerable to the criticism of subjectivism, since it is then left to decision makers to decide for themselves whether there is a perceived discriminatory difference or not.

The conclusion of this author's analysis, therefore, is that neither the 'protected characteristics' nor the 'social perception' approaches are internally consistent. Each appears to need something of the other to function. One is too 'internal', the other too 'external'. To make sense, the 'protected characteristics' needs to employ a relevancy or contextual requirement of social significance. To make sense, the 'social perception' approach does not need to apply a criterion of innate or immutable characteristics, but it does need a principle of non-discrimination. Until the proponents of each reconstructs them, so they are free of inconsistency, there will be no real resolution or possible unification.

It would seem, on the basis of the above analysis, that the most likely 'map' for how such reconstruction could be achieved would be as follows. The 'protected characteristics' approach would need to give up the idea that the three-part *Acosta/Ward* categorisation is exhaustive and accept that the characteristics needed to identify a PSG can also include groups that are both cognisable and set apart by the rest of society. It would need to ensure that the decision as to which potential groups qualify as a PSG was made in all cases by reference to the particular societal context. As now, it would apply to its analysis a human rights approach based on the principle of non-discrimination. The 'social perception' approach, for its part, would need to accept that a PSG can also include those based on protected characteristics, but would need to ensure, in applying its concept of difference (being 'set apart' from the rest of society) that the group concerned was the subject of discrimination.[284] In order to ensure objective norms were being applied when assessing whether an element of discrimination was involved, this approach would need to draw on non-discrimination norms in the most concrete form in which they are found in treaty law—in IHRL.

---

[282] See e.g. *Applicant S* (n 39) para 34; and Guide to Refugee Law in Australia (n 58) 23–25.
[283] As appears to have been applied to some degree by the Australian High Court in *Applicant A* (n 37) and *Applicant S* (n 39).
[284] Two examples of statutory attempt at unification that avoid the cumulative approach of Article 10(d) of the QD (recast) are section 8(d) of the Irish Refugee Protection Act 2015 Revised and section 5L of the Australian Migration Act 1958 (CtH) (post December 2014). However, the latter specifies bespoke criteria for a person who is a member of a family group (section 5K). For an alternative approach, see Goodwin-Gill and McAdam (n 13) 117–19. They advocate a 'sociological approach' but also apply the principle of non-discrimination.

### 3.4.5 Agreed key features

The great emphasis placed in this analysis so far on the clash between the 'protected characteristics' and 'social perception' approaches, whilst inevitable given the state of the literature, must not, however, be allowed to obscure a very important fact. Despite these divergences, and also irrespective of whether a human rights approach or a non-human rights approach has been taken, a consensus appears to have formed around a number of key features. UNHCR guidance, the case law, and wider literature[285] have identified the following as essential features of the PSG notion.

#### 3.4.5.1 Limits

As noted by Aleinikoff, notwithstanding differences in approaches, there has been convergence around the view that 'some limiting principle be identified to ensure that the "social group" ground not be all-encompassing'.[286] He notes several reasons that have been given: that the Convention was not intended to provide protection to all victims of persecution, only to those who come within one of the five reasons; that as a matter of legal logic, the social group cannot be read so broadly that it renders the other reasons superfluous; and that an overly broad definition would undermine the balance between protection and limited state obligations implicit in the Convention.

#### 3.4.5.2 Independence of the persecution

In order to avoid tautology or circularity, to qualify as a PSG it must be possible to identify the group independently of the persecution.[287] However, it has been widely agreed that the discrimination which lies at the heart of many persecutory acts can assist in defining the PSG, sometimes very considerably. The UNHCR Guidelines cite the famous example given by McHugh J in *Applicant A* of left-handed men who, whilst not ordinarily constituting a PSG, might be 'if they were persecuted because they were left-handed' and as a result 'would no doubt quickly become recognisable in their society as a particular social group'.[288] MPSG can be established by reference to discrimination from state actors or non-state actors of persecution.[289]

However, it is doubtful that rejection of identification independently of the persecution as a requirement entails acceptance of what the USCIS Asylum Office, the Board, and some Circuit courts in the US have identified as a criterion of 'particularity'.[290] One possible source of support for making this a requirement is that it could be said to comport with an ordinary meaning of 'particular'. That is how the Australian High Court understood it in *Applicant A*.[291] However, as Anker's analysis makes clear, a 'particularity' requirement lacks coherence and tends to collapse into a flawed 'social

---

[285] See on all three, Foster (n 177) 5–6.
[286] Zimmermann and Mahler (n 1) 391; Aleinikoff (n 38) 285; Hathaway and Foster (n 48) 424–25.
[287] Aleinikoff (n 38) 271; Hathaway and Foster (n 48) 425; Goodwin-Gill and McAdam (n 13) 106–07.
[288] UNHCR Guidelines No 2 (n 58) para 14; *Applicant A* (n 37); Aleinikoff (n 38) 286.
[289] Hathaway and Foster (n 48) 373–76.
[290] Anker (n 1) §§5.43–5.44, 516–36; see also Hathaway and Foster (n 48) 425. The BIA's construction of particularity was found reasonable by the 9th Circuit in *Reyes v Lynch* [2016] 842 F.3d 1125, paras 1131 and 1136, cited by Goodwin- Goodwin-Gill and McAdam (n 13) 105.
[291] *Applicant A* (n 37). Per Brennan CJ: 'the ordinary meaning of the words used, a "particular group" is a group identifiable by any characteristic common to the members of the group'. See above p. 618.

visibility' requirement.[292] It can also sometimes rely on the mistaken notion that a PSG is not such unless it is shown that each and every member of it is subject to or at risk of persecution.[293]

*3.4.5.3 Cohesiveness, interdependence, and homogeneity?*
The UNHCR Guidelines[294] and leading cases have rejected cohesiveness as a criterion of a PSG,[295] albeit accepting that a PSG cannot normally consist in a disparate collection of individuals.[296] Nor is it necessary for such a group to possess the attributes of interdependence, organisation, homogeneity, voluntary association, or consciousness of being a group.[297] Neither Article 10(d) of the QD in the European context nor best state practice globally (as evidenced by case law at least) impose any such requirements.

Nevertheless, that is not to say that groups that have such characteristics are excluded and indeed some PSGs embody them fully.

It is also clear that self-identity as a MPSG is not a universal prerequisite. One example given is that in the 1930s many German citizens of Jewish ethnicity did not identify themselves as 'Jews', but as Germans. This did not prevent their being members 'of a particular social group' and persecuted for that reason (as well as for reasons of race and religion).[298]

*3.4.5.4 Size?*
Size is not a criterion as such.[299] It is clear that relatively small groups can also qualify as PSGs. Leading decisions have given the example of families. By the same token, there is nothing in principle to prevent the size of the PSG being large and even to comprise a majority of the population (as can happen in some countries with women). However, size may be relevant to the assessment of whether the putative PSG exists in any particular case and/or whether there is the requisite causal nexus. For example, if a group is too narrowly drawn, that may mean that it is not definable independently of the asserted risk of 'being persecuted'. The need for a causal nexus to be established

---

[292] Anker (n 1) §5.43, 520.
[293] For a critique of this notion, see Aleinikoff (n 38) 288; Hathaway and Foster (n 48) 441, citing Baroness Hale in *Fornah* (n 2) para 113.
[294] UNHCR Guidelines No 2 (n 58) para 15. *Islam* (n 54); *MIMA v Khawar* [2002] 210 CLR 1 (Aus HC), para 33.
[295] Early US case law sometimes sought to impose a cohesion requirement: see e.g. *Luis Alonzo Sanchez-Trujillo and Luis Armando Escobar-Nieto v INS* [1986] 801 F.2d 1571: see further Aleinikoff (n 38) 278–79. Anker (n 1) §5.44, 527 notes that some Board decisions still apply it.
[296] It may be different if a disparate group of individuals is perceived by persecutors to be a group: see below section 3.4.5.6 on doctrine of attribution.
[297] See Foster (n 177) 5–6. Discounting the necessity of voluntary association is not inconsistent with the *Acosta/Ward* framework as that recognises there can be at least one category of PSG that lacks this characteristic.
[298] *Applicant A* (n 37) para 296. A more recent example would be mixed race Hutu/Tutsi individuals who were at risk if they looked like members of the persecuted group.
[299] UNHCR Guidelines No 2 (n 58) paras 18–19. In relation to the position in the US, Anker (n 1) §5.41, 510 writes: '[c]onsistent with the *eiusdem generis* approach adopted by the Board, particular social groups may be as large as the groups encompassed by other grounds (an entire race, for example) or as small as a nuclear family'. A case exemplifying this view is *Perdomo v Holder* [2010] 611 F.3d 662, para 669. See also Hathaway and Foster (n 48) 425–26.

between this group and the persecution may be more easily achieved in relation to sub-categories of large groups.[300] On the other hand, some leading cases have seen it not to matter particularly whether a large group or a sub-category of it is identified. In *Fornah*, for example, one of the issues ventilated was whether the appropriate PSG was 'women', 'women at risk of FGM', or some other variant of this group.[301]

*3.4.5.5 A contextual requirement?*
Close attention has been paid throughout this chapter to what has been termed the relevancy or 'contextual requirement'. This refers to the attempt, especially in some leading common law cases,[302] to enunciate, as a further indice of the definition of a PSG, considerations of historical time and place. This requirement considers that whether any particular group can constitute a PSG *in fact* must always be evaluated in the context of historical time and place. It is this author's view that without such a context, the concept would lack any real limits. In the nature of human societies, certain groups can occupy very different positions in the social and political hierarchy, sometimes having great but at other times no real significance. For example, in a society in which both sexes are in general accorded equal treatment, it may make little sense to identify either of them as a PSG; but the same will not be true where there are significant inequalities between the sexes. The contextual requirement also offers an explanation for why there must be an open-ended approach to which groups can qualify as PSGs. As stated by the UNHCR Guidelines on MPSG, 'there is no "closed list" of what groups may constitute a "particular social group" .... Rather, the term ... should be read in an evolutionary manner, open to the diverse and changing nature of groups in various societies and evolving international human rights norms'.[303] This insight is now incorporated into the QD (recast). The opening words of the main paragraph in 10(1)(d) states that identification of a PSG '[d]epend[s] on the circumstances in the country of origin'.

However, it cannot unequivocally be said that there is wide agreement about such a requirement. Nor do commentators always make fully clear what they mean. Thus, as already noted, Hathaway and Foster's detailed treatment of this reason sometimes portrays the 'protected characteristics' approach as entailing that certain groups such as women, family, and children constitute a PSG per se;[304] at other times, as entailing

---

[300] Aleinikoff (n 38) 287. This is a point emphasised in the Australian case law: see e.g. *Khawar* (n 294) para 30, in which Gleeson CJ stated that in some circumstances the large size of the group might make implausible a suggestion that the group is a target of persecution and might suggest that a narrower definition of the group is necessary; and *Applicant A* (n 37) para 257 (per McHugh). This problem appears underplayed by Hathaway and Foster's 2014 treatment: see Hathaway and Foster (n 48) 436–42 (on gender).

[301] *Fornah* (n 2) paras 31, 55–58, 75–80, 114.

[302] See e.g. ibid para 13, per Lord Bingham, summarising the principles established by *Islam* (n 54) described this principle as requiring that 'to identify a social group one must first identify the society of which it forms part; a particular social group may be recognisable as such in one country but not in another'. See also paras 31, 54, 56, 71, 78, 101.

[303] UNHCR Guidelines No 2 (n 58) para 3.

[304] Hathaway and Foster (n 48) 437: 'there is nonetheless widespread recognition in Europe that women constitute a social group for Convention purposes'; ibid 449: 'In sum, family is properly understood as constituting a particular social group for Convention purposes'; ibid 451: 'recognition of age as an immutable characteristic is consistent with the straightforward *eiusdem generis* approach to social group'. In her 2012 study Foster (n 177) 21 notes that in some jurisdictions, PSG is 'explicitly defined in legislation to include

only that they 'may' or are 'capable of' constituting a PSG.[305] Their endorsement of the approach of the House of Lords in *Fornah* would appear to suggest that their considered position is to recognise a contextual requirement. That is also consistent with their treatment of, for example, the category of children. If they considered that children per se were a PSG, there would have been no point in them discussing approvingly cases in which it was considered appropriate to identify certain sub-categories of children.[306]

As regards the 'social perception' approach, of its two main versions, the one that simply requires social cognisability[307] would seem not to require any contextual criterion (and for that reason is open to the criticism of being effectively limitless). However, its other main version, which posits a difference requirement, clearly depends heavily on a contextual requirement. For the Australian High Court in *Applicant S*, '[t]he general principle is not that the group must be recognised or perceived within the society, but rather that the group must be distinguished from the rest of the society'.[308] This difference criterion writes into the identification exercise the fact that in a particular society the perceived characteristic is the subject of division. As also stated in *Applicant S*, making reference to the oft-cited example of left-handed men, such persons are not ordinarily distinguishable from the rest of the community.[309]

Whilst this author considers the contextual requirement to resonate heavily in UNHCR, judicial, and academic materials, it is clear from the earlier survey that it cannot be said to constitute an agreed principle.

### 3.4.5.6 *The doctrine of attribution*

As noted earlier, the doctrine of attribution applies in relation to all five Convention reasons. It has been significantly relied on in cases concerned with the MPSG rubric. Although (surprisingly) not mentioned in the UNHCR Guidelines on MPSG, other UNHCR guidance has seen this doctrine as applicable to MPSG cases,[310] as has case law.[311] In one respect the doctrine of attribution might be said to support the 'social perception' approach, insofar as the latter places focus on the perception of the

---

listed groups such as '[f]ormer victims of human trafficking', 'gender, sexual orientation or other membership of a particular social group', 'a group of persons of particular gender, sexual orientation, disability, class or caste', 'membership of a trade union', and 'membership of a group of persons whose defining characteristic is their belonging to the female or the male sex or having a particular sexual orientation'.

[305] Hathaway (n 19) 437: 'Widespread state practice ... now reflects the notion that women, sex or gender may constitute a particular social group'; see also 439; 446: 'As a rule ... a claim grounded in family background is properly receivable under the social group category'.

[306] Hathaway and Foster (n 48) 450: 'age-based social groups have appropriately been formulated, inter alia, as "orphaned children", "abandoned children", illegitimate children, "street children", "impoverished children", "black children", or "hei haizi" ..., and girls.' It may be they mean to endorse such groups in order to establish the causal nexus, but that is not always made clear.

[307] See above p. 631.

[308] *Applicant S* (n 39) para 27.

[309] ibid para 31.

[310] See e.g. UNHCR Guidelines No 9 (n 83) para 41.

[311] Anker (n 1) §5.44, 526 gives the example of *NLA v Holder* [2014] 744 F.3d 425, para 11, quoting *Cece v Holder* [2013] 733 F.3d 662, para 21, the shared trait of being targeted by a persecutor 'does not disqualify [an] otherwise valid social group'.

persecutor and it is well-known that persecutors may impute characteristics not held in reality. However, application of this doctrine is just as applicable within the 'protected characteristics' approach. What application of the doctrine does demonstrate, however, is that in relation to both the 'protected characteristics' and 'social perception' approaches, it expands the range of potential PSGs since as well as PSGs that actually exist, those which persecutors believe to exist must also be included. A classic example is medieval demonising of certain women as witches.[312] The difficulties this causes, in terms of giving rise to 'double construction' will be discussed in subsection 3.5 on political opinion.

*3.4.5.7 A broad approach? A non-evaluative approach?*
The above list of agreed key features does not include that the definition of MPSG needs to be broad. It is perhaps a curiosity of the literature on Convention reasons as a whole that there has rarely been consideration of whether being broad is a feature they all share. Since, as we have seen, race and nationality have generally been accepted as requiring a broad reading and religion has also been increasingly regarded as in need of such a reading, why should not MSPG and political opinion be seen in the same way? It is understandable that concern should be expressed about an 'overly broad' definition, as that would risk it collapsing into an open-ended residual reason. But that should not mean the definition should be understood as narrow. Be that as it may, there has clearly not been the same readiness to accept this as a feature of MPSG (or as we shall see, some aspects of the political opinion reason).

Nor has there been the same readiness to view the MSPG criteria as non-evaluative, that is, as it being unnecessary for establishing such membership to inquire whether individuals think or act according to a particular set of values. For example, there is no basis for a priori exclusion from the MPSG definition a terrorist group (an application based on membership of such a group may well fall to be rejected under Article 1F, but that is a different matter). It will be recalled that a non-evaluative understanding was a self-evident feature of the concepts of race and nationality. It was also noted in relation to religion that there was no qualitative criterion imposed in relation to the right to hold a religion or the sincerity or morality of any particular religious belief. A similar point will be made below in relation to the right to hold a political opinion. In the view of this author, it should also be regarded as a key feature of the MPSG reason that it similarly requires to be given a broad and non-evaluative definition. Certainly, much of the literature reflects such an approach.[313] Possibly, one reason why there has been some hesitancy about the evaluative aspect when it comes to MPSG (and why it has not been included in the list of agreed key features) stems from the introduction in the *Acosta/Ward* categories of a category comprising persons who voluntarily

---

[312] See e.g. *Applicant A* (n 37) para 265. See further Jenni Millbank and Anthea Vogl, 'Adjudicating Fear of Witchcraft Claims in Refugee Law' (2018) 45 Journal of Law and Society 370; Sara Dehm and Jenni Millbank, 'Witchcraft Accusations as Gendered Persecution in Refugee Law' (2018) 28 Social and Legal Studies 202.

[313] e.g. UNHCR Guidelines No 2 (n 58) para 4. See also Goodwin-Gill and McAdam (n 13) 102 who call for the notion to have an 'open-endedness capable of expansion' and note that '[m]any commentators have favoured a broad approach'.

associate through shared beliefs fundamental to human dignity.[314] That may represent a valid sub-category, but it cannot be taken to define features of the MPSG category as a whole.

### 3.4.6 Evaluation

As just explained, the UNHCR 'merger' solution, whilst right to seek convergence between the 'protected characteristics' and 'social perception' approaches, wrongly accepts both as internally consistent and able to stand on their own.

But whether or not this author's own tentative suggestion for reconstruction/unification is correct, there is no getting away from the fact that the current state of the jurisprudence and wider literature on the MPSG rubric identifies real problems with both approaches. Viewed in this light, there must *a fortiori* be serious doubt as to the compatibility with the refugee definition of a requirement that an applicant must show there is a PSG by applying *both* a 'protected characteristics' and a 'social perception' test.[315]

Nevertheless, as has been observed, despite adopting very different standpoints, both approaches broadly agree about a number of common features: that the PSG ground cannot be unlimited; that a PSG must exist independently of the persecution; that a PSG does not have to be cohesive or interdependent or homogeneous or associational; that a PSG does not need to be of a particular size. Even though this might seem a meagre list, the literature shows that in relation to establishing each of these points, UNHCR, judicial, governmental, and academic sources had to overcome numerous understandings to the contrary.

In the view of this author, as will be reflected in the 'suggested propositions' set out at the end of this chapter, any attempt to build a coherent definition of MPSG must include within it a contextual requirement—a criterion of relevancy that takes into account societal context.

## 3.5 Political Opinion

The Convention reason of political opinion has been seen as hard to define and somewhat different from the other reasons—as an 'odd one out'. Grahl-Madsen wrote that 'the scope of the term "political opinion" ... is not easily ascertainable'.[316] In 2008, the New Zealand RSAA said of this reason that 'all-encompassing definitions are an unhelpful distraction'.[317] In one of the most detailed studies of this reason, Dauvergne

---

[314] See above p. 597.
[315] That the two tests set out in Article 10(1)(d) are to be applied conjunctively has been confirmed by the CJEU in *Y and Z* (n 147), and Case C-652/16 *Nigyar Rauf Kaza Ahmedbekova and Rauf Emin Ogla Ahmedbekov v Zamestnik-predsedatel na Darzhavna agentsia za bezhantsite* [2018] ECLI:EU:C:2018:801. However, the CJEU has yet to rule on the implications for overall assessment of Article 10, the significance of the fact that the definition of each of the reasons set out in 10(1)(a)-(d) is couched in non-exhaustive language: ('in particular'). In the UK, the Nationality and Borders Act 2022, section 33 also prescribes that the two tests be treated as cumulative.
[316] Grahl-Madsen (n 28) 220.
[317] *Refugee Appeal No 76339* [2010] NZRSAA 386, para 87.

has observed, 'political opinion sticks out as different on this list'.[318] Next to the MPSG reason, the political opinion reason has generated the most case law and the most debate. The Michigan Guidelines on Risk For Reasons of Political Opinion state that 'the absence of an authoritative definition of "political opinion" in either the Convention or international law more generally has allowed interpretive inconsistencies to emerge, both within and among jurisdictions'.[319] This reason also poses, perhaps the most difficult challenges for attempts to find a common theme lying behind the Convention reasons.

3.5.1 Origins and *travaux préparatoires*

In 1938, the Inter-Governmental Committee on Refugees (IGCR), set up as an outgrowth of the Evian Conference process called by US President Roosevelt in July 1938, included within its category of refugee those who 'left their countries of origin (Germany, including Austria)' on account 'of their political opinions, religious beliefs and racial origin'.[320] In the inter war years, the paradigm of refugee was of course, the 'political refugee', a designation that implicitly recognised political causes for why individuals had fled their countries of origin.[321] The 1946 IRO Constitution, which included provision that no refugee with 'valid objections' should be compelled to return to his or her country of origin, listed as the first of six such categories: 'persons who were considered refugees before the outbreak of the second world war, for reasons of race, religion, nationality or political opinion provided these opinions are not in conflict with the principles of the United Nations, as laid down in the Preamble of the Charter of the United Nations'.[322] As regards the issue of whether 'prosecutions' for political offences could qualify as 'political opinion', Grahl-Madsen observed that although the IRO Manual for Eligibility Officers took a 'liberal position', it did not consider that common deserters or persons who had refused military service came within the IRO definition 'unless the event in respect of which punishment was feared had a bearing on the political opinion of the person concerned'.[323]

In the case of the 'political opinion' reason, by the time of the drafting of the 1951 Convention, there were already in place within IHRL specific rights partly covering its subject matter. The UDHR contains a non-discrimination guarantee at Article 2 that prohibits discrimination on the basis, inter alia, of 'political or other opinion'. Article 19 of the same instrument provides that '[e]veryone has the right to freedom of opinion and expression; the right includes freedom to hold opinions without

---

[318] Catherine Dauvergne, 'Toward a New Framework for Understanding Political Opinion' (2016) 37 Mich J Int'l L 243, 249.
[319] Michigan Guidelines (MGs) on Political Opinion in James C Hathaway, *The Michigan Guidelines on the International Protection of Refugees* (Michigan Publishing 2019) 110.
[320] Intergovernmental Committee for Refugees, Proceedings of the Intergovernmental Committee, Evian, July 6th to 15th 1938: Verbatim Record of the Plenary Meetings of the Committee and Resolutions (July 1938), cited in Claudena Skran, 'Historical Developments of International Refugee Law' in Zimmermann (n 1) 34.
[321] See e.g. Louise W Holborn, 'The Legal Status of Political Refugees, 1920–1938' (1938) 32(4) AJIL 680, 702; Vernant (n 30).
[322] IRO Constitution (n 31) Annex I, Part I, Sec A.
[323] Grahl-Madsen (n 28) 221.

interference and to seek, receive and impart information and ideas through any media and regardless of frontiers'.[324]

In extradition law, the notion of 'political offences' was well-established.[325] Although in common with their treatment of other Convention reasons the drafters made little comment as to the meaning of political opinion, it was stated during the discussions of the ECOSOC Social Committee that the reason should include 'diplomats thrown out of office', people 'whose political party had been outlawed', and 'individuals who fled from revolutions'.[326] It is notable that, in contrast to the wording of the first of the six 'valid objections' under the IRO Constitution, the reference to 'political opinion' was no longer made subject to the proviso that such opinion(s) be 'not in conflict with the principles of the United Nations, as laid down in the Preamble of the Charter of the United Nations'.

### 3.5.2 Article 31 and other Article 32 VCLT considerations

The limited assistance to be gained by considering the double-barrelled term 'political opinion' in its purely literal sense is self-evident. 'Opinion' is an extremely nebulous concept. The term 'political' has been given a range of dictionary definitions, some capacious.[327]

In respect of context, it might be said that there is at least an argument for considering that any definition of 'political' in Article 1A(2) must be consonant with that given to 'political' (or more precisely its opposite, 'non-political') in Article 1F(b). It might also be said that sometimes both sets of issues may need deciding in relation to one and the same applicant, e.g. if someone has been arrested for serious public order offences at a demonstration against rent rises, the question may arise as to whether the authorities will target him/her because of his/her political opinion (either actual or perceived); and the question may also arise as to whether his/her offences (assuming they are serious crimes) are political or non-political. To have two variant definitions of 'political' applicable to one and the same applicant could be seen as inconsistent.

If recourse was to be had by this route to the concept of 'political' in Article 1F(b), then it would be salient to consider the meaning given to the notion of 'political' in the international law that inspired it—that governing extradition in the context of the notion of 'political offence' (which is adjacent to the Article 1F(b) notion of 'non-political crime').[328] Extradition cases like *In re Castioni*[329] could then be seen as

---

[324] Universal Declaration of Human Rights (adopted 10 December 1948) UNGA Res 217 A(III).
[325] Lora L Deere, 'Political Offenses in the Law and Practice of Extradition' (1933) 27(2) 27 AJIL 247.
[326] ECOSOC, Summary Record of the 172nd meeting held at the Palais des Nations, Geneva, on Saturday, 12 August 1950 (24 August 1950) UN Doc E/AC.7/SR.172, paras 18–23; ECOSOC, Summary Record of the 173rd meeting held at the Palais des Nations, Geneva, on Saturday, 12 August 1950 (25 August 1950) UN Doc E/AC.7/SR.173, para 5 (cited in Hathaway (n 19) 149).
[327] Senses listed in the OED Online <https://www.oed.com> accessed 6 August 2021, include: '[i]nvolved, employed, or interested in politics; that takes a side, promotes, or follows a particular party line in political debate' and '[r]elating to or concerned with public life and affairs as involving questions of authority and government; relating to or concerned with the theory or practice of politics'.
[328] Joan Fitzpatrick, 'The Post-Exclusion Phase: Extradition, Prosecution and Expulsion' (2000) 12(1) IJRL 272; Geoff Gilbert, *Responding to International Crime* (Martinus Nijhoff 2006) ch 5; Goodwin-Gill and McAdam (n 13) 138–44.
[329] *In re Castioni* [1891] 1 QB 149, para 155.

useful reference points. It is clear from the *travaux* that the drafters, certainly in respect of non-political crime, had in mind the analogue of extradition law definitions. However, if one sought to build a bridge out of such materials, then among the objections that would arise is that prevailing interpretations—e.g. Bassiouni's concept within extradition law of a 'purely political offence'[330] and Garcia-Mora's definition of 'political offense' as an offence against the security of the state—appear to construe the notion of 'political' somewhat narrowly around the idea that it relates to a system of government, i.e. confined to state actors.[331] That (as we shall see) would impose a very restrictive paradigm.

Although in analysing the VCLT element of context, Gardiner describes it as a 'general principle ... to expect the same term to have the same meaning throughout a single instrument', he adds that this is not an absolute rule and that context can sometimes suggest different meaning of the same term.[332] '[P]olitical' in 1A(2) and [non]-'political' in 1F(b) denote two entirely different phenomena: opinions in the one context and offences in the other. This significantly undermines the value of any attempted read-across from Article 1F(b).[333]

The fact that context also covers the Preamble and that the latter identifies 'fundamental rights and freedoms' and 'non-discrimination' has led many to view the political opinion reason as having a strong international law/human rights axis. Significantly, even though not adopting a human rights approach to the refugee definition generally, Grahl-Madsen was one of the first to note that 'it seems reasonable to infer [from these features of the Preamble] that a person may justly fear persecution "for reasons of political opinion" in the sense of the Refugee Convention if he is threatened with measures of a persecutory nature because of his exercise of or his insistence on certain of the "rights" laid down in the Universal Declaration'.[334] As regards 'opinion', Article 19(1) of the ICCPR provides that '[e]veryone shall have the right to hold opinions without interference'. The ICCPR also contains a non-discrimination guarantee at Article 2 that prohibits discrimination on the basis, inter alia, of 'political or other opinion'. The Covenant's title, of course describes the rights it enshrines as 'Civil and Political'.[335] The American Convention on Human Rights (ACHR) also identifies certain rights as 'civil and political' and thereby makes clear that certainly the rights of freedom of expression, assembly, and association are inherently civil/

---

[330] Cherif M Bassiouni, *International Extradition: United States Law and Practice* (6th edn, OUP 2014).
[331] Manuel R García-Mora, 'The Nature of Political Offenses: A Knotty Problem of Extradition Law' (1962) 48 Virginia Law Rev 1226.
[332] Richard Gardiner, *Treaty Interpretation* (2nd edn, OUP 2015) 209. He cites as an example different meanings ascribed to the term 'responsibility': *Responsibilities and Obligations of States Sponsoring Persons and Entities with respect to Activities in the Area* (Advisory Opinion) (2011) ITLOS Case No 17, paras 64–71.
[333] At para 13, the MGs on Political Opinion state: '[t]he meaning of a "political" opinion should not be constrained by importing an understanding of "political" that is contextually incongruous. For example, the notion of a non-"political" crime that circumscribes exclusion under Article 1(F)(b) derives meaning from its criminal context, whereas interpretation of the nexus clause must be informed by its non-discrimination context.' See also *EMAP (Gang Violence—Convention Reason) El Salvador CG* [2022] UKUT 00335 (IAC), paras 83–86, 115–16; Geoff Gilbert, 'Exclusion' in Cathryn Costello et al (n 9) 717.
[334] Grahl-Madsen (n 28) 227.
[335] ICCPR (n 5). See also UDHR (n 324) Article 19(1) and Article 2.

political.[336] The European Convention on Human Rights (ECHR) at Article 14 identifies as one specified ground of discrimination, 'political or other opinion'.[337]

In its General Comment No 34, the UN Human Rights Committee (HRC) states that freedom of opinion and freedom of expression are 'indispensable conditions for the full development of the person. They are essential for any society.'[338] However, a clear distinction is made between the two. '[F]reedom of expression' has permissible limitations.[339] By contrast, all forms of opinion are protected. At paragraph 10, the HRC states that [a]ny form of effort to coerce the holding or not holding of any opinion is prohibited'. At paragraph 11, the Committee spells out that the scope of Article 19(2) embraces even expression that may be regarded as deeply offensive,[340] although such expression may be restricted in accordance with the provisions of Article 19(3) and Article 20.

These sources do not include a definition of either 'opinion' or 'political', nor do they address the compound concept of 'political opinion'. Further, there has been very little IHRL jurisprudence on the concept of 'political'. Such features have led Dauvergne to conclude that 'political opinion is not defined in an adjacent area of law in a way that can be easily borrowed for Refugee Convention purposes'.[341] That said, the HRC comments do lend support for giving a broad reading to the concept of 'opinion' in Article 1A(2), since the medley of political rights enshrined in, inter alia, the UDHR, ICCPR, and ECHR manifestly encompasses opinion as well as expression and, in contrast to expression, there is no restriction on the content of opinion.

Whilst, therefore, the anchorage of the 'political opinion' reason in IHRL is strong and can be said to directly assist in classic cases where a person's freedom of expression is threatened by state or quasi-state actors for overtly political reasons, it does not offer any significant help in clarifying the term's full contours. What is said below about the problems arising in relation to the 'political' component only add to the uncertainty.

Turning to Article 31(3) as well as other Article 32 VCLT considerations, UNHCR, judicial, governmental, and academic materials have contributed a number of insights to the meaning of the 'political opinion' reason. The 1979 UNHCR Handbook offers no definition of the term but does give guidance as to certain of its aspects. Built on state practice up to that time, this guidance specifies, inter alia, that the opinions concerned must be 'opinions not tolerated by the authorities, which are critical of their policies or methods' (paragraph 80). Such opinions must 'have come to the notice of the authorities or are attributed by them to the applicant' (paragraph 80); or where 'it

---

[336] American Convention on Human Rights (adopted 22 November 1969, entered into force 18 July 1978).

[337] European Convention on Human Rights (adopted 4 November 1950, entered into force 3 September 1953).

[338] HRC, General Comment No 34: Article 19 (Freedoms of Opinion and Expression) (12 September 2011) UN Doc CCPR/C/GC/34, para 2.

[339] ICCPR (n 5) Article 19(3).

[340] HRC General Comment No 34 (n 338). The Committee cites *Case of Malcolm Ross v Canada* (18 October 2000) Communication No 736/97, UN Doc CCPR/C/70/D/736/1997.

[341] Dauvergne (n 318) 295.

may be reasonable to assume that his opinions will sooner or later find expression and that the applicant will, as a result, come into conflict with the authorities' (paragraph 82); or where an applicant prior to departure '[c]onceals his political opinion' but refuses to avail himself of protection. e.g. by virtue of *sur place* activities (paragraph 83). The Handbook also notes that '[t]he relative importance or tenacity of the applicant's opinions ... will also be relevant' (paragraph 80). They further contain several paragraphs seeking to clarify the circumstances in which persons who face prosecution for political offences may be considered to have a political opinion (paragraphs 84–86). Subsequently UNHCR adopted the Goodwin-Gill definition of 'political opinion' as 'any opinion on any matter in which the machinery of State, government and policy may be engaged'.[342]

Turning to judicial materials, at least in the common law world, most have often adopted the same Goodwin-Gill definition.[343] Dauvergne's study identifies several other propositions that, through the medium of leading cases, have become part of an 'agreed terrain':[344] that a political opinion need not have been expressed outright but can be perceived from actions; that the opinion in question need not conform to the applicant's true beliefs; that this ground of persecution is also relevant in cases where the persecutor is not the state; and that while it is the victim's political opinion that must be assessed, it is what the persecutor believes, rather than the truth of the opinion, that matters.[345] However, her study of case law also identifies considerable division over the meaning of 'political' opinion. Traversing case law on five 'case clusters'—involving military conscientious objectors, people fleeing China's one-child policy, people in flight from criminal violence, people at risk because of their whistleblowing activities, and circumstances where gender and political opinion are linked—she concludes that each demonstrate gaps and differences which call for a new way forward.[346]

### 3.5.3 Key features
In light of the above application of VCLT considerations, it is possible to derive several key features of the political opinion reason.

*3.5.3.1 Concept of 'opinion'*
From the UNHCR, judicial, and academic materials it is clear that by virtue of protecting political 'opinion' rather than acts, the refugee definition encompasses diverse manifestations of the political. Opinions can be held in numerous ways. It is not necessary for Article 1A(2) purposes to express a political opinion in order

---

[342] Goodwin-Gill and McAdam (n 207) 87. UNHCR Guidelines No 1 (n 169) para 32; No 9 (n 83) para 50. See also UNHCR, 'Guidance Note on Refugee Claims relating to Victims of Organised Gangs' (2010) para 45; UNHCR, 'Written observations on the reference for a preliminary ruling of the Court of Justice of the European Union in the matter between S. and A. and Netherlands, Case C-151/22 (June 2022)' para 16, available at <https://www.refworld.org/docid/62c6d38a4.html>. Goodwin-Gill and McAdam (n 13) 119 maintain the same definition.
[343] Most explicitly in the Canadian jurisprudence: see e.g. *Ward* (n 14); *Klinko v MCI* [2000] 3 FC 327, para 33; *Olvera v Canada (MCI)* [2012] 2012 FC 1048, paras 33–34.
[344] Dauvergne (n 318) 255.
[345] ibid 264.
[346] ibid 266.

to hold or have it, albeit it will most often be evidenced by pointing to activity undertaken by an applicant.[347] Further, as already noted, in IHRL there is no permissible restriction on the mere holding of an opinion. To hold a political opinion or to express it, it is not necessary that one is a formal member of a political organisation or party or in a leadership position,[348] although, once again, being able to point to involvement in a political organisation may be valuable evidence of the opinion's existence (and relevance to the case).[349] And, to repeat, in cases in which political opinion is imputed, it is not necessary that an applicant in reality holds the perceived opinion, or indeed any political opinion at all. Also clear is that the 'opinion' concept—unless taking the form of expression of opinion—is seemingly uncircumscribed by any qualitative criteria. As noted earlier, the drafters did not make it subject to the proviso (as had the IRO Constitution's treatment of the political opinion ground) that such opinion(s) be 'not in conflict with the principles of the United Nations, as laid down in the Preamble of the Charter of the United Nations'.[350] If there are effective limits, they must be sought in the 'political' descriptor.

Dauvergne's study concludes that whilst in both IHRL and refugee law 'opinion is almost unlimited', in the latter context, 'for an opinion to be the object of a risk ... , it must have some discernible trace in the world'.[351] Her study's tentative conclusion is that '"opinion" need not trouble the analysis when there is some overt statement of it ...; the problems arise instead in the doubly constructed realm of imputation, which is doubly constructed because the decision-maker must speculate about the speculation of the persecutor'.[352]

### 3.5.3.2 Notion of 'political' opinion

In the early years the case law and wider literature on the epithet 'political' in the Article 1A(2) context featured a split between those who sought to take a restrictive[353] and those adopting a liberal approach. Although Grahl-Madsen appears to have seen his own approach as falling within the latter camp, his own seeming attempt at a definition envisaged that it 'covers persecution of persons on the simple ground that they are alleged or known to hold opinions contrary to or critical of the policies of the government or ruling party', which includes 'public expression of opinions' whether made a political offence or not.[354] Pointedly, the Canadian Supreme Court in *Ward* rejected this definition as unduly restrictive.[355]

---

[347] Anker (n 1) §5.18, 435–36.
[348] Zimmermann and Mahler (n 1) 400; UNHCR (n 342) paras 17–18.
[349] Anker (n 1) §5.18, 435–36.
[350] See above p. 640.
[351] Dauvergne (n 318) 291.
[352] ibid.
[353] Sternberg (n 38) 67, notes that US case law 'has historically suffered from an exceptionally restrictive construction. Limiting interpretations have resulted from, among other things, an austere view of the nexus requirement as well as from a highly limited view of the sort of opinions which could be characterized as political.' It is notable, however, that Anker (n 1) §§5.17–5.40 identifies current case law as taking a broader view.
[354] Grahl-Madsen (n 28) 220.
[355] *Ward* (n 14).

Gradually a more liberal approach appears to have prevailed. According to Hathaway and Foster:

> Contemporary international jurisprudence mirrors the drafters' notion that 'political opinion' can be relevant to a broad range of people in recognizing that 'the fact of non-membership in a political party' is in and of itself 'irrelevant', that political opinion 'encompasses more than electoral politics or formal political ideology or action', that where a person is affiliated with an organisation, group, or entity, it need not be characterised as or understood as a traditionally political one, and that it is irrelevant that any such group is 'loosely knit' and has 'no official title, office or status' in the home country.[356]

Their own conclusion is that 'a broad and inclusive approach to interpreting "political opinion" is vital to ensuring the ability of the refugee definition to evolve and accommodate modern refugees in need of protection'.[357] That conclusion can be said to be supported by the wording of Article 10(1)(e) of the QD (recast) which sets out a broad, non-exhaustive definition. It states that: 'the concept of political opinion shall in particular include the holding of an opinion, thought or belief on a matter related to the potential actors of persecution mentioned in Article 6 and to their policies or methods, whether or not that opinion, thought or belief has been acted upon by the applicant'.[358] Article 6 identifies, as potential actors of persecution, state as well as non-state actors.

However, despite convergence around a liberal approach, analysis of case law and the wider literature, both by Hathaway and Foster[359] and other scholars,[360] identify a number of interpretive challenges that have arisen, particularly over the meaning of 'political'.

In relation to the meaning of 'political', three main positions appear to have been articulated.

The first is that voiced by Goodwin-Gill in a formulation that was taken up by the Canadian Supreme Court in *Ward*,[361] by UNHCR in 2010,[362] and in many academic studies. As noted earlier, this formulation defines political opinion as 'any opinion on any matter in which the machinery of State, government and policy may be engaged'.[363]

A second position, whilst still making it a requirement that the opinion be in some way related to government or the state, emphasises the importance of considering matters in terms of power transactions and recognising that non-state actors of serious harm can sometimes be the object of political opinions. Expressing this

---

[356] Hathaway and Foster (n 48) 405–06.
[357] ibid 423.
[358] That this wording reflects a broad approach was confirmed by the CJEU in Case C-280/21, *PI v Migracijos departamentas prie lietuvos Respublikos vidaus reikalu miniterijos*, 12 January 2023 [2023] EUECJ C-280/21, para 26. See also EUAA, 'Practical Guide on Political Opinion' (EUAA, December 2022) 1.2; Dauvergne (n 318) 254 however, considers the Article 10(1)(e) definition unduly broad.
[359] Hathaway and Foster (n 48) 405–06, 422 and generally 405–23.
[360] The study of case law by Dauvergne (n 318) being amongst the most comprehensive.
[361] *Ward* (n 14).
[362] UNHCR, Guidance Note on Refugee Claims Relating to Victims of Organized Gangs (n 342) para 45.
[363] Goodwin-Gill and McAdam (n 207) 87.

position, the UKIAT in *Gomez* defined political opinion as being concerned with 'views which have a bearing on the major power transactions relating to government taking place in a particular society'.[364] Along similar lines, the Michigan Guidelines enunciate that:

> A 'political' opinion is an opinion about the nature, policies, or practices of a state or of an entity that has the capacity, legitimately or otherwise, to exercise societal power or authority. A relevant non-state entity is one that is institutionalized, formalized, or informally systematized and which is shown by evidence of pattern or practice to exercise *de facto* societal power or authority.[365]

Dauvergne herself considers that:

> Turning to context ought to involve considering the power dynamics that surround any expressed or imputed view, and considering how those dynamics link, or fail to link, to formal authority within the relevant state. Such an approach to context would allow for opinions to be political without touching upon state or government, but would still leave a space for considering how the formal political sector is constructed in a given society.[366]

A third position shares with the second position a focus on power transactions but considers that these can be political at all levels of society. Although stating that 'political opinion' could not be defined, the New Zealand RSAA, addressing the case of an Alevi Kurdish woman from Turkey who feared being murdered by family members in the name of honour, ventured that:

> In the particular context, a woman's actual or implied assertion of her right to autonomy and the right to control her own life may be seen as a challenge to the unequal distribution of power in her society and the structures which underpin that inequality. In our view such situation is properly characterized as 'political'.[367]

Dauvergne has commented that 'this approach is in sharp contrast to all of the other leading cases. The word "government" is not mentioned at any point in the analysis, and the focus is instead on how power is exercised in particular social contexts.'[368]

### 3.5.3.3 Importance of context

Despite divergent views having been expressed about the meaning of 'political' opinion, it is notable that most commentators attach great importance to context.

---

[364] *Gutierrez Gomez v SSHD* [2000] UKIAT 00007, para 69.
[365] MGs on Political Opinion (n 319) para 8.
[366] Dauvergne (n 318) 294.
[367] *Refugee Appeal No 76044* [2008] NZAR 719, para 84. See also paras 1, 8. For a similar view see Alice Edwards, 'Age and Gender Dimensions in International Refugee Law' in Feller et al (n 37) 46, 68.
[368] Dauvergne (n 318) 261.

Thus it appears that the Canadian Supreme Court in *Ward* was only able to overcome the difficulty that Ward's case was not concerned directly with the machinery of government by attaching significance to the fact that a view imputable to him was that innocent people should not be killed as part of a political struggle.[369] In *Gomez*, the IAT stated that '[i]n consequence of the shifting boundaries of the political in different societies and at different periods neither is it possible to identify any fixed categories of persons or bodies that will qualify as political entities'.[370] For the RSAA, in 2008 this factor was seen as so decisive as to defeat any attempt to define 'political opinion' in the abstract.[371] From Dauvergne's own attempt at definition cited earlier, it is clear that she too sees context as pivotal.

*3.5.3.4 Discretion/concealment*
As already noted,[372] the fact that a person may choose on return to conceal his or her political opinions or abstain from political activity will not preclude him or her from being recognised as a refugee, at least if one of the reasons why he would behave in this way is fear of persecution.

3.5.4 Evaluation
Despite case law and the wider literature having failed to clarify all of its aspects, some common threads can be discerned.

*3.5.4.1 Role of the concept of 'opinion'*
Even though the 'opinion' element has generally been understood as an almost unlimited concept, this has not caused particular problems in the refugee law context save in relation to cases where political opinion is imputed or attributed (the latter aspect is addressed separately below).

*3.5.4.2 Meaning of 'political'*
For interpreters the constant struggle has been to strike a balance between being over inclusive and under inclusive. As stated by Chairperson Haines in a 2010 RSAA decision:

> When interpreting the political opinion ground of the Refugee Convention there is a risk of both over-inclusion and under-inclusion. Over-inclusion because, given an unjustifiably broad interpretation, virtually any issue can be categorised as 'political'. This would collapse the five enumerated grounds in Article 1A(2) (race, religion, nationality, membership of a political social group or political opinion) into one. Too narrow a construction, on the other hand, would exclude claims which on accepted

---

[369] *Ward* (n 14) para 748.
[370] *Gomez* (n 364) para 64. To similar effect, see Case C-280/21, *PI* (n 358), para 33; *Jerez-Spring v Canada (MEI)* [1981] 2 FC 527.
[371] *Refugee Appeal No 76044* (n 367) para 87. Reaffirmed by the same tribunal in *Refugee Appeal No 76339* [2010] NZAR 386, para 88.
[372] See p. 601. See also Goodwin-Gill and McAdam (n 13) 122.

principles of treaty interpretation should be recognised as falling within the political opinion ground.[373]

Despite their differences over how to interpret the concept of 'political' in the Article 1A(2) context, the three main approaches outlined above would appear to share considerable common ground. As *Ward* demonstrates, the Goodwin-Gill approach to definition can be operated so as to overcome the main criticisms, by construing it to cover even understandings imputed to non-state actors about ongoing struggles for political change. In Canadian case law post-*Ward*, the Goodwin-Gill definition can encompass the machinery of government, indirectly as well as directly.[374] The Goodwin-Gill definition does also refer to 'policy' and it is this aspect that UNHCR has seized on in gender and sexual orientation contexts. Whilst concerned to link the political to power relationship in a society, *Gomez* still required some reference to government. The New Zealand RSAA, albeit making no mention of government, still sought to situate analysis in the context of the 'distribution of power in society'. Accordingly, it would appear possible to amalgamate these three positions by adoption of a slightly broader formulation. Of the proposals canvassed so far, the definition that best achieves this is that proffered in the Michigan Guidelines, which extends it to cover an opinion about 'the nature, policies, or practices of a state or of an entity that has the capacity, legitimately or otherwise, to exercise societal power or authority'.[375]

At the same time, it is vital that analysis does not lose sight of why reference to the machinery of government, without any qualification, is apt to mislead. Such a formulation causes no real problems when the state is the actor of persecution. However, where non-state actors are involved, such an approach risks adoption of a narrow understanding of the causal nexus. This is linked to what has become known in the literature as the 'bifurcated nexus' issue.[376] This is addressed more fully in section 4.3, but must be put in context here as well. According to Hathaway and Foster, persecution is defined as serious harm plus lack of state protection. It follows from this approach to definition that the nexus with the Convention reason may be established by linkage to *either* the serious harm or the lack of state protection. In state actor cases, the focus is on the reasons which cause them to persecute an applicant. In non-state actor cases, the political opinion can be elicited either by reference to the reason perceived by the non-state actor or to the reason which causes the state to withhold effective protection.[377] If in non-state actor cases the focus had to be solely on the reasons causing the

---

[373] *Refugee Appeal No 76339* (n 371) 86.

[374] In *Klinko* (n 343), which concerned a businessman from the Ukraine who, along with five others, made a complaint against the widespread corruption of customs officers and police, the Court said that the Goodwin-Gill/*Ward* test 'does not require that the state or machinery of state be actually engaged in the subject-matter of the opinion'. It was sufficient in order to meet the test that the state or machinery of state 'may be engaged'. For a similar recognition of indirect connection with the state, see Case C-280/21, *PI* (n 358), para 32.

[375] MGs on Political Opinion (n 319) para 8.

[376] Anker (n 1) §5.16, 430–31. See below pp. 658–659.

[377] James C Hathaway, *The Michigan Guidelines on the International Protection of Refugees* (Michigan Publishing 2019) 116 at [14]; see also James C Hathaway, 'The Michigan Guidelines on Nexus to a Convention Ground' (2002) 23(2) Michigan Journal of International Law 207.

*state* to withhold protection, there would be blatant incongruities. It could lead, for example, to an assessment that the political opinion reason was not made out even when the non-state actor in question was motivated by a strong perception that a claimant was a political opponent, but the state had no political reasons for withholding protection. Conversely, it could lead to an assessment that the political opinion reason was not made out if the state's inability to protect was motivated by political reasons, but the non-state actor had none. So, it is necessary to recognise that political opinion can be established by either route.

In a range of non-state actor cases, where the state reason for failing to protect is a political one, the focus remains (as conventionally conceived) on how state actors perceive the applicant's opinion(s). For example, where non-state actor X seeks to persecute an applicant for non-political reasons to do with a family dispute over a marriage, yet the state fails to protect for political reasons, focus will necessarily be on what the latter are, e.g. the powers that be may disapprove of interreligious marriages. However, where the political opinion-related reason for the persecution relates to a non-state actor, focus will need to be on that actor's role. For example, an organised drug cartel's motives may be solely concerned with the applicant's perceived disobedience to its regional policy, without reference to governmental machinery at all.

The question remains, though, what in such cases is the dividing line between the political and the criminal. The UNHCR Guidance Note on Refugee Claims Relating to Victims of Organized Gangs, in adopting the Goodwin-Gill definition, makes clear that opinions about such gangs/cartels can be political where there is interconnection with governmental machinery:

> It is important to consider, especially in the context of Central America, that powerful gangs, such as the Maras, may directly control society and *de facto* exercise power in the areas where they operate. The activities of gangs and certain State agents may be so closely intertwined that gangs exercise direct or indirect influence over a segment of the State or individual government officials. Where criminal activity implicates agents of the State, opposition to criminal acts may be analogous with opposition to State authorities. Such cases, thus, may under certain circumstances be properly analysed within the political opinion Convention ground.[378]

As noted by Dauvergne, however, the difficulty remains that 'many cases of individuals fleeing criminal groups fall into a murky in-between position where the group is *not* state-like, but where state protection is not possible.'[379] From the divergent views taken in the case law analysed by Dauvergne, resolution of this problem remains elusive, but it would appear that the emphasis placed in the definition offered by the Michigan Guidelines on Political Opinion, which refers to non-state actors exercising '*de facto*

---

[378] UNHCR (n 362) para 45. See also Anker (n 1) §5.26, 451–75 (on '[t]hird-generation gangs').
[379] Dauvergne (n 318) 279. She gives as examples the cases of *INS v Elias-Zacarias* [1992] 502 US 478 and *Ward* (n 14). These, she writes, 'probably would not be considered to involve gangs exercising "*de facto*... power*" or which "directly control society"'. But see *EMAP* (n 333) paras 78–86.

societal power or authority', at least alerts decision makers to the need to think about a country's societal as well as its governmental dimension.[380]

It should also be noted, given the reference immediately above to the distinction between the political and the criminal, that the criminal should not be classified as non-political purely because of the distaste of decision makers for the conduct of the criminal actors involved (we return to this matter in subsection 3.5.4.4 when discussing qualitative considerations).

At the same time, it must be recognised that even taking the broader approach to the meaning of 'political' just outlined, opinions relating to personal, or family, or local community matters will not easily qualify. If for example, a private actor seeks to persecute another private actor because of an isolated personal or family feud, it will be very difficult to ascribe any 'political' opinion for such persecution. That does not necessarily mean that the affected person might not be able to show a different Convention reason (e.g. membership of a particular social group based on family). And it may be different if there was a political backdrop to the feud. Analysis may be very fact specific.

The need for a broad reading which accommodates both state and non-state actor scenarios, has been reinforced by the definition given in Article 10(1)(d) of the Qualification Directive which states that it includes 'the holding of an opinion, thought or belief on a matter related to the potential *actors of persecution* ... and to their policies and methods' (Article 6 of the Qualification Directive accepts that actors of persecution can be either state or non-state actors).[381]

Yet in light of the continuing debates over the concept of the political it cannot be said that there is substantial agreement that the 'political opinion' reason requires a broad reading. Presently it is only the 'opinion' element that is widely accepted as having a broad meaning.

### 3.5.4.3 The contextual requirement

As noted earlier, considerable emphasis has been placed in the case law and wider literature on the importance of considering the concept of 'political' in historical time and place. In order to decide whether the 'political opinion' reason is engaged, it will be necessary to have close regard to the historical context,[382] as the boundaries between the political and the non-political are susceptible of change. Opinions considered as apolitical in one society may be seen as highly political in another, for example the violations of dress codes in a fundamentalist Muslim country as compared to the more

---

[380] This definition also matches better the insights of feminist perspectives. As Dauvergne (n 318) 289, writes, '[t]hinking through gender-related political opinion compels the decision-maker to consider how, why, and when opinions about private concerns, micro-level concerns, or matters of self-interest link up with larger social themes and thereby take on characteristics that are, to recall the words of the Second Circuit, "typical of political protest". Thus, feminist analysis brings to the question a well-developed framework for illuminating the political in the personal.'

[381] See analysis in Case C-280/21, *PI* (n 358), paras 32, 40. Dauvergne (n 318) 254 considers the Article 10(1)(e) definition a 'clumsy formulation' that is unduly broad. She comments that, '[f]or example, forming the idea that "this group is going to harm me and no one can protect me" would appear to be a political opinion under the QD. Paragraph (c) provides an illustration of how easy it is for political opinion analysis to become so open-ended as to be unwieldy.'

[382] Zimmermann and Mahler (n 1) 399. See also Case C-280/21, *PI* (n 358), para 33.

laissez-faire approach of liberal democracies.[383] Formal governmental structures and machineries may not truly reflect the shifting contours of what is political in any particular society. In theocracies, church and state may be inextricably connected. In the contemporary world criminal gangs may sometimes see themselves as wholly apolitical, but their *modus operandi* may be highly political. For example, political elites may seek to recruit them as paramilitaries. In other contexts, criminal gangs may themselves seek to gain actual control or 'capture' of (or at least exercise strong influence over) the levers of governmental power, in order to better achieve their ends. This context-specific approach to the meaning of 'political' comports well with the understanding that whether particular structures and machineries or organisations are political essentially has to do with nature of the major power transactions and prevailing power structures in a particular society.[384]

However, contrary to the view expressed in the 2008 New Zealand RSAA case,[385] a context-specific approach is not in itself a reason to eschew any attempt at definition. It does entail rejection of any absolutist definition but not one that integrates the contextual requirement into its terms.

### 3.5.4.4 Qualitative considerations

Clearly the requirement that the opinion must be 'political' imposes some limits. Yet we have seen that the 'opinion' element, at least, appears relatively unlimited. In particular, it cannot be limited to opinions that embody human rights values (such as an oppositionist's speaking out against a repressive regime) or reflect certain moral or ethical values. The right to hold opinions is absolute. Even in relation to expression of opinion, which is subject to permissible limitations, a human rights approach in fact requires a relatively non-judgmental pluralist approach that is ready to encompass opinions of myriad kinds. The Michigan Guidelines are particularly helpful in underlining such aspects, including, for example, that '[a]n opinion does not cease to be "political" because it advances the self-interest of the person seeking recognition of refugee status' (paragraph 11). These Guidelines also correctly warn against the conflation of the 'political opinion' reason with issues relating to whether conduct is persecutory:

> The scope of a 'political opinion' as defined in paras. 3–13 of these Guidelines should not be constrained to ensure that the Convention is not brought into disrepute by recognizing the refugee status of an undeserving person. In particular, risk arising from a criminal prosecution that is conceived and conducted in accordance with international law does not amount to a risk of being persecuted, and will therefore not be the basis for recognition of refugee status. Decision makers must moreover exclude serious criminals and others deemed undeserving of protection on the terms

[383] Somewhat controversially, the US Supreme Court in *Elias-Zacarias* (n 379) held that resisting forced recruitment by guerrillas did not necessarily imply political opinion.
[384] This author accepts, however, that Dauvergne (n 318) 291, is correct to find the *Gomez* formulation too open-ended. Even if historical examples can be found of government actors who lack any power, they mostly illustrate that when this happens (except in the context of state breakdown) governmental functions shift to other actors.
[385] *Refugee Appeal No 76044* (n 367) para 87.

mandated by Article 1(F) of the Convention. The combination of these safeguards suffices to protect the integrity of the Convention.[386]

There is no principled basis, therefore, for excluding from the category of 'political' opinion per se persons involved in 'bad politics', e.g. criminal or paramilitary or terrorist group activities. As noted by Dauvergne, 'there is a potentially wide range of political opinions that are morally repugnant (for example Holocaust deniers) or embrace illegal acts (for example, support for a political assassination)'.[387] To impose a value judgment that persecution carried out against an individual could not be for a Convention reason of political opinion solely because, for example, he or she held terrorist views, would have the effect of depriving the Convention reasons of their efficacy. Paradoxical though it might seem, conceptualising 'political' within Article 1A(2) in this way is consistent with IHRL. From time to time, IHRL has, of course, found no violation of a person's human rights where they have acted, for example, in support of extremist or terrorist causes or amount to 'hate speech'.[388] But that has been in the context of balancing public or community interest factors involved in assessing the proportionality of interference in the *exercise* of the right to freedom of expression; it has not been in the context of assessing whether opinion (which does not necessarily have to be expressed) qualifies as political.[389]

### 3.5.4.5 *The doctrine of attribution*
It was noted earlier that there has been a long-standing recognition in the context of the political opinion reason of the importance of the doctrine of attribution or imputability. Indeed, in the 1979 UNHCR Handbook this is the only reason in relation to which this doctrine is expressly recognised. In *RT (Zimbabwe)* the UK House of Lords noted Hathaway's formulation of it in his 1991 TLRS:

> The focus is always to be the existence of a *de facto* political attribution by the state of origin, notwithstanding the objective unimportance of the claimant's political acts, her own inability to characterise her actions as flowing from a particular political ideology, or even an explicit disavowal of the views ascribed to her by the state.[390]

It cannot be denied, as Dauvergne has highlighted, that this doctrine plants real difficulties in the path of a coherent interpretation of the political opinion reason—if not all five. It gives rise to the artificiality of what she describes as a 'doubly constructed' assessment.[391] As an example of how this extra dimension can complicate matters, consider the statement in the Michigan Guidelines that 'an "opinion" is a conscious choice

---

[386] MGs on Political Opinion (n 319) para 15.
[387] Dauvergne (n 318) 267.
[388] In the ECHR context, see e.g. 'Factsheet on Hate Speech, March 2020, Press Unit, European Court of Human Rights'. In the Inter-American context, see IACHR, InterAmerican Legal Framework Regarding the Right to Freedom of Expression (2009) OEA/Ser.L/V/II CIDH/RELE/INF.2/09.
[389] Dauvergne (n 318) 258. There is a parallel here with the right to hold a religious belief, which is likewise absolute: see above p. 609.
[390] *RT (Zimbabwe)* (n 74); Hathaway (n 19) 155–56. See also the US case, *Abdel-Rahman v Gonzales* [2007] 493 F.3d 444, paras 450–51.
[391] Dauvergne (n 318) 291.

or stance'.[392] In the case of attribution, not only does the applicant not in fact hold that opinion, but his or her persecutors may simply impute such an opinion simply because they dislike him; it may have nothing to do with choice. To preserve the notion of conscious choice may require highly artificial constructions (e.g. assuming that the persecutors perceive that he or she has made a conscious choice). However, coherence can be maintained by recognising that the Convention reasons are concerned at their core with persons who have certain characteristics, but that they also need extension to cater for the perceptions of persecutors.

*3.5.4.6 Commonality with other reasons*
The fact that this reason's 'opinion' element is seemingly unlimited means that establishing a basis in common within the threefold *Acosta/Ward* categories[393] is not straightforward. It is difficult to portray this reason as innate, since individuals may not have any political opinion, that is, they may be apolitical (although of course they can have a political opinion attributed to them nonetheless). Similarly, to portray the reason as immutable or unchangeable is problematic, since political opinions can change. Confining political opinions to ones that are fundamental to human dignity would add requirements into the refugee definition that are not specified in the text. On the other hand, if all five reasons are seen as linked by the non-discrimination norm, without reliance on the three-fold categorisation set forth in *Acosta/Ward*, there is no apparent difficulty, since the human rights approach can apply this norm in a straightforward way.

A possible further difficulty in the way of aligning political opinion with the other reasons concerns a point mentioned earlier relating to the concept of membership. As noted by Gummow J in *Applicant A v MIEA*, those of a particular race, or nationality, or who are adherents of a particular religion, might be said in each case to be members of a particular social group, but a person may not be a member of any group but still fall within the definition by reason of the fear of persecution for reasons of political opinion.[394]

Yet this objection relies overmuch on the use of the words 'membership' and 'group' in the MPSG reason. Discrimination (which is widely agreed to be the key unifying element) always arises in a societal context and whilst political opinions can sometimes be idiosyncratic and/or held by isolated individuals, what will bring them within the scope of this reason (if at all) is that they sufficiently relate to at least certain types of power relationships within a particular society.[395]

# 4 Causal Nexus ('for Reasons of')

The 'causal nexus' requirement is the second main component of the Convention reasons clause. It is dealt with last because it is only when there is an understanding

---
[392] MGs on Political Opinion (n 319) para 4.
[393] See above pp. 596–597.
[394] *Applicant A* (n 37) para 284. See also *X v MIMA* [1999] FCA 697, para 32.
[395] See above pp. 650–651.

of the subject matter of the Convention reasons that proper analysis can be made of the connective words, 'for reasons of'. Lacking this context, that terminology would be open to manifold meanings. As always VCLT considerations must be applied, although in this instance it suffices to deal with them collectively.

## 4.1 The Nature of the Causal Link

The Refugee Convention contains two different terms for the causal nexus. Article 1A(2) requires that the well-founded fear of 'being persecuted' be *'for reasons of'*. Curiously, the language of Article 33(1) uses different wording; it requires that the threat to 'life or freedom' (the apparent equivalent to 'well-founded fear of being persecuted') be *'on account of'*[396] one of the same five enumerated reasons.[397] However, it is mostly accepted that the different wording of the causal nexus does not signify a difference in meaning.[398] By these respective wordings, both articles of the Convention make plain that the persecutory treatment of which the applicant has a well-founded fear must be causally linked with the Convention reason on which the applicant is seen to rely.

It is apparent from the literature that not all countries with a significant refugee case law have devoted much attention to the nature of the causal link. As the UNHCR Guidelines No 1 note:

> In many jurisdictions, the causal link ... must be explicitly established (e.g. some Common Law States) while in other States causation is not treated as a separate question for analysis, but is subsumed within the holistic analysis of the refugee definition.[399]

In *Chen Shi Hai* Kirby J stated that:

> In the context of the expression 'for reasons of' in the Convention, it is neither practicable nor desirable to attempt to formulate 'rules' or 'principles' which can be substituted for the Convention language.
>
> In the end it is necessary for the decision-maker to return to the broad expression of the Convention, avoiding the siren song of those who would offer suggested verbal equivalents. The decision-maker must evaluate the postulated connexion between the asserted fear of persecution and the ground suggested to give rise to that fear.

---

[396] Article 33(1) prohibits refoulement to the frontiers of territories 'where his life or freedom would be threatened *on account of* his race, religion, nationality, membership of a particular social group or political opinion' (emphasis added).

[397] Within the availment clause Article 1A(2) also refers twice to 'owing to such fear'; however, the immediate linkage here is between fear of persecution and being 'outside' one's country: see Zimmermann and Mahler (n 1) 323–24.

[398] Walter Kälin, Martina Caroni, and Lukas Heim, 'Article 33, para 1' in Zimmermann (n 1) 1394. See also 'The Michigan Guidelines on Nexus to A Convention Ground (2001)' in Hathaway (ed) (2019) (n 377) 24.

[399] UNHCR Guidelines No 1 (n 169) para 20.

The decision-maker must keep in mind the broad policy of the Convention and the inescapable fact that he or she is obliged to perform a task of classification.[400]

The jurisprudence (such as it is) as to the intensity of the causation required has disclosed a number of different views. The terminologies in use (often borrowed from other areas of law such as tort law)[401] do not lend themselves to easy classification, but it is possible to discern three main views:

(i) that the Convention reason must be the sole or primary reason why the person fears persecution;
(ii) that the Convention reason must be 'at least one central' or an 'essential and significant' reason or reasons. The former wording has been favoured by the US courts.[402] The 'essential and significant' formula is now written into Australian legislation;[403] and
(iii) that the reason need only be one among several reasons. I will refer to this as the 'effective reason' or 'effective cause' test (a descriptor favoured by UK courts and tribunals). Another way this has been described (or perhaps representing a lower threshold still) is as a 'contributing cause' approach, as expressed, for example, by UNHCR in Guidelines No. 1: '[t]he Convention ground must be a relevant contributing factor, though it need not be shown to be the sole, or dominant, cause.'[404]

Both (i) and (ii) are sometimes seen in the literature to amount to a 'but for' test, although arguably the latter term requires the cause to be the sole cause.[405] Whilst the dividing line between (ii) and (iii) can be either small or non-existent, in practice there is a theoretical distinction, since a cause can be effective without being central.

As is clear from Kirby J's observations quoted above, senior courts and tribunals, at least in the common law world, have been cautious about adjudicating between competing approaches to the causal nature of the test. In the UK case of *Islam* and the Australian High Court case of *Chen*, however, the 'but for' test (which both courts appear to have seen as very similar to a 'sole cause' test) was found inappropriate to the Refugee Convention context. The appropriate test was said to require a taking into account of the context in which it was raised and of the broad policy of the Convention.[406] The House of Lords followed suit in *Fornah*, emphasising the need for

---

[400] *Chen Shi Hai* (n 76) paras 68–69.
[401] See e.g. 'Rethinking Actual Causation in Tort Law' (2017) 130 Harv L Rev 2163.
[402] For the current statutory 'one central reason' standard in the US, see *Regalado-Escobar v Holder* [2013] 717 F.3d 724; *Hernandez-Avalos v Lynch* [2015] 784 F.3d 944; *Alvarez Lagos v Barr* [2019] No 17-2291. Anker (n 1) 334 notes that a landmark US case recognising mixed motives was *In Re SP* [1996] WL 422990 BIA. See also Zimmermann and Mahler (n 1) 373.
[403] The Guide to Refugee Law in Australia (n 58) ch 5 states that, post-16 December 2014, '[t]o come within art 1A(2) as qualified by s 91R(1)(a), or s 5H(1) as qualified by s 5J, a refugee ground or grounds must constitute at least the essential and significant reason or reasons for the persecution'.
[404] Hathaway and Foster (n 48); see also Michelle Foster, 'Causation in Context: Interpreting the Nexus Clause in the Refugee Convention' (2002) 23(2) Michigan Journal of International Law 265, 340; Rodger Haines, 'Gender-related persecution' in Feller et al (n 37) 339–42; Hathaway (n 377) para 13.
[405] Hathaway and Foster (n 239) 471 state that the 'but for' test founders particularly in cases where the applicant fears persecution because of a mixture of Convention and non-Convention reasons.
[406] *Islam* (n 54); *Chen Shi Hai* (n 76).

a 'a more sophisticated approach, appropriate to the context and taking account of all the facts and circumstances relevant to the particular case'.[407]

Lord Bingham went on to observe in *Fornah* that 'the ground on which the claimant relies need not be the only or even the primary reason for the apprehended persecution. It is enough that the ground relied on is an effective reason.'[408] This formulation clearly imports rejection of a primary or 'dominant' cause test.

The language of 'effective reason' or 'effective cause' makes apparent that a remote or incidental cause cannot qualify; it must be an *effective* cause.[409] In the view of this author, to identify the test as an 'effective cause' test is to be preferred to the concept of 'contributory cause' (sometimes used as a synonym), since the latter on its face could include even peripheral or remote causes.[410] That said, most versions of the 'contributory cause' approach couple it with an insistence that it does not extend to remote or peripheral causes.

Article 9(3) of the recast Directive states:

> In accordance with point (d) of Article 2, there must be a connection between the reasons mentioned in Article 10 and the acts of persecution as qualified in paragraph 1 of this Article or the absence of protection against such acts.[411]

The wording, 'a connection between', makes apparent that the causal link between the fear of 'being persecuted' and the Convention reason does not have to be *the* sole or the dominant cause. As stated by UNHCR, '[t]he Convention ground ... need not be shown to be the sole, or dominant, cause'.[412] Both these formulations would appear akin to the 'effective cause' and 'contributory cause' approaches and, in any event, certainly do not require the cause to be the only or the dominant one.

The contributory cause understanding is also adopted by the Michigan Guidelines on Nexus to a Convention Ground. They state that '[the Convention ground] ... need only be a contributing factor to the risk of being persecuted. If, however, the Convention ground is remote to the point of irrelevance, refugee status should not be recognised.'[413] This formulation also bears out the point made earlier that proponents of the 'contributory cause' test do not intend it literally, i.e. so that it includes contributions of every possible kind albeit very minor. It excludes causes that are 'remote to the point of irrelevance'. But since this is not always made clear, the language of 'effective' cause appears more consistent with the case law and wider literature.

Thus, whilst there is still not complete consensus, the clear trend[414] is towards the view that in order to show a Convention reason it is not necessary for an applicant to show that it is the only or dominant reason why he or she faces persecution.

---

[407] *Fornah* (n 2).
[408] ibid para 17.
[409] For a summary of the jurisprudence see Zimmermann and Mahler (n 1) 372–73.
[410] The UK Supreme Court in *HJ (Iran)* (n 154) chose to identify the test as being whether there was a 'material reason' for the persecution. See ibid para 82, per Lord Rodger.
[411] The text of original Article 9 omitted the final eight words.
[412] UNHCR Guidelines No 1 (n 169).
[413] Hathaway (2019) (n 377) 32 (at footnote 13).
[414] For analysis of the evolving US position following the REAL ID Act of 2005 (which stated that an applicant 'must establish that race, religion, nationality, membership in a particular social group, or political

## 4.2 Causal Nexus and Persecutory Intent

The matter of whether persecutory intent is a requirement of the 'being persecuted' element of the definition was addressed in Chapter 6.[415] It remains necessary to consider the interrelated issue of whether in order to establish a Convention reason there is such a requirement.

Early jurisprudence, particularly that in the US, conceptualised the causal nexus inquiry as requiring evidence that the persecutor was specifically motivated to punish the applicant because of the characteristic or belief described in the enumerated reason.[416] The position in the US has since shifted, Anker noting that even though case law still references motive, 'U.S. authorities more frequently treat motive as a proxy for objective indicia of causation'.[417] Australian case law has continued to view the nexus clause as requiring proof of motive,[418] but increasingly international legal opinion has moved away from requiring persecutory intent.[419] As stated by Lord Rodger in *R (Sivakumar)*, 'the law is concerned with the reasons for the persecution and not with the motives of the persecutor'.[420] It is a curious feature of some of the common law case law that although quick to reject the notion that the reason for persecution had to manifest animus or malignant intent, it has sometimes clung on to the idea that some sort of persecutory intent is still indispensable, without recognising the inherent problems of reliance on intent of whatever coloration. The UNHCR Guidelines on Sexual Orientation[421] puts matters this way:

> Perpetrators may rationalize the violence they inflict on LGBTI individuals by reference to the intention of 'correcting', 'curing' or 'treating' the person. The focus is on the reasons for the applicant's predicament, rather than on the mind-set of the perpetrator.[422]

At the same time, whilst in Chapter 6 the notion of persecutory intent was said not to be an essential prerequisite for persecution to exist, when an individual is in fact

---

opinion was or will be at least one central reason for persecuting the applicant'), see Anker (n 1) §5.10, 401–02.

[415] See Chapter 6, section 3.9.
[416] See e.g. *Acosta* (n 14).
[417] Anker (n 1) §5.2, 402. For earlier US case law see Christian Cameron, 'Why Do You Persecute Me? Proving The Nexus Requirement For Asylum' (2014) 18(2) University of Miami International and Comparative Law Review 233.
[418] *Minister for Information v Haji Ibrahim* [2000] HCA 55, para 102. See also Guide to Refugee Law in Australia (n 58) 5; and Department of Home Affairs' Refugee Law Guidelines (2017) Section 8.3 (the author is grateful to Jane McAdam for this latter reference). However, as noted in Chapter 6, the Australian case law is not entirely unambivalent. Kirby J's statement in *Chen Shi Hai* (n 76) para 65, which clearly rejects persecutory intent as a universal requirement, does not seem to have ever been expressly disapproved.
[419] Zimmermann and Mahler (n 1) 374. Anker (n 1) §5.4, 403–04, 413 notes that focus is now on 'the effect of persecution rather than in terms of the persecutor's or victim's intent'.
[420] *R (Sivakumar) v SSHD* [2003] 2 All ER 1097, para 41.
[421] UNHCR Guidelines No 9 (n 83) para 39. See also Guidelines No 7 (n 88) paras 31–32.
[422] Whilst this formulation strongly reflects the emerging consensus on this matter, it is to be observed that it is at odds with the position taken in the 1979 UNHCR Handbook on the bipartite test for determining well-founded fear (see Chapter 11). On the phenomenon of corrective rape, see Annie Kelly et al, *Hate Crimes: The Rise of Corrective Rape in South Africa* (Action Aid 2009).

targeted for severe violations of human rights because he or she is perceived to be of, inter alia, a particular race, religion, particular social group, or to have political opinion (even if in fact he is not), then persecutory intent can be significant evidence both of the persecution and the causal nexus with a Convention reason.[423]

## 4.3 'Bifurcated Nexus'

As alluded to earlier, a particular problem that has taxed commentators seeking to elicit the meaning of the nexus requirement concerns cases in which the fear of being persecuted arises not from state actors but from non-state actors and from the inability or unwillingness of the state to protect against such persecution. This is sometimes referred to as the 'bifurcated nexus' issue. This particular term is associated with the writings of Hathaway and Foster and their version of the human rights approach which defines persecution as serious harm plus lack of state protection.[424] The expression is idiosyncratic, but the underlying reasoning has gained wide acceptance.[425] It follows from this approach that the nexus with the Convention reason may be established by linkage to *either* the serious harm *or* the lack of state protection.[426] In the latter context, the state actor need not possess a nexus-related motive.

Within this understanding, the meaning of the nexus requirement is informed by the principle of surrogacy. The latter operates to prevent a narrow reading by ensuring that those who face a real risk of serious harm at the hands of non-state actors such as criminal gangs are not excluded from qualifying as a refugee when (even though the criminal gang has no Convention reason for its acts) the basis for the unwillingness or inability of the authorities of the state to protect them is a Convention reason.[427]

The first leading case to adopt this approach was the UK House of Lords case, *Islam*.[428]

UNHCR has fully embraced it and also sought to refine it. The UNHCR Guidelines on MPSG contain the simplest explanation of this notion:

> 23. This reasoning may be summarised as follows. The causal link may be satisfied: (1) where there is a real risk of being persecuted at the hands of a non-State actor for reasons which are related to one of the Convention grounds, whether or not the failure of the State to protect the claimant is Convention related; or (2) where the risk of being persecuted at the hands of a non-State actor is unrelated to a Convention

---

[423] UNHCR Guidelines No 9 (n 83) para 39.
[424] Hathaway and Foster (n 48) 373; Anker (n 1) §5.16, 430–31.
[425] Zimmermann and Mahler (n 1) 374, note that German jurisprudence has 'especially' highlighted this feature.
[426] Hathaway (n 377) 215.
[427] See p. 415.
[428] *Islam* (n 54). In Australia, see *Chen Shi Hai* (n 76); in New Zealand, see *Refugee Appeal No 71427/99* (n 73). See also Aleinikoff (n 38) 301–03; and Karen Musalo, 'Revisiting Social Group and Nexus in Gender Asylum Claims: A Unifying Rationale for Evolving Jurisprudence' (2003) 52 DePaul Law Review 777.

ground, but the inability or unwillingness of the State to offer protection is for a Convention reason.[429]

As noted earlier,[430] this insight is now incorporated in Article 9(3) of the QD (recast), thus ensuring decision makers in EU countries recognise the scope for alternative linkages. It now reads (the relevant new words are here put in italics): 'there must be a connection between the reasons mentioned in Article 10 and the acts of persecution as qualified in paragraph 1 of this Article *or the absence of protection against such acts*.'[431]

## 4.4 Causal Nexus and the Doctrine of Attribution

As charted in the subsection on political opinion,[432] the doctrine of attribution raises difficulties in identifying the contents of the Convention reasons. As Sternberg has noted, the principle 'confer[s] upon the grounds of international protection an exceptional degree of elasticity.'[433] It follows from what has already been said about this doctrine, that satisfaction of the causal nexus requirement is not limited to those who have the actual characteristics specified. It also covers those at risk for reasons of imputed identity or protected characteristics.[434]

## 5 Conclusions

This chapter's analysis has confirmed that the requirement to have a well-founded fear of being persecuted 'for reasons of race, religion, nationality, membership of a particular social group or political opinion' is an essential element of the refugee definition. It is now widely accepted that it imposes limits on the types of persecution and on when a Convention reason can be established.

In section 1 the history and *travaux préparatoires* relating to this clause was examined. Section 2 interrogated whether the reasons are united by a common theme of non-discrimination and whether, in any event, they can be said to exhibit common features (several are identified). Doubt is expressed that the framework developed by the 'protected characteristics' approach to the particular social group reason does, as claimed, govern all five reasons.

In section 3, each of the reasons was analysed in turn by application of VCLT rules of interpretation. As regards race, general agreement was noted that it must be interpreted in a very wide sense, to include all kinds of ethnic groups and groups with a common nationality, tribal affiliation, shared language, and traditional ways and

---

[429] UNHCR, Guidelines No 2 (n 58).
[430] See above p. 656.
[431] QD (recast) (n 8) (emphasis added).
[432] See above p. 652.
[433] Sternberg (n 38) 231.
[434] As stated in Article 10(2) QD (recast) (n 8): see above p. 602.

backgrounds. With nationality, it was noted that in contrast to its legal meaning in the availment clause, its meaning in the reasons clause must span the legal and sociological and thus encompass ethnic, cultural, and linguistic groups and groups with common geographic or political origins. Such groups are not necessarily restricted to minorities. This reason also encompasses stateless persons. As regards religion, whose meaning in international law has proven opaque, growing agreement was noted that it be given a broad meaning encompassing not just its primary meaning (religion in the form of belief) but also religion as a form of identity and religion as a way of life. It must be interpreted to include the right to hold or not to hold a religious belief, the right not to be forced to follow a religion and the right to change one's religion. Selected aspects of this reason that have posed difficulties in the case law were also analysed—proselytism, the *forum internum/forum externum* distinction, doctrinal knowledge, and discretion/concealment. It was noted that whilst a human rights approach supports reading the term 'religion' broadly—so that it encompasses both the 'core' and the 'periphery' of the right to freedom of religion and extends, for example, even to atheistic beliefs—it does place some limits on the manifestation of religious belief, as can be seen, for example, in cases concerned with proselytism.

In respect of MPSG, particular attention was paid to the opposed approaches known as the 'protected characteristics' and 'social perception' approaches. Whilst commending UNHCR's attempt to treat them as alternatives—and so achieve convergence—it was concluded that neither is in fact a coherent approach on its own, as both need aspects of the other to be so. Whilst a brief 'map' is proposed for how to merge them into a single approach, the more important point is seen to be that this division has not prevented widespread agreement to coalesce around several common features that a PSG must possess: that the PSG ground cannot be unlimited; that a PSG must exist independently of the persecution feared; that a PSG does not have to be cohesive or interdependent or homogeneous or associational; and that a PSG does not need to be of a particular size.

In the analysis of political opinion, it was noted that it has been seen as the most difficult to align with the others. Despite this reason having a strong human rights underpinning in IHRL, its concept of 'opinion' is almost unlimited and its notion of 'political' has proved contentious. Three main existing approaches to the notion of 'political' were discussed, with a suggestion as to how they can be amalgamated, particularly so that non-state actor cases are properly accommodated. Also addressed were some specific problems that have arisen concerning this reason: the issue of whether it includes 'bad politics'; the implications for this reason of the doctrine of attribution; and the extent of its commonalities with the other reasons (is it indeed the 'odd one out'?).

Section 4 examined the second main requirement of the nexus clause, that there be a causal connection between the persecution and at least one enumerated reason. It was explained why the trend of interpretation is towards an effective or contributory reason test and why it is erroneous to impose a requirement of persecutory intent. The importance to the ability of the refugee definition to accommodate those at risk from non-state actors persecution was seen to necessitate what has been coined the 'bifurcated nexus'. Further observations were made on the doctrine of attribution.

## 5.1 Basic Propositions

From the analysis in this chapter, it is possible, despite the many disagreements surrounding this clause, to distil the following propositions about which there is substantial consensus.

1. The nexus clause imposes limits on the types of persecution necessary to establish refugeehood.
2. The five Convention reasons are united by a common theme. The theme most frequently identified is non-discrimination.
3. In relation to each reason, they may be either real or attributed.
4. As regards race, it must be interpreted in a very wide sense, to include all kinds of ethnic groups and groups with a common national or social origin, tribal affiliation, shared language, and traditional ways and backgrounds.
5. Religion must be understood in a broad sense to encompass not just its primary meaning (religion in the form of belief) but also religion as a form of identity and religion as a way of life. It must be interpreted to include the right to hold or not to hold a religious belief, the right not to be forced to follow a religion and the right to change one's religion.
6. The meaning of nationality in this part of the definition spans both the legal and sociological senses of the term and thus, in addition to nationals in the legal sense, it can refer to ethnic, cultural, and linguistic groups and groups with common geographic or social or political origins. This reason also encompasses stateless persons.
7. Whilst disagreements persist about whether MPSG is best interpreted by applying a 'protected characteristics' or 'social perception' approach, or by applying both, disjunctively or cumulatively, there is consensus that: the MPSG ground cannot be unlimited; that a PSG must exist independently of the persecution; that a PSG does not have to be cohesive or interdependent or homogeneous or associational; and that a PSG does not need to be of a particular size.
8. In the 'political opinion' ground, the concept of 'opinion' is almost unlimited. Although disagreement remains as to the notion of 'political', it is accepted that it must be one that can accommodate, where relevant, opinions about non-state actors.
9. In non-state actor cases, the causal connection can potentially be either with the non-state actor or the state.
10. To establish the causal nexus between the reason for persecution and the persecution, it is not necessary that a reason be the sole or dominant cause.

## 5.2 Suggested Propositions

In addition to the above list, the following propositions are ones that this study considers to be cogent.

1. Whilst the Convention reasons can be analysed without adoption of a human rights approach, the latter provides the best way of giving shape and contents to their analysis.
2. The *Acosta/Ward* framework has significant drawbacks, both for understanding the commonalities of all five reasons, and for conceptualising the MPSG reason.
3. Each reason should be given a broad meaning.
4. A non-evaluative approach should be taken to all five reasons: it is not required that a Convention reason reflects a particular moral or ethical quality.
5. As presently formulated, neither the 'protected characteristics' approach nor the 'social perception' approach to the Convention reason of membership of a particular social group is internally consistent. Until each resolves this deficiency, there will be no real resolution of the debate surrounding them.
6. As is increasingly acknowledged in the refugee law literature, in order to establish the causal nexus it is not necessary to establish persecutory intent on the part of the persecutor.

# 11
## 'Well-Founded Fear'
### ('*Craignant Avec Raison*')

| | | | |
|---|---|---|---|
| 1 Well-Founded Fear | 663 | 3.1.3 Subjective fear as a 'plus factor' | 691 |
| 1.1 'Well-Founded Fear' and a | | 3.1.4 Conclusion | 692 |
| Human Rights Approach | 665 | 4 'Well-Founded Fear': The | |
| 1.2 National Law Definitions | 667 | Objective Element | 692 |
| 2 VCLT Considerations | 668 | 4.1 The Objective Approach | 692 |
| 2.1 Origins and *Travaux Préparatoires* | 668 | 4.1.1 Perceived merits | 692 |
| 2.1.1 Early instruments | 668 | 4.1.2 Perceived demerits | 692 |
| 2.1.2 1946 IRO Constitution | 668 | 4.1.3 Evaluation | 694 |
| 2.1.3 *Travaux préparatoires* | 670 | 4.2 Commonalities Between the Bipartite | |
| 2.1.4 The ECOSOC draft | 672 | Approach's 'Objective Element' and the | |
| 2.1.5 Conclusions on origins and | | 'Objective Approach': Key Components | 695 |
| travaux préparatoires | 672 | 4.2.1 Foundation in fact | 696 |
| 2.2 Main VCLT Considerations | 673 | 4.2.2 Individual assessment | 696 |
| 2.2.1 Ordinary meaning | 673 | 4.2.3 Holistic inquiry | 697 |
| 2.2.2 Context | 675 | 4.3 Risk Assessment | 698 |
| 2.2.3 Object and purpose | 676 | 4.3.1 Temporal dimension | 698 |
| 2.2.4 Other VCLT considerations | 676 | 4.3.2 The risk component | 702 |
| 2.2.5 Conclusions on VCLT | | 4.3.3 Conclusion on objective | |
| considerations | 682 | element | 704 |
| 3 'Well-Founded Fear': The | | 4.4 Well-Founded Fear and Burden and | |
| 'Subjective Element' | 682 | Standard of Proof | 704 |
| 3.1 The Subjective Element of the | | 4.4.1 Burden of proof | 706 |
| Bipartite/Combined Subjective- | | 4.4.2 Standard of proof | 707 |
| Objective Approach | 683 | 5 Conclusions | 711 |
| 3.1.1 Perceived merits | 683 | 5.1 Basic Propositions | 712 |
| 3.1.2 Perceived demerits | 686 | 5.2 Suggested Propositions | 712 |

## 1 Well-Founded Fear

What meaning should be given to the expression 'well-founded fear' ('*craignant avec raison*' in the French) has been the subject of copious commentary.[1] Some regard it

---

[1] See e.g. Atle Grahl-Madsen, *The Status of Refugees in International Law. Volume 1: Refugee Character* (Sijthoff 1966) 173–87; Theodore N Cox, 'Well-Founded Fear of Being Persecuted: The Sources and Application of a Criterion of Refugee Status' (1984) 10 Brook J Int'l L 333; Mark Gibney, 'A Well-Founded Fear of Persecution' (1987) 10 Human Rights Quarterly 109; Humberto H Ocariz and Jorge L Lopez, 'Practical Implications of INS v. Cardoza-Fonseca: Evidencing Eligibility for Asylum under the "Well-Founded Fear of Persecution" Standard' (1988) 19 Miami Inter-Am L Rev 617, 644; James C Hathaway, *The Law of Refugee Status* (Butterworths Limited 1991) 69–97; Walter Kälin, 'Well-Founded Fear of

Persecution: A European Perspective' in Jacqueline Bhabha and Geoffrey Coll (eds), *Asylum Law and Practice in Europe and North America: A Comparative Analysis* (Federal Publications 1992) 21–35; Reinhard Marx, 'The Criteria for Determining Refugee Status in the Federal Republic of Germany' (1992) 4(2) IJRL 151; Costas Douzinas and Ronnie Warrington, 'A Well-Founded Fear of Justice: Law and Ethics in Postmodernity' in Jerry D Leonard (ed), *Legal Studies as Cultural Studies: A Reader in (Post) Modern Critical Theory* (Albany State University of New York Press 1995); Patricia Tuitt, *False Images: Law's Construction of the Refugee* (Pluto Press 1996); Jean-Yves Carlier and others, *Who Is a Refugee? A Comparative Case Law Study* (Brill 1997), where each of the national reports includes an entry on 'objective' and 'subjective' elements of fear; Dirk Vanheule, 'A Comparison of the Judicial Interpretations of the Notion of Refugee' in Jean-Yves Carlier and Dirk Vanheule (eds), *Europe and Refugees: A Challenge?* (Kluwer Law International 1997) 91–105; Elizabeth Adjin-Tettey, 'Reconsidering the Criteria for Assessing Well-Founded Fear in Refugee Law' (1997) 25(1) Manitoba Law Journal 127; UNHCR, Note on Burden and Standard of Proof in Refugee Claims (16 December 1998); Audrey Macklin, 'Truth and Consequences: Credibility Determination in the Refugee Context' (1998) International Association of Refugee Law Judges, Conference in Ottawa (Canada); Vigdis Vevstad, *Refugee Protection: A European Challenge* (Tano Aschehoug 1998) 58–62; Cécile Rousseau et al, 'The Complexity of Determining Refugeehood: A Multidisciplinary Analysis of the Decision-Making Process of the Canadian Immigration and Refugee Board' (2002) 15(1) Journal of Refugee Studies 43; Niraj Nathwani, *Rethinking Refugee Law* (Martinus Nijhoff Publishers 2003) 68–73, 148; Brian Gorlick, 'Common Burdens and Standards: Legal Elements in Assessing Claims to Refugee Status' (2003) 15 IJRL 357; Michael Kagan, 'Is Truth in the Eye of the Beholder? Objective Credibility Assessment in Refugee Status Determination' (2003) 17(3) Georgetown Immigration Law Journal 367; University of Michigan Law School, 'The Michigan Guidelines ("MGs") on Well-Founded Fear' (2004); Michael Bossin and Laila Demirdache, 'A Canadian Perspective on the Subjective Component of the Bipartite Test for "Persecution": Time for Re-evaluation' (2004) 22(1) Refugee: Canada's Journal on Refugees 108; Gregor Noll, 'Evidentiary Assessment under the Refugee Convention: Risk, Pain and the Intersubjectivity of Fear' in Gregor Noll (ed), *Proof, Evidentiary Assessment and Credibility in Asylum Procedures* (Martinus Nijhoff 2005) 141–60; Gregor Noll, 'Evidentiary Assessment and the EU Qualification Directive' (2005) New Issues in Refugee Research, Working Paper No 117; James C Hathaway and William S Hicks, 'Is There a Subjective Element in the Refugee Convention's Requirement of Well-Founded Fear?' (2005) 26(2) *Michigan Journal of International Law* 505; Bridgette A Carr, 'We Don't Need to See Them Cry: Eliminating the Subjective Apprehension Element of the Well-Founded Fear Analysis for Child Refugee Applicants' (2006) 33 Pepperdine Law Review 535; Hemme Battjes, *European Asylum Law and International Law* (Martinus Nijhoff 2006) 224–29; Guy S Goodwin-Gill and Jane McAdam, *The Refugee in International Law* (3rd edn, OUP 2007) 63–64; Hilary E Cameron, 'Risk Theory and "Subjective Fear": The Role of Risk Perception, Assessment, and Management in Refugee Status Determinations' (2008) 20(4) IJRL 567; Tillmann Löhr, 'Die Qualifikationsrichtlinie: Rückschritt hinter internationale Standards?' in Rainer Hofmann and Tillmann Löhr (eds), *Europäisches Flüchtlings—und Einwanderungsrecht, Seite 47–98* (Nomos 2008) 47–97; James A Sweeney, 'Credibility, Proof and Refugee Law' (2009) 21(4) IJRL 700; Kees Wouters, *International Legal Standards for the Protection from Refoulement* (Intersentia 2009) 83–90; Mark Symes and Peter Jorro, *Asylum Law and Practice* (2nd edn, Bloomsbury 2010) 2.1–2.67; Andreas Zimmermann and Claudia Mahler, 'Article 1A, para 2' in Andreas Zimmermann (ed), *The 1951 Convention Relating to the Status of Refugees and Its 1967 Protocol: A Commentary* (OUP 2011) 335–45; John Barnes and Allan Mackey, 'The Credo Document: Assessment of Credibility in Refugee and Subsidiary Protection Claims under the EU Qualification Directive: Judicial Criteria and Standards' in Carolus Grutter, Elspeth Guild, and Sebastiaan de Groot (eds), *Assessment of Credibility by Judges in Asylum Cases in the EU* (Oisterwiijk Wolf Legal Publishers 2013) 89; UNHCR, Beyond Proof—Credibility Assessment in EU Asylum Systems (2013); Hungarian Helsinki Committee, Credibility Assessment in Asylum Procedures—A Multidisciplinary Training Manual: Volume 1 (2013) available at <https://www.refworld.org/docid/5253bd9a4.html> accessed 13 September 2021; James C Hathaway and Michelle Foster, *The Law of Refugee Status* (2nd edn, CUP 2014); Marcelle Reneman, *EU Asylum Procedure and the Right to an Effective Remedy* (Hart Publishing 2014) 195–208; UNHCR, Summary of Deliberations on Credibility Assessment in Asylum Procedures, Expert Roundtable, 14–15 January 2015, Budapest, Hungary (5 May 2015) available at <https://www.refworld.org/docid/554c9aba4.html> accessed 13 September 2021; Louise Hooper and Livio Zilli, *Refugee Status Claims Based on Sexual Orientation and Gender Identity* (International Commission of Jurists 2016) ch 2, 55–73; Hilary E Cameron, *Refugee Law's Fact-Finding Crisis: Truth, Risk, and the Wrong Mistake* (CUP 2018); EASO, Judicial Analysis—Evidence and Credibility Assessment in the Context of the Common European Asylum System (2018); Adrienne Anderson et al, 'Imminence in Refugee and Human Rights Law: A Misplaced Notion for International Protection' (2019) 68(1) ICLQ 111; Lorne Waldman, *The Definition of Convention Refugee* (2nd edn, Lexis Nexis 2019) 105–78; Adrienne Anderson et al, 'A Well-Founded Fear of Being Persecuted... But When?' (2020) 42 Sydney L Rev 155; Guy S Goodwin-Gill and Jane McAdam (with Emma Dunlop), *The Refugee in International Law* (4th edn, OUP 2021); Grace Kim,

as the 'key'[2] or 'core'[3] or 'touchstone'[4] or 'backbone'[5] of the definition. Even if some of these descriptors go too far, it is plainly *a* key element and it furnishes the main concepts that individualise the definition, providing the necessary link between its personal and material scope.

Whilst, as explained earlier, there is no prescribed order in which to examine the key elements of the refugee definition, 'well-founded fear' denotes a quality that persecutees must have (or have attributed to them) in order to qualify. This is why this study has chosen to deal with it last, after the inquiries into the 'being persecuted' element of the definition and the closely related availment clause[6] have been addressed in full.

There have been two main axes of debates about the meaning of this expression. First, whilst it is widely agreed that the term incorporates an 'objective element', there has been a deep division over whether it also incorporates a 'subjective element'. Second, there has been considerable dispute over whether the objective element compels decision makers to apply a particular standard of proof and also some uncertainty over whether, if it does, it is one based on 'more likely than not' or on some lower standard.

In this chapter, we shall seek to analyse the expression by applying Vienna Convention on the Law of Treaties (VCLT) rules.

Before embarking on this examination, three general questions arise. The first concerns the relevance of the human rights approach. The second concerns where and how the 'well-founded fear' element fits into the definition as a whole. The third relates to the issue of risk assessment.

### 1.1 'Well-Founded Fear' and a Human Rights Approach

The first question is whether this particular element of the definition is susceptible of a human rights reading and if so to what extent? Not all have accepted that it is[7] and,

---

'Abandoning the Subjective and Objective Components of a Well-Founded Fear of Persecution' (2021) 16 Nw J L & Soc Pol'y 192; Gregor Noll, 'Credibility, Reliability and Evidential Assessment' in Cathryn Costello, Michelle Foster, and Jane McAdam (eds), *The Oxford Handbook of International Refugee Law* (OUP 2021) 607–24; Deborah Anker, *Law of Asylum in the United States* (Thomsons Reuters 2022), ch 2Michelle Foster et al, '"Time" in Refugee Status Determination in Australia and the United Kingdom: A Clear and Present Danger from Armed Conflict?' (2022) 34(2) IJRL 163.

[2] Cox (n 1) 333; UNHCR, Note on Burden and Standard of Proof in Refugee Claims (n 1) para 13; UNHCR, Interpreting Article 1 of the 1951 Convention Relating to the Status of Refugees (2001) para 11.
[3] Waldman (n 1) 105.
[4] *Camara v A-G (US)* [2009] 580 F.3d 196, 202.
[5] Wouters (n 1) 83: '[t]he element of risk stipulated by the words "well-founded fear" is the backbone of the refugee definition as well as the prohibition on refoulement'.
[6] See Chapters 6–9.
[7] e.g. Jane McAdam, *Complementary Protection in International Refugee Law* (OUP 2007) 62 considers the 'well-founded fear' element as 'captur[ing] a need for protection that is outside the realm of pure human rights assessment and which cautions against tying the concept of persecution exclusively to human rights law'. In the view of this author, that pays insufficient regard to the fact that both human rights law and the objective approach to well-founded fear apply a principle of individual assessment: see below pp. 696–697.

viewed at the level of purely textual analysis, there is no obvious human rights content to the concept of 'well-founded fear'. Nevertheless, there are several reasons why we should expect an international law/human right reading to infuse the approach to this phrase's definition to some degree. One is that, irrespective of what specific meaning is given to the term 'fear', it is something that is ascribed to persons. Under International Human Rights Law (IHRL) persons are rights-bearers. IHRL notably emphasises that all persons are entitled to the protection of basic human rights which include respect for human dignity and privacy among others and such respect may preclude decision makers from certain types or methods of inquiry into a person's fear. Thus, for example, in *A and Others*[8] the Court of Justice of the European Union (CJEU) saw the right to human dignity to preclude certain methods of questioning of an asylum applicant.

Another reason is that to hinge decisions on refugee status on inquiry into a person's state of mind (*forum internum*) sits uneasily with a human rights understanding that focuses on the likely effects on them of threatened harm rather than on the state of mind of the applicant. Without a IHRL understanding of the person there is nothing to stop decision makers attempting to be mind-readers.

A further reason is that IHRL does not in general deny human rights protection just because persons claiming to be in fear of ill-treatment harbour bad motives or *mala fides*. As stated by Hathaway, an absolutist preoccupation with the possibility of fraud ignores the basic human rights of all persons to be free to express themselves, to associate with whomever they wish, to pursue the development of their own personalities.[9] That view has particular force in the realm of refugee law, as demonstrated by leading cases in some jurisdictions expressly recognising that acting in bad faith does not necessarily preclude a person qualifying as a refugee, subject only to the exclusion clauses.[10]

Finally, if one adopts a holistic understanding of the refugee definition, and a human rights approach is taken to interpreting 'being persecuted' (which is the approach taken in this book, see Chapters 6–9), it is difficult to see how such an approach would not also need to be taken to 'well-founded fear', since the latter only makes sense as a term in relation to its object.

Even though, therefore, the analysis in this chapter endeavours to apply a human rights approach, it also seeks to recognise the important contributions made to clarification of the well-founded fear phrase by those adopting other approaches.

---

[8] Joined Cases C-148/13 to C-150/13 *A and Others v Staatssecretaris van Veiligheid en Justitie* [2014] ECLI:EU:C:2014:2406, para 53; Case C-473/16 *F v Bevándorlási és Állampolgársági Hivatal* [2018] ECLI:EU:C:2018:36, paras 35–37.

[9] Hathaway (n 1) 37; see also Hathaway and Foster (n 1) 79–90; Penelope Mathew, 'Limiting Good Faith: "Bootstrapping" Asylum Seekers and Exclusion from Refugee Protection' (2010) 29 Australian Yearbook of International Law 135.

[10] In the UK see e.g. *Mbanza v SSHD* [1996] Imm AR 136, and *Danian v SSHD* [1999] EWCA Civ 3000, two cases in which the English Court of Appeal has held that bad faith does not necessarily defeat a refugee claim; see also *Mohammed v MIMA* [1999] FCA 868, paras 24–28, now overridden by Migration Act, s 91R(3)—but see *SZJZN v MIC* [2008] FCA 519, para 35, cited by Hathaway and Foster (n 1) 85. See also p. 404 where reference is made, inter alia, to the pending preliminary reference before the CJEU, *J.F. v Bundesamt für Fremdenwesen und Asyl* (C-222/22).

A second general question loops back to the discussion in Chapter 3 of the interrelationship between the refugee definition's different elements. It concerns debates that have arisen as to whether or not the 'well-founded fear' element is the primary locus of the refugee definition.[11]

In Chapter 9, for example, a division was noted between those like the United Nations High Commissioner for Refugees (UNHCR) and Fortin, who have seen the 'well-founded fear' limb as the proper locus of analysis of protection[12] and those, like Hathaway and Foster, who consider the protection inquiry to belong in the 'being persecuted' limb and the 'internal protection' inquiry to belong in the availment clause.[13] However, as explained earlier, to the extent UNHCR and others seek to prioritise the 'well-founded fear' limb, they can only mean the 'well-founded fear of being persecuted' clause in full, since 'well-founded fear' on its own lacks any identification of its object. Perhaps capturing the point about prioritisation best of all is the observation by Goodwin-Gill and McAdam that because the refugee definition 'begins with the refugee as someone with a well-founded fear of being persecuted' this means that 'the Convention's first point of reference is the individual, particularly as a rights-holder, rather than the system of government and its efficacy or intention in relation to protection, relevant as these elements are to the well-founded fear dimension'.[14]

Another general question concerns the role of the 'well-founded fear' element in the risk assessment that is widely seen to be an integral part of the refugee definition. As we shall explain in section 4.3.2 below, the weight of the international jurisprudence favours an interpretation of 'well-founded fear' so that it incorporates something about risk assessment as well as something about the standard of proof. For that reason, the risk assessment component of the 'well-founded fear' inquiry is predominantly understood as occurring after (or 'downstream' of) the inquiry into whether the anticipated harm constitutes 'being persecuted'.[15] This view has not met with unanimous agreement, however. For example, Matthew Scott has argued that 'well-founded fear' is only about the standard of proof and is not about risk assessment. Risk assessment in his view is rather a feature of the experience of 'being persecuted'.[16] His view will be evaluated below,[17] but it can be noted here that it has not been echoed in any of the case law or other academic literature.

## 1.2 National Law Definitions

The meaning of the 'well-founded fear' element has largely been seen as difficult to codify in national or regional law—the EU Qualification Directive (QD), for example,

---

[11] See e.g. p. 441 and p. 667.
[12] See p. 441 and pp. 560–561; Julian Lehmann, *'Protection' in European Union Asylum Law* (Brill Nijhoff 2020) 85, argues that 'analysis of available protection is not a separate inquiry following the analysis of harm, but is linked to the notion of a well-founded fear'.
[13] See p. 563.
[14] Goodwin-Gill and McAdam (4th edn) (n 1) 8.
[15] Bruce Burson, 'Give Way to the Right: The Evolving Use of Human Rights in New Zealand Refugee Status Determination' in Bruce Burson and David Cantor (eds), *Human Rights and the Refugee Definition* (Brill Nijhoff 2016) 25, 37 (citing *Refugee Appeal No 74665/03* [2004] NZRSAA, para 82).
[16] Matthew Scott, *Climate Change, Disasters, and the Refugee Convention* (CUP 2020) 100–07.
[17] See below pp. 703–704.

offers no definition. However, there have been two recent attempts in the common law world to codify aspects of it, mainly relating to the standard of proof and risk assessment.[18]

## 2 VCLT Considerations

Bearing in mind the sharp differences that have arisen over whether the notion of 'well-founded fear' has a subjective as well as an objective element, it is particularly salient to consider what is disclosed by application of VCLT rules.

### 2.1 Origins and *Travaux Préparatoires*

#### 2.1.1 Early instruments

Two features of the interwar instruments bear mention. Although characterised by a generalised group approach, these instruments[19] still contained a requirement that refugees be persons who do not 'enjoy' the protection of their countries. This reflected the drafters' intention that some type of check had to be made whether that was in fact the case.[20] Second, by the time of the 1938 Convention, there was a greater concern to ensure beneficiaries were genuinely fleeing situations of persecution. Thus, Article 1, paragraph 3 of the 1938 Convention expressly excluded persons 'leaving Germany for purely personal convenience'.[21] Zimmermann and Mahler note that '[t]his formulation encompassed persons who left for economic motives, without being constrained to do so, or in order to evade taxation. It did not intend to exclude persons however, who were subjected to economic sanctions or proscriptions.'[22] Both these aspects could be said to acknowledge the relevance of a person's motives and/or individual circumstances as of some relevance, although only in secondary respects.

#### 2.1.2 1946 IRO Constitution

The immediate precursor of the phrase 'well-founded fear' was the phrase 'valid objections' set out in Annex 1 of the International Refugee Organisation (IRO)

---

[18] Section 5J of the Australian Migration Act as amended in 2014; section 32 of the UK Nationality and Borders Act 2022 (NBA). Both seek to differentiate between a test of whether an applicant fears persecution and a risk assessment of that fear. Section 32 of the NBA additionally seeks to apply a balance of probabilities standard to the former and a reasonable likelihood standard to the latter. See below n 287.

[19] League of Nations, Arrangement Relating to the Issue of Identify Certificates to Russian and Armenian Refugees (12 May 1926) 89 LNTS 47; League of Nations, Arrangement Concerning the Extension to Other Categories of Certain Measures Taken in Favour of Russian and Armenian Refugees (30 June 1928) 89 LNTS 63; League of Nations, Convention Relating to the International Status of Refugees (28 October 1933) 159 LNTS 3663; League of Nations, Provisional Arrangement concerning the Status of Refugees Coming from Germany (4 July 1936) 171 LNTS 395; League of Nations, Convention concerning the Status of Refugees Coming From Germany (10 February 1938) 192 LNTS 59.

[20] Ivor C Jackson, *The Refugee Concept in Group Situations* (Kluwer Law International 1999) 22–25.

[21] Convention concerning the Status of Refugees Coming From Germany (n 19).

[22] Zimmermann and Mahler (n 1) 306.

Constitution. This stated that no refugee with 'valid objections' should be compelled to return to his or her country of origin. This was the first time that an international refugee instrument made the individual an integral part of the refugee definition. However, in continuation of the approach taken in prior agreements, this concept was still attached to categories of refugees listed according to their countries of origin or other identifying characteristics—victims of Nazi or fascist regimes, refugees from the Saar, the Sudetenland, and German and Austrian Jews.[23]

The requirement of 'valid objections' was clearly prompted in part by concern to ensure this provision was not exploited by de facto emigrants. This was made overt in the definition contained in the introductory section of the Annex to the IRO Constitution entitled 'General Principles' at subparagraph 1(e):

> (e) It should be the concern of the Organization to ensure that its assistance is not exploited by persons in the case of whom it is clear that they are unwilling to return to their countries of origin because they prefer idleness to facing the hardships of helping in the reconstruction of their countries, or by persons who intend to settle in other countries for purely economic reasons, thus qualifying as emigrants.[24]

The first valid objection was stated in the IRO Constitution to be to '[p]ersecution, *or fear* based on reasonable grounds of persecution because of race, religion, nationality or political opinion, provided these opinions are not in conflict with the principles of the United Nations, as laid down in the Preamble of the Charter of the United Nations'.[25] This formulation clearly indicated that 'fear' was not enough; it had to be 'fear based on reasonable grounds'.

To assist in construction and application of the IRO Constitution, the IRO circulated to member governments on a confidential basis in February 1950 a Manual for Eligibility Officers. As regards valid objections derived from 'persecution or fear, based on reasonable grounds, of persecution', the Manual stated that:

> [ ... ] it is neither incumbent upon nor possible for the organization to give its own independent and objective view about the conditions at present prevailing in some countries of origin of the Displaced Persons. Fear of persecution is to be regarded as a valid objection whenever an applicant can make plausible that owing to his religious or political convictions or to his race, he is afraid of discrimination, or persecution, on returning home. Reasonable grounds are to be understood as meaning that the applicant can give a plausible and coherent account of why he fears persecution. Since fear is a subjective feeling the Eligibility Officer cannot refuse to consider the objection as valid when it is plausible.[26]

---

[23] Constitution of the International Refugee Organization (IRO) (adopted 15 December 1946, entered into force 20 August 1948) 18 UNTS 3, Annex, Section A(1) (a)–(c).
[24] ibid Annex 1.
[25] ibid Part 1, Section C, para (1)(a)(i) (emphasis added).
[26] IRO, Manual for Eligibility Officers (1950) ch IV, para 19 (cited in Cox (n 1) 340).

Thus, for the IRO, 'fear' denoted a 'subjective feeling'.[27] From the IRO perspective, a person's own 'objections statement' was to be taken as the primary basis of a determination, and if that statement expressed 'why he fears persecution' in the subjective sense, that went a considerable way to establishing his case, although it had also to be demonstrated that it was 'plausible'. The IRO interpreted 'fear based on reasonable grounds' to require, where possible, that a refugee provide documentation in support of his claim.[28]

It can be seen therefore that immediately prior to the Refugee Convention, there was a bipartite approach to 'fear'. 'Fear' was considered to be subjective, but it was also seen to require an objective element implied by the language of plausibility, directed at past and future persecution.[29] Nonetheless, in this iteration, fear in the subjective sense was the dominant criterion. To the extent that reference to 'plausibility' and 'reasonable grounds' required an objective inquiry, the Manual made clear that such an inquiry could only be a light-touch one because (in words that ring strange to modern decision makers with access to compendious Country of Origin Information (COI)) it was 'neither incumbent upon nor possible' for the IRO to 'give its own independent and objective view' about the conditions prevailing in the person's country of origin.[30]

### 2.1.3 *Travaux préparatoires*

The early drafts of the definition article of the Convention undertaken by the Ad Hoc Committee on Statelessness and Related Problems in January 1950 indicate an intention to build on the IRO definition of refugee.[31] Some nations wished to continue to include reference to categories of persons. Some delegates wished to extend protection to all persons who fear persecution—i.e. achieve a global definition. Reflecting a compromise between these two approaches, the Committee's first provisional draft included both categorical and global aspects.

The move towards rendering the definition purely global, excluding reference to national origin, was discernible in the first British proposal for Article I, the definition article. It encompassed 'persons who ... for good reasons (such as, for example, serious apprehension based on reasonable grounds of political, racial or religious persecution in the event of their going to that State) do not desire the protection of the State'.[32] According to Grahl-Madsen, 'well-founded fear' was 'a technical term, evolved by the drafters of the Refugee Convention from the clumsy phrase "persecution, or fear based on reasonable grounds of persecution" employed in Part I, section C, of Annex I to the IRO Constitution'.[33]

---

[27] Focus on the subjective element was said to 'factor in the attitude of the individual himself': see Hathaway (n 1) 67, who cites UNGA, Refugees and Stateless Persons: Report of the Secretary-General (26 October 1949) UN Doc A/C.3/527, 7.

[28] Cox (n 1) 340–41.

[29] Hathaway (n 1) 66: '[ ... ] the Organisation had competence over persons who had already suffered persecution in their home state, as well as over persons judged by the administering authorities to face a *prospective risk* of persecution were they to be returned to their own country' (emphasis added).

[30] IRO Manual (n 26) ch II, para 3.

[31] As noted by Cox (n 1) 338, the *travaux* contain 'numerous references to the IRO'.

[32] Ad Hoc Committee on Statelessness and Related Problems, *Comité spécial de l'apatridie et des problèmes connexes, Royaume-Uni: Texte remanié proposé pour l'article premier* (19 January 1950) UN Doc E/AC.32/L.2/Rev.1, 1.

[33] Grahl-Madsen (n 1) 173.

The first appearance of the phrase 'well-founded fear' appeared on 19 January 1950 in a revised draft submitted by the UK:

> In this Convention, the expression 'refugee' means, except where otherwise provided, a person who, having left the country of his ordinary residence on account of persecution or well-founded fear of persecution, either does not wish to return to that country for good and sufficient reason or is not allowed by the authorities of that country to return there and who is not a national of any other country.[34]

The reference to 'having left the country' appears to consider that the test of whether the fear is well-founded was meant to focus on what caused a person to flee. The first draft suggested by France chose the phrase 'justifiable fear of persecution', or '*crainte fonde de persécution*', wording identical to the French text of the earlier IRO Constitution.[35]

The final report of the Ad Hoc Committee to the Economic and Social Council offered a version splitting the definition into three parts:

> 1. Any person who: (a) as a result of events in Europe after 3 September 1939 and before 1 January 1951 has well-founded fear of being the victim of persecution for reasons of race, religion, nationality or political opinion; and (b) has left or, owing to such fear, is outside the country of his nationality, or if he has no nationality the country of his former habitual residence and (c) is unable or, owing to such fear, unwilling to avail himself of the protection of the country of his nationality.[36]

By referring to inability or unwillingness to return, this definition harked back to the emphasis in earlier proposals on the significance of the individual's disinclination to return to his country of origin, including the first British and the first French drafts.[37] It directed the focus of inquiry less towards the reasons why the person fled and more towards his or her reasons for desiring protection. The Israeli delegate, Mr Robinson, commented that '[a]ll the objective factors which would make it possible to characterise a person as a refugee were now known [and] contained in paragraph (1)'.[38] He went on to identify the only subjective elements of relevance as the 'horrifying memories of past persecution justifying non-return to the country of origin'.[39]

---

[34] Ad Hoc Committee on Statelessness and Related Problems, *Comité spécial de l'apatridie et des problèmes connexes, Royaume-Uni: Texte remanié proposé pour l'article premier* (n 32).

[35] The United States' first draft adhered to the category-based approach of the IRO Constitution in limiting the scope of the refugee definition to persons of particular nationality or status, but made fear alone determinative; however, this did not find favour (the US did not in the event sign the Convention, albeit because of the general reluctance of the Senate to permit United States law to be modified by international agreement).

[36] Ad Hoc Committee to the Economic and Social Council (1950) UN Doc E/AC.32/L.38, 13.

[37] The first British draft proposal, UN Doc E/AC.32/SR.6 (1950) 3, referred to a refugee as a person who 'either does not wish to return to that country for good and sufficient reason or is not allowed by the authorities of that country to return there and who is not a national of any other country'. The French draft, UN Doc E/AC.32/L.3 (1950) spoke of 'refusing to return' because of justifiable fear. See further Cox (n 1) 345.

[38] Ad Hoc Committee on Statelessness and Related Problems, First Session, Summary Record of the Eighteenth Meeting (8 February 1950) UN Doc E/AC.32/SR.18, para 10(3).

[39] Cited in Goodwin-Gill and McAdam (4th edn) (n 1) 80.

The Ad Hoc Committee shed light on the meaning of 'well-founded fear' in two official comments. In a Draft Report of 15 February 1950, it stated that 'well-founded fear' means that a person can give a 'plausible account' of why he fears persecution. In its Final Report of 17 February 1950, it stated that this meant 'that a person has either been actually a victim of persecution or can show good reasons why he fears persecution'.[40] Both comments, it can be seen, used language akin to the IRO Manual terminology. According to Zimmermann and Mahler, the second comment 'adopted an objective approach towards the assessment of the alleged past persecution ("has ... been actually a victim of persecution") while at the same time referring to a combined objective and subjective element as to future acts of persecution ("show good reason why he fears persecution")'.[41]

### 2.1.4 The ECOSOC draft

The immediate precursor to the Article 1A(2) definition was the draft revised by the United Nations Economic and Social Council (ECOSOC). It replicated most of the final report's definition although adding phrases to make explicit that a person had to show unwillingness to avail himself of the protection of the country 'for reasons other than personal convenience' (thus utilising language employed in earlier instruments).[42] According to Zimmermann and Mahler (citing Nehemiah Robinson), '[t]he broad term "well-founded fear of persecution" was incorporated to show that there were many scenarios amounting to persecution without providing at the same time for too tight limits of the definition'.[43]

### 2.1.5 Conclusions on origins and *travaux préparatoires*

Recourse to the *travaux* discloses that the decision to deploy the 'well-founded fear' notion went hand in hand with the decision to abandon the previous category or group-based criteria. At best the latter had applied a very minimal reference to individual motives, designed solely to avoid applications based purely on personal convenience. But, in the course of moving away from such criteria, the drafters perceived that it was necessary to provide more individuation. From the exchanges resulting in adoption of the phrase 'well-founded fear', it can be seen that, as under the IRO Constitution, there was a commitment to a bipartite approach that juxtaposed an individual's subjective state of mind with objective considerations. In terms of the latter, the words used were capable in ordinary usage of being understood in a broad way—e.g. the reference

---

[40] UN Ad Hoc Committee on Refugees and Stateless Persons, Report of the Ad Hoc Committee on Statelessness and Related Problems (17 February 1950) UN Doc E/1618 and UN Ad Hoc Committee on Statelessness and Related Problems, 1st Session, 5th Meeting (30 January 1950) UN Doc E/AC.32/SR.5, 39; cited in Zimmermann and Mahler (n 1) 336.

[41] Zimmermann and Mahler (n 1) 336.

[42] UNGA Res 429(V) of 14 December 1950, Annex Draft Convention Relating to the Status of Refugees; see further Zimmerman and Mahler (n 1) 310–11. Despite adhering closely to the eventual definition set out in Article 1A(2) of the 1951 Convention, the Statute of the Office of the United Nations High Commissioner for Refugees signed in December 1951 utilised the same language ('for reasons other than personal convenience') in both Article 6 A(ii) and also in its cessation clause in 6A(ii)(e).

[43] Zimmermann and Mahler (n 1) 336, citing Nehemiah Robinson, *Convention Relating to the Status of Stateless Persons: Its History and Interpretation, A Commentary* (UNHCR 1997) 40–41.

in the 1946 IRO Constitution to 'valid objections' (wording repeated in some of the Ad Hoc Committee exchanges) and the formal comment of the Committee that the phrase 'well-founded fear of persecution' meant 'that a person has either been actually a victim of persecution or can show *good reasons* why he fears persecution'.[44] At the same time, nothing was said to contradict the seemingly minimalistic understanding of these 'good reasons' considerations in the IRO Manual, i.e. as considerations which existed to check plausibility by reference to an applicant's statements with little or no independent verification.

## 2.2 Main VCLT Considerations

The stage is now set to turn to the main VCLT considerations (and the non-*travaux* aspects of Article 32 VCLT) relevant to interpreting 'well-founded fear', although it is convenient to leave aside to be addressed later two aspects of this term—that relating to forward-looking assessment and that relating to risk assessment—as these raise specific issues.

### 2.2.1 Ordinary meaning

As regards *ordinary meaning*, in purely textual terms, the 'well-founded fear' element of the definition cannot easily be taken in isolation because it prompts, inter alia, the question, 'Well-founded fear of what?' It is essentially an expression that has no ascertainable content without reference to its direct object, namely the condition of 'being persecuted'. Nonetheless, both words have to be considered for their ordinary meaning.

As regards the abstract noun, 'fear', ordinary meaning recognises more than one usage. For our purposes there are two main ones. One concerns subjective belief of danger or trepidation. In this usage, focus is on the individual's emotional state. The other concerns an anticipatory apprehension of danger. In one shape or form, both usages can be found in most dictionaries, both in the English and French[45] languages (the only two authentic languages for this Convention). Thus, to take the OED Online, its definitions include both '[t]he emotion of pain or uneasiness caused by the sense of impending danger, or by the prospect of some possible evil'[46] and '[a]pprehension or dread of something that will or may happen in the future'.[47]

In favour of reading 'fear' as trepidation might also be said to be the fact that, read as a whole, Article 1A(2) would appear to link the well-founded fear of persecution with

---

[44] UN Ad Hoc Committee on Statelessness and Related Problems, UN Docs E/1618 and E/AC.32/5 (n 40) (emphasis added).

[45] Hathaway and Hicks (n 1) 508, note that although the verb '*craindre*' in French can mean trepidation, its principal meaning concerns anticipatory apprehension of danger. They give various examples from Paul Robert and Alain Rey, *Le Grand Robert De La Langue Francaise: Dictionaire Alphabetique Et Analogique De La Langue Francaise* (2nd edn, Le Robert 1985).

[46] OED Online <https://www.oed.com> accessed 18 August 2021, sense 2(a). The OED (OUP 2nd edn, 1989) gave as one definition '[t]he emotion of pain or uneasiness caused by the sense of impending danger'.

[47] ibid, sense 3(a). The 1989 OED also gave as another of the definitions 'a particular apprehension of some future evil ... [an] apprehensive feeling towards anything regarded as a source of danger, or towards a person regarded as able to inflict injury or punishment'.

an unwillingness to avail oneself of the protection of a state,[48] and 'unwilling[ness] to avail himself' clearly refers to a person's state of mind.

Noll seeks to argue that 'there is nothing unclear about the term 'fear', and anyone would agree that it contains an emotive dimension, which is necessarily subjective'.[49] But the very fact that there are two common meanings belies this assertion.

In relation to the 'well-founded' component, though, the ordinary meaning is relatively unambiguous. Dictionary definitions more or less converge on seeing its meaning to be 'based on good evidence or reasons; having a foundation in fact or reality' or synonyms to this effect.[50] Consistent with that, even those who regard the 'well-founded fear' element to require both a subjective and an objective test, recognise that this adjectival component necessitates an objective test of some sort. For example, Dawson J in *Chan* observed that:

> The use of the adjectival expression 'well-founded' must be taken as qualifying in some way the 'fear of persecution'. It is hard to conceive of a fear which has no objective foundation at all as well-founded, no matter how genuine the fear might be. If the test were entirely subjective, the expression 'well-founded' would serve no useful purpose.[51]

As Hathaway and Foster note,[52] the qualities of being justifiable or reasonable were also clearly in the minds of the drafters who agreed that an individual is a refugee if he has a 'justifiable'[53] claim, 'good reasons'[54] to flee, and 'reasonable grounds'[55] for concern. It might also be said that the drafters' use elsewhere in Article 1A(2) of the term 'valid reasons' (in relation to persons of multiple nationality) shows a similar concern for objectivity of reasons. In the French text, the wording is '*avec raison*'.

But even if it were thought that somehow the plain wording of the 'well-founded' component warranted treating the compound expression, 'well-founded fear' as unambiguous, there remains the problem that the ordinary meaning of 'well-founded' (comprising synonyms such as 'justifiable' or 'reasonable') is extremely vague. In sum, we are left with one abstract noun ('fear') which has at least two quite different meanings and is thus (voices like Noll to the contrary) equivocal, and one adjective ('well-founded') for which the words seen at the time to define it are synonyms, not explanations. It is plain therefore that not much at all can be derived either from these two words individually or together. Hence recourse is needed to other VCLT elements for help.

---

[48] Noll (2005) (n 1) 153.
[49] ibid.
[50] OED Online <https://www.oed.com> accessed 25 August 2021.
[51] *Chan Yee Kin v MIEA* [1989] HCA 62, para 21.
[52] Hathaway and Foster (n 1) 110–11.
[53] UN Ad Hoc Committee on Refugee and Stateless Persons, Ad Hoc Committee on Statelessness and Related Problems, Corrigendum to the Proposal for a Draft Convention Submitted by France (18 January 1950) UN Doc E/AC.32/L.3/Corr.1, 1.
[54] Statement of Sir Leslie Brass of the UK, UN Doc E/AC.32/SR.18 (n 38) 6, adopted in UN Doc E/1618 (n 40) 39.
[55] UN Ad Hoc Committee on Refugees and Stateless Persons, Ad Hoc Committee on Statelessness and Related Problems, United Kingdom Draft Proposal for Article 1 (17 January 1950) UN Doc E/AC.32/2.

### 2.2.2 Context

As regards *context*, a little more emerges when these two words are read in relation to other elements of the definition, in particular: the references to 'being persecuted'; to a causal connection being required when the issue is whether someone is unwilling to avail themself of protection ('owing to such fear'); and to the causal nexus needed between 'being persecuted' and one or more enumerated Convention reasons/grounds ('reasons of'). All can be said to confirm that the fear must concern something grave enough to give rise to unwillingness to seek internal protection or (in the case of stateless persons) return.

Going outside Article 1A(2) but still working within the Convention, commentators have especially urged the significance of Article 33 and Article 1C(5)-(6). Article 33(1), which is often seen as broadly interchangeable with Article 1A(2) so far as contents are concerned,[56] makes no reference to 'well-founded fear'.[57] Likewise, Article 1C(5)-(6) identify circumstances under which refugee status must cease, without any explicit mention of 'well-founded fear' or whether a person's 'well-founded fear' still exists or not.[58] Omission of any reference to 'fear' in these provisions has been seen to reinforce the need to construe fear in an objective sense.[59] The Michigan Guidelines on Well-Founded Fear, Hathaway and Hicks, and Hathaway and Foster all invoke these provisions as evidence that fear cannot mean subjective fear.[60] However, it must be doubted that mere reference to 'internal inconsistency' between Article 1A(2) on the one hand and Article 33(1) and Article 1C(5)-(6)[61] on the other, establishes this. The same argument could, anomalously, equally support the idea that the entire 'well-founded fear' element does not have any independent role (even understood as essentially a test of objective fear) as a key element of the refugee definition. In any event, it is clear that consideration of the Convention's context, gets us only a little way.

Noll, by contrast, seeks to recruit the differences in wording between Article 1A(2) and Article 33(1), in particular the use of the concept of 'threat' in the latter, to reinforce a reading of 'fear' as subjective fear.[62] That view is to be contrasted with the more commonly expressed view that in terms of denoting risk on return, the two provisions should be treated as interchangeable.[63]

---

[56] Although issue is taken with that position in Chapter 6, section 1.4.2.
[57] Convention Relating to the Status of Refugees (adopted 28 July 1951, entered into force 22 April 1954) 189 UNTS 137, Article 33.
[58] ibid Article 1C(5)-(6).
[59] Of possible significance there is also the fact that Article 1C(5), second paragraph (which applies to statutory refugees) does not use the language of fear as such, but rather 'compelling reasons arising out of previous persecution'.
[60] MGs on Well-Founded Fear (n 1) para 5; Hathaway and Hicks (n 1) 535–36; Hathaway and Foster (n 1) 100 (on Article 1C(4)).
[61] In relation to the cessation clauses, there is a strong argument for regarding 'well-founded fear' as an implicit precondition, since they contemplate cessation of refugee status, i.e. status based on there having been a well-founded fear of being persecuted.
[62] Noll (2005) (n 1) 153–54: see also 142–43. A similar approach was taken by the US Supreme Court in *INS v Cardoza-Fonseca* [1987] 480 US 421. For fuller discussion, see Chapter 6, section 1.4.2.
[63] See Goodwin-Gill and McAdam (4th edn) (n 1) 266–67; see Chapter 6, section 1.4.2.

### 2.2.3 Object and purpose

It has mainly, although not exclusively,[64] been proponents of the 'objective approach' who have sought to invoke object and purpose. Thus, Hathaway and Foster contend that if the bipartite approach were correct and 'subjective' fear had to be seen as a necessary component of the meaning of being persecuted, that would conflict with the Convention's human rights and non-discrimination purposes.[65] Two aspects have particularly been highlighted. One is that it is contrary to the protection purposes of the Convention to hinge vital decisions about refugee status on something as variable as a person's state of mind. As stated by the Australian High Court in *Chan*, 'the object of the Convention is not to relieve fears which are all in the mind, however understandable, but to facilitate refuge for those who are in need of it'.[66] The other main aspect has been concern that such a requirement licenses discrimination. Thus, for Hathaway and Hicks, its result:

> [ ... ] is to advantage the claims of applicants whose trepidation can be readily identified by decisionmakers and to disadvantage individuals who, for whatever reason, do not project fearfulness. The disparate treatment of applicants identically situated with respect to their actual risk of being persecuted is difficult to square with the human rights-based goals of refugee law.[67]

### 2.2.4 Other VCLT considerations

In relation to Articles 31(3), 32, and 33 VCLT, the most well-known source for shedding light on the meaning of 'well-founded fear' is the 1979 UNHCR Handbook.[68] It will be recalled that this Handbook can justifiably be taken to represent state practice at least up to that date.[69] It contains passages that clearly consider the notion of 'well-founded fear' to require a bipartite approach akin to that taken in the IRO Constitution. It states, for example, that:

> To the element of fear—a state of mind and a subjective condition—is added the qualification 'well-founded'. This implies that it is not only the frame of mind of the person concerned that determines his refugee status, but that this frame of mind must be supported by an objective situation. The term 'well-founded fear' therefore

---

[64] e.g. Noll (2005) (n 1) 153–54.
[65] Hathaway and Foster (n 1) 108–10.
[66] *Chan Yee Kin* (n 51). See also Lord Goff in *R v SSSHD, Ex parte Sivakumaran and Conjoined Appeals* [1988] AC 958: '[t]he true object of the Convention is not just to assuage fear, however reasonably and plausibly entertained, but to provide a safe haven for those unfortunate people whose fear of persecution is in reality well-founded'.
[67] Hathaway and Hicks (n 1) 536; Hathaway and Foster (n 1) 109–10. See also Zimmermann and Mahler (n 1) 337–38.
[68] UNHCR, Handbook on Procedures and Criteria for Determining Refugee Status and Guidelines on International Protection under the 1951 Convention and the 1967 Protocol Relating to the Status Of Refugees (Geneva, 2019, reissued in 2019) (UNHCR Handbook or Handbook).
[69] See Chapter 1, section 6.1.1.

contains a subjective and an objective element, and in determining whether well-founded fear exists, both elements must be taken into consideration.[70]

The Handbook also states at paragraph 41 that '[a]n evaluation of the subjective element is inseparable from an assessment of the personality of the applicant'.

It must not be assumed, however, that the Handbook as a whole enunciates a clear and consistent approach to subjective fear.[71] At paragraph 41 it also states that '[f]ear must be reasonable' although '[e]xaggerated fear ... may be well-founded if, in all the circumstances of the case, such a state of mind can be regarded as justified'.[72] This seems to require that the subjective element must also be of a particular quality. Be that as it may, and without exploring precisely what the Handbook means to cover by expressions such as 'the personality of the applicant', and 'subjective fear', such references strongly convey two things. First, they confirm the view that the refugee definition requires decision makers to make an individual assessment. Second, however, they clearly go beyond that since they require that such individual assessment identify subjective fear as one of two *necessary conditions* for the existence of 'well-founded fear'.[73]

That said, it is noteworthy that the Handbook also seeks to acknowledge the need for qualifications to attach to assessment of the subjective element. Paragraph 48 recognises that 'fear of persecution' is 'usually foreign to a refugee's normal vocabulary'. It notes that a refugee 'for psychological reasons' may not be able to 'describe his experiences and situation in political terms'. Paragraph 198 states that a person 'in fear of the authorities in his own country' may feel 'afraid to speak freely and give a full and accurate account of his case'. In relation to children, it observes that:

> When the minor has not reached a sufficient degree of maturity to make it possible to establish well-founded fear in the same way as for an adult, it may be necessary to have greater regard to certain objective factors. Thus, if an unaccompanied minor finds himself in the company of a group of refugees, this may—depending on the circumstances—indicate that the minor is also a refugee.[74]

For children with parents and who wish their child to be outside the country of origin on grounds of well-founded fear of persecution, the Handbook states that 'the child himself may be presumed to have such fear'.[75]

---

[70] UNHCR Handbook (n 68) para 38; see also paras 41, 206.
[71] Hathaway and Hicks (n 1) 507 consider that various passages support 'almost every imaginable understanding of the subjective element', including e.g. paras 37–42 and 52. Another important critique of the Handbook's treatment of 'well-founded fear' is that by Noll (2005) (n 1) 141, 147–50.
[72] UNHCR Handbook (n 68) para 41.
[73] For this reason, I find it difficult to try and resolve the division of opinion in the manner chosen by Goodwin-Gill and McAdam (4th edn) (n 1) 82, namely to read what is intended as being 'not so much evidence of subjective fear, as evidence of the subjective aspects of an individual's life, including beliefs and commitments'.
[74] UNHCR Handbook (n 68) para 217. See also UNHCR, Guidelines on Policies and Procedures in dealing with Unaccompanied Children Seeking Asylum (1997) para 8.6. The approach taken in UNHCR, Note on Burden and Standard of Proof in Refugee Claims (n 1) paras 13–14 is rather more nuanced.
[75] UNHCR Handbook (n 68) para 218.

The Handbook's bipartite approach remained the 'dominant' approach in the first four decades after the Convention's signing.[76] Indeed, UNHCR still endorses this view. It has expressly reconfirmed this approach in its Guidelines on Child Asylum Claims.[77] And in a 2021 third party intervention in a Canadian case, it expressly maintains the bipartite test, even in the context of the cessation clauses (in which, as we have noted, there is no express reference to a 'well-founded fear' test of any kind).[78] However, some of its Guidelines have adopted a noncommittal or ambivalent approach to this issue.[79]

Turning to judicial materials, the UNHCR Handbook approach early on received widespread jurisprudential backing. Surveys of national case law in previous decades show that the bipartite approach mostly held sway.[80] US jurisprudence has consistently followed one or more versions of it.[81] It was endorsed by the Canadian Supreme Court in the seminal case of *Ward*.[82] At one point the German Federal Administrative

---

[76] See Hathaway and Hicks (n 1) 510; Carr (n 1) 537. As academic support for this approach, Tuitt (n 1) 81 cites Robert C Sexton, 'Political Refugees, Non-refoulement and State Practice: A Comparative Study' (1985) 18(4) Vanderbilt Journal of Transnational Law 733; Michael H Posner and Susan Kaplan, 'Who Should We Let in?' in Sarah Spencer (ed), *Strangers and Citizens: A Positive Approach to Migrants and Refugees* (Rivers Oram Press 1994) 18; Austin T Fragomen Jr, 'The Refugee: A Problem of Definition' (1970) 3(1) Case Western Reserve Journal of International Law 45, 53; Christopher Wydrzynski, 'Refugees and the Immigration Act' (1979) 25(2) McGill Law Journal 316–18; Patricia Hyndman, 'Refugees Under International Law with a Reference to the Concept of Asylum' (1986) 60 Australian Law Journal 148.

[77] UNHCR, Guidelines on International Protection (Guidelines) No 8: Child Asylum Claims under Articles 1(A)2 and 1(F) of the 1951 Convention and/or 1967 Protocol relating to the Status of Refugees (2009) UN Doc HCR/GIP/09/08, para 11. However, in the UNHCR, Guidelines on International Protection No 6: Religion-Based Refugee Claims under Article 1A(2) of the 1951 Convention and/or the 1967 Protocol relating to the Status of Refugees (2004) UN Doc HCR/GIP/04/06, it is noted that '[i]n this context, the well-founded fear need not necessarily be based on the applicant's own personal experience'.

[78] UNHCR, *Canada (MCI) v Camayo*—Memorandum of the Intervener: U.N. High Commissioner for Refugees (24 February 2021) available at:<https://www.refworld.org/docid/6040f4c34.html≥accessed 16 August 2021. As previously, this approach is seen to require exceptions. Para 28 states that 'UNHCR recognizes that the lack of subjective fear is not always a reliable indicator of the lack of the need for protection in all cases.'

[79] Contrast the UNHCR, Guidelines on International Protection No 1: Gender-Related Persecution within the context of Article 1A(2) of the 1951 Convention and/or its 1967 Protocol relating to the Status of Refugees (2002) UN Doc HCR/GIP/02/01, para 9; UNHCR Guidelines No 6 (n 77) para 14; UNHCR, Guidelines on International Protection No 7: The Application of Article 1A(2) of the 1951 Convention and/or 1967 Protocol Relating to the Status of Refugees to Victims of Trafficking and Persons at Risk of Being Trafficked (7 April 2006) UN Doc HCR/GIP/06/07, para 14; UNHCR, Guidelines on International Protection No 10: Claims to Refugee Status related to Military Service within the context of Article 1A (2) of the 1951 Convention and/or the 1967 Protocol relating to the Status of Refugees (12 November 2014) UN Doc HCR/GIP/13/10/Corr.1, para 13; UNHCR, Guidelines on International Protection No 12: Claims for refugee status related to situations of armed conflict and violence under Article 1A(2) of the 1951 Convention and/or 1967 Protocol relating to the Status of Refugees and the regional refugee definitions (2 December 2016) UN Doc HCR/GIP/16/12, para 11. In each of these the preferred wording is '[w]hat amounts to a well-founded fear of persecution will depend on the particular circumstances of each individual case'.

[80] Cox (n 1) 355–77. See also Carr (n 1) 537, who cites the following cases: *Saleh v US Department of Justice* [1992] 962 F.2d 234, 239; *Canada (AG) v Ward* [1993] 2 SCR 689, 691; *Sivakumaran* (n 66); *Re MIMA; Ex parte MIAH* [2001] HCA 22; *Zgnat'ev v MJELR* [2001] IEHC 105; *Luu the Truong v Chairman of the Refugee Status Review Bd* [2001] HCAL 3261, 45.

[81] Anker (n 1) §2.5, 68–75 citing, inter alia, *Cardoza-Fonseca* (n 62) and *Matter of Mogharrabi* [1987] 19 I&N Dec 439, paras 441–42. See also Kim (n 1) 210.

[82] *Ward* (n 80); see also *Adjei v Canada (MEI)* [1989] 2 FC 680; and *Chan v Canada (MEI)* [1995] 3 SCR 593, para 120. Waldman (n 1); Bossin and Demirdache (n 1).

Court (Germany) approved it.[83] Leading Australian cases supported it.[84] The Irish High Court embraced it.[85] UK practice indicated at least ambivalent support for it.[86] Writing in 2005, Hathaway and Hicks considered that the bipartite approach was still the 'dominant approach'.[87]

However, almost from the beginning, significant jurisprudential opposition emerged to making subjective fear a necessary condition. Zimmermann and Mahler observe that French courts never referred to the applicant's subjective state of mind when determining whether they have a well-founded fear.[88] In the leading UK case, *Sivakumaran*, Lord Keith of Kinkel remarked that:

> [ ... ] the question whether the fear of persecution held by an applicant for refugee status is well-founded is ... intended to be objectively determined by reference to the circumstances at the time prevailing in the country of the applicant's nationality. This inference is fortified by the reflection that the general purpose of the Convention is surely to afford protection and fair treatment to those for whom neither is available in their own country, and does not extend to the allaying of fears not objectively justified, however reasonable these fears may appear from the point of view of the individual in question.... Fear of persecution, in the senses of the Convention, is not to be assimilated to a fear of instant personal danger arising out of an immediately presented predicament ... the question is what might happen if he were to return to the country of his nationality.[89]

The German Federal Administrative Court from early on emphasised the need for an objective assessment of the act of a persecutor rather than an assessment of an

---

[83] *BVerwG 10 C 23.12* [2013] para 19. However, Zimmermann and Mahler (n 1) 341, also note that the German Federal Administrative Court has supported the objective approach. They cite *BVerwG 9 C 36/83* [1983] 67.

[84] e.g. *Chan Yee Kin* (n 51) para 396; *Ex parte MIAH* (n 80) para 62 (Gaudron J); *Iyer v MIMA* [2000] FCA 1788; *SDAQ v MIMIA* (2003) 129 FCR 137, para 19.

[85] *Zgnat'ev* (n 80) para 6; *Xiao v RAT* [2005] IEHC 167.

[86] e.g. in *Sivakumaran* (n 66), widely seen as endorsing a purely objective approach, Sir John Donaldson MR stated that '[t]he adjectival phrase 'well-founded' qualifies, but cannot transform, the subjective nature of the emotion'.

[87] Hathaway and Hicks (n 1) 510–11.

[88] Zimmermann and Mahler (n 1) 340. They cite *Commission des Recours des Réfugiés* (Refugee Appeal Authority, France); Case No 140222 *Straravecka* [1999]; and Case No 312811 *Chiporev* [1997].

[89] *Sivakumaran* (n 66). Hathaway and Foster (n 1) 92 appear to suggest that the UK approach supports the bipartite approach, on the strength of a passage from Lord Hope's opinion in *HJ (Iran) and HT (Cameroon) v SSHD* [2010] UKSC 31, para 17, stating that '[t]he Convention directs attention to the state of mind of the individual. It is the fear which that person has that must be examined and shown to be well-founded'. Given, however, that *Sivakumaran* has continued to be cited as authority for an objective approach and was not disapproved as such by Lord Dyson in *MA (Somalia) v SSHD* [2010] UKSC 49, it would be more accurate to describe the UK position as ambivalent. That fits more accurately with Hathaway and Foster's own statement at (n 1) 92 (footnote 9), which, after having cited a UK case openly adopting a bipartite approach (*E v SSHD* [2004] QB 531, 542), goes on to note a case in which an objective approach appears to have been taken (*Subramanian v IAT* [2000] Imm AR 173, 179). Hathaway and Foster conclude in this footnote that 'subjective fear seems traditionally to have played a relatively minor role in United Kingdom jurisprudence'. See further, Mark Symes and Peter Jorro, *Asylum Law and Practice* (LexisNexis 2003), §§2.41–2.42, 59–60.

applicant's subjective intentions.[90] Some Australian cases also supported the objective approach.[91] New Zealand strongly embraced it.[92]

Moving forward to more recent times, despite viewing the common law world to be largely[93] still in thrall to the bipartite approach, Hathaway and Foster point out that most civil law jurisprudence either does not require subjective fear or treats this requirement as being simply a means by which the applicant's individual circumstances are taken account of.[94] By strong implication, the CJEU has also adopted a purely objective approach. In *Y and Z*, the CJEU defined fear as 'being subject to acts of persecution'[95] and fear is considered 'well-founded' if it is established that there is a 'reasonable chance of its realisation in the future'.[96] An applicant must establish that he or she 'personally' has a well-founded fear but that is treated as an aspect of the individual assessment.[97] Also significant is the fact that in the context of 'horizontal judicial dialogue', the European Union Asylum Agency (EUAA) Judicial Analysis on Qualification for International Protection, produced by IARMJ-Europe, considers that this element of the definition 'concerns a risk assessment'.[98] Further, whilst the common law case law continues to largely adopt a bipartite approach, there are some decisions that strongly disavow it[99] and some exhibit an ongoing ambivalence.[100] The approach taken in common law case law to exceptions, which will be dealt with below,[101] also calls into question whether the bipartite approach is effectively adhered to.

As regards academic materials, views remain split between two main camps, albeit there is a discernible trend towards support for the objective approach. The bipartite

---

[90] *BVerwG* 9 C 36/83 [1983], cited Zimmermann and Mahler (n 1) 341; *BVerwG* 9 C 158/94 [1994], cited by Roland Bank, 'Refugee Law Jurisprudence from Germany and Human Rights' in Burson and Cantor (n 15) 163.

[91] See e.g. *Chan Yee Kin* (n 51); *MIEA v Guo Wei Rong* [1997] HCA 22.

[92] *Refugee Appeal No 72668/01* [2002] NZRSAA 11, cited Zimmermann and Mahler (n 1) 340.

[93] The common law country that continues to endorse the bipartite approach most explicitly are Canada (see Cameron, 2018 (n 1) 62); Australia (see Guide to Refugee Law in Australia: ch 3 Well-founded Fear—available at <http//www/aat.gov.au> accessed 26 January 2022 3–4); and the United States: see e.g. *Murugan v US Attorney General*, 10 F.4th 1185, 1193(11th Cir.2021), cited by Anker (n 1) §2.5, 68. New Zealand, however, continues to consistently reject it: see e.g. *K v RSAA (No 2)* [2005] NZAR 441, 450.

[94] Hathaway and Foster (n 1) 106–08. Their analysis does, however, note that some of the civil law jurisprudence still expresses itself in bipartite terms: see also ibid 92.

[95] Joined Cases C-71/11 and C-99/11 *Bundesrepublik Deutschland v Y and Z* [2012] ECLI:EU:C:2012:518, paras 51 and 72.

[96] ibid para 51. In CJEU, *Case C-255/19 SSHD v O A* [2021] ECLI:EU:C:2021:36, para 56, the Court emphasised that the concepts of 'well-founded fear' and 'protection' are 'intrinsically linked', thereby reinforcing that the assessment in relation to both elements is conceived in objective terms. See also ibid para 61. Note, however, that Noll (2005) (n 1) 155, considers that the drafting of the Qualification Directive 'does not lend itself to support a shift towards an "inherently objective" assessment'.

[97] Case C-652/16 *Nigyar Rauf Kaza Ahmedbekova and Rauf Emin Ogla Ahmedbekov v Zamestnik-predsedatel na Darzhavna agentsia za bezhantsite* [2018] ECLI:EU:C:2018:801, para 49.

[98] EASO, 'Qualification for International Protection: Judicial Analysis' (2nd edn, January 2023) 1.5.2. Formerly the European Asylum Support Office (EASO), this agency has been renamed the European Union Asylum Agency (EUAA): see Regulation (EU) 2021/2303 of the European Parliament and of the Council of 15 December 2021 on the European Union Agency for Asylum and repealing Regulation (EU) No 439/2010 [2021] OJ L 468/1.

[99] New Zealand has continued to take a strong singular objective approach: see e.g. *Refugee Appeal No 70074* [1996] NZRSAA; *Refugee Appeal No 72668/01* (n 92); *Refugee Appeal No 76044* [2008] NZAR 719; *DS (Iran)* [2016] NZIPT 800788.

[100] See e.g. Lord Walker's observations in *HJ (Iran)* (n 89).

[101] See below pp. 688–691.

approach has received some, although relatively limited support in the academic literature. Weis[102] and Melander[103] were early proponents. Those endorsing it more recently include Kourula,[104] Vanheule,[105] Marx,[106] Zahle,[107] Noll,[108] and (to a lesser extent) Goodwin-Gill and McAdam.[109]

In the other camp, support for a singular objective approach was voiced early on in the life of the Convention. Thus for Grahl-Madsen, '[t]he adjective "well-founded" suggests that it is not the frame of mind of the person concerned which is decisive for his claim to refugeehood, but that his claim should be measured with a more objective yardstick.... In fact, ... the frame of mind of the individual hardly matters at all'.[110] Others who have also rejected a bipartite approach include Hathaway,[111] Adjin-Terry,[112] Hathaway and Hicks,[113] Carlier,[114] Kälin,[115] Hailbronner,[116] Löhr,[117] Bossin and Demirdache,[118] Wouters,[119] Zimmermann and Mahler,[120] and Hathaway and Foster. As early as 2003, Hathaway and Hicks noted Walter Kälin's observation made in 1992 that 'during the last decades, a trend has developed to put the main emphasis on the objective elements'.[121] Accordingly, even though it remains that only a limited number of senior courts have expressly rejected such a requirement, the bipartite approach seems no longer to constitute the 'dominant view' in the *scholarly literature*.[122]

As regards Article 32 VCLT, whilst the *travaux* (as we saw) disclose a bipartite approach, it is abundantly clear from the various sources just described that to varying degrees academics and jurists remain split in their interpretation of the well-founded fear element.

---

[102] Paul Weis, 'The Concept of Refugee in International Law' (1960) 87(1) Journal du Droit International 928, 970.
[103] Göran Melander, 'The Protection of Refugees' (1974) 18 Scandinavian Studies in Law 151, 158.
[104] Pirkko Kourula, *Broadening the Edges: Refugee Definition and International Protection Revisited* (Kluwer Law International 1997) 91.
[105] Vanheule (n 1) 91–105.
[106] Marx (n 1) 151–70.
[107] Henrik Zahle, 'Competing Patterns For Evidentiary Assessments' in Noll (2005) (n 1) 25.
[108] Noll (2005) (n 1) 152–55.
[109] See above n 76 for other academic support for this approach cited by Tuitt (n 1) 81. Goodwin-Gill and McAdam (4th edn) (n 1) 81–82 qualify their support with the observation, at 82, that '[w]hat seems to be intended, however, is not so much evidence of subjective fear, as evidence of the subjective aspects of an individual's life, including beliefs and commitments'. They also describe the argument of Hathaway and Hicks (n 1) as 'the not unreasonable view'.
[110] Grahl-Madsen (n 1) 174.
[111] Hathaway (n 1) 69, 74.
[112] Adjin-Terry (n 1) 127–51.
[113] Hathaway and Hicks (n 1) 505–60.
[114] Carlier (n 1) 685.
[115] Kälin (n 1) 28. However, he expressed the hope that 'states, without neglecting objective factors, would take subjective factors more into account'.
[116] Hailbronner's support is inferred from the fact that (like Noll) he is one of the signatories of the MGs on Well-Founded Fear (n 1).
[117] Löhr (n 1) 47–97, cited Zimmermann and Mahler (n 1) 340.
[118] Bossin and Demirdache (n 1) 108–18.
[119] Wouters (n 1) 83–84.
[120] Zimmermann and Mahler (n 1) 338–41.
[121] Kälin (n 1) 21–35.
[122] I respectfully disagree with Anderson et al, who in their 2019 ICLQ journal article (n 1) 118, state that 'the preponderance of scholars and judges still adhere to this view'. Judges yes, scholars no.

In relation to Article 33 VCLT, it must not be forgotten that Hathaway and Hicks consider the 'equally authentic' French text to point in favour of an objective approach, although they do not dispute that in French the term *'craindre'* can also convey subjective fearfulness.[123]

Given that supplementary means of interpretation include academic materials and that we have seen these to reflect widely divergent viewpoints, Article 32 considerations appear to offer little help, at least when it comes to resolving this main debate.

### 2.2.5 Conclusions on VCLT considerations

Summarising the result of the application of VCLT rules to this element of the definition, one struggles to identify any common view. All that can really be said is that VCLT considerations appear capable of supporting both of the two main interpretations. This also means, when it comes to seeking to identify agreed propositions, that (certainly in relation to the 'fear' component of the phrase) there is no state practice in either the strict or the broad sense as to whether it requires a subjective as well as an objective element. However, as regards the 'well-founded' component, as already noted, there is wide agreement that this does denote (at least in part) an objective element. The nature and extent of this agreement will be examined separately in section 4.

## 3 'Well-Founded Fear': The 'Subjective Element'

Given that application of VCLT rules yields no clear answer to what meaning the term 'well-founded fear' possesses, it is necessary to go on to consider the competing arguments more closely. In doing so, it is important to restate precisely what the two main approaches consist of. According to the bipartite approach,[124] a key component of the well-founded fear notion is a subjective element. According to the objective approach,[125] there is no such element. Whilst some question the very terminology typically employed to distinguish 'subjective' and 'objective' elements,[126] no alternative labels have taken hold and for this reason this study continues to refer to both, these being their most commonly known labels. The focus of this next section is on whether well-founded fear has a subjective element as one of its requirements.

---

[123] As conceded also by Hathaway and Foster (n 1) 106.

[124] The term used, inter alia, by Hathaway and Hicks (n 1) and Hathaway and Foster (n 1). Zimmermann and Mahler (n 1) 338 prefer the term 'Combined Subjective-Objective' Approach'. Although their term better identifies the actual contents of the approach, 'bipartite approach' is the more frequently used term.

[125] Zimmermann and Mahler (n 1) 340.

[126] Hathaway and Hicks (n 1) 509 contend that 'persistent references in the jurisprudence and scholarly literature to such abstract concepts as objectivity and subjectivity are at least partly responsible for the conceptual confusion that, to this point, has frustrated the emergence of a shared understanding of the well-founded fear standard'. See also Noll (2005) (n 1) 144; Kim (n 1) 193, 196.

## 3.1 The Subjective Element of the Bipartite/Combined Subjective-Objective Approach

What are the main merits and demerits that have been perceived in the 'bipartite approach', focusing first of all on its 'subjective element'? Complicating the tasks of addressing this question is the fact that this approach has been understood in varying ways, some, for example, considering that it entails perceiving the subjective element 'as the more crucial one';[127] some considering that decision makers regard it as the less important element.[128] Some versions of it (e.g. the UNHCR Handbook's) appear internally inconsistent. All this makes it exceedingly difficult to place different formulations into neat categories. However, broadly speaking, it is possible to identify two versions. In the most commonly propounded one, encapsulated by the main treatment given in the UNHCR Handbook, subjective fear is a necessary but not a sufficient condition of being able to establish a well-founded fear. However, an important feature of this version is that it accepts, at least in places, that the subjective fear requirement is subject to exceptions. In the other version of the bipartite approach, subjective fear is not a necessary condition but operates as a 'top-up' in cases insufficiently established on objective grounds.[129] Although there has been little use or recognition of this latter version in the case law or academic literature, this author agrees with Hathaway and Hicks and others that it is conceptually distinct and should be treated as such.[130]

### 3.1.1 Perceived merits

As regards the main version, let us first consider points in favour of treating the subjective element as a necessary requirement (the classic bipartite approach), starting with those arising out of the earlier application of VCLT rules. One consideration is the fact that one of the ordinary meanings of 'fear' is trepidation. The linkage made in the definition between 'well-founded fear' and 'unwillingness' of a person to avail himself or herself of protection can also be said to support a focus on a person's state of mind. As regards object and purpose, it could be said that the bipartite approach does not obviously conflict with the principle of surrogacy or human rights norms. Indeed, some have seen it more congruent with such norms than the 'objective approach'.[131] It could be said to pre-eminently achieve the purpose of ensuring an individual assessment that takes full account of particular circumstances. In relation to

---

[127] Zimmermann and Mahler (n 1) 338, citing Vanheule (n 1) 91, 94 and Adjin-Terry (n 1) 505–62 *passim*. Hathaway and Foster, TLRS2 (n 1) 91 cite Robert C Sexton, 'Political Refugees, Nonrefoulement and State Practice: A Comparative Study' (1985) 18 Vanderbilt Journal of Transnational Law 731, at 733 who describes 'substantial, if not predominant, reliance on subjective elements'. Hathaway and Hicks (n 1) 510 consider that some commentators have even seen subjective fear as the exclusive criterion. They cite Cox (n 1) 349, as holding this view, but that must be doubted: see Cox (n 1) 377.
[128] e.g. Goodwin-Gill and McAdam (4th edn) (n 1) 82.
[129] In making this distinction I draw on the analysis of Hathaway and Hicks (n 1) 509, and the MGs on Well-founded Fear (n 1) 38–40.
[130] Hathaway and Hicks (n 1) 509; Hathaway and Foster (n 1) 10.
[131] Although not a proponent of the bipartite approach as such, Noll (2005) (n 1) 154, considers that construing the term 'fear' to include a 'reference to the emotive repercussions of risk in the individual' promotes human dignity, in ensuring individuals are treated as ends, not means. See generally George Kateb, *Human Dignity* (Harvard University Press 2011).

Article 31(3) and/or Article 32 VCLT, it is of considerable importance that UNHCR has continued (although fitfully) to endorse a bipartite approach, as do some senior courts and tribunals, although mainly in the common law world. Maintaining such an approach—working with the grain as it were—could be said to help ensure continuity and consistency of decision-making. As regards the *travaux*, we have seen that the drafters clearly saw themselves as building on the bipartite approach adopted by the IRO Constitution.

A recurrent theme in various formulations of the bipartite approach is that it ensures that Refugee Status Determination (RSD) is 'more personal and individualised, by allowing the refugee applicant an avenue for conveying his or her reaction to the persecution that he or she faced'.[132] It has been seen as a way of ensuring a presumptive refugee retains a form of agency in the procedure.[133] Linked to this, some commentators have seen insistence on a subjective requirement as a bulwark against a restrictive approach to the refugee definition.[134] Doubtless some have had in mind that the IRO approach, on which the drafters saw themselves as building, privileged the applicant's own testimony.[135]

It is also arguable that the bipartite approach has proven flexible and adaptable. UNHCR's 2001 note on Article 1 underlines that '[t]here are varying degrees to which each of [the subjective and objective] two elements may be important in any individual case'.[136] From the outset its main formulations (those in the UNHCR Handbook in particular) have sought to qualify insistence on proving subjective fear by identifying justified exceptions, in particular children[137] and the mentally disabled. It can be argued that applying this hybrid approach, courts and tribunals have over time refined or fashioned a number of procedural devices to accommodate cases that deviate from the norm. In particular, a coherent body of case law has built up around children such that the fears of their parents/carers or similarly situated persons/groups are attributed to them. A prime example of attribution of parental fears to a child is the Australian High Court case of *Chen Shi Hai*, which concerned two parents with a three and half year-old Chinese male infant.[138] Attribution of the fears of a group of similarly situated persons to others has not only been made in relation to children. A prime example of

---

[132] As summarised by Carr (n 1) 543. See also Noll (2005) (n 1) 141–59.
[133] Noll (2005) (n 1) 141–44: '[w]ere it not for the mentioning of 'fear', emphasising the importance of a refugee's own assessment, determination procedures could cast claimants as mere objects to be dissected by an impersonal machinery of assessment'.
[134] See e.g. Vevstad (n 1) 60, who criticises: '[t]he use by States of a restrictive interpretation which focuses on the objective element of fear'. She considers this interpretation to be 'partly guided by the policy pursed by asylum receiving countries of restricting the flow of refugees since the 1980s'. Nathwani (n 1) 68 considers that treating well-founded fear as an objective standard results in a 'significant reduction of the scope of the refugee concept'. In his understanding, the objective standard 'does not contain any subjective elements' (see Nathwani (n 1) at 148). He links this, in turn, with its dependency on a human rights approach.
[135] See above p. 670.
[136] UNHCR, Interpreting Article 1 of the 1951 Convention Relating to the Status of Refugees (n 1) para 11.
[137] UNHCR Handbook (n 68) para 218.
[138] *Chen Shi Hai v MIEA* [2000] 201 CLR 293. Justice Kirby, did, however, express concern in paras 75–81 about denying the child applicant refugee status simply because the parents' application failed.

attribution of group fears to both minor and adult applicants has been the widespread practice of prima facie recognition.[139]

Other devices that have arguably produced workable results include: equating the well-founded fear test with the making of a positive credibility finding;[140] inferring or deriving subjective fear from the surrounding circumstances;[141] or treating is as a requirement that is *de minimis* and not needing therefore to be seen as a problem.[142]

The fact that by requiring focus on the applicant's state of mind the bipartite approach endows decision makers with a degree of discretion could also be said to ensure flexibility and avoidance of strict thresholds. It has been argued that it has enabled decision makers to grant status in certain types of cases where people are fleeing from situations in which the existence of objective evidence is minimal, e.g. people fleeing from armed conflicts where reporters are prevented from having access to what is happening.[143]

The bipartite approach has also proven capable of adaptation in response to criticism. In particular, it has been argued that writing into the approach the notion of a 'reasonable person' has enabled decision makers to continue to approach cases through the lens of the individual's state of mind, albeit applying to it a reasonableness filter.[144]

Possibly, it can also be argued that even two of the main proponents of the objective approach, Hathaway and Hicks, also acknowledge some role for the subjective

---

[139] Hathaway and Hicks (n 1) 522–23.

[140] ibid 531–33. At 531, they note the following cases using this mechanism: *Ward* (n 80) (La Forest, J); *Maximilok v Canada (MCI)* [1998] FTR 461; *Mario v SSHD* [1998] UNHCR RefWorld 2004 CD-ROM, issue 13; *Mgoian v INS* [1999] 184 F.3d 1029, 1035; *Abankwah v INS* [1999] 185 E3d 18, 22; *Carranza-Hernandez v INS* [1993] 12 E3d 4. In Australia, see *Emiantor v MIMA* (Federal Court of Australia, Olney, Sundberg and Marshall JJ), 20 July 1998; *SZSSQ v MIBP* [2013] FCCA 1762, paras 38 and 48.

[141] As examples of resort to the inference mechanism Hathaway and Hicks (n 1) 513, cite the following cases: *Savchenkov v SSHD* [1994] HX/71698/94 (unpublished) (stated as being on file with authors); *Adjei* (n 82); *Al-Harbi v INS* [2001] 242 F3d 882, 890–91; and *Aguilera-Cota v INS* [1990] 914 F.2d 1375, 1378. At 525–31 they critique inferences from various types of pre-application conduct; however, the inference mechanism is also applied to the applicant's experiences or likely situation in the country of origin. See also *SZWCI v MIBP* [2015] FCCA 1809. Sometimes the inference mechanism shades into the attribution mechanism, e.g. in *S273 of 2003 v MIMIA* [2005] FMCA 983 it was suggested that in the case of minors or intellectually challenged adults, decision makers can 'derive' that such a subjective fear is held, which achieves a very similar effect to the device of attributing to such persons the subjective fear of parents or carers.

[142] e.g. Goodwin-Gill and McAdam (4th edn) (n 1) 82, who consider that 'in practice, however, decision-makers do not tend to make much of the subjective issue'. Hathaway and Hicks (n 1) 513, give as examples of such 'marginalisation': *Thompson v SSHD*, HX/78032/1996 (unpublished); *Yusuf v Canada (MEI)* [1992] 1 FC. In an early US study, Ocariz and Lopez (n 1), described the test as 'no more than formalism'. Kim (n 1) 194 considers that subjective fear is 'essentially a non-issue because the asylum seekers can prove the component by stating that they are afraid to go back to their home country'.

[143] Carr (n 1) 543–44.

[144] Hathaway and Hicks (n 1) 524–25, note its role in US cases. According to Anker (n 1) §2.6, 72, the 'Board's post-*Cardoza-Fonseca* formulation—"a reasonable person in the [applicant's] circumstances"—may resolve these concerns. 'The "subjectivity" of the standard means that the applicant's perspective—or that of a reasonable person in his or her circumstances—is the lens through which the adjudicator must evaluate the reasonableness of the applicant's flight or fear of return.' She considers that the 'reasonable person' standard ensures that protection is not provided to 'those with fanciful or neurotic fears'. She notes that Grahl-Madsen (n 1) 174, cited with approval a German case (*Bayerisches Verwaltung Ansbach Case 3719 II/58* [1959]) in which it was stated that 'well-founded fear' exists 'when a reasonable person would draw the conclusion from external facts that he would be subject to persecution in his home country.'

element, in that they have appeared to view this as established (at least for recognition purposes) by the mere act of applying for asylum.[145] That, in itself, might be said to show that a purely objective approach remains dependent on some type of subjective element.

As regards the other (minor) version of the bipartite approach, which treats subjective fear not as a necessary condition but rather as an element which, if established, can supplement or 'top-up' a claim insufficiently made out in objective terms, this position appears to be advanced in isolated passages of the UNHCR Handbook.[146] According to this understanding, '[f]ear must be reasonable. Exaggerated fear, however, may be well-founded if, in all the circumstances, such a state of mind can be regarded as justified.'[147] This appears to regard fear that has a particular quality—'reasonableness'—as a factor capable of overcoming an insufficiency of objective risk. This notion is further developed in paragraph 42 of the same Handbook by reference to the notion of 'intolerability':

> [T]he applicant's fear should be considered well-founded if he can establish, to a reasonable degree, that his continued stay in his country of origin has become intolerable to him for the reasons stated in the definition, or would for the same reasons be intolerable if he returned there.[148]

However, since it identifies subjective fear as essential in cases where objective evidence is insufficient, this formulation is best understood as a logically distinct version. In practice, though, this approach has only really performed a role as a method of accentuating the importance of individual vulnerabilities.

### 3.1.2 Perceived demerits

The bipartite approach has been seen to suffer from a number of shortcomings. Application of VCLT rules demonstrates that ordinary meaning is ambiguous, and, in any event, the bipartite approach would appear to rely unduly on interpreting the abstract noun 'fear' in isolation. The Convention's context, by contrast, indicates the need to treat the 'fear' component as inextricably tied both to the 'well-foundedness' of the fear and to the object of the fear—persecution and lack of protection. In terms of object and purpose, the fact remains that to hinge decisions on refugee status on inquiry into a person's state of mind (*forum internum*) sits uneasily with a human rights understanding that views individuals as rights-bearers and focuses on the likely effects on them of threatened harm rather than on the state of mind of the applicant. Bearing in mind the broad consensus that one of the main purposes of the Convention is 'to

---

[145] Hathaway and Hicks (n 1) 507: 'Once fear so conceived [as forward-looking expectation of risk] is voiced by the act of seeking protection, it falls to the state party assessing refugee status to determine whether that expectation is borne out by the actual circumstances of the case.' However, Hathaway and Foster (n 1) 105 (footnote 83) distance themselves from this formulation.

[146] I concur with Hathaway and Hicks (n 1) 509–10, 534, the MGs on Well-founded Fear (n 1) 38–40, and Hathaway and Foster (n 1) 110 in (at least implicitly) treating this as a distinct version of the bipartite approach.

[147] UNHCR Handbook (n 68) para 41.

[148] ibid para 42.

provide refuge to those whose home state cannot or does not afford them protection from persecution,[149] the bipartite approach, by treating subjective fear as a necessary condition, appears to distract attention away from the crucial issue of whether or not individuals will face persecution on return.

What of the notion that the subjective fear requirement can be rescued by treating it as consisting only of an individual assessment that takes into account the particular circumstances? Firstly, that (as we shall see) is already achieved within an objective approach as part of a holistic assessment of the risks individuals claim they face.[150] But secondly, thus expressed, the test does not impose a precondition of establishing subjective fear. To elide the two is to effectively concede that establishing subjective fear is not a necessary condition.

Contrary to the assertion by some that treating subjective fear as a necessary condition immunises against a restrictive approach, there are cogent reasons for considering it does precisely the opposite, since one way or another it imposes an additional burden on the applicant. Surveys done of case law have identified a very significant number of cases in which a court or tribunal has concluded that refugee status must be denied where subjective fear cannot be demonstrated, 'even where there is evidence of a genuine, objective risk'.[151] The objective approach, by contrast (as we shall see), ensures a multifaceted individual assessment, without in itself erecting such a precondition.

Treating 'subjective fear' as a necessary condition gives rise to difficulties both on the part of the applicant and the decision maker.

For applicants, it confronts them, in the words of Carr, with 'the inherent difficulty of defining, identifying and articulating their subjective apprehension. To have subjective apprehension requires not only capacity to know and actual knowledge of the objective risk, but also the ability to articulate coherently and credibly these feelings of fear to the decision maker'.[152] This articulation, Carr notes, is often extremely difficult due to cultural, educational, and language difficulties.[153] As UNHCR has itself acknowledged, '[s]ubjective elements asserted are particularly hard to prove'.[154]

For decision makers, this approach requires them to undertake an assessment of subjective apprehension in the face of the known difficulties of inquiring into an individual's state of mind.[155] As acknowledged by the Canadian Supreme Court in *Chan v Canada*, determining an applicant's subjective fear is an 'intricate task' especially when the evidence is ambiguous.[156] Seeking to inquire into a person's state of mind inevitably runs up against the fact that decision makers have limited tools for conducting such an inquiry especially given the fact that often they are considering

---

[149] *Ward* (n 80).
[150] Hathaway and Hicks (n 1) 509–10, 545, 556.
[151] e.g. Hathaway and Foster (n 1) 93–95; Carr (n 1) 545–51.
[152] Carr (n 1) 544.
[153] ibid 545.
[154] UNHCR, Note on Burden and Standard of Proof in Refugee Claims (n 1) para 20.
[155] Carr (n 1) 546; Cameron (2008) (n 1) 585. Niamh Kinchin and Davoud Mougouei, 'What Can Artificial Intelligence Do for Refugee Status Determination? A Proposal for Removing Subjective Fear' (2022) 34 IJRL 373, 375 argue that 'the future application of AI in RSD as a legitimate techno-human process depends upon the removal of the subjective element of the "well-founded fear" standard'.
[156] *Chan* (n 82).

people from different cultures and educational backgrounds and who speak a different language.[157] They are not mind readers. Decision makers are inevitably faced with cases involving applicants who for one reason or another are unable to express their fear. This carries the inherent risk of them viewing this failure as meaning that applicants have no well-founded fear, even though the evidence may demonstrate that they are objectively at risk.[158]

A further shortcoming is that the bipartite approach appears to disregard the evident fact that persons who are at real risk of persecution objectively considered may not possess a subjective fear. Examples of those who may not have subjective fear of persecution are very young children, persons lacking full mental capacity, and brave or foolhardy individuals. There is no justifiable reason why such persons should be excluded from the refugee definition. In this respect, the bipartite approach stands in conflict with the universal scope of the refugee definition, which applies to 'any person'. Instead, the bipartite approach effectively uses a non-universal reference point, namely the paradigm of fear as is likely to be held by a normal adult. In truth, there is no basis for erecting a paradigm of a person who is neither too young or too old or too sick to have or understand fear or too foolhardy or too reckless to feel fear. The fear that the definition requires applicants to show must surely be one that is realistically something all refugees have.[159] Proponents of the bipartite approach have simply not provided a satisfactory answer to this objection.

As regards the assertion that the bipartite approach has ensured a flexible approach, this is best dealt with in two parts looking firstly at this assertion at a general level and then at the various procedural devices this approach has devised to achieve flexibility.

There is nothing wrong as such with an approach to assessing well-founded fear that is flexible, so long as there are clear parameters around cases deemed to be the exception. Nor, given that assessment of refugee claims is highly fact-sensitive, is there anything wrong as such with an approach that affords an element of discretion to decision makers. But again, unless the exercise of discretion is structured and governed by transparent criteria, it can too easily descend into a recipe for subjective decision-making. As noted by Carr, among others, it has led to abuse by some decision makers.[160]

Insofar as the argument is that imposing a subjective fear requirement can assist especially in cases where there is a lack of evidence, it is true that even with the advances in human rights monitoring globally, in some cases decision makers may lack relevant COI. However, such lack is not a reason in itself to require the establishment of subjective fear. The type of holistic individual assessment undertaken within the objective approach can take account of all aspects of an individual's situation, without artificially ascribing an a priori value to subjective fear (if any exists).

In relation to the various procedural devices developed in order to overcome the evident problems associated with applying the subjective requirement uniformly, each

---

[157] Hathaway and Hicks (n 1) 512, 517; Hathaway and Foster (n 1) 95–96.
[158] Carr (n 1) 550.
[159] Grahl-Madsen (n 1) 175: '[w]e cannot find a meaningful, common denominator in the minds of refugees'.
[160] Carr (n 1) 545.

has demonstrable flaws. The device of attribution—attributing the fears of parents or others to children or incapacitated adults—is beset with problems. To take the example of attribution to young children, this device may not have any application if the child is unaccompanied and cannot thereby be attached to parents or some other adult or adults. Further, as is demonstrated by the Australian case of *Chen Shi Hai*,[161] it can mean a child's claim is not considered in its own right, even when a parent's motives are different and even when the child may be subject to distinct persecutory risks. As illustrated by female genital mutilation (FGM) cases, where a parent or guardian approves of FGM, it could lead to decision makers simply assuming the child will grow up having the same view, even though FGM would inflict persecutory harm on them.

Operating such a device is also subject to inconsistent application. Thus in the way in which it is formulated in the UNHCR Handbook's paragraphs on unaccompanied minors, it does not mean that children are excluded from having to meet the refugee definition requirements; it means rather that an intervening inquiry into capacity must be made to establish whether the child is sufficiently mature to articulate fear and only if not, does the need for attribution arise.[162] Yet such an inquiry can require decision makers to make exceedingly difficult decisions about whether a child is to be considered as sufficiently mature to be able to have a subjective fear. If, on the other hand, as is proposed in some later UNHCR materials[163] and in some case law,[164] such inquiry can be omitted, this then amounts to giving children a 'free pass' based on their minority.[165]

As regards attributing to a child—or indeed any applicant—a fear possessed by similarly situated persons, it has undoubtedly come to the aid of many refugees, but it effectively amounts to saying in respect of such a person that fear personal to them (whether subjective or objective or both) is not required because it can be presumed.[166] As Hathaway and Hicks have pointed out, there is something inherently suspect about an approach wrapped in such heavy exception-making, especially when it is applied to a majority of refugee status determinations worldwide.[167] In Hathaway and Foster's words, 'if the exceptions swallow the rule (as seems to be the case), can it really be said that there is a requirement to demonstrate subjective fear at all?'.[168]

Further, it is not just children and the mentally disabled for whom exemptions have been or might need to be devised from the subjective requirement. As noted by

---

[161] *Chen Shi Hai* (n 138).
[162] UNHCR Handbook (n 68) para 217.
[163] e.g. UNHCR Guidelines No 8 (n 77) 7, para 11: '[i]t may be the case that a child is unable to express fear when this would be expected or, conversely, exaggerates the fear. In such circumstances, decision makers must make an objective assessment of the risk that the child would face, regardless of that child's fear.'
[164] Carr (n 1) 556–57.
[165] ibid 562: 'This lack of discussion regarding capacity is further evidence that in the majority of cases, child refugee applicants are being given a free pass on the subjective apprehension element of the well-founded fear analysis.'
[166] Indeed, in prima facie determination the requirement of subjective fear is explicitly not applied even in assessing whether the group of similarly situated persons has a well-founded fear: see UNHCR Guidelines No 11: Prima Facie Recognition of Refugee Status (24 June 2015) UN Doc HCR/GIP/15/11, para 15: '[a]n individualized assessment of the element of fear would normally be rendered unnecessary in such circumstances, as being on its face self-evident from the event or situation which precipitated the flight'.
[167] Hathaway and Hicks (n 1) 522–23; see also 524.
[168] Hathaway and Foster (n 1) 104.

Zimmermann and Mahler, specific groups in relation to whom it might prove difficult to assess subjective fear include 'women, children, disabled applicants, or persons suffering from post-traumatic stress disorder', or 'similarly situated groups'.[169] In relation to women, Adjin-Terry has written that 'the duty to demonstrate trepidation particularly disadvantages women required to testify to sexual violence, as '[w]omen fleeing gender-related harms have often not been successful in communicating their subjective fear of persecution even in the face of strong objective indicators because they have difficulty relating their claims ... to asylum decision-makers who are predominantly men'.[170] Further, some of the categories just identified are porous, for example, persons suffering from post-traumatic stress disorder. That is a category that even normal adults can fall inside or outside of depending on circumstances. A wide range of circumstances can mean that even normal adults may experience psychological difficulties, in response to actual or threatened harm. It becomes increasingly difficult to see how such diverse and frequently necessary exceptions warrant preservation of the rule.

The device of equating the subjective requirement with a positive credibility assessment is heavily artificial in nature. Further, as noted by Hathaway and Hicks, the underlying premise—that fearful applicants do not lie or exaggerate in the course of relating their story—'defies common sense' and 'is fundamentally at odds with the generally accepted view that credibility is not a per se requirement for refugee status'.[171]

Treating the subjective fear requirement as something that can be inferred from the surrounding circumstances requires resort to a number of highly artificial mechanisms[172] and is at odds with the proclaimed raison d'être of the bipartite approach, which is to take full account of personal experience and state of mind. It also makes such an approach virtually indistinguishable from the objective approach.

As regards treating the subjective requirement as of relative unimportance, this does overcome many of the practical problems, but only serves to highlight the fundamental weakness in an approach which treats subjective fear as a necessary condition.

One way or another, procedural devices elevate form over substance and erect additional hurdles for applicants.[173] They insist on the test being a necessary condition but then adopt qualifications which frequently disapply it. In the author's view, it is exceedingly hard not to agree with Carr, Hathaway and Hicks,[174] and Hathaway and Foster, among others,[175] that the artificiality of such devices is too great and that they fail to overcome the root problem, namely that the bipartite approach is not coherent in itself.

It is true enough that the bipartite approach has shown itself to be adaptable. However (to focus on the most notable attempt to adapt it), the 'reasonable person'

---

[169] Zimmermann and Mahler (n 1) 339.
[170] Adjin-Terry (n 1) 132. Catherine Dauvergne, 'Women in Refugee Jurisprudence' in Costello et al (n 1) 731, however, considers that '[o]ver time, and in assessments in many Western countries, decision-makers appears to find women more believable than they find men'.
[171] Hathaway and Hicks (n 1) 533; see also Hathaway and Foster (n 1) 100–02.
[172] Hathaway and Hicks (n 1) 525–31, and Hathaway and Foster (n 1) 96–100 focus on attempt to infer fearfulness from pre-flight conduct, delay in fleeing, failure to claim asylum in an intermediate country, failure to claim promptly in the host country, and return travel.
[173] Carr (n 1) 563–64; Hathaway and Foster (n 1) 103–05.
[174] Carr (n 1) 563–64; Hathaway and Hicks (n 1) 513; Hathaway and Foster (n 1) 104–05.
[175] e.g. Jason Pobjoy, The Child in International Refugee Law (CUP 2017) 217.

standard, at least as formulated in the US case law (and hinted at in isolated passages in the UNHCR Handbook), is difficult to fathom. Insofar as it still depends as a first step on ascertaining the individual's subjective (unfiltered) fears, the reasonable person standard is vulnerable to all the criticisms made of the first stage. Insofar as its function is to act as a filter, so that 'protection is not provided to those with purely fanciful or neurotic fears',[176] this function is served by the second ('objective') stage of the bipartite approach anyway. Likewise, if the 'reasonable person' standard is based (as in a formulation of it approved by Grahl-Madsen) on 'draw[ing] conclusions from external facts',[177] then that amounts in essence to a singular objective test.[178]

It is possible to counter-argue that the objective approach is somewhat misleading inasmuch as it has at least sometimes represented that the subjective fear component still has some role, albeit confined to the fact of making an asylum application.[179] However, even if that is what is meant,[180] it remains effectively an objective test only, since it is a sine qua non of any application for recognition of refugee status that a claim has been made. In any event, as already noted, the objective approach does encompass individual assessment. Both the bipartite and the objective approach recognise an essential need for individual assessment taking into account a wide range of factors and a holistic approach to establishing well-founded fear of persecution. In examining and taking into account individual circumstances, there must be proper constraints against intrusive methods, but that is not an argument as such against any kind of individual consideration of all relevant aspects of a person's account including subjective fears. Within this framework, subjective fear is not a necessary condition, but it can still be a factor of varying significance depending on the particular circumstances of the individual case.

### 3.1.3 Subjective fear as a 'plus factor'

As regards the other (minor) version of the bipartite approach, which treats subjective fear not as a necessary condition but as a 'plus factor', this has a similar drawback to the main version, namely that it is inherently discriminatory. The discriminatory drawback of such an approach is well-captured in the Michigan Guidelines:

> Under this formulation, persons who are more timid or demonstrative, or who are simply able to articulate their trepidation in ways recognizable as such by the decision-maker, are advantaged relative to others who face the same level of actual

---

[176] Anker (n 1) 62.
[177] Grahl-Madsen (n 1) 174.
[178] Hathaway and Hicks (n 1) 525 maintain that 'in truth, the reasonable person inquiry dispenses with a requirement of subjective fear altogether. To satisfy the subjective element under this approach, the applicant need only establish an objective risk of being persecuted of a kind that would engender fear in a "reasonable person"—his or her own fear, or lack thereof, is completely irrelevant.' See also Hathaway and Foster (n 1) 104–05.
[179] See Hathaway and Hicks (n 1) 507 (cited in n 52).
[180] On the logic of Hathaway and Foster's position, it does not 'in any sense condition refugee status on the ability to show subjective fear'—see Hathaway and Foster (n 1) 92.

risk, but who are more courageous, more reserved, or whose expressions of trepidation are not identified as such.[181]

### 3.1.4 Conclusion

It is not possible to regard the issue of whether the bipartite test's insistence on a requirement of subjective fear is correct as settled one way or the other. However, it can at least be said that the bipartite approach has so far failed to respond adequately to the various criticisms ranged against it. The fact that its proponents have not really engaged with well-known criticisms that have been made over and over again, and that very often case law simply skips over the issue, would seem to suggest this approach lacks efficacy.

## 4 'Well-Founded Fear': The Objective Element

As the various critiques made of the bipartite approach demonstrate, the alternative approach has come to be known as 'the objective approach'.[182] Terminological confusion can easily arise at this point because the bipartite approach also includes an 'objective *element*', despite criticising the rejection by the 'objective approach' of a subjective fear component. Before identifying what this element is, it is important to consider the respective merits and demerits of the 'objective *approach*'.

### 4.1 The Objective Approach

#### 4.1.1 Perceived merits

The perceived merits of the 'objective approach' can largely be reprised from the earlier analysis setting out criticisms of the bipartite approach. In summary, the 'objective approach' builds on one of the ordinary meanings of the term 'fear'; it fits closely with the Convention's object(s) and purpose(s), in particular by orienting the refugee definition directly to the ultimate question of future risk; it does not impose an intervening requirement of subjective fear, with all the attendant problems to which that has given rise; it is unencumbered by the battery of procedural devices that have been pressed into service in order to prop up the bipartite approach; it fits well with IHRL in not requiring applicants to exhibit emotions they may not always have or be able to express; it does not task decision makers with having to peer into people's souls but focusses instead on the likely effects of harms upon them; and it is less dependent on the exercise of discretion.

#### 4.1.2 Perceived demerits

In terms of the perceived demerits, it is possible to discern four main themes, which sometimes overlap.[183] First, it has been portrayed as an external approach that

---

[181] MGs on Well-founded Fear (n 1) 38; see also Hathaway and Hicks (n 1) 508; Hathaway and Foster (n 1) 110.
[182] See e.g. Zimmermann and Mahler (n 1) 340.
[183] Noll (2005) (n 1) 152 also identifies as an additional problem that 'it replicates the fragmentation of the definition into 'fear' and 'well-foundedness', rather than reading the terms as an inseparable unit'.

disregards the individual circumstances of the applicant.[184] Tuitt, for example, considers that the gradual shift towards more objectively determined criteria has meant undue reliance on a concept of reasonableness which has resulted in assessments 'tainted with local perceptions and thus often failing to be context-sensitive'.[185] In a similar vein, Noll criticises Hathaway and Hick's formulation for:

> [ ... ] overlook[ing] the fact that the three occurrences of the term 'fear' in the Convention actually accord a role to the applicant's will formation on the basis of the apprehension felt by her or him. If the translation of the term 'fear' into a 'forward-looking expectation of risk' shall be deemed acceptable, then it presupposes that the ownership of the expectation is vested in the refugee. A primary consideration of refugee status determination is to give the applicant a sufficient opportunity to formulate his or her assessment of future risks as part of the claim.[186]

Second, it has been seen to impose too rigid constraints on the assessment of individual circumstances, for example, by requiring it to focus exclusively on objective factors. Noll consider that the objective approach's 'total subjugation of fear to reason disenfranchises the refugee, while framing the Northern adjudicator as a gnostic agent, capable of better understanding reality in the South or the East through its Northern institutions'.[187] He appears to suggest that the 'objective approach' entails 'a procedure that merely lets the claimant express her fear in a truncated and fragmented form (e.g. as fear being the sense of trepidation only)'.[188] Third, it has been seen to encourage an approach that treats putative refugees as objects. Thus, Noll again considers that only by understanding the term 'fear' to include a reference to 'the emotive repercussions of risk in the individual' can one 'vest ownership with the individual and ensure promotion of human dignity'. 'Dignity', he writes, is a concept 'the exigencies of which are hardly exhausted by objectivist risk calculations in this particular case'.[189] He considers that to discard an assessment of 'fear' altogether 'would bereave the applicant of presenting her or his claim. That would throw the baby out with the bathwater.'[190]

A fourth discernible theme is to view the objective approach as 'confusing to apply' and leading to inconsistency and duplication. Thus, Kim canvasses that 'objective fear analysis forces asylum seekers to present the same evidence that proves the substantive three elements of being a refugee [namely 'the persecution, the protected grounds the alien is claiming, and the nexus of causation between the persecution and the protected category'] which is redundant and unnecessary'.[191]

---

[184] See e.g. Vevstad (n 1) 58–61.
[185] Tuitt (n 1) 80–83.
[186] Noll (2005) (n 1) 153.
[187] ibid 156, also citing Tuitt (n 1). He also cites Douzinas and Warrington's critique (n 1) 209, of reliance on the notion of 'reasonable fear'.
[188] Noll (2005) (n 1) 158.
[189] ibid 154.
[190] ibid 155.
[191] Kim (n 1) 193, 196.

### 4.1.3 Evaluation

The first three criticisms can best be addressed together. The central defect with each is that they do not engage with the evident fact that the objective approach has never asserted that subjective factors are irrelevant, only that subjective fear is not a necessary requirement. Although there are certainly examples of decisions purporting to apply the objective approach that fail to take subjective factors into account,[192] there is nothing inherent in the approach per se that prevents it taking full account of 'will-formation' or emotive dimensions. In criticising Hathaway and Hicks's 'objective approach', Noll objects that it overlooks the role of 'the applicant's will-formation', whereas '[a] primary consideration of refugee status determination is to give the applicant a sufficient opportunity to formulate his or her assessment of future risks as part of the claim'.[193] Yet it is far from clear that the 'objective approach' overlooks that. Hathaway and Foster, for example, highlight the fact that under a human rights-based assessment of serious harm 'physical or psychological vulnerabilities are appropriately taken into account'.[194]

Nonetheless, it must be acknowledged that some of Hathaway and Hicks and Hathaway and Foster's formulations of the 'objective approach' are capable of being read as suggesting that subjective fear can never form any part of the individual assessment. Consider, for example, the latter duo's statement that the concept of well-founded fear 'does not *in any sense* condition refugee status on the ability to show subjective fear'.[195] In some other passages the latter seem to consider that the inherent difficulties of reliably identifying subjective fear means that inquiring into it at all is 'an inherently problematic exercise'.[196] Such formulations are too limiting. In a sexual orientation case, for example, when one is analysing whether any of the reasons why a person would conceal his or her sexuality relates to a fear of persecution, that surely may at least sometimes involve an inquiry into a number of things including that person's state of mind and feelings. As noted earlier, any inquiry into a person's state of mind or motives would have to employ methods that comport with fundamental human rights, particularly the right to human dignity. It would also have to avoid reifying subjective fear. But that does not negate that such an inquiry might be valid and necessary in certain cases, if carried out sensitively and avoiding methods incompatible with human dignity. Accentuating too sharply the dangers of analysing a person's emotional state[197] can make it hard to understand how decision makers should assess, e.g. religious or sexual orientation cases where the importance of a person's faith to their identity or way of life or their own understanding of their sexual or religious identity, may be key. It could deny applicants the opportunity to present their case fully.

---

[192] Kim's own survey notes that 'many of the circuit court cases addressing the objective component of an asylum seeker's fear often do not mention the *Mogharrabi* factors, and the proper use of the objective standard still remains unclear'. See ibid 201.
[193] Noll (2015) (n 1) 153.
[194] Hathaway and Foster (n 1) 107–08, 137.
[195] Hathaway (n 1) 92 (emphasis added).
[196] Hathaway and Foster (n 1) 96.
[197] ibid.

However, the strong thrust of most of Hathaway and Foster's analysis and actual application of the objective approach is that the individual assessment component encompasses all aspects of the applicant's circumstances, including the 'physical or psychological'.[198] Their own analysis of concealment cases, for example, clearly recognises the importance of understanding the psychological (or 'endogenous') harms that can be involved. They note with approval the New Zealand Refugee Status Authority treatment of such cases as concerned with denial of the right to a meaningful 'private life'.[199] They point out that '[m]uch the same result would be reached by focusing instead on the risk of serious psychological harm inherent in the need to conceal one's sexual identity in order to be safe'. They observe that the ' "long-term deliberate concealment" of a person's sexuality, involving denial of the "fundamental right to be what they are", can amount to the kind of threat to "mental integrity" appropriately considered within the ambit of cruel, inhuman, or degrading treatment at international law'.[200]

As regards the fourth critical theme (alleging that the objective approach breeds confusion, inconsistency, and duplication), it is unsurprising, given that application of some kind of objective element is agreed on all sides to be necessary, that national case law is sometimes inconsistent and/or fails to approach its application correctly. But it is not immediately apparent why conceptually it should cause duplication. On a holistic approach to the refugee definition, the evidence is relevant to all elements. Once it is 'presented' it is there; it is not a case of the asylum seeker having to present it more than once.[201]

## 4.2 Commonalities Between the Bipartite Approach's 'Objective Element' and the 'Objective Approach': Key Components

The distinction surmised within the bipartite approach between the 'subjective' and 'objective' elements might be thought in itself to suggest that the 'objective element' is what remains to be established after the subjective element is established. However, UNHCR materials have always made clear that what it calls the 'objective element' requires considering both the applicant's personal situation and the background evidence.[202] Again, this fuzziness of terminology makes it hard to identify what the bipartite approach understands the components of the objective element to be. However, on both the bipartite approach's exposition of the 'objective element' and the objective

---

[198] ibid 106–08, 117, 122. See also MGs on Well-Founded Fear (n 1) 38, 40: '[t]he requirement to take account of "fear" is instead treated as a general duty to give attention to an applicant's specific circumstances and personal vulnerabilities in the assessment of refugee status'.
[199] Hathaway (n 1) 287. They cite *Refugee Appeal No 74665/03* (n 15) 114, and James C Hathaway and Jason Pobjoy, 'Queer Cases Make Bad Law' (2012) 44(2) NYU Journal of International Law and Politics 315.
[200] Hathaway and Foster (n 1) 287; they cite *HJ (Iran)* (n 89) 11–12, per Lord Hope.
[201] It appears that Kim's main point is that the objective component should be understood to be just 'an evidentiary burden that refers to the likelihood of persecution'. See Kim (n 1) 194–95.
[202] e.g. UNHCR Handbook (n 68) 42; UNHCR, Note on Burden and Standard of Proof in Refugee Claims (n 1) para 18: '[w]hile by nature, an evaluation of risk of persecution is forward-looking and therefore inherently somewhat speculative, such an evaluation should be made based on factual considerations which take into account the personal circumstances of the applicant as well as the elements relating to the situation in the country of origin'. See also *Chan Yee Kin* (n 51) para 429.

approach's understanding of its own essence (at least in its most well-known academic versions), it appears to have at least four main aspects.

### 4.2.1 Foundation in fact

A main component of the objective element, from its first articulation, is that it views the establishment of the 'well-founded[ness]' of the fear as requiring something more than simply a check as to whether an applicant's statements regarding fear are plausible (as was seemingly the position under the IRO Constitution). In the language of the 1979 Handbook, to be 'well-founded' fear must be 'supported by an objective situation'.[203] As noted by Dawson J in *Chan*, well-founded 'must mean something more than plausible, for an applicant may have a plausible belief which may be demonstrated, upon facts unknown to him or her, to have no foundation'.[204] So too, for the objective approach, the objective element requires an 'objective assessment'.[205] To avoid overuse of the term 'objective', this component shall be termed that of having a 'foundation in fact'.

### 4.2.2 Individual assessment

Another key component of the objective element is that it requires taking into account not just the background information but the applicant's particular circumstances. The bipartite approach's understanding of this component is illustrated by the UNHCR Handbook formulation:

> [ … ] it will be necessary to take into account the personal and family background of the applicant, his membership of a particular racial, religious, national, social or political group, his own interpretation of his situation, and his personal experiences— in other words everything that may serve to indicate that the predominant motive for his application is fear.[206]

Reflective of state practice, Article 4(3) of the EU Qualification Directive (QD) (recast) imposes a mandatory rule on evaluation of evidence on an individual basis.[207] As noted above (despite suggestions by some critic to the contrary), the objective approach also emphasises the 'importance of understanding the applicant's particular circumstances'.[208]

---

[203] UNHCR Handbook (n 68) para 38.
[204] *Chan Yee Kin* (n 51); see also *Acosta* [1985] A-24159781 (an individual's fear 'must have a solid basis in objective facts or events').
[205] Hathaway and Foster (n 1) 108; see also 92. Kay Hailbronner and Daniel Thym, *EU Immigration and Asylum Law: A Commentary* (2nd edn, Hart Publishing 2016) 1139 describe the position of the German Federal Administrative Court as requiring the individual's fear to be 'based on objective facts in order to be well-founded'.
[206] UNHCR Handbook (n 68) para 41.
[207] Directive 2011/95/EU of the European Parliament and of the Council of 13 December 2011 on standards for the qualification of third-country nationals or stateless persons as beneficiaries of international protection, for a uniform status for refugees or for persons eligible for subsidiary protection, and for the content of the protection granted (recast) [2011] OJ L 337/9 (QD (recast)); see also Directive 2013/32/EU of the European Parliament and of the Council of 26 June 2013 on common procedures for granting and withdrawing international protection (recast) (APD (recast)) Article 10(3)(a).
[208] Hathaway and Foster (n 1) 107–08, 137.

It would seem, therefore, that fairly understood, both the bipartite approach's concept of the objective component and the objective approach endorse the principle of individual assessment. But each understands this principle's parameters very differently. Within the bipartite approach, as we have seen, it requires (subject to exceptions) not only taking subjective fear into account but treating it as a necessary condition. If an applicant fails to demonstrate subjective fear, the well-founded fear test is not met. If (but only if) the decision maker finds there is subjective fear, that finding is then carried forward into the assessment of the objective element. The purpose of the latter assessment of the objective situation is thus to 'corroborate the subjective perception of risk'.[209] Within the objective approach, by contrast, subjective fear is only one factor to be taken into account when considering individual circumstances and its absence may not be determinative. Additionally, in its main incarnations, the 'objective approach' seeks to frame its analysis by direct reference to IHRL norms and the way they view the person.

4.2.3 Holistic inquiry

The formulation in the UNHCR Handbook of the objective component of the bipartite test[210] clearly requires a holistic inquiry in which the applicant's statements are 'viewed in the context of the relevant background situation'[211] focusing on examination of information available about conditions in the country of origin. Given the far greater monitoring in the modern era of countries of origin by numerous bodies, governmental and non-governmental, there is, unsurprisingly, no repetition of the concern voiced in the IRO Manual about general difficulties of accessing such information. Further, the objectivity required is now seen to focus not on the causes of a person's flight but on the reasons why they do not wish to return.[212] In this understanding, whether the objective element test fulfils its role depends on the finesse of decision makers in approaching all the relevant evidence in the case, both particular to the applicant and to general country evidence, in a holistic way. The objective approach also encompasses the importance of a holistic approach. As developed by Hathaway and Foster, this means that 'country data is normally a critical means of both putting an applicant's evidence into context, and more generally of ensuring a complete understanding of relevant risks'.[213] Article 4 of the QD (recast), Article 4(3) in particular, encapsulates a holistic approach.[214] A fourth main aspect of the objective element, in both the bipartite approach and the objective approach, is that it also constitutes a risk assessment. This is best dealt with after discussion of the temporal dimension and then the concept of risk itself.

---

[209] Zimmermann and Mahler (n 1) 339.
[210] Which significantly, in dealing with minors, calls on decision makers to place greater emphasis on objective information: see UNHCR Handbook (n 68) 217.
[211] UNHCR Handbook (n 68) para 42.
[212] In the bipartite approach, this means that 'the applicant's fear should be considered well-founded if he can establish, to a reasonable degree, that his continued stay in his country of origin has become intolerable for him for the reasons stated in the definition, or would for the same reasons be intolerable if he returned there' (ibid para 44).
[213] Hathaway (n 1) 122.
[214] QD (recast) (n 207).

## 4.3 Risk Assessment

### 4.3.1 Temporal dimension

In earlier chapters it was found useful to conceptualise the refugee definition in terms of personal, temporal, and material scope. The temporal scope was noted to have more than one dimension, since assessment requires sometimes looking into the past, to establish whether there has been past persecution, sometimes into the immediate present, and sometimes into the future.[215] This has been eloquently put by Bruce Burson:

> On the one hand, time points backwards because refugee claims are grounded in what has happened in the past.... [RSD], however, also faces forward in time. It reaches into the future and inquires as to the predicament of the claimant in his or her country of origin. Refugee status is recognised precisely because the future there for the claimant is anticipated to be one in which some form of serious harm will accrue to him or her at some projected point in time arising from a failure of the state of origin to protect the enjoyment of his or her fundamental human rights by reason of a Convention-protected ground.[216]

Not on its own but, in conjunction with the use of the present tense 'has' and the passive present tense of the expression 'being persecuted', the 'well-founded fear' element has been seen to entail a forward-looking assessment. The definition being cast in the present tense means that a person must possess the fear presently, but fear, of its nature, concerns something ongoing. However, recourse to ordinary meaning in this regard is of limited assistance, since the object of a person's fear in the present may sometimes be limited to what pertains immediately (e.g. 'I fear the bad weather just sweeping in') but sometimes further away ('I fear what will happen when the earth's poles lose all their ice').

In terms of context, the terms of the cessation provisions set out in Article 1C(5)–(6), by making clear that refugee status can cease if a change of circumstances demonstrates that an applicant cannot continue to refuse to avail himself of protection, reinforce the forward-looking orientation of Article 1A(2). It is clearly consonant with the Convention's object and purpose (and the principle of surrogacy) to require applicants to show that their fear is a current one, as otherwise they have not demonstrated a need for international protection. UNHCR,[217] judicial,[218] and academic materials[219] are virtually united in considering that the refugee definition is forward-looking.

---

[215] See p. 403 and p. 405.
[216] Bruce Burson, 'The Concept of Time and the Assessment of Risk in Refugee Status Determination' (Kaldor Centre Annual Conference, 18 November 2016) 1.
[217] See e.g. UNHCR, Note on Burden and Standard of Proof in Refugee Claims (n 1) para 18.
[218] *Sivakumaran* (n 66); *MIMA v Respondents S152/2003* [2004] 222 CLR 1 (Aus HC) (McHugh J); *BJU15 v MIBP* [2018] FCCA 1296; BVerwG 10 C 23.12 [2013].
[219] e.g. Goodwin-Gill and McAdam (4th edn) (n 1) 57; Hathaway and Foster (n 1) 105–08; Wouters (n 1) 83; Zimmermann and Mahler (n 1) 338.

Despite sometimes confusing use of terminologies, there has also been a broad consensus that forward-looking assessment must involve a degree of speculation.[220] Given that at least in common law countries a sharp distinction is sometimes drawn between inference (which is permissible) and speculation (which is impermissible),[221] it is important to underline that the consensus in practice disapproves not of speculation per se, but only of undue or 'sheer speculation'.[222] It does not disapprove of 'reasonable speculation'[223] or 'rational speculation'. In the words of Kirby J, '[b]ecause the future can never be told with certainty, particularly perhaps in the variable and sometimes unpredictable matter of persecution, this Court endorsed a test which both permits and requires rational speculation but denies the need for proof of affirmative certainty'.[224] As stated by Goodwin-Gill and McAdam, any refugee determination is necessarily an 'essay in hypothesis, an attempt to prophesy what might happen to the applicant in the future, if returned to his or her country of origin'.[225]

Mere agreement that the 'well-founded fear' element requires a forward-looking assessment does not, however, resolve the issue of how far into the future one must look. This needs addressing next.

*4.3.1.1 The temporal dimension and reasonable foreseeability*
It cannot be said that there is consensus about any precise formulation of the temporal aspects of the forward-looking test. As already noted, considerations of ordinary meaning give no singular answer on this aspect. In terms of context, though, the fact that Article 1C(5) specifies that refugee status can only be lost if there has been a change of circumstances sufficient for an applicant to be unwilling to avail himself or herself of protection, strongly indicates that more is required than temporary or superficial change.[226] As regards, object and purpose (and considering also that in the *travaux* concern was expressed about the need to avoid definitional limits that are 'too tight'),[227] it can be inferred that whatever precise formulation is used, it must avoid being temporally narrow (confined to the immediate or imminent future), as that would conflict with the purposes of providing protection to those who need it. Conversely, it cannot be temporally indefinite, as that would entail treating persons as refugees who are not presently or foreseeably in need of international protection. As

---

[220] UNHCR, Note on Burden and Standard of Proof in Refugee Claims (n 1) para 18: '[ ... ] an evaluation of risk of persecution is forward-looking and therefore inherently somewhat speculative'. In *MIEA v Guo* [1997] 191 CLR 559, 572 the Australian High Court stated that '[c]onjecture or surmise has no part to play in determining whether a fear is well-founded'. However, it went on to clarify that what it was rejecting was confined to 'mere speculation' ('A fear of persecution is not well-founded if it is merely assumed or if it is mere speculation.').
[221] See e.g. *Cothran v Town Council of Los Gatos* [1962] 209 Cal App.2d 647; *Masters Homes Improvement Australia Pty Ltd v North East Solutions* [2017] VSCA 88.
[222] *Ganze v Canada (MEI)* [1993] FCJ 1062 (cited Hathaway and Foster (n 1) 114).
[223] *SZVKA v MIBP* [2017] 320 FLR 453, 461. See Foster et al (n 1) 172–77.
[224] Kirby J in the High Court of Australia in *MIEA v Guo* (n 220); see also *Refugee Appeal No 72668/01* (n 92).
[225] Goodwin-Gill and McAdam (4th edn) (n 1) 57.
[226] In construing equivalent cessation provisions under the QD, the CJEU has identified a principle of non-temporariness: see Joined Cases C-175/08, C-176/08, C-178/08, and C-179/08 *Salahadin Abdulla and Others* [2010] ECR I-0000, para 73.
[227] See above p. 672.

stated by Hathaway and Foster, the approach must exclude risks that amount to 'sheer speculation', situations where there is only a 'bare possibility' of harm, or where the risk is 'so slight that it could be discounted'.[228]

Turning to Article 31(3) and/or other Article 32 VCLT considerations, the UNHCR Handbook's treatment of the Article 1A(2) provisions offers little insight, but its analysis of Article 1C(5) includes the observation that changes need to be 'fundamental' and that '[a] mere—possibly transitory—change in the facts surrounding the individual refugee's fear, which does not entail such major change of circumstances, is not sufficient to make this clause applicable'.[229] EU asylum legislation has entrenched the notion of an *ex nunc* assessment that looks forward from the date of decision[230] and as noted earlier, the QD (recast) provisions on protection include a requirement of non-temporariness. As regards judicial materials, there have been varying formulations, but the CJEU has confirmed that to be effective protection must be non-temporary and the Australian case law has adopted a test of 'reasonable foreseeability'.[231] 'Reasonable foreseeability' has also been the test adopted by the Human Rights Committee in relation to the right to life (Article 6 of the International Covenant on Civil and Political Rights (ICCPR)).[232] In the academic literature especially, emphasis has been placed on the notion of durable change. Hathaway and Foster, for example, seek to draw on the significance of Article 1C(5):

> The Convention's intentionally low risk threshold of well-founded means that states can—and should—comfortably err on the side of not pre-judging the durability and efficacy of still-evolving changes, knowing that cessation of status under Article 1C(5) is available if and when the observed changes take hold.[233]

There are obvious implications of the effect of time passing on the reasonableness of the assessment. Burson, for example, considers that 'the longer the future time frame, the less predictive certainty there is and the more speculative the risk assessment becomes because of the potential for mitigation, adaptation, and other risk-reducing actions'.[234]

More recently, there has been a strong case made by Anderson and others for express jettisoning of any notion of imminence.[235] They contend that:

---

[228] Hathaway and Foster (n 1) 114–15.
[229] UNHCR Handbook (n 68) para 135.
[230] Article 46 of APD (recast) (n 207) requires that 'Member States shall ensure that an effective remedy provides for a full and ex nunc examination of both facts and points of law, including, where applicable, an examination of the international protection needs pursuant to [the QD (recast)]'.
[231] See *Abdulla* (n 226) para 73. See also e.g. *MIEA v Wu Shan Liang* [1996] 185 CLR 259, 279; *EBZ17 v MIBP* [2019] FCCA 79. See also Zimmermann and Mahler (n 1) 341–42; German Federal Administrative BVerwG 10 C 25.10 [2011]: 'A change is permanent if a prognosis indicates that the change in circumstances is stable, i.e., that the factors on which persecution was based will remain eradicated for the foreseeable future.'
[232] UN Human Rights Committee (HRC), General Comment No 36 (2019): Article 6 (Right to Life) (3 September 2019) UN Doc CCPR/C/GC/35, para 18.
[233] Hathaway and Foster (n 1) 132.
[234] Burson (n 15) 8–10.
[235] Anderson et al (2019) (n 1) 111; Anderson et al (2020) (n 1) 155.

Analysis of the 'well-founded fear' test has tended not to invoke concepts of directness of harm, necessity, or any indication of when a risk needs to eventuate. It is possible that a risk becomes more 'remote' or speculative, and thus less likely, the further into the future it is anticipated, but imminence—in the sense of timing—has not and cannot be assumed to constitute an inherent aspect of the well-founded fear test.[236]

They caution against a too-ready classification of risk as remote:

> Rather, that test would appear to be sufficiently open-textured to accommodate a longer-frame assessment of future risk. It thus appears capable of encompassing the evolving nature of many contemporary forms of slower-onset harms which may present less immediate, but no less serious, risks to human rights.[237]

They seek to identify a number of situations in which decision makers should be prepared to take a 'longer-range view': children; slow-onset impacts of climate change; armed conflict; and health deterioration.[238] For example, in relation to armed conflict, they cite, inter alia, the observations of the UNHCR Guidelines on Armed Conflict,[239] regarding armed conflicts that have a long trajectory in time.[240]

The critique of the role of imminence by Anderson et al is forcefully made. However, three caveats are needed. First, whilst their analysis helps contextualise assessment in such situations, it must be doubted that it fully overcomes the difficulty identified by Burson. In relation, for example, to armed conflicts that are protracted, it will be of course important, for example, not to overlook that even though they may go through quiet periods, they may flare up again. However, the problem for decision makers is that any assessment dependent on harm materialising a long way into the future means accepting that there are more unknown variables to be considered and this consideration must inevitably impact on the assessment of whether the risk is real as opposed to remote.

Second, it is unclear applying a human rights approach that the notion of imminence can be entirely severed from the refugee definition. Applying a human rights approach requires having regard to the case law of both human rights treaty-monitoring bodies and the regional human rights courts. In relation to the prohibition of ill-treatment under Article 7 of the ICCPR and its regional equivalents, Anderson et al themselves note in this regard that 'the notion of imminence has been referred to and used explicitly in all jurisdictions examined for this research, and, in particular, has been engaged in some cases to reject a claim for international protection'.[241] Further, whereas in relation to the prohibition of ill-treatment recourse to the concept of imminence is

---

[236] Anderson et al (2019) (n 1) 119.
[237] ibid.
[238] Anderson et al (2020) (n 1) 174–80.
[239] UNHCR Guidelines No 12 (n 79).
[240] ibid para 176. Foster et al (n 1) consider one of the reasons decision makers do not take a longer-range view to be that they rely heavily on country of origin information 'which inherently deals with the past and present'.
[241] Anderson et al (2019) (n 1) 123.

at best occasional, greater use of it has been made in the case law on the right to life.[242] Given that the logic of a human rights approach is to apply IHRL norms (save when there are cogent reasons not to), this would suggest that at least when the risk of persecution is linked predominately to the positive obligation on the state to protect the right to life, there cannot be a full rejection of the imminence criterion.

### 4.3.2 The risk component

Insofar as one of the ordinary meanings of the term 'fear' is apprehension of future harm, it might be said that risk is part of this meaning. The forward-looking assessment is an apprehension of danger or harm. Risk is a loose synonym for 'danger'[243] and 'danger' is also (as we have seen)[244] a loose synonym for the object of the well-founded fear—the condition of 'being persecuted'.[245] As regards context, bearing in mind that the 'being persecuted' requirement encompasses threats of persecution,[246] use of the language of risk to elucidate the meaning of well-founded fear of being persecuted could be said to be almost inherent in the definition's language.

With respect to Article 31(3) and/or other Article 32 VCLT considerations, although the UNHCR Handbook formulation largely eschews the language of risk, it posits that fear is well-founded when an applicant can establish that conditions in his country of origin 'for the reasons stated in the definition' would 'be intolerable if he returned there'. Further, the Handbook notes that 'the word "fear" refers not only to persons who have actually been persecuted, but also to those who wish to avoid a situation entailing the risk of persecution'.[247]

Confirming UNHCR's acknowledgment of risk as a valid concept, its 2001 note on Article 1 stated that '[t]he key to the characterisation of a person as a refugee is risk of persecution for a Convention reason'.[248] More frequent references, including in the context of well-founded fear, can be found in later Guidelines.[249]

---

[242] On Article 6, ICCPR, see *Aalbersberg v Netherlands* (12 July 2006) Communication No 1440/2005, UN Doc CCPR/C/87/D/1440/2005, para 3.4 (see also HRC, General Comment No 36 (n 232) para 12, in relation to the use of force). On Article 2 ECHR, see e.g. *Osman v United Kingdom* App No 23452/94 (ECtHR, 28 October 1998) para 116; *Paul and Audrey Edwards v United Kingdom* App No 46477/99 (ECtHR, 14 March 2002) para 55; *Mastromatteo v Italy* App No 37703/97 (ECtHR, 24 October 2002) para 68.

[243] OED Online, available at<https://www.oed.com> accessed 28 August 2021, sense 5a. Treating 'risk' and 'danger' as synonyms could be said to be written into the wording of the 1975 Convention against Torture, which in Article 3(1) refers to '... *danger* of being subjected to torture' (emphasis added). See Convention Against Torture and Other Cruel, Inhuman or Degrading Treatment or Punishment (adopted 10 December 1984, entered into force 26 June 1987) 1465 UNTS 85.

[244] See p. 445.

[245] See Chapter 6.

[246] See pp. 384–385.

[247] UNHCR Handbook (n 68) para 45. Although early Guidelines do refer to 'risk' it is rarely in the context of 'well-founded fear': see e.g. UNHCR Guidelines No 1 (n 79) para 36(x); Guidelines No 2: Membership of a particular social group within the context of Article 1A(2) of the 1951 Convention and/or its 1967 Protocol relating to the Status of Refugees (7 May 2002) UN Doc HCR/GIP/02/01, para 17; Guidelines No 4: Internal Flight or Relocation Alternative Within the Context of Article 1A(2) of the 1951 Convention and/or 1967 Protocol Relating to the Status of Refugees (23 July 2003) UN Doc HCR/GIP/03/04, paras 13 and 20; Guidelines No 7 (n 79) paras 17–18; Guidelines No 8 (n 77) para 22.

[248] UNHCR, Interpreting Article 1 of the 1951 Convention (n 136) para 7.

[249] See UNHCR Guidelines No 10 (n 79) paras 15, 19, 29, 41, 44, and 46; and Guidelines No 12 (n 79) paras 17, 18, 19, 22, 24, 25, and 28.

Recourse to the concept of risk assessment is widespread at the judicial and academic level. Summarising judicial practice up to 1997, Carlier stated that: '[f]or the applicant to have a well-founded fear of being persecuted, there must be a risk of persecution'.[250] Anker summarises the position taken on the objective element in US decisions as being that 'an applicant must present credible, direct, and specific evidence that he or she has a reasonable fear of persecution as measured by objective and subjective standards'.[251] More recently, citing in support the CJEU judgment in *Y and Z*,[252] the EUAA Judicial Analysis on Qualification for International Protection states that '[t]his element of the refugee definition concerns assessment of "the extent of the risk" of being "subject to acts of persecution" on "return to his country of origin"'.[253] The existence of a risk component is heavily endorsed in the academic literature. In his study of European asylum law, Battjes states that '[t]he first element of the definition of refugees, "well-founded fear", addresses the "risk": a standard that the person concerned will indeed incur persecution or serious harm'.[254] Wouters states that '[t]he element of risk stipulated by the words "well-founded fear" is the backbone of the refugee definition as well as the prohibition on refoulement'.[255] Zimmermann and Mahler consider that '[t]he two-parts of the notion of "well-founded fear" try to circumscribe the situation where the respective risk level is high enough so as to trigger the obligation to grant international protection by the contracting party when refuge against persecution is sought'.[256] Hathaway and Foster align the understanding of 'well-founded fear' as an objective test with 'an anticipatory, objective assessment of risk'.[257] For them, reference to risk is an integral part of the forward-looking assessment. They refer to 'the risk-oriented understanding of "fear" as forward-looking apprehension, and as mandating only a prospective appraisal of an applicant's actual risk'.[258]

Thus, it can be seen that both the bipartite approach and the objective approach see the risk component as an integral part of the 'well-founded fear' concept.

*4.3.2.1 Risk assessment: Is there a need for an alternative approach?*
Whilst the above analysis has confirmed wide acceptance that the risk component is an integral part of the well-founded fear element, it would be wrong to represent that there has been complete unanimity about this. Scott in particular has voiced doubts by reference to what the Australian and UK courts have termed the 'Anne Frank principle'. He contends that this principle demonstrates that it is incorrect to understand well-founded fear as denoting a risk that is likely to accrue in the future. He considers that the proper location of risk assessment is within the notion of 'being persecuted', as

---

[250] Carlier (n 1) 696.
[251] Anker (n 1) §2.5, 68.
[252] *Y and Z* (n 95) 51.
[253] EUAA, 'Qualification for International Protection: Judicial Analysis' (n 98) 1.5.1, citing *Y and Z* (n 95) paras 76 and 78–79.
[254] Battjes (n 1) 224.
[255] Wouters (n 1) 83.
[256] Zimmerman and Mahler (n 1) 337.
[257] Hathaway and Foster (n 1) 108; see also MGs on Well-Founded Fear (n 1) 44.
[258] Hathaway and Foster (n 1) 110. Once cast in the language of risk, the principal question is then to determine the threshold for establishing such a risk.

distinct from being a separate assessment that takes place after determining whether what the claimant fears amounts to being persecuted.[259]

He criticises Hathaway and Pobjoy who, when discussing this principle, argue that if Anne Frank could have successfully avoided detection by hiding in the attic, then 'it is entirely correct to say that she was not at real risk of being sent to the concentration camps'.[260] He considers the position taken in *HJ (Iran)* by Lord Collins to be more cogent, namely that 'it remains the threats to Jews of the concentration camp and the gas chamber which constitutes the persecution'.[261]

It is this author's view that Lord Collin's analysis is apt, but it would be wrong to regard it as demonstrating the need for a novel understanding of the location of the risk component. The Anna Frank principle, properly understood, is just a restatement of the well-known principle that persecution can consist in the threat alone of persecution and does not necessarily depend on its materialisation.[262]

Scott's argumentation is an unsafe basis on which to cast the risk assessment adrift from the 'well-founded fear' inquiry. As analysed in Chapter 6, his attempt to refute it depends on importing the concept of risk into the concept of 'being persecuted' and in the process distorting ordinary usage as well as a purposive understanding.[263]

### 4.3.3 Conclusion on objective element

From the above it can be derived that despite their diametrically opposed views regarding the 'subjective element', both the bipartite approach and the objective approach agree on the essential components of the objective element: foundation in fact; individual assessment; holistic inquiry; and risk assessment. The only clear differences in their rendering of this element are that: (i) for the objective approach the objective element is the only element; (ii) in the bipartite approach, the objective element only comes into play, subject to limited exceptions, if an applicant has first established the subjective element; and (iii) whereas for the bipartite approach subjective fear is a necessary condition, for the objective approach the existence or not of subjective fear, whilst it can be a relevant consideration, is not a necessary condition.

## 4.4 Well-Founded Fear and Burden and Standard of Proof

Having analysed the basic meaning of the concept of 'well-founded fear', it remains to consider its interrelationship with evidence assessment. In particular we need to ask, does this element of the refugee definition entail or import anything as regards either the burden or standard of proof or both?

---

[259] Scott (n 16) 96–111.
[260] ibid, 107–09; Hathaway and Pobjoy (n 199) 350.
[261] *HJ (Iran)* (n 89).
[262] See e.g. '*Qui craint de souffrir, il souffre déjà de ce quail craint*' (Michel de Montaigne, *Les Essais*); or the Dutch saying '*Een mens lijdt dikwijls het meest door het lijden dat hij vreest*' (which roughly translates as 'the worst suffering is the fear of it'). See pp. 384–385.
[263] See pp. 380–383 and pp. 385–385.

On one view, the legal criteria set out in the refugee definition and the issue of their application to decision-making and assessment of evidence need to be kept wholly separate. This is the view implicit in the 1979 UNHCR Handbook which is divided into a 'Part One' on Criteria for the determination of refugee status and 'Part Two' on Procedures for the Determination of Refugee Status. In the opening paragraph of Part Two, the Handbook states that whilst it is obvious that to enable state parties to implement the provision of the Convention and Protocol, refugees have to be 'identified':

> Such identification, i.e. the determination of refugee status, although mentioned in the 1951 Convention (cf Article 9), is not specifically regulated. In particular the Convention does not indicate what type of procedures are to be adopted for the determination of refugee status. It is therefore left to each Contracting State to establish the procedure that it considers most appropriate having regard to its particular constitutional and administrative structure.[264]

However, the terms of the refugee definition cannot be treated as entirely neutral as regards the task of evidence assessment.[265] Article 1A(2) has to be read together with Article 33(1) which prohibits refoulement to countries where refugees would be at risk. If state parties were entirely free to establish whatever procedures they chose, there would be nothing to prevent them, for example, devising status determination systems that made no allowances for the difficulties asylum-seekers can face in proving their case or that applied an unduly onerous standard of proof. Such systems would also defeat the underlying protective purposes of the Convention and rob the refugee definition of its *effet utile*. Regulation of how identification of refugees is done (to use the phraseology of the Handbook) cannot be wholly regarded as a purely national (or indeed regional) law matter. Given that the terms of the refugee definition must be accorded a broad interpretation, and that assessing 'well-founded fear' requires an objective test (either by way of a bipartite approach or an objective approach), the standard for assessing whether such fear can be shown must be one that is not too strict or so demanding that it prevents or inhibits applicants from being able to establish their claims.[266]

Hence it is both legitimate and necessary to ask whether the refugee definition either entails or implies anything as regards burden and standard of proof.

---

[264] UNHCR Handbook (n 68) para 189. See also UNHCR, Note on Burden and Standard of Proof in Refugee Claims (n 1) para 2; UNHCR, Global Consultations on International Protection, 2nd Meeting (31 May 2001) EC/GC/01/12, para 4: 'the 1951 Convention ... does not set out procedures for the determination of refugee status as such, either for individual cases or in situations of large-scale influx'.

[265] More generally, even though the Refugee Convention contains no express provisions laying down procedures, it clearly presupposes some kind of identification process, otherwise there would be no way of establishing who falls within or outside the refugee definition: see Patricia Hyndman, 'The 1951 Convention and Its Implications for Procedural Questions' (1994) 6 IHRL 246; Reinhard Marx, 'Non-Refoulement, Access to Procedures, and Responsibility for Determining Refugee Claims' (1995) 7 IJRL 401. See also François Crepeau, *Droit d'asile: de l'hospitalité aux contrôles migratoires* (Bruylant 1995) 123, cited by Vincent Chetail, 'Are Refugee Rights Human Rights? An Unorthodox Questioning of the Relations Between Refugee Law and Human Rights Law' in Ruth Rubio-Marín (ed), *Human Rights and Immigration* (OUP 2014) 51.

[266] Gorlick (n 1) 360; Cameron (2018) (n 1) 84 (who cites Reneman (n 1) 85 in the EU context).

### 4.4.1 Burden of proof

That the refugee definition states nothing specific about the issue of the burden of proof is obvious. On the other hand, the drafters could not have been unaware of the general legal position according to which he who asserts must prove. It has never been seriously disputed that in order to show one is a refugee, an applicant has to substantiate his or her application and that they cannot simply claim refugee status on the basis that the state has failed to prove it should be denied to him or her. The UNHCR position regarding this continues to be as set out in paragraph 198 of the UNHCR Handbook, that 'it is a general legal principle that the burden of proof lies on the person submitting a claim'.[267] Judicial and academic sources take the same position. In the EU asylum law context, the CJEU noted that in international protection claims, '[t]he onus is ... on the applicant to substantiate those claims in a credible manner by submitting evidence which permits the competent authority to satisfy itself that those claims are true'.[268]

Complicating matters, by the term 'burden of proof' people can understand different things. A distinction is made between the burden of producing evidence (or the evidential burden) and the burden of persuasion (the legal burden).[269] Some though have also argued that there is no need for any such terminologies.[270]

Whatever the precise terms used, it is clear that there are special features about the situation of an applicant making a claim for refugee status as compared with most other administrative law proceedings. This insight permeates the UNHCR Handbook's approach, which considers that 'whilst the burden of proof in principle rests on the applicant, the duty to ascertain and evaluate all the relevant facts is shared between the applicant and the examiner'[271] and that '[t]he requirement of evidence should thus not be too strictly applied in view of the difficulty of proof inherent in the special situation in which an applicant for refugee status finds himself'.[272] Again, the notion of a shared burden is one broadly subscribed to in judicial and academic sources.[273] There is wide agreement that the special situation of the asylum applicant may require the host state (or UNHCR where it undertakes RSD) in certain contexts to take positive steps to assist the applicant in substantiating their application. That is clearest in the case of COI where the host state authorities may be far better placed to assemble all the relevant

---

[267] UNHCR Handbook (n 68) para 196. See also UNHCR, Note on Burden and Standard of Proof in Refugee Claims (n 1) paras 5–6; UNHCR, Interpreting Article 1 (n 136) para 10.
[268] Case C-56/17 *Bahtiyar Fathi v Predsedatel na Darzhavna agentsia za bezhantsite* [2018] ECLI:EU:C:2018:803, para 90. But in Case C-238/19 *EZ v Bundesrepublik Deutschland* [2020] ECLI:EU:C:2020:945, paras 54–55, the Court's position is more circumscribed.
[269] Zahle (n 107) 22–24. The German case law refers to a burden of persuasion: see e.g. BVerwG C 31.18.0.
[270] See e.g. Aleksandra Popovic, 'Evidentiary Assessment and Non-Refoulment' in Noll (2005) (n 1) 45. Noll (2021) (n 1) 610 remarks that '[t]he term "burden of proof" is at times reserved for adversarial trials and considered less appropriate for refugee status determination to the extent that it is performed in an inquisitorial setting', but goes on to approve the observation of Kirby J in *MIMIA v QAHH of 2004* [2006] HCA 53, para 136 that: 'the forensic context still reflects the reality of the decision-making process. If a party that could be expected to present material in support of its case fails to do so, that party cannot complain if the decision-maker decides that a basis for the relief claimed has not been established.'
[271] UNHCR Handbook (n 68) para 196.
[272] ibid para 197.
[273] Madeline Garlick, 'Selected Aspects of UNHCR's Research Findings' in Grutters et al (eds), *Assessment of Credibility by Judges in Asylum Cases in the EU* (Wolf Legal Publishers 2013); Cameron (2018) (n 1) 80.

background country information bearing on the applicant's case. Whilst EU asylum law in the shape of Article 4(1) of the QD (recast) does not strictly follow the UNHCR Handbook in referring to a shared burden, it does impose a duty on member states to assess the relevant elements of an application '[i]n cooperation with the applicant'.[274] Where it properly arises, this duty must at least have an ameliorative effect in respect of an applicant being able to discharge the legal burden.

It must not be forgotten either that refugee law has recognised that determination of some relevant matters may require the burden of proof to shift to the deciding authority. For example, recital 27 of the EU QD (recast) comes close to doing that in relation to internal protection in cases '[w]here the State or agents of the State are the actors of persecution or serious harm'; in such cases, 'there should be a presumption that effective protection is not available'.[275]

4.4.2 Standard of proof
Does the notion of well-founded fear require that assessment of who is a refugee adopts a particular standard of proof? If it does, must such a standard be a lower one than the ordinary criminal (beyond reasonable doubt) and ordinary civil (balance of probabilities) standards? Whilst it is really only in common law jurisdictions that these questions have been agonised over, their implications for a global understanding of well-founded fear cannot be ignored.

On a purely textual level, Article 1A(2) does not state anything about the standard of proof. This holds true even when reading the phrase holistically with other elements of the Article 1A(2) definition or other provisions of the Convention. As regards considerations of object and purpose, their implications will need further consideration below, but whatever significance is attached to them, they cannot be read as requiring a specific formulation of this standard. Applying Article 31(3) and other VCLT considerations, whilst UNHCR considers that the standard is 'reasonable degree' of likelihood,[276] or reasonable possibility,[277] it has been careful to note that it is mainly the common law jurisprudence that has largely supported the view that there is no requirement to prove well-foundedness conclusively beyond doubt, or even that persecution is more probable than not.[278]

---

[274] According to the second sentence of Article 4(1) QD (recast) (n 207), '[i]n cooperation with the applicant, it is the duty of the Member State to assess the relevant elements of the application'. In Case C-349/20, *NB and AB v SSHD* [2022] ECLI:EU:C:2022:151, para 64, the Court ruled (apropos the identical text in the original directive) that this second sentence is mandatory. See also Case C-756/21, *X v IPAT & anr* [2023] ECLI:EU:C:2023:523, paras 48 and 53.

[275] QD (recast) (n 207). Presumably this refers to a shift in the evidential burden. In *EZ* (n 268), para 55, the CJEU consider that in relation to establishing a connection between the reasons mentioned in Article 2(d) and Article 10 of Directive 2011/95 and the prosecution and punishment which an applicant will face as a result of his or her refusal to perform military service in the circumstances referred to in Article 9(2)(e) of that directive, '[s]uch a burden of proof would be inconsistent with the detailed rules for the assessment of applications for international protection, as set out in Article 4 of Directive 2011/95'.

[276] UNHCR Handbook (n 68) 42.

[277] UNHCR, Note on Burden and Standard of Proof in Refugee Claims (n 1) para 17.

[278] ibid. However, see (n 292), explaining that in several European countries, including Germany, the jurisprudence has confirmed that the test requires something less than 50 per cent likelihood.

Such caution reflects the fact that in civil law countries the refugee definition is often applied without recourse to concepts of standard of proof.[279] Further, within EU law, in which member state national legal systems are predominantly civil law, both the burden and standard of proof are generally seen as matters for the domestic courts and tribunals to determine (the principle of procedural autonomy) so long as they do not offend the principle of equivalence and/or the principle of effectiveness.[280] In addition, even though the QD (recast) largely duplicates (at Article 2(d)) the Convention's refugee definition, it includes a detailed article on evidence assessment (Article 4); yet the EU legislator did not choose in either to specify anything about the evidentiary standard.

A further difficulty with any attempt to view the common law approach as reflective of international consensus is that even among the leading courts of common law countries, there has not been complete agreement about the precise wording of the lower standard of proof. A variety of formulations are used, e.g. 'real chance', 'reasonable degree of likelihood', 'reasonable likelihood', 'real possibility', 'serious possibility', 'real and substantial danger', 'real and substantial risk', etc. Even though some leading common law cases have taken the view that these various formulations of the test are broadly equivalent,[281] that has not always been accepted.[282] Even within one and the same jurisdiction there is not always consensus on whether the well-founded fear notion can be conceived in terms of 'real risk'.[283]

Moreover, within some common law countries, different views have been expressed about whether the lower standard has to be applied uniformly to all aspects of evidence assessment and also about whether the same standard should apply to historical as well as to future facts. In Ireland, for example, the standard of proof applied to 'past facts' is the normal civil standard, i.e. the balance of probabilities, coupled with, where appropriate, the benefit of the doubt.[284] In Canada the courts apply a 'serious possibility' standard to future events but sometimes insist that this remains a probabilistic standard.[285] In the UK Supreme Court case of *MA (Somalia)*, Lord Dyson noted

---

[279] See Carlier et al (n 1), entries for each selected country under the headings *Proof*. Drawing on the jurisprudence, Carlier states that a fixed level of risk is not required as this level varies depending on the severity of the persecution feared; see also Battjes (n 1) 224–25; UNHCR, 'Summary of Deliberations on Credibility Assessment in Asylum Procedures, Expert Roundtable in Budapest on 14–15 January 2015' (5 May 2015) paras 56–59.

[280] See e.g. Case C-234/17 *XC and Others v Generalprokuratur* [2018] ECLI:EU:C:2018:853, paras 22–25; Case C-380/17 *K and B v Staatssecretaris van Veiligheid en Justitie* [2018] ECLI:EU:C:2018:877, para 56 and the case law cited.

[281] *Sivakumaran* (n 66); *Chan Yee Kin* (n 51).

[282] See the analysis of Brooke LJ in *Karanakaran v SSHD* [2000] 3 All ER 449 of the Canadian standard of proof and the critique by the Canadian Federal Court in *Adjei* (n 82) 684 (MacGuigan JA).

[283] See e.g. the different formulations discussed by the judges in *HJ (Iran)* (n 89), cited in Hathaway and Foster (n 1) 112. Compare *RT (Zimbabwe) and others v SSHD* [2012] UKSC 38, 55.

[284] See *ON v Refugee Appeals Tribunal & Others* [2017] IEHC 13, para 63.

[285] Thus, the IRB Legal and Policy resources publication, on 'Weighing Evidence', ch 4: Standard of Proof and Burden of Proof, states at para 4.1 that: 'while claimants must establish their case on a balance of probabilities, they do not have to establish that persecution would be more likely than not'. This document refers to *Adjei* (n 82) para 98; *Alam v Canada (MCI)* [2005] FC 4, para 8; *Gebremedhin v Canada (IRC)* [2017] FC 497, para 28; *Halder v Canada (Citizenship and Immigration)* [2019] FC 922; and *Sivagnanam v Canada (Citizenship and Immigration)* [2019] FC 1540. The case law seeks to draw a distinction between the applicable standard of proof (balance of probabilities) and 'the legal test' which is 'serious possibility': see *Ndjizera v Canada (MCI)* [2013] FC 601.

the case of *GM (Eritrea)*,[286] as supporting the view that the English Court of Appeal applied the standard of a reasonable degree of likelihood to the past facts asserted to be true by applicants (in particular, that they had left Eritrea illegally). Without deciding the matter, he went on to note that 'it would be desirable for the point to be decided authoritatively by this court on another occasion'.[287] All this very much bears out Gregor Noll's observation that 'there is no single, straightforward and generally accepted yardstick'.[288] It reminds us, as well, of the description in a 2002 Canadian study of the adjudication of refugee claims as the single most complex adjudication function in contemporary Western societies.[289]

Prior to the coming into force of the Nationality and Borders Act 2022, the leading authority was *Karanakaran*, in which, drawing on Australian cases, Brooke and Sedley LJJ held that it is open to decision makers to apply a normal civil standard to some items of evidence, as long as they do not forget when they arrive at the 'end point' to carry forward any findings about which, even if considered not probable, there was uncertainty.[290] This has sometimes been seen as what is conveyed by the UNHCR Handbook's treatment of the 'benefit of the doubt' notion.[291]

At the same time, in both common law and civil law countries, there has been marked agreement, even by those countries who use probabilistic language, that it would be contrary to the Refugee Convention to require applicants to show that

---

[286] *GM (Eritrea), YT (Eritrea) and MY (Eritrea) v SSHD* [2008] EWCA Civ 833.

[287] *MS (Somalia)* [2019] EWCA Civ 1345. Any such consideration has now been foreclosed by section 32, Nationality and Borders Act 2022: see (n 18). Section 32(1) and (2) provides that:
'(1) In deciding for the purposes of Article 1(A)(2) of the Refugee Convention whether an asylum seeker's fear of persecution is well-founded, the following approach is to be taken.
(2) The decision-maker must first determine, on the balance of probabilities—
(a) whether the asylum seeker has a characteristic which could cause them to fear persecution for reasons of race, religion, nationality, membership of a particular social group or political opinion (or has such a characteristic attributed to them by an actor of persecution), and
(b) whether the asylum seeker does in fact fear such persecution in their country of nationality (or in a case where they do not have a nationality, the country of their former habitual residence) as a result of that characteristic.'
By section 32(4), it is only if these two preconditons ((a) and (b)) are met that the decision maker can go on to determine 'whether there is a reasonable likelihood' or persecution. This appears to mean that if, for example, an applicant has only established under section 32(2)(b) that he or she left Eritrea illegally to a likelihood of 49 per cent or less, that is the end of the matter. That is so, even if the decision maker thinks that, in terms of future risk, the Eritrean applicant is 90–100 per cent likely to be at risk.

[288] Noll (2005) (n 1) 2. See in the same volume, Jens Vedstad-Hansen's remark that in relation to the standard of proof, 'there seem to be rather significant differences between the various jurisdictions as to the specification of the evidentiary standard applicable in refugee status determination cases': Vevstad (n 1) 61–62. See further Noll (2021) (n 1) 610–14 who argues that 'the interaction of the burden of proof, standard of proof, and benefit of the doubt in asylum is vague and logically deficient'.

[289] Rousseau et al (n 1) 43.

[290] In *Karanakaran* (n 282), Brooke, LJ noted that when assessing the future, the decision maker had to 'reach a well-rounded decision as to whether in all the circumstances there is a serious possibility of persecution for a Convention reason'. See also *SR (Iran) v SSHD* [2007] EWCA Civ 460, para 9. In relation to determination of nationality, see, however, *MA (Ethiopia) v SSHD* [2009] EWCA Civ 289, para 78; *AS (Guinea) v SSHD & Anor* [2018] EWCA Civ 2234.

[291] UNHCR, 'Beyond Proof Credibility: Assessment in EU Asylum Systems' (2013) 246–47; IARLJ, 'Assessment of Credibility in Refugee and Subsidiary Protection Claims under the EU Qualification Directive: Judicial Criteria and Standards' in Grutters Carolus, Elspeth Guild, and De Groot Sebastiaan (eds), *Assessment of Credibility by Judges in Asylum Cases in the EU* (Wolf Legal Publishers 2013); and also *KS (benefit of the doubt)* [2014] UKUT 552 (IAC).

their 'future risk' of persecution it is at least 50 per cent likely (e.g. German courts have made reference to 'considerable probability' but insisted this is less than 50 per cent).[292] Such an approach comports with that taken by the ECtHR in risk on return cases under Article 3 ECHR. In *Saadi v Italy*, in the context of Article 3 of the European Convention on Human Rights (ECHR), the Court held that the applicant is not obliged '[to prove] that being subjected to ill-treatment is more likely than not'.[293]

It cannot be said, however, that there has been enough case law to establish that this is a point of substantial consensus. The CJEU employs the language of risk without any apparent differentiation between assessment of evidence relating to the past or the future.[294]

Enough has been said to make plain that in terms of Article 31(3) and/or Article 32 VCLT considerations, there really cannot be said to be any substantial consensus regarding the standard of proof.

Whilst, therefore, application of VCLT considerations does not warrant reading into the refugee definition anything specific about the standard of proof, it is possible to discern two widely subscribed principles at work (although they are rarely phrased using these terms): an 'ameliorative' and a 'precautionary' principle.

The ameliorative aspect resides in what Grahl-Madsen described as 'the well-known fact that a person who claims to be a refugee may have difficulties in proving his allegations'.[295] In the EU law context, Reneman links this to the principle of effectiveness: '[it] follows from the principle of effectiveness that Member States cannot require asylum applicants to prove something which is impossible or excessively difficult to prove'.[296]

The 'precautionary' aspect relates to concerns about the particularly grave consequences of 'getting it wrong' in a context in which the stakes are high: sending back persons wrongly refused international protection status could result in their death or ill-treatment. Ensuring that burdens and standards are not too onerous is a way of

---

[292] *BVerwG C 31.18* [2019]; *BVerwG 10 C 33.07* [2008] para 37; *BVerwG 1 C 31.18* [2019]; see also Gorlick (n 1) 367–69; Sweeney (n 1) 720–04; UNHCR, Summary of Deliberations on Credibility Assessment in Asylum Procedures (n 279) para 60. See also Supreme Administrative Court (SAC) of Czech Republic 5 Azs 207/2017-36 [2019]; Supreme Court (Spain), App No 1699/2015 [2015] ECLI:ES:TS:2015:5211, 9. See further *MIEA v Guo* (n 220) 572; *Lopes v Canada (MCI)* [2010] FCJ 467; *Ndjizera* (n 285).

[293] *Saadi v Italy* App No 37201/06 (ECtHR [GC], 28 February 2008) para 140. See also *Case of Velásquez Rodríguez v Honduras*, Merits, Inter-American Court of Human Rights Series C No 4 (29 July 1988).

[294] See e.g. *Y and Z* (n 95) para 80.

[295] Grahl-Madsen (n 1) 145–46; it is also this aspect that the ECtHR had in mind in *RC v Sweden* App No 41827/07 (ECtHR, 09 June 2010).

[296] Reneman (n 1) 85. In Case C-635/17 *E v Staatssecretaris van Veiligheid en Justitie* [2019] ECLI:EU:C:2018:973, Advocate-General Wahl observed that: '[ ... ] the margin of appreciation which Member States enjoy should not be used in such a way as to defeat the objective of Directive 2003/86 [on the right to family reunification], which is to adapt the procedure regarding evidence to the particular difficulties which beneficiaries of international protection are likely to face. The requirements for such evidence must be realistic and adapted to the actual situation in which the persons in question find themselves' (para 51).

recognising 'what is at stake in a mistaken denial'.[297] Both the ameliorative and precautionary concerns do perhaps provide context to ongoing efforts to explain and justify the adoption of a standard of proof lower than more likely than not—and also for there being a shared burden of proof (or a shared duty of cooperation on the applicant and respondent in certain contexts).

## 5 Conclusions

This chapter has sought to consider the meaning of 'well-founded fear' by application of VCLT rules of interpretation. It was concluded in section 2 that there is no unequivocal ordinary meaning and that application of other VCLT considerations does not resolve the matter one way or the other. Sections 3 and 4 examined the two main approaches that have been developed to seek to articulate the meaning of the 'well-founded fear' element: the 'bipartite approach' and the 'objective approach'. Analysis of the relative merits and demerits of the bipartite approach led to the conclusion that it has not dealt adequately with the main criticisms directed against it by proponents of the objective approach. The main criticisms made of the 'objective approach' were seen to overlook that it incorporates individual assessment taking into account both physical and psychological circumstances.

Notwithstanding the differences between the two main approaches, it was seen to be significant that both broadly agree that the notion of well-founded fear requires an objective test, and both broadly agree about its key components: foundation in fact; individualised assessment, taking into account, inter alia, the applicant's personal circumstances; a holistic inquiry; and forward-looking risk assessment.

As regards the risk assessment, a broad consensus was noted about the well-founded fear phrase importing in temporal terms what has become known as a 'forward-looking assessment of risk'. Substantial agreement was noted that such assessment must avoid the pitfalls of demanding certainty on the one hand and accepting mere possibilities on the other. Also widely agreed was that some elements of conjecture and speculation are unavoidable. Although there is no agreement on nomenclature, there was found to be an underlying acceptance that the risk must be reasonably foreseeable. It was concluded that in general the well-founded fear notion has not been seen to require a criterion of immediacy or imminence.

Albeit the 'well-founded fear' notion does not establish anything in particular regarding the burden and standard of proof, a wide consensus was noted that the burden of proof in one sense or the other rests on the applicant though it is shared with the decision maker in certain respects. As regards the standard of proof, it was concluded that VCLT considerations do not indicate any particular standard. At the same time, broad agreement was found to exist that the standard cannot be either too lax or too high, in view of the ameliorative and precautionary principles.

---

[297] *Varga v Canada (MCI)* [2013] FC 494, para 5 (Rennie J); *Karanakaran* (n 282) (paras 44, 17); *MIEA v Wu Shan Liang* [1996] 185 CLR 259, 293. See further Cameron (2018) (n 1) 42–78.

## 5.1 Basic Propositions

In terms of basic propositions, we can therefore derive the following:

1. The 'well-founded fear' element contains[298] an objective test encompassing: foundation in fact; individualised assessment, taking into account, inter alia, the applicant's personal circumstances; a holistic inquiry; and forward-looking risk assessment.
2. The temporal scope of the risk assessment must avoid extremes that seek to impose either a criterion of undue immediacy or imminence on the one hand or a criterion of undue protraction into the future on the other.
3. Whilst the wording of the 'well-founded fear' element does not prescribe any particular burden or standard of proof, there is a substantial consensus that the burden of proof rests on the applicant, albeit what is meant by 'burden of proof' is not always clear. However, the decision maker has a shared duty to co-operate with the applicant in substantiating his or her application.
4. In relation to the standard of proof, there is no consensus as to what it should be, save that it must avoid imposing too high or too low a threshold.

## 5.2 Suggested Propositions

Whilst lacking substantial consensus, the following emerge from analysis of the main debates that have arisen over the meaning of well-founded fear so far:

1. Although disagreements still subsist regarding whether the phrase 'well-founded fear' must incorporate a subjective test, there are cogent reasons for regarding the test as essentially an objective one.
2. Whilst there is no agreement as to the standard of proof (or standard of persuasion), it is accepted that in order not to defeat the protective purpose of the Convention, application of the well-founded fear test must apply both an ameliorative and a precautionary principle.
3. It would be contrary to the Refugee Convention to require applicants to show that their feared persecution is at least 50 per cent likely.

---

[298] Deliberately, this formulation avoids specifying whether the 'objective test is the only test or whether there is also a subjective test.

# 12
# Conclusions

| | | | | |
|---|---|---|---|---|
| Introduction | 714 | 1.10.1 Basic propositions | 722 |
| 1 Contents of the Working Definition | 715 | 1.10.2 Suggested propositions | 723 |
| 1.1 Chapter 1: The Refugee Definition | 715 | 1.11 Chapter 11: 'Well-Founded Fear' | |
| 1.1.1 Basic propositions | 715 | (*'Craignant Avec Raison'*) | 724 |
| 1.1.2 Suggested propositions | 715 | 1.11.1 Basic propositions | 724 |
| 1.2 Chapter 2: Interpretation | 716 | 1.11.2 Suggested propositions | 724 |
| 1.2.1 Suggested propositions | 716 | 2 Nature and Status | 724 |
| 1.3 Chapter 3: Approaches, Ordering, Interrelationships, Modalities | 716 | 2.1 Rationale for a Working Definition | 724 |
| 1.3.1 Key propositions | 716 | 2.2 Legal Form | 725 |
| 1.3.2 Suggested propositions | 716 | 2.3 *Lex Lata* and *De Lege Ferenda* | 725 |
| 1.4 Chapter 4: Nationality and Statelessness (*Nationalité et condition d'apatride*) | 717 | 2.4 Role of the 'Suggested Propositions' | 725 |
| | | 2.5 Framework for the Definition | 726 |
| 1.4.1 Basic propositions | 717 | 2.6 Definition as a Whole | 727 |
| 1.4.2 Suggested propositions | 717 | 2.6.1 An underlying principle or principles? | 728 |
| 1.5 Chapter 5: 'Outside the Country …' (*'Hors du pays …'*) | 717 | 2.7 Quasi-State Practice | 728 |
| 1.5.1 Basic propositions | 717 | 2.8 Implications of Existing Codification Measures | 729 |
| 1.5.2 Suggested propositions | 718 | 2.8.1 Relevance of QD (recast) | 729 |
| 1.6 Chapter 6: 'Being Persecuted' and Serious Harm (*'Être persécutée' et préjudice grave*) | 718 | 2.9 Existing Sources of Interpretive Guidance | 730 |
| 1.6.1 Basic propositions | 718 | 2.9.1 Governmental guidance | 730 |
| 1.6.2 Suggested propositions | 719 | 2.9.2 Examples of academic interpretive guidance | 731 |
| 1.7 Chapter 7: 'Being Persecuted' and Protection (*'Etre persécutée' et protection*) | 719 | 2.9.3 Examples of judicial interpretive guidance | 731 |
| 1.7.1 Basic propositions | 719 | 2.9.4 UNHCR interpretive guidance | 732 |
| 1.7.2 Suggested propositions | 720 | 2.10 Possible Drawbacks to the Working Definition Approach | 733 |
| 1.8 Chapter 8: 'Being Persecuted' and the Internal Protection Alternative (*'Etre persécutée' et l'alternative de protection à l'intérieur du pays*) | 721 | 3 How Does the Working Definition Represent Progress? | 736 |
| 1.8.1 Basic propositions | 721 | 4 How Might Greater Clarity Be Achieved? | 738 |
| 1.8.2 Suggested propositions | 721 | 4.1 UN Level | 739 |
| 1.9 Chapter 9: The Availment Clause: 'To Avail Himself of the Protection' (*'Se Réclamer de la Protection'*) | 722 | 4.2 Other Fora | 739 |
| | | 4.3 UNHCR Level | 740 |
| 1.9.1 Basic propositions | 722 | 4.3.1 UNHCR Handbook | 741 |
| 1.9.2 Suggested propositions | 722 | 4.3.2 UNHCR Guidelines on International Protection | 742 |
| 1.10 Chapter 10: Refugee Convention Reasons: 'For Reasons Of' (*'Du Fait de'*) | 722 | 4.3.3 The way forward | 743 |

## Introduction

How many more studies of the refugee definition will it take before we accept that more must be done to clarify it? If tackling all the major issues and arguments affecting this definition now requires books the length of this one, does that not show that something is up? This final chapter explores further what can and might be done about this problem.

As explained in Chapter 1, this study leaves to one side issues regarding whether the definition of refugee in Article 1A(2) is still fit for purpose or ethically sound. That is not to diminish such issues' importance, but only to concentrate on the definition itself. The basis on which this study proceeds is that this definition continues to be the cornerstone of the international protection system. A principal aim has been to interrogate its meaning and content in a contemporary context.

It is possible that readers will see the main worth of this study to reside in its analyses of different elements of the refugee definition and perhaps also in its first three chapters dealing with 'framework' matters. However, the mission from the start has been to go beyond analysis of each element in turn by trying to achieve a working definition. With that in mind, this final chapter endeavours to draw together the main themes of the book by examining four questions: (1) what basic propositions form this study's 'working definition' of key terms of the refugee definition; (2) what is their nature and status; (3) how does its working definition represent progress (if any); and (4) how might it help achieve greater clarity regarding interpretation of the Article 1A(2) definition of refugee? Undoubtedly the most important matter from the point of view of this book's main rationale is question 3. For that reason, section 2 of this chapter will be devoted to it.

In Chapter 1, reference was made to Arboleda and Hoy's prescient observation thirty years ago that to resolve the problem of lack of clarity about who is a refugee, a two-fold approach was called for:

> First, more specific criteria must be developed, in order to eliminate the ambiguities of the Convention definition as far as possible. Second, and most importantly, the Convention definition must be applied uniformly.[1]

Seen in this context, this study can only hope to have tackled resolution of the first stage of the problem. However, as they pointed out, until the first stage is resolved, there can be no second stage.[2]

It was contended in Chapter 1 that the guidance provided by the United Nations High Commissioner for Refugees (UNHCR), case law, governmental publications, and academic studies does not contain or achieve a further definition of the key elements of Article 1A(2) ready-made. Accordingly, one of the aims of the book has

---

[1] Eduardo Arb7oleda and Ian Hoy, 'The Convention Refugee Definition in the West: Disharmony of Interpretation and Application' (1993) 5 IJRL 66, 76.

[2] ibid: 'the second [stage] is predicated on the implementation of the first'. In Chapter 1 (C1P75), this study proposes a criterion of convergence rather than uniformity, the latter being seen as utopian.

been to analyse each main element of the definition with a view to eliciting what propositions could now be said to be widely agreed. In each of the chapters devoted to the definition's key elements—Chapters 4 to 11—focus was placed on analysing various sources, in accordance with the rules of interpretation set out in the Vienna Convention on the Law of Treaties (VCLT) in order to see what has been agreed and what remains unsettled. In this regard, each chapter took particular note, inter alia, of the interpretive guidance provided in the 1979 UNHCR Handbook as well as in subsequent UNHCR materials. It was explained that for the purposes of constructing a working definition, focus had to be, not on this Handbook, but on UNHCR's 'ongoing guidance', since the Refugee Convention is a living instrument. It was argued that whilst UNHCR guidance cannot be treated as dispositive, no proposition can be treated as basic if UNHCR in its ongoing guidance disputes it. The same point was made in relation to case law as contained in leading decisions of senior courts and tribunals worldwide. Governmental sources are also relevant but are presently too limited and national law-oriented to play a major role. In relation to academic sources, it was remarked that in view of their great diversity, for them to serve as a point of reference for identifying consensus, focus had to be on the preponderance of scholarly opinions.

In Chapter 1, it was also contended that despite continuing concerns about divergent interpretations of key elements of the refugee definition, a significant number of debates have now been settled and there has been considerable progress in plain sight towards achieving greater consistency and that it is now possible to give the definition greater specificity and detail.

It is time then to bring together in one place the 'basic propositions' set out at the end of each chapter on the key elements of the refuge definition, so as to assemble this study's 'working definition' of these key elements (taking each chapter in sequence). In each instance, they are accompanied by a separately headed sub-head, 'suggested propositions', which reflect the author's own views on certain key issues that remain contested.

## 1 Contents of the Working Definition

### 1.1 Chapter 1: The Refugee Definition

1.1.1 Basic propositions
The two major pillars of interpretive guidance on the refugee definition are UNHCR guidance and the case law of courts and tribunals. However, both governmental guidelines and academic materials continue to play a highly significant role.

1.1.2 Suggested propositions
Valid concerns about seeking to define key elements of the refugee definition do not and must not defeat the endeavour to achieve a correct interpretation and to develop a 'working definition'. Such concerns have force only against absolutist or fixed-list approaches to definition.

## 1.2 Chapter 2: Interpretation

### 1.2.1 Suggested propositions
In light of earlier remarks, it is not possible to identify any basic propositions relating to methods of interpretation. It is possible, however, to suggest the following:

1. Important contributions towards interpreting the meaning of key elements of the refugee definition have been made both by those who have expressly applied VCLT rules of interpretation and those who have not.
2. There is an increasing acceptance that in order to establish the true meaning of the key terms of Article 1A(2), the interpreter must actively apply VCLT rules.
3. A key feature of VCLT rules is that they confirm that treaty interpretation must strive to provide an autonomous, universally correct, meaning. Further, although not prescriptive as to outcome, they do constitute a set of generally applicable guidelines.
4. It follows that if any interpretive statements about key terms of the refugee definition are inconsistent with such rules, then they cannot be said to represent instances of the pursuit of a truly universal meaning.

## 1.3 Chapter 3: Approaches, Ordering, Interrelationships, Modalities

### 1.3.1 Key propositions
Given co-existing differences over approaches, views on interrelationship, ordering, and modalities, it cannot be said that there is any widespread agreement regarding any of these matters. In particular, it has to be recognised that important contributions to clarifying various aspects of the refugee definition have been made both by approaches to the refugee definition that apply International Human Rights Law (IHRL) norms and those that do not.

### 1.3.2 Suggested propositions
There are, however, several suggested propositions that flow from this author's own analysis, as follows:

1. The human rights approach to ascertaining the meaning of key terms of the refugee definition coheres well with VCLT rules of interpretation. It remains the dominant approach and the main criticisms made of it to date do not withstand scrutiny. Such an approach confirms that refugee law is a branch of law operating within the framework of international law. Whilst other approaches exist, it should be seen as the approach most likely to yield greater analytical clarity and appropriate resolution of new issues as they arise.
2. There is no fixed order for analysing the different elements of the refugee definition.
3. Whilst there exist differing views about which clauses or elements of the definition are key, there is a broad consensus that the definition's elements are to be understood as closely interrelated and their interpretation best approached holistically.

## 1.4 Chapter 4: Nationality and Statelessness (*Nationalité et condition d'apatride*)

### 1.4.1 Basic propositions

1. Establishing nationality or statelessness is an essential element of the refugee definition.
2. The primary framework for interpreting this element of the definition is the international law on nationality.
3. Nationality within the meaning of its main use in Article 1A(2) concerns the legal bond between the individual and the state.
4. In temporal terms, it concerns actual nationality.
5. In relation to the phrase 'not having a nationality', this can now be seen to identify stateless persons as defined in Article 1 of the Convention Relating to the Status of Stateless Persons. In parallel with the position that applies to nationals, the temporal scope of this term is actual status.
6. The effect of the second paragraph of 1A(2) is that a person of multiple nationality must have a well-founded fear of persecution in each country of nationality, unless there are 'valid reasons' for not availing himself or herself of their protection. Two obvious instances that would constitute valid reasons are non-admission and risk of refoulement to the country of persecution.
7. Assessment of inability to return requires a hypothetical inquiry into the situation a stateless person would face if returned.

### 1.4.2 Suggested propositions

1. Whilst IHLR norms have become more relevant to determination of nationality, the primary set of rules governing such determination remain those set out in the international law.
2. Treating nationality as meaning actual nationality should not be extended to embrace 'inchoate nationality' or 'potential nationality'.
3. In relation to Article 1A(2), second paragraph, dealing with multiple nationals who can show 'valid reasons' why they are not required to show a well-founded fear of persecution in each country, there is no requirement for nationality to be 'effective'.

## 1.5 Chapter 5: 'Outside the Country …' ('*Hors du pays …*')

### 1.5.1 Basic propositions

1. The 'outside the country' requirement must be construed so as to require physical absence from the territory of a country, the latter being understood in jurisdictional terms.
2. In relation to nationals, they must be outside the territory of their state.
3. '[H]abitual residence' does not require domicile or permanent residence.
4. A person can have more than one country of former habitual residence.

### 1.5.2 Suggested propositions

1. In the phrase 'country of former habitual residence', the 'country' need not be a state but must be one in which there are actors controlling the territory or a substantial part of the territory of that country.
2. As regards the temporal dimension of the concept of former habitual residence, there is no sound basis for imposing either a first or last country requirement, notwithstanding some support in both case law and the wider literature for one or the other view.
3. Despite the lack of any provision for stateless persons that parallel those of the second paragraph of Article 1A(2) (which concerns persons with multiple nationality), the arguments for treating stateless persons who have more than one country of former habitual residence as subject to analogous requirements outweigh those which favour giving stateless persons preferential treatment.
4. Whilst there is some support in the case law and academic literature for the view that in respect of stateless children born in the receiving country they can be treated for Article 1A(2) purposes as having the same country of former habitual residence as their parents, it is limited and requires a reading contrary to a proper application of VCLT rules of interpretation.

## 1.6 Chapter 6: 'Being Persecuted' and Serious Harm ('*Être persécutée*' et *préjudice grave*)

### 1.6.1 Basic propositions

1. The personal scope of the refugee definition is universal.
2. Determining whether an applicant is 'being persecuted' requires assessment relative to the individual.
3. The 'being persecuted' element requires human agency and is to be analysed in terms of acts or measures of persecution.
4. Actors of persecution can be state or non-state actors.
5. Laws and related measures (including laws of general application) can be persecutory in certain circumstances.
6. In order to rise to the level of the persecutory, harm must attain the level of sufficient seriousness or severity. Whilst discrimination can be persecutory in itself, more commonly it will not be persecutory unless established by reference to a number of cumulative harms.
7. Discrimination is not a necessary condition of 'being persecuted'.
8. Persecutory harm can be actual or threatened.
9. Persecutory harm can sometimes be indirect or derivative.
10. Acts or measures can be said to be persecutory even though directed, not at a person individually, but at a group of which the individual is a member.
11. The refugee definition allows for group persecution.
12. Among situations that can engender the phenomenon of group persecution are situations of armed conflict or generalised violence.

13. In terms of temporal scope, Article 1A(2) imposes a requirement of current persecution: it poses the hypothetical question of whether, if return were to take place now (*ex nunc*), persecution would arise.
14. It is a logical corollary of the focus in Article 1A(2) on current fear of persecution that a person can have a '*sur place*' fear, i.e. a fear arising out of events or his or her own actions that have occurred since the applicant has been outside the country of origin.
15. Past persecution does not in itself constitute 'being persecuted', but the fact that an applicant has already been subject to persecution is a serious indication of such, unless there are good reasons to consider that such persecution will not be repeated.

### 1.6.2 Suggested propositions

1. Applying VCLT rules, interpretation of the meaning of 'being persecuted' requires giving priority to 'object and purpose' considerations.
2. Application of VCLT rules confirms that the human rights approach to the 'being persecuted' element of the refugee definition is the dominant approach.
3. The meaning of 'being persecuted' is usefully elucidated by considering the modalities of persecution in terms of acts and actors of persecution.
4. Use of the phrase 'being persecuted' focuses inquiry on the predicament of the refugee.
5. The human agency necessary for an act to be persecutory must be shown to be a substantial if not a predominant cause.
6. Understanding that different types of harms can be persecutory—especially physical and related harms; psychological and related harms; socio-economic, and cultural harms; and environmental harms—is enhanced by a human rights approach.
7. Harms carried out by non-state actors only become persecutory if the state is unwilling or unable to provide effective protection against such harms.
8. As part of the consideration of material scope, it is necessary to have regard to forms of persecution that are specific to certain categories of person, especially age- and child-specific persecution; gender-specific persecution; LGBTI+-specific persecution, and disability-specific persecution. Such consideration is vital in order to ensure that 'being persecuted' element is interpreted in a way that is sensitive to individual vulnerabilities.
9. 'Persecutory intent' is not a necessary requirement of 'being persecuted'.
10. In *sur place* claims there is no requirement of 'good faith'.

## 1.7 Chapter 7: 'Being Persecuted' and Protection (*'Etre persécutée' et protection*)

### 1.7.1 Basic propositions

1. Persons are not in need of international protection if they can find protection in their home state.
2. A state has a basic duty to protect those within its jurisdiction.

3. In addition to being willing and able to provide protection, the protection provided by actors of protection must include being accessible, effective, and non-temporary.

### 1.7.2 Suggested propositions

1. Notwithstanding recent criticisms to the contrary, surrogacy is a principle underlying the refugee definition.
2. Treating protection as an integral part of the meaning of 'being persecuted' is at once consistent with VCLT rules of interpretation and with the dynamics of human rights law. It is particularly important as a way of ensuring that the refugee definition fully addresses harm emanating from non-state actors and properly recognises that connection may be made with a Convention reason either by reference to the non-state source of harm or the state's inadequate response.
3. As case law and wider learning have developed, it is clear that treating protection as an integral part of the meaning of 'being persecuted' does not entail applying misplaced notions of state responsibility and does not displace the role of individual assessment or impose undue evidential burdens on applicants. However, the notion of state responsibility as embodied in IHRL remains essential to a human rights approach to persecution and protection.
4. Whilst the notion that a state has a basic duty to protect is widely endorsed, it is only international human rights law that has given it concrete content in terms of a set of negative and positive obligations that states (or de facto state entities) must meet in order to avoid sufficiently severe violations of human rights.
5. Applying a human rights approach, protection within the meaning of Article 1A(2) must possess not just the negative quality of countering serious harm; it must also possess several positive qualities. To accord with international human rights law, these qualities entail that states have a duty to organise the governmental apparatus (and indeed all the structures through which public power is exercised), so that they are capable of securing human rights and the rule of law. In the refugee law context, the duty to protect imposed by human rights law, requires that the state protects against sufficiently severe violations of human rights.
6. There remains no consensus about whether or not states are the only entity that can provide protection under Article 1A(2). However, whichever view is taken, it is clear that no entity can meet the requirements of protection outlined above unless they exhibit the aforementioned five qualities of protection, including a stable and enduring character.
7. There is powerful judicial and academic support for the view that in assessing the threshold of the effectiveness of state actor activities, no account can be taken of the role of private civil society actors, but how that view can be reconciled with a holistic approach to assessment of well-founded fear of persecution remains moot.

## 1.8 Chapter 8: 'Being Persecuted' and the Internal Protection Alternative (*'Etre persécutée' et l'alternative de protection à l'intérieur du pays*)

### 1.8.1 Basic propositions

1. IPA analysis requires an individual assessment.
2. IPA analysis is forward-looking.
3. The IPA analysis is premised on a prior finding of well-founded fear of being persecuted for a Convention reason in the home area.
4. An IPA must, as a precondition, be safe in the sense that it is both free from a well-founded fear of persecution and accessible.
5. The conditions in the IPA must not be such as would compel an applicant to return to the home area.
6. In cases that call for an IPA analysis, the causal nexus requirement of the refugee definition is satisfied simply by virtue of an applicant being able to show a well-founded fear of being persecuted for a Convention reason in their home area.

### 1.8.2 Suggested propositions

1. The concept of IPA is an integral part of the refugee definition. It would be contrary to the principle of surrogacy if an applicant could qualify as a refugee even though he or she had a viable IPA.
2. The IPA analysis must be tied back to the refugee definition; it is not a test independent of whether an applicant has a well-founded fear of being persecuted in their country of origin.
3. An IPA must, as a precondition, be accessible (increasingly understood to mean that it must be safe practically and legally to travel to, gain admittance into, and settle in).
4. To be a viable IPA, the alternative part or parts of the country must be a place in which the applicant can settle. Settlement means stay that is more than temporary.
5. Accepting that harms at a lesser threshold than ill-treatment can establish that there is no internal protection in a <u>part of the country</u> should not mean that assessment of whether there is protection against persecution in <u>the country as a whole</u> is assessed at a lower threshold also.
6. In order to ensure that the IPA analysis is tied back to the refugee definition, it is vital that IPA analysis contains a final stage in which the assessment of risk in any putative IPA is incorporated into the overall assessment of whether there is a well-founded fear of being persecuted in the country of origin.
7. Ordinarily the refugee status determining authority has:
    (i) the burden of raising IPA as an issue;
    (ii) the duty to give notice that an IPA is under active consideration; and
    (iii) a duty to specifically identify (but not necessarily precisely) a part or parts of the country that are said to afford a viable IPA.

## 1.9 Chapter 9: The Availment Clause: 'To Avail Himself of the Protection' ('*Se Réclamer de la Protection*')

### 1.9.1 Basic propositions

1. Protection encompasses both internal and external aspects (the latter being understood as diplomatic and consular protection).
2. Internal protection (in the sense of protection within the country of origin) is a crucial component of the refugee definition.
3. Inability and unwillingness (which are both concepts expressly identified in the availment clause) are key requirements for assessing the availability of protection.
4. In terms of external protection, it remains the case that issues of inability and unwillingness on the part of applicants in relation to diplomatic and consular protection can sometimes be ones that need to be addressed in determining whether someone meets the requirements of the refugee definition.

### 1.9.2 Suggested propositions

1. The approach of reading the availment clause as connoting external protection exclusively suffers from numerous difficulties, most notably that it would entail operating two different concepts of protection within Article 1A(2). The approach of reading the clause as connoting internal protection exclusively also suffers from numerous difficulties, most notably that it involves wholesale duplication, given that all agree that an internal protection inquiry must take place within either the well-founded fear or the being persecuted elements of the definition, or both.
2. The only feasible approach is to read the availment clause as connoting both internal and external protection but to understand its internal protection dimension as being most appropriately conducted within either the well-founded fear or being persecuted elements, or both.

## 1.10 Chapter 10: Refugee Convention Reasons: 'For Reasons Of' ('*Du Fait de*')

### 1.10.1 Basic propositions

1. The nexus clause imposes limits on the types of persecution necessary to establish refugeehood.
2. The five reasons are united by a common theme. That most frequently identified is non-discrimination.
3. In relation to each reason, they may be either real or attributed.
4. As regards race, it must be interpreted in a very wide sense, to include all kinds of ethnic groups and groups with a common nationality, tribal affiliation, religious faith, shared language, and traditional ways and backgrounds.

5. Religion must be understood to encompass not just its primary meaning (religion in the form of belief) but also religion as a form of identity and religion as a way of life. It must be interpreted to include the right to hold or not to hold a religious belief, the right not to be forced to follow a religion, and the right to change one's religion.
6. The meaning of nationality in this part of the definition spans both the legal and sociological senses of the term and thus, in addition to nationality in the legal sense, covers ethnic, cultural, and linguistic groups, and groups with common geographic or political origins. This reason also encompasses stateless persons.
7. Whilst disagreements persist about whether membership of a particular social group (MPSG) is best interpreted by applying a 'protected characteristics' or 'social perception' approach, or both, disjunctively or cumulatively, there is consensus that: the MPSG ground cannot be unlimited; that a particular social group (PSG) must exist independently of the persecution; that a PSG does not have to be cohesive or interdependent or homogeneous or associational; and that a PSG does not need to be of a particular size.
8. In the 'political opinion' ground, the notion of 'opinion' is almost unlimited. Whilst disagreement remains as to the meaning of 'political' in this ground, it is accepted that it must be one that can accommodate, where relevant, opinions about non-state actors.
9. In non-state actor cases, the causal connection can potentially be either with the non-state actor or the state.
10. To establish the causal nexus between the reason for persecution and the persecution, it is not necessary that a reason be the sole or dominant cause.

### 1.10.2 Suggested propositions

1. Whilst the Convention reasons can be analysed without adoption of a human rights approach, the latter provides the best way of giving shape and contents to their analysis.
2. The *Acosta/Ward* framework has significant drawbacks, both for understanding the commonalities of all five reasons, and for conceptualising the MPSG reason.
3. Each reason should be given a broad meaning.
4. A non-evaluative approach should be taken to all five reasons: it is not required that a Convention reason reflects a particular moral or ethical quality.
5. As presently formulated, neither the 'protected characteristics' approach nor the 'social perception' approach to the Convention reason of membership of a particular social group is internally consistent. Until each resolves this deficiency, there will be no real resolution of the debate surrounding them.
6. As is increasingly acknowledged in the refugee law literature, in order to establish the causal nexus it is not necessary to establish persecutory intent on the part of the persecutor.

## 1.11 Chapter 11: 'Well-Founded Fear' ('*Craignant Avec Raison*')

### 1.11.1 Basic propositions

1. The 'well-founded fear' element contains an objective test encompassing: foundation in fact; individualised assessment (taking into account, inter alia, the applicant's personal circumstances); a holistic inquiry; and forward-looking risk assessment.
2. The temporal scope of the risk assessment must avoid extremes that seek to impose either a criterion of undue immediacy or imminence on the one hand or a criterion of undue protraction into the future on the other.
3. Whilst the wording of the 'well-founded fear' element does not prescribe any particular burden or standard of proof, there is a substantial consensus that the burden of proof (in some sense) rests on the applicant. However, the decision maker has a shared duty to cooperate with the applicant in substantiating his or her application.
4. In relation to the standard of proof, there is no consensus as to what it should be, save that it must avoid imposing too high or too low a threshold.

### 1.11.2 Suggested propositions

1. Although disagreements still subsist regarding whether the phrase 'well-founded fear' must incorporate a subjective test, there are cogent reasons for regarding the test as essentially an objective one.
2. Whilst there is no agreement as to the standard of proof (or standard of persuasion), it is accepted that, in order not to defeat the protective purpose of the Convention, application of the well-founded fear test must apply both an ameliorative and precautionary principle.
3. It would be contrary to the Refugee Convention to require applicants to show that their feared persecution it is at least 50 per cent likely.

## 2 Nature and Status

Before seeking to answer the key questions posed at the outset of this chapter, some general observations about the nature and contents of the working list set out immediately above need making.

### 2.1 Rationale for a Working Definition

As presaged in Chapter 1, the list of basic propositions set out above purports to offer a 'working definition' of the key terms of Article 1A(2) and how they are to be approached. As such, they are based on recognition that they can only attempt to elaborate on the Article 1A(2) definition: there cannot, *stricto sensu*, be a 'definition of a definition'. However, seeking the meaning of key terms in a given definition is part of the task of treaty interpretation and by self-identifying as a 'working definition', this list purposively seeks to go beyond academic and other commentaries that merely provide analyses and conclusions as to what the various elements mean without seeking to consolidate them. Unless the various conclusions drawn about key elements of the definition are consolidated, it is not really possible to gain a picture of the definition as a whole and how the different elements fit together. Nor is it possible without doing so to achieve greater clarity and certainty. The answer to the question 'Who is a refugee' should be capable of being answered by setting out in the one place '[a] refugee within the meaning of the key terms set out in Article 1A(2) is ...'.

## 2.2  Legal Form

If a working definition is to be taken seriously it must contain a significant number of basic propositions that are at least capable of being cast into legal text. This does not necessarily mean that they must set out requirements regarded as essential requirements; in some contexts, it is legitimate for legal text to proceed indicatively, as e.g. the European Union's Qualification Directive (recast) (QD) does in Article 9(2) when it notes that persecution 'can, *inter alia*, take the form of ...'.[3] Surveying the list of basic propositions in their entirety, it is submitted that there are a good number that could stand as legal text.

## 2.3  *Lex Lata* and *De Lege Ferenda*

Most of the propositions in the list above delineate the state of the law as it is, in terms of legal principles or criteria. However, a small few contain an assessment of trends in the law. In one respect, this might appear to muddle *lex lata* and *de lege ferenda*.[4] However, if the Refugee Convention is a 'living instrument' and the meaning of key terms of its refugee definition must always remain evolutionary in character (as is widely agreed), then not to note directions being taken in law and practice would risk confining any working definition to a mere snapshot frozen in time. Further, the assessment made of trends in a small number of the basic propositions (2.1.1, 2.2.1, 2.3.1, 2.8.1) is purely descriptive rather than an attempt to argue for what the law should be.

## 2.4  Role of the 'Suggested Propositions'

The working definition as set out above comprises only those propositions headed 'basic propositions'. Nevertheless, the list given above also includes sub-headings of

---

[3] Directive 2011/95/EU of the European Parliament and of the Council of 13 December 2011 on standards for the qualification of third-country nationals or stateless persons as beneficiaries of international protection, for a uniform status for refugees or for persons eligible for subsidiary protection, and for the content of the protection granted (recast) [2011] OJ L 337/9 (QD (recast)).

[4] On these concepts, see further Alan E Boyle, 'Soft Law in International Law-Making' in Malcolm D Evans (ed), *International Law* (2nd edn, OUP 2006) 142; Christine Chinkin, 'Normative Development in the International Legal System' in Dinah Shelton (ed), *Commitment and Compliance: The Role of Non-Binding Norms in the International Legal System* (OUP 2003) 21, 30.

'suggested propositions'. In contrast to the 'basic propositions', which are intended to state propositions that are the subject of substantial consensus, the suggested propositions are confined in the main to addressing the main points of disagreement that exist currently over the meaning of key terms and to offer solutions: see e.g. the proposal (*à propos* of Chapter 4) to reject the view that actual nationality can include 'inchoate nationality' and 'effective nationality'; and the proposal in Chapter 7 that treating protection as an integral part of the being persecuted element does not entail reliance on misplaced notions of state responsibility. Thus, for example, Chapter 10 on Convention reasons proposes a different way of understanding the current divide between the 'protected characteristics' and 'social perception' approaches to MPSG. In this way it is hoped that the 'suggested propositions' also serve the role of indicating possible future trends.

## 2.5 Framework for the Definition

In Chapters 1 to 3 this study has identified matters that relate to the 'framework' of the refugee definition (as distinct from its contents), including those concerned with the proper approach to definition and to interpretation, ordering, interrelationships, modalities, and the issue of whether there is a principle or principles underlying the definition as a whole.

In seeking to interpret key elements of the refugee definition, this study has attempted to apply VCLT rules in a systematic way, considering ordinary meaning, context, object and purpose etc. in relation to each key term. Such an approach is seen as a necessary part of the system of international law norms within which the refugee definition operates. Indeed, application of VCLT rules is required by customary international law.[5] If there was substantial consensus about the need to apply VCLT rules expressly, that would do much to improve consistency and quality. At the same time, in seeking to elicit common understandings of the refugee definition, this study has been at pains not to limit the sources it has trawled to those that have applied VCLT rules explicitly. As the propositions addressing the substantive meaning of key elements demonstrate, the continuing lack of agreement about such framework matters has not thwarted the development of wide accord about important aspects of the meaning of key elements. Also, concentration in the main on basic propositions pertaining to the meaning of key elements (without expressly identifying relevant VCLT considerations) could be said to help render a further definition that is more accessible in form.

What matters at root then is only whether existing understandings, for example as set out in UNHCR, judicial, governmental, or academic sources, are *consistent with* VCLT rules.[6] It is a reasonable expectation over time that the law and practice in signatory states will make more explicit reference to VCLT rules (this would reflects trends discerned by comparative law studies of other public international law treaties),[7] but

---

[5] See p. 62.
[6] In Chapter 2, pp. 119–120 and p. 126, it was concluded, in particular, that the unique approach to interpretation applied by the CJEU to European Union law is broadly consistent with VCLT rules.
[7] See Chapter 2, n 115.

it remains that the existing law and practice of such states must be considered (irrespective of whether it makes such reference) for what light they shed on levels of common understanding or their lack.

It will also remain of great importance to ensure that ongoing attempts to elicit basic propositions regarding the meaning of key terms of the refugee definition take full account of both human rights and non-human rights approaches.

## 2.6 Definition as a Whole

A significant part of Chapter 3 was devoted to the issue of how the different elements of the refugee definition fit together. What is important to carry over from the discussion there is the significant level of agreement that the different elements of the definition be seen as interlocking and interdependent, not as a set of self-contained elements. There is a significant consensus that a 'holistic' approach must be taken to the definition.

A powerful example of the interconnectivity of the refugee definition's parts is the QD (recast). It contains several articles that set out specific requirements that must be met in order to establish whether or not a person qualifies as a refugee. Whilst some of them do contain specific cross-references, see e.g. Articles 6(c) and 9(3), most stand on their own as criteria that have to be met. For example, in order to qualify as a refugee under this directive, one has to establish, inter alia, that there is an act of persecution within the meaning of Article 9(1), that there are actors of persecution within the meaning of Article 6, and that there is no actor of protection within the meaning of Article 7. Yet the Court of Justice of the European Union (CJEU) has made abundantly clear that the different articles are interconnected. Thus in *O A*, it noted in relation to the definition of refugee set out in Article 2(c) of Directive 2004/83 (which is virtually identical to Article 1A(2) of the Convention), that well-founded fear of persecution and protection are 'intrinsically linked'.[8]

Acceptance though that the various elements of the refugee definition set out in Article 1A(2) are interconnected does not entail confirmation of every particular interconnection asserted. Thus, in relation to Chapter 7, the suggested propositions include an acknowledgement that whilst treating protection as an integral part of the meaning of 'being persecuted' has considerable support in the case law and wider literature, it is not accepted by all.

Nevertheless, assent that the definition is interlocking does serve to underline the importance of ensuring that any attempts made to codify the refugee definition avoid undue compartmentalisation. Failure to do so may cause national law to diverge from the Refugee Convention. Two recent examples from the common law world where this may arise are Australia and the United Kingdom's attempts to codify the 'well-founded fear' test,[9] by dividing it into an assessment of fear on the one hand and assessment

---

[8] Case C-255/19 *SSHD v O A* [2021] ECLI:EU:C:2021:36, paras 56, 59.
[9] See Australian Migration Act, s 5J and the UK Nationality and Borders Act 2022, s 32. On the latter, see further Chapter 11, n 287.

of forward-looking risk (expressed as 'real chance' or 'reasonable likelihood') on the other.[10]

### 2.6.1 An underlying principle or principles?

Any consideration of the definition as a whole cannot omit inquiry into whether or not there can be said to be any underlying principle or principles. The main candidate for such a principle identified in the case law and wider literature is the principle of surrogacy. However, as is evident from the discussion in Chapter 7, there is a marked lack of consensus about the very notion of surrogacy; hence no basic proposition is stated concerning it. This author's own position is that surrogacy is both 'a principle underlying the refugee definition' (see 'suggested proposition 1' in Chapter 7) and one that also plays a substantive role in informing the meaning to be given to certain of the definition's individual elements.[11] It is clear that there is a need for further debate on this matter, but hopefully this study's examination of the various ways in which the principle 'permeates' the definition has helped lay more of the groundwork.

## 2.7 Quasi-State Practice

The basic propositions stated are not advanced as incarnations of 'state practice' (in its international law meaning)[12] or of 'subsequent practice' within the meaning of Article 31(3) VCLT. From the analysis made of VCLT rules in Chapter 2, refugee law currently contains very little 'subsequent practice' that meets the strict requirements of that term.[13] Be that as it may, the basic propositions can properly be said to constitute quasi-state practice or what the ILC refers to as state practice 'in the broad sense'.[14] As such they fall within the ambit of the VCLT rules in both a general and a specific sense. In a general sense, they comprise propositions that have emerged from a systematic application of VCLT rules, relating to ordinary meaning, context, object and purpose, and other Article 31 and 32 considerations. In a specific sense they describe the state of the evidence currently regarding whether there exists 'subsequent practice' within the meaning of Article 31(3)(b).[15]

There are added reasons within the specific context of the Refugee Convention for considering that the basic propositions, being drawn from a combination of UNHCR guidance, the Qualification Directive (QD), governmental guidance, case law, and supported by academic learning, should be considered to possess a degree of authority, albeit non-binding. The sine qua non of such basic propositions is that they reflect the guidance of the two main pillars of interpretive guidance on the refugee

---

[10] See Chapter 11, n 287. However, in *DQU16 v MHA* [2021] HCA 10, para 10, the Australian High Court referred to s 5J as 'largely codifying the definition of "refugee" under the Convention'.
[11] See p. 415.
[12] James Crawford, *Brownlie's Principles of Public International Law* (9th edn, OUP 2019) 21–28.
[13] See Chapter 2, section 2.6.2.
[14] See Chapter 2, n 69. Such prpositions can be said to reflect what the Australian Federal Court has referred to as 'generally accepted construction in other countries subscribing to the Convention' (*SZTEQ v Minister for Immigration and Border Protection*, [2015] FCAFC 39, para 70).
[15] See p. 99 and p. 107.

definition—UNHCR guidance and the case law—and also reflect the preponderance of academic opinion. As we saw earlier, the duty imposed on UNHCR by Article 35 to supervise the application of the Convention provides sufficient basis for it to issue guidance and (in turn) UNHCR itself has recognised the great importance of case law in helping interpret key terms of the Convention, including Article 1A(2).[16]

This means that unless propositions described as basic in fact reflect *both* UNHCR and judicial consensus, they cannot properly be endowed with some cachet of authority.[17]

## 2.8 Implications of Existing Codification Measures

Some of the propositions listed have already been included in identical or similar form in regional or national law codification measures, for example, in relation to Chapter 6, the wording of one of the propositions ('Past persecution does not in itself constitute "being persecuted", but the fact that an applicant has already been subject to persecution is a serious indication of such, unless there are good reasons to consider that such persecution will not be repeated') is almost word-for-word to be found in Article 4(4) QD (recast).[18]

As can be seen from the various critiques that have been levelled against certain attempts at codification (including at the regional level, in the QD), codification in itself does not guarantee correct interpretation; and, certainly there must always be a concern that its objective may be to impose interpretive guidance based on national (or regional) political and/or policy priorities rather than to elicit the one true (but ever-evolving) international meaning of the key terms of the Refugee Convention.[19] There is the added problem that once a state party introduces a national law provision more restrictive than the international meaning, it can be hard to amend that later. The fact that such codifications often assert that they are in accordance with the Refugee Convention cannot be conclusive of whether that is so in fact. Further, whilst such codifications may sometimes be more restrictive, national or regional codifications may sometimes, conversely, go further than what has been widely agreed within refugee law internationally. For example, Article 8 of the QD (recast) contains (for those member states who apply the concept) more demanding criteria concerning the accessibility of an IPA and settlement in an IPA than had been internationally agreed at the time of its drafting.[20]

### 2.8.1 Relevance of QD (recast)
Whilst only some of the propositions listed in this study's working definition appear in any of the existing attempts at codification or incorporation, a significant number

---

[16] See p. 53 and p. 111.
[17] See p. 51.
[18] See p. 405.
[19] See p. 22 and p. 53.
[20] As argued in Chapter 8 (p. 527, p. 534, p. 535, and p. 537), these criteria can now be said to have achieved substantial consensus.

mirror, either precisely or in broad terms, provisions of the EU QD (recast). The QD (recast) is, of course, a legal instrument binding only within the domain of EU law. However, as has been highlighted throughout this book, this directive claims to be 'based on the full and inclusive application of the [Refugee Convention]',[21] and some of its provisions represent an attempt to build on global state practice regarding the Refugee Convention. In addition to provisions of this directive that seek to provide a more detailed definition of some of the key terms of Article 1A(2), it also identifies some specific modalities of the refugee definition, in terms of acts and actors of persecution, protection against persecution, and *sur place* activities. In this regard, it goes beyond the UNHCR Handbook and subsequent Guidelines on International Protection, whose relevant parts mostly confine themselves to elucidation of the key terms of Article 1A(2) in substantive terms without considering modalities (except in relation to *sur place* claims). That does not make all or some of the provisions of the QD 'state practice' or even 'quasi-state practice' globally, but (to reiterate a point made in Chapters 1 and 2), it must not be overlooked that they do constitute relevant *evidence* of state practice, at least in the broad sense.[22] In any event, the basic propositions stated in this study seek to reflect substantial consensus reached at an international, not simply a regional level. Further, this study identifies more than one respect in which this directive fails to reflect international meaning.

## 2.9 Existing Sources of Interpretive Guidance

Existing sources of interpretive guidance were analysed in Chapter 1. In order to test this study's notion of a working definition, it is salient to compare and contrast them in outline terms with the working definition list extracted from Chapters 4 to 11. It is convenient to first address two sources seen of lesser importance before considering judicial and UNHCR sources.

### 2.9.1 Governmental guidance

It was stated in Chapters 1 and 2 that there is a need for caution in relation to guidance issued by governments; that in any event, it rather disqualifies itself through being designed to provide a national approach; and that there are presently too few accessible examples of it to represent a cross-section of state party opinion.[23] Nonetheless, it is instructive to observe that several examples of such guidance do attempt to address all or almost all key elements of the Article 1A(2) refugee definition[24] and certainly play a role as evidence of state practice.

---

[21] QD (recast) (n 3) Recital 3.
[22] See Chapter 2, n 69.
[23] See pp. 22–24 and p. 53; also see Chapter 2, n 302.
[24] See e.g. Administrative Appeals Tribunal, A Guide to Refugee Law in Australia (2021) available at <www.aat.gov.au/guide-to-refugee-law> accessed 31 December 2021. For the various governmental

### 2.9.2 Examples of academic interpretive guidance

To look at academic examples of interpretive guidance is particularly pertinent not least because leading decisions of courts and tribunals have sometimes attached significant weight to academic sources. Further, it could be said that all scholarly publications on one or more aspects of the Article 1A(2) definition seek to offer guidance on their meaning (even those who disavow efforts to offer further definitions).[25] But as already noted, such publications do not ordinarily offer an overall working definition of all the key elements of Article 1A(2). Even if one could extract a list of basic propositions similar to the one furnished in this study from the individual chapters of some of the major textbooks on refugee law, the fact that they do not themselves currently attempt an overview in the one place is a shortcoming. Separately, there are pioneering examples of guidelines produced by groups of scholars on certain aspects of the refugee definition. However, even the Michigan Guidelines[26], which represent the principal example of (mainly) academic guidance, constitute only an ad hoc set of materials on selected elements. They do not cover nationality or statelessness or the 'outside the country' elements. They do not specifically cover persecution or protection. Nor do they cover approaches to the refugee definition or the efficacy of a human rights approach per se.

### 2.9.3 Examples of judicial interpretive guidance

Chapter 1 highlighted the fact that in the past few decades case law has emerged as a major pillar of interpretive guidance on the meaning of key terms of the refugee definition. This contrasts sharply with the position obtaining in 1979 when the UNHCR Handbook was virtually the only source (outside the national sphere) of interpretive guidance. The analysis undertaken in this book's Chapters 4 to 11 bears out how instrumental such case law has been in probing and refining understandings of the refugee definition's different elements. Indubitably, therefore, just as one test of whether this study's basic propositions correctly reflect substantial consensus is whether they are consistent with *UNHCR* guidance, so another indispensable test must be whether they are consistent with *case law*. By its nature, case law in this context must concentrate on the leading decisions of senior courts and tribunals around the world that continue to be widely cited.[27]

At the same time, there must be due recognition of case law's limitations. Case law predominantly seeks to analyse specific points of law on points material to an individual case, not to provide a full coverage of the refugee definition. On a significant number of issues, case law is not united. It is also evident that leading cases do not always reflect a well-reasoned analysis of one or more elements of the refugee definition. Nevertheless, based on this study's efforts to document case law contributions, collating analyses in case law of each element in the one place would likely show

---

guidelines in use in the United States, see Deborah Anker, *Law of Asylum in the United States* (Thomsons Reuters 2022) §1.4, 18–19.

[25] See p. 37.

[26] James C Hathaway, *The Michigan Guidelines on the International Protection of Refugees* (Michigan Publishing 2019). See further p. 115 and this chapter below p. 736, p. 737, p. 738, and p. 739.

[27] See pp. 51–53, p. 72, and p. 113.

judicial consensus and/or convergence on many matters; indeed, one of the criteria for inclusion in this study's list of basic propositions is that they have met with judicial consensus.

Overwhelmingly judges speak through their judgments; it is their decisions alone that generate case law. However, the judicial pillar also encompasses the contributions made by 'horizontal judicial dialogue'. As noted in Chapter 2, there have been important recent developments within Europe in the forms this dialogue can take (beyond cross-citations and exchanges at judicial conferences and training workshops, networking, etc.), in particular the development and publication of 'Judicial Analyses' as part of the European Union Asylum Agency's (EUAA's) development of a 'Professional Development Series' (now Judicial Publications Series) for members of courts and tribunals.[28] They share with this study's basic propositions the quality of seeking to identify the law as it is rather than to impose the views of the judicial authors. However, it is still the case that they are specific to the EU law regime and there are presently no equivalent analyses at a global level.

### 2.9.4 UNHCR interpretive guidance

As was foreshadowed in Chapter 1, similarities between this study's working definition are closest with UNHCR materials, in particular the UNHCR Handbook[29] and the series of Guidelines on International Protection,[30] although, as will be reiterated in a moment, Article 35 of the Convention endows UNHCR guidance with a special status.

*2.9.4.1 Comparisons with UNHCR Handbook*

In terms of Part 1 of the Handbook, this study's working definition shares the aim of providing a comprehensive treatment of the key terms of Article 1A(2). Some of this study's basic propositions either mirror the analysis given in the Handbook or can be understood as amending and updating it. However, this study's working definition list is significantly shorter. That is largely because the Handbook's approach is sometimes not to offer a definition of a key element at all, but rather to proceed indicatively. For instance, in relation to persecution, the relevant paragraphs of the Handbook largely confine themselves to giving examples of what persecution comprises.

The Handbook does not address 'framework' issues concerned with the definitional endeavour, interpretation, or approaches to definition. Neither does this study's working definition say much about such matters (although they are addressed in some of its 'suggested propositions'). However, if this study is right in discerning an increasing trend in the wider literature towards seeing application of VCLT rules as an integral part of the definitional endeavour, that does tend to suggest that affirming such rules might become an established feature of refugee law in the foreseeable future.

---

[28] Chapter 1, n 257. The Agency was formerly called 'EASO'. These publications are available on the courts and tribunals section of the EUAA website.
[29] UNHCR, Handbook on Procedures and Criteria for Determining Refugee Status and Guidelines on International Protection under the 1951 Convention and the 1967 Protocol Relating to the Status Of Refugees (Geneva, 2019, reissued in 2019) (UNHCR Handbook or Handbook); see Chapter 1, section 6.1.1 and p. 108.
[30] See Chapter 1, section 6.1.4; this chapter, section 2.9.4.2 below; and pp. 109–110.

*2.9.4.2 Comparison with the Guidelines on International Protection*
Again, some of the basic propositions set out in this study either mirror the analyses given in one or more of the Guidelines on International Protection or can be understood as amending and updating them. For example, what is stated in the working definition as regards the internal protection alternative can be seen as updating several propositions set out in the July 2003 Guidelines on Internal Flight Alternative (IFA).[31] This study's working definition also seeks, in the suggested propositions, to resolve some of the difficulties that subsequent case law and academic commentary have found with several of the Guidelines. But principally the main substantive difference is that, in contrast to the Guidelines which up to the present have not addressed all key elements of the refugee definition, individually or collectively, this study's working list does.

## 2.10 Possible Drawbacks to the Working Definition Approach

Adverting to the discussion in Chapter 1 of the definitional endeavour, one objection that might be raised is that the working definition list set out above could act to freeze or stultify interpretive understandings. However, as explained in that chapter, this objection only works against inflexible definitions that seek to lay down a fixed list.[32] One of the reasons for describing the list as comprising a 'working definition' is precisely to convey that it is only intended to set out the law as it is presently, fully recognising that its interpretation must be evolutive. A working definition can only ever be a work in progress. But unless each generation takes stock of where the law has got to, reliance can mistakenly be placed on propositions that have not stood the test of time. Further, it is important to note that some of the basic propositions identify criteria that seek to give due recognition to the hugely fact-sensitive nature of refugee law, e.g. the proposition that '[d]etermining whether an application is "being persecuted" requires individual assessment relative to the individual'.

Another objection might be that the working definition is really just a statement of the obvious. That is certainly true inasmuch as the basic propositions are intended to set out understandings of the refugee definition that have achieved substantial consensus. However, if they are obvious, that tends to corroborate the accuracy of their inclusion as widely agreed propositions. In key respects, the search for greater clarity and simplicity has as one consequence a statement of the obvious. This is something that should be embraced, not scorned.

In any event, the working definition's contents are noticeably different from a list of basic propositions that might have been drawn up in earlier decades, for example, it differs in some respects from understandings set out in the 1979 UNHCR Handbook. It does not, for instance, endorse the notion that 'well-founded fear' comprises two requirements, subjective and objective fear. It does note, as the Handbook does not, that political opinions can relate to non-state as well as to state actors. Further, one must not confuse what is obvious within the charmed world of scholarship with what is

---
[31] See Chapter 8, sections 2.7.1 and 4.
[32] See p. 37 and p. 302.

obvious to the public at large. Achieving greater clarity must at least in good measure be concerned with the latter.

Another point of dispute might be that even if not a statement of the obvious the basic propositions set out are so short and summary as to be relatively meaningless. They leave much that remains indeterminate. Linked to this, the criticism may be raised that such a list is essentially reductive and runs the risk of being used as a substitute for more detailed and nuanced interpretive analysis.

The brevity of many of the basic propositions does not necessarily mean that they are inconsequential or lack legal effectiveness. For example, they share with the QD (recast) and some national codifications a recognition that there can be non-state actors of persecution. That short proposition, as now enshrined within EU asylum law, for example, through Article 6 of the QD (recast), has had, and continues to have, major implications for the application of the refugee definition.

It might also be argued that being relatively short and summary such propositions defeat their own purpose, which is surely to provide a meaningful elaboration of the key terms of the existing definition of refugee set out in Article 1A(2). There is a slice of truth in this argument. Plainly, to revert to the example of non-state actors of persecution, this simple concept itself requires considerable elaboration. Yet, that is part of the very process of interpretation—that it will lead to further propositions, which in turn require further layers of refinement and analysis. It is utopian to expect a working definition to render the indeterminate determinate at a stroke. Not to at least seek to distil a working definition will leave refugee law in the problematic state it is now, where lack of clarity and consistency and unity remain all too-frequent complaints.[33]

Linked to the concern about brevity it might be contended that such a list runs the risk of reductionism, shrinking further definition of key elements to the lowest common denominator. It could justly be pointed out that the lifeblood of case law and refugee scholarship is addressing new problems and, where needed, breaking new ground. The working definition project might seem anathema to that. However, the main aim of the list is to set out a digest of what has been clarified following previous disagreements; and to give a 'joined-up' view of what has been agreed. It is not to substitute for the broad and detailed contents of the refugee law on the Convention definition. Refugee law relating to Article 1A(2) cannot be reduced to what has been widely agreed; the basic propositions will and must continue to co-exist with the broader body of learning contained in the wider literature, including that which calls for new or different interpretations. Nevertheless, one of the purposes of including also 'suggested propositions' is to indicate trends regarding still-unsettled issues of interpretation, and, in that way, help enhance the reaching of more common understandings in the future. The goal is to further reduce areas of continuing uncertainty. Ultimately there is no guarantee that propositions that are described in this study as 'basic' (or a fortiori those described as 'suggested') encapsulate the true international meaning

---

[33] See p. 5. Notably, even within the EU which has made the greatest efforts to achieve a uniform interpretation of key terms of the refugee definition within the QD (recast), the position remains (in December 2021) that considerable divergences are seen to persist: see Regulation (EU) 2021/2303 of the European Parliament and of The Council of 15 December 2021 on the European Union Agency for Asylum and repealing Regulation (EU) No 439/2010, Recital (3).

currently, but in the end refugee law operates in a positivist world. At least several 'basic propositions' (if properly included) represent the triumph of learning and practice over previous interpretations now seen to be incorrect.

Another concern that might be canvassed about a working definition is that any attempt at codification plays into the hands of governments who wish to take a restrictive approach to their obligations under the Refugee Convention. So much might certainly be suggested, to take two common law examples, about recent Australian[34] and UK attempts[35] to codify the refugee definition. In the UK context, the government stated in explanatory notes to what is now the Nationality and Borders Act 2022 that it wanted to take the opportunity 'to clearly define, in a unified source, some of the key elements of the Refugee Convention'. This was seen as necessary to rectify the existing situation in which the definition 'contains broad concepts and principles, many of which are open to some degree of interpretation as to exactly what they mean in practice'.[36] A more accurate way of putting the UK government of the day's objection would have been to say that it did not like certain aspects of existing case law established by the UK senior judiciary over the past twenty-five years or so. That case law had taken a holistic approach and given key elements of the definition a settled meaning. However, as noted earlier,[37] codification per se is not restrictive; if national codifying legislation gives meanings of key terms that are unduly narrow, that is the result of political, not legal, decisions. Greater clarification of the definition's international meaning can only help make it more difficult for state parties to deviate.

Could it be argued that the basic propositions comprising this study's working definition do not in fact comport with VCLT rules of treaty interpretation? If the working definition is not in fact the result of proper application of VCLT rules, then that is a fatal malady, since, as we have seen, interpretation that at least accords with VCLT rules is necessary to all treaty interpretation. However, the contents of this definition have been arrived at through a systematic application of VCLT rules and one that has taken a unified approach to them.

Finally, it needs to be asked whether the working definition fares any better in relation to criticisms chronicled in Chapter 1 attacking focus on 'arcane disputes about how words in a treaty can be reinterpreted to fit today's challenges'.[38] Certainly one aim of the distillation of basic propositions has been to clarify points of interpretation and to establish points on which there is no longer any significant dispute. If that is what is meant by arcane, then this study pleads guilty. But surely one of the points

---

[34] In relation to the Australian Migration Act, as amended in 2014, see Linda J Kirk, 'Island Nation: The Impact of International Human Rights Law on Australian Refugee Law' in Bruce Burson and David Cantor (eds), *Human Rights and the Refugee Definition* (Brill Nijhoff 2016).

[35] UNHCR, 'Observations on the Nationality and Borders Bill, Bill 141, 2021–22' (2021) paras 133–180, available at <www.unhcr.org/uk/publications/legal/615ff04d4/> accessed 6 December 2021.

[36] UK Parliament, 'Nationality and Borders Bill. Explanatory Notes' (6 July 2021) paras 312, 315.

[37] Chapter 1, section 2.4.

[38] Alexander Betts and Paul Collier, *Refuge: Transforming a Broken Refugee System* (Penguin 2017) 6. See also Guy S Goodwin-Gill and Jane McAdam (with Emma Dunlop), *The Refugee in International Law* (4th edn, OUP 2021) 15 who seek to address early on in their book the concern that: 'Defining refugees may appear an unworthy exercise in legalism and semantics, obstructing a prompt response to the needs of people in distress.'

behind such lines of criticism is that there is too much diversity and disagreement. If that is so, then is not a working definition one path out of the arcane?

## 3  How Does the Working Definition Represent Progress?

We now come to the questions most fundamental to the rationale of this book, namely: 'Are the basic propositions clarificatory?'; 'Do they bear out the claim that a significant number of disagreements about the meaning of key terms have been effectively settled?; and 'Is it accurate to say that they are in line with the positions taken by ongoing UNHCR guidance and case law and with the preponderance of academic studies?' It is convenient to address all three questions together.

Of their nature, basic propositions about the definition cannot be expected to evidence on their face resolution of major disagreements or make reference to their origins, whether the latter be in UNHCR guidance or other sources. However, focussing on the chapters addressing each of the definition's key elements, the following can be said of each.

There has not always been clarity that nationality (within the meaning of its main use in Article 1A(2)) is concerned with the legal bond between the individual and the state or about the fact that the primary framework for interpreting the meaning of 'country of nationality' and 'not having a nationality' is the international law on nationality and statelessness. Chapter 4 notes that there were early objections to equating those 'not having a nationality' with stateless persons under CSSP54, but it is also notes that these have almost entirely fallen away. Since the meaning of these elements has never been addressed in either the UNHCR Handbook or in any of the Guidelines on International Protection or indeed in any of the Michigan Guidelines, the basic propositions for Chapter 4 stand as an important clarification of the correct position.[39] As regards multiple nationality, the position taken in paragraphs 106 and 107 of the 1979 Handbook is confirmed except for the latter's reliance on the concept of 'effective' nationality. The basic proposition in Chapter 4 stating that '[a]ssessment of inability to return requires a hypothetical inquiry into the situation a stateless person would face if returned' is an example of a proposition that was not fully agreed for a time, but about which consensus has now descended. This is exemplified by the fact that the most prominent scholar who disputed it (Hathaway) has now expressly retracted his earlier arguments to the contrary.

As regards Chapter 5, analysis therein underlines that occasional attempts to construe the meaning of 'outside the country' so as to cover some persons who have not left the territory of their country in jurisdictional terms have never gained any traction. In this regard, the basic propositions stated in this study (that the 'outside the country' requirement must be construed so as to require physical absence from the territory of a country, the latter being understood in jurisdictional terms) confirms

---

[39] Albeit the UNHCR, Handbook on Protection of Stateless Persons (Geneva, 2014) (UNHCR 2014 Handbook), contains a number of observations that are pertinent to assessment of nationality (or its lack) in the refugee context: see p. 217, p. 218, p. 228, pp. 237–238, p. 239, p. 249, p. 251, and p. 256.

that the position taken in the UNHCR Handbook at paragraph 88 is now firmly entrenched. As regards the listing as a basic proposition that for stateless persons their 'country of former habitual residence' is a wider term than 'state', Chapter 5 charts how this view has come to be widely accepted, notwithstanding isolated decisions to the contrary. The other basic proposition concerning stateless persons (that '[a] person can have more than one country of former habitual residence') is an example of a confirmation that the UNHCR Handbook's statement to this effect remains the agreed position.

In relation to Chapter 6, a number of the basic propositions enunciate points that have never really been doubted. Some simply reconfirm what is set out in the 1979 UNHCR Handbook and in subsequent UNHCR Guidelines, for example, that a person can qualify as a refugee on the basis of *sur place* activities. Others are essentially elaborations of aspects of the meaning of 'being persecuted' that have always had wide acceptance—e.g. that the 'being persecuted' element requires human agency and that persecutory harm can be actual or threatened. There are also several propositions categorised as basic that have not always been propositions voiced by or adhered to by decision makers in the past—e.g. the proposition that '[d]iscrimination is not a necessary condition of "being persecuted"', although it is assessed to now be the subject of substantial consensus. But in order to justify this assessment, Chapter 6 addresses the isolated disagreements that have arisen.

Importantly, several of the basic propositions stated in Chapter 6 are examples of conclusions arrived at only after considerable prior disagreement in the literature. Thus, as has been well-documented, there were intense debates in past decades about whether there could be non-state actors of persecution. So too, there was clearly disagreement or doubt in earlier decades over whether acts or measures could be said to be persecutory even though directed, not at a person individually, but at a group of which the individual is a member. Chapter 6 addresses these and charts how it has come about that there is now no serious dispute about these propositions.

Only a few basic propositions are set out in Chapter 7, but what is stated can fairly be said to represent key outcomes of what has been a sustained debate in the case law and wider literature about the protection element of the definition. That they are short and stated in very general terms does, however, demonstrate that there remains a need for greater clarification. As indicated in the 'suggested propositions', however, considerable developments are taking place towards achieving that, by applying a human rights approach. One obvious sticking point remains the competing understandings of state responsibility concepts when applied to refugee law.

The basic propositions set out in Chapter 8 represent ones that have weathered the various controversies that have raged over the role and place in the refugee definition of the IPA. As regards the proposition that the IPA analysis is premised on a prior finding of well-founded fear of being persecuted for a Convention reason in the home area, this is not one that has been expressly declared by all sides in the various debates, but it can still fairly be said to underline them all. The statement that for an IPA to be viable it must be one that is safe, in the sense of being free of a well-founded fear of being persecuted and that it must be accessible, are again not necessarily ones formulated in this way by all, but there is now no serious opposition to them. The same is true of the proposition that the conditions in the IPA must not be such as would compel an applicant to return to the home area. These propositions can also be gleaned from the Michigan Guidelines, but the latter mix together description of the law as it is and what these guidelines consider the correct position.

The basic propositions set out in Chapter 9 are a prime example of how, despite the literature disclosing very strong disagreements over the meaning of the availment clause—and ongoing uncertainly about its precise role—there can now be said to be acceptance on all sides of two key matters: that protection encompasses both internal and external aspects, and that internal protection is a crucial component of the refugee definition.

Several of the basic propositions forming part of Chapter 10 represent restatements of points already made in the UNHCR Handbook and some of the UNHCR Guidelines on International Protection. The basic propositions stating the meaning of race, nationality, and religion again broadly reflect the interpretations already set out in the Handbook, although the contents given to the reason of religion derives mainly from subsequent materials, including the UNHCR Guidelines, rather than from the Handbook. The proposition that reasons may be real or attributed represents a point only glancingly made in the Handbook but voiced recurrently in the UNHCR Guidelines on International Protection, among other sources. The identification of several essential features of MPSG is also in similar form to that which can be extracted from the UNHCR Guidelines, case law, and the wider literature.

The basic proposition relating to the Convention reasons being united by a common theme (and that it is most frequently identified being non-discrimination), is forged primarily out of case law, although it is consistent with UNHCR materials and the preponderance of academic studies. The two propositions stated on political opinion are not to be found in the Handbook and derive primarily from case law, albeit consistent with ongoing UNHCR guidance. Both are also to be found in the Michigan Guidelines on Political Opinion. They represent a following through of the impact of prior acceptance that persecution can emanate from non-state as well as state actors.

In relation to well-founded fear, the subject of Chapter 11, it has hopefully been shown that despite the continuing sharp divide between the 'bipartite approach' and the 'objective approach', both agree on four essential features of an objective component.

Although the above only provides illustrations, they suffice to demonstrate that this study's working definition does indeed contain a significant number of propositions that are clarificatory and/or have emerged from debates and disagreements expressed over the years. Each of the underlying chapters sets out more detail confirming this to be the case.

## 4 How Might Greater Clarity Be Achieved?

Even assuming the aforesaid basic propositions accurately reflect the existing state of learning about the meaning of key terms of the refugee definition, they still at best amount to an offer of interpretation. Other academic studies may not attempt in quite this way to draw the same dividing line between a digest of the law as it is and setting out interpretations they favour. They may not try and consolidate the state of the learning on the whole of the definition in the one place. However, the working definition proposed here remains at root an academic digest. If its contents are to have any added value, beyond the ordinary contribution of academic treatises on the refugee definition, it can only be if they are taken up, in whole or part, by sources that would command more authority. The question needs to be asked whether there are sources or mechanisms that might carry forward the project of a working definition in a more concrete way.

It is convenient to explore possibilities that might be argued to exist at the UN level or the UNHCR level and in other fora, in whatever form.

## 4.1 UN Level

At the time of writing, to expect further elaboration (or amendment) of the refugee definition at the UN treaty level is simply unrealistic. Nor is it realistic to expect other UN instruments—e.g. global compacts[40]—to address what is manifestly covered by the scope of an existing treaty. Unless driven to do so by severe global crises, e.g. wars, climate change, it is most unlikely that steps will be taken at the UN level to achieve greater unity and clarity of the refugee definition. That is not to discount, however, that UNGA might have a potential role to play in endorsing any UNHCR initiatives to achieve more up to date guidance in comprehensive form.

## 4.2 Other Fora

As already noted, there have been attempts separate from UNHCR to develop guidelines. For example, there are those that have been undertaken by individual states at the governmental (executive or quasi-judicial) level;[41] or by academics and kindred experts, most notably in the form of the Michigan Guidelines.[42] However, the international value of the former is almost limited by definition, as their purpose is to offer guidance for decision makers applying the national law in a particular country.[43] The value of academic contributions is limited in the same way as this book's working definition is limited. At best it offers a distillation of existing law and practice together with the author or authors' views on the best understanding. For reasons set out in Chapter 1, such materials can never attain the potentially authoritative status of UNHCR guidance or case law.[44]

Whilst judicial materials have been highlighted throughout this study as one of the two main pillars of modern refugee law, this has primarily been in the context of case

---

[40] See UNGA Res 73/151 (17 December 2018); Report of the United Nations High Commissioner for Refugees, Part II: Global Compact on Refugees (2 August 2018) UN Doc A/73/12.
[41] See p. 53.
[42] See pp. 115–117.
[43] There are also reasons to be cautious about the extent to which such guidance seeks interpretation in the application of the Convention: see above p. 53 and also pp. 22–23.
[44] See pp. 54–55.

law. There remains little prospect of the Convention's Article 38 mechanism being activated to refer disputes over interpretation to the International Court of Justice (ICJ) (and even if it were to occur in one or two instances, that would not get anywhere near resolving the multitude of interpretive issues). There may be scope for case law to take a more proactive approach to elaborating one or more aspects of the refugee definition, but as already noted it is not of its nature designed to interpret all elements of the refugee definition in the one place. Sometimes national (or regional) law constraints may prevent judges from directly addressing the Article 1A(2) definition in any event.[45]

A significant development in recent years has been the production within Europe by the International Association of Refugee and Migration Judges (IARMJ) of judicial analyses, including one on Qualification for International Protection for members of courts and tribunals in EU member states.[46] These analyses seek, inter alia, to provide a systematic analysis of EU asylum law. The methodology they employ features consultation with outside bodies, including judges throughout the EU but also UNHCR. They share with this study's working definition the aim of setting out the law as it is. Such analyses go beyond the materials produced by various IARMJ working parties, which have largely confined themselves to miscellaneous observations on key issues.[47] However, for the present, such analyses are confined to EU asylum law. Even assuming that IARMJ moves to producing global guidelines, which potentially could greatly enhance convergence of interpretation, they would have at most persuasive authority. Guidelines written by judges extra-curially are important as tools of persuasion, as a form of horizontal judicial dialogue, reinforcing the efficacy of the judicial pillar, but they cannot substitute for case law and it is only case law that has legal effects at the national level or—in the case of the Court of Justice of the European Union (CJEU)—at the regional level. Case law from other countries (when of course domestic law and policy makes it possible to cite it) must inevitably remain the most important source of persuasive judicial authority.

## 4.3 UNHCR Level

The UNHCR level is dealt with last to enable greater perspective as to where it fits in the range of possible alternatives. This study sees it as offering the most potential for concrete advances in achieving greater clarity.

Considerable effort, including by UNHCR, has gone into exploring possibilities as to how it might address, inter alia, the lack of clarity and agreement about the refugee definition acting under its Article 35 supervisory responsibility by devising new mechanisms such as: an annual protection reporting exercise undertaken by UNHCR

---

[45] See p. 113 and pp. 22–24.
[46] EUAA, 'Qualification for International Protection Judicial Analysis', 2nd edition (Produced by IARMJ-Europe under contract to the EUAA, January 2023). See further Chapter 2, section 3.3.2.
[47] See e.g. Kate Jastram, Anne Mactavish, and Penelope Mathew, 'Violations of Socio-Economic Rights as a Form of Persecution and as an Element of Internal Protection' (2009) IARLJ Human Rights Nexus Working Party Paper.

field offices; a 'Refugee Rights Committee' established to ensure States Parties and international organisations are held accountable for fulfilling their respective obligations under the 1951 Convention and 1967 Protocol; a Sub-Committee on Review and Monitoring established by the UNHCR Executive Committee; an independent monitoring mechanism on the implementation of the Refugee Convention (to include an 'advisory group' comprising a distinguished group of experts to advise UNHCR); and an International Judicial Commission for Refugees to provide non-binding but highly persuasive judgments on divergent interpretations of the Refugee Convention.[48]

None of these proposals has succeeded to date and there are few indications that they will prevail in the future. There would appear to be too many institutional reasons (in particular UNHCR's reliance on voluntary contributions from affluent States of the Global North and the primacy UNHCR accords to its operational responsibilities)[49] why it is unlikely to implement any of them.

However, there are valid reasons for thinking that UNHCR, through its International Protection Division, could take concrete steps to enhance the clarity and unity of the refugee definition by overhauling one or both of its existing mechanisms for providing interpretive guidance, namely the UNHCR Handbook and the UNHCR Guidelines on International Protection.

### 4.3.1 UNHCR Handbook

As was discussed in Chapter 1, when first issued in 1979, the UNHCR Handbook had immense authority. Even though drafted with little external input, it represented state practice at the time, based on twenty-five years of practical experience (1954–1979).[50] That authority was enhanced in the 1990s as courts and tribunals around the world, most grappling with the Refugee Convention for the first time, endorsed it as the primary source of reference. For some time, it was key to the progressive development of refugee law, instrumental, for example, in overcoming European continental resistance to the notion that there could only be state actors of persecution. But increasingly, having never been revised (only reissued), it has fallen out of date. It has been aptly described as now possessing only 'equivocal authority'.[51] This should be expected. Unlike the Convention which, under rules of treaty interpretation, is a 'living instrument', guidelines do not get to age gracefully. If any group of experts were to be given the task of going through the Handbook today with a view to remedying its shortcomings and bringing it up to date, the document would be a thicket of 'track changes'.

Yet, UNHCR continues to represent the Handbook as the 'first and most comprehensive interpretive instrument issued by UNHCR'[52] and to stick with the decision

---

[48] See p. 30. These proposed mechanisms have not been conceived as confined to the Article 1A(2) definition.

[49] Gil Loescher, *The UNHCR and World Politics: A Perilous Path* (OUP 2001); James Milner and Jay Ramasubramanyam, 'The Office of the United Nations High Commissioner for Refugees' in Cathryn Costello, Michelle Foster, and Jane McAdam (eds), *The Oxford Handbook of International Refugee Law* (OUP 2021) 186–201.

[50] See p. 96.

[51] ibid.

[52] e.g. in a 2007 intervention before the US Supreme Court, see *UNHCR intervention before the United States Board of Immigration Appeals in the Matter of Michelle Thomas et al (in Removal Proceedings)* (25 January 2007) Doc A-75-597-033/-034/-035/-036. The Handbook is described as 'internationally

taken in 2003 to routinely describe its Guidelines on International Protection as 'complementary' to it.[53] UNHCR has never expressly disowned any of the Handbook's provisions.

This stance looks increasingly untenable. Importantly, most of the Handbook's paragraphs do still stand up (something borne out by this study's individual chapters). Not having been challenged, there is a strong case for saying they continue to reflect state practice. But year by year, through case law and needed responses to challenges thrown up by new refugee-producing situations, some no longer withstand scrutiny. To represent the Handbook in its entirety as still authoritative is to mislead. In Chapter 1 a number of examples were given of paragraphs of Part 1 of the Handbook that must now be seen as problematic if not downright incorrect.[54]

However, it would appear entirely within the power of UNHCR to revise Part 1 of the Handbook (Part 2 on 'Procedures for the Determination of Refugee Status' is self-professedly devoted to subject matter not regulated by the Convention). States party have a legitimate interest in how this might be done, but it is for UNHCR to decide. Indeed, given its Article 35 supervisory responsibility, it could be said to be vital to UNHCR and the world that its guidelines can be looked to as reliably authoritative for today and not just for decades gone. Although Article 35 does not endow UNHCR with authority to resolve disputes about interpretation, supervision of the application of the Convention must inevitably involve taking active steps to steer the interpretive process and ensure both quality and consistency.[55] It is the view of this author that in order to ensure that any revision of Part 1 of the Handbook constitutes an authoritative source, it would be necessary for it to be done according to a structured methodology designed to achieve input from a wide range of stakeholders. More is said about this in section 4.3.3 of this chapter.

### 4.3.2 UNHCR Guidelines on International Protection

One argument to the contrary might be that the shortcomings of the Handbook have been and are increasingly being remedied incrementally since 2003 by the production of UNHCR Guidelines on International Protection. A major problem with that argument is that these Guidelines do not describe themselves as revising the Handbook. As noted above, all expressly defer to the primacy of the Handbook and describe

---

recognized as the key source of interpretation of international refugee law'. See also another intervention in January 2021 before the UK Supreme Court: UNHCR, Submission by the United Nations High Commissioner for Refugees in the case *G v G* [2021] UKSC 2020/0191, where the Handbook is listed first as interpretive guidance and its contents are 'commend[ed]' to the court. There are signs, however, that this may be changing. e.g. in its latest interventions, UNHCR simply refers to the Handbook alongside other UNHCR guidance materials: see e.g. UNHCR, 'Statement on Membership of Particular Social Group and the Best Interests of the Child in Asylum Procedures Issued in the context of the preliminary ruling reference to the Court of Justice of the European Union in the case of *K., L. v Staatssecretaris van Justitie en Veiligheid* (C-646/21)' (21 June 2023) para 2, available at <https://www.refworld.org/docid/6492f5f54.html> accessed 15 July 2023.

[53] See p. 48.
[54] See pp. 41–44.
[55] See p. 39 and p. 108.

themselves as 'complementary' to it. Additionally, some of the Guidelines would now themselves appear in need of revision.[56] To ascertain UNHCR's ongoing guidance has become a matter of consulting a range of UNHCR materials, including not just the Guidelines but also other UNHCR guidance notes, amicus curiae, and third-party interventions etc.

It would be possible for UNHCR to limit such problems, e.g. by beginning either in new Guidelines or in revisions of previous Guidelines, to make express note of relevant limitations of the Handbook, i.e. to start identifying and 'owning up to' the Handbook's shortcomings as and when appropriate. Arguably, the Handbook could in this way be preserved as having ongoing authority on a range of matters, but no longer represented as infallible. This would mean that over time it gracefully merged more into the background whilst retaining a foundational status. However, absent a radical departure from existing planning regarding Guidelines, such an enterprise would likely take an inordinate period of time. Over the past decade, Guidelines have been produced at less than one a year. Further, as noted earlier, they still fall markedly short of providing a coverage of all of the key elements of the refugee definition. Some do not address the inclusion clauses of the refugee definition at all. Moreover, coverage of aspects of the refugee definition is only part of the purpose of these Guidelines—they also seek to cover procedures as well as complementary protection and to examine more thematic aspects of each of the problems they address, e.g. trafficking. Such a process would also inevitably be piecemeal and would certainly not address the root of the problem, namely that there is no longer any one place in which UNHCR aims to set out in authoritative fashion elaboration of all the key terms of the refugee definition.

4.3.3 The way forward
Hence the only way in which UNHCR could address the existing problems of lack of clarity concerning the refugee definition would appear to be to undertake a wholesale revision of the Handbook as a specific project.

If UNHCR were to undertake such a project, one of the things it would need to do is take stock of the various criticisms that have been raised over the years of one or other of the 1979 Handbook's Part 1 paragraphs, including those summarised in this book's Chapter 1.[57] It would also, seemingly, need to collate all of its existing guidance-related materials, which are many and varied, into one place so that its own officers could be sure of all that has been said; to the outsider, seeking to identify current UNHCR guidance can sometimes seem a magical mystery tour. UNHCR would obviously seek to draw on, inter alia, existing case law, governmental guidance, and academic analyses. It would also need to consider whether to address what this study has termed 'framework' questions relating to the approach to definition and to interpretation and the relevance or otherwise of a human rights approach (should it, for example, promote the express application of the VCLT rules that are mandated by customary

---

[56] See e.g. UNHCR, 'Guidelines on International Protection (Guidelines) No 4: Internal Flight or Relocation Alternative Within the Context of Article 1A(2) of the 1951 Convention and/or 1967 Protocol Relating to the Status of Refugees' (23 July 2003) UN Doc HCR/GIP/03/04, as discussed in Chapter 8, section 2.7.1.
[57] See pp. 41–44.

international law?). It would also assist to look at any existing attempts to further elaborate key terms of the refugee definition, as one way of checking that any revised Part 1 did constitute interpretive guidance as opposed to mere illustrations. Possibly this study's working definition would provide at least one point of reference.

However, a revision project that simply consulted existing learning (whether in the form of a working definition or otherwise) would not on its own result in a document that would be received as authoritative in the same way as the UNHCR Handbook was. The latter was seen in the first place as authoritative because it codified state practice of the previous twenty-five years[58] and for a significant period after 1979 was really the only interpretive reference point. A revision of the Handbook would need therefore to take place according to a methodology that sought to achieve input from all important stakeholders and to incorporate structured consultation.

The methodology used for the Global Consultations at the turn of the Millennium and the ongoing methodology used for production of the Guidelines[59] offer some guidance on how this could be achieved, but would be unlikely to gain widespread endorsement unless made more rigorous. In particular, such a methodology would need to heed the reality that what this study has called the 'judicial pillar' has now established itself as another major shaper of interpretive guidance.[60] Adopting this substitutionist approach would (gracefully) leave the reputation of the 1979 Handbook intact as a foundational document and at the same time ensure continuity of identity. Most importantly, it would ensure that the wider world could once again safely and securely be able to treat the 'UNHCR Handbook' as authoritative in a comprehensive way. It could become again the start point (if not often also the finishing point) for interpreting key terms of the definition. It would also serve as a powerful, truly contemporary, reference point in all discussions about the 'international meaning' of key terms, thus making it that much harder for national governments to justify any restrictive national law codification(s). For various reasons—including the nature of refugee law; the rule of law; the independence of the judiciary; and the fact that the Convention is a 'living instrument'—this would not result in courts and tribunals treating such a new edition of the Handbook as binding, although it would undoubtedly enhance its persuasive value. Moreover, as emphasised earlier, the true goal of such a mechanism cannot be unanimity but only convergence. It would nevertheless go a long way to overcoming the current perception that divergent interpretations of one or more of the key elements of the refugee definition remain rife.

---

[58] ibid.
[59] Discussed at p. 47.
[60] See further Chapter 1, section 6.2 and Chapter 2, section 3.3.

# Selected Bibliography

## Books

Albanese FP and Takkenberg L, *Palestinian Refugees in International Law* (2nd edn, OUP 2020).
Aleinikoff TA and Zamore L, *The Arc of Protection: Reforming the International Refugee Regime* (Stanford University Press 2019).
Alexy R, *A Theory of Constitutional Rights* (OUP 2002).
Altman BM (ed), *International Measurement of Disability—Purpose, Method and Application* (Springer 2017).
Anker D, *Law of Asylum in the United States* (Thomson Reuters 1999).
Anker D, *Law of Asylum in the United States* (Thomson Reuters 2014).
Anker D, *Law of Asylum in the United States* (Thomson Reuters 2022).
Arbel E, Dauvergne C, and Millbank J (eds), *Gender in Refugee Law: From the Margins to the Centre* (Routledge 2014).
Arendt H, *The Origins of Totalitarianism* (Harcourt 1951).
Aust A, *Modern Treaty Law and Practice* (3rd edn, CUP 2013).
Bassiouni CM, *International Extradition: United States Law and Practice* (6th edn, OUP 2014).
Battjes H, *European Asylum Law and International Law* (Martinus Nijhoff 2006).
Beaumont PR and McEleavy PE, *The Hague Convention on International Child Abduction* (OUP 1999).
Behrman S and Kent A (eds), *Climate Refugees: Global, Local and Critical Approaches* (CUP 2022).
Ben-Naftali O (ed), *International Humanitarian Law and International Human Rights Law* (OUP 2011).
Berman H J and Greiner W R, *The Nature and Functions of Law* (Foundation Press 1980).
Bettati M, *L'Asile Politique en Question* (PUF 1985).
Betts A and Collier P, *Refuge: Transforming a Broken Refugee System* (Penguin 2017).
Bianchi A (ed), *Non-State Actors and International Law* (Routledge 2009).
Bjorge E, *The Evolutionary Interpretation of Treaties* (OUP 2014).
Boll AM, *Multiple Nationality and International Law* (Brill Nijhoff 2006).
Brownlie I, *Principles of Public International Law* (6th edn, OUP 2003).
Brownlie I, *System of the Law of Nations: State Responsibility. Part 1* (Oxford Clarendon Press 1983).
Buckley CM, Donald A, and Leach P (eds), *Towards Convergence in International Human Rights Law: Approaches of Regional and International Systems* (Brill Nijhoff 2016).
Cameron HE, *Refugee Law's Fact-Finding Crisis: Truth, Risk, and the Wrong Mistake* (CUP 2018).
Carens JH, *The Ethics of Immigration* (OUP 2013).
Carlier J, *Droit d'asile et des refugies* (Brill Nijhoff 2008).
Carlier J and Vanheule D (eds), *Europe and Refugees: A Challenge?* (Kluwer Law International 1997).
Carlier J et al, *Who Is a Refugee? A Comparative Case Law Study* (Brill 1997).
Chen L, *An Introduction to Contemporary International Law: A Policy-Oriented Perspective* (Yale University Press 1989).

Clapham A (ed), *Human Rights and Non-State Actors* (Edward Elgar 2013).
Clapham A, *Human Rights Obligations of Non-state Actors* (OUP 2006).
Collier J and Low V, *The Settlement of Disputes in International Law* (OUP 1999).
Costello C, *The Human Rights of Migrants and Refugees in European Law* (OUP 2016).
Costello C, Foster M, and McAdam J (eds), *The Oxford Handbook of International Refugee Law* (OUP 2021).
Crawford JR, *The International Law Commission's Articles on State Responsibility: Introduction, Text and Commentaries* (OUP 2002).
Crawford JR, *Brownlie's Principles of Public International Law* (8th edn, OUP 2012).
Crawford JR, *Chance, Order, Change: The Course of International Law, General Course on Public International Law (Volume 365)* (Brill 2013).
Crawford JR, *Brownlie's Principles of Public International Law* (9th edn, OUP 2019).
Crawley H, *Refugees and Gender: Law and Process* (Jordan Publishing Limited 2001).
Crepeau F, *Droit d'asile: de l'hospitalité aux contrôles migratoires* (Bruylant 1995).
Crock M and Berg L, *Immigration Refugees and Forced Migration: Law, Policy and Practice in Australia* (The Federation Press 2011).
Davidson WL, *Logic of Definition* (Michigan 1896).
Dawidowicz LS, *The War Against the Jews 1933–1945* (Bantam 1975).
de Visscher C, *Problèmes d'interprétation judiciaire en droit international public* (Pedone 1963).
Denza E, *Diplomatic Law: Commentary on the Vienna Convention on Diplomatic Relations* (4th edn, OUP 2018).
Donnelly J, *Universal Human Rights in Theory and Practice* (3rd edn, Cornell University Press 2013).
Dörr O and Schmalenbach K (eds), *Vienna Convention on the Law of Treaties* (Springer 2012).
Feller E, Türk V, and Nicholson F (eds), *Refugee Protection in International Law: UNHCR's Global Consultations on International Protection* (CUP 2003).
Foster M, *International Refugee Law and Socio-Economic Rights: Refuge from Deprivation* (CUP 2007).
Foster M and Lambert H, *International Refugee Law and the Protection of Stateless Persons* (OUP 2019).
Fripp E, *Nationality and Statelessness in the International Law of Refugee Status* (Hart Publishing 2016).
Gardiner R, *Treaty Interpretation* (OUP 2008).
Gardiner R, *Treaty Interpretation* (2nd edn, OUP 2015).
Germov R and Motta F, *Refugee Law in Australia* (OUP 2003).
Gibney MJ, *The Ethics and Politics of Asylum: Liberal Democracy and the Response to Refugees* (CUP 2014).
Gilbert G, *Responding to International Crime* (Martinus Nijhoff 2006).
Goodwin-Gill GS, *The Refugee in International Law* (1st edn, OUP 1983).
Goodwin-Gill GS, *The Refugee in International Law* (2nd edn, Clarendon Press 1996).
Goodwin-Gill GS and Lambert H (eds), *The Limits of Transnational Law: Refugee Law, Policy Harmonization and Judicial Dialogue in the European Union* (CUP 2010).
Goodwin-Gill GS and McAdam J, *The Refugee in International Law* (3rd edn, OUP 2007).
Goodwin-Gill GS and McAdam J, *The Refugee in International Law* (4th edn, OUP 2021).
Grahl-Madsen A, *Commentary on the Refugee Convention 1951* (UNHCR 1963).
Grahl-Madsen A, *The Status of Refugees in International Law. Volume 1: Refugee Character* (Sijthoff 1966).
Grahl-Madsen A, *The Status of Refugees in International Law. Volume II: Asylum, Entry and Sojourn* (Sijthoff 1972).

Guler A, Shevtsova M, and Venturi D (eds), *LGBTI Asylum Seekers and Refugees from a Legal and Political Perspective: Persecution, Asylum and Integration* (Springer 2019).
Hailbronner K and Thym D, *EU Immigration and Asylum Law: A Commentary* (2nd edn, Hart Publishing 2016).
Hart HLA, *Essays in Jurisprudence and Philosophy* (Clarendon Press 1983).
Hathaway JC, *The Law of Refugee Status* (Butterworths Limited 1991).
Hathaway JC, *The Rights of Refugees Under International Law* (CUP 2005).
Hathaway JC, *The Michigan Guidelines on the International Protection of Refugees* (Michigan Publishing 2019).
Hathaway JC, *The Rights of Refugees Under International Law* (2nd edn, CUP 2021).
Hathaway JC and Foster M, *The Law of Refugee Status* (2nd edn, CUP 2014).
Higgins R, *Problems and Process: International Law and How We Use It* (Oxford Clarendon Press 1994).
Hobbes T, *Leviathan* (Bobbs-Merrill Co 1958).
Holborn LW, *The International Refugee Organization: A Specialized Agency of the United Nations: Its History and Work 1946–1952* (OUP 1956).
Holborn LW et al, *Refugees, A Problem of Our Time: The Work of the United Nations High Commissioner for Refugees, 1951–1972* (Scarecrow Press 1975).
Holzer V, *Refugees from Armed Conflict* (Intersentia 2015).
Hooper L and Zilli L, *Refugee Status Claims Based on Sexual Orientation and Gender Identity* (International Commission of Jurists 2016).
Jackson IC, *The Refugee Concept in Group Situations* (Kluwer Law International 1999).
Jakab A, Dyevre A, and Itzcovich G (eds), *Comparative Constitutional Reasoning* (CUP 2017).
Jellinek G, *The Declaration of the Rights of Man and of Citizens: A Contribution to Modern Constitutional History* (authorized translation from the German by Max Farrand, revised by the Author, Henry Holt and Co 1901).
Jennings R and Watts A (eds), *Oppenheim's International Law* (9th edn, OUP 2008).
Joseph S, Schultz J, and Castan M, *The International Covenant on Civil and Political Rights: Cases, Materials, and Commentary* (OUP 2000).
Kälin W and Künzli J, *The Law of International Human Rights Protection* (2nd edn, OUP 2019).
Kateb G, *Human Dignity* (Harvard University Press 2011).
Kersting D and Leuoth M (eds), *Der Begriff des Flüchtlings: Rechtliche, Moralische und Politische Kontroversen. [The Concept of the Refugee: Legal, Moral and Political Controversies]* (JB Metzler 2020).
Khun TS, *The Structure of Scientific Revolution* (50th Anniversary edn, University of Chicago 2012).
Kimminich O, *Der internationale Rechtsstatus des Flüchtlings* (Heymann 1962).
Kneebone SY, Stevens D, and Baldassar L (eds), *Refugee Protection and the Role of Law: Conflicting Identities* (Routledge 2014).
Kourula P, *Broadening the Edges: Refugee Definition and International Protection Revisited* (Martinus Nijhoff 1997).
Krasner SD, *Sovereignty: Organized Hypocrisy* (Princeton University Press 1999).
Lambert H, McAdam J, and Fullerton M (eds), *The Global Reach of European Refugee Law* (CUP 2013).
Lauterpacht H, *The Development of International Law by the International Court* (Stevens 1958).
Lauterpacht H, *International Law, Being the Collected Papers of Hersch Lauterpacht, Vol 3* (CUP 1977).
Lehmann J, *'Protection' in European Union Asylum Law* (Brill Nijhoff 2020).
Loescher G, *The UNHCR and World Politics: A Perilous Path* (OUP 2001).

Marx R, *Handbuch zum Flüchtlingsschutz: Erläuterungen zur Qualifikationsrichtlinie* (2nd edn, Luchterhand Verlag GmbH 2012).
Mayblin L, *Asylum after Empire: Colonial Legacies in the Politics of Asylum Seeking* (Roman & Littlefield International 2017).
McAdam J, *Complementary Protection in International Refugee Law* (OUP 2007).
McAdam J, *Climate Change, Forced Migration and International Law* (OUP 2012).
McArthur E and Nowak M, *The United Nations Convention Against Torture: A Commentary* (OUP 2008).
McCorquodale R (ed), *International Law Beyond the State: Essays on Sovereignty, Non-State Actors and Human Rights* (CMP Publishing 2011).
McNair AD, *The Law of Treaties* (OUP 2003).
Melander G, *The Two Refugee Definitions* (University of Lund 1987).
Miller D, *Global Justice and National Responsibility* (OUP 2007).
Miller D and Straehle C (eds), *The Political Philosophy of Refuge* (CUP 2020).
Moore J, Musalo K, and Boswell RA, *Refugee Law and Policy* (Carolina Academic Press 2018).
Moraru M, Cornelisse G, and De Bruycker P (eds), *Law and Judicial Dialogue on the Return of Irregular Migrants from the European Union* (Hart Publishing 2020).
Moreno-Lax V, *Accessing Asylum in Europe: Extraterritorial Border Controls and Refugee Rights under EU Law* (OUP 2017).
Moreno-Lax V, Cantor D, and Durieux J-F (eds), *Refugee from Inhumanity? War Refugees and International Humanitarian Law* (Brill 2014).
Motz SA, *The Refugee Status of Persons with Disabilities* (Brill 2020).
Moyn S, *The Last Utopia: Human Rights in History* (Harvard University Press 2010).
Moyn S, *Not Enough: Human Rights in an Unequal World* (Harvard University Press 2018).
Nathwani N, *Rethinking Refugee Law* (Martinus Nijhoff Publishers 2003).
Nowak M, *Introduction to the International Human Rights Regime* (Martinus Nijhoff 2003).
O'Connell DP, *International Law* (2nd edn, Stevens 1970).
O'Connor JF, *Good Faith in International Law* (Dartmouth 1991).
Orakhelashvili A and Williams S (eds), *40 Years of the Vienna Convention on the Law of Treaties* (BIICL 2010).
Orford A, *International Authority and the Responsibility to Protect* (CUP 2011).
Parekh S, *Refugees and the Ethics of Forced Displacement* (Routledge 2017).
Passerin d'Entrèves A, *The Notion of the State: An Introduction to Political Theory* (OUP 1967).
Phuong C, *The International Protection of Internally Displaced Persons* (CUP 2004).
Pobjoy J, *The Child in International Refugee Law* (CUP 2017).
Posner E, *The Twilight of Human Rights Law* (OUP 2014).
Prakash SS, *Asylum and International Law* (Springer 1971).
Price ME, *Rethinking Asylum History, Purpose, and Limits* (CUP 2010).
Ramji-Nogales J, Schoenholtz AI, and Schrag PG (eds), *Refugee Roulette. Disparities in Asylum Adjudication and Proposals for Reform* (New York University Press 2009).
Reneman M, *EU Asylum Procedure and the Right to an Effective Remedy* (Hart Publishing 2014).
Robert P and Rey A, *Le Grand Robert De La Langue Francaise: Dictionaire Alphabetique Et Analogique De La Langue Française* (2nd edn, Le Robert 1985).
Robinson N, *Convention Relating to the Status of Stateless Persons: Its History and Interpretation, A Commentary* (UNHCR 1997).
Robinson R, *Definition* (OUP 1950).
Ronning CN, *Diplomatic Asylum: Legal Norms and Political Reality in Latin American Relations* (Martinus Nijhoff 1965).

Rosenne S, *Developments in the Law of Treaties, 1945–1986* (CUP 1989).
Sandberg R, *Religion, Law and Society* (CUP 2014).
Schultz J, *The Internal Protection Alternative in Refugee Law: Treaty Basis and Scope of Application under the 1951 Convention Relating to the Status of Refugees and Its 1967 Protocol* (Brill Nijhoff 2018).
Scott M, *Climate Change, Disasters, and the Refugee Convention* (CUP 2020).
Sharp M, *The Regional Law of Refugee Protection in Africa* (OUP 2018).
Shaw MN, *International Law* (2nd edn, Grotius 1986).
Shaw MN, *International Law* (5th edn, CUP 2012).
Shearer IA, *Starke's International Law* (11th edn, London Butterworths 1994).
Simeon JC (ed), *The UNHCR and the Supervision of International Refugee Law* (CUP 2013).
Simpson JH, *Refugees: Preliminary Report of a Survey* (Royal Institute of International Affairs 1938).
Sinclair I, *The Vienna Convention on the Law of Treaties* (Manchester University Press 1984).
Sitaropoulos N, *Judicial Interpretation of Refugee Status: In Search of a Principled Methodology Based on a Critical Comparative Analysis, with Special Reference to Contemporary British, French, and German Jurisprudence* (Sakkoulas 1999).
Skran C, *Refugees in Inter-War Europe: The Emergence of a Regime* (OUP 1995).
Slaughter A, *A New World Order* (Princeton University Press 2004).
Smet S, *Resolving Conflicts between Human Rights: The Judge's Dilemma* (Routledge 2017).
Soguk N, *States and Strangers: Refugees and Displacements of Statecraft* (University of Minnesota Press 1999).
Symes M and Jorro P, *Asylum Law and Practice* (LexisNexis 2003).
Symes M and Jorro P, *Asylum Law and Practice* (2nd edn, Bloomsbury 2010).
Takkenberg A and Tabhaz C, *The Collected Travaux Préparatoires of the 1951 Geneva Convention Relating to the Status of Refugees* (Dutch Refugee Council 1989).
Tuitt P, *False Images: Law's Construction of the Refugee* (Pluto Press 1996).
van Panhuys HF, *The Role of Nationality in International Law* (Sijthoff 1930).
Vermeulen B et al, *Persecution by Third Parties* (University of Nijmegen 1998).
Vernant J, *The Refugee in the Post-War World* (Yale University Press 1953).
Vevstad V, *Refugee Protection: A European Challenge* (Tano Aschehoug 1998).
Villiger ME, *Commentary on the 1969 Vienna Convention on the Law of Treaties* (Brill 2008).
Von Sternberg MR, *The Grounds of Refugee Protection in the Context of International Human Rights and Humanitarian Law: Canada and United States Case Law Compared* (Martinus Nijhoff 2002).
Waldman L, *The Definition of Convention Refugee* (2nd edn, Lexis Nexis 2019).
Walzer M, *Spheres of Justice: A Defence of Pluralism and Equality* (Basic Books 1983).
Weis P, *Nationality and Statelessness in International Law* (2nd edn, Kluwer Academic Publishers Group 1979).
Weis P (ed), *The Refugee Convention 1951* (CUP 1995).
Yeo C, *Refugee Law* (Bristol University Press 2022).
Zimmermann A (ed), *The 1951 Convention Relating to the Status of Refugees and Its 1967 Protocol: A Commentary* (OUP 2011).
Zolberg RA, Sukrke A, and Aguayo S, *Escape from Violence: Conflict and the Refugee Crisis in the Developing World* (OUP 1989).
Zoller E and Bastid S, *La Bonne Foi en Droit International Public* (Pedone 1977).

## Book Chapters

Achiume TE, 'Race, Refugees, and International Law' in Cathryn Costello, Michelle Foster, and Jane McAdam (eds), *The Oxford Handbook of International Refugee Law* (OUP 2021).

Akram SM, 'UNRWA and Palestine Refugees' in Cathryn Costello, Michelle Foster, and Jane McAdam (eds), *The Oxford Handbook of International Refugee Law* (OUP 2021).

Aleinikoff TA, 'Protected Characteristics and Social Perceptions: An Analysis of the Meaning of "Membership of a Particular Social Group"' in Erika Feller, Volker Türk, and Frances Nicholson (eds), *Refugee Protection in International Law: UNHCR's Global Consultations on International Protection* (CUP 2003).

Aleinikoff TA, 'The Mandate of the Office of the United Nations High Commissioner for Refugees' in Vincent Chetail and Céline Bauloz (eds), *Research Handbook on International Law and Migration* (Edward Elgar 2014).

Alleweldt R, 'Preamble to the 1951 Convention' in Andreas Zimmermann (ed), *The 1951 Convention Relating to the Status of Refugees and Its 1967 Protocol: A Commentary* (Oxford University Press 2011).

Alston P and Goodman R, 'Non-State Actors and Human Rights' in Philip Alston and Ryan Goodman, *International Human Rights Law* (OUP 2013).

Anderson A and Foster M, 'A Feminist Appraisal of International Refugee Law' in Cathryn Costello, Michelle Foster, and Jane McAdam (eds), *The Oxford Handbook of International Refugee Law* (OUP 2021).

Anker D and Vittor J, 'International Human Rights and US Refugee Law: Synergies and Contradictions' in Bruce Burson and David J Cantor (eds), *Human Rights and the Refugee Definition* (Brill Nijhoff 2016).

Bank R, 'Refugee Law Jurisprudence from Germany and Human Rights: Cutting Edge or Chilling Effect?' in Bruce Burson and David J Cantor (eds), *Human Rights and the Refugee Definition: Comparative Legal Practice and Theory* (Brill Nijhoff 2016).

Barnes J and Mackey A, 'The Credo Document: Assessment of Credibility in Refugee and Subsidiary Protection Claims under the EU Qualification Directive: Judicial Criteria and Standards' in Carolus Grutter, Elspeth Guild, and Sebastiaan de Groot (eds), *Assessment of Credibility by Judges in Asylum Cases in the EU* (Oisterwiijk Wolf Legal Publishers 2013).

Bayles MD, 'Definitions in Law' in James H Fetzer, David Shatz, and George N Schlesinger (eds), *Definitions and Delinability: Philosophical Perspectives* (Springer 1991).

Benhabib S and Nathwani N, 'The Ethics of International Refugee Protection' in Cathryn Costello, Michelle Foster, and Jane McAdam (eds), *The Oxford Handbook of International Refugee Law* (OUP 2021).

Blake N, 'Entitlement to Protection: A Human Rights-based Approach to Refugee Protection in the United Kingdom' in Frances Nicholson and Patrick Twomey (eds), *Current Issues of UK Asylum Law and Policy* (Routledge 1998).

Boyle AE, 'Soft Law in International Law-Making' in Malcolm D Evans (ed), *International Law* (2nd edn, OUP 2006).

Brandvoll J, 'Deprivation of Nationality: Limitations on Rendering Persons Stateless under International Law' in Alice Edwards and Laura van Waas (eds), *Nationality and Statelessness under International Law* (CUP 2014).

Burson B, 'Give Way to the Right: The Evolving Use of Human Rights in New Zealand Refugee Status Determination' in Bruce Burson and David Cantor (eds), *Human Rights and the Refugee Definition* (Brill Nijhoff 2016).

Burson B, 'Refugee Status Determination' in Cathryn Costello, Michelle Foster, and Jane McAdam (eds), *The Oxford Handbook of International Refugee Law* (OUP 2021).

Burson B and Cantor D, 'Introduction: Interpreting the Refugee Definition via Human Rights Standards' in Bruce Burson and David Cantor (eds) *Human Rights and the Refugee Definition* (Brill Nijhoff 2016).

Calhoun C, 'Civil Society and the Public Sphere' in Michael Edwards (ed), *The Oxford Handbook of Civil Society* (OUP 2011).

Cantor D, 'European Influence on Asylum Practices in Latin America: Accelerated Procedures in Colombia, Ecuador, Panama and Venezuela' in Hélène Lambert, Jane McAdam, and Maryellen Fullerton (eds), *The Global Reach of European Refugee Law* (CUP 2013).

Cantor D, 'Defining Refugees: Persecution, Surrogacy and the Human Rights Paradigm' in Bruce Burson and David Cantor (eds), *Human Rights and the Refugee Definition* (Brill Nijhoff 2016).

Carlier J, 'General Report' in Jean-Yves Carlier et al, *Who Is a Refugee? A Comparative Case Law Study* (Brill 1997).

Carlier J, 'The Geneva Refugee Convention Definition and the "Theory of the Three Scales"' in Frances Nicholson and Patrick Twomey (eds), *Refugee Rights and Realities: Evolving International Concepts and Regimes* (CUP 1999).

Cheeseman C, 'Harmonising Jurisprudence of Regional and International Human Rights Bodies: A Literature Review' in Carla M Buckley, Alice Donald, and Philip Leach (eds), *Towards Convergence in International Human Rights Law: Approaches of Regional and International Systems* (Brill Nijhoff 2017).

Chetail V, 'Are Refugee Rights Human Rights? An Unorthodox Questioning of the Relations Between Refugee Law and Human Rights Law' in Ruth Rubio-Marín (ed), *Human Rights and Immigration* (OUP 2014).

Chetail V, 'Moving Towards an Integrated Approach of Refugee Law and Human Rights Law' in Cathryn Costello, Michelle Foster, and Jane McAdam (eds), *The Oxford Handbook of International Refugee Law* (OUP 2021).

Chinkin C, 'Normative Development in the International Legal System' in Dinah Shelton (ed), *Commitment and Compliance: The Role of Non-Binding Norms in the International Legal System* (OUP 2003).

Coles G, 'The Human Rights Approach to the Solution of the Refugee Problem: A Theoretical and Practical Enquiry' in Alan E Nash (ed), *Human Rights and the Protection of Refugees under International Law* (Institute for Research on Public Policy 1988).

Coles G, 'Approaching the Refugee Problem Today' in Gil Loescher and Laila Monahan (eds), *Refugees and International Relations* (OUP 1989).

Cole G, 'Cessation' in Cathryn Costello, Michelle Foster, and Jane McAdam (eds), *The Oxford Handbook of International Refugee Law* (OUP 2021).

Costello C, 'The Outer Edges of Non-Refoulement in Europe' in Bruce Burson and David Cantor (eds), *Human Rights and the Refugee Definition* (Brill Nijhoff 2016).

Crawley H, '[En]gendering International Refugee Protection: Are We There Yet?' in Bruce Burson and David Cantor (eds), *Human Rights and the Refugee Definition* (Brill Nijhoff 2016).

Crock M, 'Protecting Refugees With Disabilities' in Cathryn Costello, Michelle Foster, and Jane McAdam (eds), *The Oxford Handbook of International Refugee Law* (OUP 2021).

Dauvergne C, 'Women in Refugee Jurisprudence' in Cathryn Costello, Michelle Foster, and Jane McAdam (eds), *The Oxford Handbook of International Refugee Law* (OUP 2021).

Denza E, 'Diplomatic Asylum' in Andreas Zimmermann (ed), *The 1951 Convention Relating to the Status of Refugees and its 1967 Protocol: A Commentary* (OUP 2011).

Dörig H, 'Asylum Qualification Directive 2011/95/EU: Articles 1–10' in Kay Hailbronner and Daniel Thym, *EU Immigration and Asylum Law: A Commentary* (2nd edn, Hart Publishing 2016).

Dörr I, 'Article 31: General Rules of Interpretation' in Oliver Dörr and Kirsten Schmalenbach (eds), *Vienna Convention on the Law of Treaties: A Commentary* (Springer 2012).

Douzinas C and Warrington R, 'A Well-Founded Fear of Justice: Law and Ethics in Postmodernity' in Jerry D Leonard (ed), *Legal Studies as Cultural Studies: A Reader in (Post) Modern Critical Theory* (Albany State University of New York Press 1995).

Edwards A, 'Age and Gender Dimensions in International Refugee Law' in Erika Feller, Volker Türk, and Frances Nicholson (eds), *Refugee Protection in International Law: UNHCR's Global Consultations on International Protection* (CUP 2003).

Edwards A, 'The Meaning of Nationality in International Law in an Era of Human Rights' in Alice Edwards and Laura van Waas (eds), *Nationality and Statelessness under International Law* (CUP 2014).

Einarsen T, 'Drafting History of the 1951 Convention and the 1967 Protocol' in Andreas Zimmermann (ed), *The 1951 Convention Relating to the Status of Refugees and its 1967 Protocol: A Commentary* (OUP 2011).

Evans MD, 'Co-existence and Confidentiality: The Experience of the Optional Protocol to the Convention Against Torture. Harmony and Human Rights: The Music of the Spheres' in Carla M Buckley, Alice Donald, and Philip Leach (eds), *Towards Convergence in International Human Rights Law: Approaches of Regional and International Systems* (Brill Nijhoff 2016).

Ferreira N and Danisi C, 'Queering International Refugee Law' in Cathryn Costello, Michelle Foster, and Jane McAdam (eds), *The Oxford Handbook of International Refugee Law* (OUP 2021).

Fischel De Andrade J, 'Regional Refugee Regimes: Latin America' in Cathryn Costello, Michelle Foster, and Jane McAdam (eds), *The Oxford Handbook of International Refugee Law* (OUP 2021).

Fitzpatrick J and Bonoan R, 'Cessation of Refugee Protection' in Erika Feller, Volker Türk, and Frances Nicholson (eds), *International Law: UNHCR's Global Consultations on International Protection* (CUP 2003).

Foster M, 'Why We Are Not There Yet: The Particular Challenge of "Particular Social Group"' in Efrat Arbel, Catherine Dauvergne, and Jenni Millbank (eds), *Gender in Refugee Law: From the Margins to the Centre* (Routledge 2014).

Foster M, 'Economic Migrant or Person in Need of Protection? Socio-Economic Rights and Persecution in International Refugee Law' in Bruce Burson and David Cantor (eds), *Human Rights and the Refugee Definition* (Brill Nijhoff 2016).

Freier LF, 'A Liberal Paradigm Shift? A Critical Appraisal of Recent Trends in Latin American Asylum Legislation' in Jean-Pierre Gauci et al (eds), *Exploring the Boundaries of Refugee Law* (Brill Nijhoff 2015).

Garlick M, 'UNHCR and the Implementation of Council Directive 2004/83/EC on Minimum Standards for the Qualification and Status of Third Country Nations or Stateless Persons as Refugees or as Persons who Otherwise Need International Protection and the Content of the Protection Granted (The EC "Qualification Directive")' in Karin Zwaan (ed), *The Qualification Directive: Central Themes, Problem Issues, and Implementation in Selected Member States* (Wolf Legal Publishers 2007).

Garlick M, 'Selected Aspects of UNHCR's Research Findings' in Grutters et al (eds), *Assessment of Credibility by Judges in Asylum Cases in the EU* (Wolf Legal Publishers 2013).

Garlick M, 'Protection in the European Union for People Fleeing Indiscriminate Violence in Armed Conflict: Article 15(c) of the EU Qualification Directive' in Volker Türk, Alice Edwards, and Cornelis Wouters (eds), *In Flight from Conflict and Violence UNHCR's Consultations on Refugee Status and Other Forms of International Protection* (CUP and UNHCR 2017).

Gibney M, 'US Foreign Policy and the Creation of Refugee Flows', in Howard Adelman (ed), *Refugee Policy: Canada and the United States* (York Lanes Press, Toronto 1991).

Gilbert G, 'Exclusion' in Cathryn Costello, Michelle Foster, and Jane McAdam (eds), *The Oxford Handbook of International Refugee Law* (OUP 2021).

Goodwin-Gill GS, 'State Responsibility and the "Good Faith" Obligation in International Law' in Malgosia Fitzmaurice and Dan Sarooshi (eds), *Issues of State Responsibility before International Judicial Institutions* (Hart Publishing 2004).

Goodwin-Gill GS, 'The Search for the One, True Meaning …', in Guy S Goodwin-Gill and Hélène Lambert (eds), *The Limits of Transnational Law: Refugee Law, Policy Harmonization and Judicial Dialogue in the European Union* (CUP 2010).

Goodwin-Gill GS, 'The International Law of Refugee Protection' in Elena Fiddian-Qasmiyeh et al (eds), *The Oxford Handbook of Refugee and Forced Migration Studies* (OUP 2014).

Goodwin-Gill GS, 'Current Challenges in Refugee Law' in Jean-Pierre Gauci et al (eds), *Exploring the Boundaries of Refugee Law* (Brill Nijhoff 2015).

Hailbronner K, 'Comments on the Right to Leave, Return and Remain' in Vera Gowlland-Debbas (ed), *The Problem of Refugees in the Light of Contemporary International Law Issues* (Martinus Nijhoff 1996).

Hailbronner K, 'Nationality' in Thomas A Aleinikoff and Vincent Chetail (eds), *Migration and International Legal Norms* (TMC Asser Press 2003).

Hailbronner K, 'Nationality in Public International Law and European Law' in Rainer Bauböck et al (eds), *Acquisition and Loss of Nationality Policies and Trends in 15 European States. Volume 1: Comparative Analyses* (Amsterdam University Press 2006).

Haines R, 'Gender-related Persecution' in Erika Feller, Volker Türk, and Frances Nicholson (eds), *Refugee Protection in International Law: UNHCR's Global Consultations on International Protection* (CUP 2003).

Hamlin R, 'The Politics of International Refugee Law and Protection' in Cathryn Costello, Michelle Foster, and Jane McAdam (eds), *The Oxford Handbook of International Refugee Law* (OUP 2021).

Harvey CJ, 'Taking Human Rights Seriously in the Asylum Context' in Frances Nicholson and Patrick Twomey (eds), *Current Issues of UK Asylum Law and Policy* (Routledge 1998).

Harvey CJ, 'Is Humanity Enough? Refugees, Asylum Seekers and the Rights Regime' in Satvinder Juss and Colin J Harvey (eds), *Contemporary Issues in Refugee Law* (Edward Elgar 2013).

Hathaway JC, 'International Refugee Law: Humanitarian Standard or Protectionist Ploy?' in Alan E Nash and John P Humphrey (eds), *Human Rights and the Protection of Refugees Under International Law. Proceedings of a Conference Held in Montreal, November 29–December 2, 1987* (The Institute for Research on Public Policy 1987).

Heintze HJ, 'Are De Facto Regimes Bound by Human Rights?' in IFSH (ed), *OSCE Yearbook 2009* (Baden-Baden 2010).

Husain R, 'International Human Rights and Refugee Law: The United Kingdom' in Bruce Burson and David Cantor (eds), *Human Rights and the Refugee Definition* (Brill Nijhoff 2016).

IARLJ, 'Assessment of Credibility in Refugee and Subsidiary Protection Claims under the EU Qualification Directive: Judicial Criteria and Standards' in Grutters Carolus, Elspeth Guild, and De Groot Sebastiaan (eds), *Assessment of Credibility by Judges in Asylum Cases in the EU* (Wolf Legal Publishers 2013).

Janmyr M and Stevens D, 'Regional Refugee Regimes: Middle East' in Cathryn Costello, Michelle Foster, and Jane McAdam (eds), *The Oxford Handbook of International Refugee Law* (OUP 2021).

Jastram K, 'Economic Harm as a Basis for Refugee Status and the Application of Human Rights Law to the Interpretation of Economic Persecution' in James C Simeon (ed), *Critical Issues in International Refugee Law: Strategies toward Interpretative Harmony* (CUP 2010).

Jubilut LL et al, 'Human Rights in Refugee Protection in Brazil' in Bruce Burson and David Cantor (eds), *Human Rights and the Refugee Definition* (Brill Nijhoff 2016).

Juss SS, 'The UNHCR Handbook and the Interface between "Soft Law" and "Hard Law" in International Refugee Law' in Satvinder S Juss and Colin Harvey (eds), *Contemporary Issues in Refugee Law* (Edward Elgar 2013).

Kälin W, 'Well-founded Fear of Persecution: A European Perspective' in Jacqueline Bhabha and Geoffrey Coll (eds), *Asylum Law and Practice in Europe and North America: A Comparative Analysis* (Federal Publications 1992).

Kälin W, 'Implementing Treaties in Domestic Law: From "Pacta Sunt Servanda" to "Anything Goes"?' in Vera Gowlland-Debbas (ed), *Multilateral Treaty-Making: The Current Status of Challenges to and Reforms Needed in the International Legislative Process* (Springer 2000).

Kälin W, 'Supervising the 1951 Convention Relating to the Status of Refugees: Article 35 and Beyond' in Erika Feller et al (eds), *Refugee Protection in International Law: UNHCR's Global Consultations on International Protection* (CUP 2003).

Kälin W, Caroni M, and Heim L, 'Article 33, para 1' in Andreas Zimmermann (ed), *The 1951 Convention Relating to the Status of Refugees and its 1967 Protocol: A Commentary* (OUP 2011).

Kirk LJ, 'Island Nation: The Impact of International Human Rights Law on Australian Refugee Law' in Bruce Burson and David Cantor (eds), *Human Rights and the Refugee Definition* (Brill Nijhoff 2016).

Klabbers J, 'The Accountability of International Organisations in Refugee and Migration Law' in Cathryn Costello, Michelle Foster, and Jane McAdam (eds), *The Oxford Handbook of International Refugee Law* (OUP 2021).

Kneebone SY, 'Moving Beyond the State: Refugees, Accountability and Protection' in Susan Y Kneebone (ed), *The Refugees Convention 50 Years On: Globalisation and International Law* (Routledge 2003, reissued 2018).

Kneebone SY, 'Refugees as Objects of Surrogate Protection: Shifting Identities' in Susan Y Kneebone, Dallal Stevens, and Loretta Baldassar (eds), *Refugee Protection and the Role of Law: Conflicting Identities* (Routledge 2014).

Kneebone SY and O'Sullivan M, 'Article 1C' in Andreas Zimmermann (ed), *The 1951 Convention Relating to the Status of Refugees and its 1967 Protocol: A Commentary* (OUP 2011).

Lambert H, 'Conclusion: Europe's Normative Power in Refugee Law' in Hélène Lambert, Jane McAdam, and Maryellen Fullerton (eds), *The Global Reach of European Refugee Law* (CUP 2013).

Lambert H, 'Customary Refugee Law' in Cathryn Costello, Michelle Foster, and Jane McAdam (eds), *The Oxford Handbook of International Refugee Law* (OUP 2021).

Lambert H, 'Stateless Refugees' in Cathryn Costello, Michelle Foster, and Jane McAdam (eds), *The Oxford Handbook of International Refugee Law* (OUP 2021).

Lauterpacht E and Bethlehem D, 'The Scope and Content of the Principle of Non-Refoulment: Opinion' in Erika Feller, Volker Türk, and Frances Nicholson (eds), *Refugee Protection in International Law: UNHCR's Global Consultations on International Protection* (CUP 2003).

Leontiev L, 'The Application of International Human Rights Law in de facto States' in Sebastian Relitz (ed), *Obstacles and Opportunities for Dialogue and Cooperation in Protracted Conflicts* (Leibniz Institute for East and Southeast European Studies 2018).

Lester E, 'National Constitutions and Refugee Protection' in Cathryn Costello, Michelle Foster, and Jane McAdam (eds), *The Oxford Handbook of International Refugee Law* (OUP 2021).

Löhr T, 'Die Qualifikationsrichtlinie: Rückschritt hinter internationale Standards?' in Rainer Hofmann and Tillmann Löhr (eds), *Europäisches Flüchtlings—und Einwanderungsrecht, Seite 47–98* (Nomos 2008).

Martin DA, 'The Refugee Concept: On Definition, Politics and the Careful Use of State Resources' in Howard Adelman (ed), *Refugee Policy: Canada and the United States* (Center Migration Studies 1991).

Marx R, 'Article 1E' in Andreas Zimmermann (ed), *The 1951 Convention Relating to the Status of Refugees and its 1967 Protocol: A Commentary* (OUP 2011).

Mathew P, 'Draft Dodger/Deserter or Dissenter? Conscientious Objection as Grounds for Refugee Status' in Satvinder Juss and Colin J Harvey (eds), *Contemporary Issues in Refugee Law* (Edward Elgar 2013).

Mathew P, 'The Shifting Boundaries and Content of Protection: The Internal Protection Alternative Revisited' in Satvinder Juss (ed), *The Ashgate Research Companion to Migration Law, Theory and Policy* (Ashgate 2013).

McAdam J, 'The Qualification Directive: An Overview' in Karin Zwaan (ed), *The Qualification Directive: Central Themes, Problem Issues and Implementation in Selected Member States* (Wolf Legal Publishers 2007).

McAdam J, 'Interpretation of the 1951 Convention' in Andreas Zimmermann (ed), *The 1951 Convention Relating to the Status of Refugees and its 1967 Protocol: A Commentary* (OUP 2011).

McAdam J, 'Complementary Protection' in Cathryn Costello, Michelle Foster, and Jane McAdam (eds), *The Oxford Handbook of International Refugee Law* (OUP 2021).

McAdam J, 'Displacement in the Context of Climate Change and Disasters' in Cathryn Costello, Michelle Foster, and Jane McAdam (eds), *The Oxford Handbook of International Refugee Law* (OUP 2021).

Melander G, 'Refugee Policy Options—Protection or Assistance' in Göran Rystad (ed), *The Uprooted: Forced Migration as an International Problem in the Post-War Era* (Lund University Press 1990).

Millbank J, 'Sexual Orientation and Gender Identity in Refugee Claims' in Cathryn Costello, Michelle Foster, and Jane McAdam (eds), *The Oxford Handbook of International Refugee Law* (OUP 2021).

Milner J and Ramasubramanyam J, 'The Office of the United Nations High Commissioner for Refugees' in Cathryn Costello, Michelle Foster, and Jane McAdam (eds), *The Oxford Handbook of International Refugee Law* (OUP 2021).

Motz SA, 'The Persecution of Disabled Persons' in Céline Bauloz et al (eds), *Seeking Asylum in the European Union: Selected Protection Issues Raised by the Second Phase of the Common European Asylum System* (Brill Nijhoff 2015).

Muntarbhorn V, 'Regional Refugee Regimes: Southeast Asia' in Cathryn Costello, Michelle Foster, and Jane McAdam (eds), *The Oxford Handbook of International Refugee Law* (OUP 2021).

Ní Ghráinne B, 'The Internal Protection Alternative' in Cathryn Costello, Michelle Foster, and Jane McAdam (eds), *The Oxford Handbook of International Refugee Law* (OUP 2021).

Noll G, 'Evidentiary Assessment under the Refugee Convention: Risk, Pain and the Intersubjectivity of Fear' in Gregor Noll (ed), *Proof, Evidentiary Assessment and Credibility in Asylum Procedures* (Martinus Nijhoff 2005).

Noll G, 'Credibility, Reliability and Evidential Assessment' in Cathryn Costello, Michelle Foster, and Jane McAdam (eds), *The Oxford Handbook of International Refugee Law* (OUP 2021).

O'Sullivan M, 'Territorial Protection: Cessation of Refugee Status and Internal Flight Alternative Compared' in Satvinder S Juss (ed), *The Ashgate Research Companion to Migration Law, Theory and Policy* (Routledge 2013).

Oellers-Frahm K, 'Article 38 of the 1951 Convention/Article IV of the 1967 Protocol' in Andreas Zimmermann (ed) *The 1951 Convention Relating to the Status of Refugees and its 1967 Protocol: A Commentary* (OUP 2011).

Perry SR, 'Immigration, Justice, and Culture' in Warren F Schwartz (ed), *Justice in Immigration* (CUP 1995).
Pobjoy J, 'Refugee Children' in Cathryn Costello, Michelle Foster, and Jane McAdam (eds), *The Oxford Handbook of International Refugee Law* (OUP 2021).
Popovic A, 'Evidentiary Assessment and Non-Refoulment' in Gregor Noll (ed), *Proof, Evidentiary Assessment and Credibility in Asylum Procedures* (Martinus Nijhoff 2005).
Posner MH and Kaplan S, 'Who Should We Let in?' in Sarah Spencer (ed), *Strangers and Citizens: A Positive Approach to Migrants and Refugees* (Rivers Oram Press 1994).
Qafisheh MM and Azarova V, 'Article 1D' in Andreas Zimmermann (ed), *The 1951 Convention Relating to the Status of Refugees and its 1967 Protocol: A Commentary* (OUP 2011).
Ramcharan BG, 'Equality and Non-Discrimination' in Louis Henkin (ed), *The International Bill of Rights: The Covenant on Civil and Political Rights* (Columbia University Press 1981).
Refinish A, 'The Changing International Legal Framework for Dealing with Non-State Actors' in Philip Alston (ed), *Non-State Actors and Human Rights* (OUP 2005).
Rorty R, 'Human Rights, Rationality, and Sentimentality' in Stephen Shute and Susan L Hurley (eds), *On Human Rights: The Oxford Amnesty Lectures 1993* (Basic Books 1993).
Saul B, 'The Responsibility of Armed Groups Concerning Displacement' in Cathryn Costello, Michelle Foster, and Jane McAdam (eds), *Oxford Handbook of International Refugee Law* (OUP 2021).
Schmahl S, 'Article 1 Protocol Relating to the Status of Refugees' in Andreas Zimmermann (ed), *The 1951 Convention Relating to the Status of Refugees and its 1967 Protocol: A Commentary* (OUP 2011).
Schmahl S, 'Article 1A, para. 1' in Andreas Zimmermann (ed), *The 1951 Convention Relating to the Status of Refugees and its 1967 Protocol: A Commentary* (OUP 2011).
Schmahl S, 'Article 1B' in Andreas Zimmermann (ed), *The 1951 Convention Relating to the Status of Refugees and its 1967 Protocol: A Commentary* (OUP 2011).
Schultz J and Einarsen T, 'The Right to Refugee Status and the Internal Protection Alternative: What Does The Law Say?' in Bruce Burson and David Cantor (eds), *Human Rights and the Refugee Definition* (Brill Nijhoff 2019).
Schultz J, 'The European Court of Human Rights and Internal Relocation: An Unduly Harsh Standard?' in Jean-Pierre Gauci, Mariagiulia Giuffrè, and Evangelia Tsourdi (eds), *Exploring the Boundaries of Refugee Law: Current Protection Challenges* (Brill Nijhoff 2015).
Schultz J, 'The Internal Protection Alternative and Its Relation to Refugee Status' in Satvinder Juss (ed), *Research Handbook on International Refugee Law* (Edward Elgar 2019).
Schwebel SM, 'May Preparatory Work Be Used to Correct Rather Than Confirm the "Clear" Meaning of a Treaty Provision?' in Jerzy Makarczyk (ed), *Theory of International Law at the Threshold of the 21st Century: Essays in Honor of Krzysztof Skubiscewski* (Kluwer Law International 1996).
Sharpe M, 'Regional Refugee Regimes: Africa' in Cathryn Costello, Michelle Foster, and Jane McAdam (eds), *The Oxford Handbook of International Refugee Law* (OUP 2021).
Shearer IA and Opeskin B, 'Nationality and Statelessness' in Brian Opeskin, Richard Perrechoud, and Jillyanne Redpath-Cross (eds), *Foundations of International Migration Law* (CUP 2012).
Simeon JC, 'Strengthening International Refugee Rights through the Enhanced Supervision of the 1951 Convention and its 1967 Protocol' in Satvinder S Juss (ed), *The Ashgate Research Companion to Migration Law, Theory and Policy* (Ashgate Publishing 2013).
Simeon JC, 'The Human Rights Bases of Refugee Protection in Canada' in Bruce Burson and David Cantor (eds), *Human Rights and the Refugee Definition* (Brill Nijhoff 2016).
Skordas A, 'Article 5 (Rights Granted Apart from this Convention)' in Andreas Zimmermann (ed), *The 1951 Convention Relating to the Status of Refugees and Its 1967 Protocol: A Commentary* (OUP 2011).

Skran C, 'Historical Developments of International Refugee Law' in Andreas Zimmermann (ed), *The 1951 Convention Relating to the Status of Refugees and its 1967 Protocol: A Commentary* (OUP 2011).

Steinbock DJ, 'The Refugee Definition as Law: Issues of Interpretation' in Frances Nicholson and Patrick Twomey (eds), *Refugee Rights and Realities: Evolving International Concepts and Regimes* (CUP 1999).

Storey H, 'Persecution: Towards a Working Definition' in Vincent Chetail and Céline Bauloz (eds), *Research Handbook on Migration and International Law* (Edward Elgar 2014).

Storey H, 'Are Those Fleeing Ukraine Refugees?' in Sergio Carrera and Meltem Ineli-Ciger (eds), *EU Response to the Large-Scale Displacement from Ukraine: An Analysis on the Temporary Protection Directive and Its Implications for the Future EU Asylum Policy* (European University Institute (EUI) 2023).

Suhrke A, 'Global Refugee Movements and Strategies of Response' in Mary M Kritz (ed), *U.S. Immigration and Refugee Policy: Global and Domestic Issues* (Lexington Books 1983).

Sztucki J, 'Who Is a refugee? The Convention Definition: Universal or Obsolete?' in Frances Nicholson and Patrick M Twomey (eds), *Refugee Rights and Realities* (CUP 1999).

Türk V, 'The Role of UNHCR in the Development of International Refugee Law' in Frances Nicholson and Patrick M Twomey (eds), *Refugee Rights and Realities* (CUP 1999).

Türk V and Dowd R, 'Protection Gaps' in Elena Fiddian-Qasmiyeh et al (eds), *The Oxford Handbook of Refugee and Forced Migration Studies* (OUP 2014).

Türk V and Nicholson F, 'Refugee Protection in International Law: An Overall Perspective' in Erika Feller, Volker Türk, and Frances Nicholson (eds), *Refugee Protection in International Law* (CUP 2003).

Tzanakopoulos A, 'Domestic Courts as the "Natural Judge" of International Law: A Change in Physiognomy' in James Crawford and Sarah Nouwen (eds), *Select Proceedings of the European Society of International Law, Vol 3* (Hart Publishing 2010).

Tzanakopoulos A, 'Judicial Dialogue as a Means of Interpretation' in Helmut Philip Aust and Georg Nolte (eds), *The Interpretation of International Law by Domestic Courts: Uniformity, Diversity, Convergence* (OUP 2016).

van Waas L, 'The Intersection of International Refugee Law and International Statelessness Law' in Cathryn Costello, Michelle Foster, and Jane McAdam (eds), *The Oxford Handbook of International Refugee Law* (OUP 2021).

Vanheule D, 'A Comparison of the Judicial Interpretations of the Notion of Refugee' in Jean-Yves Carlier and Dirk Vanheule (eds), *Europe and Refugees: A Challenge?* (Kluwer Law International 1997).

Waibel M, 'Principles of Treaty Interpretation—Developed for and Applied by National Courts' in Helmut Phillipp Aust and Georg Nolte (eds), *The Interpretation of International Law by Domestic Courts* (OUP 2016).

Wallace R, 'Internal Protection Alternative in Refugee Status Determination: Is the Risk/Protection Dichotomy Reality or Myth: A Gendered Analysis' in Satvinder Juss and Colin Harvey (eds), *Contemporary Issues in Refugee Law* (Edward Elgar 2013).

Walter Kälin, 'Internal Displacement' in Cathryn Costello, Michelle Foster, and Jane McAdam (eds), *The Oxford Handbook of International Refugee Law* (OUP 2021).

Wouters K, 'Conflict Refugees' in Cathryn Costello, Michelle Foster, and Jane McAdam (eds), *The Oxford Handbook of International Refugee Law* (OUP 2021).

Zahle H, 'Competing Patterns For Evidentiary Assessments' in Gregor Noll (ed), *Proof, Evidentiary Assessment and Credibility in Asylum Procedures* (Martinus Nijhoff 2005).

Zard M, 'Towards a Comprehensive Approach to Protecting Refugees and the Internally Displaced' in Anne Bayefsky (ed), *Human Rights and Refugees, Internally Displaced Persons and Migrant Workers* (Martinus Nijhoff 2006).

Zieck M, 'Article 35/Article III' in Andreas Zimmermann (ed), *The 1951 Convention Relating to the Status of Refugees and its 1967 Protocol: A Commentary* (OUP 2011).

Ziegler R, 'International Humanitarian Law and Refugee Protection' in Cathryn Costello, Michelle Foster, and Jane McAdam (eds), *The Oxford Handbook of International Refugee Law* (OUP 2021).

Zimmermann A and Mahler C, 'Article 1A, para 2' in Andreas Zimmermann (ed), *The 1951 Convention Relating to the Status of Refugees and Its 1967 Protocol: A Commentary* (OUP 2011).

# Journal Articles

Adjin-Tettey E, 'Reconsidering the Criteria for Assessing Well-Founded Fear in Refugee Law' (1997) 25(1) Manitoba Law Journal 127.

Aitchison SA, 'A Teleological and Child-Sensitive Interpretation of a Country of Former Habitual Residence for Stateless Children Born Outside Their Parents' Country of Nationality or Former Habitual Residence' (2022) 4 Statelessness and Citizenship Review 7.

Akram SM, 'Orientalism Revisited in Asylum and Refugee Claims' (2000) 12 IJRL 7.

Aleinikoff TA, 'State Centred Refugee Law: From Resettlement to Containment' (1992) 14(1) Michigan Journal of International Law 120.

Aleinikoff TA, 'The Meaning of Persecution in United States Asylum Law' (1991) 3(1) IJRL 5.

Alexander H and Simon J, '"Unable to Return" in the 1951 Refugee Convention: Stateless Refugees and Climate Change' (2014) 26(3) Fla J Int'l L 531.

Anderson A, 'Flawed Foundations: An Historical Evaluation of Domestic Violence Claims in the Refugee Tribunals' (2021) 45(1) MULR 1.

Anderson A et al, 'A Well-Founded Fear of Being Persecuted... But When?' (2020) 42 Sydney L Rev 155.

Anderson A et al, 'Imminence in Refugee and Human Rights Law: A Misplaced Notion for International Protection' (2019) 68(1) ICLQ 111.

Andrysek O, 'Gaps in International Protection and the Potential for Redress through Individual Complaints Procedures' (1997) 9 IJRL 392.

Anker D, 'Refugee Law, Gender and the Human Rights Paradigm' (2002) 15 Harv Hum Rts LJ 133.

Arboleda E and Hoy I, 'The Convention Refugee Definition in the West: Disharmony of Interpretation and Application' (1993) 5 IJRL 66.

Aust HP, Rodiles A, and Staubach P, 'Unity or Uniformity: Domestic Courts and Treaty Interpretation' (2014) 27 LJIL 75.

Azoria D, '"Codification by Interpretation": The International Law Commission as an Interpreter of International Law' (2020) 31(1) EJIL 171.

Bagaric M and Dimopoulos P, 'Discrimination as the Touchstone of Persecution in Refugee Law' (2007) 3 Journal of Migration and Refugee Issues 14.

Bailliet CM, 'National Case Law as a Generator of International Refugee Law: Rectifying an Imbalance within UNHCR Guidelines on International Protection' (2015) 29 Emory International Law Review 2059.

Barbour B and Gorlick B, 'Embracing the Responsibility to Protect: A Repertoire of Measures including Asylum for Potential Victims' (2008) 20 IJRL 533.

Barksy RF, 'From the 1965 Bellagio Colloquium to the 1967 Refugee Protocol' (2020) 32(2) IJRL 340.

Barutciski M, 'Tensions Between the Refugee Concept and the IDP Debate' (1998) 3 Forced Migration Review 11.
Bassiouni MC, 'A Functional Approach to "General Principles of International Law"' (1990) 11(3) Michigan Journal of International Law 768.
Batchelor CA, 'Stateless Persons: Some Gaps in International Protection' (1995) 7(2) IJRL 232.
Batchelor CA, 'UNHCR and Issues Related to Nationality' (1995) 14(3) Refugee Survey Quarterly 91.
Batchelor CA, 'Statelessness and the Problem of Resolving Nationality Status' (1998) 10(1–2) IJRL 156.
Bauer J, 'Multiple Nationality and Refugees' (2014) 47 Vanderbilt Journal of Transnational Law 905.
Beaton E, 'Against the Alienage Condition for Refugeehood' (2020) 39 Law and Philosophy 147.
Benhabib S, 'The End of the 1951 Refugee Convention? Dilemmas of Sovereignty, Territoriality, and Human Rights' (2020) 2 Jus Cogens 75.
Berman F, 'Treaty "Interpretation" in a Judicial Context' (2004) 29(2) Yale Journal of International Law 315.
Bernard LL, 'The Definition of Definition' (1941) 19 Soc F 500.
Beyleveld D and Brownsword R, 'Human Dignity, Human Rights, and Human Genetics' (1998) 61(5) The Modern Law Review 661.
Bhabha J, 'Internationalist Gatekeepers: The Tension between Asylum Advocacy and Human Rights' (2002) 15 Harv Hum Rts LJ 155.
Bossin M and Demirdache L, 'A Canadian Perspective on the Subjective Component of the Bipartite Test for "Persecution": Time for Re-evaluation' (2004) 22(1) Refugee: Canada's Journal on Refugees 108.
Brett R and Lester E, 'Refugee Law and International Humanitarian Law: Parallels, Lessons and Looking Ahead' (2001) 83(843) IRRC 713.
Brölmann CM, 'Law-Making Treaties: Form and Function in International Law' (2005) 74 Nordic Journal of International Law 383.
Buffard I and Zemanek K, 'The "Object and Purpose" of a Treaty: An Enigma' (1968) 3 Austrian Review of International and European Law 311.
Buxton R, 'A History From Across The Pond' (2012) 44 International Law and Politics 391.
Cameron C, 'Why Do You Persecute Me? Proving The Nexus Requirement For Asylum' (2014) 18(2) University of Miami International and Comparative Law Review 233.
Cameron HE, 'Risk Theory and "Subjective Fear": The Role of Risk Perception, Assessment, and Management in Refugee Status Determinations' (2008) 20(4) IJRL 567.
Campanelli D, 'The United Nations Compensation Commission (UNCC): Reflections on Its Judicial Character' (2005) 4(1) The Law & Practice of International Courts and Tribunals 107.
Cantor D, 'The Laws of War and the Protection of "War Refugees": Reflections on the Debate and its Future Directions' (2014) 12(5) Journal of International Criminal Justice 931.
Cantor D, 'Reframing Relationships: Revisiting the Procedural Standards for Refugee Status Determination in Light of Recent Human Rights Treaty Body Jurisprudence' (2015) 34(1) Refugee Survey Quarterly 79.
Cantor D, 'The IDP in International Law? Developments, Debates, Prospects' (2018) 30(2) IJRL 191.
Cantor D and Chikwanha F, 'Reconsidering African Refugee Law' (2019) 31(2/3) IJRL 182.
Carens JH, 'Who Should Get In? The Ethics of Immigration Admissions' (2006) 17(1) Ethics & International Affairs 95.
Carnahan BM, 'Treaty Review Conferences' (1987) 81(1) AJIL 226.

Carr BA, 'We Don't Need to See Them Cry: Eliminating the Subjective Apprehension Element of the Well-Founded Fear Analysis for Child Refugee Applicants' (2006) 33 Pepperdine Law Review 535.
Cary B, 'Differing Interpretations of the Membership in a Particular Social Group Category and Their Effects on Refugees' (2016) 41 Okla City U L Rev 241.
Chan JM, 'The Right to a Nationality as a Human Right: The Current Trend Towards Recognition' (1991) 12(1/2) Human Rights Law Journal 1.
Chimni BS, 'The Geopolitics of Refugee Studies: A View from the South' (1998) 11(4) JRS 350.
Clark T and Crépeau F, 'Mainstreaming Refugee Rights: The 1951 Refugee Convention and International Human Rights Law' (1999) 17(4) Netherlands Quarterly of Human Rights 389.
Coles G, 'Refugees and Human Rights' (1992) 91 Bulletin of Human Rights 63.
Compton D, 'Asylum for Persecuted Social Groups: A Closed Door Left Slightly Ajar' (1987) 62 Washington Law Review 913.
Conte C, 'What about Refugees with Disabilities? The Interplay between EU Asylum Law and the UN Convention on the Rights of Persons with Disabilities' (2016) 18 European Journal of Migration and Law 327.
Cox TN, 'Well-Founded Fear of Being Persecuted: The Sources and Application of a Criterion of Refugee Status' (1984) 10 Brook J Int'l L 333.
Crawford J, 'The Criteria for Statehood in International Law' (1976) 48(1) British Yearbook of International Law 93.
Crawford J and Hyndman P, 'Three Heresies in the Application of the Refugee Convention' (1989) 1 IJRL 152.
Crisp J, 'Refugees, Persons of Concern, and People on the Move: The Broadening Boundaries of UNHCR' (2009) 26 Refuge 1.
Crock M et al, 'Where Disability and Displacement Intersect: Asylum Seekers and Refugees with Disabilities' (2012) 24(4) IJRL 735.
Cullen A and Wheatley S, 'The Human Rights of Individuals in De Facto Regimes under the European Convention on Human Rights' (2013) 13(4) Human Rights Law Review 691.
Daley K and Kelley N, 'Particular Social Group: A Human Rights Based Approach in Canadian Jurisprudence' (2000) 12 IJRL 148.
Danchin PG, 'Of Prophets and Proselytes: Freedom of Religion and the Conflict of Rights in International Law' (2008) 49 Harv Intl LJ 249.
Dauvergne C, 'Toward a New Framework for Understanding Political Opinion' (2016) 37 Mich J Int'l L 243.
Deere LL, 'Political Offenses in the Law and Practice of Extradition' (1933) 27(2) 27 AJIL 247.
Dehm S and Millbank J, 'Witchcraft Accusations as Gendered Persecution in Refugee Law' (2018) 28 Social and Legal Studies 202.
den Heijer M, 'Diplomatic Asylum and the Assange Case' (2013) 26(2) Leiden Journal of International Law 399.
DeWind J, 'Response to Hathaway' (2007) 20(3) Journal of Refugee Studies 381.
Donnelly J, 'The Relative Universality of Human Rights' (2007) 29 Human Rights Quarterly 281.
Dowd R, 'Dissecting Discrimination in Refugee Law: An Analysis of its Meaning and its Cumulative Effect' (2011) 23(1) IJRL 28.
Durieux J, 'The Many Faces of "Prima Facie": Group-Based Evidence in Refugee Status Determination' (2008) 25 Refuge 152.
Durieux J, 'Three Asylum Paradigms' (2013) 20(2) International Journal of Minority and Group Rights 147.
Eades D, 'Applied Linguistics and Language Analysis in Asylum Seeker Cases' (2005) 26(4) Applied Linguistics 503.

Eaton J, 'The Internal Protection Alternative under European Union Law: Examining the Recast Qualification Directive' (2012) 24(4) IJRL 765.
Edwards A, 'Human Rights, Refugees, and the Right to Enjoy Asylum' (2005) 17(2) IJRL 293.
Edwards A, 'Transitioning Gender: Feminist Engagement with International Refugee Law and Policy 1950–2010' (2010) 29(2) RSQ 21.
Edwards A and Hurwitz A, 'Introductory Note to the Arusha Summary Conclusions on Complementarities between International Refugee Law, International Criminal Law, and International Human Rights Law' (2011) 23(4) IJRL 856.
Ellison CS and Gupta A, 'Unwilling Or Unable? The Failure to Conform the Nonstate Actor Standard in Asylum Claims to the Refugee Act' (2021) 52 Colum Hum Rts L Rev 441.
Feller E, 'Address to the Conference of the International Association of Refugee Law Judges' (2001) 15(3) Georgetown Immigration Law Journal 381.
Feller E, 'International Refugee Protection 50 Years on: The Protection Challenges of the Past, Present and Future' (2001) 83(843) International Review of the Red Cross 581.
Ferris E, 'Internal Displacement and the Right to Seek Asylum' (2008) 278(3) Refugee Survey Quarterly 76.
Fink C, 'Minority Rights as an International Question' (2000) 9(3) Contemporary European History 385.
Fitzpatrick J, 'Revitalizing the 1951 Refugee Convention' (1996) 9 Harv Hum Rts LJ 229.
Fitzpatrick J, 'The Post-Exclusion Phase: Extradition, Prosecution and Expulsion' (2000) 12(1) IJRL 272.
Foighel I, 'The Legal Status of the Boat People' (1979) 48 Nordisk Tidsskrift for International Relations 222.
Fong C, 'Some Legal Aspects of the Search for Admission into Other States of Persons Leaving the Indo-Chinese Peninsula in Small Boats' (1981) 52(1) British Yearbook of International Law 53.
Forlati S, 'On Court Generated State Practice: The Interpretation of Treaties as Dialogue between International Courts and States' (2015) 20 Austrian Review of International and European Law 99.
Fortin A, 'The Meaning of "Protection" in the Refugee Definition' (2000) 12(4) IJRL 548.
Foster M, 'Causation in Context: Interpreting the Nexus Clause in the Refugee Convention' (2002) 23(2) Michigan Journal of International Law 265.
Foster M et al, '"Time" in Refugee Status Determination in Australia and the United Kingdom: A Clear and Present Danger from Armed Conflict?' (2022) 34(2) IJRL 163.
Fragomen AT, 'The Refugee: A Problem of Definition' (1970) 3 Case Western Reserve Journal of International Law 45.
Frelick B, 'Down the Rabbit Hole: The Strange Logic of Internal Flight Alternative' [1999] World Refugee Survey 22.
Fresia M, 'Building Consensus within UNHCR's Executive Committee: Global Refugee Norms in the Making' (2014) 27(4) Journal of Refugee Studies 514.
Fripp E, 'Deprivation of Nationality, "The Country of His Nationality" in Article 1A(2) of the Refugee Convention, and Non-Recognition in International Law' (2016) 28(3) IJRL 453.
Fripp E, 'Nationality, Protection, and "the Country of His Nationality" as the Country of Reference for the Purposes of Article 1A(2) of the 1951 Convention Relating to the Status of Refugees' (2021) 33(2) IJRL 300.
Fripp E, 'Statelessness, Inability or Unwillingness to Return, and the "Country of his Former Habitual Residence" as the Country of Reference for the Purposes of Article 1A(2) of the 1951 Convention relating to the Status of Refugees' (2022) 34(4) IJRL 327.
Fullerton M, 'Persecution Due to Membership in a Particular Social Group: Jurisprudence in the Federal Republic of Germany' (1990) 4 Geo Imm LJ 381.

Fullerton M, 'A Comparative Look at Refugee Status Based on Persecution Due to Membership in a Particular Social Group' (1993) 26 Cornell Int'l LJ 505.
García-Mora MR, 'The Nature of Political Offenses: A Knotty Problem of Extradition Law' (1962) 48 Virginia Law Rev 1226.
Garlick M, 'International Protection in Court: The Asylum Jurisprudence of the Court of Justice of the EU and UNHCR' (2015) 34 RSQ 115.
Garvey JI, 'Toward a Reformulation of International Refugee Law' (1985) 26(2) Harv Intl LJ 483.
Geiss R, 'Failed States: Legal Aspects and Security Implications' (2004) 48 German Yearbook of International Law 457.
Genser J, 'The United Nations Security Council's Implementation of the Responsibility to Protect: A Review of Past Interventions and Recommendations for Improvement' (2018) 18(2) Chicago Journal of International Law 420.
Gibney M, 'A Well-Founded Fear of Persecution' (1987) 10 Human Rights Quarterly 109.
Gibney MJ, 'Liberal Democratic States and Responsibilities to Refugees' (1999) 93(1) American Political Science Review 169.
Gilbert G, 'UNHCR and Courts' (2016) 28 IJRL 623.
Godfrey PC, 'Defining the Social Group in Asylum Proceedings: The Expansion of the Social Group to Include a Broader Class of Refugees' (1994) 3 Journal of Law and Policy 257.
Golder B, 'Beyond Redemption? Problematising the Critique of Human Rights in Contemporary International Legal Thought' (2014) 2 London Review of International Law 77.
Goodwin-Gill GS, 'Refugee Law and the Protection of Refugees' (1989) 1(1) IJRL 2.
Goodwin-Gill GS, 'The Language of Protection' (1989) 1(1) IJRL 6.
Goodwin-Gill GS, 'Judicial Reasoning and "Social Group" after Islam and Shah' (1999) 11 IJRL 538.
Goodwin-Gill GS, 'Asylum 2001—A Convention and a Purpose' (2001) 13(1/2) IJRL 1.
Goodwin-Gill GS, 'Refugees and Responsibility in the Twenty-First Century: More Lessons Learned from the South Pacific' (2003) 12(1) Washington International Law Journal 23.
Goodwin-Gill GS, 'The Dynamic of International Refugee Law' (2013) 25(4) IJRL 651.
Goodwin-Gill GS, 'The Office of the United Nations High Commissioner for Refugees and the Sources of International Refugee Law' (2020) 69 International and Comparative Law Quarterly 1.
Gorlick B, 'Human Rights and Refugees: Enhancing Protection through International Human Rights Law' (2000) 69(2) Nordic Journal of International Law 117.
Gorlick B, 'Common Burdens and Standards: Legal Elements in Assessing Claims to Refugee Status' (2003) 15 IJRL 357.
Grahl-Madsen A, 'Protection of Refugees by their Country of Origin' (1986) 11 Yale Journal of International Law 362.
Graves M, 'From Definition to Exploration: Social Groups and Political Asylum Eligibility' (1989) 26 San Diego Law Review 739.
Greatbatch J, 'The Gender Difference: Feminist Critiques of Refugee Discourse' (1989) 1 IJRL 518.
Gunn J, 'The Complexity of Religion and the Definition of "Religion" in International Law' (2003) 16 Harv Hum Rts LJ 189.
Gunning I, 'Expanding the International Definition of Refugee: A Multicultural View' (1989) 13(1) Fordham LJ 35.
Haines R, Hathaway JC, and Foster M, 'Claims to Refugee Status Based on Voluntary but Protected Actions: Discussion Paper No. 1 Advanced Refugee Law Workshop International Association of Refugee Law Judges Auckland, New Zealand, October 2002' (2003) 15(3) IJRL 430.

Hasselbacher L, 'State Obligations Regarding Domestic Violence: The European Court of Human Rights, Due Diligence, And International Legal Minimums of Protection' (2010) 8(2) Northwestern Journal of Human Rights 190.

Hathaway JC, 'New Directions to Avoid Hard Problems: The Distortion of the Palliative Role of Refugee Protection' (1995) 8 Journal of Refugee Studies 293.

Hathaway JC, 'International Refugee Law: The Michigan Guidelines on the Internal Protection Alternative' (1999) 21(1) Michigan Journal of International Law 131.

Hathaway JC, 'The Michigan Guidelines on Nexus to a Convention Ground' (2002) 23(2) Michigan Journal of International Law 207.

Hathaway JC, 'A Forum for the Transnational Development of Refugee Law: The IARLJ's Advanced Refugee Law Workshop' (2003) 15(3) IJRL 418.

Hathaway JC, 'Forced Migration Studies: Could We Agree Just to "Date"?' (2007) 20(3) Journal of Refugee Studies 349.

Hathaway JC, 'Food Deprivation: A Basis for Refugee Status?' (2014) 81(2) Social Research 327.

Hathaway JC and Foster M, 'The Causal Connection ("Nexus") to a Convention Ground: Discussion Paper No. 3 Advanced Refugee Law Workshop International Association of Refugee Law Judges Auckland, New Zealand, October 2002' (2003) 15(3) IJRL 461.

Hathaway JC and Hicks WS, 'Is There a Subjective Element in the Refugee Convention's Requirement of Well-Founded Fear?' (2005) 26(2) Michigan Journal of International Law 505.

Hathaway JC and Pobjoy J, 'Queer Cases Make Bad Law' (2012) 44(2) NYU Journal of International Law and Politics 315.

Heiskanen V, 'Jurisdiction v. Competence: Revisiting a Frequently Neglected Distinction' (1994) 5 Finnish Yearbook of International Law 1.

Helton A, 'Persecution on Account of Membership in a Social Group as Basis for Refugee Status' (1983) 15 Columbia Human Rights Law Review 39.

Henkin L, 'Refugees and Their Human Rights' (1994) 18 Fordham International Law Journal 1079.

Hessbruegge JA, 'Human Rights Violations Arising from Conduct of Non-State Actors' (2005) 11 Buffalo Human Rights Law Review 21.

Heyman MG, 'Redefining Refugees: A Proposal for Relief of the Victims of Civil Strife' (1987) 24 San Diego L Rev 449.

Hill Jr DW, 'Estimating the Effects of Human Rights Treaties on State Behavior' (2010) 72(4) The Journal of Politics 1161.

Holborn LW, 'The Legal Status of Political Refugees, 1920–1938' (1938) 32(4) AJIL 680.

Hyndman P, 'Refugees Under International Law with a Reference to the Concept of Asylum' (1986) 60 Australian Law Journal 148.

Hyndman P, 'The 1951 Convention Definition of Refugee' (1987) 9 Human Rights Quarterly 49.

Hyndman P, 'The 1951 Convention and Its Implications for Procedural Questions' (1994) 6 IHRL 246.

Imseis A, 'Statelessness and Convention Refugee Determination: An Examination of the Palestinian Experience at the Immigration and Refugee Board of Canada' (1997) 31(2) University of British Columbia Law Review 317.

Inder C, 'The Origins of "Burden Sharing" in the Contemporary Refugee Protection Regime' (2017) 29(4) IJRL 523.

Jaeger G, 'The Definition of "Refugee": Restrictive versus Expanding Trends' [1983] World Refugee Survey 5.

Jennings R, 'Some International Law Aspects of the Refuge Question' (1939) 20 British Yearbook of International Law 98.

Kagan M, 'Is Truth in the Eye of the Beholder? Objective Credibility Assessment in Refugee Status Determination' (2003) 17(3) Georgetown Immigration Law Journal 367.
Kälin W, 'The Guiding Principles on Internal Displacement—Introduction' (1998) 10 IJRL 557.
Kälin W, 'Flight in Times of War' (2001) 83 IRRC 629.
Kälin W, 'Non-State Agents of Persecution and the Inability of the State to Protect' (2001) 15(3) Georgetown Immigration Law Journal 415.
Kashefi S, 'Human Rights: A Relative, Progressive, Regressive, and Controversial Concept' (2011) 7(2) International Zeitschrift 74.
Keith K, 'The Difficulties of "Internal Flight'" and "Internal Relocation" as Frameworks of Analysis' (2001) 15 Georgetown Immigration Law Journal 433.
Kelley N, 'Internal Flight/Relocation/Protection Alternative: Is it Reasonable?' (2002) 14(1) IJRL 4.
Kelly D, 'Revisiting the Rights of Man: Georg Jellinek on Rights and State' (2004) 22(3) Law and History Review 493.
Kelly N, 'Gender-Related Persecution: Assessing the Asylum Claims of Women' (1993) 26 Cornell International Law Journal 625.
Kim G, 'Abandoning the Subjective and Objective Components of a Well-Founded Fear of Persecution' (2021) 16 Nw J L & Soc Pol'y 192.
Kinchin N and Mougouei D, 'What Can Artificial Intelligence Do for Refugee Status Determination? A Proposal for Removing Subjective Fear' (2022) 34 IJRL 373.
Klabbers J, 'Some Problems Regarding the Object and Purpose of Treaties' (1997) 8 Finnish Yearbook of International Law 138.
Krause U, 'Colonial Roots of the 1951 Refugee Convention and its Effects on the Global Refugee Regime' (2021) 24(5) J Int Relat Dev.
Kumin J, 'Gender: Persecution in the Spotlight' (2001) 123(2) Refugees 12.
Kuosmanen J, 'What's So Special about Persecution?' (2014) 17(1) Ethical Theory and Moral Practice 129.
Kyriakides C et al, 'Introduction: The Racialized Refugee Regime' (2019) 35(1) Refuge 3.
Lambert H, 'The Conceptualisation of "Persecution" by the House of Lords: Horvath vs Secretary of State' (2001) 13(1) IJRL 16.
Lambert H, 'Comparative Perspectives on Arbitrary Deprivation of Nationality and Refugee Status' (2015) 64 Int'l & Comp LQ 1.
Lapenna E, 'Le réfugié et l'émigrant dans le cadre des droits et libertés fondamentaux' (1984) 22 AWR Bulletin 50.
LaViolette N, 'Gender-Related Refugee Claims: Expanding the Scope of the Canadian Guidelines' (2007) 19(2) IJRL 169.
Leary JW, '"Outsourcing authority?" Citation to Foreign Court Precedent in Domestic Jurisprudence & Refinement or Reinvention: The State of Reform in New York' (2006) 69(3) Albany Law Review 1.
Lee LT, 'Internally Displaced Persons and Refugees: Toward a Legal Synthesis?' (1996) 9(1) Journal of Refugee Studies 27.
Lester A, 'Non-discrimination in International Human Rights Law' (1993) 19(4) Commonwealth Law Bulletin 1653.
Lister MJ, 'Who Are Refugees?' (2013) 32(5) Law and Philosophy 645.
Lo Giacco L, 'Swinging between Finding and Justification: Judicial Citation and International Law-Making' (2017) 6 Cambridge J Int'l & Comp L 27.
Lubell N, 'Challenges in Applying Human Rights Law to Armed Conflict' (2005) 87(860) IRRC 737.

Magugliani N, 'Trafficked Adult Males as (Un)Gendered Protection Seekers: Between Presumption of Invulnerability and Exclusion from Membership of a Particular Social Group' (2022) 34(4) IJRL 353.
Marouf FE, 'The Emerging Importance of "Social Visibility" in Defining a Particular Social Group and Its Potential Impact on Asylum Claims Related to Sexual Orientation and Gender' (2008) 27 Yale Law & Policy Review 47.
Martin DA, 'Review of the Law of Refugee Status' (1993) 87(2) AJIL 335.
Martin DA, 'Major Developments in Asylum Law Over the Past Year: A Year of Dialogue Between Courts and Agencies' (2007) 84 Interpreter Releases 2069.
Marx R, 'The Criteria for Determining Refugee Status in the Federal Republic of Germany' (1992) 4(2) IJRL 151.
Marx R, 'Non-Refoulement, Access to Procedures, and Responsibility for Determining Refugee Claims' (1995) 7 IJRL 401.
Marx R, 'The Notion of Persecution by Non-State Agents in German Jurisprudence' (2001) 15 Georgetown Immigration Law Journal 447.
Marx R, 'The Criteria of Applying the "Internal Flight Alternative" Test in National Refugee Status Determination Procedures' (2002) 14 IJRL 179.
Marx R, 'Interner Schutz von Flüchtlingen nach Art. 1a Nr. 2 GFK (Art. 2 Buchst. d) RL 2011/95/EU' (2017) 13 Zeitschrift für Ausländerrecht und Ausländerpolitik 303.
Mathew P, 'Limiting Good Faith: "Bootstrapping" Asylum Seekers and Exclusion from Refugee Protection' (2010) 29 Australian Yearbook of International Law 135.
Mathew P, Hathaway JC, and Foster M, 'The Role of State Protection in Refugee Analysis: Discussion Paper No. 2 Advanced Refugee Law Workshop International Association of Refugee Law Judges Auckland, New Zealand, October 2002' (2003) 15(3) IJRL 444.
Mayblin L, 'Colonialism, Decolonisation and the Right to be Human: Britain and the 1951 Geneva Convention on the Status of Refugees' (2014) 27(3) Journal of Historical Sociology 423.
McAdam J, 'Rethinking the Origins of "Persecution" in Refugee Law' (2013) 25(4) IJRL 667.
McDonald N, 'The Role of Due Diligence in International Law' (2019) 68(4) ICLQ 1041.
McGinley GP, 'Practice as a Guide to Treaty Interpretation' (1985) 9 Fletcher Forum 211.
McLachlan C, 'The Principle of Systemic Integration and Article 31(3)(c) of the Vienna Convention' (2005) 54(2) International and Comparative Law Quarterly 279.
McVay K, 'Self-Determination in New Contexts: The Self-Determination of Refugees and Forced Migrants in International Law' (2012) 28 Merkourios-Utrecht J Int'l & Eur L 36.
Meili S, 'When Do Human Rights Treaties Help Asylum Seekers?' (2014) 51(2) Osgood Hall Law Journal 627.
Meili S, 'Do Human Rights Treaties Help Asylum-Seekers: Lessons from the United Kingdom' (2015) 48(1) Vanderbilt Journal of Transnational Law 123.
Melander G, 'The Protection of Refugees' (1974) 18 Scandinavian Studies in Law 151.
Meron T, 'On a Hierarchy of International Human Rights' (1986) 80(1) AJIL 1.
Merrills JG, 'Two Approaches to Treaty Interpretation' (1971) 4(1) The Australian Year Book of International Law Online 55.
Millbank J and Vogl A, 'Adjudicating Fear of Witchcraft Claims in Refugee Law' (2018) 45 Journal of Law and Society 370.
Moore J, 'Whither the Accountability Theory: Second-Class Status for Third-Party Refugees as a Threat to International Refugee Protection' (2001) 13(1) IJRL 32.
Moreno-Lax V, 'Systematising Systemic Integration: "War Refugees", Regime Relations, and a Proposal for a Cumulative Approach' (2014) 12(5) Journal of International Criminal Justice 907.

Moretti S, 'Keeping Up Appearances: State Sovereignty and the Protection of Refugees in Southeast Asia' (2018) 17 European Journal of East Asian Studies 1.
Moretti S, 'Southeast Asia and the 1951 Convention Relating to the Status of Refugees: Substance without Form?' (2021) 33(2) IJRL 214.
Morgenstern F, 'Diplomatic Asylum' (1951) 67(267) LQR 362.
Musalo K, 'Irreconcilable Differences? Divorcing Refugee Protections from Human Rights Norms' (1994) 15 Michigan Journal of International Law 1179.
Musalo K, 'Revisiting Social Group and Nexus in Gender Asylum Claims: A Unifying Rationale for Evolving Jurisprudence' (2003) 52 DePaul Law Review 777.
Musalo K, 'Claims for Protection Based on Religion or Belief' (2004) 16(2) IJRL 170.
Nathwani N, 'The Purpose of Asylum' (2000) 12(3) IJRL 354.
Ní Ghráinne B, 'The International Protection Alternative Inquiry and Human Rights Considerations—Irrelevant or Indispensable' (2015) 27 IJRL 29.
Noll G, 'Seeking Asylum at Embassies: A Right to Entry under International Law?' (2005) 17(3) IJRL 542.
Noll G and Fagerlund J, 'Safe Avenues to Asylum? The Actual and Potential Role of EU Diplomatic Representations in Processing Asylum Requests' (2002) Danish Centre for Human Rights 1.
North AM and Chia J, 'Towards Convergence in the Interpretation of the Refugee Convention: A Proposal for the Establishment of an International Judicial Commission for Refugees' (2006) 25 Aust YBIL 105.
O'Sullivan M, 'Acting the Part: Can Non-State Entities Provide Protection Under International Refugee Law?' (2012) 24(1) IJRL 85.
Ocariz HH and Lopez JL, 'Practical Implications of INS v. Cardoza-Fonseca: Evidencing Eligibility for Asylum under the "Well-Founded Fear of Persecution" Standard' (1988) 19 Miami Inter-Am L Rev 617.
Ogg K, 'Protection Closer to Home? A Legal Case for Claiming Asylum at Embassies and Consulates' (2014) 33(4) RSQ 81.
Okoth-Obbo G, 'Thirty Years On: A Legal Review of the 1969 OAU Convention Governing the Specific Aspects of Refugee Problems in Africa' (2001) 20(1) Refugee Survey Quarterly 79.
Orakhelashvili A, 'Restrictive Interpretation of Human Rights Treaties in the Recent Jurisprudence of the European Court of Human Rights' (2003) 14 EJIL 529.
Orgad L, 'The Preamble in Constitutional Interpretation' (2010) 8(4) International Journal of Constitutional Law 714.
Phuong C, 'Persecution by Third Parties and European Harmonization of Asylum Policies' (2001) 16 Georgetown Immigration Law Journal 81.
Phuong C, 'Persecution by Non-State Agents: Comparative Judicial Interpretations of the 1951 Refugee Convention' (2003) 4(4) European Journal of Migration and Law 521.
Piotrowicz R, 'Refugee Status and Multiple Nationality in the Indonesian Archipelago: Is there a Timor Gap?' (1996) 8 IJRL 319.
Piotrowicz R, 'Lay Kon Tje and Minister for Immigration & Ethnic Affairs: The Function and Meaning of Effective Nationality in the Assessment of Applications for Asylum' (1999) 11(2) IJRL 544.
Pirjola J, 'Shadows in Paradise—Exploring Non-Refoulement as an Open Concept' (2007) 19(4) IJRL 639.
Pittaway E and Bartolomei L, 'Refugees, Race and Gender: The Multiple Discrimination against Refugee Women' (2001) 19(6) Refuge 21.
Porcino P, 'Toward Codification of Diplomatic Asylum' (1976) 8 New York University Journal of International Law and Politics 435.

Price ME, 'Persecution Complex: Justifying Asylum Law's Preference for Persecuted People' (2006) 47(2) Harv Intl LJ 413.
Prieur M, 'Draft Convention on the International Status of Environmentally-Displaced Persons' (2008) 4 Revue Européenne de Droit de l'Environnement 395.
Reed R, 'Foreign Precedents and Judicial Reasoning: The American Debate and British Practice' (2008) 124(2) LQR 253.
Rempell S, 'Defining Persecution' (2013) 2013(1) Utah Law Rev 283.
Riveles S, 'Diplomatic Asylum as a Human Right: The Case of the Durban Six' (1989) 11(1) Human Rights Quarterly 139.
Rousseau C et al, 'The Complexity of Determining Refugeehood: A Multidisciplinary Analysis of the Decision-Making Process of the Canadian Immigration and Refugee Board' (2002) 15(1) Journal of Refugee Studies 43.
Rubinstein S, 'Toward Principles for Refuge Claims Based on Unenforced Persecutory Laws' (RefLaw, 10 November 2020).
Sands P, 'Treaty, Custom and the Cross-Fertilisation of International Law' (1998) 1(1) Yale Human Rights and Development Law Journal 85.
Scanlon TM, 'Adjusting Rights and Absolute Values' (2004) 72 Fordham Law Review 1477.
Schoenholtz AI, 'The New Refugees and the Old Treaty: Persecutors and Persecuted in the Twenty-First Century' (2015) 16 Chicago Journal of International Law 81.
Seet M, 'The Origins of UNHCR's Global Mandate on Statelessness' (2016) 28 IJRL 7.
Sexton RC, 'Political Refugees, Nonrefoulement and State Practice: A Comparative Study' (1985) 18(4) Vanderbilt Journal of Transnational Law 733.
Shacknove A, 'Who Is a refugee?' (1985) 95 Ethics 274.
Shelton D, 'Reconcilable Differences? The Interpretation of Multilingual Treaties' (1997) 20(3) Hastings International and Comparative Law Review 611.
Shelton D, 'Normative Hierarchy in International Law' (2006) 100(2) AJIL 291.
Sidhom M, 'Jong Kim Koe v Minister for Immigration and Multicultural Affairs: Federal Court Loses Sight of the Purpose of the Refugee Convention' (1998) 20(2) Sydney Law Review 315.
Sitaropoulos N, 'Refugee: A Legal Definition in Search of a Principled Interpretation by Domestic Fora' (1999) 52 RHDI 151.
Slaughter A, 'A Typology of Transjudicial Communication' (1994) 29(1) University of Richmond Law Review 99.
Slaughter A, 'Judicial Globalization' (1999) 40 Virginia Journal of International Law 1103.
Smyth C, 'The Human Rights Approach to 'Persecution' and Its Child Rights Discontents' (2021) 33(2) IJRL 238.
Spiro PJ, 'Dual Nationality and the Meaning of Citizenship' (1997) 46(4) Emory Law Journal 1411.
Spiro PJ, 'Dual Citizenship as Human Right' (2010) 8 Int'l J Const L 111.
Stahnke T, 'Proselytism and the Freedom to Change Religion in International Law' [1999] Brigham Young University Law Review 251.
Stein MA and Lord JE, 'Enabling Refugee and IDP Law and Policy: Implications of the U.N. Convention on the Rights of Persons with Disabilities' (2011) 28(2) Arizona Journal of International and Comparative Law 401.
Steinbock DJ, 'Interpreting the Refugee Definition' (1998) 45(3) UCLA Law Review 733.
Stevens D, 'What Do We Mean By Protection?' (2013) 20(1) International Journal on Minority and Group Rights 233.
Storey H, 'The Internal Flight Alternative Test: The Jurisprudence Re-examined' (1998) 10(3) IJRL 499.
Storey H, 'Armed Conflict in Asylum Law: The "War Flaw"' (2012) 31(2) Refugee Survey Quarterly 1.

Storey H, 'Consistency in Refugee Decision-Making: A Judicial Perspective' (2013) 32(4) Refugee Survey Quarterly 112.
Storey H, 'The Law of Refugee Status, 2nd edition: Paradigm Lost' (2015) 27 IJRL 348.
Storey H, 'The Meaning of "Protection" within the Refugee Definition' (2016) 35(3) Refugee Survey Quarterly 1.
Storey H, 'The Human Rights Approach: Rising Sun or Falling Star' (2021) 33(3) IJRL 379.
Storey H, 'What Constitutes Persecution? Towards a Working Definition' (2014) 25(2) IJRL 272.
Stuyt AM, 'Good Faith and Bad Faith' (1981) 28(1) Netherlands International Law Review 54.
Summers RS, 'The Principles of the Rule of Law' (1999) 74 Notre Dame Law Review 1691.
Sweeney JA, 'Credibility, Proof and Refugee Law' (2009) 21(4) IJRL 700.
Sztucki J, 'The Conclusions on the International Protection of Refugees Adopted by the Executive Committee of the UNHCR Programme' (1989) 1 IJRL 285.
Tahvanainen A, 'Hierarchy of Norms in International and Human Rights Law' (2006) 24(3) Nordisk Tidsskrift for Menneskerettigheter 191.
Tobin J, 'Assessing GLBTI Refugee Claims: Using Human Rights Law to Shift the Narrative of Persecution Within Refugee Law' (2012) 44 International Law and Politics 447.
Türk V, 'Introductory Note to UNHCR Guidelines on International Protection' (2003) 15 IJRL 303.
van Essen J, 'De Facto Regimes in International Law' (2012) 28 Merkourios-Utrecht J Int'l & Eur L 31.
van Heuven Goedhart GJ, 'The Problem of Refugees' (1953) 82 Recueil des Cours 284.
Veiter T, 'Begriffe und Definitionen zum Flüchtlingsrecht' (1983) 21 Association for the Study of the World Refugee Problem Bulletin 118.
Virally M, 'Review Essay: Good Faith in Public International Law' (1983) 77(1) AJIL 130.
Waldron J, 'Rights in Conflict' (1989) 99(3) Ethics 503.
Waldron J, 'Foreign Law and the Modern Jus Gentium' (2005) 119(1) Harv L Rev 129.
Walker K, 'Defending the 1951 Convention Definition of Refugee' (2003) 17 Geo Immigr LJ 583.
Weis P, 'Legal Aspects of the Convention of 28 July 1951 Relating to the Status of Refugees' (1953) 30 British Yearbook of International Law 480.
Weis P, 'The Concept of Refugee in International Law' (1960) 87(1) Journal du Droit International 928.
Weis P, 'The United Nations Declaration on Territorial Asylum' (1969) 7 Canadian Yearbook of International Law 92.
Weis P, 'Human Rights and Refugees' (1971) 10(1–2) Israel Yearbook on Human Rights 35.
Wellman C, 'On Conflicts between Rights' (1995) 14 Law and Philosophy 271.
Wessels J, 'HJ (Iran) and HT (Cameroon)—Reflections on a New Test for Sexuality-Based Asylum Claims in Britain' (2012) 24(4) IJRL 815.
Williams G, 'The Correlation of Allegiance and Protection' (1948) 10(1) Cambridge Law Journal 54.
Wilsher D, 'Non-State Actors and the Definition of a Refugee in the United Kingdom: Protection, Accountability or Culpability' (2003) 15(1) IJRL 68.
Wilsher D, '"Between Martyrdom and Silence": Dissent, Duress, and Persecution as the Suppression of Human Rights under the Refugee Convention' (2021) 33(1) IJRL 28.
Wolman A, 'North Korean Asylum Seekers and Dual Nationality' (2012) 24(4) IJRL 793.
Wood T, 'Interpreting and Applying Africa's Expanded Refugee Definition' (2019) 32(2/3) IJRL 290.
Wood T, 'Who Is a Refugee in Africa? A Principled Framework for Interpreting and Applying Africa's Expanded Refugee Definition' (2019) 31(2/3) IJRL 290.
Wydrzynski C, 'Refugees and the Immigration Act' (1979) 25(2) McGill Law Journal 154.

Yasseen RMK, 'L'interprétation des traités d'après la Convention de Vienne sur le Droit des Traités' (1976) 151 Recueil des Cours 78.
Zambelli P, 'Knowing Persecution: Non-State Actors and the Measure of State Protection' (2020) 32(1) IJRL 28.
Zeigler SL and Stewart KB, 'Positioning Women's Rights within Asylum Policy: A Feminist Analysis of Political Persecution' (2009) 30(2) Frontiers: Journal of Women Studies 115.
Zink KF, 'Zur Bestimmung des Begriffs "Verfolgung" im Sinne des Abkommens vom 28. Juli 1951 über die Rechtsstellung der Flüchtlinge' (1956) 2 Internationales Asyl-Colloquium.

## Reports and Other Sources

AIDA, 'Mind the Gap: An NGO Perspective on Challenges to Accessing Protection in the Common European Asylum System' (Annual Report 2013–14).
Bauler P, 'Vienna Convention on the Law of Treaties', Encyclopaedia Britannica.
Bonavero Institute of Human Rights, 'A Preliminary Human Rights Assessment of Legislative and Regulatory Responses to the COVID-19 Pandemic across 11 Jurisdictions' (May 2020) Bonavero Report No 3/2020.
Brennen E, 'RefLaw Primer: Alienage' (2021) RefLaw.
Burson B, 'The Concept of Time and the Assessment of Risk in Refugee Status Determination' (Kaldor Centre Annual Conference, 18 November 2016).
Clayton G, ' "Even If . . . ": The Use of the IPA in Asylum Decisions in the UK' (Asylum Aid, 1 July 2014).
Crawford JR, 'State Responsibility' (2006) Max Plank Encyclopaedias of International Law.
de Moffarts G, 'Refugee Status and the Internal Flight or Protection Alternative' (2002) 2 (unpublished copy on file with the author) this is an update of the 1997 paper, 'Refugee Status and the "Internal Flight Alternative" ' (Refugee and Asylum Law: Assessing the Scope for Judicial Protection: International Association of Refugee Law Judges, Second Conference, Nijmegen, January 1997) 123–38).
Dörr O, 'Nationality', Max Planck Encyclopaedias of Public International Law.
EASO, 'Annual Report on the Situation of Asylum in the European Union' (2015).
EASO, 'Qualification for International Protection (Directive 2011/95/EU): A Judicial Analysis' (December 2016).
EASO, Judicial analysis—Evidence and Credibility Assessment in the Context of the Common European Asylum System (2018).
EASO, Judicial Analysis on Ending International Protection (2nd edn, 2021).
ECRE, 'Actors of Protection and the Internal Protection Alternative: European Comparative Report' (2014).
EUAA, 'Qualification for International Protection Judicial Analysis' (2nd edition, Produced by IARMJ-Europe under contract to the EUAA, January 2023).
Editorial, 'Refugee crisis: Many migrants falsely claim to be Syrians, Germany says as EU tries to ease tensions' (*The Telegraph*, 25 September 2015).
European Legal Network on Asylum, 'Research Paper on the Application of the Concept of Internal Protection Alternative' (2000).
Explanatory Report to the Council of Europe Convention on the avoidance of statelessness in relation to State succession (19 May 2006).
Foster M, 'The "Ground with the Least Clarity": A Comparative Study of Jurisprudential Developments Relating to "Membership of a Particular Social Group" ' (2012) UNHCR Legal and Protection Policy Research Series.

Goodwin-Gill GS, 'Deprivation of Citizenship Resulting in Statelessness and its Implications in International Law: Opinion' (12 March 2014).
Goodwin-Gill GS, 'Strategy and Strategic Litigation' (Keynote Address, Global Strategic Litigation Council Annual Conference, 12 April 2022).
Hathaway JC and Foster M, 'Internal Protection/Relocation/Flight Alternative' in Erika Feller, Volker Türk, and Frances Nicholson (eds), *UNHCR Global Consultations, Refugee Protection in International Law* (UNHCR 2003).
Holzer V, 'The 1951 Refugee Convention and the Protection of Persons Fleeing Armed Conflict and Other Situations of Violence' (September 2012) UNHCR, Legal and Protection Policy Research Series, PPLA/2012/05.
IARMJ-Europe, 'Evidence and Credibility Assessment in the Context of the Common European Asylum System: Judicial Analysis' (2nd edn, 2023).
Inter-Parliamentary Union and UNHCR, Nationality and Statelessness: A Handbook for Parliamentarians No 22 (2014).
International Association of Refugee and Migration Judges, 'Judicial Criteria for Assessing Country of Origin Information (COI): A Checklist' (9 November 2006).
International Association of Refugee Law Judges, 'A Structured Approach to the Decision Making Process' (2016).
International Commission on Intervention and State Sovereignty, 'The Responsibility to Protect' (2001).
Kälin W and Schrepfer N, 'Protecting People Crossing Borders in the Context of Climate Change: Normative Gaps and Possible Approaches' (2012) UNHCR, Legal and Protection Policy Research Series, PPLA/2012/01.
Kelly A and Pattisson P, ' "A Pandemic of Abuses": Human Rights under Attack during Covid, says UN Head' (*The Guardian*, 22 February 2021).
Macklin A, 'Truth and Consequences: Credibility Determination in the Refugee Context' (1998) International Association of Refugee Law Judges, Conference in Ottawa (Canada).
Martin A et al, 'Hate Crimes: The Rise of "Corrective" Rape in South Africa' (ActionAid 2019).
Moïse Mbengue M, 'Preamble', Max Planck Encyclopaedias of International Law (2006).
O Hudson M, 'Report on Nationality, Including Statelessness' (21 February 1952) UN Doc A/CN.4.50.
Patrick PL, 'Asylum and Language Analysis' in Susan K Brown and Frank D Beans (eds), Encyclopaedia of Migration (Springer 2013).
Refugee Women's Legal Group (RWLG), 'Gender Guidelines for the Determination of Asylum Claims in the UK' (1998).
Röhl K, 'Fleeing Violence and Poverty: Non-Refoulement Obligations under the European Convention on Human Rights' (2005) UNHCR: New Issues in Refugee Research, Working Paper No 111.
Sheridan Mouton L, 'Gender-related Asylum Claims and the Social Group Calculus: Recognizing Women as a "Particular Social Group" Per Se' (The Committee on Immigration and Nationality Law of Association of the Bar of the City of New York 2003).
Spijkerboer T and Sabine J, 'Fleeing Homophobia. Asylum Claims Related to Sexual Orientation and Gender Identity in Europe' (6 September 2011).
Storey H, ' "From Nowhere to Somewhere": An Evaluation of the UNHCR 2nd Track Global Consultations on International Protection: San Remo 8-10 September 2001 Experts Roundtable on the IPA/IRA/IFA Alternative' in IARLJ Conference 2002 (Victoria University of Wellington 2003).
Storey H, 'Nationality as an Element of the Refugee Definition and the Unsettled Issues of "Inchoate Nationality" and "Effective Nationality" ' (2017) RefLaw, 1st part.

Storey H, 'Nationality as an Element of the Refugee Definition and the Unsettled Issues of "Inchoate Nationality" and "Effective Nationality"' (2019) RefLaw, 2nd part.
UNHCR, 'Beyond Proof Credibility: Assessment in EU Asylum Systems' (2013).
UNHCR, 'Summary of Deliberations on Credibility Assessment in Asylum Procedures, Expert Roundtable in Budapest on 14–15 January 2015' (5 May 2015).
UNHCR, Canada (MCI) v Camayo—Memorandum of the Intervener: U.N. High Commissioner for Refugees (24 February 2021).
Weerasinghe S, 'In Harm's Way: International Protection in the Context of Nexus Dynamics between Conflict or Violence and Disaster or Climate Change' (2018) UNHCR, Legal and Policy Protection Research Series, PPLA/2018/05.
Wood T, 'Protection and Disasters in the Horn of Africa: Norms and Practice for Addressing Cross-Border Displacement in Disaster Contexts' (The Nansen Initiative, January 2013).
Wouters K, International Legal Standards for the Protection from Refoulement (Intersentia 2009).
WTO, Panel Reports, European Communities—Measures Affecting the Approval and Marketing of Biotech Products (29 September 2006) WT/DS291/R.
Zink KF, Das Asylrecht in der Bundesrepublik Deutschland nach dem Abkommen vom 28. Juli über die Rechtsstellung der Flüchtlinge under besonder Berucksichtigung der Rechtssprechung der Verwalkungsgerichte (Dissertation, Erlangen-Nürnberg 1962).

## United Nations Documents

4 UN GAOR (29 November 1950).
4 UN GAOR, Third Committee, Summary Records (2 December 1949).
5 UN GAOR (4 December 1950).
Ad Hoc Committee on Refugees and Stateless Persons, A Study of Statelessness, United Nations, August 1949, Lake Success–New York (1 August 1949) UN Doc E/1112/Add.1.
Ad Hoc Committee on Refugees and Stateless Persons, Second Session: Summary Record of the Fortieth Meeting Held at the Palais des Nations, Geneva, on Tuesday, 22 August 1950, at 2.30 p.m. (27 September 1950) UN Doc E/AC.32/SR.40.
Ad Hoc Committee on Statelessness and Related Problems, Comité spécial de l'apatridie et des problèmes connexes, Royaume-Uni: Texte remanié proposé pour l'article premier (19 January 1950) UN Doc E/AC.32/L.2/Rev.1.
Ad Hoc Committee on Statelessness and Related Problems, Comité spécial de l'apatridie et des problèmes connexes, Texte provisoire de paragraphes a insérer dans le rapport sur la question et la suppression de l'apatridie, Proposé par le Président (13 February 1950) UN Doc E/AC.32/L.36.
Ad Hoc Committee on Statelessness and Related Problems, Comments of the Committee on the Draft Convention (10 February 1950) UN Doc E/AC.32/L.32/Add.1.
Ad Hoc Committee on Statelessness and Related Problems, First Session, Summary Record of the Eighteenth Meeting (8 February 1950) UN Doc E/AC.32/SR.18.
Ad Hoc Committee on Statelessness and Related Problems, First Session: Summary Record of the Third Meeting Held at Lake Success, New York, on Tuesday, 17 January 1950, at 3 p.m. (26 January 1950) UN Doc E/AC.32/SR.3.
Ad Hoc Committee on Statelessness and Related Problems, Seventeenth Meeting (Definition of the term 'refugee') (31 January 1951) UN Doc E/AC.32/SR.17.
Ad Hoc Committee on Statelessness and Related Problems, Thirty-third Meeting (Election of officers and preliminary discussion) (1950) UN Doc E/AC.32/SR.33.

## 772 SELECTED BIBLIOGRAPHY

Ad Hoc Committee to the Economic and Social Council (1950) UN Doc E/AC.32/L.38.
Bonaventure Rutinwa, 'Prima Facie Status and Refugee Protection' (2002) UNHCR, New Issues in Refugee Research, Working Paper No 69.
Case of Gareth Anver Prince v South Africa (31 October 2007) Communication No 1474/2006, UN Doc CCPR/C/91/D/1474/2006.
CERD General Recommendation VIII Concerning the Interpretation and Application of Article 1, Paragraphs 1 and 4 of the Convention Identification with a Particular Racial or Ethnic Group (22 August 1990) UN Doc A/45/18.
Commission of Human Rights, Resolution 2005/63: Protection of the Human Rights of Civilians in Armed Conflicts (20 April 2005) UN Doc E/CN.4/RES/2005/63.
Committee on the Rights of Persons with Disabilities, General Comment No 6 (2018) on equality and non-discrimination (26 April 2018) UN Doc CRPD/C/GC/6.
Conference of Plenipotentiaries on the Status of Refugees and Stateless Persons: Summary Record of the Twenty-second Meeting (26 November 1951) UN Doc A/CONF.2/SR.22.
Conference of Plenipotentiaries on the Status of Refugees and Stateless Persons: Summary record of the 3rd meeting, held at the Palais des Nations, Geneva, on Tuesday, 3 July 1951 (19 November 1951) UN Doc A/CONF.2/SR.3.
Conference of Plenipotentiaries on the Status of Refugees and Stateless Persons, Conference of Plenipotentiaries on the Status of Refugees and Stateless Persons: Summary Record of the Twenty-first Meeting (26 November 1951) UN Doc A/CONF.2/SR.21.
Conference of Plenipotentiaries on the Status of Refugees and Stateless Persons: Summary Record of the Nineteenth Meeting (26 November 1951) UN Doc A/CONF.2/SR.19.
Conference of Plenipotentiaries on the Status of Refugees and Stateless Persons: Summary Record of the Thirty-fourth Meeting (30 November 1951) UN Doc A/CONF.2/SR.34.
Conference of Plenipotentiaries on the Status of Refugees and Stateless Persons: Summary Record of the Twenty-third Meeting (26 November 1951) UN Doc A/CONF.2/SR.23.
Conference of Plenipotentiaries on the Status of Refugees and Stateless Persons, Conference of Plenipotentiaries on the Status of Refugees and Stateless Persons: Summary Record of the Twenty-first Meeting (26 November 1951) UN Doc A/CONF.2/SR.21.
Conference of Plenipotentiaries on the Status of Refugees and Stateless Persons, Summary Record of the Twenty-fourth Meeting (27 November 1951) UN Doc A/CONF.2/SR.24.
Conference of Plenipotentiaries on the Status of Refugees and Stateless Persons: Summary Record of the 1st Meeting, held at the Palais des Nations, Geneva, on Monday, 2 July 1951 (19 July 1951) UN Doc A/CONF.2/SR.1.
Danilo Türk, 'The New International Economic Order and the Promotion of Human Rights: Realization of Economic, Social and Cultural Rights (Preliminary Report)' (28 June 1989) UN Doc E/CN.4/Sub.2/1989/19.
Danilo Türk, 'Thee New International Economic Order and the Promotion of Human Rights: Realization of Economic, Social and Cultural Rights (Final Report)' (3 July 1992) UN Doc E/CN.4/Sub.2/1992/16.
Declaration on the Elimination of All Forms of Intolerance and of Discrimination Based on Religion or Belief (25 November 1981) UN Doc A/36/55.
Declaration on the Rights of Persons belonging to National or Ethnic, Religious and Linguistic Minorities (4 March 1994) UN Doc A/RES/48/138.
ECOSOC, Commission on Human Rights, Report of the Working Party on an International Convention on Human Rights (11 December 1947) UN Doc E/CN.4/56.
ECOSOC, Official Records, First Session, Summary Record of the Hundred and Sixtieth Meeting of the Social Committee (1950) UN Doc E/AC.7/SR.160.
ECOSOC Res 248 (IX) (6 August 1949).
ECOSOC, Res 248 (IX) B (8 August 1949).

ECOSOC Res 2011 (LXI) (2 August 1976).
ECOSOC, Summary Record of the 172nd meeting held at the Palais des Nations, Geneva, on Saturday, 12 August 1950 (24 August 1950) UN Doc E/AC.7/SR.172.
Executive Committee Conclusion No 87 (1999). See also Executive Committee Conclusions: No 39 on Refugee Women and International Protection (1985); No 54 on Refugee Women (1998); No 64 on Refugee Women and International Protection (1990); No 73 on Refugee Protection and Sexual Violence (1993); No 77(g) on General Conclusion on International Protection (1995); No 105 on Women and Girls At Risk (2006). See also No 81(t) on General Conclusion on International Protection (1997).
Executive Committee of the High Commissioner's Programme, Implementation of the 1951 Convention and the 1967 Protocol Relating to the Status of Refugees (13 October 1989).
Executive Committee of the High Commissioner's Programme, Refugee Protection and Sexual Violence No 73 (XLIV)—1993 (8 October 1993).
Final Act of the United Nations Conference of Plenipotentiaries on the Status of Refugees and Stateless Persons (1954) 189 UNTS 37.
Human Rights Council, Report of the Office of the High Commissioner on the Outcome of the Expert Consultation on the Issue of Protecting the Human Rights of Civilians in Armed Conflict (2 June 2010) UN Doc A/HRC/11/40.
ILC, 'Fourth report on peremptory norms of general international law (jus cogens) by Dire Tladi, Special Rapporteur' (2019) UN Doc A/CN.4/727.
ILC, 'Fourth report on peremptory norms of general international law (jus cogens) by Dire Tladi, Special Rapporteur' (2019) UN Doc A/CN.4/727.
ILC, 'Fragmentation of international law: difficulties arising from the diversification and expansion of international law. Report of the Study Group of the International Law Commission, finalized by Martti Koskenniemi' (13 April 2006) UN Doc A/CN.4/L.682.
ILC, Fourth report on peremptory norms of general international law (jus cogens) by Dire Tladi, Special Rapporteur (31 January 2019) UN Doc A/CN.4/727.
ILC, Guide to Practice on Reservations to Treaties (2011) UN Doc A/66/10.
ILC, Report by William Mansfield on the Interpretation of Treaties in the Light of 'any Relevant Rules of International Law Applicable in Relations Between the Parties' (Article 31 (3) (C) of The Vienna Convention on the Law of Treaties), in the Context of General Developments in International Law and Concerns of the International Community (2004).
ILC, Report of the International Law Commission Fifty-eighth session (1 May–9 June and 3 July–11 August 2006) (2006).
ILC, Report of the International Law Commission, Sixty-fifth session (6 May–7 June and 8 July–9 August 2013) (2013) UN Doc A/68/10.
ILC, Report on Responsibility of States for Internationally Wrongful Acts (12 December 2001) UNGA Res 56/83.
ILC, Report on Responsibility of States for Internationally Wrongful Acts (12 December 2001) UNGA Res 56/83.
ILC, Report on Subsequent Agreements and Subsequent Practice in Relation to the Interpretation of Treaties (2018) UN Doc A/73/10.
ILC, Second Report on Subsequent Agreements and Subsequent Practice in Relation to Treaty Interpretation (26 March 2014) UN Doc A/CN.4/671.
International Law Commission, Articles on Diplomatic Protection with commentaries (2006).
International Law Commission, Articles on Nationality of Natural Persons in Relation to the Succession of States (1999) Supplement No 10 (A/54/10).
International Refugee Organisation, Manual for Eligibility Officers (1950).
Ministerial Communiqué (8 December 2011) UN Doc HCR/MINCOMMS/2011/16.
New York Declaration for Refugees and Migrants (9 September 2016) UNGA Res 71/1.

# 774 SELECTED BIBLIOGRAPHY

Report of the Ad Hoc Committee on Refugees and Stateless Persons, Second Session, Geneva, 14 August to 25 August 1950 (25 August 1950) UN Docs E/1850 and E/AC.32/8 (1950).

Report of the International Law Commission on the work of its Forty-ninth session, 12 May–18 July 1997, Official Records of the General Assembly, Fifty-second session, Supplement No 10 (1997) UN Doc A/52/10.

Report of the United Nations Conference on Territorial Asylum (1977) UN Doc A/CONF.78/12.

Report of the United Nations High Commissioner for Refugees, Part II: Global Compact on Refugees (2 August 2018) UN Doc A/73/12.

Statute of the Office of the United Nations High Commissioner for Refugees (1950) UNGA Res 428(v).

Summary of the Committee Meeting of the Economic and Social Council, UN Doc E/AC.7/SR.160 (18 August 1950).

The Final Act of the United Nations Conference of Plenipotentiaries on the Status of Refugees and Stateless Persons (25 July 1951) UN Doc A/CONF.2/108/Rev/1.

UN Ad Hoc Committee on Refugee and Stateless Persons, Ad Hoc Committee on Statelessness and Related Problems, Corrigendum to the Proposal for a Draft Convention Submitted by France (18 January 1950) UN Doc E/AC.32/L.3/Corr.1.

UN Ad Hoc Committee on Refugees and Stateless Persons, Ad Hoc Committee on Statelessness and Related Problems, United Kingdom Draft Proposal for Article 1 (17 January 1950) UN Doc E/AC.32/2.

UN Ad Hoc Committee on Refugees and Stateless Persons, Ad Hoc Committee on Statelessness and Related Problems, First Session: Summary Record of the Second Meeting Held at Lake Success, New York, on Tuesday, 17 January 1930, at 11 a.m. (17 January 1950) UN Doc E/AC.32/SR.2.

UN Ad Hoc Committee on Refugees and Stateless Persons, Ad Hoc Committee on Statelessness and Related Problems, Status of Refugees and Stateless Persons—Memorandum by the Secretary-General (3 January 1950) E/AC.32/2.

UN Ad Hoc Committee on Refugees and Stateless Persons, Ad Hoc Committee on Statelessness and Related Problems, First Session: Summary Record of the Fourth Meeting Held at Lake Success, New York, on Wednesday, 16 January 1950, at 11 a.m. (26 January 1950) UN Doc E/AC.32/SR.4.

UN Ad Hoc Committee on Refugees and Stateless Persons, Ad Hoc Committee on Statelessness and Related Problems, First Session: Summary Record of the Twentieth Meeting Held at Lake Success, New York, on Wednesday, 1 February 1950, at 2.30. p.m. (10 February 1950) E/AC.32/SR.20.

UN Ad Hoc Committee on Refugees and Stateless Persons, Ad Hoc Committee on Statelessness and Related Problems, France: Proposal for a Draft Convention—Revision of Draft Article 12 of Document (25 January 1950) UN Doc E/AC/32/L.3.

UN Ad Hoc Committee on Refugees and Stateless Persons, Report of the Ad Hoc Committee on Statelessness and Related Problems (17 February 1950) UN Doc E/1618.

UN Ad Hoc Committee on Statelessness and Related Problems, 1st Session, 5th Meeting (30 January 1950) UN Doc E/AC.32/SR.5.

UN Ad Hoc Committee on Statelessness and Related Problems, Ad Hoc Committee on Statelessness and Related Problems, Memorandum from the Secretariat of the International refugee Organisation (30 January 1950) UN Doc E/AC/32/1/16.

UN Ad Hoc Committee on Statelessness and Related Problems, First Session: Summary Record of the Sixth Meeting Held at Lake Success, New York, on Thursday, 19 January 1950, at 11 a.m. (26 January 1950) UN Doc E/AC.32/SR.6.

SELECTED BIBLIOGRAPHY 775

UN Committee on Economic, Social and Cultural Rights, General comment No 20: Non-discrimination in economic, social and cultural rights (Art. 2, para. 2, of the International Covenant on Economic, Social and Cultural Rights) (2 July 2009) UN Doc E/C.12/GC/20.
UN Committee on Economic, Social and Cultural Rights, General Comment No 14: The Right to the Highest Attainable Standard of Health (Art. 12) (11 August 2000) UN Doc E/C.12/2000/4.
UN Committee on Economic, Social and Cultural Rights, General Comment No 21: Right of Everyone to Take Part in Cultural Life (Art 15, para 1a of the Covenant on Economic, Social and Cultural Rights) (21 December 2009) UN Doc E/C.12/GC/21.
UN Committee on Economic, Social and Cultural Rights, General Comment No 15: The Right to Water (Arts. 11 and 12 of the Covenant) (20 January 2003) UN Doc E/C.12/2002/11.
UN Committee on Economic, Social and Cultural Rights, General Comment No 3 (14 December 1990) UN Doc E/1991/23.
UN Committee on Economic, Social and Cultural Rights, General Comment No 9: The Domestic Application of the Covenant (3 December 1998) E/C.12/1998/24.
UN Committee on Economic, Social and Cultural Rights, General Comment No 13 (8 December 1999) UN Doc E/C.12/1999/10.
UN Committee on Economic, Social and Cultural Rights, General Comment No 11 (10 May 1999) UN Doc E/1992/23.
UN Committee on the Elimination of Discrimination Against Women, CEDAW General Recommendation No 19: Violence Against Women (1992).
UN Committee on the Elimination of Discrimination Against Women, CEDAW General Recommendation No 21: Equality in Marriage and Family Relations (1994).
UN Committee on the Rights of the Child, General Comment No 14 (2013) on the Right of the Child to Have his or her Best Interests Taken as a Primary Consideration (Art. 3, para. 1) (29 May 2013) UN Doc CRC/C/GC/14.
UN Committee on the Rights of the Child, General Comment No 5 (2003): General Measures of Implementation of the Convention on the Rights of the Child (27 November 2003) UN Doc CRC/GC/2003/5.
UN Conference of Plenipotentiaries on the Status of Refugees and Stateless Persons, Conference of Plenipotentiaries on the Status of Refugees and Stateless Persons: Summary Record of the Nineteenth Meeting (26 November 1951) UN Doc A/CONF.2/SR.19.
UN COVID-19 Global Humanitarian Response Plan for COVID-19 (25 March 2020).
UN Economic and Social Council, General Comment No 18: The Right to Work (Art 6 of the Covenant) (6 February 2006) UN Doc E/C.12/GC/18.
UN General Assembly, Vienna Declaration and Programme of Action (12 July 1993) UN Doc A/CONF.157/23.
UN Guiding Principles on Internal Displacement (1998) UN Doc E/CN.4/1998/53/Add.2.
UN Human Right Committee, Concluding Observations on Kosovo (Serbia) (14 August 2006) UN Doc CCPR/C/UNK/CO/1.
UN Human Rights Committee, CCPR General Comment No 27: Article 12 (Freedom of Movement) (2 November 1999) UN Doc CCPR/C/21/Rev.1/Add.9.
UN Human Rights Committee, Concluding Observations on Georgia (2007) UN Doc CCPR/C/GEO/CO/3/CRP.1.
UN Human Rights Committee, Concluding Observations on Moldova (2016) UN Doc CCPR/C/MDA/CO/3.
UN Human Rights Committee, General Comment No 18: Non-discrimination (29 March 1996) UN Doc HRI/GEN/1/Rev.2.

776 SELECTED BIBLIOGRAPHY

UN Human Rights Committee, General Comment No 20: Article 7 (Prohibition of Torture, or Other Cruel, Inhuman or Degrading Treatment or Punishment) (12 May 2004) UN Doc HRI/GEN/1/Rev.7.
UN Human Rights Committee, General Comment No 22: Article 18 (27 September 1993) UN Doc CCPR/C/21/Rev.1/Add.4.
UN Human Rights Committee, General Comment No 24 on Issues Relating to Reservations Made upon Ratification or Accession to the Covenant or the Optional Protocols thereto, or in Relation to Declarations under Article 41 of the Covenant (4 November 1994) UN Doc CCPR/C/21/Rev.1/Add.6.
UN Human Rights Committee, General Comment No 29: States of Emergency (Article 4) (31 August 2001) UN Doc CCPR/C/21/Rev.1/Add/11.
UN Human Rights Committee, General Comment No 31: Nature of the General Legal Obligation Imposed on States Parties to the Covenant (26 May 2004) UN Doc CCPR/C/21/Rev.1/Add.13.
UN Human Rights Committee, General Comment No 34: Article 19 (Freedoms of Opinion and Expression) (12 September 2011) UN Doc CCPR/C/GC/34.
UN Human Rights Committee, General Comment No 35: Article 9 Liberty and Security of person (16 December 2014) UN Doc CCPR/C/GC/35.
UN Human Rights Committee, General Comment No 36 (2019): Article 6 (Right to Life) (3 September 2019) UN Doc CCPR/C/GC/35.
UN Human Rights Council, Human Rights and Arbitrary Deprivation of Nationality: Report of the Secretary-General (14 December 2009) UN Doc A/HC/13/34.
UN, Final Act of the United Nations Conference of Plenipotentiaries on the Status of Refugees and Stateless Persons (25 July 1951) 189 UNTS 137.
UN, Third Report on the Law of Treaties, by Sir Humphrey Waldock, Special Rapporteur (1964) UN Doc A/CN.4/167 and Add.1–3.
UNGA Res 1167 (XII) (26 November 1957).
UNGA Res 1388 (XIV) (20 November 1959).
UNGA Res 1499 (XV) (5 December 1960).
UNGA Res 1671 (XVI) (11 December 1961).
UNGA Res 1673 (XVI) (18 December 1961).
UNGA Res 194 (III) (11 December 1948).
UNGA Res 2040 (XX) (7 December 1965).
UNGA Res 2294 (XXII) (11 December 1967).
UNGA Res 2594 (XXIV) (16 December 1969).
UNGA Res 2650 (XXV) (30 November 1970).
UNGA Res 2856 (XXVI) (20 December 1971) UN GAOR, Supp No 29, UN Doc A/8429.
UNGA Res 2958 (XXVII) (12 December 1972).
UNGA Res 302 (IV) (8 December 1949).
UNGA Res 31/35 (30 November 1976).
UNGA Res 3143 (XXVIII) (14 December 1973).
UNGA Res 319 (IV) (3 December 1949).
UNGA Res 32/67 (8 December 1977).
UNGA Res 3321 (XXIX), Question of diplomatic asylum (14 December 1974).
UNGA Res 34/61 (29 November 1979).
UNGA Res 3447 (XXX) (9 December 1975) UN GAOR, Supp No 34, UN Doc A/10034.
UNGA Res 3454 (XXX) (1 December 1975).
UNGA Res 36/125 (14 December 1981).
UNGA Res 428 (V) (14 December 1950) GAOR, 5th Session, Supplement No 20.
UNGA Res 429(V) (14 December 1950).

UNGA Res 44/150 (15 December 1988).
UNGA Res 48/118 (20 December 1993).
UNGA Res 64/127 (18 December 2009).
UNGA Res 73/151 (17 December 2018).
UNGA Res 73/203 (20 December 2018) on 'Identification of Customary Law'.
UNGA, 'Report of the International Law Commission: Fifty-eighth Session' (2006) UN Doc A/61/10.
UNGA, Declaration on Territorial Asylum (14 December 1967) UN Doc A/RES/2312(XXII).
UNGA, Draft Protocol relating to the Status of Stateless Persons (14 December 1950) UN Doc A/RES/429.
UNGA, Interim Report of the Special Rapporteur on Freedom of Religion or Belief (17 July 2009) UN Doc A/64/159.
UNGA, Interim Report of the Special Rapporteur on Freedom of Religion or Belief (20 August 2007) UN Doc A/62/280.
UNGA, Juxtaposition of Article 1 of the Draft Convention relating to the Status of Refugees with Chapter II, Paragraphs 6 and 7 of the Statute of the Office of the United Nations High Commissioner for Refugees: Note (21 May 1951).
UNGA, Question of Diplomatic Asylum: Report of the Secretary-General (22 September 1975).
UNGA, Refugees and Stateless Persons: Report of the Secretary-General (26 October 1949) UN Doc A/C.3/527.
UNGA, Reports of the International Law Commission on the second part of its seventeenth session 3–28 January 1966 and on its eighteenth session 4 May–19 July 1966 (1966) UN Doc A/6309/Rev.1.
UNHCR and Asylum Aid, Mapping Statelessness in the United Kingdom (2011).
UNHCR Executive Committee, Agenda for Protection (2003).
UNHCR, 'Better Protecting Refugees in the EU and Globally'.
UNHCR, 'Collection of International Instruments and Legal Texts Concerning Refugees and Others of Concern to UNHCR, vol. III: Regional Instruments: Asia, Middle East, Asia, Americas' (2007).
UNHCR, 'Expert Meeting—The Concept of Stateless Persons under International Law: Summary Conclusions' (2010) (UNHCR 2010 Prato Conclusions).
UNHCR, 'Implementation of the 1951 Convention and the 1967 Protocol Relating to the Status of Refugees – Some Basic Questions' (15 June 1992) UN Doc EC/1992/SCP/CRP.10.
UNHCR, 'Information Note on Article 1 of the 1951 Convention' (1995).
UNHCR, 'Relocating Internally as a Reasonable Alternative to Seeking Asylum (The So-Called "Internal Flight Alternative" or "Relocation Principle")' (1999) UNHCR Position Paper.
UNHCR, 'Safe at Last? Law and Practice in Selected EU Member States with Respect to Asylum-Seekers Fleeing Indiscriminate Violence' (July 2011).
UNHCR, 'UNHCR Statement on the "Ceased Circumstances" Clause of the EC Qualification Directive' (14 August 2008).
UNHCR, An Overview of Protection Issues in Europe: Legislative Trends and Positions Taken by UNHCR (September 1995) European Series Volume 1(3) 1995/09.
UNHCR, Beyond Proof—Credibility Assessment in EU Asylum Systems (2013).
UNHCR, Conclusion on International Protection No 22 (XXXII) (1981) UN Doc A/36/12/Add.121.
UNHCR, Conclusion on International Protection No 85 (XLIX) (1998) UN Doc A/53/12/Add.1.
UNHCR, Conclusion on the Civilian and Humanitarian Character of Asylum No 94 (LIII)—2002 (8 October 2002) UN Doc A/AC.96/973.

UNHCR, Conclusion on the Provision of International Protection Including Through Complementary Forms of Protection No 103 (LVI)—2005 (2005) UN Doc A/AC.96/1021.

UNHCR, Conclusion on the Provision on International Protection Including Through Complementary Forms of Protection No. 103 (LVI)—2005 (07 October 2005).

UNHCR, Conclusions on International Protection Adopted by the Executive Committee of the UNHCR Programme 1975–2017 (Conclusion No 1–114) (October 2017) UN Doc HCR/IP/3/Eng/REV. 2017.

UNHCR, Consistent and Predictable Responses to IDPs—A Review of UNHCR's Decision-Making Processes (2005).

UNHCR, Declaration of States Parties to the 1951 Convention and or Its 1967 Protocol relating to the Status of Refugees (16 January 2002) UN Doc HCR/MMSP/2001/09.

UNHCR, Division of International Protection (February 1982) UNST/HCR/063.4/R4-E.

UNHCR, Executive Committee of the High Commissioner's Programme, Conclusion on Refugee Women and International Protection No 39 (XXXVI) (18 October 1985).

UNHCR, General Conclusion on International Protection No. 99 (LV)–2004 (8 October 2004) UN Doc A/AC.96/1003.

UNHCR, Guidance Note on Refugee Claims Relating to Victims of Organized Gangs (31 March 2010).

UNHCR, Guidelines for National Refugee Legislation, with Commentary (9 December 1980) UN Doc HCR/120/41/80/GE.81-0013.

UNHCR, Guidelines on International Protection No 1: Gender-Related Persecution within the context of Article 1A(2) of the 1951 Convention and/or its 1967 Protocol relating to the Status of Refugees (2002) UN Doc HCR/GIP/02/01.

UNHCR, Guidelines on International Protection No 10: Claims to Refugee Status related to Military Service within the context of Article 1A (2) of the 1951 Convention and/or the 1967 Protocol relating to the Status of Refugees (12 November 2014) UN Doc HCR/GIP/13/10/Corr.1.

UNHCR, Guidelines on International Protection No 11: Prima Facie Recognition of Refugee Status (24 June 2015) UN Doc HCR/GIP/15/11.

UNHCR, Guidelines on International Protection No 12: Claims for Refugee Status Related to Situations of Armed Conflict and Violence under Article 1A(2) of the 1951 Convention and/or 1967 Protocol relating to the Status of Refugees and the Regional Refugee Definitions (2 December 2016) UN Doc HCR/GIP/16/12.

UNHCR, Guidelines on International Protection No 13: Applicability of Article 1D of the 1951 Convention relating to the Status of Refugees to Palestinian Refugees (December 2017) UN Doc HCR/GIP/17/13.

UNHCR, Guidelines on International Protection No 2: Membership of a Particular Social Group within the context of Article 1A(2) of the 1951 Convention and/or its 1967 Protocol relating to the Status of Refugees (7 May 2002) UN Doc HCR/GIP/02/01.

UNHCR, Guidelines on International Protection No 3: Cessation of Refugee Status under Article 1C(5) and (6) of the 1951 Convention relating to the Status of Refugees (the 'Ceased Circumstances' Clauses) (10 February 2003) UN Doc HCR/GIP/03/03.

UNHCR, Guidelines on International Protection No 4: Internal Flight or Relocation Alternative Within the Context of Article 1A(2) of the 1951 Convention and/or 1967 Protocol Relating to the Status of Refugees (23 July 2003) UN Doc HCR/GIP/03/04.

UNHCR, Guidelines on International Protection No 5: Application of the Exclusion Clauses: Article 1F of the 1951 Convention relating to the Status of Refugees (4 September 2003) UN Doc HCR/GIP/03/05.

UNHCR, Guidelines on International Protection No 6: Religion-Based Refugee Claims under Article 1A(2) of the 1951 Convention and/or the 1967 Protocol relating to the Status of Refugees (2004) UN Doc HCR/GIP/04/06.

UNHCR, Guidelines on International Protection No 7: The Application of Article 1A(2) of the 1951 Convention and/or 1967 Protocol Relating to the Status of Refugees to Victims of Trafficking and Persons at Risk of Being Trafficked (7 April 2006) UN Doc HCR/GIP/06/07.

UNHCR, Guidelines on International Protection No 8: Child Asylum Claims under Articles 1(A)2 and 1(F) of the 1951 Convention and/or 1967 Protocol relating to the Status of Refugees (2009) UN Doc HCR/GIP/09/08.

UNHCR, Guidelines on International Protection No 9: Claims to Refugee Status based on Sexual Orientation and/or Gender Identity within the context of Article 1A(2) of the 1951 Convention and/or its 1967 Protocol relating to the Status of Refugees (23 October 2012) HCR/GIP/12/01.

UNHCR, Guidelines on Policies and Procedures in Dealing with Unaccompanied Children Seeking Asylum (1997).

UNHCR, Guidelines on Statelessness No 1: The Definition of 'Stateless Person' in Article 1(1) of the 1954 Convention relating to the Status of Stateless Persons (20 February 2012) HCR/GS/12/01.

UNHCR, Guidelines on Statelessness No 4: Ensuring Every Child's Right to Acquire a Nationality through Articles 1–4 of the 1961 Convention on the Reduction of Statelessness (21 December 2012) UN Doc HCR/GS/12/04.

UNHCR, Handbook on Procedures and Criteria for Determining Refugee Status and Guidelines on International Protection under the 1951 Convention and the 1967 Protocol Relating to the Status Of Refugees (Geneva, 2019, reissued in 2019) (UNHCR 1979 Handbook or 1979 Handbook).

UNHCR, Handbook on Protection of Stateless Persons (Geneva, 2014) (UNHCR 2014 Handbook or 2014 Handbook).

UNHCR, Interpreting Article 1 of the 1951 Convention Relating to the Status of Refugees (2001).

UNHCR, Ministerial Meeting of States Parties to the 1951 Convention relating to the Status of Refugees and UNHCR's Global Consultations on International Protection: Background (2001).

UNHCR, Note on Burden and Standard of Proof in Refugee Claims (16 December 1998).

UNHCR, Note on Determination of Refugee Status under International Instruments (24 August 1977) UN Doc EC/SCP/5.

UNHCR, Note on International Protection (1994) UN Doc A/AC.96/830.

UNHCR, Note on International Protection No 62 (XLI) (1990) UN Doc A/45/12/Add.1.

UNHCR, Note on Non-Refoulement (Submitted by the High Commissioner) (23 August 1977) EC/SCP.2.

UNHCR, 'Note on the Applicability of Art. 1D of the 1951 Convention relating to the Status of Refugees to Palestinian Refugees' (October 2002).

UNHCR, Note on UNHCR's Interpretation of Article 1D of the 1951 Convention relating to the Status of Refugees and Article 12(1)(a) of the EU Qualification Directive in the context of Palestinian refugees seeking international protection (2013).

UNHCR, Population Movements Associated with the Search for Asylum and Refuge (4 December 1990) UN Doc EXCOM/WGSP/5.

UNHCR, Position on mixed Azeri-Armenian couples from Azerbaijan and the specific issue of their admission and asylum in Armenia (2003).

UNHCR, Protection—Call for Comments on: Guidelines on International Protection No 11: Prima Facie Recognition of Refugee Status (2014).

UNHCR, Refugees and Others of Concern to UNHCR: 1996 Statistical Overview (1997).

UNHCR, Regional Bureau for Europe, An Overview of Protection Issues in Western Europe: Legislative Trends and Positions Taken by UNHCR (1995) 1(3) European Series.

UNHCR, Representation Stateless Persons before U.S. Immigration Authorities (August 2017).

UNHCR, 'Statement on the concept of persecution on cumulative grounds in light of the current situation for women and girls in Afghanistan: Issued in the context of the preliminary ruling reference to the Court of Justice of the European Union in the cases of *AH and FN v. Bundesamt für Fremdenwesen und Asyl* (C-608/22 and C-609/22)' (25 May 2023).

UNHCR, 'Statement on the interpretation of Article 5(3) of the EU Qualification Directive regarding subsequent applications for international protection based on sur place religious conversion: Issued in the context of the preliminary ruling reference to the Court of Justice of the European Union in the case of *J.F. v. Bundesamt für Fremdenwesen und Asyl* (C-222/22)' (3 February 2023).

UNHCR, 'Statement on Membership of Particular Social Group and the Best Interests of the Child in Asylum Procedures Issued in the context of the preliminary ruling reference to the Court of Justice of the European Union in the case of *K., L. v. Staatssecretaris van Justitie en Veiligheid* (C-646/21)' (21 June 2023).

UNHCR, Summary of Deliberations on Credibility Assessment in Asylum Procedures, Expert Roundtable, 14–15 January 2015, Budapest, Hungary (5 May 2015) available at <https://www.refworld.org/docid/554c9aba4.html> accessed 13 September 2021.

UNHCR, The International Protection of Refugees: Interpreting Article 1 of the 1951 Convention Relating to the Status of Refugees (2001) UN Doc A/AC.96/951.

UNHCR, The State of the World's Refugees: Fifty Years of Humanitarian Action (OUP 2000).

UNHCR, UNHCR and Human Rights: A policy paper resulting from deliberations in the Policy Committee on the basis of a paper prepared by the Division of International Protection (1997) UN Doc AHC/97/325.

UNHCR, Written Submission on Behalf of the UN High Commissioner for Refugees in the UK Court of Appeal in Sepet [2001] EWCA Civ 681.

United Nations, Beijing Declaration and Platform of Action, adopted at the Fourth World Conference on Women (27 October 1995).

UNSC Res 1244 (10 June 1999) UN Doc S/RES/1244(1999).

UNSC Res 1474 (2003) UN Doc S/RES/1474(2003).

UNSC Res 688 (1991) (5 April 1991).

Yearbook of the International Law Commission 1964 Volume I (1964) UN Doc A/CN.4/SR.772, 326.

Yearbook of the International Law Commission 1964 Volume II (1965) UN Doc A/CN.4/SER.A/1964/ADD.1.

Yearbook of the International Law Commission 1966 Volume II (1967) UN Doc A/CN.4/SER.A/1966/Add.l.

Yearbook of the United Nations, 1946–47 (United Nations 1947).

# Index

*For the benefit of digital users, indexed terms that span two pages (e.g., 52–53) may, on occasion, appear on only one of those pages.*

AALCO  21
academic guidance  115–17, 731, 739
  main studies  *see* main studies on refugee definition in English
academic pillar  55
*Acosta/Ward* categories  596–99, 620–21, 627–30, 653
age  29, *see also* Convention reasons, persecution
Algeria  17
alienage  260
androcentrism  29
approaches
  case-by-case approach  134
  circumstantial approach  131, 303, 318
  conceptual approach  37–38
  evolutive approach  19, 43, 86
  human rights approach  *see* human rights approach
  indicative approach  37–38, 42–43
  integrated approach  46–47, 81–82
  literalist approach  81–82, 85–86, 130–32
  purposive approach  68
  systematic approach  83
  US subjective approach  132–34, 303
Arab Convention  22
availment
  clause  548, 572–83
  meaning  547–72

Bangkok Principles  21
benefit of the doubt  709
biases
  expatriate bias  30
  proximity bias  30, 683–92
burden sharing  89, 92

Cartagena Declaration  19–20, 213–14

case law  51–53, 72, 98–99, 111–13, 731–32, 734–35, 739–40, 743–44, *see also* judicial guidance
causal nexus  42, 46–47, 426, 431, 440–41, 524–27, 540, *see also* nexus clause
cessation  26, 45–46
Chinese refugees  16
climate change  18, *see also* natural disasters
codification  23–24, 729–30, 734, 735, 744
Cold War  27–28
colonialism  28–29
common *v* civil law  78–80, 111–12, 116, 122
comparative exercise  515–17
complementary protection  31–32, 588
concealment *see* Convention reasons, persecution
contextual requirement  613, 628–29, 635–36
Convention purpose(s)  86–93
Convention reasons
  MPSG as a reason  13–14, 42, 46–47, 86, 105, 617–38
    age and children  624
    combined alternative approach  625–26, 627, 638
    combined cumulative approach  625, 626, 627, 630–31, 638
    contextual requirement  624, 628–30
    human rights approach  618–19, 631–32
    meaning  618–22
    origins  592, 617–18
    protected characteristics  596–99, 603–4, 620–22, 624–30
    sexual orientation  623–24
    social perception  618, 621, 624–25, 630–32
    women  622, 624
  nationality as a reason  200–1, *see also* nationality

Convention reasons (*cont.*)
  non-evaluative approach  628, 637–38, 644, 651–52
  political opinion as a reason  42, 597–98
    concealment/discretion  647
    contextual requirement  646–47, 650–51
    criminal/political  649–50, 652
    human rights approach  639–40, 641–42
    meaning of 'opinion'  640, 641–42, 643–44, 647, 652–53
    meaning of 'political'  640–43, 644–46, 647, 650–51
  race as a reason  604–7
    ethnicity  606
    human rights approach  605–6
    origins  604
  religion as a reason  607–13
    concealment/discretion  612–13
    doctrinal knowledge  612
    *forum internum/forum externum*  611–12
    human rights approach  608, 609–11
    meaning  607–11
    origins  607
    proselytism  611
    right to hold  609
    right to manifest  609
country of former habitual residence  272, 287
  multiple countries  282–86
country of nationality  263, 264–72, 285
  temporal dimension  286–87
customary international law  35, 454–55

declaratory act  24
definition *see* refugee definition
derogability criterion  143, 145, 171, 176
diplomatic asylum  288, 289–93, 294
diplomatic protection  46–47, *see also* protection
displaced persons  14–15
doctrine of attribution  602–4, 609, 636–37, 652–53, 659

Eastern Europe  27–28
*Eritrea-Ethiopia Boundary Commission* case  69–70
EU asylum law  20–21, 99–100, 117–21, 125–27, 138, 171–72, 195–96, *see also* Qualification Directive

EU Qualification Directive *see* Qualification Directive
EUAA Judicial Analysis  703, 740
*euisdem generis*  76, 594–95, 619, 620, 627–28
Eurocentrism  27–28
exclusion  11, 25, 26, 31–32, 45–46
  exclusion inquiry  483, 488, 497–98, 512
extraterritoriality  30, 290–91, 293

fear  26, *see also* refugee definition
  absence of well-founded fear  538
  well-founded fear *see* well-founded fear
forced migrants  18
formalism  7–8

gender  29, *see* also Convention reasons, persecution
*Genocide* case  84–85
governmental guidance  53–54, 728, 730, 743–44

habitual residence  201–2, 215, 234, 242–45, 274, 277, 281–82, 533–34
Hong Kong  16, 275–76, 280–81
human rights approach  32, 37, 47, 48–49, 51–52, 56–57, 92, 147–70
  availment clause  559, 564–65, 569
  Convention reasons  589, 595–96
  nationality and statelessness  203n.17, 211–12, 242–43
  outside the country  262
  persecution and internal protection alternative  484–85, 505, 513–18
  persecution and protection  413, 421, 425–26, 433–35, 445–46, 448
  persecution and serious harm  309, 316, 320–21
  well-founded fear  686–87, 692–93, 701–2
human rights approaches and models
  hierarchical models  142–43, 170–72
  history  135–40
  justifications  139–40
  meaning  134, 141, 167, 168–69, 170
  New Zealand IPT model  146, 175
  non-hierarchical models  143–46, 172–76
  serious harm  149–50, 161, 176–77
  state accountability  149–50, 155–56, 193–94, 195–96, 417, 428, 453–54
  variable impact  141

humanitarian purpose 87–88
Hungary 17

IARLJ *see* IARMJ
IARMJ 114–15, 740
ill treatment 30, 324–28
inability to return 242–45
internal displacement 18, 411–12
Internal Flight Alternative 475–76, 494, 527–28
Internal Protection Alternative 54–55, 412, 423, 565, 582
  analysis 494–97, 505, 507–9
  burden of proof 540, 706–7
  burden of raising 540
  burden of specific identification 541
  duty to give notice 541
  'home area' 511, 514–15, 518–20, 523–24, 533–34
  location 185, 189–90
Internal Relocation Alternative 475–76
International Court of Justice 5–6, 39–40
international law framework 140, 157, 160, 163, 176, 179–80
International Refugee Organisation 301–2, 669–70, 672–73
interpretation 34–36, 38–40, 51–52, *see also* VCLT
  autonomous meaning 122
  cognate treaties 73–74, 100
  *euisdem generis* 105, 593, 595, 614, 619, 627–28, 629–30, 631–32
  extrinsic means of interpretation 67–68
  flexibility 126–27
  generic terms 70
  intrinsic means of interpretation 67–68
  living instrument 25, 43, 68, 69, 86
  principle of effectiveness 66, 69
  static interpretation 69
  systematic interpretation 68

judicial dialogue 113–15
  transnational judicial dialogue 113–14
judicial endorsement 138
judicial guidance 98–99, 111–15, 731–32, 739–40, 744, *see also* case law
judicial pillar 51–53

legal status 14
*lex specialis* 9

main studies on refugee definition
  in English
  Goodwin-Gill, G and McAdam, M 116–17
  Hathaway, J 115, 140, 143
  Hathaway, J and Foster, M 116, 144–46, 174–75, 217–20, 226–30, 251
  Zimmermann, A (ed) 116
mandate refugees 14
*Michigan Guidelines*
  Michigan Guidelines on the International Protection of Refugees 115–16, 731, 737–38, 739
  Michigan Guidelines on Internal Protection Alternative 482–83, 497–501, 509–13
  Michigan Guidelines on Nexus to a Convention Ground 656
  Michigan Guidelines on Political Opinion 638–39, 645–46, 649–50, 656
  Michigan Guidelines on Well-Founded Fear 695, 704
monitoring 32–33
morality 31

national transpositions 22, 23–24, 72–73, *see also* codification
nationality
  actual nationality 220–21, 252
  burden of proof 251
  country of nationality 213–14
  denationalisation 207–8, 210, 220–21, 245–48, *see also* persecution
  deprivation 210, 211, 219–20, 257
  discretionary entitlement 209
  duty of cooperation 254
  effective nationality 221, 224–30
  fraud or misrepresentation 249
  inchoate nationality 217–20
  indeterminate nationality 210, 255–56
  loss of nationality 210, 249
  meaning 200–1, 212–13, 214–15, 614–17
  misuse 248–49
  modes of acquisition 209
  multiple nationalities 222
  by operation of law 254–55
  origins 613–14
  production of passport 251
  reasonable steps 252–54
  voluntary renunciation 249–50

784   INDEX

natural disasters  18, 344, 345, 347, 359, 363–64, 383, 538–39
*Navigational Rights* case  70
nexus clause
   bifurcated nexus  658–59
   causal nexus  587, 634–35, 650–51, 653–54, 657–58, 659
   discretion/concealment  601–2
   meaning  587
   persecutory intent  657–58
non-admission  231
non-discrimination  89–90, 185, 590, 591, 595–99, 618–19, 631–32, 653
non-refoulement  93–94
   extra-territorial application  288–95
*Nottebohm* case  207

OAU Convention  19, 213–14
outside the country  263–64, 266–68, 271–72, 273, *see also* country of former habitual residence, country of nationality

Palestinian refugees  11
particularity  7, 22–24
people on the move  18
persecution  20–21, 37
   actors of  362–66
   acts of  361–62
   age-specific  355
   armed conflict  392–402
   Article 1D  458–59
   child-specific  355–58
   civil society actors  466–67
   concealment/discretion  333, 354
   cultural harm  342–44
   current  403
   de facto state entities  459–60
   definition  302–3
   denationalisation  210, 245–48, 373–75
   denial of right to return  375
   deprivation of nationality  373–75
   disability-specific  358–60
   discrimination  379–84
   duration  308, 386–91
   education-related harm  338–39
   environmental harm  344–48
   gender-specific  351–53
   group  304–5, 397–98
   health-related harm  340–42
   human agency  306, 337–38, 345–46, 361–62, 363–64, 395–96
   indirect  385–86
   individualisation  375–76, 396–97
   intensity  376–79
   laws  366–75
   life or freedom  312–14
   military service  372–73
   past  405
   persecutory intent  391–96
   persistency *see* duration
   physical harm  321–30
   predicament approach  300, 361–62, 363, 393–94, 395–96
   prosecution  369–72
   psychological harm  330–33
   sexual orientation  353–55
   singling out  312–96
   socio-economic  303–4, 333–38
   state actors  537
   sur place  403–4
   temporal scope  402–3
   threat of  384–85
persuasiveness  41
*prima facie* recognition  398–99
protection
   ability  442, 444
   accessibility  447–48
   additional requirement in own right  555–56, 566, 578–79, 581
   affirmative protection  482–83, 493, 542–43
   consular protection  547, 564–65, 568–69, 571, 573–75, 577
   diplomatic protection  491, 579–81, 583
   due diligence  418–19, 428–29, 436–38
   effectiveness  438, 447–48, 468–71
   exhaustion of local remedies  418–19, 429–30, 439
   external protection  547, 551–52, 553–54, 556–57, 560–62, 572, 573–76
   inability  548–49, 554, 577
   ineffective protectors  366
   internal protection  409, 412–13, 418, 420–21, 444, 491, 547, 554–55, 557–60, 562–63, 570–71, 576–79
   meaning  565–82
   national protection  417
   non-state actors  418–19, 432, 446–47, 466, 470

INDEX 785

non-temporariness 448, 539
positive and negative obligations 433–34, 445–46, 464
presumption of state protection 418–19, 429–30, 439
protection purpose 88–89
reasonable steps 428–29, 438, 447–48, 468
return 550, 574–75
role of individual 417–18, 421–22, 429, 438–39
soft law sources 455–56
State protection see State
surrogate protection 90–91, 379
unwillingness 13–14, 549, 577
willingness 444

Qualification Directive 300–1, 349, 426, 432, 438–40, 448, 477–78, 485–86, 502, 696, 707–8, 727, 729–30, 734, *see also* EU asylum law

reasonableness test 43–44
refoulement
  indirect refoulement 483–84, 538–39
refugee
  Article 1A(1) 34–36
  Article 1A(2) 33–34
  Article 1D 10–11
  Recommendation E 37–38
  wider meaning 17–18
refugee definition
  concept of definition 3–8
  criticisms 27–33
  'fear test' 184, 194
  holistic approach 188–89, 192, 727, 735
  interrelated elements 181–95, 727–28
  limitations 12, 25–27
  limits of Article 1A(2) 506, 521–22
  national definitions 22–24
  problems of definition 33–38
  'protection inquiry' 184–85, 189–90, 192–93
  'protection test' 184, 193–94
  risk assessment 185, 187, 190, 191, 193
  true meaning 62
  uniformity 7, 22–24, 41
  vagueness 35–36
  working definition 37–38, *see also* working definition
Refugee Status Determination 24

responsibility to protect 455–56
risk assessment 667, *see also* refugee definition, well-founded fear
  forward-looking assessment 698–99
  imminence 700–2
  reasonable foreseeability 699–702
  risk component 702–3
  speculation 699
  temporal dimension 698–704
Rome Statute 101, 308–9

scope 14, 15–16, 17–18, 196
  personal scope 20–21
serious harm
  sufficient severity 349–50, 379
standard of proof 705, 707–11
State
  accountability 460–63
  basic duty to protect 449–50, 457–58
  culpability 418–19, 454
  failed state 463–66
  protection 449
  responsibility 417, 428–29, 435–36, 453–54
  statehood 452–53
  state-individual 450–51
State practice 6, 20, 22–24, 25, 35, 47–48
  quasi-State practice 728–29
stateless person 13–14, 18, 43–44, 234–45
  stateless children 277–79
  statelessness 13–14, 205–6
statutory refugee 9–10, 13–14
subjective element 682–85
subsidiary protection 21
surrogacy
  attribution 603
  criticisms 149–50, 163–65, 194
  human rights approach 153
  internal protection alternative 484, 542
  nationality 216
  nexus clause 589, 658
  outside the country 270, 285
  protection 90, 91–92, 410–24, 463, 569, 576, 578–79
  underlying principle 196–97, 728
  well-founded fear 698

territoriality 30
territorial asylum 30, 270, 289–90, 294–95

786  INDEX

territory 267–68, 269–71, 275–76, 280–81, 289–90, 292–93
'theory of three scales' 136, 172
*Tunis and Morocco* case 207

UN Guiding Principles on Internal Displacement 506, 520–21
UNHCR
  2001 note 45–47, 136–37, 684–85, 707
  ExCom Conclusions 44–45, 96–98, 109, 358
  good offices 15–16
  Guidance Note on Organised Gangs 649
  Guidelines on International Protection 47–51, 109–10, 137–38, 732, 733, 742–43
  Guidelines on International Protection No 1 622–23, 654, 656–57
  Guidelines on International Protection No 2 596–97, 601, 603–4, 626, 633–35, 658–59
  Guidelines on International Protection No 4 478, 491, 494–97, 507–9
  Guidelines on International Protection No 6 608–9, 610–11, 613
  Guidelines on International Protection No 8 624, 678, 689
  Guidelines on International Protection No 9 623, 657
  Guidelines on International Protection No 11 689
  Handbook *see* UNHCR Handbook
  Handbook on Protection of Stateless Persons 217, 221–22
  Note on Burden and Standard of Proof 687
  persons of concern 14–15, 17
  pillar 39–40, 97–98, 107, 110–11, 125
  positions 476–77, 494
  Statute 13–15, 592
UNHCR Handbook 41–44, 741–42
  Convention reasons 593–94, 600–1, 605, 615, 619–20, 642–43
  illustrative approach 149–50, 166
  internal protection alternative 485–86, 494
  interpretive guidance 41–44, 732, 733–34, 741–42, 744
  nationality 202–3, 222–23
  outside the country 260, 267–68, 283
  persecution 302–3, 330, 334, 358, 371, 403–4
  protection 424–25, 447n.195, 449–50
  source 83, 96–98, 108–9
  well-founded fear 676–77, 686, 696, 706–7

VCLT 27, 46–47, 716, 720, 726–27, 732, 735
  any relevant rules of international law 73–74, 100–2
  Article 31 64–65, 67–68, 73–74
  Article 32 64–65, 74–76
  Article 33 76–77, 106
  Article 38 78
  consistency 78–80, 92
  context 67–68, 83–84
  customary international law 62–63, 79–80, 119, 122
  *effet utile* 66
  *euisdem generis* *see* euisdem generis
  good faith 65–66, 80
  good faith 65–66, 80, 123
  integrated/unified approach 65, 81–82, 122, 125
  law-making treaty 70–71, 84–85, 97
  object and purpose 68–70, 84–87, 91–93
  ordinary meaning 66–67, 80–82, 123
  special meaning 74, 102–3
  subsequent agreement 71–73, 93–95
  ILC Report on Subsequent Agreement 64, 72–73, 74–75, 76, 98
  subsequent practice 35, 41, 44–45, 53–54, 69, 71–73, 95–96
  *travaux* 75, 84, 103–5
  *ut regis magis valeat quam pereat* 66

well-founded fear 26
  bipartite approach 672–73, 676–79, 680–81, 683–92
  foundation in fact 696
  holistic inquiry 688, 695, 697
  human rights approach 676, 686–87, 692–66, 701–2
  individual assessment 687, 691, 693, 695, 696–97
  meaning 673–82
  objective approach 672, 680, 681, 682, 683, 692–95
  objective element 692–97
  origins 668–70, 672–73
  procedural devices 688–90

reasonable person standard  690–91
 subjective element  682–92
 subjective fear as 'plus factor'  686, 691–92
working definition
 basic propositions  724–25, 734–35, 736–38
 contents  715–24
 framework  726–27
 legal form  725
 *lex lata* and *de lege ferenda*  725
 nature and status  37–38, 724–36
 possible drawbacks  733–36

The manufacturer's authorised representative in the EU for product safety is
Oxford University Press España S.A. of el Parque Empresarial San Fernando de
Henares, Avenida de Castilla, 2 – 28830 Madrid (www.oup.es/en or product.
safety@oup.com). OUP España S.A. also acts as importer into Spain of products
made by the manufacturer.

www.ingramcontent.com/pod-product-compliance
Lightning Source LLC
Chambersburg PA
CBHW072051290825
31867CB00004B/330